VOLUMI

CW01612775

MUTUAL & FEDERAL SOUTH AFRICAN CRICKET ANNUAL 2006

Edited by COLIN BRYDEN
Statistics by Andrew Samson
Scorecards formatted by Ros Brodie

Published with the cooperation of Cricket South Africa

Publishers: Mutual & Federal Insurance Company Ltd, PO Box 1120, Johannesburg 2000

Name of publication:	Mutual & Federal South African Cricket Annual 2006
Publishers:	Mutual & Federal, 75 President Street, Johannesburg www.mf.co.za
Editor:	Colin Bryden
Production Editor:	Alison Ward, MWP Media
Typeface:	Times New Roman
Repro:	Colin Bryden Communications, MWP Media, Creda Communications
Printing:	Creda Communications, Eliot Avenue, Eppindust II, Cape Town

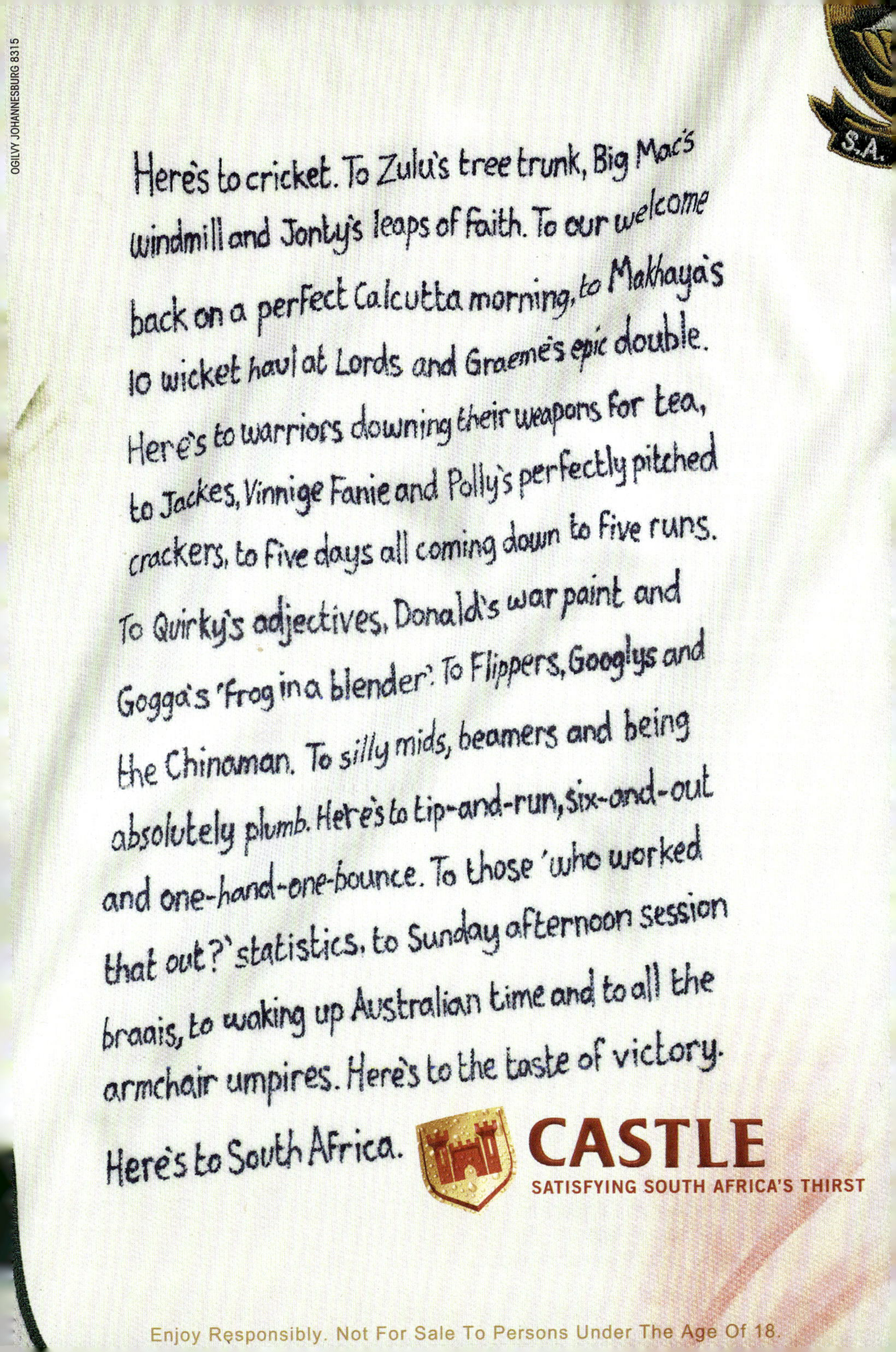
OGILVY JOHANNESBURG 8315
S.A.
Here's to cricket. To Zulu's tree trunk, Big Mac's windmill and Jonty's leaps of faith. To our welcome back on a perfect Calcutta morning, to Makhaya's 10 wicket haul at Lords and Graeme's epic double. Here's to warriors downing their weapons for tea, to Jackes, Vinnige Fanie and Polly's perfectly pitched crackers, to five days all coming down to five runs. To Quirky's adjectives, Donald's war paint and Gogga's 'frog in a blender'. To Flippers, Googlys and the Chinaman. To silly mids, beamers and being absolutely plumb. Here's to tip-and-run, six-and-out and one-hand-one-bounce. To those 'who worked that out?' statistics, to Sunday afternoon session braais, to waking up Australian time and to all the armchair umpires. Here's to the taste of victory.
Here's to South Africa.
CASTLE
SATISFYING SOUTH AFRICA'S THIRST
Enjoy Responsibly. Not For Sale To Persons Under The Age Of 18.

Contents

CONTENTS

EDITOR'S NOTES

South African cricket will go into the 2006/07 season under a new name, facing another challenging season. The decision to put the country's cricket under the name of Cricket South Africa was a sensible one given that the professional wing, established in 2002, was already known by that title, albeit with the addendum (Pty) Ltd, and was gaining an ever-increasing profile.

The principle challenge in a World Cup season is for the national team, now known officially as the Proteas, to re-establish themselves as a major force in the world game.

South Africa had a disappointing 2005/06 season in Test cricket, losing five out of six matches against Australia but were more successful in the one-day game, regaining their second position on the world rankings and clinching a one-day series victory against Australia in what has already passed into legend as the "438 game".

Off the field, there were encouraging developments.

In the year that Percy Sonn became South Africa's first President of the International Cricket Council, South Africa was awarded the hosting of the inaugural world 20-overs championship. This event, to be staged in late September 2007, should be a rousing one although the timing is not ideal, coming as it does early in the season when it will be difficult to produce the type of batsman-friendly pitches that such contests demand. Nevertheless the staging of the tournament in South Africa is a fitting reward for a country that was one of the first to embrace and bring promotional flair to the concept of short matches, introducing many new followers to cricket.

Advocate Sonn became the sixth person elected to head the ICC when he was inaugurated at the conclusion of the annual conference in London on 7 July 2006, having served as Vice-President to Ehsan Mani of Pakistan. He will serve for a minimum of two and a maximum of three years and will be the man at the helm when important decisions are made regarding cricket's future, not the least of which will be negotiations for new sponsorship and marketing agreements beyond the current contracted period which ends in 2007.

Hardly had Sonn taken office than two major issues arose. South Africa returned early from their tour of Sri Lanka, instead of playing in a triangular one-day series, because of security concerns and Pakistan forfeited a Test match against England after protesting against an accusation of ball-tampering levelled by the umpires.

CRICKET'S POPULARITY

In December 2005 it was announced that Makhaya Ntini, South Africa's outstanding fast bowler, had been found to be the most popular sports person in South Africa in the reputable BMI 2005 Sportrack survey, the first cricketer to earn this accolade.

The BMI survey found that cricket was the second most popular sport among all South Africans behind soccer, with black South Africans having become the majority of those who follow cricket.

Cricket's growing popularity was reflected in significant sponsorship agreements with three of South Africa's major companies, collectively worth many millions of rands.

In September 2005, Standard Bank affirmed its commitment to South African cricket when it announced a R106-million renewal of its sponsorship, as well as pledging an additional R19-million for development projects. The new agreement is for three years.

Under the new sponsorship agreements, Standard Bank will be the sole sponsor of the South African one-day international team and the Standard Bank Pro20 Series, while the bank committed to a new investment in the international Pro20 format. Standard Bank renewed their contract for one-day internationals and the domestic Standard Bank Cup for the 2005/06 season only.

Also in September 2005, it was announced that long-time sponsor Castle Lager would continue its support of Test cricket and the national team with a sponsorship worth R60-million over three years.

Standard Bank's relinquishing of its rights to one-day internationals and the domestic 45-overs competition opened the way for MTN, Africa's biggest cellular phone provider, to announce in May 2006 that it would sponsor one-day international and domestic matches over a two-year period, enabling Cricket South Africa to split event and team sponsorship for limited overs cricket.

CRICKET SOUTH AFRICA

Cricket South Africa (Pty) Ltd was established in 2002 as the professional arm of the United Cricket Board of South Africa. As Cricket SA gained an increasingly higher profile, the different names and logos caused a certain amount of confusion and it was a sensible decision at the annual general meeting in August 2006 to put all cricket under the banner of Cricket SA, effectively changing the name and logo of the controlling body. The company running professional cricket will continue to operate under its established name.

At the AGM, Professor Hentie van Wyk, the treasurer, reported that cricket was in good financial shape. Although a loss of R14.6-million had been budgeted, for the financial year which ended on 30 April 2006, Cricket SA had made an operating profit of R19.4-million and the United Cricket Board a profit of R6.7-million, a combined surplus of R26.1-million.

THE NATIONAL TEAM

Any season in which South Africa have to play away and at home against Australia is bound to be a tough one and so it proved yet again. There were encouraging signs on the tour of Australia when South Africa salvaged an honourable draw in the first Test. Dropped catches were a critical factor in the second Test, which Australia ended up winning reasonably comfortably, but South Africa were distinctly unlucky when weather interfered with the third Test when the Proteas had the upper hand. In an attempt to force a series-levelling win, South Africa set the world champions a target which was all too easily achieved.

The home series was most disappointing, with Australia winning all three Tests. It was the first time in more than a century that South Africa had suffered a "whitewash" at home. The third Test could have gone either way but the fact was that Australia proved much the better side over the course of the summer.

The Proteas finished the season on a reasonable note by winning a series 2-0 against New Zealand to regain fifth place on the International Cricket Council ranking list at the expense of the Kiwis. Within two months, however, they had dropped back to sixth as a result of the ICC's annual revision of the rankings, which meant that results before August 2003 were discarded. They then lost both matches in a two-Test series in Sri Lanka. The first Test was humiliating, with the Sri Lankans setting several records, but the second Test was a thriller which the home side won by one wicket. One obvious question which had to be asked was whether a single warm-up game was enough on such a demanding tour after a lay-off.

The picture was brighter in one-day games, with South Africa trouncing New Zealand at home before sharing a series in India. They failed to reach the final of a triangular series in Australia, when they were badly hit by injuries, but redeemed themselves at home against Australia.

Ashwell Prince became South Africa's 32nd Test captain and the eighth since unity when he led the side to Sri Lanka. He also became the country's first captain of colour, which may have been significant as a historical footnote, although it was hardly a matter of controversy or sensation. Prince was appointed vice-captain during the tour of Australia when Kallis had to return home early and was named vice-captain for the tour of Sri Lanka. When Graeme Smith withdrew because of injury, Prince was the obvious choice to take charge.

Much optimism has been expressed about South Africa's prospects in the World Cup in the West Indies but it will be a difficult tournament, especially as the Proteas have to play all three of the major Asian powers in Guyana, assuming the line-up for the Super Eight phase is as expected. Although a new stadium will be used for the World Cup, pitches in Guyana typically are among the slowest in the Caribbean, which will favour the Asians. It is a fact, too, that at least six of the competing teams will have strong hopes of winning the World Cup.

On a broader level, the appointment of Vintcent van der Bijl as general manager of professional cricket seemed likely to reap dividends into the future. Particularly encouraging was the involvement of former players such as Allan Donald, Gary Kirsten, Shafiek Abrahams and Denys Hobson and the development of a high performance programme to groom potential international players.

WORLD HONOURS

South Africa fared well in the selection of the World teams which played against Australia in what proved to be an anti-climactic ICC Super Series. Graeme Smith was named captain of the World Test team, while Shaun Pollock led the World one-day side.

Jacques Kallis and Mark Boucher played alongside Smith in the Test side, while Shaun Pollock was in the squad but did not make final eleven. Kallis and Makhaya Ntini joined Pollock in the one-day team, while Herschelle Gibbs was selected for the one-day squad but had to withdraw because of a knee injury.

The Super Series coincided with the ICC Player Awards function and there was a further significant honour for South Africa when Kallis was named joint ICC Cricketer of the Year, sharing the honour with Andrew Flintoff of England.

DOMESTIC CRICKET

The jury remained out on whether the franchise system had led to a significant improvement in standard at domestic level. A worrying trend continued whereby some of the country's leading players opted to take their talent abroad, although the dispensation introduced by Cricket South Africa, drawing a distinction between "South African" and "foreign" overseas players, enabled the likes of Dale Benkenstein, Martin van Jaarsveld and HD Ackerman to continue to play in this country.

For a nation not blessed with a plethora of outstanding spin bowlers, the decision of Paul Harris to play for English county Warwickshire was especially disappointing as he was undoubtedly a contender for national honours in the not-too-distant future. Kruger van Wyk, the Northerns and Titans wicketkeeper, opted to further his career in New Zealand.

EDITOR'S NOTES

Good sense finally prevailed in the dispute between Griqualand West and Cricket South Africa, with Griquas becoming part of the Central franchise. Ironically, the Eagles were hardly in need of strengthening, having proved the most successful franchise despite drawing only on players from Free State.

An anomaly in the first-class structure was the status accorded the 11 amateur teams. Most newspapers did not cover these matches yet they were accorded the same status for record purposes as Test or franchise clashes. Even more teams will be playing first-class cricket in the coming season following a decision to include the five associate unions of Cricket South Africa, as well as Namibia, in an expanded competition. There is a danger that some cheap centuries and multi-wicket hauls will be achieved against some of the weaker teams.

A similar situation existed at international level, with some of the International Cricket Council's second-tier nations being granted one-day international status. Soon after South Africa established a world record with their total against Australia, it was broken by Sri Lanka against the Netherlands in a match played on a small ground, with no television coverage and minimal media following.

RACISM

During South Africa's tour of Australia there were incidents of racist abuse from spectators during the Test matches. Cricket South Africa lodged an official complaint with the International Cricket Council, which led to the appointment of Goolam Vahanvati, the Solicitor General of India, to conduct an inquiry.

The report confirmed that premeditated and coordinated racial abuse had occurred. While it was disappointing that such incidents happened, it was encouraging that both the ICC and Cricket Australia took the matter seriously and responded appropriately.

During South Africa's tour of Sri Lanka, the Australian commentator, Dean Jones, made an inappropriate reference to Hashim Amla as a "terrorist" when he thought he was off air. Ten Sports summarily dismissed Jones and made a public apology, action which was welcomed by Cricket South Africa, who made an official complaint.

As Cricket South Africa Chief Executive Gerald Majola noted, South Africans are particularly sensitive to racial incidents, given the country's history, and it is necessary to do all that is possible to prevent further such incidents.

DRIVING TO THE TOP . . . Hashim Amla topped the domestic run-scorers and made an impressive return to international cricket   Picture: TERTIUS PICKARD, Touchline Photo

FIVE CRICKETERS OF THE YEAR

HASHIM AMLA

Hashim Amla's meteoric rise through the ranks of South Africa's batsmen encompasses three consecutive years of prolific run-making for the Dolphins in domestic cricket, culminating in his outstanding achievements last season.

Despite concerns in some quarters over his unusual technique, which includes an eye-catching semi-circular flourish in his backlift, Amla is rightly admired for his mental strength. This was showcased for the first time in senior domestic cricket when he batted for more than nine hours to record his maiden first-class century, an unbeaten 159, against a Free State attack that included Allan Donald in 2003/04.

Amla has steadily improved since that first season for the Dolphins in which he compiled 647 runs at 49.76. He followed that up in his second season with 707 runs at 54.38, and topped that last season with 893 runs at 55.81, establishing himself as the top run-scorer in the SuperSport Series.

His consistency was first rewarded at national level in 2004/05 when he played in three Tests against India and England. Although that proved to be a false start to his international career, he put that right in no uncertain terms against the touring New Zealanders earlier this year, striking a century and a half-century in the two Tests in which he played.

The fierceness of Amla's ambition to play for his country was revealed at the end of the 2004/05 season. Despite leading his team to a share of the SuperSport Series trophy as well as striking his first double-century in the final, the determined young man relinquished the captaincy after just one season, citing his desire to force his way back into the national team by focusing exclusively on his batting. It was a brave decision, largely because of the keen expectations of the Indian community in Durban, but it has been vindicated.

HASHIM MAHOMED AMLA, born in Durban on 31 March 1983, is the younger brother of Ahmed Amla, who will captain the Dolphins this season. He made his first-class debut for KwaZulu-Natal at the early age of 16 against Nasser Hussain's touring England team in 1999/2000. It was a huge step up for the captain of the Durban High School first team, but then-coach Phil Russell was not concerned: "He batted calmly for half-an-hour against Andrew Caddick, Alex Tudor and Freddie Flintoff and even then I could see he belonged in that company. Hashim has a good, analytical mind, and a strong one too, and he deserves all he has achieved."

Those early impressions proved accurate as Amla established himself both as a remorseless accumulator of runs as well as an entertainer when the opportunity presented itself. His trademark stroke is the wristy flick through the square leg region, a shot that looks to have been patented on the sub-continent. In fact, Amla had never been to India before his Test debut, and he says that his style is entirely uncoached.

Although he still favours the leg side, he has developed a complete array of strokes all round the wicket, including whipping drives through the covers off the back and front foot as well as a ferocious square cut. While he can bat stubbornly for long periods, he is more than capable of taking an attack apart. His match-winning 153 against a Cobras attack that included Charl Willoughby and Alan Dawson in February took him only 179 balls and included 23 fours.

TOP OF HIS GAME . . . Mark Boucher leaps to catch Australia's Michael Hussey in Sydney. He was a driving force in the national team   Picture: GETTY IMAGES/TOUCHLINE PHOTO

Dolphins' skipper Lance Klusener expressed many players' views when he described it as "one of the better hundreds I've seen".

Amla is a devout Muslim who honours God for his achievements. Those not of his faith will be inclined to give the bearded right-hand batsman at least some of the credit.

Patrick Compton

MARK BOUCHER

After a disappointing couple of seasons in which he failed to do justice to his undoubted talent, MARK VERDON BOUCHER finally revisited the heights of 2003/04 when he scored the last of his four Test centuries. The combination of cocksure self-belief and white-knuckled determination that characterised the start of his career was back.

For a brief time Boucher's words spoke louder than his deeds but, during the last year, he stood up to the huge challenge posed by the Australians and still maintained the feisty edge so appreciated by his team-mates.

From the first Test of the summer, in Perth, when he came to the crease at 167-5 and made a positive, confident 62 from just 77 deliveries, to the last against New Zealand at the Wanderers in May, he maintained form and fitness like almost never before.

His resilience was never better displayed than in the second Test against Australia in Durban when he presented an impenetrable barrier to Brett Lee and Shane Warne in a brave attempt to save the game and keep the series alive. Arriving at the crease on 146-5 with more than half of the final day to go, Boucher toiled until the bitter end – on a torrid pitch and through failing light – and was unbeaten on 51 when last man Makhaya Ntini had trouble in picking Warne, let alone his googly, and perished lbw within touching distance of safety.

The other side of Boucher the batsman was there for the all the world to see – and will be forever more in the greatest one-day international yet played, the famous "438" game at the Wanderers.

Never before, and almost certainly never again, will Boucher come to the crease with the total reading 299. Not in a one-day game, anyway. And certainly not in the 32nd over. During times of crisis, panic, looming defeat or even potential glory it is not about having men who can keep their cool or their emotions under control, because nobody can. It is about having men who can display the appearance of having their emotions under control.

He appeared to take no risks at all and a boundary count of just four confirmed his discretion and superb placement of the ball. When last man Ntini walked to the crease with two runs required from the final three balls, Boucher spoke to him as though enquiring about the well being of his vegetable garden. At least, that's the impression he gave the opposition.

The last of the four boundaries was the one he launched to long on against Lee to win the game with a ball to spare and register an unbeaten 50 from just 43 deliveries. The dam wall holding back his emotions was instantly demolished and the party began.

Strangely, Boucher, who was born in East London on 3 December 1976, has always been spoken of more as a batsman than a wicketkeeper. Perhaps it is because he has never been flashy behind the stumps and has become less and less so as the years pass. Like a good "fetching" flanker in rugby, the best 'keepers should be noticed as little as possible.

The lack of recognition for his glovework, and the amount of hard work he puts into it, has irked Boucher in the past but it should not. His career statistics speak for themselves. He

INDEFATIGABLE . . . a rare injury-enforced break was all that interrupted another outstanding season by Makhaya Ntini *Picture: TERTIUS PICKARD, Touchline Photo*

has claimed the second most dismissals in both Test and one-day cricket with 360 and 320 respectively behind Ian Healy (395) and Adam Gilchrist (393). And only Gilchrist has a higher rate of dismissals per match than Boucher, in either form of the game.

Two years ago he wondered whether he would ever play international cricket again having been dropped after a South African record 75 consecutive Test appearances. In 2006, for the third time, he is one of South Africa's Cricketers of the Year.

Neil Manthorp

MAKHAYA NTINI

Of all the lessons Makhaya Ntini has learned on the way to becoming one of the best fast bowlers in the world, the one instruction he has ignored has been the importance of rest and recovery.

Taking a break is something Ntini is not very good at doing. So when he was forced to return home from the tour of Australia because of injury, Ntini was in new territory. It speaks volumes for his strength and fitness that the knee injury he suffered in the second Test at Melbourne was his first serious ailment as an international cricketer.

The month-long break was a blessing, though Ntini was "angry" that it came at a time when his team-mates were suffering loss after loss in the one-day series in Australia, making him desperate to rejoin them. He was instructed to stay put, and the wisdom of that decision was seen in the return series in South Africa, and in the subsequent Tests against New Zealand.

The Test summer started perfectly for Ntini with five wickets on the first day of the first Test in Perth. It was a performance that in one respect epitomised Ntini – all hustle and bustle – but in another respect also showed how much he'd grown. He bowled with guile and a street-smartness that he hadn't hitherto shown. Who knows what could have happened had he not missed the third Test in Sydney where Graeme Smith's courageous second innings declaration was unhinged by the absence of his sole strike bowler?

Ntini showed just how much good that break did him with a sterling performance in the second one-day international against Australia in Cape Town, claiming 6-22 and eclipsing Allan Donald's mark for the best analysis by a South African in a limited overs international. He also scored perhaps the most important run of his life in that pulsating final one-dayer against the Aussies at the Wanderers when he coolly put Mark Boucher back on strike with a nudge down to third man.

Then followed a series of landmark wicket-taking hauls that culminated in him becoming the first South African to claim back-to-back ten-wicket yields in Tests, 10-178 in the third match against Australia and 10-145 in the first Test against New Zealand.

Throughout the summer he also showed willingness to experiment, and his use of a delivery from wide of the crease that can both hold its line and move away from the right-hander proved devastating. In addition he also developed the uncanny – though for the opposition wholly uncomfortable – habit of hitting batsmen, with Australians Justin Langer and Andrew Symonds and New Zealand's Hamish Marshall among those scarred by his brutal assault.

Ntini finished the lengthy 2005/06 season with 48 Test wickets, close to a third of the total number garnered by South African bowlers. In the last three years he has picked up 165 of his 269 Test wickets in just 35 matches at a rate of 4.7 wickets a Test.

BIG-MATCH TEMPERAMENT . . . Ashwell Prince's century against Australia in Sydney typified his determined approach *Picture: GETTY IMAGES/TOUCHLINE PHOTO*

From the hills of Mdingi where MAKHAYA NTINI was born on 6 July 1977, to the streets of Kingston, Jamaica, he has risen and become not only South Africa's most popular sportsmen, but also an icon wherever the game is played.

He also recognises his role as a senior player, and just as he learnt from team-mates like Donald and Shaun Pollock so Ntini has enthusiastically sought to encourage and assist newcomers to the national side. "For me as a front-liner I've been given the opportunity with the new ball to lead up front," he said after being named Man of the Series for his 20 wickets in the three Tests against New Zealand. "It has been one of the things that gives me motivation to show a youngster like Dale Steyn how it's done when you've been given an opportunity."

Makhaya Ntini, now well-rested, is steadily on the road to becoming a South African cricketing legend.

Stuart Hess

ASHWELL PRINCE

Ashwell Prince's century against Australia in the third Test at Sydney was the third and most significant of four Test hundreds made in just over a year. He finished the 2005/06 season as a senior member of the national side, whose status was underlined when he was appointed vice-captain of the touring party in Australia after Jacques Kallis was forced to return home.

Prince received the ultimate accolade in South African cricket when, having been appointed vice-captain of the Test squad to tour Sri Lanka in July 2006, he was named as South Africa's 32nd Test captain, and the eighth since 1991/92, following the withdrawal of Graeme Smith because of an ankle injury.

Born in Port Elizabeth on 28 May 1977, ASHWELL GAVIN PRINCE grew up in the Gelvandale township where his horizons were limited by apartheid. His boyhood hero was his brother Lloyd, six years older, who represented Eastern Province in four different sports under the nonracial Sacos organisation. In November 1991, however, he was inspired by the sight of Allan Donald charging in to bowl against India in Calcutta in the first match played by the new South Africa. He dared to dream that he too might play for his country.

As a boy at St Thomas Secondary School, the young Prince played 25-overs-a-side cricket, which required only natural ability and youthful exuberance. Eldine Baptiste, the former West Indian and Eastern Province bowler, gave him crucial technical advice when he started to play for the Gelvandale club.

The stocky left-hander played in the 1993 and 1994 Coca-Cola Weeks and toured England with the South African under-19 team in 1995 and India in 1995/96. He made his first-class debut for Eastern Province in the latter season and his ability was obvious, although initially he played too many strokes for his own good.

A move to Western Province two seasons later was motivated as much by the guarantee of a starting place, with the province's leading batsmen subject to Test calls, as by a financial incentive.

An innings of 92 for South Africa A against the Australians in Potchefstroom in 2001/02, after missing much of the season following a shoulder operation, proved timely. When Justin Ontong withdrew with an injury the day before the first Test at the Wanderers, Prince was called up. He made 49 in his maiden Test innings and an important 48 in South Africa's successful run chase in the third Test at Kingsmead. He played in the home Tests against Bangladesh and Sri Lanka the following season before losing his place.

HOW WAS THAT? . . . Dale Steyn celebrates after dismissing New Zealand's Jamie How as he adds pace and potency to the Proteas' attack *Picture: LEE WARREN, Touchline Photo*

Successfully playing an anchor role in one-day internationals earned Prince a recall to the Test side in the 2004/05 season. A century against Zimbabwe at Centurion was an important breakthrough, although he was not selected for South Africa's next Test match, against the West Indies in Georgetown, when the selectors decided to pick only five specialist batsmen. He played in the three remaining matches, however, and capped the series with one of eight centuries in the high-scoring fourth Test in Antigua.

In the six Tests against Australia last season, Prince's 391 runs at 32.58 put him second only to Jacques Kallis, who made 420 at 46.66. A hallmark of his play was his calm determination, especially as he struggled initially against Shane Warne's leg-spin and was the victim of at least two poor umpiring decisions. In addition to his 119 at Sydney he made 93 at the Wanderers, the first time he had passed fifty but failed to go on to a hundred in his Test career.

With the flashiness of his youth long replaced by a watchful defence, Prince was at his most dogged when he ground out a six-hour century against New Zealand at Newlands in a match in which playing for a draw was the only option after New Zealand's first innings lasted until the third morning.

Ironically, having earned his Test recall on the strength of his solid batting in one-day games, Prince ended the season out of the one-day side as the selectors opted for a more attacking approach. His one-day claims are significant, however, as in addition to his batting skills he is an outstanding fielder in the cover or point areas.

Colin Bryden

DALE STEYN

Dale Steyn may not have the figure of the archetypal fierce fast bowler, being five-foot-ten (1.78m) and lithe, but there is no doubting he has pace, skill and, most importantly, gets people out. Just ask his victims in the past season, all 69 of them, a haul of wickets bettered only once in a South African season by a home player. The legendary Vintcent van der Bijl holds the record with his 75 scalps in 1981/82.

And there will be many in the 69-Club who fell prey to Steyn's signature delivery – the ball that swings away late at high pace. The same unplayable delivery that bowled England captain Michael Vaughan on Steyn's Test debut in December 2004.

Steyn was dropped from the national side after playing just three Tests in his international baptism, which took his tally of first-class matches to a meagre ten. But in 2005/06, with the benefit of a second season of franchise cricket and some time with Essex in the county championship, he went some way to stamping his class and fulfilling the tremendous potential that led to his selection in the first place.

In nine SuperSport Series matches he took 49 wickets, a decisive contribution in the Titans' progress to the final and the eventual sharing of the title with the KZN Dolphins, and he was rightly returned to the national team for the three-Test series against New Zealand, opening the bowling for his country for the first time in Tests.

He had earlier traipsed around Australia as a replacement for the injured Andre Nel in the VB Series, playing just two matches, 90 runs being plundered in his eight overs.

He undoubtedly gained more in the dressing room, though, and by the time he returned to South Africa and domestic action for the Titans, he felt more a part of the national squad, knowing his team-mates better and feeling more comfortable in their company.

"I've really grown as a cricketer and as a person. I've played a lot more first-class cricket and I'm more confident. I know the guys much better now, the whole experience is not as nerve-wracking," Steyn said during the New Zealand series.

Armed with increased confidence, he added greater control to his kit-bag of fast bowler's weapons and Kiwi captain Stephen Fleming confirmed after the series that the 22-year-old had given his team a thoroughly uncomfortable time. "Ntini and Steyn were superb, they made us work very hard from ball one. Steyn, in particular, was pretty brutal with his away swing at pace," Fleming said.

Sixteen wickets in three Tests against New Zealand will state Steyn's claim as the new-ball successor to Shaun Pollock in no uncertain terms. The less helpful pitches of Sri Lanka lie in wait but the future of South African fast bowling surely lies in the hands of this tearaway from the Far North bushveld.

DALE WILLEM STEYN was born in the mining town of Phalaborwa on 27 June 1983, went to Merensky High School and played for Northern Province Schools in 2000 and 2001. From this unfashionable beginning, he was recruited by the Northerns Academy and played his first game for the union against Western Province in October 2003.

The fact that Steyn was not contracted when franchises were introduced the next season suggests Northerns did not expect so much so soon from the likeable lad. But a couple of Steyn's best attributes are courage and a determination to stick things out for the long haul.

Even considering the sheer pace of the man and the lethal away shape he can generate, his progress in the last 12 months has been extraordinarily rapid and he will surely soon be a fixture in the South African Test team.

Ken Borland

FIVE MUTUAL & FEDERAL CRICKET ANNUAL CRICKETERS OF THE YEAR

As at 10 May 2006

HASHIM MAHOMED AMLA (Born 31 March 1983, Durban)

Teams: KwaZulu-Natal, Dolphins and South Africa

Season	Teams	M	Inns	NO	Runs	HS	Avg	100	50	Ct	St	Balls	Runs	Wkts	Avg	RpO	BB	5I	10M
1999/00	KZN	1	1	0	1	1	1.00	0	0	0	0	0	0	0	-	-	-	0	0
2001/02	KZN/SAA/SAPres	8	12	2	516	103	51.60	1	5	7	0	18	15	1	15.00	5.00	1-10	0	0
2002/03	KZN/RestSA	7	13	1	463	108	38.58	1	3	1	0	0	0	0	-	-	-	0	0
2003/04	KZN	9	14	1	647	159	49.76	1	4	6	0	42	21	0	-	3.00	-	0	0
2004	SAA in Zim	2	3	0	92	74	30.66	0	1	6	0	12	20	0	-	10.00	-	0	0
2004/05	Dol/SA/SAA	14	22	2	1003	249	50.15	5	1	10	0	6	0	0	-	0.00	-	0	0
2004/05	SA in Ind	2	4	1	43	24	14.33	0	0	0	0	66	41	0	-	3.72	-	0	0
2005/06	SAA in SL	2	4	1	135	64*	45.00	0	1	6	0	0	0	0	-	-	-	0	0
2005/06	Dol/SA	13	22	3	1126	153	59.26	3	7	5	0	6	4	0	-	4.00	-	0	0
Totals																			
Tests		5	9	0	295	149	32.77	1	1	3	0	6	4	0	-	4.00	-	0	0
SuperSport Series		38	64	6	2823	249	48.67	7	16	21	0	48	21	0		2.62	-	0	0
All First-class		58	95	11	4026	249	47.92	11	22	41	0	150	101	1	101.00	4.04	1-10	0	0
All Limited Overs		31	31	2	661	59*	22.79	0	4	13	0	16	28	0	-	10.50	-	0	

MARK VERDON BOUCHER (Born 3 December 1976, East London)

Teams: Border, Warriors and South Africa

Season	Teams	M	Inns	NO	Runs	HS	Avg	100	50	Ct	St	Balls	Runs	Wkts	Avg	RpO	BB	5I	10M
1995/96	Bdr/BdrB	5	7	1	123	47	20.50	0	0	6	2	18	20	0	-	6.66	-	0	0
1996/97	Bdr	9	17	5	566	71	47.16	0	5	33	3	0	0	0	-	-	-	0	0
1997/98	SA in Pak	1	1	0	6	6	6.00	0	0	0	0	0	0	0	-	-	-	0	0
1997/98	Bdr/SA	8	13	0	393	80	30.23	0	4	42	3	0	0	0	-	-	-	0	0
1997/98	SA in Aus	1	1	0	55	55	55.00	0	1	0	0	0	0	0	-	-	-	0	0

Season	Teams	M	Inns	NO	Runs	HS	Avg	100	50	Ct	St	Balls	Runs	Wkts	Avg	RpO	BB	5I	10M
1998	SA in Eng	11	10	1	211	46	23.44	0	0	43	1	0	0	0	-	-	-	0	0
1998/99	Bdr/SA	10	18	3	535	100*	35.66	2	2	33	0	0	0	0	-	-	-	0	0
1998/99	SA in NZ	4	2	0	41	33	20.50	0	0	11	0	0	0	0	-	-	-	0	0
1999/00	Bdr/SA	10	14	2	598	112	49.83	2	3	37	0	0	0	0	-	-	-	0	0
1999/00	SA in Zim	1	1	0	125	125	125.00	1	0	4	0	0	0	0	-	-	-	0	0
1999/00	SA in Ind	3	5	3	85	33*	42.50	0	0	14	0	0	0	0	-	-	-	0	0
2000	SA in SL	3	6	0	111	60	18.50	0	1	6	1	0	0	0	-	-	-	0	0
2000/01	Bdr/SA	8	11	3	341	92	42.62	0	2	32	2	0	0	0	-	-	-	0	0
2000/01	SA in WI	7	12	0	238	56	19.83	0	2	23	1	0	0	0	-	-	-	0	0
2001/02	SA in Zim	2	1	0	14	14	14.00	0	0	2	1	0	0	0	-	-	-	0	0
2001/02	Bdr/SA	7	11	2	238	68*	26.44	0	1	32	1	0	0	0	-	-	-	0	0
2001/02	SA in Aus	5	9	1	372	134	46.50	1	1	10	0	0	0	0	-	-	-	0	0
2002/03	Bdr/SA	7	8	3	322	112	64.40	1	2	29	2	0	0	0	-	-	-	0	0
2002/03	SA in Ban	2	1	0	71	71	71.00	0	1	9	2	0	0	0	-	-	-	0	0
2003	SA in Eng	8	11	1	360	89	36.00	0	3	21	1	0	0	0	-	-	-	0	0
2003/04	SA in Pak	2	4	0	114	72	28.50	0	1	3	1	0	0	0	-	-	-	0	0
2003/04	SA	4	5	1	192	122*	48.00	1	0	13	0	0	0	0	-	-	-	0	0
2003/04	SA in NZ	4	6	0	101	58	16.83	0	1	10	1	0	0	0	-	-	-	0	0
2004	SA in SL	2	3	1	67	51	33.50	0	1	6	2	0	0	0	-	-	-	0	0
2004/05	War/SA/SAA	11	18	2	578	65	36.12	0	4	41	2	0	0	0	-	-	-	0	0
2004/05	SA in WI	4	5	2	112	41	37.33	0	0	12	0	8	6	1	6.00	4.50	1-6	0	0
2005/06	SA/Wor in Aus	5	10	1	158	62	17.55	0	1	16	0	0	0	0	-	-	-	0	0
2005/06	SA	6	11	1	253	63	25.30	0	2	23	0	0	0	0	-	-	-	0	0
Totals																			
Tests		94	132	17	3396	125	29.53	4	21	346	14	8	6	1	6.00	4.50	1-6	0	0
SuperSport Series		29	55	10	1901	112	42.24	3	11	110	8	0	0	0	-	-	-	0	0
All First-class		150	221	33	6380	134	33.93	8	38	511	26	26	26	1	26.00	6.00	1-6	0	0
Limited Overs Internationals		217	158	39	3175	76	26.68	0	19	303	17	0	0	0	-	-	-	0	
All Limited Overs		275	214	49	4393	98	26.62	0	27	367	25	0	0	0	-	-	-	0	

MAKHAYA NTINI (Born 6 July 1977, Mdingi)

Teams: Border, Warriors, Warwickshire and South Africa

Season	Teams	M	Inns	NO	Runs	HS	Avg	100	50	Ct	St	Balls	Runs	Wkts	Avg	RpO	BB	5I	10M
1995/96	Bdr	8	13	2	69	19*	6.27	0	0	0	0	1140	630	17	37.05	3.31	3-49	0	0
1996/97	Bdr	9	9	2	16	5	2.28	0	0	0	0	1333	847	25	33.88	3.81	6-49	1	0
1997/98	Bdr/SA	6	7	5	46	22	23.00	0	0	0	0	854	528	16	33.00	3.70	3-45	0	0
1997/98	SA in Aus	1	0	0	0	-	-	0	0	0	0	162	108	2	54.00	4.00	2-24	0	0
1998	SA in Eng	7	2	1	4	4*	4.00	0	0	2	0	1107	578	19	30.42	3.13	4-72	0	0
1998/99	Bdr/SAA	8	11	5	19	9	3.16	0	0	6	0	1031	630	18	35.00	3.66	3-51	0	0
1999/00	Bdr/BdrEP	8	13	6	89	34*	12.71	0	0	1	0	1120	582	22	26.45	3.11	4-55	0	0
2000	SA in SL	1	2	0	8	8	4.00	0	0	0	0	114	73	1	73.00	3.84	1-73	0	0
2000/01	Bdr/SA	8	5	3	27	10	13.50	0	0	3	0	1610	688	36	19.11	2.56	6-59	2	0
2000/01	SA in WI	5	6	2	47	24*	11.75	0	0	2	0	671	372	11	33.81	3.32	4-31	0	0
2001/02	SA in Zim	2	0	0	0	-	-	0	0	1	0	384	187	1	187.00	2.92	1-48	0	0
2001/02	Bdr/SA	8	12	2	148	34*	14.80	0	0	1	0	1641	987	28	35.25	3.60	6-37	1	0
2001/02	SA in Aus	2	3	0	13	9	4.33	0	0	1	0	354	185	2	92.50	3.13	2-108	0	0
2002/03	Bdr/SA	7	4	2	10	8	5.00	0	0	3	0	1552	739	42	17.59	2.85	5-19	1	0
2002/03	SA in Ban	2	1	1	0	0*	-	0	0	1	0	336	151	7	21.57	2.69	3-32	0	0
2003	SA in Eng	6	7	3	64	32*	16.00	0	0	0	0	1334	910	24	37.91	4.09	5-75	2	1
2003/04	SA in Pak	2	3	2	24	16*	24.00	0	0	0	0	498	221	4	55.25	2.66	2-45	0	0
2003/04	SA	4	3	1	40	22*	20.00	0	0	1	0	1121	620	29	21.37	3.31	5-49	3	0
2003/04	SA in NZ	3	4	0	31	21	7.75	0	0	0	0	690	343	7	49.00	2.98	3-110	0	0
2004	SA in SL	2	3	0	10	10	3.33	0	0	2	0	372	207	3	69.00	3.33	2-108	0	0
2004/05	War/SA	10	16	3	164	26	12.61	0	0	3	0	2429	1151	47	24.48	2.84	5-71	1	0
2004/05	SA in Ind	3	2	0	12	12	6.00	0	0	0	0	642	311	9	34.55	2.90	4-112	0	0
2004/05	SA in WI	4	3	0	28	16	9.33	0	0	2	0	791	437	17	25.70	3.31	7-37	2	1
2005	Warwickshire	6	8	1	74	27*	10.57	0	0	1	0	1153	721	22	32.77	3.75	5-69	1	0
2005/06	SA in Aus	3	5	1	24	12	6.00	0	0	0	0	633	330	10	33.00	3.12	5-64	1	0
2005/06	SA	6	10	3	59	17*	8.42	0	0	2	0	1391	836	39	21.43	3.60	6-100	4	2
Totals																			
Tests		67	74	21	538	32*	10.15	0	0	18	0	14241	7557	269	28.09	3.18	7-37	14	4
SuperSport Series		40	55	19	331	34*	9.19	0	0	10	0	6708	3629	124	29.26	3.24	6-37	4	0
All First-class		131	152	45	1026	34*	9.58	0	0	32	0	24463	13372	458	29.19	3.27	7-37	19	4
Limited Overs Internationals		129	31	17	147	42*	10.50	0	0	25	0	6462	4772	206	23.16	4.43	6-22	3	
All Limited Overs		184	51	23	202	42*	7.21	0	0	35	0	8844	6483	270	24.01	4.39	6-22	4	

ASHWELL GAVIN PRINCE (Born 28 May 1977, Port Elizabeth)
Teams: Eastern Province, Western Province, Western Province Boland and South Africa

Season	Teams	M	Inns	NO	Runs	HS	Avg	100	50	Ct	St	Balls	Runs	Wkts	Avg	RpO	BB	5I	10M
1995/96	EP/EPB	5	7	0	165	50	23.57	0	1	1	0	0	0	0	-	-	-	0	0
1996/97	EP/EPB	6	10	1	333	125*	37.00	1	2	5	0	0	0	0	-	-	-	0	0
1997/98	WP/EPB/SAA	7	11	0	447	116	40.63	1	2	4	0	0	0	0	-	-	-	0	0
1998/99	SAA in SL	2	2	0	17	12	8.50	0	0	3	0	0	0	0	-	-	-	0	0
1998/99	WP/SAA	10	17	1	541	133	33.81	1	3	6	0	0	0	0	-	-	-	0	0
1999/00	WP/BolWP/SAA/SAIn	11	17	1	623	117	38.93	1	5	6	0	6	3	0	-	3.00	-	0	0
2000/01	SAA in WI	4	5	0	129	69	25.80	0	1	1	0	0	0	0	-	-	-	0	0
2000/01	WP	8	14	4	539	120*	53.90	1	2	7	0	0	0	0	-	-	-	0	0
2001/02	SA/SAA	4	7	0	247	92	35.28	0	1	4	0	0	0	0	-	-	-	0	0
2002/03	SAA in Aus	2	3	0	52	32	17.33	0	0	1	0	0	0	0	-	-	-	0	0
2002/03	WP/SA/SAA	11	13	2	594	143	54.00	2	3	9	0	0	0	0	-	-	-	0	0
2003/04	WP/SAA	9	14	4	646	182*	64.60	2	3	4	0	0	0	0	-	-	-	0	0
2004	SAA in Zim	2	4	1	49	39*	16.33	0	0	2	0	0	0	0	-	-	-	0	0
2004/05	WPBol/SA/SAA	14	20	2	859	184	47.72	3	3	6	0	102	59	1	59.00	3.47	1-34	0	0
2004/05	SA in WI	3	3	0	199	131	66.33	1	0	3	0	54	22	0	-	2.44	-	0	0
2005/06	SA in Aus	4	8	0	258	119	32.25	1	0	2	0	0	0	0	-	-	-	0	0
2005/06	SA	6	11	2	361	108*	40.11	1	1	2	0	12	2	1	2.00	1.00	1-2	0	0
Totals																			
Tests		21	32	3	1089	139*	37.55	4	1	9	0	66	24	1	24.00	2.18	1-2	0	0
SuperSport Series		47	78	10	3000	184	44.11	7	18	29	0	54	28	0		3.11	-	0	0
All First-class		108	166	18	6059	184	40.93	15	27	66	0	174	86	2	43.00	2.96	1-2	0	0
Limited Overs Internationals		37	33	11	870	89*	39.54	0	3	20	0	0	0	0	-	-	-	0	
All Limited Overs		150	136	31	3369	89*	32.08	0	19	71	0	79	83	0	-	6.30	-	0	

DALE WILLEM STEYN (Born 27 June 1983, Phalaborwa)
Teams: Northerns, Titans, Essex and South Africa

Season	Teams	M	Inns	NO	Runs	HS	Avg	100	50	Ct	St	Balls	Runs	Wkts	Avg	RpO	BB	5I	10M
2003/04	Nor	2	2	1	10	10*	10.00	0	0	1	0	264	176	3	58.66	4.00	2-43	0	0
2004/05	Ttn/SA	10	13	5	63	11*	7.87	0	0	3	0	2031	1127	36	31.30	3.32	5-30	1	0
2005	Essex	6	7	2	94	82	18.80	0	1	2	0	1196	838	14	59.85	4.20	3-69	0	0
2005/06	SAA in SL	1	2	0	0	0	0.00	0	0	0	0	108	76	2	38.00	4.22	1-37	0	0
2005/06	Ttn/Nor/SA	13	16	4	140	34	11.66	0	0	1	0	2767	1425	69	20.65	3.09	5-27	4	1
Totals																			
Tests		6	9	4	60	13	12.00	0	0	2	0	1260	832	24	34.66	3.96	5-47	1	0
SuperSport Series		18	21	5	152	34	9.50	0	0	3	0	3592	1780	80	22.25	2.97	5-27	4	1
All First-class		32	40	12	307	82	10.96	0	1	7	0	6366	3642	124	29.37	3.43	5-27	5	1
Limited Overs Internationals		4	2	0	4	3	2.00	0	0	0	0	109	132	3	44.00	7.26	1-2	0	
All Limited Overs		27	8	3	13	6*	2.60	0	0	3	0	1186	900	36	25.00	4.55	5-20	1	

MUTUAL & FEDERAL SA CRICKET ANNUAL CRICKETERS OF THE YEAR

The tradition of honouring five South African Cricketers of the Year was established in the first edition of the South African Cricket Annual in 1952 by the first Editor, Geoffrey A Chettle, who marked the occasion by naming five "stalwarts who have recently left the international field", Eric and Athol Rowan, Dudley Nourse, Norman "Tufty" Mann and Geoff Chubb. Initially the honour was bestowed once only, as remains the case with the Wisden Cricketers' Almanack, but Special Tributes were introduced to recognise long-serving and exceptional performers Graeme Pollock and Mike Procter in 1977 before a system evolved whereby the five outstanding players of the season were chosen, whether or not they had received the award previously. In 2002 it was decided to restrict the award to players who played for South African-based teams.

Ackerman HM (WP)	1971
Adams PR (WP)	2002
Adcock NAT (Tvl)	1954
Alabaster JC (New Zealand)	1962
Amla HM (Dol)	2006
Armitage RLS (EP)	1982
Azharuddin M (India)	1997
Bacher A (Tvl)	1961
Barlow EJ (Tvl)	1962
and Special Tribute (WP)	1981
Barnard LJ (N Tvl)	
Special Tribute	1990
Barrington KF (England)	1965
Bath BF (Tvl)	1974
Benaud R (Australia)	1958
Benkenstein DM (Ntl)	1997
Bestall D (Ntl)	1975
Bezuidenhout SJ (EP)	1973
Biggs AL (EP)	1969
Bland KC (Rho)	1962
Boje N (FS)	2001
Bosch T (N Tvl)	1991
Botten JT (NE Tvl)	1959
Boucher MV (Bdr)	1998/2000/06
Brickett DJ (EP)	1980
Bruyns A (WP)	1972
Burke JW (Australia)	1958
Burke SF (NE Tvl)	1964
Callaghan DJ (EP)	1988
Carlstein PR (Tvl)	1963
Cheetham JE (WP)	1953
Chevalier GA (WP)	1970
Chubb GWA (Tvl)	1952
Clarke ST (W Indians/Tvl)	1984/85
Clift PB (Rho)	1979
Close DB (D Robins)	1974
Cole JM (Ntl)	1961
Compton DCS (England)	1957
Connolly AN (Australia)	1970
Cook SJ (Tvl)	1981/83
Cooper KR (Ntl)	1981
Craig ID (Australia)	1958
Cronje WJ (OFS)	1992/95/98
Cullinan DJ (WP/Bdr/Gau)	1989/96/99
Davidson AK (Australia)	1958
Davison BF (Rho)	1973
Dawson AC (WP)	2004
Day NT (Tvl/N Tvl)	1981/85
De Vaal PD (Tvl)	1971
De Villiers AB (Ttn)	2005
De Villiers PS (N Tvl)	1989/95
Dick AE (New Zealand)	1962
Dippenaar HH (Eag)	2005
Dodds PM (Ntl)	1963
Doherty MJD (GW)	1972
Donald AA (OFS)	1993/96/97/98
Drakes VC (Bdr)	2000
Dumbrill R (Ntl)	1965
Du Preez JH (Rho)	1967
Du Preez VF (N Tvl)	1982
Dyer DD (Ntl)	1974
Elworthy S (Nor)	2002
Endean WR (Tvl)	1953
Estwick RO (Tvl)	1988
Farrer WS (Bdr)	1961
Fellows-Smith JP (Tvl)	1960
Ferrandi JH (WP)	1959
Ferreira AM (N Tvl)	1978
Fletcher DAG (Rho)	1975
Fotheringham HR (Ntl/Tvl)	1977/83
and Special Tribute (Ntl)	1990

FIVE CRICKETERS OF THE YEAR

Foulkes I (Bdr)	1978
Fuller ERH (WP)	1956
Funston KJ (Tvl)	1957
Gamsy D (Ntl)	1969
Gatting MW (English XI)	1990
Gibbs HH (WP)	1999/2003/04
Gibson OD (Bdr)	1993
Gleeson JW (Australia)	1970
Goddard TL (Ntl)	1955
Greig AW (EP)	1972
Greve VS (Tvl)	1973
Griffin GM (Ntl)	1960
Gripper RA (Rho)	1968
Hall AJ (Eas)	2002
Hanley RW (EP/Tvl)	1975/84
Haysman MD (Australians)	1987
Hayward M (EP)	2000
Heine PS (Tvl)	1955
Henry O (OFS)	1993
and Special Tribute (Bol)	1986
Henwood PP (Ntl)	1974
Heron JG (Rho)	1976
Hobson DL (WP)	1975
Hudson AC (Ntl)	1992
Innes GAS (WP)	1959
Irvine BL (Ntl)	1968
Jack SD (Tvl)	1991
Jackman RD (Rho)	1973
Jefferies ST (WP)	1982
Jennings RV (Tvl)	1980
and Special Tribute	1985
Kallicharran AI (W Indians/Tvl)	1983
Kallis JH (WP/WP Bol)	1999/2000/04/05
Kaschula RH (Rho)	1972
Keith HJ (Ntl)	1955
Kirsten G (WP)	1994/95/96
Kirsten PN (WP)	1977/84
Klusener L (Ntl)	1997/99
Kourie AJ (Tvl)	1980
and Special Tribute	1987
Kuiper AP (WP)	1982/84/90
Lamb AJ (WP/OFS)	1980/88
and Special Tribute (WP)	1982
Lance HR (Tvl)	1965
Lara BC (West Indies)	1993
Lawrence GB (Rho)	1960
Le Roux FJ (N Tvl)	1979
Le Roux GS (WP)	1978/86/87
Le Roux RA (OFS)	1979
Lewis DJ (Rho)	1956
Liddle JR (WP)	1956
Lillee DK (Int Wanderers)	1976
Lindsay DT (NE Tvl)	1964
Macaulay MJ (OFS)	1964
and Special Tribute (EP)	1978
Mackay KD (Australia)	1958
Mackay-Coghill D (Tvl)	1969
Maguire JN (EP)	1990
Maile JBR (WP)	1960
Mann NBF (EP)	1952
Mansell PNF (Rho)	1955
Marshall MD (Ntl)	1994/95
Matthews CR (WP)	1991
May PBH (England)	1957
McCurdy RJ (EP)	1990
McEwan KS (WP/EP)	1983/86/87/89
and Special Tribute (EP)	1990
McGlew DJ (Ntl)	1953
McKenzie GD (Australia)	1967
McKenzie KA (Tvl)	1974/86
McKenzie ND (Nor)	2001
McKinnon AH (EP)	1959
McLean RA (Ntl)	1955
McMillan BM (WP)	1991/96
Morby-Smith L (WP)	1964
Morris RET (WP)	1978
Motz RC (New Zealand)	1962
Murray ARA (EP)	1956
Muzzell PJ (Bdr)	1969
Muzzell RK (WP)	1968
Neilson DR (Tvl)	1977
and Special Tribute	1981
Nel A (Eas/Ttn)	2004/05
Ngam M (EP)	2001
Nourse AD (Ntl)	1952
Ntini M (Bdr/War)	2001/03/04/05/06
O'Linn S (Tvl)	1960
Ontong RC (N Tvl)	
Special Tribute	1990
Page HA (Tvl)	1985
Partridge JT (Rho)	1963
Pfuhl GP (WP)	1971
and Special Tribute	1980

FIVE CRICKETERS OF THE YEAR

Pienaar RF (WP/Tvl)	1983/90
Pithey AJ (Rho)	1959
Pollock PM (EP)	1963
Pollock RG (EP/Tvl)	1961/84
and Special Tribute (EP/Tvl)	1977/87
Pollock SM (Ntl)	1996/98/2001/03
Pressdee JS (NE Tvl)	1966
Prince AG (Cob)	2006
Pringle MW (WP)	1992
Procter MJ (Ntl)	1967
and Special Tribute	1977
Rabone GO (New Zealand)	1954
Rackemann CG (Australians)	1986
Reid JR (New Zealand)	1954
Rhodes JN (Ntl)	1992/99
Rice CEB (Tvl)	1971/85/86/88
Richards BA (Ntl)	1968
and Special Tribute	1984
Richardson C (OFS)	1961
Richardson DJ (EP)	1995
Rindel MJR (N Tvl)	1989
Roberts B (Tvl)	1988
Robertson SD (Rho)	1972
Rosendorff N (OFS)	1969
Rowan AMB (Tvl)	1952
Rowan EAB (Tvl)	1952
Rowe LG (W Indians)	1984
Rudolph JA (Nor)	2003
Rushmere MW (EP)	1988
Rutherford KR (Gau)	2000
Schonegevel DJ (GW)	1968
Seeff L (WP)	1981
Shaw TG (EP)	1994
Short AM (Ntl)	1970
Simons EO (N Tvl/WP)	1985/89
Simpson RB (Australia)	1967
Smith AJS (Ntl)	1976
Smith GC (WP)	2002/03
Smith MJK (England)	1965
Smith SB (Australians)	1987
Smith VI (Ntl)	1956
Statham JB (England)	1957
Steyn DW (Ttn)	2006
Strydom S (OFS)	1966
Strydom WT (OFS)	1977
Swart PD (WP)	1975
Symcox PL (Ntl)	1998
Tayfield HJ (Ntl)	1953
Taylor MD (Australians)	1986
Titmus FJ (England)	1965
Trimborn PHJ (Ntl)	1967
Trotman EN (Bdr)	1989
Ullyett RB (Rho)	1964
Van der Bijl VAP (Ntl)	1971
and Special Tribute	1979
Van der Merwe PL (WP)	1963
Van Jaarsveld M (Nor)	2002
Van Ryneveld CB (WP)	1964
Versfeld BJ (Ntl)	1966
Waddington JE (GW)	1953
Waite JHB (Tvl)	1954
Waqar Younis (Pakistan)	1993
Wardle JH (England)	1957
Warne SK (Australia)	1994
Watson GLG (Tvl)	1970
Watson WK (EP)	1979
Waugh SR (Australia)	1994/97
Wessels KC (Australians/EP)	1987/92
White RC (Tvl)	1966
Whitfield BJ (Ntl)	1987
Wilkins CP (Bdr)	1966
Wilmot AL (EP)	1973
and Special Tribute	1980
Yachad M (N Tvl)	1985/91

SOUTH AFRICANS HONOURED BY WISDEN CRICKETERS' ALMANACK

Forty South Africans have been named as a Cricketer of the Year by Wisden. Those honoured since 1990 are:

Cook SJ	1990
Donald AA	1992
Kirsten G	2004
Klusener L	2000
Pietersen KP	2006
Pollock SM	2003
Rhodes JN	1999
Smith GC	2004
Smith RA	1990
Wessels KC	1995

TOP OF THE HEAP . . . Makhaya Ntini holds the Mutual & Federal SA Cricketer of the Year trophy for the second successive year *Picture: LEE WARREN, Touchline Photo*

NTINI TAKES TOP AWARD AGAIN

Makhaya Ntini was named the Mutual & Federal South African Cricketer of the Year for the second successive year at the third annual cricket awards banquet held at Kyalami, north of Johannesburg, on 18 May 2006. Ntini also won the Castle Test Cricketer of the Year award, while Shaun Pollock was named Standard Bank One-day International Cricketer of the Year and was honoured by his fellow players as the SA Players' Player of the Year.

Ntini was nominated in all five categories for established international players after an outstanding season in which he climbed to second in the world Test bowling rankings.

Johan van der Wath, who burst onto the international scene during the Australian tour, was named SA Newcomer of the Year, while AB de Villiers was voted SuperSport Fans' Cricketer of the Year.

The panel of Judges was chaired by Cricket South Africa's General Manager: Professional Cricket, Vintcent van der Bijl. Also on the panel were South Africa's Player of the Century Graeme Pollock, former national selector Peter Bacela, former SA fast bowler and CSA Commercial and Communications Manager, Steve Elworthy and commentator and journalist Aslam Khota.

South African Under-19 captain Dean Elgar concluded his season by being named the Under-19 Coca-Cola Cricketer of the Year.

Women's cricket teenage star, Johmari Logtenberg, was named Women's Cricketer of the Year, while Chris Liebenberg and Kevin Venter were named Blind Cricketer and Deaf Cricketer of the Year respectively. Liebenberg also received the coveted Khaya Majola Amateur Cricket Award, which recognises achievements both on and off the field.

MUTUAL & FEDERAL SOUTH AFRICAN CRICKET AWARDS

2006 MUTUAL & FEDERAL SA CRICKET AWARDS WINNERS

AMATEUR AWARDS

Standard Bank Under-13 Player of the Tournament: Keaton Jennings (Gauteng)
PG Bison Under-15 Player of the Tournament: Nicolas Loizides (WP)
Under-17 Player of the Tournament: Rilee Rossouw (Free State)
Coca-Cola Under-19 Cricketer of the Year: Dean Elgar (Free State)
Student Cricketer of the Year: Esmund van Wyk (UWC)
Club Championships Player of the Tournament: Justin Kreusch (Border)
Country Districts Cricketer of the Year: Pieter Ferreira (Gauteng)
Blind Cricketer of the Year: Chris Liebenberg (Boland)
Deaf Cricketer of the Year: Kevin Venter (Gauteng)
Intellectually Impaired Cricketer of the Year: Keegan Chetty (KZN)
SAA Provincial Associates Cricketer of the Year: Ross McMillan (KZN Inland)
SAA Provincial Amateur Cricketer of the Year: Pierre Joubert (Northerns)
Women's Cricketer of the Year: Johmari Logtenberg (KZN)
Khaya Majola Amateur Cricket Award: Chris Liebenberg (Boland)
Bakers Administrator of the Year: Clinton Saddler (EP)

PROFESSIONAL AWARDS

Operations Awards
Mutual & Federal Coach of the Year: Phil Russell (Nashua Dolphins)
Mutual & Federal Groundsman of the Year: Chris Scott (Liberty Life Wanderers)
Mutual & Federal Scorers Association of the Year: Gauteng
Mutual & Federal Umpire of the Year: Marais Erasmus

Domestic Awards
Standard Bank Cup Cricketer of the Year: Stephen Cook (Highveld Lions)
Standard Bank Pro20 Cricketer of the Year: Roger Telemachus (Gestetner Eagles)
SuperSport Series Cricketer of the Year: Hashim Amla (Nashua Dolphins)
Domestic Newcomer of the Year: Saidi Mhlongo (Nashua Dolphins)
Domestic Players' Player of the Year: Garnett Kruger (Highveld Lions)

SA International Awards
Standard Bank ODI Cricketer of the Year: Shaun Pollock
Castle Test Cricketer of the Year: Makhaya Ntini
SA Newcomer of the Year: Johan van der Wath
SA Players' Player of the Year: Shaun Pollock
SuperSport Fans' Cricketer of the Year: AB de Villiers
Mutual & Federal SA Cricketer of the Year: Makhaya Ntini

THE GREATEST ONE-DAY GAME

Cricket was taken into uncharted waters on Sunday, March 12, 2006, in the most remarkable one-day international match yet played. South Africa's successful overhauling of Australia's world record total of 434-4 enthralled and invigorated the nation.

Colin Bryden sat down with **Graeme Smith, Herschelle Gibbs** and **Mark Boucher** to find out what it was like at the heart of the drama.

After Australia's Ricky Ponting won the toss, Smith said on television he was happy to chase a target at the Wanderers because it was a difficult ground for a fielding side to defend. Initially the innings proceeded at a relatively normal rate before Ponting led an explosion of scoring.

Smith: I said (to the team) that if we could keep them to between 260 and 300 we would have done well. It was a very good wicket and the outfield was going to be very quick. I think it (the pitch) had a little bit of juice in the first six or seven overs. The ball was doing a little bit and I think games that had gone before made them a little circumspect. Gilchrist's wicket (for 55 with the total on 97) was crucial. He was just starting to get going. If he had stayed in they might have been chasing 500.

Boucher: The shots that Ricky Ponting was hitting weren't just clearing the boundary, they were going quite a way over. Taking the short boundary and the good deck into consideration, for a guy to get 164 off 100-odd balls, that's spectacular. It was unfortunate for us, but good to watch from behind (the stumps) because some of the shots he hit were unbelievable.

We could have been maybe a bit more stingy with the runs, maybe 20 or 30 less, but the guys never really just gave it to them. We still fielded pretty well and the guys were diving around in the field. The wicket was the winner of the day.

Smith: All through (the Australian innings), we did reasonably well but to go for 130 runs in our last ten overs . . . I don't think we gave up but we could have done better. It's difficult to describe what it feels like when a team goes past 400. Balls are disappearing all over the place and it's difficult to have that same intensity as when it's 50 for four and you're bowling and fielding well.

There were only 15 minutes between innings.

Smith: We had a little chat in the dressing room and said 'it's a freaky game, let's forget about the outcome, let's concentrate on the moment, let's try and win the little situations.' If you go out there and concentrate on scoring 400 you will blow your mind. We set a target of 185 in 25 overs, which at the time seemed massive. I remember looking at Hersch across the room and we had a little giggle.

Gibbs: I had the same feeling as in the 1999 World Cup when I got a hundred against Australia. You wake up and it's like someone telling you you're going to get a hundred. Graeme hit those two fours off Brett Lee in the third over and then I hit three fours off (Nathan) Bracken. I didn't want him to settle into a length like he had in the other four games. I just did it to him and one thing led to another.

When we got to about 20 overs I had a good sense about the whole thing. Graeme kept saying, 'if it's in your area go for it, otherwise just look for singles.' But singles weren't going to help at that stage.

UNFORGETTABLE . . . the South African team celebrate after achieving an against-the-odds victory in a one-day international at the Wanderers Stadium which clinched the series and rewrote the record books *Picture: GETTY IMAGES/TOUCHLINE PHOTO*

Smith: When I walked out to bat, with just a 15-minute changeover, I was maybe still feeling a little dejected but you focus on what you have to do and switch on to batting mode. The key thing was to get momentum going and we got it when I got those two fours off Brett and Herschelle hit those three fours. We started building up from there. It's the same as Australia's batting. They're a momentum side. When they get going they just go and that's why they are capable of getting big scores. Herschelle and I got going and we rode with it.

Between overs, Smith and Gibbs spoke briefly.

Smith: It was just about managing it. There were times when Herschelle would go six, four and I would remind him we've got our (target of) eight or nine an over so make sure you get the two ones now. I would know if we had only got a few ones I'd have to get a boundary in the over. There was a little talking like that but it was more playing a lot on instinct. At one stage we both looked up at the scoreboard and we said, 'Gee, we still need 310' and we had been going berserk for ten overs.

That was when we made a conscious decision to forget about the total and just play. We were beating our (over-by-over) target by about 40 runs or something. We were both in such a good zone. We had got the momentum shift and certainly for me I just hit my zone, everything was just going to go for four or six.

Gibbs: It was one of those days where everything you tried came off. But you've still got to be able to play good shots irrespective of the target. All our risks were calculated. We were very still when we hit the ball and that helped. We weren't going to allow the bowlers to settle into any line or length and we kept putting them under pressure.

Smith: You know the series is two-all, you've played some good cricket and yes, the target is massive and yes, you've got to play with freedom to chase 434 and you've got to allow yourself that freedom but I think in the back of our minds we all knew that if we conceded 434 and lost we would get slated to smithereens.

The pressure is to allow yourself to play your shots. Often you're playing under pressure and you know you have to be a bit more circumspect. Chasing 434 it's almost the other way. You've got to allow yourself to play some extraordinary shots, back yourself to go over the top or even to take on long-on at times.

Smith was out, for 90 off 55 balls, with the total on 190 in the 23rd over. Gibbs hit the next ball for six.

Gibbs: It wasn't meant to go for six. It was a bottom edge . . .

Smith: Top edge, surely.

Gibbs: No, it was a bottom edge. I swept, it came off the bottom of my bat. It went for six. It was one of those days.

Smith: The key with Herschelle was that every time we took drinks out to him we didn't want to give him instructions. The way he was going, suddenly to give him a rule was the wrong way to go.

At one stage, it seemed Gibbs would score the first double century in one-day internationals.

Gibbs: I just went with the momentum. Yes, I probably could have got 200 but it was irrelevant at that stage. If you get out, you get out. The main thing is you are trying to score nine, ten runs an over consistently.

Smith: Nella (Andre Nel) and Polly (Shaun Pollock) were on the drinks at that stage and they were asking what message I wanted to give him. I said, just give him a high five and tell him to keep going. After I got out, Herschelle was going to get us to the point where we could knock ones and get six or seven an over and hold ourselves for the last ten (overs) and then have another burst.

Gibbs was out for 175 with the total on 299 for four in the 32nd over. Boucher went out to bat with 136 needed off 109 balls.

Boucher: Because Herschelle and the guys had batted so well up front it was basically like a normal one-day game for me. You know at the Wanderers you are going to be able to hit a few out of the ground. So add 30 or so for those hits, it's pretty much a run a ball from there on in. I never actually looked at the target, just the balls left and the runs needed.

Smith: When Jacques (Kallis) and (Mark) Boucher were at the wicket, it was a crucial period. We didn't get sixes and sevens (runs an over) but that was what we looking to get without too many risks. We wanted wickets in hand at the end. It didn't actually work and we changed our tune and said to the guys, 'look, we've got so close now, just go and play.'

Boucher: We had lost a couple of wickets quickly so Jacques and I wanted to get a partnership going. We knew we could always step it up a little if we needed. The scoring got a little slower but we never panicked. The first time we thought it was maybe getting a little out of hand was when there were 50-odd required in 20-odd balls. But we always knew we still had guys who could hit the balls out of the ground.

Gibbs: Johan van der Wath played a great little innings to get momentum back in our favour. And Roger (Telemachus) too. Between them they scored about 50 runs in the space of about three or four overs.

Smith: When Boom (Van der Wath) went out to bat, I said to him, 'buddy, just go and play. Back yourself and put all rules aside. Go and hit the ball.' All the time I knew Bouchy being there at the end was crucial because of his experience. At that stage we were about 30 runs behind the balls left so we needed someone to hit it out of the ground. It was going to take one or two overs to get us ahead again and Boom gave us that.

Mark is such a good finisher and he reads the game so well. He's got good intensity at the wicket and he's such a good communicator with the people who are with him. Experience definitely comes through.

Boucher: I was a batter who was in so I knew that if I could stay to the end I could maybe do a finishing-off job with the guys at the other end taking the risks. The guys all played their part and it worked perfectly.

Smith: When Hally (Andrew Hall) went out, I said to him, 'it's going to be awfully difficult to win this game if we get nine down.' He did awesomely well to get us to the position he did. At that stage, the last ten balls, I couldn't watch. I was in the back room with the video analyst and (assistant coach) Vinnie Barnes and they were saying, 'he's running in to bowl' and you know there's a delay on the TV and I would hear the crowd. I watched the whole game but I couldn't watch those last ten balls.

Gibbs: Hally went for glory.

Smith: It was so frustrating. Bouch hit the first ball of that last over sweet and we all thought, 'that's four' and it hit Brett Lee's foot. Then Hally played a superb shot and we were all on such a high. I was running around the dressing room, the okes were all screaming and there was

Makhaya (Ntini), in the back with his gloves on and getting ready. Then next ball Hally got out. Then it all was just quiet. There was such emotion.

Boucher: When I hit that drive and Brett Lee stopped it, I said to Hally, 'it's going to be one of those games again, with what could have been and what should have been.' But I never doubted Hally. He's a guy who comes to the fore in a pressure situation and he managed to hit a four off the next ball. We should have coasted in from there (with two runs needed off four balls). But then he got out.

I was thinking of the 1999 World Cup and the run-out in the last over. I went to Makhaya and I said, 'obviously you've got to get one but it's not panic stations. If you don't hit the ball through the field, don't run. Just watch me, if I run, then run, if not just dive back into your crease.' We still had three balls to go. When Makhaya played that shot to third man and we couldn't lose the game it was almost like a win. I thought, I've been in for a while, the field is in and if he bowls in my area it's game, set and match. The last thing I wanted to do was do something silly, like try to sneak one down to third man or walk across my stumps. I had to back myself to hit the ball.

Boucher hit the fifth ball of the final over for four and South Africa had won.

Smith: I heard them say the other night on Extra Cover that bowlers are becoming null and void. I don't think so. There are going to be games like that where batters are going to have to win games with big totals. But I think a game of such emotion, of such importance, with such big scores, such a rollercoaster, that's not going to happen again. Sides will get 400 but whether both teams get it, with such emotion, I don't think it will happen again.

Gibbs: For me it was my perfect innings. I'd love to think I could bat again like that just once more before I retire.

Smith: I don't think many people will experience that. I've had a few people say maybe I should have thanked the Australians (at the after-match presentation) but you just get so caught up in the emotion you don't actually think. You're still living the game in your head, with Makhaya facing the third last ball and needing one to get Boucher on strike. There was no way we were going to think clearly.

People don't understand where we were in that position. To think you must thank people, it's the last thing on your minds. You're coming to terms with the game and chasing 434. I don't think any of us could believe. A few of the boys were close to tears.

We had put so much work in, and taken so much flak since we got back from Australia, that moment was like a massive release for us and we just wanted to be together. All the work we had put in, we just wanted to share it. It was incredible.

Gibbs: It all happened so quickly. It was like everything happened at a hundred miles an hour.

Boucher: It was a release of a lot of emotion. Going to Australia, we worked really hard, we lost a lot of our guys with injuries, we took flak from the critics and the crowds. To come back and do it in front of a packed bullring after being so close in Durban (two nights earlier), it was very emotional. I watched the highlights, you see people in the crowd crying. That's something special, you know you've touched quite a few people.

Smith: You can see how happy the country is but I don't think people understand just what it was like. The ten minutes after that game, if you could just wrap that up and have that once more in your life, that would be just unbelievable.

A shorter version of this article first appeared in the Sunday Times on 19 March 2006. It is reprinted with permission.

RECORDS SET AT THE WANDERERS ON 12 MARCH 2006

Highest team total in an ODI: South Africa 438-9 beat the previous record of 434-4 by Australia in their innings, which in turn beat the previous record of 398-5 by Sri Lanka against Kenya at Kandy in 1995/96.
Note: Sri Lanka subsequently made 443-9 against the Netherlands at Amstelveen in July 2006.

Highest total in any List A limited overs game: South Africa 438-9 equalled the 438-5 by Surrey v Glamorgan at The Oval in 2002. (see note above).

Highest total batting 2nd and winning in an ODI: South Africa 438-9 beat 332-8 by New Zealand v Australia at Christchurch in 2005/06.

Highest total batting 2nd and winning in any List A limited overs game: South Africa 438-9 beat 392-2 by Karachi v Sialkot at Sialkot in 2003/04.

Highest match aggregate in an ODI: 872 runs (for 13 wickets) beat the 693 (for 15 wickets) in the match between Pakistan and India at Karachi in 2003/04.

Highest match aggregate in any List A limited overs game: 872 runs (for 13 wickets) beat the 867 (for 15 wickets) in the match between Surrey and Glamorgan at The Oval in 2002.

Most fours in an ODI: 87 beat the 79 in the match between Pakistan and India at Peshawar 2004/05.

Most sixes in an ODI: 26 beat the 21 in the matches between Sri Lanka and Kenya at Kandy in 1995/96 and New Zealand and Australia at Christchurch in 2005/06.

Most boundaries in an ODI: 113 (87 x 4, 26 x 6) beat the 87 (79 x 4, 8 x 6) in the match between Pakistan and India at Peshawar in 2005/06.

Fastest 150 in an ODI: 99 balls by Ricky Ponting beat the 109 balls by Lou Vincent for New Zealand v Zimbabwe at Bulawayo in 2005/06.

Most runs conceded in an innings in an ODI: Mick Lewis conceded 113 runs in his 10 overs which beat the 99 conceded by Muttiah Muralitharan for Sri Lanka v Australia at Sydney in 2005/06, the previous most in 10 overs and also surpassed the 105 conceded by Martin Snedden in 12 overs for New Zealand v England at The Oval in 1983.

Most runs conceded in an innings in any List A limited overs game: Mick Lewis' 113 beat the 108 conceded by Darren Thomas (in 9 overs) for Glamorgan v Surrey at The Oval in 2002.

Fastest ODI century for South Africa: 79 balls by Herschelle Gibbs beat his own record of 84 balls v Zimbabwe at Bulawayo in 2001/02.

Highest ODI score against Australia: Herschelle Gibbs' 175 beat the 167* by Robin Smith for England at Birmingham in 1993.

THE PASSING OF TWO LEGENDS

Peter Pollock

It's pretty well accepted that the greatest five years in South African cricket history was between 1965 and 1970. That period has virtually been accorded legendary status. For certain the 1970 South African team, specifically the one that played in the Third Test at the Wanderers, will always be the benchmark against which all future SA teams will be compared. Apartheid, politics and cancelled tours cannot detract from the achievements and credentials of those whose privilege it was to be part of this incredible time in the annals of South African cricket.

Not only did the team beat the Australians in two series, winning seven out of nine matches, but they also went to England and won the rubber there in 1965. That triumph was only the second time that South Africa had won a series in England and sadly it is still only the second time ever. Also, the triumphs over Australia have not subsequently been repeated.

Indeed it was a special time. It was a time that produced heroes. A "cinderella" cricketing nation became the world's best and this will always be etched fondly in our warmest memories. Recalling and recounting those days still produces great emotion and nostalgia for those who were blessed to live through the glory of it all. Radio commentators Charles Fortune and Gerhard Viviers were in their element as they brought it all so breathlessly to life for an audience that had no television.

Making it easier for those smooth-tongued painters of vivid cricketing word pictures were some great personalities and characters, dynamic cricketers who stamped their authority with that special something that separates them unmistakably from the ordinary. Fondly and with great respect I remember two of them – Eddie Barlow and Denis Lindsay.

Eddie and I made our international debuts together against New Zealand at Kingsmead way back in December 1961. The abiding memory was the New Zealand fast bowlers almost literally tearing their hair out as Eddie brought a new dimension to opening the batting. He loved to get on with it and he had a passion for the cut. But these were cuts with a difference! He hit them over the top of the slips cordon and by the end of the series the New Zealand captain, John Reid, was employing a new fielding position – a third man half-way between slips and the boundary fence.

Not long afterwards we watched the Australians having to adopt similar tactics, because they finally accepted that they were not lucky shots but a genuine and very effective part of the Barlow repertoire. "Bunter" Barlow had arrived and the opposition needed to re-align it's thinking.

His dynamic self-belief and determination was highly infectious. Why should we fear the Aussies? They breathed the same air as us. With that positive attitude, he led the way on the tour to Australia in 1963/64. He posted his most famous double century at Adelaide in an historic partnership with my brother, Graeme, and then to complete his all-round contribution took three vital wickets at a stage when the Aussies were just starting to look like saving the match. We shared the series with the mighty Aussies, having been told in no uncertain terms when we arrived that it was going to be a wasted summer, a one-sided walk-over.

It was the start of an Aussie nightmare and Eddie played a major hand in the psychological stranglehold that the Springboks enjoyed and which Australians, even to this day, would prefer to commit to amnesia or denial. Technically there might have been better players than

GLORY DAYS . . . Eddie Barlow at first slip and wicketkeeper Denis Lindsay celebrate as England batsman Geoff Boycott is bowled during the victorious 1965 Test at Trent Bridge

Eddie but when it came to sheer application he had no peers. "If only I had your brother's talent" he once said to me, implying that a combination of his determination and application and Graeme's artistry would have dusted down the feats of even the great Sir Donald Bradman.

Eddie only managed 40 Test wickets as a bowler but that belies his all-round influence. How often did he come on and take the right wicket at the right time. He had an ability to swing the ball and had a good slower one but again it was his irrepressible enthusiasm and will to succeed that saw him often breach the enemy lines. Eddie not only talked a good game, and was never short of a positive outlook, but he lived out his cricket with the same ebullience.

He had a dynamic influence on younger players and loved a challenge, like rejuvenating Western Province cricket or getting Boland promoted. Later as a coach he had a huge impact on the Free State and particularly Hansie Cronje, who often spoke glowingly to me about Eddie's powerful contribution. Eddie spoke straight. He spoke it as it was. He did not beat around the bushes and sometimes he upset those in hierarchal places. But whether you agreed with him or not, you could always be sure that whatever view he expressed, he truly believed it was in the best interests of a game he served with the same obsessive passion that he played.

My first experience of the dynamic side of Denis Lindsay, "Sporty" as we affectionately called him, was at Chelmsford in Essex way back in 1961 when he neatly dispatched the local leg-spinner, WT Greensmith, for five sixes in one over. The Fezelas, a team of promising young potential Springboks, smashed the County team to smithereens and aggressive Lindsay hit the headlines, signposting an indomitable talent. But South Africa already had a wicketkeeper, and a very good one at that – Johnny Waite. And Denis had to "wait" to get the gloves.

He was however a good enough batsman to merit Test selection in that capacity alone. Vividly I remember the morning of the fourth Test at Adelaide in 1964. Johnny Waite, the "old pro", was feeling off colour and was reluctant to play. The team management wasn't sure what to do, whether to risk him or not. Finally, somewhat hesitantly, they went with Denis. About an hour before the start Waite was withdrawn. Denis's reaction: "He is never going to get his place back".

Perhaps Denis was irritated by the indecisiveness but his threat was typical of the attitude that made him such a valued team member and ally in arms. Physically he was not big but Denis lay down for nobody. In that match he took an incredible catch, running backwards to pouch a "skier" at round about third man, after Barry Shepherd had attempted to hook a Barlow bouncer. This was the first of Eddie's three wickets in ten balls that finally nailed the Aussie coffin.

Then in England in 1965, Trevor Goddard had made himself unavailable and there was no Tony Pithey. The team had a huge problem. There was no opening partner for Eddie Barlow, nor was there a number three! Selflessly, up to the plate stepped Denis Lindsay. His technique was not suited to the demands of top-order batting but it was the type of sacrifice that personified Denis. He literally "guts-ed" it out for the team. But his time was to come.

Finally to our shores came Bobby Simpson's Aussies and more specifically fast bowler Dave Renneberg. What a summer! There were some fine performances in that series but they all paled into insignificance as Lindsay took charge. When someone like Graeme Pollock, who had an excellent series (537 runs at average of 76.71), has to play second fiddle, then you can appreciate the magnitude of the Lindsay dominance. He scored 606 runs, averaging 86.57, but that does not even tell half the story. In the first Test he came to the crease with the Springboks at 41-5. Believe it! He top scored with 69 to get us to 199.

After trailing on the first innings by 126 runs, South Africa were 268-5 when he returned to the crease to a packed Wanderers. Still a precarious position. But 182 runs later, South Africa had amassed a total of 620 and with that Trevor Goddard bowled us to a victory by the huge margin of 233 runs. It was the first time that the Springboks had beaten Australia in a Test on South African soil. But again, all this does not do justice to the manner in which Lindsay flayed the Australian bowlers.

My one unforgettable memory of that summer is Renneberg running in, dropping it short and Denis hooking the ball deep into the stands. It was brutal stuff. It was absolutely magnificent if you were a South African. It is still a nightmare for some of those Aussies. Seldom has one man so taken a series by the scruff of the neck. Further centuries in the third and fourth Tests completed the statistical brilliance but perhaps the most astounding factor, and the one which really did separate the two teams, was that thanks to Denis, in five South African innings in the series, the Springboks doubled the score that they had made at the fall of the fifth wicket. Simply translated, it is saying that in a Test at 150-5 you are in trouble, 300 all out is not so bad. Add to that the devastating psychological affect it has on the bowlers when it happens five times in five matches!

It was a golden summer for Denis. It was not to happen again but always his presence in the team ensured that positive and competitive edge that inspires confidence in the dressing room and out there in the middle and belongs unashamedly to those who have made their mark and served the game with distinction. Denis and Eddie were salt-of-the-earth characters, the type who provide the true seasoning for any good cricketing meal. They both left an indelible mark on the game and that we can say without reservation. Their names will live forever in the annals of all that is well and truly good about South African cricket.

Peter Pollock, the author of The Thirty Tests (Don Nelson), played in 28 Test matches for South Africa, in each of which he was a team-mate of Barlow, while on 19 occasions Lindsay was also in the side. Detailed obituaries of Barlow and Lindsay can be found in the Obituaries section.

JHB BRO12184

CRICKET'S ULTIMATE PRIZE . . . Ricky Ponting after Australia won the 2003 World Cup final in Johannesburg *Picture: MICHAEL STEELE, Getty Images/Touchline Photo*

WORLD CUP CHALLENGE

Mark Baldwin

As an Englishman, it is refreshing sometimes to remind the rest of the world that the English can do trend-setting. Actually, we've a bit of a history of it. The game of cricket itself was born in England, of course, while the Cricket World Cup was . . . well, in some ways you could say it was the Twenty20 of its day.

We are all now so familiar with one-day international cricket that it is hard to believe that, back in the early 1970's, limited-overs matches between different countries was actually quite a revolutionary thing. The ODI may have started its life on Australian soil on 5 January 1971, as a sop to a Melbourne public which had just seen a third Ashes Test washed away without a ball bowled, but it was undeniably an English invention.

Australia, indeed, did not even stage another ODI of their own - following that 1971 match - until January 1975.

WORLD CUP CHALLENGE

The sponsorship of Prudential Assurance, a City of London based insurance company, was crucial to the birth of the first World Cup. The Prudential had initially supported a three-match limited-overs tournament between England and Australia during the 1972 Ashes summer in England, and this had met with enthusiastic public response.

More one-day 'Prudential Cup' series were subsequently organised during the following summers, and the company then accepted an invitation from England's Test and County Cricket Board to lend their name to the new World Cup enterprise.

An idea of a Cricket World Cup had been bounced around in the corridors of power at Lord's for several years in the early 1970s, chiefly as a result of the initial success of the one-day format both in domestic English cricket and then at international level. The popularity of the football World Cup, boosted enormously of course by England's own staging (and winning) of it in 1966, had also generated talk of a cricket equivalent.

Intriguingly, however, one of the first proposals for a World Cup tournament revolved around the possibility of organising an event to find the world champions of Test match cricket.

Derrick Robins, a self-made millionaire businessman and a member of the TCCB's 12-strong Public Relations and Promotion Sub-Committee, proposed a series of preliminary Test matches taking place across the world and culminating in a five-day 'Final' at Lord's.

This idea was put to the International Cricket Conference (as the ICC was then known) in July 1971 but it met with scant support. Financial objections were the main reason for this knock-back, but the idea of a tournament based on five-day cricket was still discussed further before, gradually, the logistics of staging a World Cup demanded that one-day matches be utilised instead.

Three ICC annual meetings in 1972, 1973 and 1974 were required before - at last - a competition involving the then six Test-playing countries plus Sri Lanka and East Africa was proposed, and accepted, for 1975.

Australia, however, remained sceptical about the event ("Do we really need it?" was the reported comment of Australian Cricket Board representatives at one meeting at Lord's) and it was only after the successful completion of the first World Cup that India and Pakistan, too, really began to embrace one-day international cricket for its own sake.

The growth of the World Cup in the 31 years since then, of course, has been huge in terms of its profile and especially in its commercial worth.

Clive Lloyd's West Indies team, who beat Australia in the thrilling 1975 final, received nothing extra from their Board by way of reward and had to settle for their £300-a-man tournament fee and a share-out of the £4000 winners prize. Compare that to the $2 million prize money which Australia's players shared for winning the 2003 World Cup.

Looking back, it is also staggering to note that the whole cost of staging the 15 matches in 1975, including the prize money, which also gifted £2000 to the runners-up and £1000 to the two losing semi-finalists, and the subsistence claims of all eight teams, was covered by Prudential's £155 000 sponsorship.

Attendances, however, were good and the final at Lord's generated gate receipts of £66 950 - then a record for a one-day match in Britain. In all, the 1975 World Cup made a profit of £200 000, which was considered fairly tidy at the time.

Yet profits of $194 million from the 2003 World Cup in South Africa, compared even to the $51 million surfeit generated by the 1999 tournament, illustrates graphically how it is now big business as much as sporting administrators who drive the decision-making on central issues like choice of venues, promotion, tournament format and duration of event.

It is in this climate that the 2007 World Cup will be the longest-running affair yet, at 47 days, although its 51 matches are three less than at the over-bloated 2003 tournament.

Huge television revenues will ensure that next year's Caribbean extravaganza will be profitable but the ICC are still taking a calculated gamble in staging the ninth World Cup in the West Indies.

Logistical problems mainly in the areas of accommodation and internal travel seem set to dog the event, with supporters of visiting countries already complaining about the inflated cost of match tickets, airline tickets and hotel rooms.

In April this year, indeed, the World Cup organising committee - officially called the ICC Cricket World Cup WI 2007 Inc - appealed to the relevant West Indian Heads of Government for assistance with the extremely high room rates being charged by some hoteliers in the region.

The managing director and chief executive of CWC 2007, Chris Dehring, wrote to Keith Mitchell, the prime minister of Grenada and also chairman of the CARICOM Sub-committee on Cricket, saying: "We are always very appreciative of the support the Heads of Government have given to this Event, without which it would be impossible to conceive of a successful Cricket World Cup".

Some hoteliers, Dehring claimed, were charging more than 300 per cent above the normal rack rate price for rooms at that time of year. He appealed to them to adhere to the recommended rate of 15 per cent above usual prices, adding that the tourism industry in the islands hosting World Cup matches could be damaged "for many years" by exorbitant charges.

"There is no doubt that visitor arrivals could be dampened because of the rates being quoted," he added. "Broadcasters, sponsors and media are also expressing serious concern and are considering modifications to their attendance, production and coverage which would also reduce the economic impact of hosting this event. In addition, negative international press could hurt our regional tourism product for many years after."

There were also fears, 10 months ahead of the 2007 World Cup, that the stadiums being used for the tournament - which, in some cases, are completely new structures and in others are undergoing major upgrading - will not be ready in time.

Dehring was forced to issue official denials that work across the region was falling behind schedule but evidence on the ground often seemed to suggest otherwise.

Antigua, Guyana and Jamaica are building new grounds while Queen's Park Oval in Trinidad, Kensington Oval in Barbados and Sabina Park in Jamaica are receiving huge facelifts. St George's in Grenada needed to be completely rebuilt, following its destruction by a hurricane, and only the impressive and recently-built Beausejour Stadium in St Lucia looked anything like ready to host the world's most important cricket event as April gave way to May.

Jamaica admitted that its new stadium construction had been delayed by cement shortages on the island but Warner Park in St Kitts, which will host South Africa's group matches, was ready in time to stage international matches during May and June 2006. Contractors working on the new Sir Vivian Richards Stadium in Antigua and on Guyana's new Providence Stadium said they were confident of completing work by the October 2006 deadline.

The history books await their chance to update the tale.

Mark Baldwin, who writes for The Times of London, is the author of The History of the Cricket World Cup (Sanctuary Publishing)

WORLD CUP RECORDS

TEAM RECORDS

SUMMARY OF RESULTS

Team	Played	Won	Lost	Tied	NR	%Won	Winner	Runner-up
Australia	58	40	17	1	0	68.96	3	2
Bangladesh	11	2	8	0	1	20.00	0	0
Canada	9	1	8	0	0	11.11	0	0
East Africa	3	0	3	0	0	0.00	0	0
England	50	31	18	0	1	63.26	0	3
India	55	31	23	0	1	57.40	1	1
Kenya	20	5	14	0	1	26.31	0	0
Namibia	6	0	6	0	0	0.00	0	0
Netherlands	11	1	10	0	0	9.09	0	0
New Zealand	52	28	23	0	1	54.90	0	0
Pakistan	53	29	22	0	2	56.86	1	1
Scotland	5	0	5	0	0	0.00	0	0
South Africa	30	19	9	2	0	63.33	0	0
Sri Lanka	46	17	27	1	1	37.77	1	0
United Arab Emirates	5	1	4	0	0	20.00	0	0
West Indies	48	31	16	0	1	65.95	2	1
Zimbabwe	42	8	31	0	3	20.51	0	0

Note: The %Won calculation excludes "No Result" matches.

HIGHEST TOTALS

398-5	(50)	Sri Lanka v Kenya	Kandy	1996
373-6	(50)	India v Sri Lanka	Taunton	1999
360-4	(50)	West Indies v Sri Lanka	Karachi	1987
359-2	(50)	Australia v India	Johannesburg	2003
340-2	(50)	Zimbabwe v Namibia	Harare	2003
338-5	(60)	Pakistan v Sri Lanka	Swansea	1983
334-4	(60)	England v India	Lord's	1975
333-9	(60)	England v Sri Lanka	Taunton	1983
330-6	(60)	Pakistan v Sri Lanka	Nottingham	1975
329-2	(50)	India v Kenya	Bristol	1999

LOWEST TOTALS

36	(18.4)	Canada v Sri Lanka	Paarl	2003
45	(40.3)	Canada v England	Manchester	1979
45	(14)	Namibia v Australia	Potchefstroom	2003
68	(31.3)	Scotland v West Indies	Leicester	1999
74	(40.2)	Pakistan v England	Adelaide	1992
84	(17.4)	Namibia v Pakistan	Kimberley	2003
86	(37.2)	Sri Lanka v West Indies	Manchester	1975
93	(36.2)	England v Australia	Leeds	1975
93	(35.2)	West Indies v Kenya	Pune	1996
94	(52.3)	East Africa v England	Birmingham	1975

WORLD CUP RECORDS

HIGHEST TOTALS BATTING SECOND

313-7	(49.2)	Sri Lanka v Zimbabwe	New Plymouth	1992 (Won)
289-4	(47.5)	Australia v New Zealand	Madras	1996 (Won)
288-9	(60)	Sri Lanka v Pakistan	Swansea	1983 (Lost)

HIGHEST MATCH AGGREGATE

652-12	(100 overs)	Sri Lanka v Kenya	Kandy	1996

LARGEST MARGINS OF VICTORY

256 runs	Australia beat Namibia	Potchefstroom	2003
202 runs	England beat India	Lord's	1975
196 runs	England beat East Africa	Birmingham	1975
10 wkts	on 6 occasions		

NARROWEST MARGINS OF VICTORY

1 run	Australia beat India	Madras	1987
1 run	Australia beat India	Brisbane	1992 (revised target)
1 wkt	West Indies beat Pakistan	Birmingham	1975
1 wkt	Pakistan beat West Indies	Lahore	1987

TIED MATCHES

Australia v South Africa	Birmingham	1999
South Africa v Sri Lanka (D/L)	Durban	2003

BATTING

HIGHEST INDIVIDUAL INNINGS

188*	G Kirsten	South Africa v United Arab Emirates	Rawalpindi	1996
183	SC Ganguly	India v Sri Lanka	Taunton	1999
181	IVA Richards	West Indies v Sri Lanka	Karachi	1987
175*	Kapil Dev	India v Zimbabwe	Tunbridge Wells	1983
172*	CB Wishart	Zimbabwe v Namibia	Harare	2003
171*	GM Turner	New Zealand v East Africa	Birmingham	1975
161	AC Hudson	South Africa v Netherlands	Rawalpindi	1996
152	SR Tendulkar	India v Namibia	Pietermaritzburg	2003
145	PA de Silva	Sri Lanka v Kenya	Kandy	1996
145	RS Dravid	India v Sri Lanka	Taunton	1999

MOST RUNS IN A TOURNAMENT

673 (avg 61.18)	SR Tendulkar (Ind)	2003
523 (avg 87.16)	SR Tendulkar (Ind)	1996
484 (avg 80.66)	ME Waugh (Aus)	1996
471 (avg 58.87)	GA Gooch (Eng)	1987
465 (avg 58.12)	SC Ganguly (Ind)	2003

WORLD CUP RECORDS

MOST RUNS

	M	Inns	NO	Runs	HS	Avg	100	50
SR Tendulkar (Ind)	33	32	3	1732	152	59.72	4	12
Javed Miandad (Pak)	33	30	5	1083	103	43.32	1	8
PA de Silva (SL)	35	32	3	1064	145	36.68	2	6
IVA Richards (WI)	23	21	5	1013	181	63.31	3	5
ME Waugh (Aus)	22	22	3	1004	130	52.84	4	4
RT Ponting (Aus)	28	27	3	998	140 *	41.58	3	2
SR Waugh (Aus)	33	30	10	978	120 *	48.90	1	6
A Ranatunga (SL)	30	29	8	969	88 *	46.14	0	7
BC Lara (WI)	25	25	3	956	116	43.45	2	6
Saeed Anwar (Pak)	21	21	4	915	113 *	53.82	3	3

MOST CENTURIES

4	SC Ganguly (Ind)
4	SR Tendulkar (Ind)
4	ME Waugh (Aus)

RECORD WICKET PARTNERSHIPS

1st	194	Saeed Anwar and Wajahatullah Wasti	Pak v NZ	Manchester	1999
2nd	318	SC Ganguly and RS Dravid	Ind v SL	Taunton	1999
3rd	237*	RS Dravid and SR Tendulkar	Ind v Ken	Bristol	1999
4th	168	LK Germon and CZ Harris	NZ v Aus	Madras	1996
5th	148	RG Twose and CL Cairns	NZ v Aus	Cardiff	1999
6th	161	MO Odumbe and AV Vadher	Ken v SL	Southampton	1999
7th	98	RR Sarwan and RD Jacobs	WI v NZ	Port Elizabeth	2003
8th	117	DL Houghton and IP Butchart	Zim v NZ	Hyderabad (Ind)	1987
9th	126*	Kapil Dev and SMH Kirmani	Ind v Zim	Tunbridge Wells	1983
10th	71	AME Roberts and J Garner	WI v Ind	Manchester	1983

BOWLING

BEST BOWLING

7-15	GD McGrath	Australia v Namibia	Potchefstroom	2003
7-20	AJ Bichel	Australia v England	Port Elizabeth	2003
7-51	WW Davis	West Indies v Australia	Leeds	1983
6-14	GJ Gilmour	Australia v England	Leeds	1975
6-23	A Nehra	India v England	Durban	2003
6-23	SE Bond	New Zealand v Australia	Port Elizabeth	2003
6-25	WPUJC Vaas	Sri Lanka v Bangladesh	Pietermaritzburg	2003
6-39	KH MacLeay	Australia v India	Nottingham	1983
5-14	GD McGrath	Australia v West Indies	Manchester	1999
5-21	AG Hurst	Australia v Canada	Birmingham	1979
5-21	PA Strang	Zimbabwe v Kenya	Patna	1996
5-21	L Klusener	South Africa v Kenya	Amstelveen	1999

HAT-TRICKS

C Sharma	India v New Zealand	Nagpur	1987
Saqlain Mushtaq	Pakistan v Zimbabwe	The Oval	1999
WPUJC Vaas	Sri Lanka v Bangladesh	Pietermaritzburg	2003
B Lee	Australia v Kenya	Durban	2003

WORLD CUP RECORDS

ECONOMICAL BOWLING

RpO					
0.40	DA Reeve	5-3-2-1	England v Pakistan	Adelaide	1992
0.50	BS Bedi	12-8-6-1	India v East Africa	Leeds	1975
0.62	M Hendrick	8-4-5-1	England v Canada	Manchester	1979
0.80	B Wood	5-2-4-0	England v India	Lord's	1975
0.80	CM Old	10-5-8-4	England v Canada	Manchester	1979
0.80	CEL Ambrose	10-4-8-2	West Indies v Scotland	Leicester	1999

(Minimum: 5 overs)

EXPENSIVE BOWLING

RpO					
11.16	RW Ali	6-0-67-0	Kenya v Sri Lanka	Kandy	1996
10.80	AR Adams	5-0-54-1	New Zealand v Zimbabwe	Bloemfontein	2003
9.85	TBM de Leede	7-0-69-2	Netherlands v Zimbabwe	Bulawayo	2003
9.70	ALF de Mel	10-0-97-1	Sri Lanka v West Indies	Karachi	1987
9.57	Z Khan	7-0-67-0	India v Australia	Johannesburg	2003

(Minimum: 5 overs)

Note: The most runs conceded in an innings is 105 by MC Snedden (12-1-105-2) for New Zealand v England at The Oval in 1983.

MOST WICKETS IN A TOURNAMENT

23 (avg 14.39)	WPUJC Vaas (SL)	2003
22 (avg 17.90)	B Lee (Aus)	2003
21 (avg 14.76)	GD McGrath (Aus)	2003
20 (avg 16.25)	GI Allott (NZ)	1999
20 (avg 18.05)	SK Warne (Aus)	1999

MOST WICKETS

	M	Balls	Runs	Wkts	Avg	RpO	BB	4I
Wasim Akram (Pak)	38	1947	1311	55	23.83	4.04	5-28	3
GD McGrath (Aus)	28	1470	935	45	20.77	3.81	7-15	2
J Srinath (Ind)	34	1700	1224	44	27.81	4.32	4-30	2
AA Donald (SA)	25	1313	913	38	24.02	4.17	4-17	2
WPUJC Vaas (SL)	21	1104	754	36	20.94	4.09	6-25	2
Imran Khan (Pak)	28	1017	655	34	19.26	3.86	4-37	2
CZ Harris (NZ)	28	1166	861	32	26.90	4.43	4-7	1
SK Warne (Aus)	17	977	624	32	19.50	3.83	4-29	4
IT Botham (Eng)	22	1332	762	30	25.40	3.43	4-31	1
M Muralitharan (SL)	21	1127	693	30	23.10	3.68	4-28	1

WICKETKEEPING

MOST DISMISSALS IN A MATCH

6 (ct 6)	AC Gilchrist	Australia v Namibia	Potchefstroom	2003
5 (ct 5)	SMH Kirmani	India v Zimbabwe	Leicester	1983
5 (ct 4, st 1)	JC Adams	West Indies v Kenya	Pune	1996
5 (ct 4, st 1)	Rashid Latif	Pakistan v New Zealand	Lahore	1996
5 (ct 4, st 1)	NR Mongia	India v Zimbabwe	Leicester	1999
5 (ct 5)	RD Jacobs	West Indies v New Zealand	Southampton	1999

MOST DISMISSALS IN A TOURNAMENT

21 (ct 21)	AC Gilchrist (Aus)	2003
17 (ct 15, st 2)	KC Sangakkara (SL)	2003
16 (ct 15, st 1)	PJL Dujon (WI)	1983
16 (ct 12, st 4)	Moin Khan (Pak)	1999
16 (ct 15, st 1)	RS Dravid (Ind)	2003

MOST DISMISSALS

	M	Ct	St	Total
AC Gilchrist (Aus)	20	33	2	35
Moin Khan (Pak)	20	23	7	30
AJ Stewart (Eng)	25	21	2	23
MV Boucher (SA)	15	22	0	22
RD Jacobs (WI)	11	21	1	22
Wasim Bari (Pak)	14	18	4	22

FIELDING

MOST CATCHES IN A MATCH

4	M Kaif	India v Sri Lanka	Johannesburg	2003

MOST CATCHES IN A TOURNAMENT

11	RT Ponting (Aus)	2003
8	A Kumble (Ind)	1996
8	DJ Cullinan (SA)	1999
8	B Lee (Aus)	2003
8	D Mongia (Ind)	2003
8	V Sehwag (Ind)	2003

MOST CATCHES

	M	Ct
RT Ponting (Aus)	28	18
CL Cairns (NZ)	28	16
ST Jayasuriya (SL)	27	15

APPEARANCES

MOST MATCHES

Wasim Akram (Pak)	38
PA de Silva (SL)	35
J Srinath (Ind)	34
Javed Miandad (Pak)	33
SR Tendulkar (Ind)	33
SR Waugh (Aus)	33

MOST TOURNAMENTS

Javed Miandad (Pak)	6 (1975-1996)

SOUTH AFRICA: WORLD CUP RECORDS

Highest total for	328-3	v Netherlands	Rawalpindi	1996
Highest total against	278-5	by West Indies	Cape Town	2003
Lowest total for	185	v Zimbabwe	Chelmsford	1999
Lowest total against	103	by England	The Oval	1999

Highest individual innings for	188*	G Kirsten	v United Arab Emirates	Rawalpindi	1996
Highest individual innings against	134*	SP Fleming	for New Zealand	Johannesburg	2003
Best bowling for	5-21	L Klusener	v Kenya	Amstelveen	1999
Best bowling against	4-29	SK Warne	for Australia	Birmingham	1999

RECORD WICKET PARTNERSHIPS

1st	186	G Kirsten and AC Hudson	v Netherlands	Rawalpindi	1996
2nd	116	G Kirsten and WJ Cronje	v United Arab Emirates	Rawalpindi	1996
3rd	145*	G Kirsten and DJ Cullinan	v United Arab Emirates	Rawalpindi	1996
4th	109	GC Smith and HH Dippenaar	v Canada	East London	2003
5th	84	JH Kallis and JN Rhodes	v Australia	Birmingham	1999
6th	77	JH Kallis and SM Pollock	v Pakistan	Nottingham	1999
7th	66	DJ Cullinan and SM Pollock	v Zimbabwe	Chelmsford	1999
8th	67	L Klusener and N Boje	v West Indies	Cape Town	2003
9th	44	L Klusener and S Elworthy	v Sri Lanka	Northampton	1999
10th	35	L Klusener and AA Donald	v Zimbabwe	Chelmsford	1999

Most dismissals in a match	4 (ct 4)	MV Boucher	v Australia	Birmingham	1999
Most catches in a match - fielder	3	HH Dippenaar	v Bangladesh	Bloemfontein	2003
Most runs in a tournament	410 (avg 68.33)	PN Kirsten			1992
Most wickets in a tournament	17 (avg 20.58)	L Klusener			1999
Most dismissals in a tournament	15 (ct 14, st 1)	DJ Richardson			1992
Most catches in a tournament - fielder	8	DJ Cullinan			1999

Most runs in a career	806 (avg 47.41)	G Kirsten
Most centuries in a career	2	HH Gibbs
Most wickets in a career	38 (avg 24.02)	AA Donald
Most dismissals in a career	22 (ct 22)	MV Boucher
Most catches in a career - fielder	11	DJ Cullinan
Most matches in a career	25	AA Donald

SOUTH AFRICA WORLD CUP CAREER RECORDS

As at 1 July 2006

Name	Years	M	Inns	NO	Runs	HS	Avg	SR	100	50	Ct	St	Balls	Runs	Wkts	Avg	RpO	BB	4I
PR Adams	1996-1996	2	1	0	10	10	10.00	71.42	0	0	0	0	108	87	3	29.00	4.83	2-45	0
N Boje	1999-2003	5	2	1	54	29	54.00	87.09	0	0	2	0	132	144	1	144.00	6.54	1-44	0
T Bosch	1992-1992	1	0	0	0	-	-	-	0	0	0	0	15	19	0	-	7.60	-	0
MV Boucher	1999-2003	15	12	4	204	49	25.50	73.91	0	0	22	0	0	0	0	-	-	-	0
WJ Cronje	1992-1999	23	20	4	476	78	29.75	80.81	0	2	10	0	444	329	8	41.12	4.44	2-17	0
DJ Cullinan	1996-1999	15	15	3	471	69	39.25	67.57	0	3	11	0	12	7	0	-	3.50	-	0
PS de Villiers	1996-1996	1	1	0	12	12	12.00	109.09	0	0	0	0	42	27	2	13.50	3.85	2-27	0
HH Dippenaar	2003-2003	6	3	0	108	80	36.00	68.35	0	1	3	0	0	0	0	-	-	-	0
AA Donald	1992-2003	25	5	2	13	7	4.33	32.50	0	0	3	0	1313	913	38	24.02	4.17	4-17	2
S Elworthy	1999-1999	8	3	0	25	23	8.33	53.19	0	0	0	0	432	262	10	26.20	3.63	2-20	0
HH Gibbs	1999-2003	15	15	2	725	143	55.76	85.49	2	4	3	0	0	0	0	-	-	-	0
AJ Hall	2003-2003	3	1	1	22	22*	-	200.00	0	0	0	0	138	103	5	20.60	4.47	2-15	0
O Henry	1992-1992	1	1	0	11	11	11.00	84.61	0	0	0	0	60	31	1	31.00	3.10	1-31	0
AC Hudson	1992-1996	12	12	0	571	161	47.58	76.85	1	4	2	0	0	0	0	-	-	-	0
JH Kallis	1996-2003	19	16	4	438	96	36.50	66.66	0	4	4	0	720	510	11	46.36	4.25	3-26	0
G Kirsten	1996-2003	21	21	4	806	188*	47.41	75.46	1	5	9	0	18	9	0	-	3.00	-	0
PN Kirsten	1992-1992	8	8	2	410	90	68.33	66.55	0	4	2	0	108	87	5	17.40	4.83	3-31	0
L Klusener	1999-2003	14	11	8	372	57	124.00	121.17	0	3	2	0	605	487	22	22.13	4.82	5-21	2
AP Kuiper	1992-1992	9	8	1	113	36	16.14	71.51	0	0	3	0	246	235	9	26.11	5.73	3-40	0
CK Langeveldt	2003-2003	1	0	0	0	-	-	-	0	0	0	0	30	24	0	-	4.80	-	0
BM McMillan	1992-1996	15	9	4	145	33*	29.00	74.74	0	0	8	0	696	433	17	25.47	3.73	3-11	0
CR Matthews	1996-1996	6	2	2	17	9*	-	68.00	0	0	1	0	357	226	7	32.28	3.79	2-30	0
M Ntini	2003-2003	6	2	0	14	14	7.00	175.00	0	0	0	0	313	176	10	17.60	3.37	4-24	1
SJ Palframan	1996-1996	6	3	0	45	28	15.00	70.31	0	0	8	0	0	0	0	-	-	-	0
RJ Peterson	2003-2003	1	0	0	0	-	-	-	0	0	1	0	36	21	0	-	3.50	-	0
SM Pollock	1996-2003	21	13	1	216	52	18.00	78.54	0	1	10	0	1110	674	23	29.30	3.64	5-36	1
MW Pringle	1992-1992	7	1	1	5	5*	-	83.33	0	0	1	0	342	236	8	29.50	4.14	4-11	1
JN Rhodes	1992-2003	24	20	3	354	43	20.82	88.05	0	0	7	0	0	0	0	-	-	-	0
DJ Richardson	1992-1992	9	5	2	66	28	22.00	66.66	0	0	14	1	0	0	0	-	-	-	0
MW Rushmere	1992-1992	3	3	0	49	35	16.33	47.57	0	0	1	0	0	0	0	-	-	-	0
GC Smith	2003-2003	3	3	0	121	63	40.33	85.81	0	1	2	0	6	10	0	-	10.00	-	0
RP Snell	1992-1992	9	4	2	24	11*	12.00	120.00	0	0	1	0	437	310	8	38.75	4.25	3-42	0
PL Symcox	1996-1996	4	2	0	25	24	12.50	104.16	0	0	0	0	240	149	6	24.83	3.72	2-22	0
KC Wessels	1992-1992	9	9	2	313	85	44.71	53.32	0	3	7	0	0	0	0	-	-	-	0
M Zondeki	2003-2003	3	1	1	1	1*	-	100.00	0	0	2	0	120	76	2	38.00	3.80	1-17	0

Section B: International Cricket

AFRO-ASIA CUP 2005

Colin Bryden

The first officially sanctioned one-day international matches between sides representing continents were played in South Africa during August 2005. The inaugural Afro-Asia Cup matches were arranged at short notice but featured many of the best players from Africa and Asia.

The Cup was played under the auspices of Afro-Asian Cricket Cooperation, a body representing the Asian Cricket Council and the Africa Cricket Association, chaired by Jagmohan Dalmiya, the former president of the Board of Control for Cricket in India and the International Cricket Council. It was announced that proceeds would be used primarily for cricket development in the two continents, with 70 percent going to the host continent and 20 percent to the visitors, with the remaining 10 percent allocated to charity. It was decided at a meeting during the tournament that sight-related charities would be the beneficiaries.

During June 2006 it was announced that a donation of R1.43-million had been made to Sight Savers International for eye care programmes in the developing world and the eradication of blindness. Sight Savers is based in West Sussex in the United Kingdom and services countries in Africa and Asia.

The new chairman of the renamed Afro-Asia Cricket Committee (AACC), Sharad Pawar, said: "This is the start of major things to come to enable the Afro-Asia Series and cricket generally to give back to humanity in the form of charity globally."

It was due to be an annual event, with Standard Chartered Bank having agreed to be sponsors for three years, with the venues alternating between Asia and Africa. No series was scheduled for 2006, however.

The series, played out of season, did not capture the imagination of the South African public, with fewer than 12 000 spectators watching the three matches, one of which was badly affected by rain. In order to fit in with the requirements of Asian television stations, the day-night matches started at the unusual time of noon in South Africa.

The matches interrupted a rare extended break for the South African players but they were well rewarded. In addition to match fees and a negotiated amount for commercial rights, there was prize money of US$200 000 at stake, with $100 000 for the series winners, $25 000 for the winners of each match, $5000 for each Man of the Match and $10 000 for the Man of the Series.

The bulk of the money was shared, with both teams winning one match before the final contest was rained off. There was a slight advantage for the Asians, however, as Shoaib Akhtar was named Man of the Match in the undecided game, while Zaheer Khan took the Man of the Series award.

The series was announced less than a month before it started and South African fast bowlers Makhaya Ntini and Andre Nel were not considered because they were on short-term English county contracts, while Andrew Hall was also playing county cricket. The first match

ALL-STAR CAST . . . Inzamam-ul-Haq leads out the Asia XI for the first official international match between teams representing continents *Picture: LEE WARREN, Touchline Photo*

coincided with a Test in Zimbabwe, ruling out the Zimbabweans, Heath Streak and Tatenda Taibu.

Graeme Smith, the South African captain, was named as the captain of the African XI but could not play in the first two matches because he was serving the last two matches of a four-game suspension for slow over-rates incurred in the West Indies earlier in the year. Shaun Pollock captained the team in Smith's absence.

It was the first time in South Africa that the new ICC regulations regarding substitutes and fielding restrictions were applied.

The squads were:

Africa: Graeme Smith (captain), Shaun Pollock (vice-captain), Boeta Dippenaar, AB de Villiers, Jacques Kallis, Ashwell Prince, Mark Boucher, Monde Zondeki, Jacques Rudolph, Nicky Boje, Justin Ontong, Dale Steyn, Justin Kemp (all South Africa), Steve Tikolo, Collins Obuya, Thomas Odoyo (Kenya), Heath Streak and Tatenda Taibu (Zimbabwe). Manager, Goolam Rajah; coach, Mickey Arthur; physiotherapist, Shane Jabaar; fitness trainer, Adrian le Roux.

Asia: Inzamam-ul-Haq (Pakistan, captain), Muttiah Muralitharan (Sri Lanka, vice-captain), Virender Sehwag, Anil Kumble, Ashish Nehra, Zaheer Khan (India), Kumar Sangakkara, Sanath Jayasuriya, Mahela Jayawardene (Sri Lanka), Mohammad Yousuf, Shahid Afridi, Abdul Razzaq, Shoaib Akhtar (Pakistan), Mohammad Ashraful and Mashrafe Bin Mortaza (Bangladesh). Manager, Sultan Rana; coach, Rumesh Ratnayake.

In the Africa team, Kemp and Steyn replaced South African Albie Morkel and Zimbabwe's Andy Blignaut, who both had injuries. The Asia team was also hit by withdrawals, with Jayawardene, Mortaza, Nehra and Zaheer Khan replacing Rahul Dravid (India), Naved-ul-Hasan (Pakistan), Irfan Pathan (India) and Chaminda Vaas (Sri Lanka). Dravid had originally been named vice-captain.

Herschelle Gibbs was not considered for the Africa team because of a knee injury, while India's Sachin Tendulkar was out of action following elbow surgery.

AFRICA v ASIA — 1st Limited Overers International

Played at SuperSport Park, Centurion on 17 August 2005 (D/N) — Toss: Asia

Umpires: SJ Davis & BR Doctrove (TV: KH Hurter) — Referee: CH Lloyd

Debuts: Afr: DW Steyn. Asia: None

Result: Africa won by 2 runs

Man of Match: Ashwell Prince

Notes: Africa substitute: JM Kemp replaced TM Odoyo after 39.5 overs of Africa's innings. Asia substitute: Mohammad Ashraful replaced M Muralitharan after 0 overs of Asia's innings.

In front of a small crowd on a chilly day, the Africa XI were soon in trouble against good bowling on a pitch which offered plenty of seam movement off a course, grassy surface.

Prince and Boucher put on 84 for the sixth wicket in what proved a crucial partnership. Prince was dropped by wicketkeeper Sangakkara off an inside edge from Muralitharan when he was on 35 during a composed, solid innings.

There were boos from the crowd of 3800 when Shoaib Akhtar sent down two fast full tosses to last batsman Steyn.

Sangakkara and Sehwag gave Asia a good start before Pollock took three wickets in the 11th over to put the Africans on top. The match swung Asia's way again when Kumble and Razzaq put on 56 for the seventh wicket. Shoaib hit Kemp for a straight six to take Asia to within six runs of victory but sliced a catch to backward point off the next delivery before Steyn produced a fast, straight delivery to gain his first one-day international wicket and seal a win for the Africans.

AFRICA	Runs	Mins	Balls	4	6
AB de Villiers lbw b Shoaib Akhtar	24	34	23	3	1
HH Dippenaar c Sehwag b Khan	14	40	23	2	-
JH Kallis c Nehra b Khan	4	27	14	-	-
JL Ontong lbw b Khan	0	2	2	-	-
AG Prince not out	78	157	113	5	-
SO Tikolo c Sangakkara b Nehra	0	5	2	-	-
†MV Boucher lbw b Muralitharan	42	83	59	3	-
*SM Pollock b Kumble	2	5	9	-	-
N Boje c Sangakkara b Shahid Afridi	3	12	13	-	-
JM Kemp lbw b Shoaib Akhtar	4	8	5	1	-
DW Steyn run out (Nehra)	3	12	10	-	-
TM Odoyo					
Extras (lb 7, w 11, nb 6)	24				
TOTAL (44.3 overs)	**198**				

ASIA	Runs	Mins	Balls	4	6
†KC Sangakkara b Kallis	35	114	80	6	-
V Sehwag c Boucher b Pollock	21	44	26	5	-
Mohammad Yousuf c Boucher b Pollock	1	4	3	-	-
Mohammad Ashraful c Tikolo b Pollock	0	2	1	-	-
*Inzamam-ul-Haq c Dippenaar b Kemp	6	22	12	-	-
Shahid Afridi c Boucher b Kallis	13	23	10	3	-
Abdul Razzaq c Boucher b Boje	38	95	77	3	-
A Kumble lbw b Kallis	24	61	48	3	-
Z Khan not out	20	38	21	1	-
Shoaib Akhtar c Ontong b Kemp	15	18	13	-	1
A Nehra b Steyn	1	5	2	-	-
M Muralitharan					
Extras (lb 2, w 16, nb 4)	22				
TOTAL (48.1 overs)	**196**				

Asia	O	M	R	W
Shoaib Akhtar	7.3	1	40	2 (6 nb)
Khan	8	0	37	3 (2 w)
Nehra	5	1	19	1
Abdul Razzaq	3	0	17	0 (1 w)
Kumble	10	0	39	1 (2 w)
Muralitharan	9	1	26	1 (1 w)
Shahid Afridi	2	0	13	1 (1 w)

Afr	O	M	R	W
Pollock	10	1	32	3 (3 nb, 1 w)
Steyn	9.1	2	40	1 (5 w)
Kemp	9	0	40	2 (1 nb, 5 w)
Kallis	10	2	42	3 (2 w)
Boje	10	1	40	1 (1 w)

Fall of Wickets	Afr	Asia
1st	39 (1)	50 (2)
2nd	44 (2)	52 (3)
3rd	44 (4)	52 (4)
4th	53 (3)	59 (5)
5th	57 (6)	89 (6)
6th	141 (7)	96 (1)
7th	152 (8)	152 (8)
8th	164 (9)	169 (7)
9th	174 (10)	193 (10)
10th	198 (11)	196 (11)

AFRICA v ASIA — 2nd Limited Overs International

Played at Sahara Stadium Kingsmead, Durban on 20 August 2005 (D/N) — Toss: Asia
Umpires: SJ Davis & BR Doctrove (TV: BG Jerling) — Referee: CH Lloyd
Debuts: Afr: None. Asia: None
Result: Asia won by 17 runs
Man of Match: Kumar Sangakkara
Notes: In Africa's innings Muralitharan captained Asia as Inzaman-ul-Haq did not field. Africa substitute: SO Tikolo replaced M Zondeki after 0 overs of Africa's innings.

The Sri Lankan pair of Sangakkara and Jayawardene played a dominant role as the Asia XI squared the series. Both hit half-centuries and they jointly accounted for seven dismissals in the field. Jayawardene held three catches in the slips and one on the boundary, while Sangakkara was responsible for a catch behind the wicket, a direct-hit run-out to dismiss De Villiers and a piece of quick thinking to account for the dangerous Kemp. He had the opportunity to run out Tikolo after the Kenyan was sent back after setting out for a run but chose to toss the ball to bowler Muralitharan when he spotted that Kemp was out of his ground at the other end.

Sehwag and Sangakkara's stand of 91 for the second wicket set up Asia for a good total and Jayawardene, Yousuf and Inzamam all made useful scores in front of a crowd of 5380.

Odoyo, after being substituted out of the first game before making an appearance, bowled his medium-pacers steadily to be the best of the African bowlers, while Tikolo went on to make top score for the Africans in a good day for the two Kenyan players.

Muralitharan captained the Asia side on the field after Inzamam strained a groin when he slipped while batting. Kallis was ruled out of the African team with a back muscle strain suffered when loading his luggage onto a van the previous day, while Kumble could not play for Asia because of a hamstring strain.

ASIA	*Runs*	*Mins*	*Balls*	*4*	*6*
V Sehwag c Boucher b Odoyo	38	78	51	4	1
Shahid Afridi lbw b Streak	6	5	2	-	1
†KC Sangakkara c Boucher b Odoyo	61	97	70	9	1
DPMD Jayawardene st Boucher b Odoyo	52	106	72	1	1
Mohammad Yousuf c Pollock b Kemp	42	57	56	3	1
*Inzamam-ul-Haq not out	32	56	31	1	1
Abdul Razzaq run out (De Villiers)	0	2	3	-	-
Shoaib Akhtar c Boucher b Streak	6	11	9	-	-
Z Khan not out	13	17	11	2	-
A Nehra					
M Muralitharan					
Extras (lb 6, w 6, nb 5)	17				
TOTAL (for 7 wkts) (50 overs)	**267**				

AFRICA	*Runs*	*Mins*	*Balls*	*4*	*6*
HH Dippenaar c Jayawardene b Shoaib Akhtar	23	49	26	3	-
†MV Boucher c Jayawardene b Khan	16	17	16	4	-
AB de Villiers run out (Sangakkara)	39	110	67	5	-
JA Rudolph c Sangakkara b Nehra	10	33	22	1	-
AG Prince run out (Abdul Razzaq)	0	3	2	-	-
JM Kemp run out (Shoaib Akhtar/Sangakkara/Murali)	38	64	57	4	1
SO Tikolo c Sehwag b Muralitharan	43	38	43	6	1
*SM Pollock b Khan	29	55	30	3	-
N Boje c Jayawardene b Shoaib Akhtar	1	5	2	-	-
HH Streak c Jayawardene b Khan	27	44	32	4	-
TM Odoyo not out	3	8	4	-	-
M Zondeki					
Extras (b 1, lb 9, w 5, nb 6)	21				
TOTAL (49.2 overs)	**250**				

Afr	*O*	*M*	*R*	*W*	
Pollock	10	3	36	0	(3 nb)
Streak	9	0	64	2	(2 w)
Zondeki	9	1	64	0	
Odoyo	10	0	45	3	(2 nb, 3 w)
Boje	4	0	24	0	
Kemp	8	0	28	1	(1 w)

Asia	*O*	*M*	*R*	*W*	
Shoaib Akhtar	10	0	50	2	(3 nb)
Khan	9.2	1	43	3	(1 w)
Nehra	8	0	33	1	
Abdul Razzaq	5	0	27	0	(2 nb)
Muralitharan	10	0	45	1	(3 w)
Shahid Afridi	7	1	42	0	(1 w)

Fall of Wickets	*Asia*	*Afr*
1st	7 (2)	23 (2)
2nd	98 (1)	50 (1)
3rd	120 (3)	71 (4)
4th	199 (5)	72 (5)
5th	225 (4)	118 (3)
6th	225 (7)	154 (6)
7th	235 (8)	192 (7)
8th	-	193 (9)
9th	-	235 (8)
10th	-	250 (10)

AFRICA v ASIA — 3rd Limited Overs International

Played at Sahara Stadium Kingsmead, Durban on 21 August 2005 (D/N) — Toss: Africa

Umpires: SJ Davis & BR Doctrove (TV: KH Hurter) — Referee: CH Lloyd

Debuts: Afr: None. Asia: None

Result: No result

Man of Match: Shoaib Akhtar

Man of Series: Zaheer Khan

Notes: Africa substitute: TM Odoyo replaced JA Rudolph after 0 overs of Asia's innings. Asia substitute: A Nehra replaced Mohammad Ashraful after 10 overs of Africa's innings.

Rain fell soon after the returning Smith won the toss. The start of play was delayed by an hour and 45 minutes. When the game started under grey skies, Shoaib bowled at express pace and the left-armed Zaheer Khan proved an ideal foil, bowling all his ten overs in one spell. Pollock chanced his arm and played some exciting strokes.

Conditions remained difficult for batsmen when the Asia XI set off in pursuit of a small target but rain ended the prospects of what might have been an interesting finish.

AFRICA	*Runs*	*Mins*	*Balls*	*4*	*6*
*GC Smith lbw b Shoaib Akhtar	0	5	5	-	-
HH Dippenaar c Jayawardene b Khan	7	31	25	1	-
JH Kallis lbw b Khan	4	57	20	-	-
JA Rudolph run out (Abdul Razzaq)	7	25	18	1	-
AG Prince c Muralitharan b Shoaib Akhtar	0	13	5	-	-
JM Kemp lbw b Khan	8	29	15	1	-
†T Taibu c Sehwag b Abdul Razzaq	10	39	32	1	-
SM Pollock not out	44	64	35	6	-
HH Streak lbw b Shahid Afridi	14	36	35	1	-
DW Steyn lbw b Muralitharan	1	3	5	-	-
M Zondeki run out (Mohammad Yousuf/Sangakkara)	0	4	2	-	-
TM Odoyo					
Extras (lb 8, w 3)	11				
TOTAL (32.5 overs)	**106**				

ASIA	*Runs*	*Mins*	*Balls*	*4*	*6*
V Sehwag b Steyn	5	8	5	1	-
Shahid Afridi c Streak b Pollock	0	14	4	-	-
†KC Sangakkara not out	1	9	6	-	-
DPMD Jayawardene not out	0	4	4	-	-
Mohammad Yousuf					
*Inzamam-ul-Haq					
Abdul Razzaq					
A Nehra					
Z Khan					
Shoaib Akhtar					
M Muralitharan					
Mohammad Ashraful					
Extras (w 1, nb 1)	2				
TOTAL (for 2 wkts) (3 overs)	**8**				

AFRO-ASIA CUP 2005

Asia	O	M	R	W	
Shoaib Akhtar	8	3	16	2	(1 w)
Khan	10	2	21	3	(2 w)
Nehra	6	1	30	0	
Abdul Razzaq	2	0	18	1	
Muralitharan	4	1	8	1	
Shahid Afridi	2.5	0	5	1	

Afr	O	M	R	W	
Pollock	2	0	6	1	
Steyn	1	0	2	1	(1 nb, 1 w)

Fall of Wickets	Afr	Asia
1st	1 (1)	7 (1)
2nd	16 (2)	7 (2)
3rd	26 (4)	-
4th	26 (3)	-
5th	26 (5)	-
6th	35 (6)	-
7th	54 (7)	-
8th	105 (9)	-
9th	106 (10)	-
10th	106 (11)	-

AFRICA v ASIA 2005/06

LIMITED OVERS INTERNATIONAL AVERAGES

AFRICA

Batting & Fielding

Name	M	Inns	NO	Runs	HS	Avg	SR	100	50	Ct	St
AG Prince	3	3	1	78	78 *	39.00	65.00	0	1	0	0
SM Pollock	3	3	1	75	44 *	37.50	101.35	0	0	1	0
AB de Villiers	2	2	0	63	39	31.50	70.00	0	0	0	0
MV Boucher	2	2	0	58	42	29.00	77.33	0	0	7	1
SO Tikolo	2	2	0	43	43	21.50	95.55	0	0	1	0
HH Streak	2	2	0	41	27	20.50	61.19	0	0	1	0
JM Kemp	3	3	0	50	38	16.66	64.93	0	0	0	0
HH Dippenaar	3	3	0	44	23	14.66	59.45	0	0	1	0
T Taibu	1	1	0	10	10	10.00	31.25	0	0	0	0
JA Rudolph	2	2	0	17	10	8.50	42.50	0	0	0	0
JH Kallis	2	2	0	8	4	4.00	23.52	0	0	0	0
N Boje	2	2	0	4	3	2.00	26.66	0	0	0	0
DW Steyn	2	2	0	4	3	2.00	26.66	0	0	0	0
JL Ontong	1	1	0	0	0	0.00	0.00	0	0	1	0
GC Smith	1	1	0	0	0	0.00	0.00	0	0	0	0
M Zondeki	2	1	0	0	0	0.00	0.00	0	0	0	0
TM Odoyo	3	1	1	3	3 *	-	75.00	0	0	0	0
Totals	36	33	3	498	78 *			0	1	12	1
			Extras	56					subs	0	
			Total	554		18.46	64.59			12	

Bowling

Name	Overs	Mdns	Runs	Wkts	Avg	RpO	BB	4I
JH Kallis	10	2	42	3	14.00	4.20	3-42	0
TM Odoyo	10	0	45	3	15.00	4.50	3-45	0
SM Pollock	22	4	74	4	18.50	3.36	3-32	0
DW Steyn	10.1	2	42	2	21.00	4.13	1-2	0
JM Kemp	17	0	68	3	22.66	4.00	2-40	0
HH Streak	9	0	64	2	32.00	7.11	2-64	0
N Boje	14	1	64	1	64.00	4.57	1-40	0
M Zondeki	9	1	64	0	-	7.11	-	0
Totals	101.1	10	463	18			3-32	0
		b/lb/pen	8	1	run outs			
		Total	471	19	24.78	4.65		

AFRO-ASIA CUP 2005

ASIA

Batting & Fielding

Name	M	Inns	NO	Runs	HS	Avg	SR	100	50	Ct	St
DPMD Jayawardene	2	2	1	52	52	52.00	68.42	0	1	5	0
KC Sangakkara	3	3	1	97	61	48.50	62.17	0	1	3	0
Inzamam-ul-Haq	3	2	1	38	32 *	38.00	88.37	0	0	0	0
A Kumble	1	1	0	24	24	24.00	50.00	0	0	0	0
Mohammad Yousuf	3	2	0	43	42	21.50	72.88	0	0	0	0
V Sehwag	3	3	0	64	38	21.33	78.04	0	0	3	0
Abdul Razzaq	3	2	0	38	38	19.00	47.50	0	0	0	0
Shoaib Akhtar	3	2	0	21	15	10.50	95.45	0	0	0	0
Shahid Afridi	3	3	0	19	13	6.33	118.75	0	0	0	0
A Nehra	3	1	0	1	1	1.00	50.00	0	0	1	0
Mohammad Ashraful	2	1	0	0	0	0.00	0.00	0	0	0	0
Z Khan	3	2	2	33	20 *	-	103.12	0	0	0	0
M Muralitharan	3	0	0	0	-	-	-	0	0	1	0
Totals	35	24	5	430	61			0	2	13	0
			Extras	41					subs	0	
			Total	471		24.78	69.69			13	

Bowling

Name	Overs	Mdns	Runs	Wkts	Avg	RpO	BB	4I
Z Khan	27.2	3	101	9	11.22	3.69	3-21	0
Shoaib Akhtar	25.3	4	106	6	17.66	4.15	2-16	0
M Muralitharan	23	2	79	3	26.33	3.43	1-8	0
Shahid Afridi	11.5	1	60	2	30.00	5.07	1-5	0
A Kumble	10	0	39	1	39.00	3.90	1-39	0
A Nehra	19	2	82	2	41.00	4.31	1-19	0
Abdul Razzaq	10	0	62	1	62.00	6.20	1-18	0
Totals	126.4	12	529	24			3-21	0
		b/lb/pen	25	6	run outs			
		Total	554	30	18.46	4.37		

ICC SUPER SERIES 2005/06

Neil Manthorp

Right from the start opinion was divided on the merits of pitting the best team in the world against the best of the rest. The wizened sporting adage that a champion team will always beat a team of champions was put to the test and it proved as right as it always has been.

South Africa's representation was huge and reflected the esteem in which so many individuals were regarded by their worldwide peers. Jonty Rhodes was an ICC XI selector on an illustrious panel chaired by Sunil Gavaskar and including Michael Atherton, Sir Richard Hadlee, Aravinda de Silva and Clive Lloyd.

The one-day squad was captained by Shaun Pollock and the Test XI by Graeme Smith, a glowing tribute and a daunting task for a 24-year-old with just two seasons experience of international captaincy.

Makhaya Ntini was also included in the one-day squad and Mark Boucher in the Test XI while Jacques Kallis and Pollock were included in both - although Pollock endured the rarity of performing 12th man duties during the Super Test. Herschelle Gibbs was picked for the one-day side but had to withdraw because of a knee injury.

As hard as Smith and Pollock's jobs were, Rhodes probably had the hardest task. It became wincingly obvious during the three-week jamboree what the driving forces were behind its inception. The first was money. The second was money. And the third was, well, money.

Gavaskar's panel wasn't so much required to select a team as to gather together the biggest names in the game, add the marquee players, make sure there was representation amongst all nations, and then reward their chosen with the largest match fees any of them had received. The fact that form and fitness were not prime concerns became an onerous burden to the contest and, finally, flattened it.

Before the players arrived in Australia the payments of $8000 for each one-day game and $25 000 for the Test - and winner-takes-all win bonuses of $125 000 per one-day match and $740 000 for the Super Test - were regarded as due reward for the world's best and reflective of the size of the occasion. But judging from the performances, it was based as much on the ICC's concern about motivating a disparate group of superstars from wildly different cultures and backgrounds.

Brian Lara hadn't played a competitive game for six months, though he was clearly dedicated. Andrew Flintoff, by contrast, had just completed a spectacular Ashes series against Australia in which England had regained the famous urn for the first time in 16 years. He, like Lara, was willing – but his body was exhausted.

Shahid Afridi slogged at every ball he faced in the one-dayers while his national captain, Inzamam-ul-Haq, had treated his original non-selection to the Test squad as a personal and national insult. He had to be coaxed into accepting his eventual call-up after Sachin Tendulkar's injury-enforced withdrawal but looked utterly disinterested in everything he did and sulked demonstrably - especially when Smith announced that he, rather than Inzi, would be fielding at first slip.

As much as the concept should, and could, have worked, it didn't. And as much as the World XI failed to unite, the Australians rallied together brilliantly after their Ashes loss and -

inspired by the notion of beating the Rest of the World and enforcing their number one ranking - did so emphatically.

Smith, Pollock and coach John Wright danced a merry political jig around the subject of the future of the Super Series afterwards but it was obvious that nobody felt it had worked. And the ludicrously expensive replica shirts on sale outside the grounds remained stubbornly unsold.

Sadly, it really was all about money and ICC chief executive Malcolm Speed's only positive comments afterwards were about the revenue numbers from global television rights. "We will have to review the possibility of repeating the Super Series," he said. "A different concept may have to be tried."

AUSTRALIA v WORLD XI — 1st Limited Overs International

Played at Telstra Dome, Melbourne on 5 October 2005 (D/N) — Toss: Australia
Umpires: Aleem Dar & SJA Taufel (TV: RE Koertzen) — Referee: RS Madugalle
Debuts: Aus: CL White. Wor: None
Result: Australia won by 93 runs
Man of Match: Shane Watson
Notes: Australia substitute: CL White replaced DR Martyn after 16 overs of World XI's innings. World XI substitute: Shahid Afridi replaced M Muralitharan after 43 overs of Australia's innings.

Adam Gilchrist and Simon Katich gave the home side a rollicking start on an awkward, "drop-in" pitch before Andrew Symonds and Mike Hussey added 36 and 32 respectively. Shaun Pollock was typically miserly but Kiwi spinner Daniel Vettori was the pick of the bowlers with 4-33.

Kumar Sangakkara was outstanding at the top of the order but Jacques Kallis, Brian Lara and Rahul Dravid all looked painfully short of form while Virender Sehwag and Shahid Afridi both played "who cares" shots across the line. The five batsmen below Sangakkara mustered 20 runs between them, rendering Andrew Flintoff's 38 redundant.

AUSTRALIA	*Runs*	*Mins*	*Balls*	*4*	*6*
†AC Gilchrist b Kallis	45	75	48	7	-
SM Katich c and b Muralitharan	58	133	79	4	-
*RT Ponting c Lara b Pollock	23	33	26	1	1
DR Martyn c Vettori b Muralitharan	0	3	3	-	-
A Symonds c Flintoff b Vettori	36	72	54	1	1
MJ Clarke c and b Vettori	6	18	16	-	-
MEK Hussey c Pietersen b Vettori	32	61	44	1	-
SR Watson c Lara b Vettori	8	15	15	-	-
B Lee not out	26	21	17	1	1
NW Bracken not out	2	10	3	-	-
GD McGrath					
CL White					
Extras (b 2, lb 6, w 6, nb 5)	19				
TOTAL (for 8 wkts) (50 overs)	**255**				

WORLD XI	*Runs*	*Mins*	*Balls*	*4*	*6*
†KC Sangakkara c Ponting b Watson	64	125	94	7	-
V Sehwag c Hussey b McGrath	6	22	10	-	-
JH Kallis lbw b McGrath	8	26	23	1	-
BC Lara c Symonds b Bracken	0	2	2	-	-
RS Dravid c Ponting b Lee	4	29	14	-	-
KP Pietersen lbw b Watson	2	10	6	-	-
A Flintoff c McGrath b Watson	38	70	52	2	1
Shahid Afridi lbw b Symonds	2	3	4	-	-
*SM Pollock run out (Watson)	5	14	12	-	-
DL Vettori c Ponting b Lee	15	31	28	-	-
Shoaib Akhtar not out	10	7	5	1	1
M Muralitharan					
Extras (lb 1, w 6, nb 1)	8				
TOTAL (41.3 overs)	**162**				

Wor	*O*	*M*	*R*	*W*	
Shoaib Akhtar	9	1	49	0	(3 nb, 1 w)
Pollock	8	1	32	1	
Flintoff	9	1	66	0	(1 nb, 3 w)
Kallis	4	0	26	1	(1 nb, 1 w)
Muralitharan	10	0	41	2	(1 w)
Vettori	10	1	33	4	

Aus	*O*	*M*	*R*	*W*	
Lee	7.3	2	31	2	(1 nb, 2 w)
McGrath	7	1	13	2	(1 w)
Bracken	8	0	36	1	(1 w)
Watson	10	0	43	3	(1 w)
Symonds	9	0	38	1	(1 w)

Fall of Wickets	*Aus*	*Wor*
1st	80 (1)	18 (2)
2nd	128 (3)	45 (3)
3rd	128 (4)	50 (4)
4th	142 (2)	75 (5)
5th	154 (6)	82 (6)
6th	206 (5)	101 (1)
7th	223 (8)	104 (8)
8th	231 (7)	118 (9)
9th	-	150 (7)
10th	-	162 (10)

AUSTRALIA v WORLD XI — 2nd Limited Overs International

Played at Telstra Dome, Melbourne on 7 October 2005 (D/N) — Toss: Australia
Umpires: DB Hair & RE Koertzen (TV: Aleem Dar) — Referee: RS Madugalle
Debuts: Aus: SR Clark. Wor: None
Result: Australia won by 55 runs
Man of Match: Adam Gilchrist
Notes: Gilchrist scored his century off 73 balls in Australia's innings. Australia substitute: CL White replaced SM Katich after 0 overs of World XI's innings. World XI substitute: CH Gayle replaced M Muralitharan after 47 overs of Australia's innings.

Gilchrist picked up where he left off two days earlier but this time he completed the job with a stunning century from just 73 deliveries, eight of which went for four and four were scythed over the ropes. Katich (47) was a virtual spectator in an opening stand of 110, Ricky Ponting (66) and Damien Martyn (54) batted with controlled aggression and Andrew Symonds pushed the total well beyond 300 with a brutal 31 from 14 balls.

Shoaib Akhtar was carved everywhere, Pollock maintained a modicum of respectability but Kallis was dispatched for 33 from just three overs.

Sangakkara and Chris Gayle slammed an astonishing 98 in 12 overs for the second wicket to take the World XI to 125-1 but they crumbled quickly thereafter and conceded the series.

AUSTRALIA	Runs	Mins	Balls	4	6
†AC Gilchrist b Sehwag	103	128	79	8	4
SM Katich b Muralitharan	47	86	71	3	-
*RT Ponting run out (Flintoff)	66	104	72	4	-
DR Martyn b Flintoff	54	65	54	5	-
A Symonds not out	31	25	14	1	2
MJ Clarke not out	17	23	15	1	-
MEK Hussey					
SR Watson					
B Lee					
NW Bracken					
SR Clark					
CL White					
Extras (lb 4, w 1, nb 5)	10				
TOTAL (for 4 wkts) (50 overs)	**328**				

WORLD XI	Runs	Mins	Balls	4	6
CH Gayle c Gilchrist b Watson	54	81	48	8	1
V Sehwag c Ponting b Lee	21	15	15	4	-
†KC Sangakkara run out (Martyn/Gilchrist)	61	84	44	9	1
JH Kallis run out (Ponting)	11	37	25	-	-
BC Lara c Symonds b Bracken	5	13	10	-	-
RS Dravid b Symonds	26	63	36	2	-
A Flintoff c Symonds b Bracken	42	47	49	3	-
KP Pietersen c Watson b Clark	16	24	22	-	1
*SM Pollock c White b Clark	15	20	16	-	-
DL Vettori not out	10	13	8	-	-
Shoaib Akhtar c Watson b Bracken	2	3	3	-	-
M Muralitharan					
Extras (lb 1, w 6, nb 3)	10				
TOTAL (45.3 overs)	**273**				

Wor	O	M	R	W	
Shoaib Akhtar	8	1	61	0	(3 nb, 1 w)
Pollock	8	0	49	0	
Flintoff	8	0	64	1	(2 nb)
Muralitharan	10	0	43	1	
Vettori	10	0	54	0	
Kallis	3	0	33	0	
Sehwag	3	0	20	1	

Aus	O	M	R	W	
Lee	8	1	47	1	(1 nb, 2 w)
Bracken	7.3	0	43	3	
Clark	9	0	55	2	
Watson	10	1	56	1	(2 nb, 1 w)
Symonds	8	0	49	1	(2 w)
White	3	0	22	0	(1 w)

Fall of Wickets	Aus	Wor
1st	110 (2)	27 (2)
2nd	173 (1)	125 (1)
3rd	276 (3)	151 (3)
4th	276 (4)	157 (5)
5th	-	157 (4)
6th	-	220 (7)
7th	-	235 (6)
8th	-	250 (8)
9th	-	267 (9)
10th	-	273 (11)

AUSTRALIA v WORLD XI — 3rd Limited Overs International

Played at Telstra Dome, Melbourne on 9 October 2005 (D/N) — Toss: Australia
Umpires: Aleem Dar & DB Hair (TV: SJA Taufel) — Referee: RS Madugalle
Debuts: Aus: None. Wor: None
Result: Australia won by 156 runs
Man of Match: Shane Watson
Man of Series: Adam Gilchrist
Notes: World XI substitute: Shahid Afridi replaced M Muralitharan after 0 overs of World XI's innings.

Ponting's measured 68 stabilised a shaky(ish) start at 58-2 but then Australia pulled so far ahead by the half-way stage that the conclusion was a formality. Mike Hussey and Shane Watson compiled an unbeaten 145 at a run-a-ball for the sixth wicket to post another intimidating total.

Pollock, finally, succumbed to the indifference around him and was clobbered for 67 in nine overs while Makhaya Ntini, given his first game, understandably looked rusty and leaked 58 from just seven overs.

Kallis' appalling lack of form didn't help the visitors' cause and if Sehwag hadn't decided - belatedly - to display some commitment, the all-stars might have been dismissed for less than a hundred. It was a sad and pathetic way for the series to end.

AUSTRALIA	Runs	Mins	Balls	4	6
†AC Gilchrist c and b Pollock	32	38	31	2	1
MJ Clarke lbw b Ntini	3	8	3	-	-
*RT Ponting c Lara b Muralitharan	68	98	84	8	1
DR Martyn lbw b Vettori	33	84	44	3	-
A Symonds c Sangakkara b Muralitharan	1	6	5	-	-
MEK Hussey not out	75	91	74	5	1
SR Watson not out	66	84	66	4	-
CL White					
B Lee					
NW Bracken					
GD McGrath					
Extras (lb 7, w 1, nb 7)	15				
TOTAL (for 5 wkts) (50 overs)	**293**				

WORLD XI	Runs	Mins	Balls	4	6
CH Gayle b Lee	0	2	2	-	-
V Sehwag run out (Watson)	37	87	40	4	1
†KC Sangakkara c Martyn b McGrath	13	14	15	2	-
JH Kallis c Hussey b Lee	2	12	10	-	-
BC Lara c Gilchrist b Lee	0	2	1	-	-
A Flintoff b Watson	21	33	25	4	-
RS Dravid c Martyn b Lee	16	48	38	1	-
*SM Pollock c White b Watson	8	44	27	1	-
DL Vettori ċ Clarke b Watson	0	3	5	-	-
Shahid Afridi c McGrath b Watson	16	11	8	2	1
M Ntini not out	0	2	0	-	-
M Muralitharan					
Extras (lb 6, w 14, nb 4)	24				
TOTAL (27.5 overs)	**137**				

Wor	O	M	R	W	
Pollock	9	0	67	1	(6 nb)
Ntini	7	0	58	1	(1 nb)
Flintoff	4.2	0	23	0	
Muralitharan	10	1	38	2	
Kallis	1.4	0	11	0	
Vettori	10	0	34	1	(1 w)
Gayle	6	0	42	0	
Sehwag	2	0	13	0	

Aus	O	M	R	W	
Lee	9	2	30	4	(3 nb, 1 w)
McGrath	6	0	26	1	
Bracken	5	0	36	0	(3 w)
Watson	7.5	0	39	4	(1 nb, 1 w)

Fall of Wickets	Aus	Wor
1st	15 (2)	0 (1)
2nd	58 (1)	20 (3)
3rd	143 (3)	27 (4)
4th	146 (5)	27 (5)
5th	148 (4)	87 (6)
6th	-	99 (2)
7th	-	119 (7)
8th	-	120 (9)
9th	-	137 (8)
10th	-	137 (10)

AUSTRALIA v WORLD XI — Only Test

Played at Sydney Cricket Ground, Sydney on 14,15,16,17 October 2005 — Toss: Australia
Umpires: RE Koertzen & SJA Taufel (TV: DB Hair) — Referee: RS Madugalle
Debuts: Aus: None. World: None
Close of play: Day 1: Aus (1) 331-6 (Gilchrist 94*, Warne 1*, 85 overs). Day 2: Aus (2) 66-1 (Hayden 27*, Ponting 17*, 20 overs). Day 3: World (2) 25-2 (Dravid 17*, Lara 0*, 8 overs).
Result: Australia won by 210 runs
Man of Match: Matthew Hayden

As many Australians noted beforehand, a Test match scheduled for six days at the SCG would need at least two rainy days if it was to go the distance. It didn't rain and the match finished inside four days with leg-spinners Shane Warne and Stuart MacGill sharing 15 of the 20 wickets.

Ponting won the toss in all four matches but the Super Test was undoubtedly influenced most by the luxury of batting first and unleashing his leg-spinners at the end of the game.

Matthew Hayden spoke before the game of how a lean Ashes series had helped him become a more patient player and he proved it by reaching 50 from 103 balls on the opening day.

The England duo of Harmison and Flintoff shared the new ball and each claimed an early wicket. When Smith ran out Simon Katich, the innings was in the balance at 163-4. At which point Gilchrist strode to the crease and dominated like only he can reaching an undefeated 94 by the close and allowing Hayden to coast to a workmanlike century.

Flintoff quickly knocked over the tail on the second morning - Gilchrist becoming the first man in Test cricket to be given out lbw by the TV umpire - but any hopes of a rally from the tourists were ended by Brett Lee and Glenn McGrath who reduced them to 43-3.

Virender Sehwag displayed some of the discipline and application he didn't bother with in the one-day series - not to mention some devastating ball-striking - and Kallis grafted a typically resilient 44. Flintoff smashed four sixes in the company of the tail-enders which put a smile on a few faces.

But a deficit of 155 was always going to be fatal, even when the home side were bundled out in their second innings. The combination of form and determination shown by Hayden and Ponting on a deteriorating pitch was patently lacking in the World XI.

After a nightmare sequence of 0, 5, 0, 5 in the Super Series, Brian Lara finally showed a glimpse of his genius while Kallis was left stranded when the last wicket fell with the total an embarrassing 144.

Warne finished with a match haul of 6-71 and his 'understudy', MacGill, collected 9-82. The World XI collected criticism and derision. And their cheques.

AUSTRALIA	*Runs*	*Mins*	*Balls*	*4*	*6*		*Runs*	*Mins*	*Balls*	*4*	*6*
JL Langer b Harmison	0	1	3	-	-	c Smith b Kallis	22	41	33	2	-
ML Hayden c Kallis b Muralitharan	111	277	180	12	-	b Harmison	77	189	120	9	-
*RT Ponting c Kallis b Flintoff	46	97	76	6	1	c Boucher b Flintoff	54	175	111	4	-
MJ Clarke c Sehwag b Vettori	39	88	68	4	-	b Harmison	5	8	8	1	-
SM Katich run out (Smith)	0	10	9	-	-	c and b Muralitharan	2	22	22	-	-
†AC Gilchrist lbw b Flintoff	94	158	111	8	4	c Kallis b Muralitharan	1	12	3	-	-
SR Watson lbw b Muralitharan	24	66	60	1	-	c Boucher b Flintoff	10	60	37	1	-
SK Warne c Kallis b Flintoff	5	29	20	-	-	c Dravid b Flintoff	7	22	19	-	-
B Lee c Smith b Flintoff	1	22	10	-	-	c Muralitharan b Harmison	3	49	28	-	-
GD McGrath run out (Dravid)	0	11	5	-	-	c Smith b Muralitharan	2	12	9	-	-
SCG MacGill not out	0	4	5	-	-	not out	0	7	5	-	-
Extras (b 5, lb 11, w 3, nb 6)	25					Extras (b 7, lb 7, nb 2)	16				
TOTAL (90 overs)	**345**					**TOTAL (65.3 overs)**	**199**				

WORLD XI	*Runs*	*Mins*	*Balls*	*4*	*6*		*Runs*	*Mins*	*Balls*	*4*	*6*
*GC Smith c Gilchrist b Lee	12	33	25	1	-	b McGrath	0	3	5	-	-
V Sehwag c Katich b Warne	76	144	82	14	-	c Gilchrist b MacGill	7	26	13	-	1
R Dravid c Gilchrist b McGrath	0	6	6	-	-	c Hayden b Warne	23	88	68	3	-
BC Lara lbw b McGrath	5	8	8	1	-	c Gilchrist b Warne	36	75	51	7	-
JH Kallis c Hayden b Warne	44	123	94	8	-	not out	39	111	86	3	1
Inzamam-ul-Haq st Gilchrist b MacGill	1	6	5	-	-	lbw b Lee	0	5	2	-	-
A Flintoff c Lee b MacGill	35	45	36	-	4	c sub (BJ Hodge) b MacGill	15	41	27	2	-
†MV Boucher c Gilchrist b Warne	0	3	2	-	-	c Hayden b Warne	17	38	43	1	-
DL Vettori not out	8	34	16	-	-	c Ponting b MacGill	0	8	5	-	-
SJ Harmison c Clarke b MacGill	1	8	8	-	-	lbw b MacGill	0	3	1	-	-
M Muralitharan c Langer b MacGill	2	7	4	-	-	st Gilchrist b MacGill	0	1	3	-	-
Extras (b 1, lb 1, w 1, nb 3)	6					Extras (b 1, lb 2, nb 4)	7				
TOTAL (47.1 overs)	**190**					**TOTAL (50 overs)**	**144**				

World	*O*	*M*	*R*	*W*		*O*	*M*	*R*	*W*	
Harmison	18	3	60	1	(2 nb, 3 w)	12.3	2	41	3	
Flintoff	18	3	59	4	(3 nb)	16	2	48	3	(1 nb)
Kallis	7	1	35	0	(1 nb)	3	1	3	1	
Muralitharan	30	3	102	2		24	5	55	3	
Vettori	17	3	73	1		10	0	38	0	(1 nb)
Aus	*O*	*M*	*R*	*W*		*O*	*M*	*R*	*W*	
McGrath	12	4	34	2		6	3	8	1	
Lee	8	1	54	1	(3 nb)	10	2	42	1	(4 nb)
Watson	6	0	38	0	(1 w)					
Warne	12	3	23	3		(3) 19	4	48	3	
MacGill	9.1	0	39	4		(4) 15	4	43	5	

Fall of Wickets

	Aus	**World**	**Aus**	**World**
1st	0 (1)	27 (1)	30 (1)	0 (1)
2nd	73 (3)	31 (3)	152 (2)	18 (2)
3rd	154 (4)	43 (4)	160 (4)	56 (3)
4th	163 (5)	134 (2)	167 (3)	69 (4)
5th	260 (2)	135 (6)	167 (5)	70 (6)
6th	323 (7)	147 (5)	170 (6)	122 (7)
7th	331 (6)	151 (8)	177 (8)	143 (8)
8th	339 (8)	183 (7)	192 (7)	144 (9)
9th	344 (9)	184 (10)	195 (10)	144 (10)
10th	345 (10)	190 (11)	199 (9)	144 (11)

21st CENTURY GAME . . . dancers entertain the crowd at the first Pro20 international to be played in South Africa *Picture: DUIF DU TOIT, Touchline Photo*

NEW ZEALAND ONE-DAY SERIES 2005/06

Colin Bryden

What was envisaged as a conventional tour, with Test matches and one-day internationals, became a one-day series only because of the difficulty of arranging a schedule to fit in with the International Cricket Council's Super Series between Australia and the Rest of the World.

South Africa won four of the five matches, with the other rained off, to gain ample recompense for their defeats in New Zealand in 2004 when the Kiwis won the last five matches of a six-match series.

New Zealand started the tour well by winning two warm-up matches against South Africa A, as well as the first 20-overs international played in South Africa. They had a good chance of winning the first 50-overs contest in Bloemfontein before a fine partnership between Justin Kemp and Shaun Pollock set the tone for the rest of the series.

A significant omission from the New Zealand team was Chris Cairns, with coach John Bracewell stating that the 35-year-old all-rounder needed to gain full match fitness by playing in domestic cricket. Cairns retired later in the season, abandoning plans to play in the 2007 World Cup.

The New Zealand squad was: Stephen Fleming (captain), Daniel Vettori (vice-captain), Andre Adams, Nathan Astle, Shane Bond, James Franklin, Hamish Marshall, James Marshall, Brendon McCullum, Craig McMillan, Kyle Mills, Jacob Oram, Jeetan Patel, Scott Styris, Lou Vincent. Coach, John Bracewell.

SOUTH AFRICA A v NEW ZEALANDERS Limited Overs Match 50 overs per side

Played at Willowmoore Park, Benoni on 14 October 2005 (D/N) — Toss: New Zealanders
Umpires: IL Howell & BG Jerling (TV: KH Hurter) — Referee: CJ Mitchley
Debuts: SAA: None. NZ: None
Result: New Zealanders won by 19 runs (D/L method), target revised to 219 in 43 overs
Man of Match: Craig McMillan
Notes: New Zealanders substitute: JS Patel replaced CD McMillan after 0 overs of South Africa A's innings.

After winning a triangular tournament in Sri Lanka, South Africa A put New Zealand under pressure, mainly through the bowling of Henderson, who gained swing and bounce. McMillan and James Marshall put the tourists on top, however, with McMillan going on to a century. Bond and Mills bowled superbly under floodlights as South Africa A could score only 22 runs off the first 13 overs. Rudolph and the hard-hitting Morkel gave the A side some faint hope before a storm brought an early end.

NEW ZEALANDERS	*Runs*	*Mins*	*Balls*	*4*	*6*
*SP Fleming lbw b Steyn	11	17	14	2	-
NJ Astle c Tsolekile b Henderson	9	15	11	2	-
L Vincent c Henderson b Steyn	7	22	10	-	1
HJH Marshall c Tsolekile b Henderson	10	31	29	1	-
CD McMillan lbw b Henderson	105	135	106	9	2
JAH Marshall c Tsolekile b Rudolph	64	112	83	4	1
†BB McCullum c De Bruyn b Henderson	2	14	8	-	-
JEC Franklin b Henderson	3	7	8	-	-
AR Adams run out (Ontong/Tsolekile)	32	26	18	3	2
KD Mills not out	10	18	13	-	-
SE Bond					
JS Patel					
Extras (lb 8, w 12)	20				
TOTAL (for 9 wkts) (50 overs)	**273**				

SOUTH AFRICA A	*Runs*	*Mins*	*Balls*	*4*	*6*
AG Puttick b Mills	0	13	10	-	-
LL Bosman c Fleming b Franklin	16	60	52	1	-
Z de Bruyn c Mills b Adams	40	107	80	2	1
*JA Rudolph not out	73	110	88	9	-
JL Ontong c Vincent b Patel	8	8	10	1	-
JA Morkel not out	48	41	28	5	3
RJ Peterson					
†TL Tsolekile					
JJ van der Wath					
T Henderson					
DW Steyn					
Extras (b 2, lb 1, w 1, nb 10)	14				
TOTAL (for 4 wkts) (43 overs)	**199**				

SAA	O	M	R	W	
Steyn	9	0	46	2	(5 w)
Henderson	10	3	38	5	
Van der Wath	8	1	48	0	(2 w)
Morkel	6	0	27	0	
Peterson	4	0	28	0	
De Bruyn	4	0	26	0	(3 w)
Rudolph	9	0	52	1	

NZ	O	M	R	W	
Bond	8	2	29	0	(1 nb)
Mills	8	0	35	1	(2 nb)
Franklin	5	1	11	1	(3 nb, 1 w)
Adams	6	0	28	1	(1 nb)
Astle	6	0	29	0	
Patel	10	0	64	1	(3 nb)

Fall of Wickets	NZ	SAA
1st	21 (2)	2 (1)
2nd	21 (1)	31 (2)
3rd	33 (3)	107 (3)
4th	42 (4)	118 (5)
5th	203 (6)	-
6th	223 (5)	-
7th	224 (7)	-
8th	231 (8)	-
9th	273 (9)	-

SOUTH AFRICA A v NEW ZEALANDERS Limited Overs Match 50 overs per side

Played at Sedgars Park, Potchefstroom on 16 October 2005 — Toss: South Africa A

Umpires: IL Howell & BG Jerling (TV: KH Hurter) — Referee: CJ Mitchley

Debuts: SAA: DJ Jacobs (LO for SAA). NZ: None

Result: New Zealanders won by 103 runs

Man of Match: Stephen Fleming

Notes: South Africa A substitute: JL Ontong replaced M Zondeki after 0 overs of South Africa A's innings.

Davy Jacobs was added to the South Africa A squad after Loots Bosman suffered a knee injury in the first game. Fleming's century was the only significant contribution from the New Zealand top order, while Van der Wath bowled well. Although Jacobs gave the A side a bright start, Bond's pace was too much for the South African second string.

NEW ZEALANDERS	Runs	Mins	Balls	4	6
NJ Astle c De Bruyn b Henderson	0	20	12	-	-
*SP Fleming c Tsolekile b Peterson	100	146	115	16	-
L Vincent c Rudolph b Van der Wath	14	34	13	1	1
HJH Marshall c De Bruyn b Zondeki	0	8	1	-	-
JDP Oram run out (Peterson)	2	13	10	-	-
CD McMillan c Tsolekile b Van der Wath	9	16	16	1	-
†BB McCullum b Van der Wath	37	81	62	1	-
KD Mills not out	47	68	48	4	-
AR Adams b Morkel	1	6	5	-	-
SE Bond c Jacobs b Van der Wath	2	12	8	-	-
JS Patel not out	9	17	10	1	-
Extras (lb 6, w 4)	10				
TOTAL (for 9 wkts) (50 overs)	**231**				

SOUTH AFRICA A	Runs	Mins	Balls	4	6
AG Puttick c Astle b Mills	1	8	6	-	-
DJ Jacobs c Vincent b Bond	26	28	20	6	-
Z de Bruyn c McCullum b Astle	20	70	44	1	-
*JA Rudolph b Adams	20	22	18	3	-
JL Ontong c Adams b Bond	37	75	72	1	-
JA Morkel run out (sub - JAH Marshall)	8	15	13	2	-
RJ Peterson run out (Marshall)	6	28	14	-	-
†TL Tsolekile c McCullum b Bond	2	12	10	-	-
JJ van der Wath not out	2	14	5	-	-
T Henderson b Bond	0	2	1	-	-
DW Steyn c Fleming b Bond	0	2	2	-	-
M Zondeki					
Extras (lb 1, w 3, nb 2)	6				
TOTAL (33.5 overs)	**128**				

SAA	O	M	R	W	
Steyn	10	1	40	0	
Henderson	8	0	44	1	
Zondeki	7	0	37	1	
Van der Wath	10	1	31	4	(2 w)
Morkel	8	0	33	1	(2 w)
Peterson	7	0	40	1	

NZ	O	M	R	W	
Bond	5.5	1	37	5	(2 w)
Mills	5	0	21	1	(1 nb, 1 w)
Adams	8	2	25	1	
Astle	10	1	26	1	
Patel	5	0	18	0	(1 nb)

Fall of Wickets	NZ	SAA
1st	15 (1)	16 (1)
2nd	68 (3)	34 (2)
3rd	80 (4)	61 (4)
4th	87 (5)	85 (3)
5th	97 (6)	97 (6)
6th	148 (2)	123 (7)
7th	196 (7)	125 (5)
8th	198 (9)	128 (8)
9th	209 (10)	128 (10)
10th	-	128 (11)

SOUTH AFRICA v NEW ZEALAND Only Pro20 International

Played at Liberty Life Wanderers Stadium, Johannesburg on 21 October 2005 (D/N) — Toss: New Zealand

Umpires: IL Howell & BG Jerling (TV: KH Hurter) — Referee: BC Broad

Debuts: SA: All (20Int). NZ: SE Bond, JAH Marshall, JDP Oram and JS Patel (All 20Int and 20), NJ Astle (20Int)

Result: New Zealand won by 5 wickets

Man of Match: Jeetan Patel

Notes: New Zealand substitute: JAH Marshall replaced JS Patel after 0 overs of New Zealand's innings. South Africa substitute: N Boje replaced JM Kemp after 5.1 overs of New Zealand's innings.

A crowd of 28 526 watched the first Pro20 international played in South Africa. Gibbs was back in the national team after recovering from a knee injury. Initially the spectators had much to cheer, urged on by dancing girls and flashing lights, as Smith and Kallis put on 84 for the first wicket, with Smith in belligerent mood before he was out off the fourth ball of the tenth over.

The foundation had been laid for an imposing total but the innings crumbled, primarily against the slower bowlers. The slow medium-paced Astle and the off-spinner Patel returned identical figures and were similarly effective as South Africa contrived to lose all their wickets for the addition of 49 runs before 20 overs had been bowled. New Zealand suffered a minor scare when three wickets fell in the space of eight balls but went on to win easily.

SOUTH AFRICA	*Runs*	*Mins*	*Balls*	*4*	*6*
*GC Smith c and b Astle	61	39	43	10	1
JH Kallis b Patel	20	43	18	1	1
HH Gibbs lbw b Patel	9	10	7	1	-
JM Kemp c and b Astle	8	11	11	1	-
†MV Boucher b Astle	4	14	8	-	-
SM Pollock c Fleming b Adams	0	3	2	-	-
AG Prince run out (Patel)	5	13	6	-	-
JA Morkel c McCullum b Patel	11	16	12	-	1
CK Langeveldt b Bond	2	5	4	-	-
M Ntini b Bond	5	8	6	1	-
A Nel not out	0	3	2	-	-
N Boje					
Extras (b 1, lb 2, w 1, nb 4)	8				
TOTAL (19.3 overs)	**133**				

NEW ZEALAND	*Runs*	*Mins*	*Balls*	*4*	*6*
*SP Fleming c Morkel b Langeveldt	31	30	25	6	-
NJ Astle b Nel	10	23	10	1	-
HJH Marshall c Boucher b Nel	3	4	3	-	-
CD McMillan c Nel b Boje	15	26	19	1	-
SB Styris b Langeveldt	24	39	28	2	-
JDP Oram not out	23	26	16	1	2
†BB McCullum not out	17	8	9	1	1
JAH Marshall					
KD Mills					
AR Adams					
SE Bond					
JS Patel					
Extras (b 1, lb 3, w 3, nb 4)	11				
TOTAL (for 5 wkts) (18 overs)	**134**				

NZ	*O*	*M*	*R*	*W*	
Bond	3.3	0	25	2	
Mills	4	0	38	0	(1 nb, 1 w)
Adams	4	0	27	1	
Astle	4	0	20	3	
Patel	4	0	20	3	(1 nb)

SA	*O*	*M*	*R*	*W*	
Pollock	3	0	16	0	(1 w)
Ntini	2	0	21	0	
Nel	4	0	19	2	
Langeveldt	2	0	14	2	(2 w)
Boje	4	0	27	1	
Morkel	2	0	13	0	
Smith	1	0	20	0	(2 nb)

Fall of Wickets	*SA*	*NZ*
1st	84 (1)	37 (2)
2nd	90 (2)	41 (3)
3rd	99 (3)	46 (1)
4th	105 (4)	80 (4)
5th	106 (6)	110 (5)
6th	110 (5)	-
7th	117 (7)	-
8th	121 (9)	-
9th	129 (8)	-
10th	133 (10)	-

SOUTH AFRICA v NEW ZEALAND — 1st Limited Overs International

Played at Goodyear Park, Bloemfontein on 23 October 2005 — Toss: New Zealand
Umpires: SA Bucknor & IL Howell (TV: KH Hurter) — Referee: BC Broad
Debuts: SA: None. NZ: None
Result: South Africa won by 2 wickets
Man of Match: Justin Kemp
Notes: New Zealand substitute: JS Patel replaced JDP Oram after 18 overs of South Africa's innings. South Africa substitute: N Boje replaced M Ntini after 20.4 overs of New Zealand's innings.

Kemp's powerful hitting enabled South Africa to stretch their unbeaten record to 15 one-day internationals after they lost half their wickets before reaching the half-way mark in their run chase. Two partnerships of 65, with Boucher and Pollock, took South Africa to the brink of victory before Pollock and Kemp both fell with only three runs needed.

Fleming played a delightful innings for New Zealand before falling to a sensational catch by Gibbs, diving to his left at backward point, and McMillan steered the tourists to what Fleming considered a reasonable target. Ntini became the first player to be substituted by South Africa under the "super-sub" system when it was considered Boje's spin would be better suited to a slow, dry surface.

Bond's first over cost 17 runs, including two wides which went to the boundary, costing five apiece, but South Africa then struggled before Boucher and Kemp came together. Kemp gave a return chance to Astle when he had made eight and promptly made the bowler pay dearly when he hit 22, including two fours and two successive sixes, off Astle's next over.

DID YOU CATCH THAT . . . Andre Nel and Ashwell Prince act like photographers, recording a great catch by Herschelle Gibbs in Bloemfontein   Picture: DUIF DU TOIT, Touchline Photo

NEW ZEALAND	*Runs*	*Mins*	*Balls*	*4*	*6*
*SP Fleming c Gibbs b Nel	45	64	48	9	-
NJ Astle c Boucher b Pollock	1	12	9	-	-
L Vincent c Boucher b Ntini	8	15	12	1	-
HJH Marshall lbw b Kallis	16	63	40	1	-
CD McMillan c Prince b Kallis	66	118	75	8	1
JDP Oram run out (Smith/Boucher)	35	68	60	2	-
†BB McCullum c Dippenaar b Nel	28	51	32	-	1
DL Vettori c Prince b Nel	1	6	3	-	-
AR Adams not out	30	26	22	1	1
KD Mills not out	1	6	1	-	-
SE Bond					
JS Patel					
Extras (b 1, lb 11, w 4, nb 2)	18				
TOTAL (for 8 wkts) (50 overs)	**249**				

SOUTH AFRICA	*Runs*	*Mins*	*Balls*	*4*	*6*
*GC Smith b Adams	19	34	24	4	-
HH Dippenaar lbw b Bond	10	12	9	2	-
JH Kallis b Mills	0	10	5	-	-
HH Gibbs c Marshall b Bond	25	88	69	-	-
AG Prince b Astle	31	52	45	5	-
†MV Boucher b Vettori	33	67	50	1	-
JM Kemp c Vincent b Patel	73	82	64	5	3
SM Pollock c Adams b Patel	37	37	29	2	1
N Boje not out	3	7	3	-	-
CK Langeveldt not out	0	5	0	-	-
A Nel					
M Ntini					
Extras (b 1, lb 4, w 13, nb 1)	19				
TOTAL (for 8 wkts) (49.3 overs)	**250**				

SA	*O*	*M*	*R*	*W*	
Pollock	10	2	43	1	
Ntini	4	0	19	1	(2 nb)
Langeveldt	10	1	48	0	(1 w)
Nel	9	0	42	3	
Kallis	9	1	45	2	(2 w)
Boje	6	0	32	0	(1 w)
Kemp	2	0	8	0	

NZ	*O*	*M*	*R*	*W*	
Bond	9.3	1	50	2	(2 w)
Mills	10	2	38	1	
Adams	6	0	28	1	
Vettori	10	0	35	1	(1 nb)
Astle	6	0	46	1	(1 w)
Patel	8	0	48	2	(1 w)

Fall of Wickets	*NZ*	*SA*
1st	7 (2)	29 (2)
2nd	18 (3)	34 (3)
3rd	70 (1)	41 (1)
4th	97 (4)	85 (5)
5th	172 (6)	117 (4)
6th	200 (5)	182 (6)
7th	204 (8)	247 (8)
8th	241 (7)	247 (7)

SOUTH AFRICA v NEW ZEALAND — 2nd Limited Overs International

Played at Sahara Park Newlands, Cape Town on 28 October 2005 (D/N) — Toss: South Africa
Umpires: SA Bucknor & IL Howell (TV: KH Hurter) — Referee: BC Broad
Debuts: SA: AG Puttick. NZ: None
Result: South Africa won by 19 runs
Man of Match: Lou Vincent
Notes: New Zealand substitute: JEC Franklin replaced SE Bond after 16 overs of New Zealand's innings. South Africa substitute: N Boje replaced JH Kallis after 7 overs of New Zealand's innings.

Andrew Puttick, who had been on South Africa's tour of Sri Lanka in 2004, earned his first full international cap in unusual circumstances when he was summonsed from a match for the Cobras in nearby Paarl. Dippenaar withdrew on the morning of the match because of a ganglion on his right wrist, which required surgery, while AB de Villiers was ruled out with a calf strain. Andrew Hall had been released to play for the Lions in Potchefstroom and could not have reached Cape Town in time.

It was an unfortunate debut for Puttick, who failed to score before being bowled by a superb, fast delivery from Bond. South Africa's top order batting was again shaky but Kallis played a watchful innings while Boucher was again in good form on a pitch of uneven bounce.

Vincent and Styris put on 64 off 53 balls for the third wicket to get New Zealand well ahead of the required rate but the rest of the batting failed until substitute Franklin joined Vincent. The Black Caps were still on target until Vincent, two runs after calling for a runner because of cramp, pulled the first ball of a new spell from Ntini to mid-wicket. He was eighth man out when 37 runs were needed off 47 balls. Langeveldt took the last two wickets.

AGGRESSIVE INTENT . . . big-hitting Justin Kemp gets fired up as the third international in Port Elizabeth heads for a thrilling finish *Picture: DUIF DU TOIT, Touchline Photo*

SOUTH AFRICA		Runs	Mins	Balls	4	6
*GC Smith b Styris		36	62	44	4	1
AG Puttick b Bond		0	8	5	-	-
HH Gibbs lbw b Mills		33	72	53	5	-
SM Pollock c Adams b Styris		0	7	5	-	-
JH Kallis c Vincent b Mills		51	120	94	2	-
AG Prince b Vettori		19	52	40	1	-
†MV Boucher c and b Mills		40	53	47	6	-
JM Kemp not out		8	18	5	1	-
CK Langeveldt c Adams b Mills		1	3	2	-	-
M Ntini b Bond		0	4	5	-	-
A Nel not out		4	1	1	1	-
N Boje						
Extras (lb 1, w 6, nb 2)		9				
TOTAL (for 9 wkts) (50 overs)		**201**				

NEW ZEALAND	Runs	Mins	Balls	4	6
*SP Fleming c Smith b Ntini	6	23	15	-	-
NJ Astle c Gibbs b Ntini	3	15	13	-	-
L Vincent c Prince b Ntini	90	168	109	9	2
SB Styris c Kemp b Nel	27	37	27	5	-
CD McMillan c Boucher b Langeveldt	3	20	15	-	-
JDP Oram c Boucher b Kemp	11	51	37	1	-
†BB McCullum st Boucher b Boje	1	9	7	-	-
DL Vettori c Smith b Boje	0	7	5	-	-
JEC Franklin c Puttick b Langeveldt	21	59	38	2	-
AR Adams lbw b Langeveldt	6	15	13	-	-
KD Mills not out	2	10	9	-	-
SE Bond					
Extras (lb 5, w 6, nb 1)	12				
TOTAL (47.5 overs)	**182**				

NZ	O	M	R	W
Mills	10	0	44	4 (2 w)
Bond	10	0	42	2 (2 nb, 2 w)
Adams	6	0	39	0
Styris	10	1	29	2 (1 w)
Vettori	10	0	31	1 (1 w)
Astle	4	0	15	0

SA	O	M	R	W
Pollock	7	0	36	0
Ntini	10	1	29	3 (1 w)
Nel	9	1	32	1 (3 w)
Langeveldt	7.5	3	35	3 (1 nb)
Kemp	6	0	19	1
Boje	8	0	26	2 (1 w)

Fall of Wickets	SA	NZ
1st	3 (2)	7 (2)
2nd	69 (1)	16 (1)
3rd	71 (4)	80 (4)
4th	74 (3)	93 (5)
5th	120 (6)	126 (6)
6th	182 (7)	129 (7)
7th	188 (5)	137 (8)
8th	196 (9)	165 (3)
9th	197 (10)	177 (10)
10th	-	182 (9)

SOUTH AFRICA v NEW ZEALAND — 3rd Limited Overs International

Played at Sahara Oval St George's, Port Elizabeth on 30 October 2005 — Toss: South Africa
Umpires: SA Bucknor & BG Jerling (TV: KH Hurter) — Referee: BC Broad
Debuts: SA: None. NZ: None
Result: South Africa won by 4 wickets
Man of Match: Herschelle Gibbs
Notes: New Zealand substitute: JDP Oram replaced CD McMillan after 28 overs of South Africa's innings. South Africa substitute: N Boje replaced A Nel after 17 overs of South Africa's innings.

Kallis withdrew because of the illness that caused him to be substituted in Cape Town, while Rudolph returned to the squad as a replacement for Dippenaar. De Villiers played after passing a fitness test.

The South African bowlers gained early assistance after Smith sent New Zealand in, with Ntini striking twice in his first spell. Fleming and Styris were mainly responsible for New Zealand making another competitive total.

De Villiers got the South African innings off to an explosive start, with Bond's first three overs costing 26, including a hooked six by De Villiers. Gibbs played a fluent innings but again there were some anxious moments. Forty-two were needed off 28 balls when Pollock joined Kemp. Nine were needed off the final over but Kemp pulled a huge six out of the ground off Bond's first ball before hooking the next for four to clinch the match and the series.

It was South Africa's 12th successive win, the second-longest winning streak behind Australia's 21 in 2003.

NEW ZEALAND	Runs	Mins	Balls	4	6
*SP Fleming run out (Kemp)	54	117	90	7	-
NJ Astle c Kemp b Ntini	11	20	20	2	-
L Vincent c Boucher b Ntini	3	10	6	-	-
HJH Marshall c Smith b Nel	7	32	18	1	-
SB Styris b Langeveldt	78	130	102	7	-
CD McMillan run out (Pollock)	19	38	24	2	-
†BB McCullum b Ntini	19	31	20	-	1
AR Adams run out (De Villiers/Boucher)	25	21	14	2	1
DL Vettori c Gibbs b Nel	6	6	4	1	-
KD Mills not out	6	8	4	1	-
SE Bond					
JDP Oram					
Extras (lb 5, w 8, nb 2)	15				
TOTAL (for 9 wkts) (50 overs)	**243**				

SOUTH AFRICA	Runs	Mins	Balls	4	6
*GC Smith c McCullum b Adams	18	32	26	2	-
AB de Villiers c McCullum b Mills	29	41	29	4	1
HH Gibbs c Marshall b Bond	81	135	94	8	1
JA Rudolph run out (Marshall)	17	65	52	2	-
AG Prince c Mills b Adams	21	30	30	1	-
†MV Boucher run out (Vincent)	24	44	33	1	-
JM Kemp not out	30	39	19	2	2
SM Pollock not out	21	23	14	2	-
CK Langeveldt					
M Ntini					
N Boje					
A Nel					
Extras (lb 2, w 1, nb 1)	4				
TOTAL (for 6 wkts) (49.2 overs)	**245**				

SA	O	M	R	W	
Pollock	10	0	23	0	(5 w)
Ntini	10	0	37	3	
Nel	10	2	47	2	
Langeveldt	10	0	76	1	(2 nb)
Kemp	7	0	40	0	
Smith	3	0	15	0	(3 w)

NZ	O	M	R	W	
Mills	10	2	45	1	(1 nb)
Bond	9.2	1	73	1	(1 w)
Adams	10	1	40	2	
Styris	10	0	32	0	
Vettori	9	0	49	0	
Astle	1	0	4	0	

Fall of Wickets	NZ	SA
1st	18 (2)	40 (1)
2nd	23 (3)	48 (2)
3rd	49 (4)	101 (4)
4th	108 (1)	150 (5)
5th	155 (6)	187 (3)
6th	203 (7)	202 (6)
7th	206 (5)	-
8th	224 (9)	-
9th	243 (8)	-

SOUTH AFRICA v NEW ZEALAND — 4th Limited Overs International

Played at Sahara Stadium Kingsmead, Durban on 4 November 2005 (D/N) Toss: South Africa
Umpires: SA Bucknor & BG Jerling (TV: KH Hurter) Referee: BC Broad
Debuts: SA: None. NZ: None
Result: No result

South Africa's winning streak came to an end but they continued unbeaten when rain fell after 20 overs of the South African innings and no further play was possible. With the series won, South Africa left out Gibbs and Boje, who were both unavailable for the forthcoming tour of India. Astle became the fourth New Zealander to play in 200 one-day internationals.

SOUTH AFRICA	Runs	Mins	Balls	4	6
AB de Villiers c McCullum b Bond	6	19	18	1	-
*GC Smith lbw b Franklin	22	60	37	4	-
JH Kallis not out	24	70	43	4	-
AG Prince not out	17	29	23	2	-
JM Kemp					
†MV Boucher					
SM Pollock					
AJ Hall					
CK Langeveldt					
M Ntini					
A Nel					
Extras (lb 4, w 5, nb 1)	10				
TOTAL (for 2 wkts) (20 overs)	**79**				

NEW ZEALAND
*SP Fleming
NJ Astle
L Vincent
SB Styris
CD McMillan
HJH Marshall
†BB McCullum
DL Vettori
JEC Franklin
KD Mills
SE Bond

NZ	O	M	R	W	
Mills	8	1	34	0	(3 w)
Bond	5	0	19	1	(1 nb, 1 w)
Franklin	5	1	18	1	(1 w)
Styris	2	0	4	0	

Fall of Wickets	SA
1st	14 (1)
2nd	52 (2)

SOUTH AFRICA v NEW ZEALAND — 5th Limited Overs International

Played at SuperSport Park, Centurion on 6 November 2005 — Toss: South Africa
Umpires: SA Bucknor & BG Jerling (TV: KH Hurter) — Referee: BC Broad
Debuts: SA: None. NZ: None
Result: South Africa won by 5 wickets (D/L method), target revised to 140 in 30 overs
Man of Match: Andrew Hall
Man of Series: Justin Kemp
Notes: New Zealand substitute: CD McMillan replaced AR Adams after 25.3 overs of New Zealand's innings. South Africa substitute: JA Morkel replaced A Nel after 22.5 overs of South Africa's innings.

Hall had career-best figures as New Zealand again failed to put together a team batting effort. Astle and Vincent put on 75 for the second wicket off 80 balls, in a stand interrupted by rain, before the innings lost momentum.

Lightning flashed nearby when South Africa started their innings under heavy cloud. With every chance of a Duckworth/Lewis calculation, Smith made sure South Africa were ahead of the target rate before he was out in the 18th over. Lightning and imminent rain stopped play when South Africa were 105-2 off 19 overs, one over short of the number needed for a result. Coach Arthur's exchange with the umpires when they took the players off earned him a fine of 25 percent of his match fee.

After a delay of more than an hour, South Africa needed only 35 off 11 overs to complete a 4-0 series win.

Langeveldt was fined 75 percent of his match fee after, for the second time in his career, being found guilty of celebrating a wicket before appealing to the umpire, while Styris was fined 25 percent for showing dissent at an umpire's decision. Surprisingly there was no action against Kyle Mills, who was captured by television cameras having a heated exchange with Smith after an appeal against the South African captain was turned down.

NEW ZEALAND	Runs	Mins	Balls	4	6
*SP Fleming c Boucher b Pollock	0	1	2	-	-
NJ Astle c Hall b Langeveldt	37	54	43	8	-
L Vincent c De Villiers b Hall	66	118	76	8	2
HJH Marshall c Boucher b Langeveldt	3	19	13	-	-
SB Styris c Boucher b Hall	19	35	31	2	-
CD McMillan lbw b Hall	9	25	16	-	-
†BB McCullum c Boucher b Hall	27	65	49	2	-
DL Vettori run out (Boucher)	0	1	1	-	-
JEC Franklin c Boucher b Nel	12	43	29	-	-
KD Mills c Prince b Ntini	19	28	24	1	1
SE Bond not out	9	24	17	-	1
AR Adams					
Extras (lb 3, w 7, nb 4)	14				
TOTAL (49.3 overs)	**215**				

SOUTH AFRICA	Runs	Mins	Balls	4	6
*GC Smith b Franklin	66	81	65	13	-
AB de Villiers c Fleming b Mills	11	46	25	2	-
JH Kallis c Fleming b Vettori	15	46	20	3	-
AG Prince st McCullum b Vettori	9	37	25	-	-
JA Morkel c Astle b Styris	5	10	12	1	-
†MV Boucher not out	22	22	22	3	-
JM Kemp not out	1	7	1	-	-
SM Pollock					
AJ Hall					
CK Langeveldt					
M Ntini					
A Nel					
Extras (lb 3, w 7, nb 1)	11				
TOTAL (for 5 wkts) (28.1 overs)	**140**				

SA	O	M	R	W	
Pollock	8	1	34	1	(2 nb, 1 w)
Ntini	8.3	0	49	1	(1 w)
Nel	9	0	46	1	(4 w)
Langeveldt	9	2	36	2	(1 nb)
Hall	10	1	23	4	(1 nb, 1 w)
Kallis	5	0	24	0	

NZ	O	M	R	W	
Mills	8	0	45	1	(1 w)
Bond	5	0	27	0	(1 w)
Franklin	4	1	19	1	(1 nb)
Styris	6	0	27	1	(1 w)
Vettori	5	0	18	2	
Astle	0.1	0	1	0	

Fall of Wickets	NZ	SA
1st	0 (1)	61 (2)
2nd	75 (2)	103 (1)
3rd	91 (4)	106 (3)
4th	134 (5)	113 (5)
5th	141 (3)	131 (4)
6th	152 (6)	-
7th	152 (8)	-
8th	185 (9)	-
9th	187 (7)	-
10th	215 (10)	-

Sahara recommends Microsoft® Windows® XP Professional.
The Power of 2
intel Core 2 Duo inside
Dual-core
Do more.
The Sahara DT725126 powered by the new Intel® Core™2 Duo processor.
With the Intel® Core™2 Duo desktop processor, you'll experience revolutionary performance, unbelieva
system responsiveness, and built in energy-efficiency – up to 40% faster and over 40% more energy effi
▶ Intel® Core™2 Duo processor E6600
4MB L2 Cache, 2.40 GHz 1066 MHz
▶ Genuine Microsoft® Windows® XP Professional
SAHARA
THE ULTIMATE IN
CRICKET SOUTH AFRICA
The official IT hardware supplier to CSA and the Proteas
www.sahara.co
Intel, the Intel logo, Intel Core and Core Inside are trademarks or registered trademarks of Intel Corporation or its subsidiaries in the United States and other countries.

NEW ZEALAND ONE-DAY SERIES 2005/06

SOUTH AFRICA v NEW ZEALAND 2005/06
LIMITED OVERS INTERNATIONAL AVERAGES

SOUTH AFRICA

Batting & Fielding

Name	M	Inns	NO	Runs	HS	Avg	SR	100	50	Ct	St
JM Kemp	5	4	3	112	73	112.00	125.84	0	1	2	0
HH Gibbs	3	3	0	139	81	46.33	64.35	0	1	3	0
MV Boucher	5	4	1	119	40	39.66	78.28	0	0	10	1
GC Smith	5	5	0	161	66	32.20	82.14	0	1	3	0
JH Kallis	4	4	1	90	51	30.00	55.55	0	1	0	0
SM Pollock	5	3	1	58	37	29.00	120.83	0	0	0	0
AG Prince	5	5	1	97	31	24.25	59.50	0	0	4	0
JA Rudolph	1	1	0	17	17	17.00	32.69	0	0	0	0
AB de Villiers	3	3	0	46	29	15.33	63.88	0	0	1	0
HH Dippenaar	1	1	0	10	10	10.00	111.11	0	0	1	0
JA Morkel	1	1	0	5	5	5.00	41.66	0	0	0	0
CK Langeveldt	5	2	1	1	1	1.00	50.00	0	0	0	0
M Ntini	5	1	0	0	0	0.00	0.00	0	0	0	0
AG Puttick	1	1	0	0	0	0.00	0.00	0	0	1	0
A Nel	5	1	1	4	4 *	-	400.00	0	0	0	0
N Boje	3	1	1	3	3 *	-	100.00	0	0	0	0
AJ Hall	2	0	0	0	-	-	-	0	0	1	0
Totals	59	40	10	862	81			0	4	26	1
			Extras	53					subs	0	
			Total	915		30.50	72.62			26	

Bowling

Name	Overs	Mdns	Runs	Wkts	Avg	RpO	BB	4I
AJ Hall	10	1	23	4	5.75	2.30	4-23	1
M Ntini	32.3	1	134	8	16.75	4.12	3-29	0
A Nel	37	3	167	7	23.85	4.51	3-42	0
N Boje	14	0	58	2	29.00	4.14	2-26	0
CK Langeveldt	36.5	6	195	6	32.50	5.29	3-35	0
JH Kallis	14	1	69	2	34.50	4.92	2-45	0
JM Kemp	15	0	67	1	67.00	4.46	1-19	0
SM Pollock	35	3	136	2	68.00	3.88	1-34	0
GC Smith	3	0	15	0	-	5.00	-	0
Totals	197.2	15	864	32			4-23	1
		b/lb/pen	25	5	run outs			
		Total	889	37	24.02	4.50		

NEW ZEALAND

Batting & Fielding

Name	M	Inns	NO	Runs	HS	Avg	SR	100	50	Ct	St
L Vincent	5	4	0	167	90	41.75	82.26	0	2	2	0
SB Styris	4	3	0	124	78	41.33	77.50	0	1	0	0
AR Adams	4	3	1	61	30 *	30.50	124.48	0	0	3	0
KD Mills	5	4	3	28	19	28.00	73.68	0	0	2	0

NEW ZEALAND ONE-DAY SERIES 2005/06

SP Fleming	5	4	0	105	54	26.25	67.74	0	1	2	0
CD McMillan	5	4	0	97	66	24.25	74.61	0	1	0	0
JDP Oram	3	2	0	46	35	23.00	47.42	0	0	0	0
BB McCullum	5	4	0	75	28	18.75	69.44	0	0	3	1
JEC Franklin	3	2	0	33	21	16.50	49.25	0	0	0	0
NJ Astle	5	4	0	52	37	13.00	61.17	0	0	1	0
HJH Marshall	4	3	0	26	16	8.66	36.61	0	0	2	0
DL Vettori	5	4	0	7	6	1.75	53.84	0	0	0	0
SE Bond	5	1	1	9	9 *	-	52.94	0	0	0	0
JS Patel	1	0	0	0	-	-	-	0	0	0	0
Totals	59	42	5	830	90			0	5	15	1
			Extras	59					subs	0	
			Total	889		24.02	69.57			15	

Bowling

Name	**Overs**	**Mdns**	**Runs**	**Wkts**	**Avg**	**RpO**	**BB**	**4I**
JEC Franklin	9	2	37	2	18.50	4.11	1-18	0
JS Patel	8	0	48	2	24.00	6.00	2-48	0
KD Mills	46	5	206	7	29.42	4.47	4-44	1
SB Styris	28	1	92	3	30.66	3.28	2-29	0
DL Vettori	34	0	133	4	33.25	3.91	2-18	0
SE Bond	38.5	2	211	6	35.16	5.43	2-42	0
AR Adams	22	1	107	3	35.66	4.86	2-40	0
NJ Astle	11.1	0	66	1	66.00	5.91	1-46	0
Totals	197	11	900	28			4-44	1
		b/lb/pen	15	2	run outs			
		Total	915	30	30.50	4.64		

SOUTH AFRICA IN INDIA 2005/06

Colin Bryden

In what was a far from ideal prelude to their Test tour of Australia, South Africa completed their obligations from the previous season by playing a five-match one-day international series in India. It was a high-profile tour, with the South Africans scheduled to play matches in some of India's most notable venues, including a first visit by a South African team to Chennai, formerly known as Madras. It also proved to be a successful tour, with South Africa sharing the series at two matches apiece, with the Chennai match rained off.

Despite efforts by Cricket South Africa and the SA Cricketers' Association to establish from the Indian police the status of Herschelle Gibbs and Nicky Boje, no clarity could be obtained and the two players, who also missed the Test tour a year earlier, decided not to tour.

The selectors picked three spin bowlers in a 15-man squad, including a new cap in Johan Botha, the Warriors off-spinner, who had a good tour with South Africa A in Sri Lanka in September and October. Robin Peterson and Justin Ontong were recalled.

The squad was: Graeme Smith (captain), Jacques Kallis (vice-captain), Johan Botha, Mark Boucher, AB de Villiers, Andrew Hall, Justin Kemp, Charl Langeveldt, Albie Morkel, Andre Nel, Makhaya Ntini, Justin Ontong, Robin Peterson, Shaun Pollock, Ashwell Prince. Manager, Goolam Rajah; coach, Mickey Arthur; assistant coach, Vincent Barnes; physiotherapist, Shane Jabaar; fitness trainer, Adrian le Roux; computer analyst, Gustav Obermeyer; team doctor, Dr Mohammed Moosajee.

HYDERABAD XI v SOUTH AFRICANS — Limited Overs Match 50 overs per side

Played at Vijay Sports Complex Ground, Amberpet, Hyderabad on 14 November 2005 — Toss: Hyderabad XI
Umpires: PK Rao & AK Srinivas
Debuts: Hyd: None. SA: None
Result: South Africans won by 8 wickets
Notes: Hyderabad XI substitute: SM Shoaib replaced A Shinde. South Africans substitute: JL Ontong replaced M Ntini.

HYDERABAD XI	*Runs*	*Mins*	*Balls*	*4*	*6*
DS Manohar c Boucher b Pollock	20	31	23	5	-
P Shashank Nag c Prince b Ntini	6	27	19	1	-
Anirudh Singh c Kemp b Nel	3	32	20	-	-
*AS Yadav c Boucher b Nel	21	76	52	2	-
D Vinay Kumar run out	18	41	31	3	-
SA Pai c Nel b Botha	19	82	59	-	-
†I Khaleel c Boucher b Nel	0	16	12	-	-
A Shinde run out	9	27	15	1	-
S Vishnuvardhan c Kallis b Botha	0	6	4	-	-
PIS Reddy c Nel b Botha	15	14	17	3	-
A Absolem not out	2	9	5	-	-
SM Shoaib					
Extras (lb 1, w 7, nb 6)	14				
TOTAL (42 overs)	**127**				

SOUTH AFRICANS	*Runs*	*Mins*	*Balls*	*4*	*6*
AB de Villiers not out	55	108	76	3	2
*GC Smith b Absolem	44	67	45	6	1
JL Ontong b Reddy	16	21	17	1	1
JH Kallis not out	10	18	16	1	-
AG Prince					
JM Kemp					
†MV Boucher					
SM Pollock					
J Botha					
CK Langeveldt					
A Nel					
M Ntini					
Extras (w 7)	7				
TOTAL (for 2 wkts) (25.5 overs)	**132**				

SA	*O*	*M*	*R*	*W*	
Pollock	6	2	20	1	(1 nb)
Ntini	6	0	16	1	(1 nb, 1 w)
Langeveldt	5	0	23	0	(1 w)
Nel	8	2	14	3	(1 nb)
Botha	10	1	34	3	(1 nb, 2 w)
Kallis	3	0	11	0	(1 nb, 1 w)
Kemp	3	1	4	0	(1 nb)
Ontong	1	0	4	0	(2 w)

Hyd	*O*	*M*	*R*	*W*	
Vishnuvardhan	4	1	23	0	
Shoaib	6	1	22	0	(1 w)
Absolem	6	0	25	1	
Reddy	6.5	1	38	1	(1 w)
Pai	2	0	13	0	
Shinde	1	0	11	0	(1 w)

Fall of Wickets	*Hyd*	*SA*
1st	25 (2)	66 (2)
2nd	29 (1)	90 (3)
3rd	39 (3)	-
4th	73 (5)	-
5th	74 (4)	-
6th	83 (7)	-
7th	103 (8)	-
8th	104 (9)	-
9th	121 (10)	-
10th	127 (6)	-

MATCH-WINNING EFFORT . . . Shaun Pollock during a great opening spell which set up a victory over India in Hyderabad *Picture: DUIF DU TOIT, Touchline Photo*

SOUTH AFRICA IN INDIA 2005/06

INDIA v SOUTH AFRICA — 1st Limited Overers International

Played at Rajiv Gandhi International Stadium, Uppal, Hyderabad on 16 November 2005 — Toss: South Africa
Umpires: K Hariharan & DJ Harper (TV: I Shivram) — Referee: JJ Crowe
Debuts: Ind: None. SA: J Botha
Result: South Africa won by 5 wickets
Man of Match: Yuvraj Singh
Notes: India substitute: G Gambhir replaced M Kartik after 10.3 overs of India's innings. South Africa substitute: JL Ontong replaced CK Langeveldt after 0 overs of South Africa's innings.

South Africa played in the first full international match to be staged at a new stadium which was already impressive, although a second tier, still to be completed, will almost double the capacity from 28 000, the maximum number who could attend.

South Africa took a firm grip on the match after Smith won the toss and made use of bowler-friendly conditions. Pollock and Ntini were superb on a pitch which offered bounce and sideways movement and only six runs were scored for the loss of three wickets in the first five overs. Nel bowled Dravid, the Indian captain, with a superb delivery which penetrated the defences of one of the most technically-correct batsmen in the world. India were forced to bring in Gambhir as a substitute but he quickly followed Dravid back to the dressing room.

The left-handed Yuvraj Singh rescued India with an outstanding century, playing some thrilling strokes as the pitch became easier for batting. Pathan helped set up the recovery, while Harbhajan frustrated the tourists with unorthodox hitting as 58 runs were scored off the last five overs. Langeveldt could not bowl his anticipated two overs at the end of the innings because of a strained left hamstring.

Smith enabled South Africa to get off to a flying start. Kallis and Prince shared a solid but slow partnership before Kemp played another free-scoring innings to seal the win.

Harbhajan was fined 25 percent of his match fee for aggressive gestures after dismissing Prince.

INDIA	*Runs*	*Mins*	*Balls*	*4*	*6*
V Sehwag c Prince b Ntini	1	6	4	-	-
SR Tendulkar c Boucher b Pollock	2	20	9	-	-
M Kaif lbw b Pollock	1	5	3	-	-
*RS Dravid b Nel	8	34	24	1	-
Yuvraj Singh run out (Kallis/Ontong)	103	192	122	10	3
G Gambhir c Boucher b Ntini	1	3	4	-	-
IK Pathan b Botha	46	78	63	6	-
†MS Dhoni run out (Nel/Boucher)	17	39	28	1	-
AB Agarkar c Kemp b Nel	21	33	27	2	-
Harbhajan Singh not out	37	16	17	4	2
RP Singh not out	1	8	2	-	-
M Kartik					
Extras (b 1, lb 3, w 4, nb 3)	11				
TOTAL (for 9 wkts) (50 overs)	**249**				

SOUTH AFRICA	*Runs*	*Mins*	*Balls*	*4*	*6*
*GC Smith b Singh	48	58	36	9	-
AB de Villiers lbw b Agarkar	7	24	16	1	-
JL Ontong c Dravid b Agarkar	11	31	23	2	-
JH Kallis not out	68	145	97	5	-
AG Prince c Sehwag b Harbhajan Singh	46	89	74	5	-
†MV Boucher c Dravid b Tendulkar	2	3	4	-	-
JM Kemp not out	46	49	49	5	-
SM Pollock					
J Botha					
A Nel					
M Ntini					
CK Langeveldt					
Extras (lb 5, w 13, nb 6)	24				
TOTAL (for 5 wkts) (48.5 overs)	**252**				

SA	*O*	*M*	*R*	*W*
Pollock	10	1	37	2 (2 nb)
Ntini	10	1	62	2 (1 w)
Nel	10	2	45	2 (1 nb)
Langeveldt	8	0	34	0 (1 w)
Botha	6	0	31	1
Kallis	6	0	36	0 (2 w)

Ind	*O*	*M*	*R*	*W*
Pathan	6	0	51	0 (1 nb)
Agarkar	9.5	1	55	2 (1 nb, 3 w)
Singh	7	1	18	1 (7 w)
Harbhajan Singh	10	0	35	1
Sehwag	3	0	18	0
Tendulkar	8	0	43	1 (2 nb, 3 w)
Yuvraj Singh	5	0	27	0 (2 nb)

Fall of Wickets	*Ind*	*SA*
1st	1 (1)	32 (2)
2nd	4 (3)	76 (3)
3rd	5 (2)	76 (1)
4th	34 (4)	165 (5)
5th	35 (6)	168 (6)
6th	110 (7)	-
7th	159 (8)	-
8th	198 (9)	-
9th	227 (5)	-

CROWD FAVOURITE . . . Graeme Smith had the spectators on his side as he pounded a century in the fourth international in Kolkata *Picture: DUIF DU TOIT, Touchline Photo*

INDIA v SOUTH AFRICA — 2nd Limited Overs International

Played at Chinnaswamy Stadium, Bangalore on 19 November 2005 (D/N) — Toss: India
Umpires: DJ Harper & AV Jayaprakash (TV: K Hariharan) — Referee: JJ Crowe
Debuts: Ind: None. SA: None
Result: India won by 6 wickets
Man of Match: Irfan Pathan
Notes: India substitute: G Gambhir replaced RP Singh after 0 overs of India's innings. South Africa substitute: JL Ontong replaced AB de Villiers after 0 overs of India's innings.

South Africa's 20-match unbeaten run came to an end in front of a packed crowd of 55 000 who created a wall of noise in a roofed, enclosed stadium. The left-armed Pathan put South Africa under early pressure before India's spinners tied up the batsman on a slow, dry pitch which yielded plenty of turn.

With dew under the floodlights always likely to be a factor, South Africa's total was not nearly enough. Tendulkar, who equalled Wasim Akram's world record of 356 one-day international appearances, went early but India romped to an easy win, with Sehwag thrilling the crowd with dashing stroke-play.

SOUTH AFRICA	Runs	Mins	Balls	4	6
AB de Villiers c Harbhajan Singh b Pathan	4	3	5	1	-
*GC Smith lbw b Pathan	3	20	10	-	-
AJ Hall c Kaif b Harbhajan Singh	32	70	43	6	-
JH Kallis c Dhoni b Pathan	2	10	8	-	-
AG Prince c Harbhajan Singh b Sehwag	30	93	69	5	-
†MV Boucher lbw b Sehwag	14	41	33	1	-
JM Kemp c Singh b Harbhajan Singh	28	57	59	3	-
SM Pollock b Yuvraj Singh	29	58	61	1	1
J Botha not out	15	15	12	3	-
M Ntini b Agarkar	1	5	3	-	-
A Nel					
JL Ontong					
Extras (b 1, lb 3, w 4, nb 3)	11				
TOTAL (for 9 wkts) (50 overs)	**169**				

INDIA	Runs	Mins	Balls	4	6
G Gambhir run out (Ontong/Boucher)	38	69	50	7	-
SR Tendulkar c sub (RJ Peterson) b Pollock	2	31	22	-	-
IK Pathan run out (Ontong)	37	85	58	4	1
V Sehwag not out	77	90	62	11	-
*RS Dravid c and b Ontong	10	35	17	-	-
Yuvraj Singh not out	4	6	6	1	-
†MS Dhoni					
AB Agarkar					
Harbhajan Singh					
M Kaif					
M Kartik					
RP Singh					
Extras (w 2, nb 1)	3				
TOTAL (for 4 wkts) (35.4 overs)	**171**				

Ind	O	M	R	W	
Pathan	6	1	23	3	
Agarkar	7	0	25	1	(1 w)
Singh	5	0	22	0	
Harbhajan Singh	10	2	33	2	(2 w)
Kartik	10	4	16	0	(1 nb)
Sehwag	8	0	29	2	(2 nb)
Yuvraj Singh	4	0	17	1	(1 w)

SA	O	M	R	W	
Pollock	6	3	10	1	
Ntini	8	1	32	0	(1 w)
Nel	5	0	31	0	(1 w)
Botha	8	1	47	0	(1 nb)
Hall	6	0	23	0	
Ontong	2.4	0	28	1	

Fall of Wickets	SA	Ind
1st	4 (1)	13 (2)
2nd	14 (2)	52 (1)
3rd	20 (4)	105 (3)
4th	57 (3)	155 (5)
5th	85 (6)	-
6th	96 (5)	-
7th	143 (7)	-
8th	158 (8)	-
9th	169 (10)	-

INDIA v SOUTH AFRICA — 3rd Limited Overs International

At MA Chidambaram Stadium, Chennai on 22 November 2005 (D/N)
No play – rain

Heavy rain started the day before and continued on the day, preventing any chance of play at the historic Chennai ground.

INDIA v SOUTH AFRICA — 4th Limited Overs International

Played at Eden Gardens, Kolkata on 25 November 2005 (D/N) — Toss: South Africa
Umpires: DJ Harper & AV Jayaprakash (TV: I Shivram) — Referee: JJ Crowe
Debuts: Ind: None. SA: None
Result: South Africa won by 10 wickets
Man of Match: Graeme Smith
Notes: India substitute: M Kartik replaced G Gambhir after 11 overs of South Africa's innings. South Africa substitute: RJ Peterson replaced A Nel after 0 overs of South Africa's innings.

South Africa gained a crushing win in the home town of Sourav Ganguly, the former Indian captain, whose axing from the one-day team was a bitter source of discontent for his supporters.

Pollock produced an excellent opening spell, gaining lateral movement off a surprisingly well-grassed pitch. Yuvraj and Kaif had a good partnership but Botha's dismissal of Yuvraj started another slide.

Smith was in majestic form as he and Hall took South Africa to victory without the loss of a wicket. Astonishingly, the crowd, estimated at 80 000, started to cheer for Smith and jeer the Indians. Afterwards, Dravid was booed during the presentation ceremony, a circumstance he accepted philosophically as part of the job of being captain of India.

INDIA	*Runs*	*Mins*	*Balls*	*4*	*6*
G Gambhir c Smith b Pollock	11	31	19	2	-
IK Pathan b Pollock	0	3	2	-	-
SR Tendulkar c Boucher b Pollock	2	17	15	-	-
V Sehwag c Boucher b Hall	30	30	21	6	-
*RS Dravid b Langeveldt	6	53	31	1	-
Yuvraj Singh lbw b Botha	53	102	78	7	-
M Kaif c Smith b Nel	46	83	63	4	-
†MS Dhoni c Botha b Hall	14	40	26	-	-
AB Agarkar b Kallis	11	22	16	1	-
Harbhajan Singh lbw b Hall	0	5	4	-	-
RP Singh not out	1	2	1	-	-
M Kartik					
Extras (lb 5, w 8, nb 1)	14				
TOTAL (45.5 overs)	**188**				

SOUTH AFRICA	*Runs*	*Mins*	*Balls*	*4*	*6*
*GC Smith not out	134	147	124	20	1
AJ Hall not out	48	147	94	4	-
JH Kallis					
AG Prince					
†MV Boucher					
JM Kemp					
SM Pollock					
JA Morkel					
RJ Peterson					
J Botha					
CK Langeveldt					
A Nel					
Extras (w 4, nb 3)	7				
TOTAL (for 0 wkts) (35.5 overs)	**189**				

SA	*O*	*M*	*R*	*W*
Pollock	10	4	25	3 (3 w)
Nel	10	1	35	1 (1 w)
Hall	6.5	0	36	3 (3 w)
Langeveldt	8	1	33	1 (1 w)
Kallis	4	0	20	1 (1 nb)
Botha	5	0	21	1
Morkel	2	0	13	0

Ind	*O*	*M*	*R*	*W*
Agarkar	5	0	41	0 (2 nb, 2 w)
Pathan	6	0	28	0
Singh	4	0	18	0 (1 w)
Harbhajan Singh	10	0	37	0
Kartik	8	1	52	0 (1 nb)
Sehwag	2.5	0	13	0 (1 w)

Fall of Wickets	*Ind*	*SA*
1st	2 (2)	-
2nd	14 (3)	-
3rd	23 (1)	-
4th	49 (4)	-
5th	71 (5)	-
6th	152 (6)	-
7th	167 (7)	-
8th	187 (9)	-
9th	187 (8)	-
10th	188 (10)	-

INDIA v SOUTH AFRICA — 5th Limited Overs International

Played at Wankhede Stadium, Mumbai on 28 November 2005 (D/N) — Toss: India

Umpires: K Hariharan & DJ Harper (TV: I Shivram) — Referee: JJ Crowe

Debuts: Ind: None. SA: None

Result: India won by 5 wickets

Man of Match: Rahul Dravid

Man of Series: Graeme Smith and Yuvraj Singh

Notes: India substitute: G Gambhir replaced RP Singh after 0 overs of India's innings. South Africa substitute: RJ Peterson replaced JM Kemp after 8 overs of India's innings.

The trend of wildly-fluctuating fortunes from match to match continued as South Africa struggled on a slow, gripping pitch. Kallis anchored the South African innings but the scoring was always too slow, despite a late burst of hitting by Pollock. Kallis could hit only five boundaries before he was caught at long-on with seven balls left in the innings.

Dravid, the villain in the eyes of the crowd in Kolkata, quickly re-established himself as a hero in Mumbai with a measured, fluent innings which took India to a comfortable win and a share of the series.

Nel was fined 20 percent of his match fee for using obscene language that was seen by television viewers.

Smith and Ontong both suffered injuries to their left hands while fielding. Smith suffered a tear to a plate over a joint of his fourth left finger and would need protection for ten to twelve days, while Ontong suffered a fractured first metacarpal of his left hand, which needed an operation.

SOUTH AFRICA IN INDIA 2005/06

SOUTH AFRICA	*Runs*	*Mins*	*Balls*	*4*	*6*
*GC Smith c Harbhajan Singh b Pathan	24	41	29	3	-
AJ Hall b Pathan	4	11	7	1	-
JH Kallis c Kaif b Pathan	91	183	146	5	-
AG Prince c Yuvraj Singh b Harbhajan Singh	9	56	32	1	-
†MV Boucher c Harbhajan Singh b Sehwag	35	69	56	-	-
JM Kemp c Yuvraj Singh b Harbhajan Singh	11	12	12	1	-
SM Pollock not out	30	19	17	4	1
J Botha not out	3	5	3	-	-
CK Langeveldt					
A Nel					
M Ntini					
RJ Peterson					
Extras (lb 4, w 8, nb 2)	14				
TOTAL (for 6 wkts) (50 overs)	**221**				

INDIA	*Runs*	*Mins*	*Balls*	*4*	*6*
G Gambhir c Kemp b Ntini	0	5	7	-	-
SR Tendulkar c Prince b Nel	30	77	44	5	-
V Sehwag lbw b Pollock	27	24	20	4	1
*RS Dravid not out	78	186	106	10	-
Yuvraj Singh c Boucher b Nel	49	78	64	7	-
†MS Dhoni c Boucher b Langeveldt	12	37	26	1	-
M Kaif not out	16	20	19	2	-
IK Pathan					
AB Agarkar					
Harbhajan Singh					
M Kartik					
RP Singh					
Extras (lb 6, w 5, nb 1)	12				
TOTAL (for 5 wkts) (47.3 overs)	**224**				

Ind	*O*	*M*	*R*	*W*	
Pathan	8	1	20	3	(1 w)
Agarkar	7	1	33	0	(3 w)
Singh	6	0	27	0	(3 w)
Kartik	10	0	58	0	(1 nb, 1 w)
Harbhajan Singh	10	0	32	2	
Sehwag	5	0	24	1	(1 nb)
Yuvraj Singh	4	0	23	0	

SA	*O*	*M*	*R*	*W*	
Pollock	9	1	49	1	(2 w)
Ntini	10	0	53	1	
Nel	10	2	35	2	(1 w)
Langeveldt	8.3	1	38	1	(1 nb, 2 w)
Botha	6	0	24	0	
Hall	4	0	19	0	

Fall of Wickets	*SA*	*Ind*
1st	6 (2)	1 (1)
2nd	36 (1)	46 (3)
3rd	77 (4)	83 (2)
4th	158 (5)	162 (5)
5th	178 (6)	201 (6)
6th	209 (3)	-

INDIA v SOUTH AFRICA 2005/06

LIMITED OVERS INTERNATIONAL AVERAGES

INDIA

Batting & Fielding

Name	M	Inns	NO	Runs	HS	Avg	SR	100	50	Ct	St
Yuvraj Singh	4	4	1	209	103	69.66	77.40	1	1	2	0
V Sehwag	4	4	1	135	77 *	45.00	126.16	0	1	1	0
Harbhajan Singh	4	2	1	37	37 *	37.00	176.19	0	0	4	0
RS Dravid	4	4	1	102	78 *	34.00	57.30	0	1	2	0
M Kaif	4	3	1	63	46	31.50	74.11	0	0	2	0
IK Pathan	4	3	0	83	46	27.66	67.47	0	0	0	0
AB Agarkar	4	2	0	32	21	16.00	74.41	0	0	0	0
MS Dhoni	4	3	0	43	17	14.33	53.75	0	0	1	0
G Gambhir	4	4	0	50	38	12.50	62.50	0	0	0	0
SR Tendulkar	4	4	0	36	30	9.00	40.00	0	0	0	0
RP Singh	4	2	2	2	1 *	-	66.66	0	0	1	0
M Kartik	4	0	0	0	-	-	-	0	0	0	0
Totals	48	35	7	792	103			1	3	13	0
			Extras	40					subs	0	
			Total	832		29.71	73.33			13	

SOUTH AFRICA IN INDIA 2005/06

Bowling

Name	Overs	Mdns	Runs	Wkts	Avg	RpO	BB	4I
IK Pathan	26	2	122	6	20.33	4.69	3-20	0
Harbhajan Singh	40	2	137	5	27.40	3.42	2-32	0
V Sehwag	18.5	0	84	3	28.00	4.46	2-29	0
SR Tendulkar	8	0	43	1	43.00	5.37	1-43	0
AB Agarkar	28.5	2	154	3	51.33	5.34	2-55	0
Yuvraj Singh	13	0	67	1	67.00	5.15	1-17	0
RP Singh	22	1	85	1	85.00	3.86	1-18	0
M Kartik	28	5	126	0	-	4.50	-	0
Totals	184.4	12	818	20			3-20	0
		b/lb/pen	13	0	run outs			
		Total	831	20	41.55	4.50		

SOUTH AFRICA

Batting & Fielding

Name	M	Inns	NO	Runs	HS	Avg	SR	100	50	Ct	St
JH Kallis	4	3	1	161	91	80.50	64.14	0	2	0	0
GC Smith	4	4	1	209	134 *	69.66	105.02	1	0	2	0
SM Pollock	4	2	1	59	30 *	59.00	75.64	0	0	0	0
JM Kemp	4	3	1	85	46 *	42.50	70.83	0	0	2	0
AJ Hall	3	3	1	84	48 *	42.00	58.33	0	0	0	0
AG Prince	4	3	0	85	46	28.33	48.57	0	0	2	0
MV Boucher	4	3	0	51	35	17.00	54.83	0	0	6	0
JL Ontong	2	1	0	11	11	11.00	47.82	0	0	1	0
AB de Villiers	2	2	0	11	7	5.50	52.38	0	0	0	0
M Ntini	3	1	0	1	1	1.00	33.33	0	0	0	0
J Botha	4	2	2	18	15 *	-	120.00	0	0	1	0
CK Langeveldt	3	0	0	0	-	-	-	0	0	0	0
JA Morkel	1	0	0	0	-	-	-	0	0	0	0
A Nel	4	0	0	0	-	-	-	0	0	0	0
RJ Peterson	2	0	0	0	-	-	-	0	0	0	0
Totals	48	27	7	775	134 *			1	2	14	0
			Extras	56					subs	1	
			Total	831		41.55	69.07			15	

Bowling

Name	Overs	Mdns	Runs	Wkts	Avg	RpO	BB	4I
SM Pollock	35	9	121	7	17.28	3.45	3-25	0
AJ Hall	16.5	0	78	3	26.00	4.63	3-36	0
JL Ontong	2.4	0	28	1	28.00	10.50	1-28	0
A Nel	35	5	146	5	29.20	4.17	2-35	0
M Ntini	28	2	147	3	49.00	5.25	2-62	0
CK Langeveldt	24.3	2	105	2	52.50	4.28	1-33	0
JH Kallis	10	0	56	1	56.00	5.60	1-20	0
J Botha	25	1	123	2	61.50	4.92	1-21	0
JA Morkel	2	0	13	0	-	6.50	-	0
Totals	179	19	817	24			3-25	0
		b/lb/pen	15	4	run outs			
		Total	832	28	29.71	4.64		

SOUTH AFRICA IN AUSTRALIA 2005/06

Colin Bryden

South Africa once again fell short when they challenged the world champions on their own turf, although the margin of two matches to nil was not an accurate reflection of the contests. Catches went down at crucial times and the weather played a role in the final Test in Sydney where South Africa made a bold declaration, which led to them losing the match, in an unsuccessful attempt to square the series.

Injuries played a role, with Jacques Kallis missing the first Test, Justin Kemp the second and third and Makhaya Ntini the third, while Andre Nel was able to bowl only seven overs in the second innings of the final Test. Boeta Dippenaar, who had finished the previous season in the Test team, could not join the side until the one-day series because he was recovering from an operation on his right wrist.

The Test tour followed two one-day series played by South Africa, the most recent of which was in India in conditions far different from those in Australia. It was far from ideal preparation.

South Africa led on the first innings in two of the Test matches but in all three matches the bowlers were unable to sustain their efforts through the second innings. In Perth, Jacques Rudolph's century enabled the tourists to earn a draw but a batting collapse in Melbourne and Australia's comfortable achievement of a generous target in Sydney meant the series ended in disappointment.

Graeme Smith, the captain, suffered an injury to his fourth left finger in the final match in India shortly before the Australian tour. He missed the first warm-up game in Perth but played in the second match before taking his place in the Test line-up. Smith took it upon himself to be the main media focal point of the South African team, making some provocative comments, which ideally needed to be backed up with results and personal success. Instead, he had a poor series, with a highest score of 39, and with Kallis missing the first Test because of an elbow tendon injury and only performing in the final Test the batting was inconsistent against a strong Australian bowling attack. Only two century partnerships were registered.

Ntini's injury in the first innings of the Melbourne Test robbed the side of much-needed firepower, although Nel bowled with energy until hampered by a foot injury in Sydney.

Injuries were a considerable factor in the one-day triangular series which followed the Tests, with both Ntini and Nel forced to return home and Kallis able to play in only one game, while Charl Langeveldt also missed matches because of injury, leaving Shaun Pollock and Andrew Hall as the only experienced bowlers. Even so, it was a major disappointment that for the first time in four tours South Africa were unable to qualify for the one-day finals.

Dippenaar was one of the leading batsmen in the tournament but the next most successful batsman was Boucher, which was an indication that not enough runs were scored by the top order.

Pollock was South Africa's outstanding bowler in the one-day games, taking 11 wickets and conceding only 3.18 runs an over. Hall bowled well and Van der Wath showed promise but part-time bowler Smith had the next-best economy rate to Pollock at 4.67.

As Malcolm Conn wrote in The Australian: "To compete against the world champions in Australia touring teams need the planets to line up. Opponents must get the most even of

Men's

"A"

U19

National Academy

Women's

breaks to prevent being out-muscled and over-run." The planets did not line up for South Africa on their 2005/06 venture.

The South African Test squad was: Graeme Smith (captain), Jacques Kallis (vice-captain), Nicky Boje, Mark Boucher, AB de Villiers, Herschelle Gibbs, Justin Kemp, Garnett Kruger, Charl Langeveldt, Andre Nel, Makhaya Ntini, Shaun Pollock, Ashwell Prince, Jacques Rudolph. Manager, Dr Mohammed Moosajee; coach, Mickey Arthur; assistant coach, Vincent Barnes; physiotherapist, Shane Jabaar; fitness trainer, Adrian le Roux; computer analyst, Gustav Obermeyer.

Kruger was the only uncapped player in the squad.

Off-spin bowler Johan Botha joined the side in time for the third Test following the injuries to Ntini and Kemp.

Long-time manager Goolam Rajah was unable to be with the team for the Test series because he had to undergo a shoulder operation. He joined the tour for the one-day series, replacing Dr Moosajee.

Botha, Boeta Dippenaar, Andrew Hall and Monde Zondeki were selected for the one-day matches, with Boje, De Villiers and the injured Ntini returning home. Nel was initially part of the squad but he too returned home when it was decided he needed four to six weeks to recover from the foot injury he suffered in the third Test. Kallis followed soon afterwards.

Nel was replaced by Dale Steyn, while Johan van der Wath, another new player at international level, also joined the side as a replacement for Kallis.

Prince was named vice-captain after Kallis went home.

The difficulties of the tour were not confined to the challenge of taking on a powerful opposition team.

There were incidents of racial abuse against the tourists, which led to an official complaint by the United Cricket Board and to the appointment by the International Cricket Council of India's Solicitor General, Goolam Vahanvati, as a one-man commission to travel to Australia, South Africa and Sri Lanka, to interview players and officials before reporting back to the ICC board meeting in March.

Vahanvati's report concluded that racial abuse took place, that it would be wrong to attribute it only to South African expatriates, that it was pre-meditated and co-ordinated and that there was a grave problem in Australia relating to crowd behaviour, particularly drunken spectators. He found that Cricket Australia, which strongly condemned the incidents, had made an appropriate response to the issue. The ICC appointed a sub-committee consisting of the chief executives of the ICC, Cricket Australia and the United Cricket Board to provide recommendations.

Johan Botha was reported for having a suspect bowling action after making his Test debut in Sydney. Although he was allowed to continue playing in the one-day series pending a bio-mechanical assessment, it was found that his action was illegal and he was then suspended from bowling in international matches.

WESTERN AUSTRALIA v SOUTH AFRICANS — First-class 3-day match

Played at WACA Ground, Perth on 5,6,7 December 2005 — Toss: South Africans
Umpires: B Bennett & IH Lock
Debuts: WA: WS Gillies (FC). SA: None
Close of play: Day 1: WA (1) 306-5 (Bandy 59*, Gillies 10*, 92 overs). Day 2: SA (2) 25-2 (Rudolph 4*, Prince 1*, 12 overs)..
Result: Western Australia won by an innings and 48 runs
Man of Match: Adam Voges

With Smith still recovering from a left finger injury and Kallis suffering from a left elbow tendon injury, Boucher led the tourists in their opening first-class match at the ground where the first Test was scheduled 11 days later.

The Proteas' lack of first-class cricket was exposed as they slumped to an innings defeat against a team that was bottom of the Australian domestic first-class log. Marcus North and Adam Voges set the Warriors on the way to a good total and none of the South Africans was able to register a half-century.

Justin Langer, the Australian Test opening batsman, decided to enforce the follow-on, reasoning that if his side could beat the tourists it would outweigh any potential benefit the South African batsmen might derive from a second chance to bat.

Beau Casson, a promising left-arm spinner, was the most successful bowler.

Boje split the webbing in his right hand while fielding.

WESTERN AUSTRALIA	*Runs*	*Mins*	*Balls*	*4*	*6*
*JL Langer b Langeveldt	21	50	36	2	1
CJL Rogers c Langeveldt b Nel	22	69	46	3	-
CJ Heron c Boucher b Pollock	13	46	30	1	-
MJ North c Boucher b Langeveldt	71	199	153	12	-
AC Voges c sub (GJ-P Kruger) b Boje	101	215	168	17	-
DC Bandy c Prince b Langeveldt	64	115	84	9	1
WS Gillies c Gibbs b Ntini	20	76	57	1	-
†L Ronchi b Langeveldt	16	26	20	3	-
B Casson not out	22	63	45	1	1
SJ Magoffin not out	24	41	27	4	-
BM Edmondson					
Extras (b 4, lb 6, w 1, nb 6)	17				
TOTAL (for 8 wkts dec) (110 overs)	**391**				

SOUTH AFRICANS	*Runs*	*Mins*	*Balls*	*4*	*6*		*Runs*	*Mins*	*Balls*	*4*	*6*
JA Rudolph c Bandy b Gillies	43	85	78	6	-	(2) c Casson b Edmondson	18	71	45	1	-
AB de Villiers b Gillies	27	81	46	4	-	(1) c Ronchi b Edmondson	7	6	6	-	1
HH Gibbs b Edmondson	25	53	35	3	-	c Ronchi b Magoffin	13	34	30	2	-
AG Prince c Magoffin b Gillies	4	14	11	-	-	c Ronchi b Magoffin	49	145	106	6	-
JM Kemp b Edmondson	13	61	56	1	-	c Voges b Casson	8	41	27	1	-
*†MV Boucher c Bandy b Edmondson	8	23	18	1	-	c Langer b Casson	14	25	17	3	-
SM Pollock c Voges b Casson	4	13	11	-	-	c Langer b Magoffin	25	35	26	5	-
N Boje not out	26	53	34	6	-	not out	25	46	39	2	-
M Ntini lbw b Casson	0	1	1	-	-	lbw b Casson	0	11	6	-	-
A Nel c Langer b Casson	0	13	11	-	-	c Langer b Casson	3	22	15	-	-
CK Langeveldt c and b Casson	14	23	18	1	1	absent hurt					
Extras (b 8, lb 6, w 1)	15					Extras (lb 1, nb 1)	2				
TOTAL (53.1 overs)	**179**					**TOTAL (52.4 overs)**	**164**				

SA	*O*	*M*	*R*	*W*	
Pollock	22	9	51	1	
Ntini	22	5	66	1	
Nel	22	3	94	1	
Langeveldt	24	3	104	4	(6 nb, 1 w)
Boje	12	2	36	1	
Kemp	8	1	30	0	

WA	*O*	*M*	*R*	*W*		*O*	*M*	*R*	*W*	
Magoffin	8	2	30	0		17	6	37	3	(1 nb)
Edmondson	12	1	48	3		12	2	41	2	
Bandy	12	4	25	0		(5) 1	0	1	0	
Gillies	11	2	41	3	(1 w)	4	0	17	0	
Casson	10.1	4	21	4		(3) 18.4	2	67	4	

Fall of Wickets

	WA	**SA**	**SA**
1st	30 (1)	71 (2)	7 (1)
2nd	51 (2)	72 (1)	23 (3)
3rd	67 (3)	84 (4)	39 (2)
4th	213 (4)	112 (3)	67 (5)
5th	253 (5)	124 (6)	95 (6)
6th	323 (6)	124 (5)	132 (7)
7th	324 (7)	136 (7)	147 (4)
8th	343 (8)	136 (9)	152 (9)
9th	-	146 (10)	164 (10)
10th	-	179 (11)	-

CRICKET AUSTRALIA CHAIRMAN'S XI v SOUTH AFRICANS — Limited Overs Match

Played at Lilac Hill Park, Perth on 9 December 2005 — Toss: South Africans

Umpires: AR Craig & IH Lock

Debuts: CAC: None. SA: None

Result: South Africans won by 8 wickets

Man of Match: Herschelle Gibbs

In his first appearance in South African colours, Kruger bowled impressively to restrict the invitation team to a total that was easily achieved, with Gibbs showing sparkling form in an unbeaten 151-run stand with Rudolph.

CRICKET AUSTRALIA CHAIRMAN'S XI	Runs	Mins	Balls	4	6
CJL Rogers c Boucher b Pollock	2	8	10	-	-
†RJ Campbell lbw b Pollock	23	24	19	4	1
MJ North run out (Gibbs)	41	78	63	6	1
AC Voges c Prince b Kruger	34	84	53	5	-
DT Christian c Boucher b Kemp	18	54	35	3	-
PC Worthington c and b Kruger	1	13	11	-	-
*JL Langer c Gibbs b Kruger	31	58	53	2	-
TJ Zoehrer c Kruger b Nel	15	34	25	1	-
DJ Wates b Kruger	11	4	4	1	1
BR Dorey not out	4	5	2	-	-
MWH Inness not out	1	2	3	-	-
BA Reid					
Extras (lb 1, w 10)	11				
TOTAL (for 9 wkts) (46 overs)	**192**				

SOUTH AFRICANS	Runs	Mins	Balls	4	6
*GC Smith c Langer b Inness	24	40	31	3	-
AB de Villiers b Inness	18	31	20	3	-
JA Rudolph not out	59	97	62	5	1
HH Gibbs not out	91	89	86	7	3
AG Prince					
JM Kemp					
†MV Boucher					
SM Pollock					
N Boje					
CK Langeveldt					
GJ-P Kruger					
M Ntini					
A Nel					
Extras (w 1)	1				
TOTAL (for 2 wkts) (35.2 overs)	**193**				

SA	O	M	R	W
Pollock	7	2	22	2
Ntini	8	1	40	0
Langeveldt	8	0	30	0
Nel	10	0	47	1 (4 w)
Kruger	8	0	33	4 (1 w)
Kemp	5	0	19	1 (1 w)

CAC	O	M	R	W
Reid	4	0	19	0
Wates	9	1	31	0
Inness	8	0	47	2
Dorey	5	1	18	0
Worthington	2	0	11	0
Zoehrer	3	0	33	0
Voges	2	0	22	0 (1 w)
Christian	2	0	11	0
Campbell	0.2	0	1	0

Fall of Wickets	CAC	SA
1st	6 (1)	39 (2)
2nd	33 (2)	42 (1)
3rd	95 (3)	-
4th	113 (4)	-
5th	117 (6)	-
6th	128 (5)	-
7th	170 (7)	-
8th	177 (8)	-
9th	189 (9)	-

WESTERN AUSTRALIA XI v SOUTH AFRICANS — 3-day Match (not First-class)

Played at James Oval, Crawley on 11,12,13 December 2005 — Toss: South Africans

Umpires: B Bennett & AR Craig

Debuts: WAXI: None. SA: None

Close of play: Day 1: WAXI (1) 26-2 (Davis 11*, 9 overs). Day 2: SA (2) 155-3 (Rudolph 72*, Prince 46*, 41 overs)

Result: Drawn

Notes: Pomersbach scored his century off 90 balls in Western Australia XI's 1st innings.

The South Africans had a largely unimpressive warm-up for the Test match against what was effectively a Western Australia second XI. After a reasonable batting performance, the South African bowlers took some heavy punishment from 20-year-old Luke Pomersbach, a grade cricketer without a State contract. The tourists were hampered by the absence for most of the innings of Ntini, who split the webbing of his left hand while fielding.

When the South Africans lost their eighth wicket in the second innings before lunch on the final day they were a precarious 212 runs ahead but Rudolph, who batted with increasing assurance, and Nel averted the danger with a stand of 175.

SOUTH AFRICANS	Runs	Mins	Balls	4	6		Runs	Mins	Balls	4	6
AB de Villiers c Ronchi b Petrie	9	27	24	1	-	(2) b Crawford	5	15	10	-	-
*GC Smith c Ronchi b Gillies	50	87	59	6	-	(1) c Johnston b Petrie	18	19	14	3	-
HH Gibbs c Clark b Heal	62	117	94	10	-	(6) b Petrie	0	10	10	-	-
JA Rudolph c Gillies b Heal	21	68	54	3	-	(3) not out	201	371	312	24	2
AG Prince retired out	68	115	115	8	2	c Ronchi b Crawford	57	141	122	5	1
JM Kemp c and b Heal	8	33	34	1	-	(4) c Davis b Crawford	10	19	16	2	-
†MV Boucher b Doropoulos	31	87	68	5	-	b Petrie	0	1	1	-	-
SM Pollock not out	11	30	24	1	-	b Petrie	9	26	16	1	-
CK Langeveldt run out (Meuleman)	12	5	8	2	-	lbw b Johnston	12	14	11	2	-
A Nel not out	0	7	1	-	-	c Heal b Davis	64	145	110	9	1
M Ntini											
GJ-P Kruger											
Extras (b 5, lb 2, w 2, nb 11)	20					Extras (b 13, lb 2, nb 4)	19				
TOTAL (for 8 wkts dec) (79 overs)	**292**					**TOTAL (for 9 wkts dec) (102 overs)**	**395**				

HEROIC EFFORT . . . Jacques Rudolph acknowledges the applause as he reaches a match-saving century in Perth *Picture: GETTY IMAGES/TOUCHLINE PHOTO*

WESTERN AUSTRALIA XI	Runs	Mins	Balls	4	6		Runs	Mins	Balls	4	6
*SW Meuleman b Pollock	1	11	9	-	-	not out	34	87	71	2	-
LM Davis c Boucher b Nel	60	144	106	7	-						
HF Brown c Gibbs b Pollock	6	22	12	1	-	(2) b Pollock	10	19	9	2	-
LA Pomersbach c Kemp b Langeveldt	145	204	128	21	3						
†L Ronchi c Boucher b Pollock	31	41	41	7	-						
WS Gillies not out	25	81	44	4	-						
TP Doropoulos not out	18	29	33	3	-						
M Johnston						(3) not out	18	66	40	7	-
AK Heal											
MW Clark											
MJ Petrie											
A Crawford											
Extras (b 4, lb 6, nb 4)	14					Extras (b 1, lb 1)	2				
TOTAL (for 5 wkts dec) (61.3 overs)	**300**					**TOTAL (for 1 wkt) (20 overs)**	**64**				

WAXI	O	M	R	W			O	M	R	W	
Clark	15	3	58	0	(1 w)	(8)	4	0	9	0	
Petrie	14	3	41	1			27	5	78	4	
Crawford	7	1	40	0	(6 nb)	(1)	18	4	108	3	(4 nb)
Gillies	13	4	50	1	(1 nb, 1 w)	(5)	13	3	38	0	
Johnston	7	4	8	0		(3)	12	1	40	1	
Heal	19	2	67	3		(4)	16	3	44	0	
Doropoulos	4	0	21	1		(9)	4	0	21	0	
Meuleman						(6)	4	0	15	0	
Pomersbach						(7)	2	1	8	0	
Davis							2	0	19	1	
SA	O	M	R	W			O	M	R	W	
Pollock	15	4	51	3			5	1	9	1	
Ntini	7	1	29	0			5	0	22	0	
Nel	12.3	3	40	1		(4)	4	1	16	0	
Langeveldt	12	0	77	1	(3 nb)	(3)	4	1	11	0	
Smith	3	0	26	0	(1 nb)						
Kruger	8	1	51	0		(5)	2	0	4	0	
Kemp	4	0	16	0							

Fall of Wickets

	SA	WAXI	SA	WAXI
1st	24 (1)	8 (1)	11 (2)	21 (2)
2nd	94 (2)	26 (3)	23 (1)	-
3rd	148 (3)	161 (2)	57 (4)	-
4th	153 (4)	218 (5)	173 (5)	-
5th	176 (6)	269 (4)	176 (6)	-
6th	257 (5)	-	176 (7)	-
7th	269 (7)	-	200 (8)	-
8th	284 (9)	-	220 (9)	-
9th	-	-	395 (10)	-

AUSTRALIA v SOUTH AFRICA — 1st Test

Played at WACA Ground, Perth on 16,17,18,19,20 December 2005 — Toss: Australia

Umpires: SA Bucknor & BR Doctrove (TV: DJ Harper) — Referee: BC Broad

Debuts: Aus: None. SA: None

Close of play: Day 1: SA (1) 38-0 (De Villiers 14*, Smith 18*, 7 overs). Day 2: Aus (2) 38-1 (Langer 15*, Lee 0*, 11 overs). Day 3: Aus (2) 310-4 (Hodge 91*, Hussey 54*, 99 overs). Day 4: SA (2) 85-2 (Gibbs 17*, Rudolph 18*, 36 overs)

Result: Match drawn

Man of Match: Brad Hodge

Kallis had not recovered fully from a left elbow tendon injury, which enabled Rudolph to play. Conditions were unusual, with light drizzle falling on the first day and the pitch not having as much pace and bounce as the WACA ground of legend.

South Africa had an excellent first day, despite dropping three catches. Ntini struck with the second ball of the second over when Hayden's attempted pull looped off a top edge and Rudolph ran from gully to backward point to hold the catch.

Ponting joined Langer and the pair shared a partnership of 111 before Langer also fell to a mistimed pull shot, Smith holding a catch at mid-off. Ponting was out to Pollock and South Africa failed to make a double breakthrough when a leaping Boucher could not hold a chance behind the wicket from Hodge off Ntini.

Hodge and Hussey seemed to be tilting the advantage in Australia's favour before the tireless Ntini dismissed both. Kemp dropped Gilchrist at first slip off Ntini but Gilchrist did not add another run before Gibbs caught him at second slip.

Langeveldt grassed a simple chance at mid-on from Lee off Nel but Australia's total was unimpressive and looked less so as De Villiers and Smith shared an attacking first wicket stand of 83. When he was on 33, De Villiers had scored 1000 Test runs in only 20 innings, only Smith (17) needing fewer for South Africa.

The Australian bowlers stuck to their task, however, and South Africa were unable to capitalise on their start despite an impressive innings by Boucher, whose run-a-ball partnership of 77 with Pollock was a highlight of the innings.

If dropped catches had not proved especially costly in the first innings, they were disastrous in the second innings. Pollock could not hide his disappointment when Gibbs at third slip could not hold an overhead chance before Langer had scored.

Hayden's dismissal shortly before the end of the second day meant South Africa were slightly ahead but it took the tourists an hour on the third morning to get rid of night-watchman Lee. Then there was a cruel blow when umpire Doctrove incorrectly no-balled Langeveldt to invalidate an excellent catch by Rudolph at square leg when Ponting was on four.

After Pollock ended a long vigil by Langer, Hodge was dropped on 13 when he edged Langeveldt wide of Kemp at third slip. De Villiers put down difficult chances at mid-wicket and slip from Hussey and Gilchrist as Australia's total mounted and Hodge, without looking particularly convincing, advanced. Ponting was later criticised for delaying his declaration until Hodge reached his double century but he left his bowlers with 132 overs, which seemed reasonable enough.

South Africa were in deep trouble when four wickets fell before lunch on the final day but Rudolph and Kemp, the latter having been the subject of some derisive comments from Warne, showed immense character as they stayed together for more than 50 overs. Rudolph reached probably the most important century of his career and was generously applauded by the Australians before play was called off.

It emerged after the match that racist comments had been directed by some spectators at Prince, substitute Kruger, Pollock, Kemp and Ntini during the third day's play. The team management reported the incidents to match referee Chris Broad and security was increased. Both Cricket Australia and the International Cricket Council condemned the incidents.

A crowd of more than 57 000 was a record for a Test in Perth.

AUSTRALIA	*Runs*	*Mins*	*Balls*	*4*	*6*		*Runs*	*Mins*	*Balls*	*4*	*6*
JL Langer c Smith b Ntini	37	136	89	6	-	b Pollock	47	180	114	8	-
ML Hayden c Rudolph b Ntini	0	5	2	-	-	c Boucher b Langeveldt	20	43	33	5	-
*RT Ponting lbw b Pollock	71	155	107	12	-	(4) c Boucher b Ntini	53	161	106	4	-
BJ Hodge c Boucher b Ntini	41	121	96	4	-	(5) not out	203	469	332	22	-
MEK Hussey c Langeveldt b Ntini	23	84	51	3	-	(6) c Boucher b Pollock	58	172	121	8	-
A Symonds b Nel	13	48	29	2	-	(7) c Gibbs b Langeveldt	25	79	49	4	-
†AC Gilchrist c Gibbs b Ntini	6	18	13	1	-	(8) c Rudolph b Nel	44	68	58	4	-
SK Warne lbw b Langeveldt	24	51	30	3	-	(9) lbw b Kemp	5	6	7	1	-
B Lee not out	19	48	29	4	-	(3) lbw b Langeveldt	32	62	53	4	-
NW Bracken c Boucher b Nel	10	11	11	2	-	not out	14	46	24	1	-
GD McGrath c Boucher b Nel	0	1	1	-	-						
Extras (b 4, lb 2, w 2, nb 6)	14					Extras (b 5, lb 4, w 1, nb 17)	27				
TOTAL (75.2 overs)	**258**					**TOTAL (for 8 wkts dec) (146.4 overs)**	**528**				

SOUTH AFRICA	*Runs*	*Mins*	*Balls*	*4*	*6*		*Runs*	*Mins*	*Balls*	*4*	*6*
AB de Villiers b Warne	68	166	109	10	-	(2) c Hodge b Warne	12	76	57	2	-
*GC Smith c Ponting b Bracken	34	91	65	5	-	(1) lbw b Bracken	30	100	65	4	-
HH Gibbs b Lee	21	58	43	4	-	c Warne b Lee	33	129	104	5	-
JA Rudolph c Langer b Lee	8	35	28	1	-	not out	102	431	283	13	-
AG Prince lbw b Warne	28	102	79	2	-	lbw b Warne	8	55	45	1	-
JM Kemp c Hodge b McGrath	7	44	29	1	-	c Ponting b Warne	55	213	166	9	-
†MV Boucher c Hayden b Warne	62	115	77	7	-	not out	13	52	39	2	-
SM Pollock b Lee	34	52	35	6	-						
A Nel not out	4	38	20	-	-						
CK Langeveldt lbw b Lee	0	1	1	-	-						
M Ntini c Hodge b Lee	12	8	10	2	-						
Extras (b 4, lb 2, nb 12)	18					Extras (b 18, lb 13, nb 3)	34				
TOTAL (81.2 overs)	**296**					**TOTAL (for 5 wkts) (126 overs)**	**287**				

SA	O	M	R	W		O	M	R	W	
Pollock	19	6	46	1		36	6	98	2	(6 nb)
Ntini	19	3	64	5		34	8	113	1	
Langeveldt	17	1	100	1	(6 nb)	31	3	117	3	(8 nb)
Nel	17.2	3	29	3		28	2	104	1	(1 w)
Kemp	3	0	13	0	(2 w)	(6) 11	0	58	1	(3 nb)
Rudolph						(5) 6.4	1	29	0	
Aus	*O*	*M*	*R*	*W*		*O*	*M*	*R*	*W*	
McGrath	18	3	59	1		24	11	39	0	(1 nb)
Lee	22.2	1	93	5	(8 nb)	31	9	83	1	(2 nb)
Bracken	12	3	46	1		(4) 19	5	37	1	
Warne	29	4	92	3		(3) 47	21	83	3	
Symonds						3	0	6	0	
Hodge						2	0	8	0	

Fall of Wickets

	Aus	SA	Aus	SA
1st	0 (2)	83 (2)	37 (2)	35 (2)
2nd	111 (1)	127 (3)	86 (3)	55 (1)
3rd	117 (3)	135 (1)	129 (1)	109 (3)
4th	180 (5)	145 (4)	184 (4)	138 (5)
5th	185 (4)	167 (6)	316 (6)	250 (6)
6th	199 (7)	187 (5)	377 (7)	-
7th	210 (6)	264 (8)	444 (8)	-
8th	243 (8)	282 (7)	451 (9)	-
9th	258 (10)	283 (10)	-	-
10th	258 (11)	296 (11)	-	-

Longest innings in the 4th innings of a Test for South Africa

Mins			
431	JA Rudolph (102*)	v Australia (Perth)	2005/06
410	B Mitchell (189*)	v England (The Oval)	1947
357	JH Kallis (101)	v Australia (Melbourne)	1997/98

All of these matches were drawn. The world record is 645 minutes by MA Atherton (185*) for England v South Africa at Johannesburg in 1995/96.

AUSTRALIA v SOUTH AFRICA — 2nd Test

Played at Melbourne Cricket Ground, Melbourne on 26,27,28,29,30 December 2005 — Toss: Australia
Umpires: Asad Rauf & SA Bucknor (TV: RL Parry) — Referee: BC Broad
Debuts: Aus: PA Jaques. SA: None
Close of play: Day 1: Aus (1) 239-8 (Hussey 23*, 89.1 overs). Day 2: SA (1) 169-2 (Gibbs 54*, Kallis 17*, 58 overs). Day 3: Aus (2) 110-2 (Hayden 45*, Hodge 17*, 37 overs). Day 4: SA (2) 99-6 (Prince 16*, Pollock 13*, 42 overs)
Result: Australia won by 184 runs
Man of Match: Michael Hussey
Notes: Symonds scored his fifty off 40 balls in Australia's 2nd innings.

Kallis returned in place of Kemp, who was ruled out because of an injured right shoulder, and Boje replaced Langeveldt to give South Africa a spin bowling option. Langer could not play for Australia because of a hamstring injury and his replacement, Phil Jaques, was out early, caught at short leg off Pollock. Before he had scored, Ponting edged Pollock at catchable height but there was no third slip in place. On 17, Ponting survived a straightforward chance to Nel at square leg off Kallis.

It was the first of three chances in the match to men who went on to make centuries.

In front of a first-day crowd of 71 910, Ponting and Hayden put Australia in a strong position before a great comeback by the South African bowlers, who reduced Australia to 248-9. Before another run was scored, Hussey, on 27, edged Pollock to second slip and Kallis could not hold what by his standards was a routine head-high chance.

Hussey and a defiant McGrath swung the match back towards Australia with a last wicket stand of 107. The left-handed Hussey played some audacious strokes, including two successive sixes off Nel, as South Africa's tactics of trying to get McGrath on strike failed.

A classic one-two from Lee produced a breakthrough after De Villiers, Gibbs and Kallis had put the tourists in a promising position. After hitting Kallis on the helmet with a bouncer, which caused the batsman to tread dangerously close to his stumps, Lee produced a fast, swinging yorker to bowl South Africa's leading batsman.

After a first-ball dismissal, Symonds was under pressure from the Australian media but he produced a fine spell of swing bowling as Australia worked their way through the South

DEVASTATING . . . Brett Lee completes a classic one-two as he bowls Jacques Kallis one ball after a vicious bouncer in Melbourne *Picture: GETTY IMAGES/TOUCHLINE PHOTO*

African batting. Symonds took the wicket of Gibbs, who was unusually subdued as he battled his way towards a century, only to be bowled off a glove when Symonds managed to get some extra bounce.

Hayden gave a sharp low return chance to Nel's left when he had 27 before going on to play an innings which put Australia in a position to push for a win. Ntini could not bowl on the fourth day because of injured left knee ligaments, which put him out of the rest of the tour. Symonds played a thrilling innings studded with sixes as he and Hayden put on 124 in only 66 minutes off 93 balls for the fifth wicket to set up a declaration which, by coincidence, gave Australia a potential 132 overs, the same number as in Perth, to force a result.

This time, Australia were not to be denied. Warne's introduction in the 14th over paid early dividends as he took wickets with his eighth and 19th deliveries, with Smith falling to McGrath in between Warne's strikes. Symonds completed a good day by dismissing Kallis and Rudolph and South Africa were doomed when Boucher was caught off bat and pad by the ever-alert Ponting.

Warne's frequent and impassioned appeals were the subject of some controversy and he gained what seemed an unjustified reward when Prince, after a defiant stand with Pollock, turned his back on a ball which went off his arm to slip, with the Australians going up in unison and winning the verdict. Afterwards, Ponting, who was a nearby witness to Prince's dismissal from silly mid-off, said his team only appealed when they thought a batsman was out. Match referee Broad said Australia had pushed the line between what was acceptable and what was not but that, according to the umpires, they had not over-stepped it.

AUSTRALIA	*Runs*	*Mins*	*Balls*	*4*	*6*		*Runs*	*Mins*	*Balls*	*4*	*6*
PA Jaques c Rudolph b Pollock	2	14	17	-	-	(2) lbw b Nel	28	64	44	3	-
ML Hayden c Smith b Pollock	65	230	177	9	-	(1) c Boucher b Kallis	137	356	242	17	2
*RT Ponting c Gibbs b Nel	117	298	198	13	-	lbw b Pollock	11	48	29	-	-
BJ Hodge c Smith b Pollock	7	30	26	1	-	c Boucher b Nel	24	80	63	3	-
MEK Hussey b Ntini	122	247	203	14	4	c Kallis b Smith	31	94	74	2	-
A Symonds c Boucher b Nel	0	1	1	-	-	c Nel b Kallis	72	69	54	5	6
†AC Gilchrist c Gibbs b Nel	2	14	7	-	-	c Prince b Kallis	0	4	1	-	-
SK Warne c Boje b Nel	9	18	14	1	-	not out	0	1	0	-	-
B Lee lbw b Ntini	4	26	16	-	-						
SCG MacGill b Ntini	4	13	11	1	-						
GD McGrath not out	11	120	56	-	-						
Extras (b 2, lb 4, w 2, nb 4)	12					Extras (b 6, lb 3, nb 9)	18				
TOTAL (119.3 overs)	**355**					**TOTAL (for 7 wkts dec) (83 overs)**	**321**				

SOUTH AFRICA	*Runs*	*Mins*	*Balls*	*4*	*6*		*Runs*	*Mins*	*Balls*	*4*	*6*
AB de Villiers lbw b McGrath	61	178	141	9	-	(2) st Gilchrist b Warne	8	64	44	1	-
*GC Smith lbw b Lee	22	62	42	2	-	(1) c Gilchrist b McGrath	25	70	53	3	-
HH Gibbs b Symonds	94	347	234	15	-	b Warne	9	18	11	2	-
JH Kallis b Lee	23	108	90	2	-	c Gilchrist b Symonds	9	39	26	2	-
AG Prince c Ponting b Warne	6	22	19	-	-	c Hayden b Warne	26	147	120	2	-
JA Rudolph b Lee	13	40	36	2	-	b Symonds	4	8	5	1	-
†MV Boucher lbw b Symonds	23	48	40	4	-	c Ponting b Warne	5	30	18	-	-
SM Pollock lbw b Symonds	9	37	21	1	-	not out	67	156	120	8	1
N Boje b Warne	12	43	27	2	-	b McGrath	13	58	38	-	1
A Nel c Hussey b MacGill	14	28	21	3	-	c Gilchrist b McGrath	2	10	7	-	-
M Ntini not out	10	12	10	2	-	b MacGill	2	5	6	-	-
Extras (b 2, lb 7, nb 15)	24					Extras (lb 6, w 1, nb 4)	11				
TOTAL (111 overs)	**311**					**TOTAL (74 overs)**	**181**				

SA	*O*	*M*	*R*	*W*		*O*	*M*	*R*	*W*	
Pollock	26	5	67	3	(2 nb)	23	5	60	1	(5 nb)
Ntini	22.3	3	70	3		8	2	17	0	
Kallis	21.5	4	69	0	(2 w)	11	0	58	3	(1 nb)
Nel	31	6	84	4	(2 nb)	20	3	71	2	
Boje	18.1	3	59	0		14	1	65	0	
Smith						7	0	41	1	(3 nb)
Aus	*O*	*M*	*R*	*W*		*O*	*M*	*R*	*W*	
McGrath	27	13	57	1	(3 nb)	15	3	44	3	
Lee	28	5	92	3	(9 nb)	11	4	23	0	(1 nb)
Symonds	20	6	50	3	(3 nb)	(4) 4	2	6	2	
Warne	21	7	62	2		(3) 28	7	74	4	(3 nb, 1 w)
MacGill	15	3	41	1		16	7	28	1	

Fall of Wickets

	Aus	**SA**	**Aus**	**SA**
1st	2 (1)	36 (2)	53 (2)	39 (2)
2nd	154 (2)	122 (1)	82 (3)	45 (1)
3rd	176 (4)	184 (4)	131 (4)	58 (3)
4th	207 (3)	192 (5)	193 (5)	64 (4)
5th	207 (6)	214 (6)	317 (1)	72 (6)
6th	213 (7)	260 (7)	321 (6)	82 (7)
7th	227 (8)	265 (3)	321 (7)	130 (5)
8th	239 (9)	281 (8)	-	166 (9)
9th	248 (10)	291 (9)	-	178 (10)
10th	355 (5)	311 (10)	-	181 (11)

AUSTRALIA v SOUTH AFRICA — 3rd Test

Played at Sydney Cricket Ground, Sydney on 2,3,4,5,6 January 2006 — Toss: South Africa
Umpires: Aleem Dar & BF Bowden (TV: RL Parry) — Referee: BC Broad
Debuts: Aus: None. SA: J Botha
Close of play: Day 1: SA (1) 230-3 (Kallis 80*, Prince 62*, 74 overs). Day 2: Aus (1) 54-3 (Ponting 13*, 14.2 overs). Day 3: SA (2) 4-1 (Smith 3*, 1.3 overs). Day 4: SA (2) 94-3 (Kallis 14*, Prince 0*, 22 overs)
Result: Australia won by 8 wickets
Man of Match: Ricky Ponting
Man of Series: Ponting

Off-spinner Botha, originally selected only for the one-day games, was picked to make his Test debut after Boje's disappointing performance in Melbourne, while Langeveldt returned in place of the injured Ntini. Langer returned for Australia in place of Jaques. It was Ponting's 100th Test.

Rain prevented any play before lunch and Smith decided to bat despite conditions being helpful to seam and swing, no doubt wary of the danger of batting last on a pitch which traditionally helped spin bowling. He and Gibbs provided a reasonable foundation before Kallis and Prince put together a partnership marked by meticulous batting in testing conditions.

Kallis survived an excellent spell by Lee on the second morning as both men made richly deserved centuries in a stand worth 219.

Despite Kallis dropping a difficult chance from Langer at second slip off Pollock, South Africa claimed three wickets before the close on the second day. There was frustration on the third day as drizzle delayed the start by an hour and Hussey survived a confident lbw appeal by Nel early in a 130-run stand with Ponting. Botha's first spell cost 25 runs in four overs but produced the wicket of Hussey who was deceived by the bowler's first "doosra".

Ponting played a fine innings but had some anxious moments as he neared his century, edging Langeveldt through a vacant second slip area when he was on 91 and then surviving an appeal for lbw off the next ball when the grounds for doubt seemed minimal.

Some thrilling stroke-play by Gilchrist enabled Australia to put on 133 for their last three wickets, restricting South Africa's lead to 92. They were in a strong position but their chances of winning were substantially reduced by rain, which allowed only 20.3 overs to be bowled on the fourth day. Gibbs made a sparkling half-century before being run out two balls before the final weather interruption of the day.

South Africa showed their determination to push for a win by going for their shots on the final morning. Even allowing for the desirability of offering Australia a carrot, Smith's declaration was generous, setting Australia to make 287 off 76 overs, on a pitch which because of the overhead conditions and the numerous stoppages had not deteriorated as much as would normally be the case in Sydney.

Langeveldt swung a ball through Langer's defences before lunch but Hayden and Ponting both batted superbly as they posted a century partnership off 97 balls. Nel, with a sore foot, was clearly struggling and even Pollock was unable to slow the scoring.

For Ponting, the match was a personal triumph as he became the first man to score two centuries in his 100th Test. Appropriately he was at the crease when Australia sealed a series victory with 15.3 overs to spare.

Further incidents of racial abuse were reported by the South Africans. Smith made an official complaint after Nel was the subject of racial taunts on the third day.

South African coach Mickey Arthur was found not to have breached the ICC Code of Conduct regarding criticism or inappropriate comment on a match-related incident or match official after comments made at a press conference about umpiring decisions. "Disappointment at an umpire's decision is allowed by both players and team officials and I am satisfied with the explanation provided by the coach," said match referee Broad.

Glenn McGrath was reprimanded for "using language that is obscene, offensive or insulting and/or the making of an obscene gesture".

Botha was reported for having a suspect bowling action. The report was made by on-field umpires Bowden and Aleem Dar, television umpire Parry and match referee Broad.

"Concerns have been raised by the match officials over the general legality of his bowling action and, in particular, his 'doosra' and quicker deliveries when viewed with the naked eye. We are therefore requesting the ICC to commission a bio-mechanical report into the bowler's action in accordance with the process introduced last year," said Broad.

Botha was allowed to continue playing until the review of his action had been completed. He had to be tested within 21 days after which the ICC had to receive a written report within another 14 days.

Botha played in the triangular one-day series before having a bio-mechanical assessment at the University of Western Australia in Perth. Following receipt of a report from the assessment team that his action was illegal, he was suspended from bowling in international cricket.

The South African team was fined for a slow over-rate on the final day, with the players fined five percent of their match fees and captain Smith ten percent.

SOUTH AFRICA	*Runs*	*Mins*	*Balls*	*4*	*6*		*Runs*	*Mins*	*Balls*	*4*	*6*
AB de Villiers c Gilchrist b Lee	2	25	18	-	-	(2) lbw b Lee	1	6	4	-	-
*GC Smith lbw b Lee	39	125	77	6	-	(1) lbw b McGrath	5	12	9	-	-
HH Gibbs b McGrath	27	64	49	5	-	run out (Hodge)	67	98	74	11	-
JH Kallis c McGrath b Symonds	111	361	275	17	-	not out	50	179	96	3	-
AG Prince lbw b Warne	119	395	271	13	-	c Ponting b MacGill	18	38	30	2	-
JA Rudolph c Gilchrist b McGrath	38	143	110	5	-	c McGrath b MacGill	4	6	7	-	-
†MV Boucher c Gilchrist b MacGill	5	31	23	-	-	st Gilchrist b MacGill	11	15	13	2	-
SM Pollock c Hodge b Lee	46	89	64	3	-	not out	26	25	21	2	1
J Botha not out	20	63	46	2	-						
A Nel c Hodge b Warne	12	8	8	2	-						
CK Langeveldt not out	1	4	3	-	-						
Extras (b 9, lb 6, nb 16)	31					Extras (b 3, lb 4, w 3, nb 2)	12				
TOTAL (for 9 wkts dec) (154.4 overs)	**451**					**TOTAL (for 6 wkts dec) (42 overs)**	**194**				

AUSTRALIA	*Runs*	*Mins*	*Balls*	*4*	*6*		*Runs*	*Mins*	*Balls*	*4*	*6*
JL Langer b Langeveldt	25	25	20	3	-	b Langeveldt	20	49	32	5	-
ML Hayden b Langeveldt	4	16	11	-	-	c Smith b Botha	90	197	134	11	-
*RT Ponting lbw b Kallis	120	257	174	12	1	not out	143	201	159	16	-
BJ Hodge c Rudolph b Nel	6	36	23	-	-	not out	27	53	42	3	-
MEK Hussey c Boucher b Botha	45	149	111	8	-						
A Symonds lbw b Nel	12	78	51	1	-						
†AC Gilchrist c Boucher b Nel	86	156	109	10	2						
SK Warne c Boucher b Nel	0	2	1	-	-						
B Lee c Smith b Kallis	17	48	40	3	-						
SCG MacGill c Nel b Pollock	29	53	21	5	-						
GD McGrath not out	1	34	12	-	-						
Extras (lb 10, w 2, nb 2)	14					Extras (lb 1, w 3, nb 4)	8				
TOTAL (95.1 overs)	**359**					**TOTAL (for 2 wkts) (60.3 overs)**	**288**				

PERFECT MATCH . . . Ricky Ponting shows his joy as Australia clinch victory in Sydney, completing a personal triumph in which he scored two centuries in his 100th Test match
Picture: GETTY IMAGES/TOUCHLINE PHOTO

Aus	*O*	*M*	*R*	*W*	*O*	*M*	*R*	*W*
McGrath	34	17	65	2	15	2	61	1 (1 nb)
Lee	30.4	7	82	3 (11 nb)	10	3	48	1 (1 nb)
Symonds	23	4	69	1 (3 nb)				
Warne	36	5	106	2	(3) 11	1	45	0 (3 w)
Hussey	2	0	12	0 (2 nb)				
MacGill	29	5	102	1	(4) 6	1	33	3
SA	*O*	*M*	*R*	*W*	*O*	*M*	*R*	*W*
Pollock	25	3	109	1 (2 nb)	14	2	55	0 (2 nb, 1 w)
Langeveldt	24	4	108	2 (1 w)	14	1	52	1 (2 nb)
Nel	24.1	3	81	4	7	0	46	0
Kallis	15	4	25	2 (1 w)	(5) 2	0	8	0
Botha	7	2	26	1	(4) 12.3	0	77	1 (1 w)
Rudolph					11	0	49	0

Fall of Wickets

	SA	**Aus**	**SA**	**Aus**
1st	16 (1)	22 (2)	4 (2)	30 (1)
2nd	69 (3)	35 (1)	6 (1)	212 (2)
3rd	86 (2)	54 (4)	92 (3)	-
4th	305 (4)	184 (5)	123 (5)	-
5th	344 (5)	222 (3)	129 (6)	-
6th	355 (7)	226 (6)	152 (7)	-
7th	394 (6)	226 (8)	-	-
8th	433 (8)	263 (9)	-	-
9th	449 (10)	322 (10)	-	-
10th	-	359 (7)	-	-

Australia's victory was the tenth against a third innings declaration in Test cricket. Previous instance involving South Africa:

Eng (395 & 174-7) bt SA (379 & 187-3*) by 3 wkts	Port Elizabeth	1948/49
Note: Eng (forf & 251-8) beat SA (248-8* & forf) by 2 wkts	Centurion	1999/00

It was the second time a team had declared both their innings and lost. Previous instance:

Eng (404 & 215-3) bt WI (526-7* & 92-2*) by 7 wkts	Port-of-Spain	1967/68

South Africa's total was the ninth highest made in the first innings of a match by a team batting first that subsequently lost.

AUSTRALIA v SOUTH AFRICA — Only Twenty20 International

Played at Woolloongabba, Brisbane on 9 January 2006 (D/N) — Toss: Australia
Umpires: BNJ Oxenford & PD Parker (TV: NS McNamara) — Referee: BC Broad
Debuts: Aus: NW Bracken, SR Clark, BJ Haddin and ML Lewis (All 20Int), SR Clark (20). SA: J Botha, HH Dippenaar, AJ Hall, GJ-P Kruger, JA Rudolph and M Zondeki (All 20Int)
Result: Australia won by 95 runs
Man of Match: Damien Martyn
Notes: Symonds scored his fifty off 25 balls in Australia's innings.

Three days after the end of the Test series, the first 20-overs international to be played in Australia attracted a sell-out crowd of 38 894, a record for the Gabba. Both sides left out leading players. On an ideal pitch for such a match, Martyn set the tone with a thrilling innings and he was unlucky to fall in seeking the boundary which would have raised his century.

Symonds clubbed the bowling mercilessly as Australia posted a total which always looked beyond the tourists, especially when Bracken quickly accounted for Dippenaar and Gibbs. Despite resting most of their first-choice bowlers, Australia won comfortably, with their fielding giving the South Africans no respite.

AUSTRALIA	*Runs*	*Mins*	*Balls*	*4*	*6*
JR Hopes c Kallis b Pollock	17	24	20	2	-
DR Martyn c Gibbs b Zondeki	96	77	56	7	5
*RT Ponting c Pollock b Botha	27	23	18	2	2
A Symonds not out	54	33	26	6	2
MJ Clarke not out	0	4	0	-	-
MEK Hussey					
SM Katich					
†BJ Haddin					
NW Bracken					
SR Clark					
ML Lewis					
Extras (b 4, lb 3, w 8)	15				
TOTAL (for 3 wkts) (20 overs)	**209**				

SOUTH AFRICA	*Runs*	*Mins*	*Balls*	*4*	*6*
*GC Smith b Hopes	22	33	26	3	-
HH Dippenaar c Haddin b Bracken	1	8	5	-	-
HH Gibbs c Clark b Bracken	0	1	2	-	-
†MV Boucher c Haddin b Clark	29	32	21	5	-
SM Pollock c Lewis b Symonds	24	21	17	2	1
JH Kallis run out (Ponting)	15	14	13	1	1
JA Rudolph not out	6	20	7	-	-
AJ Hall c Hussey b Hopes	11	6	10	1	-
J Botha c Katich b Symonds	2	4	4	-	-
GJ-P Kruger c Martyn b Lewis	3	3	5	-	-
M Zondeki b Lewis	0	1	1	-	-
Extras (w 1)	1				
TOTAL (18.3 overs)	**114**				

SA	O	M	R	W	
Pollock	4	0	34	1	(2 w)
Kruger	4	0	29	0	(2 w)
Zondeki	3	0	41	1	(3 w)
Hall	4	0	38	0	
Botha	4	0	43	1	
Kallis	1	0	17	0	

Aus	O	M	R	W	
Bracken	3	0	9	2	
Lewis	3.3	0	18	2	
Clark	4	0	35	1	
Hopes	4	0	26	2	
Symonds	4	0	26	2	(1 w)

Fall of Wickets	Aus	SA
1st	57 (1)	7 (2)
2nd	103 (3)	7 (3)
3rd	187 (2)	38 (1)
4th	-	56 (4)
5th	-	92 (5)
6th	-	92 (6)
7th	-	106 (8)
8th	-	109 (9)
9th	-	114 (10)
10th	-	114 (11)

QUEENSLAND v SOUTH AFRICANS Limited Overs Match 50 overs per side

Played at Woolloongabba, Brisbane on 10 January 2006 (D/N) Toss: South Africans
Umpires: TP Laycock & DL Orchard Referee: RG Archer
Debuts: Qld: None. SA: GJ-P Kruger (LO for SA)
Result: South Africans won by 94 runs
Notes: Queensland substitute: LM Stevens replaced MS Kasprowicz

Kruger, having spent most of the tour on the sidelines before getting a chance in the 20-overs game, made a strong claim for a full international cap with a lively and aggressive bowling spell after only Dippenaar, Rudolph and Hall had any success with the bat.

SOUTH AFRICANS	Runs	Mins	Balls	4	6
*GC Smith c Hauritz b Johnson	6	10	11	1	-
HH Dippenaar b Noffke	79	179	125	9	-
HH Gibbs c Noffke b Bichel	5	13	8	1	-
JH Kallis c Hartley b Kasprowicz	5	28	17	1	-
JA Rudolph c Hartley b Kasprowicz	50	76	62	3	-
†MV Boucher c Hartley b Johnson	10	23	28	-	-
SM Pollock c Hartley b Johnson	0	1	1	-	-
AJ Hall not out	30	45	32	1	-
J Botha run out (Hauritz)	5	20	19	-	-
GJ-P Kruger not out	0	1	0	-	-
M Zondeki					
Extras (lb 2, w 10, nb 3)	15				
TOTAL (for 8 wkts) (50 overs)	**205**				

QUEENSLAND	Runs	Mins	Balls	4	6
*JP Maher c Boucher b Kruger	0	5	9	-	-
ML Hayden c Smith b Pollock	16	28	22	1	1
CT Perren lbw b Pollock	1	11	5	-	-
SJ Paulsen b Kruger	2	13	8	-	-
BP Nash b Pollock	0	15	7	-	-
LM Stevens b Kruger	0	7	6	-	-
†CD Hartley c Pollock b Zondeki	6	30	27	1	-
AJ Bichel c Pollock b Botha	37	31	33	2	1
AA Noffke c Boucher b Zondeki	0	3	3	-	-
NM Hauritz not out	23	53	28	2	-
MG Johnson b Kallis	5	21	21	-	-
MS Kasprowicz					
Extras (b 4, lb 6, w 8, nb 3)	21				
TOTAL (27.4 overs)	**111**				

Qld	O	M	R	W	
Johnson	9	1	33	3	(4 w)
Bichel	8	1	36	1	(1 w)
Kasprowicz	10	1	35	2	(2 nb, 1 w)
Noffke	8	1	29	1	
Hauritz	10	0	43	0	
Perren	3	0	22	0	(1 nb)
Paulsen	2	0	5	0	

SA	O	M	R	W	
Pollock	8	4	22	3	(1 nb)
Kruger	7	1	18	3	(2 w)
Zondeki	6	0	32	2	(1 nb, 1 w)
Hall	4	0	22	0	(1 w)
Botha	1	0	2	1	
Kallis	1.4	0	5	1	(1 nb)

Fall of Wickets	SA	Qld
1st	15 (1)	5 (1)
2nd	26 (3)	14 (3)
3rd	44 (4)	26 (2)
4th	132 (5)	28 (4)
5th	156 (6)	28 (6)
6th	156 (7)	28 (5)
7th	180 (2)	50 (7)
8th	203 (9)	50 (9)
9th	-	100 (8)
10th	-	111 (11)

QUEENSLAND ACADEMY OF SPORT v SOUTH AFRICANS Limited Overs Match

Played at Allan Border Field, Brisbane on 13 January 2006 Toss: South Africans
Umpires: TP Laycock & NS McNamara
Debuts: QAS: None. SA: None
Result: South Africans won by 46 runs
Notes: This match was played with 12 players per side, but only 11 allowed to bat and field

South Africa were firmly in control of a low-key fixture after Kallis and Prince shared a century partnership in the style of men who wanted to play themselves into form for more demanding challenges. Simpson, the Academy team captain, bowled his off-spin capably and followed up with a hard-hitting innings.

SOUTH AFRICANS	Runs	Mins	Balls	4	6
*GC Smith c Simpson b Tate	24	68	42	3	-
HH Dippenaar b Rimmington	1	10	6	-	-
HH Gibbs b Schossow	5	6	8	1	-
JH Kallis c Irvine b Simpson	80	138	106	5	3
AG Prince run out (Le Loux)	50	88	72	4	-
JM Kemp not out	29	43	39	3	-
†MV Boucher c Bragg b Simpson	1	5	3	-	-
SM Pollock c Sullivan b Simpson	27	20	18	1	2
AJ Hall not out	4	13	9	-	-
J Botha					
GJ-P Kruger					
M Zondeki					
Extras (lb 5, w 5, nb 3)	13				
TOTAL (for 7 wkts) (50 overs)	**234**				

QUEENSLAND ACADEMY OF SPORT	Runs	Mins	Balls	4	6
NJ Kruger c Kruger b Hall	19	41	28	3	-
TG Irvine c Gibbs b Pollock	4	17	12	-	-
CA Philipson c Boucher b Pollock	0	2	3	-	-
*CP Simpson c Dippenaar b Zondeki	55	68	48	6	3
NJ Reardon c Boucher b Hall	0	1	1	-	-
MJ Buchanan c Kallis b Botha	28	90	51	1	-
DJ Tate not out	55	101	84	3	3
RN le Loux lbw b Botha	0	4	3	-	-
†MC Bragg b Hall	0	10	9	-	-
NJ Rimmington lbw b Botha	13	33	24	1	-
GJ Sullivan run out (Kallis)	3	6	2	-	-
GM Schossow					
Extras (lb 1, w 8, nb 2)	11				
TOTAL (43.3 overs)	**188**				

QAS	O	M	R	W	
Rimmington	10	0	35	1	(4 w)
Schossow	7	0	30	1	(2 nb)
Tate	10	3	30	1	(1 nb)
Sullivan	6	1	46	0	(1 w)
Simpson	10	0	40	3	
Le Loux	5	0	31	0	
Buchanan	2	0	17	0	

SA	O	M	R	W	
Pollock	8	1	24	2	
Kruger	8	0	52	0	(6 w)
Hall	7	1	23	3	(1 nb)
Kallis	6	0	40	0	(1 w)
Zondeki	5	0	15	1	(1 nb)
Botha	9	1	32	3	(1 w)
Smith	0.3	0	1	0	

Fall of Wickets	SA	QAS
1st	7 (2)	16 (2)
2nd	15 (3)	16 (3)
3rd	59 (1)	38 (1)
4th	168 (4)	38 (5)
5th	169 (5)	97 (4)
6th	172 (7)	131 (6)
7th	212 (8)	132 (8)
8th	-	133 (9)
9th	-	178 (10)
10th	-	188 (11)

AUSTRALIA v SRI LANKA — VB Series

Played at Telstra Dome, Melbourne on 13 January 2006 (D/N) — Toss: Sri Lanka
Result: Australia won by 116 runs
Man of Match: Andrew Symonds
Points: Aus: 5; SL: 0

Australia gained a crushing win in the opening match of the triangular series, with aggressive batting from Katich and the middle order setting an imposing target before Lee blasted out both Sri Lankan opening batsmen in quick succession, a blow from which the Lankans could not recover.

Australia 318-5 in 50 overs (SM Katich 60, DR Martyn 70, A Symonds 66, MJ Clarke 45*, PDRL Perera 2-45). **Sri Lanka** 202-7 in 50 overs (MG Vandort 48, DPMD Jayawardene 50, B Lee 2-29, NW Bracken 2-11).

AUSTRALIA v SOUTH AFRICA — VB Series

Played at Woolloongabba, Brisbane on 15 January 2006 (D/N) — Toss: Australia
Umpires: Aleem Dar & SJA Taufel (TV: DJ Harper) — Referee: JJ Crowe
Debuts: Aus: None. SA: GJ-P Kruger
Result: South Africa won by 5 wickets
Man of Match: Shaun Pollock
Points: Aus: 0; SA: 4
Notes: Australia substitute: JR Hopes replaced DR Martyn after 18 overs of South Africa's innings.

Australia went into the match as firm favourites but on a fast, bouncy pitch they came up against an inspired Pollock. Gilchrist played on to the first ball of the match and Katich edged Pollock to first slip in the third over. Perhaps trying to emulate his feats in the 20-overs game, Martyn danced down the pitch to Pollock and was bowled by an off-cutter.

Ponting was dropped by Boucher off Pollock when he was on seven but Zondeki dismissed the Australian captain with his first ball, holding a sharp return catch. Symonds and Clarke were caught behind off Hall, who bowled a superb spell. Hussey and Lee threatened to swing the match Australia's way before Hussey missed a full toss to give Kruger his first one-day international wicket off the fifth ball of the 44th over, just when it seemed the last five overs might prove costly. A splendid throw from third man by Pollock accounted for Lee, seeking a second run, and South Africa were left with a manageable target.

POWERFUL . . . Justin Kemp helped Mark Boucher clinch victory over Australia in Brisbane before the VB Series campaign stuttered *Picture: GETTY IMAGES/TOUCHLINE PHOTO*

South Africa's reply did not start promisingly, with Smith and Kallis out in quick succession, Kallis to a superb pick-up and direct hit by Symonds from cover point, but Dippenaar stood firm and found the ideal partner in Boucher. The wicketkeeper scored only one off his first 19 balls but then controlled the pace of the innings. Seventeen runs off the 46th over, bowled by Lee, including a four and a six by Kemp, followed by a straight six by Boucher off McGrath, put South Africa ahead on the Duckworth/Lewis chart when there was a short rain delay with just five needed to win off ten balls. When the players returned three balls were enough.

AUSTRALIA	*Runs*	*Mins*	*Balls*	*4*	*6*
†AC Gilchrist b Pollock	0	1	1	-	-
SM Katich c Smith b Pollock	0	12	7	-	-
*RT Ponting c and b Zondeki	33	61	47	6	-
DR Martyn b Pollock	12	23	18	2	-
A Symonds c Boucher b Hall	9	35	16	1	-
MJ Clarke c Boucher b Hall	8	18	14	1	-
MEK Hussey b Kruger	73	125	108	5	-
B Lee run out (Pollock/Boucher)	57	130	69	1	3
NW Bracken not out	7	26	12	-	-
SR Clark b Hall	15	9	10	1	1
GD McGrath run out (Boucher/Hall)	0	1	1	-	-
JR Hopes					
Extras (b 3, lb 3, w 4, nb 4)	14				
TOTAL (49.5 overs)	**228**				

SOUTH AFRICA	*Runs*	*Mins*	*Balls*	*4*	*6*
*GC Smith c Katich b McGrath	12	35	26	1	-
HH Dippenaar run out (Clark)	74	184	115	8	-
JH Kallis run out (Symonds)	0	4	1	-	-
HH Gibbs c Martyn b Bracken	16	26	27	2	-
AG Prince c Hussey b McGrath	19	74	41	1	-
†MV Boucher not out	63	81	62	6	1
JM Kemp not out	29	38	21	3	1
SM Pollock					
AJ Hall					
M Zondeki					
GJ-P Kruger					
Extras (b 4, lb 9, w 5)	18				
TOTAL (for 5 wkts) (48.5 overs)	**231**				

SA	*O*	*M*	*R*	*W*	
Pollock	10	2	30	3	
Kruger	9	1	43	1	(4 nb, 2 w)
Hall	9.5	1	43	3	(1 w)
Zondeki	10	2	64	1	
Kallis	6	0	23	0	
Smith	5	0	19	0	

Aus	*O*	*M*	*R*	*W*	
Lee	10	1	47	0	(3 w)
McGrath	9	0	35	2	
Bracken	8.5	1	37	1	
Clark	10	0	41	0	(2 w)
Hopes	8	0	44	0	
Symonds	3	0	14	0	

Fall of Wickets	*Aus*	*SA*
1st	0 (1)	27 (1)
2nd	4 (2)	27 (3)
3rd	29 (4)	55 (4)
4th	60 (3)	125 (5)
5th	64 (5)	162 (2)
6th	71 (6)	-
7th	194 (7)	-
8th	207 (8)	-
9th	228 (10)	-
10th	228 (11)	-

SOUTH AFRICA v SRI LANKA — VB Series

Played at Woolloongabba, Brisbane on 17 January 2006 (D/N) — Toss: South Africa
Umpires: Aleem Dar & DJ Harper (TV: PD Parker) — Referee: JJ Crowe
Debuts: SA: None. SL: None
Result: Sri Lanka won by 94 runs
Man of Match: Kumar Sangakkara
Points: SA: 0; SL: 5
Notes: South Africa substitute: JA Rudolph replaced M Zondeki after 46 overs of Sri Lanka's innings. Sri Lanka substitute: CM Bandara replaced WU Tharanga after 0 overs of South Africa's innings.

Any euphoria after the win over Australia was short-lived as South Africa returned to the Gabba for their fourth match in nine days, a circumstance which made them virtually the home side in conditions which should have suited them ideally.

There might have been a touch of hubris in Smith's decision to send Sri Lanka in, perhaps reckoning the opposition, who had yet to find form in Australia, could be brushed aside easily. This proved not to be the case as the left-handers Mubarak, with several slices of fortune, and the classy Sangakkara added 112 for the second wicket off only 114 balls.

South Africa did not help their cause by dropping Mubarak twice, while the bowlers conceded too many extras. Smith, who set a fine personal example in the field, called his men together after the Mubarak-Sangakkara stand was broken and whatever he said seemed to galvanise his men to some degree as the Lankans were pegged back to a big rather than huge total.

South Africa were unable to mount any partnerships of note and suffered two unnecessary run-outs caused by mix-ups between the batsmen, with that of Rudolph particularly disastrous. Boucher played another fine innings, this time in vain. The leg-spinner Bandara bowled well for Sri Lanka, as, almost inevitably, did Muralitharan.

SRI LANKA	Runs	Mins	Balls	4	6
WU Tharanga c Boucher b Kruger	16	23	18	2	-
J Mubarak lbw b Botha	61	112	69	9	-
†KC Sangakkara c Smith b Pollock	88	146	109	10	-
TM Dilshan c Gibbs b Zondeki	15	27	20	-	-
*MS Atapattu run out (Gibbs/Smith)	33	62	43	2	-
DPMD Jayawardene c Prince b Botha	14	21	15	1	1
RP Arnold not out	15	23	17	1	-
WPUJC Vaas not out	14	13	14	1	-
KMDN Kulasekara					
M Muralitharan					
PDRL Perera					
CM Bandara					
Extras (lb 12, w 9, nb 5)	26				
TOTAL (for 6 wkts) (50 overs)	**282**				

SOUTH AFRICA	Runs	Mins	Balls	4	6
*GC Smith lbw b Vaas	3	11	10	-	-
HH Dippenaar b Kulasekara	10	28	12	2	-
JA Rudolph run out (Mubarak/Perera)	53	80	63	8	-
HH Gibbs run out (Perera/Sangakkara/Kulasekara)	7	32	16	-	-
AG Prince c Kulasekara b Bandara	29	65	44	2	-
†MV Boucher c Dilshan b Bandara	62	96	71	3	2
JM Kemp b Bandara	10	24	21	-	-
SM Pollock c Atapattu b Vaas	4	16	9	-	-
AJ Hall b Muralitharan	4	6	9	-	-
J Botha lbw b Muralitharan	2	7	8	-	-
GJ-P Kruger not out	0	4	3	-	-
M Zondeki					
Extras (lb 1, w 3)	4				
TOTAL (44.2 overs)	**188**				

SA	O	M	R	W	
Pollock	10	1	39	1	(1 nb, 1 w)
Kruger	8	0	61	1	(4 w)
Hall	10	0	58	0	(3 nb, 1 w)
Zondeki	9	0	49	1	(1 nb, 2 w)
Botha	10	0	49	2	
Smith	3	0	14	0	

SL	O	M	R	W	
Vaas	8	2	21	2	
Perera	6	0	38	0	(1 w)
Kulasekara	6	0	24	1	(2 w)
Dilshan	6	0	29	0	
Muralitharan	9	1	34	2	
Bandara	8.2	0	31	3	
Mubarak	1	0	10	0	

Fall of Wickets	SL	SA
1st	33 (1)	8 (1)
2nd	145 (2)	30 (2)
3rd	172 (4)	57 (4)
4th	211 (3)	93 (3)
5th	244 (6)	127 (5)
6th	259 (5)	152 (7)
7th	-	179 (8)
8th	-	184 (9)
9th	-	188 (10)
10th	-	188 (6)

AUSTRALIA v SOUTH AFRICA — VB Series

Played at Telstra Dome, Melbourne on 20 January 2006 (D/N) — Toss: Australia
Umpires: MR Benson & DJ Harper (TV: PD Parker) — Referee: JJ Crowe
Debuts: Aus: BR Dorey and PA Jaques. SA: JJ van der Wath (LOI), DW Steyn (LOI for SA)
Result: Australia won by 59 runs
Man of Match: Brett Lee
Points: Aus: 5; SA: 0
Notes: Australia substitute: GB Hogg replaced PA Jaques after 20 overs of South Africa's innings. South Africa substitute: JJ van der Wath replaced DW Steyn after 18 overs of Australia's innings.

South Africa's bowling attack had been decimated by injuries to Ntini, Nel, Kallis and Langeveldt, with the result that Dale Steyn and Johan van der Wath were both rushed into action after arriving as replacements, the latter less than 24 hours after his arrival. Steyn had arrived a day earlier after it was decided that Ntini, who had been keen to return after making a rapid recovery from a knee injury, needed more time for rehabilitation.

Phil Jaques played as a one-off replacement for Katich, who had a groin strain, and the sturdy left-hander made a record score for an Australian on one-day debut – a performance which was not enough to earn him an extended stay in the squad. Steyn bowled with impressive pace early on but had a nightmare when he was recalled to the attack in the 15th over, conceding 24 runs in an over which, remarkably, included the wicket of Symonds as well as four successive boundaries by Jaques, two no-balls and a wide and a boundary by Clarke.

Steyn was substituted by Van der Wath, who made an impressive debut, squaring up Clarke and ending Jaques' fine innings with a ball which lifted to take the shoulder of the bat. The previous highest score by an Australian on one-day debut was 79 by Kepler Wessels against New Zealand in Melbourne in 1982/83.

The South Africans fought back well, with the last seven wickets falling for 73 runs in 19 overs, but they had no answer to an outstanding display of fast bowling by Lee, who took two early wickets, then came back to dismiss Dippenaar, Prince and Kemp with blistering pace. Lee's figures were his best in one-day internationals.

Pollock played delightfully but it was a convincing win for Australia, who rested wicketkeeper Adam Gilchrist for two matches, calling up Brad Haddin.

AUSTRALIA	Runs	Mins	Balls	4	6
DR Martyn b Pollock	11	11	9	2	-
PA Jaques c Boucher b Van der Wath	94	146	112	14	-
*RT Ponting c Smith b Hall	9	31	19	1	-
A Symonds c Prince b Steyn	7	23	14	1	-
MJ Clarke c Boucher b Van der Wath	34	67	44	4	-
MEK Hussey c Kruger b Hall	18	38	31	-	-
†BJ Haddin b Pollock	1	6	4	-	-
JR Hopes c Botha b Hall	38	56	47	1	-
B Lee b Smith	6	12	9	-	-
BR Dorey c Kemp b Hall	2	14	8	-	-
GD McGrath not out	2	7	6	-	-
GB Hogg					
Extras (lb 3, w 13, nb 7)	23				
TOTAL (49.2 overs)	**245**				

SOUTH AFRICA	Runs	Mins	Balls	4	6
*GC Smith c Haddin b Lee	9	19	17	1	-
HH Dippenaar b Lee	41	131	93	3	-
AJ Hall b Lee	1	9	4	-	-
HH Gibbs lbw b Hogg	39	72	53	4	1
AG Prince b Lee	21	36	27	1	1
†MV Boucher lbw b Hogg	5	23	12	-	-
JM Kemp b Lee	3	9	8	-	-
JJ van der Wath c Haddin b Hogg	0	8	6	-	-
SM Pollock c Haddin b Dorey	46	37	31	1	4
J Botha not out	15	41	25	1	-
GJ-P Kruger c Symonds b McGrath	0	6	7	-	-
DW Steyn					
Extras (b 1, lb 2, w 2, nb 1)	6				
TOTAL (47 overs)	**186**				

SA	O	M	R	W
Pollock	10	2	31	2 (1 w)
Steyn	5	0	58	1 (7 nb, 2 w)
Hall	9.2	0	35	4 (1 w)
Kruger	6	0	35	0 (2 w)
Botha	10	0	47	0
Van der Wath	5	0	21	2 (1 w)
Smith	4	0	15	1 (2 w)

Aus	O	M	R	W
Lee	10	1	22	5 (2 w)
McGrath	9	2	35	1 (1 nb)
Dorey	9	1	51	1
Hopes	7	1	28	0
Hogg	10	0	32	3
Symonds	2	0	15	0

Fall of Wickets	Aus	SA
1st	17 (1)	12 (1)
2nd	55 (3)	16 (3)
3rd	85 (4)	84 (4)
4th	172 (5)	114 (2)
5th	177 (2)	119 (5)
6th	181 (7)	123 (7)
7th	208 (6)	123 (6)
8th	221 (9)	124 (8)
9th	238 (10)	185 (9)
10th	245 (8)	186 (11)

AUSTRALIA v SRI LANKA — VB Series

Played at Sydney Cricket Ground, Sydney on 22 January 2006 (D/N) — Toss: Sri Lanka

Result: Sri Lanka won by 51 runs

Man of Match: Sanath Jayasuriya

Points: SL: 4; Aus: 0

Australia continued their rotation policy by resting McGrath from the match in his home city. Jayasuriya, playing his first match of the series after recovering from a shoulder injury, was in magnificent form, scoring his 114 off 96 balls and sharing a second-wicket stand of 163 with Sangakkara.

Sri Lanka 309-7 in 50 overs (ST Jayasuriya 114, KC Sangakkara 78, DPMD Jayawardene 56, NW Bracken 2-40).
Australia 258 in 50 overs (MJ Clarke 67, BJ Haddin 41, JR Hopes 43, PDRL Perera 2-37, CM Bandara 4-58).

SOUTH AFRICA v SRI LANKA — VB Series

Played at Adelaide Oval, Adelaide on 24 January 2006 (D/N) — Toss: South Africa

Umpires: Aleem Dar & DJ Harper (TV: SJ Davis) — Referee: JJ Crowe

Debuts: SA: None. SL: None

Result: South Africa won by 9 runs

Man of Match: Boeta Dippenaar

Points: SA: 4; SL: 0

Notes: South Africa substitute: J Botha replaced JM Kemp after 11 overs of Sri Lanka's innings. Sri Lanka substitute: CM Bandara replaced PDRL Perera after 47.2 overs of Sri Lanka's innings.

Pollock became the most capped one-day player for South Africa when he played in his 246th match for his country, one more than Jonty Rhodes. It was his 252nd match, including his appearances for the World and Africa XIs.

Dippenaar batted soundly on a scorchingly hot day but the most exciting batting for South Africa came from Gibbs.

Muralitharan claimed his 400th one-day international wicket when he had Van der Wath caught at short leg, becoming the third bowler after Wasim Akram and Waqar Younis, of Pakistan, to achieve the feat.

NEW KID ON THE BLOCK . . . Johan van der Wath, on his international debut, dismisses Phil Jaques in the Telstra Dome in Melbourne

Picture: GETTY IMAGES/TOUCHLINE PHOTO

A fifth wicket stand of 107 off 107 balls between Dilshan and Jayawardene gave Sri Lanka a good chance of winning but Jayawardene's dismissal to a yorker by Van der Wath proved a turning point. Van der Wath bowled well towards the end of the innings, while Hall produced a magnificent final two overs, which cost just five runs and brought a wicket and a run-out.

SOUTH AFRICA	*Runs*	*Mins*	*Balls*	*4*	*6*
*GC Smith st Sangakkara b Muralitharan	28	88	50	2	-
HH Dippenaar not out	125	209	145	7	-
JJ van der Wath c Arnold b Muralitharan	0	1	1	-	-
JA Rudolph c and b Dilshan	11	28	27	-	-
HH Gibbs b Perera	68	65	65	4	3
SM Pollock c Atapattu b Kulasekara	8	15	8	-	-
JM Kemp not out	6	7	4	1	-
AG Prince					
†MV Boucher					
AJ Hall					
CK Langeveldt					
J Botha					
Extras (b 2, lb 11, w 4)	17				
TOTAL (for 5 wkts) (50 overs)	**263**				

SRI LANKA	*Runs*	*Mins*	*Balls*	*4*	*6*
J Mubarak c Prince b Pollock	4	18	19	-	-
ST Jayasuriya st Boucher b Hall	37	52	30	4	2
†KC Sangakkara c and b Van der Wath	23	42	31	4	-
TM Dilshan not out	82	164	108	3	-
*MS Atapattu run out (Boucher)	23	49	40	-	-
DPMD Jayawardene b Van der Wath	52	74	52	4	-
RP Arnold b Hall	11	16	11	1	-
CM Bandara run out (Hall)	0	2	1	-	-
WPUJC Vaas c Botha b Pollock	9	8	7	-	-
M Muralitharan not out	0	5	3	-	-
KMDN Kulasekara					
PDRL Perera					
Extras (lb 6, w 5, nb 2)	13				
TOTAL (for 8 wkts) (50 overs)	**254**				

SL	*O*	*M*	*R*	*W*
Vaas	10	1	55	0
Perera	7	0	45	1
Kulasekara	9	1	35	1
Muralitharan	10	0	45	2 (1 w)
Dilshan	8	0	43	1
Jayasuriya	6	0	27	0

SA	*O*	*M*	*R*	*W*
Pollock	10	1	51	2 (1 w)
Langeveldt	10	0	62	0 (1 nb, 1 w)
Van der Wath	10	1	37	2 (1 nb)
Hall	10	1	38	2 (1 w)
Botha	9	0	53	0 (2 w)
Smith	1	0	7	0

Fall of Wickets	*SA*	*SL*
1st	72 (1)	11 (1)
2nd	72 (3)	68 (2)
3rd	101 (4)	68 (3)
4th	220 (5)	117 (5)
5th	249 (6)	224 (6)
6th	-	242 (7)
7th	-	242 (8)
8th	-	253 (9)

AUSTRALIA v SRI LANKA — VB Series

Played at Adelaide Oval, Adelaide on 26 January 2006 (D/N) — Toss: Sri Lanka

Result: Australia won by 5 wickets

Man of Match: Andrew Symonds

Points: Aus: 4; SL: 0

The Australian selectors attracted criticism when they rested the in-form captain Ponting from the Australia Day fixture at the Adelaide Oval, with Gilchrist taking over the captaincy. No Sri Lankan batsman could score more than 34 and Australia won reasonably comfortably. Katich, under pressure to score runs, made the only half-century of the match.

It was announced that Gilchrist had been fined 40 percent of his match fee for showing dissent during his team's second match against South Africa. It had not been possible to hold a hearing before he rejoined the side in Adelaide.

Sri Lanka 218-8 in 50 overs (NW Bracken 2-45, A Symonds 3-48, GB Hogg 2-35). **Australia** 219-5 in 48.3 overs (SM Katich 52, DR Martyn 46, KMDN Kulasekara 2-32, M Muralitharan 2-35).

AUSTRALIA v SRI LANKA — VB Series

Played at WACA Ground, Perth on 29 January 2006 (D/N) — Toss: Sri Lanka

Result: Australia won by 6 wickets

Man of Match: Adam Gilchrist

Points: Aus: 4; SL: 0

Ponting again stood down and stand-in captain Gilchrist delighted his home town supporters with a thrilling century, hitting 116 off 105 balls. Katich continued his form of Adelaide as he and Gilchrist put on 191 for the first wicket.

Sri Lanka 233-8 in 50 overs (DPMD Jayawardene 69, RP Arnold 56, B Lee 2-42, SR Clark 2-40). **Australia** 237-4 in 41 overs (AC Gilchrist 116, SM Katich 82, WPUJC Vaas 2-39).

SOUTH AFRICA v SRI LANKA — VB Series

Played at WACA Ground, Perth on 31 January 2006 (D/N) — Toss: Sri Lanka
Umpires: MR Benson & PD Parker (TV: RL Parry) — Referee: JJ Crowe
Debuts: SA: None. SL: None
Result: South Africa won by 5 wickets
Man of Match: Graeme Smith
Points: SA: 4; SL: 0
Notes: South Africa substitute: J Botha replaced CK Langeveldt after 45.4 overs of Sri Lanka's innings. Sri Lanka substitute: CM Bandara replaced CRD Fernando after 38.4 overs of Sri Lanka's innings.

It was a must-win match for South Africa and their prospects looked poor when Jayasuriya flayed the bowling. Smith brought himself on immediately after the second power play and bowled Mubarak. He immediately called for the final power play, taking himself off again, and returned to change the match in the first over of his second spell in the 22nd over when Prince took a good diving catch at backward point. The last nine wickets fell for 84 runs and South Africa's task was much easier than they might have expected.

Smith followed up his bowling with his best innings of the series but it was Dippenaar who took South Africa to a position where victory was virtually assured.

Muttiah Muralitharan was given an unofficial reprimand after responding with a single-finger gesture to crowd taunts. He was photographed gesturing to a man with his face painted black and "no-ball" painted across his chest. Crowds in Australia regularly chanted "no-ball" when the off-spinner was bowling during matches. Match referee Jeff Crowe acknowledged there had been substantial provocation but said players needed to keep their emotions under control.

SRI LANKA	*Runs*	*Mins*	*Balls*	*4*	*6*
J Mubarak b Smith	31	67	50	5	-
ST Jayasuriya c Prince b Smith	86	97	65	9	3
†KC Sangakkara c Kemp b Langeveldt	16	43	24	1	-
DPMD Jayawardene lbw b Smith	1	8	8	-	-
*MS Atapattu c Rudolph b Van der Wath	7	24	17	-	-
RP Arnold c Kemp b Pollock	15	43	46	1	-
TM Dilshan run out (Kemp/Van der Wath)	37	74	42	3	-
WPUJC Vaas run out (Prince/Smith)	0	2	2	-	-
KMDN Kulasekara c Kemp b Pollock	1	4	6	-	-
CM Bandara run out (Prince/Van der Wath)	11	30	22	-	1
M Muralitharan not out	1	8	6	-	-
CRD Fernando					
Extras (lb 10, w 3, nb 2)	15				
TOTAL (47.4 overs)	**221**				

SOUTH AFRICA	*Runs*	*Mins*	*Balls*	*4*	*6*
*GC Smith c Sangakkara b Muralitharan	41	70	52	4	1
HH Dippenaar c Sangakkara b Muralitharan	87	139	94	7	3
JA Rudolph st Sangakkara b Bandara	25	64	48	-	-
HH Gibbs b Muralitharan	4	12	8	-	-
†MV Boucher not out	30	52	33	1	-
JM Kemp st Sangakkara b Bandara	6	11	12	-	-
AG Prince not out	20	28	25	3	-
SM Pollock					
AJ Hall					
JJ van der Wath					
J Botha					
CK Langeveldt					
Extras (b 4, w 6, nb 1)	11				
TOTAL (for 5 wkts) (45.1 overs)	**224**				

SA	*O*	*M*	*R*	*W*	
Pollock	10	3	17	2	
Langeveldt	10	0	50	1	(2 nb, 1 w)
Hall	9	0	48	0	
Van der Wath	8.4	0	66	1	
Smith	10	0	30	3	(2 w)

SL	*O*	*M*	*R*	*W*	
Vaas	9	1	39	0	(3 w)
Arnold	1	0	11	0	
Kulasekara	5.1	0	22	0	
Muralitharan	10	0	44	3	(1 nb, 2 w)
Dilshan	7	0	44	0	
Bandara	10	0	47	2	
Jayasuriya	3	0	13	0	(1 w)

Fall of Wickets	*SL*	*SA*
1st	94 (1)	84 (1)
2nd	137 (2)	164 (3)
3rd	142 (4)	164 (2)
4th	144 (3)	175 (4)
5th	159 (5)	190 (6)
6th	179 (6)	-
7th	179 (8)	-
8th	182 (9)	-
9th	216 (10)	-
10th	221 (7)	-

AUSTRALIA v SOUTH AFRICA — VB Series

Played at Telstra Dome, Melbourne on 3 February 2006 (D/N) — Toss: Australia
Umpires: Aleem Dar & PD Parker (TV: RL Parry) — Referee: JJ Crowe
Debuts: Aus: None. SA: None
Result: Australia won by 80 runs
Man of Match: Michael Hussey
Points: Aus: 5; SA: 0
Notes: Australia substitute: JR Hopes replaced DR Martyn after 12 overs of South Africa's innings. South Africa substitute: J Botha replaced CK Langeveldt after 25 overs of Australia's innings.

Brett Lee had been due to rest in accordance with Australia's rotation policy but came back into the side when McGrath withdrew to be with his wife Jane, who had suffered a recurrence of cancer. On a pitch of uneven bounce, with a damp outfield, Pollock bowled superbly but his parsimony was not matched by his team-mates.

Symonds and Hussey both batted aggressively but South Africa were still in the hunt when Smith bowled the 47th over, which started with the total on 221. Symonds hit successive full tosses for four and six and the over cost 19. Hussey hit four successive boundaries in the next over bowled by Van der Wath as 60 were added off the last four overs.

Lee's pace again proved crucial as South Africa made a poor start and were unable to recover despite the best innings of Botha's short career.

AUSTRALIA	*Runs*	*Mins*	*Balls*	*4*	*6*
†AC Gilchrist b Hall	33	41	43	4	-
SM Katich c Pollock b Van der Wath	25	69	43	2	-
*RT Ponting c Van der Wath b Botha	53	104	63	2	1
DR Martyn c Botha b Smith	34	58	46	2	-
A Symonds run out (Van der Wath)	65	86	60	5	1
MJ Clarke run out (Prince/Smith)	1	4	2	-	-
MEK Hussey b Van der Wath	62	59	44	9	-
B Lee not out	0	3	1	-	-
GB Hogg					
SR Clark					
BR Dorey					
JR Hopes					
Extras (b 1, lb 1, w 4, nb 2)	8				
TOTAL (for 7 wkts) (50 overs)	**281**				

SOUTH AFRICA	*Runs*	*Mins*	*Balls*	*4*	*6*
*GC Smith lbw b Lee	0	2	2	-	-
HH Dippenaar c Gilchrist b Clark	9	33	23	-	-
JA Rudolph run out (Hussey)	19	58	39	1	-
HH Gibbs b Hopes	33	52	40	5	-
J Botha c Gilchrist b Lee	46	109	61	4	-
AG Prince run out (Dorey/Gilchrist)	24	47	39	2	-
JM Kemp c Hopes b Lee	20	29	30	1	-
†MV Boucher c Ponting b Lee	0	3	1	-	-
SM Pollock c sub (DR Martyn) b Symonds	16	23	17	1	-
AJ Hall not out	19	37	35	-	-
JJ van der Wath not out	8	16	14	-	1
CK Langeveldt					
Extras (w 6, nb 1)	7				
TOTAL (for 9 wkts) (50 overs)	**201**				

SA	*O*	*M*	*R*	*W*	
Pollock	10	2	20	0	
Langeveldt	6	0	50	0	(2 nb, 1 w)
Hall	10	0	56	1	(1 w)
Van der Wath	10	0	82	2	(1 w)
Smith	10	0	59	1	(1 w)
Botha	4	0	12	1	

Aus	*O*	*M*	*R*	*W*	
Lee	10	2	30	4	(1 nb, 1 w)
Clark	8	1	34	1	
Dorey	10	0	48	0	(2 w)
Hopes	6	1	16	1	
Hogg	7	0	32	0	(2 w)
Symonds	9	0	41	1	(1 w)

Fall of Wickets	*Aus*	*SA*
1st	45 (1)	0 (1)
2nd	71 (2)	13 (2)
3rd	145 (4)	48 (3)
4th	163 (3)	69 (4)
5th	167 (6)	117 (6)
6th	276 (7)	155 (7)
7th	281 (5)	156 (8)
8th	-	156 (5)
9th	-	183 (9)

AUSTRALIA v SOUTH AFRICA — VB Series

Played at Sydney Cricket Ground, Sydney on 5 February 2006 (D/N) — Toss: Australia

Umpires: Aleem Dar & PD Parker (TV: RL Parry) — Referee: JJ Crowe

Debuts: Aus: None. SA: None

Result: Australia won by 57 runs

Man of Match: Adam Gilchrist

Points: Aus: 4; SA: 0

Notes: Gilchrist scored his fifty off 29 balls in Australia's innings. Australia substitute: JR Hopes replaced SM Katich after 10.3 overs of South Africa's innings. South Africa substitute: CK Langeveldt replaced M Zondeki after 14 overs of Australia's innings.

Pollock withdrew because of a bruised heel and South Africa's depleted bowling attack took a hammering, with Gilchrist and Ponting leading the way with some brutal stroke-play. Gilchrist looked capable of a massive score before he skied an attempted pull against Langeveldt off the first ball of the 18th over.

Lee again accounted for Smith early, when the South African captain gloved the first ball of the third over down the leg-side. South Africa made a spirited attempt to chase down a daunting target but only Boucher, who played a fine innings, was able to make a half-century.

AUSTRALIA	Runs	Mins	Balls	4	6
†AC Gilchrist c Boucher b Langeveldt	88	90	66	14	-
SM Katich c Kemp b Van der Wath	11	41	17	1	-
*RT Ponting c Gibbs b Botha	72	98	61	8	-
A Symonds c Hall b Smith	7	26	12	1	-
DR Martyn run out (Smith/Boucher)	79	98	75	5	-
MJ Clarke c Rudolph b Hall	27	33	37	-	-
MEK Hussey not out	47	40	33	4	1
GB Hogg					
B Lee					
NW Bracken					
SR Clark					
JR Hopes					
Extras (lb 4, w 8, nb 1)	13				
TOTAL (for 6 wkts) (50 overs)	**344**				

SOUTH AFRICA	Runs	Mins	Balls	4	6
*GC Smith c Gilchrist b Lee	6	10	8	1	-
HH Dippenaar c Hussey b Clark	27	48	29	4	-
HH Gibbs c Gilchrist b Symonds	46	78	54	6	-
†MV Boucher c Hopes b Symonds	76	103	83	3	2
JM Kemp c Bracken b Hogg	28	43	36	3	-
AG Prince run out (Ponting)	25	45	37	-	-
JA Rudolph not out	31	50	39	2	-
JJ van der Wath not out	37	21	16	2	4
AJ Hall					
J Botha					
CK Langeveldt					
M Zondeki					
Extras (lb 7, w 2, nb 2)	11				
TOTAL (for 6 wkts) (50 overs)	**287**				

SA	*O*	*M*	*R*	*W*
Van der Wath	10	0	76	1 (1 w)
Zondeki	4	0	42	0 (2 w)
Hall	10	0	69	1 (1 w)
Langeveldt	6	0	49	1 (1 nb, 2 w)
Smith	10	0	52	1 (2 w)
Botha	10	0	52	1

Aus	*O*	*M*	*R*	*W*
Lee	6	0	31	1 (1 nb, 1 w)
Bracken	9	0	51	0 (1 w)
Clark	10	0	70	1 (1 nb)
Hopes	5	0	35	0
Symonds	10	0	42	2
Hogg	10	0	51	1

Fall of Wickets	*Aus*	*SA*
1st	65 (2)	7 (1)
2nd	138 (1)	52 (2)
3rd	168 (4)	105 (3)
4th	203 (3)	172 (5)
5th	263 (6)	199 (4)
6th	344 (5)	236 (6)

SOUTH AFRICA v SRI LANKA — VB Series

Played at Bellerive Oval, Hobart on 7 February 2006 — Toss: Sri Lanka
Umpires: MR Benson & DJ Harper (TV: RL Parry) — Referee: JJ Crowe
Debuts: SA: None. SL: None
Result: Sri Lanka won by 76 runs
Man of Match: Malinga Bandara
Points: SA: 0; SL: 5
Notes: South Africa substitute: J Botha replaced DW Steyn after 18 overs of Sri Lanka's innings. Sri Lanka substitute: CM Bandara replaced CK Kapugedera after 20 overs of South Africa's innings.

In what was effectively a semi-final, with the winners going through to the best-of-three finals, Sri Lanka took advantage of winning the toss on a slow pitch which got slower and lower as the match went on.

Steyn again proved expensive after he was given the new ball as Atapattu and Jayasuriya got their side off to a fast start, which was consolidated in a stand of 123 between Atapattu and Sangakkara. South Africa fought back well in the last 15 overs but a target of 258 was always likely to be difficult in the conditions.

Vaas struck twice in the seventh over but Smith finally found form with his only half-century of the series. The match turned when Smith slogged the leg-spinner Bandara high to mid-on at the start of the 27th over. It was the first of four wickets for Bandara, who together with Muralitharan kept a clamp on the batsmen.

SRI LANKA	Runs	Mins	Balls	4	6
*MS Atapattu c Hall b Van der Wath	80	167	122	5	-
ST Jayasuriya b Pollock	25	40	26	2	1
†KC Sangakkara c Dippenaar b Van der Wath	62	114	77	5	-
DPMD Jayawardene lbw b Hall	11	29	17	1	-
J Mubarak c Prince b Hall	14	26	19	1	-
TM Dilshan b Hall	30	39	24	2	1
CK Kapugedera b Botha	3	10	6	-	-
WPUJC Vaas c Botha b Langeveldt	5	5	5	-	-
M Muralitharan c Botha b Langeveldt	1	8	5	-	-
CRD Fernando not out	1	7	2	-	-
PDRL Perera not out	1	1	1	-	-
CM Bandara					
Extras (b 3, lb 5, w 12, nb 4)	24				
TOTAL (for 9 wkts) (50 overs)	**257**				

SOUTH AFRICA	Runs	Mins	Balls	4	6
*GC Smith c Muralitharan b Bandara	67	124	76	5	-
HH Dippenaar lbw b Vaas	9	27	21	1	-
HH Gibbs c and b Vaas	0	2	3	-	-
†MV Boucher b Fernando	24	54	36	3	-
AG Prince c and b Bandara	22	64	41	-	-
JM Kemp lbw b Bandara	0	1	1	-	-
SM Pollock c Sangakkara b Bandara	15	31	26	-	-
AJ Hall not out	18	39	30	-	-
JJ van der Wath b Muralitharan	0	3	2	-	-
J Botha c sub (CK Kapugedera) b Jayasuriya	17	22	22	1	-
CK Langeveldt c Mubarak b Dilshan	1	4	5	-	-
DW Steyn					
Extras (lb 3, w 4, nb 1)	8				
TOTAL (43.4 overs)	**181**				

SA	O	M	R	W
Pollock	10	0	35	1 (2 w)
Steyn	3	0	32	0 (4 nb)
Hall	10	0	50	3 (3 w)
Langeveldt	10	0	47	2 (2 w)
Van der Wath	9	1	41	2 (2 w)
Smith	3	0	19	0 (1 w)
Botha	5	0	25	1

SL	O	M	R	W
Vaas	7	3	17	2
Perera	6	0	40	0
Fernando	7	1	32	1 (1 nb, 1 w)
Muralitharan	8	0	28	1
Dilshan	4.4	0	23	1 (1 w)
Bandara	9	0	31	4 (1 w)
Jayasuriya	2	0	7	1 (1 w)

Fall of Wickets	SL	SA
1st	52 (2)	19 (2)
2nd	175 (3)	19 (3)
3rd	190 (1)	77 (4)
4th	207 (4)	113 (1)
5th	212 (5)	114 (6)
6th	220 (7)	137 (5)
7th	229 (8)	146 (7)
8th	241 (9)	147 (9)
9th	254 (6)	178 (10)
10th	-	181 (11)

AUSTRALIA v SRI LANKA — VB Series 1st Final

Played at Adelaide Oval, Adelaide on 10 February (D/N) — Toss: Sri Lanka

Result: Sri Lanka won by 22 runs

Man of Match: Kumar Sangakkara

McGrath was not available for the finals because of his wife's illness. Atapattu and Sangakkara provided another solid foundation for Sri Lanka before the 18-year-old Kapugedara and Dilshan gave the innings late impetus. Kapugedara scored his 38 runs off only 21 balls.

Australia's reply started to unravel when Katich did not respond to a call for a single from Ponting, with the captain out for nought to be the first of five run-out victims, four of which involved Dilshan.

It was the first time Australia had lost a match in a home finals series since South Africa beat them in the first final in 1997/98.

Sri Lanka 274-8 in 50 overs (MS Atapattu 53, KC Sangakkara 83, NW Bracken 3-61, SR Clark 2-48). **Australia** 252 in 49.1 overs (SM Katich 56, MJ Clarke 80, M Muralitharan 3-40).

AUSTRALIA v SRI LANKA — VB Series 2nd Final

Played at Sydney Cricket Ground, Sydney on 12 February 2006 (D/N) — Toss: Australia

Result: Australia won by 167 runs

Man of Match: Andrew Symonds

Australia lost their first three wickets for ten runs before Ponting and Symonds put on 237, an Australian one-day record for any wicket. Both batsmen faced only 127 balls as they turned the match around in decisive fashion to leave Sri Lanka with an almost impossible task.

Australia 368-5 in 50 overs (RT Ponting 124, A Symonds 151, MJ Clarke 54*, WPUJC Vaas 4-56). **Sri Lanka** 201 in 36 overs (DPMD Jayawardene 50, RP Arnold 64*, NW Bracken 4-30, A Symonds 2-32, GB Hogg 2-35).

AUSTRALIA v SRI LANKA — VB Series 3rd Final

Played at Woolloongabba, Brisbane on 14 February 2006 (D/N) — Toss: Sri Lanka

Result: Australia won by 9 wickets

Australia won Finals series 2-1

Man of Match: Adam Gilchrist

Man of Series: Andrew Symonds

Australia clinched the series easily despite a good batting effort by Sri Lanka. Gilchrist was in irresistible form as he reached his century off only 67 balls, the fastest by an Australian, while Katich, who had been under pressure for much of the summer, offered solid support in an opening stand of 196. Katich went on to reach his maiden one-day international century.

Sri Lanka 266-9 in 50 overs (KC Sangakkara 59, DPMD Jayawardene 86, RP Arnold 76, NW Bracken 3-44, SR Clark 2-45). **Australia** 267-1 in 45.3 overs (AC Gilchrist 122, SP Katich 107*).

AUSTRALIA v SOUTH AFRICA IN AUSTRALIA 2005/06
TEST AVERAGES

AUSTRALIA

Batting & Fielding

Name	M	Inns	NO	Runs	HS	Avg	100	50	Ct	St
RT Ponting	3	6	1	515	143 *	103.00	3	2	5	0
BJ Hodge	3	6	2	308	203 *	77.00	1	0	5	0
MEK Hussey	3	5	0	279	122	55.80	1	1	1	0
ML Hayden	3	6	0	316	137	52.66	1	2	2	0
JL Langer	2	4	0	129	47	32.25	0	0	1	0
AC Gilchrist	3	5	0	138	86	27.60	0	1	6	2
A Symonds	3	5	0	122	72	24.40	0	1	0	0
B Lee	3	4	1	72	32	24.00	0	0	0	0
NW Bracken	1	2	1	24	14 *	24.00	0	0	0	0
SCG MacGill	2	2	0	33	29	16.50	0	0	0	0
PA Jaques	1	2	0	30	28	15.00	0	0	0	0
GD McGrath	3	3	2	12	11 *	12.00	0	0	2	0
SK Warne	3	5	1	38	24	9.50	0	0	1	0
Totals	33	55	8	2016	203 *		6	7	23	2
			Extras	93				subs	0	
			Total	2109		44.87			23	

Bowling

Name	Overs	Mdns	Runs	Wkts	Avg	BB	5I	10M
A Symonds	50	12	131	6	21.83	3-50	0	0
B Lee	133	29	421	13	32.38	5-93	1	0
SK Warne	172	45	462	14	33.00	4-74	0	0
SCG MacGill	66	16	204	6	34.00	3-33	0	0
GD McGrath	133	49	325	8	40.62	3-44	0	0
NW Bracken	31	8	83	2	41.50	1-37	0	0
BJ Hodge	2	0	8	0	-	-	0	0
MEK Hussey	2	0	12	0	-	-	0	0
Totals	589	159	1646	49		5-93	1	0
		b/lb/pen	74	1	run outs			
		Total	1720	50	34.40			

SOUTH AFRICA

Batting & Fielding

Name	M	Inns	NO	Runs	HS	Avg	100	50	Ct	St
JH Kallis	2	4	1	193	111	64.33	1	1	1	0
SM Pollock	3	5	2	182	67 *	60.66	0	1	0	0
HH Gibbs	3	6	0	251	94	41.83	0	2	4	0
AG Prince	3	6	0	205	119	34.16	1	0	1	0
JA Rudolph	3	6	1	169	102 *	33.80	1	0	4	0
JM Kemp	1	2	0	62	55	31.00	0	1	0	0
GC Smith	3	6	0	155	39	25.83	0	0	5	0
AB de Villiers	3	6	0	152	68	25.33	0	2	0	0
MV Boucher	3	6	1	119	62	23.80	0	1	12	0
N Boje	1	2	0	25	13	12.50	0	0	1	0

M Ntini	2	3	1	24	12	12.00	0	0	0	0
A Nel	3	4	1	32	14	10.66	0	0	2	0
CK Langeveldt	2	2	1	1	1 *	1.00	0	0	1	0
J Botha	1	1	1	20	20 *	-	0	0	0	0
Totals	33	59	9	1590	119		3	8	31	0
			Extras	130				subs	0	
			Total	1720		34.40			31	

Bowling

Name	Overs	Mdns	Runs	Wkts	Avg	BB	5I	10M
M Ntini	83.3	16	264	9	29.33	5-64	1	0
A Nel	127.3	17	415	14	29.64	4-81	0	0
JH Kallis	49.5	8	160	5	32.00	3-58	0	0
GC Smith	7	0	41	1	41.00	1-41	0	0
J Botha	19.3	2	103	2	51.50	1-26	0	0
CK Langeveldt	86	9	377	7	53.85	3-117	0	0
SM Pollock	143	27	435	8	54.37	3-67	0	0
JM Kemp	14	0	71	1	71.00	1-58	0	0
JA Rudolph	17.4	1	78	0	-	-	0	0
N Boje	32.1	4	124	0	-	-	0	0
Totals	580.1	84	2068	47		5-64	1	0
		b/lb/pen	41	0	run outs			
		Total	2109	47	44.87			

SOUTH AFRICA IN AUSTRALIA 2005/06

FIRST-CLASS AVERAGES

Batting & Fielding

Name	M	Inns	NO	Runs	HS	Avg	100	50	Ct	St
JH Kallis	2	4	1	193	111	64.33	1	1	1	0
SM Pollock	4	7	2	211	67 *	42.20	0	1	0	0
N Boje	2	4	2	76	26 *	38.00	0	0	1	0
HH Gibbs	4	8	0	289	94	36.12	0	2	5	0
JA Rudolph	4	8	1	230	102 *	32.85	1	0	4	0
AG Prince	4	8	0	258	119	32.25	1	0	2	0
GC Smith	3	6	0	155	39	25.83	0	0	5	0
AB de Villiers	4	8	0	186	68	23.25	0	2	0	0
JM Kemp	2	4	0	83	55	20.75	0	1	0	0
MV Boucher	4	8	1	141	62	20.14	0	1	14	0
CK Langeveldt	3	3	1	15	14	7.50	0	0	2	0
A Nel	4	6	1	35	14	7.00	0	0	2	0
M Ntini	3	5	1	24	12	6.00	0	0	0	0
J Botha	1	1	1	20	20 *	-	0	0	0	0
Totals	44	80	11	1916	119		3	8	36	0
			Extras	147				subs	1	
			Total	2063		29.89			37	

Bowling

Name	Overs	Mdns	Runs	Wkts	Avg	BB	5I	10M
JH Kallis	49.5	8	160	5	32.00	3-58	0	0
M Ntini	105.3	21	330	10	33.00	5-64	1	0
A Nel	149.3	20	509	15	33.93	4-81	0	0

GC Smith	7	0	41	1	41.00	1-41	0	0
CK Langeveldt	110	12	481	11	43.72	4-104	0	0
J Botha	19.3	2	103	2	51.50	1-26	0	0
SM Pollock	165	36	486	9	54.00	3-67	0	0
JM Kemp	22	1	101	1	101.00	1-58	0	0
N Boje	44.1	6	160	1	160.00	1-36	0	0
JA Rudolph	17.4	1	78	0	-	-	0	0
Totals	690.1	107	2449	55		5-64	1	0
		b/lb/pen	51	0	run outs			
		Total	2500	55	45.45			

SOUTH AFRICA

VB SERIES AVERAGES 2005/06

Batting & Fielding

Name	**M**	**Inns**	**NO**	**Runs**	**HS**	**Avg**	**SR**	**100**	**50**	**Ct**	**St**
HH Dippenaar	8	8	1	382	125 *	54.57	71.80	1	2	1	0
MV Boucher	8	7	2	260	76	52.00	87.24	0	3	6	1
JA Rudolph	5	5	1	139	53	34.75	64.35	0	1	2	0
AG Prince	8	7	1	160	29	26.66	62.99	0	0	5	0
J Botha	7	4	1	80	46	26.66	68.96	0	0	5	0
HH Gibbs	8	8	0	213	68	26.62	80.07	0	1	2	0
AJ Hall	8	4	2	42	19 *	21.00	53.84	0	0	2	0
GC Smith	8	8	0	166	67	20.75	68.87	0	1	3	0
SM Pollock	7	5	0	89	46	17.80	97.80	0	0	1	0
JM Kemp	8	8	2	102	29 *	17.00	76.69	0	0	5	0
JJ van der Wath	6	5	2	45	37 *	15.00	115.38	0	0	2	0
CK Langeveldt	5	1	0	1	1	1.00	20.00	0	0	0	0
GJ-P Kruger	3	2	1	0	0 *	0.00	0.00	0	0	1	0
JH Kallis	1	1	0	0	0	0.00	0.00	0	0	0	0
DW Steyn	2	0	0	0	-	-	-	0	0	0	0
M Zondeki	3	0	0	0	-	-	-	0	0	1	0
Totals	95	73	13	1679	125 *			1	8	36	1
			Extras	82					subs	0	
			Total	1761		29.35	73.64			36	

Bowling

Name	**Overs**	**Mdns**	**Runs**	**Wkts**	**Avg**	**RpO**	**BB**	**4I**
SM Pollock	70	11	223	11	20.27	3.18	3-30	0
AJ Hall	78.1	2	397	14	28.35	5.07	4-35	1
JJ van der Wath	52.4	2	323	10	32.30	6.13	2-21	0
GC Smith	46	0	215	6	35.83	4.67	3-30	0
J Botha	48	0	238	5	47.60	4.95	2-49	0
CK Langeveldt	42	0	258	4	64.50	6.14	2-47	0
GJ-P Kruger	23	1	139	2	69.50	6.04	1-43	0
M Zondeki	23	2	155	2	77.50	6.73	1-49	0
DW Steyn	8	0	90	1	90.00	11.25	1-58	0
JH Kallis	6	0	23	0	-	3.83	-	0
Totals	396.5	18	2061	55			4-35	1
		b/lb/pen	51	11	run outs			
		Total	2112	66	32.00	5.32		

AUSTRALIA IN SOUTH AFRICA 2005/06

Colin Bryden

South Africa won a thrilling one-day series but lost all three Test matches against a powerful Australian team during a tour which took place almost immediately after South Africa's tour of Australia.

South Africa's one-day victory was sealed in the final match when they made a world record total of 438-9. The performances in the one-day games raised hopes for a successful Test campaign but these were dashed when South Africa lost all three matches for the first time in a home series since 1895/96 when England defeated what was then a fledgling Test nation.

As was the case in Australia, the difference between the sides was not as clear-cut as the results indicated but the fact was that at the end of the summer, South Africa had lost five out of six Tests against the world champions, with one drawn.

The first Test at Newlands was played on an unsatisfactory pitch, which had been watered two days before the match following criticism by the South African camp. What is normally one of the best Test pitches in the world offered inordinate help to seam bowlers and the match was completed inside three days.

There was controversy in the second Test at Kingsmead, where South Africa might have escaped with a draw had the umpires been more consistent in their interpretation of what constituted bad light, while the third Test at the Wanderers Stadium was a thrilling contest which could have gone either way.

The inescapable conclusion, however, was that Australia were the better side and that the pressure of playing against them almost continually over an extended period wore down South Africa's resistance.

Mickey Arthur, the South African coach, admitted as much when he equated the task as akin to a golfer having to play match after match against Tiger Woods.

Although South Africa competed successfully for extended periods during both series, Australia proved superior at the key moments and performed better in all departments.

The combined averages of the two series told a compelling story. Jacques Kallis was South Africa's most successful batsman, scoring 420 runs at 46.66 but even he could only reach 50 on three occasions, two of which, commendably, he turned into centuries. Ashwell Prince was the second highest run scorer, with 391 at 32.58. Graeme Smith had an even less productive series than in Australia, while Herschelle Gibbs was disappointing.

By contrast, four Australian batsmen averaged better than 50 over the two series, while the Australians amassed ten centuries (five by their captain Ricky Ponting) and 15 half-centuries, against four and 13 respectively by South Africa.

Australia had superior bowling resources, with Stuart Clark, who made his Test debut at the age of 30, proving a more than able replacement for Glenn McGrath, who was not available for the tour of South Africa because of the illness of his wife. Clark's control of swing, seam and bounce complemented the sheer pace of Brett Lee and the leg-spin and guile of Shane Warne.

For South Africa, in the home series, Makhaya Ntini was virtually a lone warrior with Andre Nel, recovering from injury, not the factor he had been in Australia.

To add to that, South Africa again dropped important catches.

The one-day form was encouraging, however, a year out from the World Cup. Arthur's call for brave cricket was reinforced by the successful run chase at the Wanderers and it seemed that South Africa ended the season with more depth and a more clear-cut strategy than they had started it.

Australia's one-day squad was: Ricky Ponting (captain), Adam Gilchrist (vice-captain), Nathan Bracken, Stuart Clark, Michael Clarke, Brad Hogg, Michael Hussey, Mitchell Johnson, Simon Katich, Brett Lee, Mick Lewis, Damien Martyn, Andrew Symonds and Shane Watson. Manager, Steve Bernard; coach, John Buchanan; assistant coach, Dene Hills.

Phil Jaques joined the squad after both Ponting and Symonds missed the first two one-day internationals because of injury and played in one match before returning home.

McGrath, initially unavailable for the one-day series while his wife underwent treatment for cancer, eventually withdrew from the Test series as well.

The Test squad showed six changes from the one-day party, with Matthew Hayden, Michael Kasprowicz, Justin Langer, Stuart MacGill, Shaun Tait and Shane Warne replacing Bracken, Hogg, Johnson, Katich, Lewis and Watson.

SOUTH AFRICA v AUSTRALIA — Only Pro20 International

Played at Liberty Life Wanderers Stadium, Johannesburg on 24 February 2006 (D/N) — Toss: South Africa
Umpires: M Erasmus & KH Hurter (TV: BG Jerling) — Referee: BC Broad
Debuts: SA: LL Bosman, AB de Villiers, ND McKenzie, RJ Peterson, R Telemachus and JJ van der Wath (All 20Int).
Aus: GB Hogg and SR Watson (Both 20Int)
Result: South Africa won by 2 runs
Man of Match: Graeme Smith

Experimentation and the resting of key players resulted in a 13-man South African squad which included only five of the players beaten by Sri Lanka in the final one-day international 17 days earlier. Makhaya Ntini returned after injury, while Shaun Pollock, Mark Boucher, Boeta Dippenaar, Ashwell Prince and Charl Langeveldt were all rested for the Pro20 match but included in a 14-man squad for the first three one-day internationals.

Pollock eventually played as a specialist batsman, however, after Justin Kemp failed a fitness test on an injured shoulder. Pollock felt discomfort in his right knee after bowling in the nets but was cleared by a specialist to play in the one-day series.

Two uncapped players, Loots Bosman and Thandi Tshabalala, were included in the squad, although only Bosman appeared in the match. Neil McKenzie, Robin Peterson, Justin Ontong and Roger Telemachus were recalled to international cricket although Ontong was not included in the final XI.

Australia were without Andrew Symonds (thigh strain) and Michael Hussey, who arrived on the day of the match after staying in Australia for the birth of his son.

All 32 000 tickets for the second 20-overs international to be played in South Africa were sold but rain delayed the start by two hours and kept thousands away. Those who braved the weather were rewarded, with the captains agreeing to play a full match instead of deducting overs as provided for in the playing conditions after the loss of an hour.

Bosman played the sort of attacking innings he had been picked for, while Smith put his poor form in Australia behind him with a splendidly aggressive innings and Gibbs revelled in the freedom to play his shots. Hall took two wickets in his two-over opening spell and South Africa were on course for an easy win before Hogg and Lee hit out in the closing overs. Ntini, looking rusty after a lay-off, conceded 16 runs in the final over, including a huge six by Lee off the last ball.

SOUTH AFRICA		Runs	Mins	Balls	4	6
*GC Smith	not out	89	89	58	11	1
LL Bosman	b Lewis	23	26	18	3	1
HH Gibbs	lbw b Lewis	56	46	34	4	4
SM Pollock	c Clark b Watson	2	5	3	-	-
JJ van der Wath	c Clarke b Bracken	14	10	7	1	1
†AB de Villiers	not out	0	2	0	-	-
ND McKenzie						
AJ Hall						
RJ Peterson						
R Telemachus						
M Ntini						
Extras	(b 3, lb 10, w 4)	17				
TOTAL	**(for 4 wkts) (20 overs)**	**201**				

AUSTRALIA		Runs	Mins	Balls	4	6
†AC Gilchrist	lbw b Hall	1	6	2	-	-
SM Katich	c Smith b Telemachus	39	42	22	6	1
*RT Ponting	lbw b Hall	6	11	8	1	-
DR Martyn	c De Villiers b Van der Wath	17	11	9	3	-
MJ Clarke	st De Villiers b Peterson	37	33	24	-	3
SR Watson	b Peterson	4	9	6	-	-
GB Hogg	c Smith b Hall	41	35	25	2	3
B Lee	not out	43	36	21	4	2
NW Bracken	not out	3	8	3	-	-
SR Clark						
ML Lewis						
Extras	(lb 3, w 5)	8				
TOTAL	**(for 7 wkts) (20 overs)**	**199**				

Aus	O	M	R	W	
Lee	3	0	15	0	
Bracken	4	0	44	1	(2 w)
Lewis	4	0	31	2	
Clark	4	0	25	0	
Watson	3	0	35	1	(1 w)
Hogg	2	0	38	0	(1 w)

SA	O	M	R	W	
Ntini	3	0	44	0	(1 w)
Hall	4	0	22	3	(1 w)
Telemachus	4	0	40	1	(3 w)
Van der Wath	4	0	40	1	
Smith	2	0	21	0	
Peterson	3	0	29	2	

Fall of Wickets	SA	Aus
1st	48 (2)	16 (1)
2nd	159 (3)	34 (3)
3rd	170 (4)	53 (4)
4th	191 (5)	78 (2)
5th	-	93 (6)
6th	-	124 (5)
7th	-	181 (7)

SOUTH AFRICA v AUSTRALIA — 1st Limited Overs International

Played at SuperSport Park, Centurion on 26 February 2006 — Toss: Australia
Umpires: BG Jerling & JW Lloyds (TV: KH Hurter) — Referee: BC Broad
Debuts: SA: None. Aus: None
Result: South Africa won by 6 wickets (D/L method), target revised to 204 in 41 overs
Man of Match: Graeme Smith

An agreement was reached at a meeting between the two captains and match referee Chris Broad that both teams would play the series without "super-subs" following an announcement by the International Cricket Council that the experimental system would be scrapped after March 21. As substitutes were still part of the playing conditions, they would continue to be named but would not play.

With Jacques Kallis unavailable for the first three matches because of his tennis elbow injury, South Africa suffered another blow when Charl Langeveldt broke his left index finger during fielding practice.

Australia were reduced to eleven fully fit players when captain Ponting suffered an abdominal strain while batting in the nets the day before the game, while Stuart Clark sat out because of a bruised rib. Symonds had not recovered from a thigh strain.

Smith continued his resurgence of form with an unbeaten century to lead South Africa to a convincing victory. They had been set a target of 233 in 47 overs, which was revised to 204 in 41 overs after a rain break which came immediately after Smith reached his century.

On an overcast day, rain delayed the start and caused a break during the first innings when Australia were 162-6. The tourists were in early trouble as Pollock and Ntini exploited seam-friendly conditions. Pollock also ended a century partnership between Clarke and Hussey, dismissing both men in his second spell.

With rain threatening, South Africa overcame the early loss of Dippenaar and Gibbs, the latter to brilliant fielding by Clarke at short mid-wicket, with Smith and De Villiers putting on 83 off 62 balls to put the side well ahead of the required run-rate.

ONE-DAY STAR . . . Shaun Pollock strikes with the wicket of Damien Martyn in Centurion during a season in which he reinforced his status as a key man in South Africa's one-day team

Picture: GETTY IMAGES/TOUCHLINE

AUSTRALIA	Runs	Mins	Balls	4	6
*†AC Gilchrist c Nel b Ntini	14	34	19	3	-
SM Katich b Ntini	2	13	16	-	-
DR Martyn lbw b Pollock	1	3	3	-	-
MJ Clarke c De Villiers b Pollock	53	109	82	6	-
MEK Hussey c Dippenaar b Pollock	56	102	73	4	1
SR Watson b Hall	22	62	38	1	-
GB Hogg run out (Gibbs)	13	22	16	1	-
B Lee not out	38	43	28	1	2
NW Bracken run out (Boucher/Ntini)	16	8	7	-	2
MG Johnson not out	0	3	0	-	-
ML Lewis					
Extras (b 1, lb 5, w 8)	14				
TOTAL (for 8 wkts) (47 overs)	**229**				

SOUTH AFRICA	Runs	Mins	Balls	4	6
*GC Smith not out	119	172	124	12	1
HH Dippenaar b Bracken	10	26	16	2	-
HH Gibbs run out (Clarke)	0	6	1	-	-
AB de Villiers c Gilchrist b Hogg	43	52	30	7	1
†MV Boucher run out (Katich/Lee)	4	29	17	-	-
JM Kemp not out	24	59	38	2	-
SM Pollock					
RJ Peterson					
AJ Hall					
M Ntini					
A Nel					
Extras (lb 1, w 5, nb 1)	7				
TOTAL (for 4 wkts) (37.3 overs)	**207**				

SA	O	M	R	W	
Pollock	10	1	23	3	
Ntini	9	3	42	2	(3 w)
Nel	10	0	62	0	(4 w)
Hall	8	0	36	1	
Peterson	7	0	36	0	
Smith	3	0	24	0	(1 w)

Aus	O	M	R	W	
Lee	10	0	59	0	(1 nb, 2 w)
Bracken	8	1	27	1	(2 w)
Johnson	3	0	28	0	
Lewis	3	0	25	0	(1 w)
Hogg	8	1	30	1	
Clarke	3.3	0	19	0	
Watson	2	0	18	0	

Fall of Wickets	Aus	SA
1st	4 (2)	24 (2)
2nd	5 (3)	28 (3)
3rd	25 (1)	111 (4)
4th	125 (4)	134 (5)
5th	132 (5)	-
6th	157 (7)	-
7th	208 (6)	-
8th	227 (9)	-

SOUTH AFRICA v AUSTRALIA — 2nd Limited Overs International

Played at Sahara Park Newlands, Cape Town on 3 March 2006 (D/N) — Toss: South Africa
Umpires: KH Hurter & JW Lloyds (TV: BG Jerling) — Referee: BC Broad
Debuts: SA: None. Aus: None
Result: South Africa won by 196 runs
Man of Match: Makhaya Ntini

Ntini produced the best figures by a South African in one-day internationals as South Africa gained a crushing 196-run victory, the biggest victory by a margin of runs in one-day matches between the two countries. The result confirmed Newlands as a fortress for South Africa in one-day cricket. It was their 19th win in 22 matches at the ground.

It was an impressive all-round effort by South Africa, who made an imposing total on a slow pitch. After a promising opening stand between Smith and Dippenaar, Clark slowed South Africa's progress, dismissing Smith with his third ball and not conceding a run in his first two overs.

Gibbs and Boucher put on 80 off 79 balls before Kemp and Pollock hit out towards the end of the innings. Kemp hit two successive sixes off Bracken.

Australia faced a tough task under floodlights, which became more difficult when Ntini had Gilchrist caught behind off his first ball and Jaques caught at second slip four balls later. In an inspired performance, Ntini followed up with the wickets of Martyn and Clarke. At one stage he had taken 4-4 in five overs. Martyn's was his 200th wicket in one-day internationals.

It was Australia's lowest total against South Africa and their fourth-lowest of all time.

The match had been dedicated to Nobel Peace Prize Laureate, Archbishop Desmond Tutu, and the teams played for a one-off "Strength in Diversity" trophy.

SOUTH AFRICA	Runs	Mins	Balls	4	6
*GC Smith b Clark	24	36	29	3	-
HH Dippenaar b Watson	31	60	43	6	-
HH Gibbs c and b Hogg	66	105	71	8	-
AB de Villiers b Watson	18	33	23	3	-
†MV Boucher lbw b Hogg	42	67	59	1	3
JM Kemp not out	51	72	41	1	4
SM Pollock c Clarke b Lee	38	36	27	3	2
RJ Peterson c Martyn b Clark	4	6	3	1	-
AJ Hall not out	4	12	4	-	-
A Nel					
M Ntini					
Extras (b 1, lb 5, w 5)	11				
TOTAL (for 7 wkts) (50 overs)	**289**				

AUSTRALIA	Runs	Mins	Balls	4	6
*†AC Gilchrist c Boucher b Ntini	1	5	7	-	-
SM Katich c De Villiers b Nel	16	79	48	3	-
PA Jaques c Kemp b Ntini	0	3	4	-	-
DR Martyn c Dippenaar b Ntini	4	13	9	-	-
MJ Clarke c Boucher b Ntini	1	17	15	-	-
MEK Hussey c Kemp b Nel	22	69	48	2	1
SR Watson c Boucher b Ntini	27	70	39	3	-
GB Hogg c Pollock b Peterson	6	12	8	1	-
B Lee c Dippenaar b Nel	1	4	4	-	-
NW Bracken c Boucher b Ntini	10	18	20	1	-
SR Clark not out	2	7	5	-	-
Extras (lb 1, w 2)	3				
TOTAL (34.3 overs)	**93**				

Aus	O	M	R	W
Lee	8	0	51	1 (1 w)
Bracken	10	0	45	0 (1 w)
Clark	10	2	69	2 (1 w)
Watson	10	0	46	2
Hogg	9	1	48	2 (1 w)
Clarke	3	0	24	0 (1 w)

SA	O	M	R	W
Pollock	7	4	9	0 (1 w)
Ntini	9.3	4	22	6
Nel	8	2	30	3 (1 w)
Hall	5	1	15	0
Peterson	5	1	16	1

Fall of Wickets	SA	Aus
1st	45 (1)	1 (1)
2nd	57 (2)	1 (3)
3rd	95 (4)	5 (4)
4th	175 (3)	7 (5)
5th	192 (5)	33 (2)
6th	254 (7)	57 (6)
7th	262 (8)	70 (8)
8th	-	71 (9)
9th	-	86 (10)
10th	-	93 (7)

SOUTH AFRICA v AUSTRALIA — 3rd Limited Overs International

Played at Sahara Oval St George's, Port Elizabeth on 5 March 2006 — Toss: South Africa
Umpires: BG Jerling & JW Lloyds (TV: KH Hurter) — Referee: BC Broad
Debuts: SA: None. Aus: None
Result: Australia won by 24 runs
Man of Match: Brett Lee

Ponting made his first appearance of the series, after recovering from injury, and led his team to victory in a must-win game for the tourists.

Smith sent Australia in, reasoning that St George's Park was a ground difficult to defend because of its small playing area and that in a day match it was better to chase rather than set a target.

Telemachus returned for his first appearance in more than three years, after missing 91 one-day internationals, in place of Nel, who was still struggling with a foot injury.

The South African bowlers did well to restrict Australia for most of their innings on a slow pitch which proved not to be as good for batting as expected. Ponting top-scored but after 45 overs the total was a modest 207-3. Michael Hussey played a brief but spectacular innings as the last five overs yielded 47 runs.

Ponting used Lee in short, effective bursts and South Africa were in deep trouble at 69-5 before a 119-run partnership between De Villiers, who had earlier brought off a sensational run-out, and Pollock. Sixty-seven runs were needed off 47 balls when Pollock was bowled, to be followed by De Villiers in the next over to a remarkable leaping, left-handed catch on the boundary by Hogg. Telemachus hit Lee for two sixes in an over before the end.

AUSTRALIA	Runs	Mins	Balls	4	6
†AC Gilchrist c Boucher b Pollock	25	35	33	3	-
SM Katich run out (De Villiers)	49	103	80	4	1
*RT Ponting c Peterson b Pollock	62	123	82	5	-
DR Martyn c Telemachus b Ntini	51	79	69	1	1
MJ Clarke run out (Boucher)	25	42	23	-	1
MEK Hussey c Gibbs b Hall	22	16	10	1	2
B Lee not out	6	7	3	1	-
SR Watson not out	4	5	3	-	-
GB Hogg					
NW Bracken					
SR Clark					
Extras (lb 1, w 6, nb 3)	10				
TOTAL (for 6 wkts) (50 overs)	**254**				

SOUTH AFRICA	Runs	Mins	Balls	4	6
*GC Smith c Gilchrist b Lee	10	13	12	2	-
HH Dippenaar lbw b Watson	16	75	35	2	-
HH Gibbs run out (Clark)	16	38	30	2	-
AB de Villiers c Hogg b Clarke	68	134	92	6	1
†MV Boucher c Gilchrist b Lee	5	18	11	1	-
JM Kemp c Bracken b Clark	0	5	5	-	-
SM Pollock b Watson	69	80	74	7	1
AJ Hall c Gilchrist b Lee	5	12	6	-	-
RJ Peterson c Gilchrist b Lee	3	9	5	-	-
R Telemachus lbw b Bracken	29	17	13	-	3
M Ntini not out	1	14	4	-	-
Extras (lb 3, w 2, nb 3)	8				
TOTAL (47.2 overs)	**230**				

SA	O	M	R	W
Pollock	10	1	45	2
Ntini	9	0	56	1
Telemachus	8	0	59	0 (3 nb, 4 w)
Hall	9	1	39	1
Peterson	10	1	39	0 (1 w)
Smith	4	0	15	0 (1 w)

Aus	O	M	R	W
Lee	9	2	48	4 (3 nb)
Bracken	8.2	1	40	1 (2 w)
Clark	9	0	32	1
Watson	10	0	49	2
Clarke	9	0	46	1
Hogg	2	0	12	0

Fall of Wickets	Aus	SA
1st	36 (1)	15 (1)
2nd	99 (2)	43 (3)
3rd	173 (3)	60 (2)
4th	214 (4)	68 (5)
5th	243 (6)	69 (6)
6th	244 (5)	188 (7)
7th	-	192 (4)
8th	-	197 (8)
9th	-	199 (9)
10th	-	230 (10)

SOUTH AFRICA v AUSTRALIA — 4th Limited Overs International

Played at Sahara Stadium Kingsmead, Durban on 10 March 2006 (D/N) — Toss: South Africa
Umpires: KH Hurter & JW Lloyds (TV: BG Jerling) — Referee: BC Broad
Debuts: SA: None. Aus: None
Result: Australia won by 1 wicket
Man of Match: Boeta Dippenaar
Notes: Pollock scored his fifty off 28 balls in South Africa's innings

Australia drew level in the series with a tense one-wicket win with five balls to spare. Both teams were strengthened by the return of leading all-rounders after injury, with Symonds back for Australia and Kallis for South Africa.

Left-arm opening bowler Nathan Bracken removed Smith and Gibbs and South Africa were 9-2 in the sixth over. After a bright knock by De Villiers, Dippenaar found himself virtually standing alone until he was joined by Pollock, who played a sparkling innings. Dippenaar reached his century off a relatively slow 141 balls but without his contribution South Africa might not have had a competitive total. Pollock by contrast breezed to his half-century off 28 balls. Dippenaar was out off the third ball of the final over, the first of three wickets to fall for just one run off the last four deliveries.

Gilchrist and Katich gave Australia a flying start but their dismissals sparked a collapse. Telemachus took the key wickets of Martyn and Ponting within the space of three balls but South Africa suffered a blow when Pollock had to leave the field with a back strain after bowling his first spell of five overs.

The hard-hitting Symonds revived the innings but then played a rash shot and was bowled. Lee was out off the first ball of the next over. Bracken and Clark added 23 and took their side to within six runs of victory before Hall produced a perfect reverse-swinging yorker to bowl Bracken. With rain starting to fall, Clark and Lewis scrambled a thrilling win.

SOUTH AFRICA	Runs	Mins	Balls	4	6
*GC Smith c Gilchrist b Bracken	1	6	3	-	-
HH Dippenaar c Clarke b Lee	101	220	145	9	-
HH Gibbs c Gilchrist b Bracken	1	18	10	-	-
AB de Villiers lbw b Lewis	38	63	45	4	2
JH Kallis c Hussey b Symonds	21	34	27	1	1
†MV Boucher c Gilchrist b Lewis	19	42	27	1	-
JM Kemp lbw b Clark	1	10	9	-	-
SM Pollock not out	53	45	33	8	-
R Telemachus run out (Gilchrist/Lee)	0	1	1	-	-
AJ Hall run out (Gilchrist)	0	1	0	-	-
M Ntini					
Extras (b 1, lb 3, w 2, p 5)	11				
TOTAL (for 9 wkts) (50 overs)	**246**				

AUSTRALIA	Runs	Mins	Balls	4	6
†AC Gilchrist c De Villiers b Kallis	45	93	44	8	1
SM Katich c Kallis b Hall	46	75	68	5	-
*RT Ponting c Boucher b Telemachus	7	26	17	1	-
DR Martyn c Boucher b Telemachus	1	5	7	-	-
A Symonds b Telemachus	76	96	71	9	2
MJ Clarke c Boucher b Kallis	7	42	23	1	-
MEK Hussey run out (Hall)	19	34	24	2	-
B Lee c Boucher b Ntini	6	18	8	1	-
NW Bracken b Hall	7	23	14	1	-
SR Clark not out	16	28	18	2	-
ML Lewis not out	4	7	4	-	-
Extras (b 1, lb 2, w 7, nb 3)	13				
TOTAL (for 9 wkts) (49.1 overs)	**247**				

SENSATIONAL . . . Herschelle Gibbs hammers a boundary during his match-winning innings at the Wanderers *Picture: GETTY IMAGES/TOUCHLINE PHOTO*

Aus	O	M	R	W
Lee	10	0	55	1
Bracken	10	2	36	2
Clark	10	1	49	1
Lewis	10	0	38	2
Symonds	6	0	31	1 (1 w)
Hussey	2	0	15	0
Clarke	2	0	13	0 (1 w)

SA	O	M	R	W
Pollock	5	2	22	0 (1 nb)
Ntini	10	1	50	1
Hall	9.1	1	52	2
Telemachus	10	1	34	3 (2 nb)
Kallis	9	0	46	2 (3 w)
Kemp	4	0	17	0
Smith	2	0	23	0 (4 w)

Fall of Wickets	SA	Aus
1st	1 (1)	87 (2)
2nd	9 (3)	99 (1)
3rd	81 (4)	100 (4)
4th	118 (5)	101 (3)
5th	170 (6)	140 (6)
6th	173 (7)	192 (7)
7th	245 (2)	218 (5)
8th	246 (9)	218 (8)
9th	246 (10)	241 (9)

SOUTH AFRICA v AUSTRALIA 5th Limited Overs International

Played at Liberty Life Wanderers Stadium, Johannesburg on 12 March 2006 Toss: Australia
Umpires: Aleem Dar & BG Jerling (TV: KH Hurter) Referee: BC Broad
Debuts: SA: None. Aus: None
Result: South Africa won by 1 wicket
Man of Match: Herschelle Gibbs & Ricky Ponting
Man of Series: Shaun Pollock
Notes: Gilchrist scored his fifty off 35 balls in Australia's innings. Ponting scored his century off 71 balls and his 150 off 99 balls in Australia's innings. Hussey scored his fifty off 33 balls in Australia's innings. Smith scored his fifty off 33 balls in South Africa's innings. Gibbs scored his century off 79 balls and his 150 off 100 balls in South Africa's innings.

A capacity crowd of 32 000 packed the Wanderers Stadium on a warm, sunny day to watch a sensational match. The tone was set for a high-scoring encounter when Pollock, who had bowled with miserly control at the start of the previous four Australian innings, was ruled out because of the back strain he suffered in the previous match.

Smith sent Australia in to bat on a perfect pitch, prophetically saying that it was a good ground on which to chase a target. He could not have anticipated that his team would have to pursue a world record total.

Gilchrist and Katich started normally. The total was on 14 in the fifth over when Gilchrist gave a difficult chance off Ntini to Gibbs at backward point. Two runs were scored and the next three balls went for 6,3,4.

Gilchrist thrashed a half-century but Hall took a great diving left-handed catch at mid-on to dismiss the hard-hitting left-hander with the total on 97 in the 16th over.

Instead of the scoring rate slowing down, there was a torrent of runs as Ponting played a magnificent innings. He had scored 140 off 121 balls in the 2003 World Cup final against India at the same ground but this was an even more sensational effort. Nine sixes soared over the short boundaries.

Katich helped Ponting put on 119 for the third wicket off 93 balls but even more was to come as Michael Hussey joined Ponting in a partnership which yielded 158 runs, scored at a giddying pace off only 96 deliveries.

Australia soared past the previous world record total of 398 for five, by Sri Lanka against Kenya during the 1996 World Cup, with 72 runs scored off the last five overs.

South Africa lost Dippenaar in the second over but Smith and Gibbs shared a partnership studded with boundaries. The pair matched each other shot for thrilling shot before Smith was caught at deep mid-wicket off occasional left-arm spinner Clarke. Instead of going into his shell, Gibbs hit the next ball for six.

Gibbs raced to a century off 79 balls before unleashing some of the most astonishing stroke-play in cricket history, going to 175 off only another 32 deliveries. When he tried to hit one big shot too many, the total was 299-4 and the target was attainable, with 136 needed off 99 balls.

For a while, the scoring rate was almost conventional as Boucher and Kallis consolidated, knowing that wickets in hand could set up a late explosion. Kallis and Kemp fell and the required rate threatened to get out of control again before Van der Wath thrashed three sixes in a vital short innings. Telemachus played some daring strokes, while Boucher, described by Smith as one of the best finishers of a one-day match in cricket, stayed at the crease.

It went down to the last over with seven needed and two wickets standing. A searing drive by Boucher was stopped by the boot of bowler Lee and only one run was scored. The crowd roared as Hall pulled the next ball for four but groaned when he was out next ball trying to repeat the shot. Three balls left, one to tie, two to win and last man Ntini in. The field was up to prevent a single. Lee ran in, the ball was just outside the off stump and to wild cheering Ntini nudged it through one of the few gaps for one run to third man. Boucher hammered the next ball for four to spark emotional celebrations.

AUSTRALIA	*Runs*	*Mins*	*Balls*	*4*	*6*
†AC Gilchrist c Hall b Telemachus	55	68	44	9	-
SM Katich c Telemachus b Ntini	79	134	90	9	1
*RT Ponting c Dippenaar b Telemachus	164	153	105	13	9
MEK Hussey c Ntini b Hall	81	75	51	9	3
A Symonds not out	27	22	13	3	1
B Lee not out	9	11	7	-	-
DR Martyn					
MJ Clarke					
NW Bracken					
SR Clark					
ML Lewis					
Extras (lb 4, w 5, nb 10)	19				
TOTAL (for 4 wkts) (50 overs)	**434**				

SOUTH AFRICA	*Runs*	*Mins*	*Balls*	*4*	*6*
*GC Smith c Hussey b Clarke	90	100	55	13	2
HH Dippenaar b Bracken	1	6	7	-	-
HH Gibbs c Lee b Symonds	175	142	111	21	7
AB de Villiers c Clarke b Bracken	14	43	20	1	-
JH Kallis c and b Symonds	20	22	21	1	-
†MV Boucher not out	50	77	43	4	-
JM Kemp c Martyn b Bracken	13	20	17	-	-
JJ van der Wath c Ponting b Bracken	35	20	18	1	3
R Telemachus c Hussey b Bracken	12	10	6	2	-
AJ Hall c Clarke b Lee	7	8	4	1	-
M Ntini not out	1	4	1	-	-
Extras (b 4, lb 8, w 4, nb 4)	20				
TOTAL (for 9 wkts) (49.5 overs)	**438**				

SA	*O*	*M*	*R*	*W*	
Ntini	9	0	80	1	(1 w)
Hall	10	0	80	1	(2 nb)
Van der Wath	10	0	76	0	(1 nb, 1 w)
Telemachus	10	1	87	2	(7 nb, 3 w)
Smith	4	0	29	0	
Kallis	6	0	70	0	
Kemp	1	0	8	0	

Aus	*O*	*M*	*R*	*W*	
Lee	7.5	0	68	1	(3 nb, 1 w)
Bracken	10	0	67	5	
Clark	6	0	54	0	
Lewis	10	0	113	0	(1 nb, 1 w)
Symonds	9	0	75	2	
Clarke	7	0	49	1	

Fall of Wickets	*Aus*	*SA*
1st	97 (1)	3 (2)
2nd	216 (2)	190 (1)
3rd	374 (4)	284 (4)
4th	407 (3)	299 (3)
5th	-	327 (5)
6th	-	355 (7)
7th	-	399 (8)
8th	-	423 (9)
9th	-	433 (10)

SOUTH AFRICA v AUSTRALIA — 1st Test

Played at Sahara Park Newlands, Cape Town on 16,17,18 March 2006 — Toss: South Africa
Umpires: Aleem Dar & BR Doctrove (TV: KH Hurter) — Referee: BC Broad
Debuts: SA: None. Aus: SR Clark
Close of play: Day 1: Aus (1) 63-1 (Hayden 22*, Ponting 20*, 23 overs). Day 2: SA (2) 70-3 (Kallis 31*, Prince 14*, 20 overs)
Result: Australia won by 7 wickets
Man of Match: Stuart Clark

South Africa named 14 players for the first two Tests but the Newlands party was reduced to 13 when Shaun Pollock was ruled unfit because of a sprained ligament in his right sacroiliac joint. Garnett Kruger was left out and Boeta Dippenaar named 12th man. Pollock's injury meant a recall for Andrew Hall, while Ntini and Boje returned to the side in place of the injured Langeveldt and suspended Botha from the team that played in the final Test in Sydney.

When the South Africans arrived at the ground two days before the match, they were disappointed to see what they deemed to be a pitch that was dry and would help Australia's leg-spinners. Responding to comments by coach Arthur, groundsman Christo Erasmus that evening gave the pitch what he later described as a "light sprinkle".

The first morning was overcast and the pitch was green. Smith's decision to bat first after winning the toss was questionable, although as it turned out the conditions helped the bowlers throughout.

AUSTRALIA IN SOUTH AFRICA 2005/06

Australia had been expected to play Stuart MacGill alongside Shane Warne as a two-pronged leg-spin attack but after seeing the pitch they chose Stuart Clark, a tall fast-medium pace bowler who made his debut aged 30. It proved an inspired choice. Clark, bowling at a brisk pace, getting lift and making the ball move both ways off the seam, had Smith caught behind with his ninth delivery before he had conceded a run and he followed up with the wickets of Kallis and Gibbs as South Africa struggled to 66-4 at lunch.

South Africa's batting was in disarray and the best partnership of the innings was 32 for the last wicket between Nel and Ntini.

Langer appeared to glove the second ball of the innings from Ntini to wicketkeeper Boucher but was given not out by umpire Doctrove. Langer fell before the end of an eventful day when he was trapped in front by Nel.

Hayden, who earlier held his 100th Test catch in his 80th match, became the ninth Australian to reach 7000 Test runs – and to go past Sir Donald Bradman's total of 6996 – when he was on 12.

The partnership between Hayden and Ponting on the second morning proved crucial. Although the weather was sunnier, batting conditions remained difficult and both men had some awkward moments, although the only dropped catch came when Ponting, on 61, hooked Hall to Nel at fine leg. The pair put on 154 before Kallis, who was not introduced into the attack until the 41st over, had Ponting caught at short cover shortly before lunch.

The South Africans clawed their way back into the match as Australia lost their last nine wickets for 133 runs. In the context of the match, the bold approach by Symonds, who hit out for a rapid half-century, was a calculated gamble that paid off.

South Africa's hopes plummeted when Lee dismissed De Villiers and Gibbs in his third over before Warne trapped Smith with his third delivery. Smith's evident displeasure at the decision by umpire Doctrove brought him a fine for dissent of 30 percent of his match fee.

Clark made another crucial contribution with the ninth ball of the third morning when Kallis edged a forcing shot and Gilchrist held a leaping catch behind the stumps. Despite determined efforts from Rudolph and Hall, who shared South Africa's only half-century stand of the match, Australia needed only 95 to win.

A fiery spell by Ntini restored a modicum of pride for the home team but defeat within three days was a bitter blow. There was a surprising incident when Hayden on 22 appeared to have been caught by a diving Hall at mid-wicket off Boje but stood his ground. The decision was referred to television umpire Karl Hurter who, in the absence of conclusive evidence, decided in favour of the batsman.

SOUTH AFRICA	*Runs*	*Mins*	*Balls*	*4*	*6*		*Runs*	*Mins*	*Balls*	*4*	*6*
*GC Smith c Gilchrist b Clark	19	77	58	2	-	(2) lbw b Warne	16	64	34	2	-
AB de Villiers b Kasprowicz	8	40	29	1	-	(1) c Gilchrist b Lee	7	19	12	1	-
HH Gibbs b Clark	18	70	46	3	-	b Lee	0	1	2	-	-
JH Kallis c Hayden b Clark	6	10	12	-	-	c Gilchrist b Clark	36	86	50	5	-
AG Prince c Hayden b Lee	17	105	67	1	-	c Gilchrist b Clark	27	89	64	3	-
JA Rudolph c Gilchrist b Kasprowicz	10	13	14	2	-	b Warne	41	146	112	6	-
†MV Boucher c Gilchrist b Clark	16	30	23	3	-	c Langer b Kasprowicz	2	31	21	-	-
AJ Hall c Hayden b Lee	24	73	55	3	-	not out	34	104	69	4	-
N Boje lbw b Clark	31	60	48	5	-	c and b Clark	14	17	15	3	-
A Nel lbw b Lee	18	49	31	1	1	b Clark	4	4	5	1	-
M Ntini not out	17	24	15	1	1	c Kasprowicz b Warne	6	12	6	1	-
Extras (lb 6, nb 15)	21					Extras (w 3, nb 7)	10				
TOTAL (63.5 overs)	**205**					**TOTAL (63.5 overs)**	**197**				

DAZZLING DEBUT . . . team-mates rush to congratulate Stuart Clark after he dismissed Graeme Smith, the first of nine wickets in an outstanding first Test appearance at Newlands — *Picture: GETTY IMAGES/TOUCHLINE PHOTO*

AUSTRALIA	*Runs*	*Mins*	*Balls*	*4*	*6*		*Runs*	*Mins*	*Balls*	*4*	*6*
JL Langer lbw b Nel	16	41	31	3	-	b Ntini	34	89	56	4	-
ML Hayden c Rudolph b Ntini	94	237	173	14	1	c Gibbs b Ntini	32	87	70	4	-
*RT Ponting c Hall b Kallis	74	178	112	8	1	lbw b Ntini	1	11	4	-	-
DR Martyn c Boucher b Kallis	22	81	59	3	-	not out	9	32	13	-	-
MEK Hussey c Boucher b Hall	6	31	23	-	-	not out	14	23	20	1	-
A Symonds c Nel b Boje	55	84	47	3	4						
†AC Gilchrist c Smith b Kallis	12	20	19	1	-						
SK Warne c De Villiers b Boje	7	31	18	1	-						
B Lee c Gibbs b Ntini	0	5	3	-	-						
MS Kasprowicz not out	6	28	20	-	-						
SR Clark c Gibbs b Nel	8	23	19	-	-						
Extras (lb 7, w 1)	8					Extras (lb 5)	5				
TOTAL (87.2 overs)	**308**					**TOTAL (for 3 wkts) (27.1 overs)**	**95**				

Aus	*O*	*M*	*R*	*W*		*O*	*M*	*R*	*W*	
Lee	14.5	2	37	3	(1 nb)	17	5	47	2	(2 nb, 1 w)
Kasprowicz	13	0	44	2	(10 nb)	12	0	39	1	(3 nb)
Symonds	10	2	22	0	(2 nb)					
Clark	17	3	55	5	(1 nb)	(3) 16	7	34	4	(2 w)
Warne	9	0	41	0	(1 nb)	(4) 18.5	1	77	3	(2 nb)
SA	*O*	*M*	*R*	*W*		*O*	*M*	*R*	*W*	
Ntini	21	2	76	2		(2) 10	3	28	3	
Nel	22.2	6	45	2		(1) 7	1	25	0	
Hall	16	2	66	1		5	1	16	0	
Boje	16	4	63	2		5.1	1	21	0	
Kallis	12	0	51	3	(1 w)					

Fall of Wickets

	SA	Aus	SA	Aus
1st	24 (2)	21 (1)	20 (1)	71 (2)
2nd	42 (1)	175 (3)	20 (3)	71 (1)
3rd	48 (4)	192 (2)	37 (2)	76 (3)
4th	61 (3)	214 (5)	75 (4)	-
5th	76 (6)	236 (4)	92 (5)	-
6th	104 (7)	272 (7)	108 (7)	-
7th	124 (5)	294 (6)	158 (6)	-
8th	148 (8)	294 (9)	179 (9)	-
9th	173 (9)	296 (8)	183 (10)	-
10th	205 (10)	308 (11)	197 (11)	-

SOUTH AFRICA v AUSTRALIA — 2nd Test

Played at Sahara Stadium Kingsmead, Durban on 24,25,26,27,28 March 2006 — Toss: Australia

Umpires: SA Bucknor & BR Doctrove (TV: BG Jerling) — Referee: BC Broad

Debuts: SA: None. Aus: None

Close of play: Day 1: Aus (1) 228-5 (Hussey 10*, Symonds 4*, 88 overs). Day 2: SA (1) 140-2 (De Villiers 48*, Kallis 72*, 39.2 overs). Day 3: Aus (2) 125-1 (Hayden 36*, Ponting 48*, 36 overs). Day 4: SA (2) 29-0 (De Villiers 17*, Smith 10*, 7.1 overs)

Result: Australia won by 112 runs

Man of Match: Shane Warne

Pollock returned in place of Hall on another pitch which offered encouragement to the bowlers. Hayden edged Ntini's second ball to third slip and South Africa missed a chance of a double breakthrough when Ponting, on five, gloved Ntini down the leg-side but a diving Boucher could not hold the chance.

Ponting, in partnership first with Langer and then Martyn, batted with great determination. Stroke-play was never easy and Ponting said afterwards he could recall only one other innings, against the West Indies in Bridgetown in 2002/03, in which he had to work so hard for a century. The South African bowlers could be faulted, however, for not forcing the batsmen to play enough on a tricky pitch.

Ponting was disappointed when he drove Boje to short cover to be dismissed immediately before the second new ball was due. It was duly taken and both Martyn and night-watchman Lee fell to Ntini before the close, while Symonds was struck in the face by a Ntini bouncer, requiring four stitches in his upper lip after play.

Hussey was mainly responsible for Australia stretching their total beyond 350, although Warne played a valuable, aggressive innings.

Smith drove at Lee's first ball at the start of South Africa's innings and edged a catch to third slip, while Gibbs' lack of footwork was exposed again when he was bowled for the seventh time in nine Test innings against Australia. De Villiers and Kallis counter-attacked, however, with Kallis reaching an uncommonly rapid half-century off 49 balls before the two batsmen played more cautiously as the light deteriorated.

De Villiers fell to a fine gully catch by Hayden early on the third day. Prince helped Kallis add 56 before he flicked Warne to square leg to start a slide in which seven wickets fell for 67 runs, despite Kallis completing his third Test century against Australia, the 24th of his career and his fourth in successive Tests at Kingsmead.

The second new ball proved decisive. Kallis fell to a leading edge against Clark in the second over with the new ball and Lee blasted out the last four batsmen, taking his total of Test wickets to 202. Kallis was sixth out on 255, two more than the total when Australia's sixth wicket had fallen. Australia, though, led by 102 runs.

Ponting put the match beyond South Africa's reach as he made his second century of the match, his fifth of the summer against South Africa and the 30th of his career, taking him to fifth place on the all-time list, one ahead of Bradman. Once again Ponting and Hayden shared a valuable stand with Hayden making his 26th Test century and his sixth against South Africa.

Gilchrist hit 22 in an over off Nel before the declaration.

South Africa were left with the unlikely task of scoring 410 to win. Bad light ended play shortly after tea on the fourth day but there was to be no such respite on the final day.

Ponting was unable to take the field on the fifth day because of food poisoning and initially Australia struggled to make a breakthrough. The introduction of Warne proved crucial as he dismissed De Villiers and Smith in quick succession. De Villiers was smartly stumped by Gilchrist as he stretched forward and momentarily lost his balance but Smith appeared unlucky to be given out caught at leg slip by umpire Bucknor when it seemed an attempted sweep had looped off his arm.

Warne struck another vital blow when Kallis missed a sweep and was lbw and Gibbs was the fourth man out before lunch when a lifting delivery from Clark was edged to first slip.

Prince ducked a bouncer from Clark and the ball looped from his bat handle to mid-wicket. Warne made yet another breakthrough when he ended a promising innings by Rudolph. Lee's pace was too much for Pollock.

Boucher and Boje staged a fighting stand which was ended when, with the floodlights on, Boje fell to a leaping catch by substitute fielder Clarke at short cover. Nel batted defiantly in partnership with Boucher as the light deteriorated and it seemed likely, given the precedent of the previous days, that bad light would end play at any moment.

The new ball was taken and Lee was all set to bowl the 88th over when, after a discussion with the umpires, Gilchrist brought on Symonds instead, bowling off-spin, with Warne operating from the other end.

Warne finally produced a ball that was too good for Nel and Ntini had to try to save the match. With fielders clustered around the bat, the match ended, with 5.1 overs to spare, in highly unsatisfactory circumstances from a South African point of view when umpire Doctrove gave Ntini out when replays suggested the ball might not have hit a second set of stumps.

AUSTRALIA	*Runs*	*Mins*	*Balls*	*4*	*6*		*Runs*	*Mins*	*Balls*	*4*	*6*
JL Langer c Boucher b Kallis	35	167	125	5	-	c Pollock b Boje	37	73	53	6	-
ML Hayden c De Villiers b Ntini	0	5	2	-	-	c Boucher b Ntini	102	309	217	12	-
*RT Ponting c Gibbs b Boje	103	320	225	11	-	c Boje b Pollock	116	273	187	12	2
DR Martyn c Kallis b Ntini	57	171	134	10	-	not out	15	51	37	2	-
MEK Hussey lbw b Kallis	75	228	155	10	1						
B Lee c Boucher b Ntini	0	11	7	-	-						
A Symonds lbw b Nel	13	83	53	1	-						
†AC Gilchrist c Boucher b Nel	2	11	10	-	-	(5) c Nel b Boje	24	13	9	5	-
SK Warne c De Villiers b Pollock	36	56	31	6	1						
MS Kasprowicz c De Villiers b Nel	7	15	13	-	-						
SR Clark not out	13	34	15	2	-						
Extras (b 9, lb 10, w 2, nb 7)	28					Extras (lb 5, w 1, nb 7)	13				
TOTAL (127.1 overs)	**369**					**TOTAL (for 4 wkts dec) (82.4 overs)**	**307**				

SOUTH AFRICA	*Runs*	*Mins*	*Balls*	*4*	*6*		*Runs*	*Mins*	*Balls*	*4*	*6*
*GC Smith c Langer b Lee	0	1	1	-	-	(2) c Langer b Warne	40	133	75	5	-
AB de Villiers c Hayden b Clark	50	175	137	4	-	(1) st Gilchrist b Warne	46	117	80	8	-
HH Gibbs b Kasprowicz	9	15	14	2	-	c Warne b Clark	17	55	44	2	-
JH Kallis c and b Clark	114	344	223	17	-	lbw b Warne	7	32	32	1	-
AG Prince c Symonds b Warne	33	86	61	4	-	c Hussey b Clark	7	49	37	1	-
JA Rudolph c Hussey b Warne	13	43	41	2	-	c Langer b Warne	36	81	52	7	-
†MV Boucher b Lee	19	74	43	3	-	not out	51	221	156	9	-
SM Pollock c Gilchrist b Lee	1	6	4	-	-	b Lee	4	15	14	1	-
N Boje not out	6	24	14	1	-	c sub (MJ Clarke) b Kasprowicz	48	82	64	9	-
A Nel c Hayden b Lee	5	9	7	1	-	c Hayden b Warne	14	68	46	3	-
M Ntini c Ponting b Lee	0	2	1	-	-	lbw b Warne	0	14	13	-	-
Extras (lb 3, nb 14)	17					Extras (b 5, lb 8, nb 14)	27				
TOTAL (88.4 overs)	**267**					**TOTAL (99.5 overs)**	**297**				

SA	*O*	*M*	*R*	*W*			*O*	*M*	*R*	*W*	
Pollock	32	11	73	1	(7 nb, 1 w)		19	4	55	1	(7 nb)
Ntini	24	4	81	3			15	2	62	1	
Nel	31	8	83	3	(1 w)	(4)	14	3	58	0	
Kallis	21.1	8	52	2		(5)	8	0	40	0	(1 w)
Boje	19	1	61	1		(3)	26.4	4	87	2	
Aus	*O*	*M*	*R*	*W*			*O*	*M*	*R*	*W*	
Lee	19.4	5	69	5	(6 nb)		22	6	65	1	(4 nb)
Kasprowicz	14	0	60	1	(6 nb)	(5)	12	2	51	1	(6 nb)
Warne	25	2	80	2		(4)	35.5	9	86	6	
Symonds	11	3	16	0	(2 nb)	(3)	8	0	32	0	(3 nb)
Hussey	1	0	2	0		(6)	1	0	4	0	
Clark	18	4	37	2		(2)	21	6	46	2	(1 nb)

Fall of Wickets

	Aus	**SA**	**Aus**	**SA**
1st	0 (2)	0 (1)	49 (1)	91 (1)
2nd	97 (1)	10 (3)	250 (2)	98 (2)
3rd	198 (3)	144 (2)	278 (3)	122 (4)
4th	218 (4)	200 (5)	307 (5)	122 (3)
5th	219 (6)	226 (6)	-	146 (5)
6th	253 (7)	255 (4)	-	170 (6)
7th	259 (8)	256 (8)	-	181 (8)
8th	315 (9)	257 (7)	-	253 (9)
9th	327 (10)	267 (10)	-	292 (10)
10th	369 (5)	267 (11)	-	297 (11)

SOUTH AFRICA v AUSTRALIA — 3rd Test

Played at Liberty Life Wanderers Stadium, Johannesburg on 31 March, 1,2,3,4 April 2006 — Toss: South Africa

Umpires: SA Bucknor & AL Hill (TV: KH Hurter) — Referee: BC Broad

Debuts: SA: None. Aus: None

Close of play: Day 1: SA (1) 238-6 (Prince 79*, Pollock 4*, 79 overs). Day 2: Aus (1) 246-7 (Lee 42*, Kasprowicz 0*, 58.2 overs). Day 3: SA (2) 250-8 (Boucher 55*, Nel 18*, 69 overs). Day 4: Aus (2) 248-6 (Martyn 93*, Lee 9*, 78.3 overs)

Result: Australia won by 2 wickets

Man of Match: Brett Lee

Man of Series: Stuart Clark

Notes: Langer retired hurt with his score on 0 and the total on 0-0 in Australia's 1st innings.

Jacques Kallis captained South Africa for the first time after Smith suffered what was described as a severe soft tissue injury to his left ring finger during fielding practice on the day before the game.

Hashim Amla and Dale Steyn were added to the squad for the final match but the only change was Dippenaar for Smith, although there were several switches of deployment, with Gibbs moving up to open the batting and Dippenaar batting at number three, while it was decided that Pollock would no longer use the new ball when South Africa bowled. Australia kept the same side for the third successive match.

On another late-season pitch which helped the bowlers, Prince batted with typical grit and perseverance to anchor the South African innings.

Hayden claimed a catch after Rudolph edged Warne low into the slips and after consultation between the umpires Rudolph was given out. Ironically, in view of the incident when Hayden stood his ground in Cape Town, replays were inconclusive.

Boucher's dismissal shortly before bad light ended play left South Africa potentially vulnerable to the second new ball but Prince and Boje enabled the hosts to go beyond 300. After batting for more than an hour on the second morning, to add 14 runs to his overnight score, Prince edged Lee to second slip when he was seven short of a century.

Ntini put South Africa on top with an explosive spell. Langer was playing in his 100th Test and his parents had flown from Perth for the occasion. But he ducked into Ntini's first ball

REPEAT PERFORMANCE . . .Ricky Ponting at Kingsmead completes two centuries in a match against South Africa *Picture: GETTY IMAGES/TOUCHLINE PHOTO*

of the innings and slumped to the ground after being hit on the right earpiece of his helmet. He was taken to hospital with concussion, playing no further part in the match.

Ntini claimed the first four wickets and Nel had Gilchrist caught at deep midwicket as Australia crashed to 106-5 before the imperturbable Hussey led a recovery aided by Warne and Lee. Boje's dismissal of Hussey shortly before the close was an important breakthrough.

There was yet another catching controversy when Lee edged the eighth ball of the third morning from Pollock to Dippenaar at first slip. The umpires consulted and gave Lee the benefit of the doubt, although replays showed it was a clean catch. Lee made his highest Test score before he was last man out.

Gibbs went on the attack as South Africa built on their 33-run lead and Australia were handicapped by a back injury which prevented Kasprowicz from bowling more than two overs. From a promising 100-2, however, South Africa slipped to 194-8 with Warne and Clark doing most of the damage, despite an attacking innings by Pollock, who was moved up the order.

Boucher and Nel had a valuable partnership and the match was evenly poised after three days. The fourth day started dramatically when Boucher was given not out after edging Lee to Gilchrist. He swung at the next ball and it flew off a top edge over Gilchrist for four. He hit another boundary before another attempted big hit cost him his wicket.

Australia had not scored a run towards the target of 292 when Ntini made another early strike, having Hayden caught at third slip in the third over.

Hussey, opening in place of Langer, survived confident lbw appeals by Nel and Pollock while scoring his first five runs, then an appeal for a catch behind off Ntini when he had 19, before settling to play a solid innings. Nel bowled only two overs before leaving the field ill. Ponting hooked Ntini for six but was caught off an inside edge when Kallis brought himself on.

Hussey and Martyn batted until lunch and were still together at tea as they skilfully took Australia to within 94 runs of victory in the biggest partnership of the match.

There was another twist, though, when Hussey went back to Boje and was trapped in front of his stumps by a ball which hurried through. Symonds batted like a man intent on finishing the match the same day before edging an out-swinger from Kallis and Ntini produced another inspired burst, having Gilchrist and Warne caught behind as Australia lost three wickets in the space of 16 deliveries.

When bad light ended play, Australia needed 44 more runs with an effective three wickets standing and the new ball due nine deliveries into the final day.

Nel was still ill and unable to bowl. Two runs were added before the new ball was taken. Martyn completed his 13th Test century but was then twice beaten by Pollock before he was lbw when he went back to an off-cutter. Australia still needed 34.

As in the first innings, Lee batted confidently. Clark played two bold back foot cover drives off Ntini before the fast bowler took his tenth wicket of the match when Clark tried to repeat the stroke.

For the second time in less than a year, Australia's hopes depended on Lee and Kasprowicz, who put on 59 for the last wicket in the second Test of the Ashes series in Birmingham in August 2005 before Kasprowicz was dismissed as England won by two runs. This time they were not to be denied and Lee settled the issue with a back foot punch square for four off Pollock after 61 tense minutes of play.

Langer had put his pads on as the tension mounted but Ponting said afterwards he would probably not have allowed the batsman to risk further injury.

AUSTRALIA IN SOUTH AFRICA 2005/06

SOUTH AFRICA	Runs	Mins	Balls	4	6		Runs	Mins	Balls	4	6
AB de Villiers c Martyn b Clark	12	59	45	1	-	b Clark	4	18	15	-	-
HH Gibbs b Kasprowicz	16	75	44	2	-	c Martyn b Warne	53	127	87	6	1
HH Dippenaar c Gilchrist b Clark	32	101	69	7	-	c Hayden b Clark	20	38	21	4	-
*JH Kallis b Lee	37	123	92	6	-	lbw b Clark	27	124	82	4	-
AG Prince c Langer b Lee	93	247	170	11	-	c Symonds b Warne	9	41	30	1	-
JA Rudolph c Hayden b Warne	25	62	44	4	-	(7) c Gilchrist b Clark	0	9	3	-	-
†MV Boucher lbw b Symonds	24	72	53	2	-	(8) c Gilchrist b Lee	63	135	92	9	-
SM Pollock c Ponting b Clark	8	24	17	2	-	(6) c Gilchrist b Lee	44	75	47	6	-
N Boje c Langer b Kasprowicz	43	69	46	9	-	c Symonds b Warne	4	16	14	1	-
A Nel c Martyn b Lee	0	16	8	-	-	not out	18	70	41	3	-
M Ntini not out	0	6	5	-	-	b Lee	0	2	2	-	-
Extras (lb 4, nb 9)	13					Extras (b 6, lb 4, w 1, nb 5)	16				
TOTAL (97.2 overs)	**303**					**TOTAL (71.3 overs)**	**258**				

AUSTRALIA	Runs	Mins	Balls	4	6		Runs	Mins	Balls	4	6
JL Langer retired hurt	0	4	1	-	-						
ML Hayden c Gibbs b Ntini	3	15	7	-	-	(1) c De Villiers b Ntini	0	9	7	-	-
*RT Ponting c De Villiers b Ntini	34	63	40	5	1	c Boucher b Kallis	20	50	32	1	1
DR Martyn c Nel b Ntini	21	35	23	2	1	lbw b Pollock	101	287	208	13	-
MEK Hussey lbw b Boje	73	200	153	11	-	(2) lbw b Boje	89	264	197	12	-
A Symonds lbw b Ntini	4	13	11	-	-	(5) c Boucher b Kallis	29	20	26	4	1
†AC Gilchrist c Rudolph b Nel	12	37	24	3	-	(6) c Boucher b Ntini	0	5	1	-	-
SK Warne c Pollock b Ntini	36	59	33	7	-	(7) c Boucher b Ntini	3	10	8	-	-
B Lee c Boje b Ntini	64	106	68	6	2	(8) not out	24	84	46	4	-
MS Kasprowicz c Gibbs b Pollock	2	29	17	-	-	not out	7	15	13	1	-
SR Clark not out	0	4	0	-	-	(9) c Boucher b Ntini	10	21	13	2	-
Extras (b 5, lb 14, w 2)	21					Extras (b 1, lb 9, nb 1)	11				
TOTAL (62.5 overs)	**270**					**TOTAL (for 8 wkts) (91.4 overs)**	**294**				

Aus	O	M	R	W		O	M	R	W	
Lee	24	8	57	3	(3 nb)	18.3	3	57	3	(3 nb)
Clark	28	8	81	3		18	4	64	4	
Kasprowicz	24.2	4	86	2	(4 nb)	2	0	12	0	(1 nb)
Warne	13	2	49	1		(6) 26	5	90	3	(1 nb)
Symonds	8	2	26	1	(2 nb)	(4) 5	0	18	0	
Ponting						(5) 2	1	7	0	(1 w)
SA	*O*	*M*	*R*	*W*		*O*	*M*	*R*	*W*	
Ntini	18.5	2	100	6	(1 w)	26	4	78	4	
Nel	15	2	42	1	(1 w)	2	1	4	0	
Pollock	15	2	56	1		25.4	3	81	1	(1 nb)
Kallis	10	2	43	0		18	6	44	2	
Boje	4	1	10	1		19	5	65	1	
De Villiers						1	0	12	0	

Fall of Wickets	SA	Aus	SA	Aus
1st	26 (1)	12 (2)	9 (1)	0 (1)
2nd	38 (2)	68 (4)	55 (3)	33 (3)
3rd	97 (3)	73 (3)	100 (2)	198 (2)
4th	106 (4)	89 (6)	120 (5)	228 (5)
5th	161 (6)	106 (7)	130 (4)	229 (6)
6th	233 (7)	174 (8)	140 (7)	237 (7)
7th	251 (8)	242 (5)	186 (6)	258 (4)
8th	285 (5)	260 (10)	194 (9)	275 (9)
9th	303 (10)	270 (9)	258 (8)	-
10th	303 (9)	-	258 (11)	-

South Africa: Series whitewash defeats

v England in South Africa 1895/96 (3 Tests)
v Australia in Australia 1931/32 (5 Tests)
v Australia in Australia 2001/02 (3Tests)
v Australia in South Africa 2005/06 (3 Tests)

SOUTH AFRICA v AUSTRALIA IN SOUTH AFRICA 2005/06
TEST AVERAGES

SOUTH AFRICA

Batting & Fielding

Name	M	Inns	NO	Runs	HS	Avg	100	50	Ct	St
AJ Hall	1	2	1	58	34 *	58.00	0	0	1	0
JH Kallis	3	6	0	227	114	37.83	1	0	1	0
MV Boucher	3	6	1	175	63	35.00	0	2	11	0
AG Prince	3	6	0	186	93	31.00	0	1	0	0
N Boje	3	6	1	146	48	29.20	0	0	2	0
HH Dippenaar	1	2	0	52	32	26.00	0	0	0	0
AB de Villiers	3	6	0	127	50	21.16	0	1	6	0
JA Rudolph	3	6	0	125	41	20.83	0	0	2	0
HH Gibbs	3	6	0	113	53	18.83	0	1	6	0
GC Smith	2	4	0	75	40	18.75	0	0	1	0
SM Pollock	2	4	0	57	44	14.25	0	0	2	0
A Nel	3	6	1	59	18 *	11.80	0	0	3	0
M Ntini	3	6	2	23	17 *	5.75	0	0	0	0
Totals	33	66	6	1423	114		1	5	35	0
			Extras	104				subs	0	
			Total	1527		25.45			35	

Bowling

Name	Overs	Mdns	Runs	Wkts	Avg	BB	5I	10M
M Ntini	114.5	17	425	19	22.36	6-100	1	1
JH Kallis	69.1	16	230	7	32.85	3-51	0	0
A Nel	91.2	21	257	6	42.83	3-83	0	0
N Boje	89.5	16	307	7	43.85	2-63	0	0
SM Pollock	91.4	20	265	4	66.25	1-55	0	0
AJ Hall	21	3	82	1	82.00	1-66	0	0
AB de Villiers	1	0	12	0	-	-	0	0
Totals	478.5	93	1578	44		6-100	1	1
		b/lb/pen	65	0	run outs			
		Total	1643	44	37.34			

AUSTRALIA

Batting & Fielding

Name	M	Inns	NO	Runs	HS	Avg	100	50	Ct	St
MEK Hussey	3	5	1	257	89	64.25	0	3	2	0
RT Ponting	3	6	0	348	116	58.00	2	1	2	0
DR Martyn	3	6	2	225	101	56.25	1	1	3	0
ML Hayden	3	6	0	231	102	38.50	1	1	8	0
JL Langer	3	5	1	122	37	30.50	0	0	6	0
B Lee	3	4	1	88	64	29.33	0	1	0	0
A Symonds	3	4	0	101	55	25.25	0	1	3	0
SK Warne	3	4	0	82	36	20.50	0	0	1	0
SR Clark	3	4	2	31	13 *	15.50	0	0	2	0
MS Kasprowicz	3	4	2	22	7 *	11.00	0	0	1	0

GM
HERO™
GM SUPER POWERARC BLADE
WEIGHT REDUCED
FLATTER SHOULDERS
STRONG CONTOURED EDGE
BIG SWEET SPOT AND SUBSTANTIAL TOE
FOR CONCENTRATED DRIVING POWER
The set of the handle and the extravagant bow of the blade makes the Hero™ a unique bat in the Gunn & Moore range, concentrating willow in the driving area for explosive power but light pick-up.
NEW
Graeme Smith
HERO™ 909
OSM · MENS · SMALL MENS
NEW
HERO™ 909
OSM · MENS · SMALL MENS
HERO
TREATED WITH DriGuard™ TO RESIST DAMP AND MINIMISE TOE SWELL
1160 HERO™ ORIGINAL L.E.
1260 HERO™ ORIGINAL
1560 HERO™ 909
1460 HERO™ 707
FULL SIZE - JUNIOR SIZES ALSO AVAILABLE
All Gunn & Moore English Made bats* are treated with GM DriGuard™, a water repellent solution applied to the toe of the bat to reduce th
absorption of water. This helps prevent toe swelling, making the toe less susceptible to moisture induced damage. *except polycoated ba
OPAL SPORTS
Opal Sportswear (Pty) Ltd • Telephone: (011) 613-7473

AC Gilchrist	3	5	0	50	24	10.00	0	0	11	1
Totals	33	53	9	1557	116		4	8	39	1
			Extras	86				subs	1	
			Total	1643		37.34			40	

Bowling

Name	Overs	Mdns	Runs	Wkts	Avg	BB	5I	10M
SR Clark	118	32	317	20	15.85	5-55	1	0
B Lee	116	29	332	17	19.52	5-69	1	0
SK Warne	127.4	19	423	15	28.20	6-86	1	0
MS Kasprowicz	77.2	6	292	7	41.71	2-44	0	0
A Symonds	42	7	114	1	114.00	1-26	0	0
MEK Hussey	2	0	6	0	-	-	0	0
RT Ponting	2	1	7	0	-	-	0	0
Totals	485	94	1491	60		6-86	3	0
		b/lb/pen	36	0	run outs			
		Total	1527	60	25.45			

SOUTH AFRICA v AUSTRALIA IN SOUTH AFRICA 2005/06
LIMITED OVERS INTERNATIONAL AVERAGES

SOUTH AFRICA

Batting & Fielding

Name	M	Inns	NO	Runs	HS	Avg	SR	100	50	Ct	St
SM Pollock	4	3	1	160	69	80.00	119.40	0	2	1	0
GC Smith	5	5	1	244	119 *	61.00	109.41	1	1	0	0
HH Gibbs	5	5	0	258	175	51.60	115.69	1	1	1	0
AB de Villiers	5	5	0	181	68	36.20	86.19	0	1	3	0
JJ van der Wath	1	1	0	35	35	35.00	194.44	0	0	0	0
HH Dippenaar	5	5	0	159	101	31.80	64.63	1	0	4	0
MV Boucher	5	5	1	120	50 *	30.00	76.43	0	1	9	0
JM Kemp	5	5	2	89	51 *	29.66	80.90	0	1	2	0
JH Kallis	2	2	0	41	21	20.50	85.41	0	0	1	0
R Telemachus	3	3	0	41	29	13.66	205.00	0	0	2	0
AJ Hall	5	4	1	16	7	5.33	114.28	0	0	1	0
RJ Peterson	3	2	0	7	4	3.50	87.50	0	0	1	0
M Ntini	5	2	2	2	1 *	-	40.00	0	0	1	0
A Nel	2	0	0	0	-	-	-	0	0	1	0
Totals	55	47	8	1353	175			3	7	27	0
			Extras	57					subs	0	
			Total	1410		36.15	95.55			27	

Bowling

Name	Overs	Mdns	Runs	Wkts	Avg	RpO	BB	4I
SM Pollock	32	8	99	5	19.80	3.09	3-23	0
M Ntini	46.3	8	250	11	22.72	5.37	6-22	1
A Nel	18	2	92	3	30.66	5.11	3-30	0
R Telemachus	28	2	180	5	36.00	6.42	3-34	0
AJ Hall	41.1	3	222	5	44.40	5.39	2-52	0

JH Kallis	15	0	116	2	58.00	7.73	2-46	0
RJ Peterson	22	2	91	1	91.00	4.13	1-16	0
JM Kemp	5	0	25	0	-	5.00	-	0
JJ van der Wath	10	0	76	0	-	7.60	-	0
GC Smith	13	0	91	0	-	7.00	-	0
Totals	230.4	25	1242	32			6-22	1
		b/lb/pen	15	5	run outs			
		Total	1257	37	33.97	5.44		

AUSTRALIA

Batting & Fielding

Name	M	Inns	NO	Runs	HS	Avg	SR	100	50	Ct	St
A Symonds	2	2	1	103	76	103.00	122.61	0	1	1	0
RT Ponting	3	3	0	233	164	77.66	114.21	1	1	1	0
MEK Hussey	5	5	0	200	81	40.00	97.08	0	2	3	0
SM Katich	5	5	0	192	79	38.40	63.57	0	1	0	0
B Lee	5	5	3	60	38 *	30.00	120.00	0	0	1	0
AC Gilchrist	5	5	0	140	55	28.00	95.23	0	1	8	0
SR Watson	3	3	1	53	27	26.50	66.25	0	0	0	0
MJ Clarke	5	4	0	86	53	21.50	60.13	0	1	4	0
DR Martyn	5	4	0	57	51	14.25	64.77	0	1	2	0
NW Bracken	5	3	0	33	16	11.00	80.48	0	0	1	0
GB Hogg	3	2	0	19	13	9.50	79.16	0	0	2	0
PA Jaques	1	1	0	0	0	0.00	0.00	0	0	0	0
SR Clark	4	2	2	18	16 *	-	78.26	0	0	0	0
ML Lewis	3	1	1	4	4 *	-	100.00	0	0	0	0
MG Johnson	1	1	1	0	0 *	-	-	0	0	0	0
Totals	55	46	9	1198	164			1	8	23	0
			Extras	59					subs	0	
			Total	1257		33.97	85.57			23	

Bowling

Name	Overs	Mdns	Runs	Wkts	Avg	RpO	BB	4I
NW Bracken	46.2	4	215	9	23.88	4.64	5-67	1
SR Watson	22	0	113	4	28.25	5.13	2-46	0
GB Hogg	19	2	90	3	30.00	4.73	2-48	0
A Symonds	15	0	106	3	35.33	7.06	2-75	0
B Lee	44.5	2	281	7	40.14	6.26	4-48	1
SR Clark	35	3	204	4	51.00	5.82	2-69	0
MJ Clarke	24.3	0	151	2	75.50	6.16	1-46	0
ML Lewis	23	0	176	2	88.00	7.65	2-38	0
MEK Hussey	2	0	15	0	-	7.50	-	0
MG Johnson	3	0	28	0	-	9.33	-	0
Totals	234.4	11	1379	34			5-67	2
		b/lb/pen	31	5	run outs			
		Total	1410	39	36.15	6.00		

NEW ZEALAND TEST SERIES 2005/06

Colin Bryden

A home cricket campaign that began unseasonably early with the Afro-Asia Cup in August ended later than any season in living memory when New Zealand, five months after completing a one-day series, returned to South Africa for three Test matches in April and May.

The disadvantages of playing cricket in autumn were quickly apparent, with shorter days resulting in play being lost to bad light, while early starts led to some startling assistance for bowlers and awkward problems for batsmen during morning play in the two Test matches in Gauteng.

With rugby in full swing and the weather largely cool, crowd attendances were not what they might have been at a more favourable time of year.

There was, however, some good cricket, with South Africa gaining some solace after their struggles against Australia with two wins, while the second Test at Newlands was a high-scoring draw. The result of the series enabled South Africa to swop places with New Zealand, moving up from sixth to fifth on the ICC Test rankings.

While Makhaya Ntini continued in magnificent form to take the Man of the Series award, two relative newcomers in Hashim Amla and Dale Steyn took the opportunity to assert themselves at Test level. Neither had played against Australia, so with due respect to the New Zealanders, there was no knowing how much of a difference they might have made had they played against the world champions.

Amla came into the side in place of Herschelle Gibbs in Cape Town and made an impressive century, which he followed up with a half-century at the Wanderers.

Steyn's pace and ability to swing the ball away added a new dimension to the South African bowling attack. He and Ntini made a formidable new ball pair, which Stephen Fleming, the New Zealand captain, singled out as the major difference between the teams.

The Black Caps suffered a severe blow on the first day of the tour when Shane Bond, their outstanding fast bowler, limped off the field with a knee injury after bowling ten overs against the Rest of South Africa. Every effort was made to get him fit for the Tests but he eventually had to return home without playing again.

New Zealand lacked a reliable pair of opening batsmen and four different men faced the new ball in the Tests, none with any notable success.

Much depended on Fleming, who showed his class when he made 262, a ground record and the highest score by any batsman against South Africa in South Africa, at Newlands. Fleming was the victim of a poor umpiring decision in the first Test and seemed to be unlucky again in the third Test.

Fleming apart, the best New Zealand batting came from their lower order men, with Jacob Oram and James Franklin making centuries and Daniel Vettori hitting two half-centuries.

New Zealand's bowling was seldom better than steady and they lacked a man of real pace, although the left-armed Franklin was impressive at times.

The touring squad was: Stephen Fleming (captain), Daniel Vettori (vice-captain), Nathan Astle, Shane Bond, Peter Fulton, James Franklin, Jamie How, Brendon McCullum, Hamish Marshall, Chris Martin, Kyle Mills, Jacob Oram, Michael Papps, Jeetan Patel, Scott Styris. Manager, Lindsay Crocker; coach, John Bracewell; assistant coach, Robert Carter.

Michael Mason joined the team as cover for Bond but did not play.

DEADLY DUO . . . Makhaya Ntini and Dale Steyn lead the Proteas off the field after destroying the New Zealand batting with their two-pronged pace attack at Centurion *Picture: DUIF DU TOIT, Touchline Photo*

REST OF SOUTH AFRICA v NEW ZEALANDERS First-class 4-day match

Played at Willowmoore Park, Benoni on 7,8,9,10 April 2006 Toss: Rest of South Africa
Umpires: IL Howell & BG Jerling Referee: A Barnes
Debuts: Rest: None. NZ: None
Close of play: Day 1: Rest (1) 355-3 (McKenzie 125*, Duminy 125*, 90 overs). Day 2: NZ (1) 159-2 (Fulton 36*, Fleming 96*, 35.1 overs). Day 3: Rest (2) 132-4 (Ontong 59*, McKenzie 2*, 46.2 overs)

Result: Drawn

Notes: Fleming scored his century off 98 balls in New Zealanders' 1st innings. McCullum scored his century off 93 balls in New Zealanders' 1st innings.

Bond made an early strike before Justin Ontong, Neil McKenzie and J-P Duminy took control on a slow, flat pitch. McKenzie and Duminy put on 252 for the fourth wicket before the tourists, who took only three wickets on the first day, took the last seven wickets for 40 runs on the second morning despite Bond being out of action with a swollen right knee.

Fleming played a sparkling innings, while Fulton was content to take a passive role.

Zondeki took three wickets in ten balls but McCullum hit out in what was effectively a last wicket stand of 95 with Martin.

Bad light and drizzle restricted play to 40 overs on the last day but Ontong was able to score the fifth century of the match, while Vettori bowled a long spell.

REST OF SOUTH AFRICA		Runs	Mins	Balls	4	6		Runs	Mins	Balls	4	6
SC Cook	run out (Franklin/McCullum)	13	72	49	-	-	lbw b Oram	38	106	89	5	-
AN Petersen	b Bond	2	13	13	-	-	lbw b Franklin	5	22	16	1	-
JL Ontong	lbw b Franklin	61	108	95	8	1	not out	144	320	239	20	-
*ND McKenzie	b Franklin	141	400	278	20	2	(6) c Oram b Franklin	2	30	24	-	-
J-P Duminy	c Fleming b Martin	127	264	203	18	1	c McCullum b Martin	0	2	2	-	-
DJ Jacobs	c How b Martin	4	10	10	1	-	(4) c and b Vettori	22	48	36	3	1
†TL Tsolekile	c Fleming b Oram	11	49	34	1	-	st McCullum b Vettori	13	49	36	1	-
RJ Peterson	run out (sub - JS Patel/Vettori)	1	5	2	-	-	c sub (KD Mills) b Styris	24	59	55	2	1
RK Kleinveldt	not out	4	29	16	-	-	c Fulton b Vettori	0	8	6	-	-
GJ-P Kruger	lbw b Franklin	0	1	2	-	-						
M Zondeki	lbw b Franklin	1	10	9	-	-	(10) not out	13	34	15	2	-
Extras	(lb 10, w 7, nb 13)	30					Extras (b 2, lb 6, w 1)	9				
TOTAL	**(117 overs)**	**395**					**TOTAL (for 8 wkts) (86.2 overs)**	**270**				

NEW ZEALANDERS		Runs	Mins	Balls	4	6
MHW Papps	c Petersen b Zondeki	6	25	19	1	-
JM How	lbw b Kruger	11	31	22	2	-
PG Fulton	c Tsolekile b Kruger	73	179	131	14	-
*SP Fleming	c Ontong b Zondeki	118	188	132	17	5
SB Styris	c Kruger b Zondeki	17	40	27	3	-
JDP Oram	c Tsolekile b Zondeki	0	2	1	-	-
†BB McCullum	c Tsolekile b Kleinveldt	101	145	98	7	7
DL Vettori	c Duminy b Kleinveldt	8	25	17	-	-
JEC Franklin	c Tsolekile b Peterson	5	9	12	1	-
CS Martin	not out	9	86	41	2	-
SE Bond	absent hurt					
Extras	(w 5, nb 19)	24				
TOTAL	**(80.1 overs)**	**372**				

NZ	O	M	R	W		O	M	R	W	
Bond	10	1	51	1	(5 nb, 5 w)					
Franklin	24	3	80	4	(2 nb, 1 w)	16	3	58	2	(1 w)
Oram	21	10	46	1	(1 nb)	14	4	29	1	
Martin	20	5	74	2		(1) 17.2	4	71	1	
Vettori	29	3	95	0	(1 nb)	(4) 29	4	77	3	
Styris	13	3	39	0	(1 w)	(5) 10	1	27	1	
Rest	O	M	R	W						
Kruger	17	2	101	2	(10 nb, 2 w)					
Zondeki	23	4	107	4	(3 nb, 2 w)					
Kleinveldt	23.1	7	96	2	(6 nb)					
Peterson	17	3	68	1	(1 w)					

Fall of Wickets	Rest	NZ	Rest
1st	17 (2)	21 (1)	11 (2)
2nd	42 (1)	26 (2)	69 (1)
3rd	107 (3)	209 (3)	124 (4)
4th	359 (5)	233 (4)	125 (5)
5th	363 (6)	233 (6)	132 (6)
6th	385 (7)	255 (5)	178 (7)
7th	388 (8)	270 (8)	233 (8)
8th	391 (4)	277 (9)	235 (9)
9th	391 (10)	372 (7)	-
10th	395 (11)	-	-

SOUTH AFRICA v NEW ZEALAND — 1st Test

Played at SuperSport Park, Centurion on 15,16,17,18,19 April 2006 — Toss: South Africa
Umpires: MR Benson & DJ Harper (TV: M Erasmus) — Referee: RS Madugalle
Debuts: SA: None. NZ: None
Close of play: Day 1: SA (1) 266-8 (Boje 20*, Steyn 8*, 90 overs). Day 2: SA (2) 4-0 (Smith 3*, Gibbs 0*, 1 over). Day 3: SA (2) 280-9 (Steyn 5*, Ntini 0*, 91 overs). Day 4: NZ (2) 98-7 (Marshall 24*, Vettori 18*, 30 overs)
Result: South Africa won by 128 runs
Man of Match: Makhaya Ntini

Remarkably, three players appeared in their 100th Test – Fleming, Pollock and Kallis, with Kallis having played one of his matches for the World XI in the ICC Super Series in Australia.

Taking cognisance of the early sunsets, it was decided to start play in Johannesburg and Centurion at 9.30am, half an hour earlier than the published times.

South Africa announced a squad of 16 players for the three Tests, justifying the large number on the grounds that no other cricket was being played. It was the same squad that had been named for the final Test against Australia.

Smith declared himself fit despite still feeling pain in his injured finger. He replaced Rudolph in a reshuffled top order, while Steyn was selected ahead of Nel, who was still struggling with a foot injury and who fell on a shoulder the day before the match.

Bond failed a fitness test for New Zealand and Mills shared the new ball with Franklin after Smith took the tricky decision to bat first in conditions which were always likely to help the bowlers. The tall Mills, playing in his sixth Test, achieved his best figures and gained steep lift on a slow pitch of unpredictable bounce on which the batsmen had to work hard for their runs.

Gibbs was bowled off an inside edge, betrayed yet again by a lack of footwork, but Smith and Dippenaar batted well in difficult conditions before Smith lost his balance against a ball from Franklin which slanted in to him. Dippenaar made an assured half-century before playing a weak pull to mid-wicket. Kallis, who called for treatment on his troublesome left arm early in his innings, needing a pain-killing injection, was bowled by the ball of the day, a slower inswinging yorker from Franklin.

The difficulty of batting early in the morning at the time of year were shown when South Africa lost their last two wickets for ten runs and New Zealand crashed to 45-5 on the second day. Ntini quickly claimed his 250th Test wicket when he bowled Marshall. Ntini took the first three wickets in another fine performance, although Fleming was unlucky to be given out caught and bowled when replays showed the ball had looped off his pad without making contact with his bat when he pushed forward defensively.

Boucher became the fourth player in the world to complete 350 wicketkeeping dismissals when he caught Astle off a fast Steyn out-swinger.

The tall Oram, playing his first Test since November 2004 after recovering from heel and groin injuries, led a remarkable recovery, in partnership first with the aggressive McCullum and then in a seventh wicket stand of 183 with fellow left-hander Vettori. Both men were prepared to chance their arms at times and their tactics paid off. On 56, Vettori completed the double of 2000 runs and 200 wickets in Tests.

It was Oram's highest Test score and a continuation of the form he showed against South Africa in New Zealand two years earlier. The partnership was the second highest for any wicket for New Zealand against South Africa, exceeded only by the 225 Oram put on with Chris Cairns, also for the seventh wicket, in Auckland in 2003/04.

The eventual breakthrough was made by Ntini when Vettori top-edged an attempted pull to backward point. Ntini had Franklin caught behind to complete his 12th five-wicket haul.

On another difficult morning, South Africa lost three early second innings wickets and Prince was out soon after lunch before Kallis and De Villiers stabilised the innings. De Villiers played some sparkling strokes in front of his home crowd only to fall for the third time in the nineties, to go along with three centuries, when he drove Oram to cover.

New Zealand's hopes of achieving a target of 249 were wrecked by Ntini and Steyn, who reduced them to 28-6 with a devastating new-ball assault on a cool, cloudy morning. Four of the wickets fell to Ntini, while Steyn showed more confidence and better control as he picked up the important wickets of Fleming and Styris. Marshall was clearly in pain after being hit in the ribs by Ntini but battled bravely to survive the day.

Rain and bad light disrupted play and took the game into the fifth morning, which also enabled Smith to employ Ntini and Steyn for a combined 31 of the 36 overs in the innings. Ntini completed his second successive ten-wicket haul and Steyn claimed the last two wickets for his first bag of five before the two fast bowlers left the field arm in arm.

SOUTH AFRICA	*Runs*	*Mins*	*Balls*	*4*	*6*		*Runs*	*Mins*	*Balls*	*4*	*6*
*GC Smith lbw b Franklin	45	132	91	6	-	lbw b Martin	7	13	8	-	-
HH Gibbs b Mills	6	21	19	1	-	c Styris b Franklin	2	28	21	-	-
HH Dippenaar c Fulton b Mills	52	142	96	10	-	c Fleming b Oram	16	58	39	3	-
JH Kallis b Franklin	38	126	99	7	-	c Vettori b Styris	62	203	159	8	-
AG Prince c Styris b Mills	9	34	33	1	-	c McCullum b Franklin	11	59	45	1	-
AB de Villiers b Franklin	27	87	62	3	-	c Franklin b Oram	97	235	161	13	-
†MV Boucher c Fleming b Martin	18	74	57	1	-	b Mills	21	65	46	3	-
SM Pollock c Styris b Mills	24	57	39	4	-	lbw b Vettori	10	12	10	1	-
N Boje lbw b Franklin	23	60	37	4	-	c McCullum b Astle	31	66	51	5	1
DW Steyn c Mills b Martin	13	58	45	2	-	not out	7	41	27	1	-
M Ntini not out	1	8	3	-	-	lbw b Vettori	16	34	27	3	-
Extras (b 6, lb 4, w 3, nb 7)	20					Extras (b 12, lb 2, nb 5)	19				
TOTAL (95.4 overs)	**276**					**TOTAL (98.1 overs)**	**299**				

NEW ZEALAND	*Runs*	*Mins*	*Balls*	*4*	*6*		*Runs*	*Mins*	*Balls*	*4*	*6*
HJH Marshall b Ntini	6	9	8	1	-	c Boucher b Ntini	25	168	85	1	-
PG Fulton c Boucher b Pollock	14	48	29	2	-	c Boucher b Ntini	4	9	2	1	-
*SP Fleming c and b Ntini	0	9	5	-	-	(4) c Kallis b Steyn	6	21	21	-	-
SB Styris c Gibbs b Ntini	17	22	18	3	-	(5) c Boucher b Steyn	2	10	6	-	-
NJ Astle c Boucher b Steyn	4	18	8	-	-	(6) c De Villiers b Ntini	2	8	7	-	-
JDP Oram c Pollock b Steyn	133	289	169	18	2	(7) b Ntini	2	11	8	-	-
†BB McCullum c Boje b Kallis	31	43	30	6	-	(8) c Dippenaar b Steyn	33	49	38	2	2
DL Vettori c Prince b Ntini	81	166	117	11	-	(9) c Boucher b Steyn	38	57	48	6	1
JEC Franklin c Boucher b Ntini	8	13	16	1	-	(10) not out	0	8	1	-	-
KD Mills c Boje b Pollock	12	42	35	3	-	(3) c Dippenaar b Ntini	0	1	2	-	-
CS Martin not out	1	6	3	-	-	b Steyn	0	3	4	-	-
Extras (lb 12, nb 8)	20					Extras (lb 2, nb 6)	8				
TOTAL (71.4 overs)	**327**					**TOTAL (36 overs)**	**120**				

NZ	*O*	*M*	*R*	*W*		*O*	*M*	*R*	*W*	
Mills	18	7	43	4	(3 nb)	(3) 21	5	57	1	(1 nb)
Franklin	18	3	75	4	(2 nb, 1 w)	(1) 14	2	60	2	(3 nb)
Martin	22.4	4	66	2	(1 nb, 2 w)	(2) 24	6	64	1	
Oram	14	7	27	0		17	3	44	2	
Vettori	18	2	44	0	(1 nb)	15.1	0	42	2	(1 nb)
Astle	5	2	11	0		5	1	15	1	
Styris						2	0	3	1	
SA	*O*	*M*	*R*	*W*		*O*	*M*	*R*	*W*	
Ntini	19	2	94	5		14	3	51	5	
Steyn	18.4	1	95	2		17	4	47	5	(2 nb)
Pollock	15	4	45	2	(8 nb)	5	1	20	0	(4 nb)
Kallis	9	1	41	1						
Boje	7	0	29	0						
Smith	3	1	11	0						

Fall of Wickets

	SA	NZ	SA	NZ
1st	16 (2)	8 (1)	8 (1)	5 (2)
2nd	95 (1)	12 (3)	19 (2)	5 (3)
3rd	119 (3)	32 (4)	42 (3)	17 (4)
4th	130 (5)	38 (2)	73 (5)	23 (5)
5th	177 (4)	45 (5)	140 (4)	26 (6)
6th	197 (6)	89 (7)	194 (7)	28 (7)
7th	229 (7)	272 (8)	205 (8)	73 (8)
8th	233 (8)	280 (9)	270 (6)	119 (1)
9th	274 (9)	322 (10)	276 (9)	119 (9)
10th	276 (10)	327 (6)	299 (11)	120 (11)

CAPTAIN FANTASTIC . . . Stephen Fleming reaches his century on the way to a record-breaking 262 at Newlands *Picture: TERTIUS PICKARD, Touchline Photo*

SOUTH AFRICA v NEW ZEALAND — 2nd Test

Played at Sahara Park Newlands, Cape Town on 27,28,29,30 April, 1 May 2006 — Toss: South Africa
Umpires: MR Benson & EAR de Silva (TV: M Erasmus) — Referee: RS Madugalle
Debuts: SA: None. NZ: JS Patel
Close of play: Day 1: NZ (1) 265-6 (Fleming 114*, Vettori 1*, 78 overs). Day 2: NZ (1) 535-8 (Franklin 93*, 152 overs). Day 3: SA (1) 155-2 (Amla 50*, Kallis 25*, 61.5 overs). Day 4: SA (1) 427-5 (Prince 70*, Boucher 26*, 151 overs)

Result: Match drawn

Man of Match: Stephen Fleming

South Africa's squad was reduced when Gibbs and Kruger were released, with selection convenor Haroon Lorgat saying after a meeting with Gibbs that it had been agreed that a break and a fresh start the next season would be good for the out-of-form batsman. Lorgat said Kruger had been unfortunate to have suffered a shoulder strain before the Centurion Test when he was set to make his Test debut.

Amla played in place of Gibbs, while Nel returned after Pollock withdrew on the morning of the match because of lower back pain.

Despite his performance in the first Test, Mills made way for new cap Patel, an off-spinner, as New Zealand opted for two slow bowlers. Bond bowled in the nets three days ahead of the match but when his troublesome knee was swollen and sore the following day it was decided he should return home.

Early morning dew delayed the start by 30 minutes and Smith reasoned that any help for the bowlers would happen early on what transpired to be an excellent pitch for batting.

Papps, recalled in place of Marshall, who sustained a rib injury at Centurion, shared a 50-run opening stand as the pitch played placidly, although both openers played and missed several times.

Fleming survived a confident lbw appeal by Steyn early on but then batted almost flawlessly as he scored his ninth Test century and his first against South Africa. Only Astle provided sustained support, however, and South Africa could feel reasonably pleased with their efforts on the first day.

Fog delayed the start of play on day two until 55 minutes before lunch. Earlier a portable hovercraft had been used to dry the dew. South Africa seemed to have struck a vital blow when Vettori fell early to the third delivery with the second new ball but the left-handed Franklin, with a first-class double century to his credit, joined his captain in what developed into a record stand for any wicket for New Zealand against South Africa.

Two missed chances soon after lunch cost South Africa dearly. Fleming on 136 edged Steyn to first slip where Dippenaar grassed a straightforward offering. Franklin survived a difficult chance at second slip to Kallis off Ntini when he was on 28. Two runs later there was a concerted appeal for a catch behind and in the following over Franklin was felled by an Ntini bouncer which hit him on the helmet.

Thereafter the batsmen were in control, with Fleming, who had reached his century off 190 balls, notching his third Test double century off 331 deliveries. It was not a good day for the South African bowlers, who sent down only four maidens during the 74 overs bowled.

Eventually Prince, the eighth bowler used, bowled Fleming, who edged an attempted drive into his stumps, in the last over of the day.

New Zealand continued batting on the third morning, enabling Franklin to reach a maiden Test century, and South Africa's frustration continued as Franklin and Patel added an unbeaten 58 before Fleming declared.

Patel made another useful contribution when he caught Smith off his own bowling with his third ball in Tests. Dippenaar and Amla batted soundly, however, to set the tone for a solid top-order batting performance. Amla, with a previous highest score of 25 in his first three Tests, picked his strokes judiciously, whipping the ball through the leg-side with strong wrists and playing some fine cover drives.

Amla effectively ensured that New Zealand could not win the match as he batted on serenely for much of the fourth day, with Kallis his partner in a stand that lasted more than three hours and used up 50.2 overs. Kallis became the first South African and 17th player of all time to reach 8000 Test runs when he was on 60.

Amla's century was reached shortly before lunch when he drove Vettori through the covers for his 12th boundary off the 242nd ball he faced.

Prince took over the anchor role after Amla and De Villiers were dismissed in quick succession, notching 1000 Test runs when he was on 66, and moving on to his fourth Test century on the final day.

NEW ZEALAND	*Runs*	*Mins*	*Balls*	*4*	*6*		*Runs*	*Mins*	*Balls*	*4*	*6*
MHW Papps b Nel	22	74	58	3	-	c Prince b Steyn	20	35	28	4	-
PG Fulton c Boucher b Steyn	36	93	62	7	-	c Kallis b Ntini	11	54	39	2	-
*SP Fleming b Prince	262	572	423	31	2						
SB Styris c Dippenaar b Ntini	11	37	21	1	-	(3) not out	54	130	75	9	-
NJ Astle lbw b Ntini	50	112	71	6	-	(4) c Smith b Kallis	14	60	45	2	-
JDP Oram run out (Prince/Smith)	13	61	44	1	-	(5) not out	8	51	39	1	-
†BB McCullum lbw b Ntini	5	22	14	1	-						
DL Vettori c Nel b Ntini	11	16	13	1	-						
JEC Franklin not out	122	361	268	14	1						
JS Patel not out	27	61	31	3	-						
CS Martin											
Extras (b 3, lb 15, w 1, nb 15)	34					Extras (b 1, lb 9, nb 4)	14				
TOTAL (for 8 wkts dec) (165 overs)	**593**					**TOTAL (for 3 wkts) (37 overs)**	**121**				

SOUTH AFRICA	*Runs*	*Mins*	*Balls*	*4*	*6*
*GC Smith c and b Patel	25	59	40	2	-
HH Dippenaar b Patel	47	151	111	4	-
HM Amla lbw b Vettori	149	407	317	20	-
JH Kallis c Martin b Oram	71	191	170	7	-
AG Prince not out	108	401	286	9	-
AB de Villiers c Papps b Patel	13	28	23	2	-
†MV Boucher c Fleming b Franklin	33	103	76	4	-
N Boje lbw b Franklin	0	2	1	-	-
A Nel lbw b Franklin	12	66	53	1	-
DW Steyn st McCullum b Vettori	13	57	40	2	-
M Ntini run out (Astle/McCullum)	11	15	16	1	-
Extras (b 15, lb 10, nb 5)	30				
TOTAL (188 overs)	**512**				

SA	*O*	*M*	*R*	*W*		*O*	*M*	*R*	*W*
Ntini	43	5	162	4 (2 nb)	(2)	8	2	25	1 (1 nb)
Steyn	31	4	114	1 (11 nb, 1 w)	(1)	9	3	26	1 (3 nb)
Nel	27	3	98	1 (1 nb)		10	2	41	0
Kallis	15	4	45	0 (1 nb)		5	3	5	1
Boje	29	4	89	0		5	1	14	0
Smith	17	2	61	0					
Amla	1	0	4	0					
Prince	2	0	2	1					
NZ	*O*	*M*	*R*	*W*					
Martin	20	7	62	0					
Franklin	33	5	95	3 (1 nb)					
Vettori	63	10	147	2 (2 nb)					
Patel	42	8	117	3 (1 nb)					
Styris	10	2	33	0 (1 nb)					
Oram	18	10	24	1					
Astle	2	0	9	0					

Fall of Wickets

	NZ	**SA**	**NZ**
1st	50 (1)	36 (1)	34 (1)
2nd	62 (2)	108 (2)	41 (2)
3rd	82 (4)	252 (4)	81 (4)
4th	188 (5)	344 (3)	-
5th	237 (6)	361 (6)	-
6th	259 (7)	435 (7)	-
7th	279 (8)	435 (8)	-
8th	535 (3)	462 (9)	-
9th	-	495 (10)	-
10th	-	512 (11)	-

New Zealand's 593-8 declared was the ninth highest total by a team sent in to bat in Test cricket. It was New Zealand's highest total after being sent in and the highest conceded by South Africa after sending the opposition in, beating the 462 by England at Birmingham in 1998. Highest total and previous instances involving South Africa:

Score	Team	Against	Venue	Season
735-6*	Australia	Zimbabwe	Perth	2003/04
621-5*	South Africa	New Zealand	Auckland	1998/99
604-6*	South Africa	West Indies	Centurion	2003/04

Highest 8th wicket partnerships in Tests

313	Wasim Akram and Saqlain Mushtaq	Pakistan v Zimbabwe (Sheikhupura)	1996/97
256	SP Fleming and JEC Franklin	New Zealand v South Africa (Cape Town)	2005/06
253	NJ Astle and AC Parore	New Zealand v Australia (Perth)	2001/02

SOUTH AFRICA v NEW ZEALAND — 3rd Test

Played at Liberty Life Wanderers Stadium, Johannesburg on 5,6,7 May 2006 — Toss: South Africa
Umpires: EAR de Silva & DB Hair (TV: IL Howell) — Referee: RS Madugalle
Debuts: SA: None. NZ: None
Close of play: Day 1: SA (1) 133-4 (Prince 1*, De Villiers 1*, 33 overs). Day 2: NZ (2) 214-6 (Oram 19*, Vettori 21*, 57.5 overs)..
Result: South Africa won by 4 wickets
Man of Match: Graeme Smith
Man of Series: Makhaya Ntini

Groundsman Chris Scott prepared the Test pitch under a tent, using heating fans to combat the cool weather. Pollock returned to the South African side, while Smith was again able to field at first slip, albeit with a splint protecting the injured ring finger on his left hand. Boje, initially expected to be unavailable after a fielding injury at Newlands, which required five stitches between his right thumb and forefinger, was considered for selection but was replaced by Hall in an all-seam attack.

How came into the New Zealand team in place of Fulton, who had a back injury, but lasted only two balls before being caught at third slip off Steyn. Papps fell to Ntini in the fifth over, still without a run on the board, and Styris was quickly caught at third slip.

Only Fleming stood firm against the pace of Ntini and Steyn as New Zealand were shot out for the lowest total by a visiting team in a Test at the Wanderers Stadium, three runs fewer than England in 1999/2000.

Dippenaar became the third opening batsman to be out without scoring but Smith and Amla put South Africa on top, with Smith batting aggressively to score his first Test half-century of the season. Amla batted with confidence and reached his fifty in an over during which he hit four boundaries off Franklin.

The dismissals of Kallis and Amla in successive overs before the close brought New Zealand back into the match and the South African batting collapsed on the second morning, with three wickets falling in 11 balls without a run added at one stage, with only Pollock able to make any impression.

In the conditions, a lead of 67 was useful and it looked more so when How failed again. Kallis dismissed Papps in the last over before lunch but Fleming, Styris and Astle all batted with determination.

Kallis had Fleming caught at second slip to complete a double of 8000 runs and 200 wickets in Tests, a combination previously achieved only by West Indian Garfield Sobers.

The South Africans dropped four catches, three of them difficult, with Ntini having three chances go down off his bowling.

Vettori led some stubborn resistance before Hall wrapped up the innings by taking the last two wickets off successive balls.

A target of 217 could have been tricky but Smith and Dippenaar put South Africa firmly on the way to victory, with their 69-run partnership posted inside 14 overs.

Smith reached his second half-century and then cracked Vettori for four and six before being caught behind in the next over from Franklin.

There were a few anxious moments when three wickets fell on either side of tea but Prince stood firm as South Africa won inside three days.

NEW ZEALAND	*Runs*	*Mins*	*Balls*	*4*	*6*		*Runs*	*Mins*	*Balls*	*4*	*6*
MHW Papps b Ntini	0	25	18	-	-	c Hall b Kallis	15	53	33	3	-
JM How c De Villiers b Steyn	0	6	2	-	-	lbw b Steyn	4	9	9	-	-
*SP Fleming c Boucher b Ntini	46	130	82	9	-	c De Villiers b Kallis	37	101	64	6	-
SB Styris c De Villiers b Ntini	0	8	6	-	-	c and b Steyn	42	151	104	6	-
NJ Astle c Kallis b Steyn	20	77	47	2	-	c Boucher b Steyn	45	71	56	8	-
JDP Oram lbw b Pollock	18	96	46	2	-	c Dippenaar b Steyn	27	117	80	4	-
†BB McCullum c and b Ntini	0	2	2	-	-	c Boucher b Pollock	5	22	9	1	-
DL Vettori lbw b Steyn	2	5	4	-	-	c De Villiers b Hall	60	131	91	8	-
JEC Franklin c Boucher b Hall	19	47	41	2	-	b Pollock	19	47	30	3	-
KD Mills not out	0	21	11	-	-	not out	0	6	0	-	-
CS Martin c Smith b Ntini	1	8	8	-	-	c Amla b Hall	0	1	1	-	-
Extras (lb 9, w 1, nb 3)	13					Extras (b 5, lb 17, w 3, nb 4)	29				
TOTAL (44 overs)	**119**					**TOTAL (78.5 overs)**	**283**				

SOUTH AFRICA	*Runs*	*Mins*	*Balls*	*4*	*6*		*Runs*	*Mins*	*Balls*	*4*	*6*
*GC Smith c McCullum b Franklin	63	90	63	10	-	c McCullum b Franklin	68	118	80	9	1
HH Dippenaar b Martin	0	3	1	-	-	c McCullum b Martin	37	62	48	5	-
HM Amla c Papps b Styris	56	142	92	10	-	b Mills	28	77	40	5	-
JH Kallis b Martin	9	50	39	1	-	c How b Mills	13	39	28	2	-
AG Prince c McCullum b Martin	4	28	22	-	-	not out	43	76	60	7	-
AB de Villiers c Styris b Franklin	2	15	4	-	-	b Franklin	5	11	7	1	-
†MV Boucher lbw b Franklin	0	4	5	-	-	b Franklin	6	28	17	1	-
SM Pollock not out	32	40	20	3	2	not out	6	18	8	1	-
AJ Hall lbw b Martin	5	7	6	1	-						
DW Steyn b Martin	2	11	9	-	-						
M Ntini c McCullum b Mills	8	16	8	2	-						
Extras (nb 5)	5					Extras (b 4, lb 5, w 2, nb 3)	14				
TOTAL (44 overs)	**186**					**TOTAL (for 6 wkts) (47.3 overs)**	**220**				

SA	*O*	*M*	*R*	*W*			*O*	*M*	*R*	*W*	
Ntini	16	7	35	5		(2)	17	4	44	0	
Steyn	12	3	43	3	(3 nb)	(1)	22	3	91	4	(3 nb, 1 w)
Hall	9	2	21	1	(1 w)	(4)	12.5	1	50	2	
Pollock	7	2	11	1		(5)	13	3	36	2	
Kallis						(3)	14	1	40	2	(1 nb, 2 w)
NZ	*O*	*M*	*R*	*W*			*O*	*M*	*R*	*W*	
Martin	15	2	37	5	(1 nb)		17	1	64	1	(2 w)
Franklin	13	2	87	3	(4 nb)		13.3	0	67	3	(3 nb)
Oram	4	0	20	0		(4)	2	0	8	0	
Mills	8	0	30	1		(3)	11	3	49	2	
Astle	2	0	11	0							
Styris	2	1	1	1		(5)	3	0	12	0	
Vettori						(6)	1	0	11	0	

Fall of Wickets

	NZ	**SA**	**NZ**	**SA**
1st	0 (2)	1 (2)	9 (2)	69 (2)
2nd	0 (1)	99 (1)	40 (1)	130 (1)
3rd	2 (4)	131 (4)	82 (3)	156 (3)
4th	57 (5)	131 (3)	158 (5)	167 (4)
5th	78 (3)	139 (6)	177 (4)	180 (6)
6th	78 (7)	139 (7)	190 (7)	202 (7)
7th	82 (8)	139 (5)	239 (6)	-
8th	118 (9)	145 (9)	283 (9)	-
9th	118 (6)	161 (10)	283 (8)	-
10th	119 (11)	186 (11)	283 (11)	-

Most Test wickets in a season in South Africa

Name	Season	Matches	Balls	Runs	Wkts	Avg	BB	5I
SF Barnes (Eng)	1913/14	4	1356	536	49	10.93	9-103	7
CV Grimmett (Aus)	1935/36	5	2077	642	44	14.59	7-40	5
M Ntini (SA)	2005/06	6	1391	836	39	21.43	6-100	4
M Ntini (SA)	2002/03	6	1300	612	37	16.54	5-19	1
HJ Tayfield (SA)	1956/57	5	2280	636	37	17.18	9-113	4

SOUTH AFRICA v NEW ZEALAND 2005/06
TEST AVERAGES

SOUTH AFRICA

Batting & Fielding

Name	M	Inns	NO	Runs	HS	Avg	100	50	Ct	St
HM Amla	2	3	0	233	149	77.66	1	1	1	0
AG Prince	3	5	2	175	108 *	58.33	1	0	2	0
GC Smith	3	5	0	208	68	41.60	0	2	2	0
JH Kallis	3	5	0	193	71	38.60	0	2	3	0
SM Pollock	2	4	2	72	32 *	36.00	0	0	1	0
HH Dippenaar	3	5	0	152	52	30.40	0	1	4	0
AB de Villiers	3	5	0	144	97	28.80	0	1	5	0
N Boje	2	3	0	54	31	18.00	0	0	2	0
MV Boucher	3	5	0	78	33	15.60	0	0	12	0
M Ntini	3	4	1	36	16	12.00	0	0	2	0
A Nel	1	1	0	12	12	12.00	0	0	1	0
DW Steyn	3	4	1	35	13	11.66	0	0	1	0
AJ Hall	1	1	0	5	5	5.00	0	0	1	0
HH Gibbs	1	2	0	8	6	4.00	0	0	1	0
Totals	33	52	6	1405	149		2	7	38	0
			Extras	88				subs	0	
			Total	1493		32.45			38	

Bowling

Name	Overs	Mdns	Runs	Wkts	Avg	BB	5I	10M
AG Prince	2	0	2	1	2.00	1-2	0	0
M Ntini	117	23	411	20	20.55	5-35	3	1
SM Pollock	40	10	112	5	22.40	2-36	0	0
AJ Hall	21.5	3	71	3	23.66	2-50	0	0
DW Steyn	109.4	18	416	16	26.00	5-47	1	0
JH Kallis	43	9	131	4	32.75	2-40	0	0
A Nel	37	5	139	1	139.00	1-98	0	0
HM Amla	1	0	4	0	-	-	0	0
GC Smith	20	3	72	0	-	-	0	0
N Boje	41	5	132	0	-	-	0	0
Totals	432.3	76	1490	50		5-35	4	1
		b/lb/pen	73	1	run outs			
		Total	1563	51	30.64			

NEW ZEALAND TEST SERIES 2005/06

NEW ZEALAND

Batting & Fielding

Name	M	Inns	NO	Runs	HS	Avg	100	50	Ct	St
SP Fleming	3	5	0	351	262	70.20	1	0	3	0
JEC Franklin	3	5	2	168	122 *	56.00	1	0	1	0
JDP Oram	3	6	1	201	133	40.20	1	0	0	0
DL Vettori	3	5	0	192	81	38.40	0	2	1	0
SB Styris	3	6	1	126	54 *	25.20	0	1	4	0
NJ Astle	3	6	0	135	50	22.50	0	1	0	0
PG Fulton	2	4	0	65	36	16.25	0	0	1	0
HJH Marshall	1	2	0	31	25	15.50	0	0	0	0
BB McCullum	3	5	0	74	33	14.80	0	0	7	1
MHW Papps	2	4	0	57	22	14.25	0	0	2	0
KD Mills	2	4	2	12	12	6.00	0	0	1	0
JM How	1	2	0	4	4	2.00	0	0	1	0
CS Martin	3	4	1	2	1 *	0.66	0	0	1	0
JS Patel	1	1	1	27	27 *	-	0	0	1	0
Totals	33	59	8	1445	262		3	4	23	1
			Extras	118				subs	0	
			Total	1563		30.64			23	

Bowling

Name	Overs	Mdns	Runs	Wkts	Avg	BB	5I	10M
KD Mills	58	15	179	8	22.37	4-43	0	0
SB Styris	17	3	49	2	24.50	1-1	0	0
JEC Franklin	91.3	12	384	15	25.60	4-75	0	0
CS Martin	98.4	20	293	9	32.55	5-37	1	0
JS Patel	42	8	117	3	39.00	3-117	0	0
JDP Oram	55	20	123	3	41.00	2-44	0	0
NJ Astle	14	3	46	1	46.00	1-15	0	0
DL Vettori	97.1	12	244	4	61.00	2-42	0	0
Totals	473.2	93	1435	45		5-37	1	0
		b/lb/pen	58	1	run outs			
		Total	1493	46	32.45			

SOUTH AFRICA IN SRI LANKA 2006

Patrick Compton

The tour will largely be remembered for events off the field rather than on it. Eight days after the Proteas had lost the two-Test series 2-0, Cricket South Africa abandoned the tour before the start of a triangular limited-overs tournament involving India and Sri Lanka after a bomb exploded close to the team's hotel in Colombo, killing seven people.

Announcing the tour's curtailment on August 16, CSA chief executive Gerald Majola said that reports from two security companies had agreed that the risk to the team was at an "unacceptable level" and that the Sri Lankan Government was unable to guarantee the physical security of the team given the situation in the city.

The two security companies were Nicholls, Steyn and Associates, employed by CSA, and a company from Dubai, The Olive Group, who were commissioned by the International Cricket Council to provide a second opinion.

The Indians remained in Colombo and Sri Lanka Cricket scheduled three matches between the two teams. Unfortunately, the monsoon season arrived early and after two matches were washed out, the third was cancelled and it was agreed to replay the series at a later date.

The cancellation caused controversy, with Sri Lanka Cricket objecting strongly, while the president of the International Cricket Council, Percy Sonn, arrived in Colombo three days after the Proteas had left and indicated his disapproval of the decision.

If the tour ended in frustration, fear and torrential rain, the first month provided some uninterrupted Test cricket with Sri Lanka deservedly winning the series.

South Africa, who arrived after a 10-week layoff under their first black captain, Ashwell Prince, following injuries to Graeme Smith and Jacques Kallis, could argue that their performance levels improved consistently after the first two disastrous days of the first Test. In that time they were dismissed for 169 on an excellent batting track and allowed Sri Lanka to freely build the basis of a huge reply. The Proteas' improvement culminated in a thrilling climax to a high-quality second Test which the Sri Lankans won by one wicket.

Three players were largely responsible for Sri Lanka's victory. Muttiah Muralitharan's extraordinary feats are almost taken for granted these days, but it is hard not to be awed by a record 22 wickets in a two-Test series, including two consecutive 10-wicket match hauls. This meant that he had repeated his earlier world record feat of securing 10-wicket hauls in four consecutive Test matches.

On any other occasion, Sri Lankan captain Mahela Jayawardene would surely have been named Man of the Series. The diminutive right-hander had a phenomenal run with the bat, striking the fourth highest Test score (374) in the first Test, as well as a crucial century in his team's second innings of the next match as they successfully chased down their highest fourth-innings target.

Kumar Sangakkara, with a splendid 287, was Jayawardene's partner in the world record stand of 624 in the first Test that enabled the home team to win the match by an innings and 153 runs.

For the Proteas, the one shining light was AB de Villiers who played with a freedom and aggression that underlined his growing reputation as South Africa's golden boy. The team also made a full contribution to the exciting second Test with only Jayawardene's century pry-

RECORD-BREAKER . . . Mahela Jayawardene acknowledges the applause after his epic innings of 374 against South Africa *Picture: LEE WARREN, Touchline Photo*

ing the game from their grasp. As was the case in Australia, however, dropped catches cost them dearly with five going down in the Sri Lanka second innings.

There were staunch contributions with the bat from the likes of Mark Boucher, Andrew Hall, Ashwell Prince, Herschelle Gibbs and Jacques Rudolph but no South African scored a century. Furthermore, in the main the South African attack once again lacked punch on the sub-continent, although the sometimes expensive Dale Steyn bowled with spirit and real pace to record his second five-wicket haul in Tests.

The tourists were without their chief strike bowler, Makhaya Ntini, for the last day and a half of the second Test after he suffered a strained hamstring, while left-arm spinner Nicky Boje could have helped the Proteas square the series if chances off him had gone to hand.

Nevertheless, the Sri Lankans deserved their success. They have shown under coach Tom Moody and captain Jayawardene that their flamboyant talent is now effectively mixed with the kind of grit they showed on their recent tour of England.

The South African Test squad was: Ashwell Prince (captain), Hashim Amla, Nicky Boje, Mark Boucher, AB de Villiers, Boeta Dippenaar, Herschelle Gibbs, Andrew Hall, Andre Nel, Makhaya Ntini, Shaun Pollock, Jacques Rudolph, Dale Steyn, Thandi Tshabalala. Manager, Goolam Rajah; coach, Mickey Arthur; assistant coach, Vincent Barnes; physiotherapist, Shane Jabaar; fitness trainer, Adrian le Roux; computer analyst, Gustav Obermeyer; media liaison officer, Gordon Templeton.

Smith had been named as captain but suffered an injury to his right ankle while running in Knysna the weekend before the team assembled for a training camp. He needed surgery on two torn ligaments. Kallis was not available after undergoing surgery for a long-term elbow injury. Rudolph replaced Smith in the squad.

Amla, Rudolph and Boje flew home after the Test series and the squad was supplemented by Loots Bosman, Johan van der Wath, Roger Telemachus and Robin Peterson for the one-dayers. Steyn was not selected but stayed as cover for Ntini. Mark Boucher was named captain because, according to selection convenor Haroon Lorgat, Prince was not a certainty in the one-day team. Smith, Kallis, Justin Kemp and Charl Langeveldt were not considered because of injuries.

SRI LANKAN BOARD XI v SOUTH AFRICANS First-class 3-day match

Played at Colts Ground, Havelock Park, Colombo on 22,23,24 July 2006 Toss: Sri Lankan Board XI
Umpires: SSK Gallage & CBC Rodrigo
Debuts: SLBrd: None. SA: None
Close of play: Day 1: SA (1) 351-3 (Amla 128*, Prince 15*, 90 overs). Day 2: SA (2) 43-1 (Dippenaar 22*, De Villiers 3*, 9 overs)
Result: Drawn
Notes: AB de Villiers scored his 50 in 58 mins off 46 balls in South Africans' 1st innings.

South Africa enjoyed an encouraging start to the tour with both bat and ball. After being inserted by the home team, they made a big total, thanks to centuries from Jacques Rudolph and Hashim Amla. AB de Villiers was in particularly good form, a sign of things to come, striking fluent half-centuries in each innings.

The Proteas dismissed the President' s XI for 162 in their first innings, with paceman Andre Nel leading the charge with four wickets. The three-day match eventually fizzled out into a draw but coach Mickey Arthur said he was more than happy with the preparation.

SOUTH AFRICA IN SRI LANKA 2006

SOUTH AFRICANS	Runs	Mins	Balls	4	6		Runs	Mins	Balls	4	6
HH Dippenaar lbw b Zoysa	1	2	3	-	-	(2) lbw b Zoysa	25	65	27	2	-
HH Gibbs c Vandort b Herath	38	89	48	6	-	(1) b Perera	10	23	20	2	-
JA Rudolph c Mubarak b Chandana	157	327	213	16	1	(8) lbw b Mubarak	58	99	118	6	-
HM Amla lbw b Ganegama	150	339	272	16	1	(7) b Chandana	5	16	13	-	-
*AG Prince not out	50	159	116	6	-	c Samaraweera b Chandana	20	73	41	-	-
AB de Villiers not out	50	60	46	10	-	(3) b Mubarak	75	167	104	11	-
†MV Boucher						(4) c Jayawardene b Zoysa	8	27	13	1	-
N Boje						(6) lbw b Chandana	5	18	17	1	-
A Nel						not out	20	87	44	3	-
DW Steyn											
M Ntini											
Extras (b 8, lb 2, w 1, nb 8)	19					Extras (lb 1, w 3, nb 15)	19				
TOTAL (for 4 wkts dec) (115 overs)	**465**					**TOTAL (for 8 wkts dec) (63.4 overs)**	**245**				

SRI LANKAN BOARD XI	Runs	Mins	Balls	4	6		Runs	Mins	Balls	4	6
MG Vandort b Ntini	29	104	53	3	-	not out	29	92	69	4	-
*DA Gunawardene c Boucher b Ntini	18	12	14	4	-	st Boucher b Boje	37	74	39	6	-
CK Kapugedera c Gibbs b Steyn	0	11	10	-	-	not out	11	17	14	1	1
TT Samaraweera b Nel	3	18	12	-	-						
J Mubarak c De Villiers b Nel	0	6	1	-	-						
†HAPW Jayawardene b Nel	18	39	31	2	-						
UDU Chandana not out	51	116	98	8	-						
DNT Zoysa c Boucher b Nel	16	50	30	2	1						
WCA Ganegama lbw b Boje	10	48	34	1	-						
PDRL Perera lbw b Boje	0	2	1	-	-						
HMRKB Herath absent hurt											
Extras (b 2, lb 3, w 7, nb 5)	17					Extras (lb 5, w 5, nb 2)	12				
TOTAL (46.3 overs)	**162**					**TOTAL (for 1 wkt) (20 overs)**	**89**				

SLBrd	O	M	R	W		O	M	R	W	
Zoysa	14	3	54	1	(3 nb, 1 w)	9	0	29	2	(2 nb, 1 w)
Perera	20	1	68	0	(3 nb)	8	0	45	1	(8 nb, 2 w)
Ganegama	19	3	88	1	(1 nb)	8	2	33	0	
Herath	26	3	86	1						
Chandana	24	2	115	1		(4) 22	1	80	3	(2 nb)
Mubarak	6	0	27	0		(5) 12.4	2	44	2	(2 nb)
Samaraweera	6	1	17	0	(1 nb)	(6) 4	0	13	0	(1 nb)
SA	O	M	R	W		O	M	R	W	
Ntini	11	4	32	2		5	2	21	0	(2 nb)
Steyn	10	2	40	1	(4 nb, 3 w)	5	2	15	0	
Nel	13	4	39	4		(4) 4	0	21	0	(1 w)
Boje	12.3	2	46	2	(1 nb)	(3) 5	1	27	1	
De Villiers						1	1	0	0	

Fall of Wickets

	SA	SLBrd	SA	SLBrd
1st	5 (1)	22 (2)	25 (1)	72 (2)
2nd	88 (2)	23 (3)	55 (2)	-
3rd	330 (3)	33 (4)	77 (4)	-
4th	395 (4)	37 (5)	136 (5)	-
5th	-	73 (6)	153 (6)	-
6th	-	84 (1)	159 (3)	-
7th	-	133 (8)	167 (7)	-
8th	-	162 (9)	245 (8)	-
9th	-	162 (10)	-	-
10th	-	-	-	-

SRI LANKA v SOUTH AFRICA — 1st Test

Played at Sinhalese Sports Club, Colombo on 27,28,29,30,31 July 2006 — Toss: South Africa

Umpires: MR Benson & BF Bowden (TV: EAR de Silva) — Referee: J Srinath

Debuts: SL: None. SA: None

Close of play: Day 1: SL (1) 128-2 (Sangakkara 59*, DPMD Jayawardene 55*, 26 overs). Day 2: SL (1) 485-2 (Sangakkara 229*, DPMD Jayawardene 224*, 112 overs). Day 3: SA (2) 43-0 (Rudolph 24*, Hall 13*, 15 overs). Day 4: SA (2) 311-4 (Prince 60*, Boucher 38*, 105 overs)

Result: Sri Lanka won by an innings and 153 runs

Man of Match: Mahela Jayawardene

Notes: EAR de Silva replaced MR Benson as on-field umpire on the 5th day.

After initially intending to play a four-man attack, coach Arthur and convener of selectors Lorgat changed their minds shortly before the match, including all-rounder Hall in place of Dippenaar. Hall slotted in as an opener, a role he had played with considerable success at Kanpur in India in 2004.

Prince won what was considered to be an important toss on a flawless batting surface at the SSC ground but his batsmen let him down badly, subsiding to 169 all out at tea on the first day. The Proteas lost both their openers to loose shots against paceman Dilhara Fernando by lunch but it was the dismissal shortly after the break of Rudolph, who until then had played particularly well, that signalled the start of a collapse in which eight wickets fell for just 91 runs in the afternoon.

Afterwards, the management stated that early tour nerves had contributed to the debacle, leading to some tentative batting. Fernando and Muralitharan were the main destroyers, sharing eight wickets. For the South Africans, only De Villiers embodied the "brave cricket" motto of the team.

Steyn immediately struck back for the visitors, dismissing both openers for 14, but Sangakkara was dropped and then bowled off a no-ball in one over from the fast bowler. The two lost opportunities proved hugely costly. The next wicket fell 950 balls and 11 hours and three minutes later when Sangakkara was dismissed for 287 by Andrew Hall.

Sangakkara and Jayawardene added 624 runs for the third wicket, the biggest partnership of all time for both Tests and first-class cricket. In the process they overtook the previous Test record of 576 set by Sri Lanka's Sanath Jayasuriya and Roshan Mahanama against India at the R Premadasa Stadium, Khettarama, Colombo in 1997.

Both men made their highest Test scores with Jayawardene making his first triple century and the highest Test score by a Sri Lankan, overtaking Jayasuriya's 340 scored against India in 1997/98. He fell just short of Brian Lara's world record score of 400, however, being bowled by Nel shortly after tea on the third day. Jayawardene moved into fourth place on the all-time list behind Lara (400 not out and 375) and Matthew Hayden (380).

Despite defiant batting on a still-excellent pitch, with half-centuries from Hall, Rudolph, Prince and Boucher, the South Africans had little hope of avoiding an emphatic defeat which came on the final afternoon. As usual, Muralitharan was the chief destroyer. It was his 54th five-wicket haul and the 17th time he had taken 10 wickets in a Test match.

SOUTH AFRICA	*Runs*	*Mins*	*Balls*	*4*	*6*		*Runs*	*Mins*	*Balls*	*4*	*6*
HH Gibbs b Fernando	19	72	41	3	-	(7) c and b Muralitharan	18	48	32	3	-
AJ Hall b Fernando	17	49	31	3	-	lbw b Muralitharan	64	270	177	7	-
JA Rudolph c HAPW Jayawardene b Maharoof	29	71	52	5	-	(1) c Kapugedera b Fernando	90	213	182	13	-
HM Amla st HAPW Jayawardene b Muralitharan	19	95	64			(3) lbw b Fernando	2	16	14	-	-
*AG Prince c HAPW Jayawardene b Maharoof	1	16	15	-	-	(4) c DPMD Jayawardene b Muralitharan	61	213	182	4	-
AB de Villiers c Kapugedera b Muralitharan	65	98	72	8	-	(5) lbw b Muralitharan	24	66	38	3	-
†MV Boucher c Jayasuriya b Muralitharan	4	19	9	-	-	(6) c and b Jayasuriya	85	231	160	10	-
N Boje lbw b Muralitharan	5	16	10	1	-	not out	33	138	130	2	-
A Nel lbw b Fernando	0	7	2	-	-	b Muralitharan	0	9	8	-	-
DW Steyn b Fernando	0	2	1	-	-	b Muralitharan	4	13	9	1	-
M Ntini not out	0	20	5	-	-	b Malinga	16	36	32	1	1
Extras (b 4, lb 6)	10					Extras (b 11, lb 4, w 2, nb 20)	37				
TOTAL (50.2 overs)	**169**					**TOTAL (157.2 overs)**	**434**				

SRI LANKA	*Runs*	*Mins*	*Balls*	*4*	*6*
WU Tharanga c Boucher b Steyn	7	19	10	1	-
ST Jayasuriya lbw b Steyn	4	8	6	-	-
KC Sangakkara c Boucher b Hall	287	681	457	35	-
*DPMD Jayawardene b Nel	374	767	572	43	1
TM Dilshan lbw b Steyn	45	86	67	6	-
CK Kapugedera not out	1	14	7	-	-
†HAPW Jayawardene					
MF Maharoof					
SL Malinga					
CRD Fernando					
M Muralitharan					
Extras (b 17, lb 5, w 8, nb 8)	38				
TOTAL (for 5 wkts dec) (185.1 overs)	**756**				

SL	O	M	R	W		O	M	R	W	
Malinga	10	2	38	0		16.2	0	85	1	(7 nb, 1 w)
Maharoof	9	1	32	2		15	3	48	0	(5 nb, 1 w)
Fernando	13	2	48	4		24	6	69	2	(8 nb)
Muralitharan	18.2	6	41	4		64	11	131	6	
Dilshan						4	1	10	0	
Jayasuriya						34	8	76	1	
SA	*O*	*M*	*R*	*W*						
Ntini	31	3	97	0	(1 nb)					
Steyn	26	1	129	3	(6 nb, 2 w)					
Nel	25.1	2	114	1	(1 nb, 1 w)					
Hall	25	2	99	1						
Boje	65	5	221	0						
Rudolph	7	0	45	0						
Prince	2	0	7	0	(1 w)					
De Villiers	4	0	22	0						

Fall of Wickets

	SA	SL	SA
1st	32 (2)	6 (2)	165 (1)
2nd	45 (1)	14 (1)	171 (3)
3rd	78 (3)	638 (3)	185 (2)
4th	80 (5)	751 (5)	234 (5)
5th	112 (4)	756 (4)	312 (4)
6th	128 (7)	-	350 (7)
7th	148 (8)	-	401 (6)
8th	151 (9)	-	404 (9)
9th	151 (10)	-	412 (10)
10th	169 (6)	-	434 (11)

Highest partnerships in first-class cricket

Wkt			
3rd	624	KC Sangakkara and DPMD Jayawardene, Sri Lanka v SA (Colombo-SSC)	2006
4th	577	VS Hazare and Gul Mohammad, Baroda v Holkar (Baroda)	1946/47
2nd	576	ST Jayasuriya and RS Mahanama, Sri Lanka v India (Colombo-RPS)	1997/98
4th	574*	CL Walcott and FMM Worrell, Barbados v Trinidad & Tobago (Port-of-Spain)	1945/46
1st	561	Waheed Mirza and Mansoor Akhtar, Karachi Whites v Quetta (Karachi)	1976/77
1st	555	P Holmes and H Sutcliffe, Yorkshire v Essex (Leyton)	1932
1st	554	JT Brown and J Tunnicliffe, Yorkshire v Derbyshire (Chesterfield)	1898
4th	502*	FMM Worrell and JDC Goddard, Barbados v Trinidad & Tobago (Bridgetown)	1943/44

SRI LANKA v SOUTH AFRICA — 2nd Test

Played at P Saravanamuttu Stadium, Colombo on 4,5,6,7,8 August 2006 — Toss: South Africa
Umpires: Aleem Dar & BF Bowden (TV: TH Wijewardene) — Referee: J Srinath
Debuts: SL: None. SA: None
Close of play: Day 1: SA (1) 361. Day 2: SA (2) 6-0 (Gibbs 4*, Hall 2*, 2 overs). Day 3: SA (2) 257-7 (Boucher 28*, Boje 5*, 92 overs). Day 4: SL (2) 262-5 (DPMD Jayawardene 77*, HAPW Jayawardene 2*, 72 overs)
Result: Sri Lanka won by 1 wicket
Man of Match: Mahela Jayawardene
Man of Series: Muttiah Muralitharan

An excellent pitch, with pace and bounce that offered something to both batsmen and bowlers, paved the way for a gripping Test match that was only decided in Sri Lanka's favour by the narrowest of margins on the final afternoon. The hosts therefore won the Test series 2-0.

South Africa made one change, replacing Nel with Shaun Pollock, a late arrival on tour after witnessing the birth of his daughter in Durban.

Prince called correctly for the second time, electing to bat first on another good batting surface. As at the SSC, however, South Africa made a poor start, with Gibbs trapped leg before by Chaminda Vaas for a second-ball duck and makeshift opener Hall looking all at sea against Lasith Malinga before being snapped up in the slips.

Rudolph and Amla began a partial recovery but both departed after having got starts and at 70-4 South Africa were in serious trouble. They were rescued by a fine partnership of 161 by Prince and the ever-aggressive De Villiers, who both played positively, particularly against Muralitharan whose early overs were expensive.

The two men batted through the afternoon, but were parted shortly after tea when Prince was caught behind off Muralitharan. De Villiers followed shortly afterwards in an unfortunate manner when he was adjudged caught behind for 95 off Malinga to a ball that TV replays confirmed he never touched. It was the 22-year-old's fourth 90 in his 22 Test matches and rarely can a century have been more deserved.

SOUTH AFRICA IN SRI LANKA 2006

A fluent unbeaten half-century by Pollock and a cameo by Mark Boucher saw the visitors through to what seemed a useful but by no means entirely satisfactory total.

On the second morning, however, that total was looking healthy as a revitalised Ntini grabbed four wickets and Steyn one as Sri Lanka staggered into lunch on 98-5 with their first Test heroes, Sangakkara and Jayawardene, back in the pavilion.

The hosts have added grit to their natural flair, however, and century partnerships between Chamara Kapugedera and wicketkeeper Prasanna Jayawardene, and then Chaminda Vaas and Farveez Maharoof, saw them only concede a first-innings deficit of 40.

A fighting 92 by Gibbs, who succeeded for the first time on tour, and an aggressive 65 by Boucher enabled South Africa to set Sri Lanka the formidable challenge of scoring 352 for victory.

Sri Lanka had never successfully chased a target of this size before but thanks to an explosive 73 by Jayasuriya and a measured century by the inspirational Jayawardene, they inched home by just one wicket in a thrilling climax an hour after lunch on the final day. It was the sixth-highest successful fourth-innings run chase in Test history.

Going into lunch on 333-6, just 19 short of victory, the Sri Lankans had looked odds-on favourites to reach their target comfortably. But the dismissal of Jayawardene by Boje, who captured four wickets in the innings, and a magnificent slip catch by De Villiers to get rid of Vaas, set up a nail-biting finish.

South Africa could point to bad luck – Rudolph was controversially run out in the second innings after the third umpire had ruled that the ball had earlier not gone for four - contributing to their defeat, but they also had only themselves to blame for dropping five catches and missing a stumping in the Sri Lankan second innings.

Jayawardene was named Man of the Match for his outstanding century - his second such award in the series - but Muralitharan received the man of the series award for his 22 wickets.

SOUTH AFRICA	Runs	Mins	Balls	4	6		Runs	Mins	Balls	4	6
HH Gibbs lbw b Vaas	0	1	2	-	-	c Jayasuriya b Muralitharan	92	246	190	11	1
AJ Hall c Dilshan b Malinga	0	16	9	-	-	c HAPW Jayawardene b Maharoof	32	96	63	2	1
JA Rudolph b Malinga	13	35	20	2	-	run out (Tharanga)	15	59	33	1	-
HM Amla lbw b Muralitharan	40	76	47	7	-	run out (Kapugedera/HAPW Jayawardene)	8	37	29	-	-
*AG Prince c HAPW Jayawardene b Muralitharan	86	207	144	13	-	c and b Muralitharan	17	127	76	2	-
AB de Villiers c HAPW Jayawardene b Malinga	95	182	141	18	-	c Dilshan b Muralitharan	33	79	63	5	-
†MV Boucher b Muralitharan	32	42	41	6	-	c Dilshan b Muralitharan	65	122	102	7	2
SM Pollock not out	57	106	70	5	2	c Tharanga b Muralitharan	14	31	32	1	-
N Boje c Sangakkara b Maharoof	11	33	23	2	-	c HAPW Jayawardene b Muralitharan	15	55	43	3	-
DW Steyn c Jayasuriya b Muralitharan	6	24	22	-	-	lbw b Muralitharan	0	8	7	-	-
M Ntini c Maharoof b Muralitharan	13	35	27	3	-	not out	5	21	10	1	-
Extras (w 1, nb 7)	8					Extras (b 9, lb 4, w 1, nb 1)	15				
TOTAL (89.5 overs)	**361**					**TOTAL (107.5 overs)**	**311**				

SRI LANKA	Runs	Mins	Balls	4	6		Runs	Mins	Balls	4	6
WU Tharanga c Boje b Ntini	2	12	9	-	-	c Gibbs b Ntini	0	8	7	-	-
ST Jayasuriya c Gibbs b Ntini	47	111	67	8	-	c Amla b Boje	73	130	74	9	3
KC Sangakkara c Amla b Ntini	14	36	31	3	-	c Amla b Pollock	39	83	64	8	-
*DPMD Jayawardene c Boucher b Steyn	13	47	27	2	-	c Gibbs b Boje	123	359	248	11	2
TM Dilshan b Ntini	4	10	5	1	-	c Gibbs b Boje	18	40	29	4	-
CK Kapugedera b Boje	63	89	77	9	2	c De Villiers b Boje	13	40	40	1	-
†HAPW Jayawardene b Steyn	42	91	49	6	1	lbw b Hall	30	110	79	3	-
MF Maharoof b Steyn	56	155	110	11	-	not out	29	158	118	2	-
WPUJC Vaas c Boucher b Steyn	64	161	130	10	-	c De Villiers b Hall	4	22	20	-	-
SL Malinga not out	8	17	10	2	-	(11) not out	1	4	1	-	-
M Muralitharan c Hall b Steyn	0	5	1	-	-	(10) b Hall	2	6	5	-	-
Extras (lb 1, w 2, nb 5)	8					Extras (b 4, lb 8, w 4, nb 4)	20				
TOTAL (85.1 overs)	**321**					**TOTAL (for 9 wkts) (113.3 overs)**	**352**				

SL	O	M	R	W		O	M	R	W	
Vaas	18	4	71	1		19	4	53	0	
Malinga	18	4	81	3	(3 nb, 1 w)	12	1	55	0	(1 nb)
Muralitharan	33.5	2	128	5		(4) 46.5	12	97	7	
Maharoof	15	2	52	1	(4 nb)	(3) 21	3	53	1	(1 w)
Jayasuriya	5	0	29	0		9	0	40	0	
SA	*O*	*M*	*R*	*W*		*O*	*M*	*R*	*W*	
Ntini	21	3	84	4		7.2	2	13	1	
Steyn	13.1	1	82	5	(3 nb, 2 w)	22.4	2	81	0	(2 nb, 3 w)
Pollock	16	4	52	0	(2 nb)	(4) 19	2	60	1	(2 nb)
Hall	15	7	31	0		(5) 25	3	75	3	(1 w)
Boje	20	6	71	1		(3) 39.3	11	111	4	

Fall of Wickets	SA	SL	SA	SL
1st	0 (1)	16 (1)	76 (2)	12 (1)
2nd	4 (2)	43 (3)	119 (3)	94 (3)
3rd	31 (3)	74 (4)	131 (4)	121 (2)
4th	70 (4)	85 (5)	161 (1)	164 (5)
5th	231 (5)	86 (2)	206 (5)	201 (6)
6th	256 (6)	191 (6)	207 (6)	279 (7)
7th	273 (7)	191 (7)	235 (8)	341 (4)
8th	307 (9)	308 (8)	280 (9)	348 (9)
9th	327 (10)	317 (9)	282 (10)	350 (10)
10th	361 (11)	321 (11)	311 (7)	-

Most runs in a 2-Test series

Name	Series	Season	M	Inns	NO	Runs	HS	Avg	100
ST Jayasuriya	Sri Lanka v India in SL	1997/98	2	3	0	571	340	190.33	2
WR Hammond	England v New Zealand in NZ	1932/33	2	2	1	563	336 *	563.00	2
A Flower	Zimbabwe v India in Ind	2000/01	2	4	2	540	232 *	270.00	2
DPMD Jayawardene	Sri Lanka v SA in SL	2006	2	3	0	510	374	170.00	2
ML Hayden	Australia v Zimbabwe in Aus	2003/04	2	3	1	501	380	250.50	2

Most wickets in a 2-Test series

Name	Series	Season	M	Balls	Runs	Wkts	Avg	BB	5I	10M
M Muralitharan,	Sri Lanka v SA in SL	2006	2	978	397	22	18.04	7-97	3	2
J Briggs,	England v SA in SA	1888/89	2	391	101	21	4.80	8-11	2	1
IK Pathan,	India v Zimbabwe in Zim	2005/06	2	391	237	21	11.28	7-59	3	1
A Kumble,	India v Pakistan in Ind	1998/99	2	587	312	21	14.85	10-74	2	1

Highest 4th innings totals to win a Test

418-7	West Indies beat Australia	St John's	2002/03
406-4	India beat West Indies	Port-of-Spain	1975/76
404-3	Australia beat England	Leeds	1948
369-6	Australia beat Pakistan	Hobart	1999/00
362-7	Australia beat West Indies	Georgetown	1977/78
352-9	Sri Lanka beat South Africa	Colombo-PSS	2006

SRI LANKA CRICKET DEVELOPMENT XI v SOUTH AFRICANS Limited Overs Match

Played at Sinhalese Sports Club, Colombo on 12 August 2006 Toss: South Africans
Umpires: R Martinesz & MSK Nandiweera
Debuts: SLDev: None. SA: None
Result: South Africans won by 3 wickets

SRI LANKA CRICKET DEVELOPMENT XI	Runs	Mins	Balls	4	6
*WS Jayantha c De Villiers b Nel	2	8	6	-	-
ML Udawatte c Bosman b Peterson	33	72	42	4	-
†JK Silva run out	0	4	5	-	-
MK Gajanayake c Van der Wath b Telemachus	17	45	29	3	-
LPC Silva b Van der Wath	29	47	30	1	1
WMG Ramyakumara c Van der Wath b Tshabalala	6	3	4	1	-
LHD Dilhara b Nel	16	21	18	2	-
CKB Kulasekara run out	1	4	2	-	-
HMRKB Herath not out	14	12	8	2	-
TCB Fernando not out	3	8	6	-	-
S Weerakoon					
Extras (lb 5, w 10)	15				
TOTAL (for 8 wkts) (25 overs)	**136**				

SOUTH AFRICANS	Runs	Mins	Balls	4	6
LL Bosman c JK Silva b Ramyakumara	30	62	25	3	1
HH Dippenaar c Jayantha b Dilhara	5	9	10	1	-
HH Gibbs lbw b Fernando	14	15	21	2	-
†AB de Villiers b Ramyakumara	2	6	6	-	-
*AG Prince c and b Herath	22	65	33	2	-
AJ Hall b Herath	29	27	30	4	1
RJ Peterson not out	20	22	11	1	2
JJ van der Wath st JK Silva b Herath	0	1	2	-	-
A Nel not out	9	12	11	1	-
R Telemachus					
T Tshabalala					
Extras (w 6, nb 2)	8				
TOTAL (for 7 wkts) (24.3 overs)	**139**				

SA	O	M	R	W	
Nel	5	1	15	2	(1 w)
Van der Wath	4	0	16	1	
Hall	5	0	32	0	(2 w)
Telemachus	4	0	25	1	(6 w)
Peterson	4	0	23	1	(1 w)
Tshabalala	3	0	20	1	

SLDev	O	M	R	W	
Dilhara	4.3	0	26	1	(2 w)
Fernando	4	0	33	1	(2 nb, 2 w)
Ramyakumara	5	0	23	2	(1 w)
Kulasekara	3	1	7	0	(1 w)
Herath	5	0	29	3	
Weerakoon	3	0	21	0	

Fall of Wickets	*SLDev*	*SA*
1st	8 (1)	12 (2)
2nd	8 (3)	32 (3)
3rd	55 (4)	36 (4)
4th	75 (2)	61 (1)
5th	82 (6)	100 (6)
6th	116 (7)	113 (5)
7th	118 (8)	113 (8)
8th	122 (5)	-

SRI LANKA v SOUTH AFRICA 2006: TEST AVERAGES

SRI LANKA

Batting & Fielding

Name	M	Inns	NO	Runs	HS	Avg	100	50	Ct	St
DPMD Jayawardene	2	3	0	510	374	170.00	2	0	1	0
KC Sangakkara	2	3	0	340	287	113.33	1	0	1	0
MF Maharoof	2	2	1	85	56	85.00	0	1	1	0
ST Jayasuriya	2	3	0	124	73	41.33	0	1	4	0
CK Kapugedera	2	3	1	77	63	38.50	0	1	2	0
HAPW Jayawardene	2	2	0	72	42	36.00	0	0	6	1
WPUJC Vaas	1	2	0	68	64	34.00	0	1	0	0
TM Dilshan	2	3	0	67	45	22.33	0	0	3	0
WU Tharanga	2	3	0	9	7	3.00	0	0	1	0
M Muralitharan	2	2	0	2	2	1.00	0	0	2	0
SL Malinga	2	2	2	9	8 *	-	0	0	0	0
CRD Fernando	1	0	0	0	-	-	0	0	0	0
Totals	22	28	4	1363	374		3	4	21	1
			Extras	66				subs	0	
			Total	1429		59.54			21	

Bowling

Name	Overs	Mdns	Runs	Wkts	Avg	BB	5I	10M
M Muralitharan	163	31	397	22	18.04	7-97	3	2
CRD Fernando	37	8	117	6	19.50	4-48	0	0
MF Maharoof	60	9	185	4	46.25	2-32	0	0
SL Malinga	56.2	7	259	4	64.75	3-81	0	0
WPUJC Vaas	37	8	124	1	124.00	1-71	0	0
ST Jayasuriya	48	8	145	1	145.00	1-76	0	0
TM Dilshan	4	1	10	0	-	-	0	0
Totals	405.2	72	1237	38		7-97	3	2
		b/lb/pen	38	2	run outs			
		Total	1275	40	31.87			

SOUTH AFRICA

Batting & Fielding

Name	M	Inns	NO	Runs	HS	Avg	100	50	Ct	St
SM Pollock	1	2	1	71	57 *	71.00	0	1	0	0
AB de Villiers	2	4	0	217	95	54.25	0	2	2	0
MV Boucher	2	4	0	186	85	46.50	0	2	4	0
AG Prince	2	4	0	165	86	41.25	0	2	0	0
JA Rudolph	2	4	0	147	90	36.75	0	1	0	0
HH Gibbs	2	4	0	129	92	32.25	0	1	4	0
AJ Hall	2	4	0	113	64	28.25	0	1	1	0
N Boje	2	4	1	64	33 *	21.33	0	0	1	0
HM Amla	2	4	0	69	40	17.25	0	0	3	0
M Ntini	2	4	2	34	16	17.00	0	0	0	0
DW Steyn	2	4	0	10	6	2.50	0	0	0	0
A Nel	1	2	0	0	0	0.00	0	0	0	0
Totals	22	44	4	1205	95		0	10	15	0
			Extras	70				subs	0	
			Total	1275		31.87			15	

SOUTH AFRICA IN SRI LANKA 2006

Bowling

Name	Overs	Mdns	Runs	Wkts	Avg	BB	5I	10M
DW Steyn	61.5	4	292	8	36.50	5-82	1	0
M Ntini	59.2	8	194	5	38.80	4-84	0	0
AJ Hall	65	12	205	4	51.25	3-75	0	0
N Boje	124.3	22	403	5	80.60	4-111	0	0
SM Pollock	35	6	112	1	112.00	1-60	0	0
A Nel	25.1	2	114	1	114.00	1-114	0	0
AG Prince	2	0	7	0	-	-	0	0
AB de Villiers	4	0	22	0	-	-	0	0
JA Rudolph	7	0	45	0	-	-	0	0
Totals	383.5	54	1394	24		5-82	1	0
		b/lb/pen	35	0	run outs			
		Total	1429	24	59.54			

SOUTH AFRICA IN SRI LANKA 2006: FIRST-CLASS AVERAGES

Batting & Fielding

Name	M	Inns	NO	Runs	HS	Avg	100	50	Ct	St
SM Pollock	1	2	1	71	57 *	71.00	0	1	0	0
AB de Villiers	3	6	1	342	95	68.40	0	4	3	0
JA Rudolph	3	6	0	362	157	60.33	1	2	0	0
AG Prince	3	6	1	235	86	47.00	0	3	0	0
MV Boucher	3	5	0	194	85	38.80	0	2	6	1
HM Amla	3	6	0	224	150	37.33	1	0	3	0
HH Gibbs	3	6	0	177	92	29.50	0	1	5	0
AJ Hall	2	4	0	113	64	28.25	0	1	1	0
N Boje	3	5	1	69	33 *	17.25	0	0	1	0
M Ntini	3	4	2	34	16	17.00	0	0	0	0
HH Dippenaar	1	2	0	26	25	13.00	0	0	0	0
A Nel	2	3	1	20	20 *	10.00	0	0	0	0
DW Steyn	3	4	0	10	6	2.50	0	0	0	0
Totals	33	59	7	1877	157		2	14	19	1
			Extras	108				subs	0	
			Total	1985		38.17			19	

Bowling

Name	Overs	Mdns	Runs	Wkts	Avg	BB	5I	10M
A Nel	42.1	6	174	5	34.80	4-39	0	0
M Ntini	75.2	14	247	7	35.28	4-84	0	0
DW Steyn	76.5	8	347	9	38.55	5-82	1	0
AJ Hall	65	12	205	4	51.25	3-75	0	0
N Boje	142	25	476	8	59.50	4-111	0	0
SM Pollock	35	6	112	1	112.00	1-60	0	0
AG Prince	2	0	7	0	-	-	0	0
AB de Villiers	5	1	22	0	-	-	0	0
JA Rudolph	7	0	45	0	-	-	0	0
Totals	450.2	72	1635	34		5-82	1	0
		b/lb/pen	45	0	run outs			
		Total	1680	34	49.41			

SOUTH AFRICAN INTERNATIONAL CRICKETERS

The following list contains the names of all those who have represented South Africa in Test cricket. Those who have also played in official limited overs internationals are denoted +. Those who have also played in official Pro20 internationals are denoted #.

Unofficial Test matches were played against the Australian Imperial Forces 1919/20, SB Joel's XI 1924/25, SAB England XI 1981/82, Arosa Sri Lanka and the West Indian XI 1982/83, West Indian XI 1983/84, Australian XI 1985/86 and 1986/87, English XI 1989/90 and India 2001/02 (marked *). Appearances in these unofficial Test matches are shown in brackets. A total of 299 players have appeared in official Test matches.

As at 1 September 2006.

TEST CRICKETERS

ACKERMAN Hylton Deon (HD), B Cape Town 14.2.1973.
4-2 v P in SA 1997/98; 2 v SL in SA 1997/98; (To Z 2001/02).

+ADAMS Paul Regan, B Cape Town 20.1.1977.
45-2 v E in SA 1995/96; 3 v I in I 1996/97; 2 v I in SA 1996/97; 2 v A in SA 1996/97; 2 v P in P 1997/98; 1 v A in A 1997/98; 1 v P in SA 1997/98; 2 v SL in SA 1997/98; 4 v E in E 1998; 2 v WI in SA 1998/99; 3 v NZ in NZ 1998/99; 1 v Z in SA 1999/00; 1 v Z in Z 1999/00; 4 v E in SA 1999/00; 3 v SL in SL 2000; 1 v WI in WI 2000/01; 2 v A in SA 2001/02; 2 v B in B 2002/03; 3 v E in E 2003; 2 v P in P 2003/04; 1 v WI in SA 2003/04; 1 v NZ in NZ 2003/04.

ADCOCK Neil Amwin Treharne, B Sea Point, Cape Town 8.3.1931.
26-5 v NZ in SA 1953/54; 4 v E in E 1955; 5 v E in SA 1956/57; 5 v A in SA 1957/58; 5 v E in E 1960; 2 v NZ in SA 1961/62.

AMLA Hashim Mahomed, B Durban 31.3.1983.
7-1 v I in I 2004/05; 2 v E in SA 2004/05; 2 v NZ in SA 2005/06; 2 v SL in SL 2006.

ANDERSON James Henry (Biddy), B Kimberley 26.4.1874. D Melkamer Farm, Bredasdorp, CP 11.3.1926.
1-v A in SA 1902/03.

ASHLEY William Hare (Gobo), B Mowbray, Cape Town 10.2.1862. D Plumtree, Rhodesia 14.7.1930.
1-v E in SA 1888/89.

BACHER Aron (Ali), B Johannesburg 24.5.1942.
12-3 v E in E 1965; 5 v A in SA 1966/67; 4 v A in SA 1969/70.

+BACHER Adam Marc, B Johannesburg 29.10.1973.
19-3 v I in SA 1996/97; 2 v A in SA 1996/97; 3 v P in P 1997/98; 3 v A in A 1997/98; 3 v P in SA 1997/98; 1 v SL in SA 1997/98; 1 v E in E 1998; 1 v WI in SA 1998/99; 1 v Z in SA 1999/00; 1 v Z in Z 1999/00.

BALASKAS Xenophon Constantine, B Kimberley 15.10.1910. D Hyde Park, Sandton, Johannesburg 12.5.1994.
9-2 v E in SA 1930/31; (To A 1931/32); 2 v NZ in NZ 1931/32; 1 v E in E 1935; 3 v A in SA 1935/36; 1 v E in SA 1938/39.

BARLOW Edgar John, B Pretoria 12.8.1940. D General Hospital, St Helier, Jersey, Channel Islands 30.12.2005.
30-5 v NZ in SA 1961/62; 5 v A in A 1963/64; 3 v NZ in NZ 1963/64; 5 v E in SA 1964/65; 3 v E in E 1965; 5 v A in SA 1966/67; 4 v A in SA 1969/70.

BAUMGARTNER Harold Vane, B Henley-on-Thames, Oxfordshire, England 17.11.1883. D Accra, Gold Coast 8.4.1938.
1-v E in SA 1913/14.

SOUTH AFRICAN INTERNATIONAL CRICKETERS

BEAUMONT Rolland, B Newcastle, Natal 4.2.1884. D Berea Nursing Home, Durban 25.5.1958.
5-2 v A in E 1912; 1 v E in E 1912; 2 v E in SA 1913/14.

BEGBIE Denis Warburton, B Middelburg, Transvaal 12.12.1914.
5-(To E 1947); 3 v E in SA 1948/49; 2 v A in SA 1949/50.

BELL Alexander John (Sandy), B East London 15.4.1906. D Mowbray, Cape Town 1.8.1985.
16-3 v E in E 1929; 3 v E in SA 1930/31; 5 v A in A 1931/32; 2 v NZ in NZ 1931/32; 3 v E in E 1935.

BISSET Murray, B Port Elizabeth 14.4.1876. D Salisbury, Rhodesia 24.10.1931.
3-2 v E in SA 1898/99; (To E 1901); 1 v E in SA 1909/10.

BISSETT George Finlay, B Kimberley 5.11.1905. D Botha's Hill, Natal 14.11.1965.
4-(To E 1924); 4 v E in SA 1927/28.

BLANCKENBERG James Manuel, B Claremont, Cape Town 31.12.1892. Presumed dead.
18(+2)-5 v E in SA 1913/14; (*2 v AIF 1919/20); 3 v A in SA 1921/22; 5 v E in SA 1922/23; 5 v E in E 1924.

BLAND Kenneth Colin, B Bulawayo, Rhodesia 5.4.1938.
21-5 v NZ in SA 1961/62; 4 v A in A 1963/64; 3 v NZ in NZ 1963/64; 5 v E in SA 1964/65; 3 v E in E 1965; 1 v A in SA 1966/67.

BOCK Ernest George, B Kimberley 17.9.1908. D Springs Nursing Home, Springs, Transvaal 5.9.1961.
1-v A in SA 1935/36.

+#**BOJE** Nico (Nicky), B Bloemfontein 20.3.1973.
43(+1)-(To I 1996/97); (To NZ 1998/99); 2 v I in I 1999/00; 3 v SL in SL 2000; 3 v NZ in SA 2000/01; 3 v SL in SA 2000/01; 4 v WI in WI 2000/01; 2 v I in SA 2001/02; (*1 v I 2001/02); 1 v A in A 2001/02; 1 v A in SA 2001/02; 2 v P in SA 2002/03; 2 v NZ in NZ 2003/04; 2 v SL in SL 2004; 4 v E in SA 2004/05; 2 v Z in SA 2004/05; 4 v WI in WI 2004/05; 1 v A in A 2005/06; 3 v A in SA 2005/06; 2 v NZ in SA 2005/06; 2 v SL in SL 2006.

BOND Gerald Edward (Boysie), B Cape Town 5.4.1909. D Cape Town 27.8.1965.
1-v E in SA 1938/39.

+**BOSCH** Tertius, B Vereeniging, Transvaal 14.3.1966. D Westville Hospital, Westville, Durban 14.2.2000.
1-v WI in WI 1991/92.

+#**BOTHA** Johan, B Johannesburg 2.5.1982.
1-v A in A 2005/06.

BOTTEN James Thomas (Jackie), B Pretoria 21.6.1938. D Unitas Hospital, Lyttelton, Centurion, Gauteng 14.5.2006.
3-v E in E 1965.

+#**BOUCHER** Mark Verdon, B East London 3.12.1976.
95(+1)-1 v P in P 1997/98; (To A 1997/98); 3 v P in SA 1997/98; 2 v SL in SA 1997/98; 5 v E in E 1998; 5 v WI in SA 1998/99; 3 v NZ in NZ 1998/99; 1 v Z in SA 1999/00; 1 v Z in Z 1999/00; 5 v E in SA 1999/00; 2 v I in I 1999/00; 3 v SL in SL 2000; 3 v NZ in SA 2000/01; 3 v SL in SA 2000/01; 5 v WI in WI 2000/01; 2 v Z in Z 2001/02; 2 v I in SA 2001/02; (*1 v I 2001/02); 3 v A in A 2001/02; 3 v A in SA 2001/02; 2 v B in SA 2002/03; 2 v SL in SA 2002/03; 2 v P in SA 2002/03; 2 v B in B 2002/03; 5 v E in E 2003; 2 v P in P 2003/04; 4 v WI in SA 2003/04; 3 v NZ in NZ 2003/04; 2 v SL in SL 2004; 2 v E in SA 2004/05; 2 v Z in SA 2004/05; 4 v WI in WI 2004/05; 3 v A in A 2005/06; 3 v A in SA 2005/06; 3 v NZ in SA 2005/06; 2 v SL in SL 2006. (Note: Also 1-World XI v A in A 2005/06).

BRANN William Henry, B Port Elizabeth 4.4.1899. D Port Elizabeth 22.9.1953.
3-v E in SA 1922/23.

BRISCOE Arthur Wellesley (Dooley), B Johannesburg 6.2.1911. D Kombolcha, Ethiopia (War) 22.4.1941.
2-1 v A in SA 1935/36; 1 v E in SA 1938/39.

BROMFIELD Harry Dudley (Brom), B Mossel Bay, CP 26.6.1932.
9-5 v NZ in SA 1961/62; 3 v E in SA 1964/65; 1 v E in E 1965.

BROWN Lennox Sidney, B Randfontein, Transvaal 24.11.1910. D Durban 1.9.1983.
2-1 v A in A 1931/32; 1 v NZ in NZ 1931/32.
BURGER Christopher George de Villiers, B Randfontein, Transvaal 12.7.1935.
2-v A in SA 1957/58.
BURKE Sydney Frank, B Pretoria 11.3.1934.
2-1 v NZ in SA 1961/62; 1 v E in SA 1964/65.
BUYS Isaac Daniel, B Somerset East, CC 4.2.1895. Presumed dead.
1(+1)-1 v E in SA 1922/23; (*1 v SBJ 1924/25).
CAMERON Horace Brakenridge (Jock), B Port Elizabeth 5.7.1905. D Joubert Park Hospital, Johannesburg, 2.11.1935.
26-5 v E in SA 1927/28; 4 v E in E 1929; 5 v E in SA 1930/31; 5 v A in A 1931/32; 2 v NZ in NZ 1931/32; 5 v E in E 1935.
CAMPBELL Thomas, B Edinburgh, Scotland 9.2.1882. D Milnedale Railway Siding, Natal 5.10.1924.
5-4 v E in SA 1909/10; (To A 1910/11); 1 v E in E 1912.
CARLSTEIN Peter Rudolph, B Klerksdorp, Transvaal 28.10.1938.
8-1 v A in SA 1957/58; 5 v E in E 1960; 2 v A in A 1963/64.
CARTER Claude Pagdett, B Durban 23.4.1881. D Addington Hospital, Durban 8.11.1952.
10-2 v E in E 1912; 2 v E in SA 1913/14; 3 v A in SA 1921/22; 3 v E in E 1924.
CATTERALL Robert Hector, B Port Elizabeth 10.7.1900. D Springkell Sanatorium, Kempton Park, Transvaal 3.1.1961.
24(+5)-5 v E in SA 1922/23; 5 v E in E 1924; (*5 v SBJ 1924/25); 5 v E in SA 1927/28; 5 v E in E 1929; 4 v E in SA 1930/31.
CHAPMAN Horace William, B Durban 30.6.1890. D Durban 1.12.1941.
2-1 v E in SA 1913/14; 1 v A in SA 1921/22.
CHEETHAM John Erskine (Jack), B Mowbray, Cape Town 26.5.1920. D Parktown, Johannesburg 21.8.1980.
24-1 v E in SA 1948/49; 3 v A in SA 1949/50; 5 v E in E 1951; 5 v A in A 1952/53; 2 v NZ in NZ 1952/53; 5 v NZ in SA 1953/54; 3 v E in E 1955.
CHEVALIER Grahame Anton, B Cape Town 9.3.1937.
1 v A in SA 1969/70.
CHRISTY James Alexander Joseph, B Pretoria 12.12.1904. D Addington Hospital, Durban 1.2.1971.
10-2 v E in E 1929; 1 v E in SA 1930/31; 5 v A in A 1931/32; 2 v NZ in NZ 1931/32.
CHUBB Geoffrey Walter Ashton, B East London 12.4.1911. D East London 28.8.1982.
5-v E in E 1951.
COCHRAN John Alexander Kennedy, B Johannesburg 15.7.1909. D Johannesburg 15.6.1987.
1-v E in SA 1930/31.
COEN Stanley Keppel (Shunter), B Heilbron, OFS 14.10.1902. D Entabeni Hospital, Westridge, Durban 29.1.1967.
2-v E in SA 1927/28.
COMMAILLE John McIllwaine Moore (Mick), B Cape Town 21.2.1883. D Sea Point, Cape Town 28.7.1956.
12-5 v E in SA 1909/10; (To A 1910/11); 5 v E in E 1924; 2 v E in SA 1927/28.
COMMINS John Brian, B East London 19.2.1965.
3-2 v NZ in SA 1994/95; 1 v P in SA 1994/95; (To I 1996/97).
CONYNGHAM Dalton Parry (Conky), B Durban 10.5.1897. D Durban 7.7.1979.
1(+2)-1 v E in SA 1922/23; (*2 v SBJ 1924/25).
COOK Frederick James, B Java, Dutch East Indies 1870. D near Helles, Gallipoli, Turkey (War) 30.11.1915.
1-v E in SA 1895/96.
+COOK Stephen James, B Johannesburg 31.7.1953.
3(+19)-(*3 v E XI 1981/82; *2 v SL 1982/83; *2 v WI 1982/83; *4 v WI 1983/84; *3 v A 1985/86; *4 v A 1986/87; *1 v E XI 1989/90); 2 v I in SA 1992/93; 1 v SL in SL 1993/94.

COOPER Alfred Henry Cecil, B Johannesburg 2.9.1893. D Johannesburg 18.7.1963.
1(+1)-1 v E in SA 1913/14; (*1 v AIF 1919/20).

COX Joseph Lovell, B Pietermaritzburg 28.6.1886. D Bulawayo, Rhodesia 4.7.1971.
3(+1)-(To E 1912); 3 v E in SA 1913/14; (*1 v AIF 1919/20).

CRIPPS Godfrey, B Mussoorie, India 19.10.1865. D near Adelaide, Australia 27.7.1943.
1-v E in SA 1891/92; (To E 1894).

CRISP Robert James (Bob), B Calcutta, India 28.5.1911. D Colchester, Essex, England 2.3.1994.
9-5 v E in E 1935; 4 v A in SA 1935/36.

+CRONJE Wessel Johannes (Hansie), B Bloemfontein 25.9.1969. D near George, WC 1.6.2002.
68-1 v WI in WI 1991/92; 3 v I in SA 1992/93; 3 v SL in SL 1993/94; 3 v A in A 1993/94; 3 v A in SA 1993/94; 3 v E in E 1994; 3 v NZ in SA 1994/95; 1 v P in SA 1994/95; 1 v NZ in NZ 1994/95; 1 v Z in Z 1995/96; 5 v E in SA 1995/96; 3 v I in I 1996/97; 3 v I in SA 1996/97; 3 v A in SA 1996/97; 3 v P in P 1997/98; 3 v A in A 1997/98; 2 v P in SA 1997/98; 2 v SL in SA 1997/98; 5 v E in E 1998; 5 v WI in SA 1998/99; 3 v NZ in NZ 1998/99; 1 v Z in SA 1999/00; 1 v Z in Z 1999/00; 5 v E in SA 1999/00; 2 v I in I 1999/00.

+CULLINAN Daryll John, B Kimberley 4.3.1967.
70-1 v I in SA 1992/93; 3 v SL in SL 1993/94; 3 v A in A 1993/94; 1 v E in E 1994; 3 v NZ in SA 1994/95; 1 v P in SA 1994/95; 1 v NZ in NZ 1994/95; 1 v Z in Z 1995/96; 5 v E in SA 1995/96; 3 v I in I 1996/97; 3 v I in SA 1996/97; 3 v A in SA 1996/97; 3 v P in P 1997/98; 1 v A in A 1997/98; 1 v P in SA 1997/98; 2 v SL in SA 1997/98; 5 v E in E 1998; 5 v WI in SA 1998/99; 3 v NZ in NZ 1998/99; 1 v Z in SA 1999/00; 1 v Z in Z 1999/00; 5 v E in SA 1999/00; 1 v I in I 1999/00; 3 v SL in SL 2000; 3 v NZ in SA 2000/01; 3 v SL in SA 2000/01; 5 v WI in WI 2000/01.

CURNOW Sydney Harry, B Benoni, Transvaal 16.12.1907. D Perth, Australia 28.7.1986.
7-3 v E in SA 1930/31; 4 v A in A 1931/32.

DALTON Eric Londesbrough, B Durban 2.12.1906. D Entabeni Hospital, Westridge, Durban 3.6.1981.
15-1 v E in E 1929; 1 v E in SA 1930/31; 2 v A in A 1931/32; 2 v NZ in NZ 1931/32; 4 v E in E 1935; 1 v A in SA 1935/36; 4 v E in SA 1938/39.

DAVIES Eric Quail, B King William's Town, CC 26.8.1909. D Port Alfred, CP 11.11.1976.
5-2 v A in SA 1935/36; 3 v E in SA 1938/39.

+DAWSON Alan Charles, B Cape Town 27.11.1969.
2-v B in B 2002/03.

DAWSON Oswald Charles, B Rossburgh, Durban 1.9.1919.
9-5 v E in E 1947; 4 v E in SA 1948/49.

DEANE Hubert Gouvaine (Nummy), B Eshowe, Natal (Zululand) 21.7.1895. D Lower Houghton, Johannesburg 21.10.1939.
17(+4)-5 v E in E 1924; (*4 v SBJ 1924/25); 5 v E in SA 1927/28; 5 v E in E 1929; 2 v E in SA 1930/31.

DE BRUYN Zander, B Johannesburg 5.7.1975.
3-2 v I in I 2004/05; 1 v E in SA 2004/05.

+#DE VILLIERS Abraham Benjamin (AB), B Pretoria 17.2.1984.
22-5 v E in SA 2004/05; 2 v Z in SA 2004/05; 4 v WI in WI 2004/05; 3 v A in A 2005/06; 3 v A in SA 2005/06; 3 v NZ in SA 2005/06; 2 v SL in SL 2006.

+DE VILLIERS Petrus Stephanus (Fanie), B Vereeniging, Transvaal 13.10.1964.
18-(To SL 1993/94); 3 v A in A 1993/94; 3 v A in SA 1993/94; 3 v E in E 1994; 3 v NZ in SA 1994/95; 1 v P in SA 1994/95; 1 v NZ in NZ 1994/95; (To Z 1995/96); 2 v I in I 1996/97; 2 v P in SA 1997/98.

+#DIPPENAAR Hendrik Human (Boeta), B Kimberley 14.6.1977.
37-1 v Z in SA 1999/00; 1 v Z in Z 1999/00; (To I 1999/00); (To SL 2000); 3 v NZ in SA 2000/01; 2 v SL in SA 2000/01; (To WI 2000/01); 2 v Z in Z 2001/02; 2 v I in SA 2001/02; 3 v A in A 2001/02; 1 v A in SA 2001/02; 2 v P in SA 2002/03; 2 v B in B 2002/03; 3 v E in E 2003; 2 v P in P 2003/04; 2 v SL in SL 2004; 2 v I in I 2004/05; 3 v E in SA 2004/05; 2 v WI in WI 2004/05; 1 v A in SA 2005/06; 3 v NZ in SA 2005/06; (To SL 2006).

DIXON Cecil Donovan (Dickie), B Potchefstroom, Transvaal 12.2.1891. D Illovo, Johannesburg 9.9.1969.
1(+1)-1 v E in SA 1913/14; (*1 v AIF 1919/20); (To E 1924).

+DONALD Allan Anthony, B Bloemfontein 20.10.1966.
72(+2)-(*1 v A 1986/87; *1 v E XI 1989/90); 1 v WI in WI 1991/92; 4 v I in SA 1992/93; 3 v SL in SL 1993/94; 3 v A in A 1993/94; 3 v A in SA 1993/94; 3 v E in E 1994; 1 v P in SA 1994/95; 1 v NZ in NZ 1994/95; 1 v Z in Z 1995/96; 5 v E in SA 1995/96; 2 v I in I 1996/97; 3 v I in SA 1996/97; 3 v A in SA 1996/97; 2 v P in P 1997/98; 2 v A in A 1997/98; 3 v P in SA 1997/98; 2 v SL in SA 1997/98; 5 v E in E 1998; 5 v WI in SA 1998/99; 2 v NZ in NZ 1998/99; 1 v Z in SA 1999/00; 1 v Z in Z 1999/00; 4 v E in SA 1999/00; 2 v I in I 1999/00; 2 v NZ in SA 2000/01; 1 v SL in SA 2000/01; 4 v WI in WI 2000/01; 2 v A in A 2001/02; 1 v A in SA 2001/02.

DOWER Robert Reid, B Kokstad, CC 4.6.1876. D Cape Town 15.9.1964.
1-v E in SA 1898/99.

DRAPER Ronald George, B Oudtshoorn, CP 24.12.1926.
2-v A in SA 1949/50.

DUCKWORTH Christopher Anthony Russell, B Que Que, Rhodesia 22.3.1933
2-(To E 1955); 2 v E in SA 1956/57; (To E 1960).

DUMBRILL Richard, B Wandsworth, London, England 19.11.1938.
5-3 v E in E 1965; 2 v A in SA 1966/67.

DUMINY Jacobus Petrus (Koos), B Bellville, CC 16.12.1897. D Groote Schuur Hospital, Observatory, Cape Town 31.1.1980.
3-2 v E in SA 1927/28; 1 v E in E 1929.

DUNELL Owen Robert, B Port Elizabeth 15.7.1856. D Lyons, France 21.10.1929.
2-v E in SA 1888/89.

DU PREEZ John Harcourt (Jackie), B Salisbury, Rhodesia 14.11.1942.
2-v A in SA 1966/67.

DU TOIT Jacobus Francois (Vlooi), B Jacobsdal, OFS 2.4.1869. D Lindley, OFS 10.7.1909.
1-v E in SA 1891/92.

DYER Dennis Victor, B Berea, Durban 2.5.1914. D Durban 16.6.1990.
3-v E in E 1947

+EKSTEEN Clive Edward, B Johannesburg 2.12.1966.
7-1 v SL in SL 1993/94; 2 v NZ in SA 1994/95; 1 v P in SA 1994/95; 1 v NZ in NZ 1994/95; 1 v E in SA 1995/96; 1 v I in I 1999/00.

ELGIE Michael Kelsey (Kim), B Berea, Durban 6.3.1933.
3-v NZ in SA 1961/62.

+ELWORTHY Steven, B Bulawayo, Rhodesia 23.2.1965.
4-1 v E in E 1998; 1 v NZ in NZ 1998/99; (To A 2001/02); 2 v SL in SA 2002/03.

ENDEAN William Russell, B Parkview, Johannesburg 31.5.1924. D Kingston Hospital, Kingston-upon-Thames, Surrey, England 28.6.2003.
28-1 v E in E 1951; 5 v A in A 1952/53; 2 v NZ in NZ 1952/53; 5 v NZ in SA 1953/54; 5 v E in E 1955; 5 v E in SA 1956/57; 5 v A in SA 1957/58.

FARRER William Stephen (Buster), B King William's Town, CP 8.12.1936.
6-3 v NZ in SA 1961/62; (To A 1963/64); 3 v NZ in NZ 1963/64.

FAULKNER George Aubrey, B Port Elizabeth 17.12.1881. D Walham Green, London, England 10.9.1930.
25-5 v E in SA 1905/06; 3 v E in E 1907; 5 v E in SA 1909/10; 5 v A in A 1910/11; 3 v E in E 1912; 3 v A in E 1912; 1 v E in E 1924.

FELLOWS-SMITH Jonathan Payn (Pom-Pom), B Berea, Durban 3.2.1932.
4-v E in E 1960.

FICHARDT Charles Gustav, B Bloemfontein 20.3.1870. D Rhodes Nursing Home, Muizenberg, Cape Town 30.5.1923.
2-1 v E in SA 1891/92; 1 v E in SA 1895/96.

FINLASON Charles Edward, B Camberwell, London, England 19.2.1860. D Surbiton, Surrey, England 31.7.1917.
1-v E in SA 1888/89.

FLOQUET Claude Eugene, B Aliwal North, CC 3.11.1884. D Port Elizabeth 22.11.1963.
1-v E in SA 1909/10.

FRANCIS Howard Henry, B Westbury, Clifton, Bristol, Gloucestershire, England 26.5.1868. D Sea Point, Cape Town 7.1.1936.
2-v E in SA 1898/99.

FRANCOIS Cyril Matthew (Froggy), B Lewisham, London, England 20.6.1897. D near Pretoria 26.5.1944.
5(+1)-5 v E in SA 1922/23; (*1 v SBJ 1924/25).

FRANK Charles Newton, B Jagersfontein, OFS 27.1.1891. D Bryanston, Johannesburg 25.12.1961.
3(+1)-(*1 v AIF 1919/20); 3 v A in SA 1921/22.

FRANK William Hughes Bowker, B King William's Town, CC 23.11.1872. D Durban 16.2.1945.
1-v E in SA 1895/96.

FULLER Edward Russell Henry, B Worcester, CP 2.8.1931.
7-2 v A in A 1952/53; 2 v NZ in NZ 1952/53; 2 v E in E 1955; 1 v A in SA 1957/58.

FULLERTON George Murray, B Kensington, Johannesburg 8.12.1922. D Rondebosch, Cape Town 19.11.2002.
7-2 v E in E 1947; 2 v A in SA 1949/50; 3 v E in E 1951.

FUNSTON Kenneth James, B Pretoria 3.12.1925. D Kenilworth, Cape Town 15.4.2005.
18-5 v A in A 1952/53; 2 v NZ in NZ 1952/53; 3 v NZ in SA 1953/54; 3 v E in SA 1956/57; 5 v A in SA 1957/58.

GAMSY Dennis, B Glenwood, Durban 17.2.1940.
2-(To E 1965); 2 v A in SA 1969/70.

+#GIBBS Herschelle Herman, B Green Point, Cape Town 23.2.1974.
79(+1)-2 v I in I 1996/97; 1 v I in SA 1996/97; 1 v A in SA 1996/97; 2 v A in A 1997/98; 1 v P in SA 1997/98; 4 v WI in SA 1998/99; 3 v NZ in NZ 1998/99; 5 v E in SA 1999/00; 2 v I in I 1999/00; 2 v SL in SA 2000/01; 5 v WI in WI 2000/01; 2 v Z in Z 2001/02; 2 v I in SA 2001/02; (*1 v I 2001/02); 3 v A in A 2001/02; 3 v A in SA 2001/02; 2 v B in SA 2002/03; 1 v SL in SA 2002/03; 2 v P in SA 2002/03; 2 v B in B 2002/03; 5 v E in E 2003; 2 v P in P 2003/04; 4 v WI in SA 2003/04; 3 v NZ in NZ 2003/04; 1 v SL in SL 2004; 4 v E in SA 2004/05; 2 v Z in SA 2004/05; 4 v WI in WI 2004/05; 3 v A in A 2005/06; 3 v A in SA 2005/06; 1 v NZ in SA 2005/06; 2 v SL in SL 2006.

GLEESON Robert Anthony, B Port Elizabeth 6.12.1873. D Port Elizabeth 27.9.1919.
1-v E in SA 1895/96.

GLOVER George Keyworth, B Wakefield, Yorkshire, England 13.5.1870. D Kimberley 15.11.1938.
1-(To E 1894); 1 v E in SA 1895/96.

GODDARD Trevor Leslie, B Durban 1.8.1931.
41-5 v E in E 1955; 5 v E in SA 1956/57; 5 v A in SA 1957/58; 5 v E in E 1960; 5 v A in A 1963/64; 3 v NZ in NZ 1963/64; 5 v E in SA 1964/65; 5 v A in SA 1966/67; 3 v A in SA 1969/70.

GORDON Norman (Mobil), B Boksburg, Transvaal 6.8.1911.
5-v E in SA 1938/39.

GRAHAM Robert, B Grahamstown, CC 16.9.1877. D Upperton, Eastbourne, Sussex, England 21.4.1946.
2-v E in SA 1898/99; (To E 1901).

GRIEVESON Ronald Eustace, B Johannesburg 24.8.1909. D Waverley Gardens Nursing Home, Waverley, Johannesburg 24.7.1998.
2-v E in SA 1938/39.

GRIFFIN Geoffrey Merton, B Greytown, Natal 12.6.1939.
2-v E in E 1960.

HALL Alfred Ewart, B Bolton, Lancashire, England 23.1.1896. D South Rand Hospital, The Hill, Johannesburg 1.1.1964.
7(+5)-4 v E in SA 1922/23; (*5 v SBJ 1924/25); 2 v E in SA 1927/28; 1 v E in SA 1930/31.

+#**HALL** Andrew James, B Johannesburg 31.7.1975.
19-(To SL 2000); 2 v A in SA 2001/02; 2 v SL in SA 2002/03; (To B 2002/03); 4 v E in E 2003; (To P 2003/04); 2 v WI in SA 2003/04; 2 v I in I 2004/05; 2 v E in SA 2004/05; 1 v WI in WI 2004/05; 1 v A in SA 2005/06; 1 v NZ in SA 2005/06; 2 v SL in SL 2006.

HALL Glen Gordon, B Pretoria 24.5.1938. D Ramsgate, Natal 26.6.1987.
1-v E in SA 1964/65.

HALLIWELL Ernest Austin (Barberton), B Drayton Green, Ealing, Middlesex, England 7.9.1864. D Hillbrow Nursing Home, Johannesburg 2.10.1919.
8-1 v E in SA 1891/92; (To E 1894); 3 v E in SA 1895/96; 1 v E in SA 1898/99; (To E 1901); 3 v A in SA 1902/03; (To E 1904).

HALSE Clive Gray, B Empangeni, Natal (Zululand) 28.2.1935. D Highway Hospice, Sherwood, Durban 28.5.2002.
3-v A in A 1963/64.

HANDS Philip Albert Myburgh (Pam), B Claremont, Cape Town 18.3.1890. D Parys, OFS 27.4.1951.
7(+2)-5 v E in SA 1913/14; (*2 v AIF 1919/20); 1 v A in SA 1921/22; 1 v E in E 1924.

HANDS Reginald Harry Myburgh, B Claremont, Cape Town 26.7.1888. D near Bruay, Bethune, France (War) 20.4.1918.
1-v E in SA 1913/14.

HANLEY Martin Andrew, B Aliwal North, CP 10.11.1918. D Bishopscourt, Cape Town 2.6.2000.
1-v E in SA 1948/49.

HARRIS Terence Anthony (Tony), B Kimberley 27.8.1916. D Plettenberg Bay, CP 7.3.1993.
3-2 v E in E 1947; 1 v E in SA 1948/49.

HARTIGAN Gerald Patrick Desmond, B King William's Town, CC 30.12.1884. D Addington Hospital, Durban 7.1.1955.
5-1 v A in E 1912; 1 v E in E 1912; 3 v E in SA 1913/14.

HARVEY Robert Lyon, B Swinburne, OFS 14.9.1911. D Kloof, KZN 20.7.2000.
2-v A in SA 1935/36.

HATHORN Christopher Maitland Howard (Tottie), B Pietermaritzburg 7.4.1878. D Parktown West, Johannesburg 17.5.1920.
12-(To E 1901); 3 v A in SA 1902/03; (To E 1904); 5 v E in SA 1905/06; 3 v E in E 1907; 1 v A in A 1910/11.

+**HAYWARD** Mornantau (Nantie), B Uitenhage, CP 6.3.1977.
16(+1)-(To E 1998); 3 v E in SA 1999/00; 1 v I in I 1999/00; 2 v SL in SL 2000; 2 v I in SA 2001/02; (*1 v I 2001/02); 2 v A in A 2001/02; 2 v B in SA 2002/03; 2 v P in SA 2002/03; 2 v SL in SL 2004.

HEARNE Frank, B Ealing, Middlesex, England 23.11.1858. D Groote Schuur Hospital, Observatory, Cape Town 14.7.1949.
4-1 v E in SA 1891/92; (To E 1894); 3 v E in SA 1895/96. (Note: Also 2-E v SA in SA 1888/89).

HEARNE George Alfred Lawrence, B Catford, London, England 27.3.1888. D Barberton, Transvaal 13.11.1978.
3(+1)-(*1 v AIF 1919/20); 2 v E in SA 1922/23; 1 v E in E 1924.

HEINE Peter Samuel, B Winterton, Natal 28.6.1928. D Pretoria East Hospital, Moreleta Park, Pretoria 4.2.2005.
14-4 v E in E 1955; 5 v E in SA 1956/57; 4 v A in SA 1957/58; 1 v NZ in SA 1961/62.

+**HENDERSON** Claude William, B Worcester, CP 14.6.1972.
7-2 v Z in Z 2001/02; 3 v A in A 2001/02; 2 v B in SA 2002/03.

+**HENRY** Omar, B Stellenbosch, CP 23.1.1952.
3(+2)-(*2 v A 1986/87); (To WI 1991/92); 3 v I in SA 1992/93.

HIME Charles Frederick William, B Bermuda 24.10.1869. D Pietermaritzburg 6.12.1940.
1-v E in SA 1895/96.

+**HUDSON** Andrew Charles, B Eshowe, Natal (Zululand) 17.3.1965.
35-1 v WI in WI 1991/92; 4 v I in SA 1992/93; 3 v SL in SL 1993/94; 3 v A in A 1993/94; 3 v A in SA 1993/94; 2 v E in E 1994; 2 v NZ in SA 1994/95; 1 v NZ in NZ 1994/95; 1 v Z in Z

1995/96; 5 v E in SA 1995/96; 3 v I in I 1996/97; 3 v I in SA 1996/97; 1 v A in SA 1996/97; (To P 1997/98); 3 v P in SA 1997/98.

HUTCHINSON Philip, B West Dean, Sussex, England 25.1.1862. D Durban 30.9.1925.
2-v E in SA 1888/89.

IRONSIDE David Ernest James, B Lourenco Marques, Mozambique 2.5.1925. D Heartlands Hospital, Bordesley Green, Birmingham, Warwickshire, England 21.8.2005.
3-v NZ in SA 1953/54.

IRVINE Brian Lee, B Durban 9.3.1944.
4-v A in SA 1969/70.

+JACK Steven Douglas, B Durban 4.8.1970.
2-v NZ in SA 1994/95; (To NZ 1994/95).

JOHNSON Clement Lecky (Boy), B Carbury, County Kildare, Ireland 31.3.1871. D Maraisburg, Roodepoort, Transvaal 31.5.1908.
1-(To E 1894); 1 v E in SA 1895/96.

+#KALLIS Jacques Henry, B Pinelands, CP 16.10.1975.
101(+1)-2 v E in SA 1995/96; 3 v A in SA 1996/97; 1 v P in P 1997/98; 3 v A in A 1997/98; 3 v P in SA 1997/98; 2 v SL in SA 1997/98; 5 v E in E 1998; 5 v WI in SA 1998/99; 3 v NZ in NZ 1998/99; 1 v Z in SA 1999/00; 1 v Z in Z 1999/00; 5 v E in SA 1999/00; 2 v I in I 1999/00; 3 v SL in SL 2000; 3 v NZ in SA 2000/01; 3 v SL in SA 2000/01; 5 v WI in WI 2000/01; 2 v Z in Z 2001/02; 2 v I in SA 2001/02; (*1 v I 2001/02); 3 v A in A 2001/02; 3 v A in SA 2001/02; 2 v B in SA 2002/03; 2 v SL in SA 2002/03; 2 v P in SA 2002/03; 3 v E in E 2003; 2 v P in P 2003/04; 4 v WI in SA 2003/04; 3 v NZ in NZ 2003/04; 2 v SL in SL 2004; 2 v I in I 2004/05; 5 v E in SA 2004/05; 2 v Z in SA 2004/05; 4 v WI in WI 2004/05; 2 v A in A 2005/06; 3 v A in SA 2005/06; 3 v NZ in SA 2005/06. (Note: Also 1-World XI v A in A 2005/06).

KEITH Headley James, B Dundee, Natal 25.10.1927. D Pennington, KZN 17.11.1997.
8-1 v A in A 1952/53; 4 v E in E 1955; 3 v E in SA 1956/57.

+#KEMP Justin Miles, B Queenstown, CP 2.10.1977.
4-1 v SL in SA 2000/01; 2 v WI in WI 2000/01; (To Z 2001/02); 1 v A in A 2005/06.

KEMPIS Gustav Adolph, B Port Elizabeth 4.8.1865. D Chiloane Island, Mozambique 19.5.1890.
1-v E in SA 1888/89.

+KIRSTEN Gary, B Cape Town 23.11.1967.
101(+1)-3 v A in A 1993/94; 3 v A in SA 1993/94; 3 v E in E 1994; 3 v NZ in SA 1994/95; 1 v P in SA 1994/95; 1 v NZ in NZ 1994/95; 1 v Z in Z 1995/96; 5 v E in SA 1995/96; 3 v I in I 1996/97; 3 v I in SA 1996/97; 3 v A in SA 1996/97; 3 v P in P 1997/98; 3 v A in A 1997/98; 3 v P in SA 1997/98; 2 v SL in SA 1997/98; 5 v E in E 1998; 5 v WI in SA 1998/99; 3 v NZ in NZ 1998/99; 5 v E in SA 1999/00; 2 v I in I 1999/00; 3 v SL in SL 2000; 3 v NZ in SA 2000/01; 2 v SL in SA 2000/01; 5 v WI in WI 2000/01; 2 v Z in Z 2001/02; 2 v I in SA 2001/02; (*1 v I 2001/02); 3 v A in A 2001/02; 3 v A in SA 2001/02; 2 v B in SA 2002/03; 2 v SL in SA 2002/03; 2 v P in SA 2002/03; 4 v E in E 2003; 2 v P in P 2003/04; 3 v WI in SA 2003/04; 3 v NZ in NZ 2003/04.

+KIRSTEN Peter Noel, B Pietermaritzburg 14.5.1955.
12(+19)-(*3 v E XI 1981/82; *2 v SL 1982/83; *2 v WI 1982/83; *4 v WI 1983/84; *3 v A 1985/86; *4 v A 1986/87; *1 v E XI 1989/90); 1 v WI in WI 1991/92; 4 v I in SA 1992/93; 1 v A in A 1993/94; 3 v A in SA 1993/94; 3 v E in E 1994.

+KLUSENER Lance, B Durban 4.9.1971.
49(+1)-2 v I in I 1996/97; 3 v I in SA 1996/97; 2 v A in SA 1996/97; 2 v P in P 1997/98; 2 v A in A 1997/98; 2 v P in SA 1997/98; 3 v E in E 1998; 1 v WI in SA 1998/99; 3 v NZ in NZ 1998/99; 1 v Z in SA 1999/00; 1 v Z in Z 1999/00; 5 v E in SA 1999/00; 2 v I in I 1999/00; 3 v SL in SL 2000; 3 v NZ in SA 2000/01; 2 v SL in SA 2000/01; 5 v WI in WI 2000/01; 2 v Z in Z 2001/02; 2 v I in SA 2001/02; (*1 v I 2001/02); 2 v A in A 2001/02; 1 v SL in SL 2004.

KOTZE Johannes Jacobus (Kodgee) (Boerjong), B Berg River, Hopefield District, CC 7.8.1879. D Rondebosch, Cape Town 7.7.1931.
3-(To E 1901); 2 v A in SA 1902/03; (To E 1904); 1 v E in E 1907.

+**KUIPER** Adrian Paul, B Johannesburg 24.8.1959.
1(+7)-(*2 v E XI 1981/82; *2 v SL 1982/83; *2 v WI 1983/84; *1 v E XI 1989/90); 1 v WI in WI 1991/92.
KUYS Frederick, B George, CC 21.3.1870. D Oudtshoorn, CP 12.9.1953.
1-v E in SA 1898/99.
LANCE Herbert Roy (Tiger), B Pretoria 6.6.1940.
13-2 v NZ in SA 1961/62; 3 v E in E 1965; 5 v A in SA 1966/67; 3 v A in SA 1969/70.
+#**LANGEVELDT** Charl Kenneth, B Stellenbosch, CP 17.12.1974.
6-(To Z 2001/02); (To P 2003/04); 1 v E in SA 2004/05; 2 v Z in SA 2004/05; 1 v WI in WI 2004/05; 2 v A in A 2005/06.
LANGTON Arthur Chudleigh Beaumont (Chud), B Pietermaritzburg 2.3.1912. D near Maiduguri, Nigeria (War) 27.11.1942.
15-5 v E in E 1935; 5 v A in SA 1935/36; 5 v E in SA 1938/39.
LAWRENCE Godfrey Bernard (Goofy), B Salisbury, Rhodesia 31.3.1932.
5-v NZ in SA 1961/62.
LE ROUX Frederick Louis, B Somerset East, CC 5.2.1882. D Durban 22.9.1963.
1-v E in SA 1913/14.
LEWIS Percy Tyson (Plum), B Cape Town 2.10.1884. D Durban 30.1.1976.
1-v E in SA 1913/14.
+**LIEBENBERG** Gerhardus Frederick Johannes, B Upington, CP 7.4.1972.
5-(To E 1994); 1 v SL in SA 1997/98; 4 v E in E 1998.
LINDSAY Denis Thomson, B Benoni, Transvaal 4.9.1939. D Morningside Clinic, Sandton, Johannesburg 30.11.2005.
19-3 v A in A 1963/64; 3 v NZ in NZ 1963/64; 3 v E in SA 1964/65; 3 v E in E 1965; 5 v A in SA 1966/67; 2 v A in SA 1969/70.
LINDSAY John Dixon, B Barkly East, CC 8.9.1908. D Benoni, Transvaal 31.8.1990.
3-v E in E 1947.
LINDSAY Nevil Vernon, B Harrismith, OFS 30.7.1886. D Pietermaritzburg 2.2.1976.
1(+1)-1 v A in SA 1921/22; (*1 v SBJ 1924/25).
LING William Victor Stone, B Kimberley 3.10.1891. D State Mines, Brakpan, Transvaal 26.9.1960.
6(+3)-3 v A in SA 1921/22; 3 v E in SA 1922/23; (*3 v SBJ 1924/25).
LLEWELLYN Charles Bennett (Buck), B Pietermaritzburg 26.9.1876. D Chertsey, Surrey, England 7.6.1964.
15-1 v E in SA 1895/96; 1 v E in SA 1898/99; (To E 1901); 3 v A in SA 1902/03; (To E 1904); 5 v A in A 1910/11; 2 v A in E 1912; 3 v E in E 1912.
LUNDIE Eric Balfour (Bill), B Willowvale, CC (Transkei) 15.3.1888. D near Passchendaele, Belgium (War) 12.9.1917.
1-v E in SA 1913/14.
MACAULAY Michael John, B Durban 19.4.1939.
1-v E in SA 1964/65; (To E 1965).
MANN Norman Bertram Fleetwood (Tufty), B Benoni, Transvaal 28.12.1920. D Princess Nursing Home, Hillbrow, Johannesburg 31.7.1952.
19-5 v E in E 1947; 5 v E in SA 1948/49; 5 v A in SA 1949/50; 4 v E in E 1951.
MANSELL Percy Neville Frank, B St George's, Shropshire, England 16.3.1920. D Somerset West, WC 9.5.1995.
13-2 v E in E 1951; 5 v A in A 1952/53; 2 v NZ in NZ 1952/53; 4 v E in E 1955.
MARKHAM Lawrence Anderson (Fish), B Mbabane, Swaziland 12.9.1924. D Pietermaritzburg 5.8.2000.
1-v E in SA 1948/49.
MARX Waldemar Frederick Eric, B Johannesburg 4.7.1895. D Durban 2.6.1974.
3-v A in SA 1921/22.
+**MATTHEWS** Craig Russell, B Cape Town 15.2.1965.
18-3 v I in SA 1992/93; 2 v A in A 1993/94; 3 v A in SA 1993/94; 3 v E in E 1994; 2 v NZ in SA 1994/95; 1 v NZ in NZ 1994/95; 1 v Z in Z 1995/96; 3 v E in SA 1995/96.

McCARTHY Cuan Neil, B Pietermaritzburg 24.3.1929. D Johannesburg 14.8.2000.
15-5 v E in SA 1948/49; 5 v A in SA 1949/50; 5 v E in E 1951.

McGLEW Derrick John (Jackie), B Pietermaritzburg 11.3.1929. D Craighall Park, Johannesburg 9.6.1998.
34-2 v E in E 1951; 4 v A in A 1952/53; 2 v NZ in NZ 1952/53; 5 v NZ in SA 1953/54; 5 v E in E 1955; 1 v E in SA 1956/57; 5 v A in SA 1957/58; 5 v E in E 1960; 5 v NZ in SA 1961/62.

+#McKENZIE Neil Douglas, B Johannesburg 24.11.1975.
41(+1)-3 v SL in SL 2000; 3 v NZ in SA 2000/01; 3 v SL in SA 2000/01; 5 v WI in WI 2000/01; 2 v Z in Z 2001/02; 2 v I in SA 2001/02; (*1 v I 2001/02); 3 v A in A 2001/02; 3 v A in SA 2001/02; 2 v SL in SA 2002/03; 2 v P in SA 2002/03; 2 v B in B 2002/03; 3 v E in E 2003; 2 v P in P 2003/04; 4 v WI in SA 2003/04; 2 v NZ in NZ 2003/04.

McKINNON Atholl Henry, B Port Elizabeth 20.8.1932. D Durban 2.12.1983.
8-1 v E in E 1960; 1 v NZ in SA 1961/62; 2 v E in SA 1964/65; 2 v E in E 1965; 2 v A in SA 1966/67.

McLEAN Roy Alastair, B Pietermaritzburg 9.7.1930.
40-3 v E in E 1951; 5 v A in A 1952/53; 2 v NZ in NZ 1952/53; 4 v NZ in SA 1953/54; 5 v E in E 1955; 5 v E in SA 1956/57; 4 v A in SA 1957/58; 5 v E in E 1960; 5 v NZ in SA 1961/62; 2 v E in SA 1964/65.

+McMILLAN Brian Mervin, B Welkom, OFS 22.12.1963.
38(+4)-(*3 v A 1986/87; *1 v E XI 1989/90); 4 v I in SA 1992/93; 2 v SL in SL 1993/94; 1 v A in A 1993/94; 3 v A in SA 1993/94; 3 v E in E 1994; 3 v NZ in SA 1994/95; 1 v P in SA 1994/95; 1 v Z in Z 1995/96; 5 v E in SA 1995/96; 3 v I in I 1996/97; 3 v I in SA 1996/97; 2 v A in SA 1996/97; 3 v P in P 1997/98; 3 v A in A 1997/98; 1 v E in E 1998.

McMILLAN Quintin, B Germiston, Transvaal 23.6.1904. D Robinson Hospital, Randfontein, Transvaal 3.7.1948.
13-2 v E in E 1929; 5 v E in SA 1930/31; 4 v A in A 1931/32; 2 v NZ in NZ 1931/32.

MEINTJES Douglas James, B Pretoria 9.6.1890. D Johannesburg 17.7.1979.
2(+3)-(*2 v AIF 1919/20); 2 v E in SA 1922/23; (To E 1924); (*1 v SBJ 1924/25).

MELLE Michael George, B Forest Town, Johannesburg 3.6.1930. D Betty's Bay, WC 28.12.2003.
7-2 v A in SA 1949/50; 1 v E in E 1951; 4 v A in A 1952/53; (To NZ 1952/53).

MELVILLE Alan, B Carnarvon, CC 19.5.1910. D Sabie, Transvaal 18.4.1983.
11-5 v E in SA 1938/39; 5 v E in E 1947; 1 v E in SA 1948/49.

MIDDLETON James (Bonnor), B Chester-le-Street, County Durham, England 30.9.1865. D Newlands, Cape Town 23.12.1913.
6-(To E 1894); 2 v E in SA 1895/96; 2 v E in SA 1898/99; 2 v A in SA 1902/03; (To E 1904).

MILLS Charles Henry, B Peckham, London, England 26.11.1867. D Southwark, London, England 26.7.1948.
1-v E in SA 1891/92; (To E 1894).

MILTON William Henry, B Little Marlow, Buckinghamshire, England 3.12.1854. D Cannes, France 6.3.1930.
3-2 v E in SA 1888/89; 1 v E in SA 1891/92.

MITCHELL Bruce, B Ferreira Deep Gold Mine, Johannesburg 8.1.1909. D Abbotsford, Johannesburg 2.7.1995.
42-5 v E in E 1929; 5 v E in SA 1930/31; 5 v A in A 1931/32; 2 v NZ in NZ 1931/32; 5 v E in E 1935; 5 v A in SA 1935/36; 5 v E in SA 1938/39; 5 v E in E 1947; 5 v E in SA 1948/49.

MITCHELL Frank, B Market Weighton, Yorkshire, England 13.8.1872. D Blackheath, Kent, England 11.10.1935.
3-(To E 1904); 2 v A in E 1912; 1 v E in E 1912. (Note: Also 2-E v SA in SA 1898/99).

MORKEL Denijs Paul Beck, B Plumstead, Cape Town 25.1.1906. D Nottingham, Nottinghamshire, England 6.10.1980.
16-5 v E in SA 1927/28; 5 v E in E 1929; 5 v A in A 1931/32; 1 v NZ in NZ 1931/32.

MURRAY Anton Ronald Andrew, B Grahamstown, CP 30.4.1922. D Cape Town 17.4.1995.
10-4 v A in A 1952/53; 2 v NZ in NZ 1952/53; 4 v NZ in SA 1953/54; (To E 1955).

+#**NEL** Andre, B Germiston, Transvaal 15.7.1977.
23-(To WI 2000/01).; 2 v Z in Z 2001/02; 1 v A in SA 2001/02; 1 v P in P 2003/04; 4 v WI in SA 2003/04; 2 v NZ in NZ 2003/04; (To SL 2004); 1 v E in SA 2004/05; 1 v Z in SA 2004/05; 3 v WI in WI 2004/05; 3 v A in A 2005/06; 3 v A in SA 2005/06; 1 v NZ in SA 2005/06; 1 v SL in SL 2006.

NEL John Desmond (Jack), B Cape Town 10.7.1928.
6-5 v A in SA 1949/50; 1 v A in SA 1957/58.

NEWBERRY Claude, B Port Elizabeth 1889. D France (War) aged 27, 1.8.1916.
4-v E in SA 1913/14.

NEWSON Edward Serrurier (Bob), B Sea Point, Cape Town 2.12.1910. D Durban 24.4.1988.
3-1 v E in SA 1930/31; 2 v E in SA 1938/39.

NGAM Mfuneko, B Middledrift, CP 29.1.1979.
3-1 v NZ in SA 2000/01; 2 v SL in SA 2000/01.

NICHOLSON Frank (Nipper), B Millom, Cumberland, England 17.9.1909. D Port Elizabeth 30.7.1982.
4-v A in SA 1935/36.

NICOLSON John Fairless William, B Durban 19.7.1899. D Kilkeel Hospital, County Down, Northern Ireland 13.12.1935.
3-v E in SA 1927/28.

NORTON Norman Ogilvie (Pompey), B Grahamstown, CC 11.5.1881. D Mater Dei Nursing Home, Southernwood, East London 27.6.1968.
1-v E in SA 1909/10.

NOURSE Arthur Dudley, B Durban 12.11.1910. D Durban 14.8.1981.
34-4 v E in E 1935; 5 v A in SA 1935/36; 5 v E in SA 1938/39; 5 v E in E 1947; 5 v E in SA 1948/49; 5 v A in SA 1949/50; 5 v E in E 1951.

NOURSE Arthur William (Dave), B South Norwood, Surrey, England 25.1.1879. D Provincial Hospital, Glendinningvale, Port Elizabeth 8.7.1948.
45(+7)-3 v A in SA 1902/03; 5 v E in SA 1905/06; 3 v E in E 1907; 5 v E in SA 1909/10; 5 v A in A 1910/11; 3 v A in E 1912; 3 v E in E 1912; 5 v E in SA 1913/14; (*2 v AIF 1919/20); 3 v A in SA 1921/22; 5 v E in SA 1922/23; 5 v E in E 1924; (*5 v SBJ 1924/25).

+#**NTINI** Makhaya, B Mdingi, near King William's Town, CP 6.7.1977.
69(+1)-(To A 1997/98); 2 v SL in SA 1997/98; 2 v E in E 1998; 1 v SL in SL 2000; 3 v NZ in SA 2000/01; 3 v SL in SA 2000/01; 4 v WI in WI 2000/01; 2 v Z in Z 2001/02; 2 v I in SA 2001/02; (*1 v I 2001/02); 1 v A in A 2001/02; 3 v A in SA 2001/02; 2 v B in SA 2002/03; 2 v SL in SA 2002/03; 2 v P in SA 2002/03; 2 v B in B 2002/03; 5 v E in E 2003; 2 v P in P 2003/04; 4 v WI in SA 2003/04; 3 v NZ in NZ 2003/04; 2 v SL in SL 2004; 2 v I in I 2004/05; 5 v E in SA 2004/05; 1 v Z in SA 2004/05; 4 v WI in WI 2004/05; 2 v A in A 2005/06; 3 v A in SA 2005/06; 3 v NZ in SA 2005/06; 2 v SL in SL 2006.

NUPEN Eiulf Peter (Buster), B Johannesburg 1.1.1902. D Lady Dudley Nursing Home, Johannesburg 29.1.1977.
17(+4)-2 v A in SA 1921/22; 4 v E in SA 1922/23; 2 v E in E 1924; (*4 v SBJ 1924/25); 5 v E in SA 1927/28; 3 v E in SA 1930/31; 1 v A in SA 1935/36.

OCHSE Arthur Edward (Okey), B Graaff-Reinet, CC 11.3.1870. D Middle Farm, Petit Puits, Messines Ridge, France (War) 11.4.1918.
2-v E in SA 1888/89.

OCHSE Arthur Lennox, B Graaff-Reinet, CC 11.10.1898. D Eldorado Farm, near Middelburg, CP 5.5.1949.
3-1 v E in SA 1927/28; 2 v E in E 1929.

O'LINN Sidney (Micky), B Oudtshoorn, CP 5.5.1927.
7-5 v E in E 1960; 2 v NZ in SA 1961/62.

+**ONTONG** Justin Lee, B Paarl, CP 4.1.1980.
2-1 v A in A 2001/02; 1 v I in I 2004/05.

OWEN-SMITH Harold Geoffrey Owen (Tuppy), B Rondebosch, Cape Town 18.2.1909. D Rosebank, Cape Town 28.2.1990.
5-v E in E 1929.

PALM Archibald William, B Rondebosch, Cape Town 8.6.1901. D Somerset West, CP 17.8.1966.
1-v E in SA 1927/28.

PARKER George Macdonald, B Cape Town 27.5.1899. D Thredbo, New South Wales, Australia 1.5.1969.
2-v E in E 1924.

PARKIN Durant Clifford (Dante), B Port Elizabeth 20.2.1873. D Sangster's Farm (Eagle's Crag), Albany, CP 20.3.1936.
1-v E in SA 1891/92; (To E 1894).

PARTRIDGE Joseph Titus, B Bulawayo, Rhodesia 9.12.1932. D Harare, Zimbabwe 6.6.1988.
11-5 v A in A 1963/64; 3 v NZ in NZ 1963/64; 3 v E in SA 1964/65.

PEARSE Charles Ormerod Cato (Ormy), B Pietermaritzburg 10.10.1884. D Durban 7.5.1953.
3-v A in A 1910/11.

PEGLER Sidney James, B Durban 28.7.1888. D Harewood Nursing Home, Plumstead, Cape Town 10.9.1972.
16-1 v E in SA 1909/10; 4 v A in A 1910/11; 3 v A in E 1912; 3 v E in E 1912; 5 v E in E 1924.

+#PETERSON Robin John, B Port Elizabeth 4.8.1979.
5-1 v B in B 2002/03; 1 v E in E 2003; 1 v P in P 2003/04; 1 v WI in SA 2003/04; (To SL 2004); 1 v I in I 2004/05.

PITHEY Anthony John, B Umtali, Rhodesia 17.7.1933.
17-3 v E in SA 1956/57; 2 v E in E 1960; 4 v A in A 1963/64; 3 v NZ in NZ 1963/64; 5 v E in SA 1964/65.

PITHEY David Bartlett, B Salisbury, Rhodesia 4.10.1936.
8-3 v A in A 1963/64; 3 v NZ in NZ 1963/64; 2 v A in SA 1966/67.

PLIMSOLL Jack Bruce, B Kalk Bay, Cape Town 27.10.1917. D Cape Town 11.11.1999.
1-v E in E 1947.

POLLOCK Peter Maclean, B Pietermaritzburg 30.6.1941.
28-3 v NZ in SA 1961/62; 5 v A in A 1963/64; 3 v NZ in NZ 1963/64; 5 v E in SA 1964/65; 3 v E in E 1965; 5 v A in SA 1966/67; 4 v A in SA 1969/70.

POLLOCK Robert Graeme, B Durban 27.2.1944.
23(+16)-5 v A in A 1963/64; 1 v NZ in NZ 1963/64; 5 v E in SA 1964/65; 3 v E in E 1965; 5 v A in SA 1966/67; 4 v A in SA 1969/70; (*3 v E XI 1981/82; *2 v SL 1982/83; *2 v WI 1982/83; *4 v WI 1983/84; *3 v A 1985/86; *2 v A 1986/87).

+#POLLOCK Shaun Maclean, B Port Elizabeth 16.7.1973.
102(+1)-5 v E in SA 1995/96; 3 v I in SA 1996/97; 2 v A in SA 1996/97; 3 v P in P 1997/98; 3 v A in A 1997/98; 3 v P in SA 1997/98; 2 v SL in SA 1997/98; 4 v E in E 1998; 5 v WI in SA 1998/99; 3 v NZ in NZ 1998/99; 1 v Z in SA 1999/00; 1 v Z in Z 1999/00; 5 v E in SA 1999/00; 2 v I in I 1999/00; 3 v SL in SL 2000; 3 v NZ in SA 2000/01; 3 v SL in SA 2000/01; 5 v WI in WI 2000/01; 2 v Z in Z 2001/02; 2 v I in SA 2001/02; (*1 v I 2001/02); 3 v A in A 2001/02; 1 v B in SA 2002/03; 2 v SL in SA 2002/03; 2 v P in SA 2002/03; 2 v B in B 2002/03; 4 v E in E 2003; 2 v P in P 2003/04; 4 v WI in SA 2003/04; 3 v NZ in NZ 2003/04; 2 v SL in SL 2004; 2 v I in I 2004/05; 5 v E in SA 2004/05; 1 v Z in SA 2004/05; 1 v WI in WI 2004/05; 3 v A in A 2005/06; 2 v A in SA 2005/06; 2 v NZ in SA 2005/06; 1 v SL in SL 2006.

POORE Robert Montagu, B Carysfort House, Dublin, Ireland 20.3.1866. D Boscombe, Hampshire, England 14.7.1938.
3-v E in SA 1895/96.

POTHECARY James Edward, B Cape Town 6.12.1933.
3-v E in E 1960.

POWELL Albert William (Bertie), B Kimberley 18.7.1873. D Cape Town 11.9.1948.
1-v E in SA 1898/99.

PRETORIUS Dewald, B Pretoria 6.12.1977.
4-1 v A in SA 2001/02; 3 v E in E 2003.
+#PRINCE Ashwell Gavin, B Port Elizabeth 28.5.1977.
23-3 v A in SA 2001/02; 2 v B in SA 2002/03; 2 v SL in SA 2002/03; 2 v Z in SA 2004/05; 3 v WI in WI 2004/05; 3 v A in A 2005/06; 3 v A in SA 2005/06; 3 v NZ in SA 2005/06; 2 v SL in SL 2006.
PRINCE Charles Frederick Henry, B Boshof, OFS 11.9.1874. D Wynberg, Cape Town 2.2.1949.
1-v E in SA 1898/99; (To E 1901).
+PRINGLE Meyrick Wayne, B Adelaide, CP 22.6.1966.
4-1 v WI in WI 1991/92; 2 v I in SA 1992/93; 1 v E in SA 1995/96.
PROCTER Michael John, B Durban 15.9.1946.
7(+1)-3 v A in SA 1966/67; 4 v A in SA 1969/70; (*1 v E XI 1981/82).
PROMNITZ Henry Louis Ernest, B near King William's Town, CC 23.2.1904. D East London 7.9.1983.
2-v E in SA 1927/28.
QUINN Neville Anthony, B Tweefontein, OFS 21.2.1908. D Kenilworth, Kimberley 5.8.1934.
12-4 v E in E 1929; 1 v E in SA 1930/31, 5 v A in A 1931/32; 2 v NZ in NZ 1931/32.
REID Norman, B Newlands, Cape Town 26.12.1890. D Newlands, Cape Town 6.6.1947.
1-v A in SA 1921/22.
+RHODES Jonathan Neil (Jonty), B Pietermaritzburg 27.7.1969.
52-(To WI 1991/92); 4 v I in SA 1992/93; 3 v SL in SL 1993/94; 3 v A in A 1993/94; 3 v A in SA 1993/94; 3 v E in E 1994; 3 v NZ in SA 1994/95; 1 v P in SA 1994/95; 1 v NZ in NZ 1994/95; 1 v Z in Z 1995/96; 5 v E in SA 1995/96; 1 v I in I 1996/97; 1 v A in SA 1996/97; 1 v P in P 1997/98; 1 v A in A 1997/98; 5 v E in E 1998; 5 v WI in SA 1998/99; 3 v NZ in NZ 1998/99; 1 v Z in SA 1999/00; 1 v Z in Z 1999/00; 3 v E in SA 1999/00; 3 v SL in SL 2000.
RICHARDS Alfred Renfrew, B Grahamstown, CC 14.12.1867. D Salisbury Hospital, Salisbury, Rhodesia 9.1.1904.
1-v E in SA 1895/96.
RICHARDS Barry Anderson, B Morningside, Durban 21.7.1945.
4(+6)-4 v A in SA 1969/70; (*3 v E XI 1981/82; *1 v SL 1982/83, *2 v WI 1982/83).
RICHARDS William Henry Matthews (Dicky), B Grahamstown, CC 26.3.1862. D Wynberg, Cape Town 4.1.1903.
1-v E in SA 1888/89.
+RICHARDSON David John, B Johannesburg 16.9.1959.
42(+5)-(*1 v WI 1983/84; *4 v A 1986/87); 1 v WI in WI 1991/92; 4 v I in SA 1992/93; 3 v SL in SL 1993/94; 3 v A in A 1993/94; 3 v A in SA 1993/94; 3 v E in E 1994; 3 v NZ in SA 1994/95; 1 v P in SA 1994/95; 1 v NZ in NZ 1994/95; 1 v Z in Z 1995/96; 5 v E in SA 1995/96; 3 v I in I 1996/97; 3 v I in SA 1996/97; 3 v A in SA 1996/97; 2 v P in P 1997/98; 3 v A in A 1997/98.
ROBERTSON John Benjamin, B Wynberg, Cape Town 5.6.1906. D Cape Town 5.7.1985.
3-v A in SA 1935/36.
ROSE-INNES Albert, B Port Elizabeth 16.2.1868. D East London 22.11.1946.
2-v E in SA 1888/89.
ROUTLEDGE Thomas William, B Liverpool, Lancashire, England 18.4.1867. D Billingham, County Durham, England 9.5.1927.
4-1 v E in SA 1891/92; (To E 1894); 3 v E in SA 1895/96.
ROWAN Athol Matthew Burchell, B Kensington, Johannesburg 7.2.1921. D Hermanus, WC 22.2.1998.
15-5 v E in E 1947; 5 v E in SA 1948/49; 5 v E in E 1951.
ROWAN Eric Alfred Burchell, B Johannesburg 20.7.1909. D Edenvale Hospital, Transvaal 30.4.1993.
26-5 v E in E 1935; 3 v A in SA 1935/36; 4 v E in SA 1938/39; 4 v E in SA 1948/49; 5 v A in SA 1949/50; 5 v E in E 1951.
ROWE George Alexander, B Grahamstown, CC 15.6.1874. D Pinelands, CP 8.1.1950.
5-(To E 1894); 2 v E in SA 1895/96; 2 v E in SA 1898/99; (To E 1901); 1 v A in SA 1902/03.

+#**RUDOLPH** Jacobus Andries (Jacques), B Springs, Transvaal 4.5.1981.
35(+1)-(*1 v I 2001/02); (To A 2001/02); 2 v B in B 2002/03; 5 v E in E 2003; (To P 2003/04); 4 v WI in SA 2003/04; 3 v NZ in NZ 2003/04; 2 v SL in SL 2004; 2 v I in I 2004/05; 5 v E in SA 2004/05; 2 v Z in SA 2004/05; 2 v WI in WI 2004/05; 3 v A in A 2005/06; 3 v A in SA 2005/06; 2 v SL in SL 2006.

+**RUSHMERE** Mark Weir, B Port Elizabeth 7.1.1965.
1-v WI in WI 1991/92.

SAMUELSON Sivert Vause, B York, Natal 21.11.1883. D Durban 18.11.1958.
1-v E in SA 1909/10.

+**SCHULTZ** Brett Nolan, B East London 26.8.1970.
9-2 v I in SA 1992/93; 3 v SL in SL 1993/94; 1 v Z in Z 1995/96; 1 v E in SA 1995/96; 1 v A in SA 1996/97; 1 v P in P 1997/98.

SCHWARZ Reginald Oscar, B Lee, London, England 4.5.1875. D Etaples, France (War) 18.11.1918.
20-(To E 1904); 5 v E in SA 1905/06; 3 v E in E 1907; 4 v E in SA 1909/10; 5 v A in A 1910/11; 2 v A in E 1912; 1 v E in E 1912.

SECCULL Arthur William, B King William's Town, CC 14.9.1868. D Johannesburg 20.7.1945.
1-(To E 1894); 1 v E in SA 1895/96.

SEYMOUR Michael Arthur (Kelly), B Kokstad, CP 5.6.1936.
7-4 v A in A 1963/64; 2 v E in SA 1964/65; 1 v A in SA 1969/70.

SHALDERS William Alfred, B Kimberley 12.2.1880. D Cradock, CP 18.3.1917.
12-1 v E in SA 1898/99; (To E 1901); 3 v A in SA 1902/03; (To E 1904); 5 v E in SA 1905/06; 3 v E in E 1907.

SHEPSTONE George Harold, B Pietermaritzburg 9.4.1876. D Springkell Sanatorium, Germiston, Transvaal 3.7.1940.
2-1 v E in SA 1895/96; 1 v E in SA 1898/99; (To E 1904).

SHERWELL Percy William, B Isipingo, Natal 17.8.1880. D Bulawayo, Rhodesia 17.4.1948.
13-5 v E in SA 1905/06; 3 v E in E 1907; 5 v A in A 1910/11.

SIEDLE Ivan Julian (Jack), B Berea, Durban 11.1.1903. D St.Augustine's Hospital, Bulwer, Durban 24.8.1982.
18(+3)-(*3 v SBJ 1924/25); 1 v E in SA 1927/28; 3 v E in E 1929; 5 v E in SA 1930/31; 4 v E in E 1935; 5 v A in SA 1935/36.

SINCLAIR James Hugh, B Swellendam, CC 16.10.1876. D Yeoville, Johannesburg 23.2.1913.
25-3 v E in SA 1895/96; 2 v E in SA 1898/99; (To E 1901); 3 v A in SA 1902/03; (To E 1904); 5 v E in SA 1905/06; 3 v E in E 1907; 4 v E in SA 1909/10; 5 v A in A 1910/11.

SMITH Charles James Edward, B Gamtoos River, CC 25.12.1872. D Norman Nursing Home, Joubert Park, Johannesburg 27.3.1947.
3-v A in SA 1902/03.

SMITH Frederick William, B Uitenhage, CC 31.3.1861. D Johannesburg Hospital, Parktown, Johannesburg 17.4.1914.
3-2 v E in SA 1888/89; 1 v E in SA 1895/96.

+#**SMITH** Graeme Craig, B Johannesburg 1.2.1981.
47-2 v A in SA 2001/02; 2 v B in SA 2002/03; 2 v SL in SA 2002/03; 2 v P in SA 2002/03; 2 v B in B 2002/03; 5 v E in E 2003; 2 v P in P 2003/04; 4 v WI in SA 2003/04; 3 v NZ in NZ 2003/04; 2 v SL in SL 2004; 2 v I in I 2004/05; 5 v E in SA 2004/05; 2 v Z in SA 2004/05; 4 v WI in WI 2004/05; 3 v A in A 2005/06; 2 v A in SA 2005/06; 3 v NZ in SA 2005/06. (Note: Also 1-World XI v A in A 2005/06).

SMITH Vivian Ian, B Durban 23.2.1925.
9-4 v E in E 1947; 3 v A in SA 1949/50; 1 v E in E 1955; 1 v A in SA 1957/58.

+**SNELL** Richard Peter, B Durban 12.9.1968.
5(+1)-(*1 v E XI 1989/90); 1 v WI in WI 1991/92; 2 v SL in SL 1993/94; 1 v A in A 1993/94; (To E 1994); 1 v NZ in SA 1994/95.

SNOOKE Stanley de la Courtte, B St Mark's, CC (Tembuland) (Transkei) 11.11.1878. D Wynberg, Cape Town 6.4.1959.
1-v E in E 1907.
SNOOKE Sibley John (Tip), B St Mark's, CC (Tembuland) (Transkei) 1.2.1881. D Humewood, Port Elizabeth 14.8.1966.
26-(To E 1904); 5 v E in SA 1905/06; 3 v E in E 1907; 5 v E in SA 1909/10; 5 v A in A 1910/11; 2 v A in E 1912; 3 v E in E 1912; 3 v E in SA 1922/23.
SOLOMON William Rodger Thomson, B Fort Beaufort, CC 23.4.1872. D Cradock, CP 13.7.1964.
1-v E in SA 1898/99.
STEWART Robert Burnard, B Azumgurh, India 3.9.1856. D Cala, CP 12.9.1913.
1-v E in SA 1888/89.
+STEYN Dale Willem, B Phalaborwa, Transvaal 27.6.1983.
8-3 v E in SA 2004/05; 3 v NZ in SA 2005/06; 2 v SL in SL 2006.
+STEYN Philippus Jeremia Rudolf (Rudi), B Kimberley 30.6.1967.
3-1 v NZ in SA 1994/95; 1 v P in SA 1994/95; 1 v NZ in NZ 1994/95; (To Z 1995/96).
STRICKER Louis Anthony, B Beaconsfield, Kimberley 26.5.1884. D Rondebosch, Cape Town 5.2.1960.
13-4 v E in SA 1909/10; 5 v A in A 1910/11; 2 v A in E 1912; 2 v E in E 1912.
+STRYDOM Pieter Coenraad, B Somerset East, CP 10.6.1969.
2-1 v E in SA 1999/00; 1 v I in I 1999/00.
SUSSKIND Manfred John (Fred), B Johannesburg 8.6.1891. D Johannesburg Stock Exchange, Johannesburg 9.7.1957.
5(+3)-5 v E in E 1924; (*3 v SBJ 1924/25).
+SYMCOX Patrick Leonard, B Kimberley 14.4.1960.
20-3 v SL in SL 1993/94; 2 v A in A 1993/94; (To E 1994); (To NZ 1994/95); 1 v Z in Z 1995/96; 3 v I in I 1996/97; 1 v A in SA 1996/97; 3 v P in P 1997/98; 3 v A in A 1997/98; 1 v P in SA 1997/98; (To E 1998); 3 v WI in SA 1998/99.
TABERER Henry Melville, B St Matthew's Mission, Keiskammahoek, CC 7.10.1870. D Stormfontein Farm, Colesberg, CP 5.6.1932.
1-v A in SA 1902/03.
TANCRED Augustus Bernard, B Port Elizabeth 20.8.1865. D Monte Rosa Hospital, Gardens, Cape Town 23.11.1911.
2-v E in SA 1888/89.
TANCRED Louis Joseph, B Port Elizabeth 7.10.1876. D Park Lane Nursing Home, Parktown, Johannesburg 28.7.1934.
14(+1)-(To E 1901); 3 v A in SA 1902/03; (To E 1904); 5 v E in SA 1905/06; 1 v E in E 1907; 2 v A in E 1912; 2 v E in E 1912; 1 v E in SA 1913/14; (*1 v AIF 1919/20).
TANCRED Vincent Maximillian, B Port Elizabeth 7.7.1875. D Florida, Roodepoort, Transvaal 3.6.1904.
1-v E in SA 1898/99.
TAPSCOTT George Lancelot (Dusty), B Barkly West, CC 7.11.1889. D Kimberley 13.12.1940.
1-v E in SA 1913/14.
TAPSCOTT Lionel Eric (Doodles), B Kimberley 18.3.1894. D Kenilworth, Cape Town 7.7.1934.
2-v E in SA 1922/23.
TAYFIELD Hugh Joseph (Toey), B Durban 30.1.1929. D Hillcrest, Natal 24.2.1994.
37-5 v A in SA 1949/50; (To E 1951); 5 v A in A 1952/53; 2 v NZ in NZ 1952/53; 5 v NZ in SA 1953/54; 5 v E in E 1955; 5 v E in SA 1956/57; 5 v A in SA 1957/58; 5 v E in E 1960.
TAYLOR Alistair Innes (Scotch), B Johannesburg 25.7.1925. D Randjes Estate Frail Care Centre, Highlands North, Johannesburg 7.2.2004.
1-v E in SA 1956/57.
TAYLOR Daniel, B Durban 9.1.1887. D Durban 24.1.1957.
2-v E in SA 1913/14.
TAYLOR Herbert Wilfred, B Durban 5.5.1889. D Newlands, Cape Town 8.2.1973.
42(+5)-3 v A in E 1912; 3 v E in E 1912; 5 v E in SA 1913/14; 3 v A in SA 1921/22; 5 v E in SA

1922/23; 5 v E in E 1924; (*5 v SBJ 1924/25); 5 v E in SA 1927/28; 3 v E in E 1929; 4 v E in SA 1930/31; 5 v A in A 1931/32; 1 v NZ in NZ 1931/32.

+**TERBRUGGE** David John, B Ladysmith, Natal 31.1.1977.
7-4 v WI in SA 1998/99; (To SL 2000); 1 v A in SA 2001/02; 1 v B in SA 2002/03; 1 v NZ in NZ 2003/04.

THEUNISSEN Nicolaas Hendrik Christiaan de Jong, B Colesberg, CC 4.5.1867. D Willemsdal, Transvaal 9.11.1929.
1-v E in SA 1888/89.

THORNTON George, B Skipton, Yorkshire, England 24.12.1867. D Kensington, London, England 31.1.1939.
1-v A in SA 1902/03.

TOMLINSON Denis Stanley, B Umtali, Rhodesia 4.9.1910. D Durban 11.7.1993.
1-v E in E 1935.

TRAICOS Athanasios John, B Zagazig, Egypt 17.5.1947.
3-v A in SA 1969/70. (Note: Also 1-Z v I in Z 1992/93; 2-Z v NZ in Z 1992/93; 1-Z v I in I 1992/93).

TRIMBORN Patrick Henry Joseph, B Glenwood, Durban 18.5.1940.
4-3 v A in SA 1966/67; 1 v A in SA 1969/70.

TSOLEKILE Thami Lungisa, B Cape Town 9.10.1980.
3-(To E 2003); 2 v I in I 2004/05; 1 v E in SA 2004/05.

TUCKETT Lindsay, B Durban 6.2.1919.
9-5 v E in E 1947; 4 v E in SA 1948/49.

TUCKETT Lindsay Richard (Len), B Durban 19.4.1885. D Bloemfontein 8.4.1963.
1-v E in SA 1913/14.

TWENTYMAN JONES Percy Sydney, B Beaufort West, CC 13.9.1876. D Cape Town 8.3.1954.
1-v A in SA 1902/03.

VAN DER BIJL Pieter Gerhard Vintcent, B Kenilworth, Cape Town 21.10.1907. D Kalk Bay, Cape Town 16.2.1973.
5-v E in SA 1938/39.

VAN DER MERWE Edward Alexander, B Rustenburg, Transvaal 9.11.1903. D JG Strijdom Hospital, Auckland Park, Johannesburg 26.2.1971.
2-1 v E in E 1929; (To A 1931/32); 1 v A in SA 1935/36.

VAN DER MERWE Peter Laurence, B Paarl, CP 14.3.1937.
15-3 v A in A 1963/64; 2 v NZ in NZ 1963/64; 2 v E in SA 1964/65; 3 v E in E 1965; 5 v A in SA 1966/67.

+**VAN JAARSVELD** Martin, B Klerksdorp, Transvaal 18.6.1974.
9-2 v B in SA 2002/03; 1 v SL in SA 2002/03; 1 v WI in SA 2003/04; 1 v NZ in NZ 2003/04; 2 v SL in SL 2004; 1v I in I 2004/05; 1 v E in SA 2004/05.

VAN RYNEVELD Clive Berrange, B St James, Cape Town 19.3.1928.
19-5 v E in E 1951; 5 v NZ in SA 1953/54; 5 v E in SA 1956/57; 4 v A in SA 1957/58.

VARNALS George Derek, B Durban 24.7.1935.
3-v E in SA 1964/65.

VILJOEN Kenneth George, B Windsorton, CC 14.5.1910. D Krugersdorp, Transvaal 21.1.1974.
27-3 v E in SA 1930/31; 4 v A in A 1931/32; 1 v NZ in NZ 1931/32; 4 v E in E 1935; 4 v A in SA 1935/36; 4 v E in SA 1938/39; 5 v E in E 1947; 2 v E in SA 1948/49.

VINCENT Cyril Leverton, B Johannesburg 16.2.1902. D St.Augustine's Hospital, Bulwer, Durban 24.8.1968.
25-5 v E in SA 1927/28; 4 v E in E 1929; 5 v E in SA 1930/31; 5 v A in A 1931/32; 2 v NZ in NZ 1931/32; 4 v E in E 1935.

VINTCENT Charles Henry, B Mossel Bay, CC 2.9.1866. D George, CP 28.9.1943.
3-2 v E in SA 1888/89; 1 v E in SA 1891/92.

VOGLER Albert Edward Ernest, B Swartwater, near Queenstown, CC 28.11.1876. D Fort Napier Hospital, Pietermaritzburg 9.8.1946.
15-5 v E in SA 1905/06; 3 v E in E 1907; 5 v E in SA 1909/10; 2 v A in A 1910/11.

WADE Herbert Frederick, B Durban 14.9.1905. D Inanda, Sandton, Transvaal 23.11.1980.
10-5 v E in E 1935; 5 v A in SA 1935/36.

WADE Walter Wareham (Billy), B Morningside, Durban 18.6.1914. D Morningside, Durban 31.5.2003.
11-3 v E in SA 1938/39; 5 v E in SA 1948/49; 3 v A in SA 1949/50.

WAITE John Henry Bickford, B Johannesburg 19.1.1930.
50-4 v E in E 1951; 5 v A in A 1952/53; 2 v NZ in NZ 1952/53; 5 v NZ in SA 1953/54; 5 v E in E 1955; 5 v E in SA 1956/57; 5 v A in SA 1957/58; 5 v E in E 1960; 5 v NZ in SA 1961/62; 4 v A in A 1963/64; 3 v NZ in NZ 1963/64; 2 v E in SA 1964/65.

WALTER Kenneth Alexander, B Johannesburg 5.11.1939. D Sandton Clinic, Sandton, Johannesburg 13.9.2003.
2-v NZ in SA 1961/62.

WARD Thomas Alfred, B Rawalpindi, India 2.8.1887. D East Springs Gold Mine, Transvaal 16.2.1936.
23(+2)-3 v A in E 1912; 2 v E in E 1912; 5 v E in SA 1913/14; (*2 v AIF 1919/20); 3 v A in SA 1921/22; 5 v E in SA 1922/23; 5 v E in E 1924.

WATKINS John Cecil, B Durban 10.4.1923.
15-3 v A in SA 1949/50; 5 v A in A 1952/53; 2 v NZ in NZ 1952/53; 3 v NZ in SA 1953/54; 2 v E in SA 1956/57.

WESLEY Colin (Tich), B Durban 5.9.1937.
3-v E in E 1960.

+**WESSELS** Kepler Christoffel, B Bloemfontein 14.9.1957.
16(+1)-(*1 v E XI 1989/90); 1 v WI in WI 1991/92; 4 v I in SA 1992/93; 3 v SL in SL 1993/94; 2 v A in A 1993/94; 3 v A in SA 1993/94; 3 v E in E 1994. (Note: Also 4-A v E in A 1982/83; 1-A v SL in SL 1982/83; 5-A v P in A 1983/84; 2-A v WI in WI 1983/84; 5-A v WI in A 1984/85; 6-A v E in E 1985; 1-A v NZ in NZ 1985/86; *4-A XI v SA in SA 1986/87).

WESTCOTT Richard John, B Lisbon, Portugal 19.9.1927.
5-3 v NZ in SA 1953/54; 2 v A in SA 1957/58.

WHITE Gordon Charles, B Port St Johns, CC (Transkei) 5.2.1882. D Gaza, Palestine (War) 17.10.1918.
17-(To E 1904); 5 v E in SA 1905/06; 3 v E in E 1907; 4 v E in SA 1909/10; 3 v A in E 1912; 2 v E in E 1912.

+**WILLOUGHBY** Charl Myles, B Cape Town 3.12.1974.
2-1 v B in B 2002/03; 1 v E in E 2003.

WILLOUGHBY Joseph Thomas, B Aldershot, Hampshire, England 7.11.1874. D Plumstead, Cape Town 11.3.1952.
2-v E in SA 1895/96.

WIMBLE Clarence Skelton, B Graaff-Reinet, CC 22.4.1861. D Johannesburg 28.1.1930.
1-v E in SA 1891/92.

WINSLOW Paul Lyndhurst, B Johannesburg 21.5.1929.
5-2 v A in SA 1949/50; 3 v E in E 1955.

WYNNE Owen Edgar, B Johannesburg 1.6.1919. D at sea, False Bay, CP 13.7.1975.
6-3 v E in SA 1948/49; 3 v A in SA 1949/50.

+#**ZONDEKI** Monde, B King William's Town, CP 25.7.1982.
5-1 v E in E 2003; 1 v Z in SA 2004/05; 3 v WI in WI 2004/05.

ZULCH Johan Wilhelm (Billy), B Lydenburg, Transvaal 2.1.1886. D Umkomaas, Natal 19.5.1924.
16(+2)-5 v E in SA 1909/10; 5 v A in A 1910/11; 3 v E in SA 1913/14; (*2 v AIF 1919/20); 3 v A in SA 1921/22.

SOUTH AFRICAN INTERNATIONAL CRICKETERS

SOUTH AFRICAN LIMITED OVERS INTERNATIONAL CRICKETERS WHO HAVE NOT APPEARED IN OFFICIAL TEST MATCHES

Unofficial Tests and first-class tours denoted in brackets.

ABRAHAMS Shafiek, B Port Elizabeth 4.3.1968.
BENKENSTEIN Dale Martin, B Salisbury, Rhodesia 9.6.1974.
(To NZ 1998/99).
BRYSON Rudi Edwin, B Springs, Transvaal 25.7.1968.
CALLAGHAN David John, B Queenstown, CP 1.2.1965.
(To A 1993/94); (To NZ 1994/95).
CROOKES Derek Norman, B Mariannhill, near Pinetown, Natal 5.3.1969.
(To I 1996/97).
DUMINY Jean-Paul, B Strandfontein, CP 14.4.1984.
KENT Jon Carter, B Cape Town 7.5.1979.
KOEN Louis Johannes, B Paarl, CP 28.3.1967.
#KRUGER Garnett John-Peter, B Port Elizabeth 5.1.1977.
(To A 2005/06).
#MORKEL Johannes Albertus (Albie), B Vereeniging, Transvaal 10.6.1981.
(To NZ 2003/04).
MPITSANG Phenyo Victor, B Kimberley 28.3.1980.
(To NZ 1998/99).
PALFRAMAN Steven John, B East London 12.5.1970.
(To SL 1993/94).
POTHAS Nic, B Johannesburg 18.11.1973.
PUTTICK Andrew George, B Cape Town 11.12.1980.
(To SL 2004).
RICE Clive Edward Butler, B Johannesburg 23.7.1949.
(18-3 v E XI 1981/82; 2 v SL 1982/83; 2 v WI 1982/83; 4 v WI 1983/84; 3 v A 1985/86; 4 v A 1986/87).
RINDEL Michael John Raymond, B Durban 9.2.1963.
(To NZ 1994/95); (To E 1998).
RUNDLE David Bryan, B Cape Town 25.9.1965.
(1 v E XI 1989/90); (To A 1993/94).
SHAW Timothy Gower, B Empangeni, Natal (Zululand) 5.7.1959.
(To E 1994).
SIMONS Eric Owen, B Cape Town 9.3.1962.
(To NZ 1994/95).
STEWART Errol Leslie Rae, B Durban 30.7.1969.
(To A 1993/94).
#TELEMACHUS Roger, B Stellenbosch, CP 27.3.1973.
(To SL 2000); (To WI 2000/01).
#VAN DER WATH Johannes Jacobus, B Newcastle, Natal 10.1.1978.
VAN WYK Morne Nico, B Bloemfontein 20.3.1979.
VAN ZYL Cornelius Johannes Petrus Gerthardus, B Bloemfontein 1.10.1961.
(1 v A 1985/86); (To WI 1991/92).
WILLIAMS Henry Smith, B Pniel, CP 11.6.1967.
YACHAD Mandy, B Johannesburg 17.11.1960.
(1 v WI 1983/84).

SOUTH AFRICAN INTERNATIONAL CRICKETERS

SOUTH AFRICAN PRO20 INTERNATIONAL CRICKETERS WHO HAVE NOT APPEARED IN OFFICIAL TEST MATCHES OR LIMITED OVERS INTERNATIONALS

BOSMAN Lungile Loots, B Kimberley 14.4.1977.

SOUTH AFRICAN INTERNATIONAL CRICKETERS WHO HAVE APPEARED IN UNOFFICIAL TEST MATCHES

Those who have also played in unofficial limited overs internationals are denoted +.

BILLING McGregor Edward (Max), B Port Elizabeth 12.1.1887. D Morningside, Durban 3.11.1965.
(1 v SBJ 1924/25).
BOLTON James Lardner, B Cape Town 30.1.1895. D Cape Town 1.11.1969.
(1 v SBJ 1924/25).
BUDGEN Edward Albert (Hookie), B Heidelberg, Transvaal 9.12.1884. D Port Elizabeth 6.10.1962.
(1 v AIF 1919/20).
DAVIES Marchant Starr, B Balfour, CC 31.5.1896. D Port Elizabeth 22.2.1973.
(2 v AIF 1919/20).
DUFF William Dick, B Pietermaritzburg 19.9.1890. D Johannesburg 7.10.1953.
(2 v SBJ 1924/25).
ELWORTHY Francis William, B Cambridge, Cambridgeshire, England 11.6.1893. D Johannesburg 15.3.1978.
(1 v AIF 1919/20).
+FOTHERINGHAM Henry Richard, B Empangeni, Natal (Zululand) 4.4.1953.
(7-3 v WI 1983/84; 3 v A 1985/86; 1 v E XI 1989/90).
HANDS Kenneth Charles Myburgh, B Stellenbosch, CC 22.3.1892. D Paris, France 18.11.1954.
(1 v SBJ 1924/25).
+HANLEY Rupert William (Spook), B Port Elizabeth 29.1.1952.
(2 v WI 1983/84)
HOBSON Denys Laurence, B Port Elizabeth 3.9.1951.
(4-1 v E XI 1981/82; 1 v SL 1982/83; 2 v WI 1983/84).
+JEFFERIES Stephen Thomas, B Cape Town 8.12.1959.
(11-2 v E XI 1981/82; 2 v SL 1982/83; 2 v WI 1982/83; 2 v WI 1983/84; 2 v A 1985/86; 1 v A 1986/87).
+JENNINGS Raymond Vernon, B Vanderbijlpark, Transvaal 9.8.1954.
(14-3 v E XI 1981/82; 2 v SL 1982/83; 2 v WI 1982/83; 3 v WI 1983/84; 3 v A 1985/86; 1 v E XI 1989/90).
+KOURIE Alan John, B Johannesburg 30.7.1951.
(16-3 v E XI 1981/82; 2 v SL 1982/83; 2 v WI 1982/83; 4 v WI 1983/84; 3 v A 1985/86; 2 v A 1986/87).
+LE ROUX Garth Stirling, B Kenilworth, Cape Town 4.9.1955.
(15-2 v E XI 1981/82; 2 v SL 1982/83; 2 v WI 1982/83; 2 v WI 1983/84; 3 v A 1985/86; 4 v A 1986/87).
+McEWAN Kenneth Scott, B Bedford, CP 16.7.1952.
(7-4 v WI 1983/84; 1 v A 1985/86; 2 v A 1986/87).
+McKENZIE Kevin Alexander, B Pretoria 16.7.1948.
(7-2 v WI 1982/83; 2 v A 1985/86; 3 v A 1986/87).
MUNRO Campbell, B Alicedale, CC 22.7.1899. Presumed dead.
(1 v SBJ 1924/25).
NESER Vivian Herbert (Boet), B Klerksdorp, Transvaal 16.6.1894. D Pretoria 22.12.1956.
(5 v SBJ 1924/25).

SOUTH AFRICAN INTERNATIONAL CRICKETERS

+PAGE Hugh Ashton, B Salisbury, Rhodesia 3.7.1962.
(7-3 v A 1985/86; 4 v A 1986/87).
+PIENAAR Roy Francois, B Johannesburg 17.7.1961.
(1 v E XI 1989/90).
ROBBINS Victor Clark, B Umhlali, Natal 9.1.1891. D Durban 16.6.1947.
(1 v SBJ 1924/25).
SEEFF Lawrence, B Kensington, Johannesburg 1.5.1959.
(1 v SL 1982/83).
+VAN DER BIJL Vintcent Adriaan Pieter, B Rondebosch, Cape Town 19.3.1948.
(6-3 v E XI 1981/82; 1 v SL 1982/83; 2 v WI 1982/83).
+WATSON William Kenneth, B Port Elizabeth 21.5.1955.
(3-1 v E XI 1981/82; 2 v WI 1983/84).
WHITFIELD Brian Jonathan, B Durban 14.3.1959.
(4 v A 1986/87).

SOUTH AFRICAN INTERNATIONAL CRICKETERS WHO HAVE BEEN ON FIRST-CLASS OVERSEAS TOURS WITHOUT PLAYING IN OFFICIAL OR UNOFFICIAL TEST MATCHES OR LIMITED OVERS INTERNATIONALS

BISSET Arthur Vintcent Crossley (Artie), B Kenilworth, Cape Town 15.1.1879. D Wynberg, Cape Town 8.3.1955.
(To E 1901).
CASTENS Herbert Hayton, B Pearston, CC 23.11.1864. D Fulham, London, England 18.10.1929.
(To E 1894).
COOLEY Bertram Clifford (Bib), B Durban 1874. D Durban 17.8.1935.
(To E 1901).
CROOKES Norman Samuel, B Renishaw, Natal 15.11.1935.
(To E 1965).
DAVEY Darnton Charles (Don), B Mansfield, Nottinghamshire, England 7.7.1856. D Durban 7.10.1911.
(To E 1894).
HORWOOD Stanley Ebden, B Port Elizabeth 22.7.1877. D Plumstead, Cape Town 15.8.1959.
(To E 1904).
INNES Gerald Alfred Skerten, B Wynberg, Cape Town 16.11.1931. D Cape Town 11.7.1982.
(To A and NZ 1952/53).
KEMPIS George Stephen, B Port Elizabeth 25.11.1871. D Scottburgh, Natal 17.3.1948.
(To E 1894).
LOGAN James Douglas, B Cape Town 24.6.1880. D Matjiesfontein, CP 3.1.1960.
(To E 1901).
NORTON Eric Bertram (Pop), B Carlisle Bridge, near Grahamstown, CP 5.12.1919. D Kirstenhof, Cape Town 23.2.2004.
(To A and NZ 1952/53).
OVENSTONE Douglas MacPherson, B Sea Point, Cape Town 31.7.1921.
(To E 1947).
PAYN Leslie William, B Umzinto, Natal 6.5.1915. D Scottburgh, Natal 2.5.1992.
(To E 1947).
REID Allan (Jupp), B Observatory, Cape Town 1.10.1877. D Wyncarrol Rest Home, Rosebank, Cape Town 31.10.1948.
(To E 1901).
ROBINSON Cyril Deason, B Durban 18.7.1873. D Kearsney, Natal 26.8.1948.
(To E 1907).
SEWELL Cyril Otto Hudson (Skilly), B Pietermaritzburg 19.12.1874. D Bexhill-on-Sea, Sussex, England 19.8.1951.
(To E 1894).

SOUTH AFRICAN INTERNATIONAL CRICKETERS

SMITH Harry Ernest (Blackie), B Cradock, CC 21.4.1884. D Boksburg, Transvaal 25.4.1935.
(To E 1907).
STEYN Stephen Sebastian Louis (Stodgy), B Cape Town 11.3.1905. D Cape Town 14.10.1993.
(To A 1931/32).
TSHABALALA Thandi, B Welkom, OFS 19.11.1984.
(To SL 2006).
THOMAS Alfonso Clive, B Cape Town 9.2.1977.
(To I 2004/05).
WALLACH Benjamin, B Queenstown, CC 18.9.1873. D Troyeville, Johannesburg 25.5.1935.
(To E 1904).
WILLIAMS Robert James (Bob), B Viljoensdrift, OFS 12.4.1912. D Durban 14.5.1984.
(To E 1935).

SOUTH AFRICAN UNOFFICIAL LIMITED OVERS INTERNATIONAL CRICKETERS

ARMITAGE Robert Lawrence Sugden, B Grahamstown, CP 9.7.1955. D Grahamstown, EC 9.12.2000.
BARNARD Llewellyn Jamieson (Lee), B Johannesburg 5.1.1956.
BENTLEY Robert Mulock, B Bindura, Southern Rhodesia 3.11.1958.
FERREIRA Anthonie Michal (Yogi), B Pretoria 13.4.1955.
MADSEN Trevor Roy, B Durban 22.12.1957.
MATTHEWS Brett Anthony, B Cape Town 5.7.1962.

PLAYERS WHO REPRESENTED SOUTH AFRICA IN INTERNATIONAL MATCHES UNDER THE SOUTH AFRICAN CRICKET BOARD OF CONTROL (SACBOC)

In 1956/57 Kenyan Asians (KA) toured South Africa and played three 'Test' matches against representative teams chosen by SACBOC. In 1958/59 a South African team toured East Africa and Rhodesia and played two 'Test' matches against Kenya (K) and one against East Africa (EA). BL D'Oliveira captained South Africa in five of the six international matches. A Variawa captained the side in the third 'Test' against Kenyan Asians when D'Oliveira was injured. The following players represented South Africa:

ABED Gesant (Tiny) (Western Province), B Durban 9.5.1931. D Cape Town 4.4.2003.
5-2 v KA in SA 1956/57, 2 v K in K 1958/59, 1 v EA in K 1958/59.
ABED Salie (Lobo) (Western Province), B Durban 17.11.1929.
6-3 v KA in SA 1956/57, 2 v K in K 1958/59, 1 v EA in K 1958/59.
ABRAHAMS Cecil (Western Province), B Athlone, Cape Town 8.3.1932.
6-3 v KA in SA 1956/57, 2 v K in K 1958/59, 1 v EA in K 1958/59.
ABRAHAMS Hassim (Kitel) (Transvaal), B Vrededorp, Transvaal 24.5.1938.
3-v KA in SA 1956/57.
ASMAL Dawood Ahmed (Natal), B Stanger, Natal 10.6.1937. D Durban 29.3.1991.
Toured East Africa and Rhodesia in 1958/59 - no 'Tests'.
BELL Alexander J (Western Province), emigrated to Zimbabwe - no biographical details available.
3-v KA in SA 1956/57.
BULBULIA Abdul Samad (Sam) (Transvaal), B Johannesburg 22.2.1933.
1-v KA in SA 1956/57.
BULBULIA Mohamed (Koeka) (Transvaal), B Johannesburg 5.7.1935.
1-v K in K 1958/59.
DEEDAT Ahmed Ismail (Natal), B Pietermaritzburg 6.11.1934. D Durban 15.8.1998.
4-1 v KA in SA 1956/57, 2 v K in K 1958/59, 1 v EA in K 1958/59.

SOUTH AFRICAN INTERNATIONAL CRICKETERS

DINATH Abbas (Transvaal), B Krugersdorp, Transvaal 25.11.1925, D Krugersdorp, Transvaal 14.4.1994.
1-v KA in SA 1956/57.
D'OLIVEIRA Basil Lewis (Western Province), B Signal Hill, Cape Town 4.10.1931.
5-2 v KA in SA 1956/57, 2 v K in K 1958/59, 1 v EA in K 1958/59.
GARDA Mohamed (Transvaal), B Johannesburg 15.7.1931. D Johannesburg 28.9.1997.
1-v KA in SA 1956/57.
GEORGE Amien (Western Province), B on board ship Seedebonde, Cape Town 17.9.1927. D Durban 22.6.1983.
1-v KA in SA 1956/57.
JEEWA Essop Ismail (Natal), B Durban 17.2.1928. D Durban 27.6.1995.
2-v KA in SA 1956/57, toured East Africa and Rhodesia in 1958/59 - no 'Tests'.
LANGA George (Ouboetie) (Transvaal), B Johannesburg 24.5.1925. D Johannesburg 19.10.1997.
3-2 v K in K 1958/59, 1 v EA in K 1958/59.
MALAMBA Ben Ndzima (Western Province), B Ndabeni, Cape Town 16.4.1931. D Cape Town 13.9.1999.
3-v KA in SA 1956/57, toured East Africa and Rhodesia in 1958/59 - no 'Tests'.
MEYER Cecil Andrew (Chong) (Transvaal), B Mafeking, CP 23.12.1920. D Johannesburg 26.1.2002.
1-v KA in SA 1956/57.
NEETHLING John James (Coetie) (Western Province), B Goodwood, Cape Town 20.7.1932.
3-2 v K in K 1958/59, 1 v EA in K 1958/59.
PETERSEN Eric (Western Province), B Mowbray, Cape Town 6.9.1931. D near Macassar, WC 26.8.2002.
3-2 v K in K 1958/59, 1 v EA in K 1958/59.
RAZIET Salamodien (Western Province), B Stellenbosch, CP 21.3.1932. D Stellenbosch, WC 21.7.2004.
6-3 v KA in SA 1956/57, 2 v K in K 1958/59, 1 v EA in K 1958/59.
SOLOMON Sydney Norman (Western Province), emigrated to Canada - no biographical details available.
3-2 v K in K 1958/59, 1 v EA in K 1958/59.
VARIAWA Mohamed Amien (Transvaal), B Cape Town 23.4.1927. D Potchefstroom, Transvaal 31.12.1985.
3-v KA in SA 1956/57.
WILLIAMS Owen Leslie (Western Province), B Claremont, Cape Town 8.4.1932.
2-1 v K in K 1958/59, 1 v EA in K 1958/59.

CONTRACTED PLAYERS 2006/07

Fourteen players were offered contracts by Cricket South Africa for the period May 2006 to April 2007. Graeme Smith was appointed as captain for the period, which includes the 2007 Cricket World Cup.

The contracted players were: Graeme Smith (captain), Mark Boucher, AB de Villiers, Boeta Dippenaar, Herschelle Gibbs, Andrew Hall, Jacques Kallis, Justin Kemp, Charl Langeveldt, Andre Nel, Makhaya Ntini, Shaun Pollock, Ashwell Prince and Jacques Rudolph.

SOUTH AFRICAN TEST MATCH RECORDS

As at 1 September 2006

Opponents	First Match	Played	Won	Lost	Drawn
Australia	1902/03	77	15	44	18
	Since 1991/92	*24*	*4*	*15*	*5*
Bangladesh	2002/03	4	4	0	0
England	1888/89	130	26	54	50
	Since 1991/92	*28*	*8*	*8*	*12*
India	1992/93	16	7	3	6
New Zealand	1931/32	33	18	4	11
	Since 1991/92	*16*	*9*	*2*	*5*
Pakistan	1994/95	11	5	2	4
Sri Lanka	1993/94	17	8	4	5
West Indies	1991/92	19	12	2	5
Zimbabwe	1995/96	7	6	0	1
	Total	314	101	113	100
	Since 1991/92	*142*	*63*	*36*	*43*

GROUNDS (11)

City	Venue	Dates	Tests
Port Elizabeth	St George's Park (Sahara Oval)	1888/89 to date	21
Cape Town	Newlands (Sahara Park)	1888/89 to date	40
Johannesburg	(1) The Wanderers	1895/96 to 1938/39	22
	(2) Ellis Park	1948/49 to 1953/54	6
	(3) Wanderers Stadium (Liberty Life Wanderers)	1956/57 to date	28
Durban	(1) Lord's	1909/10 to 1921/22	4
	(2) Kingsmead (Sahara Stadium)	1922/23 to date	33
Centurion	Centurion Park (SuperSport Park)	1995/96 to date	11
Bloemfontein	Springbok Park (Goodyear Park)	1999/00 to date	3
East London	Buffalo Park (Mercedes-Benz Park)	2002/03	1
Potchefstroom	North West Cricket Stadium (Sedgars Park)	2002/03	1

HIGHEST AND LOWEST INNINGS TOTAL FOR EACH CENTRE

		HIGHEST			LOWEST		
Port Elizabeth	For:	502	v England	1964/65	30	v England	1895/96
	Against:	549-7*	by Australia	1949/50	106	by Pakistan	1997/98
Cape Town	For:	620-7*	v Pakistan	2002/03	35	v England	1898/99
	Against:	593-8*	by New Zealand	2005/06	54	by Zimbabwe	2004/05
Johannesburg	For:	620	v Australia	1966/67	72	v England	1956/57
	Against:	652-7*	by Australia	2001/02	79	by New Zealand (Ellis Park)	1953/54
(Wanderers Stadium)	Against:				119	by New Zealand	2005/06
Durban	For:	658-9*	v West Indies	2003/04	99	v Australia	1949/50
	Against:	654-5	by England	1938/39	66	by India	1996/97
Centurion	For:	604-6*	v West Indies	2003/04	200	v Sri Lanka	1997/98
	Against:	381-9*	by England	1995/96	119	by Sri Lanka	2000/01
Bloemfontein	For:	563	v India	2001/02	417	v Zimbabwe	1999/00
	Against:	379	by India	2001/02	192	by Zimbabwe	1999/00

HIGHEST INDIVIDUAL SCORE FOR EACH CENTRE

Port Elizabeth	For:	196	HH Gibbs v India	2001/02
	Against:	167	AL Hassett (Australia)	1949/50
Cape Town	For:	228	HH Gibbs v Pakistan	2002/03
	Against:	262	SP Fleming (New Zealand)	2005/06
Johannesburg	For:	231	AD Nourse v Australia (The Wanderers)	1935/36
	For (Wanderers Stadium):	182	DT Lindsay v Australia	1966/67
	Against:	214	GS Blewett (Australia)	1996/97

Durban	For:	275	G Kirsten v England	1999/00
	Against:	243	E Paynter (England)	1938/39
Centurion	For:	192	HH Gibbs v West Indies	2003/04
	Against:	141	GA Hick (England)	1995/96
Bloemfontein	For:	160	JH Kallis v New Zealand	2000/01
	Against:	155	SR Tendulkar (India)	2001/02

BEST BOWLING ANALYSIS FOR EACH CENTRE

Port Elizabeth	For:	7-84	AA Donald v India	1992/93
	Against:	8-7	GA Lohmann (England)	1895/96
Cape Town	For:	7-63	AE Hall v England	1922/23
	Against:	8-11	J Briggs (England)	1888/89
Johannesburg	For:	9-113	HJ Tayfield v England	1956/57
	Against:	9-28	GA Lohmann (England) (The Wanderers)	1895/96
	Against (Wanderers Stadium):	7-61	MJ Hoggard (England)	2004/05
Durban	For:	8-69	HJ Tayfield v England	1956/57
	Against:	7-46	AR Caddick (England)	1999/00
Centurion	For:	6-39	M Zondeki v Zimbabwe	2004/05
	Against:	6-80	CA Walsh (West Indies)	1998/99
Bloemfontein	For:	6-56	SM Pollock v India	2001/02
	Against:	5-140	J Srinath (India)	2001/02

HIGHEST INNINGS TOTALS

For:	682-6*	v England	Lord's	2003
	658-9*	v West Indies	Durban	2003/04
	622-9*	v Australia	Durban	1969/70
	621-5*	v New Zealand	Auckland	1998/99
	620-7*	v Pakistan	Cape Town	2002/03
	620	v Australia	Johannesburg	1966/67
	604-6*	v West Indies	Centurion	2003/04
	600-3*	v Zimbabwe	Harare	2001/02
	595	v Australia	Adelaide	1963/64
	594-5*	v England	Birmingham	2003
Against:	756-5*	by Sri Lanka	Colombo-SSC	2006
	747	by West Indies	St John's	2004/05
	654-5	by England	Durban	1938/39
	652-7*	by Australia	Johannesburg	2001/02
	628-8*	by Australia	Johannesburg	1996/97
	608	by England	Johannesburg	1948/49
	604-9*	by England	The Oval	2003
	595	by New Zealand	Auckland	2003/04
	593-8*	by New Zealand	Cape Town	2005/06
	578	by Australia	Melbourne	1910/11

LOWEST INNINGS TOTALS

For:	30	v England	Port Elizabeth	1895/96
	30	v England	Birmingham	1924
	35	v England	Cape Town	1898/99
	36	v Australia	Melbourne	1931/32
	43	v England	Cape Town	1888/89
	45	v Australia	Melbourne	1931/32
	47	v England	Cape Town	1888/89
	58	v England	Lord's	1912
	72	v England	Johannesburg	1956/57
	72	v England	Cape Town	1956/57
Against:	54	by Zimbabwe	Cape Town	2004/05
	66	by India	Durban	1996/97
	75	by Australia	Durban	1949/50
	76	by England	Leeds	1907
	79	by New Zealand	Johannesburg	1953/54
	92	by England	Cape Town	1898/99

92	by Pakistan	Faisalabad	1997/98
95	by Sri Lanka	Cape Town	2000/01
99	by England	Lord's	1994
100	by New Zealand	Johannesburg	1953/54
100	by India	Durban	1996/97

HIGHEST FOURTH INNINGS TOTALS

For:	To win:	340-5	v Australia	Durban	(Set 335 to win)	2001/02
	To draw:	423-7	v England	The Oval	(Set 451 to win)	1947
	To lose:	335	v New Zealand	Cape Town	(Set 408 to win)	1961/62
Against:	To win:	352-9	by Sri Lanka	Colombo-PSS	(Set 352 to win)	2006
	To draw:	654-5	by England	Durban	(Set 696 to win)	1938/39
	To lose:	339	by Australia	Adelaide	(Set 378 to win)	1910/11

HIGHEST MATCH AGGREGATE

1981 runs for 35 wickets v England Durban 1938/39

(The match, originally scheduled as a "timeless" Test, lasted ten days but there was no play on one day. It was abandoned as a draw because the English team had to catch a ship home)

LOWEST MATCH AGGREGATE (Completed match)

234 runs for 29 wickets v Australia Melbourne 1931/32

(This is the world record)

LARGEST MARGINS OF VICTORY

By an innings:

For:	South Africa beat Sri Lanka at Cape Town by an innings and 229 runs	2000/01
Against:	Australia beat South Africa at Johannesburg by an innings and 360 runs	2001/02

By runs:

For:	South Africa beat England at Lord's by 356 runs	1994
Against:	Australia beat South Africa at Melbourne by 530 runs	1910/11

NARROWEST MARGINS OF VICTORY

By 1 wicket:

For:	South Africa beat England at Johannesburg	1905/06
Against:	England beat South Africa at Cape Town	1922/23
	Sri Lanka beat South Africa at Colombo-PSS	2006

By runs:

For:	South Africa beat Australia at Sydney by 5 runs	1993/94
Against:	England beat South Africa at Leeds by 23 runs	1998

MOST CENTURIES IN A MATCH (BOTH TEAMS)

8	West Indies (4) v South Africa (4)	St John's	2004/05
(This is the world record)			
7	South Africa (4) v West Indies (3)	Cape Town	2003/04

MOST CENTURIES IN A MATCH (ONE TEAM)

4	Australia v South Africa	Johannesburg	1949/50
4	South Africa v India	Calcutta	1996/97
4	South Africa v West Indies	Cape Town	2003/04
4	South Africa v West Indies	St John's	2004/05
4	West Indies v South Africa	St John's	2004/05

MOST CONSECUTIVE VICTORIES BY SOUTH AFRICA

9 v Australia (1, 2001/02), Bangladesh (2, 2002/03), Sri Lanka (2, 2002/03), Pakistan (2, 2002/03), Bangladesh (2, 2002/03)
5 v Australia (1, 1966/67), Australia (4, 1969/70)
5 v New Zealand (2, 1994/95), Pakistan (1, 1994/95), New Zealand (1, 1994/95), Zimbabwe (1, 1995/96)
5 v West Indies (5, 1998/99)

MOST CONSECUTIVE VICTORIES IN HOME MATCHES BY SOUTH AFRICA

10 v Pakistan (1, 1997/98), Sri Lanka (2, 1997/98), West Indies (5, 1998/99), Zimbabwe (1, 1999/00), England (1, 1999/00)

SOUTH AFRICAN TEST MATCH RECORDS

MOST CONSECUTIVE MATCHES WITHOUT A DEFEAT BY SOUTH AFRICA

14 v West Indies (5, 1998/99), New Zealand (3, 1998/99), Zimbabwe (1, 1999/00), Zimbabwe (1, 1999/00), England (4, 1999/00)

MOST CONSECUTIVE DEFEATS BY SOUTH AFRICA

8 v England (2, 1888/89), England (1, 1891/92), England (3, 1895/96), England (2, 1898/99)

MOST CONSECUTIVE MATCHES WITHOUT A VICTORY BY SOUTH AFRICA

28 v England (3, 1935), Australia (5, 1935/36), England (5, 1938/39), England (5, 1947), England (5, 1948/49), Australia (5, 1949/50)

BATTING

HIGHEST INDIVIDUAL INNINGS

277	GC Smith	v England	Birmingham	2003
275*	DJ Cullinan	v New Zealand	Auckland	1998/99
275	G Kirsten	v England	Durban	1999/00
274	RG Pollock	v Australia	Durban	1969/70
259	GC Smith	v England	Lord's	2003
255*	DJ McGlew	v New Zealand	Wellington	1952/53
236	EAB Rowan	v England	Leeds	1951
231	AD Nourse	v Australia	Johannesburg	1935/36
228	HH Gibbs	v Pakistan	Cape Town	2002/03
222*	JA Rudolph	v Bangladesh	Chittagong	2002/03
220	G Kirsten	v Zimbabwe	Harare	2001/02
211*	HH Gibbs	v New Zealand	Christchurch	1998/99
210	G Kirsten	v England	Manchester	1998
209	RG Pollock	v Australia	Cape Town	1966/67
208	AD Nourse	v England	Nottingham	1951
204	GA Faulkner	v Australia	Melbourne	1910/11
201	EJ Barlow	v Australia	Adelaide	1963/64
200	GC Smith	v Bangladesh	East London	2002/03

MOST RUNS IN A SERIES

Five-match series:				
732	(avg 73.20)	GA Faulkner	v Australia in Australia	1910/11
714	(avg 79.33)	GC Smith	v England in England	2003
625	(avg 69.44)	JH Kallis	v England in South Africa	2004/05
621	(avg 69.00)	AD Nourse	v England in England	1947
606	(avg 86.57)	DT Lindsay	v Australia in South Africa	1966/67
603	(avg 75.37)	EJ Barlow	v Australia in Australia	1963/64
Four-match series:				
712	(avg 178.00)	JH Kallis	v West Indies in South Africa	2003/04
583	(avg 116.60)	HH Gibbs	v West Indies in South Africa	2003/04
517	(avg 73.85)	RG Pollock	v Australia in South Africa	1969/70
Three-match series:				
427	(avg 427.00)	DJ Cullinan	v New Zealand in New Zealand	1998/99
Two-match series:				
388	(avg -)	JH Kallis	v Zimbabwe in Zimbabwe	2001/02

MOST RUNS

	Years	M	Inns	NO	Runs	HS	Avg	100	50
JH Kallis	1995-2006	101	170	27	7950	189 *	55.59	24	40
G Kirsten	1993-2004	101	176	15	7289	275	45.27	21	34
HH Gibbs	1996-2006	79	135	6	5728	228	44.40	14	22
DJ Cullinan	1993-2001	70	115	12	4554	275 *	44.21	14	20
GC Smith	2002-2006	47	82	5	3879	277	50.37	11	14
WJ Cronje	1992-2000	68	111	9	3714	135	36.41	6	23
MV Boucher	1997-2006	95	134	17	3565	125	30.47	4	23
SM Pollock	1995-2006	102	147	37	3515	111	31.95	2	15
B Mitchell	1929-1949	42	80	9	3471	189 *	48.88	8	21
AD Nourse	1935-1951	34	62	7	2960	231	53.81	9	14

HW Taylor	1912-1932	42	76	4	2936	176	40.77	7	17
JN Rhodes	1992-2000	52	80	9	2532	117	35.66	3	17
EJ Barlow	1961-1970	30	57	2	2516	201	45.74	6	15
TL Goddard	1955-1970	41	78	5	2516	112	34.46	1	18
DJ McGlew	1951-1962	34	64	6	2440	255 *	42.06	7	10
JHB Waite	1951-1965	50	86	7	2405	134	30.44	4	16
RG Pollock	1963-1970	23	41	4	2256	274	60.97	7	11
AW Nourse	1902-1924	45	83	8	2234	111	29.78	1	15
RA McLean	1951-1964	40	73	3	2120	142	30.28	5	10
ND McKenzie	2000-2004	41	65	4	2028	120	33.24	2	13
JA Rudolph	2003-2006	35	63	7	2028	222 *	36.21	5	8
AC Hudson	1992-1998	35	63	3	2007	163	33.45	4	13

Note: KC Wessels scored a total of 2788 Test runs. He is the only player to have scored 1000 Test runs for two different countries.

KC Wessels (for SA)	1992-1994	16	29	2	1027	118	38.03	2	6
KC Wessels (for Aus)	1982-1985	24	42	1	1761	179	42.95	4	9

BEST BATTING AVERAGES

(Qualification 1000 runs)

	Years	M	Inns	NO	Runs	HS	Avg	100	50
RG Pollock	1963-1970	23	41	4	2256	274	60.97	7	11
JH Kallis	1995-2006	101	170	27	7950	189 *	55.59	24	40
AD Nourse	1935-1951	34	62	7	2960	231	53.81	9	14
GC Smith	2002-2006	47	82	5	3879	277	50.37	11	14
KC Bland	1961-1966	21	39	5	1669	144 *	49.08	3	9
B Mitchell	1929-1949	42	80	9	3471	189 *	48.88	8	21
EJ Barlow	1961-1970	30	57	2	2516	201	45.74	6	15
G Kirsten	1993-2004	101	176	15	7289	275	45.27	21	34
HH Gibbs	1996-2006	79	135	6	5728	228	44.40	14	22
DJ Cullinan	1993-2001	70	115	12	4554	275 *	44.21	14	20
EAB Rowan	1935-1951	26	50	5	1965	236	43.66	3	12
DJ McGlew	1951-1962	34	64	6	2440	255 *	42.06	7	10
AB de Villiers	2004-2006	22	40	1	1607	178	41.20	3	10
GA Faulkner	1906-1924	25	47	4	1754	204	40.79	4	8
HW Taylor	1912-1932	42	76	4	2936	176	40.77	7	17

MOST CENTURIES

24	JH Kallis
21	G Kirsten
14	DJ Cullinan, HH Gibbs
11	GC Smith
9	AD Nourse
8	B Mitchell
7	DJ McGlew, RG Pollock, HW Taylor
6	EJ Barlow, WJ Cronje
5	RA McLean, JA Rudolph

CENTURY ON DEBUT

163	AC Hudson	v West Indies	Bridgetown	1991/92
222*	JA Rudolph	v Bangladesh	Chittagong	2002/03

CENTURY IN EACH INNINGS

189 and 104*	A Melville	v England	Nottingham	1947
120 and 189*	B Mitchell	v England	The Oval	1947
102 and 133	G Kirsten	v India	Calcutta	1996/97

FOUR CENTURIES IN SUCCESSIVE INNINGS

A Melville	103	v England	Durban	1938/39
	189 and 104*	v England	Nottingham	1947
	117	v England	Lord's	1947

SOUTH AFRICAN TEST MATCH RECORDS

FIVE CENTURIES IN SUCCESSIVE MATCHES

JH Kallis	158 and 44	v West Indies	Johannesburg	2003/04
	177	v West Indies	Durban	2003/04
	73 and 130*	v West Indies	Cape Town	2003/04
	130*	v West Indies	Centurion	2003/04
	92 and 150*	v New Zealand	Hamilton	2003/04

CENTURY BEFORE LUNCH

HGO Owen-Smith		v England	Leeds (third day)	1929

Note: BA Richards was 94* on the first day of the match v Australia Durban 1969/70

FASTEST CENTURIES

80 minutes	JH Sinclair (104)	v Australia	Cape Town	1902/03
95 minutes	PW Sherwell (115)	v England	Lord's	1907

Note: The fastest recorded for South Africa in terms of balls faced:

95 balls	DT Lindsay (131)	v Australia	Johannesburg	1966/67
95 balls	JN Rhodes (103*)	v West Indies	Centurion	1998/99
95 balls	SM Pollock (111)	v Sri Lanka	Centurion	2000/01
100 balls	L Klusener (102*)	v India	Cape Town	1996/97

FASTEST FIFTIES

32 minutes (31 balls)	WJ Cronje (82)	v Sri Lanka	Centurion	1997/98

Note: The fastest recorded for South Africa in terms of balls faced:

24 balls	JH Kallis (54)	v Zimbabwe	Cape Town	2004/05

(This is the world record)

SLOWEST CENTURY

545 minutes	DJ McGlew (105)	v Australia	Durban	1957/58

YOUNGEST PLAYER TO SCORE A DOUBLE-CENTURY

21 years 259 days	GC Smith (200)	v Bangladesh	East London	2002/03

YOUNGEST PLAYER TO SCORE A CENTURY

19 years 318 days	RG Pollock (122)	v Australia	Sydney	1963/64

OLDEST PLAYER TO SCORE A CENTURY

42 years 295 days	AW Nourse (111)	v Australia	Johannesburg	1921/22

CENTURIES AGAINST FIVE OR MORE OPPONENTS

9	G Kirsten	vs Australia, Bangladesh, England, India, New Zealand, Pakistan, Sri Lanka, West Indies and Zimbabwe.
8	HH Gibbs	vs Australia, Bangladesh, England, India, New Zealand, Pakistan, West Indies and Zimbabwe.
	JH Kallis	vs Australia, Bangladesh, England, India, New Zealand, Pakistan, West Indies and Zimbabwe.
6	GC Smith	vs Bangladesh, England, New Zealand, Pakistan, West Indies and Zimbabwe.
5	WJ Cronje	vs Australia, England, India, New Zealand and Sri Lanka.
	DJ Cullinan	vs England, India, New Zealand, Sri Lanka and West Indies.
	JA Rudolph	vs Australia, Bangladesh, New Zealand, Sri Lanka and West Indies.

Note: WR Endean, DJ McGlew and JHB Waite all scored centuries against Australia, England and New Zealand, the only opponents of South Africa during the times of their careers.

CARRYING BAT THROUGH A COMPLETED INNINGS

AB Tancred	26*	(47)	v England	Cape Town	1888/89
JW Zulch	43*	(103)	v England	Cape Town	1909/10
TL Goddard	56*	(99)	v Australia	Cape Town	1957/58
DJ McGlew	127*	(292)	v New Zealand	Durban	1961/62
G Kirsten	100*	(239)	v Pakistan	Faisalabad	1997/98

RECORD WICKET PARTNERSHIPS

1st	368	GC Smith and HH Gibbs	v Pakistan	Cape Town	2002/03
2nd	315*	HH Gibbs and JH Kallis	v New Zealand	Christchurch	1998/99
3rd	429*	JA Rudolph and HH Dippenaar	v Bangladesh	Chittagong	2002/03
4th	249	JH Kallis and G Kirsten	v West Indies	Durban	2003/04
5th	267	JH Kallis and AG Prince	v West Indies	St John's	2004/05

6th	200	RG Pollock and HR Lance	v Australia	Durban	1969/70
7th	246	DJ McGlew and ARA Murray	v New Zealand	Wellington	1952/53
8th	150	ND McKenzie and SM Pollock	v Sri Lanka	Centurion	2000/01
	150	G Kirsten and M Zondeki	v England	Leeds	2003
9th	195	MV Boucher and PL Symcox (This is the world record)	v Pakistan	Johannesburg	1997/98
10th	103	HGO Owen-Smith and AJ Bell	v England	Leeds	1929

BOWLING

SEVEN WICKETS IN AN INNINGS

9-113	HJ Tayfield	v England	Johannesburg	1956/57
8-53	GB Lawrence	v New Zealand	Johannesburg	1961/62
8-64	L Klusener	v India	Calcutta (on Test debut)	1996/97
8-69	HJ Tayfield	v England	Durban	1956/57
8-70	SJ Snooke	v England	Johannesburg	1905/06
8-71	AA Donald	v Zimbabwe	Harare	1995/96
7-23	HJ Tayfield	v Australia	Durban	1949/50
7-29	GF Bissett	v England	Durban	1927/28
7-37	M Ntini	v West Indies	Port-of-Spain	2004/05
7-63	AE Hall	v England	Cape Town (on Test debut)	1922/23
7-65	SJ Pegler	v England	Lord's	1912
7-81	HJ Tayfield	v Australia	Melbourne	1952/53
7-84	GA Faulkner	v England	The Oval	1912
7-84	AA Donald	v India	Port Elizabeth	1992/93
7-87	SM Pollock	v Australia	Adelaide	1997/98
7-91	JT Partridge	v Australia	Sydney	1963/64
7-94	AEE Vogler	v England	Johannesburg	1909/10
7-95	WH Ashley	v England	Cape Town (on f-c debut)	1888/89
7-128	AEE Vogler	v England	Lord's	1907
7-128	PR Adams	v Pakistan	Lahore	2003/04

TEN WICKETS IN A MATCH

13-132	M Ntini	v West Indies	Port-of-Spain	2004/05
13-165	HJ Tayfield	v Australia	Melbourne	1952/53
13-192	HJ Tayfield	v England	Johannesburg	1956/57
12-127	SJ Snooke	v England	Johannesburg	1905/06
12-139	AA Donald	v India	Port Elizabeth	1992/93
12-181	AEE Vogler	v England	Johannesburg	1909/10
11-112	AE Hall	v England	Cape Town (on Test debut)	1922/23
11-113	AA Donald	v Zimbabwe	Harare	1995/96
11-127	AA Donald	v England	Johannesburg	1999/00
11-150	EP Nupen	v England	Johannesburg	1930/31
11-196	SF Burke	v New Zealand	Cape Town (on Test debut)	1961/62
10-87	PM Pollock	v England	Nottingham	1965
10-88	A Nel	v West Indies	Bridgetown	2004/05
10-106	PR Adams	v Bangladesh	Chittagong	2002/03
10-108	PS de Villiers	v Pakistan	Johannesburg	1994/95
10-116	CB Llewellyn	v Australia	Johannesburg	1902/03
10-123	PS de Villiers	v Australia	Sydney	1993/94
10-145	M Ntini	v New Zealand	Centurion	2005/06
10-147	SM Pollock	v India	Bloemfontein	2001/02
10-178	M Ntini	v Australia	Johannesburg	2005/06
10-220	M Ntini	v England	Lord's	2003

HAT-TRICK

GM Griffin	v England	Lord's	1960

Note: EJ Barlow took a hat-trick and went on to take four wickets in five balls for the Rest of the World v England at Leeds, 1970, but the Test match status of this match was later revoked.

SOUTH AFRICAN TEST MATCH RECORDS

MOST WICKETS IN A SERIES

Five-match series:			
37 (avg 17.18)	HJ Tayfield	v England in South Africa	1956/57
36 (avg 21.75)	AEE Vogler	v England in South Africa	1909/10
33 (avg 19.78)	AA Donald	v England in England	1998
30 (avg 28.10)	HJ Tayfield	v Australia in Australia	1952/53
Four-match series:			
29 (avg 21.37)	M Ntini	v West Indies in South Africa	2003/04
26 (avg 13.57)	MJ Procter	v Australia in South Africa	1969/70
Three-match series:			
25 (avg 17.92)	CB Llewellyn	v Australia in South Africa	1902/03
Two-match series:			
16 (avg 20.18)	Q McMillan	v New Zealand in New Zealand	1931/32
16 (avg 14.12)	SM Pollock	v India in South Africa	2001/02

MOST WICKETS

	Years	M	Balls	Runs	Wkts	Avg	BB	5I	10M
SM Pollock	1995-2006	102	23172	9253	395	23.42	7-87	16	1
AA Donald	1992-2002	72	15519	7344	330	22.25	8-71	20	3
M Ntini	1998-2006	69	14597	7751	274	28.28	7-37	14	4
JH Kallis	1995-2006	101	13529	6304	199	31.67	6-54	4	0
HJ Tayfield	1949-1960	37	13568	4405	170	25.91	9-113	14	2
PR Adams	1995-2004	45	8850	4405	134	32.87	7-128	4	1
TL Goddard	1955-1970	41	11736	3226	123	26.22	6-53	5	0
PM Pollock	1961-1970	28	6522	2806	116	24.18	6-38	9	1
NAT Adcock	1953-1962	26	6391	2195	104	21.10	6-43	5	0
N Boje	2000-2006	43	8620	4265	100	42.65	5-62	3	0
PS de Villiers	1993-1998	18	4805	2063	85	24.27	6-23	5	2
A Nel	2001-2006	23	4959	2503	84	29.79	6-32	3	1
CL Vincent	1927-1935	25	5851	2631	84	31.32	6-51	3	0
GA Faulkner	1906-1924	25	4227	2180	82	26.58	7-84	4	0
L Klusener	1996-2004	49	6887	3033	80	37.91	8-64	1	0
BM McMillan	1992-1998	38	6048	2537	75	33.82	4-65	0	0

BEST BOWLING AVERAGES

(Qualification 50 wickets)

	Years	M	Balls	Runs	Wkts	Avg	BB	5I	10M
NAT Adcock	1953-1962	26	6391	2195	104	21.10	6-43	5	0
AA Donald	1992-2002	72	15519	7344	330	22.25	8-71	20	3
AEE Vogler	1906-1911	15	2764	1455	64	22.73	7-94	5	1
SM Pollock	1995-2006	102	23172	9253	395	23.42	7-87	16	1
PM Pollock	1961-1970	28	6522	2806	116	24.18	6-38	9	1
PS de Villiers	1993-1998	18	4805	2063	85	24.27	6-23	5	2

ALL-ROUND PLAY

BEST PERFORMANCES IN A MATCH

JH Sinclair	110 runs (106 & 4) and 9 wickets (6-26 & 3-63)	v England	Cape Town	1898/99
CB Llewellyn	94 runs (90 & 4*) and 9 wickets (6-92 & 3-124)	v Australia	Johannesburg	1902/03
GA Faulkner	201 runs (78 & 123) and 8 wickets (5-120 & 3-40)	v England	Johannesburg	1909/10
PS de Villiers	66 runs (66*) and 10 wickets (6-81 & 4-27)	v Pakistan	Johannesburg	1994/95
SM Pollock	100 runs (70* & 30) and 8 wickets (2-55 & 6-50)	v Pakistan	Durban	1997/98
JH Kallis	198 runs (110 & 88*) and 7 wickets (2-34 & 5-90)	v West Indies	Cape Town	1998/99
JH Kallis	139 runs (139*) and 7 wickets (2-26 & 5-21)	v Bangladesh	Potchefstroom	2002/03

3000 RUNS AND 300 WICKETS

	M	Runs	Avg	Wkts	Avg
SM Pollock	102	3515	31.95	395	23.42

SOUTH AFRICAN TEST MATCH RECORDS

2000 RUNS AND 100 WICKETS

	M	Runs	Avg	Wkts	Avg
TL Goddard	41	2516	34.46	123	26.22
JH Kallis	101	7950	55.59	199	31.67

1000 RUNS AND 50 WICKETS

	M	Runs	Avg	Wkts	Avg
N Boje	43	1312	25.23	100	42.65
GA Faulkner	25	1754	40.79	82	26.58
L Klusener	49	1906	32.86	80	37.91
BM McMillan	38	1968	39.36	75	33.82
JH Sinclair	25	1069	23.23	63	31.68

200 RUNS AND 20 WICKETS IN A SERIES

	M	Runs	Avg	Wkts	Avg		
GA Faulkner	5	545	60.55	29	21.89	v England in South Africa	1909/10
TL Goddard	5	235	23.50	25	21.12	v England in England	1955
TL Goddard	5	294	32.66	26	16.23	v Australia in South Africa	1966/67
MJ Procter	4	209	34.83	26	13.57	v Australia in South Africa	1969/70
JH Kallis	5	267	29.66	20	19.75	v West Indies in West Indies	2000/01
SM Pollock	5	302	75.50	20	23.20	v West Indies in West Indies	2000/01

WICKETKEEPING

MOST DISMISSALS IN AN INNINGS

6 (ct 6)	DT Lindsay	v Australia	Johannesburg	1966/67
6 (ct 6)	MV Boucher	v Pakistan	Port Elizabeth	1997/98
6 (ct 6)	MV Boucher	v Sri Lanka	Cape Town	1997/98
6 (ct 6)	MV Boucher	v Zimbabwe	Centurion	2004/05

MOST DISMISSALS IN A MATCH

9 (ct 9)	DJ Richardson	v India	Port Elizabeth	1992/93
9 (ct 8,st 1)	MV Boucher	v Pakistan	Port Elizabeth	1997/98
8 (ct 8)	DT Lindsay	v Australia	Johannesburg	1966/67
8 (ct 8)	DJ Richardson	v Sri Lanka	Colombo-SSC	1993/94
8 (ct 8)	MV Boucher	v India	Bloemfontein	2001/02
8 (ct 8)	MV Boucher	v Sri Lanka	Centurion	2002/03
8 (ct 8)	MV Boucher	v Zimbabwe	Centurion	2004/05
7 (ct 5,st 2)	JHB Waite	v New Zealand	Port Elizabeth	1953/54
7 (ct 4,st 3)	JHB Waite	v New Zealand	Cape Town	1961/62
7 (ct 7)	DT Lindsay	v Australia	Port Elizabeth	1969/70
7 (ct 7)	DJ Richardson	v Pakistan	Johannesburg	1994/95
7 (ct 7)	DJ Richardson	v New Zealand	Auckland	1994/95
7 (ct 7)	MV Boucher	v Sri Lanka	Cape Town	1997/98
7 (ct 7)	MV Boucher	v England	Lord's	1998
7 (ct 7)	MV Boucher	v England	Johannesburg	1999/00
7 (ct 7)	MV Boucher	v India	Mumbai	1999/00
7 (ct 6,st 1)	MV Boucher	v Sri Lanka	Durban	2000/01
7 (ct 5,st 2)	MV Boucher	v Bangladesh	Chittagong	2002/03
7 (ct 7)	MV Boucher	v England	Nottingham	2003
7 (ct 7)	MV Boucher	v New Zealand	Centurion	2005/06

MOST DISMISSALS IN A SERIES

Five-match series:

26 (ct 23,st 3)	JHB Waite	v New Zealand in South Africa	1961/62
26 (ct 25, st 1)	MV Boucher	v England in England	1998
24 (ct 24)	DT Lindsay	v Australia in South Africa	1966/67
23 (ct 16,st 7)	JHB Waite	v New Zealand in South Africa	1953/54

Four-match series:

16 (ct 16)	DJ Richardson	v India in South Africa	1992/93
Three-match series:			
18 (ct 17,st 1)	MV Boucher	v Pakistan in South Africa	1997/98
17 (ct 17)	DJ Richardson	v Sri Lanka in Sri Lanka	1993/94
16 (ct 16)	DJ Richardson	v New Zealand in South Africa	1994/95
Two-match series:			
13 (ct 13)	MV Boucher	v Sri Lanka in South Africa	1997/98
13 (ct 12, st 1)	MV Boucher	v Zimbabwe in South Africa	2004/05

MOST DISMISSALS

	Years	M	Ct	St	Total	Dis/M
MV Boucher	1997-2006	95	348	14	362	3.81
DJ Richardson	1992-1998	42	150	2	152	3.61
JHB Waite	1951-1965	50	124	17	141*	2.82
DT Lindsay	1963-1970	19	57	2	59*	3.10
HB Cameron	1927-1935	26	39	12	51	1.96

Notes: *Waite did not keep wicket in one of his 50 matches. He did not take a catch on that occasion.
Lindsay was in the field for four of his 19 matches and took three catches there. These are included above.

3000 RUNS AND 300 DISMISSALS

	M	Runs	Avg	Ct	St	Total
MV Boucher	95	3565	30.47	348	14	362

1000 RUNS AND 100 DISMISSALS

	M	Runs	Avg	Ct	St	Total
DJ Richardson	42	1359	24.26	150	2	152
JHB Waite	50	2405	30.44	124	17	141

1000 RUNS AND 50 DISMISSALS

	M	Runs	Avg	Ct	St	Total
HB Cameron	26	1239	30.21	39	12	51
DT Lindsay	19	1130	37.66	57	2	59

A CENTURY AND SIX DISMISSALS IN AN INNINGS

182 and 6 ct	DT Lindsay	v Australia	Johannesburg	1966/67

NO BYES CONCEDED IN A TOTAL OF OVER 500

595	MV Boucher	v New Zealand	Auckland	2003/04
559-9*	WW Wade	v England	Cape Town	1938/39
543-5*	MV Boucher	v West Indies	Georgetown	2004/05
531	DT Lindsay	v England	Johannesburg	1964/65
520	JHB Waite	v Australia	Melbourne	1952/53

Note: DJ Richardson conceded one bye, the 545th run of the innings, when Australia scored 628-8* at Johannesburg, 1996/97.

NO BYES CONCEDED IN A FIVE-TEST SERIES

MV Boucher	v West Indies in South Africa (the first such instance in Test cricket)	1998/99

Note: 2431 runs were scored without a bye being conceded by Boucher, a world record, between the second innings against England at Leeds in 1998 and the second innings against New Zealand at Auckland in 1998/99.

FIELDING

MOST CATCHES IN AN INNINGS

4	AEE Vogler	v England	Durban	1909/10
4	AW Nourse	v England	Durban	1922/23
4	B Mitchell	v Australia	Melbourne	1931/32
4	TL Goddard	v Australia	Sydney	1963/64
4	AJ Traicos	v Australia	Durban (on Test debut)	1969/70

4	AC Hudson	v India	Cape Town	1992/93
4	HH Gibbs	v West Indies	Durban	1998/99
4	G Kirsten	v England	Cape Town	1999/00

MOST CATCHES IN A MATCH

6	AEE Vogler	v England	Durban	1909/10
6	B Mitchell	v Australia	Melbourne	1931/32

MOST CATCHES IN A SERIES

12	AEE Vogler	v England in South Africa	1909/10
12	B Mitchell	v England in South Africa	1930/31
12	TL Goddard	v England in South Africa	1956/57

MOST CATCHES

Name	Years	M	Ct	Name	Years	M	Ct
JH Kallis	1995-2006	101	94	BM McMillan	1992-1998	38	49
G Kirsten	1993-2004	101	83	TL Goddard	1955-1970	41	48
HH Gibbs	1996-2006	79	72	AW Nourse	1902-1924	45	43
SM Pollock	1995-2006	102	68	WR Endean	1951-1958	28	41 *
DJ Cullinan	1993-2001	70	67	ND McKenzie	2000-2004	41	37
B Mitchell	1929-1949	42	56	AC Hudson	1992-1998	35	36
GC Smith	2002-2006	47	56	EJ Barlow	1961-1970	30	35

Note: * Endean's catches include three when he kept wicket.

MISCELLANEOUS

MOST APPEARANCES

102	SM Pollock	68	WJ Cronje	43	N Boje
101	JH Kallis	52	JN Rhodes	42	B Mitchell
101	G Kirsten	50	JHB Waite	42	DJ Richardson
95	MV Boucher	49	L Klusener	42	HW Taylor
79	HH Gibbs	47	GC Smith	41	TL Goddard
72	AA Donald	45	PR Adams	41	ND McKenzie
70	DJ Cullinan	45	AW Nourse	40	RA McLean
69	M Ntini				

Most consecutive appearances:

75	MV Boucher	1997/98-2004
60	JH Kallis	1997/98-2002/03
53	G Kirsten	1993/94-1998/99

MOST CAPTAINCIES

Matches			Won	Lost	Drawn	%Won
53	WJ Cronje	1993/94-1999/00	27	11	15	50.94
39	GC Smith	2002/03-2005/06	15	12	12	38.46
26	SM Pollock	2000-2002/03	14	5	7	53.84
18	HW Taylor	1913/14-1924	1	10	7	5.55
16	KC Wessels	1991/92-1994	5	3	8	31.25
15	JE Cheetham	1952/53-1955	7	5	3	46.66
15	AD Nourse	1948/49-1951	1	9	5	6.66
14	DJ McGlew	1955-1961/62	4	6	4	28.57
13	TL Goddard	1963/64-1964/65	1	2	10	7.69
13	PW Sherwell	1905/06-1910/11	5	6	2	38.46
12	HG Deane	1927/28-1930/31	2	4	6	16.66
10	A Melville	1938/39-1947	0	4	6	0.00
10	HF Wade	1935-1935/36	1	4	5	10.00

Other captains with three or more Test wins:

4	A Bacher	1969/70	4	0	0	100.00
5	SJ Snooke	1909/10	3	2	0	60.00
8	PL van der Merwe	1965-1966/67	4	1	3	50.00

South Africa have had 32 Test captains in total and 8 since 1991/92.

SOUTH AFRICAN TEST MATCH RECORDS

COACHES

		Played	Won	Lost	Drawn	%Won
MJ Procter	1991/92-1994	17	5	4	8	29.41
RA Woolmer	1994/95-1999	44	21	9	14	47.72
GX Ford	1999/00-2001/02	33	16	8	9	48.48
EO Simons	2001/02-2004	24	14	5	5	58.33
RV Jennings	2004/05	13	5	3	5	38.46
JM Arthur	2005/06-2006	11	2	7	2	18.18

PLAYERS WHO HAVE APPEARED FOR TWO COUNTRIES

F Hearne	E v SA in SA 1888/89(2); SA v E in SA 1891/92(1), 1895/96(3).
F Mitchell	E v SA in SA 1898/99(2); SA v E in E 1912(1), SA v A in E 1912(2).
AJ Traicos	SA v A in SA 1969/70 (3); Z v I in Z 1992/93(1), Z v NZ in Z 1992/93(2),Z v I in I 1992/93(1).
KC Wessels	A v E in A 1982/83(4), A v SL in SL 1982/83(1), A v P in A 1983/84(5), A v WI in WI 1983/84(2), A v WI in A 1984/85(5), A v E in E 1985(6), A v NZ in NZ 1985/86(1); SA v WI in WI 1991/92(1), SA v I in SA 1992/93(4), SA v SL in SL 1993/94(3), SA v A in A 1993/94(2), SA v A in SA 1993/94(3), SA v E in E 1994(3).

Note: MV Boucher, JH Kallis and GC Smith represented the World XI against Australia in Sydney in 2005/06.

YOUNGEST PLAYERS ON DEBUT

Yrs	Days	Player	Against	Venue	Date	Born
18	340	PR Adams	v England	Port Elizabeth	26/12/1995	20/1/1977
19	1	AE Ochse	v England	Port Elizabeth	12/3/1889	11/3/1870
19	50	WA Shalders	v England	Cape Town	1/4/1899	10/2/1880
19	120	JH Sinclair	v England	Port Elizabeth	13/2/1896	16/10/1876
19	123	PR Carlstein	v Australia	Port Elizabeth	28/2/1958	28/10/1938
19	158	CB Llewellyn	v England	Johannesburg	2/3/1896	26/9/1876
19	252	MG Melle	v Australia	Johannesburg	10/2/1950	3/6/1930
19	267	CN McCarthy	v England	Durban	16/12/1948	24/3/1929
19	282	RG Pollock	v Australia	Brisbane	6/12/1963	27/2/1944
19	308	EP Nupen	v Australia	Durban	5/11/1921	1/1/1902
19	329	GH Shepstone	v England	Johannesburg	2/3/1896	8/4/1876
19	347	JM Blanckenberg	v England	Johannesburg	13/12/1913	31/12/1893

OLDEST PLAYERS ON DEBUT

Yrs	Days	Player	Against	Venue	Date	Born
40	295	O Henry	v India	Durban	13/11/1992	23/1/1952
40	56	GWA Chubb	v England	Nottingham	7/6/1951	12/4/1911
39	105	SJ Cook	v India	Durban	13/11/1992	31/7/1953
38	272	JD Lindsay	v England	Nottingham	7/6/1947	8/9/1908

OLDEST PLAYERS

Yrs	Days	Player	Against	Venue	Date	Born
45	207	AW Nourse	England	The Oval	19/8/1924	25/1/1879
44	317	JMM Commaille	England	Cape Town	4/1/1928	21/2/1883
43	118	CP Carter	England	The Oval	19/8/1924	23/4/1881
42	301	HW Taylor	New Zealand	Christchurch	1/3/1932	5/5/1889
42	197	GA Faulkner	England	Lord's	1/7/1924	17/12/1881

Note: The age given is that on the last day of their final Test.

FATHERS AND SONS WHO WERE BOTH TEST PLAYERS

F Hearne and GAL Hearne	AW Nourse and AD Nourse	LR Tuckett and L Tuckett
JD Lindsay and DT Lindsay	PM Pollock and SM Pollock	

BROTHERS WHO WERE TEST PLAYERS

3 - AB, LJ and VM Tancred

2 - PAM and RHM Hands (A third brother, KCM Hands, appeared for "South Africa" in the unofficial Tests in 1924/25)

G and PN Kirsten	AR and WHM Richards	GL and LE Tapscott
AJ and DB Pithey	AMB and EAB Rowan	D and HW Taylor
PM and RG Pollock	SD and SJ Snooke	HF and WW Wade

ON THE FIELD THROUGHOUT AN ENTIRE MATCH

DJ McGlew	v New Zealand	Wellington	1952/53
HH Gibbs	v New Zealand	Christchurch	1998/99

SOUTH AFRICA versus AUSTRALIA

Season	Venue	SA captain	Aus captain	Played	Won	Lost	Drawn
1902/03	South Africa	HM Taberer (a)	J Darling	3	0	2	1
1910/11	Australia	PW Sherwell	C Hill	5	1	4	0
1912	England	F Mitchell (b) (g)	SE Gregory	3	0	2	1
1921/22	South Africa	HW Taylor	HL Collins	3	0	1	2
1931/32	Australia	HB Cameron	WM Woodfull	5	0	5	0
1935/36	South Africa	HF Wade	VY Richardson	5	0	4	1
1949/50	South Africa	AD Nourse	AL Hassett	5	0	4	1
1952/53	Australia	JE Cheetham	AL Hassett	5	2	2	1
1957/58	South Africa	DJ McGlew (c)	ID Craig	5	0	3	2
1963/64	Australia	TL Goddard	R Benaud (d)	5	1	1	3
1966/67	South Africa	PL van der Merwe	RB Simpson	5	3	1	1
1969/70	South Africa	A Bacher	WM Lawry	4	4	0	0
1993/94	Australia	KC Wessels (e)	AR Border	3	1	1	1
1993/94	South Africa	KC Wessels	AR Border	3	1	1	1
1996/97	South Africa	WJ Cronje	MA Taylor	3	1	2	0
1997/98	Australia	WJ Cronje	MA Taylor	3	0	1	2
2001/02	Australia	SM Pollock	SR Waugh	3	0	3	0
2001/02	South Africa	MV Boucher	SR Waugh	3	1	2	0
2005/06	Australia	GC Smith	RT Ponting	3	0	2	1
2005/06	South Africa	GC Smith (f)	RT Ponting	3	0	3	0
		Tests in South Africa		42	10	23	9
		Tests in Australia		32	5	19	8
		Tests in England		3	0	2	1
		Total		77	15	44	18

Notes:
(a) JH Anderson (2nd) and EA Halliwell (3rd) also captained South Africa
(b) LJ Tancred (3rd) also captained South Africa
(c) CB van Ryneveld (2nd,3rd,4th,5th) also captained South Africa
(d) RB Simpson (2nd,3rd,4th,5th) also captained Australia
(e) WJ Cronje (3rd) also captained South Africa
(f) JH Kallis (3rd) also captained South Africa
(g) Triangular Tournament between Australia, England and South Africa

HIGHEST INNINGS TOTALS

For South Africa:

In South Africa:	622-9*	Durban (2nd Test)	1969/70
In Australia:	595	Adelaide (4th Test)	1963/64

For Australia:

In South Africa:	652-7*	Johannesburg (1st Test)	2001/02
In Australia:	578	Melbourne (4th Test)	1910/11

LOWEST INNINGS TOTALS

For South Africa:

In South Africa:	85	Johannesburg (2nd Test)	1902/03
In Australia:	36 and 45	Melbourne (5th Test)	1931/32

(The aggregate of 81 for two innings is the lowest in Test cricket)

For Australia:

In South Africa:	75	Durban (3rd Test)	1949/50
In Australia:	111	Sydney (2nd Test)	1993/94

LARGEST MARGINS OF VICTORY

By an innings:

South Africa beat Australia at Durban by an innings and 129 runs	1969/70
Australia beat South Africa at Johannesburg by an innings and 360 runs	2001/02

SOUTH AFRICAN TEST MATCH RECORDS

By runs:

South Africa beat Australia at Port Elizabeth by 323 runs	1969/70
Australia beat South Africa at Melbourne by 530 runs	1910/11

NARROWEST MARGINS OF VICTORY

By runs:

South Africa beat Australia at Sydney by 5 runs	1993/94

By wickets:

Australia beat South Africa at Port Elizabeth by 2 wickets	1996/97

BATTING

INDIVIDUAL CENTURIES

For South Africa (46):

114	EJ Barlow (5)	Brisbane	1963/64
109		Melbourne	1963/64
201		Adelaide	1963/64
127		Cape Town	1969/70
110		Johannesburg	1969/70
126	KC Bland	Sydney	1963/64
122	WJ Cronje	Johannesburg	1993/94
162*	WR Endean	Melbourne	1952/53
204	GA Faulkner (3)	Melbourne	1910/11
115		Adelaide	1910/11
122*		Manchester	1912
152	CN Frank	Johannesburg	1921/22
104	HH Gibbs	Durban	2001/02
102	AC Hudson	Cape Town	1993/94
102	BL Irvine	Port Elizabeth	1969/70
101	JH Kallis (3)	Melbourne	1997/98
111		Sydney	2005/06
114		Durban	2005/06
108*	G Kirsten (2)	Adelaide	1997/98
153		Sydney	2001/02
182	DT Lindsay (3)	Johannesburg	1966/67
137		Durban	1966/67
131		Johannesburg	1966/67
108	DJ McGlew (2)	Johannesburg	1957/58
105		Durban	1957/58
231	AD Nourse (2)	Johannesburg	1935/36
114		Cape Town	1949/50
111	AW Nourse	Johannesburg	1921/22
122	RG Pollock (5)	Sydney	1963/64
175		Adelaide	1963/64
209		Cape Town	1966/67
105		Port Elizabeth	1966/67
274		Durban	1969/70
119	AG Prince	Sydney	2005/06
140	BA Richards (2)	Durban	1969/70
126		Port Elizabeth	1969/70
143	EAB Rowan	Durban	1949/50
102*	JA Rudolph	Perth	2005/06
101	JH Sinclair (2)	Johannesburg	1902/03
104		Cape Town	1902/03
103	SJ Snooke	Adelaide	1910/11
111	KG Viljoen	Melbourne	1931/32
115	JHB Waite (2)	Johannesburg	1957/58
134		Durban	1957/58
105	JW Zulch (2)	Adelaide	1910/11
150		Sydney	1910/11

For Australia (87):

159*	WW Armstrong (2)	Johannesburg	1902/03
132		Melbourne	1910/11
132	W Bardsley (3)	Sydney	1910/11
121		Manchester	1912
164		Lord's	1912
122	R Benaud (2)	Johannesburg	1957/58
100		Johannesburg	1957/58
214	GS Blewett	Johannesburg	1996/97
169	BC Booth (2)	Brisbane	1963/64
102*		Sydney	1963/64
226	DG Bradman (4)	Brisbane	1931/32
112		Sydney	1931/32
167		Melbourne	1931/32
299*		Adelaide	1931/32
121	WA Brown	Cape Town	1935/36
189	JW Burke	Cape Town	1957/58
109	AG Chipperfield	Durban	1935/36
203	HL Collins	Johannesburg	1921/22
112	JHW Fingleton (3)	Cape Town	1935/36
108		Johannesburg	1935/36
118		Durban	1935/36
204*	AC Gilchrist (2)	Johannesburg	2001/02
138*		Cape Town	2001/02
119	JM Gregory	Johannesburg	1921/22
178	RN Harvey (8)	Cape Town	1949/50
151*		Durban	1949/50
100		Johannesburg	1949/50
116		Port Elizabeth	1949/50
109		Brisbane	1952/53
190		Sydney	1952/53
116		Adelaide	1952/53
205		Melbourne	1952/53
112	AL Hassett (3)	Johannesburg	1949/50
167		Port Elizabeth	1949/50
163		Adelaide	1952/53
131	ML Hayden (6)	Adelaide	2001/02
138		Melbourne	2001/02
105		Sydney	2001/02
122		Johannesburg	2001/02
137		Melbourne	2005/06
102		Durban	2005/06
203*	BJ Hodge	Perth	2005/06
142	C Hill (3)	Johannesburg	1902/03
191		Sydney	1910/11
100		Melbourne	1910/11
122	MEK Hussey	Melbourne	2005/06
114	C Kelleway (2)	Manchester	1912
102		Lord's	1912
116	JL Langer (2)	Adelaide	2001/02
126		Sydney	2001/02
157	WM Lawry	Melbourne	1963/64
101	SJE Loxton	Johannesburg	1949/50
137	CG Macartney (2)	Sydney	1910/11
116		Durban	1921/22
124*	DR Martyn (4)	Adelaide	2001/02
117		Sydney	2001/02
133		Johannesburg	2001/02
101		Johannesburg	2005/06
149	SJ McCabe (2)	Durban	1935/36
189*		Johannesburg	1935/36

154	CC McDonald	Adelaide	1952/53
118 & 101*	J Moroney (2)	Johannesburg	1949/50
111	AR Morris (2)	Johannesburg	1949/50
157		Port Elizabeth	1949/50
105	RT Ponting (7)	Melbourne	1997/98
100*		Cape Town	2001/02
117		Melbourne	2005/06
120 & 143*		Sydney	2005/06
103 & 116		Durban	2005/06
127	KE Rigg	Sydney	1931/32
142	J Ryder	Cape Town	1921/22
153	RB Simpson	Cape Town	1966/67
134	KR Stackpole	Cape Town	1966/67
170	MA Taylor (2)	Melbourne	1993/94
169*		Adelaide	1997/98
159	VT Trumper (2)	Melbourne	1910/11
214*		Adelaide	1910/11
113*	ME Waugh (4)	Durban	1993/94
116		Port Elizabeth	1996/97
100		Sydney	1997/98
115*		Adelaide	1997/98
164	SR Waugh (2)	Adelaide	1993/94
160		Johannesburg	1996/97
161	WM Woodfull	Melbourne	1931/32

Note: DG Bradman made centuries in the four matches in which he batted in the 1931/32 series. He was injured and did not bat in the 5th Test.

CENTURY ON DEBUT IN THE SERIES

For South Africa:			
114	EJ Barlow	Brisbane	1963/64
102*	JA Rudolph	Perth	2005/06
For Australia:			
142	C Hill	Johannesburg	1902/03
132	W Bardsley	Sydney	1910/11
226	DG Bradman	Brisbane	1931/32
127	KE Rigg	Sydney	1931/32
109	AG Chipperfield	Durban	1935/36
112	AL Hassett	Johannesburg	1949/50
101	SJE Loxton	Johannesburg	1949/50
169	BC Booth	Brisbane	1963/64
170	MA Taylor	Melbourne	1993/94
164	SR Waugh	Adelaide	1993/94
214	GS Blewett	Johannesburg	1996/97
105	RT Ponting	Melbourne	1997/98
116	JL Langer	Adelaide	2001/02
203*	BJ Hodge	Perth	2005/06

HIGHEST INDIVIDUAL INNINGS

For South Africa:	In South Africa:	274	RG Pollock	Durban	1969/70
	In Australia:	204	GA Faulkner	Melbourne	1910/11
For Australia:	In South Africa:	214	GS Blewett	Johannesburg	1996/97
	In Australia:	299*	DG Bradman	Adelaide	1931/32

MOST RUNS IN A SERIES

		Runs	Matches		
For South Africa:	In South Africa:	606	5	DT Lindsay (Avg 86.57)	1966/67
	In Australia:	732	5	GA Faulkner (Avg 73.20)	1910/11
For Australia:	In South Africa:	660	5	RN Harvey (Avg 132.00)	1949/50
	In Australia:	834	5	RN Harvey (Avg 92.66)	1952/53

SOUTH AFRICAN TEST MATCH RECORDS

CARRYING BAT THROUGH A COMPLETED INNINGS

For South Africa:	TL Goddard	56*	(99)	Cape Town	1957/58
For Australia:	WW Armstrong	159*	(309)	Johannesburg	1902/03
	MA Taylor	169*	(350)	Adelaide	1997/98

RECORD WICKET PARTNERSHIPS

For South Africa:				
1st	176	DJ McGlew and TL Goddard	Johannesburg	1957/58
2nd	173	LJ Tancred and CB Llewellyn	Johannesburg	1902/03
3rd	341	EJ Barlow and RG Pollock	Adelaide	1963/64
4th	219	JH Kallis and AG Prince	Sydney	2005/06
5th	129	JHB Waite and WR Endean	Johannesburg	1957/58
6th	200	RG Pollock and HR Lance	Durban	1969/70
7th	221	DT Lindsay and PL van der Merwe	Johannesburg	1966/67
8th	124	AW Nourse and EA Halliwell	Johannesburg	1902/03
9th	85	RG Pollock and PM Pollock	Cape Town	1966/67
10th	74	BM McMillan and PL Symcox	Adelaide	1997/98
For Australia:				
1st	233	WA Brown and JHW Fingleton	Cape Town	1935/36
2nd	275	CC McDonald and AL Hassett	Adelaide	1952/53
3rd	242	C Kelleway and W Bardsley	Lord's	1912
4th	169	MA Taylor and ME Waugh	Melbourne	1993/94
5th	385	SR Waugh and GS Blewett	Johannesburg	1996/97
6th	317	DR Martyn and AC Gilchrist	Johannesburg	2001/02
7th	160	R Benaud and GD McKenzie	Sydney	1963/64
8th	83	AG Chipperfield and CV Grimmett	Durban	1935/36
9th	78	DG Bradman and WJ O'Reilly	Adelaide	1931/32
	78	KD Mackay and I Meckiff	Johannesburg	1957/58
10th	107	MEK Hussey and GD McGrath	Melbourne	2005/06

BOWLING

SEVEN WICKETS IN AN INNINGS

For South Africa:			
7-23	HJ Tayfield	Durban	1949/50
7-81	HJ Tayfield	Melbourne	1952/53
7-87	SM Pollock	Adelaide	1997/98
7-91	JT Partridge	Sydney	1963/64
For Australia:			
7-34	JV Saunders	Johannesburg	1902/03
7-40	CV Grimmett	Johannesburg	1935/36
7-56	SK Warne	Sydney	1993/94
7-83 & 7-116	CV Grimmett	Adelaide	1931/32
7-100	CV Grimmett	Durban	1935/36

TEN WICKETS IN A MATCH

For South Africa:			
13-165	HJ Tayfield	Melbourne	1952/53
10-116	CB Llewellyn	Johannesburg	1902/03
10-123	PS de Villiers	Sydney	1993/94
10-178	M Ntini	Johannesburg	2005/06
For Australia:			
14-199	CV Grimmett	Adelaide	1931/32
13-173	CV Grimmett	Durban	1935/36
12-128	SK Warne	Sydney	1993/94
11-24	H Ironmonger	Melbourne	1931/32
11-109	SK Warne	Sydney	1997/98
10-88	CV Grimmett	Cape Town	1935/36
10-110	CV Grimmett	Johannesburg	1935/36

SOUTH AFRICAN TEST MATCH RECORDS

HAT-TRICKS

For South Africa:	No instance.		
For Australia:	TJ Matthews (2)	Manchester	1912
	(He achieved the hat-trick in each innings on the second afternoon)		
	LF Kline	Cape Town	1957/58

MOST WICKETS IN A SERIES

		Wickets	Matches		
For South Africa:	In South Africa:	26	5	TL Goddard (Avg 16.23)	1966/67
		26	4	MJ Procter (Avg 13.57)	1969/70
	In Australia:	30	5	HJ Tayfield (Avg 28.10)	1952/53
For Australia:	In South Africa:	44	5	CV Grimmett (Avg 14.59)	1935/36
	In Australia:	37	5	WJ Whitty (Avg 17.08)	1910/11

WICKETKEEPING

MOST DISMISSALS IN AN INNINGS

For South Africa:	6 (ct 6)	DT Lindsay	Johannesburg	1966/67
For Australia:	6 (ct 6)	ATW Grout	Johannesburg (on Test debut)	1957/58

MOST DISMISSALS IN A MATCH

For South Africa:	8 (ct 8)	DT Lindsay	Johannesburg	1966/67
For Australia:	8 (ct 7,st 1)	HB Taber	Johannesburg (on Test debut)	1966/67

MOST DISMISSALS IN A SERIES

For South Africa:	24 (ct 24)	DT Lindsay	in South Africa	1966/67
For Australia:	21 (ct 13,st 8)	RA Saggers	in South Africa	1949/50

FIELDING

MOST CATCHES IN AN INNINGS

For South Africa:	4	B Mitchell	Melbourne	1931/32
	4	TL Goddard	Sydney	1963/64
	4	AJ Traicos	Durban (on Test debut)	1969/70
For Australia:	5	VY Richardson	Durban (equal Test record)	1935/36

MOST CATCHES IN A MATCH

For South Africa:	6	B Mitchell	Melbourne	1931/32
For Australia:	6	VY Richardson	Durban	1935/36

MOST CATCHES IN A SERIES

For South Africa:	9	WR Endean	in Australia	1952/53
For Australia:	13	RB Simpson	in South Africa	1957/58

SOUTH AFRICA versus BANGLADESH

Season	Venue	SA captain	Ban captain	Played	Won	Lost	Drawn
2002/03	South Africa	SM Pollock (a)	Khaled Mashud	2	2	0	0
2002/03	Bangladesh	GC Smith	Khaled Mahmud	2	2	0	0
		Total		4	4	0	0

Note: (a) MV Boucher (1st) also captained South Africa

HIGHEST INNINGS TOTALS

For South Africa:			
In South Africa:	529-4*	East London (1st Test)	2002/03
In Bangladesh:	470-2*	Chittagong (1st Test)	2002/03
For Bangladesh:			
In South Africa:	252	East London (1st Test)	2002/03
In Bangladesh:	237	Chittagong (1st Test)	2002/03

SOUTH AFRICAN TEST MATCH RECORDS

LOWEST INNINGS TOTALS

For South Africa:

In South Africa:	None		
In Bangladesh:	330	Dhaka (2nd Test)	2002/03

For Bangladesh:

In South Africa:	107	Potchefstroom (2nd Test)	2002/03
In Bangladesh:	102	Dhaka (2nd Test)	2002/03

LARGEST MARGINS OF VICTORY

By an innings:

South Africa beat Bangladesh at Potchefstroom by an innings and 160 runs 2002/03

BATTING

INDIVIDUAL CENTURIES

For South Africa (7):

177*	HH Dippenaar	Chittagong	2002/03
114	HH Gibbs	Potchefstroom	2002/03
139*	JH Kallis	Potchefstroom	2002/03
150	G Kirsten (2)	East London	2002/03
160		Potchefstroom	2002/03
222*	JA Rudolph	Chittagong	2002/03
200	GC Smith	East London	2002/03

For Bangladesh (nil):

HIGHEST INDIVIDUAL INNINGS

For South Africa:	In South Africa:	200	GC Smith	East London	2002/03
	In Bangladesh:	222*	JA Rudolph	Chittagong	2002/03
For Bangladesh:	In South Africa:	71	Al Sahariar	East London	2002/03
	In Bangladesh:	75	Habibul Bashar	Chittagong	2002/03

MOST RUNS IN A SERIES

		Runs	Matches		
For South Africa:	In South Africa:	310	2	G Kirsten (Avg 155.00)	2002/03
	In Bangladesh:	293	2	JA Rudolph (Avg 293.00)	2002/03
For Bangladesh:	In South Africa:	146	2	Al Sahariar (Avg 36.50)	2002/03
	In Bangladesh:	182	2	Habibul Bashar (Avg 45.50)	2002/03

RECORD WICKET PARTNERSHIPS

For South Africa:

1st	87	GC Smith and HH Gibbs	East London	2002/03
2nd	272	GC Smith and G Kirsten	East London	2002/03
3rd	429*	JA Rudolph and HH Dippenaar	Chittagong	2002/03
4th	12	JA Rudolph and ND McKenzie	Dhaka	2002/03
5th	107	JA Rudolph and MV Boucher	Dhaka	2002/03
6th	49	MV Boucher and SM Pollock	Dhaka	2002/03
7th	45	SM Pollock and RJ Peterson	Dhaka	2002/03
8th	30	RJ Peterson and AC Dawson	Dhaka	2002/03
9th	36	RJ Peterson and PR Adams	Dhaka	2002/03
10th	0	PR Adams and M Ntini	Dhaka	2002/03

For Bangladesh:

1st	52	Hannan Sarkar and Al Sahariar	Potchefstroom	2002/03
2nd	131	Javed Omar and Habibul Bashar	Chittagong	2002/03
3rd	66	Habibul Bashar and Sanwar Hossain	East London	2002/03
4th	37	Sanwar Hossain and Khaled Mashud	East London	2002/03
5th	22	Khaled Mashud and Rafiqul Islam	Potchefstroom	2002/03
6th	35	Khaled Mashud and Alok Kapali	East London	2002/03
7th	24	Alok Kapali and Mohammad Salim	Dhaka	2002/03
8th	27	Mohammad Salim and Mohammad Rafique	Dhaka	2002/03
9th	16	Mohammad Salim and Tapash Baisya	Dhaka	2002/03
10th	26	Mohammad Salim and Mashrafe Mortaza	Chittagong	2002/03

SOUTH AFRICAN TEST MATCH RECORDS

BOWLING

BEST BOWLING IN AN INNINGS

For South Africa:	5-19	M Ntini	East London	2002/03
For Bangladesh:	6-77	Mohammad Rafique	Dhaka	2002/03

TEN WICKETS IN A MATCH

For South Africa:	10-106	PR Adams	Chittagong	2002/03
For Bangladesh:	No instance. The best performance is			
	6-77	Mohammad Rafique	Dhaka	2002/03

MOST WICKETS IN A SERIES

		Wickets	Matches		
For South Africa:	In South Africa:	12	2	M Ntini (Avg 15.00)	2002/03
	In Bangladesh:	12	2	PR Adams (Avg 14.91)	2002/03
For Bangladesh:	In South Africa:	4	2	Talha Jubair (Avg 54.25)	2002/03
	In Bangladesh:	6	1	Mohammad Rafique (Avg 12.83)	2002/03

SOUTH AFRICA versus ENGLAND

Season	Venue	SA captain	Eng captain	Played	Won	Lost	Drawn
1888/89	South Africa	OR Dunell (a)	CA Smith (b)	2	0	2	0
1891/92	South Africa	WH Milton	WW Read	1	0	1	0
1895/96	South Africa	EA Halliwell (c)	Lord Hawke (d)	3	0	3	0
1898/99	South Africa	M Bisset	Lord Hawke	2	0	2	0
1905/06	South Africa	PW Sherwell	PF Warner	5	4	1	0
1907	England	PW Sherwell	RE Foster	3	0	1	2
1909/10	South Africa	SJ Snooke	HDG Leveson Gower (e)	5	3	2	0
1912	England	F Mitchell (f) (n)	CB Fry	3	0	3	0
1913/14	South Africa	HW Taylor	JWHT Douglas	5	0	4	1
1922/23	South Africa	HW Taylor	FT Mann	5	1	2	2
1924	England	HW Taylor	AER Gilligan (g)	5	0	3	2
1927/28	South Africa	HG Deane	RT Stanyforth (h)	5	2	2	1
1929	England	HG Deane	JC White (i)	5	0	2	3
1930/31	South Africa	EP Nupen (j)	APF Chapman	5	1	0	4
1935	England	HF Wade	RES Wyatt	5	1	0	4
1938/39	South Africa	A Melville	WR Hammond	5	0	1	4
1947	England	A Melville	NWD Yardley	5	0	3	2
1948/49	South Africa	AD Nourse	FG Mann	5	0	2	3
1951	England	AD Nourse	FR Brown	5	1	3	1
1955	England	JE Cheetham (k)	PBH May	5	2	3	0
1956/57	South Africa	CB van Ryneveld (l)	PBH May	5	2	2	1
1960	England	DJ McGlew	MC Cowdrey	5	0	3	2
1964/65	South Africa	TL Goddard	MJK Smith	5	0	1	4
1965	England	PL van der Merwe	MJK Smith	3	1	0	2
1994	England	KC Wessels	MA Atherton	3	1	1	1
1995/96	South Africa	WJ Cronje	MA Atherton	5	1	0	4
1998	England	WJ Cronje	AJ Stewart	5	1	2	2
1999/00	South Africa	WJ Cronje	N Hussain	5	2	1	2
2003	England	GC Smith	MP Vaughan (m)	5	2	2	1
2004/05	South Africa	GC Smith	MP Vaughan	5	1	2	2
		Tests in South Africa		73	17	28	28
		Tests in England		57	9	26	22
		Total		130	26	54	50

Notes:
(a) WH Milton (2nd) also captained South Africa
(b) MP Bowden (2nd) also captained England
(c) AR Richards (3rd) also captained South Africa
(d) TC O'Brien (1st) also captained England
(e) FL Fane (4th,5th) also captained England
(f) LJ Tancred (2nd,3rd) also captained South Africa
(g) JWHT Douglas (4th) also captained England

(h) GTS Stevens (5th) also captained England
(i) AW Carr (4th,5th) also captained England
(j) HG Deane (2nd,3rd) and HB Cameron (4th,5th) also captained South Africa
(k) DJ McGlew (3rd,4th) also captained South Africa
(l) DJ McGlew (2nd) also captained South Africa
(m) N Hussain (1st) also captained England
(n) Triangular Tournament between Australia, England and South Africa

HIGHEST INNINGS TOTALS

For South Africa:			
In South Africa:	572-7	Durban (3rd Test)	1999/00
In England:	682-6*	Lord's (2nd Test)	2003
For England:			
In South Africa:	654-5	Durban (5th Test)	1938/39
In England:	604-9*	The Oval (5th Test)	2003

LOWEST INNINGS TOTALS

For South Africa:			
In South Africa:	30	Port Elizabeth (1st Test)	1895/96
In England:	30	Birmingham (1st Test)	1924
For England:			
In South Africa:	92	Cape Town (2nd Test)	1898/99
In England:	76	Leeds (2nd Test)	1907

LARGEST MARGINS OF VICTORY

By an innings:

South Africa beat England at Lord's by an innings and 92 runs	2003
England beat South Africa at Cape Town by an innings and 202 runs	1888/89

By runs:

South Africa beat England at Lord's by 356 runs	1994
England beat South Africa at Cape Town by 312 runs	1956/57

NARROWEST MARGINS OF VICTORY

By runs:

South Africa beat England at Johannesburg by 17 runs	1956/57
England beat South Africa at Leeds by 23 runs	1998

By wickets:

South Africa beat England at Johannesburg by 1 wicket	1905/06
England beat South Africa at Cape Town by 1 wicket	1922/23
England beat South Africa at Durban by 2 wickets	1948/49
(The winning run, a leg bye, was scored off the last possible ball of the match)	
England beat South Africa at Centurion by 2 wickets	1999/00

(England declared their first innings at 0-0 and South Africa forfeited their second innings, the only occasion an innings has been forfeited in Test cricket)

BATTING

INDIVIDUAL CENTURIES

For South Africa (84):

138	EJ Barlow	Cape Town	1964/65
144*	KC Bland (2)	Johannesburg	1964/65
127		The Oval	1965
108	MV Boucher	Durban	1999/00
120	RH Catterall (3)	Birmingham	1924
120		Lord's	1924
119		Durban	1927/28
126	WJ Cronje	Nottingham	1998
108	DJ Cullinan (2)	Johannesburg	1999/00
120		Cape Town	1999/00
117	EL Dalton (2)	The Oval	1935
102		Johannesburg	1938/39
109	AB de Villiers	Centurion	2004/05
110	HH Dippenaar	Port Elizabeth	2004/05

116*	WR Endean	Leeds	1955
123	GA Faulkner	Johannesburg	1909/10
179	HH Gibbs (3)	Birmingham	2003
183		The Oval	2003
161		Johannesburg	2004/05
112	TL Goddard	Johannesburg	1964/65
102	CMH Hathorn	Johannesburg	1905/06
132	JH Kallis (5)	Manchester	1998
105		Cape Town	1999/00
162		Durban	2004/05
149		Cape Town	2004/05
136*		Centurion	2004/05
110	G Kirsten (5)	Johannesburg	1995/96
210		Manchester	1998
275		Durban	1999/00
108		Lord's	2003
130		Leeds	2003
104	PN Kirsten	Leeds	1994
174	L Klusener	Port Elizabeth	1999/00
104*	DJ McGlew (2)	Manchester	1955
133		Leeds	1955
142	RA McLean (3)	Lord's	1955
100		Durban	1956/57
109		Manchester	1960
100*	BM McMillan	Johannesburg	1995/96
103	A Melville (4)	Durban	1938/39
189 & 104*		Nottingham	1947
117		Lord's	1947
123	B Mitchell (7)	Cape Town	1930/31
164*		Lord's	1935
128		The Oval	1935
109		Durban	1938/39
120 & 189*		The Oval	1947
120		Cape Town	1948/49
120	AD Nourse (7)	Cape Town	1938/39
103		Durban	1938/39
149		Nottingham	1947
115		Manchester	1947
112		Cape Town	1948/49
129*		Johannesburg	1948/49
208		Nottingham	1951
129	HGO Owen-Smith	Leeds +	1929
154	AJ Pithey	Cape Town	1964/65
137	RG Pollock (2)	Port Elizabeth	1964/65
125		Nottingham	1965
117	JN Rhodes	Lord's	1998
156*	EAB Rowan (2)	Johannesburg	1948/49
236		Leeds	1951
115	PW Sherwell	Lord's +	1907
141	IJ Siedle	Cape Town	1930/31
106	JH Sinclair	Cape Town +	1898/99
277	GC Smith (2)	Birmingham	2003
259		Lord's	2003
109	HW Taylor (7)	Durban	1913/14
176		Johannesburg	1922/23
101		Johannesburg	1922/23
102		Durban	1922/23
101		Johannesburg	1927/28
121		The Oval	1929
117		Cape Town	1930/31
125	PGV van der Bijl	Durban	1938/39

124	KG Viljoen	Manchester	1935
125	WW Wade	Port Elizabeth	1948/49
113	JHB Waite	Manchester	1955
105	KC Wessels	Lord's	1994
147	GC White (2)	Johannesburg	1905/06
118		Durban	1909/10
108	PL Winslow	Manchester +	1955

Notes: (a) + His maiden first-class century.
(b) A Melville scored centuries in three successive innings in 1947 and had made a century in his previous Test innings in 1938/39.

For England (108):

120	R Abel	Cape Town	1888/89
148*	LEG Ames (2)	The Oval	1935
115		Cape Town	1938/39
185*	MA Atherton (3)	Johannesburg	1995/96
103		Birmingham	1998
108		Port Elizabeth	1999/00
148*	KF Barrington (2)	Durban	1964/65
121		Johannesburg	1964/65
117	G Boycott	Port Elizabeth	1964/65
104	LC Braund	Lord's	1907
116	MA Butcher (2)	Leeds	1998
106		Nottingham	2003
163	DCS Compton (7)	Nottingham	1947
208		Lord's	1947
115		Manchester	1947
113		The Oval	1947
114		Johannesburg	1948/49
112		Nottingham	1951
158		Manchester	1955
101	MC Cowdrey (3)	Cape Town	1956/57
155		The Oval	1960
105		Nottingham	1965
104	D Denton	Johannesburg	1909/10
172	ER Dexter	Johannesburg	1964/65
119	JWHT Douglas	Durban	1913/14
219	WJ Edrich (3)	Durban	1938/39
189		Lord's	1947
191		Manchester	1947
143	FL Fane	Johannesburg	1905/06
142	A Flintoff	Lord's	2003
129	CB Fry	The Oval	1907
106	PA Gibb (2)	Johannesburg	1938/39
120		Durban	1938/39
138*	WR Hammond (6)	Birmingham	1929
101*		The Oval	1929
136*		Durban	1930/31
181		Cape Town	1938/39
120		Durban	1938/39
140		Durban	1938/39
122	TW Hayward	Johannesburg	1895/96
132	EH Hendren (2)	Leeds	1924
142		The Oval	1924
110	GA Hick (2)	Leeds	1994
141		Centurion	1995/96
124	AJL Hill	Cape Town +	1895/96
187	JB Hobbs (2)	Cape Town	1909/10
211		Lord's	1924
105	N Hussain (3)	Lord's	1998
146*		Durban	1999/00
116		Nottingham	2003

100	L Hutton (4)	Leeds	1947
158		Johannesburg	1948/49
123		Johannesburg	1948/49
100		Leeds	1951
110*	DJ Insole	Durban	1956/57
102	M Leyland (2)	Lord's	1929
161		The Oval	1935
136*	FG Mann	Port Elizabeth	1948/49
138	PBH May (3)	Leeds	1951
112		Lord's	1955
117		Manchester	1955
102	CP Mead (3)	Johannesburg	1913/14
117		Port Elizabeth	1913/14
181		Durban	1922/23
122*	PH Parfitt	Johannesburg	1964/65
108*	JM Parks	Durban	1964/65
117 & 100	E Paynter (3)	Johannesburg	1938/39
243		Durban	1938/39
175	G Pullar	The Oval	1960
152	W Rhodes	Johannesburg	1913/14
117	PE Richardson	Johannesburg	1956/57
108	RWV Robins	Manchester	1935
140 & 111	CAG Russell (2)	Durban	1922/23
137	RT Simpson	Nottingham	1951
121	MJK Smith	Cape Town	1964/65
119	RH Spooner	Lord's	1912
164	AJ Stewart	Manchester	1998
126	AJ Strauss (3)	Port Elizabeth	2004/05
136		Durban	2004/05
147		Johannesburg	2004/05
122	H Sutcliffe (6)	Lord's	1924
102		Johannesburg	1927/28
114		Birmingham	1929
100		Lord's	1929
104 & 109*		The Oval	1929
100*	MW Tate	Lord's	1929
124	GP Thorpe (2)	The Oval	2003
118*		Durban	2004/05
219	ME Trescothick (3)	The Oval	2003
132		Durban	2004/05
180		Johannesburg	2004/05
122	GE Tyldesley (2)	Johannesburg	1927/28
100		Durban	1927/28
112	JT Tyldesley	Cape Town	1898/99
112	BH Valentine	Cape Town	1938/39
156	MP Vaughan	Birmingham	2003
132*	PF Warner	Johannesburg	1898/99
195	C Washbrook	Johannesburg	1948/49
111	AJ Watkins	Johannesburg	1948/49
134*	H Wood	Cape Town +	1891/92
115*	FE Woolley (3)	Johannesburg	1922/23
134*		Lord's	1924
154		Manchester	1929
113	RES Wyatt (2)	Manchester	1929
149		Nottingham	1935

Note: + His maiden first-class century.

CENTURY ON DEBUT IN THE SERIES

For South Africa:

105	KC Wessels	Lord's	1994
277	GC Smith	Birmingham	2003

SOUTH AFRICAN TEST MATCH RECORDS

For England:

132*	PF Warner	Johannesburg (on Test debut)	1898/99
104	LC Braund	Lord's	1907
119	RH Spooner	Lord's	1912
119	JWHT Douglas	Durban	1913/14
117 & 100	E Paynter	Johannesburg	1938/39
106	PA Gibb	Johannesburg (on Test debut)	1938/39
163	DCS Compton	Nottingham	1947
138	PBH May	Leeds (on Test debut)	1951
117	PE Richardson	Johannesburg	1956/57
126	AJ Strauss	Port Elizabeth	2004/05

HIGHEST INDIVIDUAL INNINGS

For South Africa:	In South Africa:	275	G Kirsten	Durban	1999/00
	In England:	277	GC Smith	Birmingham	2003
For England:	In South Africa:	243	E Paynter	Durban	1938/39
	In England:	219	ME Trescothick	The Oval	2003

MOST RUNS IN A SERIES

		Runs	Matches		
For South Africa:	In South Africa:	625	5	JH Kallis (Avg 69.44)	2004/05
	In England:	714	5	GC Smith (Avg 79.33)	2003
For England:	In South Africa:	656	5	AJ Strauss (Avg 72.88)	2004/05
	In England:	753	5	DCS Compton (Avg 94.12)	1947

CARRYING BAT THROUGH A COMPLETED INNINGS

For South Africa:	AB Tancred	26*	(47)	Cape Town	1888/89
	JW Zulch	43*	(103)	Cape Town	1909/10
For England:	PF Warner	132*	(237)	Johannesburg (on Test debut)	1898/99

RECORD WICKET PARTNERSHIPS

For South Africa:

1st	338	GC Smith and HH Gibbs	Birmingham	2003
2nd	257	GC Smith and G Kirsten	Lord's	2003
3rd	319	A Melville and AD Nourse	Nottingham	1947
4th	214	HW Taylor and HG Deane	The Oval	1929
5th	192	G Kirsten and MV Boucher	Durban	1999/00
6th	171	JHB Waite and PL Winslow	Manchester	1955
7th	123	HG Deane and EP Nupen	Durban	1927/28
8th	150	G Kirsten and M Zondeki	Leeds	2003
9th	137	EL Dalton and ACB Langton	The Oval	1935
10th	103	HGO Owen-Smith and AJ Bell	Leeds	1929

For England:

1st	359	L Hutton and C Washbrook	Johannesburg	1948/49
2nd	280	PA Gibb and WJ Edrich	Durban	1938/39
3rd	370	WJ Edrich and DCS Compton	Lord's	1947
4th	197	WR Hammond and LEG Ames	Cape Town	1938/39
5th	237	DCS Compton and NWD Yardley	Nottingham	1947
6th	206*	KF Barrington and JM Parks	Durban	1964/65
7th	115	JWHT Douglas and MC Bird	Durban	1913/14
8th	154	CW Wright and HR Bromley-Davenport	Johannesburg	1895/96
9th	99	A Flintoff and SJ Harmison	The Oval	2003
10th	92	CAG Russell and AER Gilligan	Durban	1922/23

BOWLING

EIGHT WICKETS IN AN INNINGS

For South Africa:

9-113	HJ Tayfield	Johannesburg	1956/57
8-69	HJ Tayfield	Durban	1956/57
8-70	SJ Snooke	Johannesburg	1905/06

(The best in England is 7-65 by SJ Pegler at Lord's, 1912)

For England:

9-28	GA Lohmann	Johannesburg	1895/96
9-57	DE Malcolm	The Oval	1994
9-103	SF Barnes (b)	Johannesburg	1913/14
8-7	GA Lohmann	Port Elizabeth	1895/96
8-11	J Briggs	Cape Town	1888/89
8-29	SF Barnes	The Oval	1912
8-56	SF Barnes (a)	Johannesburg	1913/14
8-59	C Blythe	Leeds	1907

Note: (a) in the first innings (b) in the second innings of the same match.

TEN WICKETS IN A MATCH

For South Africa:

13-192	HJ Tayfield	Johannesburg	1956/57
12-127	SJ Snooke	Johannesburg	1905/06
12-181	AEE Vogler	Johannesburg	1909/10
11-112	AE Hall	Cape Town (on Test debut)	1922/23
11-127	AA Donald	Johannesburg	1999/00
11-150	EP Nupen	Johannesburg	1930/31
10-87	PM Pollock	Nottingham	1965
10-220	M Ntini	Lord's	2003

For England:

17-159	SF Barnes	Johannesburg	1913/14
15-28	J Briggs	Cape Town	1888/89
15-45	GA Lohmann	Port Elizabeth	1895/96
15-99	C Blythe	Leeds	1907
14-144	SF Barnes	Durban	1913/14
13-57	SF Barnes	The Oval	1912
13-91	JJ Ferris	Cape Town	1891/92
12-71	GA Lohmann	Johannesburg	1895/96
12-89	JH Wardle	Cape Town	1956/57
12-101	R Tattersall	Lord's	1951
12-112	AV Bedser	Manchester	1951
12-130	G Geary	Johannesburg	1927/28
12-171	AP Freeman	Manchester	1929
12-205	MJ Hoggard	Johannesburg	2004/05
11-90	AER Gilligan	Birmingham	1924
11-97	JB Statham	Lord's	1960
11-110	SF Barnes	Lord's	1912
11-118	C Blythe	Cape Town	1905/06
10-104	C Blythe	Cape Town	1909/10
10-105	SF Barnes	Durban	1913/14
10-115	SF Barnes	Leeds	1912
10-119	JC Laker	The Oval	1951
10-122	ARC Fraser	Nottingham	1998
10-138	DE Malcolm	The Oval	1994
10-175	DVP Wright	Lord's	1947
10-207	AP Freeman	Leeds	1929

HAT-TRICKS

For South Africa:	GM Griffin	Lord's	1960
For England:	GA Lohmann	Port Elizabeth	1895/96
	TWJ Goddard	Johannesburg	1938/39

MOST WICKETS IN A SERIES

		Wickets	Matches		
For South Africa:	In South Africa:	37	5	HJ Tayfield (Avg 17.18)	1956/57
	In England:	33	5	AA Donald (Avg 19.78)	1998
For England:	In South Africa:	49	4	SF Barnes (Avg 10.93)	1913/14
	In England:	34	3	SF Barnes (Avg 8.29)	1912

SOUTH AFRICAN TEST MATCH RECORDS

WICKETKEEPING

MOST DISMISSALS IN AN INNINGS

For South Africa:	5 (ct 5)	MV Boucher	Lord's	1998
	5 (ct 5)	MV Boucher	Johannesburg	1999/00
For England:	6 (ct 6)	RC Russell	Johannesburg	1995/96

MOST DISMISSALS IN A MATCH

For South Africa:	7 (ct 7)	MV Boucher	Lord's	1998
	7 (ct 7)	MV Boucher	Johannesburg	1999/00
	7 (ct 7)	MV Boucher	Nottingham	2003
For England:	11 (ct 11)	RC Russell	Johannesburg	1995/96
	(This is the world record)			

MOST DISMISSALS IN A SERIES

For South Africa:	26 (ct 25,st 1)	MV Boucher	in England	1998
For England:	27 (ct 25,st 2)	RC Russell	in South Africa	1995/96

FIELDING

MOST CATCHES IN AN INNINGS

For South Africa:	4	AEE Vogler	Durban	1909/10
	4	AW Nourse	Durban	1922/23
	4	G Kirsten	Cape Town	1999/00
For England:	No fielder has taken 4 catches in an innings.			

MOST CATCHES IN A MATCH

For South Africa:	6	AEE Vogler	Durban	1909/10
For England:	5	WR Hammond	Durban	1938/39
	5	JT Ikin	Manchester	1951

MOST CATCHES IN A SERIES

For South Africa:	12	AEE Vogler	in South Africa	1909/10
	12	B Mitchell	in South Africa	1930/31
	12	TL Goddard	in South Africa	1956/57
For England:	12	JT Ikin	in England	1951

SOUTH AFRICA versus INDIA

Season	**Venue**	**SA captain**	**Ind captain**	**Played**	**Won**	**Lost**	**Drawn**
1992/93	South Africa	KC Wessels	M Azharuddin	4	1	0	3
1996/97	India	WJ Cronje	SR Tendulkar	3	1	2	0
1996/97	South Africa	WJ Cronje	SR Tendulkar	3	2	0	1
1999/00	India	WJ Cronje	SR Tendulkar	2	2	0	0
2001/02	South Africa	SM Pollock	SC Ganguly	2	1	0	1
2004/05	India	GC Smith	SC Ganguly	2	0	1	1
		Tests in South Africa		9	4	0	5
		Tests in India		7	3	3	1
		Total		16	7	3	6

HIGHEST INNINGS TOTALS

For South Africa:			
In South Africa:	563	Bloemfontein (1st Test)	2001/02
In India:	510-9*	Kanpur (1st Test)	2004/05
For India:			
In South Africa:	410	Johannesburg (3rd Test)	1996/97
In India:	466	Kanpur (1st Test)	2004/05

SOUTH AFRICAN TEST MATCH RECORDS

LOWEST INNINGS TOTALS

For South Africa:			
In South Africa:	235	Durban (1st Test)	1996/97
In India:	105	Ahmedabad (1st Test)	1996/97
For India:			
In South Africa:	66	Durban (1st Test)	1996/97
In India:	113	Mumbai (1st Test)	1999/00

LARGEST MARGINS OF VICTORY

By an innings:	
South Africa beat India at Bangalore by an innings and 71 runs	1999/00
By runs:	
South Africa beat India at Calcutta by 329 runs	1996/97
India beat South Africa at Kanpur by 280 runs	1996/97

BATTING

INDIVIDUAL CENTURIES

For South Africa (15):			
135	WJ Cronje	Port Elizabeth	1992/93
153*	DJ Cullinan (2)	Calcutta	1996/97
122*		Johannesburg	1996/97
107	HH Gibbs (2)	Bloemfontein	2001/02
196		Port Elizabeth	2001/02
163	AJ Hall	Kanpur	2004/05
146	AC Hudson	Calcutta	1996/97
121	JH Kallis	Kolkata	2004/05
102 & 133	G Kirsten (3)	Calcutta	1996/97
103		Cape Town	1996/97
102*	L Klusener (2)	Cape Town	1996/97
108		Bloemfontein	2001/02
103*	BM McMillan	Cape Town	1996/97
118	KC Wessels	Durban	1992/93
For India (12):			
103	PK Amre	Durban	1992/93
109	M Azharuddin (4)	Calcutta	1996/97
163*		Kanpur	1996/97
115		Cape Town	1996/97
102		Bangalore	1999/00
148	RS Dravid	Johannesburg	1996/97
129	Kapil Dev	Port Elizabeth	1992/93
105	V Sehwag (2)	Bloemfontein	2001/02
164		Kanpur	2004/05
111	SR Tendulkar (3)	Johannesburg	1992/93
169		Cape Town	1996/97
155		Bloemfontein	2001/02

CENTURY ON DEBUT IN THE SERIES

For South Africa:			
118	KC Wessels	Durban	1992/93
163	AJ Hall	Kanpur	2004/05
For India:			
103	PK Amre	Durban (on Test debut)	1992/93
105	V Sehwag	Bloemfontein (on Test debut)	2001/02

HIGHEST INDIVIDUAL INNINGS

For South Africa:	In South Africa:	196	HH Gibbs	Port Elizabeth	2001/02
	In India:	163	AJ Hall	Kanpur	2004/05
For India:	In South Africa:	169	SR Tendulkar	Cape Town	1996/97
	In India:	164	V Sehwag	Kanpur	2004/05

SOUTH AFRICAN TEST MATCH RECORDS

MOST RUNS IN A SERIES

		Runs	Matches		
For South Africa:	In South Africa:	316	2	HH Gibbs (Avg 79.00)	2001/02
	In India:	322	3	G Kirsten (Avg 53.66)	1996/97
For India:	In South Africa:	277	3	RS Dravid (Avg 55.40)	1996/97
	In India:	388	3	M Azharuddin (Avg 77.60)	1996/97

RECORD WICKET PARTNERSHIPS

For South Africa:				
1st	236	AC Hudson and G Kirsten	Calcutta	1996/97
2nd	212	G Kirsten and DJ Cullinan	Calcutta	1996/97
3rd	130	JH Kallis and ND McKenzie	Bloemfontein	2001/02
4th	105	HH Gibbs and HH Dippenaar	Port Elizabeth	2001/02
5th	164	JH Kallis and L Klusener	Bangalore	1999/00
6th	144	AJ Hall and Z de Bruyn	Kanpur	2004/05
7th	121	L Klusener and MV Boucher	Bloemfontein	2001/02
8th	147*	BM McMillan and L Klusener	Cape Town	1996/97
9th	60	PS de Villiers and AA Donald	Ahmedabad	1996/97
10th	74	BM McMillan and AA Donald	Durban	1996/97
For India:				
1st	218	V Sehwag and G Gambhir	Kanpur	2004/05
2nd	171	D Dasgupta and RS Dravid	Port Elizabeth	2001/02
3rd	60*	RS Dravid and SR Tendulkar	Kolkata	2004/05
4th	145	RS Dravid and SC Ganguly	Johannesburg	1996/97
5th	220	SR Tendulkar and V Sehwag	Bloemfontein	2001/02
6th	222	SR Tendulkar and M Azharuddin	Cape Town	1996/97
7th	76	RS Dravid and J Srinath	Johannesburg	1996/97
8th	161	M Azharuddin and A Kumble	Calcutta	1996/97
9th	80	VVS Laxman and A Kumble	Port Elizabeth	2001/02
10th	52	AB Agarkar and M Kartik	Mumbai	1999/00

BOWLING

SEVEN WICKETS IN AN INNINGS

For South Africa:			
8-64	L Klusener	Calcutta	1996/97
7-84	AA Donald	Port Elizabeth	1992/93
For India:			
7-87	Harbhajan Singh	Kolkata	2004/05

TEN WICKETS IN A MATCH

For South Africa:			
12-139	AA Donald	Port Elizabeth	1992/93
10-147	SM Pollock	Bloemfontein	2001/02
For India:			
10-153	BK Venkatesh Prasad	Durban	1996/97

MOST WICKETS IN A SERIES

		Wickets	Matches		
For South Africa:	In South Africa:	20	4	AA Donald (Avg 19.70)	1992/93
		20	3	AA Donald (Avg 15.95)	1996/97
	In India:	14	3	PR Adams (Avg 20.28)	1996/97
For India:	In South Africa:	18	4	A Kumble (Avg 25.94)	1992/93
		18	3	J Srinath (Avg 28.72)	1996/97
	In India:	17	3	J Srinath (Avg 20.94)	1996/97

SOUTH AFRICAN TEST MATCH RECORDS

WICKETKEEPING

MOST DISMISSALS IN AN INNINGS

For South Africa:	5 (ct 5)	DJ Richardson	Port Elizabeth	1992/93
	5 (ct 5)	MV Boucher	Mumbai	1999/00
For India:	5 (ct 5)	NR Mongia	Durban	1996/97

MOST DISMISSALS IN A MATCH

For South Africa:	9 (ct 9)	DJ Richardson	Port Elizabeth	1992/93
For India:	8 (ct 8)	NR Mongia	Durban	1996/97

MOST DISMISSALS IN A SERIES

For South Africa:	16 (ct 16)	DJ Richardson	in South Africa	1992/93
For India:	14 (ct 14)	NR Mongia	in South Africa	1996/97

FIELDING

MOST CATCHES IN AN INNINGS

For South Africa:	4	AC Hudson	Cape Town	1992/93
For India:	3	VVS Laxman	Mumbai	1999/00
	3	W Jaffer	Bangalore	1999/00

MOST CATCHES IN A MATCH

For South Africa:	4	BM McMillan	Port Elizabeth	1992/93
	4	AC Hudson	Cape Town	1992/93
For India:	3	J Srinath	Cape Town	1992/93
	3	V Rathour	Durban	1996/97
	3	RS Dravid	Cape Town	1996/97
	3	M Azharuddin	Johannesburg	1996/97
	3	VVS Laxman	Mumbai	1999/00
	3	W Jaffer	Bangalore	1999/00
	3	VVS Laxman	Port Elizabeth	2001/02
	3	V Sehwag	Port Elizabeth	2001/02

Note: VVS Laxman took 3 catches as a substitute at Kanpur 1996/97.

MOST CATCHES IN A SERIES

For South Africa:	8	BM McMillan	in South Africa	1992/93
	8	BM McMillan	in India	1996/97
For India:	6	M Azharuddin	in South Africa	1992/93
	6	RS Dravid	in South Africa	1996/97

SOUTH AFRICA versus NEW ZEALAND

Season	Venue	SA captain	NZ captain	Played	Won	Lost	Drawn
1931/32	New Zealand	HB Cameron	ML Page	2	2	0	0
1952/53	New Zealand	JE Cheetham	WM Wallace	2	1	0	1
1953/54	South Africa	JE Cheetham	GO Rabone (a)	5	4	0	1
1961/62	South Africa	DJ McGlew	JR Reid	5	2	2	1
1963/64	New Zealand	TL Goddard	JR Reid	3	0	0	3
1994/95	South Africa	WJ Cronje	KR Rutherford	3	2	1	0
1994/95	New Zealand	WJ Cronje	KR Rutherford	1	1	0	0
1998/99	New Zealand	WJ Cronje	DJ Nash	3	1	0	2
2000/01	South Africa	SM Pollock	SP Fleming	3	2	0	1
2003/04	New Zealand	GC Smith	SP Fleming	3	1	1	1
2005/06	South Africa	GC Smith	SP Fleming	3	2	0	1
		Tests in South Africa		19	12	3	4
		Tests in New Zealand		14	6	1	7
		Total		33	18	4	11

Note: (a) B Sutcliffe (4th,5th) also captained New Zealand

SOUTH AFRICAN TEST MATCH RECORDS

HIGHEST INNINGS TOTALS

For South Africa:			
In South Africa:	512	Cape Town (2nd Test)	2005/06
In New Zealand:	621-5*	Auckland (1st Test)	1998/99
For New Zealand:			
In South Africa:	593-8*	Cape Town (2nd Test)	2005/06
In New Zealand:	595	Auckland (2nd Test)	2003/04

LOWEST INNINGS TOTALS

For South Africa:			
In South Africa:	148	Johannesburg (2nd Test)	1953/54
In New Zealand:	223	Dunedin (2nd Test)	1963/64
For New Zealand:			
In South Africa:	79	Johannesburg (4th Test)	1953/54
In New Zealand:	138	Dunedin (2nd Test)	1963/64

LARGEST MARGINS OF VICTORY

By an innings:

South Africa beat New Zealand at Wellington by an innings and 180 runs	1952/53

By runs:

South Africa beat New Zealand at Johannesburg by 132 runs	1953/54
New Zealand beat South Africa at Johannesburg by 137 runs	1994/95

NARROWEST MARGINS OF VICTORY

By runs:

South Africa beat New Zealand at Durban by 30 runs	1961/62

BATTING

INDIVIDUAL CENTURIES

For South Africa (29):

149	HM Amla	Cape Town	2005/06
122*	XC Balaskas	Wellington	1931/32
103	JAJ Christy	Christchurch	1931/32
112	WJ Cronje (2)	Cape Town	1994/95
101		Auckland	1994/95
275*	DJ Cullinan (2)	Auckland	1998/99
152		Wellington	1998/99
100	HH Dippenaar	Johannesburg	2000/01
116	WR Endean	Auckland	1952/53
211*	HH Gibbs (2)	Christchurch	1998/99
120		Wellington	1998/99
148*	JH Kallis (3)	Christchurch	1998/99
160		Bloemfontein	2000/01
150*		Hamilton	2003/04
128	G Kirsten (2)	Auckland	1998/99
137		Hamilton	2003/04
255*	DJ McGlew (3)	Wellington	1952/53
127*		Durban	1961/62
120		Johannesburg	1961/62
120	ND McKenzie	Port Elizabeth	2000/01
101	RA McLean (2)	Durban	1953/54
113		Cape Town	1961/62
113	B Mitchell	Christchurch	1931/32
109	ARA Murray	Wellington	1952/53
108*	AG Prince	Cape Town	2005/06
109	DJ Richardson	Cape Town	1994/95
154*	JA Rudolph	Auckland	2003/04
125*	GC Smith	Wellington	2003/04
101	JHB Waite	Johannesburg	1961/62

For New Zealand (14):

109	PT Barton	Port Elizabeth	1961/62
158	CL Cairns	Auckland	2003/04
262	SP Fleming	Cape Town	2005/06
122*	JEC Franklin	Cape Town	2005/06
101	PGZ Harris	Cape Town	1961/62
119*	JDP Oram (2)	Hamilton	2003/04
133		Centurion	2005/06
107	GO Rabone	Durban	1953/54
135	JR Reid (2)	Cape Town	1953/54
142		Johannesburg	1961/62
138	BW Sinclair	Auckland	1963/64
150	MS Sinclair	Port Elizabeth	2000/01
170	SB Styris	Auckland	2003/04
100	HG Vivian	Wellington	1931/32

CENTURY ON DEBUT IN THE SERIES

For South Africa:

103	JAJ Christy	Christchurch	1931/32
113	B Mitchell	Christchurch	1931/32
255*	DJ McGlew	Wellington	1952/53
109	ARA Murray	Wellington	1952/53
149	HM Amla	Cape Town	2005/06

For New Zealand:

100	HG Vivian	Wellington	1931/32
119*	JDP Oram	Hamilton	2003/04

HIGHEST INDIVIDUAL INNINGS

For South Africa:	In South Africa:	160	JH Kallis	Bloemfontein	2000/01
	In New Zealand:	275*	DJ Cullinan	Auckland	1998/99
For New Zealand:	In South Africa:	262	SP Fleming	Cape Town	2005/06
	In New Zealand:	170	SB Styris	Auckland	2003/04

MOST RUNS IN A SERIES

		Runs	Matches		
For South Africa:	In South Africa:	426	5	DJ McGlew (Avg 60.85)	1961/62
	In New Zealand:	427	3	DJ Cullinan (Avg 427.00)	1998/99
For New Zealand:	In South Africa:	546	5	JR Reid (Avg 60.66)	1961/62
	In New Zealand:	321	3	SB Styris (Avg 80.25)	2003/04

CARRYING BAT THROUGH A COMPLETED INNINGS

For South Africa:	DJ McGlew	127*	(292)	Durban	1961/62
For New Zealand:	No instance.				

RECORD WICKET PARTNERSHIPS

For South Africa:

1st	196	JAJ Christy and B Mitchell	Christchurch	1931/32
2nd	315*	HH Gibbs and JH Kallis	Christchurch	1998/99
3rd	183	G Kirsten and DJ Cullinan	Auckland	1998/99
4th	171	GC Smith and G Kirsten	Wellington	2003/04
5th	141	DJ Cullinan and JN Rhodes	Auckland	1998/99
6th	126*	DJ Cullinan and SM Pollock	Auckland	1998/99
7th	246	DJ McGlew and ARA Murray	Wellington	1952/53
8th	136	ND McKenzie and N Boje	Port Elizabeth	2000/01
9th	60	PM Pollock and NAT Adcock	Port Elizabeth	1961/62
10th	47	DJ McGlew and HD Bromfield	Port Elizabeth	1961/62

For New Zealand:

1st	126	GO Rabone and ME Chapple	Cape Town	1953/54
2nd	90	MJ Horne and NJ Astle	Auckland	1998/99
3rd	125	MH Richardson and SB Styris	Auckland	2003/04

4th	171	BW Sinclair and SN McGregor	Auckland	1963/64
5th	174	JR Reid and JEF Beck	Cape Town	1953/54
6th	100	HG Vivian and FT Badcock	Wellington	1931/32
7th	225	CL Cairns and JDP Oram	Auckland	2003/04
8th	256	SP Fleming and JEC Franklin	Cape Town	2005/06
9th	87	JDP Oram and PJ Wiseman	Hamilton	2003/04
10th	57	SB Doull and RP de Groen	Johannesburg	1994/95

BOWLING

SEVEN WICKETS IN AN INNINGS

For South Africa:

8-53	GB Lawrence	Johannesburg	1961/62

For New Zealand: No instance. The best performance is

6-60	JR Reid	Dunedin	1963/64

TEN WICKETS IN A MATCH

For South Africa:

11-196	SF Burke	Cape Town (on Test debut)	1961/62
10-145	M Ntini	Centurion	2005/06

For New Zealand:

11-180	CS Martin	Auckland	2003/04

MOST WICKETS IN A SERIES

		Wickets	Matches		
For South Africa:	In South Africa:	28	5	GB Lawrence (Avg 18.28)	1961/62
	In New Zealand:	16	2	Q McMillan (Avg 20.18)	1931/32
For New Zealand:	In South Africa:	22	5	AR MacGibbon (Avg 20.63)	1953/54
		22	5	JC Alabaster (Avg 28.04)	1961/62
	In New Zealand:	18	2	CS Martin (Avg 16.66)	2003/04

WICKETKEEPING

MOST DISMISSALS IN AN INNINGS

For South Africa:	4 (9 instances)	JHB Waite 4, DJ Richardson 3, MV Boucher 2
For New Zealand:	4 (5 instances)	AE Dick 3, AC Parore 2

MOST DISMISSALS IN A MATCH

For South Africa:	7 (ct 5,st 2)	JHB Waite	Port Elizabeth	1953/54
	7 (ct 4,st 3)	JHB Waite	Cape Town	1961/62
	7 (ct 7)	DJ Richardson	Auckland	1994/95
	7 (ct 7)	MV Boucher	Centurion	2005/06
For New Zealand:	7 (ct 6,st 1)	AE Dick	Durban	1961/62

MOST DISMISSALS IN A SERIES

For South Africa:	26 (ct 23,st 3)	JHB Waite	in South Africa	1961/62
For New Zealand:	23 (ct 21,st 2)	AE Dick	in South Africa	1961/62

FIELDING

MOST CATCHES IN AN INNINGS

For South Africa:	3	WR Endean	Johannesburg	1953/54
	3	DJ McGlew	Cape Town	1953/54
	3	G Kirsten	Durban	1994/95
	3	DJ Cullinan	Auckland	1994/95
For New Zealand:	3	PGZ Harris	Cape Town	1961/62
	3	GT Dowling	Port Elizabeth	1961/62
	3	MD Crowe	Johannesburg	1994/95

MOST CATCHES IN A MATCH

For South Africa:	5	WR Endean	Johannesburg	1953/54
For New Zealand:	4	PGZ Harris	Cape Town	1961/62
	4	GT Dowling	Port Elizabeth	1961/62
	4	MD Crowe	Johannesburg	1994/95

MOST CATCHES IN A SERIES

For South Africa:	9	WR Endean	in South Africa	1953/54
	9	HD Bromfield	in South Africa	1961/62
For New Zealand:	8	B Sutcliffe	in South Africa	1953/54

SOUTH AFRICA versus PAKISTAN

Season	Venue	SA captain	Pak captain	Played	Won	Lost	Drawn
1994/95	South Africa	WJ Cronje	Salim Malik	1	1	0	0
1997/98	Pakistan	WJ Cronje	Saeed Anwar	3	1	0	2
1997/98	South Africa	WJ Cronje (a)	Rashid Latif (b)	3	1	1	1
2002/03	South Africa	SM Pollock	Waqar Younis	2	2	0	0
2003/04	Pakistan	GC Smith	Inzamam-ul-Haq (c)	2	0	1	1
		Tests in South Africa		6	4	1	1
		Tests in Pakistan		5	1	1	3
		Total		11	5	2	4

Notes: (a) G Kirsten (1st) also captained South Africa
(b) Aamir Sohail (1st, 2nd) also captained Pakistan
(c) Yousuf Youhana (1st) also captained Pakistan

HIGHEST INNINGS TOTALS

For South Africa:			
In South Africa:	620-7*	Cape Town (2nd Test)	2002/03
In Pakistan:	403	Rawalpindi (1st Test)	1997/98
For Pakistan:			
In South Africa:	329	Johannesburg (1st Test)	1997/98
In Pakistan:	456	Rawalpindi (1st Test)	1997/98

LOWEST INNINGS TOTALS

For South Africa:			
In South Africa:	225	Durban (2nd Test)	1997/98
In Pakistan:	214	Faisalabad (3rd Test)	1997/98
For Pakistan:			
In South Africa:	106	Port Elizabeth (3rd Test)	1997/98
In Pakistan:	92	Faisalabad (3rd Test)	1997/98

LARGEST MARGINS OF VICTORY

By an innings:

South Africa beat Pakistan at Cape Town by an innings and 142 runs 2002/03

By runs:

South Africa beat Pakistan at Johannesburg by 324 runs 1994/95

NARROWEST MARGINS OF VICTORY

By runs:

Pakistan beat South Africa at Durban by 29 runs 1997/98

BATTING

INDIVIDUAL CENTURIES

For South Africa (7):

228	HH Gibbs	Cape Town	2002/03
105	JH Kallis	Durban	2002/03
100*	G Kirsten (2)	Faisalabad	1997/98
118		Faisalabad	2003/04

113	BM McMillan	Johannesburg	1994/95
151	GC Smith	Cape Town	2002/03
108	PL Symcox	Johannesburg	1997/98
For Pakistan (8):			
115	Ali Naqvi	Rawalpindi *	1997/98
128*	Azhar Mahmood (3)	Rawalpindi + *	1997/98
136		Johannesburg	1997/98
132		Durban	1997/98
128	Imran Farhat	Faisalabad	2003/04
118	Saeed Anwar	Durban	1997/98
135	Taufeeq Umar (2)	Cape Town	2002/03
111		Lahore	2003/04

Notes: (a) + His maiden first-class century.

(b) * Ali Naqvi and Azhar Mahmood provided the first instance of two players scoring centuries on their Test debuts in the same innings.

CENTURY ON DEBUT IN THE SERIES

For South Africa:			
113	BM McMillan	Johannesburg	1994/95
For Pakistan:			
115	Ali Naqvi	Rawalpindi (on Test debut)	1997/98
128*	Azhar Mahmood	Rawalpindi (on Test debut)	1997/98

HIGHEST INDIVIDUAL INNINGS

For South Africa:	In South Africa:	228	HH Gibbs	Cape Town	2002/03
	In Pakistan:	118	G Kirsten	Faisalabad	2003/04
For Pakistan:	In South Africa:	136	Azhar Mahmood	Johannesburg	1997/98
	In Pakistan:	128*	Azhar Mahmood	Rawalpindi	1997/98
		128	Imran Farhat	Faisalabad	2003/04

MOST RUNS IN A SERIES

		Runs	Matches		
For South Africa:	In South Africa:	264	2	HH Gibbs (Avg 132.00)	2002/03
	In Pakistan:	271	2	G Kirsten (Avg 90.33)	2003/04
For Pakistan:	In South Africa:	327	3	Azhar Mahmood (Avg 65.40)	1997/98
	In Pakistan:	313	2	Taufeeq Umar (Avg 78.25)	2003/04

CARRYING BAT THROUGH A COMPLETED INNINGS

For South Africa:	G Kirsten	100*	(239)	Faisalabad	1997/98
For Pakistan:	No instance.				

RECORD WICKET PARTNERSHIPS

For South Africa:				
1st	368	GC Smith and HH Gibbs	Cape Town	2002/03
2nd	114	G Kirsten and JH Kallis	Rawalpindi	1997/98
3rd	122	G Kirsten and JH Kallis	Durban	2002/03
4th	108	HH Gibbs and G Kirsten	Faisalabad	2003/04
5th	90	G Kirsten and JH Kallis	Faisalabad	2003/04
6th	157	JN Rhodes and BM McMillan	Johannesburg	1994/95
7th	106	SM Pollock and DJ Richardson	Rawalpindi	1997/98
8th	124	G Kirsten and PL Symcox	Faisalabad	1997/98
9th	195	MV Boucher and PL Symcox	Johannesburg	1997/98
10th	71	PS de Villiers and AA Donald	Johannesburg	1994/95
For Pakistan:				
1st	137	Taufeeq Umar and Imran Farhat	Faisalabad	2003/04
2nd	116	Taufeeq Umar and Younis Khan	Cape Town	2002/03
3rd	121	Taufeeq Umar and Inzamam-ul-Haq	Cape Town	2002/03
4th	93	Asif Mujtaba and Inzamam-ul-Haq	Johannesburg	1994/95
5th	99	Asim Kamal and Shoaib Malik	Lahore	2003/04
6th	144	Inzamam-ul-Haq and Moin Khan	Faisalabad	1997/98

7th	35	Salim Malik and Wasim Akram	Johannesburg	1994/95
8th	40	Inzamam-ul-Haq and Kabir Khan	Johannesburg	1994/95
9th	80	Azhar Mahmood and Shoaib Akhtar	Durban	1997/98
10th	151	Azhar Mahmood and Mushtaq Ahmed	Rawalpindi	1997/98

BOWLING

BEST BOWLING IN AN INNINGS

For South Africa:

7-128	PR Adams	Lahore	2003/04

For Pakistan:

6-78	Mushtaq Ahmed	Durban	1997/98
6-78	Waqar Younis	Port Elizabeth	1997/98

TEN WICKETS IN A MATCH

For South Africa:

10-108	PS de Villiers	Johannesburg	1994/95

For Pakistan:

10-133	Waqar Younis	Port Elizabeth	1997/98

MOST WICKETS IN A SERIES

		Wickets	Matches		
For South Africa:	In South Africa:	16	3	AA Donald (Avg 16.37)	1997/98
	In Pakistan:	10	3	SM Pollock (Avg 23.20)	1997/98
		10	2	PR Adams (Avg 34.20)	2003/04
For Pakistan:	In South Africa:	16	3	Waqar Younis (Avg 22.12)	1997/98
	In Pakistan:	14	3	Mushtaq Ahmed (Avg 27.57)	1997/98

WICKETKEEPING

MOST DISMISSALS IN AN INNINGS

For South Africa:	6 (ct 6)	MV Boucher	Port Elizabeth	1997/98
For Pakistan:	4 (ct 4)	Moin Khan	Johannesburg	1994/95

MOST DISMISSALS IN A MATCH

For South Africa:	9 (ct 8, st 1)	MV Boucher	Port Elizabeth	1997/98
For Pakistan:	6 (ct 6)	Moin Khan	Johannesburg	1994/95

MOST DISMISSALS IN A SERIES

For South Africa:	18 (ct 17, st 1)	MV Boucher	in South Africa	1997/98
For Pakistan:	6 (ct 6)	Moin Khan	in South Africa	1994/95

FIELDING

MOST CATCHES IN AN INNINGS

For South Africa:	3	HH Gibbs	Faisalabad	2003/04
For Pakistan:	4	Taufeeq Umar	Faisalabad	2003/04

MOST CATCHES IN A MATCH

For South Africa:	3 (6 instances)	GC Smith 2, AM Bacher 1, HH Gibbs 1, JH Kallis 1, ND McKenzie 1		
For Pakistan:	6	Taufeeq Umar	Faisalabad	2003/04

MOST CATCHES IN A SERIES

For South Africa:	5	GC Smith	in South Africa	2002/03
For Pakistan:	9	Taufeeq Umar	in Pakistan	2003/04

SOUTH AFRICA versus SRI LANKA

Season	Venue	SA captain	SL captain	Played	Won	Lost	Drawn
1993/94	Sri Lanka	KC Wessels	A Ranatunga	3	1	0	2
1997/98	South Africa	WJ Cronje	A Ranatunga	2	2	0	0
2000	Sri Lanka	SM Pollock	ST Jayasuriya	3	1	1	1
2000/01	South Africa	SM Pollock	ST Jayasuriya	3	2	0	1
2002/03	South Africa	SM Pollock	ST Jayasuriya (a)	2	2	0	0
2004	Sri Lanka	GC Smith	MS Atapattu	2	0	1	1
2006	Sri Lanka	AG Prince	DPMD Jayawardene	2	0	2	0
		Tests in South Africa		7	6	0	1
		Tests in Sri Lanka		10	2	4	4
		Total		17	8	4	5

Note: (a) MS Atapattu (2nd) also captained Sri Lanka

Note: The grounds in Colombo are shown as SSC - Sinhalese Sports Club and PSS P Saravanamuttu Stadium.

HIGHEST INNINGS TOTALS

For South Africa:

In South Africa:	504-7*	Cape Town (2nd Test)	2000/01
In Sri Lanka:	495	Colombo-SSC (2nd Test)	1993/94

For Sri Lanka:

In South Africa:	323	Centurion (2nd Test)	2002/03
In Sri Lanka:	756-5*	Colombo-SSC (1st Test)	2006

LOWEST INNINGS TOTALS

For South Africa:

In South Africa:	200	Centurion (2nd Test)	1997/98
In Sri Lanka:	169	Colombo-SSC (1st Test)	2006

For Sri Lanka:

In South Africa:	95	Cape Town (2nd Test)	2000/01
In Sri Lanka:	119	Colombo-SSC (2nd Test)	1993/94

LARGEST MARGINS OF VICTORY

By an innings:

South Africa beat Sri Lanka at Cape Town by an innings and 229 runs	2000/01
Sri Lanka beat South Africa at Colombo-SSC by an innings and 153 runs	2006

By runs:

South Africa beat Sri Lanka at Cape Town by 70 runs	1997/98
Sri Lanka beat South Africa at Colombo-SSC by 313 runs	2004

NARROWEST MARGINS OF VICTORY

By runs:

South Africa beat Sri Lanka at Kandy by 7 runs	2000

By wickets:

Sri Lanka beat South Africa at Colombo-PSS by 1 wicket	2006

BATTING

INDIVIDUAL CENTURIES

For South Africa (12):

122	WJ Cronje	Colombo-SSC	1993/94
102	DJ Cullinan (5)	Colombo-PSS	1993/94
113		Cape Town	1997/98
103		Centurion	1997/98
114*		Galle	2000
112		Cape Town	2000/01

180	G Kirsten	Durban	2000/01
118*	L Klusener	Kandy	2000
103	ND McKenzie	Centurion	2000/01
111	SM Pollock	Centurion	2000/01
101*	JN Rhodes	Moratuwa	1993/94
102	JA Rudolph	Galle	2004
For Sri Lanka (11):			
120	MS Atapattu	Kandy	2000
148	ST Jayasuriya	Galle	2000
167	DPMD Jayawardene (5)	Galle	2000
101*		Colombo-SSC	2000
237		Galle	2004
374		Colombo-SSC	2006
123		Colombo-PSS	2006
131	A Ranatunga	Moratuwa	1993/94
232	KC Sangakkara (2)	Colombo-SSC	2004
287		Colombo-SSC	2006
104*	HP Tillakaratne	Centurion	2002/03

CENTURY ON DEBUT IN THE SERIES

For South Africa:			
101*	JN Rhodes	Moratuwa	1993/94
102	JA Rudolph	Galle	2004
For Sri Lanka:			
131	A Ranatunga	Moratuwa	1993/94
167	DPMD Jayawardene	Galle	2000

HIGHEST INDIVIDUAL INNINGS

For South Africa:	In South Africa:	180	G Kirsten	Durban	2000/01
	In Sri Lanka:	122	WJ Cronje	Colombo-SSC	1993/94
For Sri Lanka:	In South Africa:	104*	HP Tillakaratne	Centurion	2002/03
	In Sri Lanka:	374	DPMD Jayawardene	Colombo-SSC	2006

MOST RUNS IN A SERIES

		Runs	Matches		
For South Africa:	In South Africa:	284	2	DJ Cullinan (Avg 71.00)	1997/98
	In Sri Lanka:	275	3	L Klusener (Avg 68.75)	2000
For Sri Lanka:	In South Africa:	235	3	KC Sangakkara (Avg 39.16)	2000/01
	In Sri Lanka:	510	2	DPMD Jayawardene (Avg 170.00)	2006

RECORD WICKET PARTNERSHIPS

For South Africa:				
1st	165	JA Rudolph and AJ Hall	Colombo-SSC	2006
2nd	108	GC Smith and M van Jaarsveld	Colombo-SSC	2004
3rd	140	HH Gibbs and JH Kallis	Centurion	2002/03
4th	116	G Kirsten and WJ Cronje	Centurion	1997/98
5th	161	AG Prince and AB de Villiers	Colombo-PSS	2006
6th	124	L Klusener and MV Boucher	Kandy	2000
7th	132	MV Boucher and SM Pollock	Centurion	2002/03
8th	150	ND McKenzie and SM Pollock	Centurion	2000/01
9th	45	N Boje and PR Adams	Kandy	2000
10th	43	L Klusener and M Hayward	Kandy	2000
For Sri Lanka:				
1st	193	MS Atapattu and ST Jayasuriya	Galle	2000
2nd	103	ST Jayasuriya and RP Arnold	Colombo-SSC	2000
3rd	624	KC Sangakkara and DPMD Jayawardene	Colombo-SSC	2006
4th	118	RS Mahanama and A Ranatunga	Centurion	1997/98
5th	121	PA de Silva and A Ranatunga	Moratuwa	1993/94
6th	105	CK Kapugedera and HAPW Jayawardene	Colombo-PSS	2006
7th	62	DPMD Jayawardene and MF Maharoof	Colombo-PSS	2006

8th	170	DPMD Jayawardene and WPUJC Vaas	Galle	2004
9th	48	GP Wickramasinghe and M Muralitharan	Cape Town	1997/98
10th	42	HP Tillakaratne and M Muralitharan	Centurion	2002/03

BOWLING

BEST BOWLING IN AN INNINGS

For South Africa:			
6-30	SM Pollock	Cape Town	2000/01
For Sri Lanka:			
7-84	M Muralitharan	Galle	2000

BEST BOWLING IN A MATCH

For South Africa:			
9-106	BN Schultz	Colombo-SSC	1993/94
For Sri Lanka:			
13-171	M Muralitharan	Galle	2000

MOST WICKETS IN A SERIES

		Wickets	Matches		
For South Africa:	In South Africa:	14	2	AA Donald (Avg 18.35)	1997/98
	In Sri Lanka:	20	3	BN Schultz (Avg 16.30)	1993/94
For Sri Lanka:	In South Africa:	16	2	M Muralitharan (Avg 25.00)	1997/98
	In Sri Lanka:	26	3	M Muralitharan (Avg 18.46)	2000

WICKETKEEPING

MOST DISMISSALS IN AN INNINGS

For South Africa:	6 (ct 6)	MV Boucher	Cape Town	1997/98
For Sri Lanka:	5 (ct 5)	RS Kaluwitharana	Centurion	2000/01

MOST DISMISSALS IN A MATCH

For South Africa:	8 (ct 8)	DJ Richardson	Colombo-SSC	1993/94
	8 (ct 8)	MV Boucher	Centurion	2002/03
For Sri Lanka:	5 (ct 2, st 3)	RS Kaluwitharana	Cape Town	1997/98
	5 (ct 5)	RS Kaluwitharana	Centurion	2000/01

MOST DISMISSALS IN A SERIES

For South Africa:	17 (ct 17)	DJ Richardson	in Sri Lanka	1993/94
For Sri Lanka:	9 (ct 9)	KC Sangakkara	in Sri Lanka	2000

SOUTH AFRICA versus WEST INDIES

Season	Venue	SA captain	WI captain	Played	Won	Lost	Drawn
1991/92	West Indies	KC Wessels	RB Richardson	1	0	1	0
1998/99	South Africa	WJ Cronje	BC Lara	5	5	0	0
2000/01	West Indies	SM Pollock	CL Hooper	5	2	1	2
2003/04	South Africa	GC Smith	BC Lara	4	3	0	1
2004/05	West Indies	GC Smith	S Chanderpaul	4	2	0	2
		Tests in South Africa		9	8	0	1
		Tests in West Indies		10	4	2	4
		Total		19	12	2	5

HIGHEST INNINGS TOTALS

For South Africa:			
In South Africa:	658-9*	Durban (2nd Test)	2003/04
In West Indies:	588-6*	St John's (4th Test)	2004/05

For West Indies:

In South Africa:	427	Cape Town (3rd Test)	2003/04
In West Indies:	747	St John's (4th Test)	2004/05

LOWEST INNINGS TOTALS

For South Africa:

In South Africa:	195	Port Elizabeth (2nd Test)	1998/99
In West Indies:	141	Kingston (5th Test)	2000/01

For West Indies:

In South Africa:	121	Port Elizabeth (2nd Test)	1998/99
In West Indies:	140	St John's (4th Test)	2000/01

LARGEST MARGINS OF VICTORY

By an innings:

South Africa beat West Indies at Bridgetown by an innings and 86 runs	2004/05

By runs:

South Africa beat West Indies at Centurion by 351 runs	1998/99
West Indies beat South Africa at Kingston by 130 runs	2000/01

BATTING

INDIVIDUAL CENTURIES

For South Africa (30):

100	MV Boucher (2)	Centurion	1998/99
122*		Cape Town	2003/04
168	DJ Cullinan (3)	Cape Town	1998/99
103		Port-of-Spain	2000/01
134		Bridgetown	2000/01
178	AB de Villiers (2)	Bridgetown	2004/05
114		St John's	2004/05
142	HH Gibbs (3)	Durban	2003/04
142		Cape Town	2003/04
192		Centurion	2003/04
163	AC Hudson	Bridgetown	1991/92
110	JH Kallis (7)	Cape Town	1998/99
158		Johannesburg	2003/04
177		Durban	2003/04
130*		Cape Town	2003/04
130*		Centurion	2003/04
109*		Georgetown	2004/05
147		St John's	2004/05
134	G Kirsten (3)	Centurion	1998/99
150		Georgetown	2000/01
137		Durban	2003/04
106*	SM Pollock	Bridgetown	2000/01
131	AG Prince	St John's	2004/05
103*	JN Rhodes	Centurion	1998/99
101	JA Rudolph	Cape Town	2003/04
132	GC Smith (5)	Johannesburg	2003/04
139		Centurion	2003/04
148		Port-of-Spain	2004/05
104		Bridgetown	2004/05
126		St John's	2004/05

For West Indies (18):

107	DJJ Bravo	St John's	2004/05
109	S Chanderpaul (3)	Durban	2003/04
203*		Georgetown	2004/05
127		St John's	2004/05
116	CH Gayle (3)	Cape Town	2003/04
107		Centurion	2003/04
317		St John's	2004/05

213	WW Hinds	Georgetown	2004/05
113*	RD Jacobs	Bridgetown	2000/01
202	BC Lara (4)	Johannesburg	2003/04
115		Cape Town	2003/04
196		Port-of-Spain	2004/05
176		Bridgetown	2004/05
114	RR Sarwan (4)	Durban	2003/04
119		Centurion	2003/04
107*		Port-of-Spain	2004/05
127		St John's	2004/05
105*	DR Smith	Cape Town	2003/04

CENTURY ON DEBUT IN THE SERIES

For South Africa:			
163	AC Hudson	Bridgetown (on Test debut)	1991/92
132	GC Smith	Johannesburg	2003/04
For West Indies:			
105*	DR Smith	Cape Town (on Test debut)	2003/04

HIGHEST INDIVIDUAL INNINGS

For South Africa:	In South Africa:	192	HH Gibbs	Centurion	2003/04
	In West Indies:	178	AB de Villiers	Bridgetown	2004/05
For West Indies:	In South Africa:	202	BC Lara	Johannesburg	2003/04
	In West Indies:	317	CH Gayle	St John's	2004/05

MOST RUNS IN A SERIES

		Runs	Matches		
For South Africa:	In South Africa:	712	4	JH Kallis (Avg 178.00)	2003/04
	In West Indies:	505	4	GC Smith (Avg 84.16)	2004/05
For West Indies:	In South Africa:	531	4	BC Lara (Avg 66.37)	2003/04
	In West Indies:	450	4	S Chanderpaul (Avg 90.00)	2004/05

RECORD WICKET PARTNERSHIPS

For South Africa:				
1st	301	GC Smith and HH Gibbs	Centurion	2003/04
2nd	146	G Kirsten and JH Kallis	Georgetown	2000/01
3rd	251	HH Gibbs and JH Kallis	Cape Town	2003/04
4th	249	JH Kallis and G Kirsten	Durban	2003/04
5th	267	JH Kallis and AG Prince	St John's	2004/05
6th	92	JN Rhodes and SM Pollock	Port Elizabeth	1998/99
7th	92	JH Kallis and MV Boucher	Centurion	1998/99
8th	146	MV Boucher and JH Kallis	Cape Town	2003/04
9th	132	SM Pollock and AA Donald	Bridgetown	2000/01
10th	41	RJ Peterson and M Ntini	Johannesburg	2003/04
For West Indies:				
1st	126	CH Gayle and D Ganga	Cape Town	2003/04
2nd	331	CH Gayle and RR Sarwan	St John's	2004/05
3rd	160	S Chanderpaul and BC Lara	Durban	1998/99
4th	284	WW Hinds and S Chanderpaul	Georgetown	2004/05
5th	116	BC Lara and CL Hooper	Bridgetown	2000/01
	116	S Chanderpaul and RO Hinds	Georgetown	2004/05
6th	130	S Chanderpaul and DJJ Bravo	St John's	2004/05
7th	81	RD Jacobs and NAM McLean	Centurion	1998/99
8th	65	RD Jacobs and NAM McLean	Cape Town	1998/99
9th	71	RD Jacobs and M Dillon	Port-of-Spain	2000/01
10th	64	RD Jacobs and M Dillon	Cape Town	1998/99

SOUTH AFRICAN TEST MATCH RECORDS

BOWLING

SEVEN WICKETS IN AN INNINGS

For South Africa:			
7-37	M Ntini	Port-of-Spain	2004/05
For West Indies:			
7-84	FA Rose	Durban	1998/99

TEN WICKETS IN A MATCH

For South Africa:			
13-132	M Ntini	Port-of-Spain	2004/05
10-88	A Nel	Bridgetown	2004/05
For West Indies:	No instance. The best performance is		
8-79	CEL Ambrose	Port Elizabeth	1998/99

MOST WICKETS IN A SERIES

		Wickets	Matches		
For South Africa:	In South Africa:	29	5	SM Pollock (Avg 16.65)	1998/99
		29	4	M Ntini (Avg 21.37)	2003/04
	In West Indies:	20	5	JH Kallis (Avg 19.75)	2000/01
		20	5	SM Pollock (Avg 23.20)	2000/01
For West Indies:	In South Africa:	22	4	CA Walsh (Avg 18.90)	1998/99
	In West Indies:	25	5	CA Walsh (Avg 19.68)	2000/01

WICKETKEEPING

MOST DISMISSALS IN AN INNINGS

For South Africa:	5 (ct 5)	MV Boucher	Kingston	2000/01
For West Indies:	4 (ct 4)	RD Jacobs	Cape Town	1998/99
	4 (ct 4)	RD Jacobs	Centurion	1998/99
	4 (ct 4)	RD Jacobs	Cape Town	2003/04

MOST DISMISSALS IN A MATCH

For South Africa:	6 (ct 6)	DJ Richardson	Bridgetown	1991/92
	6 (ct 6)	MV Boucher	Kingston	2000/01
For West Indies:	6 (ct 6)	RD Jacobs	Port-of-Spain	2000/01

MOST DISMISSALS IN A SERIES

For South Africa:	18 (ct 18)	MV Boucher	in West Indies	2000/01
For West Indies:	21 (ct 21)	RD Jacobs	in West Indies	2000/01

FIELDING

MOST CATCHES IN AN INNINGS

For South Africa:	4	HH Gibbs	Durban	1998/99
For West Indies:	4	CL Hooper	Port Elizabeth	1998/99

MOST CATCHES IN A MATCH

For South Africa:	4	HH Gibbs	Durban	1998/99
	4	G Kirsten	St John's	2000/01
	4	ND McKenzie	St John's	2000/01
For West Indies:	5	BC Lara	Bridgetown	1991/92
	5	CL Hooper	Port Elizabeth	1998/99

MOST CATCHES IN A SERIES

For South Africa:	10	WJ Cronje	in South Africa	1998/99
	10	DJ Cullinan	in West Indies	2000/01
For West Indies:	8	CL Hooper	in South Africa	1998/99

SOUTH AFRICA versus ZIMBABWE

Season	Venue	SA captain	Zim captain	Played	Won	Lost	Drawn
1995/96	Zimbabwe	WJ Cronje	A Flower	1	1	0	0
1999/00	South Africa	WJ Cronje	ADR Campbell	1	1	0	0
1999/00	Zimbabwe	WJ Cronje	A Flower	1	1	0	0
2001/02	Zimbabwe	SM Pollock	HH Streak	2	1	0	1
2004/05	South Africa	GC Smith	T Taibu	2	2	0	0
		Tests in South Africa		3	3	0	0
		Tests in Zimbabwe		4	3	0	1
		Total		7	6	0	1

HIGHEST INNINGS TOTALS

For South Africa:	600-3*	Harare (1st Test)	2001/02
For Zimbabwe:	419-9*	Bulawayo (2nd Test)	2001/02

LOWEST INNINGS TOTALS

For South Africa:	346	Harare (Only Test)	1995/96
For Zimbabwe:	54	Cape Town (1st Test)	2004/05

LARGEST MARGINS OF VICTORY

By an innings:

South Africa beat Zimbabwe at Harare by an innings and 219 runs 1999/00

BATTING

INDIVIDUAL CENTURIES

For South Africa (9):

125	MV Boucher	Harare	1999/00
147	HH Gibbs	Harare	2001/02
135	AC Hudson	Harare	1995/96
115	JH Kallis (3)	Harare	1999/00
157*		Harare	2001/02
189*		Bulawayo	2001/02
220	G Kirsten	Harare	2001/02
139*	AG Prince	Centurion	2004/05
121	GC Smith	Cape Town	2004/05

For Zimbabwe (2):

142 & 199*	A Flower (2)	Harare	2001/02

CENTURY ON DEBUT IN THE SERIES

For South Africa:

135	AC Hudson	Harare	1995/96
147	HH Gibbs	Harare	2001/02
121	GC Smith	Cape Town	2004/05

HIGHEST INDIVIDUAL INNINGS

For South Africa:	In South Africa:	139*	AG Prince	Centurion	2004/05
	In Zimbabwe:	220	G Kirsten	Harare	2001/02
For Zimbabwe:	In South Africa:	85	GJ Whittall	Bloemfontein	1999/00
		85	HH Streak	Centurion	2004/05
	In Zimbabwe:	199*	A Flower	Harare	2001/02

MOST RUNS IN A SERIES

		Runs	Matches		
For South Africa:	In Zimbabwe:	388	2	JH Kallis (Avg -)	2001/02
For Zimbabwe:	In Zimbabwe:	422	2	A Flower (Avg 211.00)	2001/02

SOUTH AFRICAN TEST MATCH RECORDS

RECORD WICKET PARTNERSHIPS

For South Africa:				
1st	256	HH Gibbs and G Kirsten	Harare	2001/02
2nd	199	G Kirsten and JH Kallis	Harare	2001/02
3rd	181	JH Kallis and ND McKenzie	Bulawayo	2001/02
4th	100	JH Kallis and WJ Cronje	Harare	1999/00
5th	60	AC Hudson and JN Rhodes	Harare	1995/96
6th	119	AG Prince and JH Kallis	Centurion	2004/05
7th	142	AG Prince and N Boje	Centurion	2004/05
8th	148	MV Boucher and SM Pollock	Harare	1999/00
9th	79	BM McMillan and AA Donald	Harare	1995/96
10th	54	MV Boucher and PR Adams	Bloemfontein	1999/00
For Zimbabwe:				
1st	152	ADR Campbell and DD Ebrahim	Bulawayo	2001/02
2nd	51	MH Dekker and ADR Campbell	Harare	1995/96
3rd	98	DD Ebrahim and H Masakadza	Cape Town	2004/05
4th	186	H Masakadza and A Flower	Harare	2001/02
5th	97	A Flower and GJ Whittall	Harare	1995/96
6th	17	A Flower and GJ Whittall	Harare	2001/02
7th	58	HH Streak and E Chigumbura	Centurion	2004/05
8th	76	HH Streak and AM Blignaut	Centurion	2004/05
9th	75	A Flower and TJ Friend	Harare	2001/02
10th	47	A Flower and DT Hondo	Harare	2001/02

BOWLING

SEVEN WICKETS IN AN INNINGS

For South Africa:			
8-71	AA Donald	Harare	1995/96
For Zimbabwe:	No instance. The best performance is		
5-101	BC Strang	Harare	1995/96

TEN WICKETS IN A MATCH

For South Africa:			
11-113	AA Donald	Harare	1995/96
For Zimbabwe:	No instance. The best performance is		
5-105	ACI Lock	Harare	1995/96

MOST WICKETS IN A SERIES

		Wickets	Matches		
For South Africa:	In South Africa	11	2	JH Kallis (Avg 9.63)	2004/05
	In Zimbabwe:	11	1	AA Donald (Avg 10.27)	1995/96
		11	2	CW Henderson (Avg 32.09)	2001/02
For Zimbabwe:	In South Africa	6	2	AG Cremer (Avg 32.00)	2004/05
	In Zimbabwe:	6	2	TJ Friend (Avg 46.33)	2001/02

SOUTH AFRICA TEST CAREER RECORDS

As at 1 September 2006

Name	Years	M	Inns	NO	Runs	HS	Avg	100	50	Ct	St	Balls	Runs	Wkts	Avg	RpO	BB	5I	10M
HD Ackerman	1998-1998	4	8	0	161	57	20.12	0	1	1	0	0	0	0	-	-	-	0	0
PR Adams	1995-2004	45	55	15	360	35	9.00	0	0	29	0	8850	4405	134	32.87	2.98	7-128	4	1
NAT Adcock	1953-1962	26	39	12	146	24	5.40	0	0	4	0	6391	2195	104	21.10	2.06	6-43	5	0
HM Amla	2004-2006	7	13	0	364	149	28.00	1	1	6	0	6	4	0	-	4.00	-	0	0
WH Ashley	1889-1889	1	2	0	1	1	0.50	0	0	0	0	173	95	7	13.57	3.29	7-95	1	0
A Bacher	1965-1970	12	22	1	679	73	32.33	0	6	10	0	0	0	0	-	-	-	0	0
AM Bacher	1996-1999	19	33	1	833	96	26.03	0	5	11	0	6	4	0	-	4.00	-	0	0
XC Balaskas	1930-1938	9	13	1	174	122*	14.50	1	0	5	0	1572	806	22	36.63	3.07	5-49	1	0
EJ Barlow	1961-1970	30	57	2	2516	201	45.74	6	15	35	0	3021	1362	40	34.05	2.70	5-85	1	0
HV Baumgartner	1913-1913	1	2	0	19	16	9.50	0	0	1	0	166	99	2	49.50	3.57	2-99	0	0
R Beaumont	1912-1914	5	9	0	70	31	7.77	0	0	2	0	6	0	0	-	0.00	-	0	0
DW Begbie	1948-1950	5	7	0	138	48	19.71	0	0	2	0	160	130	1	130.00	4.87	1-38	0	0
AJ Bell	1929-1935	16	23	12	69	26*	6.27	0	0	6	0	3342	1567	48	32.64	2.81	6-99	4	0
M Bisset	1899-1910	3	6	2	103	35	25.75	0	0	2	1	0	0	0	-	-	-	0	0
GF Bissett	1927-1928	4	4	2	38	23	19.00	0	0	0	0	989	469	25	18.76	2.84	7-29	2	0
JM Blanckenberg	1913-1924	18	30	7	455	59	19.78	0	2	9	0	3888	1817	60	30.28	2.80	6-76	4	0
KC Bland	1961-1966	21	39	5	1669	144*	49.08	3	9	10	0	394	125	2	62.50	1.90	2-16	0	0
EG Bock	1935-1935	1	2	2	11	9*	-	0	0	0	0	138	91	0	-	3.95	-	0	0
N Boje	2000-2006	43	62	10	1312	85	25.23	0	4	18	0	8620	4265	100	42.65	2.96	5-62	3	0
GE Bond	1938-1938	1	1	0	0	0	0.00	0	0	0	0	16	16	0	-	6.00	-	0	0
T Bosch	1992-1992	1	2	2	5	5*	-	0	0	0	0	237	104	3	34.66	2.63	2-61	0	0
J Botha	2006-2006	1	1	1	20	20*	-	0	0	0	0	117	103	2	51.50	5.28	1-26	0	0
JT Botten	1965-1965	3	6	0	65	33	10.83	0	0	1	0	828	337	8	42.12	2.44	2-56	0	0
MV Boucher	1997-2006	95	134	17	3565	125	30.47	4	23	348	14	8	6	1	6.00	4.50	1-6	0	0
WH Brann	1922-1923	3	5	0	71	50	14.20	0	1	2	0	0	0	0	-	-	-	0	0
AW Briscoe	1935-1938	2	3	0	33	16	11.00	0	0	1	0	0	0	0	-	-	-	0	0
HD Bromfield	1961-1965	9	12	7	59	21	11.80	0	0	13	0	1810	599	17	35.23	1.98	5-88	1	0
LS Brown	1931-1932	2	3	0	17	8	5.66	0	0	0	0	318	189	3	63.00	3.56	1-30	0	0
CGD Burger	1958-1958	2	4	1	62	37*	20.66	0	0	1	0	0	0	0	-	-	-	0	0
SF Burke	1962-1965	2	4	1	42	20	14.00	0	0	0	0	660	257	11	23.36	2.33	6-128	2	1

SOUTH AFRICA TEST CAREER RECORDS

Name	Years	M	Inns	NO	Runs	HS	Avg	100	50	Ct	St	Balls	Runs	Wkts	Avg	RpO	BB	5I	10M
ID Buys	1922-1922	1	2	1	4	4*	4.00	0	0	0	0	144	52	0	-	2.16	-	0	0
HB Cameron	1927-1935	26	45	4	1239	90	30.21	0	10	39	12	0	0	0	-	-	-	0	0
T Campbell	1910-1912	5	9	3	90	48	15.00	0	0	7	1	0	0	0	-	-	-	0	0
PR Carlstein	1958-1964	8	14	1	190	42	14.61	0	0	3	0	0	0	0	-	-	-	0	0
CP Carter	1912-1924	10	15	5	181	45	18.10	0	0	2	0	1475	694	28	24.78	2.82	6-50	2	0
RH Catterall	1922-1931	24	43	2	1555	120	37.92	3	11	12	0	342	162	7	23.14	2.84	3-15	0	0
HW Chapman	1914-1921	2	4	1	39	17	13.00	0	0	1	0	126	104	1	104.00	4.95	1-51	0	0
JE Cheetham	1949-1955	24	43	6	883	89	23.86	0	5	13	0	6	2	0	-	2.00	-	0	0
GA Chevalier	1970-1970	1	2	1	0	0*	0.00	0	0	1	0	253	100	5	20.00	2.37	3-68	0	0
JAJ Christy	1929-1932	10	18	0	618	103	34.33	1	5	3	0	138	92	2	46.00	4.00	1-15	0	0
GWA Chubb	1951-1951	5	9	3	63	15*	10.50	0	0	0	0	1425	577	21	27.47	2.42	6-51	2	0
JAK Cochran	1931-1931	1	1	0	4	4	4.00	0	0	0	0	138	47	0	-	2.04	-	0	0
SK Coen	1927-1928	2	4	2	101	41*	50.50	0	0	1	0	12	7	0	-	3.50	-	0	0
JMM Commaille	1910-1927	12	22	1	355	47	16.90	0	0	1	0	0	0	0	-	-	-	0	0
JB Commins	1994-1995	3	6	1	125	45	25.00	0	0	2	0	0	0	0	-	-	-	0	0
DP Conyngham	1923-1923	1	2	2	6	3*	-	0	0	1	0	366	103	2	51.50	1.68	1-40	0	0
FJ Cook	1896-1896	1	2	0	7	7	3.50	0	0	0	0	0	0	0	-	-	-	0	0
SJ Cook	1992-1993	3	6	0	107	43	17.83	0	0	0	0	0	0	0	-	-	-	0	0
AHC Cooper	1913-1913	1	2	0	6	6	3.00	0	0	1	0	0	0	0	-	-	-	0	0
JL Cox	1913-1914	3	6	1	17	12*	3.40	0	0	1	0	576	245	4	61.25	2.55	2-74	0	0
G Cripps	1892-1892	1	2	0	21	18	10.50	0	0	0	0	15	23	0	-	9.20	-	0	0
RJ Crisp	1935-1936	9	13	1	123	35	10.25	0	0	3	0	1428	747	20	37.35	3.13	5-99	1	0
WJ Cronje	1992-2000	68	111	9	3714	135	36.41	6	23	33	0	3800	1288	43	29.95	2.03	3-14	0	0
DJ Cullinan	1993-2001	70	115	12	4554	275*	44.21	14	20	67	0	120	71	2	35.50	3.55	1-10	0	0
SH Curnow	1930-1932	7	14	0	168	47	12.00	0	0	5	0	0	0	0	-	-	-	0	0
EL Dalton	1929-1939	15	24	2	698	117	31.72	2	3	5	0	864	490	12	40.83	3.40	4-59	0	0
EQ Davies	1936-1939	5	8	3	9	3	1.80	0	0	0	0	768	481	7	68.71	3.75	4-75	0	0
AC Dawson	2003-2003	2	1	0	10	10	10.00	0	0	0	0	252	117	5	23.40	2.78	2-20	0	0
OC Dawson	1947-1949	9	15	1	293	55	20.92	0	1	10	0	1294	578	10	57.80	2.68	2-57	0	0
HG Deane	1924-1931	17	27	2	628	93	25.12	0	3	8	0	0	0	0	-	-	-	0	0
Z de Bruyn	2004-2004	3	5	1	155	83	38.75	0	1	0	0	216	92	3	30.66	2.55	2-32	0	0
AB de Villiers	2004-2006	22	40	1	1607	178	41.20	3	10	29	1	198	99	2	49.50	3.00	2-49	0	0
PS de Villiers	1993-1998	18	26	7	359	67*	18.89	0	2	11	0	4805	2063	85	24.27	2.57	6-23	5	2
HH Dippenaar	1999-2006	37	60	5	1715	177*	31.18	3	7	27	0	12	1	0	-	0.50	-	0	0
CD Dixon	1914-1914	1	2	0	0	0	0.00	0	0	1	0	240	118	3	39.33	2.95	2-62	0	0
AA Donald	1992-2002	72	94	33	652	37	10.68	0	0	18	0	15519	7344	330	22.25	2.83	8-71	20	3

SOUTH AFRICA TEST CAREER RECORDS

Name	Years	M	Inns	NO	Runs	HS	Avg	100	50	Ct	St	Balls	Runs	Wkts	Avg	RpO	BB	5I	10M
RR Dower	1899-1899	1	2	0	9	9	4.50	0	0	2	0	0	0	0	-	-	-	0	0
RG Draper	1950-1950	2	3	0	25	15	8.33	0	0	0	0	0	0	0	-	-	-	0	0
CAR Duckworth	1957-1957	2	4	0	28	13	7.00	0	0	3	0	0	0	0	-	-	-	0	0
R Dumbrill	1965-1966	5	10	0	153	36	15.30	0	0	3	0	816	336	9	37.33	2.47	4-30	0	0
JP Duminy	1927-1929	3	6	0	30	12	5.00	0	0	2	0	60	39	1	39.00	3.90	1-17	0	0
OR Dunell	1889-1889	2	4	1	42	26*	14.00	0	0	1	0	0	0	0	-	-	-	0	0
JH du Preez	1967-1967	2	2	0	0	0	0.00	0	0	2	0	144	51	3	17.00	2.12	2-22	0	0
JF du Toit	1892-1892	1	2	2	2	2*	-	0	0	1	0	85	47	1	47.00	3.31	1-47	0	0
DV Dyer	1947-1947	3	6	0	96	62	16.00	0	1	0	0	0	0	0	-	-	-	0	0
CE Eksteen	1993-2000	7	11	2	91	22	10.11	0	0	5	0	1536	494	8	61.75	1.92	3-12	0	0
MK Elgie	1961-1962	3	6	0	75	56	12.50	0	1	4	0	66	46	0	-	4.18	-	0	0
S Elworthy	1998-2002	4	5	1	72	48	18.00	0	0	1	0	867	444	13	34.15	3.07	4-66	0	0
WR Endean	1951-1958	28	52	4	1630	162*	33.95	3	8	41	0	0	0	0	-	-	-	0	0
WS Farrer	1962-1964	6	10	2	221	40	27.62	0	0	2	0	0	0	0	-	-	-	0	0
GA Faulkner	1906-1924	25	47	4	1754	204	40.79	4	8	20	0	4227	2180	82	26.58	3.09	7-84	4	0
JP Fellows-Smith	1960-1960	4	8	2	166	35	27.66	0	0	2	0	114	61	0	-	3.21	-	0	0
CG Fichardt	1892-1896	2	4	0	15	10	3.75	0	0	2	0	0	0	0	-	-	-	0	0
CE Finlason	1889-1889	1	2	0	6	6	3.00	0	0	0	0	12	7	0	-	3.50	-	0	0
CE Floquet	1910-1910	1	2	1	12	12*	12.00	0	0	0	0	48	24	0	-	3.00	-	0	0
HH Francis	1899-1899	2	4	0	39	29	9.75	0	0	1	0	0	0	0	-	-	-	0	0
CM Francois	1922-1923	5	9	1	252	72	31.50	0	1	5	0	684	225	6	37.50	1.97	3-23	0	0
CN Frank	1921-1921	3	6	0	236	152	39.33	1	0	0	0	0	0	0	-	-	-	0	0
WHB Frank	1896-1896	1	2	0	7	5	3.50	0	0	0	0	58	52	1	52.00	5.37	1-52	0	0
ERH Fuller	1953-1957	7	9	1	64	17	8.00	0	0	3	0	1898	668	22	30.36	2.11	5-66	1	0
GM Fullerton	1947-1951	7	13	0	325	88	25.00	0	3	10	2	0	0	0	-	-	-	0	0
KJ Funston	1952-1958	18	33	1	824	92	25.75	0	5	7	0	0	0	0	-	-	-	0	0
D Gamsy	1970-1970	2	3	1	39	30*	19.50	0	0	5	0	0	0	0	-	-	-	0	0
HH Gibbs	1996-2006	79	135	6	5728	228	44.40	14	22	72	0	6	4	0	-	4.00	-	0	0
RA Gleeson	1896-1896	1	2	1	4	3	4.00	0	0	2	0	0	0	0	-	-	-	0	0
GK Glover	1896-1896	1	2	1	21	18*	21.00	0	0	0	0	65	28	1	28.00	2.58	1-28	0	0
TL Goddard	1955-1970	41	78	5	2516	112	34.46	1	18	48	0	11736	3226	123	26.22	1.64	6-53	5	0
N Gordon	1938-1939	5	6	2	8	7*	2.00	0	0	1	0	1966	807	20	40.35	2.46	5-103	2	0
R Graham	1899-1899	2	4	0	6	4	1.50	0	0	2	0	240	127	3	42.33	3.17	2-22	0	0
RE Grieveson	1939-1939	2	2	0	114	75	57.00	0	1	7	3	0	0	0	-	-	-	0	0
GM Griffin	1960-1960	2	4	0	25	14	6.25	0	0	0	0	432	192	8	24.00	2.66	4-87	0	0

SOUTH AFRICA TEST CAREER RECORDS

Name	Years	M	Inns	NO	Runs	HS	Avg	100	50	Ct	St	Balls	Runs	Wkts	Avg	RpO	BB	5I	10M
AE Hall	1923-1931	7	8	2	11	5	1.83	0	0	4	0	2361	886	40	22.15	2.25	7-63	3	1
AJ Hall	2002-2006	19	30	4	735	163	28.26	1	3	15	0	2838	1511	39	38.74	3.19	3-1	0	0
GG Hall	1965-1965	1	1	0	0	0	0.00	0	0	0	0	186	94	1	94.00	3.03	1-94	0	0
EA Halliwell	1892-1902	8	15	0	188	57	12.53	0	1	10	2	0	0	0	-	-	-	0	0
CG Halse	1964-1964	3	3	3	30	19*	-	0	0	1	0	587	260	6	43.33	2.65	3-50	0	0
PAM Hands	1913-1924	7	12	0	300	83	25.00	0	2	3	0	37	18	0	-	2.91	-	0	0
RHM Hands	1914-1914	1	2	0	7	7	3.50	0	0	0	0	0	0	0	-	-	-	0	0
MA Hanley	1949-1949	1	1	0	0	0	0.00	0	0	0	0	232	88	1	88.00	2.27	1-57	0	0
TA Harris	1947-1949	3	5	1	100	60	25.00	0	1	1	0	0	0	0	-	-	-	0	0
GPD Hartigan	1912-1914	5	10	0	114	51	11.40	0	1	0	0	252	141	1	141.00	3.35	1-72	0	0
RL Harvey	1936-1936	2	4	0	51	28	12.75	0	0	0	0	0	0	0	-	-	-	0	0
CMH Hathorn	1902-1911	12	20	1	325	102	17.10	1	0	5	0	0	0	0	-	-	-	0	0
M Hayward	1999-2004	16	17	8	66	14	7.33	0	0	4	0	2821	1609	54	29.79	3.42	5-56	1	0
F Hearne	1892-1896	4	8	0	121	30	15.12	0	0	2	0	62	40	2	20.00	3.87	2-40	0	0
GAL Hearne	1922-1924	3	5	0	59	28	11.80	0	0	3	0	0	0	0	-	-	-	0	0
PS Heine	1955-1962	14	24	3	209	31	9.95	0	0	8	0	3890	1455	58	25.08	2.24	6-58	4	0
CW Henderson	2001-2002	7	7	0	65	30	9.28	0	0	2	0	1962	928	22	42.18	2.83	4-116	0	0
O Henry	1992-1993	3	3	0	53	34	17.66	0	0	2	0	427	189	3	63.00	2.65	2-56	0	0
CFW Hime	1896-1896	1	2	0	8	8	4.00	0	0	0	0	55	31	1	31.00	3.38	1-20	0	0
AC Hudson	1992-1998	35	63	3	2007	163	33.45	4	13	36	0	0	0	0	-	-	-	0	0
P Hutchinson	1889-1889	2	4	0	14	11	3.50	0	0	3	0	0	0	0	-	-	-	0	0
DEJ Ironside	1953-1954	3	4	2	37	13	18.50	0	0	1	0	986	275	15	18.33	1.67	5-51	1	0
BL Irvine	1970-1970	4	7	0	353	102	50.42	1	2	2	0	0	0	0	-	-	-	0	0
SD Jack	1994-1995	2	2	0	7	7	3.50	0	0	1	0	462	196	8	24.50	2.54	4-69	0	0
CL Johnson	1896-1896	1	2	0	10	7	5.00	0	0	1	0	140	57	0	-	2.44	-	0	0
JH Kallis	1995-2006	101	170	27	7950	189*	55.59	24	40	94	0	13529	6304	199	31.67	2.79	6-54	4	0
HJ Keith	1953-1957	8	16	1	318	73	21.20	0	2	9	0	108	63	0	-	3.50	-	0	0
JM Kemp	2001-2005	4	6	0	80	55	13.33	0	1	3	0	479	222	9	24.66	2.78	3-33	0	0
GA Kempis	1889-1889	1	2	1	0	0*	0.00	0	0	0	0	168	76	4	19.00	2.71	3-53	0	0
G Kirsten	1993-2004	101	176	15	7289	275	45.27	21	34	83	0	349	142	2	71.00	2.44	1-0	0	0
PN Kirsten	1992-1994	12	22	2	626	104	31.30	1	4	8	0	54	30	0	-	3.33	-	0	0
L Klusener	1996-2004	49	69	11	1906	174	32.86	4	8	34	0	6887	3033	80	37.91	2.64	8-64	1	0
JJ Kotze	1902-1907	3	5	0	2	2	0.40	0	0	3	0	413	243	6	40.50	3.53	3-64	0	0
AP Kuiper	1992-1992	1	2	0	34	34	17.00	0	0	1	0	0	0	0	-	-	-	0	0
F Kuys	1899-1899	1	2	0	26	26	13.00	0	0	0	0	60	31	2	15.50	3.10	2-31	0	0

SOUTH AFRICA TEST CAREER RECORDS

Name	Years	M	Inns	NO	Runs	HS	Avg	100	50	Ct	St	Balls	Runs	Wkts	Avg	RpO	BB	5I	10M
HR Lance	1962-1970	13	22	1	591	70	28.14	0	5	7	0	948	479	12	39.91	3.03	3-30	0	0
CK Langeveldt	2005-2006	6	4	2	16	10	8.00	0	0	2	0	999	593	16	37.06	3.56	5-46	1	0
ACB Langton	1935-1939	15	23	4	298	73*	15.68	0	2	8	0	4199	1827	40	45.67	2.61	5-58	1	0
GB Lawrence	1961-1962	5	8	0	141	43	17.62	0	0	2	0	1334	512	28	18.28	2.30	8-53	2	0
FL le Roux	1914-1914	1	2	0	1	1	0.50	0	0	0	0	54	24	0	-	2.66	-	0	0
PT Lewis	1913-1913	1	2	0	0	0	0.00	0	0	0	0	0	0	0	-	-	-	0	0
GFJ Liebenberg	1998-1998	5	8	0	104	45	13.00	0	0	1	0	0	0	0	-	-	-	0	0
DT Lindsay	1963-1970	19	31	1	1130	182	37.66	3	5	57	2	0	0	0	-	-	-	0	0
JD Lindsay	1947-1947	3	5	2	21	9*	7.00	0	0	4	1	0	0	0	-	-	-	0	0
NV Lindsay	1921-1921	1	2	0	35	29	17.50	0	0	1	0	0	0	0	-	-	-	0	0
WVS Ling	1921-1923	6	10	0	168	38	16.80	0	0	1	0	18	20	0	-	6.66	-	0	0
CB Llewellyn	1896-1912	15	28	1	544	90	20.14	0	4	7	0	2292	1421	48	29.60	3.71	6-92	4	1
EB Lundie	1914-1914	1	2	1	1	1	1.00	0	0	0	0	285	107	4	26.75	2.24	4-101	0	0
MJ Macaulay	1965-1965	1	2	0	33	21	16.50	0	0	0	0	275	73	2	36.50	1.58	1-10	0	0
CN McCarthy	1948-1951	15	24	15	28	5	3.11	0	0	6	0	3499	1510	36	41.94	2.58	6-43	2	0
DJ McGlew	1951-1962	34	64	6	2440	255*	42.06	7	10	18	0	32	23	0	-	4.31	-	0	0
ND McKenzie	2000-2004	41	65	4	2028	120	33.24	2	13	37	0	72	63	0	-	5.25	-	0	0
AH McKinnon	1960-1966	8	13	7	107	27	17.83	0	0	1	0	2546	925	26	35.57	2.17	4-128	0	0
RA McLean	1951-1964	40	73	3	2120	142	30.28	5	10	23	0	4	1	0	-	1.50	-	0	0
BM McMillan	1992-1998	38	62	12	1968	113	39.36	3	13	49	0	6048	2537	75	33.82	2.51	4-65	0	0
Q McMillan	1929-1932	13	21	4	306	50*	18.00	0	1	8	0	2021	1243	36	34.52	3.69	5-66	2	0
NBF Mann	1947-1951	19	31	1	400	52	13.33	0	1	3	0	5796	1920	58	33.10	1.98	6-59	1	0
PNF Mansell	1951-1955	13	22	2	355	90	17.75	0	2	15	0	1506	736	11	66.90	2.93	3-58	0	0
LA Markham	1949-1949	1	1	0	20	20	20.00	0	0	0	0	104	72	1	72.00	4.15	1-34	0	0
WFE Marx	1921-1921	3	6	0	125	36	20.83	0	0	0	0	228	144	4	36.00	3.78	3-85	0	0
CR Matthews	1992-1995	18	25	6	348	62*	18.31	0	1	4	0	3980	1502	52	28.88	2.26	5-42	2	0
DJ Meintjes	1923-1923	2	3	0	43	21	14.33	0	0	3	0	246	115	6	19.16	2.80	3-38	0	0
MG Melle	1950-1953	7	12	4	68	17	8.50	0	0	4	0	1667	851	26	32.73	3.06	6-71	2	0
A Melville	1938-1949	11	19	2	894	189	52.58	4	3	8	0	0	0	0	-	-	-	0	0
J Middleton	1896-1902	6	12	5	52	22	7.42	0	0	1	0	1064	442	24	18.41	2.49	5-51	2	0
CH Mills	1892-1892	1	2	0	25	21	12.50	0	0	1	0	140	83	2	41.50	3.55	2-83	0	0
WH Milton	1889-1892	3	6	0	68	21	11.33	0	0	2	0	79	48	2	24.00	3.64	1-5	0	0
B Mitchell	1929-1949	42	80	9	3471	89*	48.88	8	21	56	0	2519	1380	27	51.11	3.28	5-87	1	0
F Mitchell	1912-1912	3	6	0	28	12	4.66	0	0	0	0	0	0	0	-	-	-	0	0
DPB Morkel	1927-1932	16	28	1	663	88	24.55	0	4	13	0	1704	821	18	45.61	2.89	4-93	0	0

SOUTH AFRICA TEST CAREER RECORDS

Name	Years	M	Inns	NO	Runs	HS	Avg	100	50	Ct	St	Balls	Runs	Wkts	Avg	RpO	BB	5I	10M
ARA Murray	1952-1954	10	14	1	289	109	22.23	1	1	3	0	2374	710	18	39.44	1.79	4-169	0	0
A Nel	2001-2006	23	25	6	135	18*	7.10	0	0	9	0	4959	2503	84	29.79	3.02	6-32	3	1
JD Nel	1949-1957	6	11	0	150	38	13.63	0	0	1	0	0	0	0	-	-	-	0	0
C Newberry	1913-1914	4	8	0	62	16	7.75	0	0	3	0	558	268	11	24.36	2.88	4-72	0	0
ES Newson	1930-1939	3	5	1	30	16	7.50	0	0	3	0	874	265	4	66.25	1.81	2-58	0	0
M Ngam	2000-2001	3	1	1	0	0*	-	0	0	1	0	392	189	11	17.18	2.89	3-26	0	0
F Nicholson	1935-1936	4	8	1	76	29	10.85	0	0	3	0	0	0	0	-	-	-	0	0
JFW Nicolson	1928-1928	3	5	0	179	78	35.80	0	1	0	0	24	17	0	-	4.25	-	0	0
NO Norton	1910-1910	1	2	0	9	7	4.50	0	0	0	0	90	47	4	11.75	3.13	4-47	0	0
AD Nourse	1935-1951	34	62	7	2960	231	53.81	9	14	12	0	20	9	0	-	2.70	-	0	0
AW Nourse	1902-1924	45	83	8	2234	111	29.78	1	15	43	0	3234	1553	41	37.87	2.88	4-25	0	0
M Ntini	1998-2006	69	78	23	572	32*	10.40	0	0	18	0	14597	7751	274	28.28	3.18	7-37	14	4
EP Nupen	1921-1936	17	31	7	348	69	14.50	0	2	9	0	4159	1788	50	35.76	2.57	6-46	5	1
AE Ochse	1889-1889	2	4	0	16	8	4.00	0	0	0	0	0	0	0	-	-	-	0	0
AL Ochse	1928-1929	3	4	1	11	4*	3.66	0	0	1	0	649	362	10	36.20	3.34	4-79	0	0
S O'Linn	1960-1961	7	12	1	297	98	27.00	0	2	4	0	0	0	0	-	-	-	0	0
JL Ontong	2002-2004	2	4	1	57	32	19.00	0	0	1	0	185	133	1	133.00	4.31	1-79	0	0
HGO Owen-Smith	1929-1929	5	8	2	252	129	42.00	1	1	4	0	156	113	0	-	4.34	-	0	0
AW Palm	1927-1927	1	2	0	15	13	7.50	0	0	1	0	0	0	0	-	-	-	0	0
GM Parker	1924-1924	2	4	2	3	2*	1.50	0	0	0	0	366	273	8	34.12	4.47	6-152	1	0
DC Parkin	1892-1892	1	2	0	6	6	3.00	0	0	1	0	130	82	3	27.33	3.78	3-82	0	0
JT Partridge	1963-1965	11	12	5	73	13*	10.42	0	0	6	0	3684	1373	44	31.20	2.23	7-91	3	0
COC Pearse	1910-1911	3	6	0	55	31	9.16	0	0	1	0	144	106	3	35.33	4.41	3-56	0	0
SJ Pegler	1910-1924	16	28	5	356	35*	15.47	0	0	5	0	2989	1572	47	33.44	3.15	7-65	2	0
RJ Peterson	2003-2004	5	6	1	159	61	31.80	0	1	4	0	785	403	8	50.37	3.08	3-46	0	0
AJ Pithey	1957-1965	17	27	1	819	154	31.50	1	4	3	0	12	5	0	-	2.50	-	0	0
DB Pithey	1963-1967	8	12	1	138	55	12.54	0	1	6	0	1424	577	12	48.08	2.43	6-58	1	0
JB Plimsoll	1947-1947	1	2	1	16	8*	16.00	0	0	0	0	237	143	3	47.66	3.62	3-128	0	0
PM Pollock	1961-1970	28	41	13	607	75*	21.67	0	2	9	0	6522	2806	116	24.18	2.58	6-38	9	1
RG Pollock	1963-1970	23	41	4	2256	274	60.97	7	11	17	0	414	204	4	51.00	2.95	2-50	0	0
SM Pollock	1995-2006	102	147	37	3515	111	31.95	2	15	68	0	23172	9253	395	23.42	2.39	7-87	16	1
RM Poore	1896-1896	3	6	0	76	20	12.66	0	0	3	0	9	4	1	4.00	2.66	1-4	0	0
JE Pothecary	1960-1960	3	4	0	26	12	6.50	0	0	2	0	828	354	9	39.33	2.56	4-58	0	0
AW Powell	1899-1899	1	2	0	16	11	8.00	0	0	2	0	20	10	1	10.00	3.00	1-10	0	0
D Pretorius	2002-2003	4	4	1	22	9	7.33	0	0	0	0	570	430	6	71.66	4.52	4-115	0	0

SOUTH AFRICA TEST CAREER RECORDS

Name	Years	M	Inns	NO	Runs	HS	Avg	100	50	Ct	St	Balls	Runs	Wkts	Avg	RpO	BB	5I	10M
AG Prince	2002-2006	23	36	3	1254	139*	38.00	4	3	9	0	78	31	1	31.00	2.38	1-2	0	0
CFH Prince	1899-1899	1	2	0	6	5	3.00	0	0	0	0	0	0	0	-	-	-	0	0
MW Pringle	1992-1995	4	6	2	67	33	16.75	0	0	0	0	652	270	5	54.00	2.48	2-62	0	0
MJ Procter	1967-1970	7	10	1	226	48	25.11	0	0	4	0	1514	616	41	15.02	2.44	6-73	1	0
HLE Promnitz	1927-1927	2	4	0	14	5	3.50	0	0	2	0	528	161	8	20.12	1.82	5-58	1	0
NA Quinn	1929-1932	12	18	3	90	28	6.00	0	0	1	0	2922	1145	35	32.71	2.35	6-92	1	0
N Reid	1921-1921	1	2	0	17	11	8.50	0	0	0	0	126	63	2	31.50	3.00	2-63	0	0
JN Rhodes	1992-2000	52	80	9	2532	117	35.66	3	17	34	0	12	5	0	-	2.50	-	0	0
AR Richards	1896-1896	1	2	0	6	6	3.00	0	0	0	0	0	0	0	-	-	-	0	0
BA Richards	1970-1970	4	7	0	508	140	72.57	2	2	3	0	72	26	1	26.00	2.16	1-12	0	0
WHM Richards	1889-1889	1	2	0	4	4	2.00	0	0	0	0	0	0	0	-	-	-	0	0
DJ Richardson	1992-1998	42	64	8	1359	109	24.26	1	8	150	2	0	0	0	-	-	-	0	0
JB Robertson	1935-1936	3	6	1	51	17	10.20	0	0	2	0	738	321	6	53.50	2.60	3-143	0	0
A Rose-Innes	1889-1889	2	4	0	14	13	3.50	0	0	2	0	128	89	5	17.80	4.17	5-43	1	0
TW Routledge	1892-1896	4	8	0	72	24	9.00	0	0	2	0	0	0	0	-	-	-	0	0
AMB Rowan	1947-1951	15	23	6	290	41	17.05	0	0	7	0	5193	2084	54	38.59	2.40	5-68	4	0
EAB Rowan	1935-1951	26	50	5	1965	236	43.66	3	12	14	0	19	7	0	-	2.21	-	0	0
GA Rowe	1896-1902	5	9	3	26	13*	4.33	0	0	4	0	998	456	15	30.40	2.74	5-115	1	0
JA Rudolph	2003-2006	35	63	7	2028	222*	36.21	5	8	22	0	664	432	4	108.00	3.90	1-1	0	0
MW Rushmere	1992-1992	1	2	0	6	3	3.00	0	0	0	0	0	0	0	-	-	-	0	0
SV Samuelson	1910-1910	1	2	0	22	15	11.00	0	0	1	0	108	64	0	-	3.55	-	0	0
BN Schultz	1992-1997	9	8	2	9	6	1.50	0	0	2	0	1733	749	37	20.24	2.59	5-48	2	0
RO Schwarz	1906-1912	20	35	8	374	61	13.85	0	1	18	0	2639	1417	55	25.76	3.22	6-47	2	0
AW Seccull	1896-1896	1	2	1	23	17*	23.00	0	0	1	0	60	37	2	18.50	3.70	2-37	0	0
MA Seymour	1963-1970	7	10	3	84	35	12.00	0	0	2	0	1458	588	9	65.33	2.41	3-80	0	0
WA Shalders	1899-1907	12	23	1	355	42	16.13	0	0	3	0	48	6	1	6.00	0.75	1-6	0	0
GH Shepstone	1896-1899	2	4	0	38	21	9.50	0	0	2	0	115	47	0	-	2.45	-	0	0
PW Sherwell	1906-1911	13	22	4	427	115	23.72	1	1	20	16	0	0	0	-	-	-	0	0
IJ Siedle	1928-1936	18	34	0	977	141	28.73	1	5	7	0	19	7	1	7.00	2.21	1-7	0	0
JH Sinclair	1896-1911	25	47	1	1069	106	23.23	3	3	9	0	3598	1996	63	31.68	3.32	6-26	1	0
CJE Smith	1902-1902	3	6	1	106	45	21.20	0	0	2	0	0	0	0	-	-	-	0	0
FW Smith	1889-1896	3	6	1	45	12	9.00	0	0	2	0	0	0	0	-	-	-	0	0
GC Smith	2002-2006	47	82	5	3879	277	50.37	11	14	56	0	1247	724	8	90.50	3.48	2-145	0	0
VI Smith	1947-1957	9	16	6	39	11*	3.90	0	0	3	0	1655	769	12	64.08	2.78	4-143	0	0
RP Snell	1992-1994	5	8	1	95	48	13.57	0	0	1	0	1025	538	19	28.31	3.14	4-74	0	0

SOUTH AFRICA TEST CAREER RECORDS

Name	Years	M	Inns	NO	Runs	HS	Avg	100	50	Ct	St	Balls	Runs	Wkts	Avg	RpO	BB	5I	10M
SD Snooke	1907-1907	1	1	0	0	0	0.00	0	0	2	0	0	0	0	-	-	-	0	0
SJ Snooke	1906-1923	26	46	1	1008	103	22.40	1	5	24	0	1620	702	35	20.05	2.60	8-70	1	1
WRT Solomon	1899-1899	1	2	0	4	2	2.00	0	0	1	0	0	0	0	-	-	-	0	0
RB Stewart	1889-1889	1	2	0	13	9	6.50	0	0	2	0	0	0	0	-	-	-	0	0
DW Steyn	2004-2006	8	13	4	70	13	7.77	0	0	2	0	1631	1124	32	35.12	4.13	5-47	2	0
PJR Steyn	1995-1995	3	6	0	127	46	21.16	0	0	0	0	0	0	0	-	-	-	0	0
LA Stricker	1910-1912	13	24	0	344	48	14.33	0	0	3	0	174	105	1	105.00	3.62	1-36	0	0
PC Strydom	2000-2000	2	3	0	35	30	11.66	0	0	1	0	36	27	0	-	4.50	-	0	0
MJ Susskind	1924-1924	5	8	0	268	65	33.50	0	4	1	0	0	0	0	-	-	-	0	0
PL Symcox	1993-1998	20	27	1	741	108	28.50	1	4	5	0	3561	1603	37	43.32	2.70	4-69	0	0
HM Taberer	1902-1902	1	1	0	2	2	2.00	0	0	0	0	60	48	1	48.00	4.80	1-25	0	0
AB Tancred	1889-1889	2	4	1	87	29	29.00	0	0	2	0	0	0	0	-	-	-	0	0
LJ Tancred	1902-1913	14	26	1	530	97	21.20	0	2	3	0	0	0	0	-	-	-	0	0
VM Tancred	1899-1899	1	2	0	25	18	12.50	0	0	0	0	0	0	0	-	-	-	0	0
GL Tapscott	1913-1913	1	2	0	5	4	2.50	0	0	1	0	0	0	0	-	-	-	0	0
LE Tapscott	1923-1923	2	3	1	58	50*	29.00	0	1	0	0	12	2	0	-	1.00	-	0	0
HJ Tayfield	1949-1960	37	60	9	862	75	16.90	0	2	26	0	13568	4405	170	25.91	1.94	9-113	14	2
AI Taylor	1956-1956	1	2	0	18	12	9.00	0	0	0	0	0	0	0	-	-	-	0	0
D Taylor	1914-1914	2	4	0	85	36	21.25	0	0	0	0	0	0	0	-	-	-	0	0
HW Taylor	1912-1932	42	76	4	2936	176	40.77	7	17	19	0	342	156	5	31.20	2.73	3-15	0	0
DJ Terbrugge	1998-2004	7	8	5	16	4*	5.33	0	0	4	0	1012	517	20	25.85	3.06	5-46	1	0
NHCD Theunissen	1889-1889	1	2	1	2	2*	2.00	0	0	0	0	80	51	0	-	3.82	-	0	0
G Thornton	1902-1902	1	1	1	1	1*	-	0	0	1	0	24	20	1	20.00	5.00	1-20	0	0
DS Tomlinson	1935-1935	1	1	0	9	9	9.00	0	0	0	0	60	38	0	-	3.80	-	0	0
AJ Traicos	1970-1970	3	4	2	8	5*	4.00	0	0	4	0	470	207	4	51.75	2.64	2-70	0	0
PHJ Trimborn	1967-1970	4	4	2	13	11*	6.50	0	0	7	0	747	257	11	23.36	2.06	3-12	0	0
TL Tsolekile	2004-2004	3	5	0	47	22	9.40	0	0	6	0	0	0	0	-	-	-	0	0
L Tuckett	1947-1949	9	14	3	131	40*	11.90	0	0	9	0	2104	980	19	51.57	2.79	5-68	2	0
LR Tuckett	1914-1914	1	2	1	0	0*	0.00	0	0	2	0	120	69	0	-	3.45	-	0	0
PS Twentyman Jones	1902-1902	1	2	0	0	0	0.00	0	0	0	0	0	0	0	-	-	-	0	0
PGV van der Bijl	1938-1939	5	9	0	460	125	51.11	1	2	1	0	0	0	0	-	-	-	0	0
EA van der Merwe	1929-1936	2	4	1	27	19	9.00	0	0	3	0	0	0	0	-	-	-	0	0
PL van der Merwe	1963-1967	15	23	2	533	76	25.38	0	3	11	0	79	22	1	22.00	1.67	1-6	0	0
M van Jaarsveld	2002-2004	9	15	2	397	73	30.53	0	3	11	0	42	28	0	-	4.00	-	0	0
CB van Ryneveld	1951-1958	19	33	6	724	83	26.81	0	3	14	0	1554	671	17	39.47	2.59	4-67	0	0
GD Varnals	1964-1965	3	6	0	97	23	16.16	0	0	0	0	12	2	0	-	1.00	-	0	0

SOUTH AFRICA TEST CAREER RECORDS

Name	Years	M	Inns	NO	Runs	HS	Avg	100	50	Ct	St	Balls	Runs	Wkts	Avg	RpO	BB	5I	10M
KG Viljoen	1930-1949	27	50	2	1365	124	28.43	2	9	5	0	48	23	0	-	2.87	-	0	0
CL Vincent	1927-1935	25	38	12	526	60	20.23	0	2	27	0	5851	2631	84	31.32	2.69	6-51	3	0
CH Vintcent	1889-1892	3	6	0	26	9	4.33	0	0	1	0	369	193	4	48.25	3.13	3-88	0	0
AEE Vogler	1906-1911	15	26	6	340	65	17.00	0	2	20	0	2764	1455	64	22.73	3.15	7-94	5	1
HF Wade	1935-1936	10	18	2	327	40*	20.43	0	0	4	0	0	0	0	-	-	-	0	0
WW Wade	1938-1950	11	19	1	511	125	28.38	1	3	15	2	0	0	0	-	-	-	0	0
JHB Waite	1951-1965	50	86	7	2405	134	30.44	4	16	124	17	0	0	0	-	-	-	0	0
KA Walter	1961-1961	2	3	0	11	10	3.66	0	0	3	0	495	197	6	32.83	2.38	4-63	0	0
TA Ward	1912-1924	23	42	9	459	64	13.90	0	2	19	13	0	0	0	-	-	-	0	0
JC Watkins	1949-1957	15	27	1	612	92	23.53	0	3	12	0	2805	816	29	28.13	1.74	4-22	0	0
C Wesley	1960-1960	3	5	0	49	35	9.80	0	0	1	0	0	0	0	-	-	-	0	0
KC Wessels	1992-1994	16	29	2	1027	118	38.03	2	6	12	0	0	0	0	-	-	-	0	0
RJ Westcott	1954-1958	5	9	0	166	62	18.44	0	1	0	0	32	22	0	-	4.12	-	0	0
GC White	1906-1912	17	31	2	872	147	30.06	2	4	10	0	498	301	9	33.44	3.62	4-47	0	0
CM Willoughby	2003-2003	2	0	0	0	-	-	0	0	0	0	300	125	1	125.00	2.50	1-47	0	0
JT Willoughby	1896-1896	2	4	0	8	5	2.00	0	0	0	0	275	159	6	26.50	3.46	2-37	0	0
CS Wimble	1892-1892	1	2	0	0	0	0.00	0	0	0	0	0	0	0	-	-	-	0	0
PL Winslow	1950-1955	5	9	0	186	108	20.66	1	0	1	0	0	0	0	-	-	-	0	0
OE Wynne	1948-1950	6	12	0	219	50	18.25	0	1	3	0	0	0	0	-	-	-	0	0
M Zondeki	2003-2005	5	4	0	82	59	20.50	0	1	1	0	692	438	16	27.37	3.79	6-39	1	0
JW Zulch	1910-1921	16	32	2	983	150	32.76	2	4	4	0	24	28	0	-	7.00	-	0	0
Career Records including the match for the World XI v Australia in 2005/06																			
MV Boucher	1997-2006	96	136	17	3582	125	30.10	4	23	350	14	8	6	1	6.00	4.50	1-6	0	0
JH Kallis	1995-2006	102	172	28	8033	189*	55.78	24	40	98	0	13589	6342	200	31.71	2.80	6-54	4	0
GC Smith	2002-2006	48	84	5	3891	277	49.25	11	14	59	0	1247	724	8	90.50	3.48	2-145	0	0
The following players also appeared for other countries:																			
Australia																			
KC Wessels	1982-1985	24	42	1	1761	179	42.95	4	9	18	0	90	42	0	-	2.80	-	0	0
England																			
F Hearne	1889-1889	2	2	0	47	27	23.50	0	0	1	0	0	0	0	-	-	-	0	0
F Mitchell	1899-1899	2	4	0	88	41	22.00	0	0	2	0	0	0	0	-	-	-	0	0
Zimbabwe																			
AJ Traicos	1992-1993	4	6	2	11	5	2.75	0	0	4	0	1141	562	14	40.14	2.95	5-86	1	0

SOUTH AFRICAN LIMITED OVERS INTERNATIONAL RECORDS

As at 1 July 2006.

SUMMARY OF RESULTS

Opponents	First Match	Played	Won	Lost	Tied	NR
Australia	1991/92	65	28	34	3	0
Bangladesh	2002/03	7	7	0	0	0
Canada	2002/03	1	1	0	0	0
England	1991/92	34	21	11	1	1
Holland	1995/96	1	1	0	0	0
India (a)	1991/92	50	30	18	0	2
Kenya	1996/97	8	8	0	0	0
New Zealand (a)	1991/92	45	27	14	0	4
Pakistan	1991/92	41	28	13	0	0
Sri Lanka	1991/92	43	20	21	1	1
United Arab Emirates	1995/96	1	1	0	0	0
West Indies	1991/92	38	26	11	0	1
Zimbabwe	1991/92	21	18	2	0	1
	Total	355	216	124	5	10

Note (a): Excludes one match abandoned without a ball bowled.

CAPTAINS

		Played	Won	Lost	Tied	NR	%Won	Toss Won	Lost
CEB Rice	1991-92	3	1	2	0	0	33.33	1	2
KC Wessels	1991-94	52	20	30	0	2	40.00	24	28
WJ Cronje	1993-99	138	99	35	1	3	73.33	72	66
SM Pollock	1999-2004	92	59	29	3	1	64.83	49	43
GC Smith	2002-05	68	35	28	1	4	54.68	33	35
MV Boucher	2003/04	1	1	0	0	0	100.00	0	1
N Boje	2004/05	1	1	0	0	0	100.00	0	1

COACHES

		Played	Won	Lost	Tied	NR	%Won
MJ Procter	1991-94	56	24	30	0	2	44.44
RA Woolmer	1994-99	117	83	30	1	3	72.80
GX Ford	1999-2002	83	52	28	2	1	63.41
EO Simons	2002-04	62	33	26	1	2	55.00
RV Jennings	2004/05	15	12	1	1	1	85.71
JM Arthur	2005/06	22	12	9	0	1	57.14

Note: the %Won calculation excludes 'No Result' matches.

SUMMARY OF RESULTS WHEN BATTING FIRST OR SECOND

	Played	Won	Lost	Tied	NR
Batting first	170	103	60	2	5
Batting second	185	113	64	3	5

SOUTH AFRICAN LIMITED OVERS INTERNATIONAL RECORDS

HIGHEST INNINGS TOTALS

FOR

438-9	(49.5)	v Australia	Johannesburg	2005/06
363-3	(50)	v Zimbabwe	Bulawayo	2001/02
354-3	(50)	v Kenya	Cape Town	2001/02
329-6	(50)	v Zimbabwe	Durban	2004/05
328-3	(50)	v Holland	Rawalpindi (WC)	1995/96
326-3	(50)	v Australia	Port Elizabeth	2001/02
324-4	(50)	v New Zealand	Centurion	2000/01
321-2	(50)	v United Arab Emirates	Rawalpindi (WC)	1995/96
321-8	(50)	v Pakistan	Nairobi	1996/97
320-7	(50)	v India	Nagpur	1999/00
317-6	(50)	v Sri Lanka	Centurion	2002/03
316-5	(50)	v Kenya	Colombo-RPS	2002/03
314-7	(50)	v New Zealand	Verwoerdburg	1994/95
314-3	(50)	v Pakistan	Sharjah	1995/96
311-9	(50)	v Sri Lanka	Lahore	1997/98
311-7	(50)	v England	East London	2004/05
310-6	(50)	v Australia	Bloemfontein	1996/97
310-6	(49.4)	v West Indies	Johannesburg	2003/04
306-6	(50)	v New Zealand	Johannesburg (WC)	2002/03
305-8	(50)	v Kenya	Nairobi	1996/97
303-5	(50)	v Zimbabwe	Harare	1995/96
302-7	(50)	v Sri Lanka	East London	2000/01
301-3	(50)	v India	Kochi	1999/00
301-8	(50)	v Bangladesh	Potchefstroom	2002/03
301-7	(50)	v Zimbabwe	Johannesburg	2004/05
300-6	(50)	v New Zealand	Brisbane	1997/98

AGAINST

434-4	(50)	by Australia	Johannesburg	2005/06
344-6	(50)	by Australia	Sydney	2005/06
335-6	(50)	by Pakistan	Port Elizabeth	2002/03
330-7	(49.1)	by Australia	Port Elizabeth	2001/02
310	(48.5)	by India	Nagpur	1999/00
308-8	(50)	by Sri Lanka	Colombo-SSC	2004
307-4	(50)	by India	Dhaka	2002/03
304-2	(50)	by West Indies	Johannesburg	2003/04
304-8	(50)	by England	East London	2004/05
302-7	(49.4)	by India	Kochi	1999/00
300-3	(45)	by West Indies	Centurion	2003/04

LOWEST INNINGS TOTALS

(Excludes reduced overs matches)

FOR

69	(28)	v Australia	Sydney	1993/94
101	(26.5)	v Pakistan	Sharjah	1999/00
106	(38.3)	v Australia	Sydney	2001/02
107	(32.1)	v England	Lord's	2003
117	(48)	v India	Nairobi	1999/00
123	(46.2)	v Australia	Wellington	1994/95
129	(41.4)	v England	East London	1995/96
140-9	(50)	v West Indies	Cape Town	1992/93

144-9	(50)	v Australia	Cape Town	1999/00
147-7	(50)	v New Zealand	Hobart	1993/94
AGAINST				
54	(23.2)	by West Indies	Cape Town	2003/04
93	(31.3)	by Bangladesh	Birmingham	2004
93	(34.3)	by Australia	Cape Town	2005/06
98	(34)	by Sri Lanka	Colombo-RPS	1993/94
103	(25.1)	by Kenya	Nairobi	1996/97
103	(41)	by England	The Oval (WC)	1999
105	(36)	by Sri Lanka	Bloemfontein	1997/98
108	(35.1)	by Bangladesh	Bloemfontein (WC)	2002/03
109	(32.3)	by Pakistan	Johannesburg	1994/95
110	(35.2)	by Sri Lanka	Northampton (WC)	1999
Note: The lowest in South Africa is:				
36	(18.4)	Canada v Sri Lanka	Paarl (WC)	2002/03

HIGHEST TOTALS BATTING SECOND BY SOUTH AFRICA

438-9	(49.5)	v Australia (won)	Johannesburg	2005/06
(This is the world record)				
310-6	(49.4)	v West Indies (won)	Johannesburg	2003/04
297-5	(48.1)	v West Indies (won)	Lahore	1997/98
289-5	(48.5)	v New Zealand (won)	Kimberley	2000/01
287-6	(50)	v Australia (lost)	Sydney	2005/06
288-2	(46.4)	v India (won)	New Delhi	1991/92
283-4	(46.4)	v England (won)	Dhaka	1998/99
280-4	(48.2)	v India (won)	Johannesburg	2001/02
276-3	(48)	v England (won)	Centurion	1995/96
275-9	(49)	v West Indies (lost)	Cape Town (WC)	2002/03

HIGHEST TOTALS BATTING SECOND AGAINST SOUTH AFRICA

330-7	(49.1)	by Australia (won)	Port Elizabeth	2001/02
310	(48.5)	by India (lost)	Nagpur	1999/00
304-8	(50)	by England (lost)	East London	2004/05
302-7	(49.4)	by India (won)	Kochi	1999/00
300-3	(45)	by West Indies (won)	Centurion	2003/04
298-9	(50)	by New Zealand (lost)	Brisbane	1997/98
287-5	(49)	by Australia (won)	Centurion	1996/97
283-6	(49.5)	by India (won)	Vadodara	1999/00
283	(49.5)	by West Indies (lost)	Bridgetown	2004/05
272-5	(49.4)	by Australia (won)	Leeds (WC)	1999

HIGHEST MATCH AGGREGATES

872-13	(99.5)	South Africa v Australia	Johannesburg	2005/06
(This is the world record)				
656-10	(99.1)	South Africa v Australia	Port Elizabeth	2001/02
631-12	(100)	Australia v South Africa	Sydney	2005/06
630-17	(98.5)	India v South Africa	Nagpur	1999/00
615-15	(100)	South Africa v England	East London	2004/05
614-8	(99.4)	South Africa v West Indies	Johannesburg	2003/04
603-10	(99.4)	India v South Africa	Kochi	1999/00
598-15	(100)	South Africa v New Zealand	Brisbane	1997/98
597-7	(95)	South Africa v West Indies	Centurion	2003/04
590-13	(98.1)	South Africa v West Indies	Lahore	1997/98

SOUTH AFRICAN LIMITED OVERS INTERNATIONAL RECORDS

LOWEST TOTAL BATTING FIRST AND WINNING BY SOUTH AFRICA

129	(41.4)	v England (won by 14 runs)	East London	1995/96

LOWEST MATCH AGGREGATES

(Excludes reduced overs matches)

187-11	(49.2)	Bangladesh v South Africa	Birmingham	2004
211-15	(62.3)	South Africa v Sri Lanka	Bloemfontein	1997/98
213-12	(57.1)	Australia v South Africa	Sydney	2001/02
217-10	(47.1)	South Africa v Bangladesh	Bloemfontein (WC)	2002/03
218-13	(52.3)	England v South Africa	Lord's	2003
229-11	(64.5)	South Africa v Pakistan	Cape Town	1997/98
237-12	(70.4)	South Africa v India	Nairobi	1999/00
241-19	(78)	Australia v South Africa	Sydney	1993/94
244-20	(85.2)	South Africa v England	East London	1995/96
247-17	(89.4)	Australia v South Africa	Wellington	1994/95

Note: The lowest in South Africa is:

73-11	(23.2)	Canada v Sri Lanka	Paarl (WC)	2002/03

(This is the world record)

LARGEST MARGINS OF VICTORY

By runs	209	v West Indies	Cape Town	2003/04
	208	v Kenya	Cape Town	2001/02
	202	v Kenya	Nairobi	1996/97
	196	v Australia	Cape Town	2005/06
	177	v Sri Lanka	Centurion	2002/03
	176	v Kenya	Colombo-RPS	2002/03
	169	v United Arab Emirates	Rawalpindi (WC)	1995/96
	168	v Bangladesh	Potchefstroom	2002/03
	165	v Zimbabwe	Johannesburg	2004/05
	160	v Holland	Rawalpindi (WC)	1995/96
By wickets	10	v India	Sharjah	1999/00
	10	v Bangladesh	Benoni	2002/03
	10	v Kenya	Potchefstroom (WC)	2002/03
	10	v Bangladesh	Bloemfontein (WC)	2002/03
	10	v India	Kolkata	2005/06

NARROWEST MARGINS OF VICTORY

By runs	1	v New Zealand	Hobart	1997/98
	1	v England	Cape Town	1999/00
	1	v West Indies	Bridgetown	2004/05
	2	v New Zealand	Brisbane	1997/98
By wickets	1	v Australia	Johannesburg	2005/06
	2	v Australia	Faridabad	1996/97
	2	v New Zealand	Napier	1998/99
	2	v England	East London	1999/00
	2	v India	Faridabad	1999/00
	2	v West Indies	Colombo-SSC	2002/03
	2	v New Zealand	Bloemfontein	2005/06

LARGEST MARGINS OF DEFEAT

By runs	182	by Pakistan	Port Elizabeth	2002/03
	153	by India	Dhaka	2002/03
	107	by West Indies	Kingston	1991/92
	103	by Australia	Sydney	1993/94

By wickets	10	by West Indies	Port-of-Spain	1991/92
	9	by West Indies	Bloemfontein	1992/93
	9	by England	Bloemfontein	1999/00
	9	by New Zealand (D/L method)	Johannesburg (WC)	2002/03

Note: The largest margin of victory by runs in South Africa is:

256	Australia v Namibia	Potchefstroom (WC)	2002/03

Note: The largest margin of victory by wickets in South Africa (in addition to the 3 cases above) is:

10	India v Kenya	Bloemfontein	2001/02
10	Sri Lanka v Bangladesh	Pietermaritzburg (WC)	2002/03

NARROWEST MARGINS OF DEFEAT

By runs	1	by Australia	Bloemfontein	1993/94
	2	by India	Calcutta	1993/94
By wickets	1	by Australia	Durban	2005/06
	2	by Sri Lanka	Nairobi	1996/97
	2	by Zimbabwe	Durban	1999/00

TIED MATCHES

v Australia	Birmingham (WC)	1999
v Australia	Melbourne-Colonial	2000
v Australia	Potchefstroom	2001/02
v Sri Lanka (D/L method)	Durban (WC)	2002/03
v England	Bloemfontein	2004/05

MOST SUCCESSIVE VICTORIES

12	England (1), Zimbabwe (3), West Indies (5), New Zealand (3)	2004/05-2005/06

Note: South Africa went 20 matches without defeat v England (6), Zimbabwe (3), West Indies (5), New Zealand (5) and India (1) in 2004/05 and 2005/06. This sequence included a tie and 2 no results.

MOST SUCCESSIVE DEFEATS

10	Australia (2), England (2), Australia and Pakistan (3 each)	1993/94-1994/95
10	New Zealand (5), Sri Lanka (5)	2003/04-2004

BATTING

HIGHEST INDIVIDUAL INNINGS

FOR				
188*	G Kirsten	v United Arab Emirates	Rawalpindi (WC)	1995/96
175	HH Gibbs	v Australia	Johannesburg	2005/06
169*	DJ Callaghan	v New Zealand	Verwoerdburg	1994/95
161	AC Hudson	v Holland	Rawalpindi (WC)	1995/96
153	HH Gibbs	v Bangladesh	Potchefstroom	2002/03
143	HH Gibbs	v New Zealand	Johannesburg (WC)	2002/03
139	JH Kallis	v West Indies	Johannesburg	2003/04
134*	GC Smith	v India	Kolkata	2005/06
133*	G Kirsten	v India	Johannesburg	2001/02
131*	ND McKenzie	v Kenya	Cape Town	2001/02
AGAINST				
164	RT Ponting	for Australia	Johannesburg	2005/06
152*	CH Gayle	for West Indies	Johannesburg	2003/04
150	S Chanderpaul	for West Indies	East London	1998/99
141*	SC Ganguly	for India	Nairobi	2000/01

135	Salim Elahi	for Pakistan	Port Elizabeth	2002/03
134*	SP Fleming	for New Zealand	Johannesburg (WC)	2002/03
132	CH Gayle	for West Indies	Bridgetown	2004/05
129	RT Ponting	for Australia	Bloemfontein	2001/02
127	SC Ganguly	for India	Johannesburg	2001/02
124	MS Atapattu	for Sri Lanka	Durban (WC)	2002/03

MOST CENTURIES

16	HH Gibbs
13	JH Kallis, G Kirsten
6	GC Smith
4	HH Dippenaar
3	DJ Cullinan

THREE SUCCESSIVE CENTURIES

HH Gibbs	116 v Kenya; 116* v India; 153 v Bangladesh	2002/03

Equalled world record with Zaheer Abbas (Pak) and Saeed Anwar (Pak).

FIVE SUCCESSIVE FIFTIES

JN Rhodes	69 v New Zealand; 61*, 50, 75* and 53 v Sri Lanka	2000/01

FASTEST CENTURY

79 balls	HH Gibbs (175)	v Australia	Johannesburg	2005/06

FASTEST FIFTIES

19 balls	MV Boucher (51*)	v Kenya	Cape Town	2001/02
19 balls	JM Kemp (53*)	v Zimbabwe	Durban	2004/05

MOST RUNS

	Years	M	Inns	NO	Runs	HS	Avg	SR	100	50
JH Kallis	1996-2006	226	216	39	7966	139	45.00	70.79	13	56
G Kirsten	1993-2003	185	185	19	6798	188 *	40.95	71.98	13	45
HH Gibbs	1996-2006	185	184	13	6117	175	35.77	82.07	16	25
JN Rhodes	1992-2003	245	220	51	5935	121	35.11	81.05	2	33
WJ Cronje	1992-2000	188	175	31	5565	112	38.64	76.49	2	39
DJ Cullinan	1993-2000	138	133	16	3860	124	32.99	70.37	3	23
L Klusener	1996-2004	171	137	50	3576	103 *	41.10	89.89	2	19
GC Smith	2002-2006	90	89	5	3389	134 *	40.34	79.07	6	19
HH Dippenaar	1999-2006	96	84	13	3190	125 *	44.92	68.03	4	24
MV Boucher	1998-2006	215	156	39	3117	76	26.64	80.33	0	19
SM Pollock	1996-2006	253	165	58	2702	75	25.25	85.94	0	11
AC Hudson	1991-1997	89	88	1	2559	161	29.41	64.47	2	18

BEST BATTING AVERAGES

(Qualification 1000 runs)

	Years	M	Inns	NO	Runs	HS	Avg	SR	100	50
JH Kallis	1996-2006	226	216	39	7966	139	45.00	70.79	13	56
HH Dippenaar	1999-2006	96	84	13	3190	125 *	44.92	68.03	4	24
L Klusener	1996-2004	171	137	50	3576	103 *	41.10	89.89	2	19
G Kirsten	1993-2003	185	185	19	6798	188 *	40.95	71.98	13	45
GC Smith	2002-2006	90	89	5	3389	134 *	40.34	79.07	6	19

SOUTH AFRICAN LIMITED OVERS INTERNATIONAL RECORDS

BEST BATTING STRIKE RATES

(Qualification 1000 runs)

	Years	M	Inns	NO	Runs	HS	Avg	SR	100	50
L Klusener	1996-2004	171	137	50	3576	103 *	41.10	89.89	2	19
N Boje	1995-2005	113	69	18	1410	129	27.64	89.29	2	4
SM Pollock	1996-2006	253	165	58	2702	75	25.25	85.94	0	11
HH Gibbs	1996-2006	185	184	13	6117	175	35.77	82.07	16	25
JN Rhodes	1992-2003	245	220	51	5935	121	35.11	81.05	2	33

MOST RUNS IN A CALENDAR YEAR

	Year	M	Inns	NO	Runs	HS	Avg	SR	100	50
G Kirsten	2000	36	36	3	1467	115	44.45	73.20	2	13

RECORD WICKET PARTNERSHIPS

FOR				
1st	235	G Kirsten and HH Gibbs v India	Kochi	1999/00
2nd	207	G Kirsten and ND McKenzie v Kenya	Cape Town	2001/02
3rd	172 *	HH Gibbs and JH Kallis v Sri Lanka	Kimberley	2002/03
4th	232	DJ Cullinan and JN Rhodes v Pakistan	Nairobi	1996/97
5th	183 *	JH Kallis and JN Rhodes v Pakistan	Durban	1997/98
6th	137	WJ Cronje and SM Pollock v Zimbabwe	Johannesburg	1996/97
7th	114	MV Boucher and L Klusener v India	Nagpur	1999/00
8th	91	DM Benkenstein and L Klusener v West Indies	Cape Town	1998/99
9th	61	SM Pollock and J Botha v Australia	Melbourne-Colonial	2005/06
10th	67 *	JA Morkel and M Ntini v New Zealand	Napier	2003/04
AGAINST				
1st	200	ME Trescothick and VS Solanki for England	The Oval	2003
2nd	257	Salim Elahi and Abdul Razzaq for Pakistan	Port Elizabeth	2002/03
3rd	175	DM Jones and ME Waugh for Australia	Sydney	1993/94
4th	226	S Chanderpaul and CL Hooper for West Indies	East London	1998/99
5th	148 *	Ijaz Ahmed and Basit Ali for Pakistan	Faisalabad	1994/95
6th	124	CD McMillan and CZ Harris for New Zealand	Adelaide	1997/98
7th	123	MEK Hussey and B Lee for Australia	Brisbane	2005/06
8th	119	PR Reiffel and SK Warne for Australia	Port Elizabeth	1993/94
9th	80 *	Arshad Laeeq and SF Dukanwala for United Arab Emirates	Rawalpindi (WC)	1995/96
10th	72	Abdul Razzaq and Waqar Younis for Pakistan	Durban	1997/98

BOWLING

BEST BOWLING IN AN INNINGS

FOR				
6-22	M Ntini	v Australia	Cape Town	2005/06
6-23	AA Donald	v Kenya	Nairobi	1996/97
6-35	SM Pollock	v West Indies	East London	1998/99
6-49	L Klusener	v Sri Lanka	Lahore	1997/98
5-20	SM Pollock	v England	Johannesburg	1999/00
5-21	L Klusener	v Kenya	Amstelveen (WC)	1999
5-21	N Boje	v Australia	Cape Town	2001/02
5-24	L Klusener	v Australia	Melbourne	1997/98
5-25	L Klusener	v Pakistan	Cape Town	1997/98
5-29	AA Donald	v India	Calcutta	1991/92

AGAINST

5-6	SB Joshi	for India	Nairobi	1999/00
5-16	Wasim Akram	for Pakistan	East London	1992/93
5-19	AJ Bichel	for Australia	Sydney	2001/02
5-22	B Lee	for Australia	Melbourne-Colonial	2005/06
5-25	Waqar Younis	for Pakistan	Durban	1992/93
5-26	DNT Zoysa	for Sri Lanka	Colombo-RPS	2004
5-38	Waqar Younis	for Pakistan	Tangier	2002
5-44	M Muralitharan	for Sri Lanka	Colombo-RPS	2000
5-61	UDU Chandana	for Sri Lanka	Colombo-SSC	2004
5-67	NW Bracken	for Australia	Johannesburg	2005/06

Note: The best in South Africa is:

7-4-15-7	GD McGrath	Australia v Namibia	Potchefstroom (WC)	2002/03

HAT-TRICK

CK Langeveldt	v West Indies	Bridgetown	2004/05

ECONOMICAL BOWLING

(5 overs or more)

FOR

Runs per over

0.87	SM Pollock	8-4-7-3	v Zimbabwe	Port Elizabeth	1999/00
0.90	SM Pollock	10-4-9-1	v Pakistan	Rawalpindi	2003/04
1.00	PS de Villiers	5-2-5-0	v West Indies	Bombay	1993/94
1.11	WJ Cronje	9-2-10-3	v West Indies	Cape Town	1998/99
1.20	MW Pringle	5-3-6-1	v West Indies	Port-of-Spain	1991/92
1.20	SM Pollock	5-2-6-0	v Bangladesh	Potchefstroom	2002/03
1.220	SM Pollock	9.5-1-12-3	v Pakistan	Durban	2002/03
1.224	SM Pollock	8.1-3-10-3	v Kenya	Nairobi	1999/00
1.25	CR Matthews	8-5-10-4	v Australia	Durban	1993/94
1.25	PS de Villiers	8-1-10-2	v England	East London	1995/96
1.25	SM Pollock	8-3-10-2	v Sri Lanka	Northampton (WC)	1999

AGAINST

0.60	SB Joshi	10-6-6-5	for India	Nairobi	1999/00
1.09	PAJ DeFreitas	11-4-12-1	for England	Manchester	1994
1.20	GR Larson	10-5-12-2	for New Zealand	Hobart	1993/94
1.25	TM Moody	8-3-10-1	for Australia	Melbourne	1997/98
1.28	D Gough	7-2-9-2	for England	Lord's	2003
1.30	GD McGrath	10-1-13-2	for Australia	Cape Town	1999/00
1.33	CJ McDermott	6-2-8-1	for Australia	Sydney	1993/94
1.50	M Muralitharan	8-1-12-1	for Sri Lanka	Tangier	2002
1.54	SD Udal	11-2-17-1	for England	Manchester	1994
1.55	D Gough	9-2-14-2	for England	Durban	2004/05

EXPENSIVE BOWLING

(5 overs or more)

FOR

Runs per over

11.66	JH Kallis	6-0-70-0	v Australia	Johannesburg	2005/06
11.60	DW Steyn	5-0-58-1	v Australia	Melbourne-Colonial	2005/06
10.50	A Nel	6-0-63-0	v West Indies	Centurion	2003/04
10.40	JH Kallis	5-0-52-0	v New Zealand	Cape Town	2000/01
10.00	JH Kallis	5-0-50-0	v Pakistan	Durban	1997/98
9.40	M Hayward	5-0-47-1	v Sri Lanka	Galle	2000

9.20	AA Donald	5-0-46-0	v New Zealand	Kimberley	2000/01
9.20	M Ntini	5-0-46-0	v Pakistan	Tangier	2002
9.05	M Ntini	9.1-0-83-1	v Australia	Port Elizabeth	2001/02
9.00	JM Kemp	5-0-45-0	v Kenya	Kimberley	2001/02
9.00	JH Kallis	5-0-45-1	v New Zealand	Wellington-WS	2003/04

AGAINST

11.30	ML Lewis	10-0-113-0	for Australia	Johannesburg	2005/06

(This is the world record for 10 overs)

10.83	J Srinath	6-0-65-0	for India	Nagpur	1999/00
10.50	KD Mills	6-1-63-0	for New Zealand	Auckland	2003/04
10.42	TJ Friend	7-0-73-1	for Zimbabwe	Bulawayo	2001/02
10.00	P Utseya	6-0-60-0	for Zimbabwe	Durban	2004/05
9.00	SR Clark	6-0-54-0	for Australia	Johannesburg	2005/06
8.75	AC Dale	8-1-70-0	for Australia	Bloemfontein	1996/97
8.68	B Lee	7.5-0-68-1	for Australia	Johannesburg	2005/06
8.66	Arshad Laiq	6-0-52-0	for United Arab Emirates	Rawalpindi (WC)	1995/96
8.60	NC McGarrell	5-0-43-2	for West Indies	Johannesburg	1998/99
8.60	Alok Kapali	5-0-43-0	for Bangladesh	Potchefstroom	2002/03

MOST WICKETS

	Years	M	Balls	Runs	Wkts	Avg	RpO	BB	4I
SM Pollock	1996-2006	253	13204	8234	342	24.07	3.74	6-35	15
AA Donald	1991-2003	164	8561	5926	272	21.78	4.15	6-23	13
M Ntini	1998-2006	128	6420	4714	205	22.99	4.40	6-22	9
JH Kallis	1996-2006	226	8044	6452	199	32.42	4.81	5-30	4
L Klusener	1996-2004	171	7336	5751	192	29.95	4.70	6-49	7
WJ Cronje	1992-2000	188	5357	3966	114	34.78	4.44	5-32	2
N Boje	1995-2005	113	4457	3351	95	35.27	4.51	5-21	3
PS de Villiers	1992-1997	83	4422	2636	95	27.74	3.57	4-27	2
CR Matthews	1991-1997	56	3003	1975	79	25.00	3.94	4-10	3
PL Symcox	1993-1999	80	3991	2762	72	38.36	4.15	4-28	1

BEST BOWLING AVERAGES

(Qualification 50 wickets)

	Years	M	Balls	Runs	Wkts	Avg	RpO	BB	4I
AA Donald	1991-2003	164	8561	5926	272	21.78	4.15	6-23	13
M Ntini	1998-2006	128	6420	4714	205	22.99	4.40	6-22	9
SM Pollock	1996-2006	253	13204	8234	342	24.07	3.74	6-35	15
CR Matthews	1991-1997	56	3003	1975	79	25.00	3.94	4-10	3
PS de Villiers	1992-1997	83	4422	2636	95	27.74	3.57	4-27	2

MOST ECONOMICAL BOWLING

(Qualification 600 balls)

	Years	M	Balls	Runs	Wkts	Avg	RpO	BB	4I
PS de Villiers	1992-1997	83	4422	2636	95	27.74	3.57	4-27	2
SM Pollock	1996-2006	253	13204	8234	342	24.07	3.74	6-35	15
CR Matthews	1991-1997	56	3003	1975	79	25.00	3.94	4-10	3
EO Simons	1994-1995	23	1212	810	33	24.54	4.00	4-42	1
PL Symcox	1993-1999	80	3991	2762	72	38.36	4.152	4-28	1
AA Donald	1991-2003	164	8561	5926	272	21.78	4.153	6-23	13

MOST WICKETS IN A CALENDAR YEAR

	Year	M	Balls	Runs	Wkts	Avg	RpO	BB	4I
SM Pollock	2000	38	1989	1319	61	21.62	3.97	5-20	3

WICKETKEEPING

MOST DISMISSALS IN A MATCH

FOR				
5 (ct 5)	DJ Richardson	v Pakistan	Johannesburg	1994/95
5 (ct 5)	DJ Richardson	v Zimbabwe	Harare	1995/96
5 (ct 5)	MV Boucher	v England	Johannesburg	1999/00
5 (ct 5)	MV Boucher	v Australia	Durban	1999/00
5 (ct 5)	MV Boucher	v Pakistan	Colombo-SSC	2000
5 (ct 5)	MV Boucher	v Bangladesh	Dhaka	2002/03
5 (ct 5)	MV Boucher	v New Zealand	Centurion	2005/06
AGAINST				
6 (ct 6)	AC Gilchrist	for Australia	Cape Town	1999/00
5 (ct 5)	A Flower	for Zimbabwe	Harare	1995/96
5 (ct 5)	CMW Read	for England	Lord's	2003
5 (ct 5)	BB McCullum	for New Zealand	Napier	2003/04

Note: The best in South Africa (in addition to the case above) is:

6 (ct 6)	AC Gilchrist	Australia v Namibia	Potchefstroom (WC)	2002/03

MOST DISMISSALS

	Years	M	Ct	St	Total
MV Boucher	1998-2006	215	296	16	312
DJ Richardson	1991-1998	122	148	17	165

FIELDING

MOST CATCHES IN A MATCH

FOR				
5	JN Rhodes	v West Indies	Bombay	1993/94
4	KC Wessels	v West Indies	Kingston	1991/92
4	AG Prince	v West Indies	Port-of-Spain	2004/05

AGAINST

Three catches have been taken against South Africa on nine occasions.

Note: The best in South Africa is:

4	CL Hooper	West Indies v Pakistan	Durban	1992/93
4	M Kaif	India v Sri Lanka	Johannesburg (WC)	2002/03

MOST CATCHES

	Years	M	Ct
JN Rhodes	1992-2003	245	105
SM Pollock	1996-2006	253	94
JH Kallis	1996-2006	226	90
HH Gibbs	1996-2006	185	77
WJ Cronje	1992-2000	188	73
DJ Cullinan	1993-2000	138	62
G Kirsten	1993-2003	185	61 *

* Also took one stumping.

SOUTH AFRICAN LIMITED OVERS INTERNATIONAL RECORDS

MOST APPEARANCES

253	SM Pollock	185	HH Gibbs	138	DJ Cullinan
245	JN Rhodes	185	G Kirsten	128	M Ntini
226	JH Kallis	171	L Klusener	122	DJ Richardson
215	MV Boucher	164	AA Donald	113	N Boje
188	WJ Cronje				

RECORDS AGAINST INDIVIDUAL COUNTRIES

SOUTH AFRICA versus AUSTRALIA

HIGHEST INNINGS TOTALS

For South Africa:	438-9	(49.5)	Johannesburg	2005/06
For Australia:	434-4	(50)	Johannesburg	2005/06

LOWEST INNINGS TOTALS

For South Africa:	69	(28)	Sydney	1993/94
For Australia:	93	(34.3)	Cape Town	2005/06

HIGHEST INDIVIDUAL INNINGS

For South Africa:	175	HH Gibbs	Johannesburg	2005/06
For Australia:	164	RT Ponting	Johannesburg	2005/06

INDIVIDUAL CENTURIES

For South Africa (9):			
112	WJ Cronje (2)	Johannesburg	1993/94
100*		Peshawar	1994/95
101	HH Dippenaar	Durban	2005/06
101	HH Gibbs (2)	Leeds (WC)	1999
175		Johannesburg	2005/06
104*	JH Kallis	Perth	2001/02
112*	G Kirsten (2)	Melbourne	1993/94
105*		Indore	1996/97
119*	GC Smith	Centurion	2005/06
For Australia (11):			
103	MG Bevan (2)	Centurion	1996/97
106		Melbourne-Colonial	2000
100	AC Gilchrist (2)	Sydney	1997/98
105		Durban	2001/02
104*	DR Martyn	Brisbane	2001/02
129	RT Ponting (2)	Bloemfontein	2001/02
164		Johannesburg	2005/06
107	ME Waugh (2)	Sydney	1993/94
115*		Port Elizabeth	1996/97
120*	SR Waugh (2)	Leeds (WC)	1999
114*		Melbourne-Colonial	2000

BEST BOWLING IN AN INNINGS

For South Africa:	6-22	M Ntini	Cape Town	2005/06
For Australia:	5-19	AJ Bichel	Sydney	2001/02

SOUTH AFRICAN LIMITED OVERS INTERNATIONAL RECORDS

FIVE WICKETS IN AN INNINGS

For South Africa (5):			
6.3-0-21-5	N Boje	Cape Town	2001/02
7.1-0-24-5	L Klusener	Melbourne	1997/98
9.3-4-22-6	M Ntini	Cape Town	2005/06
9.2-1-36-5	SM Pollock	Birmingham (WC)	1999
9.5-0-40-5	RP Snell	Melbourne	1993/94
For Australia (3):			
6.3-0-19-5	AJ Bichel	Sydney	2001/02
10-0-67-5	NW Bracken	Johannesburg	2005/06
10-1-22-5	B Lee	Melbourne-Colonial	2005/06

RECORD WICKET PARTNERSHIPS

South Africa				
1st	118	AC Hudson and G Kirsten	Indore	1996/97
2nd	187	GC Smith and HH Gibbs	Johannesburg	2005/06
3rd	149	WJ Cronje and DJ Cullinan	Centurion	1996/97
4th	131 *	JH Kallis and JN Rhodes	Port Elizabeth	2001/02
5th	134	WJ Cronje and JN Rhodes	Sydney	1997/98
6th	119	AB de Villiers and SM Pollock	Port Elizabeth	2005/06
7th	87 *	MV Boucher and L Klusener	Johannesburg	1999/00
8th	71	L Klusener and N Boje	Johannesburg	2001/02
9th	61	SM Pollock and J Botha	Melbourne-Colonial	2005/06
10th	40	PL Symcox and AA Donald	Sydney	1997/98
Australia				
1st	170	AC Gilchrist and ML Hayden	Durban	2001/02
2nd	126	AC Gilchrist and RT Ponting	Sydney	1997/98
3rd	175	DM Jones and ME Waugh	Sydney	1993/94
4th	222	MG Bevan and SR Waugh	Melbourne-Colonial	2000
5th	124	MG Bevan and MJ Slater	Gauhati	1996/97
6th	109	A Symonds and MEK Hussey	Melbourne-Colonial	2005/06
7th	123	MEK Hussey and B Lee	Brisbane	2005/06
8th	119	PR Reiffel and SK Warne	Port Elizabeth	1993/94
9th	57	IJ Harvey and AJ Bichel	Perth	1997/98
10th	45 *	MG Bevan and AC Dale	East London	1996/97

SOUTH AFRICA versus BANGLADESH

HIGHEST INNINGS TOTALS

For South Africa:	301-8	(50)	Potchefstroom	2002/03
For Bangladesh:	211	(49.3)	Dhaka	2002/03

LOWEST INNINGS TOTALS

For South Africa:	261-5	(50)	Dhaka	2002/03
For Bangladesh:	93	(31.3)	Birmingham	2004

HIGHEST INDIVIDUAL INNINGS

For South Africa:	153	HH Gibbs	Potchefstroom	2002/03
For Bangladesh:	71	Alok Kapali	Dhaka	2002/03

INDIVIDUAL CENTURIES

For South Africa (1):

153	HH Gibbs	Potchefstroom	2002/03

For Bangladesh: No instance.

SOUTH AFRICAN LIMITED OVERS INTERNATIONAL RECORDS

BEST BOWLING IN AN INNINGS

For South Africa:	4-24	SM Pollock	Kimberley	2002/03
	4-24	M Ntini	Bloemfontein	2002/03
For Bangladesh:	4-65	Talha Jubair	Potchefstroom	2002/03

FIVE WICKETS IN AN INNINGS

No instance.

RECORD WICKET PARTNERSHIPS

South Africa				
1st	155 *	GC Smith and HH Gibbs	Benoni	2002/03
2nd	101	GC Smith and JA Rudolph	Dhaka	2002/03
3rd	107	HH Gibbs and JH Kallis	Potchefstroom	2002/03
4th	105 *	HH Dippenaar and ND McKenzie	Dhaka	2002/03
5th	18	JA Rudolph and ND McKenzie	Dhaka	2002/03
6th	69 *	ND McKenzie and SM Pollock	Dhaka	2002/03
7th	2	HH Dippenaar and L Klusener	Potchefstroom	2002/03
8th	12	L Klusener and ELR Stewart	Potchefstroom	2002/03
9th	2 *	ELR Stewart and AA Donald	Potchefstroom	2002/03
10th		No partnership		
Bangladesh				
1st	26	Javed Omar and Hannan Sarkar	Benoni	2002/03
2nd	58	Mohammad Ashraful and Habibul Bashar	Dhaka	2002/03
3rd	68	Habibul Bashar and Sanwar Hossain	Kimberley	2002/03
4th	29	Mohammad Ashraful and Alok Kapali	Dhaka	2002/03
5th	55	Alok Kapali and Khaled Mahmud	Dhaka	2002/03
6th	23	Tushar Imran and Khaled Mashud	Bloemfontein (WC)	2002/03
7th	41	Alok Kapali and Mohammad Salim	Dhaka	2002/03
8th	60	Khaled Mashud and Tapash Baisya	Potchefstroom	2002/03
9th	37	Tapash Baisya and Manjural Islam	Benoni	2002/03
10th	13	Khaled Mashud and Nazmul Hossain	Birmingham	2004

SOUTH AFRICA versus ENGLAND

HIGHEST INNINGS TOTALS

For South Africa:	311-7	(50)	East London	2004/05
For England:	304-8	(50)	East London	2004/05

LOWEST INNINGS TOTALS

For South Africa:	107	(32.1)	Lord's	2003
For England:	103	(41)	The Oval (WC)	1999

HIGHEST INDIVIDUAL INNINGS

For South Africa:	118	HH Gibbs	Durban	2004/05
For England:	116	KP Pietersen	Centurion	2004/05

INDIVIDUAL CENTURIES

For South Africa (6):

100	HH Gibbs (2)	Cape Town	2004/05
118		Durban	2004/05
107	JH Kallis	The Oval	2003
116	G Kirsten	Centurion	1995/96
105	GC Smith (2)	Port Elizabeth	2004/05
115*		East London	2004/05

For England (5):

108*	KP Pietersen (3)	Bloemfontein	2004/05
100*		East London	2004/05
116		Centurion	2004/05
106	VS Solanki	The Oval	2003
114*	ME Trescothick	The Oval	2003

BEST BOWLING IN AN INNINGS

For South Africa:	5-20	SM Pollock	Johannesburg	1999/00
For England:	4-19	AR Caddick	Johannesburg	1999/00

FIVE WICKETS IN AN INNINGS

For South Africa (1):

9-1-20-5	SM Pollock	Johannesburg	1999/00

For England: No instance.

RECORD WICKET PARTNERSHIPS

South Africa

1st	156	AC Hudson and G Kirsten	Centurion	1995/96
2nd	90	GC Smith and JH Kallis	East London	2004/05
3rd	143	JH Kallis and HH Gibbs	Cape Town	2004/05
4th	145 *	JH Kallis and JA Rudolph	Manchester	2003
5th	117	GC Smith and JM Kemp	East London	2004/05
6th	74	WJ Cronje and MV Boucher	Johannesburg	1999/00
7th	69	SM Pollock and PL Symcox	Birmingham	1998
8th	71	M van Jaarsveld and PR Adams	Birmingham	2003
9th	30	BM McMillan and PS de Villiers	East London	1995/96
10th	26 *	L Klusener and AA Donald	Manchester	1998

England

1st	200	ME Trescothick and VS Solanki	The Oval	2003
2nd	87	VS Solanki and MP Vaughan	Lord's	2003
3rd	114	ME Trescothick and A McGrath	Manchester	2003
4th	100	MP Vaughan and A Flintoff	Birmingham	2003
5th	92	KP Pietersen and PD Collingwood	Bloemfontein	2004/05
6th	112	NH Fairbrother and AJ Hollioake	Dhaka	1998/99
7th	104	KP Pietersen and AF Giles	Centurion	2004/05
8th	53	KP Pietersen and Kabir Ali	Centurion	2004/05
9th	15	Kabir Ali and AG Wharf	Centurion	2004/05
10th	24	CMW Read and AD Mullally	Johannesburg	1999/00

SOUTH AFRICA versus INDIA

HIGHEST INNINGS TOTALS

For South Africa:	320-7	(50)	Nagpur	1999/00
For India:	310	(48.5)	Nagpur	1999/00

LOWEST INNINGS TOTALS

For South Africa:	117	(48)	Nairobi	1999/00
For India:	147	(49.4)	Port Elizabeth	1992/93

HIGHEST INDIVIDUAL INNINGS

For South Africa:	134*	GC Smith	Kolkata	2005/06
For India:	141*	SC Ganguly	Nairobi	2000/01

SOUTH AFRICAN LIMITED OVERS INTERNATIONAL RECORDS

INDIVIDUAL CENTURIES

For South Africa (9):

106	DJ Cullinan	Jaipur	1996/97
111	HH Gibbs (2)	Kochi	1999/00
116*		Colombo-RPS	2002/03
108	AC Hudson	Bloemfontein	1992/93
106	G Kirsten (4)	Sharjah	1995/96
115*		Sharjah	1995/96
115		Kochi	1999/00
133*		Johannesburg	2001/02
134*	GC Smith	Kolkata	2005/06

For India (10):

105*	SC Ganguly (3)	Jamshedpur	1999/00
141*		Nairobi	2000/01
127		Johannesburg	2001/02
105	SV Manjrekar	New Delhi	1991/92
114	WV Raman	Verwoerdburg	1992/93
109	RJ Shastri	New Delhi	1991/92
114	SR Tendulkar (3)	Mumbai	1996/97
122		Vadodara	1999/00
101		Johannesburg	2001/02
103	Yuvraj Singh	Hyderabad	2005/06

BEST BOWLING IN AN INNINGS

For South Africa:	5-29	AA Donald	Calcutta	1991/92
For India:	5-6	SB Joshi	Nairobi	1999/00

FIVE WICKETS IN AN INNINGS

For South Africa (4):

10-0-32-5	WJ Cronje	Cape Town	1992/93
8.4-0-29-5	AA Donald	Calcutta	1991/92
8.4-0-42-5	L Klusener	Bloemfontein	1996/97
9.5-1-37-5	SM Pollock	Centurion	2001/02

For India (1):

10-6-6-5	SB Joshi	Nairobi	1999/00

RECORD WICKET PARTNERSHIPS

South Africa

1st	235	G Kirsten and HH Gibbs	Kochi	1999/00
2nd	178 *	HH Gibbs and JH Kallis	Colombo-RPS	2002/03
3rd	113	DJ Cullinan and WJ Cronje	Jaipur	1996/97
4th	154	G Kirsten and WJ Cronje	Sharjah	1995/96
5th	107	ND McKenzie and MV Boucher	Dhaka	2002/03
6th	84 *	JH Kallis and JM Kemp	Hyderabad	2005/06
7th	114	MV Boucher and L Klusener	Nagpur	1999/00
8th	88	DJ Richardson and PL Symcox	Mumbai	1996/97
9th	20	N Boje and R Telemachus	Nairobi	2000/01
10th	21 *	DJ Richardson and AA Donald	Mohali	1993/94

India

1st	193	SC Ganguly and SR Tendulkar	Johannesburg	2001/02
2nd	180	SR Tendulkar and RS Dravid	Nagpur	1999/00
3rd	88	SC Ganguly and RS Dravid	Jamshedpur	1999/00
4th	105	RS Dravid and M Azharuddin	Port Elizabeth	1996/97

5th	110 *	M Kaif and D Mongia	Dhaka	2002/03
6th	92	AD Jadeja and RR Singh	Kochi	1999/00
7th	51	AD Jadeja and NR Mongia	Mumbai	1996/97
8th	39	Yuvraj Singh and AB Agarkar	Hyderabad	2005/06
9th	29	Yuvraj Singh and Harbhajan Singh	Hyderabad	2005/06
10th	62	AD Jadeja and J Srinath	Sharjah	1999/00

SOUTH AFRICA versus KENYA

HIGHEST INNINGS TOTALS

For South Africa:	354-3	(50)	Cape Town	2001/02
For Kenya:	229-7	(50)	Kimberley	2001/02

LOWEST INNINGS TOTALS

For South Africa:	220-7	(50)	Nairobi	1999/00
For Kenya:	103	(25.1)	Nairobi	1996/97

HIGHEST INDIVIDUAL INNINGS

For South Africa:	131*	ND McKenzie	Cape Town	2001/02
For Kenya:	69	SO Tikolo	Colombo-RPS	2002/03

INDIVIDUAL CENTURIES

For South Africa (3):

116	HH Gibbs	Colombo-RPS	2002/03
124	G Kirsten	Cape Town	2001/02
131*	ND McKenzie	Cape Town	2001/02

For Kenya: No instance.

BEST BOWLING IN AN INNINGS

For South Africa:	6-23	AA Donald	Nairobi	1996/97
For Kenya:	2-24	AO Suji	Nairobi	1999/00
	2-24	TM Odoyo	Benoni	2001/02

FIVE WICKETS IN AN INNINGS

For South Africa (2):

9-0-23-6	AA Donald	Nairobi	1996/97
8.3-3-21-5	L Klusener	Amstelveen (WC)	1999

For Kenya: No instance.

RECORD WICKET PARTNERSHIPS

South Africa

1st	159	GC Smith and HH Gibbs	Colombo-RPS	2002/03
2nd	207	G Kirsten and ND McKenzie	Cape Town	2001/02
3rd	89	JH Kallis and ND McKenzie	Benoni	2001/02
4th	77 *	ND McKenzie and MV Boucher	Cape Town	2001/02
5th	101	JN Rhodes and WJ Cronje	Nairobi	1996/97
6th	17 *	L Klusener and JL Ontong	Colombo-RPS	2002/03
7th	49	SM Pollock and MV Boucher	Nairobi	1999/00
8th	13 *	MV Boucher and S Elworthy	Nairobi	1999/00
9th	29 *	WJ Cronje and PS de Villiers	Nairobi	1996/97
10th		No partnership		

Kenya

1st	66	KO Otieno and RD Shah	Amstelveen (WC)	1999
2nd	26	RD Shah and DO Obuya	Benoni	2001/02

3rd	64	RD Shah and SO Tikolo	Kimberley	2001/02
4th	55	SO Tikolo and MO Odumbe	Benoni	2001/02
5th	106	MO Odumbe and TM Odoyo	Kimberley	2001/02
6th	60	SO Tikolo and TM Odoyo	Nairobi	1999/00
7th	27	HS Modi and AO Suji	Cape Town	2001/02
8th	31	AY Karim and M Sheikh	Amstelveen (WC)	1999
9th	19	TM Odoyo and PJC Ongondo	Potchefstroom (WC)	2002/03
10th	12	MA Suji and JO Angara	Amstelveen (WC)	1999

SOUTH AFRICA versus NEW ZEALAND

HIGHEST INNINGS TOTALS

For South Africa:	324-4	(50)	Centurion	2000/01
For New Zealand:	298-9	(50)	Brisbane	1997/98

LOWEST INNINGS TOTALS

For South Africa:	147-7	(50)	Hobart	1993/94
For New Zealand:	134	(39.5)	Cape Town	1994/95

HIGHEST INDIVIDUAL INNINGS

For South Africa:	169*	DJ Callaghan	Verwoerdburg	1994/95
For New Zealand:	134*	SP Fleming	Johannesburg (WC)	2002/03

INDIVIDUAL CENTURIES

For South Africa (11):

105*	N Boje (2)	Potchefstroom	2000/01
129		Centurion	2000/01
169*	DJ Callaghan	Verwoerdburg	1994/95
143	HH Gibbs	Johannesburg (WC)	2002/03
111	JH Kallis (3)	Perth	1997/98
100		Dunedin	1998/99
100		Auckland	1998/99
103	G Kirsten (2)	Brisbane	1997/98
101		Kimberley	2000/01
103*	L Klusener	Auckland	1998/99
107*	JN Rhodes	Perth	2001/02

For New Zealand (6):

100*	NJ Astle	Auckland	1998/99
102*	CL Cairns	Brisbane	2001/02
134*	SP Fleming (2)	Johannesburg (WC)	2002/03
108		Christchurch	2003/04
108	AC Parore	Verwoerdburg	1994/95
103	RG Twose	Cape Town	2000/01

BEST BOWLING IN AN INNINGS

For South Africa:	5-31	M Ntini	Melbourne	2001/02
For New Zealand:	4-35	GI Allott	Dunedin	1998/99

FIVE WICKETS IN AN INNINGS

For South Africa (1):

10-0-31-5	M Ntini	Melbourne	2001/02

For New Zealand: No instance.

SOUTH AFRICAN LIMITED OVERS INTERNATIONAL RECORDS

RECORD WICKET PARTNERSHIPS

South Africa				
1st	176	G Kirsten and HH Gibbs	Birmingham (WC)	1999
2nd	172	G Kirsten and JH Kallis	Kimberley	2000/01
3rd	139 *	JH Kallis and HH Dippenaar	Melbourne	2001/02
4th	145	JH Kallis and DJ Cullinan	Auckland	1998/99
5th	138	JN Rhodes and MV Boucher	Perth	2001/02
6th	97 *	JN Rhodes and SM Pollock	Perth	2001/02
7th	65	JM Kemp and SM Pollock	Bloemfontein	2005/06
8th	69 *	L Klusener and S Abrahams	Cape Town	2000/01
9th	22 *	SM Pollock and M Ntini	Christchurch	2003/04
10th	67 *	JA Morkel and M Ntini	Napier	2003/04
New Zealand				
1st	114	MJ Greatbatch and RT Latham	Auckland (WC)	1991/92
2nd	140 *	SP Fleming and NJ Astle	Johannesburg (WC)	2002/03
3rd	126	HJH Marshall and SB Styris	Dunedin	2003/04
4th	150	RG Twose and CL Cairns	Cape Town	2000/01
5th	106	AC Parore and SA Thomson	Verwoerdburg	1994/95
6th	124	CD McMillan and CZ Harris	Adelaide	1997/98
7th	84 *	CL Cairns and AC Parore	Brisbane	2001/02
8th	69	AC Parore and DJ Nash	Brisbane	1997/98
9th	47 *	AC Parore and DL Vettori	Perth	2001/02
10th	29 *	AC Parore and SE Bond	Hobart	2001/02

SOUTH AFRICA versus PAKISTAN

HIGHEST INNINGS TOTALS

For South Africa:	321-8	(50)	Nairobi	1996/97
For Pakistan:	335-6	(50)	Port Elizabeth	2002/03

LOWEST INNINGS TOTALS

For South Africa:	101	(26.5)	Sharjah	1999/00
For Pakistan:	109	(32.3)	Johannesburg	1994/95

HIGHEST INDIVIDUAL INNINGS

For South Africa:	124	DJ Cullinan	Nairobi	1996/97
For Pakistan:	135	Salim Elahi	Port Elizabeth	2002/03

INDIVIDUAL CENTURIES

For South Africa (9):			
110*	DJ Cullinan (2)	Sharjah	1995/96
124		Nairobi	1996/97
110*	HH Dippenaar	Lahore	2003/04
114	HH Gibbs	Tangier	2002
109*	JH Kallis	Durban	1997/98
118*	G Kirsten (2)	Nairobi	1996/97
102*		Paarl	2002/03
121	JN Rhodes	Nairobi	1996/97
106	MJR Rindel	Johannesburg	1994/95
For Pakistan (6):			
111	Aamir Sohail	Karachi (WC)	1995/96
112	Abdul Razzaq	Port Elizabeth	2002/03

110	Ijaz Ahmed (2)	Rawalpindi	1994/95
114*		Durban	1994/95
107	Javed Miandad	East London	1992/93
135	Salim Elahi	Port Elizabeth	2002/03

BEST BOWLING IN AN INNINGS

For South Africa:	5-25	L Klusener	Cape Town	1997/98
For Pakistan:	5-16	Wasim Akram	East London	1992/93

FIVE WICKETS IN AN INNINGS

For South Africa (3):

8.4-1-41-5	JH Kallis	Cape Town	2002/03
7.1-1-25-5	L Klusener (2)	Cape Town	1997/98
10-0-47-5		Sharjah	1999/00

For Pakistan (3):

10-0-25-5	Waqar Younis (2)	Durban	1992/93
10-0-38-5		Tangier	2002
6.1-0-16-5	Wasim Akram	East London	1992/93

RECORD WICKET PARTNERSHIPS

South Africa

1st	190	G Kirsten and MJR Rindel	Johannesburg	1994/95
2nd	145	AC Hudson and WJ Cronje	Johannesburg	1994/95
3rd	105	ND McKenzie and WJ Cronje	Sharjah	1999/00
4th	232	DJ Cullinan and JN Rhodes	Nairobi	1996/97
5th	183 *	JH Kallis and JN Rhodes	Durban	1997/98
6th	88	JN Rhodes and DJ Richardson	Durban	1994/95
7th	99	JN Rhodes and SM Pollock	Durban	2002/03
8th	45 *	L Klusener and MV Boucher	Nottingham (WC)	1999
9th	28 *	RP Snell and CR Matthews	Durban	1994/95
10th	38 *	AC Dawson and M Ntini	Lahore	2003/04

Pakistan

1st	123	Imran Nazir and Shahid Afridi	Sharjah	1999/00
2nd	257	Salim Elahi and Abdul Razzaq	Port Elizabeth	2002/03
3rd	136 *	Ijaz Ahmed and Salim Malik	Durban	1994/95
4th	165	Javed Miandad and Asif Mujtaba	East London	1992/93
5th	148 *	Ijaz Ahmed and Basit Ali	Faisalabad	1994/95
6th	47	Inzamam-ul-Haq and Abdul Razzaq	Sharjah	1999/00
7th	55	Asif Mujtaba and Wasim Akram	Johannesburg	1994/95
	55	Moin Khan and Azhar Mahmood	Nottingham (WC)	1999
8th	81 *	Salim Malik and Aaqib Javed	Sharjah	1995/96
9th	46	Wasim Akram and Waqar Younis	East London	2002/03
10th	72	Abdul Razzaq and Waqar Younis	Durban	1997/98

SOUTH AFRICA versus SRI LANKA

HIGHEST INNINGS TOTALS

For South Africa:	317-6	(50)	Centurion	2002/03
For Sri Lanka:	308-8	(50)	Colombo-SSC	2004

LOWEST INNINGS TOTALS

For South Africa:	154	(46.1)	Colombo-RPS	1993/94
For Sri Lanka:	98	(34)	Colombo-RPS	1993/94

SOUTH AFRICAN LIMITED OVERS INTERNATIONAL RECORDS

HIGHEST INDIVIDUAL INNINGS

For South Africa:	125*	HH Dippenaar	Adelaide	2005/06
For Sri Lanka:	124	MS Atapattu	Durban (WC)	2002/03

INDIVIDUAL CENTURIES

For South Africa (6):			
125*	HH Dippenaar	Adelaide	2005/06
108*	HH Gibbs	Kimberley	2002/03
113*	JH Kallis (3)	Dhaka	1998/99
100*		Paarl	2000/01
101		Colombo-SSC	2004
120*	ND McKenzie	East London	2000/01
For Sri Lanka (2):			
123*	MS Atapattu (2)	Benoni	2002/03
124		Durban (WC)	2002/03

BEST BOWLING IN AN INNINGS

For South Africa:	6-49	L Klusener	Lahore	1997/98
For Sri Lanka:	5-26	DNT Zoysa	Colombo-RPS	2004

FIVE WICKETS IN AN INNINGS

For South Africa (2):			
10-0-49-6	L Klusener	Lahore	1997/98
8.2-0-37-5	M Ntini	Cape Town	2000/01
For Sri Lanka (3):			
9.1-0-61-5	UDU Chandana	Colombo-SSC	2004
10-0-44-5	M Muralitharan	Colombo-RPS	2000
8-0-26-5	DNT Zoysa	Colombo-RPS	2004

RECORD WICKET PARTNERSHIPS

South Africa				
1st	150	G Kirsten and AJ Hall	Galle	2000
2nd	111	HH Dippenaar and JH Kallis	Paarl	2000/01
3rd	172 *	HH Gibbs and JH Kallis	Kimberley	2002/03
4th	119	HH Dippenaar and HH Gibbs	Adelaide	2005/06
5th	100	ND McKenzie and MV Boucher	East London	2000/01
6th	100	PL Symcox and JN Rhodes	Nottingham	1998
7th	101	HH Dippenaar and MV Boucher	Tangier	2002
8th	51	SM Pollock and L Klusener	Colombo-RPS	2004
9th	44	L Klusener and S Elworthy	Northampton (WC)	1999
10th	51	RP Snell and PS de Villiers	Colombo-RPS	1993/94
Sri Lanka				
1st	110	RS Mahanama and UC Hathurusingha	Kandy	1993/94
	110	ST Jayasuriya and RS Kaluwitharana	Paarl	2000/01
2nd	129	DA Gunawardene and MS Atapattu	Colombo-SSC	2000
3rd	140	MS Atapattu and PA de Silva	Benoni	2002/03
4th	152	MS Atapattu and PA de Silva	Durban (WC)	2002/03
5th	120	KC Sangakkara and RP Arnold	Galle	2000
6th	93	KC Sangakkara and UDU Chandana	Colombo-RPS	2004
7th	93	SKL de Silva and HDPK Dharmasena	Lahore	1997/98
8th	36 *	HDPK Dharmasena and WPUJC Vaas	Lahore	1997/98
9th	55	HDPK Dharmasena and DK Liyanage	Lahore	1997/98
10th	29	RP Arnold and PW Gunaratne	Kimberley	2002/03

SOUTH AFRICAN LIMITED OVERS INTERNATIONAL RECORDS

SOUTH AFRICA versus WEST INDIES

HIGHEST INNINGS TOTALS

For South Africa:	310-6	(49.4)	Johannesburg	2003/04
For West Indies:	304-2	(50)	Johannesburg	2003/04

LOWEST INNINGS TOTALS

For South Africa:	140-9	(50)	Cape Town	1992/93
For West Indies:	54	(23.2)	Cape Town	2003/04

HIGHEST INDIVIDUAL INNINGS

For South Africa:	139	JH Kallis	Johannesburg	2003/04
For West Indies:	152*	CH Gayle	Johannesburg	2003/04

INDIVIDUAL CENTURIES

For South Africa (9):

123	HH Dippenaar	Bridgetown	2004/05
125	HH Gibbs (4)	Port Elizabeth	1998/99
104		St John's	2000/01
107		Bridgetown	2000/01
101		The Oval	2004
107	JH Kallis (3)	St George's	2000/01
109*		Cape Town	2003/04
139		Johannesburg	2003/04
103	GC Smith	Kingston	2004/05

For West Indies (11):

150	S Chanderpaul	East London	1998/99
152*	CH Gayle (2)	Johannesburg	2003/04
132		Bridgetown	2004/05
105	CL Hooper (2)	Lahore	1997/98
108		East London	1998/99
111*	BC Lara (3)	Bloemfontein	1992/93
111		Karachi (WC)	1995/96
116		Cape Town (WC)	2002/03
122	PV Simmons (2)	Kingston	1991/92
104		Port-of-Spain	1991/92
103	PA Wallace	Dhaka	1998/99

BEST BOWLING IN AN INNINGS

For South Africa:	6-35	SM Pollock	East London	1998/99
For West Indies:	4-44	KLT Arthurton	Bloemfontein	1998/99

FIVE WICKETS IN AN INNINGS

For South Africa (3):

7.3-0-30-5	JH Kallis	Dhaka	1998/99
9.5-0-62-5	CK Langeveldt	Bridgetown	2004/05
10-2-35-6	SM Pollock	East London	1998/99

For West Indies: No instance.

RECORD WICKET PARTNERSHIPS

South Africa

1st	131	GC Smith and HH Dippenaar	Kingston	2004/05
2nd	194	HH Dippenaar and JH Kallis	Bridgetown	2004/05
3rd	162	HH Gibbs and WJ Cronje	Port Elizabeth	1998/99

4th	132	AG Prince and JM Kemp	Port-of-Spain	2004/05
5th	162 *	JH Kallis and JA Rudolph	Cape Town	2003/04
6th	94	WJ Cronje and DM Benkenstein	Bloemfontein	1998/99
7th	62	DM Benkenstein and MV Boucher	Cape Town	1998/99
8th	91	DM Benkenstein and L Klusener	Cape Town	1998/99
9th	36 *	L Klusener and PL Symcox	Centurion	1998/99
10th	17	CR Matthews and PR Adams	Karachi (WC)	1995/96
West Indies				
1st	193	CH Gayle and S Chanderpaul	Johannesburg	2003/04
2nd	138	S Chanderpaul and BC Lara	Karachi (WC)	1995/96
3rd	108	S Chanderpaul and RR Sarwan	Centurion	2003/04
4th	226	S Chanderpaul and CL Hooper	East London	1998/99
5th	67	CL Hooper and MN Samuels	St George's	2000/01
6th	63 *	RL Powell and RR Sarwan	Cape Town (WC)	2002/03
7th	46	AL Logie and DL Haynes	Christchurch (WC)	1991/92
8th	49 *	CO Browne and IDR Bradshaw	Kingston	2004/05
9th	30	RN Lewis and CEL Ambrose	Bloemfontein	1998/99
10th	47	RN Lewis and RD King	Bloemfontein	1998/99

SOUTH AFRICA versus ZIMBABWE

HIGHEST INNINGS TOTALS

For South Africa:	363-3	(50)	Bulawayo	2001/02
For Zimbabwe:	256-8	(50)	Johannesburg	1996/97

LOWEST INNINGS TOTALS

For South Africa:	185	(47.2)	Chelmsford (WC)	1999
For Zimbabwe:	124	(40.1)	Harare	2001/02

HIGHEST INDIVIDUAL INNINGS

For South Africa:	127	BM McMillan	Harare	1995/96
For Zimbabwe:	91	GW Flower	Nairobi	1999/00

INDIVIDUAL CENTURIES

For South Africa (5):

125	HH Gibbs	Bulawayo	2001/02
125*	JH Kallis	Canterbury	2003
101*	L Klusener	Nairobi	1999/00
127	BM McMillan	Harare	1995/96
117	GC Smith	Durban	2004/05

For Zimbabwe: No instance.

BEST BOWLING IN AN INNINGS

For South Africa:	4-17	CW Henderson	Harare	2001/02
For Zimbabwe:	4-25	HH Streak	Harare	1995/96

FIVE WICKETS IN AN INNINGS

No instance.

RECORD WICKET PARTNERSHIPS

South Africa

1st	154	GC Smith and HH Gibbs	Cardiff	2003
2nd	112	KC Wessels and PN Kirsten	Canberra (WC)	1991/92
3rd	137	GC Smith and JA Rudolph	Southampton	2003

4th	134	GC Smith and HH Gibbs	Durban	2004/05
5th	123	DJ Cullinan and WJ Cronje	Centurion	1996/97
6th	137	WJ Cronje and SM Pollock	Johannesburg	1996/97
7th	82	JH Kallis and L Klusener	Durban	1999/00
8th	43	SM Pollock and L Klusener	Chelmsford (WC)	1999
9th	14	PL Symcox and PS de Villiers	Harare	1995/96
10th	35	L Klusener and AA Donald	Chelmsford (WC)	1999
Zimbabwe				
1st	99	NC Johnson and GW Flower	Nairobi	1999/00
2nd	109	DD Ebrahim and TJ Friend	Canterbury	2003
3rd	54	ADR Campbell and A Flower	Bulawayo	2001/02
4th	60	ADR Campbell and CB Wishart	Bulawayo	2001/02
5th	93	GW Flower and DL Houghton	Johannesburg	1996/97
6th	67	BRM Taylor and HH Streak	Port Elizabeth	2004/05
7th	91	A Flower and GJ Whittall	Durban	1999/00
8th	50 *	ADR Campbell and HH Streak	Harare	1995/96
9th	44 *	HH Streak and RW Price	Southampton	2003
10th	15	P Utseya and CB Mpofu	Johannesburg	2004/05

SOUTH AFRICA versus OTHER COUNTRIES

INDIVIDUAL CENTURIES

For South Africa (2):

188*	G Kirsten	v United Arab Emirates	Rawalpindi (WC)	1995/96
161	AC Hudson	v Holland	Rawalpindi (WC)	1995/96

Against South Africa: No instance.

FIVE WICKETS IN AN INNINGS

No instance.

SOUTH AFRICA LIMITED OVERS INTERNATIONAL CAREER RECORDS

As at 1 July 2006

Name	Years	M	Inns	NO	Runs	HS	Avg	SR	100	50	Ct	St	Balls	Runs	Wkts	Avg	RpO	BB	4I
S Abrahams	2000-2000	1	1	1	16	16*	-	61.53	0	0	1	0	60	40	0	-	4.00	-	0
PR Adams	1996-2003	24	9	5	66	33*	16.50	53.22	0	0	7	0	1109	815	29	28.10	4.40	3-26	0
AM Bacher	1997-2005	13	13	0	270	56	20.76	57.56	0	1	4	0	108	64	3	21.33	3.55	2-36	0
DM Benkenstein	1998-2002	23	20	3	305	69	17.94	65.87	0	1	3	0	65	44	4	11.00	4.06	3-5	0
N Boje	1995-2005	113	69	18	1410	129	27.64	89.29	2	4	33	0	4457	3351	95	35.27	4.51	5-21	3
T Bosch	1992-1992	2	0	0	0	-	-	-	0	0	0	0	51	66	0	-	7.76	-	0
J Botha	2005-2006	11	6	3	98	46	32.66	74.80	0	0	6	0	438	361	7	51.57	4.94	2-49	0
MV Boucher	1998-2006	215	156	39	3117	75	26.64	80.33	0	19	296	16	0	0	0	-	-	-	0
RE Bryson	1997-1997	7	4	3	32	17*	32.00	123.07	0	0	1	0	378	323	7	46.14	5.12	2-34	0
DJ Callaghan	1992-2000	29	25	6	493	169*	25.94	68.00	1	0	6	0	444	365	10	36.50	4.93	3-32	0
SJ Cook	1991-1993	4	4	0	67	35	16.75	56.77	0	0	1	0	0	0	0	-	-	-	0
WJ Cronje	1992-2000	188	175	31	5565	112	38.64	76.49	2	39	73	0	5357	3966	114	34.78	4.44	5-32	2
DN Crookes	1994-2000	32	23	3	296	54	14.80	71.84	0	1	20	0	1221	1011	25	40.44	4.96	3-30	0
DJ Cullinan	1993-2000	138	133	16	3860	124	32.99	70.37	3	23	62	0	174	124	5	24.80	4.27	2-30	0
AC Dawson	1998-2004	19	7	4	69	23*	23.00	102.98	0	0	2	0	901	715	21	34.04	4.76	4-49	1
AB de Villiers	2005-2006	17	17	0	339	68	19.94	75.16	0	1	7	0	0	0	0	-	-	-	0
PS de Villiers	1992-1997	83	36	15	170	20*	8.09	79.06	0	0	15	0	4422	2636	95	27.74	3.57	4-27	2
HH Dippenaar	1999-2006	96	84	13	3190	125*	44.92	68.03	4	24	32	0	0	0	0	-	-	-	0
AA Donald	1991-2003	164	40	18	95	13	4.31	34.05	0	0	28	0	8561	5926	272	21.78	4.15	6-23	13
J-P Duminy	2004-2004	5	5	0	29	22	5.80	51.78	0	0	2	0	84	62	1	62.00	4.42	1-28	0
CE Eksteen	1991-1994	6	2	2	6	6*	-	24.00	0	0	3	0	222	181	2	90.50	4.89	1-26	0
S Elworthy	1998-2002	39	16	8	100	23	12.50	62.50	0	0	9	0	1702	1235	44	28.06	4.35	3-17	0
HH Gibbs	1996-2006	185	184	13	6117	175	35.77	82.07	16	25	77	0	0	0	0	-	-	-	0
AJ Hall	1999-2006	68	46	11	761	81	21.74	72.82	0	2	23	0	2406	1848	65	28.43	4.60	4-23	2
M Hayward	1998-2002	21	5	1	12	4	3.00	42.85	0	0	4	0	993	858	21	40.85	5.18	4-31	1
CW Henderson	2001-2001	4	0	0	0	-	-	-	0	0	0	0	217	132	7	18.85	3.64	4-17	1
O Henry	1992-1992	3	3	1	20	11	10.00	76.92	0	0	1	0	149	125	2	62.50	5.03	1-31	0
AC Hudson	1991-1997	89	88	1	2559	161	29.41	64.47	2	18	18	0	6	3	0	-	3.00	-	0
SD Jack	1994-1995	2	2	0	7	6	3.50	87.50	0	0	3	0	108	86	3	28.66	4.77	2-41	0
JH Kallis	1996-2006	226	216	39	7966	139	45.00	70.79	13	56	90	0	8044	6452	199	32.42	4.81	5-30	4
JM Kemp	2001-2006	51	39	12	888	30	32.88	92.40	0	7	24	0	881	678	19	35.68	4.61	3-20	0

SOUTH AFRICA LIMITED OVERS INTERNATIONAL CAREER RECORDS

Name	Years	M	Inns	NO	Runs	HS	Avg	SR	100	50	Ct	St	Balls	Runs	Wkts	Avg	RpO	BB	4I
JC Kent	2002-2002	2	0	0	0	-	-	-	0	0	1	0	48	57	0	-	7.12	-	0
G Kirsten	1993-2003	185	185	19	6798	188*	40.95	71.98	13	45	61	1	30	23	0	-	4.60	-	0
PN Kirsten	1991-1994	40	40	6	1293	97	38.02	56.04	0	9	11	0	183	152	6	25.33	4.98	3-31	0
L Klusener	1996-2004	171	137	50	3576	103*	41.10	89.89	2	19	35	0	7336	5751	192	29.95	4.70	6-49	7
LJ Koen	1997-2000	5	5	0	82	28	16.40	48.52	0	0	3	0	0	0	0	-	-	-	0
GJ-P Kruger	2006-2006	3	2	1	0	0*	0.00	0.00	0	0	1	0	138	139	2	69.50	6.04	1-43	0
AP Kuiper	1991-1996	25	23	7	539	63*	33.68	81.41	0	3	3	0	588	518	18	28.77	5.28	3-33	0
CK Langeveldt	2001-2006	29	5	1	7	3	1.75	50.00	0	0	1	0	1352	1102	38	29.00	4.89	5-62	2
GFJ Liebenberg	1995-1998	4	4	0	94	39	23.50	47.23	0	0	0	0	0	0	0	-	-	-	0
ND McKenzie	2000-2003	59	51	10	1580	131*	38.53	69.69	2	9	19	0	46	27	0	-	3.52	-	0
BM McMillan	1991-1998	78	52	16	841	127	23.36	73.06	1	0	42	0	3623	2589	70	36.98	4.28	4-32	1
CR Matthews	1991-1997	56	22	9	141	26	10.84	69.80	0	0	10	0	3003	1975	79	25.00	3.94	4-10	3
JA Morkel	2004-2005	8	6	1	63	23*	12.60	73.25	0	0	1	0	264	212	7	30.28	4.81	2-23	0
PV Mpitsang	1999-1999	2	1	1	1	1*	-	100.00	0	0	0	0	60	63	2	31.50	6.30	2-49	0
A Nel	2001-2006	45	7	5	12	4*	6.00	42.85	0	0	12	0	2184	1716	58	29.58	4.71	4-39	1
M Ntini	1998-2006	128	30	16	147	42*	10.50	66.51	0	0	25	0	6420	4714	205	22.99	4.40	6-22	9
JL Ontong	2001-2005	20	11	1	98	32	9.80	61.63	0	0	10	0	538	396	9	44.00	4.41	3-30	0
SJ Palframan	1996-1996	7	4	0	55	28	13.75	68.75	0	0	9	0	0	0	0	-	-	-	0
RJ Peterson	2002-2006	26	10	1	98	36	10.88	66.66	0	0	4	0	912	717	10	71.70	4.71	2-26	0
SM Pollock	1996-2006	253	165	58	2702	75	25.25	85.94	0	11	94	0	13204	8234	342	24.07	3.74	6-35	15
N Pothas	2000-2000	3	1	0	24	24	24.00	58.53	0	0	4	1	0	0	0	-	-	-	0
AG Prince	2002-2006	34	30	10	792	89*	39.60	66.33	0	2	20	0	0	0	0	-	-	-	0
MW Pringle	1992-1994	17	8	3	48	13*	9.60	85.71	0	0	2	0	870	604	22	27.45	4.16	4-11	1
AG Puttick	2005-2005	1	1	0	0	0	0.00	0.00	0	0	1	0	0	0	0	-	-	-	0
JN Rhodes	1992-2003	245	220	51	5935	121	35.11	81.05	2	33	105	0	14	4	0	-	1.71	-	0
CEB Rice	1991-1991	3	2	0	26	14	13.00	70.27	0	0	0	0	138	114	2	57.00	4.95	1-46	0
DJ Richardson	1991-1998	122	77	33	868	53	19.72	66.76	0	1	148	17	0	0	0	-	-	-	0
MJR Rindel	1994-1999	22	22	1	575	106	27.38	66.70	1	2	8	0	270	242	6	40.33	5.37	2-15	0
JA Rudolph	2003-2006	43	37	6	1157	81	37.32	68.62	0	7	11	0	24	26	0	-	6.50	-	0
DB Rundle	1994-1994	2	2	0	6	6	3.00	54.54	0	0	3	0	96	95	5	19.00	5.93	4-42	1
MW Rushmere	1992-1992	4	4	0	78	35	19.50	44.82	0	0	1	0	0	0	0	-	-	-	0
BN Schultz	1992-1992	1	0	0	0	-	-	-	0	0	0	0	54	35	1	35.00	3.88	1-35	0
TG Shaw	1991-1994	9	6	4	26	17*	13.00	74.28	0	0	2	0	504	298	9	33.11	3.54	2-19	0
EO Simons	1994-1995	23	18	4	217	24	15.50	73.55	0	0	6	0	1212	810	33	24.54	4.00	4-42	1
GC Smith	2002-2006	90	89	5	3389	134*	40.34	79.07	6	19	36	0	686	655	10	65.50	5.72	3-30	0

SOUTH AFRICA LIMITED OVERS INTERNATIONAL CAREER RECORDS

Name	Years	M	Inns	NO	Runs	HS	Avg	SR	100	50	Ct	St	Balls	Runs	Wkts	Avg	RpO	BB	4I
RP Snell	1991-1996	42	28	8	322	63	16.10	97.57	0	2	7	0	2095	1574	44	35.77	4.50	5-40	3
ELR Stewart	1993-2002	6	6	2	61	23*	15.25	52.13	0	0	5	0	0	0	0	-	-	-	0
DW Steyn	2006-2006	2	0	0	0	-	-	-	0	0	0	0	48	90	1	90.00	11.25	1-58	0
PJR Steyn	1995-1995	1	1	0	4	4	4.00	28.57	0	0	0	0	0	0	0	-	-	-	0
PC Strydom	2000-2000	10	8	3	48	34	9.60	51.06	0	0	3	0	252	206	2	103.00	4.90	1-18	0
PL Symcox	1993-1999	80	54	13	694	61	16.92	83.91	0	3	23	0	3991	2762	72	38.36	4.15	4-28	1
R Telemachus	1998-2006	36	15	3	73	29	6.08	77.65	0	0	4	0	1870	1532	54	28.37	4.91	4-43	1
DJ Terbrugge	2000-2000	4	2	1	5	5	5.00	35.71	0	0	0	0	126	105	4	26.25	5.00	4-20	1
JJ van der Wath	2006-2006	7	6	2	80	37*	20.00	140.35	0	0	2	0	376	399	10	39.90	6.36	2-21	0
M van Jaarsveld	2002-2004	11	7	1	124	45	20.66	73.37	0	0	4	0	31	18	2	9.00	3.48	1-0	0
MN van Wyk	2003-2003	1	1	0	17	17	17.00	85.00	0	0	0	0	0	0	0	-	-	-	0
CJPG van Zyl	1992-1992	2	2	1	3	3*	3.00	27.27	0	0	0	0	108	93	0	-	5.16	-	0
KC Wessels	1991-1994	55	54	4	1627	90	32.54	51.66	0	12	30	0	12	11	0	-	5.50	-	0
HS Williams	1999-2000	7	2	1	8	7	8.00	72.72	0	0	2	0	329	228	9	25.33	4.15	3-38	0
CM Willoughby	2000-2003	3	2	0	0	0	0.00	0.00	0	0	0	0	168	148	2	74.00	5.28	2-39	0
M Yachad	1991-1991	1	1	0	31	31	31.00	40.25	0	0	1	0	0	0	0	-	-	-	0
M Zondeki	2002-2006	9	2	2	4	3*	-	133.33	0	0	3	0	402	350	8	43.75	5.22	2-46	0

Career Records including the matches for Africa and the World XI

Name	Years	M	Inns	NO	Runs	HS	Avg	SR	100	50	Ct	St	Balls	Runs	Wkts	Avg	RpO	BB	4I
N Boje	1995-2005	115	71	18	1414	129	26.67	88.70	2	4	33	0	4541	3415	96	35.57	4.51	5-21	3
MV Boucher	1998-2006	217	158	39	3175	76	26.68	80.27	0	19	303	17	0	0	0	-	-	-	0
AB de Villiers	2005-2006	19	19	0	402	68	21.15	74.30	0	1	7	0	0	0	0	-	-	-	0
HH Dippenaar	1999-2006	99	87	13	3234	125*	43.70	67.89	4	24	33	0	0	0	0	-	-	-	0
JH Kallis	1996-2006	231	221	39	7995	139	43.92	70.47	13	56	90	0	8156	6564	203	32.33	4.82	5-30	4
JM Kemp	2001-2006	54	42	12	938	80	31.26	90.36	0	7	24	0	983	746	22	33.90	4.55	3-20	0
M Ntini	1998-2006	129	31	17	147	42*	10.50	66.51	0	0	25	0	6462	4772	206	23.16	4.43	6-22	9
JL Ontong	2001-2005	21	12	1	98	32	8.90	60.86	0	0	11	0	538	396	9	44.00	4.41	3-30	0
SM Pollock	1996-2006	259	171	59	2805	75	25.04	85.70	0	11	96	0	13486	8456	348	24.29	3.76	6-35	15
AG Prince	2002-2006	37	33	11	870	89*	39.54	66.21	0	3	20	0	0	0	0	-	-	-	0
JA Rudolph	2003-2006	45	39	6	1174	8[illegible]	35.57	68.01	0	7	11	0	24	26	0	-	6.50	-	0
GC Smith	2002-2006	91	90	5	3389	134*	39.87	78.97	6	19	36	0	686	655	10	65.50	5.72	3-30	0
DW Steyn	2005-2006	4	2	0	4	3	2.00	26.66	0	0	0	0	109	132	3	44.00	7.26	1-2	0
M Zondeki	2002-2006	11	3	2	4	3*	4.00	80.00	0	0	3	0	456	414	8	51.75	5.44	2-46	0

The following player also appeared for Australia:

Name	Years	M	Inns	NO	Runs	HS	Avg	SR	100	50	Ct	St	Balls	Runs	Wkts	Avg	RpO	BB	4I
KC Wessels	1983-1985	54	51	3	1740	107	36.25	59.08	1	14	19	0	737	655	18	36.38	5.33	2-16	0

SOUTH AFRICA A IN SRI LANKA 2005

South Africa A had a successful tour of Sri Lanka, highlighted by an unbeaten run in a triangular one-day series against Sri Lanka A and New Zealand A.

The tourists lost the four-day series but it was a close-run thing and they were hampered by a lack of preparation caused by rain. In the one-day series, South Africa A won all four of their qualifying matches in a fine team effort, with coach Vincent Barnes giving all the touring party a chance to play, before sweeping to victory in the final against New Zealand A.

The squad for the four-day series was: Jacques Rudolph (Eagles, captain), Paul Adams (Cobras), Hashim Amla (Dolphins), Johan Botha (Warriors), Zander de Bruyn (Titans), Jean-Paul Duminy (Cobras), Tyron Henderson (Warriors), Garnett Kruger (Lions), Justin Ontong (Lions), Andrew Puttick (Cobras), Dale Steyn (Titans), Thami Tsolekile (Cobras), Johan van der Wath (Eagles) and Monde Zondeki (Cobras). Coach, Vincent Barnes; assistant coach and manager, Barney Mohammed; physiotherapist, Ian Repton.

There were two changes to the squad originally chosen. Albie Morkel and Alfonso Thomas, both of the Titans, withdrew because of ankle injuries. They were replaced by Henderson and Kruger. Duminy suffered a recurrence of a hand injury during the side's two-day opening match and returned home. He was not replaced.

For the one-day matches, Loots Bosman (Eagles) and Robin Peterson (Warriors) replaced Adams and Amla, while Morkel joined the side after recovering from injury.

The only newcomers to South Africa A cricket were Botha, Henderson and Steyn.

SL CRICKET DEVELOPMENT XI v SOUTH AFRICA A — Not First-class 2-day Match

Played at De Soysa Stadium, Moratuwa on 4,5 September 2005 — Toss: Sri Lanka Cricket Development XI
Umpires: MWDP de Silva & PG Liyanage
Close of play: Day 1: No play
Result: Drawn

SOUTH AFRICA A	*Runs*	*Mins*	*Balls*	*4*	*6*
*JA Rudolph lbw b Perera	37	91	86	7	-
AG Puttick c Kandamby b Perera	11	70	38	-	-
HM Amla c Kandamby b Herath	19	78	52	2	-
J-P Duminy lbw b Zoysa	20	45	49	1	-
Z de Bruyn retired out	19	37	27	3	-
JL Ontong retired out	26	30	29	5	-
†TL Tsolekile not out	7	30	32	-	-
JJ van der Wath not out	15	16	14	1	1
PR Adams					
M Zondeki					
DW Steyn					
J Botha					
T Henderson					
GJ-P Kruger					
Extras (b 3, lb 6, nb 9)	18				
TOTAL (for 6 wkts dec) (53 overs)	**172**				

SL CRICKET DEVELOPMENT XI	*Runs*	*Mins*	*Balls*	*4*	*6*
HE Vithana c Steyn b Zondeki	6	27	24	-	-
S Kalavitigoda c Puttick b Kruger	9	41	22	2	-
MA Sandaruwan c Tsolekile b Adams	41	80	56	7	-
SHT Kandamby c Kruger b Henderson	30	51	41	4	2
MDK Perera c Amla b Adams	0	4	2	-	-
CK Kapugedera c Puttick b Adams	2	17	15	-	-
WMG Ramyakumara c Tsolekile b Botha	17	32	21	3	-
†JK Silva c Amla b Ontong	0	3	3	-	-
DNT Zoysa c Puttick b Ontong	1	11	6	-	-
*HMRKB Herath not out	22	34	25	3	-
ABT Lakshitha not out	11	25	22	2	-
Extras (b 4, w 2, nb 3)	9				
TOTAL (for 9 wkts) (39 overs)	**148**				

SLC	*O*	*M*	*R*	*W*	
Zoysa	7	1	21	1	(2 nb)
Lakshitha	6	0	31	0	(2 nb)
Ramyakumara	10	1	29	0	(5 nb)
Perera	15	2	51	2	
Herath	14	4	27	1	
Kandamby	1	0	4	0	

SAA	*O*	*M*	*R*	*W*	
Zondeki	5	2	13	1	
Van der Wath	4	1	14	0	
Kruger	4	1	13	1	(1 w)
Steyn	3	1	15	0	(3 nb)
Adams	6	0	18	3	(1 w)
Henderson	4	0	19	1	
Ontong	6	0	28	2	
Botha	6	1	18	1	
Rudolph	1	0	6	0	

Fall of Wickets	SAA	SLA
1st	51 (2)	14 (1)
2nd	61 (1)	27 (2)
3rd	98 (4)	85 (4)
4th	116 (3)	86 (5)
5th	144 (5)	91 (3)
6th	152 (6)	93 (6)
7th	-	94 (8)
8th	-	106 (9)
9th	-	122 (7)

SOUTH AFRICA A IN SRI LANKA 2005

SRI LANKA A v SOUTH AFRICA A — 1st A-Test

Played at Nondescripts, Colombo on 7,8,9 September 2005 — Toss: Sri Lanka A
Umpires: PT Manuel & BBJ Nandakumar — Referee: UC Hathurusingha
Debuts: SLA: RACG Jayaweera, WU Tharanga and CG Wijesinghe (All FC for SLA). SAA: J Botha and DW Steyn (Both FC for SAA)
Close of play: Day 1: SLA (1) 16-1 (Tharanga 2*, Daniel 5*, 6 overs). Day 2: SAA (2) 108-6 (Tsolekile 26*, Botha 4*, 42 overs)..
Result: Sri Lanka A won by 6 wickets

South Africa A failed to capitalise on a good start after being sent in, with Zander de Bruyn a sparkling exception as the rest of the middle order batting folded to left-arm spinner Sajeewa Weerakoon.

South Africa A took a small first innings lead despite an aggressive half-century by Kaushal Lokuarachchi but Sri Lanka A took control through another fine spell by Weerakoon. Any prospects the tourists had of winning the match were blown away by an attacking innings by the left-handed Avishka Gunawardene as the Sri Lankans won with a day to spare.

SOUTH AFRICA A	Runs	Mins	Balls	4	6		Runs	Mins	Balls	4	6
AG Puttick c Wijesinghe b Lokuarachchi	41	110	78	7	-	(2) b Perera	1	14	10	-	-
*JA Rudolph c Jayawardene b Dilhara	28	87	58	4	-	(1) c Tharanga b Weerakoon	35	112	72	5	-
HM Amla lbw b Jayaweera	15	42	34	1	-	b Weerakoon	35	76	43	4	-
Z de Bruyn not out	100	208	154	14	1	c Jayawardene b Weerakoon	0	9	7	-	-
JL Ontong b Weerakoon	40	49	44	8	-	st Jayawardene b Weerakoon	0	1	2	-	-
†TL Tsolekile b Weerakoon	0	9	2	-	-	c Mubarak b Lokuarachchi	31	134	103	2	-
JJ van der Wath c Daniel b Weerakoon	0	2	5	-	-	c Jayawardene b Jayaweera	4	31	34	-	-
J Botha c Lokuarachchi b Weerakoon	14	95	70	1	-	lbw b Weerakoon	41	126	86	6	-
PR Adams lbw b Lokuarachchi	1	6	7	-	-	not out	21	32	18	3	-
M Zondeki c and b Weerakoon	1	13	9	-	-	lbw b Weerakoon	0	5	3	-	-
DW Steyn c Wijesinghe b Weerakoon	0	8	5	-	-	lbw b Weerakoon	0	2	2	-	-
Extras (b 1, lb 1, nb 3)	5					Extras (b 1, lb 1, nb 3)	5				
TOTAL (77.2 overs)	**245**					**TOTAL (62.4 overs)**	**173**				

SRI LANKA A	Runs	Mins	Balls	4	6		Runs	Mins	Balls	4	6
*DA Gunawardene c Van der Wath b Zondeki	0	1	3	-	-	b Ontong	83	155	97	11	1
WU Tharanga c Puttick b Zondeki	12	40	27	1	-	b Zondeki	6	18	15	-	-
GI Daniel lbw b Botha	48	130	74	7	1	c Tsolekile b Steyn	35	101	65	3	1
J Mubarak c Tsolekile b Van der Wath	46	74	55	6	2	not out	37	67	53	4	1
CG Wijesinghe b Zondeki	29	89	68	2	-	c Puttick b Botha	8	12	8	1	-
†HAPW Jayawardene c Tsolekile b Botha	0	2	3	-	-	not out	16	18	19	2	-
LHD Dilhara c Botha b Steyn	3	5	5	-	-						
KS Lokuarachchi not out	53	106	72	6	1						
S Weerakoon c and b Adams	0	5	2	-	-						
RACG Jayaweera c Amla b Adams	5	7	6	1	-						
PDRL Perera lbw b Adams	8	28	15	1	-						
Extras (b 2, lb 5, nb 8, pen 5)	20					Extras (b 4, lb 8, nb 3)	15				
TOTAL (53.4 overs)	**224**					**TOTAL (for 4 wkts) (42.2 overs)**	**200**				

SLA	O	M	R	W		O	M	R	W	
Perera	14	4	40	0		9	0	42	1	(2 nb)
Jayaweera	11	4	54	1	(2 nb)	15	2	33	1	
Dilhara	10	3	28	1		(4) 4	0	17	0	(1 nb)
Weerakoon	22.2	4	59	6	(1 nb)	(3) 22.4	6	47	7	
Lokuarachchi	18	4	56	2		12	3	32	1	
Daniel	2	0	6	0						
SAA	O	M	R	W		O	M	R	W	
Zondeki	13	4	54	3		6	0	27	1	
Van der Wath	11	3	39	1	(1 nb)	(4) 5	0	25	0	(2 nb)
Steyn	9	0	39	1	(7 nb)	(2) 9	2	37	1	(1 nb)
Adams	10.4	1	37	3		(5) 3	0	16	0	
Botha	7	0	35	2		(3) 12.2	1	53	1	
De Bruyn	3	0	8	0						
Ontong						(6) 7	1	30	1	

Fall of Wickets

	SAA	SLA	SAA	SLA
1st	68 (2)	4 (1)	9 (2)	15 (2)
2nd	79 (1)	32 (2)	71 (3)	118 (3)
3rd	95 (3)	111 (4)	73 (4)	156 (1)
4th	157 (5)	123 (3)	73 (5)	171 (5)
5th	157 (6)	123 (6)	78 (1)	-
6th	157 (7)	126 (7)	89 (7)	-
7th	231 (8)	189 (5)	147 (6)	-
8th	238 (9)	190 (9)	171 (8)	-
9th	243 (10)	196 (10)	173 (10)	-
10th	245 (11)	224 (11)	173 (11)	-

SRI LANKA A v SOUTH AFRICA A — 2nd A-Test

Played at Rangiri Dambulla International Stadium, Dambulla on 14,15,16 September 2005 — Toss: South Africa A
Umpires: AG Dissanayake & R Martinesz — Referee: ADNR de Alwis
Debuts: SLA: None. SAA: T Henderson (FC for SAA)
Close of play: Day 1: SAA (1) 71-1 (Rudolph 42*, Amla 15*, 17 overs). Day 2: SLA (2) 169-6 (Gunawardene 72*, Dilhara 0*, 35 overs)..

Result: Match drawn

Notes: The match was originally scheduled for 4 days at Kandy beginning on 13 September but was switched and reduced to a 3-day game because of rain. Gunawardene retired hurt with his score on 24 and the total on 34-1 in Sri Lanka A's 2nd innings and returned at the fall of the 4th wicket.

The South Africans had a frustrating time in Kandy, where the second four-day match was due to be played. Rain prevented the team from practising and made the Asgiriya Stadium ground unplayable. Eventually it was decided to move the fixture to Dambulla and it was played over three days. In order to get in some practice, the team undertook a bus trip of more than two hours to Dambulla the day before the game – no accommodation was available until after the first day's play – and the team bus was involved in a head-on collision on the way back. None of the players were injured.

A damp pitch delayed the start and South Africa A's seam bowlers did well to restrict the home side. Despite another fine display by Weerakoon, who took his tally of wickets to 19 in three innings, South Africa A played themselves into a good position with half the Sri Lankan batsmen out in the second innings with the team only 67 runs ahead. Gunawardene and Dilhara effected a recovery. Set 219 to win, South Africa A were in deep trouble before Amla and Botha played them to safety.

SRI LANKA A	*Runs*	*Mins*	*Balls*	*4*	*6*
*DA Gunawardene c Amla b Zondeki	12	21	15	3	-
WU Tharanga b De Bruyn	72	198	109	11	-
GI Daniel b Henderson	13	44	31	3	-
J Mubarak c Tsolekile b Zondeki	18	23	18	4	-
CG Wijesinghe c Tsolekile b Zondeki	1	21	10	-	-
†HAPW Jayawardene c Amla b Kruger	9	20	17	1	-
KS Lokuarachchi c Tsolekile b De Bruyn	14	27	19	3	-
LHD Dilhara c Zondeki b Henderson	39	52	34	7	-
S Weerakoon c Tsolekile b De Bruyn	0	8	7	-	-
RACG Jayaweera not out	17	28	15	3	-
PDRL Perera lbw b Henderson	1	21	16	-	-
Extras (lb 8, nb 2)	10				
TOTAL (48 overs)	**206**				

	Runs	*Mins*	*Balls*	*4*	*6*
c Rudolph b Ontong	111	232	154	16	-
c Amla b Zondeki	9	21	11	1	-
c Amla b Zondeki	1	12	6	-	-
b Kruger	16	60	33	2	-
lbw b Kruger	10	33	19	2	-
b Botha	29	61	33	4	-
b Botha	21	46	31	2	-
c Amla b Botha	51	84	53	6	1
c Puttick b Ontong	0	4	4	-	-
run out	0	2	2	-	-
not out	6	23	15	1	-
Extras (b 8, lb 3, w 1)	12				
TOTAL (60 overs)	**266**				

SOUTH AFRICA A	*Runs*	*Mins*	*Balls*	*4*	*6*
AG Puttick b Dilhara	11	50	26	2	-
*JA Rudolph c Jayawardene b Weerakoon	83	220	152	11	-
HM Amla st Jayawardene b Weerakoon	21	44	27	4	-
Z de Bruyn lbw b Weerakoon	5	19	10	1	-
JL Ontong lbw b Dilhara	12	60	45	1	-
†TL Tsolekile b Perera	4	40	30	1	-
J Botha b Weerakoon	28	89	56	5	-
T Henderson b Lokuarachchi	50	57	30	3	4
PR Adams b Weerakoon	21	36	23	3	-
M Zondeki c Lokuarachchi b Weerakoon	4	10	4	1	-
GJ-P Kruger not out	1	2	1	-	-
Extras (b 2, lb 6, w 1, nb 5)	14				
TOTAL (66.3 overs)	**254**				

	Runs	*Mins*	*Balls*	*4*	*6*
(2) lbw b Dilhara	2	18	6	-	-
(1) c Jayawardene b Perera	3	25	21	-	-
not out	64	224	146	5	-
c Tharanga b Jayaweera	17	43	38	3	-
b Jayaweera	0	7	5	-	-
c Jayawardene b Jayaweera	7	12	9	1	-
not out	30	152	133	3	-
Extras (lb 1, w 3)	4				
TOTAL (for 5 wkts) (58 overs)	**127**				

SAA	O	M	R	W		O	M	R	W	
Zondeki	12	1	52	3		12	0	54	2	(1 w)
Kruger	8	1	43	1		(3) 6	0	33	2	
Henderson	15	4	42	3	(1 nb)	(2) 10	2	38	0	
De Bruyn	11	0	51	3	(1 nb)	10	0	46	0	
Botha	2	0	10	0		12	1	42	3	
Adams						4	0	26	0	
Ontong						6	1	16	2	
SLA	*O*	*M*	*R*	*W*		*O*	*M*	*R*	*W*	
Perera	12	0	61	1		(2) 10	2	27	1	(1 w)
Jayaweera	11	1	37	0		(4) 5	0	19	3	
Dilhara	13	2	44	2	(4 nb, 1 w)	(1) 6	2	19	1	(1 w)
Weerakoon	22.3	6	66	6	(1 nb)	(3) 20	7	31	0	
Lokuarachchi	8	1	38	1		17	3	30	0	(1 w)

Fall of Wickets	SLA	SAA	SLA	SAA
1st	20 (1)	46 (1)	33 (2)	5 (2)
2nd	54 (3)	90 (3)	35 (3)	6 (1)
3rd	75 (4)	104 (4)	57 (5)	45 (4)
4th	87 (5)	129 (5)	66 (4)	45 (5)
5th	99 (6)	148 (6)	115 (6)	53 (6)
6th	126 (7)	148 (2)	169 (7)	-
7th	171 (2)	220 (8)	248 (8)	-
8th	177 (9)	242 (7)	249 (9)	-
9th	190 (8)	253 (9)	249 (10)	-
10th	206 (11)	254 (10)	266 (1)	-

SRI LANKA U-23 v SOUTH AFRICA A — Limited Overs Match 50 overs per side

Played at Police Park, Colombo on 19 September 2005 — Toss: South Africa A

Umpires: PG Liyanage & MSK Nandiweera

Debuts: SLU23: None. SAA: J Botha, Z de Bruyn, T Henderson, AG Puttick and DW Steyn (All LO for SAA)

Result: South Africa A won by 174 runs

Notes: Bosman scored his fifty off 35 balls in South Africa A's innings. Puttick scored his century off 85 balls in South Africa A's innings. South Africa A substitute: T Henderson replaced LL Bosman after 0 overs of Sri Lanka Under-23's innings. Sri Lanka Under-23 substitute: AD Mathews replaced DT Kottehewa after 0 overs of Sri Lanka Under-23's innings.

SOUTH AFRICA A	Runs	Mins	Balls	4	6
AG Puttick c Varuna b Perera	143	170	121	15	1
LL Bosman c Gunawardene b Kottehewa	96	100	72	11	4
JL Ontong b Kottehewa	71	92	63	3	3
*JA Rudolph not out	38	47	34	4	-
Z de Bruyn not out	24	24	17	3	-
RJ Peterson					
†TL Tsolekile					
JJ van der Wath					
J Botha					
GJ-P Kruger					
DW Steyn					
T Henderson					
Extras (lb 3, w 6, nb 7)	16				
TOTAL (for 3 wkts) (50 overs)	**388**				

SRI LANKA UNDER-23	Runs	Mins	Balls	4	6
D Udagamsuriya c Tsolekile b Henderson	10	41	39	1	-
MA Sandaruwan c Henderson b Botha	15	94	57	-	-
NMNP Nawela run out	39	102	64	3	-
KD Gunawardene lbw b Botha	7	22	18	-	-
CK Kapugedera b Henderson	77	85	64	10	2
*†JK Silva st Tsolekile b Rudolph	16	28	19	1	-
MDK Perera c Tsolekile b De Bruyn	0	3	2	-	-
AD Mathews not out	16	42	27	1	-
KGN Randika not out	4	16	14	-	-
HWU Varuna					
CW Vidanapathirana					
DT Kottehewa					
Extras (b 2, lb 9, w 15, nb 4)	30				
TOTAL (for 7 wkts) (50 overs)	**214**				

SLU23	O	M	R	W	
Vidanapathirana	9	0	72	0	(2 w)
Varuna	8	0	72	0	(2 nb, 1 w)
Perera	10	0	63	1	(3 w)
Kottehewa	10	0	88	2	(3 nb)
Randika	7	0	54	0	(2 nb)
Sandaruwan	6	0	36	0	

SAA	O	M	R	W	
Steyn	7	1	31	0	(3 nb, 3 w)
Henderson	7	1	13	2	(1 nb, 1 w)
Van der Wath	8	1	32	0	(1 w)
Kruger	5	0	13	0	(1 w)
Botha	6	1	11	2	
Peterson	8	0	48	0	(3 w)
Ontong	1	0	5	0	
Rudolph	4	0	19	1	
De Bruyn	4	0	31	1	

Fall of Wickets	SAA	SLU23
1st	177 (2)	22 (1)
2nd	289 (1)	54 (2)
3rd	333 (3)	80 (4)
4th	-	103 (3)
5th	-	152 (6)
6th	-	153 (7)
7th	-	201 (5)

SRI LANKA A v SOUTH AFRICA A — Sri Lanka Triangular Tournament

Played at R Premadasa Stadium, Colombo on 21 September 2005 — Toss: South Africa A

Umpires: AG Dissanayake & PT Manuel — Referee: UC Hathurusingha

Debuts: SLA: None. SAA: None

Result: South Africa A won by 10 wickets

Points: SAA: 6; SLA: 0

Notes: South Africa A substitute: JA Morkel replaced RJ Peterson after 17 overs of Sri Lanka A's innings. Sri Lanka A substitute: MG Vandort replaced S Weerakoon after 6.4 overs of Sri Lanka A's innings.

Dale Steyn produced a sensational display of fast bowling as Sri Lanka A were bowled out for 45 before Puttick and Bosman needed only 4.5 overs to take the tourists to a 10-wicket win.

SRI LANKA A	Runs	Mins	Balls	4	6
*DA Gunawardene lbw b Steyn	0	1	1	-	-
WU Tharanga c Tsolekile b Steyn	6	36	15	-	-
S Kalavitigoda c Botha b Henderson	1	6	6	-	-
J Mubarak b Steyn	1	6	5	-	-
BMAJ Mendis c Tsolekile b Henderson	11	54	35	1	-
MG Vandort b Steyn	0	8	4	-	-
†HAPW Jayawardene c De Bruyn b Steyn	2	8	9	-	-
MF Maharoof c De Bruyn b Van der Wath	2	51	28	-	-
LHD Dilhara c Bosman b Morkel	8	27	16	2	-
KS Lokuarachchi c Tsolekile b Morkel	2	16	11	-	-
DNT Zoysa not out	0	7	3	-	-
S Weerakoon					
Extras (lb 1, w 9, nb 2)	12				
TOTAL (21.5 overs)	**45**				

SOUTH AFRICA A	Runs	Mins	Balls	4	6
AG Puttick not out	19	27	21	4	-
LL Bosman not out	22	27	12	3	1
*JA Rudolph					
Z de Bruyn					
JL Ontong					
JA Morkel					
JJ van der Wath					
T Henderson					
†TL Tsolekile					
J Botha					
DW Steyn					
RJ Peterson					
Extras (w 2, nb 4)	6				
TOTAL (for 0 wkts) (4.5 overs)	**47**				

SAA	O	M	R	W	
Steyn	7	1	20	5	(1 nb, 2 w)
Henderson	8	4	14	2	(4 w)
Van der Wath	4	3	1	1	(1 w)
Morkel	2.5	1	9	2	(1 nb, 2 w)

SLA	O	M	R	W	
Zoysa	2.5	0	31	0	(4 nb, 1 w)
Maharoof	2	0	16	0	(1 w)

Fall of Wickets	SLA	SAA
1st	0 (1)	-
2nd	1 (3)	-
3rd	4 (4)	-
4th	20 (2)	-
5th	20 (6)	-
6th	24 (7)	-
7th	28 (5)	-
8th	40 (9)	-
9th	41 (8)	-
10th	45 (10)	-

At R Premadasa Stadium, Colombo, 22 September 2005. Sri Lanka A 251-6 in 50 overs (WU Tharanga 31, J Mubarak 59, MF Maharoof 32*, LHD Dilhara 57*, DR Tuffey 2-59, JS Patel 2-41). **New Zealand A** 239-9 in 50 overs (JM How 36, MS Sinclair 51, PG Fulton 56, J Mubarak 5-59). **Sri Lanka A won by 12 runs**. Points: Sri Lanka A 5, New Zealand A 1.

NEW ZEALAND A v SOUTH AFRICA A — Sri Lanka Triangular Tournament

Played at Sinhalese Sports Club, Colombo on 24 September 2005 — Toss: South Africa A

Umpires: PG Liyanage & R Martinesz — Referee: UC Hathurusingha

Debuts: NZA: None. SAA: None

Result: South Africa A won by 6 wickets

Points: NZA: 0; SAA: 6

Notes: New Zealand A substitute: JM How replaced IE O'Brien after 41.4 overs of New Zealand A's innings. South Africa A substitute: JL Ontong replaced DW Steyn after 0 overs of South Africa A's innings.

The South African bowlers again set up a comfortable win, with both pace bowlers and spinners proving effective. Puttick played well as South Africa A again took full points.

NEW ZEALAND A	Runs	Mins	Balls	4	6
MHW Papps c Tsolekile b Henderson	7	33	19	1	-
JD Ryder c Tsolekile b Steyn	5	20	12	-	-
MS Sinclair c Tsolekile b Morkel	29	81	53	3	-
*PG Fulton c De Bruyn b Van der Wath	5	24	21	-	-
JAH Marshall st Tsolekile b Peterson	32	89	56	2	-
CZ Harris c Puttick b Botha	9	32	26	-	-
†GJ Hopkins c Van der Wath b Botha	26	47	30	2	-
JM How not out	31	61	55	1	-
DR Tuffey b Peterson	10	15	16	1	-
JS Patel run out	1	4	1	-	-
CS Martin c and b Van der Wath	1	5	2	-	-
IE O'Brien					
Extras (b 1, lb 2, w 10)	13				
TOTAL (48.3 overs)	**169**				

SOUTH AFRICA A	Runs	Mins	Balls	4	6
AG Puttick not out	87	152	98	17	-
LL Bosman c Ryder b Martin	12	17	12	3	-
T Henderson c Harris b Tuffey	0	2	1	-	-
JL Ontong c How b Tuffey	4	12	7	-	-
*JA Rudolph lbw b Harris	13	27	28	2	-
Z de Bruyn not out	45	90	69	6	-
JA Morkel					
RJ Peterson					
†TL Tsolekile					
JJ van der Wath					
J Botha					
DW Steyn					
Extras (lb 5, w 4, nb 3)	12				
TOTAL (for 4 wkts) (35.2 overs)	**173**				

SAA	O	M	R	W
Steyn	8	0	22	1 (3 w)
Henderson	6	1	15	1 (3 w)
Van der Wath	6.3	1	17	2
Morkel	8	0	35	1 (1 w)
Peterson	10	0	43	2 (2 w)
Botha	10	0	34	2 (1 w)

NZA	O	M	R	W
Tuffey	6	1	28	2 (1 nb)
Martin	8	1	47	1 (1 w)
Patel	10	0	50	0 (2 nb, 1 w)
Harris	9	3	17	1
Ryder	1	0	17	0 (1 w)
How	1.2	0	9	0

Fall of Wickets	NZA	SAA
1st	15 (2)	17 (2)
2nd	19 (1)	18 (3)
3rd	26 (4)	39 (4)
4th	66 (3)	71 (5)
5th	88 (6)	-
6th	108 (5)	-
7th	145 (7)	-
8th	163 (9)	-
9th	166 (10)	-
10th	169 (11)	-

At Moratuwa, 25 September 2005. New Zealand A 238-6 in 50 overs (JM How 56, JAH Marshall 68, CZ Harris 35*). **Sri Lanka A** 166 in 35 overs (DA Gunawardene 34, KS Lokuarachchi 33*, CS Martin 6-24, CZ Harris 2-46). **New Zealand A won by 72 runs**. Points: New Zealand A 6, Sri Lanka A 0.

SRI LANKA A v SOUTH AFRICA A Sri Lanka Triangular Tournament

Played at Colts Ground, Havelock Park, Colombo on 27 September 2005 Toss: Sri Lanka A
Umpires: WA Senanayake & MG Silva Referee: MAWR Madurasinghe
Debuts: SLA: None. SAA: None
Result: South Africa A won by 4 wickets
Points: SAA: 5; SLA: 1
Notes: Sri Lanka A substitute: MMM Suraj replaced SHT Kandamby after 12.5 overs of South Africa A's innings. South Africa A substitute: JL Ontong replaced DW Steyn after 22 overs of South Africa A's innings.

South Africa A ensured they would be playing in the final and eliminated the host nation with another convincing win. The Sri Lankans relied on their lower order to enable them to make a competitive total but it was not enough as Van der Wath, Rudolph and Ontong all batted well on a spin-friendly pitch.

SRI LANKA A	Runs	Mins	Balls	4	6
GI Daniel c Tsolekile b Van der Wath	15	27	20	3	-
*DA Gunawardene c Bosman b Van der Wath	34	68	43	5	1
WU Tharanga c Morkel b Botha	12	67	33	1	-
J Mubarak c Rudolph b Steyn	5	10	11	1	-
SHT Kandamby c Tsolekile b Zondeki	13	40	29	1	-
†HAPW Jayawardene c Tsolekile b Morkel	1	4	2	-	-
KS Lokuarachchi c Zondeki b Peterson	24	35	27	3	-
MF Maharoof not out	58	93	72	5	-
WMG Ramyakumara c Steyn b Peterson	26	40	44	1	1
LHD Dilhara b Steyn	22	19	15	1	2
S Weerakoon not out	4	16	5	-	-
MMM Suraj					
Extras (b 4, lb 5, w 10, nb 1)	20				
TOTAL (for 9 wkts) (50 overs)	**234**				

SOUTH AFRICA A	Runs	Mins	Balls	4	6
AG Puttick c Jayawardene b Maharoof	17	43	27	1	-
LL Bosman c Tharanga b Dilhara	1	7	5	-	-
JJ van der Wath c Maharoof b Weerakoon	51	51	40	4	5
*JA Rudolph not out	66	146	114	3	1
JL Ontong b Weerakoon	60	81	61	3	2
Z de Bruyn b Weerakoon	5	13	11		-
JA Morkel run out	9	5	3	2	-
J Botha not out	16	28	24	1	-
RJ Peterson					
†TL Tsolekile					
M Zondeki					
DW Steyn					
Extras (lb 2, w 7, nb 1)	10				
TOTAL (for 6 wkts) (47.2 overs)	**235**				

SAA	O	M	R	W
Steyn	10	1	55	2 (1 nb)
Zondeki	10	1	39	1 (2 w)
Van der Wath	9	0	49	2 (4 w)
Morkel	5	0	15	1 (1 w)
Botha	10	0	41	1 (2 w)
Peterson	6	0	26	2

SLA	O	M	R	W
Ramyakumara	6	0	34	0 (3 w)
Dilhara	2	0	17	1 (3 w)
Maharoof	6	0	34	1 (1 w)
Weerakoon	10	0	55	3
Lokuarachchi	10	0	38	0
Suraj	4	0	29	0
Mubarak	9.2	2	26	0 (1 nb)

Fall of Wickets	SLA	SAA
1st	31 (1)	5 (2)
2nd	64 (2)	57 (1)
3rd	69 (4)	77 (3)
4th	82 (3)	185 (5)
5th	85 (6)	195 (6)
6th	104 (5)	205 (7)
7th	119 (7)	-
8th	169 (9)	-
9th	201 (10)	-

NEW ZEALAND A v SOUTH AFRICA A Sri Lanka Triangular Tournament

Played at R Premadasa Stadium, Colombo on 28 September 2005 Toss: New Zealand A
Umpires: JWK Boteju & R Martinesz Referee: MAWR Madurasinghe
Debuts: NZA: None. SAA: None
Result: South Africa A won by 1 wicket
Points: NZA: 1; SAA: 5
Notes: New Zealand A substitute: BP Martin replaced JAH Marshall after 36 overs of South Africa A's innings. South Africa A substitute: JL Ontong replaced M Zondeki after 12.1 overs of South Africa A's innings.

Despite playing below their best, South Africa A were able to stay unbeaten in the one-day games, winning by one wicket with one ball to spare. South Africa A seemed headed for defeat before Botha and Henderson put on 85 for the eighth wicket. Both men were out in quick succession but Tsolekile and Kruger put on an unbeaten 29 for the last wicket.

NEW ZEALAND A	Runs	Mins	Balls	4	6
MHW Papps c Tsolekile b Kruger	14	38	21	2	-
JM How c Tsolekile b Zondeki	9	28	21	-	-
MS Sinclair c Peterson b Rudolph	64	105	87	7	-
*PG Fulton lbw b Peterson	43	69	54	7	-
JAH Marshall not out	56	85	70	-	1
CZ Harris run out	13	23	18	-	-
†GJ Hopkins c Peterson b Rudolph	0	1	1	-	-
JEC Franklin lbw b Rudolph	7	15	14	1	-
JS Patel c Tsolekile b Rudolph	12	15	11	-	-
CS Martin not out	4	3	2	1	-
IE O'Brien					
BP Martin					
Extras (lb 4, w 11, nb 2)	17				
TOTAL (for 8 wkts) (50 overs)	**239**				

SOUTH AFRICA A	Runs	Mins	Balls	4	6
AG Puttick c Hopkins b Franklin	11	40	30	1	-
LL Bosman c Hopkins b Harris	41	103	63	5	1
JA Morkel c How b CS Martin	13	18	16	2	-
*JA Rudolph b O'Brien	0	4	1	-	-
JL Ontong c Hopkins b Harris	26	61	44	2	-
Z de Bruyn c and b Harris	12	36	32	-	-
J Botha b CS Martin	32	82	41	2	-
RJ Peterson lbw b Franklin	1	14	15	-	-
T Henderson c Sinclair b Patel	54	58	43	6	1
†TL Tsolekile not out	13	21	12	1	-
GJ-P Kruger not out	18	15	10	1	1
M Zondeki					
Extras (b 1, lb 2, w 6, nb 10)	19				
TOTAL (for 9 wkts) (49.5 overs)	**240**				

SAA	O	M	R	W
Zondeki	4	0	24	1 (2 nb, 2 w)
Henderson	6	1	19	0 (1 w)
Kruger	7	0	24	1 (1 w)
Morkel	6	0	45	0 (2 w)
Botha	9	0	37	0 (1 w)
Peterson	10	0	46	1 (3 w)
Rudolph	8	0	40	4 (1 w)

NZA	O	M	R	W
CS Martin	10	0	54	2 (2 nb, 1 w)
Franklin	8	0	40	2 (6 nb, 2 w)
O'Brien	8.5	0	50	1
Harris	10	1	26	3 (2 w)
Patel	10	0	42	1 (1 nb)
BP Martin	3	0	25	0 (1 nb, 1 w)

Fall of Wickets	NZA	SAA
1st	23 (2)	36 (1)
2nd	35 (1)	55 (3)
3rd	127 (4)	55 (4)
4th	160 (3)	91 (2)
5th	195 (6)	113 (5)
6th	195 (7)	119 (6)
7th	211 (8)	122 (8)
8th	232 (9)	207 (7)
9th	-	211 (9)

NEW ZEALAND A v SOUTH AFRICA A — Sri Lanka Triangular Tournament Final

Played at Sinhalese Sports Club, Colombo on 1 October 2005 — Toss: South Africa A
Umpires: R Martinesz & MG Silva — Referee: UC Hathurusingha
Debuts: NZA: None. SAA: None
Result: South Africa A won by 6 wickets
Notes: New Zealand A substitute: BP Martin replaced MHW Papps after 23 overs of South Africa A's innings. South Africa A substitute: JL Ontong replaced DW Steyn after 22.2 overs of South Africa A's innings.

Opening batsman Papps batted through the New Zealand A innings but the Kiwis were unable to dominate a well-balanced bowling attack in which Henderson and Morkel claimed three wickets apiece.

Bosman and captain Rudolph set up South Africa's win with a third wicket stand of 78 and there was another good partnership between Rudolph and Ontong as South Africa A won with 7.2 overs to spare.

NEW ZEALAND A	Runs	Mins	Balls	4	6
MHW Papps not out	106	206	135	8	1
JM How c Tsolekile b Henderson	11	31	23	1	-
MS Sinclair c Tsolekile b Henderson	16	37	25	2	-
*PG Fulton c Tsolekile b Henderson	2	3	3	-	-
JAH Marshall lbw b Morkel	12	28	20	2	-
CZ Harris lbw b Botha	33	73	73	-	-
†GJ Hopkins c Bosman b Morkel	25	24	17	2	1
JEC Franklin c Bosman b Morkel	2	2	2	-	-
JS Patel not out	0	3	0	-	-
IE O'Brien					
CS Martin					
BP Martin					
Extras (lb 4, w 5)	9				
TOTAL (for 7 wkts) (50 overs)	**216**				

SOUTH AFRICA A	Runs	Mins	Balls	4	6
AG Puttick c Hopkins b Franklin	1	18	10	-	-
LL Bosman c How b BP Martin	48	106	66	8	-
JJ van der Wath b CS Martin	13	26	17	2	-
*JA Rudolph c Hopkins b Franklin	68	108	79	10	-
JL Ontong not out	54	78	70	4	1
Z de Bruyn not out	17	29	17	2	-
JA Morkel					
RJ Peterson					
†TL Tsolekile					
J Botha					
T Henderson					
DW Steyn					
Extras (w 13, nb 3)	16				
TOTAL (for 4 wkts) (42.4 overs)	**217**				

SAA	O	M	R	W
Steyn	8	1	46	0 (2 w)
Henderson	10	2	29	3 (2 w)
Van der Wath	4	0	23	0
Morkel	9	0	34	3 (1 w)
Peterson	10	1	26	0
Botha	6	0	31	1
Rudolph	3	0	23	0

NZA	O	M	R	W
CS Martin	6	0	39	1 (6 w)
Franklin	10	2	35	2 (2 nb)
Harris	9.4	1	55	0 (2 w)
O'Brien	4	0	24	0
Patel	7	0	36	0 (1 nb)
BP Martin	6	0	28	1

Fall of Wickets	NZA	SAA
1st	30 (2)	12 (1)
2nd	69 (3)	37 (3)
3rd	71 (4)	115 (2)
4th	90 (5)	168 (4)
5th	157 (6)	-
6th	205 (7)	-
7th	208 (8)	-

SOUTH AFRICA A IN SRI LANKA 2005/06: A-TEST AVERAGES

SRI LANKA A

Batting & Fielding

Name	M	Inns	NO	Runs	HS	Avg	100	50	Ct	St
DA Gunawardene	2	4	0	206	111	51.50	1	1	0	0
KS Lokuarachchi	2	3	1	88	53 *	44.00	0	1	2	0
J Mubarak	2	4	1	117	46	39.00	0	0	1	0
LHD Dilhara	2	3	0	93	51	31.00	0	1	0	0
WU Tharanga	2	4	0	99	72	24.75	0	1	2	0
GI Daniel	2	4	0	97	48	24.25	0	0	1	0
HAPW Jayawardene	2	4	1	54	29	18.00	0	0	6	2
CG Wijesinghe	2	4	0	48	29	12.00	0	0	2	0
RACG Jayaweera	2	3	1	22	17 *	11.00	0	0	0	0
PDRL Perera	2	3	1	15	8	7.50	0	0	0	0
S Weerakoon	2	3	0	0	0	0.00	0	0	1	0
Totals	22	39	5	839	111		1	4	15	2
			Extras	57				subs	0	
			Total	896		26.35			15	

Bowling

Name	Overs	Mdns	Runs	Wkts	Avg	BB	5I	10M
S Weerakoon	87.3	23	203	19	10.68	7-47	3	1
LHD Dilhara	33	7	108	4	27.00	2-44	0	0
RACG Jayaweera	42	7	143	5	28.60	3-19	0	0
KS Lokuarachchi	55	11	156	4	39.00	2-56	0	0
PDRL Perera	45	6	170	3	56.66	1-27	0	0
GI Daniel	2	0	6	0	-	-	0	0
Totals	264.3	54	786	35		7-47	3	1
		b/lb/pen	13	0	run outs			
		Total	799	35	22.82			

SOUTH AFRICA A

Batting & Fielding

Name	M	Inns	NO	Runs	HS	Avg	100	50	Ct	St
T Henderson	1	1	0	50	50	50.00	0	1	0	0
HM Amla	2	4	1	135	64 *	45.00	0	1	6	0
Z de Bruyn	2	4	1	122	100 *	40.66	1	0	0	0
J Botha	2	4	1	113	41	37.66	0	0	1	0
JA Rudolph	2	4	0	149	83	37.25	0	1	1	0
PR Adams	2	3	1	43	21 *	21.50	0	0	1	0
AG Puttick	2	4	0	55	41	13.75	0	0	3	0
JL Ontong	2	4	0	52	40	13.00	0	0	0	0
TL Tsolekile	2	4	0	42	31	10.50	0	0	7	0
JJ van der Wath	1	2	0	4	4	2.00	0	0	1	0
M Zondeki	2	3	0	5	4	1.66	0	0	1	0
DW Steyn	1	2	0	0	0	0.00	0	0	0	0

SOUTH AFRICA A IN SRI LANKA 2005

GJ-P Kruger	1	1	1	1	1 *	-	0	0	0	0
Totals	22	40	5	771	100 *		1	3	21	0
			Extras	28				subs	0	
			Total	799		22.82			21	

Bowling

Name	Overs	Mdns	Runs	Wkts	Avg	BB	5I	10M
JL Ontong	13	2	46	3	15.33	2-16	0	0
M Zondeki	43	5	187	9	20.77	3-52	0	0
J Botha	33.2	2	140	6	23.33	3-42	0	0
GJ-P Kruger	14	1	76	3	25.33	2-33	0	0
PR Adams	17.4	1	79	3	26.33	3-37	0	0
T Henderson	25	6	80	3	26.66	3-42	0	0
Z de Bruyn	24	0	105	3	35.00	3-51	0	0
DW Steyn	18	2	76	2	38.00	1-37	0	0
JJ van der Wath	16	3	64	1	64.00	1-39	0	0
Totals	204	22	853	33		3-37	0	0
		b/lb/pen	43	1	run outs			
		Total	896	34	26.35			

SOUTH AFRICA A: SRI LANKA TRIANGULAR SERIES AVERAGES

Batting & Fielding

Name	M	Inns	NO	Runs	HS	Avg	SR	100	50	Ct	St
JA Rudolph	5	4	1	147	68	49.00	66.21	0	2	1	0
JL Ontong	5	4	1	144	60	48.00	79.12	0	2	0	0
J Botha	5	2	1	48	32	48.00	73.84	0	0	1	0
AG Puttick	5	5	2	135	87 *	45.00	72.58	0	1	1	0
Z de Bruyn	5	4	2	79	45 *	39.50	61.24	0	0	3	0
JJ van der Wath	4	2	0	64	51	32.00	112.28	0	1	2	0
LL Bosman	5	5	1	124	48	31.00	78.48	0	0	4	0
T Henderson	4	2	0	54	54	27.00	122.72	0	1	0	0
JA Morkel	5	2	0	22	13	11.00	115.78	0	0	1	0
RJ Peterson	5	1	0	1	1	1.00	6.66	0	0	2	0
GJ-P Kruger	1	1	1	18	18 *	-	180.00	0	0	0	0
TL Tsolekile	5	1	1	13	13 *	-	108.33	0	0	15	1
DW Steyn	4	0	0	0	-	-	-	0	0	1	0
M Zondeki	2	0	0	0	-	-	-	0	0	1	0
Totals	60	33	10	849	87 *			0	7	32	1
			Extras	63					subs	0	
			Total	912		39.65	77.25			32	

Bowling

Name	Overs	Mdns	Runs	Wkts	Avg	RpO	BB	4I
T Henderson	30	8	77	6	12.83	2.56	3-29	0
JA Rudolph	11	0	63	4	15.75	5.72	4-40	1
DW Steyn	33	3	143	8	17.87	4.33	5-20	1
JJ van der Wath	23.3	4	90	5	18.00	3.82	2-17	0
JA Morkel	30.5	1	138	7	19.71	4.47	3-34	0
GJ-P Kruger	7	0	24	1	24.00	3.42	1-24	0
RJ Peterson	36	1	141	5	28.20	3.91	2-26	0
M Zondeki	14	1	63	2	31.50	4.50	1-24	0
J Botha	35	0	143	4	35.75	4.08	2-34	0
Totals	220.2	18	882	42			5-20	2
		b/lb/pen	21	2	run outs			
		Total	903	44	20.52	409		

EMERGING PLAYERS IN AUSTRALIA

Robin Peterson took a South African Emerging Players team to victory in the final of a four-team tournament in Brisbane, Australia, in July 2006, hitting an unbeaten 148 off 124 balls, with 11 fours and eight sixes against Australia's Centre of Excellence team. The South Africans won by one wicket off the last ball of the match.

Alviro Petersen made two centuries earlier in the tournament, 137 not out off 64 balls in a 20-over match against New Zealand Emerging Players and 110 not out off 117 balls against a Karnataka XI from India.

The South African touring party was: Neil McKenzie (Lions, captain), Loots Bosman (Eagles), Alviro Petersen (Lions), J-P Duminy (Cape Cobras), Albie Morkel (Titans), Justin Ontong (Lions), Robin Peterson (Warriors), Thami Tsolekile (Cobras), Garnett Kruger (Lions), Monde Zondeki (Cobras), Thandi Tshabalala (Eagles), Davey Jacobs (Eagles), Alfonso Thomas (Titans), Johan van der Wath (Eagles), Morne van Wyk (Eagles). Coach, Corrie van Zyl; assistant coach, Allan Donald; physiotherapist, Brandon Jackson. Charl Langeveldt was picked but withdrew because of a groin injury and was not replaced.

Twenty-over matches

Brisbane, 10 Jul 2006: SA Emerging Players168-7 in 20 overs (LL Bosman 25, MN van Wyk 34, JA Morkel 49*; BM Edmondson 2-48, B Casson 2-24, AC Voges 2-31). **Australia Centre of Excellence** 172-4 in 20 overs (SE Marsh 38, TD Paine 69*, AC Voges 41*; JJ van der Wath 2-36). **Australia Centre of Excellence won by 6 wickets.**

Brisbane, 10 Jul 2006: SA Emerging Players 214-2 in 20 overs (LL Bosman 20, AN Petersen 137*, ND McKenzie 43*). **NZ Emerging Players** 193-5 in 20 overs (JD Ryder 67, PD McGlashan 45*; RJ Peterson 2-49, JL Ontong 2-23). **SA Emerging Players won by 21 runs.**

Brisbane, 11 Jul 2006: SA Emerging Players 183-5 in 20 overs (LL Bosman 55, AN Petersen 45, JL Ontong 23*; R Vinay Kumar 2-32, C Raghu 2-33). **Karnataka XI** 152-5 in 20 overs (G Dhiman 54, SN Amit 20, C Raghu 23; AC Thomas 2-31). **SA Emerging Players won by 31 runs.**

Fifty-over matches

Brisbane, 12 Jul 2006: SA Emerging Players 200-8 in 50 overs (MN van Wyk 27, JA Morkel 33, RJ Peterson 46*; MR Gillespie 3-51). **NZ Emerging Players** 201-7 in 48 overs (JAH Marshall 104*, WC McSkimming 36; JJ van der Wath 3-46). **NZ Emerging Players won by 3 wickets.**

Brisbane, 14 Jul 2006: SA Emerging Players 213 in 47.5 overs (MN van Wyk 28, LL Bosman 54, J-P Duminy 56; BM Edmondson 2-64, DE Bollinger 2-39, AA Noffke 3-23). **Australia Centre of Excellence** 217-9 in 48.2 overs (SE Marsh 118*; JJ van der Wath 3-51, AC Thomas 3-40, M Zondeki 3-42). **Australia Centre of Excellence won by 1 wicket.**

Brisbane, 15 Jul 2006: Karnataka XI 189 in 42.3 overs (B Chipli 87, DA Chougule 40; GJ-P Kruger 4-24, RJ Peterson 4-33). **SA Emerging Players** 183-2 in 40.3 overs (AN Petersen 110*, ND McKenzie 49*). **SA Emerging Players won by 8 wickets (D/L method), target revised to 183 in 47 overs.**

Brisbane, 17 Jul 2006: SA Emerging Players 185-8 in 40 overs (ND McKenzie 63, J-P Duminy 43, TL Tsolekile 38; WC McSkimming 3-37, MR Gillespie 2-24). **NZ Emerging Players** 118 in 30.4 overs (NL McCullum 49; GJ-P Kruger 3-13, AC Thomas 2-6, T Tshabalala 2-40). **SA Emerging Players won by 67 runs.**

Brisbane, 18 Jul 2006: Australia Centre of Excellence 241 in 50 overs (CJ Ferguson 56, GJ Bailey 88, PM Siddle 26; AC Thomas 2-64, M Zondeki 3-34, JA Morkel 2-41). **SA Emerging Players** 241-8 in 50 overs (DJ Jacobs 47, MN van Wyk 57, J-P Duminy 44, JL Ontong 27, JA Morkel 29; PM Siddle 3-55, BM Edmondson 2-19). **Tied.**

EMERGING PLAYERS IN AUSTRALIA

Brisbane, 20 Jul 2006: Karnataka XI 164 in 46.5 overs (DA Chougule 86*, B Akhil 25; JJ van der Wath 2-24, GJ-P Kruger 3-30, M Zondeki 2-15, RJ Peterson 2-40). **SA Emerging Players** 103 in 30.1 overs (DJ Jacobs 25, AN Petersen 37; R Vinay Kumar 4-20, C Ragavendra 3-21). **Karnataka XI won by 61 runs.**

Final

Brisbane, 21 Jul 2006: Australia Centre of Excellence 266 in 49.4 overs (CJ Ferguson 54, AJ Finch 88, AJ Crosthwaite 44; JJ van der Wath 4-36, GJ-P Kruger 2-41). SA Emerging Players 268-9 in 50 overs (DJ Jacobs 28, JL Ontong 28, RJ Peterson 148*; BM Edmondson 2-62, DE Bollinger 3-37, PM Siddle 2-33, B Casson 2-36). **SA Emerging Players won by 1 wicket.**

SOUTH AFRICA EMERGING PLAYERS 50-OVER AVERAGES

Batting & Fielding

Name	M	Inns	NO	Runs	HS	Avg	SR	100	50	Ct	St
RJ Peterson	5	4	2	221	148 *	110.50	118.18	1	0	0	0
AN Petersen	6	6	1	170	110 *	34.00	82.12	1	0	6	0
J-P Duminy	6	5	0	162	56	32.40	63.03	0	1	4	0
MN van Wyk	5	5	0	141	57	28.20	65.27	0	1	10	0
ND McKenzie	7	7	1	152	63	25.33	52.41	0	1	2	0
DJ Jacobs	6	6	0	139	47	23.16	81.76	0	0	4	0
TL Tsolekile	3	2	0	39	38	19.50	105.40	0	0	5	1
LL Bosman	4	4	0	73	54	18.25	68.86	0	1	1	0
JL Ontong	5	5	0	80	28	16.00	50.95	0	0	3	0
JA Morkel	6	5	0	78	33	15.60	76.47	0	0	2	0
JJ van der Wath	6	6	0	54	18	9.00	63.52	0	0	2	0
M Zondeki	5	4	2	2	1 *	1.00	28.57	0	0	2	0
GJ-P Kruger	6	2	0	2	2	1.00	11.76	0	0	0	0
AC Thomas	4	3	3	10	5 *	-	55.55	0	0	1	0
T Tshabalala	3	2	2	3	2 *	-	42.85	0	0	1	0
Totals	77	66	11	1326	148 *			2	4	43	1
			Extras	67					subs	0	
			Total	1393		25.32	71.17			43	

Bowling

Name	Overs	Mdns	Runs	Wkts	Avg	RpO	BB	4I
GJ-P Kruger	54.3	7	180	13	13.84	3.30	4-24	1
M Zondeki	47.5	6	168	10	16.80	3.51	3-34	0
JJ van der Wath	51	10	205	12	17.08	4.01	4-36	1
AC Thomas	33	6	146	8	18.25	4.42	3-40	0
RJ Peterson	48	2	206	8	25.75	4.29	4-33	1
JL Ontong	4	0	27	1	27.00	6.75	1-18	0
T Tshabalala	25.4	0	141	3	47.00	5.49	2-40	0
JA Morkel	52	1	286	5	57.20	5.50	2-41	0
Totals	316	32	1359	60			4-24	3
		b/lb/pen	37	5	run outs			
		Total	1396	65	21.47	4.41		

HONG KONG SIXES 2005

Gerald Dros of the Titans led the South African team in the Hong Kong Cricket Sixes tournament in October 2005 with slightly more success than the team achieved under his leadership in the 2004 event, when they finished seventh of the eight teams. South Africa again failed to reach the Cup semi-finals but reached the Plate final before losing to Pakistan.

South Africa's hopes were effectively sunk on the first day when they lost to both India and Pakistan in pool games. They beat the eventual finalists, the West Indies, in their final pool match and then defeated Australia in a Plate semi-final.

Adam Bacher was the only member of the squad to have played at full international level. Bacher, Ahmed Amla, Tyron Henderson and Eugene Moleon played in the tournament for the first time.

The squad was: Dros (Titans, captain), Amla (Dolphins), Bacher (Lions), Goolam Bodi (Titans), William Hantam (Cobras), Henderson (Warriors), Moleon (Lions). Manager, Oupa Nkagisang (North West).

SCORES IN BRIEF

Saturday 22 October

Pool 2

Pakistan 66-5 in 5 overs (T Henderson 3-0) beat **South Africa** 55-4 (GH Bodi 27) by 11 runs.

South Africa 57-2 in 5 overs (T Henderson 25*) lost to **India** 59-0 in 3.4 overs (SB Bangar 32rtd) by 6 wickets.

Sunday 23 October

Pool 2

South Africa 86-1 in 5 overs (GH Bodi 34rtd, T Henderson 31rtd) beat **West Indies** 69-4 in 5 overs (R Kelly 24) by 17 runs.

Plate semi-final

Australia 62-4 in 5 overs (LGL Buchanan 34rtd) lost to **South Africa** 65-2 in 3.4 overs (G Dros 34rtd, N Reardon 2-4) by 4 wickets.

Plate final

Pakistan 91-2 in 5 overs (Moin Khan 32rtd, Mohammad Hafeez 24*, WC Hantam 2-21) beat South Africa 50-4 in 5 overs (Mohammad Hafeez 2-5, Riaz Afridi 2-1) by 41 runs.

Final

West Indies 72-1 in 5 overs (LMP Simmons 31rtd) lost to **India** 76-2 in 4.3 overs (RR Singh 34rtd) by 4 wickets.

SOUTH AFRICAN WOMEN INTERNATIONAL RECORDS

TESTS

RESULTS

Opponents	Played	Won	Lost	Drawn
England	6	0	2	4
India	1	0	1	0
New Zealand	3	0	1	2
Total	10	0	4	6

Highest innings totals:

For:	316	v England (Shenley)	2003
Against:	497	by England (Shenley)	2003

Lowest innings totals:

For:	89	v New Zealand (Durban)	1971/72
Against:	168	by New Zealand (Durban)	1971/72

Highest individual innings:

For:	105*	Y van Mentz v England (Cape Town)	1960/61
Against:	177	SC Taylor for England (Shenley)	2003

Most runs in a career:

256 (Avg 25.60)	JA Gove	1960-71
240 (Avg 34.28)	E Hurly	1960/61
239 (Avg 39.83)	AL Hodgkinson	2001-03

Best bowling in an innings:

For:	6-39	J McNaughton v England (Durban)	1960/61
Against:	5-24	J Lord for New Zealand (Durban)	1971/72

Best bowling in a match:

For:	7-76	L Ward v New Zealand (Johannesburg)	1971/72
Against:	8-52	J Saulbrey for New Zealand (Durban)	1971/72

Most wickets in a career:

27 (Avg 17.29)	L Ward	1960-71
12 (Avg 18.41)	G Williamson	1971/72
9 (Avg 31.55)	JA Gove	1960-71

Most dismissals in a match:

4 (ct 4)	C Gildenhuys v New Zealand (Johannesburg)	1971/72

Most dismissals in a career:

9 (ct 9)	C Gildenhuys	1971/72

Most catches (fielders) in a match:

3	JA Gove v England (Port Elizabeth)	1960/61
3	JA Gove v England (Durban)	1960/61
3	B Botha v New Zealand (Cape Town)	1971/72
3	AL Hodgkinson v England (Taunton)	2003

Most catches (fielders) in a career:

10	JA Gove	1960-71

Most appearances:

7	JA Gove	1960-71
7	L Ward	1960-71

Most captaincies:

4	SN Nefdt	1960/61

RECORD WICKET PARTNERSHIPS

1st	59	C Gildenhuys and D Moe v New Zealand (Cape Town)	1971/72
2nd	117	B Williams and D Moe v New Zealand (Johannesburg)	1971/72
3rd	50	CS Cowan and AL Hodgkinson v England (Shenley)	2003
4th	94*	JA Gove and B Botha v New Zealand (Johannesburg)	1971/72
5th	138	J Logtenberg and C van der Westhuizen v England (Shenley)	2003
6th	77	AL Hodgkinson and Y van der Merwe v England (Shenley)	2003
7th	74	Y van Mentz and A Jackson v England (Cape Town)	1960/61
8th	67	SN Nefdt and JA Gove v England (Port Elizabeth)	1960/61
9th	107	B Botha and M Payne v New Zealand (Cape Town)	1971/72
10th	24	AE Smith and LZ Jacobs v England (Shenley)	2003

LIMITED OVERS INTERNATIONALS

RESULTS

Opponents	Played	Won	Lost	NR
Australia	6	0	6	0
Denmark	1	1	0	0
England	22	6	15	1
India	7	2	4	1
Ireland	6	5	0	1
Netherlands	1	1	0	0
New Zealand	4	0	4	0
Pakistan	1	1	0	0
Sri Lanka	2	1	1	0
West Indies	4	2	2	0
Total	54	19	32	3

Highest innings totals:

For:	258-7 (50)	v Pakistan (Vadodara)	1997/98
Against:	300-4 (50)	by England (Potchefstroom)	2004/05

Highest innings total batting second and winning:

For:	254-8 (50)	v England (Taunton)	1997

(This is a world record in Women's Limited Overs Internationals)

Lowest innings totals:

For:	80 (43.1)	v India (Patna)	1997/98
	80 (34.3)	v India (Pretoria)	2004/05
Against:	82 (34.4)	by Ireland (Belfast)	1997

SOUTH AFRICAN WOMEN INTERNATIONAL RECORDS

Highest individual innings:

For:	101*	L Olivier v Ireland (Christchurch)	2000/01
Against:	108*	EC Drumm for New Zealand (Lincoln)	2000/01

Most runs in a career:

1045 (Avg 24.30)	M Terblanche	1997-2005
838 (Avg 34.91)	L Olivier	1997-2000
464 (Avg 25.77)	J Logtenberg	2003-2005

Best bowling in an innings:

For:	4-4	CE Eksteen v Ireland (Belfast)	1997
Against:	5-7	RJ Pullar for New Zealand (Hamilton)	1998/99

Most wickets in a career:

28 (Avg 30.82)	CE Eksteen	1997-2003
26 (Avg 25.46)	AE Smith	2003-2005
22 (Avg 25.40)	C-Z Brits	2002-2005

Most dismissals in a match:

5 (ct 5)	S Pillay v England (Port Elizabeth)	2003/04

Most dismissals in a career:

34 (ct 23, st 11)	M Terblanche	1997-2005

Most catches (fielders) in a match:

3	KA Laing v India (Potchefstroom)	2001/02

Most catches (fielders) in a career:

9	KA Laing	1997-2001
9	AL Hodgkinson	2000-2005

Most appearances:

50	M Terblanche	1997-2005
36	CE Eksteen	1997-2003
32	AL Hodgkinson	2000-2005

Most captaincies:

26	K Price	1997-2000

RECORD WICKET PARTNERSHIPS

1st	133*	L Olivier and AA Burger v Ireland (Dublin)	1997
2nd	136	J Logtenberg and M Terblanche v England (Bristol)	2003
3rd	115	KA Laing and A Hodgkinson v India (Lenasia)	2001/02
4th	74	AA Burger and CE Eksteen v Australia (Lincoln)	2000/01
5th	73	KA Laing and M Terblanche v Ireland (Belfast)	1997
6th	90	SA Fritz and CS Terblanche v Ireland (Centurion)	2004/05
7th	94	CE Eksteen and A Kuylaars v England (Taunton)	2000
8th	55*	A Taai and C van der Westhuizen v England (Klerksdorp)	2004/05
9th	66*	K Price and Y van der Merwe v India (Christchurch)	2000/01
10th	29	A Kuylaars and LP Lewis v New Zealand (Christchurch)	1998/99

SOUTH AFRICAN WOMEN: TEST CAREER RECORDS

As at 1 September 2006

Name	M	Inns	NO	Runs	HS	Avg	100	50	Ct	St	Balls	Runs	Wkts	Avg	BB	5I	10M
J Barnard	3	6	0	93	31	15.50	0	0	1	0	86	65	3	21.66	2-25	0	0
B Botha	3	6	2	139	72	34.75	0	1	3	0	6	6	0	-	-	0	0
C-Z Brits	3	6	0	124	61	20.66	0	1	2	0	507	255	6	42.50	2-68	0	0
B Cairncross	3	6	0	65	24	10.83	0	0	1	0	0	0	0	-	-	0	0
CS Cowan	2	4	0	54	23	13.50	0	0	1	0	0	0	0	-	-	0	0
CE Eksteen	1	2	0	42	25	21.00	0	0	1	0	228	64	2	32.00	2-64	0	0
C Gildenhuys	3	6	0	184	94	30.66	0	2	9	0	0	0	0	-	-	0	0
JA Gove	7	14	4	256	51*	25.60	0	1	10	0	683	284	9	31.55	3-57	0	0
AL Hodgkinson	3	6	0	239	95	39.83	0	2	3	0	0	0	0	-	-	0	0
P Hollett	4	7	0	71	21	10.14	0	0	1	0	102	59	1	59.00	1-46	0	0
E Hurly	4	8	1	240	96*	34.28	0	1	0	0	6	6	0	-	-	0	0
J Irwin	3	6	0	40	20	6.66	0	0	0	0	42	22	0	-	-	0	0
A Jackson	2	2	0	35	24	17.50	0	0	0	0	144	59	2	29.50	1-6	0	0
L-S Jacobs	2	3	2	4	3*	4.00	0	0	0	0	276	178	4	44.50	2-72	0	0
M Jones	1	1	0	0	0	0.00	0	0	0	0	0	0	0	-	-	0	0
M Katz	2	3	0	46	29	15.33	0	0	1	0	0	0	0	-	-	0	0
P Klesser	1	2	1	4	4	4.00	0	0	1	0	0	0	0	-	-	0	0
K-A Laing	1	2	0	16	9	8.00	0	0	1	0	144	72	1	72.00	1-72	0	0
E Lambert	2	4	0	65	34	16.25	0	0	1	0	0	0	0	-	-	0	0
B Lang	3	6	0	177	58	29.50	0	2	4	0	462	124	2	62.00	1-31	0	0
J Logtenberg	2	4	0	96	74	24.00	0	1	0	0	126	63	1	63.00	1-47	0	0
M Lotter	1	2	0	10	10	5.00	0	0	0	0	0	0	0	-	-	0	0
J McNaughton	3	6	1	45	28	9.00	0	0	4	0	276	116	6	19.33	6-39	1	0
D Moe	3	6	0	108	39	18.00	0	0	1	0	270	98	1	98.00	1-51	0	0
N Ndzundzu	1	2	1	8	8	8.00	0	0	0	0	36	24	0	-	-	0	0
SN Nefdt	4	8	1	211	68	30.14	0	2	0	0	174	108	2	54.00	1-16	0	0
M Payne	5	5	1	39	33	9.75	0	0	2	0	814	324	8	40.50	2-31	0	0
DJ Reid	1	2	1	50	36	50.00	0	0	1	0	36	19	0	-	-	0	0
W Skog	3	4	3	19	11*	19.00	0	0	1	0	420	126	3	42.00	1-24	0	0
AE Smith	2	4	2	65	24*	32.50	0	0	0	0	180	118	1	118.00	1-37	0	0
M Terblanche	3	6	0	103	41	17.16	0	0	3	0	0	0	0	-	-	0	0

Y van der Merwe	3	6	1	79	52*	15.80	0	1	1	0	462	230	3	76.66	2-81	0	0
C van der Westhuizen	2	4	0	159	83	39.75	0	1	0	0	240	116	3	38.66	2-49	0	0
Y van Mentz	4	8	2	186	105*	31.00	1	0	0	0	565	250	8	31.25	4-95	0	0
J van Zyl	1	1	0	6	6	6.00	0	0	1	0	0	0	0	-	-	0	0
SD van Zyl	2	4	1	58	37	19.33	0	0	0	0	258	121	1	121.00	1-63	0	0
S Viljoen	1	2	0	88	71	44.00	0	1	0	0	0	0	0	-	-	0	0
L Ward	7	11	2	52	17*	5.77	0	0	1	0	1420	467	27	17.29	6-48	3	0
D Weyers	3	4	0	6	5	1.50	0	0	3	0	660	204	5	40.80	3-33	0	0
B Williams	2	4	0	162	100	40.50	1	0	2	0	120	49	0	-	-	0	0
G Williamson	3	4	1	14	9	4.66	0	0	2	0	686	221	12	18.41	3-28	0	0
D Wood	1	1	1	3	3*	-	0	0	0	0	0	0	0	-	-	0	0

SOUTH AFRICAN WOMEN: LIMITED OVERS INTERNATIONAL CAREER RECORDS

As at 1 September 2006

Name	M	Inns	NO	Runs	HS	Avg	100	50	Ct	St	Balls	Runs	Wkts	Avg	RpO	BB	4I
E Akehurst	8	8	1	109	35*	15.57	0	0	2	0	168	84	1	84.00	3.00	1-24	0
J Barnard	8	8	0	122	32	15.25	0	0	0	0	108	85	2	42.50	4.72	2-33	0
SM Benade	3	3	0	21	17	7.00	0	0	1	0	0	0	0	-	-	-	0
AL Bezuidenhout	6	5	3	21	17	10.50	0	0	0	0	60	53	1	53.00	5.30	1-40	0
C-Z Brits	22	18	3	399	72	26.60	0	3	3	0	799	559	22	25.40	4.19	4-37	1
AA Burger	18	16	3	259	52*	19.92	0	1	6	0	0	0	0	-	-	-	0
D Carr	2	1	0	3	3	3.00	0	0	0	0	60	55	0	-	5.50	-	0
HA Davies	25	23	0	432	64	18.78	0	1	2	0	646	430	15	28.66	3.99	4-23	1
L de Beer	9	5	2	11	6	3.66	0	0	2	0	304	186	6	31.00	3.67	3-10	0
B Dermota	3	1	0	0	0	0.00	0	0	0	0	12	8	0	-	4.00	-	0
CE Eksteen	36	30	3	435	62	16.11	0	1	7	0	1486	863	28	30.82	3.48	4-4	1
SA Fritz	18	16	1	237	48	15.80	0	0	6	0	466	365	15	24.33	4.69	4-36	1
AL Hodgkinson	32	31	4	443	52*	16.40	0	1	9	0	114	59	1	59.00	3.10	1-18	0
D Hughes	2	0	0	0	-	-	0	0	0	0	78	37	1	37.00	2.84	1-17	0
APC Kilowan	13	7	2	68	16	13.60	0	0	2	0	426	309	4	77.25	4.35	1-18	0
L Korkie	7	5	0	20	12	4.00	0	0	1	0	24	22	0	-	5.50	-	0
A Kotze	15	12	5	95	30	13.57	0	0	2	0	623	394	8	49.25	3.79	2-14	0
A Kuylaars	23	18	6	205	74*	17.08	0	2	6	0	338	233	10	23.30	4.13	3-26	0

Name	M	Inns	NO	Runs	HS	Avg	100	50	Ct	St	Balls	Runs	Wkts	Avg	RpO	BB	4I
K-A Laing	23	22	4	385	91*	21.38	0	3	9	0	378	207	8	25.87	3.28	3-4	0
LP Lewis	9	4	4	13	6*	-	0	0	1	0	335	237	10	23.70	4.24	4-20	1
J Logtenberg	19	19	1	464	76	25.77	0	4	4	0	174	153	4	38.25	5.27	2-38	0
M Lotter	1	1	0	0	0	0.00	0	0	0	0	0	0	0	-	-	-	0
N Ndzundzu	16	6	4	14	5*	7.00	0	0	3	0	564	304	8	38.00	3.23	2-16	0
L Olivier	28	28	4	838	101*	34.91	1	7	3	0	180	95	4	23.75	3.16	2-10	0
S Pillay	12	10	2	50	11*	6.25	0	0	11	2	48	16	1	16.00	2.00	1-16	0
K Price	26	17	5	109	22	9.08	0	0	5	0	952	482	20	24.10	3.03	3-14	0
T Reeves	4	4	0	20	14	5.00	0	0	2	0	0	0	0	-	-	-	0
DJ Reid	29	25	5	275	56	13.75	0	1	2	0	408	289	12	24.08	4.25	3-7	0
R Scheepers	1	1	0	5	5	5.00	0	0	1	0	0	0	0	-	-	-	0
LH Sing	1	0	0	0	-	-	0	0	0	0	0	0	0	-	-	-	0
AE Smith	19	18	2	243	38	15.18	0	0	2	0	996	662	26	25.46	3.98	4-19	1
A Stears	2	1	1	5	5*	-	0	0	0	0	0	0	0	-	-	-	0
R Stoop	4	4	1	70	36*	23.33	0	0	0	0	96	73	0	-	4.56	-	0
H Strydom	8	8	1	122	46	17.42	0	0	2	0	140	127	3	42.33	5.44	3-33	0
K Swart	3	1	0	0	0	0.00	0	0	0	0	72	33	2	16.50	2.75	2-23	0
A Taai	7	6	2	38	22*	9.50	0	0	0	0	118	73	1	73.00	3.71	1-22	0
CS Terblanche	10	9	2	104	41*	14.85	0	0	4	0	72	70	1	70.00	5.83	1-36	0
M Terblanche	50	48	5	1045	81	24.30	0	5	23	11	0	0	0	-	-	-	0
Y van der Merwe	18	10	5	111	42*	22.20	0	0	3	0	776	576	14	41.14	4.45	3-25	0
C van der Westhuizen	18	16	5	125	25*	11.36	0	0	3	0	799	464	8	58.00	3.48	2-26	0
SD van Zyl	18	10	2	85	21	10.62	0	0	2	0	654	445	11	40.45	4.08	4-23	1
S Viljoen	17	14	2	204	54*	17.00	0	1	3	0	228	166	5	33.20	4.36	3-27	0
E Webber	1	1	0	6	6	6.00	0	0	0	0	0	0	0	-	-	-	0

SOUTH AFRICA UNDER-19 IN INDIA 2005/06

The Coca-Cola South Africa Under-19 squad played in a six-nation Afro-Asian Under-19 tournament in Vishakhapatnam, India, in November 2005. The team was captained by Free State left-hander and left-arm orthodox spinner, Dean Elgar, and coached by former national team coach, Ray Jennings.

The tournament provided an opportunity for the South African players to experience Asian conditions ahead of the Under-19 World Cup in Sri Lanka in February 2006, although in the event only four of the players participated in both tournaments. The Indian experience proved tough going for the South Africans, who lost four of their five matches.

The Coca-Cola South Africa Under-19 squad was: Dean Elgar (Free State, captain), Sean Adair (Eastern Province), Pieter Daneel (Boland), Richard das Neves (Gauteng), Sean Hendrieck (Western Province), Ryan Jaftha (Western Province), Tom Khoza (Northerns), Adrian Kritzinger (Western Province), Katlego Molutsi (Gauteng), Griffin Nieuwoudt (Free State), Siyabulela Nkosana (Eastern Province), Abdul Haq Razzak (KwaZulu-Natal), Mthokozisi Shezi (KwaZulu-Natal), CJ van der Schyff (Free State). Manager, Jay Naidoo; coach, Ray Jennings.

South Africa started their campaign well with a comfortable win against their African neighbours, Zimbabwe, but they were then outplayed by India.

There was an encouraging batting performance, led by Pieter Daneel, against Pakistan but it was not enough to stop the Pakistanis from winning by four wickets with 8.1 overs to spare. In the last two matches, South Africa's batting crumbled against Sri Lanka and Bangladesh. The heat took its toll and Shezi and Van der Schyff both had to be taken to hospital and put on drips after suffering dehydration.

Daneel was the most successful South African batsman, scoring 220 runs at an average of 73.33. Elgar was the only other player to top 100 runs. Shezi topped the bowling averages with five at 25.20 while Razzak took most wickets, six at 31.33. Das Neves, who took four wickets at 32.00, had the best economy rate, conceding 3.04 runs an over.

SOUTH AFRICA U-19 v ZIMBABWE U-19 — Afro-Asia Under-19 Cup

Played at Trishna Stadium, Visakhapatnam on 19 November 2005
Toss: Zimbabwe Under-19
Umpires: Rasheed Bhatti & ND Withana
Referee: S Chaturvedi
Result: South Africa Under-19 won by 8 wickets
Points: SA: 6; Zim: 0
Notes: South Africa Under-19 substitute: K Molutsi replaced S Nkosana

ZIMBABWE UNDER-19	Runs	Mins	Balls	4	6
AT Chiranda b Shezi	4	9	9	1	-
KD Samunderu lbw b Khoza	74	145	98	9	-
CJ Chibhabha c Nkosana b Shezi	1	8	6	-	-
*SC Williams c Kritzinger b Shezi	0	2	3	-	-
†TV Mufambisi b Van der Schyff	22	22	20	1	-
P Masvaure c Das Neves b Razak	10	55	39	1	-
RS Higgins c Hendrieck b Razak	1	6	3	-	-
G Querl run out (Das Neves)	6	18	15	1	-
VT Chaitezvi c Elgar b Khoza	16	25	29	3	-
AG Cremer run out (Das Neves)	10	14	12	1	-
IA Nicolson not out	3	7	8	-	-
Extras (lb 7, w 17, nb 2)	26				
TOTAL (40 overs)	**173**				

SOUTH AFRICA UNDER-19	Runs	Mins	Balls	4	6
S Hendrieck c Masvaure b Cremer	19	49	29	1	-
P Daneel not out	66	132	106	7	-
G Nieuwoudt run out (Mufambisi)	14	19	14	2	-
*D Elgar not out	48	62	63	6	-
A Kritzinger					
R Das Neves					
†K Molutsi					
CJ van der Schyff					
M Shezi					
AH Razak					
TR Khoza					
S Nkosana					
Extras (b 7, lb 5, w 9, nb 6)	27				
TOTAL (for 2 wkts) (34.2 overs)	**174**				

SA	*O*	*M*	*R*	*W*	
Van der Schyff	6	1	31	1	(7 w)
Shezi	6	0	29	3	(1 nb)
Nkosana	4	0	21	0	(7 w)
Das Neves	8	3	25	0	(1 w)
Razak	10	2	33	2	(1 w)
Khoza	6	0	27	2	(1 nb, 1 w)

Zim	*O*	*M*	*R*	*W*	
Nicolson	3	0	25	0	(4 nb, 3 w)
Querl	2	0	13	0	(1 w)
Higgins	9	1	40	0	(5 w)
Samunderu	5	0	21	0	
Cremer	9	0	45	1	(2 nb)
Williams	6.2	0	18	0	

Fall of Wickets	*Zim*	*SA*
1st	10 (1)	55 (1)
2nd	12 (3)	91 (3)
3rd	12 (4)	-
4th	47 (5)	-
5th	94 (6)	-
6th	104 (7)	-
7th	133 (8)	-
8th	146 (2)	-
9th	165 (9)	-
10th	173 (10)	-

INDIA U-19 v SOUTH AFRICA U-19 — Afro-Asia Under-19 Cup

Played at ACA-VDCA Stadium, Visakhapatnam on 20 November 2005 — Toss: India Under-19
Umpires: O Chirombe & ND Withana — Referee: S Chaturvedi
Result: India Under-19 won by 102 runs
Points: Ind: 6; SA: 0
Notes: India Under-19 substitute: RA Jadeja replaced an unknown player

INDIA UNDER-19	*Runs*	*Mins*	*Balls*	*4*	*6*
G Dhiman c Kritzinger b Jaftha	6	8	9	1	-
TM Srivastava c Adair b Jaftha	15	36	15	2	-
CA Pujara c Adair b Van der Schyff	15	23	17	3	-
*R Shukla c Jaftha b Das Neves	39	69	55	3	2
M Tehlan lbw b Das Neves	23	77	57	2	-
DB Das not out	66	105	77	5	-
P Chawla lbw b Jaftha	54	81	62	6	-
SS Bandekar not out	11	11	10	-	-
†PR Shah					
S Nadeem					
VY Mahesh					
RA Jadeja					
Extras (b 2, lb 4, w 16, nb 2)	24				
TOTAL (for 6 wkts) (50 overs)	**253**				

SOUTH AFRICA UNDER-19	*Runs*	*Mins*	*Balls*	*4*	*6*
G Nieuwoudt c Srivastava b Mahesh	1	12	7	-	-
P Daneel c Shah b Dhiman	26	59	35	3	-
S Hendrieck run out (Chawla)	2	38	23	-	-
*D Elgar c Jadeja b Chawla	32	69	48	4	1
A Kritzinger c Shah b Bandekar	4	30	16	-	-
R Das Neves c Srivastava b Bandekar	6	9	7	1	-
†SR Adair c Nadeem b Chawla	3	28	23	-	-
CJ van der Schyff st Shah b Nadeem	53	42	40	5	3
R Jaftha c Dhiman b Chawla	8	5	6	2	-
AH Razak not out	2	31	13	-	-
TR Khoza c Chawla b Nadeem	0	1	2	-	-
Extras (lb 2, w 12)	14				
TOTAL (36.4 overs)	**151**				

SA	*O*	*M*	*R*	*W*	
Van der Schyff	9	0	51	1	(4 w)
Jaftha	10	0	53	3	
Khoza	7	0	44	0	(1 nb, 6 w)
Nieuwoudt	1	0	8	0	(2 w)
Das Neves	10	3	22	2	(1 w)
Razak	10	1	43	0	(1 nb)
Elgar	3	0	26	0	(3 w)

Ind	*O*	*M*	*R*	*W*	
Mahesh	8	0	36	1	(7 w)
Dhiman	7	2	19	1	(3 w)
Bandekar	7	2	22	2	(1 w)
Chawla	8	2	28	3	(1 w)
Nadeem	5.4	0	31	2	
Jadeja	1	0	13	0	

Fall of Wickets	*Ind*	*SA*
1st	7 (1)	6 (1)
2nd	40 (3)	32 (3)
3rd	40 (2)	38 (2)
4th	103 (4)	59 (5)
5th	108 (5)	75 (6)
6th	237 (7)	81 (4)
7th	-	94 (7)
8th	-	104 (9)
9th	-	151 (8)
10th	-	151 (11)

PAKISTAN U-19 v SOUTH AFRICA U-19 — Afro-Asia Under-19 Cup

Played at Port Trust Golden Jubilee Stadium, Visakhapatnam on 22 November 2005 — Toss: Pakistan Under-19
Umpires: SN Bandekar & O Chirombe — Referee: SS Patil
Result: Pakistan Under-19 won by 4 wickets
Points: Pak: 5; SA: 1

SOUTH AFRICA UNDER-19	*Runs*	*Mins*	*Balls*	*4*	*6*
S Hendrieck c Sarfraz Ahmed b Haseeb Amjad	12	60	38	-	-
P Daneel not out	91	195	139	9	-
G Nieuwoudt c Imad Wasim b Haseeb Amjad	8	14	9	2	-
*D Elgar b Jamshed Ahmed	8	25	23	1	-
A Kritzinger c Sarfraz Ahmed b Usman Malik	19	40	44	1	-
R Das Neves st Sarfraz Ahmed b Imad Wasim	6	5	5	1	-
†SR Adair not out	59	46	49	6	2
AH Razak					
R Jaftha					
M Shezi					
S Nkosana					
Extras (b 1, lb 8, w 12, nb 7)	28				
TOTAL (for 5 wkts) (50 overs)	**231**				

PAKISTAN UNDER-19	*Runs*	*Mins*	*Balls*	*4*	*6*
Ali Khan c Hendrieck b Razak	39	49	35	7	-
Mohammad Faheem c Daneel b Shezi	9	23	16	2	-
Sharjeel Khan c Adair b Shezi	0	1	1	-	-
Jamshed Ahmed c Shezi b Das Neves	27	33	23	2	1
Ali Asad not out	79	123	82	11	-
*†Sarfraz Ahmed c Das Neves b Razak	52	85	70	6	1
Saadullah Ghauri c Elgar b Jaftha	11	14	14	2	-
Imad Wasim not out	5	12	10	1	-
Haseeb Amjad					
Usman Malik					
Mohammad Talha					
Extras (lb 2, w 9, nb 1)	12				
TOTAL (for 6 wkts) (41.5 overs)	**234**				

Pak	O	M	R	W		SA	O	M	R	W		Fall of Wickets	SA	Pak
Mohammad Talha	7	0	30	0	(4 nb, 3 w)	Jaftha	10	0	57	1	(1 nb, 1 w)	1st	58 (1)	31 (2)
Jamshed Ahmed	9	1	50	1	(1 nb, 3 w)	Shezi	9.5	1	54	2	(3 w)	2nd	67 (3)	31 (3)
Haseeb Amjad	10	1	49	2	(3 w)	Das Neves	10	0	41	1	(1 w)	3rd	90 (4)	78 (1)
Ali Khan	4	0	15	0	(2 w)	Razak	7	0	48	2	(2 w)	4th	135 (5)	82 (4)
Imad Wasim	10	0	41	1	(2 nb, 1 w)	Nkosana	3	0	18	0	(1 w)	5th	144 (6)	198 (6)
Usman Malik	10	0	37	1		Elgar	2	0	14	0	(1 w)	6th	-	219 (7)

SOUTH AFRICA U-19 v SRI LANKA U-19 — Afro-Asia Under-19 Cup

Played at ACA-VDCA Stadium, Visakhapatnam on 23 November 2005 — Toss: South Africa Under-19
Umpires: O Chirombe & Rasheed Bhatti — Referee: S Chaturvedi
Result: Sri Lanka Under-19 won by 8 wickets
Points: SL: 6; SA: 0

SOUTH AFRICA UNDER-19	Runs	Mins	Balls	4	6
S Hendrieck lbw b Gunasinghe	0	2	2	-	-
P Daneel run out (Karunaratne)	16	56	30	1	-
G Nieuwoudt b Perera	8	9	6	2	-
*D Elgar b Weerasinghe	25	64	44	3	-
†SR Adair b Perera	0	2	1	-	-
R Das Neves lbw b Perera	0	5	3	-	-
A Kritzinger c Fernando b Pathirana	42	109	72	5	1
CJ van der Schyff c Perera b Weerasinghe	6	28	26	-	-
AH Razak st De Zoysa b Weerasinghe	1	9	10	-	-
TR Khoza b Perera	8	46	42	1	-
M Shezi not out	1	13	12	-	-
Extras (b 1, lb 5, w 10)	16				
TOTAL (41.2 overs)	**123**				

SRI LANKA UNDER-19	Runs	Mins	Balls	4	6
FDM Karunaratne c and b Razak	39	75	63	6	1
†RSSS de Zoysa c and b Razak	28	57	38	3	-
SC Serasinghe not out	28	52	39	3	-
SH Fernando not out	29	34	34	3	-
PDMA Cooray					
*AD Mathews					
SS Pathirana					
KPSP Karunanayake					
NLTC Perera					
DRF Weerasinghe					
C Gunasinghe					
Extras (w 3)	3				
TOTAL (for 2 wkts) (29 overs)	**127**				

SL	O	M	R	W		SA	O	M	R	W		Fall of Wickets	SA	SL
Gunasinghe	5	0	18	1	(2 w)	Van der Schyff	3	0	17	0	(1 w)	1st	0 (1)	56 (2)
Perera	8	1	30	4	(4 w)	Shezi	6	1	21	0	(1 w)	2nd	12 (3)	83 (1)
Karunanayake	8	1	27	0	(3 w)	Das Neves	10	0	34	0		3rd	46 (2)	-
Weerasinghe	10	1	24	3	(1 w)	Razak	8	0	44	2		4th	46 (5)	-
Pathirana	9.2	4	17	1		Khoza	2	0	11	0	(1 w)	5th	53 (6)	-
Serasinghe	1	0	1	0								6th	61 (4)	-
												7th	78 (8)	-
												8th	80 (9)	-
												9th	121 (10)	-
												10th	123 (7)	-

BANGLADESH U-19 v SOUTH AFRICA U-19 — Afro-Asia Under-19 Cup

Played at Port Trust Golden Jubilee Stadium, Visakhapatnam on 25 November 2005 — Toss: Bangladesh Under-19
Umpires: O Chirombe & Rasheed Bhatti — Referee: SS Patil
Result: Bangladesh Under-19 won by 8 wickets
Points: Ban: 6; SA: 0

SOUTH AFRICA UNDER-19	Runs	Mins	Balls	4	6
G Nieuwoudt lbw b Kamrul Islam	0	9	7	-	-
P Daneel b Nabil Samad	21	46	32	3	-
†SR Adair b Saqibul Hasan	13	48	29	1	-
*D Elgar b Nabil Samad	7	17	14	1	-
A Kritzinger c Nazmul Hossain b Mehrab Hossain	8	60	42	-	-
K Molutsi b Suhrawadi Shuvo	23	36	34	3	-
R Das Neves lbw b Mehrab Hossain	0	5	7	-	-
CJ van der Schyff b Suhrawadi Shuvo	2	16	11	-	-
R Jaftha st Mushfiqur Rahim b Mehrab Hossain	0	1	2	-	-
AH Razak not out	1	15	15	-	-
M Shezi b Suhrawadi Shuvo	1	12	12	-	-
Extras (lb 9, w 2, p 5)	16				
TOTAL (34.3 overs)	**92**				

BANGLADESH UNDER-19	Runs	Mins	Balls	4	6
Mehdi Hasan not out	35	80	48	7	-
Tamim Iqbal run out (Jaftha)	0	7	0	-	-
Saqibul Hasan b Das Neves	30	47	28	6	-
Marshall Ayub not out	8	25	24	2	-
Mehrab Hossain					
*†Mushfiqur Rahim					
Suhrawadi Shuvo					
Nazmul Hossain					
Dolar Mahmud					
Nabil Samad					
Kamrul Islam					
Extras (lb 5, w 15)	20				
TOTAL (for 2 wkts) (16.4 overs)	**93**				

SOUTH AFRICA UNDER-19 IN INDIA 2005/06

Ban	O	M	R	W	
Dolar Mahmud	5	1	14	0	
Kamrul Islam	4	1	18	1	(1 w)
Nabil Samad	6	2	13	2	
Saqibul Hasan	7	2	20	1	(1 w)
Mehrab Hossain	7	3	7	3	
Suhrawadi Shuvo	5.3	2	6	3	

SA	O	M	R	W	
Van der Schyff	5	0	30	0	(6 w)
Shezi	2	0	22	0	(7 w)
Jaftha	2	0	10	0	(1 w)
Das Neves	4	2	6	1	(1 w)
Razak	3.4	1	20	0	

Fall of Wickets	SA	Ban
1st	1 (1)	2 (2)
2nd	39 (2)	66 (3)
3rd	45 (3)	-
4th	47 (4)	-
5th	84 (6)	-
6th	85 (7)	-
7th	90 (5)	-
8th	90 (9)	-
9th	90 (8)	-
10th	92 (11)	-

SOUTH AFRICA: AFRO-ASIA UNDER-19 CUP 2005/06 AVERAGES

Batting & Fielding

Name	M	Inns	NO	Runs	HS	Avg	SR	100	50	Ct	St
P Daneel	5	5	2	220	91 *	73.33	64.32	0	2	1	0
D Elgar	5	5	1	120	48 *	30.00	62.50	0	0	2	0
SR Adair	4	4	1	75	59 *	25.00	73.52	0	1	3	0
K Molutsi	2	1	0	23	23	23.00	67.64	0	0	0	0
CJ van der Schyff	4	3	0	61	53	20.33	79.22	0	1	0	0
A Kritzinger	5	4	0	73	42	18.25	41.95	0	0	2	0
S Hendrieck	4	4	0	33	19	8.25	35.86	0	0	2	0
G Nieuwoudt	5	5	0	31	14	6.20	72.09	0	0	0	0
R Jaftha	3	2	0	8	8	4.00	100.00	0	0	1	0
TR Khoza	3	2	0	8	8	4.00	18.18	0	0	0	0
AH Razak	5	3	2	4	2 *	4.00	10.52	0	0	2	0
R Das Neves	5	4	0	12	6	3.00	54.54	0	0	2	0
M Shezi	4	2	1	2	1 *	2.00	8.33	0	0	1	0
S Nkosana	2	0	0	0	-	-	-	0	0	1	0
Totals	56	44	7	670	91 *			0	4	17	0
			Extras	101					subs	0	
			Total	771		20.83	56.20			17	

Bowling

Name	Overs	Mdns	Runs	Wkts	Avg	RpO	BB	4I
M Shezi	23.5	2	126	5	25.20	5.28	3-29	0
R Jaftha	22	0	120	4	30.00	5.45	3-53	0
AH Razak	38.4	4	188	6	31.33	4.86	2-33	0
R Das Neves	42	8	128	4	32.00	3.04	2-22	0
TR Khoza	15	0	82	2	41.00	5.46	2-27	0
CJ van der Schyff	23	1	129	2	64.50	5.60	1-31	0
G Nieuwoudt	1	0	8	0	-	8.00	-	0
S Nkosana	7	0	39	0	-	5.57	-	0
D Elgar	5	0	40	0	-	8.00	-	0
Totals	177.3	15	860	23			3-29	0
		b/lb/pen	20	3	run outs			
		Total	880	26	33.84	4.95		

2006 UNDER-19 WORLD CUP

The South African team at the 2006 Under-19 World Cup had a disappointing campaign, failing to reach the championship phase and losing to Nepal in the semi-finals of the Plate competition. The team had two training camps, in Durban and Pretoria, and two practice matches in the two weeks leading up to their departure, as well as two practice matches in Sri Lanka but were unable to find form when it mattered.

The Coca-Cola South African Under-19 squad was: Dean Elgar (Free State, captain), Craig Alexander (Western Province), Pieter Daneel (Boland), Richard das Neves (Gauteng), Craig Kieswetter (Western Province), Richard Levi (Western Province), Grant Mokoena (Border), Wayne Parnelle (Eastern Province), Romano Ramoo (Border), Mafinki Serame (North West), Mthokozisi Shezi (KwaZulu-Natal), Malusi Siboto (Western Province), Jean Symes (Gauteng), Brett Thompson (Eastern Province). Manager, Jay Naidoo; coach, Ray Jennings; technical analyst, Anton Ferreira; team doctor, Dr Mohammed Nasir Jaffer; physiotherapist, Terry-Jill Malherbe.

Sixteen teams participated in the tournament, which was staged at five grounds in Colombo. South Africa were drawn in a tough group, together with Australia, the West Indies and the United States. With only two teams going through to the championship phase, defeats against Australia and the West Indies consigned them to playing in the Plate competition.

Elgar led by example to be the team's leading batsman. He and opening batsman Daneel were responsible for five of the eight half-centuries scored by the South Africans. Alexander was the most impressive bowler and it was a blow when he broke down in the match against Nepal. The all-rounder, Symes, was another who had a satisfactory tournament.

Pakistan became the first side to retain the title, beating India in a low-scoring final.

Warm-up matches

At De Zoysa Stadium, Moratuwa, 2 February 2006: New Zealand U-19 187 in 46.2 overs (MP Ellison 35, W Parnelle 2-27, MP Siboto 2-42, R Das Neves 2-44, NM Serame 2-40). **South Africa U-19** 190-5 in 40.5 overs (B Thompson 30, RE Levi 90*, G Mokoena 34, C Munro 2-35). **South Africa U-19 won by 5 wickets**.

At Colombo Colts Cricket Club, Colombo, 3 February 2006: England U-19 259-8 in 50 overs (V Chopra 51, M Nelson 42, W Parnelle 2-54, D Elgar 2-44, J Symes 2-46). **South Africa U-19** 243-8 in 50 overs (D Elgar 61, P Daneel 62, R Ramoo 56*). **England U-19 won by 16 runs**.

AUSTRALIA U-19 v SOUTH AFRICA U-19 — Under-19 World Cup Group B

Played at Sinhalese Sports Club, Colombo on 5 February 2006 — Toss: South Africa Under-19
Umpires: GA Baxter & EAR de Silva — Referee: RS Mahanama
Result: Australia Under-19 won by 175 runs
Man of Match: Tom Cooper
Points: Aus: 2; SA: 0
Notes: Finch scored his fifty off 35 balls in Australia Under-19's innings. Australia Under-19 substitute: WD Sheridan replaced TLW Cooper after 0 overs of South Africa Under-19's innings. South Africa Under-19 substitute: J Symes replaced M Siboto after 28 overs of Australia Under-19's innings.

Australia, the only country to have won the Cup twice, lost both their warm-up matches against Pakistan and India but found form when it mattered. Australia lost their first two wickets for four runs but Cooper made the first century of the tournament, sharing century stands for the third and fourth wickets, as the 1988 and 2002 champions posted a target that proved far beyond the reach of the South Africans.

Alexander was the one bowler who posed a constant threat to Australia's dominance as he finished with 4-47, while Thompson chipped in with the wickets of Cooper and Finch, who put on 120 for the fourth wicket.

AUSTRALIA UNDER-19	Runs	Mins	Balls	4	6
UT Khawaja lbw b Alexander	2	9	6	-	-
TLW Cooper c Das Neves b Thompson	104	148	134	12	1
TD Stray c Kieswetter b Alexander	0	2	3	-	-
*MC Henriques c and b Das Neves	37	69	34	5	2
AJ Finch c Parnelle b Thompson	74	55	57	4	5
DA Warner c Serame b Alexander	54	45	42	6	2
†MS Wade c Das Neves b Alexander	16	21	13	2	-
S Keen c Elgar b Parnelle	9	10	8	1	-
B Cutting run out (Parnelle)	2	5	3	-	-
JP McNamara not out	1	3	1	-	-
JM Bird					
WD Sheridan					
Extras (b 2, lb 4, w 10, nb 1)	17				
TOTAL (for 9 wkts) (50 overs)	**316**				

SOUTH AFRICA UNDER-19	Runs	Mins	Balls	4	6
B Thompson lbw b Henriques	11	21	18	2	-
P Daneel b Henriques	6	31	14	-	-
RE Levi c Wade b Cutting	20	29	18	3	1
*D Elgar b Keen	14	38	24	3	-
R Ramoo b Keen	11	27	19	2	-
†C Kieswetter lbw b Keen	0	13	3	-	-
J Symes not out	34	79	61	2	1
R Das Neves c Wade b Cutting	4	5	2	1	-
W Parnelle run out (Finch)	10	57	43	-	-
CJ Alexander b Henriques	0	4	4	-	-
NM Serame run out (Henriques)	1	5	3	-	-
MP Siboto					
Extras (lb 9, w 16, nb 5)	30				
TOTAL (34 overs)	**141**				

SA	O	M	R	W
Alexander	10	0	47	4 (6 w)
Parnelle	9	0	58	1
Siboto	5	0	37	0 (1 nb, 1 w)
Elgar	1	0	6	0
Das Neves	8	0	67	1 (1 w)
Serame	8	0	40	0 (1 w)
Symes	5	0	36	0 (1 w)
Thompson	4	0	19	2

Aus	O	M	R	W
Henriques	8	1	37	3 (2 nb, 4 w)
Bird	5	0	23	0 (3 w)
Cutting	5	0	24	2 (2 nb, 2 w)
Keen	6	1	10	3 (3 w)
Sheridan	4	0	14	0 (1 nb, 2 w)
McNamara	6	1	24	0 (1 w)

Fall of Wickets	Aus	SA
1st	4 (1)	23 (1)
2nd	4 (3)	32 (2)
3rd	104 (4)	60 (3)
4th	224 (5)	73 (4)
5th	234 (2)	79 (5)
6th	280 (7)	80 (6)
7th	312 (8)	85 (8)
8th	313 (6)	135 (9)
9th	316 (9)	135 (10)
10th	-	141 (11)

SOUTH AFRICA U-19 v USA U-19 — Under-19 World Cup Group B

Played at P Saravanamuttu Stadium, Colombo on 7 February 2006
Toss: United States of America Under-19
Umpires: BR Doctrove & BB Pradhan
Referee: RS Mahanama
Result: South Africa Under-19 won by 162 runs
Man of Match: Craig Kieswetter
Points: SA: 2; USA: 0
Notes: United States of America Under-19 substitute: Sumon Bari replaced AR Deopersaud after 0 overs of United States of America Under-19's innings.

Elgar and Kieswetter added 153 for the sixth wicket with good attacking batting after South Africa made a shaky start. Alexander again impressed with the ball, taking two wickets in his first over and another in his next to plunge the tournament debutants into early trouble in their reply. Das Neves ran through the lower order.

SOUTH AFRICA UNDER-19	Runs	Mins	Balls	4	6
B Thompson c and b NK Patel	10	23	16	1	-
P Daneel c Deopersaud b NK Patel	24	61	52	-	-
G Mokoena c NK Patel b MK Patel	29	67	51	3	-
RE Levi c Audain b MK Patel	19	39	34	2	-
*D Elgar c MK Patel b Rajp	79	99	73	7	-
R Ramoo run out (Rajp)	1	3	3	-	-
†C Kieswetter c Deopersaud b Punoo	80	75	66	6	3
J Symes c Audain b Deopersaud	8	4	3	2	-
R Das Neves not out	6	7	3	1	-
CJ Alexander not out	0	2	0	-	-
M Shezi					
Extras (lb 3, w 18)	21				
TOTAL (for 8 wkts) (50 overs)	**277**				

USA UNDER-19	Runs	Mins	Balls	4	6
Sumon Bari b Alexander	0	1	1	-	-
R Timbawala c and b Shezi	6	45	21	1	-
†AL Dodson b Alexander	0	1	1	-	-
*H Punoo lbw b Alexander	0	8	5	-	-
MK Patel run out	10	52	39	1	-
NK Patel c sub (NM Serame) b Das Neves	2	14	12	-	-
RA Deane c Shezi b Das Neves	9	32	22	2	-
DO Nathaniel b Das Neves	41	55	39	4	3
AA Kirton c Elgar b Das Neves	2	17	16	-	-
DL Audain not out	11	17	13	1	-
A Rajp lbw b Das Neves	3	7	8	-	-
AR Deopersaud					
Extras (lb 11, w 18, nb 2)	31				
TOTAL (29.1 overs)	**115**				

USA	O	M	R	W	
Audain	5	0	26	0	(7 w)
NK Patel	10	3	26	2	(4 w)
Punoo	10	0	62	1	(2 w)
MK Patel	7	0	34	2	
Rajp	9	0	51	1	(1 w)
Deopersaud	6	0	44	1	(3 w)
Kirton	3	0	31	0	

SA	O	M	R	W	
Alexander	8	2	26	3	(2 nb, 4 w)
Shezi	6	0	17	1	(4 w)
Das Neves	9.1	1	29	5	(1 w)
Mokoena	2	0	19	0	(2 w)
Symes	4	0	13	0	(1 w)

Fall of Wickets	SA	USA
1st	27 (1)	0 (1)
2nd	56 (2)	0 (3)
3rd	94 (3)	1 (4)
4th	100 (4)	31 (2)
5th	101 (6)	38 (6)
6th	254 (7)	40 (5)
7th	264 (8)	76 (7)
8th	271 (5)	94 (9)
9th	-	107 (8)
10th	-	115 (11)

SOUTH AFRICA U-19 v WEST INDIES U-19 — Under-19 World Cup Group B

Played at P Saravanamuttu Stadium, Colombo on 10 February 2006 — Toss: West Indies Under-19
Umpires: PT Manuel & Nadeem Ghauri — Referee: RS Mahanama
Result: West Indies Under-19 won by 7 wickets
Man of Match: Leon Johnson
Points: SA: 0; WI: 2
Notes: South Africa Under-19 substitute: G Mokoena replaced M Shezi after 37 overs of South Africa Under-19's innings.

With a place in the Super League at stake, the West Indies won comfortably, mainly through a fine innings by their captain, Johnson, who added 148 for the third wicket with Jason Mohammed after the West Indies lost two early wickets.

South Africa were unable to score enough runs, despite making a solid start after play was delayed following overnight rain. Daneel, who struggled with cramp during the later stages of his innings, made 90, but Das Neves was the only other player to reach 30.

SOUTH AFRICA UNDER-19	Runs	Mins	Balls	4	6
J Symes c Perkins b Narine	25	56	46	3	-
P Daneel c Bachan b Searles	90	184	125	6	-
RE Levi c Singh b Brooks	9	37	31	-	1
*D Elgar run out (Narine)	1	3	1	-	-
R Ramoo st Perkins b Narine	3	8	11	-	-
†C Kieswetter c Mohammed b Bachan	14	21	33	1	-
G Mokoena c Perkins b Brooks	1	6	9	-	-
R Das Neves c Singh b Searles	32	48	39	3	-
W Parnelle not out	7	8	4	1	-
CJ Alexander not out	1	5	3	-	-
NM Serame					
M Shezi					
Extras (b 5, lb 9, w 14, nb 2)	30				
TOTAL (for 8 wkts) (50 overs)	**213**				

WEST INDIES UNDER-19	Runs	Mins	Balls	4	6
†W Perkins lbw b Alexander	6	1	3	1	-
ADS Fletcher lbw b Parnelle	1	13	9	-	-
*LR Johnson c Kieswetter b Parnelle	83	130	100	11	1
J Mohammed not out	76	158	126	11	-
G Singh not out	34	39	25	4	2
KA Pollard					
SSJ Brooks					
JPR Searles					
KAJ Roach					
SP Narine					
R Bachan					
Extras (lb 7, w 7, nb 4)	18				
TOTAL (for 3 wkts) (43.1 overs)	**218**				

WI	O	M	R	W	
Searles	10	0	56	2	(9 w)
Roach	10	1	44	0	(1 nb, 2 w)
Narine	10	2	29	2	(1 nb, 2 w)
Bachan	10	1	27	1	(1 w)
Brooks	10	0	43	2	

SA	O	M	R	W	
Alexander	8	1	51	1	(4 nb, 1 w)
Parnelle	10	1	31	2	(1 w)
Das Neves	8	0	46	0	(1 w)
Serame	10	0	45	0	(1 w)
Symes	7.1	0	38	0	(3 w)

Fall of Wickets	SA	WI
1st	64 (1)	6 (1)
2nd	108 (3)	17 (2)
3rd	109 (4)	165 (3)
4th	115 (5)	-
5th	143 (6)	-
6th	148 (7)	-
7th	200 (2)	-
8th	204 (8)	-

SCOTLAND U-19 v SOUTH AFRICA U-19 — Under-19 World Cup Plate Quarter-final

Played at Nondescripts, Colombo on 14 February 2006 — Toss: Scotland Under-19
Umpires: GA Baxter & Nadeem Ghauri — Referee: AG Hurst
Result: South Africa Under-19 won by 185 runs
Man of Match: Jean Symes
Notes: Levi scored his fifty off 22 balls in South Africa Under-19's innings. Scotland Under-19 substitute: RKP Cannon replaced RT Routray after 18.1 overs of Scotland Under-19's innings.

The South Africans hit the highest total of the tournament before securing an easy win. Symes and Daneel shared a century opening stand before Elgar and Levi thrashed the bowling, with Levi playing a thrilling innings.

SOUTH AFRICA UNDER-19	Runs	Mins	Balls	4	6
J Symes run out (MacLennan)	63	90	76	7	-
P Daneel c Berrington b Routray	59	124	65	7	-
B Thompson b Iqbal	0	3	4	-	-
RE Levi c Routray b Iqbal	51	24	23	5	4
*D Elgar run out (Hislop)	86	89	73	10	-
G Mokoena b Iqbal	13	25	19	2	-
†C Kieswetter c MacLennan b Berrington	26	37	25	2	1
W Parnelle c Iqbal b Farid	13	17	17	-	1
M Shezi not out	0	1	1	-	-
MP Siboto					
NM Serame					
Extras (b 3, lb 2, w 18, nb 3)	26				
TOTAL (for 8 wkts) (50 overs)	**337**				

SCOTLAND UNDER-19	Runs	Mins	Balls	4	6
†AHJ Hislop c Parnelle b Shezi	3	20	17	-	-
G Goudie c Shezi b Symes	59	94	70	8	-
MM Iqbal run out (Symes)	11	41	22	2	-
RD Berrington b Siboto	0	2	1	-	-
*K Farid run out (Siboto)	4	13	11	1	-
RKP Cannon b Symes	6	32	21	1	-
SK MacLennan c Kieswetter b Parnelle	0	3	2	-	-
UA Mohammed c Kieswetter b Parnelle	0	2	2	-	-
AS Mehmond c and b Symes	12	30	29	1	-
CS MacLeod b Serame	16	49	41	1	-
TJ Buchan not out	22	30	29	3	-
RT Routray					
Extras (lb 2, w 16, nb 1)	19				
TOTAL (40.4 overs)	**152**				

Scot	O	M	R	W
Goudie	4	0	23	0 (5 w)
Routray	9	0	48	1 (1 nb, 4 w)
MacLeod	5	0	44	0 (1 nb, 3 w)
Buchan	2	0	21	0 (3 w)
Mohammed	5	0	37	0
Berrington	8	0	36	1 (2 w)
Iqbal	10	1	47	3
Farid	3	0	37	1 (1 nb, 1 w)
Mehmond	4	0	39	0

SA	O	M	R	W
Parnelle	9	1	22	2 (3 w)
Shezi	8	1	38	1 (2 w)
Siboto	6	1	27	1 (1 nb, 2 w)
Symes	10	0	38	3 (4 w)
Serame	7.4	0	25	1 (1 w)

Fall of Wickets	SA	Scot
1st	134 (1)	12 (1)
2nd	134 (3)	74 (3)
3rd	193 (4)	75 (4)
4th	193 (2)	81 (5)
5th	220 (6)	93 (2)
6th	289 (7)	93 (7)
7th	336 (8)	94 (8)
8th	337 (5)	102 (6)
9th	-	122 (9)
10th	-	152 (10)

NEPAL U-19 v SOUTH AFRICA U-19

Under-19 World Cup Plate Semi-final

Played at Nondescripts, Colombo on 16 February 2006
Toss: Nepal Under-19
Umpires: Shahul Hameed & TH Wijewardene
Referee: RS Mahanama
Result: Nepal Under-19 won by 2 runs
Man of Match: K Chaugai
Notes: Nepal Under-19 substitute: S Kesari replaced Y Subedi after 25 overs of South Africa Under-19's innings. South Africa Under-19 substitute: NM Serame replaced CJ Alexander after 11 overs of Nepal Under-19's innings.

For the second time in successive tournaments, Nepal beat South Africa. Coached by former Sri Lanka batsman Roy Dias, the Nepalese held their nerve in a tight finish. South Africa, who had five wickets in hand at the end, needed 16 from the last two overs, ten from the final over and three from the last ball but could not get the crucial runs.

Elgar said: "Our fielding let us down and they got 20 or 30 more runs than they should have but there are no excuses. They were the better side today."

An injury to Alexander, South Africa's best bowler of the tournament, was a blow to the young Proteas. He had to leave the field after bowling 3.1 overs.

Nepal's spinners tied down the batsmen and by the time Elgar and Ramoo came together the asking rate was up to eight an over.

NEPAL UNDER-19	Runs	Mins	Balls	4	6
*K Chaugai st Kieswetter b Symes	59	106	81	6	1
†MK Chhetri st Kieswetter b Thompson	15	67	33	2	-
S Vesawkar c Ramoo b Symes	19	31	33	2	-
G Malla not out	46	97	72	6	-
P Khadka c Kieswetter b Symes	8	10	14	1	-
P Chaudhary c Ramoo b Siboto	18	52	47	1	-
B Regmi c Das Neves b Siboto	14	14	12	-	1
Y Subedi b Siboto	9	8	7	1	-
R Shrestha b Siboto	1	2	2	-	-
R Rauniyar					
A Bhattarai					
S Kesari					
Extras (b 1, lb 12, w 11, nb 1)	25				
TOTAL (for 8 wkts) (50 overs)	**214**				

SOUTH AFRICA UNDER-19	Runs	Mins	Balls	4	6
J Symes c Chaudhary b Bhattarai	20	43	37	2	-
P Daneel run out (Chhetri/Shrestha)	32	99	64	3	-
B Thompson c Chhetri b Regmi	31	62	53	5	-
RE Levi lbw b Regmi	3	20	12	-	-
*D Elgar not out	66	96	65	3	-
R Ramoo st Chhetri b Regmi	38	80	63	1	1
†C Kieswetter not out	3	6	6	-	-
R Das Neves					
MP Siboto					
NM Serame					
M Shezi					
CJ Alexander					
Extras (b 1, lb 2, w 16)	19				
TOTAL (for 5 wkts) (50 overs)	**212**				

SA	O	M	R	W	
Alexander	3.1	1	10	0	(1 nb)
Shezi	5	0	30	0	
Siboto	8.5	0	47	4	(5 w)
Thompson	5	0	38	1	(1 w)
Das Neves	10	2	25	0	
Symes	10	2	15	3	(2 w)
Serame	6	0	23	0	(2 w)
Elgar	2	0	13	0	

Nep	O	M	R	W	
Bhattarai	8	1	28	1	(1 w)
Khadka	10	2	36	0	(2 w)
Shrestha	8	0	52	0	
Rauniyar	4	0	20	0	(1 w)
Vesawkar	7	0	25	0	(2 w)
Regmi	10	1	31	3	(2 w)
Kesari	3	0	17	0	

Fall of Wickets	Nep	SA
1st	67 (2)	39 (1)
2nd	105 (3)	92 (2)
3rd	106 (1)	95 (3)
4th	116 (5)	99 (4)
5th	172 (6)	205 (6)
6th	195 (7)	-
7th	212 (8)	-
8th	214 (9)	-

OTHER SCORES IN BRIEF

Group A

At P Saravanamuttu Stadium, 5 February: Bangladesh won the toss. **New Zealand** 175 in 45.3 overs (Mehrab Hossain 4-29). **Bangladesh** 176-7 in 37.5 overs. Bangladesh won by three wickets.
At P Saravanamuttu Stadium, 6 February. Pakistan won the toss. **Uganda** 74 in 33.3 overs. **Pakistan** 75-2 in 12.2 overs. Pakistan won by eight wickets.
At Nondescripts Cricket Club, 7 February. Uganda won the toss. **New Zealand** 259-6 in 50 overs (T Astle 67, K Noema-Barnett 67). **Uganda** 137 in 48.4 overs (D Bartlett 5-30). New Zealand won by 122 runs.
At Nondescripts Cricket Club, 8 February. Bangladesh won the toss. **Pakistan** 170 in 43.1 (Sakib Al Hasan 4-34). **Bangladesh** 171-6 in 34.5 overs. Bangladesh won by four wickets
At Sinhalese Sports Club, 9 February. Uganda won the toss. **Bangladesh** 255 in 49.4 overs (Mushfiqur Rahim 64, R Semanda 4-43). **Uganda** 84 in 33.4 overs. Bangladesh won by 171 runs.
At Sinhalese Sports Club, 10 February. Pakistan won the toss. **New Zealand** 77 in 24 overs (Anwer Ali Khan 5-34). **Pakistan** 78-2 in 9 overs. Pakistan won by eight wickets.

Group B

At Nondescripts Cricket Club, 6 February. West Indies won the toss. **West Indies** 302-7 in 50 overs (W Perkins 133, Gajanand Singh 65). **United States** 215 in 45.4 overs (H Punoo 65). West Indies won by 87 runs.
At Sinhalese Sports Club, 8 February. Australia won the toss. **Australia** 251 in 47.5 overs (U Khawaja 77). **West Indies** 238 in 48 overs (J Mohammad 57). Australia won by 13 runs.
At P Saravanamuttu Stadium, 9 February. Australia won the toss. **United States** 148 in 42.5 overs (J Holland 4-39). **Australia** 149-6 in 24.1 overs. Australia won by four wickets.

Group C

At R Premadasa Stadium, 5 February. Sri Lanka won the toss. **Scotland** 186 in 49.4 overs (K Farid 76). **Sri Lanka** 187-6 in 39.5 overs (S Seerasinghe 64). Sri Lanka won by four wickets.
At R Premadasa Stadium, 6 February. India won the toss. **Namibia** 170 in 48.5 overs (D Botha 61). **India** 173-1 in 27.1 overs (G Dhiman 90*, C.Pujara 66*). India won by nine wickets.
At R Premadasa Stadium, 7 February. Sri Lanka won the toss. **Sri Lanka** 263-8 in 50 overs (D Cooray 64). **Namibia** 126 in 38.3 overs (R Weerasinghe 4-24). Sri Lanka won by 137 runs.
At R Premadasa Stadium, 8 February. India won the toss. **Scotland** 112 in 39.4 overs (Abu Nechim Ahmed 4-25). **India** 115-2 in 19 overs. India won by eight wickets.
At Colombo Cricket Club, 9 February. Namibia won the toss. **Scotland** 156 in 48 overs (N Scholtz 4-25). **Namibia** 160-3 in 36.3 overs (D Botha 55*). Namibia won by seven wickets.
At R Premadasa Stadium, 10 February. Sri Lanka won the toss. **Sri Lanka** 207 in 48.3 overs (A Mathews 52). **India** 209-6 in 47.4 overs (R Sharma 78, M Tehlan 64). India won by four wickets.

Group D

At Nondescripts Cricket Club, 5 February. Ireland won the toss. Match reduced to 44 overs per side. **Zimbabwe** 215-7 in 44 overs (D Samunderu 61). **Ireland** 97 in 29.1 overs. Zimbabwe won by 118 runs.
At Sinhalese Sports Club, 6 February. England won the toss. **England** 209-9 in 50 overs (M Ali 54). **Nepal** 132 in 45.2 overs. England won by 77 runs.
At Colombo Cricket Club, 7 February. Nepal won the toss. **Zimbabwe** 201 in 49.5 overs (R Higgins 74, P Khadra 4-28). **Nepal** 199-9 in 50 overs (K Chaugai 78). Zimbabwe won by two runs.
At Colombo Cricket Club, 8 February. Ireland won the toss. **England** 214 in 49.4 overs (R Hamilton-Brown 55, B Wright 50, N McDarby 6-50). **Ireland** 210 in 50 overs (G Wilson 69). England won by four runs.
At Nondescripts Cricket Club, 9 February. Ireland won the toss. **Nepal** 234-8 in 50 overs (S Veswarkar 82). **Ireland** 174 in 45.3 overs (E Morgan 86). Nepal won by 60 runs.
At Colombo Cricket Club, 10 February. Zimbabwe won the toss. **England** 172 in 49.5 overs. **Zimbabwe** 175-8 in 47.1 overs. Zimbabwe won by two wickets.

2006 UNDER-19 WORLD CUP

Super League quarter-finals
At P Saravanamuttu Stadium, 11 February. England won the toss. **Bangladesh** 155 in 48.2 overs. **England** 156-5 in 43.3 overs. England won by five wickets.
At R Premadasa Stadium, 11 February. India won the toss. **India** 284-9 in 50 overs (C Pujara 97, G Dhiman 74, R Sharma 50, J Searles 6-68). **West Indies** 158 in 38.5 overs (V Yomahesh 4-25). India won by 126 runs.
At Nondescripts Cricket Club, 11 February. Pakistan won the toss. **Zimbabwe** 181 in 49.3 overs(Riaz Khail 4-29). **Pakistan** 185-5 in 48 overs. Pakistan won by five wickets.
At Sinhalese Sports Club, 11 February. Sri Lanka won the toss. **Sri Lanka** 177 in 46.3 overs (M Henriques 4-22). **Australia** 178-1 in 26.1 overs (M Henriques 84*, T Cooper 79*). Australia won by nine wickets.

Super League semi-finals
At R Premadasa Stadium, 15 February. India won the toss. **India** 292-4 in 50 overs (C Pujara 129*, R Sharma 59). **England** 58 in 20.1 overs (Abu Nechim Ahmed 4-14). India won by 234 runs.
At R Premadasa Stadium, 16 February. Pakistan won the toss. **Pakistan** 287-9 in 50 overs (Riaz Kail 84, Ali Asad 69). **Australia** 124 in 32.3 overs (U Khawaja 59). Pakistan won by 163 runs.

Super League final
At R Premadasa Stadium, 19 February. Pakistan won the toss. **Pakistan** 109 in 41.1 overs (P Chawla 4-8). **India** 71 in 18.5 overs (Anwer Ali Khan 5-35). Pakistan won by 38 runs.

Super League play-off semi-finals
At Sinhalese Sports Club, 15 February. West Indies won the toss. **West Indies** 161 in 37.2 overs. **Bangladesh** 162-6 in 33.1 overs (N Pascal 4-53). Bangladesh won by four wickets.
At Sinhalese Sports Club, 16 February. Zimbabwe won the toss. **Zimbabwe** 256-8 in 50 overs (K Meth 91, G Balance 53). **Sri Lanka** 259-2 in 47.2 overs (S de Zoysa 63 rtd hurt 63, D Cooray 53*, D Karunaratne 53, H Fernando 52*). Sri Lanka won by eight wickets.

Super League play-off final (fifth place)
At Sinhalese Sports Club. 18 February. Sri Lanka won the toss. **Bangladesh** 278-8 in 50 overs (Sakib Al Hasan 67, Mehrab Hossain 66*). **Sri Lanka** 180 in 44.5 overs (D Cooray 58). Bangladesh won by 98 runs.

Plate Championship quarter-finals
At R Premadasa Stadium, 14 February. New Zealand won the toss. **Ireland** 304-9 in 50 overs (E Morgan 124, A Poynter 76, H Bennett 4-31). **New Zealand** 305-7 in 49.1 overs (T Southee 92, A de Boorder 87). New Zealand won by three wickets.
At Sinhalese Sports Club, 14 February. Namibia won the toss. **Namibia** 219-8 in 50 overs (P Grove 58, D Botha 56). **United States** 220-8 in 49 overs (H Punoo 64). United States won by two wickets.
At P Saravanamuttu Stadium, 14 February. Nepal won the toss. **Nepal** 192-9 in 50 overs (G Malla 64). **Uganda** 132 in 44.3 overs. Nepal won by 60 runs.

Plate Championship semi-finals
At P Saravanamuttu Stadium, 15 February. United States won the toss. **New Zealand** 295-8 in 50 overs (A de Boorder 100*, T Astle 59, A Rajp 5-61). **United States** 125 in 29.3 overs (H Bennett 4-16). New Zealand won by 170 runs.

Plate Championship final (9th place)
At P Saravanamuttu Stadium, 18 February. New Zealand won the toss. **New Zealand** 204 in 49.2 overs (T Astle 66). **Nepal** 205-9 in 49.4 overs (B Regmi 66). Nepal won by one wicket.

Plate Championship play-off semi-finals
At P Saravanamuttu Stadium, 16 February. Scotland won the toss. **Uganda** 214-9 in 50 overs (P Ochan 64). **Scotland** 145 in 40 overs (E Isaanez 4-20). Uganda won by 69 runs.
At Nondescripts Cricket Club, 15 February. Ireland won the toss. **Namibia** 115 in 36.3 overs (J Hall 4-29). **Ireland** 116-4 in 29.2 overs. Ireland won by six wickets.

Plate Championship play-off final (13th place)
At Nondescripts Cricket Club, 18 February. Uganda won the toss. **Uganda** 165-8 in 50 overs. **Ireland** 166-4 in 35.5 overs (E Morgan 60*). Ireland won by six wickets.

SOUTH AFRICA: UNDER-19 WORLD CUP 2006 AVERAGES

Batting & Fielding

Name	M	Inns	NO	Runs	HS	Avg	SR	100	50	Ct	St
D Elgar	5	5	1	246	86	61.50	104.23	0	3	2	0
P Daneel	5	5	0	211	90	42.20	65.93	0	2	0	0
J Symes	5	5	1	150	63	37.50	67.26	0	1	1	0
C Kieswetter	5	5	1	123	80	30.75	92.48	0	1	5	2
R Das Neves	4	3	1	42	32	21.00	95.45	0	0	4	0
RE Levi	5	5	0	102	51	20.40	86.44	0	1	0	0
W Parnelle	3	3	1	30	13	15.00	46.87	0	0	2	0
G Mokoena	3	3	0	43	29	14.33	54.43	0	0	0	0
R Ramoo	4	4	0	53	38	13.25	55.20	0	0	2	0
B Thompson	4	4	0	52	31	13.00	57.14	0	0	0	0
CJ Alexander	4	3	2	1	1 *	1.00	14.28	0	0	0	0
NM Serame	4	1	0	1	1	1.00	33.33	0	0	1	0
M Shezi	4	1	1	0	0 *	-	0.00	0	0	3	0
MP Siboto	3	0	0	0	-	-	-	0	0	0	0
Totals	58	47	8	1054	90			0	8	20	2
			Extras	126					subs	1	
			Total	1180		30.25	74.48			21	

Bowling

Name	Overs	Mdns	Runs	Wkts	Avg	RpO	BB	4I
CJ Alexander	29.1	4	134	8	16.75	4.59	4-47	1
B Thompson	9	0	57	3	19.00	6.33	2-19	0
W Parnelle	28	2	111	5	22.20	3.96	2-22	0
MP Siboto	19.5	1	111	5	22.20	5.59	4-47	1
J Symes	36.1	2	140	6	23.33	3.87	3-15	0
R Das Neves	35.1	3	167	6	27.83	4.74	5-29	1
M Shezi	19	1	85	2	42.50	4.47	1-17	0
NM Serame	31.4	0	133	1	133.00	4.20	1-25	0
D Elgar	3	0	19	0	-	6.33	-	0
G Mokoena	2	0	19	0	-	9.50	-	0
Totals	213	13	976	36			5-29	3
		b/lb/pen	39	4	run outs			
		Total	1015	40	25.37	4.76		

SOUTH AFRICA UNDER-19 INTERNATIONAL RECORDS

TESTS

RESULTS

Opponents	Played	Won	Lost	Drawn
England	8	2	2	4
India	3	1	1	1
New Zealand	3	0	2	1
Pakistan	6	0	3	3
Total	20	3	8	9

Highest innings totals:

For:	646-9*	v England (Chelmsford)	2003
Against:	528-7*	by England (Taunton)	1995

Lowest innings totals:

For:	87	v Pakistan (Bloemfontein)	1996/97
Against:	135	by India (Chandigarh)	1995/96

Highest individual innings:

For:	201*	GD Elliott v England (Cape Town)	1997/98
Against:	188*	Hasan Raza for Pakistan (Karachi)	1998/99

Best bowling in an innings:

For:	6-53	M Ntini v India (Kanpur)	1995/96
Against:	7-35	Fazl-e-Akbar for Pakistan (Bloemfontein)	1996/97

Best bowling in a match:

For:	10-99	R Munnik v Pakistan (Bloemfontein)	1996/97
Against:	12-99	Fazl-e-Akbar for Pakistan (Bloemfontein)	1996/97

RECORD WICKET PARTNERSHIPS

1st	79	MV Boucher and AG Prince v England (Worcester)	1995
2nd	144	PK Hearle and S Hofmeyr v Pakistan (East London)	1996/97
	144	AG Puttick and IJL Trott v Pakistan (Sheikhupura)	1998/99
3rd	164	HH Dippenaar and ND McKenzie v England (Leeds)	1995
4th	220	J-P Duminy and AB de Villiers v England (Worcester)	2003
5th	138	F du Plessis and ET Springer v England (Chelmsford)	2003
6th	175	AM Omar and BG Stigant v England (Taunton)	1995
7th	116	J Botha and CA Thyssen v New Zealand (Lincoln)	2000/01
8th	148	GD Elliott and MW Creed v England (Cape Town)	1997/98
9th	76	GH Bodi and W Samsodien v England (Fochville)	1997/98
	76	CA Thyssen and VD Philander v England (Chelmsford)	2003
10th	123*	CA Thyssen and WC Hantam v England (Chelmsford)	2003

SOUTH AFRICA UNDER-19 INTERNATIONAL RECORDS

LIMITED OVERS INTERNATIONALS

RESULTS

Opponents	Played	Won	Lost	NR
Americas	1	1	0	0
Australia	3	0	3	0
Bangladesh	3	2	1	0
Canada	1	1	0	0
England	8	5	2	1
India	8	3	5	0
Ireland	1	1	0	0
Kenya	1	1	0	0
Nepal	3	0	2	1
Netherlands	1	1	0	0
New Zealand	5	3	1	1
Pakistan	7	2	5	0
Scotland	2	2	0	0
Sri Lanka	3	0	3	0
Uganda	1	1	0	0
United States of America	1	1	0	0
West Indies	2	0	2	0
Zimbabwe	3	3	0	0
Total	54	27	24	3

Highest innings totals:

For:	337-8 (50)	v Scotland (Colombo-Non)	2005/06
Against:	316-9 (50)	by Australia (Colombo-SSC)	2005/06

Lowest innings totals:

For:	92 (34.3)	v Bangladesh (Visakhapatnam)	2005/06
Against:	41 (28.4)	by Canada (Auckland)	2001/02

Highest individual innings:

For:	156*	JA Rudolph v Nepal (Katunayake)	1999/00
Against:	122	SR Patel for England (Arundel)	2003

Best bowling in an innings:

For:	5-13	P Joubert v Pakistan (Kimberley)	1996/97
Against:	6-34	Ahmer Saeed for Pakistan (Paarl)	1996/97

RECORD WICKET PARTNERSHIPS

1st	138	DJ Jacobs and SC Cook v Bangladesh (Auckland)	2001/02
2nd	160	GC Smith and JA Rudolph v Nepal (Katunayake)	1999/00
3rd	110*	MJ Lumb and MN van Wyk v Scotland (Potchefstroom)	1997/98
4th	91	JG Myburgh and U Abrahams v Netherlands (Kandy)	1999/00
5th	141	DJ Jacobs and RT Bailey v New Zealand (Lincoln)	2001/02
6th	153	D Elgar and C Kieswetter v USA (Colombo-PSS)	2005/06
7th	57	AB de Villiers and CA Thyssen v England (Arundel)	2003
8th	79	G Stevens and KC Africa v Nepal (Chittagong)	2003/04
9th	47	CJ van der Schyff and AH Razak v India (Visakhapatnam)	2005/06
10th	33*	Z Homani and IK Postman v Australia (Lincoln)	2001/02

Section C: Senior Domestic Cricket

CRICKET SOUTH AFRICA

PO Box 55009, Northlands 2116.
Tel (011) 880 2810. Fax (011) 880 6578.

At the Annual General Meeting of the United Cricket Board of South Africa on 3 August 2006 it was decided to change the name of the governing body to Cricket South Africa. The professional wing will continue to be Cricket South Africa (Pty) Ltd.

In announcing the change, Gerald Majola, the Chief Executive, said market research had shown the use of two names caused confusion among stakeholders. He said: "We believe the name change will give us the opportunity to capitalise on a fresh, innovative brand for South African cricket." He stressed that the change of name would in no way reduce the commitment to unity in South African cricket. "The continued unification of South African cricket remains a major pillar of our vision and our constitution," he said.

In his presidential address to the AGM, Ray Mali called on South African cricket to design its own winning model. "South African cricket cannot design, shape or mould its cricket based on models from other countries. We need to design our own model based on the strength we derive from a diverse society."

The Treasurer, Professor Hentie van Wyk, said: "The UCBSA and CSA experienced very successful financial results for the year ended 30 April 2006 as both entities realised operating profits. The operating profits of CSA and the UCBSA were R19.4 million and R6.7 million respectively, which represents a combined surplus of R26.1 million. In view of the fact that a combined budget loss of R14.6 million was approved for the year under review the actual results are evidence of the strict financial control over operating expenses.

"Cricket revenue is like a roller coaster. We have good years and lean years. Yet there is a constant level of mostly human driven expenses and therefore we need to have a long term vision. The CSA and the UCBSA aim to achieve a combined cash reserve of at least R80 million so as to sustain the ups and downs of future income streams."

The AGM decided to extend life membership to Advocate Percy Sonn, the former President of the United Cricket Board and recently elected President of the International Cricket Council.

General Council 2006/07

President: Ray Mali. **Vice-President:** Adv Norman Arendse. **Chief Executive:** Gerald Majola. **Treasurer:** Professor Hentie van Wyk. **Members:** Xolani Boqwana (Black African representative), Leon Crawley (Free State), Dr Peter Cyster (Boland), Keke Dali (Easterns), Professor Fanie Gericke (North West), Ahmed Jinnah (Griqualand West), Tim Khumalo (Black African representative), Vuyisile Mgadle (Border), Dr Logan Naidoo (KwaZulu-Natal), Dr Mtutuzeli Nyoka (Gauteng), Gabriel Nkagisang (Black African representative), Pieter Steffens (Northerns), Raymond Uren (Eastern Province), Mohamed Ebrahim (Western Province).

CRICKET SOUTH AFRICA

Key staff

Chief Executive: Gerald Majola. **Personal Assistant to CEO:** Lesley O'Donohue. **Commercial and Finance: General Manager:** Don McIntosh. **Cricket Affairs: General Manager:** Brian Basson. **Manager: Coaching:** Anton Ferreira. **Manager: Senior Amateur Cricket:** Max Jordaan. **Manager: Operations:** Mike Gajjar. **Manager: Schools:** Niels Momberg.

UNITED CRICKET BOARD/CRICKET SOUTH AFRICA PRESIDENTS

1991-92	GF Dakin
1992-98	K Mackerdhuj
1998-2000	RC White
2000-2003	PHF Sonn
2003-	R Mali

Honorary Life Members: GF Dakin, JL Pamensky, SK Reddy, PHF Sonn.

CRICKET SOUTH AFRICA (PTY) LTD

Board of Directors

Chairperson: Ray Mali. **Vice-Chairperson:** Adv Norman Arendse. **Chief Executive:** Gerald Majola. **Treasurer:** Professor Hentie van Wyk. **Other Board members:** Paul Harris (Independent Director), Thandi Orleyn (Independent Director), Tony Irish (SA Cricketers' Association), Andy O'Connor (Eastern Titans (Pty) Ltd), Dr Logan Naidoo (KZN Cricket (Pty) Ltd), Raymond Uren (Cricket East Cape (Pty) Ltd), Charlie Robinson (Central Franchise BFN (Pty) Ltd), Prof Fanie Gericke (New Heights Cricket (Pty) Ltd), Mohamed Ebrahim (Western Cape Cricket (Pty) Ltd).

Key staff

Chief Executive: Gerald Majola. **General Manager: Professional Cricket:** Vintcent van der Bijl. **Commercial and Communications Manager:** Steve Elworthy. **Marketing Manager:** Ros Goldin. **Media Liaison Officer:** Gordon Templeton.

CSA COMPETITION WINNERS

FIRST-CLASS COMPETITIONS

CASTLE CUP/SUPERSPORT SERIES

Castle Cup

Season	Winners
1991/92	Eastern Province
1992/93	Orange Free State
1993/94	Orange Free State
1994/95	Natal
1995/96	Western Province

SuperSport Series

Season	Winners
1996/97	Natal
1997/98	Free State
1998/99	Western Province
1999/2000	Gauteng
2000/01	Western Province
2001/02	KwaZulu-Natal
2002/03	Easterns
2003/04	Western Province

SuperSport Series (Franchise)

Season	Winners
2004/05	Dolphins/Eagles (shared)
2005/06	Dolphins/Titans (shared)

PRESIDENT'S CUP

Season	Winners
1991/92	Western Province B

UCB BOWL

Season	Winners
1991/92	Eastern Transvaal
1992/93	Boland
1993/94	Transvaal B/Western Province B (shared)
1994/95	Natal B
1995/96	Griqualand West/Natal B (shared)
1996/97	Eastern Province B
1997/98	North West
1998/99	North West

UCB PROVINCIAL CUP

Season	Winners
2004/05	Griqualand West
2005/06	Northerns

LIMITED OVERS COMPETITIONS

NISSAN SHIELD/TOTAL POWER SERIES

Nissan Shield

Season	Winners	Runners-up	Margin of victory
1991/92	Orange Free State	Eastern Province	6 wickets

Total Power Series

Season	Winners	Runners-up	Margin of victory
1992/93	Orange Free State	Eastern Province	6 wickets

Matches in the above competitions were contested over 55 overs per side.

BENSON & HEDGES SERIES

Season	Winners	Runners-up	Margin of victory
1991/92	Eastern Province	Western Province	6 wickets
1992/93	Transvaal	Natal	1 run

CSA COMPETITION WINNERS

1993/94	Orange Free State	Natal	7 wickets
1994/95	Orange Free State	Eastern Province	113 runs
1995/96	Free State	Transvaal	142 runs

Matches were contested over 45 overs per side except for 1993/94 and 1994/95 when matches were contested over 50 overs per side.

STANDARD BANK LEAGUE

Season	Winners	Runners-up
1996/97	Northerns Transvaal	Western Province
1997/98	Western Province	Northerns
1998/99	Northerns	Gauteng

From 1999/2000, the Standard Bank competition was played as a single tournament.

STANDARD BANK CUP

Season	Winners	Runners-up	Margin of victory
1996/97	Natal	Western Province	2-1 (best of three)
1997/98	Gauteng	Northerns	3 wickets
1998/99	Griqualand West	Border	6 wickets
1999/2000	Boland	Eastern Province	36 runs
2000/01	KwaZulu-Natal	Northerns	3 wickets
2001/02	KwaZulu-Natal	Western Province	28 runs
2002/03	Western Province	Griqualand West	9 wickets
2003/04	Gauteng	Easterns	7 wickets
Standard Bank Cup (Franchise)			
2004/05	Eagles	Titans	7 wickets
2005/06	Eagles	Titans	2 wickets

STANDARD BANK PRO20 (Franchise)

Season	Winners	Runners-up	Margin of victory
2003/04	Eagles	Eastern Cape	7 runs (D/L Method)
2004/05	Titans	Warriors	8 wickets
2005/06	Eagles	Cape Cobras	6 wickets

UCB BOWL

Season	Winners	Season	Winners
1993/94	Orange Free State B	1999/2000	Free State B
1994/95	Natal B	2000/01	Zimbabwe Board XI
1995/96	Western Province B	2001/02	Western Province B
1996/97	Eastern Province B	2002/03	Free State B
1997/98	Northerns B	2003/04	Western Province B
1998/99	Western Province B		

UCB PROVINCIAL SHIELD

Season	Winners	Season	Winners
2004/05	Free State	2005/06	Northerns

UCB ASSOCIATES SHIELD

Season	Winners	Season	Winners
2004/05	KwaZulu-Natal Inland	2005/06	KwaZulu-Natal Inland

OTHER COMPETITIONS

UCB BOWL

Season	Winners	Season	Winners
1999/2000	Western Province B	2002/03	Western Province B
2000/01	Western Province B	2003/04	Western Province B
2001/02	Western Province B		

UCB ASSOCIATES CUP

Season	Winners	Season	Winners
2004/05	KwaZulu-Natal Inland	2005/06	KwaZulu-Natal Inland

Matches in the above competitions were played over three days but did not have first-class status.

PREVIOUS COMPETITION WINNERS

Prior to the formation of the United Cricket Board of South Africa on June 29, 1991, there were various controlling bodies for cricket in South Africa. The following is a list of winners of competitions organised by the bodies, in order of the dates on which they were first organised.

SOUTH AFRICAN CRICKET ASSOCIATION AND SOUTH AFRICAN CRICKET UNION

FIRST-CLASS COMPETITIONS

CURRIE CUP

Season	Winners	Season	Winners
1889/90	Transvaal	1958/59	Transvaal
1890/91	Kimberley	1959/60	Natal
1892/93	Western Province	1960/61	Natal
1893/94	Western Province	1962/63	Natal
1894/95	Transvaal	1963/64	Natal
1896/97	Western Province	1965/66	Natal/Transvaal (tied)
1897/98	Western Province	1966/67	Natal
1902/03	Transvaal	1967/68	Natal
1903/04	Transvaal	1968/69	Transvaal
1904/05	Transvaal	1969/70	Transvaal/Western Province (tied)
1906/07	Transvaal	1970/71	Transvaal
1908/09	Western Province	1971/72	Transvaal
1910/11	Natal	1972/73	Transvaal
1912/13	Natal	1973/74	Natal
1920/21	Western Province	1974/75	Western Province
1921/22	Transvaal/Natal/Western Province (tied)	1975/76	Natal
1923/24	Transvaal	1976/77	Natal
1925/26	Transvaal	1977/78	Western Province
1926/27	Transvaal	1978/79	Transvaal
1929/30	Transvaal	1979/80	Transvaal
1931/32	Western Province	1980/81	Natal
1933/34	Natal	1981/82	Western Province

CSA COMPETITION WINNERS

1934/35	Transvaal
1936/37	Natal
1937/38	Natal/Transvaal (tied)
1946/47	Natal
1947/48	Natal
1950/51	Transvaal
1951/52	Natal
1952/53	Western Province
1954/55	Natal
1955/56	Western Province
1982/83	Transvaal
1983/84	Transvaal
1984/85	Transvaal
1985/86	Western Province
1986/87	Transvaal
1987/88	Transvaal
1988/89	Eastern Province
1989/90	E Province/W Province (tied)
1990/91	Western Province

The Currie Cup was donated by shipping line owner Sir Donald Currie prior to the departure of the first English touring team to South Africa in 1888/89 to be awarded to the team which excelled most against the visitors. It was awarded to the Kimberley XVIII. Following the formation of the South African Cricket Association in April, 1890, it became the trophy awarded to the champion first-class team. Transvaal won the first Currie Cup championship in April, 1890, beating Kimberley in a challenge match. Kimberley won the trophy back the following season. Western Province played in a centralised tournament in Kimberley in 1892/93, with Natal and Eastern Province making their first appearance in the fourth Currie Cup tournament in Cape Town in 1893/94. The tournament was first played at various centres in 1903/04.

TRANSVAAL won the competition outright 24 times and, including ties, 28 times.
NATAL won outright 18 times and, including ties, 21 times.
WESTERN PROVINCE won outright 14 times and, including ties, 17 times.
EASTERN PROVINCE won outright once and, including a tie, twice.
GRIQUALAND WEST (previously Kimberley) won outright once.

CURRIE CUP B SECTION/BOWL

Season	Winners
1951/52	Orange Free State
1952/53	Transvaal
1954/55	Eastern Province
1955/56	Rhodesia
1958/59	Border
1959/60	Eastern Province/Transvaal B (tied)
1962/63	Transvaal B
1963/64	Rhodesia
1965/66	NE Transvaal
1966/67	NE Transvaal
1967/68	Rhodesia
1968/69	Western Province
1969/70	Transvaal B
1970/71	Rhodesia
1971/72	Northern Transvaal
1972/73	Transvaal B
1973/74	Natal B
1974/75	Transvaal B
1975/76	Orange Free State
1976/77	Transvaal B
1977/78	Northern Transvaal
1978/79	Northern Transvaal
1979/80	Natal B
1980/81	Western Province B
1981/82	Boland
1982/83	Western Province B
1983/84	Western Province B
1984/85	Transvaal B
1985/86	Boland
1986/87	Transvaal B
1987/88	Boland
1988/89	Border
1989/90	Border/W Province B (shared)
1990/91	Border/W Province B (shared)

From 1977/78-1979/80 the competition was renamed the Castle Bowl, from 1980/81-1982/83 the SAB Bowl, from 1983/84-1987/88 the Castle Bowl and 1988/89-1990/91 the Bowl.

PRESIDENT'S COMPETITION

(For 2nd XI's of major provinces)

Season	Winners
1978/79	Transvaal B

CSA COMPETITION WINNERS

LIMITED OVERS COMPETITIONS

GILLETTE CUP/DATSUN SHIELD/NISSAN SHIELD

Season	Winners	Runners-up	Margin of victory
Gillette Cup			
1969/70	Western Province	Natal	2 runs
1970/71	Western Province	Transvaal	3 wickets
1971/72	Eastern Province	Natal	31 runs
1972/73	Western Province	Eastern Province	7 wickets
1973/74	Transvaal	Natal	10 runs
1974/75	Natal	Western Province	31 runs
1975/76	Eastern Province	Western Province	128 runs
1976/77	Natal	Eastern Province	7 wickets
Datsun Shield			
1977/78	Rhodesia	Eastern Province	runs/wkts ratio
1978/79	Transvaal	Natal	76 runs
1979/80	Transvaal	Western Province	7 wickets
1980/81	Transvaal	Eastern Province	7 wickets
1981/82	Western Province	Natal	2 runs
1982/83	Transvaal	Western Province	109 runs
Nissan Shield			
1983/84	Transvaal	Western Province	89 runs
1984/85	Transvaal	Western Province	9 wickets
1985/86	Transvaal	Western Province	7 wickets
1986/87	Natal	Transvaal	faster scoring rate
1987/88	Eastern Province	Northern Transvaal	7 wickets
1988/89	Western Province	Transvaal	2-0 (best of three)
1989/90	Eastern Province	Northern Transvaal	2-0 (best of three)
1990/91	Transvaal	Eastern Province	7 wickets

Matches in the above competitions were contested over 60 overs per side from 1969/70 to 1980/81 and 55 overs per side from 1981/82 to 1990/91, except for 1986/87 when matches were contested over 50 overs per side.

BENSON & HEDGES SERIES

Season	Winners	Runners-up	Margin of victory
1981/82	Transvaal	Natal	3 wickets
1982/83	Transvaal	Western Province	6 wickets
1983/84	Natal	Eastern Province	7 wickets
1984/85	Transvaal	Northern Transvaal	7 wickets
1985/86	Western Province	Northern Transvaal	12 runs
1986/87	Western Province	Transvaal	41 runs
1987/88	Western Province	Transvaal	5 wickets
1988/89	Orange Free State	Western Province	61 runs
1989/90	Eastern Province	Natal	1 wicket
1990/91	Western Province	Natal	6 wickets

Matches were contested over 45 overs per side except for 1981/82 when matches were contested over 50 overs per side.

SOUTH AFRICAN COLOURED CRICKET BOARD AND SOUTH AFRICAN MALAY CRICKET BOARD

BARNATO TROPHY

Season	Winners	Season	Winners
1904	Western Province	1932	Western Province
1908	Western Province	1945/46	Western Province
1910	Griqualand West	1947/48	Transvaal
1912/13	Western Province	1949/50	Transvaal
1922/23	Western Province	1951/52	Western Province
1924/25	Western Province	1954/55	Western Province
1927/28	Western Province	1957/58	Western Province
1929/30	Western Province	1959/60	Eastern Province

The above tournament was administered initially by the SA Coloured Cricket Board and eventually by the SA Malay Cricket Board. This was an open tournament not restricted by race but latterly played for predominantly by Malays. No tournaments were held between 1933 and 1944 because this pioneering cricket organisation lay dormant, mainly because of the emergence of racial splinter groups - SA Coloureds (1926), SA Bantus (1932) and SA Indians (1940).

SOUTH AFRICAN COLOURED CRICKET ASSOCIATION

SIR DAVID HARRIS TROPHY

Season	Winners	Season	Winners
1926/27	Natal	1948/49	Western Province
1928/29	Western Province	1950/51	Western Province/Transvaal (shared)
1930/31	Eastern Province	1952/53	Eastern Province
1933/34	Griqualand West	1954/55	Western Province
1937/38	Western Province	1956/57	Western Province
1946/47	WP/EP/GW (triple tie)	1957/58	Western Province

The SA Coloured Cricket Association was formed by cricketers who broke away from the Barnato group in 1926. Until 1948 it was known as the SA Independent Coloured Cricket Board.

SOUTH AFRICAN BANTU CRICKET BOARD

NRC TROPHY

Season	Winners	Season	Winners
1933/34	Transvaal	1947/48	Western Province
1934/35	Transvaal	1950/51	Transvaal
1935/36	Border	1952/53	Western Province
1936/37	Border	1954/55	Western Province
1938/39	Transvaal	1956/57	Eastern Province
1940/41	Transvaal	1958/59	Eastern Province
1946/47	Transvaal		

SOUTH AFRICAN INDIAN CRICKET UNION

CHRISTOPHER TROPHY

Season	Winners	Season	Winners
1940/41	Natal	1950/51	Natal
1941/42	Natal	1952/53	Transvaal
1944/45	Natal	1954/55	Transvaal
1946/47	Transvaal	1957/58	Transvaal/Natal (shared)
1948/49	Transvaal		

After 1958 the tournaments were organised on a nonracial basis.

SOUTH AFRICAN CRICKET BOARD OF CONTROL AND SOUTH AFRICAN CRICKET BOARD

Note: SACB succeeded SACBOC on 13 November 1977.

FIRST-CLASS COMPETITIONS

DADABHAY TROPHY

Season	Winners
1971/72-1972/73	Western Province and Natal (shared) (three-day matches, home-and-away round robin played over two seasons)
1973/74	Western Province (three-day matches, home-and-away round robin played in one season)
1974/75	Transvaal

SFW TROPHY

Season	Winners	Season	Winners
1975/76	Western Province	1976/77	No competition

HOWA BOWL

Season	Winners	Season	Winners
1977/78	Western Province	1984/85	Eastern Province
1978/79	Eastern Province	1985/86	Eastern Province
1979/80	Western Province	1986/87	Western Province
1980/81	Western Province	1987/88	Western Province
1981/82	Western Province	1988/89	Western Province
1982/83	Western Province	1989/90	Western Province
1983/84	Western Province	1990/91	Western Province

LIMITED OVERS COMPETITIONS

SFW TROPHY

Season	Winners	Season	Winners
1973/74	Western Province	1974/75	Natal

CSA COMPETITION WINNERS

BENSON & HEDGES TROPHY

Season	Winners
1982/83	Western Province
1983/84	Western Province/Eastern Province (shared)
1984/85	Western Province

OTHER COMPETITIONS

DADABHAY TROPHY

Season	Venue	Winners
1950/51	Johannesburg	SA Indian Cricket Union
1952/53	Johannesburg	SA Coloured Cricket Association
1954/55	Johannesburg	SA Indian Cricket Union
1957/58	Cape Town	SA Coloured Cricket Association

The above tournaments were centralised with two-day matches being played and organised by SACBOC on an ethnic basis.

Season	Venue	Winners
1961/62	Johannesburg	Transvaal
1963/64	Port Elizabeth	Western Province
1965/66	Durban	Western Province
1967/68	Cape Town	Western Province
1969/70	Kimberley	Western Province/Transvaal (shared)

The above tournaments were centralised with two-day matches being played on an inter-provincial nonracial basis. Thereafter matches were decentralised.

Season	Winners
1970/71	Western Province and Transvaal (shared)

The above competition was contested over a single round of two-day matches.

FEATURES OF THE SEASON 2005/06

HIGHEST TOTALS

593-8*	New Zealand v South Africa	Cape Town
586-9*	Titans v Warriors	East London
543-6*	Eagles v Warriors	Bloemfontein
512-7*	Dolphins v Warriors	East London
512	South Africa v New Zealand	Cape Town
494-7*	Eagles v Cape Cobras	Bloemfontein
478-8*	Free State v Gauteng	Bloemfontein
476	Gauteng v North West	Potchefstroom
474	Lions v Warriors	East London
470	Dolphins v Titans	Durban

LOWEST TOTALS

70	Easterns v Griqualand West	Benoni
74	Boland v Western Province	Cape Town
77	Zimbabwe Under-23 v Western Province	Cape Town
81	Boland v Eastern Province	Paarl
85	Gauteng v Easterns	Johannesburg-OP
91	Eastern Province v Boland	Paarl
93	Griqualand West v Free State	Bloemfontein
93	Lions v Eagles	Bloemfontein
97	Warriors v Cape Cobras	Stellenbosch
100	Warriors v Cape Cobras	Port Elizabeth

BATTING

LEADING FIRST-CLASS AVERAGES

		M	Inns	NO	Runs	HS	Avg	SR	100	50
1	JG Myburgh (Nor)	8	16	6	808	128 *	80.80	52.43	1	7
2	G Dros (Nor)	5	9	1	565	136	70.62	84.96	2	4
3	DM Benkenstein (Dol)	10	15	5	652	151	65.20	57.19	3	1
4	M Bekker (KZN)	8	9	1	505	138	63.12	82.92	2	3
5	HM Amla (Dol/SA)	13	22	3	1126	153	59.26	58.13	3	7
6	F du Plessis (Ttn/Nor)	6	11	3	463	156	57.87	65.30	1	3
7	JL Ontong (Lio/Rest)	9	17	2	864	144 *	57.60	59.05	2	7
8	MN van Wyk (Eag)	10	17	3	786	200 *	56.14	52.15	3	1
9	PJ Koortzen (FS)	7	12	1	580	107 *	52.72	59.97	1	3
10	J Booysen (Eas)	8	13	1	602	134 *	50.16	80.48	1	4
11	ND McKenzie (Lio/Rest)	10	19	2	837	161 *	49.23	44.90	3	2
12	AM Amla (Dol)	8	13	2	531	125	48.27	54.57	1	4
13	CFK van Wyk (Ttn/Nor)	9	12	3	427	104	47.44	52.26	1	4
14	LL Gamiet (War/Bdr)	6	11	1	467	105	46.70	44.99	1	2
15	J-P Duminy (Cob/Rest)	11	20	3	782	128	46.00	48.63	2	4
16	Z de Bruyn (Ttn/Eas)	12	18	2	733	175	45.81	46.10	2	3
17	A Jacobs (War)	9	18	2	726	149	45.37	51.52	1	4
18	JA Rudolph (Eag/SA)	10	18	0	808	141	44.888	57.06	3	4
19	DJ Watson (Dol)	11	20	3	763	103	44.882	45.25	2	5
20	L Klusener (Dol)	10	13	3	428	102	42.80	80.60	2	0

(Qualification: 8 completed innings)

FEATURES OF THE SEASON 2005/06

LEADING RUN-SCORERS

1	HM Amla (Dol/SA)	1126
2	HG Kuhn (Ttn/Nor)	949
3	JL Ontong (Lio/Rest)	864
4	BL Bennett (War/Bdr)	861
5	ND McKenzie (Lio/Rest)	837
6	JG Myburgh (Nor)	808
	JA Rudolph (Eag/SA)	808
8	MN van Wyk (Eag)	786
9	J-P Duminy (Cob/Rest)	782
10	BC de Wett (War/Bdr)	769

HIGHEST INDIVIDUAL INNINGS

SP Fleming	262	New Zealand v South Africa	Cape Town
MN van Wyk	200*	Eagles v Warriors	Bloemfontein
BC de Wett	182	Border v Boland	Paarl
Z de Bruyn	175	Titans v Warriors	East London
CA Ingram	169	Eastern Province v Western Province	Port Elizabeth
D Wiese	168	Easterns v Free State	Bloemfontein
ND McKenzie	161*	Lions v Dolphins	Durban
MN van Wyk	158	Eagles v Lions	Potchefstroom
H Davids	158	Boland v Eastern Province	Port Elizabeth
CA Thyssen	157	Free State v Gauteng	Bloemfontein

CENTURY IN EACH INNINGS

W Wyngaard	132* & 101*	Western Province v Border	Cape Town
RT Ponting	103 & 116	Australia v South Africa	Durban

CENTURY ON FIRST-CLASS DEBUT

M Bekker	115	KwaZulu-Natal v Zimbabwe Under-23	Chatsworth
DM van Wyk	122*	Gauteng v Northerns	Pretoria

CENTURY ON FIRST-CLASS DEBUT IN SOUTH AFRICA

(Having previously played first-class cricket elsewhere)

BB McCullum	101	New Zealanders v Rest of South Africa	Benoni

CARRYING BAT THROUGH A COMPLETED INNINGS

AJ Seymore	135* (241)	Easterns v Northerns	Benoni
DJ Kgamadi	53* (145)	North West v Northerns	Potchefstroom

CENTURY BEFORE LUNCH

AJA Gray	102* (Day 1)	Western Province v Boland	Cape Town

WICKET PARTNERSHIPS OF 200 OR MORE

Runs	Wkt			
307	2nd	BL Bennett (122) and BC de Wett (182)	Border v Boland	Paarl
292	6th	MN van Wyk (200*) and R McLaren (140)	Eagles v Warriors	Bloemfontein
272	2nd	CA Ingram (169) and U Abrahams (100*)	Eastern Prov v Western Prov	Port Elizabeth
265	4th	N van Woerkom (146) and G Dros (136)	Northerns v Gauteng	Pretoria
256	8th	SP Fleming (262) and JEC Franklin (122*)	New Zealand v South Africa	Cape Town

252	1st	HG Kuhn (111) and F du Plessis (156)	Northerns v Gauteng	Johannesburg-WM
252	4th	ND McKenzie (141) and J-P Duminy (127)	Rest of SA v New Zealanders	Benoni
234	3rd	Z Homani (118) and W Wyngaard (132*)	Western Province v Border	Cape Town
211	3rd	DJ Watson (91*) and AM Amla (125)	Dolphins v Lions	Johannesburg
206	7th	M Bekker (138) and ZA Abrahim (103*)	KwaZulu-Natal v Boland	Chatsworth
206	3rd	B Hector (154) and DJ van Wyk (106)	Free State v Easterns	Benoni
205	3rd	HM Amla (137) and AM Amla (98)	Dolphins v Cape Cobras	Paarl
201	2nd	R Gobind (60) and HM Amla (153)	Dolphins v Cape Cobras	Durban
201	2nd	ML Hayden (102) and RT Ponting (116)	Australia v South Africa	Durban

OTHER NOTABLE PARTNERSHIPS

(Over 150 for 7th or 8th wicket, over 100 for 9th or 10th wicket)

183	7th	JDP Oram (133) and DL Vettori (81)	New Zealand v South Africa	Centurion
160	9th	R Telemachus (116) and TS Motsamai (51*)	Free State v Griqualand West	Kimberley
157	7th	JC Kent (94) and RP Symcox (87)	Dolphins v Lions	Durban
141*	9th	GE von Hoesslin (101*) and DL Brown (77*)	Border v Boland	East London
128	10th	MT Masinga (48*) and PG Thompson (66)	Gauteng v Easterns	Johannesburg-OP

CENTURIES

There were 124 first-class centuries scored during the season:

U Abrahams		100*	Eastern Province v Western Province	Port Elizabeth
ZA Abrahim		103*	KwaZulu-Natal v Boland	Chatsworth
M Akoojee	(2)	105*	North West v Griqualand West	Potchefstroom
		103	North West v Free State	Potchefstroom
WA Albertyn		101*	Boland v Eastern Province	Port Elizabeth
AM Amla		125	Dolphins v Lions	Johannesburg
HM Amla	(3)	137	Dolphins v Cape Cobras	Paarl
		153	Dolphins v Cape Cobras	Durban
		149	South Africa v New Zealand	Cape Town
DJ Bassage	(2)	108*	Western Province v Eastern Province	Port Elizabeth
		100	Cape Cobras v Eagles	Stellenbosch
M Bekker	(2)	115	KwaZulu-Natal v Zimbabwe Under-23	Chatsworth
		138	KwaZulu-Natal v Boland	Chatsworth
DM Benkenstein	(3)	117*	Dolphins v Eagles	Bloemfontein
		103	Dolphins v Eagles	Durban
		151	Dolphins v Titans	Durban
BL Bennett	(3)	126	Border v KwaZulu-Natal	East London
		150	Border v Western Province	Cape Town
		122	Border v Boland	Paarl
JA Beukes		130	Free State v Northerns	Bloemfontein-UFS
GH Bodi	(2)	143	Easterns v Gauteng	Johannesburg-OP
		140	Titans v Warriors	Benoni
J Booysen		134*	Easterns v Free State	Benoni
CC Bradfield		119	Warriors v Cape Cobras	Port Elizabeth
WL Coetsee		108*	North West v Griqualand West	Potchefstroom
SC Cook		100	Gauteng v Free State	Bloemfontein
H Davids		158	Boland v Eastern Province	Port Elizabeth
P de Bruyn		125*	Titans v Eagles	Benoni
Z de Bruyn	(2)	175	Titans v Warriors	East London
		107	Easterns v Gauteng	Benoni
C de Grandhomme		109	Zimbabwe Under-23 v Eastern Province	Port Elizabeth-GS

BC de Wett	(2)	182	Border v Boland	Paarl
		109	Warriors v Lions	East London
G Dros	(2)	136	Northerns v Gauteng	Pretoria
		130	Northerns v Griqualand West	Pretoria
F du Plessis		156	Northerns v Gauteng	Johannesburg-WM
WA Dugmore		138	Gauteng v North West	Johannesburg
J-P Duminy	(2)	128	Cape Cobras v Eagles	Bloemfontein
		127	Rest of South Africa v New Zealanders	Benoni
SP Fleming	(2)	118	New Zealanders v Rest of South Africa	Benoni
		262	New Zealand v South Africa	Cape Town
JEC Franklin		122*	New Zealand v South Africa	Cape Town
R Frylinck		100*	KwaZulu-Natal v Zimbabwe Under-23	Chatsworth
DR Gain		100	Gauteng v Free State	Johannesburg
LL Gamiet		105	Border v KwaZulu-Natal	Durban
HH Gibbs	(2)	133	Cape Cobras v Titans	Cape Town
		149	Cape Cobras v Lions	Johannesburg
R Gobind		112	KwaZulu-Natal v Border	East London
AJA Gray	(2)	112*	Western Province v Boland	Paarl
		108	Western Province v Boland	Cape Town
MJ Harris	(2)	135*	Lions v Eagles	Potchefstroom
		100	Lions v Warriors	Johannesburg
ML Hayden		102	Australia v South Africa	Durban
B Hector	(2)	102	Eagles v Cape Cobras	Bloemfontein
		154	Free State v Easterns	Benoni
Z Homani		118	Western Province v Border	Cape Town
CA Ingram		169	Eastern Province v Western Province	Port Elizabeth
A Jacobs		149	Warriors v Dolphins	East London
DJ Jacobs	(3)	128	Eagles v Titans	Benoni
		100	Eagles v Dolphins	Bloemfontein
		113*	Eagles v Lions	Bloemfontein
JH Kallis		114	South Africa v Australia	Durban
I Khan		118	Dolphins v Eagles	Bloemfontein
RK Kleinveldt		115*	Western Province v KwaZulu-Natal	Chatsworth
L Klusener	(2)	102	Dolphins v Warriors	Durban
		100*	Dolphins v Warriors	East London
PJ Koortzen		107*	Free State v North West	Bloemfontein
AK Kruger		103	Griqualand West v Free State	Kimberley
HG Kuhn	(2)	133*	Northerns v Easterns	Pretoria-TO
		111	Northerns v Gauteng	Johannesburg-WM
J le Roux	(2)	109	North West v Easterns	Potchefstroom
		110	North West v Free State	Potchefstroom
DR Martyn		101	Australia v South Africa	Johannesburg
BB McCullum		101	New Zealanders v Rest of South Africa	Benoni
ND McKenzie	(3)	161*	Lions v Dolphins	Durban
		109	Lions v Titans	Potchefstroom
		141	Rest of South Africa v New Zealanders	Benoni
AP McLaren	(2)	131	Griqualand West v Gauteng	Kimberley
		119	Griqualand West v Northerns	Pretoria
R McLaren		140	Eagles v Warriors	Bloemfontein
WB Motaung	(2)	101	Gauteng v Free State	Johannesburg
		114	Gauteng v North West	Potchefstroom
JG Myburgh		128*	Northerns v Free State	Bloemfontein-UFS

JL Ontong	(2)	102	Lions v Eagles	Bloemfontein
		144*	Rest of South Africa v New Zealanders	Benoni
JDP Oram		133	New Zealand v South Africa	Centurion
AN Petersen		140	Titans v Warriors	East London
RT Ponting	(2)	103	Australia v South Africa	Durban
	&	116	Australia v South Africa	Durban
SC Pope	(2)	102	Border v Eastern Province	East London
		101	Warriors v Lions	East London
AG Prince		108*	South Africa v New Zealand	Cape Town
JA Rudolph	(3)	133	Eagles v Warriors	Port Elizabeth
		103	Eagles v Cape Cobras	Bloemfontein
		141	Eagles v Lions	Bloemfontein
MD Sanders		103	KwaZulu-Natal v Border	Durban
AJ Seymore	(2)	135*	Easterns v Northerns	Benoni
		133	Easterns v North West	Benoni
K Smit		144	Dolphins v Warriors	East London
BD Snijman		114	Gauteng v Easterns	Benoni
FA Steyn	(2)	105	North West v Northerns	Centurion
		116	North West v Easterns	Potchefstroom
JG Strydom		123	Boland v Zimbabwe Under-23	Stellenbosch
J Symes		133	Gauteng v North West	Potchefstroom
R Telemachus		116	Free State v Griqualand West	Kimberley
CA Thyssen		157	Free State v Gauteng	Bloemfontein
M van Jaarsveld		145	Titans v Eagles	Bloemfontein
VB van Jaarsveld	(3)	105	Lions v Dolphins	Durban
		126	Lions v Warriors	East London
		125	Lions v Dolphins	Johannesburg
N van Woerkom		146	Northerns v Gauteng	Pretoria
CFK van Wyk		104	Northerns v Western Province	Cape Town
DJ van Wyk		106	Free State v Easterns	Benoni
DM van Wyk		122*	Gauteng v Northerns	Pretoria
MN van Wyk	(3)	158	Eagles v Lions	Potchefstroom
		110*	Eagles v Cape Cobras	Bloemfontein
		200*	Eagles v Warriors	Bloemfontein
GE von Hoesslin		101*	Border v Boland	East London
DJ Watson	(2)	100	Dolphins v Titans	Centurion
		103	Dolphins v Titans	Durban
D Wiese		168	Easterns v Free State	Bloemfontein
W Wyngaard	(3)	132*	Western Province v Border	Cape Town
	&	101*	Western Province v Border	Cape Town
		104*	Western Province v Boland	Cape Town

BOWLING

LEADING FIRST-CLASS AVERAGES

		M	Overs	Mdns	Runs	Wkts	Avg	RpO	BB	5I	10M
1	P Joubert (Nor)	11	266.5	88	554	47	11.78	2.07	7-32	2	0
2	SR Clark (Aus)	3	118	32	317	20	15.85	2.68	5-55	1	0
3	M de Stadler (WP)	10	353	115	841	47	17.89	2.38	5-42	1	0
4	F de Wet (Lio/NW)	8	264.2	58	776	42	18.47	2.93	7-61	3	1
5	WC Hantam (WP)	6	120	27	396	21	18.85	3.30	6-39	1	0
6	Q Friend (WP)	7	132.4	30	418	21	19.90	3.15	7-31	1	0

7	RK Kleinveldt (Cob/WP/Rest)	9	262.1	69	761	38	20.02	2.90	8-47	2	1
8	R Pietersen (GW)	7	136.1	24	493	24	20.54	3.62	6-73	1	0
9	DW Steyn (Ttn/Nor/SA)	13	461.1	95	1425	69	20.65	3.09	5-27	4	1
10	S Mhlongo (Dol/KZN)	12	257	69	774	37	20.91	3.01	5-25	1	0
11	CM Willoughby (Cob)	9	333.4	91	861	41	21.00	2.58	6-41	4	0
12	M Ntini (SA)	6	231.5	40	836	39	21.43	3.60	6-100	4	2
13	U Govender (Dol/KZN)	12	323.5	66	1008	47	21.44	3.11	6-59	2	0
14	PSE Sandri (Bol)	6	148.2	34	480	22	21.81	3.23	5-32	1	0
15	PL Harris (Ttn/Nor)	13	407.5	112	1108	50	22.16	2.71	6-54	4	0
16	N Boje (Eag/SA)	11	406.5	101	1052	47	22.38	2.58	8-93	4	1
17	RR Richards (War/Bdr)	7	187.2	50	562	24	23.41	3.00	5-30	2	0
18	FS Holtzhausen (NW)	8	209.2	40	612	26	23.53	2.92	5-25	1	0
19	A Nawab (Gau)	5	119.3	13	498	21	23.71	4.16	6-106	2	1
20	S Mjekula (War/EP)	9	182	37	594	25	23.76	3.26	5-46	1	0

(Qualification: 20 wickets)

LEADING WICKET-TAKERS

1	DW Steyn (Ttn/Nor/SA)	69
2	PL Harris (Ttn/Nor)	50
3	P Joubert (Nor)	47
	M de Stadler (WP)	47
	U Govender (Dol/KZN)	47
	N Boje (Eag/SA)	47
7	GJ-P Kruger (Lio/Rest)	45
8	F de Wet (Lio/NW)	42
9	CM Willoughby (Cob)	41
10	M Ntini (SA)	39

BEST BOWLING IN AN INNINGS

RK Kleinveldt	8-47	Cape Cobras v Warriors	Stellenbosch
N Boje	8-93	Eagles v Dolphins	Durban
N Boje	8-102	Eagles v Cape Cobras	Bloemfontein
GJ-P Kruger	8-112	Lions v Dolphins	Durban
Q Friend	7-31	Western Province v KwaZulu-Natal	Chatsworth
P Joubert	7-32	Northerns v Gauteng	Pretoria-LCD
GJ-P Kruger	7-44	Lions v Warriors	Johannesburg
AC Thomas	7-54	Titans v Cape Cobras	Cape Town
F de Wet	7-61	Lions v Cape Cobras	Cape Town
N Boje	7-75	Eagles v Titans	Bloemfontein

TEN WICKETS IN A MATCH

N Boje	12-152	Eagles v Cape Cobras	Bloemfontein
AK Kruger	11-66	Griqualand West v Easterns	Benoni
GJ-P Kruger	11-90	Lions v Warriors	Johannesburg
F de Wet	11-152	Lions v Cape Cobras	Cape Town
A Nawab	11-172	Gauteng v Northerns	Johannesburg-WM
DW Steyn	10-71	Titans v Warriors	Benoni
RK Kleinveldt	10-80	Cape Cobras v Warriors	Stellenbosch
AC Dawson	10-99	Cape Cobras v Lions	Johannesburg
M Ntini	10-145	South Africa v New Zealand	Centurion
AC Thomas	10-161	Titans v Cape Cobras	Cape Town
S Conrad	10-175	Western Province v Border	Cape Town
M Ntini	10-178	South Africa v Australia	Johannesburg

FEATURES OF THE SEASON 2005/06

HAT-TRICKS

GJ-P Kruger	Lions v Warriors	Johannesburg
M de Stadler	Western Province v Boland	Cape Town
CM Willoughby	Cape Cobras v Dolphins	Durban (a)
JP Kreusch	Warriors v Cape Cobras	Stellenbosch (b)

(a) Also took 4 wickets in 4 balls
(b) Also took 4 wickets in 5 balls

FIVE WICKETS IN AN INNINGS

There were 98 cases of 5 wickets in an innings in first-class cricket during the season:

AP Abrahams		6-36	Free State v Easterns	Bloemfontein
R Almeida		5-18	Easterns v Gauteng	Johannesburg-OP
MA Aronstam		5-82	Northerns v Western Province	Cape Town
NO Arthur		6-27	Griqualand West v Free State	Bloemfontein
BL Bennett		5-21	Border v Boland	Paarl
N Boje	(4)	8-102	Eagles v Cape Cobras	Bloemfontein
		7-75	Eagles v Titans	Bloemfontein
		8-93	Eagles v Dolphins	Durban
		5-23	Eagles v Lions	Bloemfontein
S Chatterjee		5-81	Gauteng v Griqualand West	Kimberley
SR Clark		5-55	Australia v South Africa	Cape Town
J Coetzee	(2)	5-92	Griqualand West v North West	Kimberley
		5-33	Eagles v Warriors	Bloemfontein
S Conrad	(3)	5-64	Western Province v Border	Cape Town
	&	5-111	Western Province v Border	Cape Town
		6-45	Western Province v Eastern Province	Port Elizabeth
AC Dawson		6-39	Cape Cobras v Lions	Johannesburg
GJ de Bruin	(2)	5-47	Gauteng v Easterns	Johannesburg-OP
		5-55	Gauteng v Easterns	Benoni
Z de Bruyn		5-28	Titans v Cape Cobras	Benoni
M de Stadler		5-42	Western Province v Boland	Cape Town
F de Wet	(3)	5-35	Lions v Titans	Benoni
		5-80	Lions v Dolphins	Johannesburg
		7-61	Lions v Cape Cobras	Cape Town
BC de Wett		7-95	Border v KwaZulu-Natal	Durban
D du Preez		5-33	Free State v Griqualand West	Kimberley
Q Friend		7-31	Western Province v KwaZulu-Natal	Chatsworth
R Frylinck		6-94	KwaZulu-Natal v Western Province	Chatsworth
U Govender	(2)	5-57	Dolphins v Cape Cobras	Paarl
		6-59	Dolphins v Titans	Centurion
AJ Hall		5-39	Lions v Eagles	Potchefstroom
WC Hantam		6-39	Western Province v Zimbabwe Under-23	Cape Town
PL Harris	(4)	5-32	Titans v Dolphins	Durban
		6-79	Titans v Eagles	Bloemfontein
		5-61	Titans v Lions	Potchefstroom
		6-54	Titans v Cape Cobras	Benoni
T Henderson		6-80	Warriors v Titans	Benoni
IC Hlengane		7-107	Easterns v Griqualand West	Kimberley
FS Holtzhausen		5-25	North West v Gauteng	Johannesburg
F Jardine		5-118	Western Province v Border	East London
P Joubert	(2)	6-39	Northerns v North West	Centurion
		7-32	Northerns v Gauteng	Pretoria

FEATURES OF THE SEASON 2005/06

JM Kemp		5-41	Titans v Dolphins	Centurion
RK Kleinveldt	(2)	6-57	Western Province v Eastern Province	Cape Town
		8-47	Cape Cobras v Warriors	Stellenbosch
L Klusener	(2)	5-73	Dolphins v Titans	Durban
		5-39	Dolphins v Warriors	East London
JP Kreusch		5-31	Warriors v Cape Cobras	Stellenbosch
AK Kruger	(3)	6-37	Griqualand West v Free State	Kimberley
		5-20	Griqualand West v Easterns	Benoni
	&	6-46	Griqualand West v Easterns	Benoni
GJ-P Kruger	(4)	8-112	Lions v Dolphins	Durban
		5-114	Lions v Eagles	Potchefstroom
		7-44	Lions v Warriors	Johannesburg
		5-118	Lions v Titans	Potchefstroom
B Lee		5-69	Australia v South Africa	Durban
JMM Malao		5-27	Free State v Griqualand West	Bloemfontein
CS Martin		5-37	New Zealand v South Africa	Johannesburg
MA Mashimbyi		5-32	Titans v Lions	Benoni
L Mbane		5-26	Border v Zimbabwe Under-23	East London
NE Mbhalati		5-26	Titans v Dolphins	Durban
R McLaren		6-96	Eagles v Dolphins	Bloemfontein
L Meyer		5-38	Eastern Province v Western Province	Cape Town
S Mhlongo		5-25	KwaZulu-Natal v Western Province	Cape Town
S Mjekula		5-46	Eastern Province v Zimbabwe Under-23	Port Elizabeth-GS
PV Mpitsang		5-35	Eagles v Warriors	Bloemfontein
A Mwayenga	(2)	5-41	Zimbabwe Under-23 v KwaZulu-Natal	Chatsworth
		5-67	Zimbabwe Under-23 v Boland	Stellenbosch
A Nawab	(2)	6-106	Gauteng v Northerns	Johannesburg-WM
	&	5-66	Gauteng v Northerns	Johannesburg-WM
M Ntini	(4)	6-100	South Africa v Australia	Johannesburg
		5-94	South Africa v New Zealand	Centurion
	&	5-51	South Africa v New Zealand	Centurion
		5-35	South Africa v New Zealand	Johannesburg
HH Paulse		5-65	Boland v Western Province	Paarl
AM Phangiso		5-76	Northerns v Gauteng	Johannesburg-WM
VD Philander		5-49	Cape Cobras v Titans	Cape Town
R Pietersen		6-73	Griqualand West v Easterns	Kimberley
TD Pillay		5-45	KwaZulu-Natal v Zimbabwe Under-23	Chatsworth
MN Ranger		6-30	Border v Boland	East London
RR Richards	(2)	5-30	Border v Eastern Province	Port Elizabeth
		5-53	Border v KwaZulu-Natal	East London
PSE Sandri		5-32	Boland v Eastern Province	Paarl
AJ Schultz		5-51	Free State v Gauteng	Bloemfontein
DW Steyn	(4)	5-44	Titans v Warriors	Benoni
	&	5-27	Titans v Warriors	Benoni
		5-124	Titans v Dolphins	Durban
		5-47	South Africa v New Zealand	Centurion
R Telemachus		6-85	Eagles v Warriors	Port Elizabeth
J Theron		6-47	Eastern Province v Boland	Paarl
AC Thomas		7-54	Titans v Cape Cobras	Cape Town
JJ van der Wath		5-126	Eagles v Titans	Benoni
SK Warne		6-86	Australia v South Africa	Durban

CM Willoughby	(4)	5-36	Cape Cobras v Warriors	Port Elizabeth
		6-41	Cape Cobras v Dolphins	Durban
		5-42	Cape Cobras v Eagles	Stellenbosch
		5-51	Cape Cobras v Lions	Cape Town
M Zondeki		5-67	Cape Cobras v Lions	Cape Town

ALL-ROUNDERS

CENTURY AND FIVE WICKETS IN AN INNINGS

AK Kruger	103 & 5, 1-34 & 6-37	Griqualand West v Free State	Kimberley
BL Bennett	122 & 35, 1-39 & 5-21	Border v Boland	Paarl
L Klusener	100*, 0-75 & 5-39	Dolphins v Warriors	East London

400 RUNS AND 20 WICKETS IN THE SEASON

	M	Runs	Avg	Wkts	Avg
WL Coetsee (Lio/NW)	13	581	34.17	36	34.72
L Klusener (Dol)	10	428	42.80	34	31.11
AK Kruger (Eag/GW)	10	488	28.70	27	32.48
R McLaren (Eag)	10	441	33.92	28	30.39
D Wiese (Eas)	9	526	37.57	26	28.15

WICKETKEEPING AND FIELDING

LEADING WICKETKEEPERS

		M	Ct	St	Total
1	HG Kuhn (Ttn/Nor)	14	50	2	52 *
2	MJ Harris (Lio)	10	42	0	42
3	TL Tsolekile (Cob/Rest)	11	36	1	37
4	RCC Canning (WP)	10	30	1	31
	C Linde (FS)	10	24	7	31

* includes 1 catch taken in the field.

MOST DISMISSALS IN AN INNINGS

DR Miller	6 (ct 4, st 2)	KwaZulu-Natal v Border	East London
MJ Harris	6 (ct 6)	Lions v Titans	Potchefstroom
HG Kuhn	5 (ct 5)	Northerns v Easterns	Benoni
HG Kuhn	5 (ct 5)	Northerns v North West	Centurion
AB de Villiers	5 (ct 5)	Titans v Eagles	Benoni
A Maregwede	5 (ct 5)	Zimbabwe Under-23 v KwaZulu-Natal	Chatsworth
MJ Harris	5 (ct 5)	Lions v Eagles	Potchefstroom
TA Bula	5 (ct 5)	North West v Easterns	Potchefstroom
AM Sodumo	5 (ct 5)	Warriors v Eagles	Port Elizabeth
TL Tsolekile	5 (ct 5)	Cape Cobras v Titans	Benoni
MV Boucher	5 (ct 5)	South Africa v Australia	Johannesburg

MOST DISMISSALS IN A MATCH

AB de Villiers	8 (ct 8)	Titans v Eagles	Benoni
W Bossenger	7 (ct 7)	Griqualand West v Free State	Kimberley
A Maregwede	7 (ct 7)	Zimbabwe Under-23 v KwaZulu-Natal	Chatsworth

TA Bula	7 (ct 6, st 1)	North West v Easterns	Potchefstroom
HG Kuhn	7 (ct 7)	Northerns v Griqualand West	Kimberley
TA Bula	7 (ct 7)	North West v Gauteng	Johannesburg
MV Boucher	7 (ct 7)	South Africa v New Zealand	Centurion

LEADING FIELDERS

		M	Ct
1	M van Jaarsveld (Ttn)	11	25
2	VB van Jaarsveld (Lio)	10	15
3	JA Beukes (Eag/FS)	9	14
	DJ Kgamadi (NW)	10	14
	AG Puttick (Cob)	10	14
	AJ Seymore (Ttn/Eas)	12	14
7	AN Petersen (Lio/Ttn/Nor/Rest)	10	13
8	DM Benkenstein (Dol)	10	11
	AB de Villiers (Ttn/SA)	6	11 *
	HH Gibbs (Cob/SA)	7	11
	DJ van Wyk (FS)	7	11

* Also took 8 catches in one match as a wicketkeeper.

MOST CATCHES IN AN INNINGS (FIELDERS)

M van Jaarsveld	4	Titans v Eagles	Benoni
WC Hantam	4	Western Province v Eastern Province	Port Elizabeth
A Jacobs	4	Warriors v Lions	East London

MOST CATCHES IN A MATCH (FIELDERS)

M van Jaarsveld	5	Titans v Eagles	Benoni
TD Pillay	5	KwaZulu-Natal v Western Province	Cape Town

FIRST-CLASS AVERAGES 2005/06

Name	M	Inns	NO	Runs	HS	Avg	100	50	Ct	St	Balls	Runs	Wkts	Avg	RpO	BB	5I	10M
YA Abdullah (KZN)	1	1	0	5	5	5.00	0	0	0	0	118	101	4	25.25	5.13	4-33	0	0
AP Abrahams (FS)	1	2	0	8	7	4.00	0	0	0	0	132	76	6	12.66	3.45	6-36	1	0
S Abrahams (Eas)	1	2	1	26	15	26.00	0	0	0	0	170	93	5	18.60	3.28	4-33	0	0
U Abrahams (EP)	7	12	2	354	100*	35.40	1	2	4	0	0	0	0	-	-	-	0	0
ZA Abrahim (KZN)	5	6	3	147	103*	49.00	1	0	0	0	638	274	16	17.12	2.57	3-17	0	0
HD Ackerman (Cob)	4	7	0	168	61	24.00	0	1	5	0	0	0	0	-	-	-	0	0
SR Adair (EP)	4	6	2	128	44	32.00	0	0	9	2	0	0	0	-	-	-	0	0
BC Adams (Lio/Gau)	9	15	3	272	73	22.66	0	1	2	0	528	293	1	293.00	3.32	1-71	0	0
PR Adams (Cob/WP)	9	13	4	220	47	24.44	0	0	5	0	1142	596	13	45.84	3.13	3-54	0	0
KC Africa (KZN)	6	9	1	100	33	12.50	0	0	3	0	522	278	8	34.75	3.19	4-31	0	0
M Akoojee (NW)	10	17	2	626	105*	41.73	2	2	6	0	284	181	4	45.25	3.82	1-16	0	0
WA Albertyn (Bol)	7	12	2	361	101*	36.10	1	2	4	0	764	318	13	24.46	2.49	4-33	0	0
R Almeida (Eas)	4	7	0	114	44	16.28	0	0	2	0	732	464	15	30.93	3.80	5-18	1	0
AM Amla (Dol)	8	13	2	531	125	48.27	1	4	6	0	108	66	1	66.00	3.66	1-54	0	0
HM Amla (Dol/SA)	13	22	3	1126	153	59.26	3	7	5	0	6	4	0	-	4.00	-	0	0
RG Arendse (Bol)	4	7	0	116	35	16.57	0	0	2	0	0	0	0	-	-	-	0	0
MA Aronstam (Nor)	7	14	0	473	91	33.78	0	4	1	0	1323	686	17	40.35	3.11	5-82	1	0
MC Arthur (GW)	2	4	0	36	20	9.00	0	0	1	0	0	0	0	-	-	-	0	0
NO Arthur (Eag/GW)	10	18	4	179	45	12.78	0	0	5	0	1258	725	25	29.00	3.45	6-27	1	0
NJ Astle (NZ)	3	6	0	135	50	22.50	0	1	0	0	84	46	1	46.00	3.28	1-15	0	0
R Bailey (Bol)	3	6	1	125	60	25.00	0	1	2	0	0	0	0	-	-	-	0	0
RT Bailey (Eag)	10	18	1	375	85	22.05	0	2	9	0	324	194	1	194.00	3.59	1-25	0	0
W Barresi (Eas)	3	6	0	9	5	1.50	0	0	5	0	0	0	0	-	-	-	0	0
DJ Bassage (Cob/WP)	13	24	2	660	108*	30.00	2	2	10	0	54	15	0	-	1.66	-	0	0
C Baxter (EP)	9	16	0	308	67	19.25	0	3	2	0	5	6	0	-	7.20	-	0	0
M Bekker (KZN)	8	9	1	505	138	63.12	2	3	4	0	0	0	0	-	-	-	0	0
WE Bell (EP)	3	6	0	74	27	12.33	0	0	1	0	114	99	4	24.75	5.21	3-57	0	0
DM Benkenstein (Dol)	10	15	5	652	151	65.20	3	1	11	0	1110	467	17	27.47	2.52	4-16	0	0
BL Bennett (War/Bdr)	12	21	0	861	150	41.00	3	2	8	0	494	331	10	33.10	4.02	5-21	1	0
CN Bennett (GW)	5	10	0	266	64	26.60	0	1	3	0	30	22	0	-	4.40	-	0	0
KD Bennett (Bdr)	5	7	1	150	47	25.00	0	0	1	0	121	95	1	95.00	4.71	1-47	0	0

Name	M	Inns	NO	Runs	HS	Avg	100	50	Ct	St	Balls	Runs	Wkts	Avg	RpO	BB	5I	10M
JA Beukes (Eag/FS)	9	17	0	603	130	35.47	1	3	14	0	17	19	2	9.50	6.70	1-8	0	0
AR Beukman (Nor)	1	1	1	3	3*	-	0	0	0	0	129	55	2	27.50	2.55	1-27	0	0
GH Bhayat (Lio/NW)	9	9	2	100	61*	14.28	0	1	6	0	1223	724	21	34.47	3.55	3-42	0	0
R Bhayat (NW)	7	8	1	120	44	17.14	0	0	6	0	336	257	5	51.40	4.58	2-59	0	0
AM Blignaut (Lio)	5	10	0	135	50	13.50	0	1	4	0	541	290	6	48.33	3.21	3-34	0	0
GH Bodi (Ttn/Eas)	11	18	1	705	143	41.47	2	2	6	0	77	59	1	59.00	4.59	1-5	0	0
TM Bodibe (Eas)	9	15	3	193	39*	16.08	0	0	16	3	0	0	0	-	-	-	0	0
N Boje (Eag/SA)	11	18	2	393	62	24.56	0	2	8	0	2441	1052	47	22.38	2.58	8-93	4	1
SE Bond (NZ)	1	0	0	0	-	-	0	0	0	0	60	51	1	51.00	5.10	1-51	0	0
J Booysen (Eas)	8	13	1	602	134*	50.16	1	4	6	0	6	1	0	-	1.00	-	0	0
LL Bosman (Eag/FS)	7	13	1	191	47	15.91	0	0	1	0	0	0	0	-	-	-	0	0
M Bosman (GW)	4	8	0	103	28	12.87	0	0	2	0	0	0	0	-	-	-	0	0
W Bossenger (GW)	9	18	2	509	71	31.81	0	4	22	1	18	26	1	26.00	8.66	1-26	0	0
J Botha (War)	6	12	0	281	93	23.41	0	1	2	0	148	71	4	17.75	2.87	4-71	0	0
MV Boucher (SA)	6	11	1	253	63	25.30	0	2	23	0	0	0	0	-	-	-	0	0
CC Bradfield (War/Bdr)	12	24	2	611	119	27.77	1	5	6	0	0	0	0	-	-	-	0	0
J Brooker (GW)	9	18	0	552	99	30.66	0	5	5	0	0	0	0	-	-	-	0	0
NG Brouwers (EP)	1	2	0	31	30	15.50	0	0	0	0	0	0	0	-	-	-	0	0
DL Brown (Dol)	5	6	0	188	82	31.33	0	1	14	0	0	0	0	-	-	-	0	0
DL Brown (Bdr)	3	3	1	90	77*	45.00	0	1	0	0	299	179	4	44.75	3.59	3-83	0	0
ML Bruyns (War)	4	8	0	177	54	22.12	0	2	3	0	0	0	0	-	-	-	0	0
BW Buckley (Gau)	1	2	0	52	41	26.00	0	0	0	0	0	0	0	-	-	-	0	0
TA Bula (NW)	10	14	2	343	68	28.58	0	3	26	3	0	0	0	-	-	-	0	0
S Burger (Gau)	3	5	0	70	31	14.00	0	0	1	0	508	244	12	20.33	2.88	4-11	0	0
JP Campher (NW)	6	4	2	40	17	20.00	0	0	3	0	725	547	16	34.18	4.52	3-54	0	0
RCC Canning (WP)	10	15	2	473	72	36.38	0	5	30	1	0	0	0	-	-	-	0	0
DD Carolus (EP)	3	5	1	46	16*	11.50	0	0	2	0	426	198	4	49.50	2.78	2-25	0	0
S Chatterjee (Gau)	1	1	1	1	1*	-	0	0	0	0	252	140	6	23.33	3.33	5-81	1	0
AI Chinnappa (KZN)	3	3	0	9	5	3.00	0	0	1	0	60	33	3	11.00	3.30	3-19	0	0
IM Chinyoka (ZimU23)	2	4	1	34	18*	11.33	0	0	1	0	203	122	5	24.40	3.60	2-42	0	0
N Chouhan (Nor)	7	11	1	173	93	17.30	0	1	2	0	0	0	0	-	-	-	0	0
SR Clark (Aus)	3	4	2	31	13*	15.50	0	0	2	0	708	317	20	15.85	2.68	5-55	1	0
WL Coetsee (Lio/NW)	13	22	5	581	108*	34.17	1	2	6	0	2533	1250	36	34.72	2.96	4-95	0	0
J Coetzee (Eag/GW)	10	17	3	383	56*	27.35	0	2	6	0	1529	905	36	25.13	3.55	5-33	2	0
SR Connor (Eas)	1	2	0	41	24	20.50	0	0	0	0	0	0	0	-	-	-	0	0

Name	M	Inns	NO	Runs	HS	Avg	100	50	Ct	St	Balls	Runs	Wkts	Avg	RpO	BB	5I	10M
S Conrad (Cob/WP)	6	7	2	32	11	6.40	0	0	4	0	966	575	24	23.95	3.57	6-45	3	1
SC Cook (Lio/Gau/Rest)	12	24	1	692	100	30.08	1	4	7	0	24	10	0	-	2.50	-	0	0
H Davids (Cob/Bol)	6	10	0	343	158	34.30	1	1	5	0	66	49	0	-	4.45	-	0	0
AC Dawson (Cob)	4	6	2	179	65	44.75	0	2	2	0	748	262	17	15.41	2.10	6-39	1	1
WA Deacon (Eag)	3	6	2	94	34	23.50	0	0	0	0	381	222	3	74.00	3.49	1-30	0	0
GJ de Bruin (Lio/Gau)	8	13	4	111	27	12.33	0	0	2	0	1471	911	36	25.30	3.71	5-47	2	0
P de Bruyn (Ttn/Nor)	8	11	3	337	125*	42.12	1	2	5	0	222	118	5	23.60	3.18	2-8	0	0
Z de Bruyn (Ttn/Eas)	12	18	2	733	175	45.81	2	3	8	0	904	555	17	32.64	3.68	5-28	1	0
C de Grandhomme (ZimU23)	5	10	0	279	109	27.90	1	1	4	0	452	226	5	45.20	3.00	3-26	0	0
CJ de Jager (GW)	4	8	0	185	62	23.12	0	2	0	0	0	0	0	-	-	-	0	0
HG de Kock (Eag/FS)	9	16	2	563	93	40.21	0	5	5	0	237	143	3	47.66	3.62	1-8	0	0
S de Kock (Bdr)	6	8	0	85	31	10.62	0	0	1	0	516	324	7	46.28	3.76	2-56	0	0
CD de Lange (Cob)	5	8	1	141	42	20.14	0	0	4	0	924	361	5	72.20	2.34	1-6	0	0
M de Stadler (WP)	10	11	2	146	37	16.22	0	0	4	0	2118	841	47	17.89	2.38	5-42	1	0
AB de Villiers (Ttn/SA)	7	13	0	374	98	28.76	0	3	19	0	6	12	0	-	12.00	-	0	0
F de Wet (Lio/NW)	8	11	1	85	36	8.50	0	0	2	0	1586	776	42	18.47	2.93	7-61	3	1
BC de Wett (War/Bdr)	11	22	0	769	182	34.95	2	3	4	0	880	586	13	45.07	3.99	7-95	1	0
L Dipha (EP)	1	2	0	14	9	7.00	0	0	0	0	138	74	1	74.00	3.21	1-55	0	0
HH Dippenaar (SA)	4	7	0	204	52	29.14	0	1	4	0	0	0	0	-	-	-	0	0
AG Doherty (GW)	4	8	0	308	92	38.50	0	3	1	0	60	44	0	-	4.40	-	0	0
D Donaldson (GW)	3	6	0	109	42	18.16	0	0	2	0	222	152	3	50.66	4.10	2-64	0	0
G Dros (Nor)	5	9	1	565	136	70.62	2	4	7	0	487	264	8	33.00	3.25	3-41	0	0
WA Dugmore (Gau)	3	6	0	314	138	52.33	1	2	5	0	204	143	0	-	4.20	-	0	0
J-P Duminy (Cob/Rest)	11	20	3	782	128	46.00	2	4	7	0	126	86	1	86.00	4.09	1-70	0	0
F du Plessis (Ttn/Nor)	6	11	3	463	156	57.87	1	3	7	0	366	204	8	25.50	3.34	3-31	0	0
D du Preez (Eag/FS)	6	6	0	50	23	8.33	0	0	1	0	1092	463	18	25.72	2.54	5-33	1	0
AZM Dyili (War/Bdr)	9	15	1	338	65	24.14	0	2	16	2	0	0	0	-	-	-	0	0
D Elgar (FS)	2	4	0	70	32	17.50	0	0	0	0	0	0	0	-	-	-	0	0
T Essack (KZN)	5	7	0	115	51	16.42	0	1	0	0	156	63	3	21.00	2.42	2-19	0	0
GM Ewing (ZimU23)	3	6	1	101	40	20.20	0	0	1	0	172	112	5	22.40	3.90	3-27	0	0
SG Fensham (EP)	4	7	1	94	41*	15.66	0	0	2	0	0	0	0	-	-	-	0	0
MP Fick (FS)	4	6	0	78	29	13.00	0	0	3	0	156	122	2	61.00	4.69	1-24	0	0
SP Fleming (NZ)	4	6	0	469	262	78.16	2	0	5	0	0	0	0	-	-	-	0	0
P Fojela (Bdr)	1	1	1	1	1*	-	0	0	0	0	115	72	6	12.00	3.75	4-34	0	0
H Fourie (Bol)	1	2	0	20	19	10.00	0	0	0	0	0	0	0	-	-	-	0	0

FIRST-CLASS AVERAGES 2005/06

Name	M	Inns	NO	Runs	HS	Avg	100	50	Ct	St	Balls	Runs	Wkts	Avg	RpO	BB	5I	10M
JEC Franklin (NZ)	4	6	2	173	122*	43.25	1	0	1	0	789	522	21	24.85	3.96	4-75	0	0
BL Fransman (Bol)	5	5	2	6	4*	2.00	0	0	0	0	659	379	12	31.58	3.45	3-34	0	0
Q Friend (WP)	7	9	1	131	36	16.37	0	0	3	0	796	418	21	19.90	3.15	7-31	1	0
R Frylinck (Dol/KZN)	8	10	2	261	100*	32.62	1	1	3	0	1088	564	23	24.52	3.11	6-94	1	0
PG Fulton (NZ)	3	5	0	138	73	27.60	0	1	2	0	0	0	0	-	-	-	0	0
DR Gain (Gau)	6	12	2	391	100	39.10	1	3	6	0	0	0	0	-	-	-	0	0
LL Gamiet (War/Bdr)	6	11	1	467	105	46.70	1	2	3	0	30	17	1	17.00	3.40	1-14	0	0
TN Garwe (ZimU23)	1	1	0	8	8	8.00	0	0	0	0	42	42	0	-	6.00	-	0	0
FA Geldenhuys (Bol)	1	2	0	28	24	14.00	0	0	0	0	0	0	0	-	-	-	0	0
JP Geoghegan (WP)	2	3	1	23	15	11.50	0	0	0	0	66	38	0	-	3.45	-	0	0
SG George (WP)	1	2	0	7	6	3.50	0	0	0	0	6	5	0	-	5.00	-	0	0
HH Gibbs (Cob/SA)	7	14	0	473	149	33.78	2	1	11	0	0	0	0	-	-	-	0	0
AC Gilchrist (Aus)	3	5	0	50	24	10.00	0	0	11	1	0	0	0	-	-	-	0	0
R Gobind (Dol/KZN)	10	16	2	560	112	40.00	1	3	10	0	18	1	0	-	0.33	-	0	0
U Govender (Dol/KZN)	12	12	6	27	21*	4.50	0	0	7	0	1943	1008	47	21.44	3.11	6-59	2	0
AJA Gray (WP)	10	20	3	719	112*	42.29	2	3	9	0	270	165	0	-	3.66	-	0	0
GC Grobler (Eas)	1	2	1	0	0*	0.00	0	0	0	0	96	72	3	24.00	4.50	2-28	0	0
SF Grobler (Gau)	1	1	0	3	3	3.00	0	0	1	0	72	65	1	65.00	5.41	1-61	0	0
AJ Hall (Lio/SA)	3	4	1	63	34*	21.00	0	0	2	0	509	275	10	27.50	3.24	5-39	1	0
WC Hantam (WP)	6	10	4	151	38	25.16	0	0	8	0	720	396	21	18.85	3.30	6-39	1	0
MJ Harris (Lio)	10	17	2	614	135*	40.93	2	1	42	0	0	0	0	-	-	-	0	0
PL Harris (Ttn/Nor)	13	14	2	193	47	16.08	0	0	7	0	2447	1108	50	22.16	2.71	6-54	4	0
IJ Harvey (Cob)	5	8	0	131	51	16.37	0	1	3	0	258	100	5	20.00	2.32	2-13	0	0
TN Harvey (KZN)	2	4	0	37	19	9.25	0	0	1	0	0	0	0	-	-	-	0	0
DL Haupt (WP)	1	0	0	0	-	-	0	0	0	0	126	81	1	81.00	3.85	1-57	0	0
W Hauptfleisch (KZN)	2	4	0	59	50	14.75	0	1	0	0	24	17	0	-	4.25	-	0	0
ML Hayden (Aus)	3	6	0	231	102	38.50	1	1	8	0	0	0	0	-	-	-	0	0
M Hayward (Dol)	6	6	2	55	33	13.75	0	0	3	0	958	485	16	30.31	3.03	3-64	0	0
WD Hayward (Bol)	3	5	0	73	47	14.60	0	0	0	0	0	0	0	-	-	-	0	0
B Hector (Eag/FS)	12	20	2	768	154	42.66	2	5	9	0	0	0	0	-	-	-	0	0
JM Henderson (Eag)	1	0	0	0	-	-	0	0	0	0	12	7	0	-	3.50	-	0	0
T Henderson (War)	8	15	3	108	44*	9.00	0	0	4	0	1515	651	22	29.59	2.57	6-80	1	0
JS Hermitage (NW)	5	6	1	61	17	12.20	0	0	2	0	488	350	9	38.88	4.30	3-85	0	0
ND Hewer (KZN)	4	3	2	35	23*	35.00	0	0	1	0	576	328	11	29.81	3.41	4-31	0	0
WR Hinkel (Bdr)	1	1	1	18	18*	-	0	0	1	0	163	66	6	11.00	2.42	4-42	0	0

Name	M	Inns	NO	Runs	HS	Avg	100	50	Ct	St	Balls	Runs	Wkts	Avg	RpO	BB	5I	10M
IC Hlengane (Eas)	9	12	4	55	23	6.87	0	0	4	0	1030	594	19	31.26	3.46	7-107	1	0
DL Hobson (Bol)	1	2	1	15	11*	15.00	0	0	1	0	90	85	0	-	5.66	-	0	0
FPG Holtzhausen (GW)	3	6	0	143	54	23.83	0	2	4	0	305	200	1	200.00	3.93	1-22	0	0
FS Holtzhausen (NW)	8	12	4	334	69*	41.75	0	3	5	0	1256	612	26	23.53	2.92	5-25	1	0
Z Homani (WP)	7	13	1	383	118	31.91	1	1	3	0	0	0	0	-	-	-	0	0
T Hove (ZimU23)	1	1	0	2	2	2.00	0	0	1	0	0	0	0	-	-	-	0	0
JM How (NZ)	2	3	0	15	11	5.00	0	0	2	0	0	0	0	-	-	-	0	0
GE Howell (EP)	8	13	2	163	58	14.81	0	1	10	0	936	529	11	48.09	3.39	2-27	0	0
MEK Hussey (Aus)	3	5	1	257	89	64.25	0	3	2	0	12	6	0	-	3.00	-	0	0
CA Ingram (EP/FS)	6	10	0	393	169	39.30	1	1	5	0	381	234	8	29.25	3.68	4-16	0	0
A Jacobs (War)	9	18	2	726	149	45.37	1	4	9	0	6	8	0	-	8.00	-	0	0
DJ Jacobs (Eag/Rest)	11	19	2	671	128	39.47	3	2	5	0	28	19	0	-	4.07	-	0	0
F Jardine (WP)	1	1	0	14	14	14.00	0	0	0	0	299	133	6	22.16	2.66	5-118	1	0
RR Jeggels (EP)	9	15	0	396	86	26.40	0	2	3	0	0	0	0	-	-	-	0	0
P Joubert (Nor)	11	14	5	352	68	39.11	0	2	8	0	1601	554	47	11.78	2.07	7-32	2	0
JR Jumat (Nor)	1	1	1	5	5*	-	0	0	0	0	48	37	0	-	4.62	-	0	0
JH Kallis (SA)	6	11	0	420	114	38.18	1	2	4	0	673	361	11	32.81	3.21	3-51	0	0
QK Kannemeyer (Bol)	2	3	0	94	70	31.33	0	1	0	0	72	15	1	15.00	1.25	1-15	0	0
MS Kasprowicz (Aus)	3	4	2	22	7*	11.00	0	0	1	0	464	292	7	41.71	3.77	2-44	0	0
JM Kemp (Ttn)	3	4	0	109	52	27.25	0	1	4	0	132	74	5	14.80	3.36	5-41	1	0
JC Kent (Dol)	9	10	0	227	94	22.70	0	1	5	0	1068	465	17	27.35	2.61	3-77	0	0
DJ Kgamadi (NW)	10	18	2	575	84	35.93	0	4	14	0	6	4	0	-	4.00	-	0	0
I Khan (Dol/KZN)	12	21	3	717	118	39.83	1	5	4	0	618	423	10	42.30	4.10	3-38	0	0
TR Khoza (Nor)	1	0	0	0	-	-	0	0	0	0	177	89	4	22.25	3.01	3-41	0	0
RK Kleinveldt (Cob/WP/Rest)	9	14	3	291	115*	26.45	1	1	6	0	1573	761	38	20.02	2.90	8-47	2	1
L Klusener (Dol)	10	13	3	428	102	42.80	2	0	4	0	2143	1058	34	31.11	2.96	5-39	2	0
CE Knox (Gau)	3	4	2	92	47*	46.00	0	0	3	0	216	126	6	21.00	3.50	3-31	0	0
PJ Koortzen (FS)	7	12	1	580	107*	52.72	1	3	7	0	54	52	0	-	5.77	-	0	0
BB Kops (War)	3	6	4	13	8*	6.50	0	0	0	0	271	179	4	44.75	3.96	3-41	0	0
JP Kreusch (War)	8	15	0	273	85	18.20	0	1	4	0	1043	439	13	33.76	2.52	5-31	1	0
AK Kruger (Eag/GW)	10	18	1	488	103	28.70	1	2	7	0	1218	877	27	32.48	4.32	6-37	3	1
GJ-P Kruger (Lio/Rest)	8	11	3	129	33	16.12	0	0	4	0	1774	1078	45	23.95	3.64	8-112	4	1
HG Kuhn (Ttn/Nor)	14	25	2	949	133*	41.26	2	5	50	2	0	0	0	-	-	-	0	0
JM Kuiper (WP)	4	6	1	146	81*	29.20	0	1	1	0	0	0	0	-	-	-	0	0
PC Laing (Bol)	5	8	0	243	80	30.37	0	2	4	0	438	301	9	33.44	4.12	3-80	0	0

FIRST-CLASS AVERAGES 2005/06

Name	M	Inns	NO	Runs	HS	Avg	100	50	Ct	St	Balls	Runs	Wkts	Avg	RpO	BB	5I	10M
JL Langer (Aus)	3	5	1	122	37	30.50	0	0	6	0	0	0	0	-	-	-	0	0
FB Lazarus (KZN)	2	4	0	3	2	0.75	0	0	1	0	0	0	0	-	-	-	0	0
B Lee (Aus)	3	4	1	88	64	29.33	0	1	0	0	696	332	17	19.52	2.86	5-69	1	0
BW Lemmetjies (GW)	3	6	0	115	37	19.16	0	0	3	0	174	123	2	61.50	4.24	1-37	0	0
DC Lentz (Bdr)	2	2	0	23	19	11.50	0	0	0	0	0	0	0	-	-	-	0	0
HW le Roux (Gau)	4	4	0	49	25	12.25	0	0	5	0	423	296	11	26.90	4.19	4-66	0	0
J le Roux (NW)	10	17	1	545	110	34.06	2	3	3	0	48	35	1	35.00	4.37	1-1	0	0
C Linde (FS)	10	16	3	227	56	17.46	0	1	24	7	0	0	0	-	-	-	0	0
NJ Livi (Eas)	1	2	0	49	42	24.50	0	0	0	0	0	0	0	-	-	-	0	0
WP Lombard (KZN)	2	3	2	25	25*	25.00	0	0	0	0	158	77	2	38.50	2.92	1-27	0	0
DP Lotter (NW)	1	2	0	14	8	7.00	0	0	0	0	0	0	0	-	-	-	0	0
J Louw (Eag)	4	4	1	34	21	11.33	0	0	3	0	590	289	2	144.50	2.93	1-48	0	0
WJ Louw (Bol)	4	8	1	266	85	38.00	0	1	6	0	0	0	0	-	-	-	0	0
LL Lwana (Bdr)	6	6	2	53	24	13.25	0	0	3	0	462	315	11	28.63	4.09	3-6	0	0
APT Mabuya (GW)	2	3	1	18	12*	9.00	0	0	0	0	114	95	0	-	5.00	-	0	0
CS Mabuya (KZN)	2	2	0	9	5	4.50	0	0	0	0	0	0	0	-	-	-	0	0
BB McCullum (NZ)	4	6	0	175	101	29.16	1	0	8	2	0	0	0	-	-	-	0	0
ND McKenzie (Lio/Rest)	10	19	2	837	161*	49.23	3	2	10	0	54	21	0	-	2.33	-	0	0
AP McLaren (GW)	9	18	0	570	131	31.66	2	3	12	0	6	3	0	-	3.00	-	0	0
R McLaren (Eag)	10	15	2	441	140	33.92	1	3	7	0	1689	851	28	30.39	3.02	6-96	1	0
JT Mafa (Gau)	8	6	2	6	4	1.50	0	0	1	0	1163	772	25	30.88	3.98	4-46	0	0
A Magiet (WP)	1	1	0	0	0	0.00	0	0	0	0	0	0	0	-	-	-	0	0
M Mahlombe (WP)	4	3	0	22	20	7.33	0	0	1	0	336	156	11	14.18	2.78	3-11	0	0
DL Makalima (Gau)	6	11	0	248	61	22.54	0	2	4	0	102	100	0	-	5.88	-	0	0
S Makongolo (EP)	1	2	0	61	56	30.50	0	1	0	0	0	0	0	-	-	-	0	0
DJ Malan (Bol)	4	7	0	158	64	22.57	0	1	2	0	159	152	3	50.66	5.73	1-22	0	0
JMM Malao (FS)	8	8	3	38	18	7.60	0	0	2	0	1486	872	30	29.06	3.52	5-27	1	0
S Mandan (Eas)	6	10	0	228	98	22.80	0	1	2	0	0	0	0	-	-	-	0	0
L Manzini (Nor)	2	1	0	0	0	0.00	0	0	1	0	138	80	4	20.00	3.47	4-22	0	0
A Maregwede (ZimU23)	5	9	0	35	7	3.88	0	0	13	0	0	0	0	-	-	-	0	0
HJH Marshall (NZ)	1	2	0	31	25	15.50	0	0	0	0	0	0	0	-	-	-	0	0
CS Martin (NZ)	4	5	2	11	9*	3.66	0	0	1	0	816	438	12	36.50	3.22	5-37	1	0
DR Martyn (Aus)	3	6	2	225	101	56.25	1	1	3	0	0	0	0	-	-	-	0	0
MA Mashimbyi (Ttn/Nor)	12	12	2	113	41	11.30	0	0	2	0	1148	554	23	24.08	2.89	5-32	1	0
MR Masinda (WP)	1	1	0	1	1	1.00	0	0	0	0	6	8	0	-	8.00	-	0	0

Name	M	Inns	NO	Runs	HS	Avg	100	50	Ct	St	Balls	Runs	Wkts	Avg	RpO	BB	5I	10M
MT Masinga (Gau)	1	2	2	69	48*	-	0	0	1	0	54	42	0	-	4.66	-	0	0
H Matanga (ZimU23)	2	4	2	13	8	6.50	0	0	1	0	341	162	2	81.00	2.85	1-26	0	0
BM Mathebula (Lio/Gau)	6	8	4	66	18*	16.50	0	0	2	0	701	590	9	65.55	5.04	2-50	0	0
MM Matika (Bdr)	3	5	1	63	21	15.75	0	0	4	0	78	22	0	-	1.69	-	0	0
S Matsikenyeri (ZimU23)	5	10	1	151	53	16.77	0	1	3	0	126	94	1	94.00	4.47	1-18	0	0
TMK Mawoyo (ZimU23)	5	10	0	88	35	8.80	0	0	1	0	0	0	0	-	-	-	0	0
VCM Mazibuko (NW)	3	4	1	33	21	11.00	0	0	2	0	182	151	5	30.20	4.97	3-37	0	0
JT Maziya (Eas)	1	2	0	4	4	2.00	0	0	0	0	60	72	0	-	7.20	-	0	0
L Mbane (Bdr)	8	9	2	254	60	36.28	0	1	5	0	783	490	15	32.66	3.75	5-26	1	0
NE Mbhalati (Ttn/Nor)	10	12	3	32	10	3.55	0	0	0	0	1648	917	33	27.78	3.33	5-26	1	0
EE Meyer (Nor)	3	6	1	100	31	20.00	0	0	1	0	6	6	0	-	6.00	-	0	0
L Meyer (War/EP)	11	18	3	135	35*	9.00	0	0	5	0	1565	815	26	31.34	3.12	5-38	1	0
S Mhlongo (Dol/KZN)	12	12	3	61	21	6.77	0	0	3	0	1542	774	37	20.91	3.01	5-25	1	0
DR Miller (KZN)	9	12	2	301	64*	30.10	0	2	26	2	12	13	0	-	6.50	-	0	0
KD Mills (NZ)	2	4	2	12	12	6.00	0	0	1	0	348	179	8	22.37	3.08	4-43	0	0
S Mjekula (War/EP)	9	11	7	26	10	6.50	0	0	2	0	1092	594	25	23.76	3.26	5-46	1	0
B Mlambo (ZimU23)	5	10	0	237	86	23.70	0	1	2	0	0	0	0	-	-	-	0	0
PT Mofokeng (Eas)	9	9	6	15	4*	5.00	0	0	4	0	534	386	8	48.25	4.33	2-36	0	0
MJ Mokonyama (Nor)	9	11	2	263	40	29.22	0	0	4	0	0	0	0	-	-	-	0	0
EO Moleon (Lio/NW)	12	19	3	274	67	17.12	0	1	4	0	1598	707	22	32.13	2.65	3-21	0	0
K Moothosamy (Gau)	3	5	0	77	42	15.40	0	0	1	0	24	16	1	16.00	4.00	1-3	0	0
JA Morkel (Ttn/Eas)	6	8	2	451	84	75.16	0	6	3	0	1012	518	17	30.47	3.07	4-28	0	0
M Morkel (Ttn/Eas)	3	4	1	30	22	10.00	0	0	5	0	491	293	9	32.55	3.58	4-96	0	0
LN Mosena (FS)	7	13	1	322	78	26.83	0	2	8	0	0	0	0	-	-	-	0	0
JF Mostert (FS)	3	5	2	112	70	37.33	0	1	1	0	205	118	4	29.50	3.45	3-20	0	0
WB Motaung (Lio/Gau)	7	13	0	419	114	32.23	2	1	5	0	78	33	1	33.00	2.53	1-15	0	0
TS Motsamai (FS)	8	11	5	171	51*	28.50	0	1	1	0	1074	585	17	34.41	3.26	2-16	0	0
PV Mpitsang (Eag)	9	9	3	36	16*	6.00	0	0	0	0	1420	632	18	35.11	2.67	5-35	1	0
CB Mpofu (ZimU23)	4	7	1	17	10	2.83	0	0	0	0	468	308	8	38.50	3.94	3-23	0	0
R Munnik (Cob/WP)	6	9	1	265	75	33.12	0	3	1	0	120	63	3	21.00	3.15	2-14	0	0
RG Mutch (Eas)	3	5	2	89	34*	29.66	0	0	0	0	422	282	10	28.20	4.00	4-57	0	0
A Mwayenga (ZimU23)	5	9	5	70	14*	17.50	0	0	1	0	613	338	14	24.14	3.30	5-41	2	0
JG Myburgh (Nor)	8	16	6	808	128*	80.80	1	7	7	0	396	207	5	41.40	3.13	2-45	0	0
SJ Myburgh (Nor)	4	4	0	44	31	11.00	0	0	4	0	18	11	0	-	3.66	-	0	0
A Nawab (Gau)	5	6	2	44	19	11.00	0	0	3	0	717	498	21	23.71	4.16	6-106	2	1

Name	M	Inns	NO	Runs	HS	Avg	100	50	Ct	St	Balls	Runs	Wkts	Avg	RpO	BB	5I	10M
A Nel (SA)	4	7	1	71	18*	11.83	0	0	4	0	770	396	7	56.57	3.08	3-83	0	0
R Nel (EP)	1	2	0	23	23	11.50	0	0	2	0	0	0	0	-	-	-	0	0
M Ngam (War/Bdr)	7	12	3	84	27	9.33	0	0	1	0	837	612	10	61.20	4.38	4-71	0	0
FG Nkuna (Nor)	10	5	3	7	4*	3.50	0	0	2	0	1050	579	17	34.05	3.30	4-43	0	0
ET Nkwe (Lio/Gau)	8	15	2	386	98	29.69	0	3	6	0	528	379	4	94.75	4.30	2-56	0	0
E Nogabe (FS)	1	2	1	0	0*	0.00	0	0	0	0	24	22	0	-	5.50	-	0	0
NM Northcote (Bol)	1	1	1	27	27*	-	0	0	2	0	0	0	0	-	-	-	0	0
M Ntini (SA)	6	10	3	59	17*	8.42	0	0	2	0	1391	836	39	21.43	3.60	6-100	4	2
E Nyawo (Eas)	5	9	0	88	31	9.77	0	0	4	0	0	0	0	-	-	-	0	0
SP O'Connor (Eas)	10	17	1	271	41	16.93	0	0	1	0	782	547	13	42.07	4.19	4-61	0	0
AW Olivier (Bol)	1	2	0	18	10	9.00	0	0	0	0	0	0	0	-	-	-	0	0
MW Olivier (War/Bdr)	10	15	1	72	12	5.14	0	0	0	0	1359	955	26	36.73	4.21	4-68	0	0
AM Omar (Gau)	3	5	0	39	20	7.80	0	0	5	0	0	0	0	-	-	-	0	0
JL Ontong (Lio/Rest)	9	17	2	864	144*	57.60	2	7	10	0	587	306	8	38.25	3.12	3-73	0	0
JDP Oram (NZ)	4	7	1	201	133	33.50	1	0	1	0	540	198	5	39.60	2.20	2-44	0	0
A Paleker (Nor)	5	7	1	130	48	21.66	0	0	5	1	0	0	0	-	-	-	0	0
Y Pangabantu (Bdr)	5	2	2	1	1*	-	0	0	0	0	618	302	13	23.23	2.93	3-24	0	0
MHW Papps (NZ)	3	5	0	63	22	12.60	0	0	2	0	0	0	0	-	-	-	0	0
JS Patel (NZ)	1	1	1	27	27*	-	0	0	1	0	252	117	3	39.00	2.78	3-117	0	0
HH Paulse (Bol)	8	9	4	22	8*	4.40	0	0	2	0	914	635	21	30.23	4.16	5-65	1	0
GD Perry (FS)	1	2	0	1	1	0.50	0	0	0	0	78	49	1	49.00	3.76	1-49	0	0
AN Petersen (Lio/Ttn/Nor/Rest)	10	19	1	566	140	31.44	1	3	13	0	42	29	0	-	4.14	-	0	0
RJ Peterson (War/Rest)	5	10	2	161	28	20.12	0	0	1	0	802	431	8	53.87	3.22	3-151	0	0
MX Pethu (Bdr)	2	4	0	28	15	7.00	0	0	0	0	0	0	0	-	-	-	0	0
AM Phangiso (Ttn/Nor)	11	14	5	315	63	35.00	0	1	4	0	994	524	15	34.93	3.16	5-76	1	0
VD Philander (Cob/WP)	11	18	1	350	66	20.58	0	1	4	0	1945	837	31	27.00	2.58	5-49	1	0
R Pietersen (GW)	7	10	7	24	7	8.00	0	0	1	0	817	493	24	20.54	3.62	6-73	1	0
TD Pillay (Dol/KZN)	7	7	2	70	32	14.00	0	0	9	0	1027	415	18	23.05	2.42	5-45	1	0
TR Plaatjie (GW)	5	9	4	39	25	7.80	0	0	1	0	282	186	6	31.00	3.95	2-39	0	0
SM Pollock (SA)	4	8	2	129	44	21.50	0	0	3	0	790	377	9	41.88	2.86	2-36	0	0
RT Ponting (Aus)	3	6	0	348	116	58.00	2	1	2	0	12	7	0	-	3.50	-	0	0
SC Pope (War/Bdr)	10	19	2	671	102	39.47	2	3	8	0	396	249	5	49.80	3.77	2-39	0	0
E Potgieter (EP)	3	6	1	79	30	15.80	0	0	4	0	6	1	0	-	1.00	-	0	0
D Pretorius (GW)	1	1	0	1	1	1.00	0	0	2	0	156	83	1	83.00	3.19	1-83	0	0
ML Price (EP)	6	11	0	110	59	10.00	0	1	1	0	24	14	0	-	3.50	-	0	0

Name	M	Inns	NO	Runs	HS	Avg	100	50	Ct	St	Balls	Runs	Wkts	Avg	RpO	BB	5I	10M
AG Prince (SA)	6	11	2	361	108*	40.11	1	1	2	0	12	2	1	2.00	1.00	1-2	0	0
C Prinsloo (Bol)	2	4	0	80	41	20.00	0	0	0	0	0	0	0	-	-	-	0	0
AG Puttick (Cob)	10	18	2	447	70	27.93	0	4	14	0	0	0	0	-	-	-	0	0
EC Rainsford (ZimU23)	3	6	1	20	10	4.00	0	0	1	0	385	161	9	17.88	2.50	2-16	0	0
MN Ranger (Bdr)	8	11	2	343	96	38.11	0	3	7	0	858	442	14	31.57	3.09	6-30	1	0
AH Razak (Dol)	1	1	1	0	0*	-	0	0	1	0	126	126	2	63.00	6.00	1-38	0	0
BL Reddy (Eas)	2	4	0	42	16	10.50	0	0	2	0	397	237	4	59.25	3.58	3-56	0	0
R Reddy (KZN)	2	1	0	10	10	10.00	0	0	1	0	241	86	5	17.20	2.14	3-32	0	0
RA Reeves (FS)	2	3	1	73	41	36.50	0	0	1	0	60	64	2	32.00	6.40	2-25	0	0
RR Richards (War/Bdr)	7	7	2	19	12	3.80	0	0	1	0	1124	562	24	23.41	3.00	5-30	2	0
JA Rudolph (Eag/SA)	10	18	0	808	141	44.88	3	4	8	0	243	116	1	116.00	2.86	1-29	0	0
QG Samson (FS)	7	8	3	21	10	4.20	0	0	1	0	906	702	17	41.29	4.64	3-31	0	0
MD Sanders (KZN)	5	7	0	290	103	41.42	1	1	0	0	0	0	0	-	-	-	0	0
U Sandi (EP)	1	1	1	0	0*	-	0	0	0	0	60	27	1	27.00	2.70	1-27	0	0
PSE Sandri (Bol)	6	8	4	64	17*	16.00	0	0	0	0	890	480	22	21.81	3.23	5-32	1	0
AJ Schultz (FS)	2	2	2	2	2*	-	0	0	1	0	150	105	5	21.00	4.20	5-51	1	0
MR Sekhoto (Lio/Gau)	6	11	1	236	80	23.60	0	1	6	0	72	67	3	22.33	5.58	2-42	0	0
BK Sekonyane (FS)	8	8	0	57	20	7.12	0	0	3	0	1158	708	24	29.50	3.66	4-80	0	0
PM Selowa (KZN)	2	2	0	35	19	17.50	0	0	3	0	0	0	0	-	-	-	0	0
WE September (Bol)	8	14	4	263	63*	26.30	0	1	8	0	882	552	15	36.80	3.75	3-35	0	0
AJ Seymore (Ttn/Eas)	12	20	1	732	135*	38.52	2	2	14	0	12	4	0	-	2.00	-	0	0
SR Sibande (FS)	1	2	0	11	6	5.50	0	0	1	0	0	0	0	-	-	-	0	0
LF Simpson (WP)	4	5	1	3	2	0.75	0	0	0	0	299	182	7	26.00	3.65	3-22	0	0
Y Singh (Lio/Gau)	3	4	3	44	17*	44.00	0	0	0	0	468	169	3	56.33	2.16	2-30	0	0
M Slwana (EP)	5	8	0	87	34	10.87	0	0	14	0	0	0	0	-	-	-	0	0
D Smit (Dol)	6	7	0	85	35	12.14	0	0	19	0	0	0	0	-	-	-	0	0
K Smit (Dol/KZN)	9	12	0	338	144	28.16	1	0	5	0	12	8	0	-	4.00	-	0	0
GC Smith (SA)	5	9	0	283	68	31.44	0	2	3	0	120	72	0	-	3.60	-	0	0
MBA Smith (War/Bdr)	6	9	0	146	39	16.22	0	0	5	0	72	25	0	-	2.08	-	0	0
BD Snijman (Lio/Gau)	11	21	1	585	114	29.25	1	2	8	0	274	182	9	20.22	3.98	4-26	0	0
AM Sodumo (War/Bdr)	11	19	2	267	77*	15.70	0	2	27	3	0	0	0	-	-	-	0	0
GC Stevens (Bol)	3	5	0	48	18	9.60	0	0	1	0	325	157	4	39.25	2.89	2-22	0	0
DW Steyn (Ttn/Nor/SA)	13	16	4	140	34	11.66	0	0	1	0	2767	1425	69	20.65	3.09	5-27	4	1
FA Steyn (Lio/NW)	10	18	1	556	116	32.70	2	2	10	0	18	17	0	-	5.66	-	0	0
RA Stroh (NW)	7	11	1	243	52	24.30	0	1	5	0	756	428	18	23.77	3.39	4-24	0	0

Name	M	Inns	NO	Runs	HS	Avg	100	50	Ct	St	Balls	Runs	Wkts	Avg	RpO	BB	5I	10M
GM Strydom (ZimU23)	5	9	0	182	56	20.22	0	2	3	0	451	253	8	31.62	3.36	3-29	0	0
HM Strydom (NW)	1	2	1	24	17	24.00	0	0	1	0	0	0	0	-	-	-	0	0
JG Strydom (Cob/Bol)	7	13	1	421	123	35.08	1	1	1	0	0	0	0	-	-	-	0	0
SB Styris (NZ)	4	7	1	143	54*	23.83	0	1	4	0	240	115	3	38.33	2.87	1-1	0	0
SP Summers (Bol)	1	2	0	21	21	10.50	0	0	0	0	90	53	1	53.00	3.53	1-39	0	0
WC Swan (Bol)	9	16	0	427	93	26.68	0	4	2	0	210	149	1	149.00	4.25	1-54	0	0
RP Symcox (Dol)	4	5	0	111	87	22.20	0	1	3	0	624	292	1	292.00	2.80	1-52	0	0
J Symes (Gau)	3	5	0	185	133	37.00	1	0	4	0	171	101	2	50.50	3.54	2-13	0	0
A Symonds (Aus)	3	4	0	101	55	25.25	0	1	3	0	252	114	1	114.00	2.71	1-26	0	0
R Telemachus (Eag/FS)	6	10	4	215	116	35.83	1	0	5	0	844	509	16	31.81	3.61	6-85	1	0
FD Telo (Cob/WP)	6	11	0	398	72	36.18	0	3	0	0	0	0	0	-	-	-	0	0
DJ Terbrugge (Lio/Gau)	3	5	1	97	31	24.25	0	0	1	0	570	322	6	53.66	3.38	2-38	0	0
J Theron (EP)	6	7	1	52	15	8.66	0	0	1	0	735	387	16	24.18	3.15	6-47	1	0
J Theunissen (Eas)	1	2	0	22	22	11.00	0	0	0	0	0	0	0	-	-	-	0	0
AC Thomas (Ttn/Nor)	8	11	2	191	42*	21.22	0	0	2	0	1404	683	26	26.26	2.91	7-54	1	1
PG Thompson (Gau)	2	3	0	76	66	25.33	0	1	3	0	198	147	2	73.50	4.45	2-46	0	0
CA Thyssen (Eag/FS)	8	12	2	384	157	38.40	1	1	3	0	156	103	2	51.50	3.96	2-27	0	0
G Toyana (Ttn/Eas)	14	20	1	383	55	20.15	0	2	9	0	180	86	1	86.00	2.86	1-30	0	0
ES Tsamaisi (GW)	2	3	2	10	7*	10.00	0	0	0	0	66	59	2	29.50	5.36	1-25	0	0
T Tshabalala (Eag/FS)	6	6	2	48	25	12.00	0	0	0	0	789	515	13	39.61	3.91	4-129	0	0
TL Tsolekile (Cob/Rest)	11	18	1	378	91	22.23	0	1	36	1	0	0	0	-	-	-	0	0
LL Tsotsobe (EP)	5	6	2	33	12*	8.25	0	0	1	0	738	395	14	28.21	3.21	4-38	0	0
ANW Tweedie (Dol)	5	6	2	25	19	6.25	0	0	2	0	795	404	16	25.25	3.04	4-74	0	0
AM van den Berg (Eas)	3	6	0	70	32	11.66	0	0	4	0	318	182	5	36.40	3.43	3-32	0	0
F van der Merwe (NW)	3	1	0	6	6	6.00	0	0	0	0	324	206	4	51.50	3.81	2-69	0	0
JJ van der Wath (Eag)	4	8	0	160	52	20.00	0	2	0	0	576	312	6	52.00	3.25	5-126	1	0
M van Jaarsveld (Ttn)	11	18	2	618	145	38.62	1	4	25	0	30	10	1	10.00	2.00	1-1	0	0
VB van Jaarsveld (Lio)	10	18	1	670	126	39.41	3	3	15	0	0	0	0	-	-	-	0	0
HA van Straaten (Eas)	7	11	0	191	68	17.36	0	1	5	0	0	0	0	-	-	-	0	0
N van Woerkom (Nor)	2	4	0	308	146	77.00	1	2	1	0	72	43	1	43.00	3.58	1-13	0	0
CFK van Wyk (Ttn/Nor)	9	12	3	427	104	47.44	1	4	23	3	6	7	1	7.00	7.00	1-7	0	0
DJ van Wyk (FS)	7	10	0	351	106	35.10	1	1	11	0	0	0	0	-	-	-	0	0
DM van Wyk (Gau)	7	12	5	513	122*	73.28	1	4	22	5	0	0	0	-	-	-	0	0
JM van Wyk (Bol)	3	5	1	71	33*	17.75	0	0	0	0	282	205	5	41.00	4.36	2-45	0	0
MN van Wyk (Eag)	10	17	3	786	200*	56.14	3	1	17	1	0	0	0	-	-	-	0	0

Name	M	Inns	NO	Runs	HS	Avg	100	50	Ct	St	Balls	Runs	Wkts	Avg	RpO	BB	5I	10M
MA Vermeulen (ZimU23)	4	8	0	128	47	16.00	0	0	4	0	48	34	1	34.00	4.25	1-17	0	0
DL Vettori (NZ)	4	6	0	200	81	33.33	0	2	2	0	931	416	7	59.42	2.68	3-77	0	0
GE von Hoesslin (Bdr)	8	13	2	319	101*	29.00	1	1	17	1	9	9	1	9.00	6.00	1-9	0	0
N Wagner (Nor)	4	2	1	29	20	29.00	0	0	0	0	512	245	14	17.50	2.87	4-39	0	0
L-R Walters (Bol)	8	15	2	258	56	19.84	0	1	16	1	0	0	0	-	-	-	0	0
MD Walters (WP)	1	1	0	0	0	0.00	0	0	1	0	0	0	0	-	-	-	0	0
SK Warne (Aus)	3	4	0	82	36	20.50	0	0	1	0	766	423	15	28.20	3.31	6-86	1	0
DJ Watson (Dol)	11	20	3	763	103	44.88	2	5	3	0	14	4	0	-	1.71	-	0	0
D Wiese (Eas)	9	15	1	526	168	37.57	1	2	4	0	1203	732	26	28.15	3.65	4-48	0	0
D Willemse (War/EP)	6	7	1	191	58	31.83	0	1	4	0	786	386	9	42.88	2.94	4-56	0	0
M Williamson (WP)	7	14	2	205	44	17.08	0	0	7	0	5	4	0	-	4.80	-	0	0
CM Willoughby (Cob)	9	12	5	24	13*	3.42	0	0	1	0	2002	861	41	21.00	2.58	6-41	4	0
WR Wingfield (KZN)	4	5	2	214	70	71.33	0	1	0	0	54	30	0	-	3.33	-	0	0
W Wyngaard (Cob/WP)	11	20	4	578	132*	36.12	3	1	6	0	0	0	0	-	-	-	0	0
M Zondeki (Cob/Rest)	11	17	5	78	26*	6.50	0	0	2	0	1789	943	31	30.41	3.16	5-67	1	0

SOUTH AFRICAN FIRST-CLASS RECORDS

(a) The symbol * denotes an innings declared, an unbroken partnership, or a not out innings, as appropriate.
(b) The Currie Cup was superseded by the Castle Cup in 1991/92. Both are denoted by '(CC)'. Castle Cup also includes Currie Cup where applicable. In 1996/97 the competition became the SuperSport Series (SS). The Castle Bowl is denoted by (CB), the SAA Provincial Challenge (previously the UCB Provincial Cup) by (PC) and the UCB Bowl by (UB).
(c) Matches denoted (SACB) are three-day matches played between 1971/72 and 1990/91 under the auspices of the South African Cricket Board of Control and its successor, the South African Cricket Board. These matches were granted first-class status retrospectively following the formation of the United Cricket Board of South Africa in 1991.
(d) As at 10 May 2006. Career records do not include the 2006 English season.

TEAM RECORDS

HIGHEST INNINGS TOTALS

In South Africa (600 or more):

754	KwaZulu-Natal v Northerns (SS)	Durban	2001/02
676	MCC v Griqualand West	Kimberley	1938/39
664-6*	Natal v Western Province (CC)	Durban	1936/37
663-6*	South Africa v Arosa Sri Lanka	Cape Town	1982/83
658-9*	South Africa v West Indies (2nd Test)	Durban	2003/04
654-5	England v South Africa (5th Test)	Durban	1938/39
652-7*	Australia v South Africa (1st Test)	Johannesburg	2001/02
640-5*	Gauteng v Griqualand West (SS)	Kimberley	1999/00
628-8*	Australia v South Africa (1st Test)	Johannesburg	1996/97
622-9*	South Africa v Australia (2nd Test)	Durban	1969/70
620-7*	South Africa v Pakistan (2nd Test)	Cape Town	2002/03
620	South Africa v Australia (1st Test)	Johannesburg	1966/67
620	Australians v Griqualand West	Kimberley	1966/67
618-4*	South Africa v Rest of South Africa	Johannesburg	1964/65
618	West Indians v Free State	Bloemfontein	2003/04
612-8*	Dolphins v Eagles (SS)	Bloemfontein	2004/05
609	Transvaal v Orange Free State (CC)	Johannesburg	1934/35
608-6*	Transvaal v Natal	Johannesburg	1939/40
608	England v South Africa (2nd Test)	Johannesburg	1948/49
604-6*	South Africa v West Indies (4th Test)	Centurion	2003/04
603	Griqualand West v Western Province (CC)	Kimberley	1929/30
602-9*	Transvaal v Northern Transvaal (CC)	Johannesburg	1993/94
602	Griqualand West v Rhodesia (CC)	Kimberley	1929/30
601	Western Province v Border (CC)	Cape Town	1929/30

Overseas:

747	West Indies v South Africa (4th Test)	St John's	2004/05
692	South Africans v Cambridge University	Cambridge	1901
682-6*	South Africa v England (2nd Test)	Lord's	2003
621-5*	South Africa v New Zealand (1st Test)	Auckland	1998/99
613-8*	South Africans v Sussex	Hove	1994
611	South Africans v Nottinghamshire	Nottingham	1904
604-9*	England v South Africa (5th Test)	The Oval	2003
600-3*	South Africa v Zimbabwe (1st Test)	Harare	2001/02
600-8*	Western Australia v South Africans	Perth	2001/02

LOWEST INNINGS TOTALS

In South Africa (40 or less):

16 and 18 (a)	Border v Natal (CC)	East London	1959/60
23	Border v Natal (CC)	East London	1920/21
29	Griqualand West v Transvaal (CC)	Johannesburg	1950/51
30	South Africa v England (1st Test)	Port Elizabeth	1895/96
31	Griqualand West v Natal (CC)	Johannesburg	1906/07
34	Griqualand West v Transvaal (CC)	Port Elizabeth	1902/03

34 (b)	Border v Eastern Province (CC)	East London	1946/47
34	Eastern Province v Natal (CC)	Port Elizabeth	1980/81
35	South Africa v England (2nd Test)	Cape Town	1898/99
36	Eastern Province v Transvaal (CC)	Port Elizabeth	1937/38
37	Eastern Province v Western Province (CC)	Port Elizabeth	1933/34
37	Orange Free State v Transvaal (CC)	Bloemfontein	1936/37
38	Transvaal v Western Province (SACB)	Cape Town	1981/82
39	Natal v Western Province (SACB)	Cape Town	1981/82
40	Eastern Province v Orange Free State (CC)	Durban	1910/11
40	Orange Free State v Transvaal B (CC)	Johannesburg	1960/61

Note: (a) Border's 1959/60 aggregate is a world record.
(b) Border were set only 42 to win. This is the lowest target in first-class cricket for a losing team to be set.

Overseas:

30	South Africa v England (1st Test)	Birmingham	1924
32	Derbyshire v South Africans	Derby	1947
36	Scotland v South Africans	Glasgow	1924
36	South Africa v Australia (5th Test) (First innings. They were dismissed for 45 in the second innings.)	Melbourne	1931/32
40	Gloucestershire v South Africans	Clifton	1901

HIGHEST FOURTH INNINGS TOTALS

654-5 (set 696)	England v South Africa (5th Test)	Durban	1938/39
529-9 (set 579)	Combined XI v South Africans	Perth	1963/64
500-7 (and won)	SA Universities v Western Province	Stellenbosch	1978/79
447 (lost by 111)	Orange Free State v Transvaal (CC)	Bloemfontein	1926/27
443-4 (and won)	Free State v KwaZulu-Natal (SS)	Durban	1999/00
442 (lost by 44)	South Africans v New South Wales	Sydney	1910/11
438-8 (and won)	Free State v West Indians	Bloemfontein	1998/99

MATCH AGGREGATES

Highest:

In South Africa:	1981 for 35 wickets	South Africa v England (5th Test)	Durban	1938/39
In SuperSport Series:	1529 for 18 wickets	Northerns v Griqualand West	Centurion	2001/02
SA teams abroad:	1744 for 40 wickets	New South Wales v South Africans	Sydney	1910/11

Lowest (for completed matches):

In South Africa:	198 for 22 wickets	Eastern Province v Transvaal (CC)	Port Elizabeth	1937/38
SA teams abroad:	234 for 29 wickets	Australia v South Africa (5th Test)	Melbourne	1931/32

DURATION OF MATCHES

Longest:

10 days (no play on 8th)	South Africa v England (5th Test)	Durban	1938/39
7 days (play each day)	Transvaal v Kimberley (CC)	Johannesburg	1890/91

Shortest:

Two matches have begun and been completed on the same day:

Transvaal v Orange Free State (CC)	Johannesburg	1906/07
Eastern Province v Orange Free State (CC)	Port Elizabeth	1912/13

MOST RUNS SCORED IN A SINGLE DAY

By one side:

618 for 4 wickets	South Africa v Rest of South Africa	Johannesburg	1964/65

By both sides:

616 for 16 wickets	Transvaal v Orange Free State (CC)	Johannesburg	1929/30

Note: The following instance occurred during a two-day match where the hours of play were extended:

By both sides:

665 for 20 wickets	Transvaal v Rest of South Africa	Johannesburg	1911/12

FEWEST RUNS SCORED IN A SINGLE DAY

By one side:

138 for 5 wickets	South Africa v England (5th Test)	Port Elizabeth (1st day)	1956/57

By both sides:

122 for 8 wickets	South Africa v England (5th Test)	Port Elizabeth (3rd day)	1956/57

SOUTH AFRICAN FIRST-CLASS RECORDS

LARGEST MARGINS OF VICTORY

By an innings and:

374 runs	MCC beat Orange Free State	Bloemfontein	1913/14
360 runs	Australia beat South Africa (1st Test)	Johannesburg	2001/02
359 runs (a)	Western Province beat Griqualand West (CC)	Johannesburg	1906/07

Note: (a) In 1906/07 Griqualand West were beaten three times in ten days by an innings and more than 300 runs.

By runs:

530	Australia beat South Africa (4th Test)	Melbourne	1910/11
411	Rhodesia beat International Wanderers	Salisbury	1972/73
398	Western Province beat Boland (PC)	Cape Town	2005/06
386	Transvaal beat Griqualand West (CC)	Johannesburg	1929/30

VICTORY LOSING ONLY ONE WICKET

Rhodesia (549-1*) beat Orange Free State (252 & 235) (CC)	Bloemfontein	1967/68
Transvaal (325-1*) beat Northern Transvaal (97 & 173) (CC)	Pretoria	1980/81
Transvaal (362-1*) beat Arosa Sri Lanka (122 & 200)	Johannesburg	1982/83

VICTORY AFTER FOLLOWING ON

Transvaal (122 & 288) beat Natal (254 & 79) (CC) by 77 runs	Cape Town	1897/98
South Africans (95 & 281) beat Kent (273 & 101) by two runs	Catford	1907
Orange Free State (163 & 298) beat Western Province (393 & 44) (CC) by 24 runs	Cape Town	1926/27
Natal (115 & 458) beat Transvaal (370 & 190) by 13 runs	Durban	1932/33
Transvaal B (293 & 362) beat North-Eastern Transvaal (468 & 87) (CC) by 100 runs	Johannesburg	1962/63
Natal B (121 & 413) beat Orange Free State (319 & 196) (CC) by 19 runs	Bloemfontein	1975/76
Natal B (205 & 456-8*) beat Border (403-6* & 222) (CB) by 36 runs	East London	1988/89

CLOSE FINISHES

Tied matches:

Worcestershire v South Africans	Worcester	1901
Middlesex v South Africans	Lord's	1904
Western Province v Eastern Province (SACB)	Cape Town	1984/85
Eastern Province B v Boland (CB)	Grahamstown	1985/86
Natal B v Eastern Province B (CB)	Pietermaritzburg	1985/86

Note: The last two instances occurred in consecutive matches played by Eastern Province B.

Victory by one wicket:

There have been 37 occasions in which South African teams have been involved.

Victory by 10 runs or less:

There have been 38 occasions in which South African teams have been involved.

LOWEST INNINGS TOTAL TO INCLUDE A CENTURY

170 (ML Bruyns 102*)	Border v Northerns (SS)	Centurion	2001/02
172 (G Boycott 107)	Northern Transvaal v Rhodesia	Pretoria	1971/72
177 (JH Sinclair 106)	South Africa v England (2nd Test)	Cape Town	1898/99
World record:			
143 (CEB Rice 105*)	Nottinghamshire v Hampshire	Bournemouth	1981

HIGHEST INNINGS TOTAL NOT TO INCLUDE A CENTURY

517	South Africa v Australia	Adelaide (highest score 87)	1997/98
512	South Africans v South Australia	Adelaide (highest score 97)	1931/32
503	Transvaal v Orange Free State (CC)	Bloemfontein (highest score 91)	1903/04

BATTING

HIGHEST INDIVIDUAL INNINGS

337*	DJ Cullinan	Transvaal v Northern Transvaal (CC)	Johannesburg	1993/94
317	CH Gayle	West Indies v South Africa (4th Test)	St John's	2004/05
307*	TN Lazard	Boland v Western Province	Worcester	1993/94
306*	EAB Rowan	Transvaal v Natal	Johannesburg	1939/40
304*	AW Nourse	Natal v Transvaal	Johannesburg	1919/20
300	DCS Compton	MCC v North-Eastern Transvaal	Benoni	1948/49

Note: The highest score by a South African is 356 by BA Richards, for South Australia v Western Australia at Perth, 1970/71 (he scored 325 runs in a day).

SOUTH AFRICAN FIRST-CLASS RECORDS

HIGHEST MAIDEN CENTURIES

261*	SSL Steyn	Western Province v Border (CC)	Cape Town	1929/30
240	WFE Marx	Transvaal v Griqualand West (CC)	Johannesburg	1920/21

(On debut in first-class cricket - a world record until 1993/94)

DOUBLE CENTURIES

Players who have scored most double centuries:

8 G Kirsten — 6 AD Nourse

7 AW Nourse — 5 EJ Barlow, RG Pollock, EAB Rowan

Note: BA Richards scored six double centuries in all first-class cricket, only one of them in South Africa.

EJ Barlow scored six double centuries in all first-class cricket, including five for South African teams, three of them in South Africa and two in Australia. PN Kirsten scored eight double centuries in all first-class cricket, two of them in South Africa.

Two double centuries in the same innings:

AD Nourse 240, IJ Siedle 207	Natal v Western Province (CC)	Durban	1936/37
(This was Siedle's last innings in first-class cricket)			
TL Goddard 222, HM Ackerman 200*	North-Eastern Transvaal v Western Province (CC)	Cape Town	1966/67

CENTURY ON FIRST-CLASS DEBUT

(Notable instances and current players)

240	WFE Marx	Tvl v GW (CC)	Johannesburg	1920/21
183*	R Watson-Smith	Bdr v OFS (CC)	Bloemfontein	1969/70
	(Watson-Smith scored 125* in his next innings for Bdr v GW (CC) at East London and thus scored 308 runs in his first two innings without being dismissed - a world record)			
+122*	JM Henderson	Bol B v OFS B (UB)	Bloemfontein	1994/95
112	A Jacobs	NW v WP B (UB)	Potchefstroom	1997/98
187	GC Smith	UCB Inv XI v GW	Kimberley	1999/00
106	ET Nkwe	Gau v Eas (SS)	Johannesburg	2002/03
115	M Bekker	KZN v Zim U23 (PC)	Chatsworth	2005/06
122*	DM van Wyk	Gau v Nor (PC)	Pretoria	2005/06

+ Second innings.

DOUBLE CENTURY AND CENTURY IN A MATCH

210	112*	AM Bacher	Tvl v GW (SS)	Kimberley	1996/97
200*	171	HH Gibbs	SA v Ind A	Nagpur	1996/97

CENTURIES IN EACH INNINGS

(Current players)

105	102*	HH Dippenaar	FS v KZN (SS)	Durban	1998/99
131	129	JDC Bryant	EP v WP (SS)	Cape Town	1999/00
100	115	CM Spearman	NZ v NW	Potchefstroom	2000/01
142	199*	A Flower	Zim v SA	Harare	2001/02
105	101*	JA Beukes	FS v Bdr (SS)	East London	2001/02
182*	158*	M van Jaarsveld	Nor v GW (SS)	Centurion	2001/02
122	110*	JM Henderson	NW v Gau (SS)	Potchefstroom	2002/03
156*	113	SC Pope	War v Eag (SS)	East London	2004/05
134	123	SC Cook	Gau v Bdr (PC)	East London	2004/05
115	127*	JG Myburgh	Nor v KZN (PC)	Durban	2004/05
149	109*	AN Petersen	Nor v FS (PC)	Pretoria	2004/05
132*	101*	W Wyngaard	WP v Bdr (PC)	Cape Town	2005/06
120	143*	RT Ponting	Aus v SA	Sydney	2005/06
103	116	RT Ponting	Aus v SA	Durban	2005/06

FOUR OR MORE CENTURIES IN SUCCESSIVE INNINGS

Six centuries:

MJ Procter (Rhodesia 1970/71) equalled the world record held jointly by CB Fry (1901) and DG Bradman (1938/39). 119 v Natal B (CC) at Bulawayo; 129 v Transvaal B (CC) at Salisbury; 107 v Orange Free State (CC) at Bloemfontein; 174 v North-Eastern Transvaal (CC) at Pretoria; 106 v Griqualand West (CC) at Kimberley and 254 v Western Province at Salisbury.

SOUTH AFRICAN FIRST-CLASS RECORDS

Four centuries:

DG Bradman (New South Wales and Australia, all v South Africa)	1931/32
PBH May (MCC)	1956/57
PN Kirsten (WP and SA Universities) (he scored six centuries in seven innings)	1976/77

Note: KS McEwan for Essex in 1977, SJ Cook for Somerset in 1989.

YOUNGEST PLAYER TO SCORE A CENTURY

16 years 304 days	DJ Cullinan (106*)	Border v Natal B (CB)	East London	1983/84

YOUNGEST PLAYER TO SCORE A DOUBLE CENTURY

17 years 122 days	JG Myburgh (203)	Northerns B v Easterns (UB)	Pretoria	1997/98

MOST CENTURIES IN A SEASON

6 BA Richards (Natal/SA) 1969/70, MJ Procter (Rhodesia) 1970/71 and PN Kirsten (WP/SA Universities) 1976/77

MOST CENTURIES IN A CAREER

+ Denotes current player

AJ Lamb	89	PN Kirsten	57
BA Richards	80	BF Davison	53
KS McEwan	74	MJ Procter	48
KC Wessels	66	CEB Rice	48
SJ Cook	64	CL Smith	47
RG Pollock	64	G Kirsten	46
RA Smith	61	BL D'Oliveira	45
South African first-class cricket only:			
RG Pollock	61	SJ Cook	36
G Kirsten	46	+JH Kallis	35
AD Nourse	41	BA Richards	33
DJ Cullinan	39	+HH Gibbs	31
AW Nourse	38	B Mitchell	30
EJ Barlow	37	EAB Rowan	30
PN Kirsten	37	HW Taylor	30
Currie Cup/Castle Cup/SuperSport Series only:			
RG Pollock	35	KC Wessels	22
SJ Cook	32	DJ Cullinan	20
PN Kirsten	29	EJ Barlow	20
BA Richards	26		

CARRYING BAT THROUGH A COMPLETED INNINGS

(Current players)

DJ Watson	103*	(246)	Ntl B v FS B (UB)	Durban	1995/96
JM Henderson	117*	(235)	Bol v FS (SS)	Stellenbosch	1998/99
CC Bradfield	64*	(149)	EP v Nor (SS)	Port Elizabeth	2000/01
ML Bruyns	102*	(170)	Bdr v Nor (SS)	Centurion	2001/02
ML Bruyns	110*	(251)	War v WP Bol (SS)	East London	2004/05
AJ Seymore	135*	(241)	Eas v Nor (PC)	Benoni	2005/06
DJ Kgamadi	53*	(145)	NW v Nor (PC)	Potchefstroom	2005/06

Note: DJ McGlew carried his bat four times, EW Warner three times, ML Bruyns, TL Goddard, E Mall and JH van den Berg twice each.

MOST RUNS IN A SEASON

By a home player:

	M	Inns	NO	Runs	HS	Avg	100	50	Season
HD Ackerman (WP)	16	29	2	1373	202 *	50.85	5	6	1997/98
BA Richards (Ntl)	12	18	2	1285	186 *	80.31	4	8	1973/74
M van Jaarsveld (Nor)	11	19	2	1268	182 *	74.58	5	5	2001/02
BA Richards (Ntl)	10	19	1	1247	197	69.27	5	5	1972/73
BA Richards (Ntl)	10	18	2	1172	169	73.25	6	3	1969/70
SJ Cook (Tvl)	13	21	2	1142	201 *	60.10	4	5	1982/83
HM Amla (Dol)	13	22	3	1126	153	59.26	3	7	2005/06

AB de Villiers (Ttn)	14	25	3	1122	151	51.00	3	5	2004/05
RG Pollock (EP)	10	19	5	1097	167 *	78.35	5	4	1974/75
BA Richards (Ntl)	8	15	1	1089	219	77.78	4	4	1971/72
PN Kirsten (WP)	9	15	1	1074	173 *	76.71	6	1	1976/77
HH Dippenaar (FS)	11	21	3	1070	147	59.44	4	6	1998/99
BA Richards (Ntl)	11	21	4	1051	159	61.82	3	5	1975/76
KC Bland (Rho)	10	18	3	1048	151 *	69.86	3	7	1964/65
Z de Bruyn (Eas)	10	17	1	1048	266 *	65.50	3	5	2003/04
RG Pollock (EP)	8	14	2	1043	196	86.91	3	5	1968/69
SJ Cook (Tvl)	11	21	3	1016	166	56.44	2	6	1983/84
DT Lindsay (NE Tvl)	10	14	0	1014	216	72.42	4	4	1966/67
RG Pollock (EP)	10	19	4	1013	194	67.53	3	5	1975/76
AM Bacher (Tvl)	10	19	2	1012	210	59.52	4	3	1996/97
RF Pienaar (Tvl)	11	20	4	1010	152 *	63.12	3	6	1989/90
RG Pollock (EP)	9	16	0	1005	274	62.81	4	4	1969/70
HM Amla (Dol)	14	22	2	1003	249	50.15	5	1	2004/05
Note also:									
RG Pollock (Tvl)	8	11	1	961	233	96.10	5	3	1978/79
MJ Procter (Rho)	8	8	0	956	254	119.50	6	0	1970/71
AD Nourse (Ntl)	5	6	1	846	260 *	169.20	4	0	1936/37
JH Kallis (WP)	5	7	2	817	177	163.40	5	1	2003/04

BA Richards played domestic cricket in Australia in 1970/71, returning to South Africa for one match at the end of the season. In all, he played the same number of innings as in 1973/74, but had an even better record:

In Australia (South Australia)	10	16	2	1538	356	109.85	6	3	
In SA (Transvaal Inv XI)	1	2	0	207	140	103.50	1	1	
Total	11	18	2	1745	356	109.06	7	4	
Currie Cup/Castle Cup/SuperSport Series only:									
BA Richards (Ntl)	8	15	1	1089	219	77.78	4	4	1971/72
BA Richards (Ntl)	8	16	1	1064	197	70.93	4	5	1972/73
Z de Bruyn (Eas)	9	15	1	1015	266 *	72.50	3	5	2003/04
By touring players:									
JR Reid (New Zealand)	17	30	2	1915	203	68.39	7	9	1961/62
For South African teams abroad:									
In Australia and New Zealand:									
EJ Barlow	18	32	2	1900	209	63.33	6	8	1963/64
In England:									
B Mitchell	23	37	4	2014	189 *	61.03	8	8	1947

FAST SCORING

Fastest 300:					
181 mins	DCS Compton	(300)	MCC v North-Eastern Transvaal	Benoni	1948/49
Fastest 200s:					
144 mins	DCS Compton	(300)	MCC v North-Eastern Transvaal	Benoni	1948/49
165 mins	L Hutton	(202)	MCC v Eastern Province	Port Elizabeth	1938/39
Fastest 100s:					
53 mins	MG Francis	(115*)	Orange Free State v Griqualand West	Bloemfontein	1927/28
55 mins	GL Tapscott	(111)	Rest of South Africa v Transvaal	Johannesburg	1911/12
60 mins	SJ Snooke	(121)	Western Province v Griqualand West (CC)	Johannesburg	1906/07
Fastest 50s:					
14 mins	SJ Pegler	(50)	South Africans v Tasmania	Launceston	1910/11
14 mins	HB Cameron	(56)	Transvaal v Orange Free State (CC)	Johannesburg	1934/35
16 mins	PGV van der Bijl	(51*)	Western Province v Eastern Province (CC)	Cape Town	1937/38

Note:

HW Taylor scored 250* in 225 minutes, Natal v Transvaal (CC) at Johannesburg, 1912/13.

MG Francis scored 115* in 66 minutes, Orange Free State v Griqualand West at Bloemfontein, 1927/28.

MJ Procter increased his score from 100 to 150 in 12 minutes, Western Province v Australians at Cape Town, 1969/70.

IR Redpath increased his score from 101 to 152 in 12 minutes, Australians v Orange Free State at Bloemfontein, 1969/70.

FB Touzel increased his score from 50 to 100 in 9 minutes, off 14 balls, Western Province B v Griqualand West (UB) at Kimberley (6x6, 2x4, 1x3, 1x2, 1x1), 1993/94 (Scored in contrived circumstances to expedite a declaration).

The fastest known century in terms of balls faced is 55 by JM Kemp, Northerns v Easterns (PC) at Centurion, 2004/05.

SOUTH AFRICAN FIRST-CLASS RECORDS

CENTURY BEFORE LUNCH

(Current players)

HH Gibbs	(163*)	WP v Ntl (SS)	Cape Town	1996/97
		(Score increased from 47* to 163* on second morning)		
CS Baugh	(158*)	WI v FS	Bloemfontein	2003/04
		(Innings started on fourth morning, 108* at lunch)		
CH Gayle	(145)	WI v Eas	Benoni	2003/04
		(Innings started on first morning, 110* at lunch)		
AJA Gray	(108)	WP v Bol (PC)	Cape Town	2005/06
		(Innings started on first morning, 102* at lunch)		

Note: BA Richards hit a century before lunch on nine occasions during his career. RG Draper (GW) hit centuries before lunch in three successive Currie Cup matches 1951/52-1952/53.

MOST SIXES IN AN INNINGS

13	FB Touzel	(128*)	Western Province B v Griqualand West (UB)	Kimberley	1993/94
			(Scored in contrived circumstances to expedite a declaration)		
10	HR Lance	(122)	Transvaal v Eastern Province (CC)	Johannesburg	1966/67
10	EA Brandes	(165*)	Zimbabwe Board XI v Griqualand West (UB)	Kimberley	1994/95
10	G Dros	(130)	Northerns v Griqualand West (PC)	Pretoria	2005/06
9	PJ Heather	(109*)	Transvaal v Border (CC)	Durban	1910/11
9	MJ Procter	(155)	Western Province v Australians	Cape Town	1969/70
9	SM Skeete	(119)	Eastern Transvaal v Border B (UB)	Springs	1994/95
9	AP Kuiper	(117*)	Boland v Free State (SS)	Paarl	1996/97
9	H Pangarker	(128*)	Western Province B v Natal B (UB)	Cape Town	1997/98
9	JM Kemp	(188)	Eastern Province v North West (SS)	Port Elizabeth	2000/01

HITS FOR SIX OFF CONSECUTIVE BALLS

5	DT Lindsay	off WT Greensmith	Fezelas v Essex	Chelmsford	1961
5	MJ Procter	off AA Mallett	Western Province v Australians	Cape Town	1969/70
5	JM Kemp	off M Strydom	Eastern Province v North West (SS)	Port Elizabeth	2000/01

MOST RUNS OFF AN OVER

34 (646666)	FB Touzel off FJJ Viljoen	Western Province B v Griqualand West (UB)	Kimberley	1993/94
	(Scored in contrived circumstances to expedite a declaration)			
32 (666644)	IR Redpath off N Rosendorff	Australians v Orange Free State	Bloemfontein	1969/70
31 (1)	MH Bowditch and			
(66666)	MJ Procter off AA Mallett	Western Province v Australians	Cape Town	1969/70
31 (666661)	JM Kemp off M Strydom	Eastern Province v North West (SS)	Port Elizabeth	2000/01
30 (444666)	HB Cameron off H Verity	South Africans v Yorkshire	Sheffield	1935
30 (446646)	PL Winslow off JT Ikin	South Africans v Lancashire	Manchester	1955
30 (066666)	DT Lindsay off WT Greensmith	Fezelas v Essex	Chelmsford	1961
30 (246666)	JD du Toit off CE Eksteen	Boland v Transvaal	Vereeniging	1989/90

Note: For South Africa v Australia (3rd Test) at Cape Town in 1902/03, JH Sinclair hit 34 (44624464) off eight successive balls.

MOST BOUNDARIES IN AN INNINGS

Fours	Sixes				
53	0	AW Nourse (304*)	Ntl v Tvl	Johannesburg	1919/20

SLOW SCORING

Slowest 100s:

545 mins DJ McGlew	(105)	South Africa v Australia (3rd Test)	Durban	1957/58
488 mins PE Richardson	(117)	England v South Africa (1st Test)	Johannesburg	1956/57
484 mins DJ Schonegevel	(114*)	Griqualand West v Northern Transvaal (CC)	Kimberley	1972/73

Slowest 50s:

333 mins BA Young	(51)	New Zealand v South Africa (2nd Test)	Durban	1994/95
313 mins DJ McGlew	(70)	South Africa v Australia (4th Test)	Johannesburg	1957/58
296 mins BM White	(76)	Border v Northerns (SS)	Centurion	1999/00

SOUTH AFRICAN FIRST-CLASS RECORDS

Longest period before opening score:

101 mins	GI Allott	New Zealand v South Africa (1st Test)	Auckland	1998/99
	(He was out for 0. The longest known instance in first-class cricket of a player scoring 0)			
96 mins	DJ Watson	KwaZulu-Natal v Boland (SS)	Durban	2002/03
	(He went on to make 129 in 419 minutes)			
87 mins	VR Hogg	Zimbabwe-Rhodesia B v Natal B (CB)	Pietermaritzburg	1979/80
	(He was out for 0. The longest known instance in first-class cricket of a player scoring 0 until the innings by GI Allott, above)			
73 mins	BJ Versfeld	Natal v Transvaal (CC)	Durban	1965/66
	(He went on to make 100 in 350 minutes and 201* in 559 minutes)			

Note: B Mitchell (58) for South Africa v Australia (1st Test) at Brisbane in 1931/32 did not add to his score for 90 minutes

RECORD WICKET PARTNERSHIPS

In South Africa:

1st	424	IJ Siedle (174) and JFW Nicolson (252*)	Natal v OFS (CC)	Bloemfontein	1926/27
2nd	441	CC Bradfield (196) and JDC Bryant (234*)	Eastern Province v North West (SS)	Potchefstroom	2002/03
3rd	400	RT Simpson (130*) and DCS Compton (300)	MCC v NE Transvaal	Benoni	1948/49
	361	DJ Jacobs (218) and RT Bailey (148)	Eagles v Dolphins (SS)	Bloemfontein	2004/05
4th	342	EAB Rowan (195) and PJM Gibb (203)	Transvaal v NE Transvaal (CC)	Johannesburg	1952/53
5th	385	SR Waugh (160) and GS Blewett (214)	Australia v South Africa	Johannesburg	1996/97
	355	AJ Lamb (294) and JJ Strydom (107)	OFS v Eastern Province (CC)	Bloemfontein	1987/88
6th	317	DR Martyn (133) and AC Gilchrist (204*)	Australia v South Africa	Johannesburg	2001/02
	292	MN van Wyk (200*) and R McLaren (140)	Eagles v Warriors (SS)	Bloemfontein	2005/06
7th	299	B Mitchell (159) and A Melville (153)	Transvaal v Griqualand West (CC)	Kimberley	1946/47
8th	256	SP Fleming (262) and JEC Franklin (122*)	New Zealand v South Africa	Cape Town	2005/06
	222	SSL Steyn (261*) and DPB Morkel (114)	Western Province v Border (CC)	Cape Town	1929/30
9th	221	NV Lindsay (160*) and GR McCubbin (97)	Transvaal v Rhodesia	Bulawayo	1922/23
	217	AW Nourse (112*) and BC Cooley (113)	Natal v Western Province (CC)	Johannesburg	1906/07
10th	174	HR Lance (168) and D Mackay-Coghill (58*)	Transvaal v Natal (CC)	Johannesburg	1965/66
	174	AC Thomas (106*) and GA Roe (66)	North West v Griqualand West (SS)	Kimberley	2000/01

For South African teams abroad:

1st	338	GC Smith (277) and HH Gibbs (179)	SA v England	Birmingham	2003
2nd	315*	HH Gibbs (211*) and JH Kallis (148*)	SA v New Zealand	Christchurch	1998/99
3rd	429*	JA Rudolph (222*) and HH Dippenaar (177*)	SA v Bangladesh	Chittagong	2002/03
4th	242	WJ Cronje (145) and DJ Cullinan (113)	SA v Queensland	Brisbane	1993/94
5th	267	JH Kallis (147) and AG Prince (131)	SA v West Indies	St John's	2004/05
6th	187	EL Dalton (157) and Q McMillan (86)	SA v Kent	Canterbury	1929
7th	246	DJ McGlew (255*) and ARA Murray (109)	SA v New Zealand	Wellington	1952/53
8th	156	GC White (162*) and RO Schwarz (71)	SA v Gloucestershire	Bristol	1907
9th	268	JB Commins (164) and N Boje (102)	SA A v Mashonaland	Harare	1994/95
10th	103	HGO Owen-Smith (129) and AJ Bell (26*)	SA v England	Leeds	1929
	103	JA Morkel (94) and CK Langeveldt (37*)	SA A v Zimbabwe A	Bulawayo	2004

BATSMEN WHO HAVE SCORED 10000 RUNS IN A CAREER

+ Denotes current player

	Career	M	Inns	NO	Runs	HS	Avg	100	50
AJ Lamb	1972-95	467	772	108	32502	294	48.94	89	166
BA Richards	1964-82	339	576	58	28358	356	54.74	80	152
BF Davison	1967-87	467	766	79	27453	189	39.96	53	148
KS McEwan	1972-91	428	705	67	26628	218	41.73	74	122
CEB Rice	1969-93	482	766	123	26331	246	40.95	48	137
RA Smith	1980-2003	426	717	87	26155	209 *	41.51	61	131
KC Wessels	1973-99	316	539	50	24738	254	50.58	66	132
PN Kirsten	1973-96	327	568	59	22635	271	44.46	57	107
MJ Procter	1965-88	401	667	58	21936	254	36.01	48	109
SJ Cook	1972-94	270	475	57	21143	313 *	50.58	64	87
RG Pollock	1960-86	262	437	54	20940	274	54.67	64	99
BL D'Oliveira	1961-80	367	575	91	19490	227	40.26	45	101
EJ Barlow	1959-82	283	493	28	18212	217	39.16	43	86
CL Smith	1977-91	269	466	60	18028	217	44.40	47	88

G Kirsten	1987-2003	221	387	42	16670	275	48.31	46	79
AW Greig	1965-78	350	579	45	16660	226	31.19	26	97
DJ Cullinan	1983-2004	246	417	54	16261	337 *	44.79	44	79
RC Ontong	1972-94	367	604	87	15234	204 *	29.46	20	78
AW Nourse	1896-1935	228	371	39	14216	304 *	42.81	38	60
+JH Kallis	1993-	188	306	42	14069	200	53.29	40	76
NG Featherstone	1967-81	329	528	54	13922	147	29.37	12	88
HW Taylor	1909-35	206	339	26	13105	250 *	41.86	30	64
AD Nourse	1931-52	175	269	27	12472	260 *	51.53	41	54
+HH Gibbs	1990-	171	294	12	12460	228	44.18	31	53
HM Ackerman	1963-81	234	409	33	12219	208	32.49	20	60
DJ McGlew	1947-66	190	299	34	12170	255 *	45.92	27	68
WJ Cronje	1987-99	184	310	33	12103	251	43.69	32	57
EAB Rowan	1929-53	157	258	17	11710	306 *	48.58	30	54
SH Martin	1925-49	267	457	31	11511	191 *	27.02	13	68
CB Llewellyn	1894-1912	267	461	34	11425	216	26.75	18	52
B Mitchell	1925-49	173	281	30	11395	195	45.39	30	55
TL Goddard	1952-69	179	298	20	11289	222	40.60	26	54
RA McLean	1949-65	200	318	19	10969	207	36.68	22	65
CP Wilkins	1962-82	198	357	21	10966	156	32.63	18	61
RF Pienaar	1977-98	199	346	27	10896	153	34.15	18	62
A Melville	1928-48	190	295	15	10598	189	37.85	25	53
South African first-class cricket only:									
RG Pollock	1960-86	246	410	53	20070	274	56.21	61	95
G Kirsten	1987-2003	221	387	42	16670	275	48.31	46	79
DJ Cullinan	1983-2004	229	388	50	15136	337 *	44.78	39	76
PN Kirsten	1973-96	220	386	34	14882	271	42.27	37	74
EJ Barlow	1959-82	208	367	20	14406	212	41.51	37	66
AW Nourse	1896-1935	228	371	39	14216	304 *	42.81	38	60
SJ Cook	1972-94	199	351	38	13539	228	43.25	36	60
HW Taylor	1909-35	197	324	25	12669	250 *	42.37	30	63
+JH Kallis	1993-	165	270	38	12590	200	54.26	35	70
AD Nourse	1931-52	175	269	27	12472	260 *	51.53	41	54
Currie Cup/Castle Cup/SuperSport Series only:									
RG Pollock	1960-86	157	261	34	12409	233	54.66	35	64
PN Kirsten	1973-96	170	300	19	11835	271	42.11	29	57
SJ Cook	1972-94	163	289	33	11307	201 *	44.16	32	48
KC Wessels	1973-99	114	195	23	8487	197	49.34	22	45
HR Fotheringham	1971-89	132	220	21	7981	184	40.10	19	44
EJ Barlow	1959-82	122	217	11	7881	212	38.25	20	35
DJ Cullinan	1983-2004	111	194	26	7737	337 *	46.05	20	40
CEB Rice	1969-93	164	259	43	7714	150 *	35.71	11	41
BA Richards	1964-82	79	140	15	7551	219	60.40	26	36
MW Rushmere	1983-99	119	207	25	7074	188	38.86	17	34

BOWLING

BEST BOWLING IN AN INNINGS

TEN WICKETS

O M R W				
12-2-26-10	AEE Vogler	EP v GW (CC)	Johannesburg	1906/07
23.5-7-59-10	ST Jefferies	WP v OFS (CC)	Cape Town	1987/88

NINE WICKETS (outstanding instances)

9-19	AMB Rowan	Tvl v Aus	Johannesburg	1949/50
9-22	MG Melle	SA v Tasmania	Launceston	1952/53
9-23	WP Howell	Aus v WP	Cape Town	1902/03
9-23	JT Botten	NE Tvl v GW (CC)	Pretoria	1958/59
9-28	GA Lohmann	Eng v SA (2nd Test)	Johannesburg	1895/96
9-29	JT Botten	NE Tvl v Rho (CC)	Pretoria	1963/64

9-32	JM Gregory	AIF v Ntl	Durban	1919/20
9-32	AF Hagemann	Bdr v GW (CC)	Kimberley	1960/61
9-46	VA Barnes	WP v Ntl (SACB)	Ladysmith	1983/84
9-48	EP Nupen	Tvl v GW (CC)	Johannesburg	1931/32
9-52	MH Bowditch	WP v Ntl (CC)	Cape Town	1965/66
	(The first occasion Bowditch had bowled in first class cricket. He had played in one match previously)			
9-53	Q McMillan	SA v S Australia	Adelaide	1931/32
9-54	K McLaren	GW v Ntl B (CC)	Umzinto	1973/74
9-56	MJ Horton	Worcestershire v SA	Worcester	1955
9-57	N Edwards	Tvl v Ntl (SACB)	Tongaat	1984/85
9-57	DE Malcolm	Eng v SA (3rd Test)	The Oval	1994
9-64	RJ Crisp	WP v Ntl (CC)	Durban	1933/34
9-64	DL Hobson	WP v EP (CC)	Cape Town	1978/79
9-71	MJ Procter	Rho v Tvl (CC)	Bulawayo	1972/73
9-72	GJ Parsons	Bol v Tvl B (CB)	Johannesburg	1984/85
EIGHT WICKETS (outstanding instances)				
8-7	GA Lohmann	Eng v SA (1st Test)	Port Elizabeth	1895/96
8-8	MG Melle	Tvl v GW (CC)	Johannesburg	1950/51
8-11	J Briggs	Eng v SA (2nd Test)	Cape Town	1888/89
8-12	RW Norden	Tvl v Rho (CC)	Johannesburg	1904/05
8-13	DPB Morkel	SA v W Australia	Perth	1931/32
8-18	JJ Kotze	Tvl v GW (CC)	Port Elizabeth	1902/03
8-20	JL Cox	Ntl v Tvl (CC)	Durban	1910/11
8-22	GM Gilder	SA A v Worcestershire	Worcester	1996
8-24	AEE Vogler	EP v OFS (CC)	Johannesburg	1906/07
8-25	GA Rowe	WP v SWD (CC)	Mossel Bay	1904/05
8-28	FTM Drummer	WP v Bdr (CC)	East London	1966/67
8-29	SF Barnes	Eng v SA (3rd Test)	The Oval	1912
8-29	VA Barnes	WP v Ntl (SACB)	Durban	1982/83
8-29	VA Barnes	Tvl v WP (SACB)	Johannesburg	1985/86
8-31	WP Howell	Aus v WP	Cape Town	1902/03
	(Howell took 9-23 in the second innings)			
8-31	RJ Crisp	WP v GW (CC)	Johannesburg	1931/32
	(The other two batsmen were absent)			
8-32	L Tuckett	OFS v GW (CC)	Kimberley	1951/52
8-34	S Haigh	Lord Hawke's XI v Cape Colony	Cape Town	1898/99
8-34	AJ Bell	WP v EP (CC)	Cape Town	1929/30
8-34	L Klusener	Ntl v WP (CC)	Durban	1995/96
8-35	GK Glover	GW v EP (CC)	Cape Town	1893/94
8-35	JT Botten	Fezelas v Gloucestershire	Bristol	1961
8-35	VAP van der Bijl	Ntl v WP (CC)	Pietermaritzburg	1971/72
8-35	M Rampersad	Ntl v Tvl (SACB)	Johannesburg	1984/85
SEVEN WICKETS (outstanding instances)				
7- 4	WA Henderson	NE Tvl v OFS (CC)	Bloemfontein	1937/38
7- 9	JT Partridge	Rho v Bdr (CC)	Bulawayo	1959/60
7-10	AC King	Ntl v GW (CC)	Johannesburg	1906/07
7-11	SF Burke	OFS v EP (CC)	Port Elizabeth	1958/59
7-11	GM Griffin	Ntl v Bdr (CC)	East London	1959/60
SIX WICKETS (outstanding instances)				
6-1	VI Smith	SA v Derbyshire	Derby	1947
6-3	TL Goddard	Ntl v Bdr (CC)	East London	1959/60
6-7	AER Gilligan	Eng v SA (1st Test)	Birmingham	1924
6-7	AL Adams	WP v EP (SACB)	Cape Town	1979/80
6-8	JP McNally	GW v EP (CC)	Kimberley	1934/35
FIVE WICKETS (outstanding instances)				
5-2	S Elworthy	Nor v GW (SS)	Centurion	1997/98
5-4	E Amod	Tvl v EP (SACB)	Port Elizabeth	1977/78
5-5	AJ Kourie	Tvl v EP (CC)	Johannesburg	1986/87
5-6	JJ Kotze	WP v GW (CC)	Johannesburg	1906/07
5-6	H Ironmonger	Aus v SA (5th Test)	Melbourne	1931/32

5-6	Y Thomas	WP v Tvl (SACB)	Cape Town	1982/83
5-6	CW Henderson	WP v Nor (SS)	Centurion	2000/01
5-7	AS Kennedy	MCC v Bdr	East London	1922/23

BEST BOWLING IN A MATCH

17 WICKETS				
17-54	WP Howell	Aus v WP	Cape Town	1902/03
17-159	SF Barnes	Eng v SA (2nd Test)	Johannesburg	1913/14
16 WICKETS				
16-38	AEE Vogler	EP v GW (CC)	Johannesburg	1906/07
16-136	EP Nupen	Tvl v GW (CC)	Johannesburg	1931/32
15 WICKETS				
15-28	J Briggs	Eng v SA (2nd Test)	Cape Town	1888/89
15-45	GA Lohmann	Eng v SA (1st Test)	Port Elizabeth	1895/96
15-49	JT Botten	NE Tvl v GW (CC)	Pretoria	1958/59
15-68	GK Glover	GW v EP (CC)	Cape Town	1893/94
15-68	AMB Rowan	Tvl v Aus	Johannesburg	1949/50
15-99	C Blythe	Eng v SA (2nd Test)	Leeds	1907
14 WICKETS				
14-58	AEE Vogler	EP v OFS (CC)	Johannesburg	1906/07
14-59	AF Hagemann	Bdr v GW (CC)	Kimberley	1960/61
14-79	DW McCosh	N Tvl B v EP B (CB)	Port Elizabeth	1988/89
14-86	JM Gregory	AIF v Ntl	Durban	1919/20
14-96	JH Wardle	MCC v OFS	Bloemfontein	1956/57
14-101	JT Partridge	Rho v Ntl	Salisbury	1961/62
14-111	VAP van der Bijl	Ntl v N Tvl (CC)	Pretoria	1981/82
14-113	DL Hobson	WP v Ntl (CC)	Cape Town	1975/76
14-115	AE Hall	Tvl v Ntl (CC)	Johannesburg	1926/27
14-119	J Mercer	Glamorgan v SA	Pontypridd	1929
14-126	HJ Tayfield	SA v Hampshire	Southampton	1955
14-144	SF Barnes	Eng v SA (4th Test)	Durban	1913/14
14-153	VI Smith	Ntl v EP (CC)	Durban	1955/56
14-154	DLC McCay	WP v Ntl B (CC)	Cape Town	1966/67
14-199	CV Grimmett	Aus v SA (4th Test)	Adelaide	1931/32
13 WICKETS (outstanding instances)				
13-53	VAP van der Bijl	Ntl v WP (CC)	Pietermaritzburg	1971/72
13-56	VA Barnes	SACBOC XI v President's XI	Cape Town	1987/88
13-57	SF Barnes	Eng v SA (3rd Test)	The Oval	1912
13-59	JE Waddington	GW v Bdr (CC)	Kimberley	1947/48
13-61	AJ Bell (All 13 were bowled)	WP v EP (CC)	Cape Town	1929/30
12 WICKETS (outstanding instances)				
12-33	RW Norden	Tvl v Rho (CC)	Johannesburg	1904/05
12-47	P Joubert	Nor v EP (SS)	Port Elizabeth	2003/04
12-53	RW Hanley	Tvl v EP (CC)	Johannesburg	1983/84
12-56	MG Melle	SA v Tasmania	Launceston	1952/53
12-58	GV Wienand	Bdr v EP (CC)	East London	1946/47
12-59	SF Burke	NE Tvl v Tvl B (CC)	Johannesburg	1963/64
11 WICKETS (outstanding instances)				
11-24	H Ironmonger	Aus v SA (5th Test)	Melbourne	1931/32
11-33	VAP van der Bijl	Ntl v SAU	Durban	1975/76
11-37	JJ Kotze	Tvl v GW (CC)	Port Elizabeth	1902/03
11-45	SD Snooke	WP v Bdr (CC)	Durban	1910/11
11-45	AA Jones	N Tvl v OFS (CC)	Pretoria	1972/73
11-45	A Jabaar	WP v Ntl (SACB)	Cape Town	1977/78
10 WICKETS (outstanding instances)				
10-15	AL Adams	WP v EP (SACB)	Cape Town	1979/80
10-30	MG Melle	Tvl v GW (CC)	Johannesburg	1950/51
10-31	PS Hubbard	Bdr v EP (CC)	East London	1936/37
10-33	VA Barnes	WP v Ntl (SACB)	Cape Town	1988/89

10-34	D Govindjee	EP v Tvl (SACB)	Port Elizabeth	1981/82
10-35	S Draai	EP v Tvl (SACB)	Johannesburg	1979/80

MOST WICKETS IN A DAY

16-38	AEE Vogler	EP v GW (CC)	Johannesburg	1906/07
15-28	J Briggs	Eng v SA (2nd Test)	Cape Town	1888/89
14-96	JH Wardle	MCC v OFS	Bloemfontein	1956/57
14-113	DL Hobson	WP v Ntl (CC)	Cape Town	1975/76

FOUR WICKETS WITH CONSECUTIVE BALLS

S Haigh	MCC v The Army	Roberts Heights	1905/06
AF Borland	Ntl v GW (CC)	Kimberley	1926/27
RJ Crisp	WP v GW (CC)	Johannesburg	1931/32
RJ Crisp	WP v Ntl (CC)	Durban	1933/34
WA Henderson	NE Tvl v OFS (CC)	Bloemfontein	1937/38
(He went on to take five wickets in six balls)			
CM Willoughby	Cob v Dol (SS)	Durban	2005/06

HAT-TRICK IN BOTH INNINGS OF A MATCH

TJ Matthews	Aus v SA (1st Test)	Manchester	1912

HAT-TRICKS

(Current players)

CW Henderson	Bol v Warwickshire	Paarl	1994/95
M Ntini	Bdr v FS (SS)	Bloemfontein	1999/00
GJ-P Kruger	EP v SL	Port Elizabeth	2000/01
GJ Kruis	GW v KZN (SS)	Durban	2000/01
M Ntini	Bdr v FS (SS)	Bloemfontein	2001/02
CM Willoughby	WP v EP (SS)	Cape Town	2001/02
RP Symcox	Dol v Lio (SS)	Johannesburg	2004/05
GJ-P Kruger	Lio v War (SS)	Johannesburg	2005/06
M de Stadler	WP v Bol (PC)	Cape Town	2005/06
CM Willoughby	Cob v Dol (SS)	Durban	2005/06
JP Kreusch	War v Cob (SS)	Stellenbosch	2005/06

Note: RJ Crisp performed this feat three times. Those who have done it twice are AF Borland, GA Faulkner, TL Goddard, TWJ Goddard, S Haigh, JJ Kotze, TJ Matthews (in the same match), M Ntini, VI Smith, HJ Tayfield, CJ van Heerden and CM Willoughby.

MOST WICKETS IN A SEASON

By home players (55 or more):

	M	Runs	Wkts	Avg	BB	5I	10M	Season
VAP van der Bijl (Ntl)	11	1119	75	14.92	8-47	10	4	1981/82
DW Steyn (Ttn/Nor)	13	1425	69	20.65	5-27	4	1	2005/06
VAP van der Bijl (Ntl)	13	1084	65	16.67	7-24	3	1	1975/76
JT Partridge (Rho)	11	1064	64	16.62	7-69	4	0	1962/63
VAP van der Bijl (Ntl)	12	1037	64	16.20	7-45	3	1	1973/74
JT Botten (NE Tvl)	7	664	63	10.53	9-23	7	2	1958/59
AJ Kourie (Tvl)	13	1501	63	23.82	7-79	5	0	1982/83
MJ Procter (Rho)	11	1049	60	17.48	9-71	4	2	1972/73
JN Maguire (EP)	10	903	60	15.05	6-48	6	2	1989/90
VC Drakes (Bdr)	10	979	60	16.31	5-26	3	0	1999/00
MJ Procter (Ntl)	8	936	59	15.86	7-77	7	2	1976/77
ST Jefferies (WP)	12	1386	58	23.89	6-91	3	0	1982/83
ST Clarke (Tvl)	10	738	58	12.72	5-8	6	1	1984/85
HJ Tayfield (Ntl/Tvl)	9	1036	56	18.50	9-113	6	2	1956/57
VC Drakes (Bdr)	9	820	56	14.64	5-35	5	0	1998/99
AEE Vogler (EP/Tvl)	9	580	55	10.54	10-26	7	2	1906/07
Currie Cup/Castle Cup/SuperSport Series only:								
VC Drakes (Bdr)	10	979	60	16.31	5-26	3	0	1999/00
MJ Procter (Ntl)	8	936	59	15.86	7-77	7	2	1976/77
ST Clarke (Tvl)	10	738	58	12.72	5-8	6	1	1984/85

SOUTH AFRICAN FIRST-CLASS RECORDS

By touring players (100 or more):								
R Benaud (Australia)	18	2056	106	19.39	7-46	11	2	1957/58
SF Barnes (England)	12	1117	104	10.74	9-103	13	5	1913/14
For South African teams abroad:								
In Australia and New Zealand:								
HJ Tayfield	17	2196	84	26.14	7-71	6	1	1952/53
In England:								
SJ Pegler	34	2885	189	15.26	7-31	17	3	1912

BEST BOWLING ON DEBUT

Eight or more wickets in an innings:

9-52	MH Bowditch	WP v Ntl (CC)	Cape Town	1965/66
9-122	GG Hall	SAU v WP	Cape Town	1960/61
8-64	WB Gadsden	Ntl v Tvl	Durban	1928/29
8-89	LW Payn	Ntl v OFS (CC)	Bloemfontein	1936/37

12 wickets in a match:

13-146	(4-24 & 9-122)	GG Hall	SAU v WP	Cape Town	1960/61
13-204	(7-82 & 6-122)	JHD Piton	Tvl v Kimberley (CC)	Johannesburg	1890/91
		(His second match. He did not bowl in his first match)			
12-120	(9-52 & 3-68)	MH Bowditch	WP v Ntl (CC)	Cape Town	1965/66
		(His second match. He did not bowl in his first match)			

BOWLERS WHO HAVE TAKEN 400 WICKETS IN A CAREER

+ Denotes current player

	Career	M	Runs	Wkts	Avg	BB	5I	10M
MJ Procter	1965-88	401	27679	1417	19.53	9-71	70	15
AA Donald	1985-2003	316	27680	1216	22.76	8-37	68	9
CB Llewellyn	1894-1912	267	23715	1013	23.41	9-55	82	20
NV Radford	1978-95	296	26707	994	26.86	9-70	48	7
CEB Rice	1969-93	482	20922	930	22.49	7-62	23	1
PB Clift	1971-87	319	21610	876	24.66	8-17	26	2
HJ Tayfield	1945-62	187	18890	864	21.86	9-113	67	16
AW Greig	1965-78	350	24702	856	28.85	8-25	33	8
RC Ontong	1972-94	367	26487	845	31.34	8-67	33	4
GS le Roux	1975-88	239	17800	838	21.24	8-107	35	3
VAP van der Bijl	1967-82	156	12692	767	16.54	8-35	46	12
+SM Pollock	1991-	177	14811	634	23.36	7-33	22	2
AM Ferreira	1974-91	245	17708	583	30.37	8-38	18	2
EJ Barlow	1959-82	283	13785	571	24.14	7-24	16	2
BL D'Oliveira	1961-80	367	15126	551	27.45	6-29	17	2
TL Goddard	1952-69	179	11563	534	21.65	6-3	24	1
SH Martin	1925-49	267	15063	532	28.31	8-24	21	6
+CW Henderson	1990-	146	15447	507	30.46	7-57	16	0
S Elworthy	1987-2003	138	13687	494	27.70	7-65	18	4
JH Sinclair	1892-1911	130	10530	492	21.40	8-32	33	10
PM Pollock	1958-71	127	10620	485	21.89	7-19	27	2
ST Jefferies	1978-93	142	13204	478	27.62	10-59	19	4
AH McKinnon	1952-68	111	9937	470	21.14	7-37	38	9
CE Eksteen	1985-2003	142	14034	468	29.98	7-29	17	1
+M Ntini	1995-	131	13372	458	29.19	7-37	19	4
GA Faulkner	1902-24	118	7826	449	17.42	7-26	33	8
WK Watson	1974-91	143	11034	446	24.73	7-50	16	0
+GJ Smith	1993-	141	12233	445	27.48	8-53	17	2
+CM Willoughby	1994-	120	11052	444	24.89	7-56	17	3
O Henry	1973-93	131	11151	443	25.17	7-22	22	3
+N Boje	1990-	159	14128	439	32.18	8-93	20	2
+L Klusener	1993-	144	12091	433	27.92	8-34	17	4
MW Pringle	1985-2000	119	10876	429	25.35	7-60	15	3
PS de Villiers	1985-97	102	9553	427	22.37	7-80	23	3
SJ Pegler	1908-30	103	8324	425	19.58	8-54	32	5

AJ Kourie	1970-88	127	9869	421	23.44	8-113	24	3
IA Greig	1974-91	253	13023	419	31.08	7-43	10	2
TG Shaw	1980-96	138	12118	417	29.05	7-79	15	2
RW Hanley	1970-86	113	8491	408	20.81	7-31	23	3
NAT Adcock	1952-62	99	6989	405	17.25	8-39	19	4
+M Hayward	1995-	120	11567	404	28.63	6-31	9	2
South African first-class cricket only:								
HJ Tayfield	1945-62	187	18890	864	21.86	9-113	67	16
VAP van der Bijl	1967-82	135	11402	681	16.74	8-35	41	11
AA Donald	1985-2003	174	16443	675	24.36	8-37	33	4
MJ Procter	1965-88	137	11021	569	19.36	9-71	27	10
+SM Pollock	1991-	154	12895	564	22.86	7-33	21	2
TL Goddard	1952-69	176	11311	522	21.66	6-3	24	1
AH McKinnon	1952-68	111	9937	470	21.14	7-37	38	9
CE Eksteen	1985-2003	142	14034	468	29.98	7-29	17	1
JH Sinclair	1892-1911	123	9848	468	21.04	8-40	32	10
PM Pollock	1958-71	117	9708	463	20.96	7-19	27	2
Currie Cup/Castle Cup/SuperSport Series only:								
VAP van der Bijl	1968-82	109	9395	572	16.42	8-35	36	9
MJ Procter	1965-88	110	9120	471	19.36	9-71	26	10
CEB Rice	1969-93	164	7975	396	20.13	7-62	11	1
CE Eksteen	1985-2003	115	11897	386	30.82	7-29	15	1
AJ Kourie	1970-88	107	8364	378	22.12	8-113	21	3
O Henry	1977-93	103	8937	375	23.83	7-82	19	2
+CW Henderson	1990-2003	92	10062	374	26.90	7-57	12	0
S Elworthy	1987-2002	98	9407	366	25.70	7-65	15	4
MW Pringle	1985-2000	90	8245	366	22.52	7-60	14	3
GS le Roux	1975-88	83	7125	365	19.52	7-40	16	2

ALL-ROUND PLAY

100 RUNS AND 10 WICKETS IN A MATCH

AE Trott	101*	7-74 & 4-66	Lord Hawke's XI v Tvl	Johannesburg	1898/99
GA Faulkner	42 & 68*	6-72 & 4-94	Tvl v WP (CC)	Cape Town	1908/09
GA Faulkner	54 & 73	5-32 & 5-106	SA v Queensland	Brisbane	1910/11
XC Balaskas	132	5-87 & 6-43	GW v EP (CC)	Kimberley	1929/30
XC Balaskas	101	6-142 & 6-93	GW v WP (CC)	Kimberley	1929/30
(In successive matches)					
LS Brown	63 & 37	6-89 & 4-54	NE Tvl v Tvl (CC)	Springs	1937/38
JR Liddle	31 & 77	7-97 & 5-115	OFS v Rho (CC)	Bulawayo	1951/52
PNF Mansell	94* & 13*	7-71 & 3-79	Rho v NE Tvl (CC)	Pretoria	1951/52
ARA Murray	78 & 44*	5-77 & 5-54	EP v Bdr	East London	1953/54
JPD Flanagan	98 & 17	8-113 & 2-86	Tvl B v Ntl B (CC)	Johannesburg	1968/69
CEB Rice	90 & 11	7-62 & 4-50	Tvl v WP (CC)	Johannesburg	1975/76
AL Barnes	107	6-50 & 5-47	Tvl v EP (SACB)	Johannesburg	1975/76
I Foulkes	130	3-62 & 7-54	Bdr v EP B (CB)	East London	1977/78
PD de Vaal	100*	3-32 & 7-94	E Tvl v W Tvl (UB)	Potchefstroom	1991/92
MJG Davis	60 & 46	8-37 & 4-47	N Tvl B v W Tvl (UB)	Potchefstroom	1994/95
N Boje	104* & 9*	5-84 & 6-34	FS v Nor (SS)	Bloemfontein	1997/98
J Botha	80 & 74*	5-72 & 5-66	Bdr v Gau (PC)	East London	2004/05

Note: MJ Procter scored 108 and took 7-35 & 6-38 for Gloucestershire v Worcestershire at Cheltenham, 1977 and scored 73 & 35 and took 7-16 & 7-60 for Gloucestershire v Worcestershire at Cheltenham, 1980.
RC Ontong scored 130 and took 5-39 & 8-67 for Glamorgan v Nottinghamshire at Nottingham, 1985.

500 RUNS AND 50 WICKETS IN A SEASON

By home players:	Runs	Avg	Wkts	Avg	Season
AEE Vogler	505	36.07	55	10.54	1906/07
PNF Mansell	571	43.92	52	17.63	1951/52
MJ Procter	695	40.88	52	16.01	1971/72
MJ Procter	870	48.33	60	17.48	1972/73

SOUTH AFRICAN FIRST-CLASS RECORDS

By touring players:

JR Reid	1012	37.48	51	19.54	1953/54
R Benaud	817	51.06	106	19.39	1957/58
AK Davidson	813	54.20	72	15.13	1957/58

4000 RUNS AND 200 WICKETS IN A CAREER

The following list, which is alphabetical, covers those who have made 4000 runs and taken 200 wickets in South African domestic cricket or for South African teams overseas. Some of the players have also played in overseas domestic cricket and these are marked *. + Denotes current player.

	Runs	Wickets
EJ Barlow *	14406	444
+N Boje *	5851	412
PJ Botha	4982	217
DN Crookes	5690	218
PD de Vaal	4208	240
GA Faulkner *	5525	402
AM Ferreira *	4976	248
TL Goddard *	11164	522
O Henry *	4470	427
+JH Kallis *	12590	290
+L Klusener *	5519	419
AJ Kourie	4470	421
PNF Mansell	4598	299
BM McMillan *	6899	293
B Mitchell	11395	249
AW Nourse	14216	305
RC Ontong *	4281	311
+SM Pollock*	5582	564
MJ Procter *	7203	569
CEB Rice *	9009	451
EO Simons	4264	330
JH Sinclair *	4262	468
PD Swart *	4068	299
PL Symcox	4206	264
JF Venter	5066	241

WICKETKEEPING

MOST DISMISSALS IN AN INNINGS

7 (ct 7,st 0)	MS Smith	Ntl v Bdr (CC)	East London	1959/60
7 (ct 6,st 1)	N Kirsten	Bdr v Rho (CC)	East London	1959/60
7 (ct 6,st 1)	RJ East	OFS v WP B (CB)	Cape Town	1984/85
7 (ct 4,st 3)	F Abrahams	EP v Ntl (SACB)	Durban	1986/87
7 (ct 6,st 1)	A Coetzee	EP v Tvl (SACB)	Lenasia	1987/88
7 (ct 7,st 0)	DJ Richardson	EP v OFS (CC)	Bloemfontein	1988/89
7 (ct 5,st 2)	N White	WP v Ntl (SACB)	Cape Town	1989/90
7 (ct 7,st 0)	PJL Radley	OFS v WP (CC)	Cape Town	1990/91
7 (ct 7,st 0)	P Kirsten	GW v W Tvl (UB)	Potchefstroom	1993/94
7 (ct 7,st 0)	HM de Vos	W Tvl v E Tvl (UB)	Potchefstroom	1993/94
7 (ct 7,st 0)	GJ Hopkins	NZA v SAA	Centurion	2004/05
7 (ct 7,st 0)	TL Tsolekile	WP Bol v Dol (SS)	Durban	2004/05

MOST DISMISSALS IN A MATCH

11 (ct 10,st 1)	IA Healy	Aus v N Tvl	Verwoerdburg	1993/94
11 (ct 11,st 0)	RC Russell (The world Test record)	Eng v SA (2nd Test)	Johannesburg	1995/96
10 (ct 10,st 0)	RV Jennings	Tvl v Arosa Sri Lanka	Johannesburg	1982/83
10 (ct 10,st 0)	DA Murray	WI XI v SA	Port Elizabeth	1983/84
10 (ct 8,st 2)	RJ Ryall	WP v Tvl (CC)	Cape Town	1984/85
10 (ct 10,st 0)	SJ Rixon	Aus XI v SA	Johannesburg	1985/86
10 (ct 10,st 0)	RV Jennings	Tvl v N Tvl (CC)	Verwoerdburg	1986/87
10 (ct 10,st 0)	SJ Rixon	Aus XI v SA	Johannesburg	1986/87
10 (ct 10,st 0)	RV Jennings	Tvl v OFS (CC)	Johannesburg	1986/87
10 (ct 9,st 1)	A Coetzee	EP v Tvl (SACB)	Lenasia	1987/88
10 (ct 10,st 0)	DJ Richardson	EP v OFS (CC)	Bloemfontein	1988/89
10 (ct 9,st 1)	DJ Richardson	EP v N Tvl (CC)	Verwoerdburg	1989/90
10 (ct 10,st 0)	HM de Vos	W Tvl v E Tvl (UB)	Potchefstroom	1993/94
10 (ct 10,st 0)	MO Johnston	Tvl B v Bol B (UB)	Randjesfontein	1995/96
10 (ct 10,st 0)	J Burger	GW v N Tvl B (UB)	Kimberley	1995/96
10 (ct 10,st 0)	MN van Wyk	FS v Bdr (SS)	Bloemfontein	2000/01
10 (ct 9,st 1)	D Jennings	Eas v GW (SS)	Benoni	2001/02

HIGHEST INNINGS WITHOUT BYES

600-3*	A Flower	Zim v SA (1st Test)	Harare	2001/02
595	MV Boucher	SA v NZ (2nd Test)	Auckland	2003/04
589	DP Marais	Ntl v Aus	Pietermaritzburg	1957/58

MOST DISMISSALS IN A SEASON

By home players:

65 (ct 57,st 8)	RV Jennings (Tvl)	1982/83
55 (ct 49,st 6)	RV Jennings (Tvl)	1984/85
52 (ct 50,st 2) *	HG Kuhn (Ttn/Nor)	2005/06
51 (ct 51,st 0)	DL Brown (Dol)	2004/05
50 (ct 49,st 1)	DL Brown (KZN)	2003/04
48 (ct 43,st 5)	TL Tsolekile (WP)	2003/04
47 (ct 45,st 2)	RJ Ryall (WP)	1990/91
46 (ct 45,st 1)	DT Lindsay (NE Tvl)	1966/67
46 (ct 45,st 1)	NT Day (N Tvl)	1984/85
45 (ct 43,st 2)	AJS Smith (Ntl)	1975/76
45 (ct 42,st 3)	MV Boucher (Bdr)	1997/98

* Includes 1 catch taken as a fielder.

Currie Cup/Castle Cup/SuperSport Series only:

51 (ct 51,st 0)	DL Brown (Dol)	2004/05
50 (ct 49,st 1)	DL Brown (KZN)	2003/04
46 (ct 45,st 1)	NT Day (N Tvl)	1984/85
46 (ct 40,st 6)	RV Jennings (Tvl)	1984/85
44 (ct 42,st 2)	RV Jennings (N Tvl)	1990/91

By touring players:

55 (ct 42, st 13)	AE Dick (NZ)	1961/62

WICKETKEEPERS WHO HAVE DISMISSED 200 BATSMEN IN A CAREER

+ Denotes current player. Some of the catches may have been taken while the player was not keeping wicket.

	Career	M	Ct	St	Total
RV Jennings	1973-92	159	567	54	621
DJ Richardson	1977-97	200	579	40	619
+MV Boucher	1995-	150	511	26	537
JHB Waite	1948-65	199	427	84	511
+N Pothas	1993-	146	398	36	434
RJ Ryall	1980-94	123	384	38	422
NT Day	1975-91	105	312	29	341
SJ Palframan	1990-2002	102	313	28	341
DT Lindsay	1958-73	124	292	41	333
AJS Smith	1971-83	103	309	11	320
GP Pfuhl	1967-79	95	280	34	314
D Gamsy	1958-72	93	278	33	311
B McBride	1980-94	87	280	30	310
RJ East	1973-89	96	288	8	296
+W Bossenger	1996-	78	252	14	266
+TL Tsolekile	1999-	77	246	20	266
BL Irvine	1962-76	157	240	7	247
ELR Stewart	1988-2002	98	232	8	240
HB Cameron	1924-35	107	155	69	224
PJL Radley	1989-98	68	190	17	207

South African first-class cricket only:

	Career	M	Ct	St	Total
RV Jennings	1973-92	159	567	54	621
DJ Richardson	1977-97	200	579	40	619
+MV Boucher	1995-	149	509	26	535
JHB Waite	1948-65	199	427	84	511
RJ Ryall	1980-94	123	384	38	422
NT Day	1975-91	105	312	29	341
SJ Palframan	1990-2002	102	313	28	341
DT Lindsay	1958-73	118	284	38	322

AJS Smith	1971-83	102	308	11	319
GP Pfuhl	1967-79	95	280	34	314
Currie Cup/Castle Cup/SuperSport Series only:					
RV Jennings	1973-92	137	490	48	538
RJ Ryall	1980-94	111	354	34	388
DJ Richardson	1977-97	119	318	26	344
NT Day	1975-91	101	308	29	337
SJ Palframan	1990-2002	84	271	22	293

FIELDING

MOST CATCHES IN AN INNINGS

6	J Seymour	Kent v SA	Canterbury	1904

MOST CATCHES IN A MATCH

7	SP de Vigne	NE Tvl v OFS (CC)	Benoni	1950/51
7	A Barrow	Tvl B v N Tvl B (CB)	Pietersburg	1982/83
7	CB Lambert	N Tvl v Bol (CC)	Paarl	1994/95

MOST CATCHES IN A SEASON

By home players:		
25	M van Jaarsveld (Ttn)	2005/06
24	NC Johnson (WP)	2000/01
22	GFJ Liebenberg (FS)	2003/04
21	MJ Procter (Rho)	1972/73
21	AJ Kourie (Tvl)	1984/85
21	LJ Koen (Bol)	1999/00
21	GFJ Liebenberg (FS)	1999/00
By touring players:		
29	W Rhodes (England)	1913/14

FIELDERS WHO HAVE HELD 200 CATCHES IN A CAREER

+ Denotes current player. Some of the catches may have been taken when they occasionally kept wicket.

	Career	M	Ct
CEB Rice	1969-93	482	401
AJ Lamb	1972-95	467	371
BA Richards	1964-82	339	367
KS McEwan	1972-91	428	359 *
AW Greig	1965-78	350	345
BF Davison	1967-87	467	338
EJ Barlow	1959-82	283	335
MJ Procter	1965-88	401	325
NG Featherstone	1967-81	329	277
KC Wessels	1973-99	316	268
RG Pollock	1960-86	262	248
DJ Cullinan	1983-2004	246	245
RA Smith	1980-2003	426	233
B Mitchell	1925-49	173	228
NC Johnson	1989-2004	161	218
CP Wilkins	1962-82	198	211 **

* Also took 7 stumpings
** Also took 6 stumpings

South African first-class cricket only:

EJ Barlow	1959-82	208	237
DJ Cullinan	1983-2004	229	237
RG Pollock	1960-86	246	237
B Mitchell	1925-49	173	228

FIRST-CLASS CAREER RECORDS

As at 10 May 2006, excluding first-class matches in England in 2006.

Name	Debut	M	Inns	NO	Runs	HS	Avg	100	50	Ct	St	Balls	Runs	Wkts	Avg	RpO	BB	5I	10M
YA Abdullah	2005/06	1	1	0	5	5	5.00	0	0	0	0	118	101	4	25.25	5.13	4-33	0	0
AP Abrahams	1999/00	4	4	1	23	14	7.66	0	0	1	0	328	223	9	24.77	4.07	6-36	1	0
S Abrahams	2003/04	12	17	4	84	15	6.46	0	0	1	0	1311	801	20	40.05	3.66	4-33	0	0
U Abrahams	1998/99	23	43	3	923	134 *	23.07	2	4	11	0	47	40	0	-	5.10	-	0	0
ZA Abrahim	1995/96	56	80	20	972	103 *	16.20	1	2	15	0	9894	4647	160	29.04	2.81	6-53	4	0
HD Ackerman	1993/94	139	228	22	8600	202 *	41.74	22	48	107	0	102	57	0	-	3.35	-	0	0
SR Adair	2005/06	4	6	2	128	44	32.00	0	0	9	2	0	0	0	-	-	-	0	0
BC Adams	2004/05	13	23	4	515	73	27.10	0	3	4	0	792	483	5	96.60	3.65	3-47	0	0
PR Adams	1995/96	126	136	51	1471	61 *	17.30	0	1	67	0	25396	12532	380	32.97	2.96	9-79	16	3
KC Africa	2004/05	11	14	1	156	33	12.00	0	0	6	0	1224	716	17	42.11	3.50	4-31	0	0
M Akoojee	2004/05	14	25	2	694	105 *	30.17	2	2	7	0	440	332	6	55.33	4.52	1-16	0	0
WA Albertyn	2001/02	23	40	7	642	101 *	19.45	1	2	16	0	3458	1619	55	29.43	2.80	4-29	0	0
R Almeida	1998/99	13	21	3	257	44	14.27	0	0	5	0	2238	1279	29	44.10	3.42	5-18	1	0
AM Amla	1997/98	63	107	12	2876	125	30.27	4	17	39	0	516	340	6	56.66	3.95	2-53	0	0
HM Amla	1999/00	58	95	11	4026	249	47.92	11	22	41	0	150	101	1	101.00	4.04	1-10	0	0
RG Arendse	1997/98	31	52	3	1074	95	21.91	0	5	30	0	6	15	0	-	15.00	-	0	0
MA Aronstam	2003/04	17	32	1	1115	201 *	35.96	2	6	7	0	2097	1140	33	34.54	3.26	5-37	2	0
MC Arthur	1998/99	7	14	1	108	21	8.30	0	0	4	0	54	50	0	-	5.55	-	0	0
NO Arthur	2004/05	15	23	6	276	45	16.23	0	0	6	0	2219	1235	38	32.50	3.33	6-27	1	0
AM Bacher	1993/94	112	201	11	7283	210	38.33	18	33	99	0	1169	528	10	52.80	2.71	2-24	0	0
R Bailey	1998/99	17	28	3	403	60	16.12	0	1	8	0	6	14	0	-	14.00	-	0	0
RT Bailey	2003/04	28	52	6	1321	148	28.71	1	8	18	0	504	308	4	77.00	3.66	3-42	0	0
W Barresi	2004/05	4	8	0	68	57	8.50	0	1	5	0	0	0	0	-	-	-	0	0
DJ Bassage	2003/04	24	44	5	1387	108 *	35.56	3	7	22	0	54	15	0	-	1.66	-	0	0
C Baxter	2003/04	15	28	0	530	86	18.92	0	4	8	0	5	6	0	-	7.20	-	0	0
F Behardien	2004/05	3	5	0	122	60	24.40	0	1	3	0	300	177	6	29.50	3.54	3-48	0	0
M Bekker	2005/06	8	9	1	505	138	63.12	2	3	4	0	0	0	0	-	-	-	0	0
WE Bell	2004/05	6	12	1	155	48 *	14.09	0	0	2	0	244	203	9	22.55	4.99	3-57	0	0
DM Benkenstein	1993/94	140	203	26	8075	259	45.62	21	41	105	0	4780	2219	68	32.63	2.78	4-16	0	0
BL Bennett	2001/02	26	49	1	1338	150	27.87	3	4	17	0	626	416	12	34.66	3.98	5-21	1	0

Name	Debut	M	Inns	NO	Runs	HS	Avg	100	50	Ct	St	Balls	Runs	Wkts	Avg	RpO	BB	5I	10M
CN Bennett	2005/06	5	10	0	266	64	26.60	0	1	3	0	30	22	0	-	4.40	-	0	0
KD Bennett	2005/06	5	7	1	150	47	25.00	0	0	1	0	121	95	1	95.00	4.71	1-47	0	0
JA Beukes	1997/98	52	93	6	2687	135 *	30.88	4	14	63	0	47	34	2	17.00	4.34	1-8	0	0
AR Beukman	2005/06	1	1	1	3	3 *	-	0	0	0	0	129	55	2	27.50	2.55	1-27	0	0
GH Bhayat	2002/03	16	20	7	141	61 *	10.84	0	1	11	0	1938	1212	32	37.87	3.75	3-39	0	0
R Bhayat	2004/05	8	10	2	125	44	15.62	0	0	7	0	336	257	5	51.40	4.58	2-59	0	0
AM Blignaut	1997/98	56	89	5	2303	194	27.41	2	14	38	0	8052	4819	133	36.23	3.59	5-73	3	0
GH Bodi	1996/97	48	74	10	2010	143	31.40	4	8	23	0	3788	2385	58	41.12	3.77	6-63	2	0
TM Bodibe	2004/05	13	21	4	254	39 *	14.94	0	0	22	3	0	0	0	-	-	-	0	0
N Boje	1990/91	159	235	44	6260	116	32.77	5	36	93	0	32906	14128	439	32.18	2.57	8-93	20	2
J Booysen	2003/04	15	22	2	774	134 *	38.70	1	4	16	0	12	2	0	-	1.00	-	0	0
LL Bosman	1997/98	73	131	8	3558	140	28.92	3	20	43	0	570	342	8	42.75	3.60	3-25	0	0
M Bosman	2004/05	9	15	0	281	106	18.73	1	0	5	0	36	45	0	-	7.50	-	0	0
W Bossenger	1996/97	78	138	18	3689	124 *	30.74	4	24	252	14	102	69	4	17.25	4.05	3-16	0	0
J Botha	2000/01	34	60	8	1585	93	30.48	0	10	22	0	4004	2068	75	27.57	3.09	6-42	3	1
MV Boucher	1995/96	150	221	33	6380	134	33.93	8	38	511	26	26	26	1	26.00	6.00	1-6	0	0
CC Bradfield	1993/94	90	169	11	5299	196	33.53	9	29	64	0	49	24	0	-	2.93	-	0	0
J Brooker	1998/99	29	54	1	1494	115	28.18	2	8	23	0	84	65	0	-	4.64	-	0	0
NG Brouwers	1998/99	13	21	2	350	59	18.42	0	2	13	0	1648	622	22	28.27	2.26	6-57	1	0
DL Brown (Dol)	1998/99	35	51	9	1273	152 *	30.30	2	5	123	3	0	0	0	-	-	-	0	0
DL Brown (Bdr)	2005/06	3	3	1	90	77 *	45.00	0	1	0	0	299	179	4	44.75	3.59	3-83	0	0
ML Bruyns	1993/94	118	196	8	6550	153	34.84	17	32	149	4	642	271	6	45.16	2.53	2-3	0	0
BW Buckley	2005/06	1	2	0	52	41	26.00	0	0	0	0	0	0	0	-	-	-	0	0
TA Bula	2001/02	32	50	12	759	68	19.97	0	4	88	4	0	0	0	-	-	-	0	0
S Burger	2001/02	11	16	3	306	55 *	23.53	0	2	5	0	1834	928	35	26.51	3.03	5-78	1	0
JP Campher	2005/06	6	4	2	40	17	20.00	0	0	3	0	725	547	16	34.18	4.52	3-54	0	0
RCC Canning	2004/05	14	22	2	617	72	30.85	0	6	41	1	0	0	0	-	-	-	0	0
DD Carolus	2003/04	8	13	2	79	16 *	7.18	0	0	3	0	1386	651	22	29.59	2.81	5-61	1	0
S Chatterjee	2005/06	1	1	1	1	1 *	-	0	0	0	0	252	140	6	23.33	3.33	5-81	1	0
AI Chinnappa	2005/06	3	3	0	9	5	3.00	0	0	1	0	60	33	3	11.00	3.30	3-19	0	0
N Chouhan	2000/01	13	22	1	378	93	18.00	0	2	4	0	445	313	5	62.60	4.22	2-41	0	0
WL Coetsee	2003/04	27	47	8	1082	108 *	27.74	1	7	11	0	4687	2487	65	38.26	3.18	4-95	0	0
J Coetzee	2004/05	15	25	5	525	56 *	26.25	0	2	8	0	2445	1387	61	22.73	3.40	7-42	3	0
SR Connor	2005/06	1	2	0	41	24	20.50	0	0	0	0	0	0	0	-	-	-	0	0
S Conrad	1998/99	16	23	7	251	60	15.68	0	2	6	0	2676	1485	37	40.13	3.32	6-45	3	1

FIRST-CLASS CAREER RECORDS

Name	Debut	M	Inns	NO	Runs	HS	Avg	100	50	Ct	St	Balls	Runs	Wkts	Avg	RpO	BB	5I	10M
SC Cook	2000/01	42	79	4	2283	135	30.44	6	9	16	0	25	14	0	-	3.36	-	0	0
H Davids	2000/01	34	63	4	1685	158	28.55	2	11	26	0	355	210	6	35.00	3.54	3-11	0	0
AC Dawson	1992/93	98	127	27	2196	143	21.96	1	13	47	0	18482	7756	305	25.42	2.51	6-18	12	2
WA Deacon	2003/04	14	22	5	465	59	27.35	0	3	1	0	2735	1465	39	37.56	3.21	4-46	0	0
GJ de Bruin	2003/04	15	20	5	166	27	11.06	0	0	4	0	2768	1768	68	26.00	3.83	6-90	5	0
P de Bruyn	1995/96	67	108	14	3369	202	35.84	8	15	59	0	6086	2870	102	28.13	2.82	6-38	3	0
Z de Bruyn	1995/96	87	147	18	5506	266 *	42.68	13	26	54	0	7606	4397	117	37.58	3.46	6-120	2	0
CJ de Jager	2005/06	4	8	0	185	62	23.12	0	2	0	0	0	0	0	-	-	-	0	0
HG de Kock	2004/05	13	24	2	680	93	30.90	0	5	6	0	303	176	4	44.00	3.48	1-8	0	0
S de Kock	2004/05	7	8	0	85	31	10.62	0	0	1	0	648	388	9	43.11	3.59	2-56	0	0
CD de Lange	1997/98	40	63	6	1433	109	25.14	1	6	22	0	7720	3449	83	41.55	2.68	7-48	3	1
M de Stadler	2004/05	14	17	5	227	37	18.91	0	0	4	0	2730	1071	66	16.22	2.35	5-18	3	0
AB de Villiers	2003/04	38	70	3	2773	178	41.38	5	18	68	2	174	77	2	38.50	2.65	2-49	0	0
F de Wet	2001/02	12	17	2	161	36	10.73	0	0	4	0	2276	1185	55	21.54	3.12	7-61	3	1
BC de Wett	2000/01	25	47	3	1204	182	27.36	2	4	11	0	1050	734	17	43.17	4.19	7-95	1	0
L Dipha	2001/02	5	10	0	103	22	10.30	0	0	2	0	250	156	3	52.00	3.74	2-13	0	0
HH Dippenaar	1995/96	110	185	17	7022	200 *	41.79	21	30	83	0	19	13	0	-	4.10	-	0	0
N Dladla	2000/01	7	7	3	43	14	10.75	0	0	0	0	687	397	12	33.08	3.46	3-41	0	0
AG Doherty	2004/05	5	10	0	308	92	30.80	0	3	1	0	60	44	0	-	4.40	-	0	0
D Donaldson	2005/06	3	6	0	109	42	18.16	0	0	2	0	222	152	3	50.66	4.10	2-64	0	0
G Dros	1993/94	81	140	18	4022	136	32.96	4	22	97	0	2325	1203	39	30.84	3.10	5-17	1	0
WA Dugmore	2001/02	13	25	0	933	138	37.32	2	6	15	0	330	236	1	236.00	4.29	1-35	0	0
J-P Duminy	2001/02	28	44	9	1900	128	54.28	6	10	21	0	737	435	10	43.50	3.54	4-89	0	0
F du Plessis	2003/04	13	24	3	836	156	39.80	1	6	10	0	539	317	15	21.13	3.52	4-39	0	0
D du Preez	2003/04	15	19	1	359	89	19.94	0	3	4	0	2510	1179	43	27.41	2.81	5-33	2	0
WJ du Toit	1998/99	18	28	4	301	42	12.54	0	0	4	0	3014	1600	46	34.78	3.18	7-82	2	0
AZM Dyili	2004/05	11	18	2	357	65	22.31	0	2	20	3	0	0	0	-	-	-	0	0
D Elgar	2005/06	2	4	0	70	32	17.50	0	0	0	0	0	0	0	-	-	-	0	0
T Essack	2005/06	5	7	0	115	51	16.42	0	1	0	0	156	63	3	21.00	2.42	2-19	0	0
W Euley	2003/04	7	12	0	284	50	23.66	0	1	16	2	0	0	0	-	-	-	0	0
SG Fensham	2005/06	4	7	1	94	41 *	15.66	0	0	2	0	0	0	0	-	-	-	0	0
MP Fick	2005/06	4	6	0	78	29	13.00	0	0	3	0	156	122	2	61.00	4.69	1-24	0	0
P Fojela	2004/05	5	1	1	1	1 *	-	0	0	1	0	481	259	13	19.92	3.23	4-34	0	0
H Fourie	2004/05	3	6	0	152	45	25.33	0	0	0	0	138	78	3	26.00	3.39	3-16	0	0
BL Fransman	2003/04	9	12	4	32	14	4.00	0	0	4	0	1205	682	25	27.28	3.39	5-36	1	0

FIRST-CLASS CAREER RECORDS

Name	Debut	M	Inns	NO	Runs	HS	Avg	100	50	Ct	St	Balls	Runs	Wkts	Avg	RpO	BB	5I	10M
Q Friend	2002/03	28	31	8	530	51	23.04	0	1	10	0	3959	2114	80	26.42	3.20	7-31	3	0
R Frylinck	2005/06	8	10	2	261	100 *	32.62	1	1	3	0	1088	564	23	24.52	3.11	6-94	1	0
DR Gain	1996/97	33	61	4	1503	100	26.36	1	11	26	0	48	37	0	-	4.62	-	0	0
LL Gamiet	1995/96	49	84	7	1979	116	25.70	2	7	35	0	30	17	1	17.00	3.40	1-14	0	0
FA Geldenhuys	2005/06	1	2	0	28	24	14.00	0	0	0	0	0	0	0	-	-	-	0	0
JP Geoghegan	2005/06	2	3	1	23	15	11.50	0	0	0	0	66	38	0	-	3.45	-	0	0
SG George	2005/06	1	2	0	7	6	3.50	0	0	0	0	6	5	0	-	5.00	-	0	0
HH Gibbs	1990/91	171	294	12	12460	228	44.18	31	53	137	0	138	78	3	26.00	3.39	2-14	0	0
R Gobind	2001/02	24	41	4	1235	119	33.37	2	7	25	1	18	1	0	-	0.33	-	0	0
U Govender	2004/05	17	15	9	33	21 *	5.50	0	0	8	0	2877	1507	68	22.16	3.14	6-59	3	0
AJA Gray	2004/05	11	22	3	799	112 *	42.05	2	3	10	0	270	165	0	-	3.66	-	0	0
GC Grobler	2005/06	1	2	1	0	0 *	0.00	0	0	0	0	96	72	3	24.00	4.50	2-28	0	0
SF Grobler	2005/06	1	1	0	3	3	3.00	0	0	1	0	72	65	1	65.00	5.41	1-61	0	0
AJ Hall	1995/96	109	160	21	4649	163	33.44	5	31	79	0	18641	8647	334	25.88	2.78	6-77	12	1
WC Hantam	2004/05	7	12	4	197	38	24.62	0	0	9	0	890	472	24	19.66	3.18	6-39	1	0
MJ Harris	2003/04	25	43	7	1250	135 *	34.72	2	3	80	3	0	0	0	-	-	-	0	0
PL Harris	1998/99	32	38	8	485	47	16.16	0	0	14	0	6670	3134	109	28.75	2.81	6-54	5	0
IJ Harvey	1993/94	154	254	23	7559	209 *	32.72	11	44	106	0	23240	11199	410	27.31	2.89	8-101	15	2
TN Harvey	2005/06	2	4	0	37	19	9.25	0	0	1	0	0	0	0	-	-	-	0	0
DL Haupt	2005/06	1	0	0	0	-	-	0	0	0	0	126	81	1	81.00	3.85	1-57	0	0
W Hauptfleisch	2004/05	3	6	1	161	67 *	32.20	0	2	0	0	78	41	0	-	3.15	-	0	0
M Hayward	1995/96	120	135	49	981	55 *	11.40	0	1	35	0	21482	11567	404	28.63	3.23	6-31	9	2
WD Hayward	2004/05	4	7	0	75	47	10.71	0	0	1	0	0	0	0	-	-	-	0	0
B Hector	2001/02	29	54	6	1853	200 *	38.60	5	8	14	0	6	3	0	-	3.00	-	0	0
JM Henderson	1994/95	64	118	9	3389	143 *	31.09	7	16	29	0	3017	1555	29	53.62	3.09	3-13	0	0
T Henderson	1998/99	67	108	15	1603	81	17.23	0	5	21	0	12358	5417	203	26.68	2.63	6-56	6	0
JS Hermitage	2005/06	5	6	1	61	17	12.20	0	0	2	0	488	350	9	38.88	4.30	3-85	0	0
ND Hewer	2005/06	4	3	2	35	23 *	35.00	0	0	1	0	576	328	11	29.81	3.41	4-31	0	0
WR Hinkel	2001/02	16	26	5	555	100	26.42	1	2	9	0	2289	1234	46	26.82	3.23	6-85	1	1
IC Hlengane	2005/06	9	12	4	55	23	6.87	0	0	4	0	1030	594	19	31.26	3.46	7-107	1	0
DL Hobson	2005/06	1	2	1	15	11 *	15.00	0	0	1	0	90	85	0	-	5.66	-	0	0
FPG Holtzhausen	2005/06	3	6	0	143	54	23.83	0	2	4	0	305	200	1	200.00	3.93	1-22	0	0
FS Holtzhausen	2004/05	10	16	4	404	69 *	33.66	0	3	5	0	1451	739	30	24.63	3.05	5-25	1	0
Z Homani	2001/02	20	34	2	757	118	23.65	1	2	42	3	0	0	0	-	-	-	0	0
GE Howell	2004/05	10	17	3	347	80 *	24.78	0	3	10	0	1119	604	15	40.26	3.23	4-38	0	0

FIRST-CLASS CAREER RECORDS

Name	Debut	M	Inns	NO	Runs	HS	Avg	100	50	Ct	St	Balls	Runs	Wkts	Avg	RpO	BB	5I	10M
CA Ingram	2004/05	9	14	0	429	169	30.64	1	1	5	0	513	317	8	39.62	3.70	4-16	0	0
A Jacobs	1997/98	62	110	14	3454	197	35.97	8	15	78	0	408	260	3	86.66	3.82	1-2	0	0
DJ Jacobs	2001/02	43	80	4	3148	218	41.42	11	11	42	1	34	20	0	-	3.52	-	0	0
F Jardine	2005/06	1	1	0	14	14	14.00	0	0	0	0	299	133	6	22.16	2.66	5-118	1	0
RR Jeggels	2004/05	13	23	0	590	86	25.65	0	2	7	0	0	0	0	-	-	-	0	0
P Joubert	1995/96	53	76	26	1413	112 *	28.26	1	7	29	0	8949	3504	156	22.46	2.34	7-32	6	1
JR Jumat	2005/06	1	1	1	5	5 *	-	0	0	0	0	48	37	0	-	4.62	-	0	0
JH Kallis	1993/94	188	306	42	14069	200	53.29	40	76	158	0	22168	10236	334	30.64	2.77	6-54	7	0
QK Kannemeyer	2005/06	2	3	0	94	70	31.33	0	1	0	0	72	15	1	15.00	1.25	1-15	0	0
JM Kemp	1996/97	81	132	14	4225	188	35.80	8	21	88	0	9363	4393	165	26.62	2.81	6-56	5	0
JC Kent	1997/98	61	92	8	2995	178 *	35.65	6	15	53	0	6471	3195	100	31.95	2.96	6-77	1	0
DJ Kgamadi	2004/05	13	24	2	632	84	28.72	0	4	18	0	6	4	0	-	4.00	-	0	0
I Khan	2003/04	31	50	7	1694	150	39.39	2	12	11	0	2559	1467	38	38.60	3.43	6-43	1	0
TR Khoza	2005/06	1	0	0	0	-	-	0	0	0	0	177	89	4	22.25	3.01	3-41	0	0
RK Kleinveldt	2002/03	19	29	6	555	115 *	24.13	1	2	13	0	3502	1723	62	27.87	2.96	8-47	2	1
L Klusener	1993/94	144	199	42	5731	174	36.50	10	29	78	0	25226	12091	433	27.92	2.87	8-34	17	4
CE Knox	2005/06	3	4	2	92	47 *	46.00	0	0	3	0	216	126	6	21.00	3.50	3-31	0	0
PJ Koortzen	1996/97	52	98	5	2744	164	29.50	4	10	40	0	1477	943	15	62.86	3.83	3-60	0	0
BB Kops	2001/02	24	39	14	225	25	9.00	0	0	7	0	3336	2171	61	35.59	3.90	5-36	3	0
JP Kreusch	1999/00	27	48	1	959	91	20.40	0	6	18	0	2002	957	34	28.14	2.86	5-31	1	0
AK Kruger	2000/01	30	52	7	1087	158	24.15	2	4	14	0	3967	2533	66	38.37	3.83	6-37	3	1
GJ-P Kruger	1997/98	66	81	25	696	58	12.42	0	2	17	0	11876	6621	222	29.82	3.34	8-112	9	2
HG Kuhn	2004/05	16	28	2	1045	133 *	40.19	2	5	57	5	0	0	0	-	-	-	0	0
JM Kuiper	2005/06	4	6	1	146	81 *	29.20	0	1	1	0	0	0	0	-	-	-	0	0
PC Laing	2005/06	5	8	0	243	80	30.37	0	2	4	0	438	301	9	33.44	4.12	3-80	0	0
CK Langeveldt	1997/98	59	71	24	681	56	14.48	0	1	16	0	10221	5122	174	29.43	3.00	5-19	5	1
FB Lazarus	2003/04	3	6	0	11	8	1.83	0	0	1	0	48	31	0	-	3.87	-	0	0
BW Lemmetjies	1998/99	13	22	4	348	41 *	19.33	0	0	5	0	1148	749	13	57.61	3.91	4-27	0	0
DC Lentz	2005/06	2	2	0	23	19	11.50	0	0	0	0	0	0	0	-	-	-	0	0
HW le Roux	2005/06	4	4	0	49	25	12.25	0	0	5	0	423	296	11	26.90	4.19	4-66	0	0
J le Roux	2004/05	14	25	2	764	110	33.21	3	5	5	0	54	40	1	40.00	4.44	1-1	0	0
C Linde	2004/05	15	24	4	456	56	22.80	0	2	33	12	0	0	0	-	-	-	0	0
NJ Livi	2005/06	1	2	0	49	42	24.50	0	0	0	0	0	0	0	-	-	-	0	0
WP Lombard	2004/05	3	5	4	38	25 *	38.00	0	0	1	0	170	84	2	42.00	2.96	1-27	0	0
DP Lotter	2005/06	1	2	0	14	8	7.00	0	0	0	0	0	0	0	-	-	-	0	0

Name	Debut	M	Inns	NO	Runs	HS	Avg	100	50	Ct	St	Balls	Runs	Wkts	Avg	RpO	BB	5I	10M
J Louw	2000/01	60	86	12	1484	124	20.05	1	7	26	0	10502	5563	175	31.78	3.17	6-51	6	0
WJ Louw	2004/05	7	14	1	341	85	26.23	0	1	6	0	0	0	0	-	-	-	0	0
LL Lwana	2004/05	7	7	3	59	24	14.75	0	0	3	0	516	341	11	31.00	3.96	3-6	0	0
APT Mabuya	2001/02	5	9	3	70	27	11.66	0	0	4	0	363	261	3	87.00	4.31	2-27	0	0
CS Mabuya	2005/06	2	2	0	9	5	4.50	0	0	0	0	0	0	0	-	-	-	0	0
ND McKenzie	1994/95	132	222	25	8174	175	41.49	20	43	99	0	528	312	5	62.40	3.54	1-6	0	0
AP McLaren	1998/99	32	60	3	1862	164	32.66	6	6	46	3	6	3	0	-	3.00	-	0	0
R McLaren	2003/04	23	35	4	1017	140	32.80	1	6	14	0	3746	1849	60	30.81	2.96	6-96	3	0
JT Mafa	1997/98	32	30	10	86	19 *	4.30	0	0	11	0	4707	2901	82	35.37	3.69	6-62	1	0
A Magiet	2004/05	2	2	0	8	8	4.00	0	0	1	0	18	0	3	0.00	0.00	3-0	0	0
M Mahlombe	2005/06	4	3	0	22	20	7.33	0	0	1	0	336	156	11	14.18	2.78	3-11	0	0
DL Makalima	1997/98	36	63	3	1278	78	21.30	0	6	20	0	156	128	0	-	4.92	-	0	0
S Makongolo	2005/06	1	2	0	61	56	30.50	0	1	0	0	0	0	0	-	-	-	0	0
DJ Malan	2005/06	4	7	0	158	64	22.57	0	1	2	0	159	152	3	50.66	5.73	1-22	0	0
H Malan	2004/05	1	1	0	26	26	26.00	0	0	2	0	0	0	0	-	-	-	0	0
JMM Malao	2001/02	21	21	9	81	18	6.75	0	0	5	0	4973	2539	80	31.73	3.06	5-27	4	0
S Mandan	2004/05	9	15	0	274	98	18.26	0	1	4	0	12	24	0	-	12.00	-	0	0
L Manzini	2005/06	2	1	0	0	0	0.00	0	0	1	0	138	80	4	20.00	3.47	4-22	0	0
MA Mashimbyi	2003/04	21	28	4	446	61	18.58	0	2	4	0	2258	1296	34	38.11	3.44	5-32	1	0
MR Masinda	2005/06	1	1	0	1	1	1.00	0	0	0	0	6	8	0	-	8.00	-	0	0
MT Masinga	2005/06	1	2	2	69	48 *	-	0	0	1	0	54	42	0	-	4.66	-	0	0
BM Mathebula	2003/04	10	15	6	121	31	13.44	0	0	2	0	1069	864	17	50.82	4.84	5-56	1	0
MM Matika	2003/04	13	23	3	522	107	26.10	1	2	12	0	84	30	0	-	2.14	-	0	0
VCM Mazibuko	2005/06	3	4	1	33	21	11.00	0	0	2	0	182	151	5	30.20	4.97	3-37	0	0
JT Maziya	2004/05	4	6	1	18	8	3.60	0	0	0	0	90	107	0	-	7.13	-	0	0
L Mbane	2004/05	13	16	2	399	64	28.50	0	2	7	0	1529	880	26	33.84	3.45	5-26	1	0
NE Mbhalati	2002/03	32	36	16	78	10	3.90	0	0	2	0	4964	2646	90	29.40	3.19	5-26	1	0
EE Meyer	2001/02	8	16	1	363	73	24.20	0	1	3	0	6	6	0	-	6.00	-	0	0
L Meyer	2001/02	15	26	4	256	38	11.63	0	0	6	0	1921	994	31	32.06	3.10	5-38	1	0
S Mhlongo	2004/05	15	13	4	68	21	7.55	0	0	4	0	2039	999	45	22.20	2.93	5-25	1	0
DR Miller	2005/06	9	12	2	301	64 *	30.10	0	2	26	2	12	13	0	-	6.50	-	0	0
S Mjekula	2004/05	11	14	8	37	10	6.16	0	0	2	0	1296	681	31	21.96	3.15	5-46	1	0
PT Mofokeng	2004/05	13	13	9	31	10 *	7.75	0	0	5	0	810	576	10	57.60	4.26	2-36	0	0
MJ Mokonyama	2002/03	14	20	5	471	92	31.40	0	2	5	0	0	0	0	-	-	-	0	0
EO Moleon	1996/97	45	74	10	1015	67	15.85	0	2	16	0	7053	3612	99	36.48	3.07	5-60	2	0

FIRST-CLASS CAREER RECORDS

Name	Debut	M	Inns	NO	Runs	HS	Avg	100	50	Ct	St	Balls	Runs	Wkts	Avg	RpO	BB	5I	10M
K Moothosamy	2004/05	6	10	0	156	42	15.60	0	0	2	0	24	16	1	16.00	4.00	1-3	0	0
JA Morkel	1999/00	43	61	13	2113	204 *	44.02	3	15	16	0	7067	3595	114	31.53	3.05	6-36	3	0
M Morkel	2003/04	10	12	4	117	44 *	14.62	0	0	8	0	1752	1048	37	28.32	3.58	6-66	3	0
LN Mosena	2005/06	7	13	1	322	78	26.83	0	2	8	0	0	0	0	-	-	-	0	0
JF Mostert	2005/06	3	5	2	112	70	37.33	0	1	1	0	205	118	4	29.50	3.45	3-20	0	0
WB Motaung	2003/04	15	28	1	912	116	33.77	3	3	11	0	78	33	1	33.00	2.53	1-15	0	0
TS Motsamai	2003/04	17	23	10	282	51 *	21.69	0	1	3	0	1832	988	24	41.16	3.23	2-16	0	0
PV Mpitsang	1997/98	60	72	29	268	23	6.23	0	0	10	0	9614	4406	144	30.59	2.74	5-24	4	0
R Munnik	1997/98	35	56	4	1522	138	29.26	1	11	21	0	3286	1845	61	30.24	3.36	4-58	0	0
RG Mutch	2005/06	3	5	2	89	34 *	29.66	0	0	0	0	422	282	10	28.20	4.00	4-57	0	0
JG Myburgh	1997/98	46	84	14	2955	203	42.21	6	17	27	0	1083	573	11	52.09	3.17	2-45	0	0
SJ Myburgh	2005/06	4	4	0	44	31	11.00	0	0	4	0	18	11	0	-	3.66	-	0	0
A Nawab	2005/06	5	6	2	44	19	11.00	0	0	3	0	717	498	21	23.71	4.16	6-106	2	1
A Nel	1996/97	81	90	31	824	44	13.96	0	0	30	0	16207	7408	290	25.54	2.74	6-25	12	1
R Nel	2004/05	5	10	0	224	59	22.40	0	2	4	0	0	0	0	-	-	-	0	0
M Ngam	1997/98	38	49	8	316	35	7.70	0	0	13	0	6050	3146	99	31.77	3.12	4-25	0	0
FG Nkuna	2004/05	13	5	3	7	4 *	3.50	0	0	2	0	1434	756	20	37.80	3.16	4-43	0	0
ET Nkwe	2002/03	23	40	4	947	106	26.30	1	5	17	0	1938	1232	22	56.00	3.81	5-78	1	0
E Nogabe	2005/06	1	2	1	0	0 *	0.00	0	0	0	0	24	22	0	-	5.50	-	0	0
NM Northcote	2005/06	1	1	1	27	27 *	-	0	0	2	0	0	0	0	-	-	-	0	0
M Ntini	1995/96	131	152	45	1026	34 *	9.58	0	0	32	0	24463	13372	458	29.19	3.27	7-37	19	4
E Nyawo	2005/06	5	9	0	88	31	9.77	0	0	4	0	0	0	0	-	-	-	0	0
SP O'Connor	1997/98	21	34	1	431	41	13.06	0	0	4	0	1918	1185	27	43.88	3.70	4-61	0	0
AW Olivier	2005/06	1	2	0	18	10	9.00	0	0	0	0	0	0	0	-	-	-	0	0
MW Olivier	2004/05	12	18	2	103	16	6.43	0	0	1	0	1684	1130	31	36.45	4.02	4-68	0	0
AM Omar	1995/96	14	19	2	261	50	15.35	0	1	33	4	0	0	0	-	-	-	0	0
JL Ontong	1997/98	80	134	7	4655	166	36.65	9	29	60	0	7574	4030	89	45.28	3.19	4-66	0	0
JM Otto	2000/01	18	32	2	1062	143	35.40	2	5	16	0	6	3	0	-	3.00	-	0	0
A Paleker	1997/98	16	26	5	484	70 *	23.04	0	1	17	1	66	41	0	-	3.72	-	0	0
Y Pangabantu	2005/06	5	2	2	1	1 *	-	0	0	0	0	618	302	13	23.23	2.93	3-24	0	0
HH Paulse	2004/05	10	12	4	36	8 *	4.50	0	0	2	0	1136	778	26	29.92	4.10	5-65	1	0
GD Perry	2005/06	1	2	0	1	1	0.50	0	0	0	0	78	49	1	49.00	3.76	1-49	0	0
AN Petersen	2000/01	45	84	4	2876	150 *	35.95	7	13	42	0	144	83	3	29.33	3.66	2-7	0	0
RJ Peterson	1998/99	67	108	14	2387	130	25.39	4	7	28	0	12505	6443	175	36.84	3.09	6-67	8	1
MX Pethu	2005/06	2	4	0	28	15	7.00	0	0	0	0	0	0	0	-	-	-	0	0

FIRST-CLASS CAREER RECORDS

Name	Debut	M	Inns	NO	Runs	HS	Avg	100	50	Ct	St	Balls	Runs	Wkts	Avg	RpO	BB	5I	10M
AM Phangiso	2004/05	16	21	8	410	63	31.53	0	1	6	0	1264	685	17	40.29	3.25	5-76	1	0
VD Philander	2003/04	18	29	2	808	168	29.92	1	3	7	0	2876	1218	51	23.88	2.54	5-49	1	0
R Pietersen	2005/06	7	10	7	24	7	8.00	0	0	1	0	817	493	24	20.54	3.62	6-73	1	0
TD Pillay	2004/05	12	11	4	74	32	10.57	0	0	13	0	1988	878	27	32.51	2.64	5-45	1	0
TR Plaatjie	2004/05	6	10	5	60	25	12.00	0	0	1	0	330	241	6	40.16	4.38	2-39	0	0
SM Pollock	1991/92	177	254	52	6613	150 *	32.73	6	32	125	0	37298	14811	634	23.36	2.38	7-33	22	2
SC Pope	1992/93	109	200	19	5958	156 *	32.91	12	27	81	2	2525	1501	48	31.27	3.56	7-62	2	0
E Potgieter	2004/05	5	10	3	272	73	38.85	0	3	7	0	6	1	0	-	1.00	-	0	0
D Pretorius	1997/98	68	72	19	509	43	9.60	0	0	18	0	11569	6413	232	27.64	3.32	6-49	7	0
ML Price	2001/02	11	20	1	439	97	23.10	0	4	6	0	84	60	0	-	4.28	-	0	0
AG Prince	1995/96	108	166	18	6059	184	40.93	15	27	66	0	174	86	2	43.00	2.96	1-2	0	0
C Prinsloo	2004/05	3	6	0	157	50	26.16	0	1	1	0	0	0	0	-	-	-	0	0
AG Puttick	2000/01	54	94	11	3520	250 *	42.40	6	19	73	2	0	0	0	-	-	-	0	0
MN Ranger	2004/05	14	20	4	558	96	34.87	0	4	12	0	1326	638	19	33.57	2.88	6-30	1	0
AH Razak	2005/06	1	1	1	0	0 *	-	0	0	1	0	126	126	2	63.00	6.00	1-38	0	0
BL Reddy	2000/01	18	28	5	544	109	23.65	1	1	10	0	2409	1136	34	33.41	2.82	5-39	1	0
R Reddy	2005/06	2	1	0	10	10	10.00	0	0	1	0	241	86	5	17.20	2.14	3-32	0	0
RA Reeves	2005/06	2	3	1	73	41	36.50	0	0	1	0	60	64	2	32.00	6.40	2-25	0	0
RR Richards	2005/06	7	7	2	19	12	3.80	0	0	1	0	1124	562	24	23.41	3.00	5-30	2	0
JA Rudolph	1997/98	90	161	10	6159	222 *	40.78	17	28	66	0	3206	1788	44	40.63	3.34	5-87	2	0
QG Samson	2004/05	9	11	5	29	10	4.83	0	0	3	0	1230	961	20	48.05	4.68	3-31	0	0
MD Sanders	1998/99	21	36	2	1188	103	34.94	1	8	7	0	66	43	0	-	3.90	-	0	0
U Sandi	2005/06	1	1	1	0	0 *	-	0	0	0	0	60	27	1	27.00	2.70	1-27	0	0
PSE Sandri	2003/04	11	16	8	87	17 *	10.87	0	0	3	0	1564	927	31	29.90	3.55	5-32	1	0
AJ Schultz	2004/05	4	3	2	7	5	7.00	0	0	1	0	330	228	6	38.00	4.14	5-51	1	0
MR Sekhoto	2001/02	15	24	5	587	81	30.89	0	3	15	0	72	67	3	22.33	5.58	2-42	0	0
BK Sekonyane	2004/05	13	15	4	121	24 *	11.00	0	0	4	0	1704	1025	36	28.47	3.60	4-45	0	0
PM Selowa	2005/06	2	2	0	35	19	17.50	0	0	3	0	0	0	0	-	-	-	0	0
WE September	2003/04	9	15	4	271	63 *	24.63	0	1	8	0	1074	665	18	36.94	3.71	3-35	0	0
AJ Seymore	1993/94	86	156	5	4870	174	32.25	8	28	77	0	46	43	0	-	5.60	-	0	0
SR Sibande	2002/03	8	13	0	137	69	10.53	0	1	2	0	0	0	0	-	-	-	0	0
LF Simpson	2005/06	4	5	1	3	2	0.75	0	0	0	0	299	182	7	26.00	3.65	3-22	0	0
Y Singh	2003/04	6	8	5	75	17 *	25.00	0	0	0	0	1022	461	15	30.73	2.70	4-82	0	0
M Slwana	2004/05	8	14	3	177	37	16.09	0	0	29	0	0	0	0	-	-	-	0	0
D Smit	2004/05	11	12	0	129	35	10.75	0	0	41	1	60	10	1	10.00	1.00	1-10	0	0

FIRST-CLASS CAREER RECORDS

Name	Debut	M	Inns	NO	Runs	HS	Avg	100	50	Ct	St	Balls	Runs	Wkts	Avg	RpO	BB	5I	10M
K Smit	2004/05	11	15	0	461	144	30.73	1	1	7	0	54	30	0	-	3.33	-	0	0
WJ Smit	1994/95	25	39	0	1014	104	26.00	1	7	16	0	68	42	0	-	3.70	-	0	0
GC Smith	1999/00	83	144	10	6720	311	50.14	19	23	113	0	1615	971	11	88.27	3.60	2-145	0	0
MBA Smith	2003/04	16	28	1	485	70	17.96	0	1	19	0	218	118	0	-	3.24	-	0	0
BD Snijman	2003/04	17	33	2	1025	114	33.06	2	4	11	0	322	215	9	23.88	4.00	4-26	0	0
AM Sodumo	2002/03	24	39	4	716	77 *	20.45	0	4	81	9	0	0	0	-	-	-	0	0
GC Stevens	2005/06	3	5	0	48	18	9.60	0	0	1	0	325	157	4	39.25	2.89	2-22	0	0
DW Steyn	2003/04	32	40	12	307	82	10.96	0	1	7	0	6366	3642	124	29.37	3.43	5-27	5	1
FA Steyn	2004/05	11	20	1	582	116	30.63	2	2	10	0	18	17	0	-	5.66	-	0	0
RA Stroh	2004/05	11	19	1	380	91	21.11	0	2	12	0	1158	701	28	25.03	3.63	6-84	1	0
HM Strydom	2005/06	1	2	1	24	17	24.00	0	0	1	0	0	0	0	-	-	-	0	0
JG Strydom	2000/01	41	75	4	2312	151	32.56	4	14	34	0	96	49	0	-	3.06	-	0	0
SP Summers	2004/05	4	6	1	200	74	40.00	0	2	0	0	132	85	1	85.00	3.86	1-39	0	0
WC Swan	2003/04	11	19	1	536	93	29.77	0	5	3	0	210	149	1	149.00	4.25	1-54	0	0
RP Symcox	2002/03	17	21	3	383	87	21.27	0	2	17	0	2474	1182	29	40.75	2.86	4-13	0	0
J Symes	2005/06	3	5	0	185	133	37.00	1	0	4	0	171	101	2	50.50	3.54	2-13	0	0
R Telemachus	1994/95	74	99	22	1214	116	15.76	1	2	19	0	11780	6140	227	27.04	3.12	6-21	7	0
FD Telo	2005/06	6	11	0	398	72	36.18	0	3	0	0	0	0	0	-	-	-	0	0
DJ Terbrugge	1994/95	67	81	32	627	40 *	12.79	0	0	18	0	13067	5551	219	25.34	2.54	6-58	6	0
J Theron	2005/06	6	7	1	52	15	8.66	0	0	1	0	735	387	16	24.18	3.15	6-47	1	0
J Theunissen	2005/06	1	2	0	22	22	11.00	0	0	0	0	0	0	0	-	-	-	0	0
AC Thomas	1998/99	54	82	18	1830	119 *	28.59	2	7	20	0	10357	4557	173	26.34	2.63	7-54	8	1
PG Thompson	2003/04	3	5	0	77	66	15.40	0	1	3	0	351	221	5	44.20	3.77	3-41	0	0
CA Thyssen	2003/04	19	28	5	796	157	34.60	1	4	6	0	528	305	5	61.00	3.46	2-14	0	0
G Toyana	1995/96	66	104	7	2201	113	22.69	1	11	45	0	318	172	1	172.00	3.24	1-30	0	0
ES Tsamaisi	2001/02	4	6	2	26	13	6.50	0	0	0	0	246	140	5	28.00	3.41	2-36	0	0
T Tshabalala	2003/04	17	23	5	219	34	12.16	0	0	4	0	2352	1420	39	36.41	3.62	5-72	1	0
TL Tsolekile	1999	77	104	13	2289	101 *	25.15	1	11	246	20	0	0	0	-	-	-	0	0
LL Tsotsobe	2004/05	8	10	3	34	12 *	4.85	0	0	2	0	1283	679	30	22.63	3.17	7-44	1	0
ANW Tweedie	1997/98	37	48	15	614	85 *	18.60	0	1	8	0	6337	3342	123	27.17	3.16	5-50	2	0
AM van den Berg	1999	27	47	1	935	103	20.32	1	4	12	0	2059	980	30	32.66	2.85	5-49	1	0
F van der Merwe	1999/00	15	18	6	122	24 *	10.16	0	0	4	0	2969	1721	49	35.12	3.47	5-45	4	0
JJ van der Wath	1996/97	53	83	14	1734	113 *	25.13	2	10	20	0	9134	4413	153	28.84	2.89	6-37	8	0
M van Jaarsveld	1994/95	136	232	22	9235	262 *	43.97	25	40	167	0	1081	550	13	42.30	3.05	2-30	0	0
VB van Jaarsveld	2003/04	21	36	3	1149	126	34.81	3	9	23	0	18	11	0	-	3.66	-	0	0

Name	Debut	M	Inns	NO	Runs	HS	Avg	100	50	Ct	St	Balls	Runs	Wkts	Avg	RpO	BB	5I	10M
PM van Niekerk	2002/03	1	1	0	5	5	5.00	0	0	0	0	306	157	3	52.33	3.07	3-79	0	0
HA van Straaten	2005/06	7	11	0	191	68	17.36	0	1	5	0	0	0	0	-	-	-	0	0
N van Woerkom	2004/05	3	6	0	384	146	64.00	1	3	1	0	198	137	3	45.66	4.15	1-13	0	0
CFK van Wyk	2000/01	48	73	13	1750	104	29.16	1	9	148	8	18	9	1	9.00	3.00	1-7	0	0
DJ van Wyk	2004/05	10	14	0	392	106	28.00	1	1	16	0	0	0	0	-	-	-	0	0
DM van Wyk	2005/06	7	12	5	513	122 *	73.28	1	4	22	5	0	0	0	-	-	-	0	0
JM van Wyk	1998/99	16	27	5	227	35	10.31	0	0	2	0	2215	1266	34	37.23	3.42	3-27	0	0
MN van Wyk	1996/97	68	116	15	3754	200 *	37.16	8	17	151	7	78	36	2	18.00	2.76	2-25	0	0
GE von Hoesslin	2004/05	12	21	2	418	101 *	22.00	1	1	23	3	9	9	1	9.00	6.00	1-9	0	0
N Wagner	2005/06	4	2	1	29	20	29.00	0	0	0	0	512	245	14	17.50	2.87	4-39	0	0
L-R Walters	2004/05	10	19	3	316	56	19.75	0	1	21	1	0	0	0	-	-	-	0	0
MD Walters	2005/06	1	1	0	0	0	0.00	0	0	1	0	0	0	0	-	-	-	0	0
DJ Watson	1993/94	112	188	17	6312	220	36.91	11	36	65	0	215	89	4	22.25	2.48	2-7	0	0
D Wiese	2005/06	9	15	1	526	168	37.57	1	2	4	0	1203	732	26	28.15	3.65	4-48	0	0
D Willemse	2004/05	8	11	1	228	58	22.80	0	1	5	0	1206	622	18	34.55	3.09	4-56	0	0
M Williamson	2005/06	7	14	2	205	44	17.08	0	0	7	0	5	4	0	-	4.80	-	0	0
CM Willoughby	1994/95	120	137	56	354	17 *	4.37	0	0	30	0	24988	11052	444	24.89	2.65	7-56	17	3
WR Wingfield	1997/98	43	68	14	1936	146 *	35.85	1	10	20	0	2202	1080	23	46.95	2.94	2-18	0	0
W Wyngaard	2004/05	15	27	4	671	132 *	29.17	3	1	10	0	0	0	0	-	-	-	0	0
M Zondeki	2000/01	47	66	18	422	59	8.79	0	1	16	0	7560	4116	133	30.94	3.26	6-39	3	0

SOUTH AFRICAN LIMITED OVERS RECORDS

As at 22 April 2006.

Note: These records are based on List A Limited Overs matches as per the Association of Cricket Statisticians and Historians. Matches included in List A are: Limited Overs Internationals, other international matches (e.g. Commonwealth Games and 'A' team internationals), domestic limited overs tournaments and matches involving major first-class teams against international touring teams. Only matches with a scheduled duration of at least 40 overs are included. All matches played in South Africa or by South African teams abroad are included.

ABBREVIATIONS

LOI .... Limited Overs International
WC .... World Cup
NS .... Gillette Cup/Datsun Shield/Nissan Shield/Total Power Series
SB .... Benson & Hedges Series/Standard Bank Cup & League
Prov .... South African Airways Provincial Challenge
Oth .... Other Limited Overs matches

TEAM RECORDS

HIGHEST INNINGS TOTALS

438-9	(49.5)	South Africa v Australia (LOI)	Johannesburg	2005/06
434-4	(50)	Australia v South Africa (LOI)	Johannesburg	2005/06
388-3	(50)	South Africa A v Sri Lanka Under-23 (Oth)	Colombo-PP	2005/06
378-5	(60)	Transvaal v Griqualand West (NS)	Kimberley	1977/78
372-5	(60)	Eastern Province v Border (NS)	East London	1974/75
364-2	(55)	Natal v Eastern Transvaal CD (NS)	Witbank	1991/92
363-3	(55)	Natal v Border CD (NS)	King William's Town	1990/91
363-3	(50)	South Africa v Zimbabwe (LOI)	Bulawayo	2001/02
361-2*	(54.4)	Natal v SA African XI (NS)	Durban	1975/76
360-4	(60)	Western Province v Border (NS)	East London	1970/71
359-2	(50)	Australia v India (WC)	Johannesburg	2002/03
355-7	(60)	Western Province v Eastern Province (NS)	Johannesburg	1969/70
354-9	(55)	Transvaal v Griqualand West (NS)	Kimberley	1983/84
354-6	(50)	South Africans v Zimbabwe CD (Oth)	Harare	1995/96
354-3	(50)	South Africa v Kenya (LOI)	Cape Town	2001/02
351-3	(50)	India v Kenya (LOI)	Paarl	2001/02
345-9	(60)	Eastern Province v Griqualand West (NS)	Kimberley	1972/73
345-2*	(51)	Eastern Province v SA African XI (NS)	Port Elizabeth	1976/77
344-6	(50)	Australia v South Africa (LOI)	Sydney	2005/06
342	(58)	Eastern Province v Western Province (NS)	Johannesburg	1969/70
341-3	(50)	Transvaal v Western Transvaal (SB)	Potchefstroom	1994/95
335-6	(50)	Pakistan v South Africa (LOI)	Port Elizabeth	2002/03
333-6	(55)	Western Province v Griqualand West (NS)	Cape Town	1969/70
332-5	(55)	Transvaal v Eastern Province (NS)	Johannesburg	1982/83
330-7	(49.1)	Australia v South Africa (LOI)	Port Elizabeth	2001/02
The highest total in a 45 over match is:				
327-3	(45)	Northerns v North West (SB)	Centurion	2003/04

LOWEST INNINGS TOTALS

36	(18.4)	Canada v Sri Lanka (WC)	Paarl	2002/03
43	(19.5)	Pakistan v West Indies (LOI)	Cape Town	1992/93
45	(14)	Namibia v Australia (WC)	Potchefstroom	2002/03
45	(21.4)	Sri Lanka A v South Africa A (Oth)	Colombo-RPS	2005/06
46	(20.1)	Natal CD v Eastern Province (NS)	Empangeni	1990/91
47	(32.1)	Border v Western Province (SB)	East London	1991/92

SOUTH AFRICAN LIMITED OVERS RECORDS

51	(18.3)	Bangladeshis v SA President's XI (Oth)	Pietermaritzburg	2000/01
54	(20.1)	West Indies XI v South Africa (Oth)	Pretoria	1983/84
54	(23.2)	West Indies v South Africa (LOI)	Cape Town	2003/04
56	(23.4)	Western Province v Border (SB)	East London	1998/99
57	(27.2)	Bangladeshis v SA President's XI (Oth)	Durban	2000/01
58	(37)	Griqualand West v Northern Transvaal (SB)	Kimberley	1995/96
60	(34)	Northern Tvl CD v Eastern Province (NS)	Pietersburg	1992/93
61	(30.3)	Border v Northern Transvaal (NS)	Pretoria	1981/82
61	(15.4)	Transvaal v Eastern Transvaal (SB)	Johannesburg	1994/95
63	(29.3)	Border v Natal (NS)	Durban	1980/81
63	(20.5)	Boland v Western Province (NS)	Stellenbosch	1990/91
64	(33.4)	Orange Free State v Natal (NS)	Bloemfontein	1982/83
64	(29.1)	Boland v Western Province (SB)	Paarl	1998/99
69	(28)	South Africa v Australia (LOI)	Sydney	1993/94
69	(31)	Boland v Gauteng (SB)	Paarl	1998/99

HIGHEST TOTALS BATTING SECOND

438-9	(49.5)	(Won)	South Africa v Australia (LOI)	Johannesburg	2005/06
342	(58)	(Lost)	Eastern Province v Western Province (NS)	Johannesburg	1969/70
330-7	(49.1)	(Won)	Australia v South Africa (LOI)	Port Elizabeth	2001/02
327-7	(48.4)	(Won)	South African XI v Australians (Oth)	Johannesburg	1966/67
310	(49.5)	(Lost)	Australian XI v South Africa (Oth)	Port Elizabeth	1986/87
310	(48.5)	(Lost)	India v South Africa (LOI)	Nagpur	1999/00
310-6	(49.4)	(Won)	South Africa v West Indies (LOI)	Johannesburg	2003/04
308-2	(43.3)	(Won)	Lions v Warriors (SB)	Potchefstroom	2004/05

LOWEST TOTALS BATTING FIRST AND WINNING

107	(41.2)	Western Province beat Orange Free State (SB)	Cape Town	1992/93
126-7	(45)	Easterns beat Western Province (SB)	Cape Town	1998/99
129	(41.4)	South Africa beat England (LOI)	East London	1995/96
132	(36.1)	Western Province beat Natal (NS)	Johannesburg	1969/70
133	(45)	Eastern Province beat Natal (SB)	Durban	1992/93
140-9	(50)	South Africa beat West Indies (LOI)	Cape Town	1992/93

HIGHEST MATCH AGGREGATES

872-13	(99.5)	South Africa v Australia (LOI)	Johannesburg	2005/06
697-17	(118)	Eastern Province v Western Province (NS)	Johannesburg	1969/70
656-10	(99.1)	South Africa v Australia (LOI)	Port Elizabeth	2001/02
650-15	(98.4)	South African XI v Australians (Oth)	Johannesburg	1966/67
641-11	(100)	Western Transvaal v Transvaal (SB)	Potchefstroom	1994/95
631-12	(100)	Australia v South Africa (LOI)	Sydney	2005/06
630-17	(98.5)	India v South Africa (LOI)	Nagpur	1999/00
626-16	(99.5)	South Africa v Australian XI (Oth)	Port Elizabeth	1986/87

LARGEST MARGINS OF VICTORY

By runs

283	Natal beat SA African XI (NS)	Durban	1975/76
269	Eastern Province beat Natal CD (NS)	Empangeni	1990/91
256	Australia beat Namibia (WC)	Potchefstroom	2002/03
247	Natal beat Border (NS)	Durban	1980/81
245	Western Province beat Border (NS)	East London	1970/71
244	Eastern Province beat SA African XI (NS)	Port Elizabeth	1976/77
239	Transvaal beat Griqualand West (NS)	Kimberley	1977/78
226	Eastern Province beat Northern Tvl CD (NS)	Pietersburg	1992/93
220	South Africa A beat West Indies A (Oth)	Durban	1997/98
219	Natal beat Western Transvaal (SB)	Fochville	1995/96

By wickets

10 Achieved on 15 occasions in South African Limited Overs matches.

The only case in a Benson & Hedges/Standard Bank Cup match (excluding reduced overs matches) is:

Titans beat Dolphins (SB)	Centurion	2005/06

SOUTH AFRICAN LIMITED OVERS RECORDS

NARROWEST MARGINS OF VICTORY

By runs

1	Orange Free State beat Western Province (NS)	Bloemfontein	1992/93
1	Transvaal beat Natal (SB)	Durban	1992/93
1	Australia beat South Africa (LOI)	Bloemfontein	1993/94
1	Griqualand West beat Free State (SB)	Bloemfontein	1996/97
1	Border beat Western Province (SB)	Cape Town	1997/98
1	South Africa beat New Zealand (LOI)	Hobart	1997/98
1	South Africa beat England (LOI)	Cape Town	1999/00
1	Eastern Province beat Boland (SB)	Port Elizabeth	2000/01
1	Australia A beat South Africa A (Oth)	Perth	2002/03
1	South Africa beat West Indies (LOI)	Bridgetown	2004/05

By wickets

1 Achieved on 32 occasions in South African Limited Overs matches. 19 of these were in Benson & Hedges/Standard Bank Cup matches.

TIED MATCHES

Griqualand West v Rhodesia (NS)	Kimberley (a)	1978/79
Transvaal v Natal (NS)	Johannesburg (b)	1980/81
Natal v Northern Transvaal (NS)	Durban (c)	1991/92
Wellington v South Africans (Oth)	Wellington	1994/95
Transvaal v Natal (SB)	Johannesburg	1995/96
Free State v Northern Transvaal (SB)	Centurion	1995/96
Zimbabwe v India (LOI)	Paarl	1996/97
Boland v North West (SB)	Paarl	1998/99
Australia v South Africa (WC)	Birmingham	1999
South Africa v Australia (LOI)	Melbourne-Colonial	2000
Eastern Province v Sri Lankans (Oth)	Port Elizabeth	2000/01
Eastern Province v Easterns (SB)	Port Elizabeth	2000/01
Eastern Province v Northerns (SB)	Centurion (d)	2001/02
Border v Northerns (SB)	East London (d)	2001/02
South Africa v Australia (LOI)	Potchefstroom	2001/02
Sri Lanka v South Africa (D/L Method) (WC)	Durban	2002/03
England v South Africa (LOI)	Bloemfontein	2004/05
Free State v Easterns (D/L Method) (Prov)	Benoni	2005/06
Cape Cobras v Dolphins (D/L Method) (SB)	Durban	2005/06

(a) Awarded to Griqualand West who had the higher scoring rate over the first 20 overs.
(b) Awarded to Transvaal by virtue of losing fewer wickets.
(c) Awarded to Natal by virtue of losing fewer wickets.
(d) Consecutive matches for Northerns.

BATTING

HIGHEST INDIVIDUAL INNINGS

222*	RG Pollock	Eastern Province v Border (NS)	East London	1974/75
202*	A Barrow	Natal v SA African XI (NS)	Durban	1975/76
188*	G Kirsten	South Africa v United Arab Emirates (WC)	Rawalpindi	1995/96
186	EJ Barlow	Western Province v Eastern Province (NS)	Johannesburg	1969/70
175	HH Gibbs	South Africa v Australia (LOI)	Johannesburg	2005/06
169*	DJ Callaghan	South Africa v New Zealand (LOI)	Verwoerdburg	1994/95
169	RG Pollock	Eastern Province v Western Province (NS)	Johannesburg	1969/70
169	CEB Rice	Transvaal v Griqualand West (NS)	Kimberley	1977/78
167*	PR Carlstein	Transvaal v North-Eastern Transvaal (NS)	Pretoria	1970/71
166*	MC Venter	North West v Natal (SB)	Fochville	1997/98
164*	SJ Cook	Transvaal v Border (NS)	East London	1978/79
164	BJ Hodge	Australia A v South Africa A (Oth)	Perth	2002/03
164	RT Ponting	Australia v South Africa (LOI)	Johannesburg	2005/06
161	AC Hudson	South Africa v Holland (WC)	Rawalpindi	1995/96

SOUTH AFRICAN LIMITED OVERS RECORDS

MOST CENTURIES IN A CAREER

+ Denotes current player

+HH Gibbs	19
G Kirsten	18
SJ Cook	16
+JH Kallis	16
RG Pollock	12
MJR Rindel	11
KC Wessels	11
Benson & Hedges/Standard Bank Cup:	
MJR Rindel	9
+AM Bacher	7
+DJ Watson	6
KC Wessels	6

The most centuries by a South African in all List A limited overs matches is 27 by RA Smith.

CARRYING BAT THROUGH AN INNINGS

(Team all out)

BJ Whitfield	72*	(174)	Natal v Transvaal (NS)	Durban	1984/85
HH Gibbs	59*	(101)	South Africa v Pakistan (LOI)	Sharjah *	1999/00
AG Puttick	101*	(192)	Western Province Boland v Dolphins (SB)	Cape Town	2004/05

* 1 batsman retired hurt.

MOST RUNS IN A SEASON

	M	Inns	NO	Runs	HS	Avg	100	50	Season
KC Wessels (EP)	28	28	5	1347	127 *	58.56	3	7	1992/93
MJR Rindel (Nor)	22	22	2	1119	144 *	55.95	3	6	1997/98
HH Gibbs (WP)	22	22	5	1007	153	59.23	3	5	2002/03
SJ Cook (Tvl)	20	20	2	1004	144 *	55.77	5	2	1982/83
GC Smith (WP)	16	16	1	982	117 *	65.46	1	9	2001/02
JH Kallis (WP)	25	24	2	966	86	43.90	0	11	1996/97
JM Kemp (Ttn)	24	23	5	943	102	52.38	1	8	2004/05
Benson & Hedges/Standard Bank Cup:									
MJR Rindel (Nor)	13	13	2	785	144 *	71.36	2	4	1997/98
MJR Rindel (NT)	14	14	1	766	121	58.92	3	4	1996/97
GC Smith (WP)	12	12	1	738	117 *	67.09	1	7	2001/02
KR Rutherford (Gau)	13	13	4	667	130 *	74.11	1	5	1997/98
DJ Watson (Ntl)	12	12	0	624	93	52.00	0	8	1996/97

FASTEST CENTURIES

(in balls faced where known)

49 balls	AP Kuiper (117)	South Africa v English XI (Oth)	Bloemfontein	1989/90
57 balls	RP Snell (122)	Transvaal v Griqualand West (SB)	Kimberley	1994/95

RG Pollock scored a century in 57 minutes for Eastern Province v SA African XI (NS) at Port Elizabeth, 1976/77.

FASTEST FIFTIES

(in balls faced where known)

19 balls	MV Boucher (51*)	South Africa v Kenya (LOI)	Cape Town	2001/02
19 balls	JA Morkel (67*)	South Africa A v New Zealand A (Oth)	Johannesburg	2004/05
19 balls	JM Kemp (53*)	South Africa v Zimbabwe (LOI)	Durban	2004/05
Benson & Hedges/Standard Bank Cup:				
21 balls	JM Kemp (64*)	Northerns v North West	Centurion	2003/04

RECORD WICKET PARTNERSHIPS

1st	274	KC Wessels and PG Amm	Eastern Province v Natal CD (Empangeni) (NS)	1990/91
	240	RF Pienaar and MJR Rindel	Northerns v Free State (Bloemfontein) (SB)	1998/99
2nd	257	Salim Elahi and Abdul Razzaq	Pakistan v South Africa (Port Elizabeth) (LOI)	2002/03
	211*	HR Fotheringham and RF Pienaar	Transvaal v Orange Free State (Johannesburg) (SB)	1988/89
3rd	303*	A Barrow and HR Fotheringham	Natal v SA African XI (Durban) (NS)	1975/76
	243	AM Bacher and ND McKenzie	Transvaal v North West (Fochville) (SB)	1996/97

4th	232	DJ Cullinan and JN Rhodes	South Africa v Pakistan (Nairobi) (LOI)	1996/97
	181	ND McKenzie and G Dros	Northerns v North West (Centurion) (SB)	2000/01
5th	183*	JH Kallis and JN Rhodes	South Africa v Pakistan (Durban) (LOI)	1997/98
	144	PC Strydom and SC Pope	Border v North West (East London) (SB)	1998/99
6th	173	PH Williams and D Bestall	Natal v Transvaal (Durban) (NS)	1979/80
	158	DR Laing and N Pothas	Transvaal v Eastern Province (Johannesburg) (SB)	1995/96
7th	128*	D du Preez and R Telemachus	Free State v Griqualand West (Kimberley) (Prov)	2005/06
	126	DR Laing and AJ Hall	Transvaal v Eastern Province (Port Elizabeth) (SB)	1996/97
8th	119	PR Reiffel and SK Warne	Australia v South Africa (Port Elizabeth) (LOI)	1993/94
	88	FJC Cronje and IL Howell	Border v Boland (Stellenbosch) (SB)	1993/94
9th	80*	Arshad Laeeq and SF Dukanwala	United Arab Emirates v South Africa (Rawalpindi) (WC)	1995/96
	76	AP Kuiper and CR Matthews	Western Province v Impalas (Cape Town) (SB)	1987/88
10th	102*	TA Bula and F de Wet	North West v Free State (Potchefstroom) (Prov)	2005/06
	78*	CE Eksteen and EW Kidwell	Gauteng v Griqualand West (Johannesburg) (SB)	1998/99

BATSMEN WHO HAVE SCORED 5000 RUNS IN A CAREER

+ Denotes current player.

	Career	M	Inns	NO	Runs	HS	Avg	100	50
+JH Kallis	1994-	294	281	46	10122	139	43.07	16	73
G Kirsten	1988-2003	294	289	27	9586	188 *	36.58	18	58
WJ Cronje	1988-99	282	263	48	9093	120	42.29	8	65
+HH Gibbs	1990-	288	279	22	8791	175	34.20	19	43
JN Rhodes	1988-2002	352	320	65	8492	121	33.30	2	50
PN Kirsten	1973-96	254	251	23	8433	134 *	36.98	8	61
KC Wessels	1974-98	214	211	23	8299	146	44.14	11	58
DJ Cullinan	1984-2004	305	292	35	8057	127 *	31.35	7	45
SJ Cook	1972-94	215	210	20	7591	164 *	39.95	16	47
RF Pienaar	1979-99	204	197	16	5960	135	32.92	6	44
AC Hudson	1985-2000	206	204	7	5884	161	29.86	4	41
AP Kuiper	1979-98	228	215	41	5554	118	31.91	4	31
+HH Dippenaar	1995-	172	154	23	5460	125 *	41.67	7	37
MW Rushmere	1985-99	189	176	31	5455	139	37.62	6	35
MJR Rindel	1986-2001	185	174	18	5432	144 *	34.82	11	31
+GC Smith	1999-	136	134	9	5198	134 *	41.58	9	34
+L Klusener	1991-	255	208	75	5189	142 *	39.01	3	25
DJ Callaghan	1984-2002	209	193	38	5107	169 *	32.94	2	32
Leading run-scorers in Benson & Hedges/Standard Bank Cup:									
KC Wessels	1986-98	109	107	15	4651	124	50.55	6	38
+AM Bacher	1994-	113	109	8	4017	158 *	39.77	7	25
MJR Rindel	1986-2001	123	116	16	3961	144 *	39.61	9	24
RF Pienaar	1981-99	138	134	12	3950	124 *	32.37	3	32
DJ Callaghan	1984-2002	143	135	25	3874	107 *	35.21	1	30
All List A limited overs matches:									
AJ Lamb	1972-95	484	463	63	15658	132 *	39.14	19	98
RA Smith	1981-2003	443	423	60	14927	167 *	41.12	27	81
CEB Rice	1970-93	479	444	83	13474	169	37.32	11	79
KC Wessels	1974-98	337	331	30	12503	146	41.53	15	90
KS McEwan	1972-91	409	396	42	11866	162 *	33.51	16	69

BOWLING

BEST BOWLING

7-15	GD McGrath	Australia v Namibia (WC)	Potchefstroom	2002/03
7-20	AJ Bichel	Australia v England (WC)	Port Elizabeth	2002/03
7-21	PP Henwood	Natal v Border (NS)	East London	1972/73
7-27	DL Hobson	Western Province v Northern Transvaal (NS)	Pretoria	1974/75
6-8	EO Simons	Western Province v Eastern Province CD (NS)	Cradock	1990/91
6-9	FD Stephenson	West Indies XI v South Africa (Oth)	Durban	1982/83
6-13	EAE Baptiste	Eastern Province v Northern Tvl CD (NS)	Pietersburg	1992/93

6-16	RJ Peterson	Eastern Province v Namibia (SB)	Port Elizabeth	2002/03
6-17	PN Kirsten	Western Province v Northern Transvaal (NS)	Cape Town	1983/84
6-17	PC Strydom	Border v Western Province (SB)	East London	2001/02
6-19	HK Olonga	Zimbabwe v England (LOI)	Cape Town	1999/00
6-20	JM Kemp	Eastern Province v Free State (SB)	Port Elizabeth	2000/01
6-21	GS le Roux	South Africa v Australian XI (Oth)	Cape Town	1986/87
6-22	RW Hanley	South Africa v West Indies XI (Oth)	Pretoria	1983/84
6-22	BN Schultz	Eastern Province v Transvaal (SB)	Johannesburg	1995/96
6-22	M Ntini	South Africa v Australia (LOI)	Cape Town	2005/06
6-23	AA Donald	South Africa v Kenya (LOI)	Nairobi	1996/97
6-23	GJ-P Kruger	Eastern Province v North West (SB)	Port Elizabeth	1999/00
6-23	A Nehra	India v England (WC)	Durban	2002/03
6-23	SE Bond	New Zealand v Australia (WC)	Port Elizabeth	2002/03
6-24	CM Willoughby	South Africa A v Barbados (Oth)	Bridgetown	2000/01
6-24	ANW Tweedie	Dolphins v Titans (SB)	Pietermaritzburg	2005/06
6-25	GM Gilder	Natal v North West (SB)	Fochville	1997/98
6-25	WPUJC Vaas	Sri Lanka v Bangladesh (WC)	Pietermaritzburg	2002/03

HAT-TRICKS

DL Hobson	Western Province v Northern Transvaal (NS)	Pretoria	1974/75
GS le Roux	Western Province v Transvaal (SB)	Cape Town	1982/83
RW Hanley	South Africa v West Indies XI (Oth)	Pretoria	1983/84
NV Radford	Transvaal v Natal (NS)	Durban	1984/85
BC Fourie	Impalas v Natal (SB)	Durban	1988/89
S Jacobs	Transvaal v Northern Transvaal CD (NS)	Nelspruit	1989/90
PA Rayment	Western Province v Orange Free State (SB)	Cape Town	1990/91
EO Simons	Western Province v Border (SB)	East London	1991/92
Waqar Younis	Pakistan v New Zealand (LOI)	East London	1994/95
BN Schultz	Eastern Province v Transvaal (SB)	Johannesburg	1995/96
M Hayward	Eastern Province v Western Province (SB)	Cape Town	1996/97
DJJ de Vos	Northerns v Easterns (SB)	Benoni	1998/99
M Hayward	Eastern Province v KwaZulu-Natal (SB)	Durban	1998/99
RE Veenstra	KwaZulu-Natal v Gauteng (SB)	Durban	1999/00
GJ Smith	Northerns v Border (SB)	East London	2000/01
WA Albertyn	Boland v Northerns (SB)	Centurion	2001/02
WPUJC Vaas	Sri Lanka v Bangladesh (WC)	Pietermaritzburg	2002/03
B Lee	Australia v Kenya (WC)	Durban	2002/03
CK Langeveldt	South Africa v West Indies (LOI)	Bridgetown	2004/05

ECONOMICAL BOWLING

(5 overs or more)

RpO					
0.16	6-5-1-0	PA Rayment	Eastern Province v Transvaal (SB)	Johannesburg	1987/88
0.18	5.2-4-1-3	PWE Rawson	Natal v Transvaal (SB)	Durban	1994/95
0.33	6-5-2-2	CEB Rice	Natal v Western Transvaal (NS)	Potchefstroom	1992/93
0.41	12-8-5-0	RH Kaschula	Rhodesia v Northern Transvaal (NS)	Pretoria	1972/73
0.44	9-5-4-1	GR Dilley	Natal v Impalas (SB)	Pietermaritzburg	1985/86
0.50	8-6-4-1	RA Woolmer	Natal v SA African XI (NS)	Durban	1975/76
0.53	7.3-5-4-5	MJ Procter	Natal v Border (NS)	Durban	1980/81
0.54	11-6-6-1	RW Hanley	Transvaal v Border (NS)	East London	1982/83
0.54	11-6-6-4	S Jacobs	Transvaal v Natal CD (NS)	Empangeni	1991/92
0.57	7-4-4-1	CM Old	Northern Transvaal v Western Province (NS)	Cape Town	1981/82

EXPENSIVE BOWLING

(5 overs or more)

RpO					
11.66	6-0-70-0	JH Kallis	South Africa v Australia (LOI)	Johannesburg	2005/06
11.60	5-0-58-1	DW Steyn	South Africa v Australia (LOI)	Melbourne-Colonial	2005/06
11.60	5-0-58-2	AK Kruger	Griqualand West v Easterns (Prov)	Kimberley	2005/06
11.57	7-0-81-0	MA Suji	Kenya v India (LOI)	Paarl	2001/02

11.30	10-0-113-0	ML Lewis	Australia v South Africa (LOI)	Johannesburg	2005/06
11.20	5-0-56-0	CJ van Heerden	Impalas v Natal (SB)	Durban	1984/85
10.83	6-0-65-0	J Srinath	India v South Africa (LOI)	Nagpur	1999/00
10.80	5-0-54-0	S Jacobs	Transvaal v Natal (SB)	Johannesburg	1990/91
10.80	5-0-54-1	AR Adams	New Zealand v Zimbabwe (WC)	Bloemfontein	2002/03
10.57	7-0-74-1	GD Watson	Australians v South African XI (Oth)	Johannesburg	1966/67
10.50	6-0-63-0	A Nel	South Africa v West Indies (LOI)	Centurion	2003/04
10.50	6-1-63-0	KD Mills	New Zealand v South Africa (LOI)	Auckland	2003/04
10.42	7-0-73-1	TJ Friend	Zimbabwe v South Africa (LOI)	Bulawayo	2001/02
10.42	7-1-73-0	VD Philander	Western Province Boland v Warriors (SB)	Port Elizabeth	2004/05
In Benson & Hedges/Standard Bank Cup matches the most expensive off 9 overs is:					
9.33	9-0-84-3	LB Taylor	Natal v Western Province	Cape Town	1983/84

MOST WICKETS IN A SEASON

	M	Balls	Runs	Wkts	Avg	BB	RpO	4I	Season
M Ntini (Bdr)	20	1089	677	39	17.35	3.73	4-24	2	2002/03
SM Pollock (Ntl)	27	1343	934	36	25.94	4.17	4-33	1	1996/97
GS le Roux (WP)	20	1071	756	35	21.60	4.23	6-21	3	1986/87
ST Jefferies (WP)	21	1144	657	33	19.90	3.44	4-31	1	1982/83
CEB Rice (Tvl)	20	857	638	33	19.33	4.46	5-43	3	1986/87
AP Kuiper (WP)	15	728	472	33	14.30	3.89	5-47	3	1988/89
AA Donald (FS)	26	1458	799	33	24.21	3.28	4-8	1	1992/93
R Telemachus (Bol)	18	874	591	33	17.90	4.05	4-43	1	1997/98
SM Pollock (KZN)	21	1012	540	33	16.36	3.20	4-18	2	2002/03
Benson & Hedges/Standard Bank Cup:									
EO Simons (WP)	16	657	405	30	13.50	3.69	4-17	2	1996/97
JC Kent (KZN)	14	662	500	26	19.23	4.53	4-29	1	2000/01
FD Stephenson (OFS)	12	636	287	25	11.48	2.70	4-14	3	1994/95

BOWLERS WHO HAVE TAKEN 200 WICKETS IN A CAREER

+ Denotes current player.

	Career	M	Balls	Runs	Wkts	Avg	RpO	BB	4I
+SM Pollock	1992-	342	16952	10442	443	23.57	3.69	6-35	17
AA Donald	1985-2003	304	15303	10103	436	23.17	3.96	6-23	19
EO Simons	1983-98	193	9351	6110	283	21.59	3.92	6-8	20
+L Klusener	1991-	255	10700	8240	271	30.40	4.62	6-49	9
+M Ntini	1995-	179	8598	6273	265	23.67	4.37	6-22	11
+JH Kallis	1994-	294	10158	7973	259	30.78	4.70	5-30	5
CR Matthews	1987-99	176	8726	5523	243	22.72	3.79	5-11	8
S Elworthy	1988-2002	193	9157	6325	234	27.02	4.14	4-23	4
MW Pringle	1987-2001	174	8480	5638	221	25.51	3.98	6-30	9
CEB Rice	1970-93	196	7495	4822	216	22.32	3.86	5-43	6
+AC Dawson	1993-	150	7173	4778	213	22.43	3.99	5-13	8
+R Telemachus	1994-	150	7262	5366	206	26.04	4.43	5-54	2
+N Boje	1993-	224	9516	6732	204	33.00	4.24	5-21	9
DN Crookes	1990-2004	176	6970	5086	200	25.43	4.37	5-37	10
Leading wicket-takers in Benson & Hedges/Standard Bank Cup:									
EO Simons	1983-98	125	5585	3609	182	19.82	3.87	4-3	12
MW Pringle	1987-2001	133	6289	4255	168	25.32	4.05	6-30	7
+AC Dawson	1993-	113	5393	3489	167	20.89	3.88	5-13	6
DN Crookes	1990-2004	118	4653	3325	151	22.01	4.28	5-37	9
RE Bryson	1988-2001	112	5275	3970	151	26.29	4.51	4-17	7
All List A limited overs matches:									
AA Donald	1985-2003	458	22857	14942	684	21.84	3.92	6-15	38
+SM Pollock	1992-	388	19218	11845	526	22.51	3.69	6-21	23
CEB Rice	1970-93	479	17738	11705	517	22.64	3.95	6-18	25
NV Radford	1980-98	351	16821	11268	484	23.28	4.01	7-19	15
GS le Roux	1975-88	250	12201	7549	378	19.97	3.71	6-21	21

SOUTH AFRICAN LIMITED OVERS RECORDS

ALL-ROUND PLAY

100 RUNS AND 4 WICKETS IN A MATCH

104* & 4-39	N Rosendorff	Orange Free State v Natal (NS)	Durban	1978/79
103 & 4-11	MI Gidley	Griqualand West v Easterns (SB)	Benoni	1996/97
121 & 4-42	JF Kloppenburg	Holland v Namibia (WC)	Bloemfontein	2002/03

500 RUNS AND 20 WICKETS IN A SEASON

	Runs	Avg	Wkts	Avg	Season
CEB Rice (Tvl)	510	72.85	23	23.08	1985/86
WJ Cronje (OFS)	830	41.50	24	24.37	1992/93
DJ Callaghan (EP)	632	52.66	22	21.22	1999/00
GC Smith (WP)	982	65.46	20	22.60	2001/02
JM Kemp (Ttn)	943	52.38	23	30.69	2004/05

2000 RUNS AND 100 WICKETS IN A CAREER

+ Denotes current player.

	Runs	Wickets		Runs	Wickets
+N Boje	2824	199	+L Klusener	5168	270
DJ Callaghan	5107	140	AP Kuiper	5554	197
WJ Cronje	9093	148	BM McMillan	3425	185
DN Crookes	2846	200	+SM Pollock	3719	441
+AJ Hall	3135	175	CEB Rice	4681	216
+JH Kallis	10086	257	EO Simons	2207	283
+JM Kemp	3385	153			

WICKETKEEPING

MOST DISMISSALS IN A MATCH

8 (ct 5, st 3)	SJ Palframan	Boland v Easterns (SB)	Paarl	1997/98
7 (ct 7, st 0)	I Mitchell	Border v Western Province (SB)	East London	1998/99
6 (ct 3, st 3)	AJS Smith	Natal v Border (NS)	East London	1972/73
6 (ct 6, st 0)	W Bossenger	Griqualand West v Northern Transvaal (SB)	Centurion	1996/97
6 (ct 6, st 0)	AC Gilchrist	Australia v South Africa (LOI)	Cape Town	1999/00
6 (ct 3, st 3)	SJ Palframan	Boland v Gauteng (SB)	Paarl	2002/03
6 (ct 6, st 0)	AC Gilchrist	Australia v Namibia (WC)	Potchefstroom	2002/03

MOST DISMISSALS IN A SEASON

36 (ct 35, st 1)	DJ Richardson (EP)	1992/93
35 (ct 34, st 1)	MV Boucher (Bdr)	2002/03
31 (ct 29, st 2)	ELR Stewart (KZN)	2000/01
30 (ct 28, st 2)	RV Jennings (Tvl)	1982/83
30 (ct 29, st 1)	RJ Ryall (WP)	1990/91
30 (ct 25, st 5)	SJ Palframan (Bol)	1997/98
30 (ct 22, st 8)	TL Tsolekile (WP)	2001/02
Benson & Hedges/Standard Bank Cup:		
31 (ct 29,st 2)	ELR Stewart (KZN)	2000/01
28 (ct 24,st 4)	SJ Palframan (Bol)	1997/98
28 (ct 20,st 8)	TL Tsolekile (WP)	2001/02

WICKETKEEPERS WHO HAVE DISMISSED 100 BATSMEN IN A CAREER

+ Denotes current player. Some of the catches may have been taken while the player was not keeping wicket.

	Career	M	Ct	St	Total
+MV Boucher	1995-	275	367	25	392
DJ Richardson	1979-97	280	315	29	344
RV Jennings	1978-92	148	187	18	205
RJ Ryall	1979-94	145	189	11	200
SJ Palframan	1991-2002	125	165	29	194
ELR Stewart	1990-2002	144	130	7	137

+TL Tsolekile	1998-	77	120	14	134
+W Bossenger	1996-	92	109	10	119
NT Day	1977-91	91	107	9	116
+N Pothas	1993-	108	91	22	113
+MN van Wyk	1997-	107	95	9	104
Benson & Hedges/Standard Bank Cup:					
SJ Palframan	1991-2002	104	135	25	160
RJ Ryall	1982-94	98	123	5	128
ELR Stewart	1990-2002	114	102	7	109
+W Bossenger	1996-	79	92	10	102

In all List A limited Overs matches, the leading five South African wicketkeepers are as above.

FIELDING

MOST CATCHES IN A MATCH

5	AJ Kourie	Transvaal v Western Province (NS)	Johannesburg	1979/80
5	JN Rhodes	South Africa v West Indies (LOI)	Bombay	1993/94
5	KC Jackson	Boland v Natal (SB)	Durban	1995/96
4	CR Matthews	Western Province v Northern Transvaal (NS)	Verwoerdburg	1988/89
4	KC Wessels	South Africa v West Indies (LOI)	Kingston	1991/92
4	CL Hooper	West Indies v Pakistan (LOI)	Durban	1992/93
4	EO Simons	Western Province v Transvaal (SB)	Johannesburg	1995/96
4	ML Bruyns	Natal v Boland (SB)	Durban	1997/98
4	ND McKenzie	Northerns v Gauteng (SB)	Johannesburg	1999/00
4	M Kaif	India v Sri Lanka (WC)	Johannesburg	2002/03
4	DM Benkenstein	Dolphins v Western Province Boland (SB)	Durban	2004/05
4	AG Prince	South Africa v West Indies (LOI)	Port-of-Spain	2004/05
4	DPMD Jayawardene	Asia v Africa (LOI)	Durban	2005/06
4	D Wiese	Easterns v Griqualand West (Prov)	Kimberley	2005/06

MOST CATCHES IN A SEASON

17	DJ Cullinan (WP)	1987/88
17	SM Pollock (KZN)	2002/03
15	LJ Koen (Bol)	1999/00

FIELDERS WHO HAVE HELD 100 CATCHES IN A CAREER

+ Denotes current player. Some of the catches may have been taken when they occasionally kept wicket.

	Career	M	Ct
JN Rhodes	1988-2002	352	152
DJ Cullinan	1984-2004	305	146
+HH Gibbs	1990-	288	130
+SM Pollock	1992-	342	130
+JH Kallis	1994-	294	110
KC Wessels	1974-1998	214	103
Leading fielders in Benson & Hedges/Standard Bank Cup:			
DJ Cullinan	1984-2004	118	64
LJ Koen	1990-2001	111	59
NC Johnson	1989-2004	97	53
All List A limited overs matches:			
CEB Rice	1970-93	479	175
RA Smith	1981-2003	443	159
JN Rhodes	1988-2004	372	158
DJ Cullinan	1984-2004	331	154
KC Wessels	1974-98	337	151

LIMITED OVERS CAREER RECORDS

As at 2 April 2006.

Note: These career records are based on List A Limited Overs matches as per the Association of Cricket Statisticians and Historians. Matches included in List A are: Limited Overs Internationals, other international matches (e.g. Commonwealth Games and 'A' team internationals), domestic limited overs tournaments and matches involving major first-class teams against international touring teams.

Strike rates are based on matches where details of balls faced are available. An asterisk indicates that details of balls faced are not available for the player's full career.

Name	Debut	M	Inns	NO	Runs	HS	Avg	SR	100	50	Ct	St	Balls	Runs	Wkts	Avg	RpO	BB	4I
YA Abdullah	2005/06	6	1	0	7	7	7.00	87.50	0	0	1	0	180	125	5	25.00	4.16	2-17	0
AP Abrahams	2001/02	13	6	3	30	14 *	10.00	52.63	0	0	2	0	223	207	6	34.50	5.56	2-38	0
S Abrahams	2004/05	10	4	2	18	13 *	9.00	42.85	0	0	2	0	384	321	11	29.18	5.01	3-32	0
U Abrahams	2000/01	28	25	4	383	73	18.23	75.09	0	3	2	0	0	0	0	-	-	-	0
ZA Abrahim	1998/99	64	32	16	191	26	11.93	67.97	0	0	9	0	2726	2207	79	27.93	4.85	4-15	3
HD Ackerman	1993/94	147	140	21	3968	114 *	33.34	68.00	1	28	53	0	48	52	0	-	6.50	-	0
SR Adair	2005/06	4	2	0	50	32	25.00	92.59	0	0	5	2	0	0	0	-	-	-	0
BC Adams	2004/05	13	10	2	174	48	21.75	61.05	0	0	4	0	388	312	4	78.00	4.82	2-26	0
MQ Adams	2005/06	2	2	1	44	23 *	44.00	86.27	0	0	1	0	83	77	5	15.40	5.56	3-53	0
PR Adams	1995/96	61	19	9	94	33 *	9.40	56.62	0	0	17	0	2552	1839	72	25.54	4.32	3-12	0
KC Africa	2004/05	10	10	2	170	48	21.25	61.59	0	0	0	0	383	329	9	36.55	5.15	4-48	1
M Akoojee	2004/05	14	13	1	421	76	35.08	79.13	0	3	3	0	90	89	1	89.00	5.93	1-47	0
WA Albertyn	2001/02	29	18	6	225	58 *	18.75	74.50	0	1	7	0	1183	898	31	28.96	4.55	4-31	1
R Almeida	1998/99	10	6	0	18	8	3.00	50.00	0	0	1	0	396	328	11	29.81	4.96	3-35	0
AM Amla	1999/00	67	62	7	1555	107 *	28.27	66.82	1	9	22	0	42	42	1	42.00	6.00	1-9	0
HM Amla	2001/02	31	31	2	661	59 *	22.79	67.10	0	4	13	0	16	28	0	-	10.50	-	0
RG Arendse	2001/02	23	17	6	459	74	41.72	64.73	0	3	5	0	0	0	0	-	-	-	0
MA Aronstam	2002/03	13	13	1	423	120 *	35.25	69.91	1	2	8	0	385	302	10	30.20	4.70	2-22	0
MC Arthur	2004/05	4	4	0	76	63	19.00	67.85	0	1	0	0	0	0	0	-	-	-	0
NO Arthur	2004/05	13	7	4	33	19	11.00	43.42	0	0	3	0	594	439	12	36.58	4.43	4-19	1
AM Bacher	1994/95	137	132	8	4523	158 *	36.47	70.13	7	28	46	0	1961	1443	47	30.70	4.41	3-20	0
R Bailey	2000/01	14	10	1	117	18	13.00	60.00	0	0	3	0	0	0	0	-	-	-	0

LIMITED OVERS CAREER RECORDS

Name	Debut	M	Inns	NO	Runs	HS	Avg	SR	100	50	Ct	St	Balls	Runs	Wkts	Avg	RpO	BB	4I
RT Bailey	2003/04	26	21	4	398	68	23.41	66.89	0	2	5	0	63	69	1	69.00	6.57	1-38	0
W Barresi	2004/05	3	3	0	20	19	6.66	33.33	0	0	2	0	0	0	0	-	-	-	0
DJ Bassage	2004/05	12	12	0	329	81	27.41	68.25	0	3	4	0	0	0	0	-	-	-	0
C Baxter	2002/03	16	15	1	500	85	35.71	65.01	0	4	6	0	0	0	0	-	-	-	0
F Behardien	2004/05	6	3	0	50	37	16.66	92.59	0	0	2	0	300	286	5	57.20	5.72	3-41	0
M Bekker	2005/06	8	7	1	174	66 *	29.00	83.25	0	2	2	0	0	0	0	-	-	-	0
NA Bell	2005/06	1	0	0	0	-	-		0	0	0	0	54	65	0	-	7.22	-	0
WE Bell	2004/05	9	7	2	89	19 *	17.80	60.95	0	0	2	0	210	156	10	15.60	4.45	3-26	0
DM Benkenstein	1992/93	197	174	43	4388	107 *	33.49	75.16 *	1	23	70	0	1904	1514	61	24.81	4.77	4-16	3
BL Bennett	2004/05	10	10	0	134	42	13.40	54.47	0	0	3	0	80	77	2	38.50	5.77	2-22	0
CN Bennett	2005/06	6	6	0	51	23	8.50	65.38	0	0	1	0	0	0	0	-	-	-	0
KD Bennett	2005/06	5	5	1	114	53	28.50	56.71	0	1	2	0	0	0	0	-	-	-	0
JA Beukes	1997/98	77	69	3	2151	127	32.59	69.09	2	14	25	0	60	41	2	20.50	4.10	2-23	0
ER Bezuidenhout	2005/06	1	0	0	0	-	-		0	0	1	0	6	12	0	-	12.00	-	0
GH Bhayat	2003/04	14	7	3	51	24	12.75	63.75	0	0	6	0	615	523	13	40.23	5.10	2-29	0
R Bhayat	2004/05	8	6	2	166	76	41.50	99.40	0	1	1	0	72	88	1	88.00	7.33	1-28	0
AM Blignaut	1997/98	77	60	9	914	63 *	17.92	94.81 *	0	6	17	0	3263	2931	69	42.47	5.38	4-43	2
GH Bodi	1999/00	66	59	5	1517	112 *	28.09	77.24	3	10	16	0	1434	1223	39	31.35	5.11	5-46	2
TM Bodibe	2004/05	13	8	5	50	19 *	16.66	37.03	0	0	13	3	0	0	0	-	-	-	0
N Boje	1993/94	235	160	44	3088	129	26.62	86.25 *	2	12	69	0	10074	7125	217	32.83	4.24	5-21	9
J Booysen	2004/05	14	12	1	314	67	28.54	115.01	0	2	5	0	42	58	0	-	8.28	-	0
LL Bosman	1997/98	99	96	9	2734	99 *	31.42	82.10	0	16	21	0	85	77	1	77.00	5.43	1-36	0
M Bosman	2004/05	9	9	1	165	37	20.62	82.91	0	0	0	0	108	67	4	16.75	3.72	3-31	0
W Bossenger	1996/97	92	73	29	1390	157 *	31.59	70.84	1	4	109	10	63	75	0	-	7.14	-	0
J Botha	2001/02	50	36	11	477	46	19.08	66.25	0	0	12	0	1967	1438	39	36.87	4.38	4-32	1
MV Boucher	1995/96	275	214	49	4393	98	26.62	80.75 *	0	27	367	25	0	0	0	-	-	-	0
CC Bradfield	1998/99	72	72	4	1691	109 *	24.86	56.97 *	1	7	16	0	66	84	4	21.00	7.63	2-17	0
J Brooker	2000/01	31	29	3	336	45	12.92	78.87	0	0	12	0	26	32	0	-	7.38	-	0
NG Brouwers	2000/01	10	3	1	21	15	10.50	77.77	0	0	4	0	324	292	5	58.40	5.40	2-38	0
DL Brown (Dol)	2000/01	32	24	8	337	53	21.06	74.39	0	1	32	0	0	0	0	-	-	-	0
DL Brown (Bdr)	2004/05	8	5	1	74	32 *	18.50	59.20	0	0	1	0	300	270	7	38.57	5.40	3-48	0
ML Bruyns	1993/94	121	115	17	2998	111	30.59	67.66 *	1	18	58	5	432	379	13	29.15	5.26	2-27	0
BW Buckley	2005/06	1	1	0	27	27	27.00	75.00	0	0	0	0	0	0	0	-	-	-	0
TA Bula	2001/02	26	16	5	276	76 *	25.09	92.61	0	1	18	4	0	0	0	-	-	-	0
S Burger	2002/03	11	7	1	77	28	12.83	74.03	0	0	4	0	452	370	17	21.76	4.91	5-44	1

LIMITED OVERS CAREER RECORDS

Name	Debut	M	Inns	NO	Runs	HS	Avg	SR	100	50	Ct	St	Balls	Runs	Wkts	Avg	RpO	BB	4I
JP Campher	2005/06	3	2	1	18	15	18.00	60.00	0	0	0	0	84	96	3	32.00	6.85	2-36	0
RCC Canning	2004/05	15	13	3	331	65	33.10	87.56	0	2	18	3	0	0	0	-	-	-	0
DD Carolus	2004/05	16	10	5	39	14 *	7.80	56.52	0	0	3	0	770	620	21	29.52	4.83	4-49	1
S Chatterjee	2005/06	10	2	2	12	10 *	-	48.00	0	0	1	0	297	254	12	21.16	5.13	4-27	1
AI Chinnappa	2005/06	3	3	0	20	14	6.66	42.55	0	0	0	0	60	46	2	23.00	4.60	1-13	0
N Chouhan	2005/06	3	3	0	50	39	16.66	65.78	0	0	1	0	0	0	0	-	-	-	0
WL Coetsee	2002/03	34	24	3	399	130 *	19.00	92.14	1	0	16	0	1417	1106	32	34.56	4.68	4-20	1
J Coetzee	2004/05	13	12	3	255	42	28.33	79.19	0	0	1	0	601	428	19	22.52	4.27	4-17	1
S Conrad	2005/06	2	0	0	0	-	-		0	0	0	0	108	76	4	19.00	4.22	2-31	0
SC Cook	2001/02	38	38	5	1673	116 *	50.69	75.73	2	16	7	0	0	0	0	-	-	-	0
H Davids	2000/01	55	54	5	1277	122 *	26.06	67.56	1	8	20	0	312	273	5	54.60	5.25	3-44	0
AC Dawson	1993/94	150	80	26	893	52 *	16.53	76.58	0	1	34	0	7173	4778	213	22.43	3.99	5-13	8
WA Deacon	2000/01	36	23	6	526	112	30.94	87.66	1	4	11	0	1662	1268	40	31.70	4.57	4-39	1
GJ de Bruin	2001/02	17	9	5	108	36	27.00	106.93	0	0	2	0	751	599	18	33.27	4.78	3-40	0
P de Bruyn	1999/00	66	48	10	976	74 *	25.68	72.70 *	0	7	27	0	2394	1883	54	34.87	4.71	4-28	1
Z de Bruyn	1995/96	93	83	17	2212	113 *	33.51	68.71 *	2	12	22	0	2038	1828	60	30.46	5.38	5-44	1
CJ de Jager	2005/06	4	4	0	157	70	39.25	94.01	0	1	1	0	0	0	0	-	-	-	0
HG de Kock	2004/05	13	13	0	492	107	37.84	67.95	1	1	1	0	24	40	1	40.00	10.00	1-40	0
S de Kock	2004/05	11	7	2	57	32 *	11.40	62.63	0	0	4	0	426	321	14	22.92	4.52	3-38	0
CD de Lange	1999/00	57	46	10	868	66	24.11	72.03	0	4	11	0	2553	1778	49	36.28	4.17	3-17	0
M de Stadler	2000/01	24	11	5	52	20	8.66	55.31	0	0	1	0	1152	885	38	23.28	4.60	4-35	2
AB de Villiers	2003/04	36	35	2	1087	102	32.93	80.10	1	7	21	0	0	0	0	-	-	-	0
F de Wet	2001/02	24	10	7	117	56 *	39.00	142.68	0	1	4	0	1063	819	23	35.60	4.62	3-56	0
BC de Wett	2000/01	30	26	4	526	62 *	23.90	58.31	0	2	8	0	83	38	4	9.50	2.74	3-19	0
L Dipha	2004/05	5	4	0	78	68	19.50	60.46	0	1	1	0	66	81	1	81.00	7.36	1-35	0
HH Dippenaar	1995/96	172	154	23	5460	125 *	41.67	70.93 *	7	37	57	0	6	2	0	-	2.00	-	0
N Dladla	2001/02	7	4	1	11	5 *	3.66	50.00	0	0	1	0	258	199	5	39.80	4.62	2-26	0
AG Doherty	2005/06	4	4	0	95	51	23.75	68.84	0	1	1	0	0	0	0	-	-	-	0
D Donaldson	2005/06	9	7	2	157	50 *	31.40	72.01	0	1	4	0	330	351	8	43.87	6.38	4-22	1
G Dros	1993/94	126	112	22	3428	124	38.08	81.74 *	5	20	54	0	1132	1006	34	29.58	5.33	3-21	0
WA Dugmore	2001/02	16	15	3	375	82 *	31.25	85.81	0	1	3	0	90	81	1	81.00	5.40	1-32	0
J-P Duminy	2002/03	32	27	2	731	88	29.24	71.66	0	7	7	0	286	224	5	44.80	4.69	1-7	0
F du Plessis	2003/04	17	15	3	535	114	44.58	81.92	1	3	5	0	366	293	9	32.55	4.80	4-47	1
D du Preez	2004/05	17	13	7	280	88 *	46.66	134.61	0	2	2	0	849	654	18	36.33	4.62	2-30	0
WJ du Toit	2000/01	16	13	7	109	21 *	18.16	74.14	0	0	3	0	670	486	16	30.37	4.35	4-49	1

LIMITED OVERS CAREER RECORDS

Name	Debut	M	Inns	NO	Runs	HS	Avg	SR	100	50	Ct	St	Balls	Runs	Wkts	Avg	RpO	BB	4I
AZM Dyili	2004/05	18	17	2	301	51	20.06	86.00	0	1	8	5	0	0	0	-	-	-	0
D Elgar	2005/06	2	2	0	50	26	25.00	69.44	0	0	0	0	0	0	0	-	-	-	0
T Essack	2005/06	5	4	0	54	30	13.50	68.35	0	0	3	0	138	81	5	16.20	3.52	3-23	0
W Euley	2003/04	16	14	3	372	88	33.81	106.28	0	2	16	0	0	0	0	-	-	-	0
SG Fensham	2005/06	6	4	1	57	35	19.00	58.16	0	0	2	0	0	0	0	-	-	-	0
AR Fernandez	2005/06	1	1	0	4	4	4.00	133.33	0	0	0	0	0	0	0	-	-	-	0
MP Fick	2005/06	6	6	1	97	57	19.40	96.03	0	1	0	0	136	143	3	47.66	6.30	2-16	0
P Fojela	2004/05	2	2	0	22	21	11.00	78.57	0	0	0	0	60	55	0	-	5.50	-	0
H Fourie	2004/05	5	5	1	169	93	42.25	90.86	0	1	0	0	72	64	1	64.00	5.33	1-44	0
BL Fransman	2003/04	17	4	2	17	14 *	8.50	60.71	0	0	6	0	732	592	27	21.92	4.85	6-40	3
Q Friend	2001/02	28	12	2	59	20	5.90	67.81	0	0	9	0	1282	937	33	28.39	4.38	3-36	0
R Frylinck	2004/05	13	9	4	311	82 *	62.20	119.61	0	3	0	0	354	282	14	20.14	4.77	5-39	1
DR Gain	1997/98	20	18	4	511	95 *	36.50	68.37 *	0	4	6	0	18	17	0	-	5.66	-	0
LL Gamiet	1999/00	63	58	12	1271	134 *	27.63	74.02	1	6	10	0	0	0	0	-	-	-	0
FA Geldenhuys	2005/06	1	1	0	0	0	0.00	0.00	0	0	0	0	0	0	0	-	-	-	0
JP Geoghegan	2005/06	4	4	0	116	77	29.00	113.72	0	1	1	0	102	116	3	38.66	6.82	3-47	0
SG George	2005/06	6	3	0	36	22	12.00	90.00	0	0	4	0	186	119	6	19.83	3.83	3-35	0
HH Gibbs	1990/91	288	279	22	8791	175	34.20	79.48 *	19	43	130	0	66	57	2	28.50	5.18	1-16	0
R Gobind	2000/01	17	16	1	307	73	20.46	63.29	0	1	2	0	0	0	0	-	-	-	0
U Govender	2004/05	6	0	0	0	-	-		0	0	0	0	166	169	3	56.33	6.10	2-26	0
AJA Gray	2004/05	9	9	0	225	70	25.00	65.21	0	1	2	0	0	0	0	-	-	-	0
AJ Hall	1994/95	208	166	31	4076	129 *	30.19	77.46 *	3	23	58	0	8341	6199	228	27.18	4.45	4-23	7
WC Hantam	2004/05	18	15	5	203	53	20.30	61.32	0	1	6	0	746	616	23	26.78	4.95	5-31	2
MJ Harris	2002/03	25	22	5	473	60	27.82	85.07	0	3	27	4	0	0	0	-	-	-	0
PL Harris	2002/03	20	4	1	23	10	7.66	37.70	0	0	11	0	864	661	17	38.88	4.59	3-37	0
IJ Harvey	1993/94	291	254	25	5369	96	23.44	98.38 *	0	25	79	0	13035	9529	434	21.95	4.38	5-19	30
TN Harvey	2005/06	3	2	0	11	11	5.50	84.61	0	0	0	0	0	0	0	-	-	-	0
DL Haupt	2005/06	5	1	1	3	3 *	-	42.85	0	0	1	0	198	128	6	21.33	3.87	4-21	1
W Hauptfleisch	2004/05	2	2	0	47	41	23.50	67.14	0	0	2	0	42	43	1	43.00	6.14	1-43	0
M Hayward	1995/96	133	39	20	202	19 *	10.63	75.09	0	0	26	0	5838	4842	183	26.45	4.97	5-37	10
WD Hayward	2004/05	1	1	0	18	18	18.00	90.00	0	0	0	0	0	0	0	-	-	-	0
B Hector	2001/02	32	31	2	1076	126	37.10	74.72	1	8	11	0	210	223	4	55.75	6.37	2-34	0
JM Henderson	1994/95	42	42	1	1047	108 *	25.53	58.54 *	1	5	12	0	438	361	7	51.57	4.94	2-40	0
T Henderson	1998/99	74	57	16	1041	126 *	25.39	112.41	1	6	14	0	3321	2291	91	25.17	4.13	5-5	2
JS Hermitage	2005/06	3	1	1	0	0 *	-		0	0	1	0	64	36	5	7.20	3.37	3-16	0

LIMITED OVERS CAREER RECORDS

Name	Debut	M	Inns	NO	Runs	HS	Avg	SR	100	50	Ct	St	Balls	Runs	Wkts	Avg	RpO	BB	4I
ND Hewer	2003/04	3	3	2	13	6 *	13.00	35.13	0	0	0	0	120	57	5	11.40	2.85	3-24	0
WR Hinkel	2001/02	6	5	0	103	40	20.60	70.06	0	0	1	0	144	102	6	17.00	4.25	4-31	1
IC Hlengane	2005/06	8	4	2	36	17	18.00	55.38	0	0	2	0	265	172	6	28.66	3.89	3-25	0
DL Hobson	2005/06	1	0	0	0	-	-		0	0	0	0	0	0	0	-	-	-	0
FPG Holtzhausen	2005/06	4	2	1	47	29	47.00	77.04	0	0	2	0	84	63	1	63.00	4.50	1-18	0
FS Holtzhausen	2004/05	11	8	1	159	49 *	22.71	69.73	0	0	8	0	502	435	12	36.25	5.19	3-30	0
Z Homani	2002/03	9	8	0	139	44	17.37	63.76	0	0	5	0	0	0	0	-	-	-	0
GE Howell	2004/05	11	8	1	256	115 *	36.57	121.90	1	1	7	0	414	276	9	30.66	4.00	4-13	1
CA Ingram	2004/05	9	9	2	303	73 *	43.28	91.81	0	4	0	0	168	138	7	19.71	4.92	2-13	0
A Jacobs	1995/96	88	84	5	2514	118	31.82	79.30	5	11	46	2	124	129	4	32.25	6.24	2-22	0
DJ Jacobs	2001/02	43	42	4	994	101 *	26.15	77.35	1	5	30	5	0	0	0	-	-	-	0
F Jardine	2004/05	2	2	2	48	27 *	-	96.00	0	0	1	0	108	84	0	-	4.66	-	0
RR Jeggels	2004/05	13	11	1	176	71	17.60	69.29	0	1	3	0	0	0	0	-	-	-	0
C Jonker	2005/06	1	1	0	5	5	5.00	25.00	0	0	0	0	30	46	1	46.00	9.20	1-46	0
P Joubert	1996/97	68	39	11	573	58 *	20.46	74.89 *	0	3	18	0	3189	2257	79	28.56	4.24	4-82	1
JR Jumat	2005/06	1	0	0	0	-	-		0	0	1	0	0	0	0	-	-	-	0
JH Kallis	1994/95	321	307	48	10977	155 *	42.38	70.04 *	19	76	118	0	10881	8504	278	30.58	4.68	5-30	6
QK Kannemeyer	2005/06	9	6	2	66	29 *	16.50	62.26	0	0	0	0	216	176	3	58.66	4.88	1-15	0
JM Kemp	1997/98	180	152	44	3849	107 *	35.63	84.98	2	26	76	0	5973	4698	163	28.82	4.71	6-20	8
JC Kent	1998/99	100	83	16	1922	115 *	28.68	77.87	1	13	38	0	3665	3024	80	37.80	4.95	4-29	1
DJ Kgamadi	2004/05	13	13	1	344	79	28.66	67.98	0	3	5	0	0	0	0	-	-	-	0
I Khan	2001/02	34	30	2	463	58	16.53	60.44	0	2	8	0	574	481	7	68.71	5.02	2-31	0
RK Kleinveldt	2002/03	21	16	3	237	54 *	18.23	102.15	0	1	4	0	895	678	23	29.47	4.54	4-29	1
L Klusener	1991/92	274	221	80	5440	142 *	38.58	88.44 *	3	27	68	0	11480	8857	288	30.75	4.62	6-49	9
CE Knox	2005/06	3	1	0	29	29	29.00	65.90	0	0	0	0	54	59	1	59.00	6.55	1-43	0
PJ Koortzen	1997/98	58	57	7	1543	134	30.86	78.16	2	9	18	0	493	432	7	61.71	5.25	3-37	0
BB Kops	2001/02	9	1	0	9	9	9.00	100.00	0	0	1	0	216	254	8	31.75	7.05	5-42	1
JP Kreusch	1999/00	43	41	6	1285	119 *	36.71	72.39	3	7	17	0	992	782	21	37.23	4.72	3-21	0
AK Kruger	2001/02	26	24	1	355	55	15.43	73.95	0	1	8	0	1013	949	28	33.89	5.62	4-20	1
GJ-P Kruger	1999/00	82	20	13	69	20 *	9.85	77.52	0	0	11	0	3627	2859	117	24.43	4.72	6-23	6
LA Kruger	2005/06	1	1	0	0	0	0.00	0.00	0	0	0	0	6	21	1	21.00	21.00	1-21	0
HG Kuhn	2004/05	11	11	1	425	113 *	42.50	76.43	2	2	8	1	0	0	0	-	-	-	0
JM Kuiper	2005/06	3	3	1	61	29	30.50	112.96	0	0	1	0	0	0	0	-	-	-	0
PC Laing	2005/06	4	3	0	23	16	7.66	60.52	0	0	1	0	156	138	9	15.33	5.30	4-42	2
CK Langeveldt	1997/98	113	43	13	205	33 *	6.83	57.42	0	0	18	0	5272	3914	165	23.72	4.45	5-7	8

LIMITED OVERS CAREER RECORDS

Name	Debut	M	Inns	NO	Runs	HS	Avg	SR	100	50	Ct	St	Balls	Runs	Wkts	Avg	RpO	BB	4I
FB Lazarus	2004/05	4	4	1	76	52 *	25.33	52.77	0	1	1	0	42	36	1	36.00	5.14	1-18	0
BW Lemmetjies	2004/05	6	5	2	52	31	17.33	106.12	0	0	4	0	51	63	5	12.60	7.41	4-25	1
DC Lentz	2005/06	2	2	0	13	13	6.50	65.00	0	0	0	0	0	0	0	-	-	-	0
HW le Roux	2005/06	4	3	2	35	22 *	35.00	94.59	0	0	0	0	162	127	1	127.00	4.70	1-28	0
J le Roux	2004/05	14	14	4	442	128 *	44.20	100.45	2	1	3	0	0	0	0	-	-	-	0
RE Levi	2004/05	3	3	0	37	16	12.33	49.33	0	0	0	0	0	0	0	-	-	-	0
C Linde	2004/05	16	14	3	228	58	20.72	91.93	0	2	21	5	0	0	0	-	-	-	0
NJ Livi	2005/06	3	2	0	12	12	6.00	75.00	0	0	0	0	0	0	0	-	-	-	0
WP Lombard	2004/05	4	2	1	50	25 *	50.00	57.47	0	0	1	0	72	64	1	64.00	5.33	1-31	0
J Louw	2000/01	65	49	10	749	72	19.20	81.32	0	3	7	0	2955	2333	103	22.65	4.73	5-27	8
WJ Louw	2004/05	8	7	1	162	57 *	27.00	84.81	0	1	8	0	0	0	0	-	-	-	0
LL Lwana	2004/05	7	3	0	13	10	4.33	34.21	0	0	0	0	210	188	3	62.66	5.37	1-28	0
APT Mabuya	2005/06	2	1	0	6	6	6.00	120.00	0	0	0	0	42	29	0	-	4.14	-	0
CS Mabuya	2005/06	2	2	0	17	16	8.50	65.38	0	0	0	0	0	0	0	-	-	-	0
ND McKenzie	1995/96	175	155	28	4604	131 *	36.25	70.62	7	28	55	0	255	248	4	62.00	5.83	2-19	0
AP McLaren	2000/01	35	33	3	517	50	17.23	76.02	0	1	11	3	0	0	0	-	-	-	0
R McLaren	2003/04	26	16	5	337	55	30.63	63.94	0	1	10	0	815	632	18	35.11	4.65	4-43	1
JT Mafa	1999/00	30	5	3	12	9 *	6.00	60.00	0	0	6	0	1108	950	35	27.14	5.14	4-34	3
A Magiet	2004/05	5	5	0	51	41	10.20	44.34	0	0	1	0	66	64	1	64.00	5.81	1-39	0
M Mahlombe	2005/06	4	2	1	8	8 *	8.00	47.05	0	0	2	0	90	59	4	14.75	3.93	3-34	0
DL Makalima	1999/00	56	50	7	880	74	20.46	71.37	0	4	12	0	18	37	1	37.00	12.33	1-17	0
S Makongolo	2004/05	1	1	0	12	12	12.00	35.29	0	0	0	0	0	0	0	-	-	-	0
DJ Malan	2005/06	5	5	0	90	42	18.00	69.76	0	0	0	0	6	13	0	-	13.00	-	0
H Malan	2005/06	2	1	0	2	2	2.00	33.33	0	0	1	0	0	0	0	-	-	-	0
JMM Malao	2001/02	26	11	7	20	7 *	5.00	32.25	0	0	9	0	1025	779	20	38.95	4.56	3-40	0
S Mandan	2004/05	7	6	1	167	115 *	33.40	91.25	1	0	0	0	0	0	0	-	-	-	0
L Manzini	2005/06	8	2	1	2	2 *	2.00	33.33	0	0	1	0	168	156	3	52.00	5.57	2-44	0
MA Mashimbyi	2003/04	15	9	4	134	40	26.80	81.70	0	0	3	0	620	525	18	29.16	5.08	4-57	1
MR Masinda	2005/06	1	0	0	0	-	-		0	0	0	0	36	36	1	36.00	6.00	1-36	0
MT Masinga	2004/05	3	1	1	1	1 *	-	50.00	0	0	0	0	156	130	5	26.00	5.00	2-28	0
BM Mathebula	2004/05	3	2	2	11	10 *	-	110.00	0	0	0	0	102	71	2	35.50	4.17	1-20	0
MM Matika	2004/05	7	7	0	116	41	16.57	64.08	0	0	2	0	78	83	2	41.50	6.38	1-20	0
VCM Mazibuko	2003/04	11	4	1	46	24 *	15.33	73.01	0	0	1	0	208	199	9	22.11	5.74	4-26	1
JT Maziya	2004/05	4	2	0	23	16	11.50	43.39	0	0	0	0	0	0	0	-	-	-	0
L Mbane	2004/05	15	8	3	24	10	4.80	61.53	0	0	4	0	361	273	4	68.25	4.53	2-31	0

LIMITED OVERS CAREER RECORDS

Name	Debut	M	Inns	NO	Runs	HS	Avg	SR	100	50	Ct	St	Balls	Runs	Wkts	Avg	RpO	BB	4I
NE Mbhalati	2002/03	37	5	3	15	6	7.50	38.46	0	0	6	0	1631	1312	47	27.91	4.82	3-26	0
EE Meyer	1996/97	6	6	1	55	19 *	11.00	47.41	0	0	1	0	0	0	0	-	-	-	0
L Meyer	2001/02	23	15	4	157	37	14.27	74.76	0	0	5	0	705	641	19	33.73	5.45	4-33	1
S Mhlongo	2004/05	8	4	4	3	3 *	-	20.00	0	0	3	0	276	177	9	19.66	3.84	5-29	1
DR Miller	2005/06	7	7	0	81	29	11.57	87.09	0	0	7	2	6	7	0	-	7.00	-	0
S Mjekula	2004/05	11	6	2	25	11 *	6.25	78.12	0	0	3	0	440	313	13	24.07	4.26	4-50	1
PT Mofokeng	2004/05	9	4	1	25	16	8.33	44.64	0	0	3	0	336	334	10	33.40	5.96	2-39	0
BT Mokonyama	2004/05	3	2	0	7	4	3.50	24.13	0	0	0	0	12	7	0	-	3.50	-	0
MJ Mokonyama	2002/03	17	10	1	61	18	6.77	53.98	0	0	2	0	0	0	0	-	-	-	0
EO Moleon	1997/98	50	38	13	508	68	20.32	86.54	0	1	12	0	2168	1706	43	39.67	4.72	4-42	1
K Moothosamy	2004/05	8	7	2	61	19	12.20	62.88	0	0	5	0	0	0	0	-	-	-	0
JA Morkel	1999/00	81	61	18	1059	79	24.62	96.80	0	4	12	0	3598	2692	89	30.24	4.48	4-23	1
M Morkel	2005/06	8	2	1	37	35	37.00	148.00	0	0	3	0	307	265	9	29.44	5.17	4-41	1
LN Mosena	2005/06	6	6	1	190	70	38.00	77.86	0	2	2	0	0	0	0	-	-	-	0
JF Mostert	2004/05	3	1	1	2	2 *	-	66.66	0	0	2	0	96	96	3	32.00	6.00	2-10	0
WB Motaung	2004/05	11	10	1	193	52	21.44	60.50	0	1	3	0	50	72	0	-	8.64	-	0
TS Motsamai	2003/04	16	7	2	47	18	9.40	57.31	0	0	3	0	653	535	17	31.47	4.91	3-54	0
PV Mpitsang	1998/99	45	17	9	49	20 *	6.12	42.24	0	0	1	0	1908	1436	36	39.88	4.51	4-22	1
R Munnik	1998/99	36	29	8	512	109	24.38	72.11	1	1	8	0	839	720	29	24.82	5.14	4-50	1
RG Mutch	2005/06	2	0	0	0	-	-		0	0	1	0	54	52	2	26.00	5.77	1-21	0
JG Myburgh	1999/00	51	47	7	1229	95	30.72	66.93	0	6	11	0	993	861	14	61.50	5.20	2-27	0
SJ Myburgh	2005/06	4	4	1	128	90 *	42.66	83.11	0	1	1	0	0	0	0	-	-	-	0
A Nawab	2005/06	9	2	1	7	5	7.00	77.77	0	0	4	0	426	312	11	28.36	4.39	3-25	0
AL Ndlovu	2005/06	1	1	0	5	5	5.00	29.41	0	0	0	0	0	0	0	-	-	-	0
A Nel	1997/98	143	52	30	225	21 *	10.22	65.78	0	0	34	0	7089	4919	202	24.35	4.16	6-27	7
R Nel	2004/05	6	6	0	173	64	28.83	70.04	0	1	2	0	18	30	1	30.00	10.00	1-30	0
M Ngam	1999/00	37	10	7	13	4	4.33	39.39	0	0	5	0	1432	1154	42	27.47	4.83	4-20	3
FG Nkuna	2004/05	16	2	0	1	1	0.50	5.26	0	0	2	0	522	390	16	24.37	4.48	3-30	0
ET Nkwe	2002/03	27	18	4	262	87	18.71	77.28	0	1	8	0	726	690	17	40.58	5.70	4-11	2
M Ntini	1995/96	184	51	23	202	42 *	7.21	64.74	0	0	35	0	8844	6483	270	24.01	4.39	6-22	11
E Nyawo	2005/06	4	1	0	11	11	11.00	61.11	0	0	0	0	0	0	0	-	-	-	0
SP O'Connor	2003/04	17	11	4	144	31 *	20.57	62.88	0	0	2	0	668	603	14	43.07	5.41	4-36	1
MW Olivier	2004/05	11	3	1	25	14 *	12.50	80.64	0	0	0	0	401	422	22	19.18	6.31	5-40	2
AM Omar	2003/04	25	13	5	62	13 *	7.75	62.00	0	0	30	7	0	0	0	-	-	-	0
JL Ontong	1998/99	110	92	9	1973	84	23.77	71.33 *	0	16	51	0	2657	2034	48	42.37	4.59	3-29	0

LIMITED OVERS CAREER RECORDS

Name	Debut	M	Inns	NO	Runs	HS	Avg	SR	100	50	Ct	St	Balls	Runs	Wkts	Avg	RpO	BB	4I
M Oosthuizen	2005/06	1	1	0	2	2	2.00	40.00	0	0	0	0	18	28	0	-	9.33	-	0
JM Otto	2000/01	41	40	5	1036	124	29.60	85.33	2	2	15	0	122	122	4	30.50	6.00	2-43	0
A Paleker	2000/01	21	11	1	262	51	26.20	75.50	0	1	7	0	0	0	0	-	-	-	0
Y Pangabantu	2004/05	8	2	1	5	5	5.00	41.66	0	0	2	0	258	199	7	28.42	4.62	3-33	0
HH Paulse	2005/06	4	1	0	1	1	1.00	14.28	0	0	0	0	132	109	3	36.33	4.95	2-16	0
GD Perry	2005/06	1	0	0	0	-	-		0	0	0	0	30	27	1	27.00	5.40	1-27	0
AN Petersen	2001/02	50	47	4	1141	115*	26.53	79.40	1	6	14	0	78	60	2	30.00	4.61	1-20	0
RJ Peterson	1999/00	99	69	6	1682	101	26.69	82.97	1	9	31	0	3863	2856	93	30.70	4.43	6-16	3
MX Pethu	2005/06	2	0	0	0	-	-		0	0	1	0	12	13	0	-	6.50	-	0
AM Phangiso	2004/05	17	12	3	76	21	8.44	53.90	0	0	3	0	426	289	6	48.16	4.07	2-18	0
VD Philander	2004	16	13	3	134	33*	13.40	74.86	0	0	3	0	582	522	10	52.20	5.38	3-49	0
R Pietersen	2005/06	5	0	0	0	-	-		0	0	0	0	240	246	6	41.00	6.15	3-51	0
TD Pillay	2004/05	14	4	2	27	14*	13.50	72.97	0	0	1	0	468	344	12	28.66	4.41	3-30	0
TR Plaatjie	2005/06	4	1	0	7	7	7.00	70.00	0	0	0	0	137	139	6	23.16	6.08	2-23	0
SM Pollock	1992/93	388	260	77	4716	134*	25.77	85.49*	2	21	140	0	19218	11845	526	22.51	3.69	6-21	23
SC Pope	1992/93	106	96	11	2660	98*	31.29	72.69*	0	21	43	3	1306	973	29	33.55	4.47	4-38	1
E Potgieter	2004/05	7	6	0	125	31	20.83	61.27	0	0	1	0	3	4	0	-	8.00	-	0
D Pretorius	1998/99	56	21	6	38	7*	2.53	44.18	0	0	8	0	2712	2049	95	21.56	4.53	5-32	4
ML Price	2002/03	10	8	0	166	69	20.75	56.08	0	1	1	0	120	107	4	26.75	5.35	3-25	0
AG Prince	1996/97	150	136	31	3369	89*	32.08	70.89	0	19	71	0	79	83	0	-	6.30	-	0
C Prinsloo	2004/05	12	12	0	404	100	33.66	69.65	1	2	4	0	0	0	0	-	-	-	0
AG Puttick	1999/00	65	63	11	1564	143	30.07	68.32	4	5	40	4	0	0	0	-	-	-	0
MN Ranger	2004/05	11	10	2	150	56*	18.75	57.03	0	1	4	0	372	246	13	18.92	3.96	4-42	1
BL Reddy	2000/01	36	19	7	180	28	15.00	65.69	0	0	7	0	1512	1098	33	33.27	4.35	3-10	0
R Reddy	2005/06	3	1	0	7	7	7.00	58.33	0	0	0	0	89	62	0	-	4.17	-	0
RA Reeves	2005/06	2	2	0	36	34	18.00	116.12	0	0	0	0	0	0	0	-	-	-	0
RR Richards	2005/06	5	3	1	13	7	6.50	92.85	0	0	0	0	156	98	8	12.25	3.76	3-13	0
MF Richardson	2005/06	1	1	0	69	69	69.00	60.52	0	1	0	0	0	0	0	-	-	-	0
JA Rudolph	2000/01	100	92	17	3445	134*	45.93	73.08	3	23	29	0	238	230	6	38.33	5.79	4-40	1
QG Samson	2004/05	8	0	0	0	-	-		0	0	1	0	252	217	12	18.08	5.16	4-25	1
MD Sanders	2003/04	10	9	0	163	53	18.11	52.75	0	1	2	0	12	11	0	-	5.50	-	0
PSE Sandri	2004/05	8	1	1	2	2*	-	100.00	0	0	1	0	312	222	5	44.40	4.26	2-27	0
AJ Schultz	2004/05	3	0	0	0	-	-		0	0	1	0	126	91	2	45.50	4.33	1-28	0
MR Sekhoto	2001/02	13	11	4	124	26*	17.71	52.54	0	0	2	0	0	0	0	-	-	-	0
BK Sekonyane	2002/03	10	5	4	43	16*	43.00	97.72	0	0	1	0	306	252	7	36.00	4.94	4-38	1

LIMITED OVERS CAREER RECORDS

Name	Debut	M	Inns	NO	Runs	HS	Avg	SR	100	50	Ct	St	Balls	Runs	Wkts	Avg	RpO	BB	4I
PM Selowa	2005/06	2	2	0	39	27	19.50	50.00	0	0	0	0	0	0	0	-	-	-	0
WE September	2004/05	12	8	1	116	48	16.57	69.87	0	0	5	0	492	373	14	26.64	4.54	3-44	0
NM Serame	2005/06	2	1	1	1	1 *	-	100.00	0	0	0	0	108	94	1	94.00	5.22	1-46	0
AJ Seymore	1993/94	63	58	7	1840	101	36.07	65.78 *	2	13	33	0	6	7	0	-	7.00	-	0
SR Sibande	2004/05	5	4	1	13	7 *	4.33	25.49	0	0	1	0	0	0	0	-	-	-	0
LF Simpson	2005/06	1	0	0	0	-	-		0	0	0	0	42	34	2	17.00	4.85	2-34	0
Y Singh	2002/03	6	1	0	1	1	1.00	100.00	0	0	2	0	282	185	7	26.42	3.93	2-28	0
M Slwana	2004/05	6	5	3	53	24 *	26.50	68.83	0	0	10	0	0	0	0	-	-	-	0
D Smit	2004/05	7	4	1	103	43 *	34.33	79.23	0	0	8	0	0	0	0	-	-	-	0
K Smit	2004/05	8	8	0	357	75	44.62	91.77	0	5	3	0	22	22	1	22.00	6.00	1-22	0
WJ Smit	1994/95	50	44	6	1320	113	34.73	75.38	4	3	19	0	444	397	13	30.53	5.36	2-35	0
GC Smith	1999/00	142	140	10	5528	134 *	42.52	78.99 *	10	37	62	0	1610	1483	39	38.02	5.52	3-30	0
MBA Smith	2003/04	14	13	1	257	64	21.41	72.39	0	1	2	0	130	90	0	-	4.15	-	0
BD Snijman	2004/05	14	14	1	436	97	33.53	74.91	0	3	5	0	197	155	5	31.00	4.72	2-22	0
AM Sodumo	2002/03	15	10	2	24	11	3.00	30.76	0	0	18	3	0	0	0	-	-	-	0
GC Stevens	2005/06	6	5	0	77	43	15.40	70.00	0	0	2	0	267	156	6	26.00	3.50	3-18	0
DW Steyn	2004/05	27	8	3	13	6 *	2.60	33.33	0	0	3	0	1186	900	36	25.00	4.55	5-20	1
FA Steyn	2005/06	8	8	0	264	137	33.00	85.43	1	0	4	0	0	0	0	-	-	-	0
RA Stroh	2003/04	12	8	2	251	89	41.83	69.14	0	2	3	0	420	346	14	24.71	4.94	2-16	0
HM Strydom	2005/06	1	0	0	0	-	-		0	0	0	0	0	0	0	-	-	-	0
JG Strydom	1999/00	41	38	3	1010	135 *	28.85	71.17	1	3	15	0	0	0	0	-	-	-	0
SP Summers	2003/04	13	10	2	194	70	24.25	99.48	0	2	6	0	126	120	1	120.00	5.71	1-12	0
WC Swan	2003/04	12	11	6	398	96 *	79.60	75.52	0	3	7	0	72	68	2	34.00	5.66	1-22	0
RP Symcox	2003/04	10	7	2	90	50 *	18.00	88.23	0	1	2	0	201	203	3	67.66	6.05	1-6	0
R Telemachus	1994/95	150	70	27	549	53 *	12.76	74.49	0	1	29	0	7262	5366	206	26.04	4.43	5-54	2
FD Telo	2005/06	8	6	0	230	90	38.33	98.29	0	3	1	0	0	0	0	-	-	-	0
MS Templeton	2005/06	1	0	0	0	-	-		0	0	0	0	36	37	0	-	6.16	-	0
DJ Terbrugge	1997/98	69	27	16	114	16 *	10.36	51.81	0	0	10	0	3165	2191	83	26.39	4.15	4-20	4
J Theron	2005/06	7	3	2	26	15	26.00	123.80	0	0	0	0	255	228	12	19.00	5.36	4-50	1
J Theunissen	2005/06	1	1	0	10	10	10.00	62.50	0	0	0	0	0	0	0	-	-	-	0
AC Thomas	2000/01	50	31	13	322	27 *	17.88	65.05	0	0	12	0	2363	1908	60	31.80	4.84	4-31	2
PG Thompson	2005/06	1	0	0	0	-	-		0	0	0	0	54	40	3	13.33	4.44	3-40	0
CA Thyssen	2002/03	28	17	5	251	43	20.91	82.29	0	0	4	0	420	384	12	32.00	5.48	4-38	1
G Toyana	1997/98	56	44	11	578	67	17.51	65.98	0	1	8	0	118	83	3	27.66	4.22	2-18	0
J-PH Triegaardt	2005/06	2	2	0	10	10	5.00	40.00	0	0	1	0	0	0	0	-	-	-	0

LIMITED OVERS CAREER RECORDS

Name	Debut	M	Inns	NO	Runs	HS	Avg	SR	100	50	Ct	St	Balls	Runs	Wkts	Avg	RpO	BB	4I
ES Tsamaisi	2004/05	6	3	2	49	43 *	49.00	94.23	0	0	2	0	139	136	3	45.33	5.87	2-33	0
T Tshabalala	2003/04	28	10	3	27	5	3.85	41.53	0	0	6	0	1176	891	35	25.45	4.54	4-24	2
TL Tsolekile	1998/99	77	46	12	500	44	14.70	56.36	0	0	120	14	0	0	0	-	-	-	0
LL Tsotsobe	2004/05	7	3	0	6	5	2.00	50.00	0	0	0	0	308	230	8	28.75	4.48	5-28	1
ANW Tweedie	1999	43	15	10	193	70 *	38.60	78.77	0	1	6	0	1974	1577	68	23.19	4.79	6-24	5
AM van den Berg	1997/98	23	16	3	212	65	16.30	63.66	0	1	6	1	558	439	9	48.77	4.72	3-36	0
F van der Merwe	1995/96	19	11	4	39	8 *	5.57	48.14	0	0	3	0	747	686	17	40.35	5.51	3-34	0
W van der Schyff	2005/06	1	1	1	37	37 *	-	100.00	0	0	0	0	24	22	1	22.00	5.50	1-22	0
JJ van der Wath	1995/96	95	76	21	1467	91	26.67	85.09	0	9	21	0	4018	3241	123	26.34	4.83	4-31	4
M van Jaarsveld	1995/96	176	162	24	5431	123	39.35	75.37 *	8	35	96	0	542	469	9	52.11	5.19	1-0	0
VB van Jaarsveld	2002/03	29	24	3	648	68	30.85	83.50	0	5	6	0	18	17	0	-	5.66	-	0
PM van Niekerk	1999/00	8	8	0	45	21	5.62	47.87	0	0	1	0	158	126	2	63.00	4.78	1-19	0
HA van Straaten	2005/06	4	3	0	76	43	25.33	79.16	0	0	0	0	0	0	0	-	-	-	0
N van Woerkom	2004/05	2	2	0	135	86	67.50	95.07	0	1	0	0	102	91	3	30.33	5.35	3-43	0
CFK van Wyk	2000/01	65	46	24	851	90 *	38.68	74.78	0	3	63	8	0	0	0	-	-	-	0
DJ van Wyk	2004/05	12	11	1	340	62	34.00	74.23	0	3	7	0	0	0	0	-	-	-	0
DM van Wyk	2005/06	8	7	2	176	52	35.20	69.29	0	1	12	1	0	0	0	-	-	-	0
JM van Wyk	1998/99	22	15	10	85	16 *	17.00	71.42	0	0	1	0	882	735	25	29.40	5.00	3-33	0
MN van Wyk	1997/98	107	102	12	3448	150 *	38.31	77.18	7	20	95	9	123	115	7	16.42	5.60	2-28	0
GE von Hoesslin	2004/05	10	9	0	102	31	11.33	51.51	0	0	7	2	0	0	0	-	-	-	0
N Wagner	2005/06	2	0	0	0	-	-		0	0	2	0	102	77	1	77.00	4.52	1-29	0
L-R Walters	2005/06	7	4	2	19	12 *	9.50	57.57	0	0	5	2	0	0	0	-	-	-	0
MD Walters	2005/06	1	1	0	2	2	2.00	12.50	0	0	0	0	0	0	0	-	-	-	0
DJ Watson	1993/94	112	111	9	3743	142	36.69	62.14 *	6	25	35	0	49	51	2	25.50	6.24	2-22	0
D Wiese	2005/06	9	7	1	233	59	38.83	105.90	0	2	5	0	396	328	7	46.85	4.96	3-25	0
D Willemse	2004/05	11	8	4	60	20 *	15.00	60.60	0	0	2	0	348	305	5	61.00	5.25	1-5	0
M Williamson	2005/06	6	6	1	234	94	46.80	65.54	0	2	2	0	0	0	0	-	-	-	0
CM Willoughby	1994/95	148	42	22	88	11	4.40	48.88	0	0	20	0	7300	4915	183	26.85	4.03	6-16	5
WR Wingfield	1997/98	66	58	13	1479	85	32.86	65.85	0	9	18	0	1602	1300	42	30.95	4.86	4-42	1
W Wyngaard	2004/05	10	9	2	238	73	34.00	68.78	0	2	3	0	0	0	0	-	-	-	0
M Zondeki	2001/02	52	19	7	96	23	8.00	69.56	0	0	11	0	2226	1809	69	26.21	4.87	6-37	2

WHO'S WHO 2005/06

This section includes all players who appeared in domestic first-class cricket, Limited Overs Internationals, Standard Bank Cup matches, Standard Bank Pro20 matches, or on tours for South African teams during the 2005/06 season. Some players, who did not appear in 2005/06, but may re-appear in 2006/07 or are contracted to franchises for 2006/07 are also included. All details are as at 21 August 2006.

ABBREVIATIONS

B	Born	Ed	Education
RHB	Right-hand batsman	LHB	Left-hand batsman
RF	Right-arm fast bowler	LF	Left-arm fast bowler
RFM	Right-arm fast-medium bowler	LFM	Left-arm fast-medium bowler
RMF	Right-arm medium-fast bowler	LMF	Left-arm medium-fast bowler
RM	Right-arm medium bowler	LM	Left-arm medium bowler
OB	Off-break bowler	LB	Leg-break bowler
LBG	Leg-break/googly bowler	SLA	Slow left-arm bowler
SLC	Slow left-arm chinaman bowler	WK	Wicketkeeper
FC	First-Class	SS	SuperSport Series
LOI	Limited Overs International	*	not out
HSTest	Highest Test score	BBTest	Best Test bowling
HSLOI	Highest Limited Overs International score	BBLOI	Best Limited Overs International bowling
HSFC	Highest First-class score	BBFC	Best First-class bowling
HSSA	Highest First-class score in SA	BBSA	Best First-class bowling in SA
HSSS	Highest SuperSport Series score	BBSS	Best SuperSport Series bowling
HSLO	Highest Limited Overs score	BBLO	Best Limited Overs bowling
HSDLO	Highest Domestic Limited Overs score	BBDLO	Best Domestic Limited Overs bowling
HS20	Highest score in Twenty Overs matches	BB20	Best bowling in Twenty Overs matches
COY	SA Annual's Cricketer of the Year	Wisden	Wisden Cricketer of the Year

Notes:

Nicknames are only given where they are not a normal contraction of a first name.

Details of highest scores are given where the player has made 10 or more, and best bowling figures where he has taken 2 or more wickets.

Highest scores and best bowling in South Africa are only given where they are inferior to overall best performances.

Highest scores and best bowling in the SuperSport Series are only given where they are inferior to overall best performances and best performances in South Africa. They refer only to matches in the SuperSport Series (and Castle Cup and Currie Cup A Section), and do *not* include performances in the UCB Bowl or SAA Provincial Challenge (previously the UCB Provincial Cup).

Highest scores and best bowling in Limited Overs include performances in all List A matches as produced by the Association of Cricket Statisticians and Historians.

Highest scores and best bowling in Domestic Limited Overs include performances in the Gillette Cup, Datsun Shield, Nissan Shield, Total Power Series, Benson & Hedges Series, Standard Bank League and Cup, and Provincial Shield, and are only given where they are inferior to overall best Limited Overs performances.

ABDULLAH Yusuf Adam (Dol/KZN). B 17/1/83 Johannesburg. LHB LFM. Ed Dundee HS. FC debut KZN v Bdr (Dbn) 2005/06. LO debut 2005/06. BBFC 4-33 KZN v Bdr (Dbn) 2005/06. BBLO 2-17 Dol v Eag (Dbn) 2005/06. BB20 2-20 Dol v War (Dbn) 2005/06.

ABRAHAMS Andre Peter (FS). B 25/1/81 Springbok. RHB LBG. Ed Highlands North BHS, UOFS. FC debut FS v KZN (Dbn) 1999/00. HSFC 14 FS v GW (Kby) 2003/04. BBFC 6-36 FS v Eas (Bfn) 2005/06. BBSS 2-61 FS v KZN (Dbn) 1999/00. HSLO 14* FS v Eas (Bfn) 2005/06. BBLO 2-38 FS v Bol (Paarl) 2001/02. Tours: SA U-19 to World Cup 2000.

ABRAHAMS Siraag (Eas/WP). B 3/7/82 Cape Town. RHB RFM. Ed Oaklands HS. FC debut Eas v FS (Ben) 2003/04, WP debut 2005/06. WPB 2001/02. Eas 2003/04-2005/06. Ttn 2004/05. HSFC 15 Eas v Nor (Ben) 2005/06. BBFC 4-33 Eas v Nor (Ben) 2005/06. HSSS 14 Eas v KZN (Ben) 2003/04. BBSS 2-37 Eas v FS (Ben) 2003/04. HSLO 13* Eas v Nor (Cent) 2004/05. BBLO 3-32 Eas v Nor (Ben) 2005/06.

ABRAHAMS Umar (EP). B 7/2/81 Port Elizabeth. LHB RM. Ed Grey HS (PE). EP Schools 1996-99, SA Schools 1998-99. Cousin of L Meyer (EP/War 2001-2005). FC debut EPB v KZNB (Dbn) 1998/99. EP 2000/01-2002/03 and 2005/06. Gau 2003/04. EPB 1998/99. HSFC 134* Gau v WP (CT) 2003/04. HSLO 73 EP v NW (PE) 2001/02. Tours: SA U-19 to Pak 1998/99; World Cup 2000.

ABRAHIM Zahir Ahmed (Dol/KZN). B 5/6/72 Robertson. LHB RFM. Ed Langenberg SS, UWC. FC debut BolB v TvlB (Randjesfontein) 1995/96, Dol debut 2004/05, KZN debut 2004/05. GW 1997/98-2003/04, GWB 1998/99. HSFC 103* KZN v Bol (Chatsworth) 2005/06. BBFC 6-53 GW v UCB Inv (Kby) 1999/00. HSSS 57 GW v NW (Kby) 2000/01. BBSS 5-22 GW v Gau (Jhb) 2000/01. HSLO 26 GW v Eas (Ben) 2002/03. BBLO 4-15 Dol v Eag (Bfn) 2005/06. BB20 3-30 Dol v Ttn (Dbn) 2005/06.

ACKERMAN Hylton Deon (HD) (Cob). B 14/2/73 Cape Town. RHB RM. Ed Rondebosch BHS. WP Schools 1990. Son of HM Ackerman (Bdr/NET/Northants/Ntl/WP/WPB 1963-1981). FC debut WPB v ET (Spr) 1993/94, Cob debut 2005/06. Gau 2003/04. Lio 2004/05. WP 1993/94-2002/03, WPB 1993/94. Leicestershire 2005-2006. Tests: 4 (1997/98). HSTest 57 v Pak (Dbn) 1997/98. HSFC 309* Leicestershire v Glamorgan (Cardiff) 2006. HSSA 202* WP v Nor (Cent) 1997/98. HSLO 114* Leicestershire v Sussex (Hove) 2005. HSDLO 92 WP v Nor (Cent) 2000/01. HS20 87 Leicestershire v Durham (Chester-le-Street) 2006. Tours: SA to Zim 2001/02; SAA to Eng 1996; SL 1998/99; Zim 2004; SA U-24 to SL 1995/96.

ADAIR Sean Robin (EP) B 26/12/86 Johannesburg. RHB WK. Ed Grey HS (PE), NMMU. EP Schools 2004. Son of RW Adair (TvlB 1977-1987). FC debut EP v Bdr (EL) 2005/06. HSFC 44 EP v Bdr (EL) 2005/06. HSLO 32 EP v Nor (Pta) 2005/06. Tours: SA U-19 to India 2005/06.

ADAMS Brendon Claude (Lio/Gau). B 10/3/84 Paarl. LHB SLA. Ed Paarl BHS, UNISA. FC debut Bol v EP (Paarl) 2004/05, Lio debut 2005/06, Gau debut 2005/06. Bol 2004/05. HSFC 73 Gau v NW (Potch) 2005/06. BBFC 3-47 Bol v NW (Paarl) 2004/05. HSSS 12 Lio v Eag (Potch) 2005/06. HSLO 48 Gau v Eas (Jhb) 2005/06. BBLO 2-26 Bol v Nor (Paarl) 2004/05.

ADAMS Moegamat *Qaasim* (WP) B 29/4/84 Cape Town. LHB RM. Ed Tafelberg HS. WP Schools 2002. No FC, LO debut 2005/06. HSLO 23* WP v ZimU23 (CT) 2005/06. BBLO 3-53 WP v ZimU23 (CT) 2005/06.

ADAMS Paul Regan (Cob/WP). B 20/1/77 Cape Town. RHB SLC. Ed Plumstead HS. FC debut WPB v Eas (Spr) 1995/96, WP same season, WPBol debut 2004/05. Tests: 45 (1995/96-2003/04). LOIs: 24 (1995/96-2003). HSTest 35 v Aus (CT) 2001/02. BBTest 7-128 v Pak (Lahore) 2003/04. HSLOI 33* v Eng (Birmingham) 2003. BBLOI 3-26 v Eng (EL) 1995/96. HSFC 61* WP v Bol (CT) 2000/01. BBFC 9-79 SA v Kent (Canterbury) 2003. BBSA 7-69 WP v GW (CT) 1997/98. HSLO 33* SA v Eng (Birmingham) 2003. BBLO 3-12 WP v KZN (Dbn) 1998/99. HS20 17* WPBol v Eag (Bfn) 2004/05. BB20 3-19 WPBol v Dol (Dbn) 2004/05. Tours: SA to Aus 1997/98; Ban 2002/03; Eng 1998, 2003; Ind 1996/97; NZ 1998/99, 2003/04; Pak 1997/98, 2003/04; SL 2000; Zim 1999/00; WI 2000/01; Ken 1999/00; Mor 2002; Shar 1995/96; World Cup 1996; SAA to Eng 1996; SL 2005/06; Zim 2004. COY 2002.

AFRICA Keegan Clint (KZN). B 6/4/85 Johannesburg. RHB RMF. Ed King Edward VII, Hilton College. KZN Schools 2003, SA Schools 2003. FC debut KZN v Eas (Ben) 2004/05. HSFC 33 KZN v EP (Chatsworth) 2005/06. BBFC 4-31 KZN v ZimU23 (Chatsworth) 2005/06. HSLO 48 KZN v Bol (Stb) 2005/06. BBLO 4-48 KZN v FS (Dbn) 2004/05. Tours: SA U-19 to World Cup 2004.

AKOOJEE Muhammad (NW). B 21/11/84 Klerksdorp. RHB LB. Ed Milner HS, Potch Univ. NW Schools 2001-02. Son of I Akoojee (Tvl SACB 1975-1984). FC debut NW v GW (Potch) 2004/05. HSFC 105* NW v GW (Potch) 2005/06. HSLO 76 NW v Eas (Potch) 2005/06.

ALBERTYN Wallace Andrew (Cob/Bol). B 26/5/81 Alberton. RHB RMF. Ed Paul Roos Gymnasium. Bol Schools 1997-99. FC debut Bol v Gau (Paarl) 2001/02. Cob LO debut 2005/06. HSFC 101* Bol v EP (PE) 2005/06. BBFC 4-29 Bol v Eas (Paarl) 2003/04 & Bol v WP (CT) 2004/05. HSSS 30 Bol v KZN (Paarl) 2003/04. HSLO 58* Bol v Nor (Paarl) 2005/06. BBLO 4-31 Bol v Nor (Cent) 2001/02.

ALMEIDA Renato (Eas). B 9/4/77 Salisbury, Rhodesia. RHB RFM. Ed John Orr Tech. FC debut Gau v Bdr (EL) 1998/99, Eas debut 2004/05. Gau 1998/99. HSFC 44 Eas v NW (Potch) 2005/06. BBFC 5-18 Eas v Gau (Jhb) 2005/06. HSSS 13* Gau v Bol (Jhb) 1998/99. BBSS 2-64 Gau v Bdr (EL) 1998/99. BBLO 3-35 Eas v Nor (Cent) 2004/05.

AMLA Ahmed Mahomed (Dol). B 15/9/79 Durban. RHB LB. Ed Tongaat SS, Univ of Natal. KZN Schools 1997. Brother of HM Amla (KZN/Dol/SA 1999-2005). FC debut NtlB v WPB (CT) 1997/98, KZN debut 1999/00, Dol debut 2004/05. HSFC 125 Dol v Lio (Jhb) 2005/06. BBFC 2-53 KZN v Eng (Dbn) 1999/00. HSLO 107* SAA v SLA (Potch) 2003/04. HSDLO 90 KZN v Nor (Cent) 2002/03. HS20 47 Dol v War (PE) 2004/05. BB20 2-30 Dol v Eag (Bfn) 2004/05. Tours: SAA to Aus 2002/03, Zim 2002/03; SA U-19 to Pak 1998/99.

AMLA Hashim Mahomed (Dol/SA/SAA). B 31/3/83 Durban. RHB RM. Ed Durban HS. KZN Schools 1999-2000, SA Schools 2000. Brother of AM Amla (KZN/KZNB/Dol 1997-2005). FC debut KZN v Eng (Dbn) 1999/00, Dol debut 2004/05. Tests: 7 (2004/05-2006). HSTest 149 v NZ (CT) 2005/06. HSFC 249 Dol v Eag (Bfn) 2004/05. HSLO 59* KZN v FS (Bfn) 2003/04. HS20 56 Dol v Lio (Dbn) 2004/05. Tours: SA to Ind 2004/05; SL 2006; SAA to SL 2005/06; Zim 2004. SA U-19 to NZ 2000/01; World Cup 2002 (capt). COY 2006.

ARENDSE Rayno Garth (Bol). B 8/12/78 Worcester. RHB RM. Ed Esselen Park SS. FC debut Bol v SL (Paarl) 1997/98. FS 2001/02-2003/04. Bol 1997/98 and 2004/05-2005/06. HSFC 95 FS v NW (Potch) 2001/02. HSLO 74 Bol v GW (Kby) 2004/05.

ARONSTAM Maurice Albert (Nor). B 21/12/80 Pretoria. RHB LB. Ed Pretoria BHS, Pretoria Univ. Nor Schools 1999. FC debut Nor v Gau (Cent) 2003/04, Ttn debut 2004/05. LO debut 2002/03. HSFC 201* Nor v Bol (Paarl) 2003/04. BBFC 5-37 Nor v Eas (Cent) 2004/05. BBSS 2-13 Nor v Eas (Cent) 2003/04. HSLO 120* Nor v FS (Bfn) 2005/06. BBLO 2-22 Nor v Eas (Cent) 2002/03.

ARTHUR Mario Charles (GW). B 25/2/72 Kimberley. RHB RM. Ed Floors SS. Brother of NO Arthur (GW/Eag 2004-2005). FC debut GWB v NorB (Cent) 1998/99, GW debut 2004/05. HSFC 21 GW v EP (PE) 2004/05. HSLO 63 GW v WP (Kby) 2004/05.

ARTHUR Nathan Oswald (Eag/GW). B 29/3/77 Kimberley. RHB SLA. Ed Floors SS. Brother of MC Arthur (GW/GWB 1998-2005). FC debut GW v NW (Potch) 2004/05, Eag debut 2005/06. HSFC 45 GW v Eas (Kby) 2005/06. BBFC 6-27 GW v FS (Bfn) 2005/06. HSLO 19 GW v WP (Kby) 2004/05. BBLO 4-19 GW v Nor (Kby) 2005/06. Hockey (EP/GW 1998-2004).

BACHER Adam Marc (Lio). B 29/10/73 Johannesburg. RHB RM. Ed King Edward VII, UNISA. Tvl Schools 1990-91. Nephew of A Bacher (Tvl/TvlB/SA 1959-1973, former UCBSA MD), brother of M Bacher (TvlB/NTB 1983-1984). FC debut TvlB v NtlB (Dbn) 1993/94, Tvl debut 1994/95, Lio debut 2004/05. Tests: 19 (1996/97-1999/00). LOIs: 13 (1996/97-2004/05). HSTest 96 v Aus (Cent) 1996/97 & v Pak (Sheikhupura) 1997/98. HSLOI 56 v Zim (Jhb) 2004/05. BBLOI 2-36 v Zim (Dbn) 2004/05. HSFC 210 Tvl v GW (Kby) 1996/97. BBFC 2-24 Gau v NW (Jhb) 2001/02. HSLO 158* Lio v War (Potch) 2004/05. BBLO 3-20 Rest v SAA (Pta) 2002/03. BBDLO 3-24 Gau v Eas (Jhb) 2003/04. HS20 65 Lio v Ttn (Cent) 2004/05. BB20 3-14 Lio v Dol (Dbn) 2004/05. Tours: SA to Aus 1997/98; Eng 1998; Pak 1997/98; Zim 1999/00; SAA to Aus 2002/03; SA U-24 to SL 1995/96.

BAILEY Rupert (Bol). B 20/2/80 Paarl. LHB LBG. Ed Paarl BHS. Bol Schools 1997. FC debut Bol v WI (Paarl) 1998/99. Eas 2001/02-2003/04. Bol 1998/99 and 2004/05-2005/06. LO for Northerns 2000/01. HSFC 60 Bol v KZN (Chatsworth) 2005/06. HSSS 28 Eas v Nor (Ben) 2001/02. HSLO 18 Bol v KZN (Chatsworth) 2005/06.

BAILEY Ryan Tyrone (Eag). B 8/9/82 Cape Town. RHB RM. Ed Rondebosch BHS. WP Schools 1999-2000. FC debut NW v Bdr (Potch) 2003/04, Eag debut 2004/05. NW 2003/04. HSFC 148 Eag v Dol (Bfn) 2004/05. BBFC 3-42 NW v Bdr (Potch) 2003/04. HSLO 68 Eag v Lio (Jhb) 2005/06. HS20 30* Eag v Cob (Paarl) 2005/06. Tours: SA U-19 to World Cup 2002.

BARRESI Wesley (Eas). B 3/5/84 Johannesburg. RHB WK. Ed Springs BHS. FC debut Eas v Nor (Cent) 2004/05. HSFC 57 Eas v Nor (Cent) 2004/05. HSLO 19 Eas v Nor (Cent) 2004/05.

BASSAGE Derrin James (Cob/WP). B 4/12/78 Pietermaritzburg. LHB WK. Ed Hilton College, UNISA. FC debut WP v NW (CT) 2003/04, WPBol debut 2004/05. HSFC 108* WP v EP (PE) 2005/06 & 108 WPBol v Dol (CT) 2004/05. HSSS 108 WPBol v Dol (CT) 2004/05. HSLO 81 Cob v Dol (Dbn) 2005/06. HS20 20 WPBol v Ttn (CT) 2004/05.

BAXTER Chad (EP). B 23/2/83 East London. RHB RM. Ed St Andrew's College (Gtn). EP Schools 1999-2001, SA Schools 2000-01. FC debut Bol v KZN (Paarl) 2003/04, EP debut 2004/05. Bol 2003/04. LO debut 2002/03. HSFC 86 Bol v EP (PE) 2003/04. HSLO 85 Bol v GW (Paarl) 2002/03. Tours: SA U-19 to NZ 2000/01; World Cup 2002.

BEHARDIEN Farhaan (WP). B 9/10/83 Johannesburg. RHB RMF. Ed Westerford HS, UCT. FC debut WP v EP (PE) 2004/05. HSFC 60 WP v EP (PE) 2004/05. BBFC 3-48 WP v EP (PE) 2004/05. HSLO 37 WP v Bdr (EL) 2005/06. BBLO 3-41 WP v NW (CT) 2004/05.

BEKKER Martin (KZN). B 15/5/85 Durban. RHB RM. Ed Westville BHS, UNISA. FC debut KZN v ZimU23 (Chatsworth) 2005/06, scoring 115. HSFC 138 KZN v Bol (Chatsworth) 2005/06. HSLO 66* KZN v WP (Chatsworth) 2005/06.

BELL Nicholas Anthony (Gau). B 10/2/85 Bloemfontein. RHB LFM. Ed Randpark HS, Univ of Jhb. No FC, LO debut 2005/06.

BELL Warren Eldrid (EP). B 23/7/86 Port Elizabeth. LHB RMF. Ed Bertram HS, Grey HS (PE). EP Schools 2003-04. FC debut EP v Bol (Paarl) 2004/05. HSFC 48* EP v GW (PE) 2004/05. BBFC 3-57 EP v Bdr (PE) 2005/06. HSLO 19* EP v NW (Potch) 2004/05 & 19 EP v Bol (Paarl) 2004/05. BBLO 3-26 EP v ZimU23 (PE) 2005/06.

BENKENSTEIN Dale Martin (Dol). B 9/6/74 Salisbury, Rhodesia. RHB RM/OB. Ed Durban HS, Michaelhouse. Ntl Schools 1990-92(C), SA Schools 1992(C). Son of MM Benkenstein (Rhod/Z-RB/NtlB 1970-1980), brother of BR Benkenstein (NtlB 1993/94) and BN Benkenstein (NtlB/GW 1994-1996). FC debut Ntl v EP (Dbn) 1993/94, Dol debut 2004/05. Durham 2005-2006. LOIs: 23 (1998/99-2002/03). HSLOI 69 v WI (CT) 1998/99. BBLOI 3-5 v Ken (Colombo-RPS) 2002/03. HSFC 259 KZN v Nor (Dbn) 2001/02. BBFC 4-16 Dol v War (Dbn) 2005/06. HSLO 107* Ntl v NW (Foch) 1997/98. BBLO 4-16 Durham v Surrey (Chester-le-Street) 2005. BBDLO 4-23 Ntl v Bdr (EL) 1996/97. HS20 56* Durham v Lancashire (Chester-le-Street) 2006. BB20 3-10 Durham v Yorkshire (Leeds) 2005. Tours: SA to Ban 1998/99; Ind 1999/00; NZ 1998/99; SL 2002/03; Ken 1999/00; Shar 1999/00; World Cup 1999 (did not play); SAA to SL 1998/99 (capt); WI 2000/01 (capt); SA U-24 to SL 1995/96 (capt). COY 1997.

BENNETT Bevan Leon (War/Bdr). B 9/9/81 East London. RHB LB. Ed Selborne College. Bdr Schools 1998-99. Twin brother of KD Bennett (Bdr 2005/06). FC debut Bdr v FS (Bfn) 2001/02, War debut 2004/05. HSFC 150 Bdr v WP (CT) 2005/06. BBFC 5-21 Bdr v Bol (Paarl) 2005/06. HSSS 85 Bdr v Gau (EL) 2001/02. HSLO 42 Bdr v WP (CT) 2005/06. BBLO 2-22 Bdr v Bol (EL) 2005/06. Hockey (SA U-21 to World Cup in Aus 2001).

BENNETT Clive Neil (GW) B 10/10/79 Kimberley. RHB LB. Ed Floors SS, UNISA. GW Schools 1996. FC debut GW v Gau (Kby) 2005/06. HSFC 64 GW v Eas (Kby) 2005/06. HSLO 23 GW v Eas (Kby) 2005/06. Hockey (GW 1999-2004).

BENNETT Kevin Dean (Bdr). B 9/9/81 East London. RHB RM. Ed Selborne College, Rhodes, UPE & UNISA. Twin Brother of BL Bennett (Bdr/War 2001-2005). FC debut Bdr v ZimU23 (EL) 2005/06. HSFC 47 Bdr v KZN (Dbn) 2005/06. HSLO 53 Bdr v KZN (Dbn) 2005/06. Hockey (Bdr/EP 2000-2005).

BEUKES Jonathan Alan (Eag/FS). B 15/3/79 Kimberley. LHB OB. Ed Grey College (Bfn). FS Schools 1994-97(C). Son of AP Beukes (GW/OFS 1970-1986). FC debut FS v Ntl (Bfn) 1997/98, Eag debut 2004/05. Scotland (LO) 2005. HSFC 135* Eag v Dol (Bfn) 2004/05. HSLO 127 FS v NW (Potch) 2005/06. BBLO 2-23 Scotland v Yorkshire (Edinburgh) 2005. HS20 57 Eag v Lio (Potch) 2004/05.

BEUKMAN Albert Rossouw (Nor) B 29/5/84 Pretoria. LHB RMF. Ed Zwartkop HS, Pretoria Univ. FC debut Nor v NW (Cent) 2005/06.

BEZUIDENHOUT Enver Robert (FS) B 29/5/81 George. LHB RM. Ed Outeniqua HS, Central UT. No FC, LO debut 2005/06.
BHAYAT Goolam Hussain (Lio/NW). B 16/10/83 Lichtenburg. RHB RMF. Ed Hoerskool Lichtenburg. Brother of R Bhayat (NW 2004-2005). FC debut NW v EP (Potch) 2002/03, Lio debut 2004/05. HSFC 61* NW v Nor (Cent) 2005/06. BBFC 3-39 Lio v Dol (Jhb) 2004/05. HSSS 19* NW v GW (Kby) 2003/04. HSLO 24 NW v Gau (Jhb) 2005/06. BBLO 2-29 NW v EP (Potch) 2004/05. BB20 2-26 Lio v Eag (Bfn) 2003/04.
BHAYAT Riyaadh (NW). B 30/12/86 Johannesburg. RHB RMF. Ed Hoerskool Lichtenburg, Potch Univ. NW Schools 2003-04. Brother of GH Bhayat (NW/Lio 2002-2005). FC debut NW v Bol (Paarl) 2004/05. HSFC 44 NW v Nor (Cent) 2005/06. BBFC 2-59 NW v Eas (Ben) 2005/06. HSLO 76 NW v FS (Potch) 2005/06,
BLIGNAUT Arnoldus Mauritius *(Andy)* (Lio). B 1/8/78 Salisbury, Rhodesia. LHB RFM. Ed Falcon College, Eaglesvale. FC debut Mashonaland A v Mashonaland (Har) 1997/98, Lio debut 2005/06. Mashonaland 1997/98-2004/05. Mashonaland A 1997/98-2000/01. Durham 2004. Tasmania 2004/05. Tests: 19 for Zim (2000/01-2005/06). LOIs: 51 for Zim (1999/00-2005/06). HSTest 92 v WI (Har) 2001. BBTest 5-73 v Ban (Byo) 2000/01. HSLOI 63* v Ken (Byo) 2002/03. BBLOI 4-43 v WI (Har) 2003/04. HSFC 194 Mashonaland v Manicaland (Mutare) 2003/04. BBFC 5-73 Zim v Ban (Byo) 2000/01. HSSA 61 Zim v SA (CT) 2004/05. BBSA 3-34 Lio v Ttn (Ben) 2005/06. HSSS 50 Lio v Ttn (Ben) 2005/06. HSLO 63* Zim v Kenya (Byo) 2002/03. BBLO 4-43 Zim v WI (Har) 2003/04. HS20 61* Lio v Dol (Potch) 2005/06. BB20 2-31 Lio v Cob (CT) 2005/06. Tours: Zim to Aus 2003/04; Eng 2003; SA 2004/05; WI 1999/00; Ken 1999/00; Shar 2002/03; Sing 1999; World Cup 2003; ZimA to SL 1999/00.
BODI Goolam Hussain (Ttn/Eas). B 4/1/79 Hathuran, India. LHB SLC. Ed Azaadville SS. Gau Schools 1996-97, SA Schools 1997. FC debut TvlB v WPB (CT) 1996/97, Ttn debut 2004/05, Eas debut 2004/05. KZN 1999/00-2003/04. Tvl/TvlB 1996/97. HSFC 143 Eas v Gau (Jhb) 2005/06. BBFC 6-63 KZN v Gau (Dbn) 2000/01. HSSS 140 Ttn v War (Ben) 2005/06. HSLO 112* Ttn v Lio (Ben) 2004/05. BBLO 5-46 KZN v EP (Dbn) 2000/01. HS20 47 Ttn v WPBol (CT) 2004/05. SA U-19 v Eng U-19 1997/98; World Cup in SA 1998.
BODIBE Tumelo Mphunzi (Eas). B 22/6/87 Vosloorus. RHB WK. Ed Ellinge HS. Eas Schools 2004. FC debut Eas v Nor (Cent) 2004/05. HSFC 39* Eas v FS (Ben) 2005/06. HSLO 19* Eas v NW (Potch) 2005/06.
BOJE Nico (Nicky) (Eag/SA/Afr). B 20/3/73 Bloemfontein. LHB SLA. Ed Grey College (Bfn). OFS Schools 1989-91(C), SA Schools 1989(T)-90-91(C). Brother of EHL Boje (OFSB 1989-1990). FC debut OFSB v NtlB (Pmb) 1990/91, OFS same season, Eag debut 2004/05. Nottinghamshire 2002. Tests: 43 (1999/00-2006). LOIs: 115 (113 for SA 1995/96-2005/06, 1 as capt; 2 for Africa 2005/06). HSTest 85 v Ind (Bangalore) 1999/00. BBTest 5-62 v SL (Colombo-SSC) 2000. HSLOI 129 v NZ (Cent) 2000/01. BBLOI 5-21 v Aus (CT) 2001/02. HSFC 116 FS v WP (Bfn) 1998/99. BBFC 8-93 Eag v Dol (Dbn) 2005/06. HSLO 129 SA v NZ (Cent) 2000/01. BBLO 5-21 SA v Aus (CT) 2001/02. HSDLO 79* OFS v NT (Bfn) 1994/95. BBDLO 4-18 OFS v EP (Bfn) 1993/94. HS20 38* Eag v Lio (Bfn) 2003/04. BB20 3-31 Eag v Dol (Dbn) 2005/06. Tours: SA to Aus 2000, 2001/02, 2005/06; Ban 1998/99; Eng 2003, 2004; Ind 1996/97, 1999/00; NZ 1998/99, 2003/04; SL 2000, 2002/03, 2004, 2006; WI 2000/01, 2004/05; Zim 1995/96; Ken 1996/97, 2000/01; Mor 2002; Shar 1999/00; Sing 2000; World Cup 1999, 2003; SAA to Aus 2002/03; Eng 1996; SL 1998/99; Zim 1994/95; SA U-24 to SL 1995/96. COY 2001.
BOOYSEN Jaco (Eas). B 10/3/85 Witbank. RHB RM. Ed HTS Witbank, Pretoria Univ. Eas Schools 2002, SA Schools 2002. FC debut Eas v EP (PE) 2003/04. HSFC 134* Eas v FS (Ben) 2005/06. HSSS 37* Eas v EP (PE) 2003/04. HSLO 67 Eas v GW (Kby) 2005/06. Tours: SA U-19 to Eng 2003; World Cup 2004.
BOSMAN Lungile Loots (Eag/FS/SA/SAA). B 14/4/77 Kimberley. RHB RM. Ed Tshireleco HS. GW Schools 1994-95. Cousin of M Bosman (GW 2004-2005). SA 20Int 2005/06. FC debut GW v FS (Bfn) 1997/98, Eag debut 2004/05, FS debut 2005/06. GW 1997/98-2003/04. HSFC 140 GW v WP (Kby) 2002/03. BBFC 3-25 GW v Pak (Kby) 1997/98. BBSS 2-69 GW v Gau (Kby) 1999/00. HSLO 99* GW v EP (PE) 2003/04. HS20 104 Eag v Lio (Potch) 2004/05. Tours: SA to SL 2006; SAA to SL 1998/99; 2005/06; Zim 2004.
BOSMAN Mbulelo (GW). B 31/1/82 Kimberley. RHB RMF. Ed Kimberley Tech HS. GW Schools 2000. Cousin of LL Bosman (GW/Eag/FS/SA 1997-2005). FC debut GW v NW (Potch) 2004/05. HSFC 106 GW v WP (Kby) 2004/05. HSLO 37 GW v Bol (Kby) 2004/05. BBLO 3-31 GW v WP (Kby) 2004/05.
BOSSENGER Wendell (GW). B 23/10/76 Cape Town. RHB LB WK. Ed Wynberg BHS. WP Schools 1994. FC debut GW v Bol (Paarl) 1996/97. HSFC 124* GW v KZN (Kby) 1997/98 & GW v Gau (Kby) 2001/02. BBFC 3-16 GW v NW (Kby) 2003/04. HSLO 157* GW v NW (Potch) 2005/06.
BOTHA Johan (War/SA/SAA). B 2/5/82 Johannesburg. RHB OB. Ed Grey HS (PE). EP Schools 1998-2000(C), SA Schools 1999-2000(C). FC debut EP v Bdr (PE) 2000/01, War debut 2004/05, Bdr debut 2004/05. EP 2000/01-2003/04. Tests: 1 (2005/06). LOIs: 11 (2005/06). HSTest 20* v Aus (Sydney) 2005/06. HSLOI 46 v Aus (Melbourne-Col) 2005/06. BBLOI 2-49 v SL (Brisbane) 2005/06. HSFC 93 War v Eag (Bfn) 2005/06. BBFC 6-42 EP v Nor (PE) 2003/04. HSLO 46 SA v Aus (Melbourne-Col) 2005/06. BBLO 4-32 EP v KZN (Dbn) 2001/02. HSDLO 28 EP v Nam (PE) 2002/03. HS20 13* War v Lio (EL) 2004/05. BB20 2-12 War v Eag (PE) 2004/05. Tours: SA to Aus 2005/06; Ind 2005/06; SAA to SL 2005/06; SA U-19 to NZ 2000/01; World Cup 2000.
BOUCHER Mark Verdon (SA/Afr). B 3/12/76 East London. RHB RM WK. Ed Selborne College. Bdr Schools 1993-94(C), SA Schools 1994. FC debut BdrB v NtlB (Dbn) 1995/96, Bdr same season, War debut 2004/05. Tests: 96 (95 for SA 1997/98-2006, 4 as capt; 1 for World 2005/06). LOIs: 217 (215 for SA 1997/98-2005/06, 1 as capt; 2 for Africa 2005/06). HSTest 125 v Zim (Harare) 1999/00. HSLOI 76 v Aus (Sydney) 2005/06. HSFC 134 SA v WA (Perth) 2001/02. HSSA 122* SA v WI (CT) 2003/04. HSSS 112 Bdr v Gau (Jhb) 1999/00 & Bdr v Bol (Paarl) 2002/03. HSLO 98 Bdr v Nor (Cent)

2002/03. HS20 57* EC v Dol (Dbn) 2003/04. Tours: SA to Aus 1997/98, 2000, 2001/02, 2005/06; Ban 1998/99, 2002/03; Eng 1998, 2003, 2004; Ind 1999/00, 2005/06; NZ 1998/99, 2003/04; Pak 1997/98, 2003/04; SL 2000, 2002/03, 2004, 2006; WI 2000/01, 2004/05; Zim 1999/00, 2001/02; Ken 1999/00, 2000/01; Mor 2002; Shar 1999/00; World Cup 1999, 2003. SA U-19 to Eng 1995; Ind 1995/96. COY 1998, 2000, 2006. Squash (Bdr/SA U-19).
BRADFIELD Carl Crispin (War/Bdr). B 18/1/75 Grahamstown. LHB RM. Ed Grey HS (PE), Kingswood College, UPE. EP Schools 1992-93, SA Schools 1993. FC debut EPB v GW (Kby) 1993/94, War debut 2004/05, Bdr debut 2004/05. EP 1996/97-2003/04, EPB 1993/94-1997/98. HSFC 196 EP v NW (Potch) 2002/03. HSLO 109* EP v Gau (PE) 2003/04. BBLO 2-17 Huntingdonshire Board XI v Oxfordshire (Challow & Childrey) 2001.
BROOKER Jason (GW). B 16/1/77 Kimberley. RHB RMF. Ed Floors SS. GW Schools 1993. Brother of FC Brooker (GW/GWB/Nor 1992-2000). FC debut GWB v NorB (Cent) 1998/99, GW debut 2000/01. HSFC 115 GW v NW (Potch) 2004/05. HSSS 110 GW v NW (Kby) 2003/04. HSLO 45 GW v Bol (Kby) 2004/05. Hockey (GW).
BROUWERS Nigel Grant (EP). B 4/9/76 Port Elizabeth. LHB SLA. EP Schools 1995. FC debut EPB v KZNB (Dbn) 1998/99, EP debut 2004/05. EPB 1998/99. Nor 2000/01. HSFC 59 Nor v FS (Cent) 2000/01. BBFC 6-57 EPB v GWB (PE) 1998/99. BBSS 3-43 Nor v GW (Cent) 2000/01. HSLO 15 EP v Bol (Paarl) 2004/05. BBLO 2-38 Nor v EP (PE) 2000/01.
BROWN Darryl Lewis (Bdr). B 25/3/83 East London. RHB RMF. Ed Selborne College. Bdr Schools 2001. FC debut Bdr v Bol (EL) 2005/06. LO debut 2004/05. HSFC 77* Bdr v Bol (EL) 2005/06. BBFC 3-83 Bdr v WP (EL) 2005/06. HSLO 32* Bdr v KZN (EL) 2005/06. BBLO 3-48 Bdr v KZN (EL) 2005/06. Hockey (SA U-18 2001).
BROWN Duncan Loudon (Dol). B 23/6/79 Durban. RHB WK. Ed Westville BHS, UNISA. Ntl Schools 1996-97. FC debut KZNB v NW (Foch) 1998/99, KZN debut 1999/00, Dol debut 2004/05. HSFC 152* KZN v Bol (Paarl) 2003/04. HSLO 53 Dol v Lio (Jhb) 2005/06.
BRUYNS Mark Lloyd (War). B 8/11/73 Pietermaritzburg. RHB RM WK. Ed Maritzburg College. Ntl Schools 1990-91. Nephew of A Bruyns (WP/Ntl 1965-1976). FC debut NtlB v BdrB (EL) 1993/94, Bdr debut 2001/02, War debut 2004/05. KZN 1993/94-2000/01, NtlB 1993/94-1996/97. HSFC 153 Bdr v GW (EL) 2002/03. BBFC 2-3 KZN v EP (PE) 1998/99. HSLO 111 Ntl v Gau (Jhb) 1997/98. BBLO 2-27 War v WPBol (PE) 2004/05. HS20 35 War v Cob (EL) 2005/06. Tours: SAA to SL 1998/99; WI 2000/01; SA U-24 to SL 1995/96.
BUCKLEY Brandon Wade (Gau). B 5/3/83 Johannesburg. LHB. Ed St John's College, Univ of Jhb. Gau Schools 2001. FC debut Gau v Nor (Pta) 2005/06. HSFC 41 Gau v Nor (Pta) 2005/06. HSLO 27 Gau v Eas (Jhb) 2005/06.
BULA Thandisizwe Andrew (*Thando*) (NW). B 1/1/81 Whittlesea. RHB WK. Ed Queen's College, Potch BHS. Bdr Schools 1999. FC debut NW v Bol (Potch) 2001/02, Lio debut 2004/05. HSFC 68 NW v Gau (Potch) 2005/06. HSSS 60* NW v WP (CT) 2003/04. HSLO 76* NW v FS (Potch) 2005/06.
BURGER Shane (Gau). B 31/8/82 Johannesburg. RHB RFM. Ed Northcliff HS. FC debut Gau v Bdr (EL) 2001/02. HSFC 55* Gau v Nor (Jhb) 2004/05. BBFC 5-78 Gau v FS (Jhb) 2001/02. HSSS 35 Gau v Nor (Cent) 2002/03. HSLO 28 Gau v FS (Jhb) 2004/05. BBLO 5-44 Gau v Eas (Jhb) 2005/06.
CAMPHER Jaco Pieter (Lio/NW). B 9/10/85 Klerksdorp. RHB LF. Ed Klerksdorp HS, NW Univ. FC debut NW v GW (Potch) 2005/06, Lio Pro20 debut 2005/06. HSFC 17 NW v GW (Kby) 2005/06. BBFC 3-54 NW v Gau (Potch) 2005/06. HSLO 15 NW v Gau (Jhb) 2005/06. BBLO 2-36 NW v Nor (Potch) 2005/06.
CANNING Ryan Clement Cavanagh (Cob/WP). B 22/2/84 Cape Town. RHB WK. Ed Fairbairn College. WP Schools 2001. FC debut WP v EP (PE) 2004/05, Cob LO debut 2005/06. HSFC 72 WP v Bol (CT) 2005/06. HSLO 65 WP v Bol (CT) 2004/05 & WP v Bol (Paarl) 2005/06.
CAROLUS Deon Dean (EP). B 10/7/78 Port Elizabeth. RHB RFM. Ed Chapman SS. FC debut EP v Bol (Paarl) 2003/04. War LO 2004/05. HSFC 16* EP v Bdr (PE) 2005/06. BBFC 5-61 EP v NW (Potch) 2004/05. HSLO 14* EP v GW (PE) 2004/05. BBLO 4-49 EP v NW (Potch) 2004/05.
CHATTERJEE Saurab (Lio/Gau). B 15/12/72 Calcutta, India. RHB RMF. Ed Kalighat HS, Calcutta Univ. FC debut Gau v GW (Kby) 2005/06, Lio LO debut 2005/06. BBFC 5-81 Gau v GW (Kby) 2005/06. HSLO 10* Gau v NW (Jhb) 2005/06. BBLO 4-27 Lio v Cob (CT) 2005/06.
CHINNAPPA Anley Isaac (KZN). B 9/2/82 Phoenix, Durban. RHB LB. Ed Trenance Manor SS, Ntl Univ, Dbn UT. FC debut KZN v EP (Chatsworth) 2005/06. BBFC 3-19 KZN v EP (Chatsworth) 2005/06. HSLO 14 KZN v WP (CT) 2005/06.
CHOUHAN Neeten (Nor). B 3/4/83 Harare, Zimbabwe. LHB LBG. Ed Prince Edward HS, Tshwane UT. FC debut Mashonaland A v Midlands (Kwekwe) 2000/01, Nor debut 2005/06. Mashonaland A 2000/01. Zimbabwe Academy 2001/02. HSFC 93 Nor v Eas (Pta) 2005/06. BBFC 2-41 Zimbabwe Academy v Manicaland (Mutare) 2001/02. HSLO 39 Nor v NW (Potch) 2005/06.
COETSEE Werner Loubser (Lio/NW). B 16/3/83 Bethlehem. RHB OB. Ed Klerksdorp HS, Potch Univ. NW Schools 1999-2001, SA Schools 2001(T). FC debut NW v Gau (Jhb) 2003/04, Lio debut 2004/05. LO debut 2002/03. HSFC 108* NW v GW (Potch) 2005/06. BBFC 4-95 Lio v Eag (Potch) 2005/06. HSSS 70* Lio v War (Potch) 2004/05. HSLO 130* NW v GW (Potch) 2005/06. BBLO 4-20 NW v WP (CT) 2004/05.
COETZEE Jandre (Eag/GW). B 15/1/84 Springbok. LHB LF. Ed Hoerskool Namakwaland. SACD Schools 2001, GW Schools 2002. FC debut GW v NW (Potch) 2004/05, Eag debut 2005/06. HSFC 56* GW v NW (Potch) 2005/06. BBFC 7-42 GW v WP (Kby) 2004/05. BBSS 5-33 Eag v War (Bfn) 2005/06. HSLO 42 GW v NW (Potch) 2004/05. BBLO 4-17 GW v Eas (Ben) 2005/06.
CONNOR Shaun Ralph (Eas). B 5/6/86 Bloemfontein. RHB. Ed Hoerskool Oosterlig. FC debut Eas v NW (Potch) 2005/06. HSFC 24 Eas v NW (Potch) 2005/06.

CONRAD Siraaj (Cob/WP). B 25/2/78 Cape Town. RHB OB. Ed Groenvlei SS, Wynberg BHS. FC debut WPB v NorB (Cent) 1998/99, WP debut 2004/05, Cob debut 2005/06. Gau 2001/02-2003/04. WPB 1998/99. HSFC 60 Gau v Bdr (EL) 2003/04. BBFC 6-45 WP v EP (PE) 2005/06. BBSS 2-68 Gau v Bdr (EL) 2001/02. BBLO 2-31 WP v Bol (CT) 2005/06.
COOK Stephen Craig (Lio/Gau/Rest). B 29/11/82 Johannesburg. RHB RM. Ed King Edward VII. Gau Schools 1999-2000, SA Schools 2000. Son of SJ Cook (Tvl/TvlB/Som/SA 1972-1994). FC debut Gau v GW (Jhb) 2000/01, Lio debut 2004/05. HSFC 135 Gau v WP (CT) 2003/04. HSLO 116* Lio v Ttn (Cent) 2005/06. HS20 45 Lio v Dol (Potch) 2005/06. Tours: SA U-19 to NZ 2000/01; World Cup 2002.
DAVIDS Henry (Cob/Bol). B 19/1/80 Stellenbosch. RHB RMF. Ed Stellenbosch HS. SACD Schools 1996, Bol Schools 1997-98. FC debut Bol v NZ (Paarl) 2000/01, WPBol debut 2004/05. HSFC 158 Bol v EP (PE) 2005/06. BBFC 3-11 Bol v EP (Paarl) 2004/05. HSSS 124 Bol v Nor (Cent) 2000/01. HSLO 122* Bol v GW (Kby) 2003/04. BBLO 3-44 Bol v EP (Paarl) 2005/06. HS20 22* WPBol v Ttn (Cent) 2003/04.
DAWSON Alan Charles (Cob). B 27/11/69 Cape Town. RHB RMF. Ed SACS. FC debut WP v EP (CT) 1992/93, WPBol debut 2004/05. Tests: 2 (2002/03). LOIs: 19 (1998/99-2004). HSTest 10 v Ban (Dhaka) 2002/03. BBTest 2-20 v Ban (Dhaka) 2002/03. HSLOI 23* v Pak (Lahore) 2003/04. BBLOI 4-49 v Ind (Dhaka) 2002/03. HSFC 143 WP v Bdr (EL) 1998/99. BBFC 6-18 WPB v FSB (CT) 1995/96. BBSS 6-39 Cob v Lio (Jhb) 2005/06. HSLO 52* WP v KZN (Dbn) 2001/02. BBLO 5-13 WP v GW (Kby) 2000/01. BB20 4-18 Cob v War (EL) 2005/06. Tours: SA to Ban 1998/99, 2002/03; Eng 2003, 2004; Pak 2003/04; SL 2002/03, 2004; Ken 1999/00; World Cup 1999 (did not play); SAA to SL 1998/99, Zim 2002/03. COY 2004.
DEACON Wycliffe Andrew (*Cliffie*) (Eag/FS). B 23/6/80 Kroonstad. LHB LFM. Ed Steynsrus Hoerskool, Grey College (Bfn), UOFS. FS Schools 1997-98(C). FC debut FS v EP (Bfn) 2003/04, Eag debut 2004/05. LO debut 2000/01. HSFC 59 FS v WP (Bfn) 2003/04. BBFC 4-46 Eag v WPBol (Bfn) 2004/05. HSLO 112 FS v Eas (Bfn) 2001/02. BBLO 4-39 FS v WP (Bfn) 2003/04. HS20 27 Eag v EC (EL) 2003/04. BB20 3-10 Eag v Ttn (Cent) 2003/04.
DE BRUIN Gerhardus Johannes (Lio/Gau). B 18/8/82 Alberton. RHB RFM. Ed Marais Viljoen HS (Alberton), RAU. Gau Schools 2000, SA Schools 2000. FC debut Gau v WP (CT) 2003/04, Lio debut 2005/06. Lio Pro20 debut 2004/05. LO debut 2001/02. HSFC 27 Gau v NW (Jhb) 2005/06. BBFC 6-90 Gau v Nor (Jhb) 2004/05. HSSS 24 Lio v Cob (Jhb) 2005/06. BBSS 4-47 Lio v Cob (CT) 2005/06. HSLO 36 Gau v FS (Jhb) 2004/05. BBLO 3-40 Gau v Bdr (EL) 2004/05. BB20 2-1 Lio v Eag (Bfn) 2005/06. Tours: SA U-19 to NZ 2000/01.
DE BRUYN Pierre (Ttn/Nor). B 31/3/77 Pretoria. RHB RFM Occ WK. Ed Zwartkop Hoerskool, Pretoria Technikon. NT Schools 1993-95. Twin brother of E de Bruyn (NorB 1997/98). FC debut NTB v TvlB (Jhb) 1995/96, Eas debut 1999/00, Ttn debut 2004/05. Nor 1995/96-1998/99 and 2005/06, NorB 1995/96-1998/99. HSFC 202 NorB v GWB (Cent) 1998/99. BBFC 6-38 NTB v BolB (Paarl) 1995/96. HSSS 185 Eas v Nor (Ben) 2001/02. BBSS 4-34 Eas v Bol (Paarl) 2000/01. HSLO 74* Eas v Gau (Jhb) 2003/04. BBLO 4-28 Eas v NW (Ben) 1999/00. HS20 27* Ttn v Lio (Cent) 2004/05. BB20 4-11 Ttn v War (Ben) 2005/06.
DE BRUYN Zander (Ttn/Eas/SAA). B 5/7/75 Johannesburg. RHB RFM. Ed Hoerskool Helpmekaar, Randburg Hoerskool. Tvl Schools 1992-94, SA Schools 1994. FC debut TvlB v NTB (Jhb) 1995/96, Eas debut 2002/03, Ttn debut 2004/05. Gau 1996/97-2001/02, TvlB 1995/96-1996/97. Worcestershire 2005. Tests: 3 (2004/05). HSTest 83 v Ind (Kanpur) 2004/05. BBTest 2-32 v Ind (Kolkata) 2004/05. HSFC 266* Eas v GW (Kby) 2003/04. BBFC 6-120 TvlB v WPB (CT) 1996/97. BBSS 5-28 Ttn v Cob (Ben) 2005/06. HSLO 113* Surrey Board XI v Huntingdonshire (Cheam) 2001. BBLO 5-44 Eas v WP (CT) 2003/04. HSDLO 104* Gau v Eas (Ben) 1997/98. HS20 37* Ttn v Lio (Jhb) 2004/05. BB20 3-27 Ttn v War (Cent) 2004/05. Tours: SA to Ind 2004/05; SAA to SL 2005/06; Zim 2004.
DE JAGER Christoffel Johannes (GW). B 31/5/83 Brits. RHB OB WK. Ed Brits HS. FC debut GW v Gau (Kby) 2005/06. HSFC 62 GW v Gau (Kby) 2005/06. HSLO 70 GW v Gau (Jhb) 2005/06.
DE KOCK Hendrik Gabriel *(Riel)* (Eag/FS). B 12/12/83 Pretoria. RHB LB. Ed Grey College (Bfn), UFS. FS Schools 2001-02(C), SA Schools 2001-02 (C). FC debut FS v KZN (Dbn) 2004/05, Eag debut 2005/06. HSFC 93 FS v Gau (Bfn) 2005/06. HSLO 107 FS v Gau (Jhb) 2005/06. Tours: SA U-19 to Eng 2003; World Cup 2002.
DE KOCK Shaun (War/Bdr). B 7/5/85 East London. LHB SLA. Ed Cambridge HS. Bdr Schools 2002-03. FC debut Bdr v Gau (EL) 2004/05, War LO debut 2005/06. HSFC 31 Bdr v KZN (EL) 2005/06. BBFC 2-56 Bdr v Bol (EL) 2005/06. HSLO 32* Bdr v Bol (EL) 2005/06. BBLO 3-38 Bdr v EP (PE) 2005/06.
DE LANGE Con de Wet (Cob). B 11/2/81 Bellville. RHB SLA. Ed Worcester Gymnasium. Bol Schools 1996-99, (C) in 1998 and 1999, SA Schools 1999. Nephew of CPL de Lange (NT/NTB 1981-1986). FC debut Bol v SL (Paarl) 1997/98, WPBol debut 2004/05. HSFC 109 Bol v Eas (Paarl) 2003/04. BBFC 7-48 Bol v Gau (Randjesfontein) 2003/04. HSLO 66 Bol v EP (PE) 2002/03. BBLO 3-17 Bol v Eas (Paarl) 1999/00. Tours: SA U-19 to Pak 1998/99.
DE STADLER Mark (WP). B 6/7/75 Cape Town. RHB RM. Ed Crestway SS, Peninsula Tech. FC debut WP v EP (PE) 2004/05, WPBol debut same season. LO debut 2000/01. HSFC 37 WP v Nor (CT) 2005/06. BBFC 5-18 WP v NW (CT) 2004/05. HSLO 20 WP v Bol (CT) 2004/05. BBLO 4-35 WP v EP (PE) 2003/04.
DE VILLIERS Abraham Benjamin (AB) (Ttn/SA/Afr). B 17/2/84 Pretoria. RHB RM WK. Ed Afrikaanse Hoer Seunskool, Pretoria Univ. Nor Schools 2000-02, SA Schools 2001-02. FC debut Nor v WP (Cent) 2003/04, Ttn debut 2004/05. Tests: 22 (2004/05-2006). LOIs: 19 (17 for SA 2004/05-2005/06; 2 for Africa 2005/06). HSTest 178 v WI (Bridgetown) 2004/05. BBTest 2-49 v WI (St John's) 2004/05. HSLOI 68 v Aus (PE) 2005/06. HSFC 178 SA v WI (Bridgetown) 2004/05. BBFC 2-49 SA v WI (St John's) 2004/05. HSSA 151 Ttn v WPBol (Ben) 2004/05. HSLO 102 Ttn v WPBol (Cent) 2004/05. HS20

91* Ttn v Lio (Cent) 2005/06. Tours: SA to Aus 2005/06; Ind 2005/06; SL 2006; WI 2004/05; SAA to Zim 2004; SA U-19 to Eng 2003. COY 2005.

DE WET Friedel (Lio/NW). B 26/6/80 Durban. RHB RFM. Ed Grenswag Hoer, Pretoria Tech. NW Schools 1998. FC debut Nor v GW (Cent) 2001/02, NW debut 2004/05, Lio debut 2005/06. Nor 2001/02-2002/03. Lio Pro20 2004/05. HSFC 36 Lio v Ttn (Ben) 2005/06. BBFC 7-61 Lio v Cob (CT) 2005/06. HSLO 56* NW v FS (Potch) 2005/06. BBLO 3-56 Lio v Cob (Potch) 2005/06. BB20 2-25 Lio v Ttn (Cent) 2004/05.

DE WETT Burton Christopher (War/Bdr). B 25/12/80 East London. LHB LBG. Ed Selborne College, Bdr Tech. Bdr Schools 1996-98. FC debut NW v WP (Potch) 2000/01, Bdr debut 2001/02, War debut 2004/05. NW 2000/01. HSFC 182 Bdr v Bol (Paarl) 2005/06. BBFC 7-95 Bdr v KZN (Dbn) 2005/06. HSSS 109 War v Lio (EL) 2005/06. BBSS 4-112 War v Lio (EL) 2005/06. HSLO 62* War v Ttn (EL) 2004/05. BBLO 3-19 Bdr v KZN (Dbn) 2005/06. HS20 16 War v Dol (PE) 2004/05.

DIPHA Lazola (EP). B 17/10/82 Port Elizabeth. RHB RFM. Ed Grey HS (PE), UPE. EP Schools 1999-2000, SA Schools 2000. FC debut EP v GW (PE) 2001/02. HSFC 22 EP v Bol (Paarl) 2004/05. BBFC 2-13 EP v GW (PE) 2004/05. HSSS 17 EP v GW (PE) 2001/02. HSLO 68 EP v Bol (Paarl) 2004/05.

DIPPENAAR Hendrik Human (Boeta) (Eag/SA/Afr). B 14/6/77 Kimberley. RHB OB. Ed Grey College (Bfn). OFS Schools 1992-95, SA Schools 1995(T). FC debut FS v Eng (Bfn) 1995/96, Eag debut 2004/05. Tests: 37 (1999/00-2005/06). LOIs: 99 (96 for SA 1999/00-2005/06; 3 for Africa 2005/06). HSTest 177* v Ban (Chittagong) 2002/03. HSLOI 125* v SL (Adelaide) 2005/06. HSFC 200* FS v Bol (Bfn) 1999/00. HSLO 125* SA v SL (Adelaide) 2005/06. HSDLO 111 FS v GW (Bfn) 2003/04. HS20 28 Eag v Lio (Bfn) 2003/04. Tours: SA to Aus 2000, 2001/02, 2005/06; Ban 2002/03; Eng 2003; Ind 1999/00, 2004/05; NZ 2003/04; Pak 2003/04; SL 2000, 2002/03, 2004, 2006; WI 2000/01, 2004/05; Zim 1999/00, 2001/02; Ken 1999/00, 2000/01; Mor 2002; Sing 2000; World Cup 2003; SAA to Zim 2004; SA U-19 to Eng 1995; Ind 1995/96. COY 2005.

DLADLA Nhlanhla (*Lucky*) (KZN). B 9/8/80 Pietermaritzburg. RHB RFM. Ed Maritzburg College, Varsity College. FC debut KZN v SL (Pmb) 2000/01. HSFC 14 KZN v Nor (Dbn) 2004/05. BBFC 3-41 KZN v GW (Kby) 2002/03. HSSS 11* KZN v WP (Dbn) 2002/03. BBLO 2-26 KZN v Bdr (Dbn) 2001/02.

DOHERTY Allan Gavin (GW). B 6/8/82 Kimberley. RHB SLC. Ed Kimberley BHS, UPE. GW Schools 1999-2000. Son of MJD Doherty (GW 1964-1984). FC debut GW v Bol (Kby) 2004/05. HSFC 92 GW v Eas (Kby) 2005/06. HSLO 51 GW v Gau (Jhb) 2005/06.

DONALDSON Donovan (GW). B 17/4/86 Klerksdorp. LHB RMF. Ed Northern Cape HS. GW Schools 2003-04. FC debut GW v Eas (Ben) 2005/06. HSFC 42 GW v Eas (Ben) 2005/06. BBFC 2-64 GW v Gau (Kby) 2005/06. HSLO 50* GW v FS (Kby) 2005/06. BBLO 4-22 GW v Nor (Kby) 2005/06. Rugby (GW Craven Week 2004).

DROS Gerald (Ttn/Nor). B 2/4/73 Pretoria. RHB RM. Ed St Alban's, Pretoria Univ. NT Schools 1990-92(C), SA Schools 1992. FC debut NTB v TvlB (Jhb) 1993/94, NT same season. Ttn LO debut 2004/05. HSFC 136 Nor v Gau (Pta) 2005/06. BBFC 5-17 Nor v Bol (Paarl) 2003/04. HSSS 100* Nor v Gau (Jhb) 2000/01. HSLO 124 Ireland v Hertfordshire (Bishop's Stortford) 2003. BBLO 3-21 Nor v Bdr (EL) 2000/01. HSDLO 105* Nor v GW (Cent) 1999/00. HS20 35 Ttn v Eag (Bfn) 2003/04. Tours: SAA to Aus 2002/03 (capt); WI 2000/01.

DUGMORE Warren Alan (Lio/Gau). B 27/2/77 Johannesburg. LHB SLA. Ed King Edward VII, RAU. Tvl Schools 1993-94. FC debut Gau v Bol (Paarl) 2001/02. Lio LO debut 2005/06. HSFC 138 Gau v NW (Jhb) 2005/06. HSSS 100 Gau v NW (Potch) 2002/03. HSLO 82* Gau v GW (Jhb) 2001/02.

DUMINY Jean-Paul *(JP)* (Cob/SAA/Rest). B 14/4/84 Strandfontein. LHB OB. Ed Plumstead HS. USSASA U-17 2000, WP Schools 2001, SA Schools 2000(T). FC debut WP v EP (CT) 2001/02, WPBol debut 2004/05. LOIs: 5 (2004). HSLOI 22 v SL (Colombo-RPS) 2004. HSFC 128 Cob v Eag (Bfn) 2005/06. BBFC 4-89 WP v Bdr (Bellville) 2002/03. HSLO 88 WP v Eas (CT) 2003/04. HS20 67* Cob v Dol (CT) 2005/06. Tours: SA to SL 2004; Eng 2004; SAA to SL 2005/06; SA U-19 to Eng 2003.

DU PLESSIS Francois *(Faf)* (Ttn/Nor). B 13/7/84 Pretoria. RHB LB. Ed Afrikaanse Hoer Seunskool. Nor Schools 2000-02. FC debut Nor v Gau (Cent) 2003/04, Ttn debut 2005/06. HSFC 156 Nor v Gau (Jhb) 2005/06. BBFC 4-39 Nor v FS (Pta) 2004/05. HSSS 38 Nor v EP (PE) 2003/04. HSLO 114 Nor v EP (Pta) 2005/06. BBLO 4-47 Nor v Eas (Cent) 2005/06. Tours: SA U-19 to Eng 2003.

DU PREEZ Dillon (Eag/FS). B 11/8/81 Queenstown. RHB RMF. Ed HTS Louis Botha. FS Schools 1999-2000. FC debut FS v WI (Bfn) 2003/04, Eag debut 2004/05. HSFC 89 FS v Gau (Jhb) 2004/05. BBFC 5-33 FS v GW (Kby) 2005/06. HSSS 31 Eag v Dol (Bfn) 2004/05. BBSS 4-46 Eag v Ttn (Bfn) 2004/05. HSLO 88* FS v GW (Kby) 2005/06. BBLO 2-30 FS v Eas (Ben) 2005/06. BB20 2-2 Eag v Ttn (Bfn) 2005/06.

DU TOIT Willem Johannes (Bol). B 18/3/81 Cape Town. RHB RF. Ed Paul Roos Gymnasium. Bol Schools 1996-99, SA Schools 1998. FC debut Bol v EP (Paarl) 1998/99. HSFC 42 Bol v KZN (Dbn) 2002/03. BBFC 7-82 Bol v Eas (Paarl) 2000/01. HSLO 21* Bol v EP (PE) 2002/03. BBLO 4-49 Bol v KZN (Paarl) 2001/02. Tours: SA U-19 to Pak 1998/99.

DYILI Athenkosi Ziphozihle Madoda (War/Bdr). B 17/7/84 King William's Town. LHB WK. Ed Dale College. Bdr Schools 2001-02. FC debut Bdr v FS (Bfn) 2004/05, War debut 2005/06. HSFC 65 Bdr v WP (CT) 2005/06. HSSS 39 War v Eag (Bfn) 2005/06. HSLO 51 War v Lio (PE) 2005/06. HS20 23 War v Lio (Jhb) 2005/06.

ELGAR Dean (FS). B 11/6/87 Welkom. LHB SLA. Ed St Dominic's. FS Schools 2004-05, SA Schools 2005(C). FC debut FS v Nor (Pta) 2005/06. HSFC 32 FS v Eas (Bfn) 2005/06 & FS v Eas (Bfn) 2005/06. HSLO 26 FS v Eas (Bfn) 2005/06. Tours: SA U-19 to Ind 2005/06 (capt); World Cup 2006 (capt).

ESSACK Tahir (KZN). B 7/1/82 Durban. RHB RM. Ed Maritzburg College, Ntl Univ (Pmb). FC debut KZN v ZimU23 (Chatsworth) 2005/06. Pro20 debut 2003/04. HSFC 51 KZN v Bol (Paarl) 2005/06. BBFC 2-19 KZN v Bol (Paarl) 2005/06. HSLO 30 KZN v Bdr (EL) 2005/06. BBLO 3-23 KZN v Bdr (EL) 2005/06.
EULEY Wesley (WP). B 10/10/79 Cape Town. LHB WK. Ed Grassy Park. WP Schools 1998. FC debut Bol v KZN (Paarl) 2003/04. WP LO debut 2005/06. WPBol LO 2004/05. HSFC 50 Bol v Eas (Ben) 2003/04. HSLO 88 Bol v Nor (Paarl) 2003/04.
FENSHAM Stephen Geoff (EP). B 17/9/85 Port Elizabeth. RHB OB. Ed Grey HS (PE), NMMU. Son of RG Fensham (EP/EPB 1979-1983), grandson of GF Dakin (EP 1952-1962, former UCBSA President), nephew of G Dakin (EPB 1985/86) and WG Fensham (EPB 1981/82). FC debut EP v WP (CT) 2005/06. HSFC 41* EP v ZimU23 (PE) 2005/06. HSLO 35 EP v Bol (Paarl) 2005/06.
FERNANDEZ Ashley Ryan (WP). B 31/1/82 Cape Town. LHB RM. Ed Fish Hoek HS, UWC. WP Schools 2001. No FC, LO debut 2005/06.
FICK Marthinus Philippus *(Thinie)* (FS). B 25/7/83 Potchefstroom. LHB RM. Ed Grey College (Bfn), UFS. FS Schools 2001. FC debut FS v NW (Bfn) 2005/06. HSFC 29 FS v NW (Bfn) 2005/06. HSLO 57 FS v GW (Bfn) 2005/06. BBLO 2-16 FS v GW (Bfn) 2005/06.
FOJELA Phaphama (Bdr). B 28/8/84 King William's Town. RHB RFM. Ed Mzontsundu HS. Bdr Schools 2002. FC debut Bdr v FS (Bfn) 2004/05. BBFC 4-34 Bdr v EP (PE) 2005/06. HSLO 21 Bdr v EP (PE) 2005/06.
FOURIE Henri (Bol). B 13/4/79 Ermelo. RHB RM. Ed Strand HS. FC debut Bol v WP (CT) 2004/05. HSFC 45 Bol v WP (CT) 2004/05. BBFC 3-16 Bol v WP (CT) 2004/05. HSLO 93 Bol v GW (Kby) 2004/05.
FRANSMAN Bardo Llewellyn (Bol). B 3/3/79 Worcester. RHB RMF. Ed Esselen Park SS. FC debut Bol v FS (Bfn) 2003/04. HSFC 14 Bol v NW (Paarl) 2004/05. BBFC 5-36 Bol v NW (Paarl) 2004/05. BBSS 3-59 Bol v FS (Bfn) 2003/04. HSLO 14* Bol v EP (PE) 2005/06. BBLO 6-40 Bol v WP (Paarl) 2005/06.
FRIEND Quinton (Cob/WP). B 16/2/82 Bellville. RHB RFM. Ed Westcliff HS. FC debut WP v KZN (Dbn) 2002/03, WPBol debut 2004/05. LO debut 2001/02. HSFC 51 WPBol v Ttn (Ben) 2004/05. BBFC 7-31 WP v KZN (Chatsworth) 2005/06. BBSS 6-114 WPBol v Lio (Paarl) 2004/05. HSLO 20 WPBol v War (PE) 2004/05. BBLO 3-36 WPBol v War (PE) 2004/05. BB20 2-29 WPBol v Dol (CT) 2003/04. Tours: SAA to Aus 2002/03.
FRYLINCK Robert (Dol/KZN). B 27/9/84 Durban. RHB RFM. Ed Westville BHS. FC debut KZN v WP (Chatsworth) 2005/06, Dol same season. LO debut 2004/05. HSFC 100* KZN v ZimU23 (Chatsworth) 2005/06. BBFC 6-94 KZN v WP (Chatsworth) 2005/06. BBSS 2-38 Dol v Ttn (Cent) 2005/06. HSLO 82* KZN v ZimU23 (Chatsworth) 2005/06. BBLO 5-39 KZN v Gau (Dbn) 2004/05. HS20 29 Dol v Lio (Potch) 2005/06. Hockey (KZN U-21 2003).
GAIN Douglas Robert (Gau). B 29/12/76 Johannesburg. RHB RM. Ed Hilton College, RAU. Ntl Schools 1994-95(C), SA Schools 1995(C). FC debut TvlB v EPB (Jhb) 1996/97, Tvl debut 1996/97. Bol 1998/99-1999/00. Gau 1996/97-1997/98 and 2003/04-2005/06, TvlB 1996/97. HSFC 100 Gau v FS (Jhb) 2005/06. HSSS 79 Bol v Nor (Cent) 1998/99. HSLO 95* Gau v FS (Bfn) 2005/06. Tours: SA U-19 to Ind 1995/96 (capt).
GAMIET Laden Liep (War/Bdr). B 23/1/78 East London. RHB RM. Ed Selborne College. Bdr Schools 1994-95. FC debut BdrB v WPB (EL) 1995/96, Bdr debut 1999/00, War debut 2004/05. BdrB 1995/96-1996/97. NorB 1997/98. HSFC 116 Bdr v NW (Potch) 2003/04. HSLO 134* Bdr v WP (EL) 2005/06. HS20 16 EC v Eag (EL) 2003/04. SA U-19 v Pak U-19 1996/97. Hockey (Bdr Schools 1994-95).
GELDENHUYS Francois Arnoldus (Bol). B 31/12/82 Pietersburg. RHB RM WK. Ed Afrikaanse Hoer Seunskool, Nor Schools 2000. FC debut Bol v EP (PE) 2005/06. HSFC 24 Bol v EP (PE) 2005/06.
GEOGHEGAN John Patrick (WP). B 21/2/83 Johannesburg. RHB RMF. Ed King Edward VII, UCT. Gau Schools 2000. FC debut WP v EP (PE) 2005/06. HSFC 15 WP v Bol (CT) 2005/06. HSLO 77 WP v Bol (CT) 2005/06. BBLO 3-47 WP v KZN (CT) 2005/06.
GEORGE Stephen Glen (WP). B 17/1/84 Cape Town. LHB OB. Ed Rockland HS, Cape Tech. FC debut WP v EP (CT) 2005/06. HSLO 22 WP v EP (CT) 2005/06. BBLO 3-35 WP v EP (CT) 2005/06.
GIBBS Herschelle Herman (Cob/SA). B 23/2/74 Green Point, Cape Town. RHB RFM/LB. Ed Diocesan College. WP Schools 1989-92, SA Schools 1991-92. FC debut WPB v TvlB (CT) 1990/91, WP same season, WPBol debut 2004/05. Tests: 79 (1996/97-2006). LOIs: 185 (1996/97-2005/06). HSTest 228 v Pak (CT) 2002/03. HSLOI 175 v Aus (Jhb) 2005/06. HSFC 228 SA v Pak (CT) 2002/03. BBFC 2-14 SAA v Somerset (Taunton) 1996. HSSS 203 WP v KZN (Dbn) 2002/03. HSLO 175 SA v Aus (Jhb) 2005/06. HSDLO 110* WP v FS (Bfn) 1997/98. HS20 56 SA v Aus (Jhb) 2005/06. Tours: SA to Aus 1997/98, 2001/02, 2005/06; Ban 2002/03; Eng 2003, 2004; Ind 1996/97, 1999/00; NZ 1998/99, 2003/04; Pak 2003/04; SL 2002/03, 2004, 2006; WI 2000/01, 2004/05; Zim 2001/02; Ken 1996/97, 1999/00; Mor 2002; Shar 1999/00; World Cup 1999, 2003; SAA to Eng 1996; SL 1998/99. COY 1999, 2003, 2004. Rugby (SA Schools 1992).
GOBIND Rivash (Dol/KZN). B 20/4/82 Durban. LHB RMF Occ WK. Ed Effingham SS. KZN Schools 1998-99, SA Schools 1999. Brother of V Gobind (KZN 2004/05). FC debut KZN v Nor (Dbn) 2001/02, Dol debut 2004/05. LO debut 2000/01. HSFC 119 KZN v Eas (Ben) 2004/05. HSSS 93 Dol v Cob (Dbn) 2005/06. HSLO 73 KZN v Bdr (Dbn) 2005/06. Tours: SA U-19 to NZ 2000/01 (capt), World Cup 2000.
GOVENDER Ugasen (Dol/KZN). B 17/12/83 Tongaat. RHB RF. Ed Verulam SS, Michaelhouse. KZN Schools 2000-02. FC debut KZN v Gau (Dbn) 2004/05, Dol same season. HSFC 21* KZN v WP (CT) 2005/06. BBFC 6-59 Dol v Ttn (Cent) 2005/06. BBLO 2-26 KZN v Gau (Dbn) 2004/05. Volleyball (SA U-17 1998, KZN U-19 2000).

GRAY Alistair John Alec (WP). B 8/7/82 Johannesburg. RHB LB. Ed Westerford HS, UCT. WP Schools 2000. FC debut WP v Bol (CT) 2004/05. HSFC 112* WP v Bol (Paarl) 2005/06. HSLO 70 WP v Bol (CT) 2005/06.

GROBLER Gerhardus Cornelius *(Neil)* (Eas). B 6/9/87 Heidelberg. RHB RMF. Ed Dr EG Jansen, Boksburg. Eas Schools 2005. FC debut Eas v Gau (Jhb) 2005/06. BBFC 2-28 Eas v Gau (Jhb) 2005/06.

GROBLER Stephanus Frederick (Gau). B 11/11/82 Pretoria. RHB LB. Ed Hoerskool Roodepoort. FC debut Gau v Nor (Jhb) 2005/06.

HALL Andrew James (Lio/SA). B 31/7/75 Johannesburg. RHB RFM. Ed Hoerskool Alberton. Tvl Schools 1993. FC debut Tvl v ZimA (Jhb) 1995/96, Lio debut 2004/05. Eas 2001/02-2003/04. Gau 1994/95 (LO only) and 1995/96-2000/01, TvlB 1995/96-1996/97. LO debut 1994/95. Worcestershire 2003-2004, Kent 2005-2006. Tests: 19 (2001/02-2006). LOIs: 68 (1998/99-2005/06). HSTest 163 v Ind (Kanpur) 2004/05. BBTest 3-1 v SL (Jhb) 2002/03. HSLOI 81 v SL (Galle) 2000. BBLOI 4-23 v NZ (Cent) 2005/06. HSFC 163 SA v Ind (Kanpur) 2004/05. BBFC 6-77 Eas v WP (Ben) 2002/03. HSSA 153 Eas v NW (Ben) 2001/02. HSLO 129* Gau v Bdr (EL) 1999/00. BBLO 4-23 SA v NZ (Cent) 2005/06. BBDLO 4-58 Gau v Nor (Jhb) 1999/00. HS20 59 Ttn v WPBol (Cent) 2003/04. BB20 3-15 Kent v Sussex (Hove) 2006. Tours: SA to Aus 2000, 2005/06; Ban 2002/03; Eng 2003; Ind 2004/05, 2005/06; Pak 2003/04; SL 2000, 2006; WI 2004/05; Ken 2000/01; Sing 2000; World Cup 2003. COY 2002.

HANTAM William Chesney (Cob/WP). B 21/9/83 Cape Town. LHB LMF. Ed Sarepta SS, UWC. WP Schools 2001, SA Schools 2001. FC debut WP v Bol (CT) 2004/05, Pro20 debut 2003/04. WPBol LO debut 2004/05. HSFC 38 WP v ZimU23 (CT) 2005/06. BBFC 6-39 WP v ZimU23 (CT) 2005/06. HSLO 53 WP v Bol (Paarl) 2005/06. BBLO 5-31 WP v KZN (CT) 2005/06. HS20 15 WPBol v Eag (Bfn) 2004/05. BB20 3-25 WPBol v War (CT) 2004/05. Tours: SA U-19 to Eng 2003.

HARRIS Matthew Justin (Lio). B 19/2/81 Johannesburg. LHB WK. Ed King Edward VII, Wits Univ. Gau Schools 1998. FC debut SAAc v SLA (Potch) 2003/04, Gau same season, Lio debut 2004/05. LO debut 2002/03. HSFC 135* Lio v Eag (Potch) 2005/06. HSLO 60 Gau v KZN (Dbn) 2004/05. HS20 35 Lio v War (EL) 2004/05.

HARRIS Paul Lee (Ttn/Nor). B 2/11/78 Salisbury, Rhodesia. RHB SLA. Ed Fish Hoek HS, CT College of Education. FC debut WPB v EPB (PE) 1998/99, Nor debut 2002/03, Ttn debut 2004/05. WP 2000/01-2001/02, WPB 1998/99. Warwickshire 2006. HSFC 47 Nor v NW (Potch) 2005/06. BBFC 6-54 Ttn v Cob (Ben) 2005/06. HSSS 35 Ttn v War (Cent) 2004/05. HSLO 10 Nor v GW (Cent) 2003/04. BBLO 3-37 Nor v NW (Cent) 2003/04. BB20 2-23 Ttn v Chilaw (Leicester) 2005.

HARVEY Ian Joseph (Cob). B 10/4/72 Wonthaggi, Victoria, Australia. RHB RM. Ed Wonthaggi Technical College. FC debut Vic v NSW (Sydney) 1993/94, Cob debut 2005/06. Victoria 1993/94-2004/05. Gloucestershire 1999-2003 and 2006. Yorkshire 2004-2005. LOIs: 73 for Aus (1997/98-2003/04). HSLOI 48* v WI (Kingston) 2002/03. BBLOI 4-16 v Ban (Darwin) 2003. HSFC 209* Yorkshire v Somerset (Leeds) 2005. BBFC 8-101 AusA v SAA (Adelaide) 2002/03. HSSA 51 Cob v Dol (Paarl) 2005/06. BBSA 2-13 Cob v Ttn (CT) 2005/06. HSLO 112 Gloucestershire v Somerset (Taunton) 2006. BBLO 5-19 Gloucestershire v Northamptonshire (Bristol) 2000. HSDLO 55 Cob v Dol (CT) 2005/06. BBDLO 2-23 Cob v Ttn (Cent) 2005/06. HS20 109 Yorkshire v Derbyshire (Leeds) 2005. BB20 3-28 Gloucestershire v Northamptonshire (Bristol) 2003. Tours: Aus to Eng 2001; Ind 2000/01 (x 2), 2003/04; NZ 1999/00; SA 1999/00, 2001/02; SL 2003/04; WI 2002/03; Zim 2003/04; Ken 2000/01; Shar 1998/99; World Cup 2003; AusA to SA 2001/02. Wisden 2004.

HARVEY Timothy Neil (KZN). B 9/12/82 Harrismith. RHB RM. Ed Durban HS, UNISA. KZN Schools 2000. Son of NH Harvey (Ntl/NtlB 1972-1983). FC debut KZN v ZimU23 (Chatsworth) 2005/06. HSFC 19 KZN v Bdr (EL) 2005/06. HSLO 11 KZN v Bdr (EL) 2005/06.

HAUPT Dale Linton (WP). B 7/5/84 Cape Town. LHB LFM. Ed Malibu HS. WP Schools 2002. FC debut WP v Bdr (CT) 2005/06. Nephew of CA Haupt (Oxfordshire LO 1999-2001). BBLO 4-21 WP v ZimU23 (CT) 2005/06.

HAUPTFLEISCH Warryn (KZN). B 15/12/81 Durban. RHB RM. Ed Glenwood HS. KZN Schools 1998-99, SA Schools 1998. FC debut KZN v Nor (Dbn) 2004/05. HSFC 67* KZN v Nor (Dbn) 2004/05. HSLO 41 KZN v Nor (Dbn) 2004/05. Tours: SA U-19 to NZ 2000/01.

HAYWARD Mornantau (*Nantie*) (Dol). B 6/3/77 Uitenhage. RHB RF. Ed Daniel Pienaar Technical HS. EP Schools 1994-95, SA Schools 1995. FC debut EPB v Zim Brd (Harare) 1995/96, Dol debut 2005/06. EP 1996/97-2003/04. EPB 1995/96. War 2004/05. Worcestershire 2003. Middlesex 2004-2005. Tests: 16 (1999/00-2004). LOIs: 21 (1998-2001/02). HSTest 14 v Aus (Melbourne) 2001/02. BBTest 5-56 v Pak (Dbn) 2002/03. BBLOI 4-31 v Ind (Sharjah) 1999/00. HSFC 55* EP v Bol (PE) 1997/98. BBFC 6-31 EP v Eas (PE) 1999/00. HSLO 19* EP v WP (CT) 1996/97. BBLO 5-37 EP v KZN (Dbn) 1998/99. BB20 3-21 Worcestershire v Somerset (Worcester) 2003. Tours: SA to Aus 2000, 2001/02; Eng 1998; Ind 1999/00; SL 2000, 2004; Shar 1999/00; Sing 2000; SA U-19 to Ind 1995/96. COY 2000. Baseball (EP).

HAYWARD Warren Douglas (Bol). B 15/5/84 Johannesburg. LHB LB. Ed Paarl Valley HS. Bol Schools 2001-02. FC debut Bol v NW (Paarl) 2004/05. HSFC 47 Bol v KZN (Paarl) 2005/06. HSLO 18 Bol v GW (Kby) 2004/05.

HECTOR Benjamin (Eag/FS). B 5/8/79 Durban. RHB RM. Ed Kearsney College, Stell Univ. Ntl Schools 1997(C). Son of AR Hector (Tvl/TvlB/EP 1962-1970), nephew of RG Hector (NT 1967-1972). FC debut Bol v Gau (Paarl) 2001/02, Eag debut 2004/05, FS debut 2004/05. Bol 2001/02-2002/03. GW 2003/04. HSFC 200* FS v Gau (Jhb) 2004/05. HSSS 143* GW v KZN (Dbn) 2003/04. HSLO 126 GW v FS (Bfn) 2003/04. BBLO 2-34 GW v FS (Bfn) 2003/04.

HENDERSON James Michael (Eag). B 6/8/75 Worcester. LHB OB. Ed Worcester Gymnasium, Cape Technikon. Bol Schools 1991-93(C). Brother of CW Henderson (Bol//WP/WPB/Leic/SA 1990-2006). FC debut BolB v OFSB (Bfn) 1994/95, scoring 122*, Eag debut 2004/05, FS debut 2004/05. Bol 1994/95 and 1997/98-2001/02, BolB 1994/95-1995/96.

TvlB 1996/97. NW 2002/03-2003/04. HSFC 143* NW v Gau (Jhb) 2003/04. BBFC 3-13 Bol v FS (Stb) 1998/99. HSLO 108* NW v Bol (Paarl) 2003/04. BBLO 2-40 Bol v GW (Kby) 1998/99.

HENDERSON Tyron (War/SAA). B 1/8/74 Durban. RHB RFM. Ed Durban HS, Univ Dbn Westville. Ntl Schools 1992. Grandson of JK Henderson (NET 1950/51), great nephew of WA Henderson (NET 1937-1946). FC debut Bdr v Bol (EL) 1998/99, War debut 2004/05. Kent 2006. HSFC 81 Bdr v Gau (Jhb) 1999/00. BBFC 6-56 Bdr v FS (Bfn) 2000/01. HSLO 126* Bdr v GW (Kby) 2003/04. BBLO 5-5 Bdr v WP (EL) 1998/99. HS20 85 EC v Lio (Potch) 2003/04. BB20 3-11 War v Ttn (Ben) 2005/06. Tours: SAA to SL 2005/06.

HERMITAGE John Stephan (NW). B 20/6/86 Secunda. RHB OB. Ed Richards Bay HS. KZN Schools 2004, SA Schools 2004. FC debut NW v Nor (Cent) 2005/06. HSFC 17 NW v Nor (Cent) 2005/06 & NW v Eas (Ben) 2005/06. BBFC 3-85 NW v Gau (Potch) 2005/06. BBLO 3-16 NW v FS (Bfn) 2005/06.

HEWER Nicolas David (KZN). B 6/7/84 Durban. RHB RMF. Ed Glenwood HS. FC debut KZN v Bol (Chatsworth) 2005/06. LO debut 2003/04. Dol Pro20 2003/04. HSFC 23* KZN v Bol (Chatsworth) 2005/06. BBFC 4-31 KZN v WP (CT) 2005/06. BBLO 3-24 KZN v Bol (Stb) 2005/06.

HINKEL Warwick Robert (Bdr). B 18/6/81 East London. RHB LB. Ed Hudson Park HS. Bdr Schools 1997-99. FC debut Bdr v Bol (EL) 2001/02. HSFC 100 Bdr v Eas (Ben) 2004/05. BBFC 6-85 Bdr v FS (Bfn) 2004/05. HSSS 49 Bdr v Gau (EL) 2003/04. BBSS 3-11 Bdr v Bol (Paarl) 2002/03. HSLO 40 Bdr v Gau (EL) 2004/05. BBLO 4-31 Bdr v Nor (EL) 2004/05.

HLENGANE Israel Christopher (Eas). B 28/7/88 Johannesburg. LHB SLA. Ed Johan Jurgens HS. Eas Schools 2005. FC debut Eas v Nor (Ben) 2005/06. HSFC 23 Eas v FS (Bfn) 2005/06. BBFC 7-107 Eas v GW (Kby) 2005/06. HSLO 17 Eas v Gau (Jhb) 2005/06. BBLO 3-25 Eas v Nor (Ben) 2005/06.

HOBSON Denys Leon (Bol). B 21/4/83 Jansenville. RHB RMF. Ed Grey HS (PE), Stell Univ. EP Schools 2001. Nephew of DL Hobson (EP/WP/WPB/SA 1970-1984) and AL Hobson (GW/EP/EPB/WP/WPB 1982-1997), cousin of IB Hobson (Ntl/NtlB 1988-1994) and MR Hobson (Ntl/NtlB/EPB/Bdr/Tvl/TvlB/NTB 1985-1995). FC debut Bol v Bdr (Paarl) 2005/06. HSFC 11* Bol v Bdr (Paarl) 2005/06.

HOLTZHAUSEN Frans Petrus Gert (GW). B 6/12/80 Vryburg. RHB OB. Ed Diamantveld HS, Stell Univ. Brother of FS Holtzhausen (NW 2004-2005). FC debut GW v NW (Potch) 2005/06. HSFC 54 GW v Nor (Kby) 2005/06. HSLO 29 GW v FS (Kby) 2005/06.

HOLTZHAUSEN Frederick Stephanus *(Frikkie)* (NW). B 17/4/85 Hartswater. RHB RMF. Ed Diamantveld HS, Potch Univ. GW Schools 2001-03. Brother of FPG Holtzhausen (GW 2005/06). FC debut NW v WP (CT) 2004/05. HSFC 69* NW v FS (Potch) 2005/06. BBFC 5-25 NW v Gau (Jhb) 2005/06. HSLO 49* NW v GW (Potch) 2004/05. BBLO 3-30 NW v Eas (Potch) 2005/06.

HOMANI Zwelibanzi (*Bob*) (WP). B 12/12/83 Port Elizabeth. RHB WK. Ed Grey HS (PE), Muir College. EP Schools 1999-2001, SA Schools 1999-2001. FC debut EP v WP (CT) 2001/02, WP debut 2005/06. EP 2001/02-2004/05. HSFC 118 WP v Bdr (CT) 2005/06. HSSS 40 EP v WP (CT) 2001/02. HSLO 44 WP v Bol (CT) 2005/06. Tours: SA U-19 to NZ 2000/01; World Cup 2000, 2002.

HOWELL Grant Edwin (EP). B 10/2/84 Queenstown. RHB LB. Ed Dale College, UPE. Bdr Schools 2001-02. Son of IL Howell (EP/EPB/Bdr 1981-1997 and FC Umpire), nephew of DH Howell (WPB/EP/EPB/Tvl/TvlB/Bdr 1976-1991), great nephew of HC Howell (WP 1949-1954). FC debut EP v WP (PE) 2004/05. HSFC 80* EP v Bol (Paarl) 2004/05. BBFC 4-38 EP v Bol (Paarl) 2004/05. HSLO 115* EP v ZimU23 (PE) 2005/06. BBLO 4-13 EP v Bol (PE) 2005/06. Hockey (EP U-21 2004).

INGRAM Colin Alexander (EP/FS). B 3/7/85 Port Elizabeth. LHB LB. Ed Woodridge College. EP Schools 2001-03, SA Schools 2003(C)(S). FC debut FS v Bdr (Bfn) 2004/05, EP debut 2005/06. HSFC 169 EP v WP (PE) 2005/06. BBFC 4-16 EP v Bol (PE) 2005/06. HSLO 73* EP v Bdr (EL) 2005/06. BBLO 2-13 EP v Bol (PE) 2005/06.

JACOBS Arno (War). B 13/3/77 Potchefstroom. LHB RM WK. Ed Hoer Volkskool (Potch), Potch Univ. WT Schools 1993-95. Brother of S Jacobs (Gau/TvlB 1987-1999). FC debut NW v WPB (Potch) 1997/98, scoring 112. War debut 2004/05, EP debut 2003/04. NW 1997/98-2002/03. HSFC 197 NW v Bdr (Potch) 2001/02. HSLO 118 NW v Eas (Potch) 2002/03. BBLO 2-22 NW v Eas (Potch) 2002/03. HS20 45 War v WPBol (CT) 2004/05.

JACOBS David Johan *(Davy)* (Eag/SAA/Rest). B 4/11/82 Klerksdorp. RHB RM WK. Ed Hoer Volkskool (Potch), Klerksdorp HS, Potch Univ. NW Schools 1998-2000. FC debut NW v Bol (Potch) 2001/02, Eag debut 2004/05. NW 2001/02-2003/04. HSFC 218 Eag v Dol (Bfn) 2004/05. HSLO 101* Eag v War (PE) 2004/05. HS20 47 Eag v EC (EL) 2003/04. Tours: SA U-19 to World Cup 2002.

JARDINE Faghme (WP). B 26/1/81 Cape Town. LHB SLA. Ed Wynberg BHS, UWC. WP Schools 1998. FC debut WP v Bdr (EL) 2005/06. LO debut 2004/05. HSFC 14 WP v Bdr (EL) 2005/06. BBFC 5-118 WP v Bdr (EL) 2005/06. HSLO 27* WP v Bol (CT) 2004/05.

JEGGELS Riaan Ruche (EP). B 10/9/81 Port Elizabeth. RHB. Ed Gelvandale HS. FC debut EP v WP (PE) 2004/05. HSFC 86 EP v Bol (PE) 2005/06. HSLO 71 EP v Nor (Pta) 2005/06.

JONKER Christiaan (NW). B 24/9/86 Rustenburg. RHB RMF. Ed Bergsig HS, NW Univ. NW Schools 2004. No FC, LO debut 2005/06.

JOUBERT Pierre (Nor). B 2/5/78 Pretoria. RHB RFM. Ed Eldoraigne HS. NT Schools 1993-96, SA Schools 1995-96. FC debut NTB v TvlB (Jhb) 1995/96, NT debut 1996/97. HSFC 112* Nor v WP (Cent) 2001/02. BBFC 7-32 Nor v Gau (Pta) 2005/06. BBSS 6-19 Nor v EP (PE) 2003/04. HSLO 58* Nor v NW (Potch) 2005/06. BBLO 4-82 Suffolk v Devon

(Exmouth) 2003. BBDLO 3-23 Nor v Gau (Jhb) 1998/99. Tours: SA U-19 to Eng 1995; Ind 1995/96. SA U-19 v Pak U-19 1996/97.

JUMAT Jeandre Ryan (Nor). B 29/1/87 Cape Town. LHB RMF. Ed Waterkloof HS, Tshwane UT. Nor Schools 2005. FC debut Nor v FS (Pta) 2005/06. Rugby (Nor Craven Week 2005).

KALLIS Jacques Henry (SA/Afr). B 16/10/75 Pinelands, Cape Town. RHB RFM. Ed Wynberg BHS. WP Schools 1992-93, SA Schools 1993. FC debut WPB v WT (Potch) 1993/94, WP debut 1994/95, WPBol debut 2004/05. Middlesex 1997. Glamorgan 1999. Tests: 102 (101 for SA 1995/96-2005/06, 1 as capt; 1 for World 2005/06). LOIs: 231 (226 for SA 1995/96-2005/06; 2 for Africa 2005/06; 3 for World 2005/06). HSTest 189* v Zim (Byo) 2001/02. BBTest 6-54 v Eng (Leeds) 2003. HSLOI 139 v WI (Jhb) 2003/04. BBLOI 5-30 v WI (Dhaka) 1998/99. HSFC 200 SA v Derbyshire (Derby) 2003. BBFC 6-54 SA v Eng (Leeds) 2003. BBSA 6-60 WP v Bol (Paarl) 1999/00. HSSA 177 SA v WI (Dbn) 2003/04. HSSS 146 WP v Tvl (CT) 1995/96. HSLO 155* Glamorgan v Surrey (Pontypridd) 1999. BBLO 5-30 SA v WI (Dhaka) 1998/99. HSDLO 116* WP v EP (PE) 1994/95. BBDLO 5-47 WP v EP (CT) 2000/01. HS20 50 WPBol v Ttn (Cent) 2003/04. Tours: SA to Aus 1997/98, 2000, 2001/02, 2005/06; Ban 1998/99; Eng 1998, 2003, 2004; Ind 1999/00, 2004/05, 2005/06; NZ 1998/99, 2003/04, Pak 1997/98, 2003/04; SL 2000, 2002/03, 2004; WI 2000/01, 2004/05; Zim 1999/00, 2001/02; Ken 1999/00, 2000/01; Mor 2002; Shar 1995/96, 1999/00; Sing 2000; World Cup 1996, 1999, 2003; SAA to Eng 1996; SA U-24 to SL 1995/96. COY 1999, 2000, 2004, 2005.

KANNEMEYER Quinton Kurt (Bol). B 31/5/84 Vredenburg. RHB RMF. Ed Vredenburg HS. Bol Schools 2002. FC debut Bol v EP (Paarl) 2005/06. HSFC 70 Bol v EP (Paarl) 2005/06. HSLO 29* Bol v KZN (Stb) 2005/06.

KEMP Justin Miles (Ttn/SA/Afr). B 2/10/77 Queenstown. RHB RFM. Ed Queen's College, UPE. Bdr Schools 1995. Son of JW Kemp (Bdr 1975-1976), grandson of JM Kemp (Bdr 1947/48), cousin of DJ Callaghan (EP/EPB/GW/Nott 1983-2002). FC debut EPB v NW (Potch) 1996/97, Nor debut 2003/04, Ttn debut 2004/05. EP 1997/98-2002/03, EPB 1996/97. Worcestershire 2003, Kent 2005-2006. Tests: 4 (2000/01-2005/06). LOIs: 54 (51 for SA 2000/01-2005/06; 3 for Africa 2005/06). HSTest 55 v Aus (Perth) 2005/06. BBTest 3-33 v SL (Cent) 2000/01. HSLOI 80 v Eng (EL) 2004/05. BBLOI 3-20 v Ind (Dbn) 2001/02. HSFC 188 EP v NW (PE) 2000/01. BBFC 6-56 EP v Bdr (PE) 2000/01. HSLO 107* Nor v GW (Cent) 2003/04. BBLO 6-20 EP v FS (PE) 2000/01. HS20 85* Ttn v Dol (Ben) 2004/05. BB20 3-19 Ttn v WPBol (CT) 2004/05. Tours: SA to Aus 2001/02, 2005/06; Ind 2005/06; WI 2000/01, 2004/05; Zim 2001/02; SAA to Aus 2002/03; WI 2000/01; Zim 2004; SA U-19 to Ind 1995/96.

KENT Jon Carter (Dol). B 7/5/79 Cape Town. RHB RMF. Ed Durban HS, UNISA. Ntl Schools 1996-97, SA Schools 1997. FC debut NtlB v NorB (Cent) 1997/98, KZN debut 1998/99, Dol debut 2004/05. Scotland (LO) 2003. LOIs: 2 (2001/02). HSFC 178* KZN v EP (Dbn) 2000/01. BBFC 6-77 KZN v Eas (Ben) 2000/01. HSLO 115* Scotland v Sussex (Hove) 2003. BBLO 4-29 KZN v EP (Dbn) 2000/01. HSDLO 78 Dol v War (Pmb) 2004/05. HS20 32* Dol v Lio (Potch) 2005/06. BB20 4-25 Dol v Ttn (Dbn) 2003/04. Tours: SAA to Zim 2002/03. SA U-19 v Eng U-19 1997/98; World Cup in SA 1998. Hockey (Ntl U-18 1996-97).

KGAMADI Diphaphany *Jimmy* (NW). B 7/10/83 Klerksdorp. RHB LB. Ed Milner HS. NW Schools 1999-2002. FC debut NW v GW (Potch) 2004/05. HSFC 84 NW v Gau (Jhb) 2005/06. HSLO 79 NW v FS (Bfn) 2005/06.

KHAN Imraan (Dol/KZN). B 27/4/84 Durban. LHB OB. Ed Orient, Durban HS. KZN Schools 1999-2001(C), SA Schools 2001 (C). FC debut KZN v Bol (Paarl) 2003/04, Dol debut 2004/05. LO debut 2001/02. HSFC 150 Dol v Ttn (Cent) 2004/05. BBFC 6-43 KZN v Eas (Ben) 2003/04. HSLO 58 Dol v Ttn (Dbn) 2004/05 & Dol v Eag (Dbn) 2004/05. BBLO 2-31 Dol v Lio (Jhb) 2004/05. HS20 22 Dol v WPBol (CT) 2003/04. BB20 2-15 Dol v Eag (Bfn) 2004/05. Tours: SA U-19 to Eng 2003(capt); NZ 2000/01; World Cup 2002.

KHOZA Tom Rhulani (Nor). B 20/7/87 Pretoria. RHB OB. Ed Saulridge HS, Tshwane UT. FC debut Nor v GW (Pta) 2005/06. BBFC 3-41 Nor v GW (Pta) 2005/06. Tours: SA U-19 to Ind 2005/06.

KLEINVELDT Rory Keith (Cob/WP/Rest). B 15/3/83 Cape Town. RHB RMF. Ed Plumstead HS, Abbott's College. WP Schools 2000-01, SA Schools 2001. Cousin of W Wyngaard (WP/Cob 2004-2005). FC debut WP v Bdr (Bellville) 2002/03, WPBol debut 2004/05. HSFC 115* WP v KZN (Chatsworth) 2005/06. BBFC 8-47 Cob v War (Stb) 2005/06. HSSS 92 WPBol v Ttn (Ben) 2004/05. HSLO 54* Cob v Ttn (Paarl) 2005/06. BBLO 4-29 Cob v Eag (Bfn) 2005/06. HS20 46 Cob v War (EL) 2005/06. BB20 3-18 WPBol v EC (PE) 2003/04 & WPBol v War (CT) 2004/05. Tours: SA U-19 to World Cup 2002.

KLUSENER Lance (Dol). B 4/9/71 Durban. LHB RFM. Ed Durban HS. FC debut NtlB v BdrB (EL) 1993/94, Ntl same season, Dol debut 2004/05. Nottinghamshire 2002. Middlesex 2004. Northamptonshire 2006. Tests: 49 (1996/97-2004). LOIs: 171 (1995/96-2004). HSTest 174 v Eng (PE) 1999/00. BBTest 8-64 v Ind (Calcutta) 1996/97, on debut. HSLOI 103* v NZ (Auckland) 1998/99. BBLOI 6-49 v SL (Lahore) 1997/98. HSFC 174 SA v Eng (PE) 1999/00. BBFC 8-34 Ntl v WP (Dbn) 1995/96. HSSS 108* Dol v Eag (Dbn) 2004/05. HSLO 142* SA v Northamptonshire (Northampton) 1998. BBLO 6-49 SA v SL (Lahore) 1997/98. HSDLO 91 Ntl v WT (Foch) 1995/96. BBDLO 4-19 Ntl v OFS (Bfn) 1994/95. HS20 72* Northamptonshire v Nottinghamshire (Nottingham) 2006. BB20 2-13 Dol v EC (Dbn) 2003/04. Tours: SA to Aus 1997/98, 2000, 2001/02; Eng 1998, 2004; Ind 1996/97, 1999/00; NZ 1998/99, 2003/04; Pak 1997/98; SL 2000, 2002/03, 2004; WI 2000/01; Zim 1999/00, 2001/02; Ken 1999/00, 2000/01; Mor 2002; Shar 1999/00; Sing 2000; World Cup 1999, 2003; SAA to Eng 1996; SA U-24 to SL 1995/96. COY 1997, 1999. Wisden 2000.

KNOX Craig Elton (Gau). B 18/7/81 East London. RHB RFM. Ed Stirling HS. Bdr Schools 1998. FC debut Gau v FS (Jhb) 2005/06. HSFC 47* Gau v Eas (Ben) 2005/06. BBFC 3-31 Gau v NW (Potch) 2005/06. HSLO 29 Gau v Nor (Jhb) 2005/06.

WHO'S WHO 2005/06

KOORTZEN Petrus Johannes (*Pieter*) (FS/Eag). B 24/9/79 Kimberley. RHB OB. Ed Diamantveld HS. SACD Schools 1993, GW Schools 1994-96. FC debut GW v WP (Kby) 1996/97. FS debut 2005/06, Eag LO debut 2005/06. GW 1996/97-2004/05, GWB 1998/99. HSFC 164 GW v NW (Kby) 2001/02. BBFC 3-60 GWB v EPB (PE) 1998/99. BBSS 2-78 GW v WP (Kby) 1996/97. HSLO 134 GW v NW (Kby) 2000/01. BBLO 3-37 GW v Nor (Kby) 2000/01.

KOPS Brent Bjorn (War). B 1/11/82 Port Elizabeth. RHB LF. Ed St Thomas SS. EP Schools 2000. FC debut EP v Nor (Cent) 2001/02, War debut 2004/05. HSFC 25 EP v Bol (Paarl) 2003/04. BBFC 5-36 EP v Nor (PE) 2003/04. BBLO 5-42 War v Dol (Pmb) 2004/05. BB20 2-19 EC v Eag (EL) 2003/04. Tours: SA U-19 to World Cup 2002.

KREUSCH Justin Peter (War). B 27/9/79 East London. RHB RM. Ed Selborne College, Rhodes Univ. Bdr Schools 1996-97(C). FC debut Bdr v Gau (Jhb) 1999/00, War debut 2004/05. HSFC 91 Bdr v Gau (EL) 2003/04. BBFC 5-31 War v Cob (Stb) 2005/06. HSLO 119* War v Eag (Bfn) 2005/06. BBLO 3-21 Bdr v Eas (EL) 2002/03. HS20 73 War v Ttn (Ben) 2005/06. BB20 3-23 War v Dol (Dbn) 2005/06.

KRUGER Alan Kevin (Eag/GW). B 16/2/81 Kimberley. RHB RMF. Ed Floors SS. GW Schools 1997-98. Brother of LA Kruger (GW LO 2005/06). FC debut GW v Ban (Kby) 2000/01, Eag debut 2005/06. HSFC 158 GW v EP (PE) 2004/05. BBFC 6-37 GW v FS (Kby) 2005/06. HSSS 56 GW v NW (Kby) 2003/04. BBSS 4-87 GW v Eas (Ben) 2001/02. HSLO 55 GW v EP (PE) 2004/05. BBLO 4-20 GW v EP (PE) 2004/05.

KRUGER Garnett John-Peter (Lio/SA/SAA/Rest). B 5/1/77 Port Elizabeth. RHB RFM. Ed Gelvandale HS, Russel Road College. FC debut EPB v Eas (Ben) 1997/98, Gau debut 2003/04, Lio debut 2004/05. EP 1999/00-2002/03, EPB 1997/98-1998/99. LOIs: 3 (2005/06). HSFC 58 SAA v Wind Isl (Arnos Vale) 2000/01. BBFC 8-112 Lio v Dol (Dbn) 2005/06. HSSA 33 Lio v Eag (Potch) 2005/06. HSLO 20* EP v WP (CT) 2002/03. BBLO 6-23 EP v NW (PE) 1999/00. HS20 12* Lio v Eag (Potch) 2004/05. Tours: SA to Aus 2005/06; SAA to SL 2005/06; WI 2000/01; Zim 2004.

KRUGER Lee Alwyn (GW). B 6/3/83 Kimberley. RHB RM. Ed Floors SS. Brother of AK Kruger (GW/Eag 2000-2005). No FC, LO debut 2005/06.

KUHN Heino Gunther (Ttn/Nor). B 1/4/84 Piet Retief. RHB WK. Ed Afrikaanse Hoer Seunskool. Nor Schools 2002. FC debut Nor v FS (Pta) 2004/05, Ttn debut 2005/06. HSFC 133* Nor v Eas (Pta) 2005/06. HSSS 96 Ttn v Eag (Bfn) 2005/06. HSLO 113* Nor v Gau (Jhb) 2005/06.

KUIPER James Morris (WP). B 23/10/86 Johannesburg. LHB RM. Ed Diocesan College, UCT. WP Schools 2004. Son of JL Kuiper (SAU 1973-1974), nephew of AP Kuiper (WP/WPB/Bol/SA/Derb 1977-1997). FC debut WP v EP (PE) 2005/06. HSFC 81* WP v Bol (CT) 2005/06. HSLO 29 WP v Bdr (EL) 2005/06.

LAING Peter Charles (Bol). B 5/10/84 Johannesburg. RHB RFM. Ed St Stithian's, Stell Univ. FC debut Bol v ZimU23 (Stb) 2005/06. HSFC 80 Bol v Bdr (Paarl) 2005/06. BBFC 3-80 Bol v KZN (Paarl) 2005/06. HSLO 16 Bol v EP (Paarl) 2005/06. BBLO 4-42 Bol v KZN (Stb) 2005/06.

LANGEVELDT Charl Kenneth (Lio/SA). B 17/12/74 Stellenbosch. RHB RFM. Ed Luckhoff SS. FC debut Bol v Nor (Cent) 1997/98, Lio debut 2004/05. Bol 1997/98-2002/03. Bdr 2003/04. Somerset 2005. Tests: 6 (2004/05-2005/06). LOIs: 29 (2001/02-2005/06). HSTest 10 v WI (Georgetown) 2004/05. BBTest 5-46 v Eng (CT) 2004/05. BBLOI 5-62 v WI (Bridgetown) 2004/05. HSFC 56 Bol v EP (PE) 1999/00. BBFC 5-19 Bol v FS (Paarl) 2000/01. HSLO 33* SAA v SL (Potch) 2002/03. BBLO 5-7 SA Pres v Ban (Pmb) 2000/01. HSDLO 20 Bdr v Nor (EL) 2003/04. BBDLO 5-35 Bol v WP (Paarl) 1999/00. BB20 2-14 SA v NZ (Jhb) 2005/06. Tours: SA to Aus 2001/02, 2005/06; Eng 2003, 2004; Ind 2005/06; Pak 2003/04; SL 2004; WI 2004/05; Zim 2001/02; World Cup 2003, SAA to Aus 2002/03; WI 2000/01; Zim 2004.

LAZARUS Fabian Brent (KZN). B 12/10/81 Durban. RHB RM. Ed Arena Park SS. FC debut KZN v WP (CT) 2003/04. HSLO 52* KZN v FS (Dbn) 2004/05. Volleyball (KZN 1999-2000).

LEMMETJIES Bradley William (GW). B 18/8/77 Kimberley. RHB LB. Ed Floors SS. FC debut GWB v NorB (Cent) 1998/99, GW debut 2004/05. HSFC 41* GW v NW (Potch) 2004/05. BBFC 4-27 GW v Bol (Kby) 2004/05. HSLO 31 GW v WP (Kby) 2004/05. BBLO 4-25 GW v Gau (Jhb) 2005/06.

LENTZ Donovan Craig (Bdr). B 20/7/82 Port Elizabeth. RHB RMF. Ed Dale College. Bdr Schools 1999-2000. FC debut Bdr v EP (PE) 2005/06. HSFC 19 Bdr v EP (PE) 2005/06. HSLO 13 Bdr v Bol (EL) 2005/06.

LE ROUX Heinrich Wilhelm (Gau). B 25/5/84 Durban. RHB RMF. Ed Afrikaanse Hoer Seunskool, Pretoria Univ. Nor Schools 2001-02, SA Schools 2002. FC debut Gau v FS (Bfn) 2005/06. HSFC 25 Gau v NW (Potch) 2005/06. BBFC 4-66 Gau v FS (Jhb) 2005/06. HSLO 22* Gau v Bol (Paarl) 2005/06. Tours: SA U-19 to Eng 2003. His mother, Ingrid, represented SA at netball and his aunt, Annelie Kloppers, represented South Africa at netball and hockey.

LE ROUX Juan (NW). B 21/12/83 Klerksdorp. RHB RM. Ed Klerksdorp HS. NW Schools 2001-02. FC debut NW v GW (Potch) 2004/05. Lio Pro20 2004/05. HSFC 110 NW v FS (Potch) 2005/06. HSLO 128* NW v Eas (Potch) 2005/06. HS20 12 Lio v War (EL) 2004/05.

LEVI Richard Ernst (Cob). B 14/1/88 Johannesburg. RHB RM. Ed Wynberg BHS. WP Schools 2004, SA Schools 2004. No FC, LO debut 2004/05. HSLO 16 Cob v Ttn (Cent) 2005/06. Tours: SA U-19 to World Cup 2006.

LINDE Corne (FS). B 19/7/81 Bloemfontein. RHB WK. Ed Grey College (Bfn), UFS. FS Schools 1998-99. Brother of H Linde (FSB 1995/96). FC debut FS v KZN (Dbn) 2004/05. HSFC 56 FS v Gau (Bfn) 2005/06. HSLO 58 FS v Gau (Jhb) 2004/05. Hockey (FS U-18 1998).

LIVI Ncamile Jacob (Eas). B 11/12/87 Springs, Transvaal. RHB RFM. Ed Esibonelwesihle HS. Eas Schools 2005. FC debut Eas v NW (Potch) 2005/06. HSFC 42 Eas v NW (Potch) 2005/06. HSLO 12 Eas v FS (Ben) 2005/06.

LOMBARD Wayne Patrick (KZN). B 1/11/85 Nelspruit. RHB OB. Ed Uplands College. FC debut KZN v Gau (Dbn) 2004/05. HSFC 25* KZN v EP (PE) 2005/06. HSLO 25* KZN v Bol (Chatsworth) 2005/06 & 25 KZN v FS (Dbn) 2004/05.

LOTTER Devan Pierre (NW). B 3/2/83 Klerksdorp. RHB OB. Ed Klerksdorp HS. NW Schools 2001. FC debut NW v Gau (Jhb) 2005/06.

LOUW Johann (Eag). B 12/4/79 Cape Town. RHB RMF. Ed Hoerskool Fraserburg, UPE. FC debut GW v Nor (Cent) 2000/01, Eag debut 2005/06. GW 2000/01-2002/03. EP 2003/04. Dol 2004/05. Northamptonshire 2004-2005. Middlesex 2006. HSFC 124 EP v Bol (PE) 2003/04. BBFC 6-51 Northamptonshire v Essex (Northampton) 2005. BBSA 6-108 GW v Bdr (EL) 2002/03. HSLO 72 GW v Nor (Kby) 2000/01. BBLO 5-27 EP v Bdr (EL) 2003/04 & Northamptonshire v Warwickshire (Northampton) 2004. HS20 17 Northamptonshire v Worcestershire (Luton) 2004. BB20 4-18 Middlesex v Hampshire (Southgate) 2006.

LOUW Willem Johannes *(Wimpie)* (Bol). B 21/10/80 Johannesburg. RHB OB. Ed Hoerskool President. FC debut Bol v NW (Paarl) 2004/05. HSFC 85 Bol v KZN (Chatsworth) 2005/06. HSLO 57* Bol v KZN (Chatsworth) 2005/06.

LWANA Lwando Lennox (Bdr). B 26/12/83 Pirie Mission, near King William's Town. RHB RFM. Ed Forbes Grant. Bdr Schools 2001-02. FC debut Bdr v FS (Bfn) 2004/05. HSFC 24 Bdr v KZN (Dbn) 2005/06. BBFC 3-6 Bdr v ZimU23 (EL) 2005/06. HSLO 10 Bdr v EP (PE) 2005/06.

MABUYA Anthony Phakamile Tebogo (GW). B 15/7/77 Kimberley. RHB SLA. Ed Tshireleco HS. GW Schools 1995. FC debut GW v KZN (Kby) 2001/02. HSFC 27 GW v KZN (Kby) 2002/03. BBFC 2-27 GW v EP (PE) 2001/02.

MABUYA Cedric Sakhumuzi (KZN). B 20/5/88 Durban. RHB OB. Ed Durban HS. KZN Schools 2004-05, SA Schools 2004. FC debut KZN v EP (Chatsworth) 2005/06. HSLO 16 KZN v WP (CT) 2005/06

McKENZIE Neil Douglas (Lio/SA/Rest). B 24/11/75 Johannesburg. RHB RM. Ed King Edward VII, RAU. Tvl Schools 1993(C)-94(C), SA Schools 1993-94(C). Son of KA McKenzie (NET/Tvl/TvlB/SA 1966-1986). FC debut TvlB v EPB (PE) 1994/95, Lio debut 2004/05. Gau 1995/96-1998/99, TvlB 1995/96. Nor 1999/00-2003/04. Tests: 41 (2000-2003/04). LOIs: 59 (1999/00-2003/04). HSTest 120 v NZ (PE) 2000/01. HSLOI 131* v Ken (CT) 2001/02. HSFC 175 Nor v Gau (Cent) 1999/00. HSLO 131* SA v Ken (CT) 2001/02. BBLO 2-19 Gau v GW (Kby) 1997/98. HSDLO 118 Tvl v NW (Foch) 1996/97. HS20 85* Lio v Eag (Bfn) 2005/06. Tours: SA to Aus 2000, 2001/02; Eng 2003; Ban 2002/03; Ind 1999/00; NZ 2003/04; Pak 2003/04; SL 2000; WI 2000/01; Zim 2001/02; Ken 2000/01; Shar 1999/00; Sing 2000; SAA to Zim 2002/03, 2004; SA U-19 to Eng 1995(C). COY 2001.

McLAREN Adrian Peter (GW). B 21/4/80 Kimberley. RHB WK. Ed Kimberley BHS. GW Schools 1996-98. Son of K McLaren (GW 1971-1984), nephew of P McLaren (GW 1977-1994), cousin of R McLaren (FS/Eag 2003-2005). FC debut GWB v NorB (Cent) 1998/99, GW debut 1999/00. HSFC 164 GW v Bol (Kby) 2004/05. HSSS 134 GW v NW (Kby) 2001/02. HSLO 50 GW v NW (Potch) 2004/05. Hockey (GW).

McLAREN Ryan (Eag). B 9/2/83 Kimberley. LHB RMF. Ed Grey College (Bfn), FS Univ. FS Schools 1999-2001, SA Schools 2001. Son of P McLaren (GW 1977-1994), nephew of K McLaren (GW 1971-1984), cousin of AP McLaren (GW/GWB 1998-2005). FC debut FS v Eas (Ben) 2003/04, Eag debut 2004/05. HSFC 140 Eag v War (Bfn) 2005/06. BBFC 6-96 Eag v Dol (Bfn) 2005/06. HSLO 55 FS v Eas (Bfn) 2003/04. BBLO 4-43 Eag v Lio (Jhb) 2005/06. HS20 10 Eag v Dol (Bfn) 2004/05. BB20 2-21 Eag v Ttn (Bfn) 2005/06. Tours: SA U-19 to World Cup 2002. Hockey (SA Schools 2001).

MAFA Johnson Tumelo (Gau). B 5/2/78 Johannesburg. RHB RFM. Ed Sparrow School. Tvl Schools 1996. FC debut Gau v SL (Jhb) 1997/98. HSFC 19* Gau v Eas (Jhb) 2002/03. BBFC 6-62 Gau v GW (Jhb) 2000/01. BBLO 4-34 Gau v NW (Jhb) 2005/06.

MAGIET Achmat (WP). B 8/2/83 Cape Town. RHB OB. Ed SACS, Abbott's College. WP Schools 2001. Nephew of MR Magiet (WP SACB 1971-1980, former Convenor National Selectors), nephew of S Magiet (WP SACB 1971-1990), cousin of R Magiet (WP/WPB/Bol 1998-2004). FC debut WP v NW (CT) 2004/05. BBFC 3-0 WP v NW (CT) 2004/05. HSLO 41 WP v EP (PE) 2004/05.

MAHLOMBE Mondli (WP). B 11/11/85 Cape Town. RHB RFM. Ed Masiyile SS. WP Schools 2003-04. FC debut WP v EP (CT) 2005/06. HSFC 20 WP v Bol (Paarl) 2005/06. BBFC 3-11 WP v EP (CT) 2005/06. BBLO 3-34 WP v EP (CT) 2005/06.

MAKALIMA Dumisa Liko (Lio/Gau). B 29/12/80 King William's Town. RHB OB. Ed Dale College. Bdr Schools 1996-97. FC debut Bdr v FS (EL) 1997/98, Gau debut 2005/06, Lio LO debut 2005/06. Bdr 1997/98-2001/02 and 2004/05, EP 2002/03-2003/04. War 2004/05. HSFC 78 Bdr/EP v SLA (PE) 1999/00. HSSS 73 Bdr v EP (PE) 2001/02. HSLO 74 EP v NW (Potch) 2003/04. Scored 302 for EPB v FSB (Bfn) 2003/04 in a UCB Bowl match (not first-class). Tours: SA U-19 to World Cup 2000.

MAKONGOLO Sithembile *(Wiza)* (EP). B 21/4/85 Middledrift. RHB OB. Ed Dale College. Bdr Schools 2001-03. FC debut EP v Bdr (PE) 2005/06. Bdr LO 2004/05. HSFC 56 EP v Bdr (PE) 2005/06. HSLO 12 Bdr v FS (Bfn) 2004/05. Hockey (SA U-16 2001).

MALAN Dawid Johannes (Bol). B 3/9/87 Roehampton, London. LHB LB. Ed Paarl BHS. Bol Schools 2004-05. Son of DJ Malan (WPB/NTB 1978-1981). FC debut Bol v Bdr (Paarl) 2005/06. Middlesex 20 2006. HSFC 64 Bol v Bdr (Paarl) 2005/06. HSLO 42 Bol v EP (PE) 2005/06. HS20 11 Middlesex v Surrey (The Oval) 2006.

MALAN Heinrich (Nor). B 6/4/81 Pretoria. RHB RM. Ed Waterkloof HS, Pretoria Univ. Nor Schools 1998-99. FC debut EasNor v Zim (Ben) 2004/05, Nor LO debut 2005/06. HSFC 26 EasNor v Zim (Ben) 2004/05. Rugby (Nor Craven Week 1999).

MALAO Jacob Moses Malekane (FS). B 19/1/72 Soweto. LHB SLA. Ed Pafogans HS. FC debut NW v Eas (Ben) 2001/02, FS debut 2005/06. NW 2001/02. Eas 2003/04. Eag 2004/05. HSFC 18 FS v GW (Kby) 2005/06. 5-27 FS v GW (Bfn) 2005/06. HSSS 15* Eag v Dol (Bfn) 2004/05. BBSS 5-50 Eas v Bol (Paarl) 2003/04. BBLO 3-40 Eag v Ttn (Bfn) 2004/05. BB20 2-32 Eag v War (Bfn) 2004/05.

MANDAN Sharad (Eas). B 8/8/85 Johannesburg. D 2/7/06 Boksburg. LHB LB. Ed Wordsworth HS. Eas Schools 2001-03. FC debut Eas v KZN (Ben) 2004/05. HSFC 98 Eas v GW (Kby) 2005/06. HSLO 115* Eas v FS (Bfn) 2005/06.
MANZINI Lucas (Nor). B 7/3/85 Pretoria. RHB RMF. Ed Jafta Mahlangu HS. FC debut Nor v GW (Kby) 2005/06. BBFC 4-22 Nor v GW (Kby) 2005/06. BBLO 2-44 Nor v GW (Pta) 2005/06.
MASHIMBYI Mandla Abednigo (Nor/Ttn). B 10/11/80 Phalaborwa. RHB RMF. Ed Nkateko HS and Prosperitus HS. SACD Schools 1998. FC debut GW v EP (Kby) 2003/04, Ttn debut 2005/06, Nor debut 2005/06. GW 2003/04. Eag 2004/05. FS 2004/05. HSFC 61 GW v Bol (Paarl) 2003/04. BBFC 5-32 Ttn v Lio (Ben) 2005/06. HSLO 40 GW v NW (Potch) 2003/04. BBLO 4-57 Nor v Bol (Paarl) 2005/06.
MASINDA Mthetheli *Ronald* (WP). B 18/7/83 Port Elizabeth. RHB SLA. Ed Cape Town HS. WP Schools 2001. FC debut WP v KZN (Chatsworth) 2005/06.
MASINGA Michael Thuli (Gau). B 12/1/84 Johannesburg. LHB RMF. Ed Queens HS. Gau Schools 2001-02. FC debut Gau v Eas (Jhb) 2005/06. HSFC 48* Gau v Eas (Jhb) 2005/06. LO debut 2004/05. BBLO 2-28 Gau v Bdr (EL) 2004/05.
MATHEBULA Brian Michael (Lio/Gau). B 26/6/85 Tembisa. RHB RFM. Ed Jeppe BHS. Gau Schools 2003. FC debut Gau v Bol (Randjesfontein) 2003/04, Lio debt 2005/06. HSFC 31 Gau v FS (Jhb) 2004/05. BBFC 5-56 Gau v Eas (Ben) 2003/04. HSSS 18* Lio v Cob (Jhb) 2005/06. HSLO 10* Gau v KZN (Dbn) 2004/05.
MATIKA Michael Mhlanguli (Bdr). B 26/4/83 King William's Town. RHB OB. Ed Forbes Grant, Dale College. Bdr Schools 2000-01. FC debut SAAc v SLA (Potch) 2003/04, Bdr same season. HSFC 107 Bdr v FS (Bfn) 2004/05. HSSS 23 Bdr v NW (Potch) 2003/04. HSLO 41 Bdr v KZN (EL) 2004/05.
MAZIBUKO Vusi Cornelius McKenzie (Lio/NW). B 5/8/85 Carletonville. RHB RMF. Ed Potchefstroom BHS. NW Schools 2002. FC debut NW v Gau (Jhb) 2005/06, Lio LO debut 2005/06. LO debut 2003/04. HSFC 21 NW v Nor (Potch) 2005/06. BBFC 3-37 NW v Gau (Jhb) 2005/06. HSLO 24* NW v Gau (Jhb) 2005/06. BBLO 4-26 NW v Gau (Jhb) 2005/06.
MAZIYA Julias Thembinkosi (Eas). B 21/7/83 Springs. RHB OB. Ed Esibonelwesihle HS. Eas Schools 2001. FC debut Eas v KZN (Ben) 2004/05. HSLO 16 Eas v NW (Potch) 2005/06.
MBANE Lundi (War/Bdr). B 10/10/82 Mdantsane. RHB RFM. Ed Green Point. Bdr Schools 2001. FC debut Bdr v KZN (EL) 2004/05, War LO debut 2005/06. HSFC 64 Bdr v Gau (EL) 2004/05. BBFC 5-26 Bdr v ZimU23 (EL) 2005/06. HSLO 10 Bdr v EP (EL) 2005/06. BBLO 2-31 War v Eag (Bfn) 2005/06.
MBHALATI Nkateko *Ethy* (Ttn/Nor). B 18/11/81 Tzaneen. RHB RFM. Ed Majeje HS, Pretoria Tech. FC debut Nor v EP (PE) 2002/03, Ttn debut 2004/05. HSFC 10 Ttn v Eag (Ben) 2005/06. BBFC 5-26 Ttn v Dol (Dbn) 2005/06. BBLO 3-26 Nor v EP (Cent) 2003/04. BB20 3-22 Ttn v Lio (Cent) 2004/05.
MEYER Esias Engelbertus *(Sys)* (Nor) B 18/4/78 Bethal. RHB WK. Ed Ermelo HS. SACD Schools 1995. FC debut GW v KZN (Kby) 2001/02, Nor debut 2005/06. GW 2001/02-2002/03. LO for Eas 1996/97. HSFC 73 GW v KZN (Kby) 2001/02. HSLO 19* Eas v FS (Vga) 1996/97.
MEYER Lyall (War/EP). B 23/3/82 Port Elizabeth. LHB RFM. Ed Alexander Road HS. EP Schools 2000. Cousin of U Abrahams (EP/EPB/Gau 1998-2005). FC debut EP v Nor (Cent) 2001/02, War debut 2005/06. War LO 2004/05. HSFC 38 EP v WP (PE) 2004/05. BBFC 5-38 EP v WP (CT) 2005/06. HSSS 35* War v Lio (EL) 2005/06. BBSS 4-97 War v Eag (PE) 2005/06. HSLO 37 EP v WP (PE) 2005/06. BBLO 4-33 EP v Bdr (PE) 2005/06. HS20 14* War v Lio (Jhb) 2005/06. BB20 2-26 War v Lio (Jhb) 2005/06. Hockey (SA U-21).
MHLONGO Saidi (Dol/KZN). B 21/9/83 Stanger. RHB LMF. Ed Stanger SS. KZN Schools 2001-02. FC debut KZN v FS (Dbn) 2004/05, Dol debut 2005/06. HSFC 21 KZN v WP (CT) 2005/06. BBFC 5-25 KZN v WP (CT) 2005/06. HSSS 19* Dol v War (EL) 2005/06. BBSS 4-38 Dol v Cob (Dbn) 2005/06. BBLO 5-29 KZN v WP (CT) 2005/06.
MILLER Duncan Rooney (KZN). B 13/10/76 Durban. RHB WK. Ed Northwood HS, UNISA. FC debut KZN v WP (Chatsworth) 2005/06. HSFC 64* KZN v WP (CT) 2005/06. HSLO 29 KZN v Bol (Chatsworth) 2005/06.
MJEKULA Sinethemba (War/EP). B 16/10/83 King William's Town. RHB RFM. Ed Amantinde HS. FC debut EP v WP (PE) 2004/05, War debut 2005/06. HSFC 10 EP v WP (PE) 2005/06. BBFC 5-46 EP v ZimU23 (PE) 2005/06. BBSS 3-65 War v Dol (Dbn) 2005/06. HSLO 11* EP v Bol (Paarl) 2005/06. BBLO 4-50 EP v WP (CT) 2005/06.
MOFOKENG Petros Tsepo (Eas). B 22/5/83 Johannesburg. RHB LMF. Ed Esibonelwesihle HS. Eas Schools 2001. FC debut Eas v KZN (Ben) 2004/05. HSFC 10* Eas v Nor (Cent) 2004/05. BBFC 2-36 Eas v GW (Ben) 2005/06. HSLO 16 Eas v Gau (Jhb) 2005/06. BBLO 2-39 Eas v FS (Bfn) 2005/06.
MOKONYAMA Bernard Tshedi *(Bennie)* (Nor). B 2/5/86 Pretoria. RHB OB. Ed St Alban's, Pretoria Univ. Nor Schools 2003-04. Brother of MJ Mokonyama (Nor 2002-2005). No FC, LO debut 2004/05. Hockey (N Gau U-18 2004).
MOKONYAMA Matsobane *James* (Nor). B 13/2/81 Pretoria. RHB OB. Ed St Alban's. Nor Schools 1997-99. Brother of BT Mokonyama (Nor LO 2004-2005). FC debut Nor v Gau (Cent) 2002/03. HSFC 92 Nor v Eas (Cent) 2004/05. HSSS 27 Nor v Gau (Cent) 2002/03. HSLO 18 Nor v FS (Pta) 2004/05.
MOLEON Eugene Owen (Lio/NW). B 2/3/77 Cape Town. RHB RFM. Ed Garlandale HS. WP Schools 1995. FC debut WPB v Eas (CT) 1996/97, NW debut 2001/02. Lio debut 2005/06. WPB 1996/97-1998/99, WP (LO only) 1997/98. Lio LO debut 2004/05. HSFC 67 Lio v Cob (Jhb) 2005/06. BBFC 5-60 NW v Gau (Jhb) 2001/02. HSLO 68 NW v Nor (Potch) 2001/02. BBLO 4-42 NW v GW (Potch) 2003/04. BB20 4-9 Lio v War (Jhb) 2005/06. Tours: SA U-19 to Ind 1995/96.
MOOTHOSAMY Khaalid (Gau). B 18/9/84 Johannesburg. RHB OB. Ed King Edward VII. Gau Schools 2002. FC debut Gau v Nor (Jhb) 2004/05. HSFC 42 Gau v Nor (Pta) 2005/06. HSLO 19 Gau v Nor (Pta) 2005/06. Hockey (Gau U-18 2001).
MORKEL Johannes Albertus (*Albie*) (Ttn/Eas/SA/SAA). B 10/6/81 Vereeniging. LHB RMF. Ed Hoerskool Vereeniging. SACD Schools 1997, Gau Schools 1998, SA Schools 1998. Brother of M Morkel (Eas/Ttn 2003-2005). FC debut Eas v Nor

(Ben) 1999/00, Ttn debut 2004/05. LOIs: 8 (2003/04-2005/06). HSLOI 23* v NZ (Napier) 2003/04. BBLOI 2-23 v Zim (Jhb) 2004/05. HSFC 204* Ttn v WPBol (Paarl) 2004/05. BBFC 6-36 Eas v GW (Kby) 1999/00. HSLO 79 SAA v AusA (Perth) 2002/03. BBLO 4-23 Eas v FS (Bfn) 1999/00. HSDLO 52 Eas v Nor (Cent) 2005/06. HS20 46* Ttn v War (Ben) 2005/06. BB20 2-29 Ttn v Eag (Cent) 2004/05. Tours: SA to Ind 2005/06; NZ 2003/04; SAA to Aus 2002/03; SL 2005/06; Zim 2002/03, 2004; SA U-19 to World Cup 2000.

MORKEL Morne (Ttn/Eas). B 6/10/84 Vereeniging. LHB RFM. Ed Hoerskool Vereeniging. Gau Schools 2002. Brother of JA Morkel (Eas/Ttn/SA 1999-2005). FC debut Eas v WI (Ben) 2003/04, Ttn debut 2004/05. HSFC 44* Eas v WI (Ben) 2003/04. BBFC 6-66 EasNor v Zim (Ben) 2004/05. BBSS 5-122 Ttn v WPBol (Paarl) 2004/05. HSLO 35 Eas v Nor (Cent) 2005/06. BBLO 4-41 Ttn v Cob (Paarl) 2005/06. BB20 2-17 Ttn v Cob (Cent) 2005/06.

MOSENA Lefa Nelson (FS). B 18/3/87 Bloemfontein. RHB. Ed St Andrew's College (Bfn). FS Schools 2003-05. FC debut FS v Gau (Bfn) 2005/06. HSFC 78 FS v Gau (Jhb) 2005/06. HSLO 70 FS v Eas (Bfn) 2005/06. Rugby (FS Craven Week 2005). Soccer (SA U-16 2003).

MOSTERT Johan Francois (FS). B 14/3/86 Pretoria. LHB OB. Ed Klerksdorp HS, UFS. NW Schools 2003-04. FC debut FS v Nor (Bfn) 2005/06. LO debut 2004/05. HSFC 70 FS v Nor (Pta) 2005/06. BBFC 3-20 FS v GW (Bfn) 2005/06. BBLO 2-10 FS v GW (Bfn) 2005/06.

MOTAUNG William Buti (Lio/Gau). B 29/12/79 Krugersdorp. RHB RMF. Ed Musupatsela HS, Wits Technikon. Gau Schools 1997. FC debut Gau v Eas (Ben) 2003/04, Lio debut 2004/05. HSFC 116 Lio v War (PE) 2004/05. HSLO 52 GNW v Zim (Potch) 2004/05.

MOTSAMAI Tello *Sylvester* (FS). B 21/9/82 Bloemfontein. RHB RFM. Ed Comm-Tech HS. FS Schools 2000-01. FC debut FS v KZN (Dbn) 2003/04. HSFC 51* FS v GW (Kby) 2005/06. BBFC 2-16 FS v Gau (Bfn) 2005/06. HSSS 23 FS v Bol (Bfn) 2003/04. HSLO 18 FS v Eas (Bfn) 2005/06. BBLO 3-54 FS v GW (Kby) 2005/06.

MPITSANG Phenyo *Victor* (Eag). B 28/3/80 Kimberley. RHB RFM. Ed Grey College (Bfn). FS Schools 1996-97, SA Schools 1997(T). FC debut FS v Bdr (EL) 1997/98, Eag debut 2004/05. LOIs: 2 (1998/99-1999/00). BBLOI 2-49 v WI (Bfn) 1998/99. HSFC 23 FS v WP (CT) 2000/01. BBFC 5-24 FS v NW (Bfn) 2000/01. HSLO 20* FS v KZN (Dbn) 1999/00. BBLO 4-22 FS v Bdr (Bfn) 2001/02. BB20 2-24 Eag v War (PE) 2005/06. Tours: SA to NZ 1998/99; Ken 1999/00; SAA to WI 2000/01. SA U-19 v Pak U-19 1996/97; Eng U-19 1997/98; World Cup in SA 1998.

MUNNIK Renier (Cob/WP). B 7/1/78 Cape Town. RHB RFM. Ed Hoerskool Tygerberg. WP Schools 1994-96, SA Schools 1996. FC debut WPB v NtlB (CT) 1997/98, WP debut 1998/99, Cob debut 2005/06. WPBol LO debut 2004/05. HSFC 138 WPB v GWB (Kby) 1998/99. BBFC 4-58 WP v Nor (Cent) 2000/01. HSSS 87 WP v FS (Bfn) 2002/03. HSLO 109 WP v KZN (Chatsworth) 2005/06. BBLO 4-50 WP v Gau (Jhb) 2000/01. HS20 26* WPBol v Ttn (CT) 2004/05. SA U-19 v Pak U-19 1996/97.

MUTCH Robert Grant (Eas). B 3/9/84 Johannesburg. LHB LFM. Ed Sunward HS. FC debut Eas v GW (Kby) 2005/06. HSFC 34* Eas v Gau (Ben) 2005/06. BBFC 4-57 Eas v GW (Kby) 2005/06.

MYBURGH Johannes Gerhardus (Ttn/Nor). B 22/10/80 Pretoria. RHB OB. Ed Pretoria BHS. Nor Schools 1997-98, SA Schools 1997. Brother of SJ Myburgh (Nor 2005/06). FC debut NorB v WPB (Cent) 1997/98, Nor debut 1999/00, Ttn debut 2004/05. HSFC 203 NorB v Eas (Pta) 1997/98, the youngest South African to score a first-class double century at 17 years, 122 days. BBFC 2-45 Nor v FS (Bfn) 2005/06. HSSS 68 Nor v EP (PE) 2000/01. HSLO 95 Nor v Eas (Cent) 2000/01. BBLO 2-27 Nor v KZN (Dbn) 2000/01. HS20 17 Ttn v Cob (Cent) 2005/06. BB20 3-16 Ttn v Chilaw (Leicester) 2005. Tours: SA U-19 to Pak 1998/99; World Cup 2000. SA U-19 v Eng U-19 1997/98; World Cup in SA 1998.

MYBURGH Stephanus Johannes (Nor). B 28/2/84 Pretoria. LHB OB. Ed Pretoria BHS, Tshwane UT. Brother of JG Myburgh (Nor/NorB/Ttn 1997-2005). FC debut Nor v NW (Potch) 2005/06. HSFC 31 Nor v Gau (Jhb) 2005/06. HSLO 90* Nor v GW (Pta) 2005/06.

NAWAB Ahmed (Gau). B 15/6/83 Johannesburg. RHB OB. Ed King Edward VII, Univ of Jhb. FC debut Gau v GW (Kby) 2005/06. HSFC 19 Gau v Nor (Jhb) 2005/06. BBFC 6-106 Gau v Nor (Jhb) 2005/06. BBLO 3-25 Gau v Nor (Pta) 2005/06.

NDLOVU Abraham Lepho (Nor). B 25/2/86 Mamelodi, Pretoria. RHB OB. Ed CBC Pretoria, Pretoria Univ. Nor Schools 2003-04. No FC, Lo debut 2005/06.

NEL Andre (Eas/SA). B 15/7/77 Germiston. RHB RFM. Ed Dr EG Jansen, Boksburg. FC debut Eas v TvlB (Ben) 1996/97, Ttn debut 2004/05. Northamptonshire 2003. Essex 2005. Tests: 23 (2001/02-2006). LOIs: 45 (2000/01-2005/06). HSTest 18* v Aus (Jhb) 2005/06 & 18 v Aus (CT) 2005/06. BBTest 6-32 v WI (Bridgetown) 2004/05. BBLOI 4-39 v Pak (Rawalpindi) 2003-04. HSFC 44 Eas v FS (Ben) 2000/01. BBFC 6-25 Eas v Gau (Jhb) 2001/02. HSLO 21* Eas v Bol (Ben) 2003/04. BBLO 6-27 Eas v GW (Ben) 2000/01. HS20 12 Northamptonshire v Worcestershire (Worcester) 2003. BB20 2-19 Ttn v Lio (Cent) 2003/04 & SA v NZ (Jhb) 2005/06. Tours: SA to Aus 2005/06; Eng 2003; Ind 2005/06; NZ 2003/04; Pak 2003/04; SL 2004, 2006; WI 2000/01, 2004/05; Zim 2001/02; SAA to Aus 2002/03; Zim 2002/03. COY 2004, 2005.

NEL Ruan (EP). B 13/10/84 Springs. LHB SLA. Ed Framesby HS. EP Schools 2002. FC debut EP v WP (PE) 2004/05. HSFC 59 EP v WP (PE) 2004/05. HSLO 64 EP v Bol (Paarl) 2004/05. Rugby (EP U-18 2001).

NGAM Mfuneko (War/Bdr). B 29/1/79 Middledrift. RHB RF. Ed Douglas Mbopha. EP Schools 1996-97, SA Schools 1997 (R). FC debut EPB v NorB (PE) 1997/98, War debut 2005/06, Bdr debut 2005/06. Dol 2004/05. EP 1999/00-2003/04. War Pro20 debut 2004/05. Tests: 3 (2000/01). BBTest 3-26 v SL (CT) 2000/01. HSFC 35 EP v Bol (PE) 2003/04. BBFC 4-25 EPB v GWB (PE) 1998/99. BBSS 4-71 War v Dol (Dbn) 2005/06. BBLO 4-20 SA Pres v Ban (Dbn) 2000/01. BBDLO 4-26 EP v Bol (PE) 2000/01. BB20 2-22 War v Lio (EL) 2004/05. Tours: SAA to WI 2000/01. COY 2001.

NKUNA Francis Gradwell *(Frans)* (Nor). B 3/4/86 Pretoria. RHB RF. Ed Jafta Mahlangu HS. Nor Schools 2002-04, SA Schools 2002-04. FC debut Nor v Bdr (EL) 2004/05. BBFC 4-43 Nor v FS (Pta) 2005/06. BBLO 3-30 Nor v EP (Pta) 2005/06. Tours: SA U-19 to Eng 2003.

NKWE Enoch Thabiso (Lio/Gau). B 8/2/83 Johannesburg. RHB RMF. Ed St Stithian's. Gau Schools 1999-2001. FC debut Gau v Eas (Jhb) 2002/03, scoring 106, Lio debut 2004/05. HSFC 106 Gau v Eas (Jhb) 2002/03. BBFC 5-78 Gau v EP (Jhb) 2002/03. HSLO 87 Gau v NW (Potch) 2005/06. BBLO 4-11 Lio v Ttn (Jhb) 2004/05. HS20 15 Lio v Eag (Bfn) 2003/04.

NOGABE Eugene (FS). B 31/1/81 Bloemfontein. RHB RMF. Ed Kagisho HS. USSASA U-17 Schools 1998, FS Schools 1999. FC debut FS v Gau (Jhb) 2005/06.

NORTHCOTE Nicholas Michael (Bol). B 5/1/81 Cape Town. RHB WK. Ed Fairbairn College, Stell Univ. FC debut Bol v ZimU23 (Stb) 2005/06. HSFC 27* Bol v ZimU23 (Stb) 2005/06.

NTINI Makhaya (War/SA). B 6/7/77 Mdingi. RHB RF. Ed Dale College, EL Technical College. Bdr Schools 1994-95, SA Schools 1995. FC debut Bdr v Eng (EL) 1995/96, War debut 2004/05. Warwickshire 2005. Tests: 69 (1997/98-2006). LOIs: 129 (128 for SA 1997/98-2005/06, 1 for World 2005/06). HSTest 32* v Eng (Leeds) 2003. BBTest 7-37 v WI (Port-of-Spain) 2004/05. HSLOI 42* v NZ (Napier) 2003/04. BBLOI 6-22 v Aus (CT) 2005/06, the best LOI figures for SA. HSFC 34* Bdr v Gau (Jhb) 1999/00 & SA v Ind (Cent) 2001/02. BBFC 7-37 SA v WI (Port-of-Spain) 2004/05. BBSA 6-37 Bdr v FS (Bfn) 2001/02. HSSS 34* Bdr v Gau (Jhb) 1999/00. HSLO 42* SA v NZ (Napier) 2003/04. BBLO 6-22 SA v Aus (CT) 2005/06. BBDLO 5-38 Bdr v NW (Foch) 1997/98. BB20 2-26 EC v Eag (EL) 2003/04. Tours: SA to Aus 1997/98, 2000, 2001/02, 2005/06; Ban 2002/03; Eng 1998, 2003, 2004; Ind 2004/05, 2005/06; NZ 2003/04; Pak 2003/04; SL 2000, 2002/03, 2004, 2006; WI 2000/01, 2004/05; Zim 2001/02; Ken 2000/01; Mor 2002; Shar 1999/00; Sing 2000; World Cup 2003; SA U-19 to Eng 1995; Ind 1995/96. COY 2001, 2003, 2004, 2005, 2006.

NYAWO Ephrahim (Eas). B 4/4/83 Springs. RHB RM. Ed Tlakula, Esibonelwesihle HS. Eas Schools 2001. FC debut Eas v Gau (Jhb) 2005/06. HSFC 31 Eas v Gau (Jhb) 2005/06. HSLO 11 Eas v Nor (Cent) 2005/06.

O'CONNOR Sean Patrick (Eas). B 21/1/77 Johannesburg. RHB RM. Ed CBC Boksburg, UNISA. Eas Schools 1993-95, (C) in 1994. Son of AG O'Connor (FC Umpire). FC debut Eas v WPB (Ben) 1997/98. HSFC 41 Eas v NW (Potch) 2005/06. BBFC 4-61 Eas v Gau (Jhb) 2005/06. HSLO 31* Eas v Gau (Ben) 2004/05. BBLO 4-36 Eas v GW (Kby) 2005/06.

OLIVIER Aidan William (Bol). B 21/10/84 Stellenbosch. LHB OB WK. Ed Luckhoff SS. FC debut Bol v Bdr (Paarl) 2005/06. HSFC 10 Bol v Bdr (Paarl) 2005/06.

OLIVIER Mario Wicus (Bdr/War). B 3/11/82 Pretoria. RHB RFM. Ed HTS John Vorster, Brackenfell HS. WP Schools 2001. FC debut Bol v WP (CT) 2004/05, War debut 2005/06, Bdr debut 2005/06. Bol 2004/05. HSFC 16 Bol v GW (Kby) 2004/05. BBFC 4-68 Bdr v EP (EL) 2005/06. HSSS 12 War v Dol (EL) 2005/06. BBSS 4-71 War v Cob (PE) 2005/06. HSLO 14* War v Eag (EL) 2005/06. BBLO 5-40 Bol v WP (CT) 2004/05.

OMAR Ahmed Mahomed (Gau). B 7/5/77 Johannesburg. RHB WK. Ed Topaz SS. Tvl Schools 1994, SA Schools 1994. FC debut TvlB v NTB (Jhb) 1995/96, Gau debut 2003/04, Lio debut 2004/05. HSFC 50 Lio v Eag (Bfn) 2004/05. HSLO 13* Gau v WP (Jhb) 2003/04. Tours: SA U-19 to Eng 1995.

ONTONG Justin Lee (Lio/SA/SAA/Afr/Rest). B 4/1/80 Paarl. RHB OB/LB. Ed Paarl Gymnasium. Bol Schools 1996-97. FC debut Bol v Ntl (Paarl) 1997/98, Lio debut 2004/05. Bol 1997/98-2003/04. Tests: 2 (2001/02-2004/05). LOIs: 21 (20 for SA 2000/01-2005/06; 1 for Africa 2005/06). HSTest 32 v Aus (Sydney) 2001/02. HSLOI 32 v Zim (Harare) 2001/02. BBLOI 3-30 v Ken (Colombo-RPS) 2002/03. HSFC 166 Bol v EP (PE) 2003/04. BBFC 4-66 Bol v Bdr (Paarl) 2002/03. HSLO 84 Bol v Gau (Paarl) 2002/03. BBLO 3-29 Bol v Gau (Paarl) 2002/03. HS20 30 Lio v WPBol (CT) 2003/04. Tours: SA to Aus 2001/02; Ind 2004/05, 2005/06; SL 2002/03; WI 2000/01, 2004/05; Zim 2001/02; Mor 2002; SAA to Aus 2002/03; SL 2005/06; WI 2000/01; Zim 2002/03; SA U-19 to Pak 1998/99.

OOSTHUIZEN Marius (Eas). B 21/10/79 Empangeni. RHB RMF. Ed Jan de Klerk. No FC, LO debut 2005/06.

OTTO Johannes *Marthinus* (Gau). B 4/9/80 Pretoria. RHB RM. Ed Randburg Hoerskool, RAU. Gau Schools 1997-98. FC debut Gau v KZN (Jhb) 2000/01. Lio LO 2004/05. HSFC 143 Gau v Bol (Paarl) 2001/02. HSLO 124 Gau v Nor (Jhb) 2004/05. BBLO 2-43 Gau v Nor (Jhb) 2004/05. HS20 31 Lio v WPBol (Jhb) 2004/05.

PALEKER Allahudien (Nor). B 1/1/78 Cape Town. RHB OB WK. Ed Cravenby SS, UWC. FC debut WPB v EPB (Bellville) 1997/98, Nor debut 2000/01. WPB 1997/98. HSFC 70* Nor v Eas (Cent) 2004/05. HSSS 38* Nor v Eas (Cent) 2000/01. HSLO 51 Nor v Eas (Cent) 2004/05.

PANGABANTU Yanda *(Lucky)* (Bdr). B 8/4/81 King William's Town. RHB RFM. Ed Mzontsundu HS, Bdr Tech. FC debut Bdr v ZimU23 (EL) 2005/06. LO debut 2004/05. BBFC 3-24 Bdr v EP (EL) 2005/06. BBLO 3-33 Bdr v WP (CT) 2005/06.

PAULSE Hillroy Henrico (Bol). B 6/9/85 Paarl. RHB RF. Ed New Orleans SS, Paarl. Bol Schools 2003-04, SA Schools 2004. FC debut Bol v WP (CT) 2004/05. BBFC 5-65 Bol v WP (Paarl) 2005/06. BBLO 2-16 Bol v Bdr (EL) 2005/06.

PERRY Garret Dwayne (FS). B 14/7/80 Virginia. RHB OB. Ed Virginia Volkskool, Hentie Cilliers HS, UFS. FC debut FS v Eas (Bfn) 2005/06. Rugby (FS Craven Week 1997-98).

PETERSEN Alviro Nathan (Ttn/Lio/Nor/Rest). B 25/11/80 Port Elizabeth. RHB RM. Ed Gelvandale HS, Otto du Plessis HS, Eastern Cape Training College. FC debut Nor v WP (Cent) 2000/01, Lio debut 2005/06. Nor 2000/01-2005/06. Ttn 2004/05-2005/06. HSFC 150* Nor v NW (Cent) 2002/03. BBFC 2-7 Nor v Eas (Ben) 2001/02. HSLO 115* Ttn v Eag (Cent) 2004/05. HS20 78* Ttn v War (Cent) 2004/05.

PETERSON Robin John (War/SA/SAA/Rest). B 4/8/79 Port Elizabeth. LHB SLA. Ed Alexander Road HS, UPE. EP Schools 1996-97, SA Schools 1996 (T)-97. FC debut EPB v NW (Foch) 1998/99, EP same season, War debut 2004/05. Tests: 5 (2002/03-2004/05). LOIs: 26 (2002/03-2005/06). HSTest 61 v Ban (Dhaka) 2002/03. BBTest 3-46 v Ban (Dhaka)

2002/03. HSLOI 36 v WI (Cent) 2003/04. BBLOI 2-26 v Pak (Faisalabad) 2003/04. HSFC 130 EP v Gau (Jhb) 2002/03. BBFC 6-67 EP v Bdr (EL) 1999/00. HSLO 101 EP v Bdr (PE) 2001/02. BBLO 6-16 EP v Nam (PE) 2002/03. HS20 42 EC v Eag (EL) 2003/04. BB20 2-21 War v Dol (PE) 2004/05. Tours: SA to Ban 2002/03; Eng 2003, 2004; Ind 2004/05, 2005/06; NZ 2003/04; Pak 2003/04; SL 2002/03, 2004, 2006; SAA to SL 2005/06; WI 2000/01; World Cup 2003. SA U-19 v Pak U-19 1996/97; Eng U-19 1997/98; World Cup in SA 1998.

PETHU Moses Xolani (Bdr). B 23/1/84 East London. RHB OB. Ed Hudson Park HS, Walter Sisulu Univ. Bdr Schools 2000-02. FC debut Bdr v KZN (Dbn) 2005/06. HSFC 15 Bdr v WP (EL) 2005/06.

PHANGISO Aaron Mpho (Ttn/Nor). B 21/1/84 Garankuwa. RHB SLA. Ed CBC Pretoria. Nor Schools 2002, SA Schools 2002. FC debut Nor v Gau (Jhb) 2004/05, Ttn debut 2005/06. HSFC 63 Nor v GW (Kby) 2005/06. BBFC 5-76 Nor v Gau (Jhb) 2005/06. HSSS 18 Ttn v Dol (Cent) 2005/06. HSLO 21 Ttn v Dol (Pmb) 2005/06. BBLO 2-18 Nor v FS (Pta) 2005/06. BB20 2-16 Ttn v Eag (Bfn) 2005/06. Tours: SA U-19 to Eng 2003.

PHILANDER Vernon Darryl (Cob/WP). B 24/6/85 Bellville. RHB RMF. Ed Ravensmead SS. WP Schools 2001-03, SA Schools 2002-03. FC debut WP v KZN (CT) 2003/04, WPBol debut 2004/05. HSFC 168 WP v GW (Kby) 2004/05. BBFC 5-49 Cob v Ttn (CT) 2005/06. HSSS 69 WPBol v Ttn (Paarl) 2004/05. HSLO 33* Cob v Dol (Dbn) 2005/06. BBLO 3-49 WP v GW (Kby) 2004/05. HS20 40 WPBol v Dol (Dbn) 2004/05. BB20 2-17 Cob v War (EL) 2005/06. Tours: SA U-19 to Eng 2003; World Cup 2004.

PIETERSEN Ruan (GW). B 10/2/88 Kimberley. RHB LFM. Ed Northern Cape HS. GW Schools 2004-05, SA Schools 2005. Brother of C Pietersen (GW/Northants 2001-2006). FC debut GW v NW (Potch) 2005/06. BBFC 6-73 GW v Eas (Kby) 2005/06. BBLO 3-51 GW v FS (Bfn) 2005/06.

PILLAY Tyron Duncan (Dol/KZN). B 18/11/84 Durban. RHB LB. Ed Stanger SS. KZN Schools 2002. FC debut KZN v Eas (Ben) 2004/05, Dol same season. Pro20 debut 2003/04. HSFC 32 KZN v Bdr (EL) 2005/06. BBFC 5-45 KZN v ZimU23 (Chatsworth) 2005/06. BBSS 2-43 Dol v WPBol (CT) 2004/05. HSLO 14* KZN v Eas (Ben) 2004/05. BBLO 3-30 KZN v ZimU23 (Chatsworth) 2005/06. BB20 2-33 Dol v EC (Dbn) 2003/04.

PLAATJIE Tsherolo *Revelation* (GW). B 11/6/82 Kimberley. RHB RF. Ed Louis Botha HS. FC debut GW v NW (Potch) 2004/05. HSFC 25 GW v FS (Bfn) 2005/06. BBFC 2-39 GW v FS (Kby) 2005/06. BBLO 2-23 GW v Eas (Ben) 2005/06.

POLLOCK Shaun Maclean (SA/Afr) B 16/7/73 Port Elizabeth. RHB RFM. Ed Northwood HS, Ntl Univ (Dbn). Ntl Schools 1991, SA Schools 1991. Son of PM Pollock (EP/SA 1958-1971), nephew of RG Pollock (EP/Tvl/SA 1960-1986), cousin of AG Pollock (Tvl/TvlB/Eas 1991-1997) and GA Pollock (Tvl/TvlB/NorB/Eas 1991-2000). FC debut NtlB v WPB (Pmb) 1991/92, Ntl debut 1992/93, Dol debut 2004/05. Warwickshire 1996 and 2002. Tests: 102 (1995/96-2006, 26 as capt). LOIs: 259 (253 for SA 1995/96-2005/06, 92 as capt; 3 for Africa 2005/06, 2 as capt; 3 for World 2005/06, 3 as capt). HSTest 111 v SL (Cent) 2000/01. BBTest 7-87 v Aus (Adelaide) 1997/98. HSLOI 75 v Zim (Jhb) 1996/97. BBLOI 6-35 v WI (EL) 1998/99. HSFC 150* Warwickshire v Glamorgan (Birmingham) 1996. BBFC 7-33 Ntl v Bdr (EL) 1995/96. HSSA 113* SA v Ind (Cent) 2001/02. HSSS 92 KZN v Gau (Jhb) 1998/99. HSLO 134* KZN v EP (Dbn) 2003/04. BBLO 6-21 Warwickshire v Leicestershire (Birmingham) 1996. BBDLO 3-20 KZN v GW (Kby) 2003/04. HS20 59 Dol v Ttn (Ben) 2004/05. BB20 2-10 Dol v WPBol (CT) 2003/04. Tours: SA to Aus 1997/98, 2000 (capt), 2001/02 (capt), 2005/06; Ban 2002/03; Eng 1998, 2003, 2004; Ind 1999/00, 2004/05, 2005/06; NZ 1998/99, 2003/04; Pak 1997/98, 2003/04; SL 2000 (capt), 2002/03 (capt), 2004, 2006; WI 2000/01 (capt), 2004/05; Zim 1999/00, 2001/02 (capt); Ken 1999/00, 2000/01 (capt); Mor 2002 (capt); Shar 1995/96, 1999/00; Sing 2000 (capt); World Cup 1996, 1999, 2003 (capt); SA U-24 to SL 1995/96. COY 1996, 1998, 2001, 2003. Wisden 2003.

POPE Steven Charles (War/Bdr). B 15/11/72 East London. RHB LB Occ WK. Ed Queen's College, Dale College, St Andrew's College (Gtn), UPE. Bdr Schools 1989-90, EP Schools 1991. Son of CWS Pope (Bdr 1966-1978), nephew of KS McEwan (EP/Ess/WP/ WAus/Bdr/SA 1971-1991), cousin of ACR Birch (EP 2004/05). FC debut EP v OFS (Bfn) 1992/93, Bdr debut 1995/96, War debut 2004/05. EP 1992/93-1994/95, EPB 1993/94-1994/95. HSFC 156* War v Eag (EL) 2004/05. BBFC 7-62 Bdr v FS (EL) 1995/96. HSLO 98* Bdr v Nor (EL) 2001/02. BBLO 4-38 Bdr v NZ (Alice) 2000/01. BBDLO 2-25 Bdr v KZN (Dbn) 2001/02. HS20 34 EC v WPBol (CT) 2003/04.

POTGIETER Etienne (EP). B 9/6/82 Ladysmith. RHB LB. Ed PE Tech. FC debut EP v GW (PE) 2004/05. HSFC 73 EP v NW (Potch) 2004/05. HSLO 31 EP v WP (PE) 2005/06.

PRETORIUS Dewald (GW). B 6/12/77 Pretoria. RHB RF. Ed Hoerskool Dr Viljoen. FS Schools 1996-97. FC debut FS v Pak (Bfn) 1997/98, GW debut 2005/06. FS 1997/98-2003/04. Durham 2003. Warwickshire 2004-2005.Tests: 4 (2001/02-2003). BBTest 4-115 v Eng (Birmingham) 2003. HSFC 43 FS v WP (Bfn) 1998/99. BBFC 6-49 SAA v IndA (Bfn) 2001/02. BBSS 5-24 FS v Gau (Jhb) 2001/02. BBLO 5-32 Warwickshire v Kent (Canterbury) 2005. BBDLO 4-39 FS v GW (Kby) 1999/00. HS20 22 Warwickshire v Worcestershire (Worcester) 2005. BB20 2-22 Warwickshire v Glamorgan (Swansea) 2005. Tours: SA to Eng 2003; SAA to Aus 2002/03.

PRICE Michael Lynn (EP). B 6/10/81 Grahamstown. RHB OB. Ed St Andrew's College (Gtn), UPE. Son of DL Price (Bdr 1964/65), nephew of JMG Price (Bdr 1955-1965), brother of JD Price (BdrB 1994/95). FC debut EP v GW (PE) 2001/02. HSFC 97 EP v GW (PE) 2004/05. HSSS 52 EP v GW (PE) 2001/02. HSLO 69 EP v ZimU23 (PE) 2005/06. BBLO 3-25 EP v WP (PE) 2004/05. Tours: SA U-19 to NZ 2000/01. Tennis (EP).

PRINCE Ashwell Gavin (Cob/SA/Afr). B 28/5/77 Port Elizabeth. LHB OB. Ed St Thomas SS, UPE. FC debut EPB v GW (PE) 1995/96, WP debut 1997/98, WPBol debut 2004/05. EP 1995/96-1996/97, EPB 1995/96-1997/98. Tests: 23 (2001/02-2006, 2 as capt). LOIs: 37 (34 for SA 2002/03-2005/06; 3 for Africa 2005/06). HSTest 139* v Zim (Cent) 2004/05. HSLOI 89* v WI (Port-of-Spain) 2004/05. HSFC 184 WPBol v Lio (Paarl) 2004/05. HSLO 89* SA v WI (Port-of-Spain) 2004/05.

HSDLO 77 WPBol v Eag (Bfn) 2004/05. HS20 37 WPBol v Dol (CT) 2003/04. Tours: SA to Aus 2005/06; Ind 2005/06; NZ 2003/04; SL 2006 (capt); WI 2004/05; SAA to Aus 2002/03; SL 1998/99; WI 2000/01; Zim 2002/03, 2004 (capt); SA U-19 to Eng 1995; Ind 1995/96. COY 2006.

PRINSLOO Clifford (Bol). B 12/12/84 Pretoria. RHB OB. Ed Waterkloof HS, Stell Univ. FC debut Bol v GW (Kby) 2004/05. HSFC 50 Bol v GW (Kby) 2004/05. HSLO 100 Bol v WP (CT) 2004/05.

PUTTICK Andrew George (Cob/SA/SAA). B 11/12/80 Cape Town. LHB WK. Ed Rondebosch BHS. WP Schools 1996-98, SA Schools 1998 (T). FC debut WP v EP (PE) 2000/01, WPBol debut 2004/05. LO debut 1999/00. LOIs: 1 (2005/06). HSFC 250* WP v GW (CT) 2003/04. HSLO 143 SAA v SLU23 (Colombo-PP) 2005/06. HSDLO 113* WP v EP (CT) 2002/03. HS20 86 WPBol v Dol (Dbn) 2004/05. Tours: SA to SL 2004; SAA to SL 2005/06; SA U-19 to Pak 1998/99; World Cup 2000. SA U-19 v Eng U-19 1997/98.

RANGER Murray Neil (War/Bdr). B 18/4/84 Stutterheim. RHB RM. Ed Dale College, Rhodes/Fort Hare Univ. Bdr Schools 2002. Son of RBC Ranger (Bdr 1976-1985). FC debut Bdr v FS (Bfn) 2004/05. War Pro20 debut 2005/06. HSFC 96 Bdr v EP (EL) 2005/06. BBFC 6-30 Bdr v Bol (EL) 2005/06. HSLO 56* Bdr v Bol (EL) 2005/06. BBLO 4-42 Bdr v Bol (EL) 2005/06.

RAZAK Abdul Hack (Dol). B 14/1/87 Durban. RHB LB. Ed Durban HS, UKZN (Westville). KZN Schools 2004. FC debut Dol v Ttn (Cent) 2005/06. Tours: SA U-19 to India 2005/06.

REDDY Brendon Leigh (Ttn/Eas). B 6/11/83 Durban. RHB RFM. Ed Springs BHS, Veritus College (Springs). Eas Schools 1999-2002, SA Schools 2002. FC debut Eas v Nor (Cent) 2000/01, Ttn debut 2005/06. Ttn Pro20 2003/04. HSFC 109 Eas v GW (Ben) 2001/02. BBFC 5-39 Eas v Nor (Cent) 2003/04. HSLO 28 Eas v GW (Kby) 2001/02. BBLO 3-10 Eas v KZN (Dbn) 2003/04. HS20 10 Ttn v Lio (Cent) 2003/04 BB20 3-27 Ttn v Eag (Bfn) 2003/04. Tours: SA U-19 to World Cup 2002.

REDDY Ravi (KZN). B 4/10/82 Durban. RHB OB. Ed Dr AD Lazarus, UKZN (Dbn). FC debut KZN v Bol (Chatsworth) 2005/06. HSFC 10 KZN v Bol (Chatsworth) 2005/06. BBFC 3-32 KZN v EP (PE) 2005/06.

REEVES Ryan Ashley (FS). B 16/6/83 Durban. RHB RFM. Ed Michaelhouse, Central UT. Nephew of AD Hall (NtlB/GW 1985-1989). FC debut FS v Eas (Ben) 2005/06. HSFC 41 FS v Gau (Jhb) 2005/06. BBFC 2-25 FS v Eas (Ben) 2005/06. HSLO 34 FS v Eas (Ben) 2005/06

RICHARDS Rowan Ronaldo (Bdr/War). B 8/7/84 East London. LHB LFM. Ed John Bisseker SS. FC debut Bdr v EP (PE) 2005/06, War same season. HSFC 12 Bdr v WP (CT) 2005/06. BBFC 5-30 Bdr v EP (PE) 2005/06. BBLO 3-13 Bdr v WP (CT) 2005/06.

RICHARDSON Mathew Frank (Bdr). B 6/9/85 Port Elizabeth. RHB RMF. Ed Rondebosch BHS, Rhodes Univ. No FC, LO debut 2005/06. HSLO 69 Bdr v WP (EL) 2005/06.

RUDOLPH Jacobus Andries (Jacques) (Eag/SA/SAA/Afr). B 4/5/81 Springs. LHB LBG. Ed Afrikaanse Hoer Seunskool. Nor Schools 1996-99(C), SA Schools 1997-99(C). FC debut NorB v WPB (Cent) 1997/98, Eag debut 2005/06. Nor 1999/00-2003/04, Nor B 1997/98-1998/99. Ttn 2004/05. Tests: 35 (2002/03-2006). LOIs: 45 (43 for SA 2002/03-2005/06; 2 for Africa 2005/06). HSTest 222* v Ban (Chittagong) 2002/03, on debut. HSLOI 81 v Ban (Dhaka) 2002/03. HSFC 222* SA v Ban (Chittagong) 2002/03. HSSA 164 Nor v EP (Cent) 2001/02. BBFC 5-87 NorB v GWB (Cent) 1998/99. BBSS 2-13 Nor v EP (PE) 2000/01. HSLO 134* SAA v Ken (Laudium) 2001/02. BBLO 4-40 SAA v NZA (Colombo-RPS) 2005/06. HSDLO 133 Nor v NW (Cent) 2003/04. HS20 71 Ttn v WPBol (Cent) 2003/04. Tours: SA to Aus 2001/02, 2005/06; Ban 2002/03; Eng 2003, 2004; Ind 2004/05; NZ 2003/04; Pak 2003/04; SL 2004, 2006; WI 2004/05; SAA to SL 2005/06 (capt); Zim 2002/03; SA U-19 to Pak 1998/99; World Cup 2000. SA U-19 v Eng U-19 1997/98; World Cup in SA 1998. COY 2003.

SAMSON Quinton Godfrey (FS). B 28/12/84 Bloemfontein. RHB LMF. Ed HTS Louis Botha, UFS. FS Schools 2002. FC debut FS v Bdr (Bfn) 2004/05. HSFC 10 FS v Gau (Jhb) 2005/06. BBFC 3-31 FS v NW (Bfn) 2005/06. BBLO 4-25 FS v Nor (Pta) 2005/06. Athletics (FS 2002).

SANDERS Mark David (KZN). B 10/7/79 Durban. RHB LB. Ed Kloof HS, UNISA. FC debut KZNB v NorB (Dbn) 1998/99. KZN 2002/03 and 2004/05-2005/06, KZNB 1998/99. Bol 2003/04. HSFC 103 KZN v Bdr (Dbn) 2005/06. HSSS 87 Bol v EP (Paarl) 2003/04. HSLO 53 KZN v Bol (Chatsworth) 2005/06.

SANDI Unathi (EP). B 26/3/80 Port Elizabeth. RHB RFM. Ed Newell HS. Cousin of L Masikazana (EP/EPB 1993-1999). FC debut EP v Bdr (PE) 2005/06.

SANDRI Pepler Sacto Emiliano (Bol). B 14/1/83 Cape Town. RHB RMF. Ed Paarl BHS, Stell Univ. Bol Schools 2001. FC debut Bol v Eas (Ben) 2003/04. HSFC 17* Bol v KZN (Chatsworth) 2005/06 & Bol v WP (Paarl) 2005/06. BBFC 5-32 Bol v EP (Paarl) 2005/06. BBSS 2-100 Bol v EP (Paarl) 2003/04. BBLO 2-27 Bol v ZimU23 (Stb) 2005/06.

SCHULTZ Ashley John (FS). B 24/12/85 Bloemfontein. RHB RMF. Ed Dr Blok SS, Central UT. FS Schools 2002-03. FC debut FS v Eas (Bfn) 2004/05. BBFC 5-51 FS v Gau (Bfn) 2005/06.

SEKHOTO Mpho Remofiloe (Lio/Gau). B 2/3/82 Johannesburg. RHB. Ed King Edward VII. FC debut Eas v EP (Ben) 2001/02, Lio debut 2005/06, Gau debut 2005/06. Eas 2001/02-2002/03. HSFC 81 SAAc v SLA (Potch) 2003/04. BBFC 2-42 Gau v Nor (Pta) 2005/06. HSSS 63* Eas v Nor (Ben) 2001/02. HSLO 26* Gau v Nor (Pta) 2005/06.

SEKONYANE Bennett Kagisho (FS). B 11/10/82 Kimberley. RHB RF. Ed Northern Cape HS. GW Schools 1998-2000. FC debut Bdr v FS (Bfn) 2004/05, FS debut 2005/06. Bdr 2004/05. Bdr LO debut 2002/03. HSFC 24* Bdr v KZN (EL) 2004/05. BBFC 4-45 Bdr v Eas (Ben) 2004/05. HSLO 16* Bdr v FS (Bfn) 2004/05. BBLO 4-38 FS v NW (Potch) 2005/06.

SELOWA Phillimon *Mpho* (KZN). B 3/8/86 Pretoria. LHB WK. Ed St Alban's, CBC Pretoria. Nor Schools 2004. FC debut KZN v Bdr (Dbn) 2005/06. HSFC 19 KZN v Bol (Paarl) 2005/06. HSLO 27 KZN v WP (CT) 2005/06. Hockey (SA U-18 2004).

SEPTEMBER Waylain Edwin (Bol). B 20/9/84 Paarl. RHB SLA. Ed New Orleans SS, Paarl. Bol Schools 2001-03, SA Schools 2002(T)-03. FC debut Bol v EP (Paarl) 2003/04. HSFC 63* Bol v WP (Paarl) 2005/06. BBFC 3-35 Bol v Bdr (Paarl) 2005/06. BBSS 3-113 Bol v EP (Paarl) 2003/04. HSLO 48 Bol v Gau (Paarl) 2005/06. BBLO 3-44 Bol v EP (Paarl) 2005/06. Tours: SA U-19 to World Cup 2004.

SERAME Nkululeko Molale *(Mafinki)* (NW). B 26/1/87 Klerksdorp. RHB OB. Ed Milner HS. NW Schools 2003-05, SA Schools 2004(T)-05. No FC, LO debut 2005/06. Tours: SA U-19 to World Cup 2006.

SEYMORE Andre Johan (Ttn/Eas). B 16/2/75 Rustenburg. RHB. Ed Hendrik Verwoerd HS, UNISA. NT Schools 1991-93, SA Schools 1992-93. FC debut NT v Barbados (Vbg) 1993/94, Ttn debut 2005/06, Eas debut 2000/01. NT 1993/94-1996/97, NTB 1994/95. Gau 1997/98-2000/01. HSFC 174 Eas v Nor (Cent) 2000/01. HSLO 101 NT v FS (Bfn) 1996/97.

SIBANDE Sipho Reginald (FS). B 6/4/82 Virginia. RHB OB. Ed Welkom HS, FS Tech. FS Schools 1999-2000. FC debut FS v WP (Bfn) 2002/03. HSFC 69 FS v KZN (Dbn) 2004/05.

SIMPSON Lucian Frederick (WP). B 20/5/80 Somerset West. RHB LF. Ed Gordon HS, Peninsula Tech. FC debut WP v KZN (Chatsworth) 2005/06. BBFC 3-22 WP v KZN (Chatsworth) 2005/06. BBLO 2-34 WP v KZN (Chatsworth) 2005/06.

SINGH Yadene (Lio/Gau). B 25/5/80 Durban. RHB RMF. Ed Effingham SS, London Guildhall Univ. FC debut KZN v Bdr (Dbn) 2003/04, Lio debut 2005/06, Gau debut 2005/06. KZN 2003/04-2004/05. KZN LO debut 2002/03. HSFC 17* Lio v War (EL) 2005/06. BBFC 4-82 KZN v FS (Dbn) 2004/05. BBSS 2-30 Lio v War (EL) 2005/06. BBLO 2-28 KZN v FS (Dbn) 2004/05. BB20 2-13 Lio v War (Jhb) 2005/06.

SLWANA Mpumelelo (EP). B 20/12/85 Port Elizabeth. RHB WK. Ed Grey HS (PE), PE Tech. EP Schools 2002-03, SA Schools 2003. FC debut EP v WP (PE) 2004/05. HSFC 37 EP v WP (PE) 2004/05. HSLO 24* EP v WP (CT) 2005/06. Tours: SA U-19 to World Cup 2004. Hockey (EP U-21 2004).

SMIT Daryn (Dol). B 28/1/84 Durban. RHB WK. Ed Northwood HS. KZN Schools 2001. FC debut KZN v Eas (Ben) 2004/05, Dol debut 2005/06. Pro20 debut 2003/04. HSFC 35 Dol v War (Dbn) 2005/06. HSLO 43* KZN v Nor (Dbn) 2004/05. Tours: SA U-19 to Eng 2003.

SMIT Kyle (Dol/KZN). B 22/9/81 Durban. RHB RM. Ed Kingsway. FC debut KZN v Bdr (EL) 2004/05, Dol debut 2005/06. Dol Pro20 debut 2004/05. HSFC 144 Dol v War (EL) 2005/06. HSLO 75 KZN v ZimU23 (Chatsworth) 2005/06. HS20 76 Dol v Eag (Dbn) 2005/06.

SMIT Willem Johannes (*Wiaan*) (Bol). B 1/8/74 Calvinia. RHB RM. Ed Paarl Gymnasium, Stell Univ. Bol Schools 1990-92(C). FC debut Bol v Tvl (Jhb) 1994/95. Bol 1994/95 and 2001/02-2004/05 (and LO 2005/06). BolB 1994/95-1995/96. FS 1997/98-2000/01. WPBol Pro20 2004/05. HSFC 104 Bol v Gau (Randjesfontein) 2003/04. HSLO 113 Bol v FS (Paarl) 2004/05. BBLO 2-35 FS v Eas (Bfn) 1998/99. HS20 21 WPBol v Ttn (CT) 2004/05.

SMITH Graeme Craig (SA). B 1/2/81 Johannesburg. LHB OB. Ed King Edward VII. Gau Schools 1998-99(C), SA Schools 1998-99. FC debut UCB Inv v GW (Kby) 1999/00, scoring 187, the second highest score on first-class debut by a South African, WP debut 2000/01, WPBol debut 2004/05. Gau LO 1999/00. Somerset 2005. Tests: 48 (47 for SA 2001/02-2005/06, 39 as capt, 1 for World 2005/06 as capt). LOIs: 91 (90 for SA 2001/02-2005/06, 68 as capt; 1 for Africa as capt). HSTest 277 v Eng (Birmingham) 2003, the highest Test score for SA. BBTest 2-145 v WI (St John's) 2004/05. HSLOI 134* v Ind (Kolkata) 2005/06. BBLOI 3-30 v SL (Perth) 2005/06. HSFC 311 Somerset v Leicestershire (Taunton) 2005. HSSA 200 SA v Ban (EL) 2002/03 & WPBol v Lio (Jhb) 2004/05. HSLO 134* SA v Ind (Kolkata) 2005/06. BBLO 3-30 SA v SL (Perth) 2005/06. HSDLO 117* WP v NW (CT) 2001/02. BBDLO 3-35 WP v FS (Bfn) 2001/02. HS20 105 Somerset v Northamptonshire (Taunton) 2005. BB20 3-23 WPBol v Lio (CT) 2003/04. Tours: SA to Aus 2005/06 (capt); Ban 2002/03 (capt); Eng 2003 (capt), 2004 (capt); Ind 2004/05 (capt), 2005/06 (capt); NZ 2003/04 (capt); Pak 2003/04 (capt); SL 2002/03, 2004 (capt); WI 2004/05 (capt); Mor 2002; World Cup 2003; SAA to WI 2000/01; Zim 2002/03 (capt); SA U-19 to World Cup 2000. COY 2002, 2003. Wisden 2004.

SMITH Michael Bruce Argo (War/Bdr). B 5/5/80 King William's Town. RHB OB. Ed Dale College, Selborne College. Bdr Schools 1998. FC debut Bdr v Nor (Cent) 2003/04, War debut 2005/06. HSFC 70 Bdr v FS (Bfn) 2004/05. HSSS 39 War v Ttn (EL) 2005/06. HSLO 64 Bdr v Bol (EL) 2005/06. HS20 49 War v Cob (EL) 2005/06.

SNIJMAN Blake Douglas (Lio/Gau). B 28/10/85 Krugersdorp. RHB RM. Ed King Edward VII, Wits Univ. Gau Schools 2002-03, SA Schools 2003. FC debut Gau v Eas (Ben) 2003/04, Lio debut 2005/06. HSFC 114 Gau v Eas (Ben) 2005/06. BBFC 4-26 Gau v NW (Jhb) 2005/06. HSSS 64 Gau v Eas (Ben) 2003/04. HSLO 97 GNW v Zim (Potch) 2004/05. BBLO 2-22 Gau v GW (Kby) 2005/06.

SODUMO Abongile Mzimkhulu (War/Bdr). B 16/6/82 King William's Town. RHB WK. Ed Dale College. Bdr Schools 2000. FC debut Bdr v GW (EL) 2002/03, War debut 2004/05. HSFC 77* War v Ttn (EL) 2005/06. HSLO 11 Bdr v KZN (EL) 2004/05. HS20 12 War v Eag (PE) 2004/05.

STEVENS Godfrey Cyril (Bol). B 24/6/86 Porterville. LHB SLA. Ed New Orleans SS, Paarl. Bol Schools 2003-04. FC debut Bol v WP (CT) 2005/06. HSFC 18 Bol v EP (PE) 2005/06. BBFC 2-22 Bol v EP (PE) 2005/06. HSLO 43 Bol v WP (CT) 2005/06. BBLO 3-18 Bol v Bdr (Paarl) 2005/06. Tours: SA U-19 to World Cup 2004.

STEYN Dale Willem (Ttn/Nor/SA/SAA/Afr). B 27/6/83 Phalaborwa. RHB RF. Ed Merensky HS. Northern Prov Schools 2000-2001. FC debut Nor v WP (Cent) 2003/04, Ttn debut 2004/05. Essex 2005. Tests: 8 (2004/05-2006). LOIs: 4 (2 for SA 2005/06; 2 for Africa 2005/06). HSTest 13 v NZ (Cent) 2005/06 & v NZ (CT) 2005/06. BBTest 5-47 v NZ (Cent) 2005/06. HSFC 82 Essex v Durham (Chester-le-Street) 2005. BBFC 5-27 Ttn v War (Ben) 2005/06. HSSA 34 Ttn v Cob (Ben) 2005/06. BBLO 5-20 SAA v SLA (Colombo-RPS) 2005/06. BBDLO 3-19 Ttn v Eag (Bfn) 2005/06. BB20 2-10 Ttn v WPBol (CT) 2004/05. Tours: SA to Aus 2005/06; SL 2006; SAA to SL 2005/06. COY 2006.

STEYN Frederik Adriaan *(Driaan)* (Lio/NW). B 15/1/82 Klerksdorp. RHB Occ WK. Ed Klerksdorp HS, Potch Univ. NW Schools 2000, SACD Schools 2001. FC debut NW v GW (Potch) 2004/05, Lio debut 2005/06. HSFC 116 NW v Eas (Potch) 2005/06. HSLO 137 NW v Gau (Potch) 2005/06.

STROH Richard Allan (NW). B 2/3/81 Johannesburg. RHB RF. Ed Potchefstroom BHS, Potch Univ. FC debut NW v GW (Potch) 2004/05, LO debut 2003/04. HSFC 91 NW v Bol (Paarl) 2004/05. BBFC 6-84 NW v GW (Potch) 2004/05. HSLO 89 NW v Bol (Paarl) 2004/05. BBLO 2-16 NW v Gau (Jhb) 2005/06. Hockey (NW 2000-04).

STRYDOM Heinrich Marthinus (NW). B 9/8/82 Pretoria. RHB. Ed Potchefstroom Gimnasium, NW Univ. FC debut NW v Eas (Ben) 2005/06. HSFC 17 NW v Eas (Ben) 2005/06.

STRYDOM Johannes *Gerhardus* (Cob/Bol). B 6/9/79 Cape Town. LHB RM. Ed Paul Roos Gymnasium. Bol Schools 1995-97. FC debut Bol v WP (CT) 2000/01, WPBol debut 2004/05. LO debut 1999/00. HSFC 151 Bol v Eas (Paarl) 2003/04. HSLO 135* Bol v WP (Paarl) 2001/02.

SUMMERS Shane Pervus (Bol). B 9/10/81 Vredenburg. RHB RM. Ed Weston HS. FC debut FS v Gau (Jhb) 2004/05, Bol debut 2005/06. FS 2004/05. FS LO debut 2003/04. HSFC 74 FS v Gau (Jhb) 2004/05. HSLO 70 Bol v Bdr (EL) 2005/06.

SWAN Warren Clive (Bol). B 30/5/83 Johannesburg. RHB OB. Ed St John's College, Stell Univ. Gau Schools 1999-2001. FC debut Bol v EP (Paarl) 2003/04. HSFC 93 Bol v Bdr (EL) 2005/06. HSSS 65* Bol v EP (Paarl) 2003/04. HSLO 96* Bol v WP (CT) 2005/06.

SYMCOX Russel Patrick (Dol). B 28/1/83 Kimberley. LHB RMF. Ed Hilton College. KZN Schools 2000. Son of PL Symcox (GW/NT/NTB/ Ntl/NtlB/SA 1977-1999), grandson of RL Symcox (GW 1957-1962 and FC Umpire). FC debut KZN v GW (Kby) 2002/03, Dol debut 2004/05. HSFC 87 Dol v Lio (Dbn) 2005/06. BBFC 4-13 KZN v FS (Dbn) 2003/04. HSLO 50* Dol v Lio (Jhb) 2005/06. HS20 18 Dol v War (PE) 2004/05. BB20 2-29 Dol v Ttn (Ben) 2004/05.

SYMES Jean (Gau). B 13/11/86 Johannesburg. LHB SLA. Ed St John's College. Gau Schools 2003-05(C), SA Schools 2005. FC debut Gau v Eas (Jhb) 2005/06. HSFC 133 Gau v NW (Potch) 2005/06. BBFC 2-13 Gau v Eas (Jhb) 2005/06. Tours: SA U-19 to World Cup 2006.

TELEMACHUS Roger (Eag/FS/SA). B 27/3/73 Stellenbosch. RHB RFM. Ed Cloetesville HS (Stell). WP Schools 1992. FC debut BolB v BdrB (EL) 1994/95, Eag debut 2004/05, FS debut 2005/06. Bol 1994/95-1998/99, BolB 1994/95. WP 1999/00-2003/04. Eag Pro20 debut 2003/04, FS LO debut 2004/05. LOIs: 36 (1997/98-2005/06). HSLOI 29 v Aus (PE) 2005/06. BBLOI 4-43 v SL (Jhb) 1997/98. HSFC 116 FS v GW (Kby) 2005/06. BBFC 6-21 Bol v GW (Paarl) 1996/97. HSSS 46* Bol v EP (PE) 1995/96 & 46 WP v KZN (CT) 1999/00. HSLO 53* FS v GW (Kby) 2005/06. BBLO 5-54 Bol v EP (PE) 1996/97. HS20 34 Eag v War (PE) 2005/06. BB20 4-25 Eag v Lio (Bfn) 2005/06. Tours: SA to Aus 2000; SL 2000, 2006; WI 2000/01; Ken 2000/01; Mor 2002; Sing 2000; SAA to Eng 1996; SA U-24 to SL 1995/96.

TELO Filipe *Dominic* (Cob/WP). B 4/3/86 Cape Town. RHB RM. Ed Wynberg BHS. WP Schools 2003-04. FC debut WP v Bol (Paarl) 2005/06, Cob same season. HSFC 72 WP v Bdr (EL) 2005/06. HSSS 26 Cob v Lio (CT) 2005/06. HSLO 90 WP v Bdr (EL) 2005/06. HS20 48 Cob v Lio (CT) 2005/06.

TEMPLETON Mark Sean (Gau). B 14/12/82 Johannesburg. LHB RM. Ed Jeppe BHS. No FC. Lo debut 2005/06.

TERBRUGGE David John (Lio/Gau). B 31/1/77 Ladysmith. RHB RFM. Ed St Stithian's, RAU. Tvl Schools 1992-94, SA Schools 1993-94. FC debut TvlB v EPB (PE) 1994/95, Tvl debut 1996/97, Lio debut 2004/05. Tests: 7 (1998/99-2003/04). LOIs: 4 (1999/00-2000). BBTest 5-46 v Ban (EL) 2002/03. BBLOI 4-20 v Pak (Colombo-SSC) 2000. HSFC 40* Lio v Dol (Dbn) 2004/05. BBFC 6-58 Gau v Bol (Jhb) 2001/02. HSLO 16* Gau v EP (Jhb) 1999/00. BBLO 4-20 SA v Pak (Colombo-SSC) 2000. BBDLO 4-31 Gau v WP (Jhb) 2000/01. BB20 4-20 Lio v WPBol (Jhb) 2004/05. Tours: SA to Aus 2000; NZ 2003/04; SL 2000; Sing 2000; SA U-19 to Eng 1995.

THERON Juan (EP). B 24/7/85 Vereeniging. RHB RMF. Ed Grey HS (PE), UFS. EP Schools 2003. FC debut EP v KZN (PE) 2005/06. HSFC 15 EP v Bol (Paarl) 2005/06. BBFC 6-47 EP v Bol (Paarl) 2005/06. HSLO 15 EP v Nor (Pta) 2005/06. BBLO 4-50 EP v Bol (Paarl) 2005/06.

THEUNISSEN Jaco (Eas). B 31/7/86 Boksburg. RHB WK. Ed Dr EG Jansen, Boksburg. FC debut Eas v NW (Potch) 2005/06. HSFC 22 Eas v NW (Potch) 2005/06. HSLO 10 Eas v NW (Potch) 2005/06.

THOMAS Alfonso Clive (Ttn/Nor). B 9/2/77 Cape Town. RHB RFM. Ed Ravensmead SS, Parow HS. FC debut WPB v NW (CT) 1998/99, Nor debut 2003/04, Ttn debut 2004/05. WPB 1998/99. NW 2000/01-2002/03. HSFC 119* NW v Nor (Cent) 2002/03. BBFC 7-54 Ttn v Cob (CT) 2005/06. HSLO 27* Ttn v WPBol (CT) 2004/05. BBLO 4-31 Nor v Gau (Cent) 2003/04. BB20 3-20 Ttn v Eag (Bfn) 2003/04. Tours: SA to Ind 2004/05; SAA to Zim 2004.

THOMPSON Patrick Grant (Gau). B 2/11/76 Randfontein. RHB LFM. Ed Jeppe BHS. FC debut Gau v Bol (Randjesfontein) 2003/04. HSFC 66 Gau v Eas (Jhb) 2005/06. BBFC 3-41 Gau v Bol (Randjesfontein) 2003/04. BBLO 3-40 Gau v Eas (Jhb) 2005/06. Hockey (SA Country Districts 2003-04).

THYSSEN Craig Andre (Eag/FS). B 25/3/84 Port Elizabeth. RHB RFM. Ed Grey HS (PE). EP Schools 2000-02, SA Schools 2000-02. FC debut EP v GW (Kby) 2003/04, FS debut 2004/05, Eag debut 2004/05. LO debut 2002/03. HSFC 157 FS v Gau (Bfn) 2005/06. BBFC 2-14 EP v KZN (PE) 2003/04. HSSS 60* EP v Eas (PE) 2003/04. HSLO 43 FS v NW (Potch) 2005/06. BBLO 4-38 FS v NW (Bfn) 2005/06. HS20 31 Eag v Ttn (Cent) 2004/05. BB20 2-19 Eag v WPBol (Bfn) 2004/05. Tours: SA U-19 to Eng 2003; NZ 2000/01.

TOYANA Geoffrey (Ttn/Eas). B 27/2/74 Soweto. LHB OB. Ed Orlando HS. FC debut SA Inv v Eng (Soweto) 1995/96, Eas debut 2002/03, Ttn debut 2004/05. Gau 1997/98-2001/02, TvlB 1995/96-1996/97. HSFC 113 Eas v Bol (Paarl) 2003/04. HSLO 67 Eas v KZN (Ben) 2002/03. BBLO 2-18 Eas v Bdr (Ben) 2003/04.

TRIEGAARDT Jean-Pierre Horatio (GW). B 10/3/84 Cape Town. RHB WK. Ed Floors SS. GW Schools 2003. No FC, LO debut 2005/06. HSLO 10 GW v FS (Kby) 2005/06. Hockey (GW).

TSAMAISI Elton Selby (GW). B 8/12/80 Kimberley. RHB RMF. Ed St Boniface HS. GW Schools 1998-99. FC debut GW v KZN (Kby) 2001/02. HSFC 13 GW v Bdr (Kby) 2004/05. BBFC 2-36 GW v Bdr (Kby) 2004/05. HSLO 43* GW v WP (Kby) 2004/05. BBLO 2-33 GW v EP (PE) 2004/05. Tours: SA U-19 to Pak 1998/99.

TSHABALALA Thandi (Eag/FS). B 19/11/84 Welkom. RHB OB. Ed Thotagauta. FS Schools 2001. FC debut FS v KZN (Dbn) 2003/04, Eag debut 2004/05. HSFC 34 FS v Gau (Jhb) 2004/05. BBFC 5-72 FS v Bdr (Bfn) 2004/05. HSSS 25 Eag v Lio (Potch) 2005/06. BBSS 4-129 Eag v Lio (Potch) 2005/06. BBLO 4-24 FS v Gau (Jhb) 2004/05 & Eag v Cob (CT) 2005/06. BB20 4-13 Eag v Lio (Potch) 2004/05. Tours: SA to SL 2006.

TSOLEKILE Thami Lungisa (Cob/SAA/Rest). B 9/10/80 Cape Town. RHB OB WK. Ed Pinelands HS. WP Schools 1997-99, (C) in 1998-99, SA Schools 1998(C)-99(C, but did not play). FC debut SAAc v Ire (Dublin) 1999, WP debut 1999/00, WPBol debut 2004/05. Tests: 3 (2004/05). HSTest 22 v Eng (PE) 2004/05. HSFC 101* WPBol v Ttn (Ben) 2004/05. HSLO 44 WP v GW (CT) 1999/00. HS20 52 WPBol v Eag (Bfn) 2004/05. Tours: SA to Eng 2003; Ind 2004/05; SAA to Aus 2002/03; SL 2005/06; Zim 2002/03, 2004; SA U-19 to Pak 1998/99 (capt); World Cup 2000 (capt).

TSOTSOBE Lonwabo Lennox (EP). B 7/3/84 Port Elizabeth. RHB LF. Ed Die Heuwel, Westering HS. FC debut EP v Bol (Paarl) 2004/05, taking 7-44. HSFC 12* EP v KZN (Chatsworth) 2005/06. BBFC 7-44 EP v Bol (Paarl) 2004/05. BBLO 5-28 EP v Bdr (EL) 2005/06.

TWEEDIE Andrew Neil Walter (Dol). B 27/11/75 Durban. RHB RFM. Ed Kearsney College, Ntl Technikon. Ntl Schools 1993. FC debut NtlB v WPB (CT) 1997/98, KZN debut 2000/01, Dol debut 2004/05. HSFC 85* Dol v Ttn (Dbn) 2004/05. BBFC 5-50 KZN v GW (Kby) 2002/03. HSLO 70* KZN v WA (Perth) 2000/01. BBLO 6-24 Dol v Ttn (Pmb) 2005/06. HSDLO 29 KZN v NW (Potch) 2003/04. HS20 10 Dol v Eag (Bfn) 2004/05. BB20 2-31 Dol v War (Dbn) 2005/06.

VAN DEN BERG Adolf Matthys (*Aldo*) (Eas). B 9/3/78 Randfontein. RHB OB. Ed Jan Viljoen, Randfontein. Tvl Schools 1995-96, SA Schools 1996. FC debut SAAc v Ire (Dublin) 1999, Eas debut 1999/00. Gau LO 1997/98-1998-99. HSFC 103 Eas v IndA (Ben) 2001/02. BBFC 5-49 Eas v Bol (Ben) 2003/04. HSSS 76 Eas v EP (PE) 2002/03. HSLO 65 Eas v FS (Bfn) 2005/06. BBLO 3-36 Eas v FS (Bfn) 2005/06.

VAN DER MERWE Francois (*Sweis*) (NW). B 5/7/76 Kempton Park. RHB RMF. Ed Klerksdorp HS. NW Schools 1994. FC debut NW v GW (Potch) 1999/00. LO debut 1995/96. HSFC 24* NW v Bdr (Potch) 2000/01. BBFC 5-45 NW v Gau (Jhb) 2003/04. BBLO 3-34 NW v GW (Potch) 2003/04.

VAN DER SCHYFF Wilhelmus (FS). B 8/1/85 Bloemfontein. RHB RM. Ed Grey College (Bfn), UFS. FS Schools 2002-03. No FC, LO debut 2005/06. HSLO 37* FS v GW (Bfn) 2005/06. Rugby (FS Craven Week 2003).

VAN DER WATH Johannes Jacobus (Eag/SA/SAA). B 10/1/78 Newcastle. RHB RFM. Ed Ermelo HS. SACD Schools 1994-95, Eas Schools 1996, SA Schools 1996. FC debut Eas v TvlB (Ben) 1996/97, FS debut 1997/98, Eag debut 2004/05. Sussex 2005. LOIs: 7 (2005/06). HSLOI 37* v Aus (Sydney) 2005/06. BBLOI 2-21 v Aus (Melbourne-Col) 2005/06. HSFC 113* FS v KZN (Bfn) 2001/02. BBFC 6-37 FS v Bol (Bfn) 2001/02. HSLO 91 FS v GW (Bfn) 2000/01 & Eag v Dol (Dbn) 2004/05. BBLO 4-31 SAA v NZ (Potch) 2005/06. BBDLO 4-35 Eag v War (EL) 2005/06. HS20 28* Eag v EC (EL) 2003/04. BB20 2-11 Eag v Lio (Potch) 2004/05. Tours: SA to Aus 2005/06, SL 2006; SAA to SL 2005/06. SA U-19 v Pak U-19 1996/97.

VAN JAARSVELD Martin (Ttn). B 18/6/74 Klerksdorp. RHB OB. Ed Warmbaths, Pretoria Univ. SACD Schools 1990-91, NT Schools 1992. FC debut NTB v NtlB (Dbn) 1994/95, NT debut 1995/96, Ttn debut 2004/05. Northamptonshire 2004. Kent 2005-2006. Tests: 9 (2002/03-2004/05). LOIs: 11 (2002/03-2004). HSTest 73 v WI (Jhb) 2003/04. HSLOI 45 v Eng (Birmingham) 2003. HSFC 262* Kent v Glamorgan (Cardiff) 2005. BBFC 2-30 SAA v SLA (Potch) 2003/04. HSSA 238* Nor v GW (Kby) 1999/00. HSLO 123 NT v EP (Cent) 1996/97. HS20 75 Kent v Leicestershire (Leicester) 2006. Tours: SA to Eng 2003, 2004; Ind 2004/05; NZ 2003/04; SL 2004; SAA to Aus 2002/03; SL 1998/99; Zim 2002/03. COY 2002.

VAN JAARSVELD Vaughn Bernard (Lio). B 2/2/85 Johannesburg. LHB RM. Ed King Edward VII. Gau Schools 2000-03, SA Schools 2003. FC debut Gau v Nor (Cent) 2003/04, Lio debut 2004/05. Gau LO debut 2002/03. HSFC 126 Lio v War (EL) 2005/06. HSLO 68 Gau v EP (PE) 2003/04 & Lio v Ttn (Jhb) 2004/05. HS20 64 Lio v WPBol (Jhb) 2004/05. Tours: SA U-19 to World Cup 2004.

VAN NIEKERK Pieter Michiel (NW). B 20/10/79 Johannesburg. LHB SLA. Ed Hoerskool Zeerust, Potch Univ. NW Schools 1995-97. FC debut NW v Gau (Potch) 2002/03. LO debut 1999/00. BBFC 3-79 NW v Gau (Potch) 2002/03. HSLO 21 NW v Bol (Paarl) 2003/04.

VAN STRAATEN Herman Antonie (Eas). B 1/2/84 Vereeniging. RHB OB. Ed Gen JBM Hertzog. Eas Schools 2002. FC debut Eas v GW (Ben) 2005/06. HSFC 68 Eas v NW (Potch) 2005/06. HSLO 43 Eas v GW (Ben) 2005/06.

VAN WOERKOM Nicholas (Nor). B 28/3/81 Nelspruit. RHB RM. Ed Pretoria BHS, Pretoria Univ. Nor Schools 1999. FC debut Nor v Gau (Jhb) 2004/05. HSFC 146 Nor v Gau (Pta) 2005/06. HSLO 86 Nor v Gau (Jhb) 2004/05. BBLO 3-43 Nor v Eas (Cent) 2004/05.

VAN WYK Cornelius Francoius *Kruger* (Ttn/Nor). B 7/2/80 Wolmaransstad. RHB WK. Ed Afrikaanse Hoer Seunskool, Pretoria Univ. Nor Schools 1996-97. FC debut Nor v GW (Cent) 2000/01, Ttn debut 2004/05. HSFC 104 Nor v WP (CT) 2005/06. HSSS 74* Ttn v Lio (Ben) 2005/06. HSLO 90* Nor v NW (Potch) 2005/06. HS20 24 Ttn v Chilaw (Leicester) 2005. Hockey (Nor).

VAN WYK Divan Jaco (FS). B 25/2/85 Bloemfontein. RHB RM WK. Ed Grey College (Bfn), UFS. FS Schools 2002-03(C), SA Schools 2003(C). Brother of MN van Wyk (FS/Eag/SA 1996-2005). FC debut FS v KZN (Dbn) 2004/05. HSFC 106 FS v Eas (Ben) 2005/06. HSLO 62 FS v Gau (Jhb) 2004/05. Tours: SA U-19 to World Cup 2004 (capt). Rugby (FS U-18 2003).
VAN WYK Diaan Marinus (Gau). B 19/1/81 Roodepoort. RHB WK. Ed Hoerskool Roodepoort, Univ of Jhb. FC debut Gau v Nor (Pta) 2005/06, scoring 122*. HSFC 122* Gau v Nor (Pta) 2005/06. HSLO 52 Gau v Nor (Jhb) 2005/06.
VAN WYK Jacques Merlin (Bol). B 27/1/78 Stellenbosch. RHB RFM. Ed Kylemore SS, Stellenbosch College. FC debut Bol v FS (Stb) 1998/99, WPBol debut 2004/05. HSFC 35 Bol v GW (Kby) 2002/03. BBFC 3-27 Bol v EP (Paarl) 2004/05. BBSS 3-95 Bol v KZN (Dbn) 2002/03. HSLO 16* Bol v GW (Kby) 2004/05. BBLO 3-33 Bol v Gau (Paarl) 2002/03.
VAN WYK Morne Nico (Eag). B 20/3/79 Bloemfontein. RHB SLA WK. Ed Grey College (Bfn). FS Schools 1995-97, SA Schools 1997. Brother of DJ van Wyk (FS 2004-2005). FC debut FS v Bdr (Bfn) 1996/97 (as substitute), Eag debut 2004/05. LOIs: 1 (2003). HSLOI 17 v Eng (Lord's) 2003. HSFC 200* Eag v War (Bfn) 2005/06. BBFC 2-25 FS v Eas (Ben) 2000/01. HSLO 150* FS v Gau (Bfn) 2002/03. BBLO 2-28 FS v Gau (Bfn) 2000/01 & FS v Eas (Ben) 2000/01. HS20 80* Eag v WPBol (Bfn) 2004/05. Tours: SA to Eng 2003; SAA to Aus 2002/03; Zim 2004. SA U-19 v Eng U-19 1997/98; World Cup in SA 1998.
VON HOESSLIN Garreth Edward (Bdr). B 19/4/85 East London. RHB WK. Ed Selborne College. Bdr Schools 2003. FC debut Bdr v Nor (EL) 2004/05. HSFC 101* Bdr v Bol (EL) 2005/06. HSLO 31 Bdr v EP (PE) 2005/06. Hockey (Bdr 2003).
WAGNER Neil (Nor). B 13/3/86 Pretoria. RHB RMF. Ed Afrikaanse Hoer Seunskool, Pretoria Univ. Nor Schools 2003-04. FC debut Nor v NW (Potch) 2005/06. HSFC 20 Nor v NW (Potch) 2005/06. BBFC 4-39 Nor v NW (Potch) 2005/06.
WALTERS Lee-Roy (Bol). B 3/12/86 Paarl. RHB WK. Ed Paarl BHS, UWC. Bol Schools 2003-04. FC debut Bol v WP (CT) 2004/05. HSFC 56 Bol v Bdr (Paarl) 2005/06. HSLO 12* Bol v Nor (Paarl) 2005/06.
WALTERS Martin Dennis (WP). B 12/3/85 East London. RHB RMF. Ed Selborne College, Harrow S, UCT. Bdr Schools 2001-03. FC debut WP v KZN (Chatsworth) 2005/06. In 2004 he was the leading run-scorer in schools cricket in England with 1204 runs (avg 109.45) for Harrow.
WATSON Douglas James (Dol). B 15/5/73 Pietermaritzburg. RHB RM. Ed Maritzburg College. Ntl Schools 1991, SA Schools 1991. FC debut NtlB v BdrB (EL) 1993/94, Ntl same season, Dol debut 2004/05. HSFC 220 KZN v NW (Potch) 1999/00. BBFC 2-7 Ntl v Bdr (EL) 1997/98. HSLO 142 Dol v Ttn (Cent) 2004/05. BBLO 2-22 Ntl v FS (Dbn) 1997/98. HS20 48 Dol v War (Dbn) 2005/06. Tours: SAA to WI 2000/01.
WIESE David (Eas). B 18/5/85 Roodepoort. RHB RFM. Ed Witbank HS, Pretoria Univ. Mpumalanga Schools 2003. FC debut Eas v Nor (Ben) 2005/06. HSFC 168 Eas v FS (Bfn) 2005/06. BBFC 4-48 Eas v Gau (Jhb) 2005/06. HSLO 59 Eas v GW (Ben) 2005/06. BBLO 3-25 Eas v GW (Ben) 2005/06.
WILLEMSE Darryl (War/EP). B 15/5/79 Vereeniging. RHB OB. Ed Victoria Park HS, UPE. FC debut EP v WP (PE) 2004/05, War debut 2005/06. HSFC 58 EP v KZN (PE) 2005/06. BBFC 4-56 EP v KZN (Chatsworth) 2005/06. HSSS 34 War v Eag (PE) 2005/06. HSLO 20* EP v WP (PE) 2004/05. Hockey (EP U-18 1997).
WILLIAMSON Myles (WP). B 3/1/84 Cape Town. RHB RM. Ed Rosebank College. FC debut WP v KZN (Chatsworth) 2005/06. HSFC 44 WP v Bdr (CT) 2005/06. HSLO 94 WP v KZN (Chatsworth) 2005/06.
WILLOUGHBY Charl Myles (Cob). B 3/12/74 Cape Town. LHB LFM. Ed Wynberg BHS, Stell Univ. WP Schools 1992. FC debut Bol v Tvl (Jhb) 1994/95, WP debut 2000/01, WPBol debut 2004/05. Bol 1994/95-1999/00, BolB 1994/95-1995/96. Leicestershire 2005. Somerset 2006. Tests: 2 (2002/03-2003). LOIs: 3 (1999/00-2002/03). BBLOI 2-39 v Pak (Sharjah) 1999/00. HSFC 47 Somerset v Worcestershire (Taunton) 2006. HSSA 17* Bol v NW (Paarl) 1999/00 & 17 WP v KZN (CT) 2000/01. BBFC 7-56 WP v Nor (Cent) 2003/04. HSLO 12* Somerset v Middlesex (Bath) 2006. HSDLO 11 Bol v NT (Cent) 1996/97. BBLO 6-24 SAA v Bar (Bridgetown) 2000/01. BBDLO 5-39 Bol v Gau (Jhb) 1999/00. BB20 4-9 WPBol v Dol (Dbn) 2004/05. Tours: SA to Ban 2002/03; Eng 2003; Shar 1999/00; SAA to WI 2000/01; Zim 2004.
WINGFIELD Wade Richard (KZN). B 17/12/77 Scottburgh. RHB RM. Ed Durban HS, Ntl Technikon. Ntl Schools 1994-95, SA Schools 1995. FC debut NtlB v WPB (CT) 1997/98, Dol debut 2004/05. KZN 1998/99-2000/01 and 2004/05-2005/06 (and LO 1997/98), KZNB 1997/98-1998/99. EP 2002/03-2003/04. HSFC 146* EP v Bol (Paarl) 2003/04. BBFC 2-18 NtlB v NW (Dbn) 1997/98. BBSS 2-36 KZN v Gau (Jhb) 2000/01. HSLO 85 Dol v WPBol (Dbn) 2004/05. BBLO 4-42 KZN v FS (Dbn) 1999/00. HS20 44 Dol v EC (Dbn) 2003/04. BB20 2-23 Dol v Lio (Jhb) 2003/04. Tours: SA U-19 to Ind 1995/96. SA U-19 v Pak U-19 1996/97.
WYNGAARD Warren (Cob/WP). B 5/11/80 Cape Town. RHB OB WK. Ed Cathkin HS. WP Schools 1997-98. Cousin of RK Kleinveldt (WP/WPBol 2002-2005). FC debut WP v EP (PE) 2004/05. HSFC 132* WP v Bdr (CT) 2005/06. HSSS 22 Cob v Dol (Dbn) 2005/06. HSLO 73 WP v EP (PE) 2004/05.
ZONDEKI Monde (Cob/WP/SA/SAA/Rest/Afr). B 25/7/82 King William's Town. RHB RF. Ed Dale College. Bdr Schools 1997-2000. FC debut Bdr v NZ (EL) 2000/01, Cob debut 2005/06, WP LO debut 2005/06. Bdr 200/01-2004/05. War 2004/05. Tests: 5 (2003-2004/05). LOIs: 11 (9 for SA 2002/03-2005/06; 2 for Africa 2005/06). HSTest 59 v Eng (Leeds) 2003. BBTest 6-39 v Zim (Cent) 2004/05. BBLOI 2-46 v Zim (PE) 2004/05. HSFC 59 SA v Eng (Leeds) 2003. BBFC 6-39 SA v Zim (Cent) 2004/05. HSSA 27 Bdr v Gau (EL) 2001/02 & Bdr v NW (Potch) 2003/04. BBSS 5-67 Cob v Lio (CT) 2005/06. HSLO 23 SAA v SL (Potch) 2002/03 & SAA v SLA (Ben) 2003/04. BBLO 6-37 SAA v SLA (Cent) 2003/04. HSDLO 19 Bdr v WP (EL) 2002/03. BBDLO 4-32 Bdr v Bol (EL) 2001/02. BB20 2-19 EC v Eag (EL) 2003/04. Tours: SA to Aus 2005/06; Eng 2003, WI 2004/05; World Cup 2003; SAA to SL 2005/06; SA U-19 to NZ 2000/01.

SHARED SPOILS . . . skippers Martin van Jaarsveld and Lance Klusener with the SuperSport Series trophy after the final *Picture: TERTIUS PICKARD, Touchline Photo*

SUPERSPORT SERIES 2005/06

DOLPHINS v TITANS — SuperSport Series Final

Played at Sahara Stadium Kingsmead, Durban on 6,7,8,9,10 April 2006 — Toss: Titans
Umpires: M Erasmus & S Wadvalla (TV: MZ Nanabhay) — Referee: CJ Mitchley
Debuts: Dol: None. Ttn: None
Close of play: Day 1: Ttn (1) 70-4 (Kemp 16*, Toyana 4*, 26 overs). Day 2: Dol (2) 99-0 (Watson 52*, Khan 39*, 27 overs). Day 3: Dol (2) 176-1 (Watson 88*, HM Amla 0*, 53.1 overs). Day 4: Ttn (2) 11-0 (Kuhn 3*, Bodi 4*, 4.2 overs)
Result: Match drawn
Man of Match: Dale Benkenstein
Notes: Kuhn remained on 17 for 84 minutes (53 balls) during the Titans' 2nd innings.

As they stood waiting for the post-match presentation to begin, neither Martin van Jaarsveld nor Lance Klusener looked as if they took any pleasure out of the fact that the stalemate that the final had dwindled to meant they would share the premier title in domestic cricket.

Unsurprisingly, calls rang out for a return to the old-fangled idea of awarding the championship to the team that finished on top of the log and it was decided later that in future the title would be decided on a league basis only.

The last day's play was entirely without fizz. The Titans were reluctant to chase the target of 378, and in the field the Dolphins went through the motions joylessly.

It was scarcely believable that, four days earlier, 14 wickets had fallen on a pitch of almost as much bounce and movement as the outrageously lithe Ethy Mbhalati, claimed a career-best 5-26. The Dolphins would have sunk without trace without half-centuries by Doug Watson and Ahmed Amla.

Justin Kemp and Geoff Toyana took the Titans to within sight of the lead on the second morning before Toyana scooped Dale Benkenstein's first delivery of the match to extra cover.

Two balls later Benkenstein reached far to his left in a deliberate attempt to deflect Albie Morkel's meaty drive onto the stumps at the non-striker's end. The ball scooted behind Benkenstein's ankles on its way to its mark and Kemp was artfully run out. Morkel's clean hitting earned the visitors a lead of 93.

The Dolphins were 99-0 when bad light ended play and they forged ahead to 176-1, 83 ahead, in the 26.1 overs the light allowed on a third day that was memorable chiefly for the disturbing appearance of Paul Harris with his head shaved. "Some of his mates decided the Arno Carstens look had to go," Titans coach Richard Pybus said of his previously hirsute left-arm spinner.

The gritty Watson reached his century on the fourth morning but the Titans took four wickets in the session to go to lunch the happier team. Then Benkenstein delivered an innings redolent with experience and class that, with the help of support of varying quality and intent from what was left of the Dolphins' order, made the game safe for the home side.

Benkenstein, who batted for almost five hours for his 151, eventually skied a drive to mid-on to give Dale Steyn a hard-earned five-wicket haul.

And so to the fifth day, which saw 62.4 overs bowled in which the Titans scored 159 runs and lost two wickets.

Telford Vice

SUPERSPORT SERIES 2005/06

DOLPHINS	Runs	Mins	Balls	4	6		Runs	Mins	Balls	4	6
DJ Watson b Mbhalati	50	153	93	6	-	lbw b Thomas	103	325	236	14	-
I Khan b Steyn	10	26	19	1	-	c Kuhn b Steyn	71	233	144	9	-
HM Amla b Mbhalati	16	46	29	3	-	c Kemp b Steyn	4	27	24	1	-
AM Amla c Morkel b Steyn	58	153	115	11	-	c Van Jaarsveld b Morkel	2	18	10	-	-
DM Benkenstein run out (De Bruyn)	4	8	4	1	-	c Harris b Steyn	151	298	202	21	4
K Smit c Kuhn b Mbhalati	7	12	7	1	-	c De Bruyn b Steyn	13	42	36	2	-
†DL Brown c Van Jaarsveld b Mbhalati	0	2	2	-	-	c Van Jaarsveld b Harris	39	76	52	3	-
*L Klusener b Steyn	11	38	25	2	-	c Van Jaarsveld b Steyn	22	31	21	2	1
S Mhlongo c Kuhn b Morkel	6	32	16	1	-	c Kuhn b Harris	1	24	15	-	-
U Govender c Kuhn b Mbhalati	0	4	3	-	-	(11) not out	0	14	8	-	-
M Hayward not out	5	17	8	-	-	(10) c De Bruyn b Thomas	33	62	32	4	2
Extras (b 2, lb 3, w 1, nb 3)	9					Extras (b 12, lb 5, w 6, nb 8)	31				
TOTAL (53 overs)	**176**					**TOTAL (128.4 overs)**	**470**				

TITANS	Runs	Mins	Balls	4	6		Runs	Mins	Balls	4	6
†HG Kuhn lbw b Hayward	20	53	36	3	-	c Brown b Hayward	37	156	121	6	-
GH Bodi c Brown b Hayward	11	42	23	2	-	run out (Klusener)	17	100	50	1	-
*M van Jaarsveld c Brown b Govender	6	54	32	-	-	not out	72	203	140	8	-
Z de Bruyn c Brown b Mhlongo	4	10	6	1	-	not out	15	147	96	2	-
JM Kemp run out (Benkenstein)	52	165	113	7	1						
G Toyana c Hayward b Benkenstein	54	128	78	7	-						
JA Morkel c Hayward b Govender	79	144	93	15	1						
AC Thomas lbw b Govender	6	46	28	1	-						
PL Harris lbw b Mhlongo	18	51	29	3	-						
DW Steyn lbw b Klusener	1	16	12	-	-						
NE Mbhalati not out	0	24	10	-	-						
Extras (b 4, lb 7, w 1, nb 6)	18					Extras (b 12, lb 11, w 1, nb 5)	29				
TOTAL (75.4 overs)	**269**					**TOTAL (for 2 wkts) (67 overs)**	**170**				

Ttn	O	M	R	W		O	M	R	W
Steyn	14.4	3	44	3 (3 nb)		36.4	7	124	5 (2 nb, 1 w)
Thomas	7	1	34	0		23	6	79	2
Morkel	13.2	4	42	1	(4)	25	5	88	1
Mbhalati	12	3	26	5	(3)	16	2	60	0 (5 nb)
De Bruyn	2	0	9	0	(6)	5	1	37	0
Harris	1	0	2	0	(5)	23	5	65	2 (1 nb, 1 w)
Kemp	3	0	14	0 (1 w)					
Dol	O	M	R	W		O	M	R	W
Klusener	23	6	75	1 (2 nb)		16	1	40	0 (1 nb, 1 w)
Hayward	17	3	47	2		15	4	36	1 (1 nb)
Govender	16.4	1	68	3 (1 nb, 1 w)	(4)	9	1	20	0
Mhlongo	17	5	64	2 (3 nb)	(3)	12	3	22	0 (3 nb)
Benkenstein	2	1	4	1		15	3	29	0

Fall of Wickets

	Dol	Ttn	Dol	Ttn
1st	25 (2)	37 (2)	176 (2)	56 (2)
2nd	52 (3)	38 (1)	186 (3)	93 (1)
3rd	105 (1)	46 (4)	189 (4)	-
4th	109 (5)	54 (3)	228 (1)	-
5th	120 (6)	161 (6)	256 (6)	-
6th	120 (7)	161 (5)	335 (7)	-
7th	155 (8)	196 (8)	363 (8)	-
8th	164 (4)	238 (9)	384 (9)	-
9th	164 (10)	247 (10)	458 (10)	-
10th	176 (9)	269 (7)	470 (5)	-

SUPERSPORT SERIES 2005/06

	P	W	L	D	Bat	Bowl	Pts
Dolphins	10	5	0	5	41.26	32	123.26
Titans	10	4	1	5	33.58	36	109.58
Cape Cobras	10	5	4	1	23.66	28	101.66
Lions	10	3	4	3	37.46	34	101.46
Eagles	10	3	4	3	26.86	25	81.86
Warriors	10	0	7	3	20.76	28	48.76

LEADING BATTING AVERAGES

		M	Inns	NO	Runs	HS	Avg	SR	100	50
1	DM Benkenstein (Dol)	10	15	5	652	151	65.20	57.19	3	1
2	HH Gibbs (Cob)	3	6	0	352	149	58.66	64.11	2	0
3	JA Rudolph (Eag)	7	12	0	683	141	56.91	59.39	3	4
4	MN van Wyk (Eag)	10	17	3	786	200*	56.14	52.15	3	1
5	HM Amla (Dol)	11	19	3	893	153	55.81	60.01	2	6
6	AM Amla (Dol)	8	13	2	531	125	48.27	54.57	1	4

7	P de Bruyn (Ttn)	7	10	3	333	125*	47.57	39.45	1	2
8	JL Ontong (Lio)	8	15	1	659	102	47.07	58.37	1	6
9	ND McKenzie (Lio)	9	17	2	694	161*	46.26	44.43	2	2
10	A Jacobs (War)	9	18	2	726	149	45.37	51.52	1	4
11	DJ Watson (Dol)	11	20	3	763	103	44.88	45.25	2	5
12	Z de Bruyn (Ttn)	10	16	2	620	175	44.28	43.63	1	3
13	J-P Duminy (Cob)	10	18	3	655	128	43.66	46.68	1	4
14	DJ Jacobs (Eag)	10	17	2	645	128	43.00	65.88	3	2
15	L Klusener (Dol)	10	13	3	428	102	42.80	80.60	2	0
16	HG Kuhn (Ttn)	6	10	1	373	96	41.44	45.43	0	2
17	MJ Harris (Lio)	10	17	2	614	135*	40.93	52.25	2	1
18	VB van Jaarsveld (Lio)	10	18	1	670	126	39.41	64.79	3	3
19	M van Jaarsveld (Ttn)	11	18	2	618	145	38.62	46.71	1	4
20	I Khan (Dol)	10	18	2	615	118	38.43	51.25	1	4

(Qualification: 6 completed innings)

JA Morkel (Ttn) scored 381 runs and was dismissed only 4 times (avg 95.25).

LEADING BOWLING AVERAGES

	Name	M	Overs	Mdns	Runs	Wkts	Avg	RPO	BB	5I	10M
1	N Boje (Eag)	6	276	80	613	40	15.32	2.22	8-93	4	1
2	AC Dawson (Cob)	4	124.4	48	262	17	15.41	2.10	6-39	1	1
3	DW Steyn (Ttn)	9	316.3	71	893	49	18.22	2.82	5-27	3	1
4	F de Wet (Lio)	5	190.2	44	567	31	18.29	2.97	7-61	3	1
5	RK Kleinveldt (Cob)	5	147.5	43	379	20	18.95	2.56	8-47	1	1
6	CM Willoughby (Cob)	9	333.4	91	861	41	21.00	2.58	6-41	4	0
7	PL Harris (Ttn)	11	379.5	104	1053	49	21.48	2.77	6-54	4	0
8	S Mhlongo (Dol)	5	127	36	387	18	21.50	3.04	4-38	0	0
9	U Govender (Dol)	9	250.5	50	718	32	22.43	2.86	6-59	2	0
10	GJ-P Kruger (Lio)	7	278.4	55	977	43	22.72	3.50	8-112	4	1
11	ANW Tweedie (Dol)	5	132.3	30	404	16	25.25	3.04	4-74	0	0
12	VD Philander (Cob)	10	286.5	76	729	28	26.03	2.54	5-49	1	0
13	EO Moleon (Lio)	8	179.2	60	446	17	26.23	2.48	3-21	0	0
14	AC Thomas (Ttn)	7	213	62	638	24	26.58	2.99	7-54	1	1
15	Z de Bruyn (Ttn)	10	104.4	22	405	15	27.00	3.86	5-28	1	0
16	GJ de Bruin (Lio)	4	129.2	23	437	16	27.31	3.37	4-47	0	0
17	JC Kent (Dol)	9	178	48	465	17	27.35	2.61	3-77	0	0
18	DM Benkenstein (Dol)	10	185	52	467	17	27.47	2.52	4-16	0	0
19	NE Mbhalati (Ttn)	9	239.4	60	847	29	29.20	3.53	5-26	1	0
20	T Henderson (War)	8	252.3	67	651	22	29.59	2.57	6-80	1	0

(Qualification: 15 wickets)

LEADING WICKETKEEPERS

		M	Ct	St	Total
1	MJ Harris (Lio)	10	42	0	42
2	TL Tsolekile (Cob)	10	32	1	33
3	AM Sodumo (War)	10	23	3	26

4	HG Kuhn (Ttn)	6	19	2	21
5	D Smit (Dol)	6	19	0	19

LEADING FIELDERS

		M	Ct
1	M van Jaarsveld (Ttn)	11	25
2	VB van Jaarsveld (Lio)	10	15
3	AG Puttick (Cob)	10	14
4	DM Benkenstein (Dol)	10	11
5	ND McKenzie (Lio)	9	10
6	RT Bailey (Eag)	10	9
	JA Beukes (Eag)	5	9
	A Jacobs (War)	9	9
	JL Ontong (Lio)	8	9
10	AN Petersen (Lio/Ttn)	8	8

CAPE COBRAS

Western Province Boland (Pty) Ltd, PO Box 23401, Claremont 7735.
Tel 021 657 2003, fax 021 657 2020.
Chief Executive: Andre Odendaal.
Physical Address: 1st floor, Slade House, Boundary Terraces, 1 Mariendahl Lane, Newlands, Cape Town.
Grounds: Sahara Park Newlands, Cape Town; Boland Park, Paarl.
Website: www.wccricket.co.za
Affiliates: Western Province Cricket Association, Boland Cricket Board.
Squad: Thami Tsolekile (captain), Derrin Bassage, Con de Lange, Jean-Paul Duminy, Quinton Friend, Benji Hector, Rory Kleinveldt, Vernon Philander, Andrew Puttick, Dominic Telo, Charl Willoughby, Monde Zondeki. One-day contracts only: Henry Davids, Alan Dawson, Adam Bacher. CSA contracted players: Graeme Smith, Ashwell Prince, Herschelle Gibbs, Jacques Kallis. Not contracted but available through sponsorship deal: Paul Adams.

REVIEW OF THE SEASON 2005/06

Michael Owen-Smith

SUPERSPORT SERIES: P10 W5 L4 D1 (third)
CAPTAIN: TL Tsolekile (10)
STANDARD BANK CUP: P10 W0 L8 T1 NR1 (sixth)
STANDARD BANK PRO20: P7 W4 L3 (beaten finalists)

The 2006/07 season will be a defining one for the Cape Cobras (as the Western Cape franchise is now known) if they are to get back among the big guns of South African domestic cricket. Last season's results were almost identical to the previous one as far as the two most important competitions (from a cricket point of view) were concerned. They again finished third in the SuperSport Series and were left to rue their poor harvest of batting bonus points and rock bottom of the Standard Bank where they failed to win a single match.

In the lucrative Pro20 they were probably fortunate that their semi-final was reduced to a seven-overs smash. The Australian professional, Ian Harvey, was recruited specifically to be an impact player who could change the course of limited overs contests but his only contribution was to play a match-winning innings in that semi-final against the Titans.

Harvey was not surprisingly dropped for the final few rounds of the SuperSport Series after indifferent form – he averaged only 16.37 with the bat – and will not be returning to fulfil the second summer of his initial contract. With most of the professional contracts coming up for renewal, new coach Shukri Conrad had the ideal opportunity to clean out the ranks and, apart from the nationally contracted quartet, only 12 players have been offered full contracts for next season plus another three on one-day terms.

The latter trio includes both veteran Alan Dawson, who only played four first-class games last summer in a sensible bid to get his body through the season, plus new recruit Adam Bacher, who has retired from first-class cricket.

CAPE COBRAS

Dawson will not be easily replaced in the four-day format although the seam bowling was easily the best department for the Cobras last season. Charl Willoughby, now a Kolpak player, again reached the 40-wicket mark (41 at 21.00) and the two newcomers, Vernon Philander and Monde Zondeki took 28 and 27 respectively.

The balance of the attack was badly disrupted by a mid-season injury to the improving all-rounder, Con de Lange, and the complete loss of form of Paul Adams. The latter is starting a new career in the financial world this year but he will still be available for the Cobras on a regular basis. South African cricket can certainly ill afford to lose one of its few spinners with a proven international record.

What the Cobras have got to do is sort out their top order batting. Fruitless attempts were made to sign an experienced batsman after a disastrous season in which the previously reliable opening combination of Andrew Puttick and Derrin Bassage struck a lean summer and Thami Tsolekile also under-performed.

J-P Duminy alone performed up to expectations and it was significant that Herschelle Gibbs, who was available for three matches while the Proteas were in India, scored two of the four centuries. The Cobras won as many matches as any team but their batting points were way off the pace (only the Warriors did worse) and this cost them the chance of contesting the final.

Philander, who has the ability to do more with the bat, was clearly the emerging talent of the season and much is also expected of Dominic Telo who came to light in the limited overs competitions and is one to watch for the future.

Playing first-class matches at Paarl was again a problem and, after a three-day match in the amateur competition had been abandoned on the second day, the remaining matches were moved to Stellenbosch where far better results were achieved.

FRANCHISE RECORDS

Highest innings totals:			
For:	509	v Lions (Paarl)	2004/05
Against:	524-4*	by Titans (Benoni)	2004/05
Lowest innings totals:			
For:	151	v Titans (Benoni)	2005/06
Against:	97	by Warriors (Stellenbosch)	2005/06
Highest individual innings:			
For:	206	AG Puttick v Warriors (East London)	2004/05
Against:	236*	M van Jaarsveld for Titans (Benoni)	2004/05
Most runs in a season:			
749 (Avg 46.81)		AG Puttick	2004/05
Most runs in a career:			
1196 (Avg 37.37)		AG Puttick	2004-05
Most 100s in a career:			
3		J-P Duminy	2004-05
Best bowling in an innings:			
For:	8-47	RK Kleinveldt v Warriors (Stellenbosch)	2005/06
Against:	8-102	N Boje for Eagles (Bloemfontein)	2005/06
Best bowling in a match:			
For:	10-80	RK Kleinveldt v Warriors (Stellenbosch)	2005/06
Against:	12-152	N Boje for Eagles (Bloemfontein)	2005/06
Most wickets in a season:			
43 (Avg 26.65)		CM Willoughby	2004/05
Most wickets in a career:			
84 (Avg 23.89)		CM Willoughby	2004-05
Most dismissals (wicketkeepers) in an innings:			
7 (ct 7)		TL Tsolekile v Dolphins (Durban)	2004/05

CAPE COBRAS

Most dismissals (wicketkeepers) in a match:		
7 (ct 7)	TL Tsolekile v Dolphins (Durban)	2004/05
7 (ct 7)	TL Tsolekile v Eagles (Bloemfontein)	2004/05
Most dismissals (wicketkeepers) in a season:		
33 (ct 32, st 1)	TL Tsolekile	2005/06
Most dismissals (wicketkeepers) in a career:		
65 (ct 64, st 1)	TL Tsolekile	2004-05
Most catches (fielders) in an innings:		
3	GC Smith, J-P Duminy, HH Gibbs and HD Ackerman	
Most catches (fielders) in a match:		
No fielder has taken more than 3 catches in a match.		
Most catches (fielders) in a season:		
14	AG Puttick	2005/06
Most catches (fielders) in a career:		
26 (plus 1 stumping)	AG Puttick	2004-05
Most appearances:		
20	AG Puttick	2004-05
Most captaincies:		
12	TL Tsolekile	2004-05

RECORD WICKET PARTNERSHIPS

1st	128	GC Smith and AG Puttick v Lions (Johannesburg)	2004/05
2nd	164	GC Smith and JG Strydom v Lions (Johannesburg)	2004/05
3rd	137	DJ Bassage and J-P Duminy v Eagles (Bloemfontein)	2005/06
4th	183	AG Prince and TL Tsolekile v Lions (Paarl)	2004/05
5th	112*	J-P Duminy and TL Tsolekile v Lions (Johannesburg)	2005/06
6th	126	TL Tsolekile and VD Philander v Titans (Paarl)	2004/05
7th	148	TL Tsolekile and RK Kleinveldt v Titans (Benoni)	2004/05
8th	86	TL Tsolekile and Q Friend v Titans (Benoni)	2004/05
9th	76	AC Dawson and M Zondeki v Eagles (Stellenbosch)	2005/06
10th	56	TL Tsolekile and M Zondeki v Eagles (Bloemfontein)	2005/06

PERFORMANCES AGAINST OTHER TEAMS

HIGHEST AND LOWEST TOTALS

Opponents	Highest Total For		Lowest Total For	
Dolphins	346	2004/05	176	2004/05
Eagles	371-7*	2004/05	206	2004/05
Lions	509	2004/05	153	2005/06
Titans	431-7*	2004/05	151	2005/06
Warriors	482-9*	2004/05	198	2005/06

BEST INDIVIDUAL PERFORMANCES

Opponents	Highest score		Best bowling (innings)		Best bowling (match, 8+)	
Dolphins	112	J-P Duminy, 2004/05	6-41	CM Willoughby, 2005/06	8-86	AC Dawson, 2004/05
Eagles	128	J-P Duminy, 2005/06	5-42	CM Willoughby, 2005/06	-	
Lions	200	GC Smith, 2004/05	6-39	AC Dawson, 2005/06	10-99	AC Dawson, 2005/06
Titans	133	HH Gibbs, 2005/06	5-49	VD Philander, 2005/06	9-55	VD Philander, 2005/06
Warriors	206	AG Puttick, 2004/05	8-47	RK Kleinveldt, 2005/06	10-80	RK Kleinveldt, 2005/06

CAPE COBRAS SUPERSPORT SERIES AVERAGES 2005/06

Batting & Fielding

Name	M	Inns	NO	Runs	HS	Avg	100	50	Ct	St
HH Gibbs	3	6	0	352	149	58.66	2	0	4	0
AC Dawson	4	6	2	179	65	44.75	0	2	2	0
J-P Duminy	10	18	3	655	128	43.66	1	4	6	0
JG Strydom	2	3	0	120	82	40.00	0	1	0	0

CAPE COBRAS

AG Puttick	10	18	2	447	70	27.93	0	4	14	0
DJ Bassage	10	18	1	465	100	27.35	1	2	6	0
H Davids	2	3	0	78	30	26.00	0	0	1	0
PR Adams	7	11	4	168	38 *	24.00	0	0	4	0
HD Ackerman	4	7	0	168	61	24.00	0	1	5	0
TL Tsolekile	10	16	1	354	91	23.60	0	1	32	1
FD Telo	1	2	0	44	26	22.00	0	0	0	0
CD de Lange	5	8	1	141	42	20.14	0	0	4	0
RK Kleinveldt	5	8	0	151	88	18.87	0	1	2	0
VD Philander	10	16	1	258	46	17.20	0	0	4	0
IJ Harvey	5	8	0	131	51	16.37	0	1	3	0
W Wyngaard	2	4	0	49	22	12.25	0	0	0	0
M Zondeki	10	15	4	64	26 *	5.81	0	0	2	0
CM Willoughby	9	12	5	24	13 *	3.42	0	0	1	0
S Conrad	1	1	0	0	0	0.00	0	0	0	0
R Munnik	1	1	0	0	0	0.00	0	0	0	0
Totals	111	181	24	3848	149		4	17	90	1
			Extras	348				subs	0	
			Total	4196		26.72			90	

Bowling

Name	**Overs**	**Mdns**	**Runs**	**Wkts**	**Avg**	**BB**	**5I**	**10M**
AC Dawson	124.4	48	262	17	15.41	6-39	1	1
RK Kleinveldt	147.5	43	379	20	18.95	8-47	1	1
IJ Harvey	43	13	100	5	20.00	2-13	0	0
CM Willoughby	333.4	91	861	41	21.00	6-41	4	0
R Munnik	7	0	24	1	24.00	1-24	0	0
VD Philander	286.5	76	729	28	26.03	5-49	1	0
M Zondeki	275.1	56	836	27	30.96	5-67	1	0
PR Adams	139	19	451	9	50.11	3-54	0	0
CD de Lange	154	44	361	5	72.20	1-6	0	0
J-P Duminy	21	3	86	1	86.00	1-70	0	0
DJ Bassage	9	2	15	0	-	-	0	0
S Conrad	3	0	21	0	-	-	0	0
Totals	1544.1	395	4125	154		8-47	8	2
		b/lb/pen	123	8	run outs			
		Total	4248	162	26.22			

MATCH REPORTS AND SCORECARDS

Warriors v Cape Cobras, Port Elizabeth, 20-22 October 2005. Cape Cobras won by 8 wickets.

CAPE COBRAS v DOLPHINS — SuperSport Series

Played at Boland Park, Paarl on 27,28,29,30 October 2005 — Toss: Dolphins
Umpires: M Gajjar & S Wadvalla — Referee: MR Magiet
Debuts: Cob: None. Dol: None
Close of play: Day 1: Dol (1) 308-3 (HM Amla 118*, Benkenstein 9*, 97 overs). Day 2: Cob (1) 109-1 (Strydom 58*, De Lange 8*, 33 overs). Day 3: Cob (1) 301-7 (Philander 28*, Adams 17*, 129 overs).
Result: Match drawn
Man of Match: Hashim Amla
Points: Cob: 4.02 (bat 3.02, bowl 1, match 0); Dol: 5.28 (bat 4.28, bowl 1, match 0)
Notes: Munnik replaced Puttick who was called up to the national team.

With the two first innings consuming more than 300 overs between them, there was never going to be much chance of a result. The Amla brothers put on 205 for the third wicket off 378 balls for a new franchise wicket record while Govender achieved his best first-class return and Benkenstein his best in South African domestic first-class cricket.

Puttick was withdrawn from the Cobras line-up on the second morning to enable him to make an 11th hour one-day debut for the Proteas against New Zealand.

DOLPHINS	*Runs*	*Mins*	*Balls*	*4*	*6*		*Runs*	*Mins*	*Balls*	*4*	*6*
DJ Watson b Philander	39	103	70	7	-	lbw b Munnik	52	219	158	7	-
I Khan c Puttick b De Lange	36	123	79	5	-	c and b De Lange	27	110	78	3	-
HM Amla lbw b Philander	137	362	273	17	-	not out	58	151	129	8	-
AM Amla b Adams	98	245	192	15		not out	15	41	39	2	-
DM Benkenstein c Tsolekile b Willoughby	23	100	75	3	-						
JC Kent lbw b Philander	48	175	135	6	-						
†D Smit c Tsolekile b Zondeki	3	40	28	-	-						
RP Symcox lbw b Adams	1	17	11	-	-						
*L Klusener run out (Duminy/Tsolekile)	35	105	95	2	-						
TD Pillay c Harvey b Philander	0	9	5	-	-						
U Govender not out	0	1	1	-	-						
Extras (b 1, lb 6, w 1, nb 4)	12					Extras (b 1, lb 1, w 1, nb 2)	5				
TOTAL (160 overs)	**432**					**TOTAL (for 2 wkts) (67 overs)**	**157**				

CAPE COBRAS	*Runs*	*Mins*	*Balls*	*4*	*6*
DJ Bassage c Smit b Kent	39	105	67	5	-
JG Strydom lbw b Benkenstein	82	259	188	9	-
CD de Lange b Benkenstein	29	134	93	3	-
J-P Duminy c Smit b Benkenstein	2	29	17	-	-
IJ Harvey c Symcox b Govender	51	173	118	2	-
*†TL Tsolekile c Smit b Govender	31	176	131	1	-
R Munnik lbw b Govender	0	4	3	-	-
VD Philander lbw b Benkenstein	30	130	90	3	-
PR Adams not out	38	157	116	4	-
M Zondeki b Govender	8	27	22	-	-
CM Willoughby b Govender	0	5	1	-	-
AG Puttick					
Extras (b 5, lb 11, w 1, nb 5)	22				
TOTAL (140.1 overs)	**332**				

Cob	*O*	*M*	*R*	*W*		*O*	*M*	*R*	*W*
Willoughby	22	7	63	1		8	1	26	0
Zondeki	26	3	69	1 (4 nb)		8	2	14	0 (2 nb)
Philander	27	8	80	4	(4)	11	3	29	0
Harvey	7	2	15	0					
De Lange	45	13	98	1	(3)	19	7	34	1 (1 w)
Adams	33	5	100	2 (1 w)	(5)	5	0	13	0
Bassage					(6)	9	2	15	0
Munnik					(7)	7	0	24	1

Dol	*O*	*M*	*R*	*W*
Klusener	31	4	100	0 (4 nb, 1 w)
Symcox	19	2	49	0
Kent	18	6	31	1
Govender	27.1	6	57	5 (1 nb)
Pillay	13	4	34	0
Watson	2	0	4	0
Benkenstein	30	14	41	4

Fall of Wickets

	Dol	**Cob**	**Dol**
1st	76 (1)	89 (1)	55 (2)
2nd	86 (2)	152 (3)	129 (1)
3rd	291 (4)	159 (2)	-
4th	341 (3)	162 (4)	-
5th	341 (5)	251 (5)	-
6th	351 (7)	251 (7)	-
7th	355 (8)	252 (6)	-
8th	429 (9)	305 (8)	-
9th	431 (6)	324 (10)	-
10th	432 (10)	332 (11)	-

CAPE COBRAS v TITANS — SuperSport Series

Played at Sahara Park Newlands, Cape Town on 3,4,5,6 November 2005 — Toss: Titans

Umpires: MW Brown & S George — Referee: WA Diedricks

Debuts: Cob: None. Ttn: None

Close of play: Day 1: Cob (1) 110-4 (Duminy 3*, Harvey 0*, 38 overs). Day 2: Cob (2) 185-2 (Gibbs 56*, Duminy 31*, 48 overs). Day 3: Ttn (2) 133-5 (P de Bruyn 13*, Van Wyk 19*, 47 overs).

Result: Cape Cobras won by 230 runs

Man of Match: Herschelle Gibbs

Points: Cob: 15.2 (bat 1.20, bowl 4, match 10); Ttn: 4 (bat 0.00, bowl 4, match 0)

Rain produced a lively pitch on the first two days with the result that Thomas and Philander both produced their best innings analysis in first-class cricket. Thomas went on to record his first ten-wicket haul in a match. Puttick and Bassage's opening partnership of 92 almost turned out to be match-winning in the context of the proceedings.

Gibbs then took the match away from the Titans with his second innings century and Philander further improved his best innings analysis to give him 9-55 in the match.

CAPE COBRAS	Runs	Mins	Balls	4	6		Runs	Mins	Balls	4	6
AG Puttick c Van Wyk b Thomas	48	129	99	9	-	c Petersen b Mbhalati	53	153	97	6	-
DJ Bassage lbw b Steyn	39	132	80	5	-	lbw b Z de Bruyn	39	96	80	7	-
HH Gibbs c Seymore b Thomas	9	25	8	1	-	b Steyn	133	292	190	19	2
J-P Duminy c P de Bruyn b Steyn	23	126	71	3	-	lbw b Steyn	35	66	59	5	-
CD de Lange c Seymore b Mbhalati	4	14	15	-	-	(8) not out	22	53	33	2	1
IJ Harvey c Seymore b Thomas	4	15	9	-	-	(5) c P de Bruyn b Z de Bruyn	13	27	17	2	-
*†TL Tsolekile lbw b Thomas	1	9	8	-	-	(6) c and b Harris	36	69	54	5	-
VD Philander lbw b Thomas	8	19	13	1	-	(7) lbw b Thomas	17	46	46	2	-
AC Dawson c Van Jaarsveld b Thomas	0	2	2	-	-	c Seymore b Thomas	0	12	4	-	-
M Zondeki c Van Wyk b Thomas	3	34	31	-	-	c Van Jaarsveld b Thomas	1	10	7	-	-
CM Willoughby not out	2	3	2	-	-	b Steyn	1	12	7	-	-
Extras (b 4, lb 7, w 1, nb 7)	19					Extras (b 7, lb 9, w 2, nb 4)	22				
TOTAL (55.1 overs)	**160**					**TOTAL (98.2 overs)**	**372**				

TITANS	Runs	Mins	Balls	4	6		Runs	Mins	Balls	4	6
AN Petersen c Gibbs b Dawson	21	57	50	4	-	lbw b Zondeki	20	74	48	2	-
AJ Seymore c Gibbs b Willoughby	0	4	1	-	-	c Duminy b Philander	36	54	46	6	-
*M van Jaarsveld c Tsolekile b Willoughby	20	56	37	2	1	lbw b Philander	9	25	15	2	-
Z de Bruyn c Puttick b Philander	23	63	40	4	-	b Philander	9	24	12	1	-
GH Bodi c Puttick b Willoughby	6	26	18	-	-	b Philander	21	81	56	2	-
P de Bruyn c Gibbs b Harvey	6	24	15	1	-	c De Lange b Zondeki	14	105	91	-	-
†CFK van Wyk lbw b Harvey	0	3	3	-	-	not out	57	120	70	9	-
AC Thomas c Tsolekile b Philander	6	28	14	1	-	c Tsolekile b Willoughby	20	60	47	2	-
PL Harris lbw b Philander	0	2	2	-	-	c and b Dawson	0	3	1	-	-
DW Steyn c Bassage b Philander	10	16	9	1	-	c Tsolekile b Willoughby	3	5	6	-	-
NE Mbhalati not out	1	2	1	-	-	b Philander	4	6	7	1	-
Extras (lb 9, w 1)	10					Extras (lb 2, nb 4)	6				
TOTAL (31.4 overs)	**103**					**TOTAL (65.5 overs)**	**199**				

Ttn	O	M	R	W		O	M	R	W
Steyn	17.1	4	32	2 (1 nb, 1 w)	(3)	17.2	5	52	3
Thomas	22	3	54	7 (6 nb)	(1)	29	4	107	3 (1 nb)
Mbhalati	12	4	43	1	(2)	14	2	68	1 (3 nb)
Z de Bruyn	4	1	20	0		9	1	37	2
Harris						20	3	74	1
P de Bruyn						9	0	18	0 (2 w)
Cob	O	M	R	W		O	M	R	W
Willoughby	12	2	33	3 (1 w)		14	4	41	2
Zondeki	4	0	22	0	(3)	15	3	69	2 (3 nb)
Dawson	9	4	20	1	(2)	11	3	31	1
Harvey	4	2	13	2					
Philander	2.4	0	6	4	(4)	22.5	6	49	5 (1 nb)
De Lange					(5)	3	1	7	0

Fall of Wickets	**Cob**	**Ttn**	**Cob**	**Ttn**
1st	92 (1)	1 (2)	71 (2)	53 (2)
2nd	92 (2)	45 (1)	130 (1)	67 (1)
3rd	105 (3)	45 (3)	197 (4)	71 (3)
4th	110 (5)	69 (5)	225 (5)	87 (4)
5th	120 (6)	84 (6)	299 (6)	108 (5)
6th	127 (7)	84 (7)	342 (7)	135 (6)
7th	139 (8)	86 (4)	354 (3)	190 (8)
8th	139 (9)	86 (9)	361 (9)	191 (9)
9th	158 (10)	102 (10)	369 (10)	194 (10)
10th	160 (4)	103 (8)	372 (11)	199 (11)

Lions v Cobras, Johannesburg, 10-13 November 2005. Cape Cobras won by 6 wickets.

Eagles v Cape Cobras, Bloemfontein, 17-20 November 2005. Eagles won by 10 wickets.

Dolphins v Cape Cobras, Durban, 23-26 February 2006. Dolphins won by 6 wickets.

CAPE COBRAS v WARRIORS — SuperSport Series

Played at University Oval, Coetzenburg, Stellenbosch on 2,3,4 March 2006 — Toss: Warriors
Umpires: M Erasmus & IW Shine — Referee: WA Diedricks
Debuts: Cob: None. War: None
Close of play: Day 1: Cob (1) 77-1 (Puttick 40*, Duminy 30*, 25 overs). Day 2: War (2) 134-6 (Jacobs 62*, Sodumo 1*, 49 overs).
Result: Cape Cobras won by 7 wickets
Man of Match: Rory Kleinveldt
Points: Cob: 15.96 (bat 1.96, bowl 4, match 10); War: 4 (bat 0.00, bowl 4, match 0)
Notes: Kreusch took a hat-trick in Cape Cobras' 1st innings. His victims were Ackerman, Zondeki, Conrad. He also took 4 wickets in 5 balls to end the Cape Cobras' 1st innings.

The Warriors surprisingly chose to bat first and were bowled out in a ball short of 40 overs with Kleinveldt taking his best first-class return and the best since the start of the franchise.

A 101-run partnership for the second wicket between Puttick and Duminy gave the Cobras a winning lead before Kreusch abruptly ended the innings with his first hat-trick and four wickets in five balls. It was also the first time that he took five wickets in an innings.

Jacobs held out stubbornly for over four hours in the Warriors' second innings but the match was over before tea on the third day.

WARRIORS	Runs	Mins	Balls	4	6		Runs	Mins	Balls	4	6
BL Bennett lbw b Kleinveldt	10	77	53	-	-	c Willoughby b Zondeki	6	30	25	-	-
*CC Bradfield c Tsolekile b Kleinveldt	12	35	29	2	-	b Willoughby	0	4	1	-	-
BC de Wett lbw b Kleinveldt	0	4	2	-	-	lbw b Zondeki	2	38	30	-	-
A Jacobs c Puttick b Kleinveldt	23	61	40	3	-	c Tsolekile b Adams	90	262	177	12	-
J Botha c Bassage b Kleinveldt	16	60	51	2	-	lbw b Zondeki	1	5	3	-	-
SC Pope c Puttick b Kleinveldt	16	45	28	3	-	b Zondeki	30	96	64	4	-
JP Kreusch lbw b Willoughby	2	14	17	-	-	c Puttick b Philander	31	49	44	3	-
†AM Sodumo c Tsolekile b Kleinveldt	5	16	9	1	-	b Kleinveldt	9	90	64	-	-
T Henderson b Willoughby	5	8	5	1	-	c Philander b Adams	2	8	4	-	-
L Meyer not out	0	5	2	-	-	b Kleinveldt	1	19	15	-	-
BB Kops b Kleinveldt	0	1	3	-	-	not out	8	16	12	2	-
Extras (b 2, lb 6)	8					Extras (lb 11, w 2)	13				
TOTAL (39.5 overs)	**97**					**TOTAL (73.1 overs)**	**193**				

CAPE COBRAS	Runs	Mins	Balls	4	6		Runs	Mins	Balls	4	6
AG Puttick c Pope b Kops	56	168	122	9	-	lbw b Henderson	13	38	30	2	-
DJ Bassage lbw b Kops	0	5	1	-	-	c Jacobs b Kops	9	26	19	2	-
J-P Duminy c and b Meyer	64	251	178	6	1	not out	38	113	75	7	-
HD Ackerman c Meyer b Kreusch	31	157	113	3	-	b Meyer	23	74	60	2	-
VD Philander c Kreusch b Kops	21	29	30	2	-	not out	4	24	16	1	-
*†TL Tsolekile lbw b Kreusch	7	21	16	-	-						
RK Kleinveldt c Kreusch b Meyer	0	9	5	-	-						
PR Adams not out	0	12	4	-	-						
M Zondeki lbw b Kreusch	0	1	1	-	-						
S Conrad lbw b Kreusch	0	1	1	-	-						
CM Willoughby c Bennett b Kreusch	0	1	2	-	-						
Extras (b 4, lb 4, w 5, nb 6)	19					Extras (b 4, lb 1, w 4)	9				
TOTAL (77.5 overs)	**198**					**TOTAL (for 3 wkts) (33.2 overs)**	**96**				

Cob	O	M	R	W			O	M	R	W	
Willoughby	13	5	22	2			23	3	53	1	(1 w)
Zondeki	5	2	9	0			19	5	39	4	(1 w)
Kleinveldt	14.5	1	47	8			14.1	6	33	2	
Philander	7	4	11	0			10	1	24	1	
Conrad							3	0	21	0	
Adams							4	0	12	2	
War	O	M	R	W			O	M	R	W	
Henderson	23	8	46	0	(1 nb)		10	2	24	1	
Kops	14	3	41	3	(4 w)		11	1	41	1	(4 w)
Meyer	19	6	49	2		(4)	6.2	3	13	1	
Kreusch	16.5	7	31	5	(3 nb, 1 w)	(3)	6	0	13	0	
De Wett	5	0	23	0	(2 nb)						

Fall of Wickets	War	Cob	War	Cob
1st	18 (2)	2 (2)	1 (2)	21 (2)
2nd	20 (3)	103 (1)	7 (1)	28 (1)
3rd	38 (1)	154 (3)	9 (3)	75 (4)
4th	55 (4)	182 (5)	15 (5)	-
5th	80 (5)	195 (6)	86 (6)	-
6th	87 (6)	198 (7)	132 (7)	-
7th	87 (7)	198 (4)	169 (8)	-
8th	97 (9)	198 (9)	175 (4)	-
9th	97 (8)	198 (10)	176 (9)	-
10th	97 (11)	198 (11)	193 (10)	-

CAPE COBRAS

Titans v Cape Cobras, Benoni, 9-12 March 2006. Titans won by an innings and 5 runs.

CAPE COBRAS v EAGLES — SuperSport Series

Played at University Oval, Coetzenburg, Stellenbosch on 16,17,18 March 2006 — Toss: Cape Cobras
Umpires: MW Brown & M Erasmus — Referee: WA Diedricks
Debuts: Cob: None. Eag: None
Close of play: Day 1: Cob (1) 139-3 (Bassage 75*, Ackerman 6*, 47 overs). Day 2: Eag (2) 67-1 (Beukes 36*, Hector 16*, 26 overs)..
Result: Cape Cobras won by 10 wickets
Man of Match: Derrin Bassage
Points: Cob: 16.94 (bat 2.94, bowl 4, match 10); Eag: 3 (bat 0.00, bowl 3, match 0)

The second match in a row at Stellenbosch finished before tea on the third day with the visiting batsmen again failing to deal with the Cobras seam attack. The Eagles were bowled out inside 47 overs after being put into bat in spite of the home side being handicapped by a hamstring injury to Dawson.

Dawson did make up, contributing a rare half-century and a 76-run partnership for the ninth-wicket with Zondeki after Bassage had scored a match-winning century. The Cobras were left with a winning target of only nine runs in 139 overs.

EAGLES	*Runs*	*Mins*	*Balls*	*4*	*6*		*Runs*	*Mins*	*Balls*	*4*	*6*
RT Bailey lbw b Willoughby	0	2	3	-	-	(2) lbw b Willoughby	7	45	32	1	-
JA Beukes c Philander b Kleinveldt	21	98	58	3	-	(1) c Tsolekile b Zondeki	46	185	127	5	-
B Hector lbw b Willoughby	0	1	1	-	-	lbw b Zondeki	25	145	107	2	-
DJ Jacobs c Tsolekile b Dawson	12	27	21	2	-	c Tsolekile b Philander	6	36	22	1	-
*†MN van Wyk lbw b Willoughby	3	14	9	-	-	not out	42	149	82	5	-
LL Bosman lbw b Kleinveldt	2	30	26	-	-	lbw b Kleinveldt	0	5	5	-	-
R McLaren c Tsolekile b Zondeki	38	127	76	7	-	b Kleinveldt	22	48	38	5	-
JJ van der Wath c Puttick b Willoughby	52	63	50	9	-	lbw b Zondeki	2	22	17	-	-
R Telemachus b Willoughby	9	23	24	2	-	c Ackerman b Philander	18	34	29	3	-
T Tshabalala c Puttick b Philander	7	24	11	1	-	(11) absent hurt					
PV Mpitsang not out	0	5	2	-	-	(10) b Philander	0	1	1	-	-
Extras (lb 5)	5					Extras (b 5, lb 9, nb 1)	15				
TOTAL (46.5 overs)	**149**					**TOTAL (76.3 overs)**	**183**				

CAPE COBRAS	*Runs*	*Mins*	*Balls*	*4*	*6*		*Runs*	*Mins*	*Balls*	*4*	*6*
AG Puttick b Mpitsang	2	14	10	-	-	not out	8	7	8	2	-
DJ Bassage b McLaren	100	312	208	17	-	not out	1	7	1	-	-
H Davids c Beukes b Telemachus	30	85	68	4	-						
J-P Duminy b Tshabalala	21	64	56	3	-						
HD Ackerman lbw b McLaren	31	118	83	5	-						
VD Philander c sub (LN Mosena) b Mpitsang	14	93	54	2	-						
*†TL Tsolekile c Beukes b Mpitsang	11	78	65	-	-						
RK Kleinveldt c sub (LN Mosena) b McLaren	11	57	32	1	-						
AC Dawson c Telemachus b Beukes	65	107	71	12	-						
M Zondeki not out	26	64	44	3	-						
CM Willoughby b Telemachus	0	5	1	-	-						
Extras (lb 4, w 1, nb 8)	13					Extras	0				
TOTAL (114 overs)	**324**					**TOTAL (for 0 wkts) (1.3 overs)**	**9**				

Cob	*O*	*M*	*R*	*W*		*O*	*M*	*R*	*W*	
Willoughby	19	7	42	5		23	4	43	1	
Dawson	9.5	5	10	1						
Kleinveldt	11.1	1	53	2		19	7	44	2	
Zondeki	6	0	35	1		(2) 17	3	46	3	(1 nb)
Philander	0.5	0	4	1		(4) 14.3	6	23	3	
Duminy						(5) 3	1	13	0	
Eag	*O*	*M*	*R*	*W*		*O*	*M*	*R*	*W*	
Van der Wath	9	2	29	0						
Mpitsang	31	10	75	3		(1) 1	0	4	0	
McLaren	28	9	61	3	(1 nb)	(2) 0.3	0	5	0	
Telemachus	26	6	77	2	(6 nb)					
Tshabalala	5	1	14	1						
Bailey	13	2	53	0	(1 nb, 1 w)					
Beukes	2	0	11	1						

Fall of Wickets

	Eag	**Cob**	**Eag**	**Cob**
1st	0 (1)	13 (1)	27 (2)	-
2nd	0 (3)	75 (3)	84 (1)	-
3rd	15 (4)	122 (4)	87 (3)	-
4th	24 (5)	178 (5)	106 (4)	-
5th	31 (6)	194 (2)	107 (6)	-
6th	52 (2)	217 (6)	152 (7)	-
7th	117 (8)	218 (7)	162 (8)	-
8th	131 (9)	247 (8)	183 (9)	-
9th	145 (7)	323 (9)	183 (10)	-
10th	149 (10)	324 (11)	-	-

CAPE COBRAS v LIONS — SuperSport Series

Played at Sahara Park Newlands, Cape Town on 23,24,25,26 March 2006 — Toss: Cape Cobras
Umpires: MW Brown & S George — Referee: S Naidoo
Debuts: Cob: None. Lio: None
Close of play: Day 1: Cob (1) 16-2 (Davids 7*, Duminy 4*, 7.5 overs). Day 2: Lio (2) 121-2 (Cook 51*, McKenzie 45*, 45 overs). Day 3: Cob (2) 174-6 (Tsolekile 14*, Kleinveldt 19*, 60 overs).
Result: Lions won by 25 runs
Man of Match: Friedel de Wet
Points: Cob: 5.06 (bat 1.06, bowl 4, match 0); Lio: 17.14 (bat 3.14, bowl 4, match 10)

Both franchises started the match with a chance of reaching the final, depending on events in the corresponding fixture between the Titans and the Dolphins. In the end victory would have seen the Cobras through at the expense of the Titans had Kleinveldt's last-gasp onslaught been carried through to the conclusion.

The Lions appeared to have the match wrapped up when the Cobras collapsed to 148-6 in pursuit of a victory target of 298 in 163 overs. But Kleinveldt put up a Custer-like stand to smash 88 off 95 balls (including four sixes) before perishing against the second new ball.

De Wet achieved his best first-class match analysis of 11-152 (also his first haul of ten wickets or more) while Willoughby and Zondeki bowled unchanged throughout the morning session and again after lunch until the conclusion of the Lions second innings on the third day (a total of 26.4 overs between them). Zondeki completed his first five-wicket return in SuperSport Series cricket.

LIONS	*Runs*	*Mins*	*Balls*	*4*	*6*		*Runs*	*Mins*	*Balls*	*4*	*6*
SC Cook b Willoughby	4	12	11	-	-	c Kleinveldt b Willoughby	63	241	165	5	-
AN Petersen c Adams b Zondeki	52	131	97	7	-	lbw b Zondeki	16	55	39	1	-
JL Ontong lbw b Willoughby	1	8	5	-	-	lbw b Zondeki	0	2	1	-	-
*ND McKenzie b Zondeki	31	113	68	4	-	c Davids b Willoughby	47	134	110	5	1
VB van Jaarsveld st Tsolekile b Adams	55	131	98	5	-	c Kleinveldt b Zondeki	51	128	70	5	2
†MJ Harris c Tsolekile b Philander	2	14	11	-	-	b Willoughby	1	9	7	-	-
ET Nkwe lbw b Kleinveldt	14	57	38	1	-	c Puttick b Willoughby	4	21	13	-	-
WL Coetsee not out	55	149	80	1	-	lbw b Zondeki	1	6	5	-	-
EO Moleon c Zondeki b Adams	15	46	42	-	-	b Zondeki	0	3	2	-	-
F de Wet c Tsolekile b Adams	6	19	18	-	-	c Tsolekile b Willoughby	0	25	15	-	
GJ de Bruin c Bassage b Kleinveldt	6	27	28	1	-	not out	0	15	8	-	-
Extras (lb 9, w 1, nb 6)	16					Extras (lb 4, w 1, nb 5)	10				
TOTAL (81.4 overs)	**257**					**TOTAL (71.4 overs)**	**193**				

CAPE COBRAS	*Runs*	*Mins*	*Balls*	*4*	*6*		*Runs*	*Mins*	*Balls*	*4*	*6*
AG Puttick c Harris b De Wet	0	8	7	-	-	(3) b De Wet	5	9	11	1	-
DJ Bassage c Harris b De Wet	4	13	9	1	-	(1) c Ontong b De Wet	3	20	18	-	-
H Davids c Ontong b De Wet	23	74	56	3	-	(2) lbw b Moleon	25	127	73	3	-
J-P Duminy c Petersen b De Wet	45	158	116	6	-	lbw b De Wet	59	171	134	6	-
FD Telo c Van Jaarsveld b Moleon	18	72	46	2	-	c Cook b Coetsee	26	67	51	1	1
*†TL Tsolekile c Harris b De Wet	10	40	30	1	-	c Harris b De Wet	25	102	83	1	-
VD Philander c Cook b Moleon	31	68	47	6	-	c Petersen b De Bruin	6	33	19	1	-
RK Kleinveldt c Van Jaarsveld b De Bruin	1	4	2	-	-	c Cook b De Bruin	88	127	95	8	4
PR Adams c and b De Wet	0	5	6	-	-	c Van Jaarsveld b De Bruin	12	51	26	1	-
M Zondeki c Harris b De Wet	8	27	16	1	-	lbw b De Bruin	0	2	1	-	-
CM Willoughby not out	0	4	3	-	-	not out	1	10	1	-	-
Extras (w 7, nb 6)	13					Extras (lb 9, w 1, nb 12)	22				
TOTAL (55.2 overs)	**153**					**TOTAL (83.2 overs)**	**272**				

Cob	*O*	*M*	*R*	*W*		*O*	*M*	*R*	*W*	
Willoughby	16	6	36	2		23	3	51	5	
Zondeki	14	0	52	2	(3 nb)	22.4	8	67	5	(1 nb, 1 w)
Kleinveldt	14.4	3	57	2	(1 nb)	9	3	24	0	(2 nb)
Philander	23	4	49	1	(2 nb, 1 w)	8	2	20	0	(2 nb)
Adams	14	2	54	3		9	2	27	0	
Lio	*O*	*M*	*R*	*W*		*O*	*M*	*R*	*W*	
De Wet	23	6	61	7	(4 nb, 1 w)	25	1	91	4	(6 nb)
De Bruin	18	4	61	1	(1 w)	16.2	1	47	4	(3 nb)
Nkwe	6	1	18	0	(1 nb, 1 w)	5	0	26	0	(3 nb, 1 w)
Moleon	6.2	1	10	2	(1 nb)	21	12	43	1	
Coetsee	2	1	3	0		15	2	47	1	
Ontong						1	0	9	0	

Fall of Wickets

	Lio	**Cob**	**Lio**	**Cob**
1st	6 (1)	4 (1)	35 (2)	8 (1)
2nd	10 (3)	7 (2)	35 (3)	14 (3)
3rd	96 (2)	60 (3)	126 (4)	76 (2)
4th	97 (4)	98 (5)	145 (1)	130 (5)
5th	105 (6)	109 (4)	153 (6)	132 (4)
6th	143 (7)	126 (6)	161 (7)	148 (7)
7th	189 (5)	127 (8)	162 (8)	197 (6)
8th	222 (9)	128 (9)	162 (9)	255 (9)
9th	230 (10)	150 (10)	180 (10)	255 (10)
10th	257 (11)	153 (7)	193 (5)	272 (8)

JOINT CHAMPIONS . . . the Dolphins players pose with the SuperSport Series trophy. They topped the league table but had to share the title with the Titans after the final in Durban ended in a draw
Picture: TERTIUS PICKARD, Touchline Photo

DOLPHINS

KZN Cricket (Pty) Ltd, PO Box 47266, Greyville 4023.
Tel 031 335 4200. Fax: 031 332 5288.
Chief Executive: Cassim Docrat
Physical Address: Sahara Stadium Kingsmead, 2 Kingsmead Way, Durban.
Ground: Sahara Stadium Kingsmead.
Website: www.dolphinscricket.co.za
Affiliates: KwaZulu-Natal Cricket Board.
Contracted players: Ahmed Amla (captain), Hashim Amla, Dale Benkenstein, Duncan Brown, Ugasen Govender, Jon Kent, Imraan Khan, Lance Klusener, Johann Louw, Tyron Pillay, Kyle Smit, Russel Symcox, Andrew Tweedie, Doug Watson. Rookies: Yusuf Abdullah, Robbie Frylinck, Saidi Mhlongo. CSA contracted players: Andrew Hall, Shaun Pollock.
Coach: Graham Ford.

REVIEW OF THE SEASON 2005/06

Patrick Compton

SUPERSPORT SERIES: P11 W5 L0 D6 (joint winners)
CAPTAIN: L Klusener (10), DM Benkenstein (1)
STANDARD BANK CUP: P11 W4 L5 T1 NR1 (semi-finalists)
STANDARD BANK PRO20: P5 W2 L3 (fifth)

The Nashua Dolphins enjoyed another successful first-class season, sharing the SuperSport Series trophy for the second consecutive year. They were unable, however, to achieve the same level of success in limited overs cricket, with the team failing to qualify for the finals of the Standard Bank Cup and the Standard Bank Pro20 competition.

Overall, the Dolphins could argue that their cup was half full, rather than half empty. Under the increasingly assured captaincy of Lance Klusener, the Durban-based franchise topped the SuperSport Series log, winning five of their ten pool matches and remaining unbeaten throughout the season - the only team to do so. They were unable to cap this effort, however, by winning their home final against the Nashua Titans, the five-day match eventually ending in a tame draw.

Still, it was a satisfying enough climax to the season, and a fitting end also to the impressive career of 62-year-old Phil Russell who completed his second two-year stint as Dolphins' coach. A Derbyshire professional, Russell had been involved with KwaZulu-Natal cricket since 1977. During his 29-year association with the union, he filled the roles of coach, groundsman, director of professional cricket and stadium manager. Russell has been succeeded by former Dolphins and Proteas coach Graham Ford.

Klusener, who began a two-year contract with Northamptonshire at the end of the South African season, was expected to return to Durban for the 2006/07 season, but declined to continue as captain. With former skipper Dale Benkenstein also reluctant to take on the captaincy again, the job was given to Ahmed Amla, the elder brother of Hashim, who captained the team for one season in 2004/05. The Dolphins were strengthened by the signing of Proteas all-rounder Andrew Hall and seam bowler Johann Louw, whose previous stint with the franchise was shortened when he opted for a Kolpak contract with Northamptonshire.

Klusener's reluctance to stay on as captain was influenced by more volatility in the administration of the union, with the president, Logan Naidoo, publicly slating the captain, selectors and team in extravagant terms after their semi-final loss to the Titans in the Standard Bank Cup.

This tremor was followed, at the end of the season, by something closer to an earthquake with the resignation of the union's chief executive, Enver Mall, a former national selector who had been in the job for only a year. He quit the day after the SuperSport Series final. It had long been apparent that he did not command the support of the union's executive.

The first-class season began slowly for the Dolphins with two draws against the Lions and the Cobras but their season caught fire when they managed a rare away victory against the Eagles, their first in Bloemfontein since January 1988. Centuries by man of the match Imraan Khan and Benkenstein led to a ten-wicket triumph after 16 wickets fell on the final day.

Victory against perennial losers the Warriors enabled the Dolphins to top the table at the half-way stage of the competition, a position they maintained to the end with further victories against the Warriors, the Cobras and the Lions.

One of the most encouraging developments was the progress of the Dolphins' young, home-grown pace bowlers, with Ugasen Govender and Saidi Mhlongo doing particularly well.

Govender, the team's leading wicket-taker with 32 at 22.43, did enough to suggest that he could take the new ball next season, while the left-arm Mhlongo, after being introduced in the second half of the SuperSport Series, showed good discipline and stamina as well as a valuable ability to swing the ball both ways.

It was the consistent batting, however, that proved to be the team's most enduring achievement, with Benkenstein (652 runs at 65.20) topping the averages and five of the Dolphins' batsmen featuring in the top 15. Hashim Amla enjoyed another prolific season with the bat, scoring the most runs (893) and earning himself a call-up for the second Test against New Zealand at Newlands, an occasion he celebrated with his first Test century.

Dolphins' batsmen were also responsible for the fastest 50 and 100 of the season, with Ahmed Amla scoring 50 in 39 balls against the Lions at the Wanderers and Klusener cracking a century in 79 balls against the Warriors at Kingsmead.

FRANCHISE RECORDS

Honours:

SuperSport Series (2): 2004/05 (shared), 2005/06 (shared)

Highest innings totals:			
For:	612-8*	v Eagles (Bloemfontein)	2004/05
Against:	541-9*	by Eagles (Bloemfontein)	2004/05
Lowest innings totals:			
For:	176	v Titans (Durban)	2005/06
Against:	165	by Warriors (Port Elizabeth)	2004/05
Highest individual innings:			
For:	249	HM Amla v Eagles (Bloemfontein)	2004/05
Against:	218	DJ Jacobs for Eagles (Bloemfontein)	2004/05
Most runs in a season:			
893 (Avg 55.81)		HM Amla	2005/06
Most runs in a career:			
1600 (Avg 55.17)		HM Amla	2004-05

DOLPHINS

Most 100s in a career:			
5		HM Amla	2004-05
Best bowling in an innings:			
For:	6-59	U Govender v Titans (Centurion)	2005/06
Against:	8-93	N Boje for Eagles (Durban)	2005/06
Best bowling in a match:			
For:	8-108	ANW Tweedie v Warriors (Port Elizabeth)	2004/05
Against:	9-161	GJ-P Kruger for Lions (Durban)	2005/06
Most wickets in a season:			
36 (Avg 32.19)		L Klusener	2004/05
Most wickets in a career:			
70 (Avg 31.67)		L Klusener	2004-05
Most dismissals (wicketkeepers) in an innings:			
5 (ct 5)		DL Brown v Western Province Boland (Durban)	2004/05
5 (ct 5)		DL Brown v Lions (Johannesburg)	2004/05
5 (ct 5)		DL Brown v Warriors (Durban)	2004/05
Most dismissals (wicketkeepers) in a match:			
7 (ct 7)		DL Brown v Western Province Boland (Durban)	2004/05
7 (ct 7)		DL Brown v Warriors (Durban)	2004/05
Most dismissals (wicketkeepers) in a season:			
51 (ct 51)		DL Brown	2004/05
Most dismissals (wicketkeepers) in a career:			
65 (ct 65)		DL Brown	2004-05
Most catches (fielders) in an innings:			
3		RP Symcox v Titans (Durban)	2004/05
3		DM Benkenstein v Cape Cobras (Durban)	2005/06
Most catches (fielders) in a match:			
4		RP Symcox v Titans (Durban)	2004/05
Most catches (fielders) in a season:			
12		JC Kent	2004/05
Most catches (fielders) in a career:			
21		DM Benkenstein	2004-05
Most appearances:			
22		DJ Watson	2004-05
Most captaincies:			
12		L Klusener	2004-05

RECORD WICKET PARTNERSHIPS

1st	176	DJ Watson and I Khan v Titans (Durban)	2005/06
2nd	201	R Gobind and HM Amla v Cape Cobras (Durban)	2005/06
3rd	211	DJ Watson and AM Amla v Lions (Johannesburg)	2005/06
4th	193	HM Amla and DM Benkenstein v Warriors (Port Elizabeth)	2004/05
5th	296	HM Amla and JC Kent v Eagles (Bloemfontein)	2004/05
6th	103	HM Amla and SM Pollock v Western Province Boland (Durban)	2004/05
7th	157	JC Kent and RP Symcox v Lions (Durban)	2005/06
8th	108	DL Brown and L Klusener v Western Province Boland (Durban)	2004/05
9th	81	L Klusener and ANW Tweedie v Warriors (Durban)	2005/06
10th	64	M Ngam and ANW Tweedie v Titans (Durban)	2004/05

PERFORMANCES AGAINST OTHER TEAMS

HIGHEST AND LOWEST TOTALS

Opponents	Highest Total For		Lowest Total For	
Cape Cobras	432	2005/06	214	2005/06
Eagles	612-8*	2004/05	300	2004/05
Lions	471-6	2004/05	182	2004/05
Titans	470	2005/06	176	2005/06
Warriors	512-7*	2005/06	223	2004/05

BEST INDIVIDUAL PERFORMANCES

Opponents	Highest score		Best bowling (innings)		Best bowling (match, 8+)	
Cape Cobras	153	HM Amla, 2005/06	5-57	U Govender, 2005/06	-	
Eagles	249	HM Amla, 2004/05	6-122	L Klusener, 2004/05	-	
Lions	125	AM Amla, 2005/06	5-87	U Govender, 2004/05	-	
Titans	151	DM Benkenstein, 2005/06	6-59	U Govender, 2005/06	-	
Warriors	144	K Smit, 2005/06	5-39	L Klusener, 2005/06	8-108	ANW Tweedie, 2004/05

DOLPHINS SUPERSPORT SERIES AVERAGES 2005/06

Batting & Fielding

Name	M	Inns	NO	Runs	HS	Avg	100	50	Ct	St
DM Benkenstein	10	15	5	652	151	65.20	3	1	11	0
HM Amla	11	19	3	893	153	55.81	2	6	4	0
AM Amla	8	13	2	531	125	48.27	1	4	6	0
DJ Watson	11	20	3	763	103	44.88	2	5	3	0
R Gobind	3	5	0	217	93	43.40	0	2	2	0
L Klusener	10	13	3	428	102	42.80	2	0	4	0
I Khan	10	18	2	615	118	38.43	1	4	3	0
K Smit	6	8	0	256	144	32.00	1	0	3	0
DL Brown	5	6	0	188	82	31.33	0	1	14	0
JC Kent	9	10	0	227	94	22.70	0	1	5	0
RP Symcox	4	5	0	111	87	22.20	0	1	3	0
M Hayward	6	6	2	55	33	13.75	0	0	3	0
D Smit	6	7	0	85	35	12.14	0	0	19	0
R Frylinck	1	1	0	8	8	8.00	0	0	0	0
S Mhlongo	5	6	1	36	19 *	7.20	0	0	3	0
ANW Tweedie	5	6	2	25	19	6.25	0	0	2	0
U Govender	9	9	5	3	2	0.75	0	0	5	0
TD Pillay	1	1	0	0	0	0.00	0	0	0	0
AH Razak	1	1	1	0	0 *	-	0	0	1	0
Totals	121	169	29	5093	153		12	25	91	0
			Extras	237				subs	2	
			Total	5330		38.07			93	

Bowling

Name	Overs	Mdns	Runs	Wkts	Avg	BB	5I	10M
S Mhlongo	127	36	387	18	21.50	4-38	0	0
U Govender	250.5	50	718	32	22.43	6-59	2	0
ANW Tweedie	132.3	30	404	16	25.25	4-74	0	0
JC Kent	178	48	465	17	27.35	3-77	0	0
DM Benkenstein	185	52	467	17	27.47	4-16	0	0
M Hayward	159.4	32	485	16	30.31	3-64	0	0
L Klusener	357.1	80	1058	34	31.11	5-39	2	0
R Frylinck	26	6	64	2	32.00	2-38	0	0
I Khan	83	12	343	8	42.87	3-38	0	0
AH Razak	21	1	126	2	63.00	1-38	0	0
AM Amla	18	1	66	1	66.00	1-54	0	0
RP Symcox	104	20	292	1	292.00	1-52	0	0
K Smit	1	1	0	0	-	-	0	0
DJ Watson	2.2	0	4	0	-	-	0	0
TD Pillay	13	4	34	0	-	-	0	0
Totals	1658.3	373	4913	164		6-59	4	0
		b/lb/pen	145	6	run outs			
		Total	5058	170	29.75			

MATCH REPORTS AND SCORECARDS

DOLPHINS v LIONS — SuperSport Series

Played at Sahara Stadium Kingsmead, Durban on 20,21,22,23 October 2005 — Toss: Dolphins
Umpires: JD Cloete & S Wadvalla — Referee: WA Diedricks
Debuts: Dol: None. Lio: None
Close of play: Day 1: Lio (1) 207-2 (Ontong 59*, McKenzie 65*, 66.2 overs). Day 2: Dol (1) 132-3 (Amla 50*, Benkenstein 25*, 31 overs). Day 3: Lio (2) 116-1 (Cook 41*, Ontong 34*, 37 overs).
Result: Match drawn
Man of Match: Garnett Kruger
Points: Dol: 7.84 (bat 5.84, bowl 2, match 0); Lio: 8.16 (bat 4.16, bowl 4, match 0)
Notes: Van Jaarsveld scored his century off 94 balls in Lions' 2nd innings.

Most of the honours went to the visitors in this drawn match, with Neil McKenzie striking an unbeaten 161 and paceman Garnett Kruger capturing a career-best 8-112 with a tremendous performance in the Dolphins' first innings. Vaughn van Jaarsveld made his first SuperSport Series hundred in the Lions' second innings.

The pitch eventually proved too good for a positive result, however, with Kruger lacking the bowling support he needed.

Despite being behind the eight-ball, the Dolphins saved the game comfortably enough with Hashim Amla, Jon Kent and Russel Symcox striking half-centuries in the home team's first innings, and veteran opener Doug Watson compiling an unbeaten 70 on the final day.

LIONS	*Runs*	*Mins*	*Balls*	*4*	*6*		*Runs*	*Mins*	*Balls*	*4*	*6*
SC Cook c Watson b Kent	26	95	72	5	-	c Kent b Govender	45	185	133	5	-
BD Snijman c Benkenstein b Kent	48	138	91	9	-	lbw b Khan	35	119	82	6	-
JL Ontong c Khan b Klusener	68	200	128	8	-	lbw b Govender	35	41	33	5	1
*ND McKenzie not out	161	447	329	18	2	lbw b Govender	0	2	1	-	-
VB van Jaarsveld c Smit b Klusener	0	9	7	-	-	c Hayward b Khan	105	149	98	13	3
†MJ Harris c Govender b Hayward	40	108	69	6	-	not out	49	148	102	7	-
WL Coetsee c Smit b Khan	42	87	56	7	-	not out	6	19	16	-	-
BC Adams c Smit b Hayward	9	38	24	1	-						
DJ Terbrugge c Kent b Klusener	31	42	40	4	1						
GJ-P Kruger											
BM Mathebula											
Extras (lb 12, w 3, nb 8)	23					Extras (lb 2, w 1, nb 5)	8				
TOTAL (for 8 wkts dec) (134.4 overs)	**448**					**TOTAL (for 5 wkts dec) (77 overs)**	**283**				

DOLPHINS	*Runs*	*Mins*	*Balls*	*4*	*6*		*Runs*	*Mins*	*Balls*	*4*	*6*
DJ Watson lbw b Kruger	14	34	31	3	-	not out	70	186	158	10	-
I Khan c Ontong b Kruger	25	59	39	5	-	c Harris b Kruger	9	21	12	1	-
R Gobind b Kruger	10	63	31	1	-	(4) lbw b Coetsee	6	18	18	-	-
HM Amla c Harris b Kruger	60	130	86	10	-	(3) c Kruger b Coetsee	40	89	57	2	-
DM Benkenstein c Terbrugge b Kruger	34	73	51	7	-	not out	37	55	51	6	-
JC Kent c McKenzie b Kruger	94	192	138	17	-						
†D Smit b Kruger	0	21	13	-	-						
RP Symcox lbw b Terbrugge	87	165	140	12	-						
*L Klusener not out	42	54	38	6	1						
M Hayward b Kruger	5	13	8	1	-						
U Govender run out (Cook/Harris)	0	27	11	-	-						
Extras (b 2, lb 8, nb 11)	21					Extras (b 1, nb 2)	3				
TOTAL (95.5 overs)	**392**					**TOTAL (for 3 wkts) (49 overs)**	**165**				

DOLPHINS

Dol	O	M	R	W		O	M	R	W	
Klusener	21.4	3	89	3	(4 nb, 1 w)	15	4	40	0	(3 nb, 1 w)
Hayward	22	6	74	2		11	2	16	0	
Symcox	25	6	76	0	(1 nb, 1 w)	(4) 11	4	34	0	
Govender	22	4	71	0	(2 nb, 1 w)	(3) 13	3	28	3	(1 nb)
Kent	20	5	41	2	(1 nb)	(6) 10	1	60	0	
Benkenstein	6	0	18	0						
Khan	18	5	67	1		(5) 17	0	103	2	
Lio	*O*	*M*	*R*	*W*		*O*	*M*	*R*	*W*	
Kruger	29	4	112	8		12	2	49	1	
Terbrugge	27	7	82	1	(2 nb)	6	1	13	0	
Mathebula	13	0	99	0	(9 nb)	6	1	33	0	(2 nb)
Coetsee	13.5	1	50	0		11	2	33	2	
Snijman	3	0	13	0						
Adams	8	1	23	0		(5) 14	2	36	0	
McKenzie	2	1	3	0						

Fall of Wickets

	Lio	Dol	Lio	Dol
1st	74 (1)	34 (1)	64 (2)	15 (2)
2nd	91 (2)	48 (2)	117 (3)	95 (3)
3rd	218 (3)	82 (3)	117 (4)	107 (4)
4th	218 (5)	151 (5)	126 (1)	-
5th	289 (6)	164 (4)	263 (5)	-
6th	372 (7)	182 (7)	-	-
7th	398 (8)	339 (6)	-	-
8th	448 (9)	357 (8)	-	-
9th	-	372 (10)	-	-
10th	-	392 (11)	-	-

Cape Cobras v Dolphins, Paarl, 27-30 October 2005. Match drawn.
Eagles v Dolphins, Bloemfontein, 3-5 November 2005. Dolphins won by 10 wickets.

DOLPHINS v TITANS — SuperSport Series

Played at Sahara Stadium Kingsmead, Durban on 10,11,12,13 November 2005 — Toss: Dolphins
Umpires: BG Jerling & MZ Nanabhay — Referee: MR Magiet
Debuts: Dol: None. Ttn: None
Close of play: Day 1: Ttn (1) 195-5 (P de Bruyn 52*, Van Wyk 33*, 67.4 overs). Day 2: Ttn (2) 6-0 (Seymore 1*, Bodi 1*, 2.3 overs). Day 3: Ttn (2) 246-5 (P de Bruyn 19*, Van Wyk 0*, 96.3 overs).
Result: Match drawn
Man of Match: Paul Harris
Points: Dol: 5.98 (bat 1.98, bowl 4, match 0); Ttn: 7.48 (bat 3.48, bowl 4, match 0)

Another drawn match, and another game in which the Dolphins were largely on the back foot. Responding to the Titans' modest first-innings total of 274, the Dolphins collapsed from 151-2 to 199 all out thanks to some poor batting and a rare five-wicket haul in the first innings from a spinner at Kingsmead.

If Paul Harris's five-wicket haul put the Titans in control, they were finally unable to turn their superiority into what would have been a deserved victory, with bad light bringing play to a close on the final day with the Dolphins eight down and needing another 91 for victory in 14.5 overs.

TITANS	Runs	Mins	Balls	4	6		Runs	Mins	Balls	4	6
GH Bodi c Smit b Tweedie	16	41	34	3	-	(2) c Symcox b Kent	47	179	106	7	-
AJ Seymore c HM Amla b Klusener	25	56	37	5	-	(1) c Smit b Symcox	91	263	217	16	-
*M van Jaarsveld c Smit b Klusener	4	18	7	1	-	c Tweedie b Klusener	32	103	84	5	-
Z de Bruyn lbw b Benkenstein	48	144	113	5	-	run out (HM Amla)	39	127	105	3	-
G Toyana c Benkenstein b Klusener	7	19	16	1	-	b Klusener	0	10	6	-	-
P de Bruyn c Smit b Govender	65	235	170	8	-	not out	19	108	61	1	-
†CFK van Wyk c Govender b Klusener	33	84	66	5	-	not out	0	11	8	-	-
AC Thomas c Smit b Tweedie	24	79	64	4	-						
PL Harris c HM Amla b Klusener	21	53	24	4	-						
DW Steyn not out	10	11	5	2	-						
NE Mbhalati run out (Klusener/Smit)	0	7	5	-	-						
Extras (lb 5, w 2, nb 14)	21					Extras (lb 7, w 3, nb 8)	18				
TOTAL (87.5 overs)	**274**					**TOTAL (for 5 wkts dec) (96.3 overs)**	**246**				

DOLPHINS	*Runs*	*Mins*	*Balls*	*4*	*6*		*Runs*	*Mins*	*Balls*	*4*	*6*
DJ Watson c Z de Bruyn b Mbhalati	23	73	41	2	-	lbw b P de Bruyn	59	205	153	9	-
I Khan run out (P de Bruyn)	80	258	186	11	-	lbw b Thomas	0	8	5	-	-
HM Amla b Mbhalati	0	8	5	-	-	c Bodi b Harris	30	108	69	5	-
AM Amla b Harris	52	103	85	9	-	lbw b Harris	36	161	126	4	-
DM Benkenstein c P de Bruyn b Harris	2	7	7	-	-	not out	43	174	115	7	-
JC Kent c Toyana b Harris	6	8	5	1	-	c Van Jaarsveld b Steyn	1	4	2	-	-
†D Smit c Van Wyk b Steyn	0	10	9	-	-	c Bodi b Mbhalati	10	28	23	2	-
RP Symcox b Harris	4	30	16	-	-	lbw b Thomas	10	35	29	1	-
*L Klusener c Harris b Steyn	21	25	18	5	-	st Van Wyk b Harris	19	29	18	3	1
ANW Tweedie c Toyana b Harris	1	7	5	-	-	not out	0	1	0	-	-
U Govender not out	0	3	2	-	-						
Extras (b 4, nb 6)	10					Extras (b 9, lb 5, w 4, nb 5)	23				
TOTAL (62.1 overs)	**199**					**TOTAL (for 8 wkts) (89.1 overs)**	**231**				

Dol	*O*	*M*	*R*	*W*		*O*	*M*	*R*	*W*	
Klusener	18	3	73	5	(9 nb, 1 w)	24.3	7	41	2	(1 nb, 2 w)
Tweedie	20.5	6	61	2	(1 nb)	14	6	19	0	
Symcox	16	2	34	0	(1 nb)	(5) 16	0	52	1	(2 nb)
Govender	12	0	56	1	(2 nb, 1 w)	(3) 17	0	56	0	(5 nb, 1 w)
Benkenstein	14	3	33	1		(6) 16	3	38	0	
Kent	7	3	12	0	(1 nb)	(7) 4	1	14	1	
Khan						(4) 5	1	19	0	
Ttn	*O*	*M*	*R*	*W*		*O*	*M*	*R*	*W*	
Steyn	13.1	2	48	2	(1 nb)	17	8	44	1	(1 nb)
Thomas	16	5	41	0	(5 nb)	17	5	45	2	(2 w)
Mbhalati	12	1	44	2		(4) 17	4	56	1	(3 nb, 2 w)
Harris	15	4	32	5		(3) 33.1	9	58	3	
P de Bruyn	5	1	20	0		(6) 4	1	8	1	
Z de Bruyn	1	0	10	0						
Bodi						(5) 1	0	6	0	(1 nb)

Fall of Wickets	**Ttn**	**Dol**	**Ttn**	**Dol**
1st	38 (1)	65 (1)	124 (2)	8 (2)
2nd	44 (2)	68 (3)	180 (1)	80 (3)
3rd	49 (3)	151 (4)	186 (3)	124 (1)
4th	66 (5)	155 (5)	188 (5)	166 (4)
5th	138 (4)	161 (6)	245 (4)	167 (6)
6th	195 (7)	162 (7)	-	180 (7)
7th	215 (6)	175 (8)	-	199 (8)
8th	264 (8)	189 (2)	-	231 (9)
9th	264 (9)	199 (10)	-	-
10th	274 (11)	199 (9)	-	-

DOLPHINS v WARRIORS — SuperSport Series

Played at Sahara Stadium Kingsmead, Durban on 17,18,19,20 November 2005 — Toss: Dolphins

Umpires: S George & KH Hurter — Referee: NC Pretorius

Debuts: Dol: None. War: None

Close of play: Day 1: Dol (1) 88-2 (HM Amla 38*, AM Amla 6*, 20.2 overs). Day 2: Dol (1) 326 all out. Day 3: War (2) 189-8 (Pope 46*, Ngam 0*, 76 overs).

Result: Dolphins won by 9 wickets

Man of Match: Lance Klusener

Points: Dol: 18.52 (bat 4.52, bowl 4, match 10); War: 5.82 (bat 1.82, bowl 4, match 0)

Notes: Klusener scored his century off 79 balls in Dolphins' 1st innings.

After showing better form away from home, the Dolphins finally got off the mark at Kingsmead with a crushing nine-wicket victory over an inexperienced Warriors team to move to the top of the SuperSport Series log at the half-way stage of the competition.

The Dolphins never looked back after medium-pacer Dale Benkenstein recorded his best first-class figures to send the Warriors tumbling to 191 all out on the first day.

Skipper Lance Klusener thoroughly deserved his man-of-the-match award, striking a blistering century in 79 balls to earn his team a crucial first-innings lead of 135. He also captured five wickets in the match.

WARRIORS	*Runs*	*Mins*	*Balls*	*4*	*6*		*Runs*	*Mins*	*Balls*	*4*	*6*
CC Bradfield lbw b Klusener	2	29	22	-	-	(2) c Benkenstein b Govender	17	83	52	2	-
*ML Bruyns c AM Amla b Tweedie	0	6	2	-	-	(1) lbw b Tweedie	4	10	8	1	-
BC de Wett b Tweedie	9	38	26	2	-	c Khan b Klusener	69	255	200	11	-
A Jacobs c Benkenstein b Govender	37	103	63	8	-	b Kent	10	51	36	2	-
MBA Smith c Symcox b Govender	33	125	89	5	-	lbw b Govender	22	38	29	2	-
SC Pope not out	74	133	93	8	2	b Govender	49	151	115	8	-
†AM Sodumo lbw b Benkenstein	10	47	32	2	-	lbw b Klusener	0	9	6	-	-
T Henderson b Benkenstein	0	1	1	-	-	c Kent b Klusener	9	12	14	2	-
MW Olivier c Tweedie b Benkenstein	7	17	17	1	-	c Smit b Govender	4	14	9	1	-
M Ngam c Watson b Benkenstein	0	16	12	-	-	c HM Amla b Klusener	0	9	6	-	-
S Mjekula lbw b Tweedie	1	10	5	-	-	not out	0	12	8	-	-
Extras (lb 5, w 8, nb 5)	18					Extras (lb 4, nb 4)	8				
TOTAL (59.3 overs)	**191**					**TOTAL (80 overs)**	**192**				

DOLPHINS	Runs	Mins	Balls	4	6		Runs	Mins	Balls	4	6
DJ Watson c Sodumo b Olivier	22	32	36	3	-	b Olivier	0	2	4	-	-
I Khan lbw b Ngam	15	72	31	2	-	not out	13	54	32	2	-
HM Amla c Sodumo b Mjekula	82	196	122	14	-	not out	42	51	42	7	-
AM Amla c Pope b Ngam	8	42	29	1	-						
DM Benkenstein c Mjekula b Henderson	5	27	21	-	-						
JC Kent b Mjekula	10	41	24	2	-						
†D Smit c Sodumo b Mjekula	35	149	99	5	-						
RP Symcox c Sodumo b Ngam	9	41	32	1	-						
*L Klusener c Smith b Henderson	102	116	83	12	5						
ANW Tweedie b Ngam	19	44	26	3	-						
U Govender not out	1	7	1	-	-						
Extras (lb 3, w 6, nb 9)	18					Extras (lb 4)	4				
TOTAL (83.2 overs)	**326**					**TOTAL (for 1 wkt) (13 overs)**	**59**				

Dol	O	M	R	W	O	M	R	W
Klusener	15	2	57	1 (3 nb)	25	10	47	4 (3 nb)
Tweedie	14.3	3	45	3 (2 w)	8	2	23	1
Symcox	6	2	20	0	11	4	27	0
Govender	12	5	30	2 (1 nb, 2 w)	18	5	42	4 (1 nb)
Kent	6	1	18	0 (1 nb)	(6) 10	3	19	1
Benkenstein	6	1	16	4	(5) 7	1	19	0
Khan					1	0	11	0
War	O	M	R	W	O	M	R	W
Henderson	20.2	7	50	2				
Olivier	16	1	76	1 (4 nb)	(1) 7	2	23	1
Ngam	22	1	71	4 (1 nb, 1 w)	(2) 4	1	22	0
Mjekula	15	3	65	3 (5 w)	(3) 2	0	10	0
De Wett	5	1	23	0				
Pope	5	0	38	0				

Fall of Wickets

	War	Dol	War	Dol
1st	0 (2)	26 (1)	10 (1)	4 (1)
2nd	9 (1)	63 (2)	38 (2)	-
3rd	18 (3)	98 (4)	66 (4)	-
4th	80 (4)	105 (5)	99 (5)	-
5th	112 (5)	138 (6)	164 (3)	-
6th	159 (7)	164 (3)	168 (7)	-
7th	159 (8)	180 (8)	178 (8)	-
8th	173 (9)	239 (7)	187 (9)	-
9th	184 (10)	320 (10)	190 (10)	-
10th	191 (11)	326 (9)	192 (6)	-

DOLPHINS v CAPE COBRAS — SuperSport Series

Played at Sahara Stadium Kingsmead, Durban on 23,24,25,26 February 2006 — Toss: Cape Cobras
Umpires: JD Cloete & IW Shine — Referee: CJ Mitchley
Debuts: Dol: None. Cob: None
Close of play: Day 1: Dol (1) 29-1 (Gobind 12*, Amla 7*, 11.3 overs). Day 2: Cob (2) 41-0 (Puttick 17*, Bassage 20*, 12 overs). Day 3: Cob (2) 195-7 (Dawson 12*, Adams 13*, 76 overs).
Result: Dolphins won by 6 wickets
Man of Match: Hashim Amla
Points: Dol: 16.28 (bat 2.28, bowl 4, match 10); Cob: 6.32 (bat 2.32, bowl 4, match 0)
Notes: Willoughby took a hat-trick in Dolphins' 1st innings. His victims were Mhlongo, Gobind, Hayward. He also took 4 wickets in 4 balls when he dismissed Watson with the first ball of Dolphins' 2nd innings.

The Dolphins blooded two youngsters, pace bowler Saidi Mhlongo, who showed considerable promise, and batsman Kyle Smit. It turned out to be a high-quality thriller with Hashim Amla striking a magnificent 153 to earn his team an exciting six-wicket victory on the final day.

The match was too close to call until Amla's entrance, with the bowlers generally holding sway on a well-grassed pitch in cloudy conditions. The Cobras' left-arm swing bowler Charl Willoughby was particularly impressive, capturing 6-41 in the Dolphins' first innings (including his second first-class hat-trick) in which opener Rivash Gobind ground out a stubborn 93 in 260 balls.

With the Dolphins facing a tough victory target of 279, Willoughby dismissed Doug Watson with his first ball (becoming the fifth man in SA cricket history to take four wickets in four balls), but there was nothing he could do to stem the flow of runs from an inspired Amla.

CAPE COBRAS	Runs	Mins	Balls	4	6		Runs	Mins	Balls	4	6
AG Puttick c Brown b Mhlongo	8	45	29	2	-	c Benkenstein b Mhlongo	18	69	52	1	-
DJ Bassage c Klusener b Mhlongo	5	42	29	1	-	c Brown b Mhlongo	20	58	37	2	-
W Wyngaard c Brown b Kent	22	101	71	2	-	b Hayward	10	103	52	1	-
J-P Duminy lbw b Mhlongo	52	161	123	9	-	c Benkenstein b Mhlongo	11	29	25	2	-
HD Ackerman c Gobind b Kent	11	31	20	2	-	c Gobind b Mhlongo	61	156	106	11	-
*†TL Tsolekile c Govender b Hayward	7	66	48	-	-	lbw b Benkenstein	0	5	2	-	-
VD Philander b Benkenstein	20	50	28	3	-	c Govender b Kent	27	96	83	4	-
AC Dawson not out	37	98	66	7	-	not out	60	156	103	9	-
PR Adams b Klusener	24	56	38	4	-	c Brown b Kent	24	108	81	1	1
M Zondeki b Klusener	5	10	10	1	-	c Benkenstein b Hayward	3	22	9	-	-
CM Willoughby b Govender	1	15	9	-	-	not out	13	15	13	3	-
Extras (lb 8, w 3, nb 13)	24					Extras (b 7, lb 5, w 6, nb 11)	29				
TOTAL (76.2 overs)	**216**					**TOTAL (for 9 wkts dec) (92 overs)**	**276**				

DOLPHINS	Runs	Mins	Balls	4	6		Runs	Mins	Balls	4	6
DJ Watson c Adams b Dawson	8	27	23	1	-	lbw b Willoughby	0	1	1	-	-
R Gobind c Adams b Willoughby	93	384	260	12	-	c Puttick b Dawson	60	229	174	8	-
HM Amla c Ackerman b Dawson	12	44	36	1	-	run out (Puttick/Tsolekile)	153	252	179	23	-
K Smit b Adams	48	113	81	8	-	c Dawson b Willoughby	23	48	23	2	-
DM Benkenstein c Tsolekile b Willoughby	21	60	58	4	-	(6) not out	11	12	11	1	-
JC Kent c Tsolekile b Willoughby	0	3	3	-	-						
†DL Brown c Ackerman b Dawson	23	108	88	1	-						
*L Klusener c Ackerman b Willoughby	0	7	3	-	-	(5) not out	30	36	20	1	2
S Mhlongo b Willoughby	0	8	6	-	-						
U Govender not out	0	8	2	-	-						
M Hayward b Willoughby	0	1	1	-	-						
Extras (b 4, lb 3, w 1, nb 1)	9					Extras (lb 1, w 1, nb 1)	3				
TOTAL (93.2 overs)	**214**					**TOTAL (for 4 wkts) (68 overs)**	**280**				

Dol	*O*	*M*	*R*	*W*		*O*	*M*	*R*	*W*	
Hayward	9	2	17	1	(2 w)	(2) 17	1	74	2	(1 nb)
Klusener	14	2	51	2	(4 nb, 1 w)	(1) 22	6	59	0	(6 nb, 2 w)
Mhlongo	18	4	47	3	(8 nb)	17	5	38	4	(1 nb)
Govender	13.2	3	33	1		11	3	36	0	(3 nb)
Benkenstein	10	2	37	1		(6) 9	4	19	1	
Kent	12	4	23	2	(1 nb)	(5) 16	7	38	2	
Cob	*O*	*M*	*R*	*W*		*O*	*M*	*R*	*W*	
Willoughby	24.2	10	41	6	(1 w)	18	5	65	2	
Dawson	21	5	43	3		15	2	59	1	
Philander	12	1	44	0	(1 nb)	(4) 18	1	62	0	(1 nb)
Zondeki	16	5	27	0		(3) 11	1	65	0	(1 w)
Adams	20	3	52	1		5	1	25	0	
Duminy						1	0	3	0	

Fall of Wickets

	Cob	**Dol**	**Cob**	**Dol**
1st	22 (2)	17 (1)	41 (2)	0 (1)
2nd	22 (1)	36 (3)	43 (1)	201 (2)
3rd	88 (3)	125 (4)	56 (4)	230 (3)
4th	107 (5)	161 (5)	105 (3)	264 (4)
5th	114 (4)	161 (6)	110 (6)	-
6th	130 (6)	212 (7)	157 (5)	-
7th	151 (7)	213 (8)	157 (7)	-
8th	201 (9)	213 (9)	223 (9)	-
9th	207 (10)	214 (2)	253 (10)	-
10th	216 (11)	214 (11)	-	-

DOLPHINS v EAGLES

SuperSport Series

Played at Sahara Stadium Kingsmead, Durban on 2,3,4,5 March 2006

Toss: Eagles

Umpires: M Gajjar & LH Matroos

Referee: S Naidoo

Debuts: Dol: None. Eag: None

Close of play: Day 1: Dol (1) 165-5 (Benkenstein 23*, Khan 15*, 68 overs). Day 2: Dol (1) 202-6 (Benkenstein 43*, Brown 0*, 80 overs). Day 3: Eag (1) 167-4 (Jacobs 48*, Bosman 1*, 48 overs).

Result: Match drawn

Points: Dol: 5.06 (bat 4.06, bowl 1, match 0); Eag: 4.34 (bat 1.34, bowl 3, match 0)

This drawn match was ruined by rain and bad light, with 112 overs lost on the first two days and no play possible on the last. The two highlights were Dale Benkenstein's fine century, his 20th overall and his second of the season, and left-arm spinner Nicky Boje's career-best 8-93 in the Dolphins' first innings.

DOLPHINS	Runs	Mins	Balls	4	6
DJ Watson lbw b Boje	36	120	80	7	-
R Gobind run out (Jacobs/Van Wyk)	48	230	169	5	-
HM Amla c Van Wyk b McLaren	30	70	58	5	-
K Smit c Van Wyk b Boje	8	21	17	1	-
DM Benkenstein c Rudolph b Boje	103	255	173	12	-
JC Kent c and b Boje	0	3	1	-	-
I Khan c Rudolph b Boje	31	94	80	5	-
†DL Brown c McLaren b Boje	44	59	38	6	1
*L Klusener lbw b Boje	32	75	71	3	1
ANW Tweedie not out	4	19	12	-	-
S Mhlongo c Van Wyk b Boje	3	15	14	-	-
Extras (lb 4, w 5, nb 6)	15				
TOTAL (117.5 overs)	**354**				

EAGLES	Runs	Mins	Balls	4	6
RT Bailey b Klusener	23	37	30	4	-
B Hector b Mhlongo	17	79	57	1	-
JA Rudolph run out (Benkenstein/Klusener)	62	142	87	12	-
DJ Jacobs not out	48	124	95	7	1
†MN van Wyk b Khan	5	16	16	-	-
LL Bosman not out	1	6	8	-	-
*N Boje					
R McLaren					
AK Kruger					
J Louw					
PV Mpitsang					
Extras (b 5, lb 1, nb 5)	11				
TOTAL (for 4 wkts) (48 overs)	**167**				

Eag	O	M	R	W	
Mpitsang	28	6	79	0	(1 nb, 1 w)
Louw	13	4	43	0	(1 nb)
McLaren	24	5	85	1	(1 nb)
Kruger	14	3	50	0	(3 nb)
Boje	38.5	8	93	8	
Dol	*O*	*M*	*R*	*W*	
Klusener	14	2	44	1	(1 nb)
Tweedie	11	1	32	0	
Khan	5	1	17	1	
Mhlongo	5	1	19	1	(3 nb)
Kent	5	0	19	0	(1 nb)
Benkenstein	7	1	30	0	
Smit	1	1	0	0	

Fall of Wickets

	Dol	Eag
1st	61 (1)	33 (1)
2nd	106 (3)	62 (2)
3rd	119 (4)	158 (3)
4th	131 (2)	166 (5)
5th	131 (6)	-
6th	202 (7)	-
7th	283 (8)	-
8th	347 (9)	-
9th	348 (5)	-
10th	354 (11)	-

Warriors v Dolphins, East London, 9-12 March 2006. Dolphins won by an innings and 29 runs.
Lions v Dolphins, Johannesburg, 16-19 March 2006. Dolphins won by 7 wickets.
Titans v Dolphins, Centurion, 23-26 March 2006. Match drawn.

(A report on the SuperSport Series final between the Dolphins and the Titans appears in the section, SuperSport Series, on Page 399)

EAGLES

Central Cricket Franchise Bfn (Pty) Ltd, PO Box 4357, Bloemfontein 9300.
Tel: 051 447 5715. Fax: 051 447 2208.
Chief Executive: Johan van Heerden.
Physical Address: Goodyear Park, Att Horak Ave, Willows, Bloemfontein.
Grounds: Goodyear Park, Bloemfontein; De Beers Diamond Oval, Kimberley.
Website: www.eaglescricket.com
Affiliates: Free State Cricket Union, Griqualand West Cricket Union.
Squad: Ryan Bailey, Jonathan Beukes, Nicky Bojé, Loots Bosman, Cliffie Deacon, Dillon du Preez, Davy Jacobs, Ryan McLaren, Victor Mpitsang, Roger Telemachus, Thandi Tshabalala, Johan van der Wath, Morné van Wyk. CSA contracted: Boeta Dippenaar, Jacques Rudolph. Coach, Corrie van Zyl. Fitness trainer, Sarel Cilliers.

REVIEW OF THE SEASON 2005/06

Johann de Jager

SUPERSPORT SERIES: P10 W3 L4 D3 (fifth)
CAPTAIN: N Boje (6), MN van Wyk (4)
STANDARD BANK CUP: P12 W8 L3 NR1 (winners)
STANDARD BANK PRO20: P7 W6 L1 (winners)

For a second consecutive season, the Eagles walked away with two of the three national titles available to franchises. They won the Standard Bank Cup for the second time in a row and added the Standard Bank Pro20 title for a second time after winning the inaugural competition in 2003/04. At that stage they had won or shared five of the six possible titles since the introduction of the franchise system.

The Eagles did not allow themselves to be unsettled by several off-field happenings.

The start of the season saw the end of a long innings by main sponsor Goodyear, the tyre manufacturers, who had been on board since the 1980s. The company retained their naming rights to Goodyear Park, however.

After initially reaching an agreement with a company offering a product in opposition to that of a national sponsor, the franchise was able to sign up Gestetner, who at the end of the season announced their ongoing involvement.

There was more positive news at the end of the season when it was announced that Griqualand West would join the Central franchise as equal partners. Bloemfontein will be the administrative centre and matches will be played in Bloemfontein and Kimberley.

The Goodyear Park pitch was under scrutiny following the resignation of groundsman Nico Pretorius the previous season. The strip did not receive enough attention during the off-season in the absence of a full-time curator, leading to a somewhat embarrassing situation.

EAGLES

There were some murmurings after South Africa's one-day match against New Zealand. Then the Eagles' first SuperSport encounter was stopped after the first ball of the seventh over for the pitch to be fixed because the area around the southern crease was unstable, making it difficult for the bowlers. A large chunk of the problem area was replaced before play could continue. Pretorius was later re-employed as consultant.

With a sliced budget, some alleged discrepancies were discovered as the administration tried to find ways of cutting costs. This culminated in the resignation of the long-serving chief executive, Seppie Lusardi.

The season started poorly for the Eagles as the defending joint-champions lost their first three SuperSport Series matches. Although they managed to beat the Cobras in their fifth and final match of the first round of fixtures, their hopes of catching up in the second half of the season were hit by two drawn matches which were affected by rain.

Victories over the Lions and Warriors saw them finish above only the Warriors in the first-class competition.

In one-day cricket, however, the Eagles remained the team to beat. The Eagles won six of their ten group matches in the Standard Bank Cup and in a repeat of the previous season beat the Lions in the semi-finals before defeating the Titans to lift the trophy.

A confident Eagles team won four of their five round robin Pro20 matches before again defeating the Lions at the semi-final stage, then beating the Cobras in the final at home to earn an invitation to play in an international 20-overs competition in England.

Several Eagles players made their mark at national level, although only Boeta Dippenaar and Jacques Rudolph were awarded national contracts.

In a rare achievement by a spinner, Nicky Boje topped the national SuperSport Series averages with 40 wickets in six matches at an average of 15.32. He twice achieved career-best performances, took 36 wickets in his last four matches and earned a recall to the national side.

All-rounder Johan van der Wath showed his worth after Jacques Kallis was injured in Australia, while veteran Roger Telemachus enjoyed a well-earned "second life" after outstanding franchise performances. Van der Wath was named The Eagles' most valuable player and Telemachus the players' player of the season at the end-of-season awards function.

Big hitter Loots Bosman did not disappoint when he represented South Africa in a Pro20 international against Australia. Still the only man to score a Pro20 century, he hit the fastest fifty of the season, off 22 balls, against the Lions.

Spinner Thandi Tshabalala was in the Pro20 squad and at the end of the season was selected for the Test tour of Sri Lanka, while left-arm seam bowler Cliffie Deacon, again the pick of the bowlers in the domestic Pro 20, was unlucky to be injured on the day he received a call-up for the national Pro20 team following an injury to Charl Langeveldt.

Benji Hector and Craig Thyssen were released from their contracts. Thyssen returned home to Port Elizabeth to play for the Warriors and Hector signed for the Cape Cobras.

FRANCHISE RECORDS

Honours:

SuperSport Series (1): 2004/05 (shared)
Standard Bank Cup (2): 2004/05, 2005/06
Standard Bank Pro20 (2): 2003/04, 2005/06

Highest innings totals:

For:	543-6*	v Warriors (Bloemfontein)	2005/06
Against:	612-8*	by Dolphins (Bloemfontein)	2004/05

EAGLES

Lowest innings totals:

For:	148	v Lions (Bloemfontein)	2004/05
Against:	93	by Lions (Bloemfontein)	2005/06

Highest individual innings:

For:	218	DJ Jacobs v Dolphins (Bloemfontein)	2004/05
Against:	249	HM Amla for Dolphins (Bloemfontein)	2004/05

Most runs in a season:

867 (Avg 43.35)	DJ Jacobs	2004/05

Most runs in a career:

1517 (Avg 48.93)	MN van Wyk	2004-05

Most 100s in a career:

5	DJ Jacobs	2004-05
5	MN van Wyk	2004-05

Best bowling in an innings:

For:	8-93	N Boje v Dolphins (Durban)	2005/06
Against:	6-79	PL Harris for Titans (Bloemfontein)	2005/06

Best bowling in a match:

For:	12-152	N Boje v Cape Cobras (Bloemfontein)	2005/06
Against:	9-141	PL Harris for Titans (Bloemfontein)	2005/06

Most wickets in a season:

40 (Avg 15.32)	N Boje	2005/06

Most wickets in a career:

52 (Avg 19.57)	N Boje	2004-05

Most dismissals (wicketkeepers) in an innings:

4 (ct 4)	MN van Wyk v Dolphins (Durban)	2004/05
4 (ct 4)	MN van Wyk v Titans (Bloemfontein)	2004/05

Most dismissals (wicketkeepers) in a match:

7 (ct 7)	MN van Wyk v Dolphins (Durban)	2004/05

Most dismissals (wicketkeepers) in a season:

38 (ct 34, st 4)	MN van Wyk	2004/05

Most dismissals (wicketkeepers) in a career:

56 (ct 51, st 5)	MN van Wyk	2004-05

Most catches (fielders) in an innings:

No fielder has taken more than 2 catches in an innings.

Most catches (fielders) in a match:

No fielder has taken more than 3 catches in a match.

Most catches (fielders) in a season:

9	RT Bailey	2005/06
9	JA Beukes	2005/06

Most catches (fielders) in a career:

16	JA Beukes	2004-05

Most appearances:

21	RT Bailey, DJ Jacobs and MN van Wyk	2004-05

Most captaincies:

11	N Boje	2004-05

RECORD WICKET PARTNERSHIPS

1st	100	DJ Jacobs and GFJ Liebenberg v Titans (Centurion)	2004/05
2nd	196	RT Bailey and JA Rudolph v Lions (Bloemfontein)	2005/06
3rd	361	DJ Jacobs and RT Bailey v Dolphins (Bloemfontein)	2004/05
4th	215	JA Beukes and MN van Wyk v Dolphins (Bloemfontein)	2004/05
5th	96	MN van Wyk and N Boje v Cape Cobras (Bloemfontein)	2005/06
6th	292	MN van Wyk and R McLaren v Warriors (Bloemfontein)	2005/06
7th	107	N Boje and JJ van der Wath v Warriors (Bloemfontein)	2004/05
8th	143	MN van Wyk and R McLaren v Lions (Potchefstroom)	2005/06
9th	60	R McLaren and T Tshabalala v Lions (Potchefstroom)	2005/06
10th	46 *	WA Deacon and JMM Malao v Dolphins (Bloemfontein)	2004/05

EAGLES

PERFORMANCES AGAINST OTHER TEAMS

HIGHEST AND LOWEST TOTALS

Opponents	Highest Total For		Lowest Total For	
Cape Cobras	494-7*	2005/06	149	2005/06
Dolphins	541-9*	2004/05	186	2005/06
Lions	418-9*	2004/05	148	2004/05
Titans	427-8*	2004/05	192	2005/06
Warriors	543-6*	2005/06	320	2004/05

BEST INDIVIDUAL PERFORMANCES

Opponents	Highest score		Best bowling (innings)		Best bowling (match, 8+)	
Cape Cobras	121	HH Dippenaar, 2004/05	8-102	N Boje, 2005/06	12-152	N Boje, 2005/06
Dolphins	218	DJ Jacobs, 2004/05	8-93	N Boje, 2005/06	8-93	N Boje, 2005/06
Lions	158	MN van Wyk, 2005/06	5-23	N Boje, 2005/06	9-129	N Boje, 2005/06
Titans	149	DJ Jacobs, 2004/05	7-75	N Boje, 2005/06	-	
Warriors	200*	MN van Wyk, 2005/06	6-85	R Telemachus, 2005/06	-	

EAGLES SUPERSPORT SERIES AVERAGES 2005/06

Batting & Fielding

Name	M	Inns	NO	Runs	HS	Avg	100	50	Ct	St
JA Rudolph	7	12	0	683	141	56.91	3	4	6	0
MN van Wyk	10	17	3	786	200 *	56.14	3	1	17	1
DJ Jacobs	10	17	2	645	128	43.00	3	2	5	0
R McLaren	10	15	2	441	140	33.92	1	3	7	0
B Hector	7	12	1	298	102	27.09	1	1	7	0
R Telemachus	5	8	4	99	27 *	24.75	0	0	4	0
N Boje	6	9	1	193	62	24.12	0	2	4	0
WA Deacon	3	6	2	94	34	23.50	0	0	0	0
JA Beukes	5	9	0	205	58	22.77	0	1	9	0
RT Bailey	10	18	1	375	85	22.05	0	2	9	0
JJ van der Wath	4	8	0	160	52	20.00	0	2	0	0
LL Bosman	6	11	1	143	47	14.30	0	0	1	0
CA Thyssen	4	7	1	80	33	13.33	0	0	2	0
T Tshabalala	5	6	2	48	25	12.00	0	0	0	0
J Louw	4	4	1	34	21	11.33	0	0	3	0
HG de Kock	1	1	0	7	7	7.00	0	0	0	0
PV Mpitsang	9	9	3	36	16 *	6.00	0	0	0	0
NO Arthur	1	1	1	1	1 *	-	0	0	0	0
J Coetzee	1	0	0	0	-	-	0	0	0	0
D du Preez	1	0	0	0	-	-	0	0	0	0
JM Henderson	1	0	0	0	-	-	0	0	0	0
AK Kruger	1	0	0	0	-	-	0	0	0	0
Totals	111	170	25	4328	200 *		11	18	74	1
			Extras	305				subs	2	
			Total	4633		31.95			76	

Bowling

Name	Overs	Mdns	Runs	Wkts	Avg	BB	5I	10M
JA Beukes	2.5	0	19	2	9.50	1-8	0	0
J Coetzee	24.1	6	60	5	12.00	5-33	1	0
N Boje	276	80	613	40	15.32	8-93	4	1
HG de Kock	6	1	20	1	20.00	1-8	0	0
R McLaren	281.3	58	851	28	30.39	6-96	1	0

EAGLES

R Telemachus	114.4	20	359	11	32.63	6-85	1	0
T Tshabalala	117.3	18	445	13	34.23	4-129	0	0
PV Mpitsang	236.4	58	632	18	35.11	5-35	1	0
D du Preez	28	5	91	2	45.50	2-53	0	0
JJ van der Wath	96	16	312	6	52.00	5-126	1	0
NO Arthur	22	2	67	1	67.00	1-34	0	0
WA Deacon	63.3	11	222	3	74.00	1-30	0	0
JA Rudolph	40.3	4	116	1	116.00	1-29	0	0
J Louw	98.2	21	289	2	144.50	1-48	0	0
RT Bailey	54	9	194	1	194.00	1-25	0	0
JM Henderson	2	0	7	0	-	-	0	0
DJ Jacobs	4.4	2	19	0	-	-	0	0
CA Thyssen	8	2	33	0	-	-	0	0
AK Kruger	14	3	50	0	-	-	0	0
Totals	1490.2	316	4399	134		8-93	9	1
		b/lb/pen	137	8	run outs			
		Total	4536	142	31.94			

MATCH REPORTS AND SCORECARDS

Titans v Eagles, Benoni, 20-23 October 2005. Titans won by 92 runs.
Lions v Eagles, Potchefstroom, 27-30 October 2005. Lions won by 6 wickets.

EAGLES v DOLPHINS — SuperSport Series

Played at Goodyear Park, Bloemfontein on 3,4,5 November 2005 — Toss: Eagles
Umpires: SB Lambson & GH Pienaar — Referee: A Barnes
Debuts: Eag: None. Dol: None
Close of play: Day 1: Eag (1) 259-8 (McLaren 50*, Telemachus 17*, 69 overs). Day 2: Dol (1) 349-4 (Benkenstein 71*, Kent 23*, 96 overs)..
Result: Dolphins won by 10 wickets
Man of Match: Imraan Khan
Points: Eag: 5.5 (bat 3.50, bowl 2, match 0); Dol: 19.32 (bat 5.32, bowl 4, match 10)

The rematch of the previous season's finalists was interrupted after 6.1 overs for repairs to be made at the southern end of the pitch. When play resumed, the Eagles suffered their third consecutive defeat in the series.

Century-maker Imraan Khan made the home team pay with his second first-class century after he was dropped on four by Davy Jacobs at second slip. Jacobs, celebrating his 23rd birthday, earlier scored his tenth first-class century.

Experienced Dale Benkenstein also scored a century to help the visitors to a match-winning first innings total, something the Eagles had been unable to do in their first three encounters.

EAGLES	*Runs*	*Mins*	*Balls*	*4*	*6*		*Runs*	*Mins*	*Balls*	*4*	*6*
RT Bailey c Smit b Kent	34	125	62	5	-	lbw b Tweedie	1	6	6	-	-
JA Beukes c Smit b Klusener	2	14	6	-	-	b Kent	41	137	97	5	-
LL Bosman c Benkenstein b Hayward	4	11	11	1	-	c and b Khan	46	115	66	7	-
DJ Jacobs b Benkenstein	100	233	158	15	1	b Khan	0	8	1	-	-
†MN van Wyk lbw b Govender	11	57	41	2	-	lbw b Benkenstein	8	39	24	1	-
*N Boje lbw b Govender	0	11	6	-	-	(7) b Khan	4	10	8	1	-
R McLaren c Smit b Klusener	52	146	103	6	1	(6) lbw b Kent	3	15	16	-	-
JJ van der Wath b Klusener	2	5	5	-	-	b Tweedie	33	92	71	4	-
WA Deacon run out (Klusener)	17	18	14	4	-	c Smit b Klusener	34	82	69	5	-
R Telemachus lbw b Tweedie	21	79	53	3	-	not out	2	13	6	-	-
T Tshabalala not out	8	24	11	1	-	b Tweedie	0	9	4	-	-
Extras (lb 2, nb 22)	24					Extras (lb 2, nb 12)	14				
TOTAL (74.4 overs)	**275**					**TOTAL (59.2 overs)**	**186**				

DOLPHINS	Runs	Mins	Balls	4	6		Runs	Mins	Balls	4	6
DJ Watson c Jacobs b McLaren	35	106	75	7	-	not out	14	27	19	3	-
I Khan c Beukes b Boje	118	264	197	17	-	not out	16	27	21	2	-
HM Amla c Bailey b McLaren	64	138	105	11	-						
AM Amla c and b Boje	21	53	45	3	-						
DM Benkenstein not out	117	264	200	12	1						
JC Kent lbw b Telemachus	37	106	79	5	-						
†D Smit c Jacobs b McLaren	6	43	35	1	-						
*L Klusener b McLaren	14	18	10	3	-						
ANW Tweedie b Boje	1	33	20	-	-						
U Govender b McLaren	0	11	12	-	-						
M Hayward lbw b McLaren	0	10	2	-	-						
Extras (b 4, w 2, nb 12)	18					Extras (nb 1)	1				
TOTAL (128 overs)	**431**					**TOTAL (for 0 wkts) (6.3 overs)**	**31**				

Dol	O	M	R	W		O	M	R	W
Hayward	5.4	0	28	1					
Klusener	17	1	77	3 (7 nb)	(1)	12	2	49	1 (7 nb)
Govender	14	4	48	2 (9 nb)		4	0	15	0 (1 nb)
Tweedie	13.4	3	29	1 (2 nb)	(2)	14.2	4	49	3 (4 nb)
Kent	6	0	20	1 (4 nb)	(4)	10	6	17	2
Watson	0.2	0	0	0					
Khan	10	0	41	0	(5)	13	2	38	3
Benkenstein	8	3	30	1	(6)	6	3	16	1
Eag	O	M	R	W		O	M	R	W
Van der Wath	23	3	91	0 (3 nb, 1 w)					
Deacon	14	2	61	0 (4 nb)	(1)	3.3	1	19	0
McLaren	28	4	96	6 (4 nb, 1 w)	(2)	3	0	12	0 (1 nb)
Boje	37	14	76	3					
Telemachus	16	2	56	1 (1 nb)					
Tshabalala	10	0	47	0					

Fall of Wickets	Eag	Dol	Eag	Dol
1st	10 (2)	102 (1)	1 (1)	-
2nd	16 (3)	225 (3)	96 (3)	-
3rd	95 (1)	230 (2)	96 (4)	-
4th	138 (5)	269 (4)	96 (2)	-
5th	144 (6)	366 (6)	102 (6)	-
6th	200 (4)	384 (7)	111 (7)	-
7th	203 (8)	410 (8)	113 (5)	-
8th	222 (9)	416 (9)	184 (9)	-
9th	262 (7)	417 (10)	184 (8)	-
10th	275 (10)	431 (11)	186 (11)	-

Warriors v Eagles, Port Elizabeth, 10-13 November 2005. Match drawn.

EAGLES v CAPE COBRAS — SuperSport Series

Played at Goodyear Park, Bloemfontein on 17,18,19,20 November 2005 — Toss: Cape Cobras
Umpires: M Gajjar & BG Jerling — Referee: CJ Mitchley
Debuts: Eag: None. Cob: None
Close of play: Day 1: Eag (1) 19-0 (Bailey 13*, Hector 5*, 11 overs). Day 2: Eag (1) 191-1 (Hector 79*, Rudolph 53*, 79 overs). Day 3: Cob (2) 21-0 (Puttick 13*, Bassage 5*, 10 overs).
Result: Eagles won by 10 wickets
Man of Match: Nicky Boje
Points: Eag: 16.66 (bat 2.66, bowl 4, match 10); Cob: 3.02 (bat 3.02, bowl 0, match 0)

Nicky Boje may have missed the Proteas' tour to India but he struck like an Indian cobra as he collected 12-152 in the match, including a career best 8-102, which he later bettered against the Dolphins in Durban. The left-arm spinner, who claimed his 400th first-class wicket, was mainly responsible for the Eagles winning for the first time in the season against a side which had won three of their previous four matches.

Centuries by Hector, Rudolph and Van Wyk provided the platform for Boje's second innings performance when he could bowl with the security of a big first innings lead achieved.

CAPE COBRAS	Runs	Mins	Balls	4	6		Runs	Mins	Balls	4	6
AG Puttick c Van Wyk b Du Preez	8	33	25	1	-	b Boje	14	49	34	3	-
DJ Bassage c Boje b Du Preez	2	8	7	-	-	lbw b Boje	65	218	167	7	-
HH Gibbs c Thyssen b Boje	33	114	83	4	-	lbw b Boje	0	3	5	-	-
J-P Duminy c Van Wyk b Telemachus	25	57	38	4	-	b Boje	128	293	227	13	-
IJ Harvey run out (Thyssen/Van Wyk)	3	26	14	-	-	c Van Wyk b Telemachus	2	22	19	-	-
*†TL Tsolekile b Mpitsang	91	226	176	13	-	run out (Jacobs/Van Wyk)	3	20	15	-	-
VD Philander c Hector b McLaren	46	133	110	9	-	lbw b Boje	0	2	1	-	-
CD de Lange c and b Boje	5	24	21	-	-	b Boje	2	9	5	-	-
RK Kleinveldt lbw b Boje	2	3	2	-	-	c Van Wyk b Boje	0	15	9	-	-
PR Adams c Jacobs b Boje	0	1	2	-	-	b Boje	23	44	36	4	-
M Zondeki not out	4	45	30	1	-	not out	0	8	3	-	-
Extras (b 2, lb 12, w 3, nb 15)	32					Extras (b 4, lb 5, w 2, nb 5)	16				
TOTAL (82.1 overs)	**251**					**TOTAL (86 overs)**	**253**				

EAGLES	Runs	Mins	Balls	4	6		Runs	Mins	Balls	4	6
RT Bailey lbw b Adams	51	184	161	7	-	not out	12	3	4	3	-
B Hector c Zondeki b Philander	102	421	311	12	-	not out	0	3	0	-	-
JA Rudolph c Harvey b Zondeki	103	285	211	12	-						
DJ Jacobs c and b De Lange	7	6	6	-	1						
†MN van Wyk not out	110	253	201	9	1						
*N Boje c Adams b Duminy	62	105	75	10	1						
R McLaren run out (De Lange)	9	45	41	-	-						
CA Thyssen run out (Tsolekile)	1	16	10	-	-						
R Telemachus not out	27	39	30	3	-						
D du Preez											
PV Mpitsang											
Extras (b 9, lb 2, w 3, nb 8)	22					Extras	0				
TOTAL (for 7 wkts dec) (173 overs)	**494**					**TOTAL (for 0 wkts) (0.4 overs)**	**12**				

Eag	O	M	R	W			O	M	R	W	
Mpitsang	13.1	5	18	1	(5 nb)		6	1	21	0	(2 nb, 1 w)
Du Preez	12	1	53	2			16	4	38	0	(1 w)
Telemachus	14	0	43	1	(5 nb, 2 w)	(6)	16	3	48	1	(3 nb)
McLaren	20	3	68	1	(5 nb, 1 w)	(5)	6	0	19	0	
Boje	21	10	50	4		(3)	39	9	102	8	
Rudolph	2	1	5	0		(4)	3	0	16	0	
Cob	O	M	R	W			O	M	R	W	
Zondeki	18	3	62	1	(4 nb)		0.4	0	12	0	
Kleinveldt	32	12	55	0	(1 nb)						
Philander	32	10	73	1							
De Lange	47	10	125	1							
Adams	24	2	96	1							
Harvey	3	2	2	0							
Duminy	17	2	70	1	(3 nb, 1 w)						

Fall of Wickets

	Cob	**Eag**	**Cob**	**Eag**
1st	4 (2)	95 (1)	26 (1)	-
2nd	17 (1)	246 (2)	26 (3)	-
3rd	70 (4)	253 (4)	163 (2)	-
4th	83 (5)	283 (3)	171 (5)	-
5th	85 (3)	379 (6)	185 (6)	-
6th	172 (7)	412 (7)	185 (7)	-
7th	193 (8)	422 (8)	195 (8)	-
8th	195 (9)	-	201 (9)	-
9th	195 (10)	-	248 (10)	-
10th	251 (6)	-	253 (4)	-

EAGLES v TITANS

SuperSport Series

Played at Goodyear Park, Bloemfontein on 23,24,25,26 February 2006

Toss: Titans

Umpires: SB Lambson & MZ Nanabhay

Referee: A Barnes

Debuts: Eag: None. Ttn: None

Close of play: Day 1: Ttn (1) 294-4 (Van Jaarsveld 130*, Toyana 1*, 100 overs). Day 2: Eag (1) 248-6 (Boje 50*, McLaren 12*, 62 overs). Day 3: No play.

Result: Match drawn

Man of Match: Martin van Jaarsveld

Points: Eag: 4.6 (bat 3.60, bowl 1, match 0); Ttn: 7.88 (bat 3.88, bowl 4, match 0)

It was a cruel game for all-rounder Deacon, who suffered a back injury on the first day. He returned from a doctor to hear he had been asked to join the national Pro20 squad – an invitation his injury prevented him from accepting.

The final session of a match badly hit by rain was as exciting as a Pro20 match as the unselfish Martin van Jaarsveld, who scored his 9000th first-class run, passed up the opportunity to score a second century in the match when he set the home team a target of 176 runs in 25 overs. Davy Jacobs made an explosive start to the chase before a flurry of wickets gave the Titans hope of victory.

Spin bowlers again played a prominent role, with impressive performances by Boje and Harris.

TITANS	Runs	Mins	Balls	4	6		Runs	Mins	Balls	4	6
†HG Kuhn c Rudolph b Boje	96	245	217	11	-	lbw b Mpitsang	2	37	31	-	-
AJ Seymore lbw b Deacon	10	35	24	2	-	c Hector b Arthur	11	101	71	-	-
*M van Jaarsveld lbw b Mpitsang	145	434	331	19	1	not out	70	141	117	8	-
GH Bodi lbw b Boje	28	42	40	5	-	not out	31	77	63	1	2
P de Bruyn lbw b Boje	7	90	51	1	-						
G Toyana c Bailey b Boje	16	72	46	1	-						
JA Morkel c Hector b Boje	0	3	4	-	-						
PL Harris c Van Wyk b Boje	1	18	9	-	-						
M Morkel not out	3	19	8	-	-						
MA Mashimbyi lbw b Mpitsang	5	8	10	1	-						
NE Mbhalati lbw b Boje	0	5	2	-	-						
Extras (b 6, lb 10, w 1, nb 11)	28					Extras (nb 2)	2				
TOTAL (121.5 overs)	**339**					**TOTAL (for 2 wkts dec) (46.4 overs)**	**116**				

EAGLES	Runs	Mins	Balls	4	6		Runs	Mins	Balls	4	6
RT Bailey b M Morkel	43	49	37	7	-	st Kuhn b Harris	6	21	8	-	-
B Hector c Mashimbyi b JA Morkel	17	73	53	2	-	(6) c M Morkel b De Bruyn	4	9	4	-	-
JA Rudolph lbw b Harris	70	170	118	10	-	c JA Morkel b De Bruyn	52	74	58	4	1
DJ Jacobs lbw b Harris	20	53	39	2	-	(2) c Kuhn b JA Morkel	45	62	45	5	1
†MN van Wyk run out (De Bruyn)	14	38	18	3	-	(4) c M Morkel b Harris	15	25	12	1	1
*N Boje c Van Jaarsveld b Harris	50	113	86	6	1	(5) c M Morkel b Harris	5	9	6	1	-
CA Thyssen lbw b Harris	0	2	3	-	-	(8) run out (Mashimbyi/De Bruyn)	2	3	3	-	-
R McLaren c M Morkel b Harris	21	114	76	-	-	(9) not out	0	10	8	-	-
WA Deacon b Mbhalati	20	43	38	5	-	(7) not out	3	20	7	-	-
PV Mpitsang b Harris	0	4	3	-	-						
NO Arthur not out	1	10	7	-	-						
Extras (b 5, lb 4, w 2, nb 13)	24					Extras (b 4, lb 5, w 1, nb 1)	11				
TOTAL (77.3 overs)	**280**					**TOTAL (for 7 wkts) (25 overs)**	**143**				

Eag	O	M	R	W			O	M	R	W	
Deacon	11	2	37	1	(6 nb)						
Mpitsang	24	5	67	2		(1)	11	5	15	1	
McLaren	30	10	76	0	(5 nb, 1 w)	(2)	3	1	2	0	(2 nb)
Boje	36.5	8	75	7		(3)	14	2	36	0	
Arthur	10	0	33	0		(4)	12	2	34	1	
Bailey	10	1	35	0		(5)	4	0	12	0	
Jacobs						(6)	2.4	1	17	0	
Ttn	O	M	R	W			O	M	R	W	
M Morkel	18	2	69	1	(9 nb)		3	0	23	0	(1 nb, 1 w)
Mbhalati	9	1	45	1	(2 nb)	(4)	1	0	11	0	
Harris	30.3	7	79	6		(2)	12	3	62	3	
JA Morkel	9	2	31	1	(2 w)	(3)	6	0	28	1	
Mashimbyi	3	0	12	0	(1 nb)						
De Bruyn	2	0	4	0		(5)	2	0	8	2	
Bodi	4	0	22	0	(1 nb)	(6)	1	0	2	0	
Van Jaarsveld	2	0	9	0							

Fall of Wickets

	Ttn	Eag	Ttn	Eag
1st	24 (2)	54 (1)	4 (1)	35 (1)
2nd	212 (1)	80 (2)	44 (2)	89 (2)
3rd	251 (4)	129 (4)	-	128 (4)
4th	288 (5)	154 (5)	-	134 (3)
5th	327 (6)	212 (3)	-	134 (5)
6th	327 (7)	212 (7)	-	139 (6)
7th	331 (3)	250 (6)	-	141 (8)
8th	331 (8)	276 (9)	-	-
9th	336 (10)	277 (10)	-	-
10th	339 (11)	280 (8)	-	-

Dolphins v Eagles, Durban, 2-5 March 2006. Match drawn.

EAGLES v LIONS — SuperSport Series

Played at Goodyear Park, Bloemfontein on 9,10,11,12 March 2006 — Toss: Eagles

Umpires: JD Cloete & MZ Nanabhay — Referee: MR Magiet

Debuts: Eag: None. Lio: None

Close of play: Day 1: Eag (1) 299-5 (Bosman 0*, Boje 0*, 99 overs). Day 2: Lio (1) 251-4 (Ontong 73*, Moleon 0*, 83 overs). Day 3: Eag (2) 135-3 (Jacobs 56*, Van Wyk 28*, 46 overs).

Result: Eagles won by 129 runs

Man of Match: Nicky Boje

Points: Eag: 15.08 (bat 4.08, bowl 1, match 10); Lio: 5.68 (bat 3.68, bowl 2, match 0)

The home team's spin twins, Nicky Boje and promising youngster Thandi Tshabalala, made good use of favourable conditions on the last day to send the Lions tumbling to defeat after the visitors had taken a first innings lead, mainly through the batting of Petersen and Ontong.

The match ended in time for the players to watch television coverage of South Africa's record one-day international run chase against Australia at the Wanderers.

EAGLES	Runs	Mins	Balls	4	6		Runs	Mins	Balls	4	6
RT Bailey run out (Ontong/Harris)	85	245	187	11	-	c Harris b Moleon	12	40	39	1	-
B Hector b Kruger	8	13	11	2	-	b Coetsee	15	50	36	2	-
JA Rudolph b Ontong	141	363	288	23	-	c and b Moleon	7	30	22	1	-
DJ Jacobs c Blignaut b Coetsee	17	26	22	2	-	not out	113	249	203	10	2
†MN van Wyk c Harris b Coetsee	25	111	77	2	-	c Blignaut b Coetsee	41	172	137	3	-
LL Bosman run out (McKenzie)	9	40	36	-	-	lbw b Coetsee	7	12	9	1	-
*N Boje run out (Ontong)	25	47	42	5	-	not out	32	43	27	4	1
R McLaren c Petersen b Coetsee	0	2	1	-	-						
J Louw b Ontong	4	15	13	-	-						
T Tshabalala not out	3	9	4	-	-						
PV Mpitsang lbw b Ontong	1	4	7	-	-						
Extras (b 5, lb 2, w 5, nb 11)	23					Extras (b 19, lb 5, nb 5)	29				
TOTAL (112.5 overs)	**341**					**TOTAL (for 5 wkts dec) (78 overs)**	**256**				

LIONS	*Runs*	*Mins*	*Balls*	*4*	*6*		*Runs*	*Mins*	*Balls*	*4*	*6*
SC Cook lbw b Boje	25	70	60	2	-	lbw b Boje	17	41	29	4	-
AN Petersen c Bosman b Bailey	96	166	152	12	2	c Rudolph b Boje	0	6	1	-	-
JL Ontong c Van Wyk b Mpitsang	102	361	231	11	-	c Rudolph b Mpitsang	8	18	17	2	-
*ND McKenzie b Boje	10	36	32	1	-	(5) lbw b Tshabalala	12	66	42	1	-
VB van Jaarsveld lbw b Boje	33	118	99	4	-	(6) c Bailey b Boje	0	2	1	-	-
EO Moleon b Mpitsang	15	103	82	1	-	(9) c Hector b Boje	5	29	32	-	-
†MJ Harris c Bailey b Boje	6	21	24	-	-	lbw b Tshabalala	2	18	15	-	-
AM Blignaut st Van Wyk b Tshabalala	12	62	33	-	-	(4) run out (Bailey)	4	3	2	1	-
WL Coetsee not out	41	81	59	6	-	(8) b Tshabalala	11	36	48	1	-
GJ-P Kruger c Hector b Tshabalala	1	10	9	-	-	c McLaren b Boje	16	33	24	2	-
Y Singh c Hector b McLaren	11	25	16	2	-	not out	0	7	1	-	-
Extras (b 14, lb 3, nb 6)	23					Extras (b 6, lb 7, w 5)	18				
TOTAL (131.5 overs)	**375**					**TOTAL (35.2 overs)**	**93**				

Lio	*O*	*M*	*R*	*W*		*O*	*M*	*R*	*W*
Kruger	14	1	53	1 (6 nb)		8	1	43	0 (5 nb)
Singh	9	4	32	0 (1 nb)					
Blignaut	12	2	41	0 (2 nb, 1 w)	(6)	7	2	10	0
Moleon	10	3	28	0 (2 nb)	(2)	17	6	44	2
Coetsee	40	9	96	3	(3)	28	6	79	3
Ontong	25.5	5	73	3	(4)	16	2	48	0
McKenzie	1	0	6	0	(5)	2	0	8	0
Petersen	1	0	5	0					
Eag	*O*	*M*	*R*	*W*		*O*	*M*	*R*	*W*
Mpitsang	22	4	53	2 (1 nb)	(3)	3	2	4	1
Louw	20	5	44	0 (1 nb)	(1)	3	0	22	0 (1 w)
Boje	43	10	106	4	(2)	16.2	7	23	5
Tshabalala	22	4	77	2		11	4	29	3
McLaren	13.5	2	43	1 (3 nb)					
Bailey	9	2	25	1 (1 nb)					
Rudolph	2	0	10	0	(5)	2	1	2	0

Fall of Wickets

	Eag	**Lio**	**Eag**	**Lio**
1st	13 (2)	58 (1)	24 (1)	9 (2)
2nd	209 (1)	163 (2)	30 (2)	30 (3)
3rd	231 (4)	187 (4)	40 (3)	34 (4)
4th	299 (3)	251 (5)	191 (5)	35 (1)
5th	299 (5)	299 (6)	205 (6)	35 (6)
6th	330 (6)	300 (3)	-	44 (7)
7th	330 (8)	305 (7)	-	66 (5)
8th	337 (7)	340 (8)	-	69 (8)
9th	337 (9)	344 (10)	-	82 (9)
10th	341 (11)	375 (11)	-	93 (10)

Cape Cobras v Eagles, Stellenbosch, 16-18 March 2006. Cape Cobras won by 10 wickets.

EAGLES v WARRIORS — SuperSport Series

Played at Goodyear Park, Bloemfontein on 23,24,25,26 March 2006 — Toss: Eagles
Umpires: JD Cloete & M Erasmus — Referee: MR Magiet
Debuts: Eag: None. War: None
Close of play: Day 1: Eag (1) 273-5 (Van Wyk 83*, McLaren 8*, 98 overs). Day 2: War (1) 89-4 (Botha 8*, Peterson 3*, 26 overs). Day 3: War (2) 216-8 (Botha 92*, Ngam 0*, 63.3 overs).
Result: Eagles won by an innings and 173 runs
Man of Match: Ryan McLaren
Points: Eag: 17.62 (bat 3.62, bowl 4, match 10); War: 2 (bat 0.00, bowl 2, match 0)

An unbeaten first career double century by Van Wyk and a maiden first-class century by McLaren put the home team in a commanding position against a Warriors team, missing several regular players, which was arguably the weakest fielded by a franchise. The umpires vetoed an attempt by the Warriors to use Johan Botha, banned from bowling because of his spin-bowling action, as a seamer. Botha later had a chance to notch a century but accepted an offer to go off for bad light on the third day when on 92, only to be dismissed early the next morning.

Left-arm seamer Jandre Coetzee, making his first appearance at first-class franchise level, started his career impressively by taking five wickets in the first innings. Henderson batted at number eleven for the Warriors, apparently for disciplinary reasons.

EAGLES

EAGLES	Runs	Mins	Balls	4	6
RT Bailey b Peterson	26	82	65	3	-
JA Beukes b Peterson	58	95	66	7	1
B Hector c Botha b Olivier	53	189	153	8	-
DJ Jacobs c Sodumo b Meyer	24	54	45	2	2
*†MN van Wyk not out	200	501	365	20	1
HG de Kock lbw b Meyer	7	79	46	1	-
R McLaren st Sodumo b De Wett	140	290	210	19	1
R Telemachus not out	6	9	6	1	-
J Coetzee					
T Tshabalala					
PV Mpitsang					
Extras (lb 6, w 4, nb 19)	29				
TOTAL (for 6 wkts dec) (157 overs)	**543**				

WARRIORS	Runs	Mins	Balls	4	6		Runs	Mins	Balls	4	6
BL Bennett b McLaren	46	91	63	8	-	(2) c Bailey b McLaren	9	45	30	-	-
CC Bradfield b Coetzee	14	61	37	1	-	(1) lbw b McLaren	0	1	2	-	-
BC de Wett lbw b Tshabalala	2	52	36	-	-	run out (Tshabalala)	54	133	79	6	-
AZM Dyili c Hector b De Kock	5	30	14	-	-	(6) c Telemachus b Mpitsang	39	121	86	4	-
J Botha c Bailey b McLaren	15	59	36	1	-	lbw b Mpitsang	93	255	155	9	1
*RJ Peterson c Bailey b Coetzee	13	40	24	2	-	(4) c Beukes b McLaren	3	13	7	-	-
†AM Sodumo lbw b Coetzee	2	3	3	-	-	lbw b Mpitsang	0	3	3	-	-
L Meyer not out	2	41	16	-	-	b Mpitsang	5	27	26	1	-
MW Olivier c Telemachus b Coetzee	9	14	16	1	-	lbw b Mpitsang	0	17	9	-	-
M Ngam c Van Wyk b McLaren	4	5	3	1	-	b McLaren	14	23	16	3	-
T Henderson c McLaren b Coetzee	4	14	9	-	-	not out	4	14	8	1	-
Extras (b 4, lb 1, w 4, nb 10)	19					Extras (lb 1, w 1, nb 12)	14				
TOTAL (41.1 overs)	**135**					**TOTAL (68.1 overs)**	**235**				

War	O	M	R	W			O	M	R	W	
Henderson	25	7	70	0	(2 nb)						
Ngam	22	3	78	0	(1 nb, 1 w)						
Meyer	24	7	81	2	(3 nb, 1 w)						
Peterson	36	7	109	2							
Olivier	17	3	79	1	(3 nb, 1 w)						
De Wett	30	7	104	1	(3 nb, 1 w)						
Bennett	3	0	16	0	(2 nb)						
Eag	*O*	*M*	*R*	*W*			*O*	*M*	*R*	*W*	
Mpitsang	10	1	43	0	(4 nb)	(3)	13	3	35	5	(4 nb)
Coetzee	15.1	5	33	5	(1 w)		9	1	27	0	
McLaren	10	2	31	3	(2 w)	(1)	17.1	4	50	4	(1 nb, 1 w)
Telemachus	3	1	6	0	(4 nb)	(5)	8	0	38	0	(5 nb)
Tshabalala	2	0	9	1	(2 nb, 1 w)	(4)	16	3	72	0	(2 nb)
De Kock	1	0	8	1			5	1	12	0	

Fall of Wickets

	Eag	War	War
1st	78 (1)	55 (2)	0 (1)
2nd	89 (2)	67 (1)	30 (2)
3rd	133 (4)	73 (3)	39 (4)
4th	191 (3)	82 (4)	115 (3)
5th	242 (6)	112 (6)	202 (6)
6th	534 (7)	114 (7)	202 (7)
7th	-	114 (5)	212 (8)
8th	-	125 (9)	216 (9)
9th	-	129 (10)	217 (5)
10th	-	135 (11)	235 (10)

LIONS

New Heights Cricket (Pty) Ltd, PO Box 55309, Northlands 2116.
Tel: 011 788 1008. Fax: 011 880 6229.
Chief Executive: Alan Kourie.
Physical Address: The Wanderers, Corlett Drive, Illovo.
Grounds: Wanderers Stadium, Johannesburg; Sedgars Park, Potchefstroom.
Website: www.highveldstrikers.co.za
Email: general@cricketgauteng.co.za
Affiliates: Gauteng Strikers Cricket Board, North West Cricket Association.
Squad: Neil McKenzie (captain), Jaco Campher, Werner Coetsee, Stephen Cook, Friedel de Wet, Matthew Harris, Tyron Henderson, Garnett Kruger, Eugene Moleon, Enoch Nkwe, Justin Ontong, Alviro Petersen, Blake Snijman, Vaughn van Jaarsveld. CSA contracted player: Charl Langeveldt. Coach, Gordon Parsons.

REVIEW OF THE SEASON 2005/06

Trevor Stevens

SUPERSPORT SERIES: P10 W3 L4 D3 (fourth)
CAPTAIN: ND McKenzie (9), JL Ontong (1)
STANDARD BANK CUP: P11 W5 L2 NR4 (semi-finalists)
STANDARD BANK PRO20: P6 W2 L4 (semi-finalists)

Same story, different season. The Highveld Lions started all three domestic competitions with aplomb, much like the previous season, but faltered in the latter stages of all three formats and again failed to get their hands on a piece of silverware. They had to settle for a fourth place finish in the SuperSport Series, only 0.2 points behind the third-placed Cobras, and were knocked out of both limited overs competitions by the Eagles in the play-off stages.

They were serious contenders in all three competitions, yet couldn't find the type of form that saw them dominate the domestic season in the early exchanges.

"I'll never be satisfied with a season where we don't win a trophy," said Lions chief executive Alan Kourie. "One must remember, however, that it was Gordon Parsons's first season in charge of the team, and it takes some time to understand the players and the thinking of the captain. Next season there will be better things to come."

Parsons, the former Lions assistant coach, was in his first year in charge since taking over the reins from Shukri Conrad, who moved to the Cobras, at the end of last season. He had to work with a relatively inexperienced squad as national call-ups and injuries, particularly in the bowling department, hampered his team's campaign.

The captaincy of Neil McKenzie, who must have come close to a national recall after producing several scores of substance with the bat, was a highlight of their season, while Matthew Harris hit back-to-back centuries early on, Vaughn van Jaarsveld compiled the first three hundreds of his first-class career, and Friedel de Wet almost single-handedly carried the

Lions attack in the absence of the players on national duty, picking up 31 wickets in just five matches. Justin Ontong was a consistent run-scorer, although he failed to turn promising half-centuries into hundreds more regularly.

On the national front the decision to keep Garnett Kruger on the sidelines for all six Tests against Australia was a bizarre one from the national selectors, as the speedster was in the form of his life when he received a recall to the South African Test squad. Kruger, who picked up an incredible 43 wickets in just seven SuperSport Series matches, should have been released to his franchise to play first-class cricket if he was surplus to the national team requirements on home soil.

Andrew Hall still couldn't command a regular spot in the Test squad but at one stage was the spearhead of the South African one-day attack as injuries cut through the national squad in Australia and Charl Langeveldt also made regular appearances for his country before a hand injury cut short his season.

In the SuperSport Series the Lions, who won two of their first three matches, were in contention for a place in the final for most of the competition before some unfavourable results in the second half of the format. The Lions, who had to do without Adam Bacher in the four-day competition as the veteran batsman wanted to concentrate on limited overs cricket and his business interests, gained the second most batting and bowling bonus points but three wins were never going to be enough for a final berth.

The Lions lost two of their most experienced players when Hall decided to move to the Dolphins, while Bacher took up a contract to play one-day cricket for the Cape Cobras. On the plus side, Warriors all-rounder Tyron Henderson signed for the Johannesburg-based franchise.

In the Standard Bank Cup the Lions' first three matches were washed out but the Lions managed to secure a home semi-final before being outplayed by the Eagles in front of their home fans. Lions opener Stephen Cook was the leading batsman by some way in the limited overs competition, scoring 567 runs at an incredible average of 81.00 thanks to one hundred and five half-centuries in 10 innings.

In the Standard Bank Pro20 Series, the Lions also started on a high note, winning their opening two matches but couldn't muster another victory before they were knocked out in the semi-finals by the Eagles, who they had beaten in the preliminary stages.

FRANCHISE RECORDS

Highest innings totals:			
For:	499-9*	v Dolphins (Johannesburg)	2004/05
Against:	509	by Western Province Boland (Paarl)	2004/05
Lowest innings totals:			
For:	93	v Eagles (Bloemfontein)	2005/06
Against:	136	by Warriors (Johannesburg)	2005/06
Highest individual innings:			
For:	180	HD Ackerman v Western Province Boland (Paarl)	2004/05
Against:	200	GC Smith for Western Province Boland (Johannesburg)	2004/05
Most runs in a season:			
698 (Avg 43.62)		AM Bacher	2004/05
Most runs in a career:			
1286 (Avg 45.92)		JL Ontong	2004-05
Most 100s in a career:			
3		ND McKenzie	2004-05
3		VB van Jaarsveld	2004-05

LIONS

Best bowling in an innings:

For:	8-112	GJ-P Kruger v Dolphins (Durban)	2005/06
Against:	6-39	AC Dawson for Cape Cobras (Johannesburg)	2005/06

Best bowling in a match:

For:	11-90	GJ-P Kruger v Warriors (Johannesburg)	2005/06
Against:	10-99	AC Dawson for Cape Cobras (Johannesburg)	2005/06

Most wickets in a season:

43 (Avg 22.72) GJ-P Kruger 2005/06

Most wickets in a career:

65 (Avg 28.89) GJ-P Kruger 2004-05

Most dismissals (wicketkeepers) in an innings:

6 (ct 6) MJ Harris v Titans (Potchefstroom) 2005/06

Most dismissals (wicketkeepers) in a match:

7 (ct 6, st 1) MJ Harris v Warriors (Port Elizabeth) 2004/05

Most dismissals (wicketkeepers) in a season:

42 (ct 42) MJ Harris 2005/06

Most dismissals (wicketkeepers) in a career:

57 (ct 55, st 2) MJ Harris 2004-05

Most catches (fielders) in an innings:

3	ND McKenzie v Warriors (Johannesburg)	2005/06
3	WL Coetsee v Cape Cobras (Johannesburg)	2005/06

Most catches (fielders) in a match:

No fielder has taken more than 3 catches in a match.

Most catches (fielders) in a season:

15 VB van Jaarsveld 2005/06

Most catches (fielders) in a career:

19 VB van Jaarsveld 2004-05

Most appearances:

19 ND McKenzie 2004-05

Most captaincies:

14 ND McKenzie 2004-05

RECORD WICKET PARTNERSHIPS

1st	178	WB Motaung and AM Bacher v Dolphins (Johannesburg)	2004/05
2nd	134	SC Cook and JL Ontong v Titans (Potchefstroom)	2005/06
3rd	130	JL Ontong and ND McKenzie v Warriors (Johannesburg)	2005/06
4th	144	ND McKenzie and HD Ackerman v Dolphins (Durban)	2004/05
5th	137	VB van Jaarsveld and MJ Harris v Dolphins (Durban)	2005/06
6th	196	HD Ackerman and ET Nkwe v Western Province Boland (Paarl)	2004/05
7th	143	MJ Harris and EO Moleon v Cape Cobras (Johannesburg)	2005/06
8th	90	ET Nkwe and EO Moleon v Dolphins (Johannesburg)	2005/06
9th	113 *	AJ Hall and DJ Terbrugge v Dolphins (Durban)	2004/05
10th	55	MJ Harris and GJ-P Kruger v Eagles (Potchefstroom)	2005/06

PERFORMANCES AGAINST OTHER TEAMS

HIGHEST AND LOWEST TOTALS

Opponents	Highest total		Lowest total	
Cape Cobras	362	2004/05	193	2005/06
Dolphins	499-9*	2004/05	249	2005/06
Eagles	390	2005/06	93	2005/06
Titans	413	2005/06	137	2005/06
Warriors	474	2005/06	175	2004/05

BEST INDIVIDUAL PERFORMANCES

Opponents	Highest score		Best bowling (innings)		Best bowling (match, 8+)	
Cape Cobras	180	HD Ackerman, 2004/05	7-61	F de Wet, 2005/06	11-152	F de Wet, 2005/06
Dolphins	161*	ND McKenzie, 2005/06	8-112	GJ-P Kruger, 2005/06	9-161	GJ-P Kruger, 2005/06
Eagles	135*	MJ Harris, 2005/06	5-39	AJ Hall, 2005/06	8-167	GJ-P Kruger, 2005/06
Titans	129	HD Ackerman, 2004/05	5-31	AJ Hall, 2004/05	8-87	F de Wet, 2005/06
Warriors	126	VB van Jaarsveld, 2005/06	7-44	GJ-P Kruger, 2005/06	11-90	GJ-P Kruger, 2005/06

LIONS SUPERSPORT SERIES AVERAGES 2005/06

Batting & Fielding

Name	M	Inns	NO	Runs	HS	Avg	100	50	Ct	St
JL Ontong	8	15	1	659	102	47.07	1	6	9	0
ND McKenzie	9	17	2	694	161 *	46.26	2	2	10	0
MJ Harris	10	17	2	614	135 *	40.93	2	1	42	0
VB van Jaarsveld	10	18	1	670	126	39.41	3	3	15	0
AN Petersen	4	8	0	281	96	35.12	0	3	5	0
DJ Terbrugge	1	1	0	31	31	31.00	0	0	1	0
SC Cook	10	20	1	541	92	28.47	0	4	7	0
Y Singh	2	3	2	28	17 *	28.00	0	0	0	0
WL Coetsee	8	13	3	272	55 *	27.20	0	1	4	0
BD Snijman	4	8	1	165	48	23.57	0	0	2	0
ET Nkwe	4	7	0	141	98	20.14	0	1	2	0
GJ-P Kruger	7	10	3	129	33	18.42	0	0	3	0
EO Moleon	8	14	1	212	67	16.30	0	1	3	0
GJ de Bruin	4	7	3	60	24	15.00	0	0	0	0
GH Bhayat	1	1	0	15	15	15.00	0	0	0	0
AM Blignaut	5	10	0	135	50	13.50	0	1	4	0
BC Adams	3	5	0	42	12	8.40	0	0	0	0
F de Wet	5	9	0	72	36	8.00	0	0	1	0
FA Steyn	1	2	0	16	9	8.00	0	0	0	0
MR Sekhoto	1	2	0	13	13	6.50	0	0	0	0
WB Motaung	1	2	0	0	0	0.00	0	0	0	0
AJ Hall	1	1	0	0	0	0.00	0	0	0	0
BM Mathebula	3	3	3	20	18 *	-	0	0	1	0
Totals	110	193	23	4810	161 *		8	23	109	0
			Extras	362				subs	0	
			Total	5172		30.42			109	

Bowling

Name	Overs	Mdns	Runs	Wkts	Avg	BB	5I	10M
F de Wet	190.2	44	567	31	18.29	7-61	3	1
AJ Hall	42	5	122	6	20.33	5-39	1	0
GJ-P Kruger	278.4	55	977	43	22.72	8-112	4	1
EO Moleon	179.2	60	446	17	26.23	3-21	0	0
GJ de Bruin	129.2	23	437	16	27.31	4-47	0	0
WL Coetsee	292.4	62	819	23	35.60	4-95	0	0
JL Ontong	97.5	15	306	8	38.25	3-73	0	0
AM Blignaut	90.1	17	290	6	48.33	3-34	0	0
Y Singh	47	17	97	2	48.50	2-30	0	0
BM Mathebula	58.5	8	308	4	77.00	2-50	0	0
ET Nkwe	43	6	188	2	94.00	2-56	0	0
DJ Terbrugge	33	8	95	1	95.00	1-82	0	0
SC Cook	4	0	10	0	-	-	0	0
ND McKenzie	9	3	21	0	-	-	0	0
BD Snijman	4	0	21	0	-	-	0	0
AN Petersen	6	1	24	0	-	-	0	0
GH Bhayat	16	4	65	0	-	-	0	0
BC Adams	36	4	123	0	-	-	0	0
Totals	1557.1	332	4916	159		8-112	8	2
		b/lb/pen	141	6	run outs			
		Total	5057	165	30.64			

MATCH REPORTS AND SCORECARDS

Dolphins v Lions, Durban, 20-23 October 2005. Match drawn.

LIONS v EAGLES — SupperSport Series

Played at Sedgars Park, Potchefstroom on 27,28,29,30 October 2005 — Toss: Eagles
Umpires: M Erasmus & LH Matroos — Referee: CJ Mitchley
Debuts: Lio: None. Eag: None
Close of play: Day 1: Lio (1) 124-4 (McKenzie 31*, Adams 11*, 37 overs). Day 2: Eag (2) 47-3 (Tshabalala 0*, Jacobs 5*, 16 overs). Day 3: Lio (2) 22-0 (Cook 10*, Snijman 12*, 6 overs).
Result: Lions won by 6 wickets
Man of Match: Matthew Harris
Points: Lio: 18.38 (bat 4.38, bowl 4, match 10); Eag: 4.62 (bat 1.62, bowl 3, match 0)
Notes: Henderson replaced Rudolph who was called up to the national team

The Lions recorded their first win of the season over the joint title-holders after establishing a massive first innings lead of 209 runs, thanks to an unbeaten maiden century by wicketkeeper Matthew Harris and a five-wicket haul from Andrew Hall. A glorious hundred from Morne van Wyk in the second innings was not enough for the visitors as Garnett Kruger claimed five wickets and Stephen Cook made a half-century to guide their side to victory.

EAGLES	Runs	Mins	Balls	4	6		Runs	Mins	Balls	4	6
RT Bailey c Harris b Kruger	6	11	9	1	-	c Van Jaarsveld b Kruger	17	63	45	2	-
JA Beukes c Harris b Hall	17	42	33	1	1	b Kruger	7	34	28	1	-
JA Rudolph c Harris b Kruger	17	38	22	2	-	b Hall	10	12	9	2	-
DJ Jacobs c Van Jaarsveld b Hall	0	10	5	-	-	(5) b Kruger	55	95	69	11	-
*†MN van Wyk b Coetsee	24	70	50	3	-	(6) b Coetsee	158	285	249	23	-
LL Bosman c Harris b Hall	47	62	49	9	-	(7) c and b Coetsee	11	20	20	2	-
JJ van der Wath b Hall	0	8	4	-	-	(8) c Harris b Kruger	18	61	52	3	-
R McLaren not out	36	111	80	4	-	(9) c McKenzie b Kruger	50	156	94	6	1
WA Deacon b Hall	1	12	8	-	-	(10) not out	19	35	30	3	-
T Tshabalala c Ontong b Coetsee	25	87	74	3	-	(4) lbw b Coetsee	5	59	24	-	-
PV Mpitsang c Harris b Kruger	0	6	6	-	-	lbw b Coetsee	5	30	21	1	-
JM Henderson											
Extras (lb 6, w 2)	8					Extras (b 13, lb 12, w 1)	26				
TOTAL (56.4 overs)	**181**					**TOTAL (106.5 overs)**	**381**				

LIONS	Runs	Mins	Balls	4	6		Runs	Mins	Balls	4	6
SC Cook c Van Wyk b McLaren	33	83	76	6	-	c McLaren b Deacon	65	162	126	5	-
BD Snijman c Van Wyk b McLaren	9	48	24	1	-	lbw b Van der Wath	19	55	33	4	-
JL Ontong c Bailey b Tshabalala	30	78	52	6	-	(4) lbw b Tshabalala	36	59	33	3	2
*ND McKenzie c Beukes b Deacon	77	254	186	10	-	(5) not out	20	43	37	3	-
VB van Jaarsveld lbw b Tshabalala	1	9	6	-	-	(6) not out	9	31	25	-	-
BC Adams c Van Wyk b McLaren	11	27	33	1	-	(3) b Tshabalala	12	34	32	1	-
AJ Hall lbw b McLaren	0	3	3	-	-						
†MJ Harris not out	135	303	223	14	-						
WL Coetsee b Tshabalala	26	45	29	5	-						
GH Bhayat lbw b Tshabalala	15	47	35	3	-						
GJ-P Kruger c and b Beukes	33	37	34	5	-						
Extras (lb 4, w 3, nb 13)	20					Extras (b 6, lb 1, w 1, nb 4)	12				
TOTAL (114.5 overs)	**390**					**TOTAL (for 4 wkts) (47 overs)**	**173**				

Lio	O	M	R	W			O	M	R	W	
Kruger	19.4	6	53	3	(1 w)		31	6	114	5	(1 w)
Hall	16	2	39	5	(1 w)		26	3	83	1	
Bhayat	6	1	35	0		(4)	10	3	30	0	
Coetsee	15	4	48	2		(3)	31.5	7	95	4	
Adams							5	0	27	0	
Ontong							3	1	7	0	
Eag	O	M	R	W			O	M	R	W	
Van der Wath	6	2	20	0			11	0	35	1	
Deacon	26	4	75	1	(1 nb)		9	2	30	1	(1 w)
McLaren	24	5	79	4	(1 w)	(4)	5	0	24	0	
Mpitsang	4.3	3	10	0	(1 nb)						
Tshabalala	33.3	3	129	4	(11 nb)	(3)	18	3	68	2	(4 nb)
Rudolph	13	0	30	0							
Bailey	7	2	35	0	(2 w)						
Beukes	0.5	0	8	1							
Henderson						(5)	2	0	7	0	
Jacobs						(6)	2	1	2	0	

Fall of Wickets

	Eag	Lio	Eag	Lio
1st	6 (1)	33 (2)	21 (2)	51 (2)
2nd	37 (2)	59 (1)	32 (3)	75 (3)
3rd	41 (3)	98 (3)	42 (1)	140 (4)
4th	41 (4)	108 (5)	91 (4)	151 (1)
5th	112 (6)	128 (6)	139 (5)	-
6th	112 (5)	128 (7)	160 (7)	-
7th	112 (7)	244 (4)	213 (8)	-
8th	120 (9)	295 (9)	356 (6)	-
9th	180 (10)	335 (10)	356 (9)	-
10th	181 (11)	390 (11)	381 (11)	-

LIONS v WARRIORS — SuperSport Series

Played at Liberty Life Wanderers Stadium, Johannesburg on 3,4,5 November 2005 — Toss: Warriors

Umpires: JD Cloete & M Gajjar — Referee: DT Lindsay

Debuts: Lio: None. War: None

Close of play: Day 1: Lio (1) 93-2 (Ontong 43*, McKenzie 23*, 22 overs). Day 2: Lio (1) 316 all out..

Result: Lions won by 10 wickets

Man of Match: Garnett Kruger

Points: Lio: 18.32 (bat 4.32, bowl 4, match 10); War: 6.24 (bat 2.24, bowl 4, match 0)

Notes: Kruger took a hat-trick in Warriors' 1st innings. His victims were Sodumo, Henderson, Olivier.

Garnett Kruger grabbed seven wickets in the first innings, including a hat-trick, to send the Eastern Cape side tumbling, before a hundred by Matthew Harris, his second in successive innings, and half-centuries from Justin Ontong and Neil McKenzie gave the home side a 104-run first innings lead.

Kruger followed up his first innings heroics with another four wickets as the Warriors were rolled over before the Lions knocked off the winning runs without losing a wicket.

WARRIORS	Runs	Mins	Balls	4	6		Runs	Mins	Balls	4	6
CC Bradfield c and b Kruger	1	23	21	-	-	c Ontong b Kruger	0	18	16	-	-
MBA Smith c Ontong b Mathebula	13	68	50	3	-	c Harris b De Bruin	4	11	7	1	-
BC de Wett c Van Jaarsveld b Kruger	36	98	68	6	-	lbw b Mathebula	16	74	58	2	-
A Jacobs c Harris b De Bruin	53	129	103	9	1	c Kruger b Moleon	31	112	71	5	-
*RJ Peterson c Ontong b Kruger	0	4	3	-	-	c Harris b Kruger	27	75	49	2	-
JP Kreusch c McKenzie b Kruger	17	35	26	3	-	c Snijman b Moleon	2	8	3	-	-
†AM Sodumo c Harris b Kruger	54	94	62	8	-	lbw b Moleon	9	18	17	2	-
J Botha c McKenzie b Mathebula	26	82	65	3	-	lbw b Coetsee	26	48	30	4	-
T Henderson c Cook b Kruger	0	2	1	-	-	c Harris b Kruger	2	10	9	-	-
MW Olivier c McKenzie b Kruger	0	2	1	-	-	c Harris b Kruger	2	9	12	-	-
RR Richards not out	2	22	13	-	-	not out	0	23	9	-	-
Extras (lb 2, w 2, nb 6)	10					Extras (b 1, lb 5, w 2, nb 9)	17				
TOTAL (67.5 overs)	**212**					**TOTAL (45.2 overs)**	**136**				

LIONS	Runs	Mins	Balls	4	6		Runs	Mins	Balls	4	6
SC Cook c Smith b Henderson	16	27	20	3	-	not out	6	30	21	1	-
BD Snijman run out (Botha/Sodumo)	5	11	9	1	-	not out	27	30	23	4	-
JL Ontong lbw b Botha	74	188	128	11	1						
*ND McKenzie c Henderson b Peterson	50	146	115	9	1						
VB van Jaarsveld c Henderson b Botha	1	5	3	-	-						
†MJ Harris c Peterson b Botha	100	205	143	12	1						
WL Coetsee c Jacobs b Olivier	22	31	26	4	-						
EO Moleon lbw b Olivier	0	17	14	-	-						
GJ-P Kruger b Botha	0	17	12	-	-						
GJ de Bruin lbw b Olivier	16	113	86	-	-						
BM Mathebula not out	0	5	1	-	-						
Extras (b 8, lb 17, nb 7)	32					Extras	0				
TOTAL (91.4 overs)	**316**					**TOTAL (for 0 wkts) (7.2 overs)**	**33**				

Lio	O	M	R	W		O	M	R	W	
Kruger	21	11	44	7		17	6	46	4	(2 nb)
De Bruin	18	3	56	1	(1 nb)	9	1	30	1	(5 nb)
Mathebula	11.5	3	50	2	(5 nb, 2 w)	8	2	17	1	(2 nb, 2 w)
Moleon	4	1	20	0		9	1	24	3	
Coetsee	13	2	40	0		2.2	0	13	1	
War	O	M	R	W		O	M	R	W	
Henderson	14	3	41	1		4	1	8	0	
Richards	3	0	24	0		3.2	0	25	0	
Kreusch	12	3	46	0	(2 nb)					
Olivier	21	7	57	3	(5 nb)					
Botha	24.4	7	71	4						
Peterson	17	2	52	1						

Fall of Wickets

	War	Lio	War	Lio
1st	2 (1)	9 (2)	4 (2)	-
2nd	29 (2)	30 (1)	8 (1)	-
3rd	77 (3)	160 (4)	44 (3)	-
4th	77 (5)	161 (5)	84 (4)	-
5th	105 (6)	170 (3)	90 (6)	-
6th	146 (4)	211 (7)	104 (7)	-
7th	197 (7)	215 (8)	104 (5)	-
8th	197 (9)	226 (9)	109 (9)	-
9th	197 (10)	316 (10)	111 (10)	-
10th	212 (8)	316 (6)	136 (8)	-

LIONS v CAPE COBRAS — SuperSport Series

Played at Liberty Life Wanderers Stadium, Johannesburg on 10,11,12,13 November 2005 — Toss: Lions
Umpires: KH Hurter & S Wadvalla — Referee: S Naidoo
Debuts: Lio: None. Cob: None
Close of play: Day 1: Lio (1) 247-8 (Moleon 17*, De Bruin 0*, 92.4 overs). Day 2: Cob (1) 231-5 (Gibbs 118*, Philander 18*, 68.3 overs). Day 3: Lio (2) 262-6 (Harris 83*, Moleon 51*, 80 overs).
Result: Cape Cobras won by 6 wickets
Man of Match: Alan Dawson
Points: Lio: 7.38 (bat 3.38, bowl 4, match 0); Cob: 17.5 (bat 4.50, bowl 3, match 10)

Veteran swing bowler Alan Dawson rolled back the years to give Cobras coach Shukri Conrad a victory over his former team in their own backyard. Dawson picked up ten wickets in the match, while the Cape outfit took advantage of Herschelle Gibbs not being with the national team in India, as the flamboyant batsman compiled a stunning first innings century.

It wasn't a walk in the park for the visitors who had to chase down 271 batting last – which they did with six wickets in the bank.

LIONS	Runs	Mins	Balls	4	6		Runs	Mins	Balls	4	6
SC Cook lbw b Zondeki	92	326	236	15	-	c Puttick b Dawson	18	84	65	3	-
BD Snijman c De Lange b Dawson	9	50	37	2	-	c Gibbs b Dawson	13	21	15	2	-
MR Sekhoto c Bassage b Dawson	13	40	33	2	-	c Tsolekile b Dawson	0	4	3	-	-
*ND McKenzie c Duminy b Harvey	16	86	66	1		c Tsolekile b Philander	35	97	57	8	-
VB van Jaarsveld c Puttick b Philander	37	87	69	5	-	c Bassage b Harvey	40	61	42	8	-
†MJ Harris c Tsolekile b Dawson	12	35	28	2	-	c Tsolekile b Dawson	84	249	169	13	-
WL Coetsee lbw b Willoughby	18	36	21	4	-	b Philander	14	28	24	3	-
EO Moleon c Puttick b Dawson	25	94	65	6	-	c Tsolekile b Dawson	67	270	193	11	1
GJ-P Kruger c Tsolekile b Zondeki	28	48	31	4	1	c Duminy b Dawson	7	39	24	1	-
GJ de Bruin c Philander b Willoughby	24	66	40	4	-	lbw b Willoughby	4	17	11	1	-
BM Mathebula not out	18	26	27	3	-	not out	2	13	9	-	-
Extras (lb 1, w 2, nb 4)	7					Extras (b 1, lb 10, nb 1)	12				
TOTAL (108.1 overs)	**299**					**TOTAL (101.5 overs)**	**296**				

CAPE COBRAS	Runs	Mins	Balls	4	6		Runs	Mins	Balls	4	6
AG Puttick c Harris b Kruger	5	16	15	1	-	c Van Jaarsveld b Coetsee	70	171	149	9	1
DJ Bassage b Kruger	22	76	52	4	-						
HH Gibbs b Kruger	149	319	221	23	-	c Snijman b Coetsee	28	52	42	4	1
J-P Duminy c Harris b Mathebula	23	56	48	4	-	(5) not out	64	117	99	9	-
IJ Harvey lbw b De Bruin	10	15	18	2	-	(4) lbw b Kruger	15	40	22	2	-
*†TL Tsolekile c and b Coetsee	11	46	49	-	-	not out	45	104	66	6	-
VD Philander c and b Coetsee	28	97	77	2	1						
CD de Lange c Mathebula b De Bruin	28	33	32	3	-	(2) c Van Jaarsveld b Kruger	42	66	47	7	-
AC Dawson c McKenzie b De Bruin	17	33	25	3	-						
M Zondeki c Coetsee b De Bruin	0	13	7	-	-						
CM Willoughby not out	0	10	1	-	-						
Extras (lb 11, w 10, nb 11)	32					Extras (lb 6, w 1, nb 2)	9				
TOTAL (89 overs)	**325**					**TOTAL (for 4 wkts) (70.3 overs)**	**273**				

Cob	O	M	R	W		O	M	R	W
Willoughby	26.1	7	97	2 (1 w)		21	2	81	1
Zondeki	19	6	64	2 (3 nb, 1 w)	(3)	19	5	48	0 (1 nb)
Dawson	30	16	60	4	(2)	28.5	13	39	6
Philander	22	6	58	1		17	5	61	2
De Lange	1	1	0	0	(6)	8	1	32	0
Harvey	10	1	19	1 (1 nb)	(5)	8	1	24	1
Lio	O	M	R	W		O	M	R	W
Kruger	25	3	93	3 (3 nb, 1 w)		20	1	95	2 (2 nb, 1 w)
De Bruin	25	5	64	4 (3 nb)		12	1	59	0
Coetsee	15	3	50	2	(4)	26.3	5	71	2
Mathebula	14	0	87	1 (5 nb, 4 w)	(3)	6	2	22	0
Moleon	9	3	12	0 (1 w)		5	1	19	0
Snijman	1	0	8	0					
Cook					(6)	1	0	1	0

Fall of Wickets

	Lio	Cob	Lio	Cob
1st	25 (2)	8 (1)	14 (2)	78 (2)
2nd	43 (3)	69 (2)	14 (3)	128 (3)
3rd	98 (4)	128 (4)	54 (1)	153 (4)
4th	163 (5)	142 (5)	87 (4)	161 (1)
5th	180 (6)	175 (6)	109 (5)	-
6th	202 (1)	247 (7)	126 (7)	-
7th	202 (7)	295 (8)	269 (6)	-
8th	247 (9)	308 (3)	281 (9)	-
9th	269 (8)	313 (10)	292 (10)	-
10th	299 (10)	325 (9)	296 (8)	-

Titans v Lions, Benoni, 17-20 November 2005. Titans won by 109 runs.
Warriors v Lions, East London, 23-26 February 2006. Match drawn.

LIONS v TITANS — SuperSport Series

Played at Sedgars Park, Potchefstroom on 2,3,4,5 March 2006 — Toss: Titans
Umpires: JD Cloete & S Wadvalla — Referee: NC Pretorius
Debuts: Lio: None. Ttn: None
Close of play: Day 1: Lio (1) 382-6 (Harris 42*, 96 overs). Day 2: Ttn (1) 251-4 (Bodi 62*, Toyana 22*, 83 overs). Day 3: Lio (2) 94-2 (Ontong 32*, McKenzie 17*, 22 overs).
Result: Match drawn
Man of Match: Justin Ontong
Points: Lio: 7.74 (bat 5.74, bowl 2, match 0); Ttn: 6.84 (bat 3.84, bowl 3, match 0)

The two Gauteng rivals shared the spoils after both teams scored in excess of 400 runs in the first innings. Neil McKenzie recorded a sparkling century, while Garnett Kruger and spinner Paul Harris grabbed five-wicket hauls for their respective teams.

The Titans were in with a chance on the final day, but the Lions' tail wagged stubbornly and the Titans were set an improbable 290 from 29 overs on the final afternoon.

LIONS	Runs	Mins	Balls	4	6		Runs	Mins	Balls	4	6
SC Cook c P de Bruyn b Mbhalati	60	189	154	7	-	lbw b Z de Bruyn	33	77	58	5	-
WB Motaung c Kuhn b Morkel	0	14	10	-	-	c Du Plessis b Mbhalati	0	8	6	-	-
JL Ontong c Morkel b Mbhalati	77	134	90	11	-	b Harris	92	330	231	10	-
*ND McKenzie c Kuhn b Morkel	109	216	166	15	1	b Harris	40	101	85	8	-
VB van Jaarsveld c Bodi b Harris	54	105	77	5	1	c Toyana b Mbhalati	14	39	27	1	-
†MJ Harris b Mbhalati	44	110	74	8	-	st Kuhn b Harris	2	23	16	-	-
WL Coetsee c Van Jaarsveld b Harris	7	35	25	-	-	lbw b Morkel	10	20	15	2	-
AM Blignaut c Kuhn b Morkel	2	8	7	-	-	c Van Jaarsveld b Harris	1	6	8	-	-
EO Moleon c sub (JG Myburgh) b Morkel	3	22	15	-	-	c Du Plessis b Harris	1	39	21	-	-
F de Wet c Van Jaarsveld b Mbhalati	4	41	30	-	-	b Bodi	8	108	68	-	-
GJ-P Kruger not out	18	22	12	4	-	not out	23	78	58	4	-
Extras (b 1, lb 8, w 8, nb 18)	35					Extras (b 4, lb 11, w 19, nb 23)	57				
TOTAL (106.5 overs)	**413**					**TOTAL (94.5 overs)**	**281**				

TITANS	Runs	Mins	Balls	4	6		Runs	Mins	Balls	4	6
†HG Kuhn c Harris b Ontong	84	246	155	10	1	not out	30	45	44	4	-
F du Plessis b Kruger	22	27	23	3	-	not out	14	45	24	-	-
*M van Jaarsveld c Harris b Kruger	0	1	1	-	-						
Z de Bruyn c Harris b De Wet	55	146	109	9	-						
GH Bodi c Harris b De Wet	70	214	161	8	-						
G Toyana lbw b Kruger	24	126	93	1	-						
P de Bruyn not out	76	182	136	8	1						
PL Harris c Van Jaarsveld b Kruger	8	56	36	-	-						
M Morkel c Harris b Blignaut	4	7	8	1	-						
MA Mashimbyi c Harris b Kruger	41	76	59	7	-						
NE Mbhalati b De Wet	0	26	11	-	-						
Extras (b 4, lb 4, w 1, nb 12)	21					Extras (nb 2)	2				
TOTAL (130 overs)	**405**					**TOTAL (for 0 wkts) (11 overs)**	**46**				

Ttn	O	M	R	W		O	M	R	W	
Mbhalati	23.5	7	90	4	(7 nb, 1 w)	(2) 19	6	69	2	(10 nb)
Morkel	26	4	96	4	(11 nb, 2 w)	(1) 24	3	78	1	(13 nb, 1 w)
Mashimbyi	9	1	36	0	(1 w)					
Z de Bruyn	12	1	38	0		11	3	53	1	(1 w)
Harris	30	5	109	2	(4 w)	(3) 40	14	61	5	(13 w)
Du Plessis	1	0	6	0						
P de Bruyn	5	1	29	0						
Bodi						(5) 0.5	0	5	1	
Lio	*O*	*M*	*R*	*W*		*O*	*M*	*R*	*W*	
Kruger	37	5	118	5	(9 nb)	3	0	19	0	(2 nb)
De Wet	28	8	76	3	(3 nb)	5	1	22	0	
Blignaut	14	2	53	1	(1 w)					
Moleon	23	8	48	0		(3) 3	2	5	0	
Coetsee	18	1	59	0						
Ontong	10	0	43	1						

Fall of Wickets

	Lio	Ttn	Lio	Ttn
1st	1 (2)	23 (2)	6 (2)	-
2nd	135 (3)	23 (3)	72 (1)	-
3rd	160 (1)	132 (4)	138 (4)	-
4th	269 (5)	197 (1)	162 (5)	-
5th	360 (4)	262 (6)	172 (6)	-
6th	382 (7)	271 (5)	195 (7)	-
7th	387 (6)	296 (8)	196 (8)	-
8th	387 (8)	303 (9)	224 (9)	-
9th	390 (9)	381 (10)	230 (3)	-
10th	413 (10)	405 (11)	281 (10)	-

Eagles v Lions, Bloemfontein, 9-12 March 2006. Eagles won by 129 runs.

LIONS v DOLPHINS

SuperSport Series

Played at Liberty Life Wanderers Stadium, Johannesburg on 16,17,18,19 March 2006 — Toss: Dolphins

Umpires: M Gajjar & SB Lambson — Referee: MR Magiet

Debuts: Lio: None. Dol: None

Close of play: Day 1: Lio (1) 199-4 (Van Jaarsveld 116*, Harris 23*, 57.4 overs). Day 2: Dol (1) 238-4 (AM Amla 43*, Smit 0*, 65 overs). Day 3: Lio (2) 249 all out.

Result: Dolphins won by 7 wickets

Man of Match: Ahmed Amla

Points: Lio: 7.38 (bat 3.38, bowl 4, match 0); Dol: 17.32 (bat 3.32, bowl 4, match 10)

Notes: AM Amla scored his fifty off 39 balls in Dolphins' 2nd innings.

The Amla brothers stole the show at the Bullring as the Dolphins maintained their unbeaten run in the competition with a seven-wicket win. Hashim was run out for 99 – ironically with his brother at the other end – in the first innings, while Ahmed made up for the earlier mix-up with a hundred in the second innings at better than a run a ball as the coastal side marched to the win, having lost two early wickets after being set a tricky 253 runs to win on the final day.

LIONS	Runs	Mins	Balls	4	6		Runs	Mins	Balls	4	6
SC Cook c Brown b Tweedie	1	5	7	-	-	b Klusener	0	3	5	-	-
AN Petersen c Benkenstein b Klusener	2	30	9	-	-	c Klusener b Tweedie	4	8	5	1	-
JL Ontong c AM Amla b Tweedie	5	8	10	1	-	lbw b Hayward	68	121	79	13	-
*ND McKenzie b Benkenstein	41	176	115	7	-	c AM Amla b Klusener	0	5	5	-	-
VB van Jaarsveld c Klusener b Mhlongo	125	233	171	26	-	b Klusener	4	30	12	-	-
†MJ Harris c Mhlongo b Klusener	45	147	93	7	-	b Mhlongo	21	67	44	3	-
ET Nkwe lbw b Hayward	1	10	5	-	-	lbw b Tweedie	98	197	136	11	2
AM Blignaut b Klusener	10	45	32	1	-	c Benkenstein b Hayward	4	13	11	1	-
EO Moleon c Klusener b Tweedie	10	40	29	1	-	c Brown b Hayward	29	111	73	5	-
F de Wet c HM Amla b Tweedie	1	43	23	-	-	c AM Amla b Benkenstein	7	23	22	1	-
GJ de Bruin not out	8	23	16	-	-	not out	2	33	22	-	-
Extras (b 1, lb 13, nb 6)	20					Extras (b 1, lb 3, w 3, nb 5)	12				
TOTAL (84 overs)	**269**					**TOTAL (68.1 overs)**	**249**				

DOLPHINS	Runs	Mins	Balls	4	6		Runs	Mins	Balls	4	6
DJ Watson c Van Jaarsveld b De Bruin	1	12	11	-	-	not out	91	240	160	16	-
I Khan c Harris b De Bruin	56	162	123	9	-	c Van Jaarsveld b De Wet	15	44	27	2	-
HM Amla run out (Blignaut/Petersen)	99	158	120	18	1	lbw b De Wet	1	8	8	-	-
AM Amla lbw b De Wet	43	107	76	6	1	c McKenzie b De Bruin	125	175	119	24	-
DM Benkenstein c Moleon b De Wet	32	89	65	7	-	not out	13	10	11	3	-
K Smit c Van Jaarsveld b De Wet	5	20	14	1	-						
†DL Brown c Harris b De Bruin	0	3	3	-	-						
*L Klusener c Harris b De Wet	0	14	4	-	-						
ANW Tweedie c Ontong b De Bruin	0	2	1	-	-						
S Mhlongo c Harris b De Wet	7	24	17	1	-						
M Hayward not out	12	18	13	2	-						
Extras (lb 4, nb 7)	11					Extras (lb 2, w 1, nb 7)	10				
TOTAL (73.2 overs)	**266**					**TOTAL (for 3 wkts) (53 overs)**	**255**				

Dol	*O*	*M*	*R*	*W*		*O*	*M*	*R*	*W*	
Klusener	22	5	62	3	(3 nb)	11	3	40	3	(3 nb)
Tweedie	21	5	74	4		15.1	0	72	2	
Hayward	14	2	36	1		18	3	64	3	(1 w)
Mhlongo	16	5	56	1	(3 nb)	12	4	37	1	(2 nb, 1 w)
Benkenstein	11	5	27	1		12	4	32	1	
Lio	*O*	*M*	*R*	*W*		*O*	*M*	*R*	*W*	
De Wet	21.2	3	80	5	(7 nb)	19	4	70	2	(6 nb, 1 w)
De Bruin	20	8	62	4		11	0	58	1	
Moleon	10	3	37	0		(4) 4	0	26	0	
Blignaut	9	1	37	0		(3) 3	0	17	0	
Nkwe	5	0	25	0		(6) 11	2	49	0	(1 nb)
Ontong	5	0	18	0		(7) 3	0	17	0	
Petersen	3	1	3	0		(5) 2	0	16	0	

Fall of Wickets	**Lio**	**Dol**	**Lio**	**Dol**
1st	3 (1)	1 (1)	0 (1)	24 (2)
2nd	9 (3)	160 (2)	4 (2)	30 (3)
3rd	13 (2)	165 (3)	5 (4)	241 (4)
4th	146 (4)	237 (5)	29 (5)	-
5th	209 (5)	238 (4)	98 (6)	-
6th	213 (7)	239 (7)	114 (3)	-
7th	239 (8)	243 (6)	122 (8)	-
8th	252 (6)	244 (9)	212 (9)	-
9th	260 (9)	244 (8)	225 (10)	-
10th	269 (10)	266 (10)	249 (7)	-

Cobras v Lions, Cape Town, 23-26 March 2006. Lions won by 25 runs.

TITANS

Easterns Titans (Pty) Ltd, PO Box 7706 Centurion 0046.
Tel 012 663 1005. Fax 012 663 3329.
Chief Executive Officer: Elise Lombard.
Physical Address: SuperSport Park, cnr South and West Avenues, Centurion.
Website: www.titans.cricket.co.za
Grounds: SuperSport Park, Centurion; Willowmoore Park, Benoni.
Affiliates: Northerns Cricket Union, Eastern Cricket Union.
Contracted players: Martin van Jaarsveld (captain), Goolam Bodi, Pierre de Bruyn, Gerald Dros, Paul Harris, Heino Kuhn, Ethy Mbhalati, Albie Morkel, Johan Myburgh, Brendon Reddy, Dale Steyn, Alfonso Thomas, Geoffrey Toyana. CSA contracted players: AB de Villiers, Justin Kemp, Andre Nel.

REVIEW OF THE SEASON 2005/06

Christo Buchner

SUPERSPORT SERIES: P11 W4 L1 D6 (joint winners)
CAPTAIN: M van Jaarsveld (11)
STANDARD BANK CUP: P12 W8 L3 NR1 (beaten finalists)
STANDARD BANK PRO20: P6 W4 L2 (semi-finalists)

The Titans again had to wait until the tail end of the season to put some silverware in their trophy cabinet, sharing the SuperSport Series honours with the Dolphins after a drawn final in Durban.

Set an unlikely 378 for victory on the final day, the visitors still needed 208 to win from 36 overs when play was abandoned. Having finished second on the log, the Titans were, however, more than happy to get one hand on the most prestigious local trophy and take half of the overall price money of R700 000.

Considering the strong squad assembled at the Centurion franchise, it was a season that again promised much but did not produce all the goods.

The Titans ended runners-up in the Standard Bank one-day competition to the Eagles and were disappointingly knocked out of the Pro 20-series in the semi-finals by the Cobras.

The Pro20 elimination was somewhat farcical. While the Cobras were raring to go when the skies eventually cleared on the reserve day, the feeling existed that the Titans were just waiting for the match to be called off, so that they could advance to the final because of their higher log placing.

It turned out to be a seven-over slog in which the Titans were caught stone cold. Having also succumbed to the Eagles for a second successive year in the Standard Bank Cup final the Titans were handed the "choker" tag.

The performance in the SuperSport final relieved the pressure on the side and the new coach, Richard Pybus, who took over from Dave Nosworthy at the start of this season, said: "'It was a very satisfactory season in which we made two finals and played some good cricket. With

JOINT CHAMPIONS . . . after finishing second on the log, the Titans had a great first day in the SuperSport Series final in Durban but eventually had to settle for a share of the trophy after the Dolphins earned a draw *Picture: TERTIUS PICKARD, Touchline Photo*

this having been my first season at the Titans it was all part of a growing process, for me and the players. 'I don't foresee many changes and am sure we will keep the core of players we have at our disposal."

Injuries and the unavailability of key players through national duty meant the Titans battled to have a settled squad throughout the season. Despite this, their strength in depth enabled them to be the most consistent side in all competitions.

Justin Kemp, who was appointed captain for the season, only played in the last three matches. Martin van Jaarsveld, initially appointed as a caretaker captain, ended up holding the reins for the season. Having left the Titans towards the end of the previous season to become a Kolpak player in England, he was lured back after a change to the definition of "overseas players" who were South African citizens not attempting to qualify to play at international level for another country.

The Titans won four of their ten SuperSport Series matches and they were all at their second home ground, Willowmoore Park, Benoni, which became somewhat of a fortress for the Titans. The only home match they could not win was against the Dolphins at SuperSport Park.

The lanky left-arm spinner, Paul Harris, ended up the joint leading wicket-taker along with Dale Steyn in the SuperSport Series with 49 scalps.

The Titans lost their opening batsman Alviro Petersen midway through the season in somewhat controversial fashion, while Kruger van Wyk opted to play in New Zealand.

The Titans had a new president in Andy O'Connor, who cut his cricketing teeth at Easterns. He took over the reigns during April 2006 from Jesse Chellen, who succeeded Brandon Foot in August 2005.

FRANCHISE RECORDS

Honours:

SuperSport Series (1): 2005/06 (shared)

Highest innings totals:			
For:	586-9*	v Warriors (East London)	2005/06
Against:	470	by Dolphins (Durban)	2005/06
Lowest innings totals:			
For:	103	v Cape Cobras (Cape Town)	2005/06
Against:	105	by Warriors (Benoni)	2005/06
Highest individual innings:			
For:	236*	M van Jaarsveld v Western Province Boland (Benoni)	2004/05
Against:	151	DM Benkenstein for Dolphins (Durban)	2005/06
Most runs in a season:			
741 (Avg 74.10)		Z de Bruyn	2004/05
Most runs in a career:			
1361 (Avg 56.70)		Z de Bruyn	2004-05
Most 100s in a career:			
4		Z de Bruyn	2004-05
Best bowling in an innings:			
For:	7-54	AC Thomas v Cape Cobras (Cape Town)	2005/06
Against:	7-75	N Boje for Eagles (Bloemfontein)	2005/06
Best bowling in a match:			
For:	10-71	DW Steyn v Warriors (Benoni)	2005/06
Against:	9-55	VD Philander for Cape Cobras (Cape Town)	2005/06
Most wickets in a season:			
49 (Avg 18.22)		DW Steyn	2005/06
49 (Avg 21.48)		PL Harris	2005/06
Most wickets in a career:			
77 (Avg 20.83)		DW Steyn	2004-05

Most dismissals (wicketkeepers) in an innings:
5 (ct 5) AB de Villiers v Eagles (Benoni) 2005/06
Most dismissals (wicketkeepers) in a match:
8 (ct 8) AB de Villiers v Eagles (Benoni) 2005/06
Most dismissals (wicketkeepers) in a season:
21 (ct 19, st 2) HG Kuhn 2005/06
Most dismissals (wicketkeepers) in a career:
24 (ct 23, st 1) AB de Villiers 2004-05
Most catches (fielders) in an innings:
4 M van Jaarsveld v Eagles (Benoni) 2005/06
Most catches (fielders) in a match:
5 M van Jaarsveld v Eagles (Benoni) 2005/06
Most catches (fielders) in a season:
25 M van Jaarsveld 2005/06
Most catches (fielders) in a career:
31 M van Jaarsveld 2004-05
Most appearances:
18 PL Harris, NE Mbhalati and M van Jaarsveld 2004-05
Most captaincies:
13 M van Jaarsveld 2004-05

RECORD WICKET PARTNERSHIPS

1st	156	AN Petersen and AB de Villiers v Dolphins (Centurion)	2004/05
2nd	317	AB de Villiers and M van Jaarsveld v Western Province Boland (Benoni)	2004/05
3rd	131	AN Petersen and Z de Bruyn v Warriors (East London)	2005/06
4th	264	JA Morkel and JM Kemp v Western Province Boland (Paarl)	2004/05
5th	152	Z de Bruyn and JA Morkel v Warriors (East London)	2005/06
6th	116*	Z de Bruyn and JA Morkel v Dolphins (Centurion)	2004/05
7th	147	DJ Cullinan and GH Bodi v Western Province Boland (Paarl)	2004/05
8th	62	G Toyana and PL Harris v Dolphins (Durban)	2004/05
9th	78	P de Bruyn and MA Mashimbyi v Lions (Potchefstroom)	2005/06
10th	63	P de Bruyn and NE Mbhalati v Eagles (Benoni)	2005/06

PERFORMANCES AGAINST OTHER TEAMS

HIGHEST AND LOWEST TOTALS

Opponents	Highest Total For		Lowest Total For	
Cape Cobras	524-4*	2004/05	103	2005/06
Dolphins	376-5*	2004/05	213	2004/05
Eagles	458-8*	2004/05	119	2004/05
Lions	405	2005/06	169	2005/06
Warriors	586-9*	2005/06	340	2005/06

BEST INDIVIDUAL PERFORMANCES

Opponents	Highest score		Best bowling (innings)		Best bowling (match, 8+)	
Cape Cobras	236*	M van Jaarsveld, 2004/05	7-54	AC Thomas, 2005/06	10-161	AC Thomas, 2005/06
Dolphins	149	Z de Bruyn, 2004/05	5-26	NE Mbhalati, 2005/06	8-90	PL Harris, 2005/06
Eagles	145	M van Jaarsveld, 2005/06	6-79	PL Harris, 2005/06	9-141	PL Harris, 2005/06
Lions	139	AN Petersen, 2004/05	5-32	MA Mashimbyi, 2005/06	-	
Warriors	175	Z de Bruyn, 2005/06	5-27	DW Steyn, 2005/06	10-71	DW Steyn, 2005/06

TITANS SUPERSPORT SERIES AVERAGES 2005/06

Batting & Fielding

Name	M	Inns	NO	Runs	HS	Avg	100	50	Ct	St
JA Morkel	5	6	2	381	84	95.25	0	5	2	0
AB de Villiers	1	2	0	103	98	51.50	0	1	8	0
CFK van Wyk	4	7	3	200	74 *	50.00	0	2	11	1
P de Bruyn	7	10	3	333	125 *	47.57	1	2	5	0
Z de Bruyn	10	16	2	620	175	44.28	1	3	6	0
HG Kuhn	6	10	1	373	96	41.44	0	2	19	2
M van Jaarsveld	11	18	2	618	145	38.62	1	4	25	0
GH Bodi	10	16	1	547	140	36.46	1	2	4	0
AN Petersen	4	7	0	222	140	31.71	1	0	3	0
AJ Seymore	6	11	0	322	91	29.27	0	2	7	0
JM Kemp	3	4	0	109	52	27.25	0	1	4	0
G Toyana	8	11	1	239	55	23.90	0	2	3	0
F du Plessis	2	3	1	41	22	20.50	0	0	2	0
AM Phangiso	3	4	1	55	18	18.33	0	0	2	0
AC Thomas	7	9	1	135	28 *	16.87	0	0	2	0
MA Mashimbyi	3	4	0	54	41	13.50	0	0	1	0
PL Harris	11	13	2	146	28	13.27	0	0	5	0
DW Steyn	9	11	2	104	34	11.55	0	0	0	0
M Morkel	2	2	1	7	4	7.00	0	0	5	0
NE Mbhalati	9	11	3	24	10	3.00	0	0	0	0
Totals	121	175	26	4633	175		5	26	114	3
			Extras	320				subs	3	
			Total	4953		33.24			117	

Bowling

Name	Overs	Mdns	Runs	Wkts	Avg	BB	5I	10M
M van Jaarsveld	5	2	10	1	10.00	1-1	0	0
JM Kemp	22	4	74	5	14.80	5-41	1	0
MA Mashimbyi	29.2	4	94	6	15.66	5-32	1	0
DW Steyn	316.3	71	893	49	18.22	5-27	3	1
PL Harris	379.5	104	1053	49	21.48	6-54	4	0
AC Thomas	213	62	638	24	26.58	7-54	1	1
Z de Bruyn	104.4	22	405	15	27.00	5-28	1	0
NE Mbhalati	239.4	60	847	29	29.20	5-26	1	0
P de Bruyn	29	3	96	3	32.00	2-8	0	0
GH Bodi	8.5	1	36	1	36.00	1-5	0	0
JA Morkel	131.4	28	436	10	43.60	3-92	0	0
M Morkel	71	9	266	6	44.33	4-96	0	0
AN Petersen	1	0	5	0	-	-	0	0
F du Plessis	1	0	6	0	-	-	0	0
AM Phangiso	2	0	11	0	-	-	0	0
Totals	1554.3	370	4870	198		7-54	12	2
		b/lb/pen	179	5	run outs			
		Total	5049	203	24.87			

MATCH REPORTS AND SCORECARDS

TITANS v EAGLES — SuperSport Series

Played at Willowmoore Park, Benoni on 20,21,22,23 October 2005 — Toss: Titans
Umpires: MW Brown & SB Lambson — Referee: CJ Mitchley
Debuts: Ttn: None. Eag: None
Close of play: Day 1: Ttn (1) 315-6 (P de Bruyn 59*, Thomas 16*, 96 overs). Day 2: Eag (1) 168-8 (Van der Wath 51*, Louw 0*, 51.3 overs). Day 3: Eag (2) 48-1 (Bailey 12*, Rudolph 25*, 24 overs).
Result: Titans won by 92 runs
Man of Match: Dale Steyn
Points: Ttn: 18.5 (bat 4.50, bowl 4, match 10); Eag: 4.84 (bat 1.84, bowl 3, match 0)
Notes: Jacobs scored his fifty off 40 balls and his century off 93 balls in Eagles' 2nd innings.

An outstanding unbeaten century by Pierre de Bruyn and 98 by AB de Villiers gave the Titans a solid platform in their first innings, to which the Eagles could only reply with a modest total, as the Titans' pace bowlers shared the wickets. With a first innings lead of 246, the Titans batted again to set up a big win despite an attacking second innings century by Davy Jacobs.

TITANS	*Runs*	*Mins*	*Balls*	*4*	*6*		*Runs*	*Mins*	*Balls*	*4*	*6*
AJ Seymore c Van Wyk b Van der Wath	52	140	105	8	-	(2) c Beukes b McLaren	38	125	87	6	-
AN Petersen c Louw b Van der Wath	12	24	18	2	-	(1) c Jacobs b McLaren	11	22	24	1	-
*M van Jaarsveld c Beukes b McLaren	0	4	2	-	-	run out (Thyssen/Louw)	70	182	147	9	-
Z de Bruyn c Beukes b Louw	17	42	39	3	-	not out	34	105	82	4	-
†AB de Villiers run out (Bailey)	98	230	159	16	-	c Bailey b Louw	5	13	9	1	-
G Toyana c Van Wyk b Mpitsang	35	92	74	5	-	not out	4	12	9	-	-
P de Bruyn not out	125	346	262	19	-						
AC Thomas lbw b Van der Wath	17	100	69	2	-						
PL Harris c Jacobs b Van der Wath	28	81	53	3	-						
DW Steyn c McLaren b Van der Wath	2	31	25	-	-						
NE Mbhalati c Louw b Rudolph	10	61	30	2	-						
Extras (b 10, lb 7, w 4, nb 21)	42					Extras (b 2, w 1, nb 4)	7				
TOTAL (136.3 overs)	**438**					**TOTAL (for 4 wkts dec) (59 overs)**	**169**				

EAGLES	*Runs*	*Mins*	*Balls*	*4*	*6*		*Runs*	*Mins*	*Balls*	*4*	*6*
RT Bailey lbw b Steyn	4	26	19	1	-	c Seymore b Harris	30	206	135	5	-
JA Beukes c Harris b Thomas	6	14	9	1	-	c De Villiers b Mbhalati	7	53	33	1	-
JA Rudolph c Van Jaarsveld b Mbhalati	26	75	47	4	-	c Seymore b Z de Bruyn	58	119	82	9	2
DJ Jacobs c Van Jaarsveld b Steyn	0	3	4	-	-	c De Villiers b Thomas	128	188	134	17	2
*†MN van Wyk c Van Jaarsveld b Mbhalati	8	16	12	2	-	hit wicket b Mbhalati	4	21	17	-	-
LL Bosman c De Villiers b Steyn	0	13	9	-	-	c Van Jaarsveld b Thomas	16	38	38	3	-
CA Thyssen c De Villiers b Steyn	2	16	11	-	-	c De Villiers b Steyn	33	84	65	4	1
JJ van der Wath c Van Jaarsveld b Thomas	52	161	109	8	1	lbw b Thomas	1	13	11	-	-
R McLaren c De Villiers b Thomas	63	134	95	8	1	c De Villiers b Steyn	1	12	3	-	-
J Louw lbw b Mbhalati	9	43	30	2	-	c De Villiers b Harris	21	39	29	2	1
PV Mpitsang not out	14	28	22	2	-	not out	16	32	18	3	-
Extras (b 4, lb 1, w 1, nb 2)	8					Extras (b 3, lb 1, w 1, nb 3)	8				
TOTAL (60.5 overs)	**192**					**TOTAL (93.4 overs)**	**323**				

Eag	*O*	*M*	*R*	*W*			*O*	*M*	*R*	*W*	
Van der Wath	42	9	126	5	(5 nb)		5	0	11	0	
McLaren	27	6	91	1	(4 nb)		11	0	31	2	
Louw	23	2	72	1	(2 nb, 2 w)	(4)	17	3	48	1	
Mpitsang	30	6	85	1	(5 nb, 1 w)	(3)	5	1	13	0	(3 nb)
Rudolph	10.3	0	29	1		(6)	6	2	15	0	
Thyssen	4	1	18	0	(1 nb, 1 w)	(7)	4	1	15	0	(1 w)
Bailey						(5)	11	2	34	0	(1 nb)
Ttn	*O*	*M*	*R*	*W*			*O*	*M*	*R*	*W*	
Steyn	21	7	56	4			20	3	62	2	(1 w)
Thomas	18	7	50	3	(1 w)		32	16	79	3	(1 nb)
Mbhalati	12.5	2	50	3	(2 nb)		13	5	37	2	
Harris	9	2	31	0			19.4	2	88	2	(2 nb)
Z de Bruyn							9	1	53	1	

Fall of Wickets

	Ttn	**Eag**	**Ttn**	**Eag**
1st	21 (2)	10 (2)	13 (1)	20 (2)
2nd	21 (3)	18 (1)	97 (2)	90 (3)
3rd	54 (4)	18 (4)	156 (3)	124 (1)
4th	114 (1)	30 (5)	162 (5)	147 (5)
5th	189 (6)	35 (6)	-	185 (6)
6th	258 (5)	43 (7)	-	280 (7)
7th	318 (8)	51 (3)	-	284 (4)
8th	370 (9)	168 (9)	-	285 (8)
9th	375 (10)	169 (8)	-	287 (9)
10th	438 (11)	192 (10)	-	323 (10)

Warriors v Titans, East London, 27-30 October 2005. Match drawn.
Cape Cobras v Titans, Newlands, 3-6 November 2005. Cape Cobras won by 230 runs.
Dolphins v Titans, Durban, 10-13 November 2005. Match drawn.

TITANS v LIONS — SuperSport Series

Played at Willowmoore Park, Benoni on 17,18,19 November 2005 — Toss: Titans
Umpires: IL Howell & LH Matroos — Referee: MR Magiet
Debuts: Ttn: None. Lio: None
Close of play: Day 1: Lio (1) 21-0 (Cook 4*, Steyn 9*, 9 overs). Day 2: Ttn (2) 141-7 (Bodi 34*, Harris 8*, 45 overs)..
Result: Titans won by 109 runs
Man of Match: Friedel de Wet
Points: Ttn: 16.5 (bat 2.50, bowl 4, match 10); Lio: 4 (bat 0.00, bowl 4, match 0)

This was a low scoring affair which led Cricket South Africa to launch an inquiry into the state of the pitch. The Lions were bundled out for under 150 in both their innings with Mandla Mashimbyi taking five wickets in the first innings after his late inclusion in the side.

The only batting of note came from Zander de Bruyn and Kruger van Wyk on the first day. It proved to be a bittersweet occasion for Van Wyk as it turned out to be his final appearance of the season in the four-day competition because when the Series resumed three months later Heino Kuhn was preferred to him as wicketkeeper.

TITANS	Runs	Mins	Balls	4	6		Runs	Mins	Balls	4	6
AJ Seymore c Cook b Kruger	7	37	24	-	-	c McKenzie b De Wet	11	25	22	1	-
AN Petersen c Blignaut b De Wet	0	7	5	-	-	b De Wet	18	32	20	4	-
*M van Jaarsveld c Moleon b Blignaut	15	51	44	3	-	c Cook b Moleon	15	50	28	3	-
Z de Bruyn c Harris b De Wet	78	247	147	14	-	b Moleon	6	35	24	1	-
GH Bodi c McKenzie b Moleon	6	90	69	-	-	b De Wet	36	140	96	6	-
P de Bruyn lbw b Moleon	4	9	7	1	-	c McKenzie b Moleon	8	17	18	1	-
†CFK van Wyk not out	74	209	163	10	-	c Harris b Kruger	23	83	63	3	-
MA Mashimbyi c Harris b Kruger	4	7	7	1	-	b Kruger	4	2	3	1	-
PL Harris c Nkwe b De Wet	0	15	14	-	-	not out	25	69	44	3	-
DW Steyn b Blignaut	21	52	35	2	-	c Harris b De Wet	0	11	8	-	-
NE Mbhalati b Blignaut	0	3	1	-		c Harris b De Wet	5	31	19	-	-
Extras (b 2, lb 1, w 2, nb 11)	16					Extras (b 3, lb 7, w 3, nb 5)	18				
TOTAL (84.1 overs)	**225**					**TOTAL (56.5 overs)**	**169**				

LIONS	Runs	Mins	Balls	4	6		Runs	Mins	Balls	4	6
SC Cook b Mashimbyi	7	96	73	-	-	b Mbhalati	7	26	25	1	-
FA Steyn c Seymore b Mbhalati	9	41	30	2	-	c Van Wyk b Steyn	7	19	7	1	-
ET Nkwe c Van Wyk b Mashimbyi	11	85	54	1	-	(5) lbw b Z de Bruyn	8	26	16	1	-
*ND McKenzie b Mbhalati	7	35	22	1	-	lbw b Steyn	38	179	126	6	-
VB van Jaarsveld lbw b Mashimbyi	0	8	5	-	-	(6) lbw b Mashimbyi	15	22	19	2	-
†MJ Harris c Petersen b Mashimbyi	0	15	9	-	-	(7) lbw b Steyn	22	60	49	3	-
BC Adams c Van Jaarsveld b Steyn	5	30	17	1	-	(3) lbw b Z de Bruyn	5	64	38	-	-
AM Blignaut c Petersen b Harris	50	90	51	6	1	b Harris	1	5	6	-	-
EO Moleon c Van Wyk b Steyn	0	1	2	-	-	not out	2	34	23	-	-
F de Wet b Mashimbyi	36	80	48	6	-	b Harris	6	14	17	-	-
GJ-P Kruger not out	0	11	11	-	-	c Van Wyk b Harris	3	13	6	-	-
Extras (b 2, lb 6, w 3, nb 12)	23					Extras (b 5, lb 5, w 2, nb 11)	23				
TOTAL (52.2 overs)	**148**					**TOTAL (54.1 overs)**	**137**				

Lio	O	M	R	W			O	M	R	W	
Kruger	23	5	63	2	(4 nb)		19	4	75	2	(2 nb, 1 w)
De Wet	22	8	52	3	(3 nb, 1 w)		17.5	6	35	5	(1 w)
Blignaut	14.1	2	34	3	(3 nb, 1 w)		8	1	24	0	(2 nb)
Moleon	16	6	36	2	(1 nb)		8	2	21	3	(1 nb, 1 w)
Adams	9	1	37	0							
McKenzie						(5)	4	2	4	0	
Ttn	O	M	R	W			O	M	R	W	
Steyn	17	6	40	2	(5 nb)		15	2	43	3	(5 nb, 1 w)
Mbhalati	19	9	44	2	(1 nb, 3 w)		12	5	25	1	(1 nb)
Mashimbyi	10.2	0	32	5	(1 nb)	(4)	7	3	14	1	
Z de Bruyn	3	0	19	0	(1 nb)	(3)	10	1	33	2	(1 nb, 1 w)
Harris	3	2	5	1			10.1	5	12	3	

Fall of Wickets

	Ttn	Lio	Ttn	Lio
1st	0 (2)	21 (2)	23 (1)	15 (2)
2nd	18 (1)	38 (1)	32 (2)	21 (1)
3rd	32 (3)	49 (3)	56 (4)	52 (3)
4th	68 (5)	49 (4)	60 (3)	63 (5)
5th	72 (6)	50 (5)	68 (6)	85 (6)
6th	156 (4)	51 (6)	128 (7)	123 (7)
7th	162 (8)	65 (7)	132 (8)	124 (8)
8th	173 (9)	65 (9)	144 (5)	124 (4)
9th	222 (10)	140 (8)	147 (10)	133 (10)
10th	225 (11)	148 (10)	169 (11)	137 (11)

TITANS

Eagles v Titans, Bloemfontein, 23-26 February 2006. Match drawn.
Lions v Titans, Potchefstroom, 2-5 March 2006. Match drawn.

TITANS v CAPE COBRAS — SuperSport Series

Played at Willowmoore Park, Benoni on 9,10,11,12 March 2006 — Toss: Cape Cobras
Umpires: GH Pienaar & S Wadvalla — Referee: CJ Mitchley
Debuts: Ttn: None. Cob: None
Close of play: Day 1: Ttn (1) 115-2 (Van Jaarsveld 57*, Z de Bruyn 7*, 36 overs). Day 2: Ttn (1) 197-4 (Bodi 22*, Toyana 1*, 70.1 overs). Day 3: Cob (2) 95-5 (Bassage 50*, Tsolekile 2*, 27 overs).
Result: Titans won by an innings and 5 runs
Man of Match: Zander de Bruyn
Points: Ttn: 17.26 (bat 3.26, bowl 4, match 10); Cob: 3.42 (bat 1.42, bowl 2, match 0)

An outstanding all-round performance by Zander de Bruyn enabled the Titans to come away with the spoils. After taking five cheap wickets with his medium pace in the Cobras' first innings, he compiled a patient top score of 60 runs as the home side grafted their way to a lead of 156.

The Cape side capitulated in their second innings, with left-arm spinner Paul Harris the destroyer in chief.

CAPE COBRAS	Runs	Mins	Balls	4	6		Runs	Mins	Balls	4	6
AG Puttick c Kuhn b Z de Bruyn	26	114	61	5	-	b Steyn	10	30	23	1	-
DJ Bassage c Phangiso b Steyn	5	19	14	-	-	c Van Jaarsveld b Harris	66	148	120	11	-
W Wyngaard c Harris b Steyn	4	8	5	1	-	lbw b Van Jaarsveld	13	46	26	1	-
J-P Duminy b Steyn	0	2	1	-	-	b Steyn	8	13	10	1	-
HD Ackerman c Van Jaarsveld b Z de Bruyn	11	34	26	2	-	b Harris	0	6	5	-	-
VD Philander c P de Bruyn b Z de Bruyn	4	31	23	1	-	lbw b Harris	0	3	4	-	-
*†TL Tsolekile c Phangiso b Z de Bruyn	37	90	67	1	3	c Van Jaarsveld b Harris	6	61	33	-	-
RK Kleinveldt c Van Jaarsveld b Z de Bruyn	39	64	42	6	1	c Kuhn b Steyn	10	40	24	-	-
PR Adams not out	17	26	17	3	-	not out	22	32	24	1	2
M Zondeki c sub (M Morkel) b Mbhalati	4	9	5	-	-	lbw b Harris	1	5	3	-	-
CM Willoughby b Mbhalati	6	8	2	-	1	c Z de Bruyn b Harris	0	1	2	-	-
Extras (b 2, lb 5, w 2, nb 9)	18					Extras (lb 2, nb 13)	15				
TOTAL (42.2 overs)	**171**					**TOTAL (43.4 overs)**	**151**				

TITANS	Runs	Mins	Balls	4	6
†HG Kuhn run out (Bassage/Adams)	41	126	87	5	-
F du Plessis c Ackerman b Zondeki	5	15	12	1	-
*M van Jaarsveld c Tsolekile b Kleinveldt	59	190	124	6	1
Z de Bruyn c Tsolekile b Philander	60	174	136	6	-
GH Bodi c Tsolekile b Zondeki	53	216	132	5	1
G Toyana c Tsolekile b Kleinveldt	39	188	126	3	-
P de Bruyn b Kleinveldt	9	47	33	-	-
AM Phangiso not out	17	90	64	-	-
PL Harris c Tsolekile b Kleinveldt	0	8	7	-	-
DW Steyn c Puttick b Willoughby	34	62	44	5	-
NE Mbhalati lbw b Willoughby	0	3	1	-	-
Extras (b 1, lb 4, w 1, nb 4)	10				
TOTAL (127 overs)	**327**				

Ttn	O	M	R	W			O	M	R	W	
Steyn	16	3	38	3	(4 nb)		17	0	67	3	(12 nb)
Mbhalati	11.2	2	69	2	(2 nb, 2 w)		2	1	4	0	
Z de Bruyn	12	3	28	5	(1 nb)		7	3	14	0	
Harris	3	0	29	0	(2 nb)	(5)	14.4	3	54	6	
P de Bruyn						(4)	2	0	9	0	
Van Jaarsveld							1	0	1	1	

Cob	O	M	R	W	
Willoughby	34	13	73	2	
Zondeki	22	1	68	2	(1 nb, 1 w)
Philander	28	9	69	1	(1 nb)
Kleinveldt	33	10	66	4	(2 nb)
Adams	10	0	46	0	

Fall of Wickets

	Cob	Ttn	Cob
1st	15 (2)	6 (2)	26 (1)
2nd	23 (3)	90 (1)	73 (3)
3rd	23 (4)	131 (3)	84 (4)
4th	40 (5)	194 (4)	86 (5)
5th	55 (6)	252 (5)	86 (6)
6th	63 (1)	274 (7)	116 (2)
7th	143 (8)	279 (6)	121 (7)
8th	144 (7)	279 (9)	147 (8)
9th	159 (10)	326 (10)	151 (10)
10th	171 (11)	327 (11)	151 (11)

TITANS v WARRIORS

SuperSport Series

Played at Willowmoore Park, Benoni on 16,17,18 March 2006 — Toss: Titans
Umpires: MZ Nanabhay & S Wadvalla — Referee: A Barnes
Debuts: Ttn: None. War: None
Close of play: Day 1: War (1) 157 all out. Day 2: Ttn (1) 318-8 (Thomas 14*, Harris 4*, 94.4 overs)..
Result: Titans won by an innings and 78 runs
Man of Match: Dale Steyn
Points: Ttn: 18.68 (bat 4.68, bowl 4, match 10); War: 4.14 (bat 1.14, bowl 3, match 0)

The visitors gave another woeful display, on the evidence of which they were out of place in a set-up supposedly matching strength against strength. Dale Steyn's pace was too much for the Warriors in both innings as he claimed the first ten-wicket haul of his career.

Goolam Bodi was the star of the show when the Titans batted, with his century ensuring his side held a substantial lead. Albie Morkel helped Bodi put on 107 for the sixth wicket after Tyron Henderson had made inroads at the top of the innings.

WARRIORS	Runs	Mins	Balls	4	6		Runs	Mins	Balls	4	6
*CC Bradfield lbw b Steyn	13	36	34	3	-	lbw b Morkel	11	44	29	2	-
BL Bennett b Steyn	35	80	44	6	-	c Kuhn b Steyn	15	39	27	3	-
JP Kreusch b De Bruyn	0	15	10	-	-	c De Bruyn b Harris	4	52	35	-	-
A Jacobs not out	83	205	149	11	2	lbw b De Bruyn	26	60	37	5	-
J Botha lbw b Harris	10	79	58	2	-	c Kuhn b Steyn	9	17	16	2	-
SC Pope c Thomas b Steyn	1	9	9	-	-	b De Bruyn	0	2	4	-	-
†AM Sodumo b Harris	9	39	22	2	-	c Kuhn b Steyn	3	21	14	-	-
T Henderson c De Bruyn b Harris	0	16	7	-	-	c sub (P de Bruyn) b Steyn	11	27	16	2	-
L Meyer c Kuhn b De Bruyn	0	11	9	-	-	c Kemp b Steyn	9	48	32	1	-
MW Olivier b Steyn	1	22	22	-	-	c Thomas b Morkel	2	27	21	-	-
M Ngam c Van Jaarsveld b Steyn	0	2	2	-	-	not out	5	11	10	1	-
Extras (lb 4, nb 1)	5					Extras (b 2, lb 4, w 1, nb 3)	10				
TOTAL (60.5 overs)	**157**					**TOTAL (39.4 overs)**	**105**				

TITANS	Runs	Mins	Balls	4	6
†HG Kuhn c Sodumo b Henderson	18	42	32	2	-
GH Bodi c Sodumo b Henderson	140	391	270	16	2
*M van Jaarsveld c Sodumo b Henderson	4	3	3	1	-
Z de Bruyn c Botha b Meyer	9	35	21	1	-
JM Kemp c Bradfield b Ngam	39	66	51	7	1
G Toyana c Jacobs b Henderson	5	20	13	-	-
JA Morkel lbw b Pope	60	108	82	11	-
AM Phangiso lbw b Henderson	16	74	58	2	-
AC Thomas c Jacobs b Meyer	28	82	58	3	-
PL Harris not out	9	57	36	1	-
DW Steyn b Henderson	1	11	5	-	-
Extras (lb 3, w 4, nb 4)	11				
TOTAL (104.1 overs)	**340**				

Ttn	O	M	R	W			O	M	R	W	
Steyn	16.5	3	44	5	(1 nb)		14.4	5	27	5	(3 nb)
Morkel	14	3	42	0			10.2	2	46	2	(1 w)
De Bruyn	14	6	41	2		(4)	5.4	1	13	2	
Harris	11	4	22	3		(3)	9	5	13	1	
Thomas	4	3	4	0							
Kemp	1	1	0	0							
War	O	M	R	W							
Henderson	28.1	7	80	6							
Ngam	17	4	64	1	(1 w)						
Olivier	9	1	45	0	(3 nb)						
Kreusch	15	3	46	0							
Meyer	23	5	61	2	(1 nb, 3 w)						
Pope	12	1	41	1							

Fall of Wickets

	War	Ttn	War
1st	23 (1)	26 (1)	30 (2)
2nd	40 (3)	30 (3)	30 (1)
3rd	58 (2)	50 (4)	60 (3)
4th	96 (5)	108 (5)	66 (4)
5th	98 (6)	123 (6)	66 (6)
6th	127 (7)	230 (7)	70 (5)
7th	145 (8)	275 (8)	80 (7)
8th	152 (9)	304 (2)	86 (8)
9th	157 (10)	337 (9)	99 (10)
10th	157 (11)	340 (11)	105 (9)

TITANS v DOLPHINS

SuperSport Series

Played at SuperSport Park, Centurion on 23,24,25,26 March 2006 — Toss: Dolphins
Umpires: SB Lambson & GH Pienaar — Referee: A Barnes
Debuts: Ttn: None. Dol: AH Razak (FC)
Close of play: Day 1: Ttn (1) 121-5 (Kemp 9*, Morkel 5*, 43 overs). Day 2: Dol (1) 149-3 (Watson 63*, Benkenstein 22*, 53 overs). Day 3: Ttn (2) 41-2 (Bodi 17*, De Bruyn 5*, 14 overs).
Result: Match drawn
Man of Match: Ugasen Govender
Points: Ttn: 5.88 (bat 2.88, bowl 3, match 0); Dol: 7.8 (bat 3.80, bowl 4, match 0)

With both sides treating this as a curtain-raiser to the final two weeks later, the Dolphins rested several key players, including their captain, Lance Klusener.

Rain played a major part on the opening day of what proved to be a drab affair, although Govender achieved his best bowling figures for the Dolphins, Doug Watson made a century and Morkel played two aggressive unbeaten innings.

TITANS	*Runs*	*Mins*	*Balls*	*4*	*6*		*Runs*	*Mins*	*Balls*	*4*	*6*
†HG Kuhn c D Smit b Kent	45	123	92	9	-	c Razak b Govender	0	3	6	-	-
GH Bodi c AM Amla b Kent	9	56	34	1	-	c Benkenstein b Frylinck	39	156	99	6	-
*M van Jaarsveld c D Smit b Govender	36	123	87	4	1	c sub (ANW Tweedie) b Frylinck	16	48	36	3	-
Z de Bruyn b Kent	6	35	24	1	-	b Kent	42	190	125	2	-
JM Kemp c K Smit b Govender	12	62	35	1	-	b Benkenstein	6	25	16	1	-
G Toyana c D Smit b Govender	0	3	4	-	-	lbw b AM Amla	55	134	112	8	-
JA Morkel not out	83	184	99	10	1	not out	75	114	74	2	5
AM Phangiso b Govender	4	15	10	1	-	c sub (ANW Tweedie) b Razak	18	25	32	-	1
AC Thomas b Govender	5	24	12	1	-	not out	28	14	10	2	3
PL Harris b Razak	26	77	65	1	2						
DW Steyn c Kent b Govender	3	27	9	-	-						
Extras (lb 3, w 1, nb 11)	15					Extras (b 2, lb 1, nb 6)	9				
TOTAL (76.4 overs)	**244**					**TOTAL (for 7 wkts dec) (84 overs)**	**288**				

DOLPHINS	*Runs*	*Mins*	*Balls*	*4*	*6*		*Runs*	*Mins*	*Balls*	*4*	*6*
DJ Watson b Steyn	100	344	241	11	-	lbw b Steyn	27	68	49	4	-
I Khan c Kemp b Thomas	2	15	11	-	-	lbw b Thomas	24	43	29	3	-
HM Amla c Kuhn b Kemp	53	137	113	7	-	not out	12	41	29	1	-
AM Amla c Kuhn b Steyn	5	12	9	-	-	not out	13	16	15	2	-
*DM Benkenstein c Van Jaarsveld b Kemp	56	117	96	8	-						
K Smit c Kuhn b Kemp	8	18	18	1	-						
JC Kent c Kemp b Harris	22	128	79	2	-						
†D Smit b Kemp	31	60	50	4	-						
R Frylinck c Kuhn b Kemp	8	24	20	-	1						
AH Razak not out	0	6	0	-	-						
U Govender b Harris	2	4	3	-	-						
Extras (lb 5, w 2, nb 6)	13					Extras (b 1, w 1, nb 2)	4				
TOTAL (105.4 overs)	**300**					**TOTAL (for 2 wkts) (20 overs)**	**80**				

Dol	*O*	*M*	*R*	*W*		*O*	*M*	*R*	*W*	
Kent	21	4	77	3	(4 nb)	(2) 17	3	34	1	(1 nb)
Govender	23.4	7	59	6	(6 nb, 1 w)	(1) 13	1	26	1	(4 nb)
Benkenstein	14	2	41	0	(1 nb)	(4) 12	2	37	1	
Frylinck	12	1	26	0		(3) 14	5	38	2	
Razak	6	0	38	1		15	1	88	1	(1 nb)
Khan						1	0	8	0	
AM Amla						12	1	54	1	
Ttn	*O*	*M*	*R*	*W*		*O*	*M*	*R*	*W*	
Steyn	21	6	64	2	(1 nb, 1 w)	4	1	13	1	(2 nb)
Thomas	19	6	46	1	(1 nb)	6	0	26	1	
Morkel	20	4	55	0						
Harris	28.4	6	78	2	(4 nb)	7	2	21	0	
Phangiso	2	0	11	0						
Kemp	15	3	41	5	(1 w)	(3) 3	0	19	0	(1 w)

Fall of Wickets

	Ttn	Dol	Ttn	Dol
1st	33 (2)	6 (2)	0 (1)	44 (2)
2nd	90 (1)	109 (3)	23 (3)	59 (1)
3rd	102 (4)	116 (4)	83 (2)	-
4th	113 (3)	207 (5)	94 (5)	-
5th	114 (6)	219 (6)	133 (4)	-
6th	141 (5)	235 (1)	210 (6)	-
7th	155 (8)	287 (8)	240 (8)	-
8th	169 (9)	298 (9)	-	-
9th	211 (10)	298 (7)	-	-
10th	244 (11)	300 (11)	-	-

(A report on the SuperSport Series final between the Dolphins and the Titans appears in the section, SuperSport Series, on Page 399)

WARRIORS

Cricket Eastern Cape (Pty) Ltd, PO Box 12327, Centrahill 6006.
Tel 041 585 1646, fax 041 586 4259.
Chief Executive: David Emslie.
Physical Address: Sahara Oval St George's, Park Drive, Port Elizabeth 6000.
Grounds: Sahara Oval St George's, Port Elizabeth; Mercedes-Benz Park, East London.
E-mail: davee@cricket.co.za or leighd@cricket.co.za
Website: www.stgeorgespark.co.za
Affiliates: Eastern Province Cricket Board, Border Cricket Board.
Contracted players: HD Ackerman, Johan Botha, Carl Bradfield, Zander de Bruyn, Burton de Wett, Mornantau Hayward, Colin Ingram, Arno Jacobs, Brent Kops, Justin Kreusch, Lyall Meyer, Mfuneko Ngam, Mario Olivier, Robin Peterson, Abongile Sodumo, Craig Thyssen, Lonwabo Tsotsobe. CSA contracted players: Mark Boucher, Makhaya Ntini. Coach, Russell Domingo; assistant coach, Piet Botha.

REVIEW OF THE SEASON 2005/06

Neale Emslie

SUPERSPORT SERIES: P10 W0 L7 D3 (sixth)
CAPTAIN: RJ Peterson (4), ML Bruyns (3), CC Bradfield (3)
STANDARD BANK CUP: P10 W3 L7 (fifth)
STANDARD BANK PRO20: P5 W0 L5 (sixth)

If there were any critics wishing to harp on the failure of the franchise system, the Warriors provided them with plenty of ammunition in the 2005/06 season. Whichever way you look at it, the summer was a failure for the Eastern Cape franchise, consisting of a long string of losses interspersed with the odd moment of success.

After two seasons, the merger of Border and EP cricket has not been successful and it will be interesting to see if the situation improves at all when the franchise's headquarters move to Sahara Oval St George's in Port Elizabeth this year.

Even in the Standard Bank Pro20 series, in which the Warriors had reached the finals in the previous two seasons, the side had no success, losing all five games.

The nadir came in a home fixture against the Eagles when they slumped to 65 all out. In front of an excellent St George's crowd of about 9 000 it was an embarrassing performance and many fans were turned off by the weak effort from the home side.

The players must take the major portion of the blame. Many were in the second year of two-year contracts with the franchise and most were found wanting.

Their first major signing for 2006/07 was HD Ackerman, a player who just failed to make the grade at the highest level but who is far superior to anyone the Warriors have had on their books, with the possible exception of Arno Jacobs.

Jacobs, an elegant left-hander, is such a classy-looking player that he seems to be a permanent under-achiever, but his 726 runs in the SuperSport Series at an average of 45.37 was a more than decent effort in a struggling side.

WARRIORS

Burton de Wett hit a vital maiden first-class century to save a four-day match against the Lions on his way to an aggregate of 506 runs (avg 28.11) and Carl Bradfield (463 runs, avg 24.36) was just behind him.

But the consistency was lacking. The Warriors struggled to make good starts and were rarely able to hold out for four days. Even when their batting came good, their bowlers lacked the skill to contain, let alone dismiss, the opposing batsmen who plundered the attack almost at will.

Tyron Henderson was the best performer with 22 wickets at 29.59 but he was 20th on the national list of averages, an indication of the lack of penetration, experience and ability in the attack.

The Warriors weren't helped by the absence of spinners Johan Botha and Robin Peterson for large parts of the season, while a player like Mfuneko Ngam seems sadly to have fallen away. He could take only nine wickets in six SuperSport matches, four of those coming in one innings.

Although he has much to learn in first-class cricket, Justin Kreusch showed his ability with several powerful one-day innings and remains the sort of player the Warriors will be aiming to develop into a fully fledged first-class cricketer over the next few seasons. He was named the franchise's player of the season, while Henderson again proved what an effective one-day and Pro20 player he is. This summer, though, he'll be plying his trade with the Highveld Lions.

It was a tough baptism for new coach Russell Domingo, who stepped into the spot vacated by Mickey Arthur. A former EP amateur coach, Domingo should be much the wiser after his first season at the top provincial level but he knows he will have to start producing the goods to keep his critics at bay.

Better news for the Warriors came in the form of a substantial R4.92 million sponsorship spread over two years from the Fidentia Group, an asset management company for whom former EP players Louis Koen, Dave Callaghan and Meyrick Pringle work.

This sponsorship was secured after the loss of previous backers DaimlerChrysler, who withdrew their sponsorship when it was decided to move the franchise to Port Elizabeth.

FRANCHISE RECORDS

Highest innings totals:			
For:	442-9*	v Titans (East London)	2005/06
Against:	586-9*	by Titans (East London)	2005/06
Lowest innings totals:			
For:	97	v Cape Cobras (Stellenbosch)	2005/06
Against:	175	by Lions (Port Elizabeth)	2004/05
Highest individual innings:			
For:	173*	A Jacobs v Dolphins (Port Elizabeth)	2004/05
Against:	206	AG Puttick for Western Province Boland (East London)	2004/05
Most runs in a season:			
827 (Avg 55.13)		A Jacobs	2004/05
Most runs in a career:			
1553 (Avg 50.09)		A Jacobs	2004-05
Most 100s in a career:			
4		A Jacobs	2004-05
4		SC Pope	2004-05
Best bowling in an innings:			
For:	6-80	T Henderson v Titans (Benoni)	2005/06
Against:	8-47	RK Kleinveldt for Cape Cobras (Stellenbosch)	2005/06
Best bowling in a match:			
For:	9-142	M Ntini v Eagles (Bloemfontein)	2004/05
Against:	11-90	GJ-P Kruger for Lions (Johannesburg)	2005/06

WARRIORS

Most wickets in a season:
27 (Avg 33.85) BB Kops 2004/05
Most wickets in a career:
44 (Avg 35.70) T Henderson 2004-05
Most dismissals (wicketkeepers) in an innings:
5 (ct 3, st 2) AM Sodumo v Lions (Port Elizabeth) 2004/05
5 (ct 5) AM Sodumo v Eagles (Port Elizabeth) 2005/06
Most dismissals (wicketkeepers) in a match:
8 (ct 6, st 2) AM Sodumo v Lions (Port Elizabeth) 2004/05
Most dismissals (wicketkeepers) in a season:
26 (ct 23, st 3) AM Sodumo 2005/06
Most dismissals (wicketkeepers) in a career:
40 (ct 35, st 5) AM Sodumo 2004-05
Most catches (fielders) in an innings:
4 A Jacobs v Lions (East London) 2005/06
Most catches (fielders) in a match:
4 A Jacobs v Lions (East London) 2005/06
Most catches (fielders) in a season:
17 A Jacobs 2004/05
Most catches (fielders) in a career:
26 A Jacobs 2004-05
Most appearances:
19 A Jacobs 2004-05
Most captaincies:
8 RJ Peterson 2004-05

RECORD WICKET PARTNERSHIPS

1st	118	ML Bruyns and CC Bradfield v Eagles (Port Elizabeth)	2005/06
2nd	158	CC Bradfield and SC Pope v Eagles (East London)	2004/05
3rd	246	ML Bruyns and A Jacobs v Titans (Centurion)	2004/05
4th	175	SC Pope and JP Kreusch v Eagles (East London)	2004/05
5th	111	A Jacobs and MV Boucher v Western Province Boland (Cape Town)	2004/05
6th	156	A Jacobs and RJ Peterson v Dolphins (Port Elizabeth)	2004/05
7th	85	RJ Peterson and BC de Wett v Titans (Centurion)	2004/05
8th	70	A Jacobs and T Henderson v Eagles (Bloemfontein)	2004/05
9th	73	A Jacobs and MW Olivier v Dolphins (East London)	2005/06
10th	48	AM Sodumo and M Hayward v Dolphins (Durban)	2004/05

PERFORMANCES AGAINST OTHER TEAMS

HIGHEST AND LOWEST TOTALS

Opponents	Highest Total For		Lowest Total For	
Cape Cobras	263	2005/06	97	2005/06
Dolphins	349	2004/05	165	2004/05
Eagles	422-9*	2004/05	135	2005/06
Lions	357	2005/06	136	2005/06
Titans	442-9*	2005/06	105	2005/06

BEST INDIVIDUAL PERFORMANCES

Opponents	Highest score		Best bowling (innings)		Best bowling (match, 8+)	
Cape Cobras	119	CC Bradfield, 2005/06	5-31	JP Kreusch, 2005/06	-	
Dolphins	173*	A Jacobs, 2004/05	4-42	M Hayward, 2004/05	-	
Eagles	156*	SC Pope, 2004/05	5-71	M Ntini, 2004/05	9-142	M Ntini, 2004/05
Lions	109	BC de Wett, 2005/06	4-35	M Zondeki, 2004/05	-	
Titans	142	ML Bruyns, 2004/05	6-80	T Henderson, 2005/06	-	

WARRIORS SUPERSPORT SERIES AVERAGES 2005/06

Batting & Fielding

Name	M	Inns	NO	Runs	HS	Avg	100	50	Ct	St
A Jacobs	9	18	2	726	149	45.37	1	4	9	0
D Willemse	1	1	0	34	34	34.00	0	0	0	0
SC Pope	6	12	1	325	101	29.54	1	1	3	0
BC de Wett	9	18	0	506	109	28.11	1	2	2	0
CC Bradfield	10	20	1	463	119	24.36	1	3	3	0
J Botha	6	12	0	281	93	23.41	0	1	2	0
RJ Peterson	4	8	2	136	28	22.66	0	0	1	0
ML Bruyns	4	8	0	177	54	22.12	0	2	3	0
AZM Dyili	1	2	0	44	39	22.00	0	0	0	0
MBA Smith	4	7	0	131	39	18.71	0	0	3	0
JP Kreusch	8	15	0	273	85	18.20	0	1	4	0
BL Bennett	4	8	0	139	46	17.37	0	0	2	0
AM Sodumo	10	19	2	267	77*	15.70	0	2	23	3
LL Gamiet	1	2	0	25	19	12.50	0	0	1	0
T Henderson	8	15	3	108	44*	9.00	0	0	4	0
L Meyer	6	11	3	62	35*	7.75	0	0	3	0
BB Kops	3	6	4	13	8*	6.50	0	0	0	0
M Ngam	6	10	2	37	14	4.62	0	0	0	0
MW Olivier	7	13	0	54	12	4.15	0	0	0	0
RR Richards	2	4	2	2	2*	1.00	0	0	0	0
S Mjekula	1	2	1	1	1	1.00	0	0	1	0
Totals	110	211	23	3804	149		4	16	64	3
			Extras	279				subs	1	
			Total	4083		21.71			65	

Bowling

Name	Overs	Mdns	Runs	Wkts	Avg	BB	5I	10M
J Botha	24.4	7	71	4	17.75	4-71	0	0
S Mjekula	17	3	75	3	25.00	3-65	0	0
T Henderson	252.3	67	651	22	29.59	6-80	1	0
JP Kreusch	173.5	47	439	13	33.76	5-31	1	0
L Meyer	160.5	31	550	15	36.66	4-97	0	0
BL Bennett	6	0	39	1	39.00	1-23	0	0
BB Kops	45.1	5	179	4	44.75	3-41	0	0
MW Olivier	142	23	636	14	45.42	4-71	0	0
SC Pope	50	7	184	4	46.00	2-39	0	0
RR Richards	30.2	11	95	2	47.50	1-11	0	0
RJ Peterson	116.4	16	363	7	51.85	3-151	0	0
M Ngam	124	16	536	9	59.55	4-71	0	0
BC de Wett	101	12	398	6	66.33	4-112	0	0
D Willemse	31	6	87	1	87.00	1-17	0	0
A Jacobs	1	0	8	0	-	-	0	0
Totals	1276	251	4311	105		6-80	2	0
		b/lb/pen	108	2	run outs			
		Total	4419	107	41.29			

MATCH REPORTS AND SCORECARDS

WARRIORS v CAPE COBRAS — SuperSport Series

Played at Sahara Oval St George's, Port Elizabeth on 20,21,22 October 2005 — Toss: Cape Cobras
Umpires: M Erasmus & MZ Nanabhay — Referee: MR Magiet
Debuts: War: None. Cob: None
Close of play: Day 1: War (1) 245-5 (Bradfield 118*, Peterson 18*, 107 overs). Day 2: War (2) 38-4 (Gamiet 17*, De Wett 8*, 18 overs)..
Result: Cape Cobras won by 8 wickets
Man of Match: Charl Willoughby
Points: War: 6.18 (bat 2.18, bowl 4, match 0), Cob: 14.22 (bat 2.22, bowl 2, match 10)

A typically solid century by left-handed opener Carl Bradfield and 87 from the elegant batsmanship of Arno Jacobs gave the Warriors a 52-run first innings lead but that's all they had to cheer about in their opening game of the season.

Cobras left-armer Charl Willoughby and Monde Zondeki ploughed through the Warriors top-order in the second innings and the home side collapsed miserably to 100 all out. The Cobras had no trouble reaching the 153 needed to win for the loss of two wickets with a day to spare.

WARRIORS	*Runs*	*Mins*	*Balls*	*4*	*6*		*Runs*	*Mins*	*Balls*	*4*	*6*
CC Bradfield run out (Strydom)	119	403	320	17	-	lbw b Zondeki	0	16	13	-	-
LL Gamiet c Duminy b Philander	6	78	59	-	-	lbw b Willoughby	19	112	72	1	-
SC Pope lbw b Philander	0	6	2	-	-	b Zondeki	0	8	6	-	-
A Jacobs b Harvey	87	224	191	12	-	c Tsolekile b Willoughby	1	3	4	-	-
JP Kreusch c Duminy b Philander	4	34	31	-	-	lbw b Willoughby	10	23	17	2	-
BC de Wett c Duminy b De Lange	1	19	21	-	-	c Bassage b De Lange	29	79	59	4	-
*RJ Peterson not out	27	84	57	4	-	not out	23	64	34	4	-
†AM Sodumo c Philander b Zondeki	6	21	17	-	-	c Harvey b Philander	0	15	15	-	-
MW Olivier c Tsolekile b Zondeki	0	7	2	-	-	c Tsolekile b Willoughby	8	20	14	2	-
M Ngam lbw b Willoughby	0	7	6	-	-	b Willoughby	0	2	2	-	-
RR Richards run out (Zondeki)	0	5	1	-	-	run out (Strydom/Willoughby)	0	6	5	-	-
Extras (b 2, lb 7, w 4)	13					Extras (lb 7, w 2, nb 1)	10				
TOTAL (117.5 overs)	**263**					**TOTAL (40.1 overs)**	**100**				

CAPE COBRAS	*Runs*	*Mins*	*Balls*	*4*	*6*		*Runs*	*Mins*	*Balls*	*4*	*6*
AG Puttick c Sodumo b Olivier	34	90	64	7	-	not out	69	135	94	12	-
DJ Bassage c Sodumo b Richards	33	53	38	7	-	b Richards	13	65	42	2	-
JG Strydom lbw b Olivier	0	4	3	-	-	st Sodumo b De Wett	38	48	35	6	-
J-P Duminy lbw b Kreusch	40	127	101	7	-	not out	17	21	25	2	-
IJ Harvey c De Wett b Olivier	33	43	28	6	-						
*†TL Tsolekile c Sodumo b Ngam	33	131	80	4	-						
VD Philander c Gamiet b Peterson	2	5	4	-	-						
CD de Lange lbw b Olivier	9	18	33	1	-						
PR Adams c De Wett b Kreusch	8	73	26	-	-						
M Zondeki not out	1	10	8	-	-						
CM Willoughby											
Extras (lb 8, w 3, nb 7)	18					Extras (lb 6, w 4, nb 6)	16				
TOTAL (for 9 wkts dec) (63 overs)	**211**					**TOTAL (for 2 wkts) (31.4 overs)**	**153**				

Cob	*O*	*M*	*R*	*W*			*O*	*M*	*R*	*W*	
Willoughby	22	5	58	1			15.1	7	36	5	
Zondeki	20.5	6	43	2	(3 w)		12	3	25	2	(1 nb, 2 w)
Philander	23	9	41	3	(1 w)		8	1	26	1	
De Lange	26	8	59	1			5	3	6	1	
Adams	15	4	26	0							
Harvey	11	5	27	1							
War	*O*	*M*	*R*	*W*			*O*	*M*	*R*	*W*	
Ngam	9	0	57	1	(7 nb, 1 w)	(3)	6	2	31	0	(6 nb, 1 w)
Richards	16	6	35	1	(2 w)		8	5	11	1	(1 w)
Olivier	19	4	71	4		(1)	6	1	44	0	(2 w)
Peterson	8	1	19	1			6.4	0	32	0	
Kreusch	11	5	21	2							
De Wett						(5)	5	0	29	1	

Fall of Wickets

	War	**Cob**	**War**	**Cob**
1st	18 (2)	61 (2)	2 (1)	57 (2)
2nd	18 (3)	66 (3)	6 (3)	117 (3)
3rd	183 (4)	83 (1)	7 (4)	-
4th	196 (5)	135 (5)	25 (5)	-
5th	206 (6)	168 (4)	54 (2)	-
6th	250 (1)	171 (7)	70 (6)	-
7th	258 (8)	188 (8)	71 (8)	-
8th	262 (9)	208 (6)	98 (9)	-
9th	263 (10)	211 (9)	98 (10)	-
10th	263 (11)	-	100 (11)	-

WARRIORS v TITANS

SuperSport Series

Played at Mercedes-Benz Park, East London on 27,28,29,30 October 2005 — Toss: Warriors
Umpires: SB Lambson & GH Pienaar — Referee: DT Lindsay
Debuts: War: None. Ttn: None
Close of play: Day 1: War (1) 277-5 (Kreusch 43*, Smith 14*, 96 overs). Day 2: Ttn (1) 121-1 (Petersen 40*, Van Jaarsveld 30*, 32.1 overs). Day 3: Ttn (1) 461-4 (De Bruyn 127*, Morkel 64*, 137 overs).
Result: Match drawn
Man of Match: Zander de Bruyn
Points: War: 4.88 (bat 3.88, bowl 1, match 0); Ttn: 6.56 (bat 4.56, bowl 2, match 0)

Solid batting by the Warriors, headed by Justin Kreusch and Abongile Sodumo, saw them post a highly respectable 442-9 declared in their first innings.

The Titans, though, replied in more impressive style, big centuries coming from Alviro Petersen and Zander de Bruyn as they raced to a lead of 144. The Warriors' batting frailties were again apparent in the second innings as they stuttered to 118-7 before rain and bad light saved them from certain defeat.

WARRIORS	*Runs*	*Mins*	*Balls*	*4*	*6*		*Runs*	*Mins*	*Balls*	*4*	*6*
ML Bruyns b Morkel	53	130	89	7	1	(2) lbw b Steyn	1	11	3	-	-
CC Bradfield c Van Jaarsveld b Steyn	52	178	122	8	-	(1) lbw b Mbhalati	9	58	42	1	-
BC de Wett c Bodi b Steyn	40	132	87	6	-	c Van Jaarsveld b Thomas	44	184	139	5	-
A Jacobs run out (Van Wyk)	34	41	37	3	2	(5) b Harris	7	41	35	1	-
*RJ Peterson c Van Wyk b Morkel	28	142	115	4	-	(7) lbw b Harris	15	21	19	3	-
JP Kreusch c Van Wyk b Thomas	85	208	158	13	1	b Mbhalati	4	13	11	1	-
MBA Smith b Harris	39	144	89	4	-	(4) c Van Wyk b Morkel	20	33	21	3	-
†AM Sodumo not out	77	127	94	9	2	not out	8	28	21	2	-
T Henderson b Harris	2	9	7	-	-	not out	3	3	3	-	-
MW Olivier c Van Wyk b Morkel	4	35	30	1	-						
M Ngam not out	8	45	31	1	-						
Extras (b 6, lb 5, nb 9)	20					Extras (b 7)	7				
TOTAL (for 9 wkts dec) (141.4 overs)	**442**					**TOTAL (for 7 wkts) (49 overs)**	**118**				

TITANS	*Runs*	*Mins*	*Balls*	*4*	*6*
AJ Seymore c Bruyns b Henderson	41	72	50	8	-
AN Petersen lbw b Henderson	140	358	289	19	1
*M van Jaarsveld lbw b Olivier	45	128	88	8	-
Z de Bruyn st Sodumo b Peterson	175	483	342	16	2
GH Bodi lbw b Peterson	17	90	77	-	-
JA Morkel c Smith b Kreusch	84	162	108	8	2
†CFK van Wyk c Sodumo b Henderson	13	29	29	1	-
AC Thomas c Bradfield b Peterson	1	18	17	-	-
PL Harris c and b Henderson	10	22	22	1	-
DW Steyn not out	19	30	23	-	2
NE Mbhalati not out	4	25	10	1	-
Extras (b 10, lb 8, w 1, nb 18)	37				
TOTAL (for 9 wkts dec) (173 overs)	**586**				

Ttn	*O*	*M*	*R*	*W*		*O*	*M*	*R*	*W*
Steyn	31	3	80	2 (7 nb)		7	3	15	1
Thomas	18	5	70	1	(7)	2	1	3	1
Mbhalati	22.4	5	73	0	(4)	11	1	33	2
Morkel	30	7	92	3 (1 nb)	(2)	4	1	12	1
Harris	39	14	111	2	(3)	21	9	47	2
Petersen	1	0	5	0 (1 nb)					
Bodi					(5)	2	1	1	0
Van Jaarsveld					(6)	2	2	0	0
War	*O*	*M*	*R*	*W*					
Henderson	50	16	120	4 (3 nb)					
Ngam	9	0	82	0 (11 nb)					
Olivier	20	1	86	1 (2 nb)					
Peterson	49	6	151	3					
Kreusch	37	4	97	1 (2 nb)					
De Wett	8	0	32	0 (1 w)					

Fall of Wickets

	War	**Ttn**	**War**
1st	91 (1)	79 (1)	1 (2)
2nd	122 (2)	165 (3)	22 (1)
3rd	165 (4)	296 (2)	48 (4)
4th	199 (3)	351 (5)	73 (5)
5th	250 (5)	503 (6)	78 (6)
6th	338 (6)	519 (7)	105 (7)
7th	371 (7)	530 (8)	115 (3)
8th	379 (9)	555 (9)	-
9th	396 (10)	563 (4)	-
10th	-	-	-

Lions v Warriors, Johannesburg, 3-5 November 2005. Lions won by 10 wickets.

WARRIORS v EAGLES

SuperSport Series

Played at Sahara Oval St George's, Port Elizabeth on 10,11,12,13 November 2005 — Toss: Warriors

Umpires: JD Cloete & M Erasmus — Referee: CJ Mitchley

Debuts: War: None. Eag: None

Close of play: Day 1: Eag (1) 329-5 (Van Wyk 45*, 96.5 overs). Day 2: War (1) 153-1 (Bradfield 67*, De Wett 9*, 68 overs). Day 3: Eag (2) 65-3 (Hector 15*, Van Wyk 22*, 17 overs).

Result: Match drawn

Man of Match: Roger Telemachus

Points: War: 4.44 (bat 2.44, bowl 2, match 0); Eag: 5.6 (bat 4.60, bowl 1, match 0)

Notes: De Wett retired hurt with his score on 9 and the total on 153-1 in Warriors' 1st innings and returned at the fall of the 7th wicket.

Despite conceding a small first innings lead of 41, the Warriors enjoyed one of their best matches of the season before bad light ended play with their score on 70-2 in 17.4 overs in pursuit of a victory target of 178 in a minimum of 34 overs.

In response to Jacques Rudolph's 133, Warriors openers Carl Bradfield and Mark Bruyns gave their side their best start of the season as first innings honours were shared. The home side then got among the Free State batsmen but they were held up long enough to be denied a chance of achieving a rare victory.

EAGLES	Runs	Mins	Balls	4	6		Runs	Mins	Balls	4	6
RT Bailey lbw b Henderson	18	60	51	2	-	c Sodumo b Henderson	0	2	2	-	-
B Hector c Sodumo b Meyer	36	165	134	5	-	run out (Kreusch/Sodumo)	21	106	69	4	-
JA Rudolph c Bruyns b Kreusch	133	241	203	19	-	b Henderson	4	2	3	1	-
DJ Jacobs c Sodumo b Kreusch	59	129	91	8	-	b Meyer	11	22	19	2	-
†MN van Wyk c Sodumo b Ngam	85	202	140	16	-	c sub (MW Olivier) b Ngam	33	84	57	5	-
CA Thyssen c Sodumo b Meyer	10	87	60	1	-	not out	32	109	83	4	1
R McLaren c Sodumo b Meyer	0	1	1	-	-	c Jacobs b Kreusch	6	31	23	1	-
*N Boje c Kreusch b Meyer	10	45	38	2	-	lbw b Willemse	5	19	13	-	-
R Telemachus lbw b Kreusch	9	47	32	2		not out	7	52	44	-	-
J Louw not out	0	16	7	-	-						
PV Mpitsang c Henderson b Ngam	0	4	3	-	-						
Extras (lb 7, w 2, nb 22)	31					Extras (lb 3, w 1, nb 13)	17				
TOTAL (123 overs)	**391**					**TOTAL (for 7 wkts dec) (50 overs)**	**136**				

WARRIORS	Runs	Mins	Balls	4	6		Runs	Mins	Balls	4	6
*ML Bruyns c Van Wyk b Telemachus	54	194	146	5	-	(2) c and b McLaren	9	26	13	-	-
CC Bradfield c Telemachus b Mpitsang	86	366	293	13	-	(1) not out	30	84	56	2	-
BC de Wett c McLaren b Telemachus	9	88	55	-	-	c Rudolph b Mpitsang	1	14	12	-	-
A Jacobs c Louw b Telemachus	3	17	11	-	-	not out	25	42	29	4	-
†AM Sodumo lbw b Boje	29	100	70	5	-						
D Willemse c Thyssen b Telemachus	34	134	99	3	-						
L Meyer b Telemachus	10	88	60	1	-						
T Henderson not out	44	85	46	5	2						
MBA Smith lbw b Telemachus	0	9	8	-	-						
JP Kreusch c Van Wyk b McLaren	25	27	26	5	-						
M Ngam run out (Thyssen)	6	19	19	1	-						
Extras (b 4, lb 16, w 3, nb 27)	50					Extras (w 1, nb 4)	5				
TOTAL (134.2 overs)	**350**					**TOTAL (for 2 wkts) (17.4 overs)**	**70**				

War	O	M	R	W		O	M	R	W
Henderson	27	8	71	1 (1 w)		17	4	32	2
Ngam	25	4	88	2 (5 nb)	(3)	10	1	43	1 (7 nb, 1 w)
Meyer	25	5	97	4 (15 nb)	(2)	6	0	28	1 (5 nb)
Kreusch	25	9	58	3 (2 nb, 1 w)	(5)	6	1	9	1 (1 nb)
Willemse	21	2	70	0	(4)	10	4	17	1
De Wett						1	0	4	0
Eag	O	M	R	W		O	M	R	W
Louw	20.2	7	49	0 (1 nb)		2	0	11	0
McLaren	24	5	60	1 (6 nb, 2 w)	(3)	7	2	18	1 (1 w)
Mpitsang	27	6	75	1 (10 nb, 1 w)	(2)	8	0	35	1 (4 nb)
Telemachus	31	8	85	6 (10 nb)		0.4	0	6	0
Boje	30	12	52	1					
Rudolph	2	0	9	0					

Fall of Wickets

	Eag	War	Eag	War
1st	44 (1)	118 (1)	0 (1)	21 (2)
2nd	130 (2)	158 (4)	4 (3)	27 (3)
3rd	269 (4)	202 (2)	29 (4)	-
4th	270 (3)	214 (5)	82 (2)	-
5th	329 (6)	261 (7)	92 (5)	-
6th	329 (7)	280 (6)	98 (7)	-
7th	357 (8)	284 (9)	103 (8)	-
8th	385 (9)	290 (3)	-	-
9th	391 (5)	335 (10)	-	-
10th	391 (11)	350 (11)	-	-

Dolphins v Warriors, Durban, 17-20 November 2005. Dolphins won by 9 wickets.

WARRIORS v LIONS

SuperSport Series

Played at Mercedes-Benz Park, East London on 23,24,25,26 February 2006 Toss: Warriors
Umpires: M Gajjar & LH Matroos Referee: MR Magiet
Debuts: War: None. Lio: None
Close of play: Day 1: War (1) 257-5 (Pope 59*, Kreusch 20*, 100.3 overs). Day 2: Lio (1) 218-4 (Van Jaarsveld 51*, Harris 1*, 58 overs). Day 3: War (2) 48-1 (Bruyns 16*, De Wett 29*, 22 overs).
Result: Match drawn
Man of Match: Burton de Wett & Steven Pope
Points: War: 5.14 (bat 3.14, bowl 2, match 0); Lio: 7.28 (bat 5.28, bowl 2, match 0)

De Wett hit his maiden first-class century to thwart the Lions' victory bid on the final day after the visitors had taken a handy 117-run first innings lead.

Pope's century bolstered the Warriors first innings but Vaughn van Jaarsveld and Alviro Petersen helped the Lions soar past that. The Warriors threatened to suffer another all-too familiar second innings collapse but De Wett and Pope added an important 75 runs for the fifth wicket and the Lions ran out of time as they chased 131 to win.

WARRIORS	Runs	Mins	Balls	4	6		Runs	Mins	Balls	4	6
*ML Bruyns run out (Ontong/Harris)	18	34	24	3	-	(2) lbw b Blignaut	38	168	116	2	-
CC Bradfield c Van Jaarsveld b Coetsee	58	235	174	9	-	(1) b De Wet	0	10	9	-	-
BC de Wett c Petersen b Nkwe	27	107	85	3	-	b Moleon	109	329	267	15	1
A Jacobs c Nkwe b Coetsee	19	56	46	3	-	c Harris b Singh	22	68	63	4	-
J Botha c Harris b Nkwe	39	147	117	5	-	c Van Jaarsveld b Singh	0	9	6	-	-
SC Pope c Harris b Blignaut	101	272	231	8	-	b Ontong	45	143	93	4	-
JP Kreusch lbw b Ontong	30	58	47	4	1	c Cook b Moleon	4	17	14	-	-
†AM Sodumo lbw b Moleon	1	5	7	-	-	c Blignaut b Moleon	0	16	9	-	-
T Henderson c Van Jaarsveld b Ontong	7	17	8	1	-	c Ontong b Coetsee	15	29	19	-	1
L Meyer not out	35	101	89	5	-	c Petersen b Ontong	0	13	15	-	-
BB Kops c Harris b De Wet	5	19	12	1	-	not out	0	1	0	-	-
Extras (lb 4, w 2, nb 11)	17					Extras (b 1, lb 2, w 1, nb 10)	14				
TOTAL (138.1 overs)	**357**					**TOTAL (100.1 overs)**	**247**				

LIONS	Runs	Mins	Balls	4	6		Runs	Mins	Balls	4	6
SC Cook lbw b Henderson	6	22	22	-	-	lbw b Meyer	17	43	28	-	-
AN Petersen c Meyer b De Wett	96	223	147	12	-	c Sodumo b Henderson	15	11	11	3	-
*JL Ontong c Jacobs b Henderson	55	98	81	7	1	(4) not out	8	20	10	-	-
ET Nkwe c Jacobs b De Wett	5	17	11	-	-						
VB van Jaarsveld c Jacobs b Meyer	126	296	205	15	3						
†MJ Harris b Henderson	49	142	99	4	-						
AM Blignaut c Jacobs b Pope	47	95	77	5	1	(3) c Bruyns b Henderson	4	9	8	-	-
WL Coetsee b Pope	19	32	21	-	1						
EO Moleon b De Wett	40	83	64	1	1						
F de Wet c Kreusch b De Wett	4	12	12	1	-						
Y Singh not out	17	54	45	1	-						
Extras (b 2, lb 2, w 2, nb 4)	10					Extras (nb 1)	1				
TOTAL (130 overs)	**474**					**TOTAL (for 3 wkts) (9.2 overs)**	**45**				

Lio	O	M	R	W			O	M	R	W	
De Wet	18.1	5	50	1			11	2	30	1	(5 nb)
Singh	21	7	35	0	(2 nb, 1 w)		17	6	30	2	(1 nb)
Blignaut	14	4	52	1	(2 nb)	(4)	9	3	22	1	(3 nb)
Moleon	19	9	34	1	(1 w)	(6)	15	2	39	3	(1 nb)
Coetsee	38	13	71	2	(1 nb)	(3)	23.1	6	64	1	
Nkwe	9	1	56	2	(6 nb)	(7)	7	2	14	0	
Ontong	19	4	55	2		(5)	15	3	36	2	
Cook							3	0	9	0	
War	O	M	R	W			O	M	R	W	
Henderson	29	4	88	3	(1 nb)		5	0	21	2	(1 nb)
Kops	18	1	90	0	(2 nb, 2 w)						
Meyer	28	3	82	1	(1 nb)	(2)	4.2	0	24	1	
Kreusch	16	3	51	0							
De Wett	26	1	112	4							
Jacobs	1	0	8	0							
Pope	12	2	39	2							

Fall of Wickets

	War	Lio	War	Lio
1st	23 (1)	24 (1)	1 (1)	19 (2)
2nd	84 (3)	115 (3)	100 (2)	25 (3)
3rd	122 (4)	124 (4)	136 (4)	45 (1)
4th	133 (2)	191 (2)	138 (5)	-
5th	209 (5)	316 (6)	213 (3)	-
6th	269 (7)	387 (5)	218 (7)	-
7th	270 (8)	395 (7)	225 (8)	-
8th	289 (9)	411 (8)	239 (6)	-
9th	343 (6)	422 (10)	247 (10)	-
10th	357 (11)	474 (9)	247 (9)	-

Cape Cobras v Warriors, Stellenbosch, 2-4 March 2006. Cape Cobras won by 7 wickets.

WARRIORS v DOLPHINS

SuperSport Series

Played at Mercedes-Benz Park, East London on 9,10,11,12 March 2006 — Toss: Dolphins

Umpires: S George & LH Matroos — Referee: A Barnes

Debuts: War: None. Dol: None

Close of play: Day 1: Dol (1) 285-5 (Smit 110*, Brown 11*, 70 overs). Day 2: War (1) 84-3 (Jacobs 20*, Botha 10*, 28.4 overs). Day 3: War (1) 287-8 (Jacobs 135*, Olivier 11*, 97 overs).

Result: Dolphins won by an innings and 29 runs

Man of Match: Lance Klusener & Kyle Smit

Points: War: 5.92 (bat 3.92, bowl 2, match 0); Dol: 19.86 (bat 5.86, bowl 4, match 10)

Klusener was at his rampaging best as he helped set up a resounding innings victory with plenty of time to spare. After contributions of 144 from Smit and 82 by Duncan Brown, the Dolphins powerhouse smashed 100 not out as the visitors swept to a big total.

Only Arno Jacobs offered resistance as Ugasen Govender and Saidi Mhlongo each took four wickets in the home side's reply. Batting again, the Warriors crumbled, Klusener taking charge with a superb performance.

DOLPHINS	*Runs*	*Mins*	*Balls*	*4*	*6*
DJ Watson c Bennett b Kreusch	19	85	47	3	-
I Khan c Sodumo b Olivier	67	117	87	8	1
HM Amla c Sodumo b Meyer	0	5	4	-	-
AM Amla c Sodumo b Bennett	55	173	113	6	1
JC Kent c Bradfield b Olivier	9	25	18	2	-
K Smit c Sodumo b Olivier	144	212	199	26	-
†DL Brown c and b Pope	82	178	145	8	1
*L Klusener not out	100	170	125	12	3
S Mhlongo not out	19	83	37	2	-
M Hayward					
U Govender					
Extras (b 4, lb 4, w 4, nb 5)	17				
TOTAL (for 7 wkts dec) (128.2 overs)	**512**				

WARRIORS	*Runs*	*Mins*	*Balls*	*4*	*6*		*Runs*	*Mins*	*Balls*	*4*	*6*
BL Bennett lbw b Hayward	0	3	4	-	-	c Brown b Klusener	18	47	31	2	-
*CC Bradfield b Govender	35	93	75	3	-	c Brown b Klusener	4	11	5	1	-
BC de Wett c Smit b Mhlongo	15	69	44	1	-	c Smit b Khan	43	143	95	4	1
A Jacobs c Watson b Mhlongo	149	369	263	19	-	c AM Amla b Kent	26	71	54	4	-
J Botha lbw b Govender	21	65	43	3	-	c Mhlongo b Klusener	25	148	105	2	
SC Pope c Kent b Hayward	8	27	17	2	-	b Mhlongo	1	4	3	-	-
JP Kreusch c Brown b Govender	26	84	63	4	-	c Mhlongo b Klusener	29	99	76	4	-
†AM Sodumo lbw b Mhlongo	19	54	41	4	-	b Mhlongo	26	70	49	3	-
L Meyer b Mhlongo	0	2	2	-	-	c Brown b Klusener	0	15	13	-	-
MW Olivier lbw b Govender	12	106	66	2	-	c Govender b Hayward	5	38	25	-	-
BB Kops not out	0	5	0	-	-	not out	0	5	2	-	-
Extras (b 4, lb 1, w 1, nb 13)	19					Extras (lb 1, nb 1)	2				
TOTAL (100.5 overs)	**304**					**TOTAL (76.1 overs)**	**179**				

War	*O*	*M*	*R*	*W*	
Kops	2.1	0	7	0	
Olivier	27	3	155	3	(2 nb, 1 w)
Meyer	25.1	2	115	1	(1 nb, 3 w)
Kreusch	29	12	67	1	(1 nb)
De Wett	21	3	71	0	
Pope	21	4	66	1	
Bennett	3	0	23	1	(1 nb)

Dol	*O*	*M*	*R*	*W*			*O*	*M*	*R*	*W*	
Hayward	17	4	60	2		(3)	14	5	33	1	
Klusener	32	11	75	0	(5 nb, 1 w)	(1)	24	8	39	5	
Govender	21	6	59	4	(5 nb)	(2)	4	1	14	0	
Mhlongo	18.5	7	74	4	(1 nb)	(5)	11.1	2	30	2	(1 nb)
Kent	8	2	19	0	(2 nb)	(4)	8	2	23	1	
Khan	4	1	12	0			9	2	27	1	
AM Amla							6	0	12	0	

Fall of Wickets

	Dol	War	War
1st	80 (1)	0 (1)	9 (2)
2nd	83 (3)	44 (3)	30 (1)
3rd	95 (2)	60 (2)	72 (4)
4th	115 (5)	111 (5)	96 (3)
5th	250 (4)	129 (6)	97 (6)
6th	344 (6)	179 (7)	145 (7)
7th	426 (7)	223 (8)	148 (5)
8th	-	223 (9)	154 (9)
9th	-	296 (10)	178 (10)
10th	-	304 (4)	179 (8)

Titans v Warriors, Benoni, 16-18 March 2006. Titans won by an innings and 78 runs.
Eagles v Warriors, Bloemfontein, 23-26 March 2006. Eagles won by an innings and 173 runs.

THE EAGLES FLY AGAIN . . . Nicky Boje and team-mates after the Eagles clinched their second successive triumph in the Standard Bank Cup, beating the Titans in the final

Picture: LEE WARREN, Touchline Photo

STANDARD BANK CUP

Ken Borland

The Eagles defended their Standard Bank Cup title but only made certain of their triumph with a strong finish to the competition. Johan van der Wath, Thandi Tshabalala and Roger Telemachus were once again key players with the ball but the Eagles' batting form was hesitant for much of the competition and they could only finish third on the log.

Forced to play an away semi-final at the Wanderers and the final in Centurion, the Eagles showed lots of nerve in beating first the Lions and then the Titans in two tight matches.

The Titans had been obvious favourites for the title, losing just two of their ten round-robin matches but the pressure of the big occasion once again saw them stumble in the final.

The Titans batsmen had been found wanting on a lively pitch against the Dolphins in their last pool game in Pietermaritzburg, being bundled out for 73, and an overly aggressive approach up front cost them dearly in the final as well.

The Titans bowlers managed to turn the final into an exciting affair in front of their home crowd but a total of 142 was always going to be insufficient.

A commanding batting display by AB de Villiers and Goolam Bodi had carried the Titans to a sweet 10-wicket victory over the Dolphins in the semi-finals, to make up for their Pietermaritzburg aberration.

Stephen Cook, with a history of success in day/night cricket, was far and away the leading run-scorer in the competition as he led the Lions to second place on the log. But despite scoring 71 in the semi-final, Cook could not quite get the Lions over the line against the Eagles, who scored a crucial 67 runs in the last six overs thanks to some long-handle hitting from Telemachus.

The Cobras managed to exceed the previous year's underachievement by once again finishing bottom of the log, this time without a win in ten matches, eight of which they lost.

Bodi, the Dolphins pair of Ahmed Amla and Andrew Tweedie, and Warriors spinner Robin Peterson were other individuals to shine, the latter three rising above their struggling team-mates.

STANDARD BANK CUP TABLE 2005/06

	P	W	L	T	NR	Bonus	Penalty	Pts	Net RR
Titans	10	7	2	0	1	1	1	39	-0.07
Lions	10	5	1	0	4	1	0	39	0.32
Eagles	10	6	3	0	1	1	0	37	0.24
Dolphins	10	4	4	1	1	2	1	31	0.31
Warriors	10	3	7	0	0	1	0	20	-0.26
Cape Cobras	10	0	8	1	1	0	0	12	-0.40

Titans finish above Lions by virtue of more wins.

STANDARD BANK CUP

LEADING BATTING AVERAGES

		M	Inns	NO	Runs	HS	Avg	SR	100	50
1	SC Cook (Lio)	10	10	3	567	116 *	81.00	81.34	1	5
2	JG Myburgh (Ttn)	12	9	5	281	59 *	70.25	72.05	0	2
3	DL Brown (Dol)	9	8	5	197	53	65.66	84.18	0	1
4	AM Amla (Dol)	11	11	3	399	71 *	49.87	68.20	0	4
5	DJ Watson (Dol)	11	11	3	395	114 *	49.37	62.69	2	2
6	T Henderson (War)	10	10	4	262	79 *	43.66	155.02	0	2
7	JP Kreusch (War)	10	10	1	389	119 *	43.22	71.24	1	2
8	RT Bailey (Eag)	9	7	3	166	68	41.50	79.42	0	1
9	L Klusener (Dol)	11	8	4	162	49 *	40.50	150.00	0	0
10	HH Dippenaar (Eag)	4	4	1	120	71 *	40.00	65.57	0	1
11	RJ Peterson (War)	8	7	0	262	90	37.42	78.67	0	2
12	AM Bacher (Lio)	10	9	1	296	93	37.00	72.01	0	1
13	M van Jaarsveld (Ttn)	12	11	2	330	111 *	36.66	83.54	1	2
14	GH Bodi (Ttn)	12	12	1	402	104 *	36.54	89.33	1	3
15	AN Petersen (Ttn)	10	10	0	365	80	36.50	83.14	0	3
16	LL Bosman (Eag)	12	12	1	398	71	36.18	78.81	0	3
17	JJ van der Wath (Eag)	11	8	3	174	70 *	34.80	91.57	0	1
18	DM Benkenstein (Dol)	11	9	2	241	87 *	34.42	93.77	0	1
19	A Jacobs (War)	10	9	2	233	54 *	33.28	67.53	0	1
20	G Dros (Ttn)	12	10	3	228	79 *	32.57	81.42	0	1

(Qualification: 3 completed innings)

LEADING BOWLING AVERAGES

		M	Overs	Mdns	Runs	Wkts	Avg	RpO	BB	4I
1	ANW Tweedie (Dol)	11	81.1	8	351	23	15.26	4.32	6-24	1
2	JJ van der Wath (Eag)	11	86.1	5	351	22	15.95	4.07	4-35	2
3	RJ Peterson (War)	8	66	1	288	15	19.20	4.36	3-46	0
4	DW Steyn (Ttn)	10	78.3	4	319	16	19.93	4.06	3-19	0
5	T Tshabalala (Eag)	9	69	1	304	15	20.26	4.40	4-24	1
6	MW Olivier (War)	5	24.5	0	185	9	20.55	7.44	5-53	1
7	CM Willoughby (Cob)	10	79	15	251	12	20.91	3.17	3-19	0
8	M Hayward (Dol)	7	39.4	4	174	8	21.75	4.38	2-5	0
9	M Morkel (Ttn)	7	43.1	4	205	9	22.77	4.74	4-41	1
10	M Zondeki (Cob)	9	59.5	3	281	12	23.41	4.69	3-34	0
11	ZA Abrahim (Dol)	10	57.2	4	268	11	24.36	4.67	4-15	1
12	NE Mbhalati (Ttn)	12	85	3	378	15	25.20	4.44	3-32	0
13	AJ Hall (Lio)	6	51.1	5	234	9	26.00	4.57	2-25	0
14	EO Moleon (Lio)	11	69.5	5	326	12	27.16	4.66	3-46	0
15	R Telemachus (Eag)	12	72	2	371	13	28.53	5.15	3-33	0
16	R McLaren (Eag)	12	70.5	4	332	11	30.18	4.68	4-43	1
17	RK Kleinveldt (Cob)	10	63.3	6	303	10	30.30	4.77	4-29	1
18	JP Kreusch (War)	10	53.1	3	247	8	30.87	4.64	3-38	0
19	BL Reddy (Ttn)	11	94	4	404	13	31.07	4.29	2-22	0
20	F de Wet (Lio)	11	77.3	11	382	12	31.83	4.92	3-56	0

(Qualification: 8 wickets)

LEADING WICKET-KEEPERS

		M	Ct	St	Total
1	MJ Harris (Lio)	11	12	2	14
2	MN van Wyk (Eag)	12	11	2	13
3	DL Brown (Dol)	9	10	0	10
	CFK van Wyk (Ttn)	10	10	0	10
5	TL Tsolekile (Cob)	10	9	0	9

LEADING FIELDERS

		M	Ct
1	HM Amla (Dol)	11	7
	AM Bacher (Lio)	10	7
3	GH Bodi (Ttn)	12	6
4	JP Kreusch (War)	10	5
	R McLaren (Eag)	12	5
	RJ Peterson (War)	8	5
	JJ van der Wath (Eag)	11	5
	M van Jaarsveld (Ttn)	12	5
9	AM Amla (Dol)	11	4
	DM Benkenstein (Dol)	11	4
	JA Beukes (Eag)	9	4
	LL Bosman (Eag)	12	4
	P de Bruyn (Ttn)	12	4
	CD de Lange (Cob)	7	4
	AJ Hall (Lio)	6	4
	A Jacobs (War)	10	4
	L Klusener (Dol)	11	4
	AN Petersen (Ttn)	10	4
	AG Puttick (Cob)	10	4

CAPE COBRAS

Lions v Cape Cobras, Potchefstroom, 25 November 2005. No result.

CAPE COBRAS v DOLPHINS — Standard Bank Cup

Played at Sahara Park Newlands, Cape Town on 27 November 2005 — Toss: Dolphins
Umpires: M Erasmus & S George — Referee: WA Diedricks
Debuts: Cob: None. Dol: None
Result: Dolphins won by 8 wickets
Man of Match: Doug Watson
Points: Dol: 4; Cob: 1
Notes: Dolphins were penalised 1 point for a slow over-rate. Cape Cobras substitute: VD Philander replaced FD Telo after 42.2 overs of Dolphins' innings. Dolphins substitute: RP Symcox replaced U Govender after 29 overs of Cape Cobras' innings.

CAPE COBRAS	Runs	Mins	Balls	4	6
AG Puttick c HM Amla b Benkenstein	53	123	95	5	-
*†TL Tsolekile b Tweedie	12	30	22	2	-
HH Gibbs c Benkenstein b Symcox	48	98	74	6	1
IJ Harvey run out (Symcox/Abrahim)	55	54	39	8	1
J-P Duminy c Klusener b Abrahim	13	30	18	1	-
RK Kleinveldt c HM Amla b Tweedie	9	14	11	1	-
VD Philander not out	5	13	7	-	-
CD de Lange c AM Amla b Tweedie	7	4	4	-	1
AC Dawson not out	0	2	0	-	-
M Zondeki					
CM Willoughby					
FD Telo					
Extras (lb 6, w 3)	9				
TOTAL (for 7 wkts) (45 overs)	**211**				

DOLPHINS	Runs	Mins	Balls	4	6
I Khan c Puttick b Willoughby	19	35	34	4	-
DJ Watson not out	101	164	150	14	-
HM Amla c Gibbs b Kleinveldt	55	94	53	6	-
AM Amla not out	31	35	31	2	1
DM Benkenstein					
JC Kent					
†D Smit					
*L Klusener					
RP Symcox					
ZA Abrahim					
ANW Tweedie					
U Govender					
Extras (b 1, lb 3, w 3, nb 1)	8				
TOTAL (for 2 wkts) (44.3 overs)	**214**				

Dol	O	M	R	W
Klusener	6	0	34	0 (1 w)
Kent	9	1	25	0 (1 w)
Tweedie	8	0	35	3
Abrahim	8	1	32	1
Govender	5	0	34	0 (1 w)
Benkenstein	5	1	22	1
Symcox	4	0	23	1

Cob	O	M	R	W
Dawson	9	0	44	0 (1 w)
Willoughby	9	1	34	1
Kleinveldt	8.3	1	42	1
Zondeki	5	0	27	0 (1 nb, 1 w)
Philander	4	0	24	0 (1 w)
De Lange	9	0	39	0

Fall of Wickets	Cob	Dol
1st	36 (2)	38 (1)
2nd	120 (1)	158 (3)
3rd	120 (3)	-
4th	172 (5)	-
5th	189 (6)	-
6th	201 (4)	-
7th	209 (8)	-

Doug Watson became the first player to make three consecutive centuries in the Standard Bank Cup. His previous innings were 114* v Warriors in Durban on November 25 and 142 v Titans at Centurion in the semi-final in 2004/05. In his two previous innings in the competition he scored 104 v Lions at Johannesburg and 23 v Western Province Boland at Durban.

The following players have each scored two consecutive Standard Bank Cup centuries: SJ Cook, DL Haynes, ND McKenzie, MJR Rindel, NC Johnson, LJ Koen, PJ Koortzen, DJ Cullinan, MN van Wyk, AG Puttick.

Warriors v Cape Cobras, Port Elizabeth, 2 December 2005. Warriors won by 41 runs.
Eagles v Cape Cobras, Bloemfontein, 9 December 2005. Eagles won by 1 wicket.
Titans v Cape Cobras, Centurion, 11 December 2005. Titans won by 2 wickets.
Dolphins v Cape Cobras, Durban, 16 December 2005. Match tied (D/L Method).

CAPE COBRAS v WARRIORS — Standard Bank Cup

Played at Boland Park, Paarl on 18 December 2005 — Toss: Warriors
Umpires: IL Howell & KH Hurter (TV: M Erasmus) — Referee: MR Magiet
Debuts: Cob: None. War: None
Result: Warriors won by 4 wickets
Man of Match: Justin Kreusch
Points: War: 5; Cob: 1
Notes: Cape Cobras substitute: JG Strydom replaced RK Kleinveldt after 16.5 overs of Cape Cobras' innings. Warriors substitute: L Mbane replaced M Ngam after 38 overs of Cape Cobras' innings.

CAPE COBRAS	Runs	Mins	Balls	4	6
AG Puttick b Henderson	9	17	15	1	-
DJ Bassage c De Kock b Kreusch	15	47	36	1	-
IJ Harvey c Smith b Kreusch	13	39	28	2	-
*†TL Tsolekile lbw b Peterson	28	83	58	1	-
H Davids c Kreusch b Ngam	2	16	12	-	-
JG Strydom c Jacobs b Henderson	63	101	73	3	-
CD de Lange b Peterson	8	11	17	1	-
VD Philander b Mbane	13	25	25	-	-
AC Dawson c and b Henderson	1	4	3	-	-
M Zondeki not out	0	4	4	-	-
CM Willoughby not out	0	2	0	-	-
RK Kleinveldt					
Extras (b 3, lb 2, w 14, nb 1)	20				
TOTAL (for 9 wkts) (45 overs)	**172**				

WARRIORS	Runs	Mins	Balls	4	6
CC Bradfield b Willoughby	16	49	42	2	-
JP Kreusch run out (De Lange/Tsolekile)	58	128	88	6	-
*RJ Peterson b Willoughby	47	93	83	5	-
A Jacobs not out	21	52	23	1	-
T Henderson c Puttick b Zondeki	9	14	11	-	-
LL Gamiet b Zondeki	11	10	12	2	-
†AZM Dyili c Tsolekile b Zondeki	4	2	3	1	-
MBA Smith not out	0	8	4	-	-
S de Kock					
L Meyer					
L Mbane					
M Ngam					
Extras (lb 2, w 5, nb 3)	10				
TOTAL (for 6 wkts) (43.5 overs)	**176**				

War	O	M	R	W	
Henderson	7	1	23	3	
Kreusch	9	2	18	2	(3 w)
Ngam	7	1	27	1	(1 nb, 3 w)
Meyer	2	0	15	0	(1 w)
Peterson	9	0	30	2	
De Kock	9	0	41	0	(1 w)
Mbane	2	0	13	1	(1 w)

Cob	O	M	R	W	
Dawson	9	1	28	0	(2 w)
Willoughby	9	1	23	2	(1 w)
Philander	7	0	39	0	(1 w)
Zondeki	8.5	0	43	3	(3 nb)
Harvey	6.1	1	22	0	(1 w)
De Lange	3.5	0	19	0	

Fall of Wickets	Cob	War
1st	17 (1)	43 (1)
2nd	34 (2)	127 (2)
3rd	41 (3)	131 (3)
4th	45 (5)	147 (5)
5th	116 (4)	161 (6)
6th	128 (7)	165 (7)
7th	169 (8)	-
8th	172 (9)	-
9th	172 (6)	-

CAPE COBRAS v LIONS

Standard Bank Cup

Played at Sahara Park Newlands, Cape Town on 23 December 2005 (D/N)

Toss: Cape Cobras

Umpires: M Gajjar & IL Howell

Referee: WA Diedricks

Debuts: Cob: None. Lio: None

Result: Lions won by 39 runs

Man of Match: Matthew Harris

Points: Lio: 6; Cob: 0

Notes: Cape Cobras substitute: R Munnik replaced CM Willoughby after 18 overs of Lions' innings. Lions substitute: F de Wet replaced SC Cook after 0 overs of Cape Cobras' innings.

LIONS	Runs	Mins	Balls	4	6
AM Bacher c Dawson b Willoughby	7	22	13	-	1
SC Cook c Harvey b Kleinveldt	25	76	55	3	-
VB van Jaarsveld c Zondeki b Willoughby	1	15	16	-	-
*ND McKenzie lbw b Willoughby	6	22	17	1	-
†MJ Harris c Kleinveldt b Dawson	56	108	74	2	1
AJ Hall c Tsolekile b Kleinveldt	0	3	2	-	-
DL Makalima c Tsolekile b Philander	8	25	15	1	-
ET Nkwe run out (Strydom)	23	40	42	3	-
WL Coetsee c Kleinveldt b Harvey	16	28	20	-	-
EO Moleon not out	5	16	9	-	-
S Chatterjee not out	2	10	9	-	-
F de Wet					
Extras (b 4, lb 3, w 2, nb 2)	11				
TOTAL (for 9 wkts) (45 overs)	**160**				

CAPE COBRAS	Runs	Mins	Balls	4	6
AG Puttick c Coetsee b De Wet	11	48	40	2	-
DJ Bassage c Harris b Hall	0	6	1	-	-
JG Strydom c Hall b Chatterjee	13	60	42	2	-
IJ Harvey c Harris b Chatterjee	9	25	14	1	-
R Munnik b Coetsee	24	71	48	3	-
*†TL Tsolekile c Harris b Moleon	2	18	14	-	-
H Davids lbw b Coetsee	19	37	35	2	-
VD Philander lbw b Moleon	6	28	21	-	-
RK Kleinveldt c De Wet b Chatterjee	18	26	17	-	2
AC Dawson not out	4	13	6	-	-
M Zondeki b Chatterjee	1	9	6	-	-
CM Willoughby					
Extras (lb 5, w 8, nb 1)	14				
TOTAL (40.3 overs)	**121**				

Cob	O	M	R	W	
Dawson	9	0	24	1	(1 w)
Willoughby	9	3	19	3	
Kleinveldt	9	2	33	2	
Zondeki	5	0	22	0	(1 nb, 1 w)
Philander	9	0	34	1	
Harvey	4	0	21	1	(1 nb)

Lio	O	M	R	W	
De Wet	9	3	21	1	(1 w)
Hall	7	1	17	1	(1 nb, 2 w)
Moleon	9	1	20	2	(2 w)
Chatterjee	6.3	0	27	4	(1 w)
Coetsee	7	1	20	2	
Nkwe	2	0	11	0	(2 w)

Fall of Wickets	Lio	Cob
1st	17 (1)	2 (2)
2nd	25 (3)	28 (1)
3rd	34 (4)	39 (3)
4th	44 (2)	44 (4)
5th	44 (6)	57 (6)
6th	70 (7)	86 (7)
7th	118 (8)	91 (5)
8th	150 (5)	113 (8)
9th	153 (9)	115 (9)
10th	-	121 (11)

CAPE COBRAS v TITANS

Standard Bank Cup

Played at Boland Park, Paarl on 30 December 2005 (D/N)

Toss: Titans

Umpires: S George & SB Lambson (TV: LH Matroos)

Referee: S Naidoo

Debuts: Cob: None. Ttn: None

Result: Titans won by 19 runs

Man of Match: Alviro Petersen

Points: Ttn: 5; Cob: 1

Notes: Cape Cobras substitute: WA Albertyn replaced CM Willoughby after 34 overs of Titans' innings. Titans substitute: F du Plessis replaced GH Bodi after 20 overs of Cape Cobras' innings.

TITANS	Runs	Mins	Balls	4	6
GH Bodi run out (Bassage/Tsolekile)	3	19	17	-	-
AN Petersen c Zondeki b Willoughby	80	125	87	13	-
*M van Jaarsveld b Zondeki	18	47	31	1	-
JG Myburgh c Tsolekile b Zondeki	30	63	48	1	1
G Dros not out	38	67	42	2	1
P de Bruyn b Zondeki	13	25	20	-	-
BL Reddy c Puttick b Dawson	4	7	4	1	-
†CFK van Wyk not out	16	27	22	1	-
DW Steyn					
M Morkel					
NE Mbhalati					
F du Plessis					
Extras (lb 3, w 2, nb 1)	6				
TOTAL (for 6 wkts) (45 overs)	**208**				

CAPE COBRAS	Runs	Mins	Balls	4	6
AG Puttick run out (Reddy)	14	34	24	3	-
DJ Bassage b Morkel	21	63	42	1	-
JG Strydom c Van Jaarsveld b Morkel	19	48	35	2	-
IJ Harvey lbw b Mbhalati	14	26	18	3	-
*†TL Tsolekile lbw b Morkel	0	1	1	-	-
H Davids c Van Wyk b Mbhalati	8	22	16	2	-
RCC Canning lbw b De Bruyn	5	18	13	-	-
WA Albertyn b Morkel	35	66	46	4	-
RK Kleinveldt not out	54	75	55	4	1
AC Dawson c Van Wyk b Dros	0	4	2	-	-
M Zondeki b Steyn	0	6	4	-	-
CM Willoughby					
Extras (lb 1, w 13, nb 5)	19				
TOTAL (41.5 overs)	**189**				

Cob	O	M	R	W	
Dawson	9	1	30	1	
Willoughby	9	2	45	1	(1 w)
Kleinveldt	8	1	43	0	
Zondeki	9	1	34	3	(1 nb)
Harvey	7	0	42	0	(1 w)
Davids	3	0	11	0	

Ttn	O	M	R	W	
Steyn	7.5	1	28	1	(1 nb, 4 w)
Reddy	7	0	24	0	(1 w)
Morkel	8	1	41	4	(2 nb, 3 w)
Mbhalati	7	0	39	2	(2 nb, 2 w)
De Bruyn	7	0	26	1	(1 w)
Du Plessis	3	0	14	0	(1 w)
Dros	2	0	16	1	

Fall of Wickets	Ttn	Cob
1st	19 (1)	26 (1)
2nd	75 (3)	58 (2)
3rd	135 (2)	74 (3)
4th	137 (4)	74 (5)
5th	159 (6)	84 (4)
6th	164 (7)	94 (6)
7th	-	95 (7)
8th	-	175 (8)
9th	-	186 (10)
10th	-	189 (11)

CAPE COBRAS v EAGLES

Standard Bank Cup

Played at Sahara Park Newlands, Cape Town on 2 January 2006
Toss: Cape Cobras
Umpires: M Erasmus & GH Pienaar
Referee: NC Pretorius
Debuts: Cob: None. Eag: None
Result: Eagles won by 35 runs
Man of Match: Thandi Tshabalala
Points: Eag: 5; Cob: 1
Notes: Cape Cobras substitute: WA Albertyn replaced CM Willoughby after 30 overs of Eagles' innings. Eagles substitute: PJ Koortzen replaced LL Bosman after 15 overs of Cape Cobras' innings.

EAGLES	Runs	Mins	Balls	4	6
JA Beukes c Tsolekile b Dawson	0	1	1	-	-
*†MN van Wyk b Willoughby	1	6	2	-	-
LL Bosman c Bassage b Harvey	71	151	100	8	1
DJ Jacobs c Davids b Zondeki	40	66	56	7	-
HH Dippenaar not out	71	118	81	6	2
D du Preez c Davids b Zondeki	2	8	5	-	-
RT Bailey not out	31	32	26	2	1
R McLaren					
WA Deacon					
R Telemachus					
T Tshabalala					
PJ Koortzen					
Extras (lb 6, w 2, nb 1)	9				
TOTAL (for 5 wkts) (45 overs)	**225**				

CAPE COBRAS	Runs	Mins	Balls	4	6
AG Puttick c Koortzen b Telemachus	28	64	51	4	-
DJ Bassage c Beukes b Deacon	5	31	22	-	-
JG Strydom c and b McLaren	13	36	21	2	-
IJ Harvey b Tshabalala	14	29	19	2	-
*†TL Tsolekile c Van Wyk b Tshabalala	18	53	42	1	-
H Davids b McLaren	31	56	43	2	-
RCC Canning c Deacon b Tshabalala	19	19	22	1	1
WA Albertyn b Tshabalala	2	10	5	-	-
RK Kleinveldt b Du Preez	36	25	19	2	3
AC Dawson b Du Preez	6	15	10	-	-
M Zondeki not out	1	6	1	-	-
CM Willoughby					
Extras (b 2, lb 3, w 9, nb 3)	17				
TOTAL (42 overs)	**190**				

Cob	O	M	R	W	
Dawson	9	0	60	1	(1 w)
Willoughby	9	3	19	1	(1 w)
Zondeki	9	1	40	2	
Kleinveldt	9	0	54	0	
Harvey	9	1	46	1	(1 nb)

Eag	O	M	R	W	
Deacon	9	2	38	1	(1 nb, 3 w)
Du Preez	9	1	43	2	(1 w)
Telemachus	6	0	31	1	(2 nb, 1 w)
McLaren	7	1	34	2	(3 w)
Tshabalala	9	1	24	4	(1 w)
Koortzen	2	0	15	0	

Fall of Wickets	Eag	Cob
1st	0 (1)	19 (2)
2nd	3 (2)	51 (1)
3rd	59 (4)	53 (3)
4th	155 (3)	72 (4)
5th	160 (6)	104 (5)
6th	-	141 (7)
7th	-	146 (6)
8th	-	148 (8)
9th	-	172 (10)
10th	-	190 (9)

DOLPHINS

DOLPHINS v WARRIORS — Standard Bank Cup

Played at Sahara Stadium Kingsmead, Durban on 25 November 2005 (D/N) — Toss: Dolphins
Umpires: KH Hurter & LH Matroos — Referee: MR Magiet
Debuts: Dol: None. War: None
Result: Dolphins won by 31 runs (D/L method), target revised to 149 in 25.1 overs
Man of Match: Doug Watson
Points: Dol: 6; War: 0
Notes: Dolphins substitute: RP Symcox replaced DJ Watson after 0 overs of Warriors' innings. Warriors substitute: L Mbane replaced M Ngam after 18 overs of Dolphins' innings.

DOLPHINS	Runs	Mins	Balls	4	6
I Khan c Bradfield b Olivier	31	62	40	3	-
DJ Watson not out	114	187	143	17	-
HM Amla lbw b Kreusch	7	22	12	-	-
AM Amla c Sodumo b Kreusch	5	8	8	1	-
DM Benkenstein c Sodumo b Kreusch	7	14	14	-	-
JC Kent b Olivier	7	13	14	1	-
†D Smit c Sodumo b Willemse	9	20	13	-	-
*L Klusener c Jacobs b Olivier	6	15	7	1	-
ANW Tweedie not out	20	26	21	2	-
ZA Abrahim					
U Govender					
RP Symcox					
Extras (b 2, lb 1, w 9, nb 2)	14				
TOTAL (for 7 wkts) (45 overs)	**220**				

WARRIORS	Runs	Mins	Balls	4	6
JP Kreusch c Klusener b Abrahim	42	64	46	7	-
*CC Bradfield c AM Amla b Abrahim	15	43	31	2	-
AZM Dyili c Smit b Tweedie	19	34	25	4	-
A Jacobs c Benkenstein b Govender	15	27	15	3	-
SC Pope lbw b Symcox	10	34	17	1	
BC de Wett not out	8	30	12	-	-
†AM Sodumo lbw b Benkenstein	0	5	5	-	-
T Henderson not out	4	3	1	1	-
D Willemse					
MW Olivier					
L Mbane					
M Ngam					
Extras (w 3, nb 1)	4				
TOTAL (for 6 wkts) (25.1 overs)	**117**				

War	O	M	R	W
Henderson	9	0	47	0
Ngam	9	1	49	0 (3 w)
Olivier	9	0	49	3 (2 nb, 5 w)
Willemse	9	0	34	1
Kreusch	9	0	38	3 (1 w)

Dol	O	M	R	W
Klusener	4	1	7	0 (1 nb, 1 w)
Kent	3	0	14	0 (1 w)
Tweedie	7	1	25	1
Abrahim	4	0	36	2
Govender	4	0	24	1 (1 w)
Symcox	2.1	0	6	1
Benkenstein	1	0	5	1

Fall of Wickets	Dol	War
1st	75 (1)	40 (2)
2nd	114 (3)	70 (1)
3rd	124 (4)	85 (3)
4th	136 (5)	99 (4)
5th	144 (6)	112 (5)
6th	166 (7)	113 (7)
7th	177 (8)	-

Cape Cobras v Dolphins, Cape Town, 27 November 2005. Dolphins won by 8 wickets.
Lions v Dolphins, Johannesburg, 2 December 2005. Lions won by 50 runs.
Titans v Dolphins, Centurion, 7 December 2005. Titans won by 6 wickets.
Warriors v Dolphins, East London, 12 December 2005. Dolphins won by 3 wickets.
Eagles v Dolphins, 14 December 2005. Eagles won by 8 runs.

DOLPHINS v CAPE COBRAS — Standard Bank Cup

Played at Sahara Stadium Kingsmead, Durban on 16 December 2005 (D/N) — Toss: Cape Cobras
Umpires: KH Hurter & MZ Nanabhay (TV: M Erasmus) — Referee: A Barnes
Debuts: Dol: None. Cob: None
Result: Tied (D/L method), target revised to 185 in 36 overs.
Man of Match: Derrin Bassage
Points: Dol: 3; Cob: 3
Notes: Cape Cobras substitute: JG Strydom replaced CM Willoughby after 15 overs of Dolphins' innings. Dolphins substitute: R Frylinck replaced M Hayward after 38 overs of Cape Cobras' innings.

CAPE COBRAS	Runs	Mins	Balls	4	6
AG Puttick c AM Amla b Tweedie	5	21	18	1	-
DJ Bassage c Symcox b Abrahim	81	152	97	10	-
IJ Harvey lbw b Tweedie	5	10	5	1	-
*†TL Tsolekile c Watson b Hayward	11	29	21	1	-
H Davids c Brown b Hayward	9	21	13	2	-
CD de Lange c Brown b Klusener	30	47	43	2	-
VD Philander not out	33	42	29	2	1
RK Kleinveldt c HM Amla b Tweedie	3	18	7	-	-
AC Dawson not out	3	3	2	-	-
M Zondeki					
CM Willoughby					
JG Strydom					
Extras (b 4, lb 4, w 4, nb 1)	13				
TOTAL (for 7 wkts) (39 overs)	**193**				

DOLPHINS	Runs	Mins	Balls	4	6
I Khan c De Lange b Dawson	13	33	20	2	-
DJ Watson c Strydom b Zondeki	55	128	88	5	-
HM Amla c Tsolekile b Zondeki	22	37	22	1	1
AM Amla c Bassage b Harvey	22	40	32	1	-
DM Benkenstein c and b Philander	18	31	17	1	-
RP Symcox lbw b Harvey	2	5	3	-	-
†DL Brown not out	27	34	25	2	1
*L Klusener run out (Puttick)	1	6	2	-	-
R Frylinck not out	18	18	8	-	2
ANW Tweedie					
ZA Abrahim					
M Hayward					
Extras (b 1, lb 2, w 2, nb 1)	6				
TOTAL (for 7 wkts) (36 overs)	**184**				

Dol	O	M	R	W
Klusener	8	1	42	1 (3 w)
Tweedie	8	0	47	3 (1 w)
Hayward	8	2	33	2
Symcox	4	0	21	0 (1 nb)
Abrahim	8	0	28	1
Benkenstein	3	0	14	0

Cob	O	M	R	W
Dawson	8	1	29	1
Willoughby	7	1	28	0
Zondeki	7	1	41	2 (1 nb, 1 w)
Kleinveldt	3	0	19	0
Harvey	7	0	40	2 (1 w)
Philander	4	0	24	1

Fall of Wickets	Cob	Dol
1st	27 (1)	28 (1)
2nd	41 (3)	60 (3)
3rd	67 (4)	104 (4)
4th	86 (5)	127 (2)
5th	137 (6)	133 (6)
6th	158 (2)	146 (5)
7th	181 (8)	151 (8)

DOLPHINS v EAGLES

Standard Bank Cup

Played at Sahara Stadium Kingsmead, Durban on 21 December 2005 (D/N) — Toss: Dolphins

Umpires: JD Cloete & BG Jerling (TV: LH Matroos) — Referee: CJ Mitchley

Debuts: Dol: None. Eag: None

Result: Eagles won by 4 wickets

Man of Match: Ryan Bailey & Ryan McLaren

Points: Eag: 5; Dol: 1

Notes: Dolphins substitute: R Frylinck replaced DJ Watson after 0 overs of Eagles' innings. Eagles substitute: R McLaren replaced T Tshabalala after 19 overs of Eagles' innings.

DOLPHINS	Runs	Mins	Balls	4	6
I Khan c Dippenaar b Deacon	23	32	33	3	-
DJ Watson c Bailey b Telemachus	11	54	33	2	-
HM Amla lbw b Telemachus	17	46	30	2	-
AM Amla not out	71	118	101	4	1
DM Benkenstein b Tshabalala	3	11	7	-	-
JC Kent c and b Van der Wath	7	12	11	1	-
†DL Brown not out	41	68	58	3	-
*L Klusener					
ANW Tweedie					
YA Abdullah					
M Hayward					
R Frylinck					
Extras (lb 1, w 5, nb 3)	9				
TOTAL (for 5 wkts) (45 overs)	**182**				

EAGLES	Runs	Mins	Balls	4	6
JA Beukes c Kent b Tweedie	8	28	26	1	-
*†MN van Wyk c Benkenstein b Abdullah	3	20	10	-	-
LL Bosman c Kent b Klusener	36	61	47	4	-
DJ Jacobs b Abdullah	0	5	6	-	-
HH Dippenaar c Brown b Hayward	6	55	28	-	-
RT Bailey not out	40	112	71	2	-
R McLaren c Hayward b Benkenstein	40	77	59	4	-
JJ van der Wath not out	23	26	24	1	1
WA Deacon					
D du Preez					
R Telemachus					
T Tshabalala					
Extras (b 3, lb 10, w 8, nb 6)	27				
TOTAL (for 6 wkts) (44.1 overs)	**183**				

Eag	O	M	R	W
Van der Wath	9	0	40	1 (2 w)
Deacon	9	1	42	1 (2 nb, 1 w)
Telemachus	9	0	41	2 (1 nb)
Du Preez	9	2	25	0
Tshabalala	9	0	33	1 (2 w)

Dol	O	M	R	W
Tweedie	8.1	2	26	1 (1 w)
Abdullah	9	1	17	2 (3 w)
Frylinck	2	0	20	0 (1 nb)
Hayward	8	0	40	1 (1 w)
Klusener	5	0	22	1 (5 nb, 3 w)
Khan	5	0	18	0
Benkenstein	7	0	27	1

Fall of Wickets	Dol	Eag
1st	28 (1)	10 (2)
2nd	50 (2)	14 (1)
3rd	68 (3)	16 (4)
4th	75 (5)	60 (3)
5th	88 (6)	62 (5)
6th	-	148 (7)

DOLPHINS v LIONS

Standard Bank Cup

Played at Sahara Stadium Kingsmead, Durban on 28 December 2005 (D/N) — Toss: Dolphins

Umpires: JD Cloete & MZ Nanabhay (TV: M Gajjar) — Referee: NC Pretorius

Debuts: Dol: None. Lio: None

Result: No result

Points: Dol: 3; Lio: 3

Notes: Lions substitute: F de Wet replaced S Chatterjee after 16 overs of Dolphins' innings.

DOLPHINS	Runs	Mins	Balls	4	6
I Khan c Harris b Moleon	29	54	51	3	-
DJ Watson b Coetsee	53	122	89	4	-
HM Amla c Harris b Hall	31	64	37	3	-
AM Amla lbw b Coetsee	39	50	38	4	-
DM Benkenstein c and b Nkwe	18	31	20	1	1
*L Klusener not out	43	35	24	1	4
†DL Brown not out	8	19	14	-	-
ANW Tweedie					
ZA Abrahim					
M Hayward					
YA Abdullah					
Extras (b 1, lb 2, w 7, nb 4)	14				
TOTAL (for 5 wkts) (45 overs)	**235**				

LIONS	Runs	Mins	Balls	4	6
SC Cook not out	13	31	19	1	-
AM Bacher not out	24	31	27	3	1
VB van Jaarsveld					
*ND McKenzie					
†MJ Harris					
AJ Hall					
DL Makalima					
ET Nkwe					
WL Coetsee					
EO Moleon					
F de Wet					
S Chatterjee					
Extras (w 5)	5				
TOTAL (for 0 wkts) (7.4 overs)	**42**				

Lio	O	M	R	W	
Hall	9	1	31	1	(2 w)
Coetsee	9	0	37	2	
Moleon	8	0	53	1	(4 w)
Chatterjee	3	0	12	0	(1 w)
De Wet	6	0	25	0	
Nkwe	7	0	46	1	(1 nb)
Bacher	1.5	0	8	0	(2 nb)
McKenzie	0.1	0	0	0	
Makalima	1	0	20	0	

Dol	O	M	R	W	
Abdullah	3	0	19	0	(3 w)
Tweedie	3	0	21	0	(2 w)
Hayward	1.4	0	2	0	

Fall of Wickets	Dol	Lio
1st	54 (1)	-
2nd	124 (3)	-
3rd	126 (2)	-
4th	174 (5)	-
5th	200 (4)	-

DOLPHINS v TITANS

Standard Bank Cup

Played at The Oval, Pietermaritzburg on 2 January 2006
Toss: Dolphins
Umpires: M Gajjar & S Wadvalla (TV: MZ Nanabhay)
Referee: A Barnes
Debuts: Dol: None. Ttn: None
Result: Dolphins won by 8 wickets
Man of Match: Andrew Tweedie
Points: Dol: 6; Ttn: 0
Notes: Titans substitute: AM Phangiso replaced NE Mbhalati after 12.4 overs of Titans' innings.

TITANS	Runs	Mins	Balls	4	6
AN Petersen b Tweedie	3	12	8	-	-
GH Bodi lbw b Tweedie	0	3	3	-	-
*M van Jaarsveld b Tweedie	2	17	11	-	-
JG Myburgh c AM Amla b Tweedie	0	1	1	-	-
G Dros c Hayward b Tweedie	21	37	26	4	-
Z de Bruyn c Benkenstein b Abdullah	1	19	15	-	-
P de Bruyn c HM Amla b Hayward	14	38	30	1	-
†CFK van Wyk lbw b Tweedie	0	2	2	-	-
AM Phangiso c Khan b Klusener	21	45	31	3	-
DW Steyn b Hayward	0	13	7	-	-
M Morkel not out	2	6	5	-	-
NE Mbhalati					
Extras (lb 5, w 4)	9				
TOTAL (23.1 overs)	**73**				

DOLPHINS	Runs	Mins	Balls	4	6
I Khan c Petersen b Steyn	0	1	1	-	-
DJ Watson not out	21	60	41	1	-
HM Amla b Morkel	10	22	17	2	-
AM Amla not out	35	36	30	6	-
DM Benkenstein					
†DL Brown					
*L Klusener					
ANW Tweedie					
ZA Abrahim					
M Hayward					
YA Abdullah					
Extras (lb 1, w 2, nb 5)	8				
TOTAL (for 2 wkts) (14.2 overs)	**74**				

Dol	O	M	R	W	
Tweedie	9	1	24	6	(1 w)
Abdullah	6	1	20	1	(1 w)
Abrahim	5	0	19	0	(1 w)
Hayward	3	0	5	2	(1 w)
Klusener	0.1	0	0	1	

Ttn	O	M	R	W	
Steyn	5	0	25	1	(2 nb, 2 w)
Morkel	6	0	33	1	(1 nb)
Z de Bruyn	2.2	0	10	0	
Phangiso	1	0	5	0	

Fall of Wickets	Ttn	Dol
1st	1 (2)	0 (1)
2nd	8 (1)	21 (3)
3rd	8 (4)	-
4th	10 (3)	-
5th	30 (6)	-
6th	38 (5)	-
7th	38 (8)	-
8th	57 (7)	-
9th	70 (10)	-
10th	73 (9)	-

EAGLES

EAGLES v TITANS — Standard Bank Cup

Played at Goodyear Park, Bloemfontein on 25 November 2005 (D/N) — Toss: Titans
Umpires: MW Brown & S Wadvalla (TV: GH Pienaar) — Referee: CJ Mitchley
Debuts: Eag: None. Ttn: None
Result: Eagles won by 21 runs (D/L method), target revised to 145 in 26 overs
Man of Match: Nicky Boje
Points: Eag: 5; Ttn: 1
Notes: Eagles substitute: PJ Koortzen replaced CA Thyssen after 34.3 overs of Eagles' innings. Titans substitute: JG Myburgh replaced NE Mbhalati after 29 overs of Eagles' innings.

EAGLES	*Runs*	*Mins*	*Balls*	*4*	*6*
†MN van Wyk c Van Wyk b Reddy	1	5	8	-	-
LL Bosman c Harris b Reddy	8	21	16	1	-
JA Rudolph c Van Wyk b Steyn	58	121	89	3	-
DJ Jacobs c Van Jaarsveld b Steyn	0	12	5	-	-
*N Boje not out	66	109	82	7	-
RT Bailey lbw b Steyn	8	8	8	1	-
PJ Koortzen not out	0	2	1	-	-
R McLaren					
JJ van der Wath					
WA Deacon					
R Telemachus					
CA Thyssen					
Extras (w 3, nb 1)	4				
TOTAL (for 5 wkts) (34.4 overs)	**145**				

TITANS	*Runs*	*Mins*	*Balls*	*4*	*6*
AN Petersen b Van der Wath	8	25	16	-	-
GH Bodi lbw b Van der Wath	0	2	2	-	-
JG Myburgh b Deacon	3	26	11	-	-
*M van Jaarsveld st Van Wyk b Boje	39	69	48	2	-
Z de Bruyn c Rudolph b Deacon	5	21	14	-	-
G Dros lbw b Boje	7	23	17	1	-
P de Bruyn c Van der Wath b Boje	14	30	20	-	-
†CFK van Wyk not out	19	27	17	2	-
BL Reddy c Koortzen b Van der Wath	14	15	9	1	-
DW Steyn not out	0	2	2	-	-
PL Harris					
NE Mbhalati					
Extras (b 1, lb 4, w 9)	14				
TOTAL (for 8 wkts) (26 overs)	**123**				

Ttn	*O*	*M*	*R*	*W*	
Steyn	6.4	0	19	3	
Reddy	7	2	22	2	(1 w)
Mbhalati	6	0	27	0	(2 w)
Z de Bruyn	4	0	21	0	(1 nb)
P de Bruyn	5	0	22	0	
Harris	3	0	16	0	
Myburgh	3	0	18	0	

Eag	*O*	*M*	*R*	*W*	
Van der Wath	6	0	22	3	(4 w)
Deacon	5	0	16	2	(1 w)
Telemachus	4	0	20	0	
McLaren	5	0	26	0	(2 w)
Boje	4	0	20	3	(1 w)
Koortzen	2	0	14	0	

Fall of Wickets	*Eag*	*Ttn*
1st	1 (1)	2 (2)
2nd	13 (2)	15 (1)
3rd	17 (4)	16 (3)
4th	135 (3)	27 (5)
5th	145 (6)	50 (6)
6th	-	85 (4)
7th	-	92 (7)
8th	-	121 (9)

Warriors v Eagles, East London, 27 November 2005. Eagles won by 6 wickets.

EAGLES v LIONS — Standard Bank Cup

Played at Goodyear Park, Bloemfontein on 30 November 2005 (D/N) — Toss: Eagles
Umpires: JD Cloete & M Gajjar — Referee: A Barnes
Debuts: Eag: None. Lio: None
Result: No result
Points: Eag: 3; Lio: 3

LIONS	*Runs*	*Mins*	*Balls*	*4*	*6*
SC Cook b Telemachus	30	41	35	4	-
AM Bacher c Van Wyk b McLaren	12	45	21	2	-
DL Makalima run out (Jacobs/Boje)	50	77	53	1	2
*ND McKenzie c Rudolph b Van der Wath	43	84	64	2	-
VB van Jaarsveld not out	21	30	17	-	-
†MJ Harris c Boje b Van der Wath	7	8	7	-	-
WL Coetsee c McLaren b Telemachus	1	6	2	-	-
EO Moleon not out	7	4	3	1	-
VCM Mazibuko					
GJ-P Kruger					
F de Wet					
Extras (lb 3, w 12, nb 4)	19				
TOTAL (for 6 wkts) (33 overs)	**190**				

EAGLES	*Runs*	*Mins*	*Balls*	*4*	*6*
†MN van Wyk not out	9	16	7	1	-
LL Bosman not out	17	16	15	3	-
JA Rudolph					
DJ Jacobs					
*N Boje					
RT Bailey					
CA Thyssen					
JJ van der Wath					
R McLaren					
WA Deacon					
R Telemachus					
Extras (lb 3, w 1, nb 1)	5				
TOTAL (for 0 wkts) (3.3 overs)	**31**				

Eag	O	M	R	W
Van der Wath	6	0	36	2 (4 w)
Deacon	6	0	36	0 (2 nb, 3 w)
Telemachus	7	0	42	2 (1 w)
McLaren	7	0	37	1 (2 nb, 3 w)
Boje	7	0	36	0 (1 w)

Lio	O	M	R	W
Kruger	2	0	15	0
De Wet	1.3	0	13	0 (1 nb, 1 w)

Fall of Wickets	Lio	Eag
1st	51 (1)	-
2nd	51 (2)	-
3rd	148 (3)	-
4th	160 (4)	-
5th	173 (6)	-
6th	182 (7)	-

Titans v Eagles, Centurion, 2 December 2005. Titans won by 2 runs.

EAGLES v WARRIORS

Standard Bank Cup

Played at Goodyear Park, Bloemfontein on 4 December 2005
Toss: Eagles
Umpires: JD Cloete & MZ Nanabhay
Referee: CJ Mitchley
Debuts: Eag: None. War: None
Result: Warriors won by 8 wickets
Man of Match: Justin Kreusch & Tyron Henderson
Points: Eag: 1; War: 5
Notes: Henderson scored his fifty off 24 balls in Warriors' innings. Eagles substitute: CA Thyssen replaced LL Bosman after 8 overs of Warriors' innings. Warriors substitute: L Mbane replaced MW Olivier after 14 overs of Eagles' innings.

EAGLES	Runs	Mins	Balls	4	6
JA Beukes c Peterson b Meyer	0	7	9	-	-
LL Bosman b Mbane	49	67	41	7	-
WA Deacon b Kreusch	57	70	52	8	-
DJ Jacobs c Jacobs b Meyer	52	102	73	3	-
*†MN van Wyk c Dyili b Peterson	26	36	37	2	-
PJ Koortzen lbw b Peterson	2	9	10	-	-
RT Bailey b Mbane	3	9	7	-	-
R McLaren c Bradfield b Meyer	3	17	14	-	-
JJ van der Wath not out	28	29	23	-	2
R Telemachus not out	22	12	10	4	-
T Tshabalala					
CA Thyssen					
Extras (b 4, lb 2, w 6, nb 6)	18				
TOTAL (for 8 wkts) (45 overs)	**260**				

WARRIORS	Runs	Mins	Balls	4	6
CC Bradfield run out (Jacobs/Van Wyk)	44	104	72	2	-
JP Kreusch not out	119	171	127	11	-
†AZM Dyili b Tshabalala	23	28	29	2	-
T Henderson not out	62	37	31	4	4
A Jacobs					
BC de Wett					
LL Gamiet					
*RJ Peterson					
L Mbane					
L Meyer					
D Willemse					
MW Olivier					
Extras (lb 2, w 5, nb 6)	13				
TOTAL (for 2 wkts) (42.5 overs)	**261**				

War	O	M	R	W
Henderson	9	0	34	0 (1 w)
Meyer	8	0	72	3 (6 nb, 1 w)
Kreusch	6	0	29	1
Olivier	2	0	27	0 (1 w)
Mbane	7	0	31	2
Peterson	9	0	39	2
Willemse	4	0	22	0 (2 w)

Eag	O	M	R	W
Van der Wath	7	2	25	0 (1 nb)
Deacon	9	0	64	0 (2 w)
Telemachus	5	0	37	0 (1 w)
McLaren	6.5	0	45	0 (1 nb, 1 w)
Thyssen	2	0	8	0
Tshabalala	9	0	62	1 (1 w)
Koortzen	4	0	18	0

Fall of Wickets	Eag	War
1st	11 (1)	130 (1)
2nd	109 (2)	174 (3)
3rd	117 (3)	-
4th	170 (5)	-
5th	178 (6)	-
6th	185 (7)	-
7th	198 (8)	-
8th	217 (4)	-

EAGLES v CAPE COBRAS

Standard Bank Cup

Played at Goodyear Park, Bloemfontein on 9 December 2005 (D/N)
Toss: Eagles
Umpires: IL Howell & SB Lambson
Referee: CJ Mitchley
Debuts: Eag: None. Cob: None
Result: Eagles won by 1 wicket
Man of Match: Ryan McLaren
Points: Eag: 5; Cob: 1
Notes: Cape Cobras substitute: VD Philander replaced H Davids after 22.2 overs of Eagles' innings. Eagles substitute: R McLaren replaced T Tshabalala after 23 overs of Eagles' innings.

CAPE COBRAS	Runs	Mins	Balls	4	6
AG Puttick b Van der Wath	2	10	7	-	-
*†TL Tsolekile lbw b Deacon	9	33	20	1	-
J-P Duminy c Beukes b Van der Wath	13	29	22	3	-
RE Levi c Van Wyk b Deacon	12	29	16	1	1
IJ Harvey c Telemachus b Du Preez	18	32	21	3	-
H Davids c Du Preez b Van der Wath	71	124	91	5	-
CD de Lange c Beukes b Koortzen	64	98	77	4	-
RK Kleinveldt c Van Wyk b Van der Wath	1	4	4	-	-
AC Dawson not out	14	17	13	1	-
M Zondeki c Koortzen b Telemachus	2	5	3	-	-
CM Willoughby not out	1	4	1	-	-
VD Philander					
Extras (lb 3, w 8, nb 5)	16				
TOTAL (for 9 wkts) (45 overs)	**223**				

EAGLES	Runs	Mins	Balls	4	6
JA Beukes b Zondeki	55	86	74	9	-
LL Bosman lbw b Willoughby	24	45	30	3	-
PJ Koortzen c Tsolekile b Kleinveldt	34	93	45	1	-
DJ Jacobs lbw b Kleinveldt	1	6	6	-	-
*†MN van Wyk c Tsolekile b Kleinveldt	0	4	2	-	-
JJ van der Wath b De Lange	16	29	30	-	1
R McLaren not out	37	68	45	2	-
CA Thyssen b Kleinveldt	18	17	14	2	1
WA Deacon c De Lange b Harvey	3	13	11	-	-
R Telemachus b Dawson	14	15	12	1	-
D du Preez not out	12	10	6	2	-
T Tshabalala					
Extras (lb 4, w 4, nb 5)	13				
TOTAL (for 9 wkts) (45 overs)	**227**				

Eag	O	M	R	W	
Van der Wath	9	1	41	4	(1 nb, 2 w)
Deacon	9	1	38	2	(1 nb, 3 w)
Telemachus	8	1	33	1	(1 nb)
Du Preez	6	0	32	1	(1 nb, 2 w)
Thyssen	4	0	20	0	
Tshabalala	6	0	35	0	(1 nb, 1 w)
Koortzen	3	0	21	1	

Cob	O	M	R	W	
Dawson	7	0	50	1	(1 nb)
Willoughby	9	1	35	1	
Harvey	9	0	46	1	(1 w)
Zondeki	7	0	42	1	(4 nb, 3 w)
Kleinveldt	9	0	29	4	
De Lange	4	0	21	1	

Fall of Wickets	Cob	Eag
1st	5 (1)	54 (2)
2nd	28 (2)	96 (1)
3rd	32 (3)	100 (4)
4th	55 (4)	100 (5)
5th	66 (5)	130 (6)
6th	198 (7)	142 (3)
7th	199 (8)	164 (8)
8th	212 (6)	177 (9)
9th	220 (10)	203 (10)

EAGLES v DOLPHINS

Standard Bank Cup

Played at Goodyear Park, Bloemfontein on 14 December 2005 (D/N)

Toss: Eagles

Umpires: MW Brown & GH Pienaar (TV: S Wadvalla)

Referee: MR Magiet

Debuts: Eag: None. Dol: None

Result: Eagles won by 8 runs

Man of Match: Johan van der Wath

Points: Eag: 5; Dol: 1

Notes: Dolphins substitute: RP Symcox replaced M Hayward after 0 overs of Dolphins' innings. Eagles substitute: R McLaren replaced HH Dippenaar after 1 over of Dolphins' innings.

EAGLES	Runs	Mins	Balls	4	6
JA Beukes c Brown b Klusener	1	21	12	-	-
LL Bosman c HM Amla b Abrahim	59	133	80	6	-
WA Deacon c HM Amla b Tweedie	14	13	12	2	-
HH Dippenaar b Tweedie	1	9	9	-	-
DJ Jacobs c Brown b Kent	24	33	24	5	-
*†MN van Wyk c Kent b Hayward	9	17	13	1	-
JJ van der Wath c Watson b Abrahim	0	1	1	-	-
CA Thyssen c Klusener b Khan	10	19	17	1	-
R Telemachus c HM Amla b Abrahim	7	17	15	1	-
D du Preez not out	5	15	11	1	-
T Tshabalala c Brown b Abrahim	4	11	9	1	-
R McLaren					
Extras (lb 4, w 7, nb 3)	14				
TOTAL (33.2 overs)	**148**				

DOLPHINS	Runs	Mins	Balls	4	6
DJ Watson c Dippenaar b Van der Wath	5	23	15	1	-
I Khan c Jacobs b Deacon	1	19	8	-	-
HM Amla c Van Wyk b Deacon	2	26	24	-	-
AM Amla c McLaren b Van der Wath	59	173	121	5	-
DM Benkenstein b Van der Wath	4	5	2	1	-
JC Kent c Beukes b Du Preez	10	53	31	1	-
†DL Brown c Van der Wath b Telemachus	20	44	37	3	-
RP Symcox b Telemachus	3	10	7	-	-
*L Klusener b Telemachus	7	17	10	1	-
ANW Tweedie b McLaren	1	7	7	-	-
ZA Abrahim not out	7	8	5	1	-
M Hayward					
Extras (lb 4, w 16, nb 1)	21				
TOTAL (44.2 overs)	**140**				

Dol	O	M	R	W	
Klusener	7	1	42	1	(2 nb, 1 w)
Tweedie	7	1	23	2	(1 w)
Hayward	7	1	22	1	
Kent	3	0	27	1	(1 nb, 1 w)
Abrahim	6.2	2	15	4	
Khan	3	0	15	1	

Eag	O	M	R	W	
Van der Wath	8.2	0	24	3	(4 w)
Deacon	9	2	27	2	(4 w)
Telemachus	9	0	33	3	
Du Preez	9	1	25	1	
McLaren	9	2	27	1	(1 nb)

Fall of Wickets	Eag	Dol
1st	19 (1)	9 (2)
2nd	36 (3)	13 (1)
3rd	45 (4)	22 (3)
4th	89 (5)	28 (5)
5th	107 (6)	63 (6)
6th	107 (7)	101 (7)
7th	126 (8)	112 (8)
8th	134 (2)	124 (9)
9th	138 (9)	127 (10)
10th	148 (11)	140 (4)

Lions v Eagles, Johannesburg, 16 December 2005. Lions won by 5 wickets.
Dolphins v Eagles, Durban, 21 December 2005. Eagles won by 4 wickets.
Cape Cobras v Eagles, Cape Town, 2 January 2006. Eagles won by 35 runs.

STANDARD BANK CUP

LIONS

LIONS v CAPE COBRAS — Standard Bank Cup

Played at Sedgars Park, Potchefstroom on 25 November 2005 (D/N) — Toss: Lions
Umpires: IL Howell & BG Jerling — Referee: A Barnes
Debuts: Lio: None. Cob: None
Result: No result
Points: Lio: 3; Cob: 3
Notes: The match was reduced to 33 overs per side before the start.

CAPE COBRAS	*Runs*	*Mins*	*Balls*	*4*	*6*	LIONS
AG Puttick c Harris b Terbrugge	1	12	7	-	-	F de Wet
*†TL Tsolekile c Terbrugge b Moleon	35	76	46	4	-	AM Bacher
HH Gibbs c Bacher b De Wet	3	12	4	-	-	VB van Jaarsveld
J-P Duminy lbw b Mazibuko	58	67	47	10	-	*ND McKenzie
IJ Harvey c Makalima b Kruger	41	43	30	6	1	†MJ Harris
FD Telo b De Wet	1	4	4	-	-	DL Makalima
CD de Lange c Bacher b Coetsee	12	19	13	1	-	WL Coetsee
VD Philander not out	20	31	19	1	-	EO Moleon
RK Kleinveldt c Bacher b De Wet	22	15	18	4	-	VCM Mazibuko
AC Dawson not out	5	11	5	-	-	GJ-P Kruger
CM Willoughby						DJ Terbrugge
Extras (lb 3, w 6, nb 1)	10					
TOTAL (for 8 wkts) (32 overs)	**208**					

Lio	*O*	*M*	*R*	*W*	
Terbrugge	6	0	29	1	(3 w)
De Wet	7	0	56	3	(1 nb)
Kruger	7	0	51	1	(2 w)
Moleon	4	0	27	1	(1 w)
Mazibuko	4	0	20	1	
Coetsee	4	0	22	1	

Fall of Wickets	*Cob*
1st	10 (1)
2nd	23 (3)
3rd	101 (2)
4th	122 (4)
5th	123 (6)
6th	159 (7)
7th	163 (5)
8th	193 (9)

Titans v Lions, Centurion, 27 November 2005. No result.
Eagles v Lions, Bloemfontein, 30 November 2005. No result.

LIONS v DOLPHINS — Standard Bank Cup

Played at Liberty Life Wanderers Stadium, Johannesburg on 2 December 2005 (D/N) — Toss: Dolphins
Umpires: MW Brown & MZ Nanabhay — Referee: NC Pretorius
Debuts: Lio: None. Dol: None
Result: Lions won by 50 runs
Man of Match: Neil McKenzie
Points: Dol: 1; Lio: 5
Notes: Dolphins substitute: RP Symcox replaced U Govender after 21 overs of Lions' innings. Lions substitute: F de Wet replaced SC Cook after 16 overs of Dolphins' innings.

LIONS	*Runs*	*Mins*	*Balls*	*4*	*6*
SC Cook run out (Symcox/Brown)	66	95	64	10	-
AM Bacher b Khan	93	137	113	12	1
*ND McKenzie not out	87	88	64	7	3
VB van Jaarsveld c Symcox b Tweedie	16	24	16	1	-
AJ Hall lbw b Abrahim	0	3	1	-	-
DL Makalima c Brown b Abrahim	13	8	8	1	1
†MJ Harris c Khan b Tweedie	4	7	5	-	-
WL Coetsee					
EO Moleon					
VCM Mazibuko					
S Chatterjee					
F de Wet					
Extras (lb 7, w 15, nb 1)	23				
TOTAL (for 6 wkts) (45 overs)	**302**				

DOLPHINS	*Runs*	*Mins*	*Balls*	*4*	*6*
I Khan c Van Jaarsveld b Hall	2	21	13	-	-
DJ Watson b Coetsee	8	7	6	2	-
HM Amla c Harris b Coetsee	8	15	12	-	-
AM Amla run out (De Wet)	59	106	94	6	1
DM Benkenstein c Makalima b De Wet	27	47	39	4	-
JC Kent b Bacher	9	17	11	2	-
†DL Brown run out (Hall)	53	77	51	3	2
RP Symcox not out	50	52	39	5	1
*L Klusener not out	17	12	6	-	2
ZA Abrahim					
ANW Tweedie					
U Govender					
Extras (b 3, lb 5, w 9, nb 2)	19				
TOTAL (for 7 wkts) (45 overs)	**252**				

Dol	O	M	R	W
Klusener	6	0	33	0 (1 w)
Kent	8	0	56	0
Tweedie	6	0	43	2 (1 w)
Govender	4	0	38	0 (3 w)
Abrahim	7	0	43	2 (1 w)
Benkenstein	5	0	24	0 (1 w)
Khan	7	0	33	1
Symcox	2	0	25	0 (1 nb)

Lio	O	M	R	W
Hall	9	0	62	1 (1 nb, 6 w)
Coetsee	8	0	33	2 (1 w)
Chatterjee	5	0	26	0 (2 w)
Moleon	7	2	28	0
De Wet	8	0	64	1
Bacher	8	0	31	1

Fall of Wickets	Lio	Dol
1st	142 (1)	11 (2)
2nd	214 (2)	19 (1)
3rd	263 (4)	19 (3)
4th	263 (5)	71 (5)
5th	283 (6)	101 (6)
6th	302 (7)	144 (4)
7th	-	222 (7)

LIONS v TITANS — Standard Bank Cup

Played at Sedgars Park, Potchefstroom on 4 December 2005 — Toss: Titans
Umpires: MW Brown & M Erasmus — Referee: MR Magiet
Debuts: Lio: None. Ttn: None
Result: Titans won by 7 wickets
Man of Match: Goolam Bodi
Points: Lio: 1; Ttn: 5
Notes: Lions substitute: F de Wet replaced SC Cook after 0 overs of Titans' innings. Titans substitute: JG Myburgh replaced DW Steyn after 31 overs of Lions' innings.

LIONS	Runs	Mins	Balls	4	6
SC Cook c Petersen b Reddy	18	41	34	2	-
AJ Hall c Bodi b P de Bruyn	74	142	98	9	-
†MJ Harris c Harris b Z de Bruyn	35	62	47	2	1
*ND McKenzie c Dros b Harris	23	43	33	4	-
VB van Jaarsveld b Reddy	20	24	17	1	1
DL Makalima not out	30	37	30	3	-
WA Dugmore run out (Z de Bruyn)	1	2	1	-	-
WL Coetsee b Z de Bruyn	8	11	7	1	-
EO Moleon not out	2	3	3	-	-
VCM Mazibuko					
S Chatterjee					
F de Wet					
Extras (lb 6, w 5)	11				
TOTAL (for 7 wkts) (45 overs)	**222**				

TITANS	Runs	Mins	Balls	4	6
GH Bodi b Hall	98	164	101	11	2
AN Petersen c and b Chatterjee	25	30	28	4	-
*M van Jaarsveld lbw b Hall	65	119	82	6	-
G Dros not out	17	24	15	1	1
Z de Bruyn not out	4	9	7	-	-
JG Myburgh					
P de Bruyn					
†CFK van Wyk					
BL Reddy					
PL Harris					
NE Mbhalati					
DW Steyn					
Extras (b 1, lb 2, w 4, nb 7)	14				
TOTAL (for 3 wkts) (37.4 overs)	**223**				

Ttn	O	M	R	W
Reddy	9	0	39	2 (2 w)
Steyn	5	0	21	0 (2 w)
Mbhalati	7	0	41	0
Z de Bruyn	9	0	32	2
P de Bruyn	9	0	49	1
Harris	6	0	34	1 (1 w)

Lio	O	M	R	W
Hall	9	0	52	2 (3 nb, 2 w)
Coetsee	7	0	44	0
Chatterjee	4	0	36	1
De Wet	9	1	43	0 (2 nb, 1 w)
Moleon	4	0	16	0
Mazibuko	2	0	16	0 (2 nb, 1 w)
Dugmore	2	0	10	0
McKenzie	0.4	0	3	0

Fall of Wickets	Lio	Ttn
1st	38 (1)	53 (2)
2nd	118 (3)	194 (3)
3rd	148 (2)	216 (1)
4th	157 (4)	-
5th	190 (5)	-
6th	191 (7)	-
7th	218 (8)	-

LIONS v WARRIORS — Standard Bank Cup

Played at Liberty Life Wanderers Stadium, Johannesburg on 9 December 2005 (D/N) — Toss: Lions
Umpires: S George & MZ Nanabhay (TV: GH Pienaar) — Referee: S Naidoo
Debuts: Lio: None. War: None
Result: Lions won by 2 wickets
Man of Match: Friedel de Wet
Points: War: 1; Lio: 5
Notes: Lions substitute: GJ de Bruin replaced S Chatterjee after 16 overs of Warriors' innings. Warriors substitute: MW Olivier replaced A Jacobs after 6 overs of Lions' innings.

WARRIORS	Runs	Mins	Balls	4	6
JP Kreusch c Bacher b De Wet	16	46	29	4	-
CC Bradfield c Bacher b De Wet	8	24	20	2	-
*RJ Peterson c Harris b Moleon	28	47	32	5	-
A Jacobs c De Wet b Moleon	7	18	16	-	-
†AZM Dyili st Harris b Coetsee	25	40	30	2	1
BC de Wett lbw b Makalima	23	57	43	2	-
LL Gamiet not out	51	79	62	6	-
T Henderson c and b Bacher	28	28	23	1	3
L Meyer b Bacher	8	9	6	1	-
L Mbane c Harris b De Bruin	1	4	2	-	-
D Willemse not out	3	12	8	-	-
MW Olivier					
Extras (b 7, lb 1, w 3, nb 1)	12				
TOTAL (for 9 wkts) (45 overs)	**210**				

LIONS	Runs	Mins	Balls	4	6
AM Bacher c De Wett b Kreusch	21	49	42	4	-
SC Cook lbw b Peterson	51	91	65	7	-
*ND McKenzie c Mbane b Kreusch	42	103	71	1	-
VB van Jaarsveld b Mbane	28	44	41	-	1
†MJ Harris st Dyili b Peterson	36	45	27	4	-
DL Makalima c Gamiet b Peterson	2	8	6	-	-
WL Coetsee run out (Peterson/Dyili)	1	9	2	-	-
BC Adams b Henderson	11	15	10	1	-
EO Moleon not out	1	8	3	-	-
F de Wet not out	1	1	1	-	-
GJ de Bruin					
S Chatterjee					
Extras (lb 4, w 13)	17				
TOTAL (for 8 wkts) (44.4 overs)	**211**				

Lio	O	M	R	W	
De Wet	9	3	21	2	
Coetsee	8	1	30	1	(1 w)
Chatterjee	4	1	19	0	(1 w)
Moleon	8	0	47	2	
De Bruin	5	0	26	1	(1 nb, 1 w)
Bacher	9	0	42	2	
Makalima	2	0	17	1	

War	O	M	R	W	
Henderson	8.4	1	35	1	
Meyer	3	0	13	0	(4 w)
Olivier	5	0	35	0	(2 w)
Kreusch	7	1	31	2	(1 w)
Mbane	7	0	28	1	(3 w)
Willemse	5	0	19	0	
Peterson	9	0	46	3	(1 w)

Fall of Wickets	War	Lio
1st	21 (2)	53 (1)
2nd	45 (1)	96 (2)
3rd	57 (4)	150 (4)
4th	66 (3)	167 (3)
5th	102 (5)	176 (6)
6th	127 (6)	189 (7)
7th	172 (8)	202 (5)
8th	189 (9)	210 (8)
9th	194 (10)	-

LIONS v EAGLES — Standard Bank Cup

Played at Liberty Life Wanderers Stadium, Johannesburg on 16 December 2005 — Toss: Lions
Umpires: S George & LH Matroos (TV: MW Brown) — Referee: WA Diedricks
Debuts: Lio: None. Eag: None
Result: Lions won by 5 wickets
Man of Match: Stephen Cook
Points: Eag: 1; Lio: 5
Notes: Eagles substitute: R McLaren replaced LL Bosman after 0 overs of Lions' innings. Lions substitute: WL Coetsee replaced S Chatterjee after 21 overs of Eagles' innings.

EAGLES	Runs	Mins	Balls	4	6
JA Beukes c Moleon b Nkwe	37	61	53	7	-
LL Bosman c Harris b De Wet	11	35	22	2	-
WA Deacon c Hall b Chatterjee	21	42	28	3	-
HH Dippenaar c Bacher b Hall	42	110	65	3	-
DJ Jacobs c Cook b Moleon	1	4	3	-	-
*†MN van Wyk c Harris b Hall	26	44	44	2	-
JJ van der Wath not out	70	59	48	4	5
CA Thyssen c McKenzie b Bacher	3	5	6	-	-
R Telemachus not out	2	8	3	-	-
D du Preez					
T Tshabalala					
R McLaren					
Extras (lb 2, w 3, nb 2)	7				
TOTAL (for 7 wkts) (45 overs)	**220**				

LIONS	Runs	Mins	Balls	4	6
AM Bacher b Du Preez	33	63	52	7	-
SC Cook not out	87	176	111	7	-
*ND McKenzie c Jacobs b McLaren	5	12	8	1	-
VB van Jaarsveld st Van Wyk b Tshabalala	5	14	10	1	-
†MJ Harris b Tshabalala	6	13	6	1	-
AJ Hall c Deacon b Tshabalala	28	35	40	1	1
DL Makalima not out	40	37	30	6	-
ET Nkwe					
WL Coetsee					
EO Moleon					
F de Wet					
S Chatterjee					
Extras (b 4, lb 1, w 12, nb 2)	19				
TOTAL (for 5 wkts) (42.3 overs)	**223**				

Lio	O	M	R	W	
De Wet	7	1	47	1	(1 nb)
Hall	9	2	47	2	(1 nb, 1 w)
Chatterjee	5	0	19	1	(1 w)
Nkwe	3	0	22	1	
Moleon	9	2	27	1	(1 w)
Bacher	8	0	38	1	
Coetsee	4	0	18	0	

Eag	O	M	R	W	
Van der Wath	8	2	24	0	(1 w)
Deacon	4.3	0	25	0	(1 nb, 1 w)
Du Preez	9	0	43	1	
McLaren	7	0	23	1	(3 w)
Telemachus	2	0	25	0	(1 nb)
Tshabalala	9	0	51	3	(2 w)
Thyssen	3	0	27	0	(1 w)

Fall of Wickets	Eag	Lio
1st	26 (2)	60 (1)
2nd	59 (1)	86 (3)
3rd	76 (3)	96 (4)
4th	77 (5)	108 (5)
5th	119 (6)	155 (6)
6th	193 (4)	-
7th	198 (8)	-

Cape Cobras v Lions, Cape Town, 23 December 2005. Lions won by 39 runs.
Dolphins v Lions, Durban, 28 December 2005. No result.
Warriors v Lions, Port Elizabeth, 2 January 2006. Lions won by 17 runs.

PROLIFIC SCORER . . . Stephen Cook on the way to a century for the Lions against the Titans at Centurion during a high-scoring season   Picture: LEE WARREN, Touchline Photo

TITANS

Eagles v Titans, Bloemfontein, 25 November 2005. Eagles won by 21 runs (D/L Method.

TITANS v LIONS — Standard Bank Cup

Played at SuperSport Park, Centurion on 27 November 2005 — Toss: Titans
Umpires: IL Howell & BG Jerling (TV: KH Hurter) — Referee: CJ Mitchley
Debuts: Ttn: None. Lio: None
Result: No result
Points: Lio: 3; Ttn: 3
Notes: Lions substitute: WL Coetsee replaced SC Cook after 1 over of Titans' innings. Titans substitute: JG Myburgh replaced PL Harris after 37 overs of Lions' innings.

LIONS	*Runs*	*Mins*	*Balls*	*4*	*6*
SC Cook not out	116	185	133	13	-
AM Bacher c Van Jaarsveld b Steyn	17	24	26	3	-
DL Makalima b Reddy	4	20	11	-	-
*ND McKenzie c Van Wyk b Mbhalati	1	9	2	-	-
VB van Jaarsveld c Harris b Mbhalati	41	69	63	2	1
†MJ Harris c Reddy b P de Bruyn	12	20	13	1	-
EO Moleon c and b Mbhalati	1	5	3	-	-
VCM Mazibuko c Reddy b Z de Bruyn	4	12	8	-	-
F de Wet b Steyn	9	16	11	1	-
GJ-P Kruger c and b Steyn	1	4	3	-	-
DJ Terbrugge					
WL Coetsee					
Extras (lb 5, w 5, nb 3)	13				
TOTAL (for 9 wkts) (45 overs)	**219**				

TITANS	*Runs*	*Mins*	*Balls*	*4*	*6*
GH Bodi lbw b Kruger	18	25	20	-	2
AN Petersen b De Wet	29	49	29	3	1
JG Myburgh not out	20	56	37	3	-
*M van Jaarsveld not out	13	32	21	2	-
G Dros					
Z de Bruyn					
P de Bruyn					
†CFK van Wyk					
BL Reddy					
DW Steyn					
NE Mbhalati					
PL Harris					
Extras (w 3)	3				
TOTAL (for 2 wkts) (17.5 overs)	**83**				

Ttn	*O*	*M*	*R*	*W*	
Steyn	9	1	37	3	(2 w)
Reddy	9	0	42	1	(1 w)
Mbhalati	9	0	42	3	
Z de Bruyn	6	0	31	1	(3 nb, 2 w)
P de Bruyn	9	0	43	1	
Harris	3	0	19	0	

Lio	*O*	*M*	*R*	*W*	
Terbrugge	2.2	0	18	0	(1 w)
Kruger	6	0	25	1	(1 w)
Mazibuko	1.4	0	13	0	(1 w)
De Wet	3	0	14	1	
Moleon	2.5	0	9	0	
Coetsee	2	0	4	0	

Fall of Wickets	*Lio*	*Ttn*
1st	29 (2)	29 (1)
2nd	51 (3)	55 (2)
3rd	58 (4)	-
4th	140 (5)	-
5th	170 (6)	-
6th	175 (7)	-
7th	192 (8)	-
8th	217 (9)	-
9th	219 (10)	-

TITANS v EAGLES — Standard Bank Cup

Played at SuperSport Park, Centurion on 2 December 2005 (D/N) — Toss: Eagles
Umpires: M Erasmus & BG Jerling — Referee: MR Magiet
Debuts: Ttn: None. Eag: None
Result: Titans won by 2 runs
Man of Match: Dale Steyn
Points: Eag: 1; Ttn: 4
Notes: Titans were penalised 1 point for a slow over-rate. Eagles substitute: CA Thyssen replaced T Tshabalala after 43.2 overs of Eagles' innings. Titans substitute: JG Myburgh replaced GH Bodi after 2 overs of Eagles' innings.

TITANS	*Runs*	*Mins*	*Balls*	*4*	*6*
AN Petersen c Van der Wath b Tshabalala	41	87	55	4	1
GH Bodi b McLaren	31	64	45	6	-
P de Bruyn c Van der Wath b Koortzen	50	82	68	2	1
*M van Jaarsveld b McLaren	4	4	5	1	-
Z de Bruyn c and b Tshabalala	0	3	2	-	-
G Dros not out	79	87	73	6	3
JA Morkel b Deacon	1	7	7	-	-
†CFK van Wyk b Van der Wath	4	20	13	-	-
BL Reddy not out	2	8	5	-	-
DW Steyn					
NE Mbhalati					
JG Myburgh					
Extras (lb 4, w 7, nb 3)	14				
TOTAL (for 7 wkts) (45 overs)	**226**				

EAGLES	*Runs*	*Mins*	*Balls*	*4*	*6*
JA Beukes b P de Bruyn	88	160	123	12	-
LL Bosman b Steyn	63	110	73	6	2
PJ Koortzen lbw b Steyn	0	2	1	-	-
DJ Jacobs b Z de Bruyn	1	17	11	-	-
*†MN van Wyk c Bodi b Reddy	34	52	40	4	-
JJ van der Wath lbw b Z de Bruyn	1	5	5	-	-
RT Bailey not out	9	29	9	1	-
WA Deacon b Steyn	0	4	4	-	-
CA Thyssen not out	10	9	8	1	-
R Telemachus					
R McLaren					
T Tshabalala					
Extras (lb 8, w 6, nb 4)	18				
TOTAL (for 7 wkts) (45 overs)	**224**				

Eag	O	M	R	W	Ttn	O	M	R	W	Fall of Wickets	Ttn	Eag
Van der Wath	9	0	41	1 (3 w)	Steyn	9	1	41	3 (1 nb, 4 w)	1st	64 (2)	140 (2)
Deacon	9	1	47	1 (1 nb, 1 w)	Reddy	9	0	56	1 (1 nb, 1 w)	2nd	104 (1)	140 (3)
Telemachus	5	0	38	0 (1 nb)	Mbhalati	8	0	44	0 (2 nb)	3rd	108 (4)	152 (4)
McLaren	5	1	35	2 (1 nb, 2 w)	Morkel	6	0	22	0	4th	109 (5)	184 (1)
Tshabalala	9	0	29	2 (1 w)	P de Bruyn	8	0	34	1	5th	171 (3)	187 (6)
Koortzen	8	0	32	1	Z de Bruyn	5	0	19	2 (1 w)	6th	173 (7)	210 (5)
										7th	210 (8)	212 (8)

Lions v Titans, Potchefstroom, 4 December 2005. Titans won by 7 wickets.

TITANS v DOLPHINS

Standard Bank Cup

Played at SuperSport Park, Centurion on 7 December 2005 (D/N)

Toss: Titans

Umpires: KH Hurter & S Wadvalla (TV: JD Cloete)

Referee: WA Diedricks

Debuts: Ttn: M Morkel (LO). Dol: None

Result: Titans won by 6 wickets

Man of Match: Martin van Jaarsveld

Points: Dol: 1; Ttn: 5

Notes: Van Jaarsveld scored his century off 94 balls in Titans' innings. Dolphins substitute: RP Symcox replaced DJ Watson after 0 overs of Titans' innings. Titans substitute: JG Myburgh replaced M Morkel after 39 overs of Dolphins' innings.

DOLPHINS	Runs	Mins	Balls	4	6
I Khan c Mbhalati b Reddy	2	6	6	-	-
DJ Watson c Petersen b Morkel	1	21	12	-	-
HM Amla c Du Plessis b Z de Bruyn	49	85	55	7	-
AM Amla c P de Bruyn b Mbhalati	15	41	36	3	-
DM Benkenstein not out	87	115	87	5	3
JC Kent lbw b Du Plessis	28	36	30	3	-
†DL Brown run out (Petersen/Van Wyk)	5	7	8	-	-
*L Klusener not out	49	43	38	4	3
ANW Tweedie					
ZA Abrahim					
U Govender					
RP Symcox					
Extras (b 1, lb 2, w 5, nb 2)	10				
TOTAL (for 6 wkts) (45 overs)	**246**				

TITANS	Runs	Mins	Balls	4	6
GH Bodi run out (HM Amla/Brown)	20	44	24	2	-
AN Petersen b Tweedie	30	28	28	3	-
*M van Jaarsveld not out	111	145	100	13	1
Z de Bruyn b Tweedie	6	17	11	-	-
G Dros c Brown b Symcox	28	51	46	2	-
JG Myburgh not out	48	60	52	5	1
F du Plessis					
†CFK van Wyk					
BL Reddy					
P de Bruyn					
NE Mbhalati					
M Morkel					
Extras (lb 1, w 1, nb 5)	7				
TOTAL (for 4 wkts) (42.4 overs)	**250**				

Ttn	O	M	R	W	Dol	O	M	R	W	Fall of Wickets	Dol	Ttn
Morkel	7	1	24	1 (1 nb, 2 w)	Klusener	6	0	43	0 (1 nb)	1st	3 (1)	44 (2)
Reddy	8	0	58	1 (2 w)	Kent	6	0	38	0 (2 nb)	2nd	13 (2)	54 (1)
Mbhalati	7	0	13	1	Tweedie	9	2	25	2	3rd	64 (4)	88 (4)
Z de Bruyn	8	0	67	1 (1 nb, 1 w)	Govender	2.4	0	36	0	4th	84 (3)	154 (5)
P de Bruyn	9	0	46	0	Abrahim	8	0	34	0 (1 w)	5th	147 (6)	-
Du Plessis	6	0	35	1	Khan	3	0	20	0	6th	155 (7)	-
					Symcox	5	0	40	1 (2 nb)			
					Benkenstein	3	0	13	0			

TITANS v CAPE COBRAS

Standard Bank Cup

Played at SuperSport Park, Centurion on 11 December 2005

Toss: Titans

Umpires: S George & SB Lambson (TV: M Erasmus)

Referee: S Naidoo

Debuts: Ttn: None. Cob: None

Result: Titans won by 2 wickets

Man of Match: Johan Myburgh

Points: Ttn: 5; Cob: 1

Notes: Cape Cobras substitute: WC Hantam replaced M Zondeki after 34.1 overs of Cape Cobras' innings. Titans substitute: JG Myburgh replaced NE Mbhalati after 42 overs of Cape Cobras' innings.

CAPE COBRAS	Runs	Mins	Balls	4	6
AG Puttick c Morkel b Reddy	12	22	20	2	-
*†TL Tsolekile c Van Wyk b Morkel	7	37	19	-	-
RE Levi c P de Bruyn b Mbhalati	16	43	38	3	-
J-P Duminy run out (Reddy)	43	96	68	2	1
IJ Harvey lbw b Mbhalati	15	16	12	3	-
H Davids run out (Van Jaarsveld/Mbhalati)	40	78	65	2	-
CD de Lange c Bodi b Van Jaarsveld	1	4	3	-	-
WC Hantam b Reddy	2	4	6	-	-
RK Kleinveldt not out	13	34	21	1	-
AC Dawson c Van Wyk b Mbhalati	0	2	2	-	-
CM Willoughby b Morkel	5	13	11	-	-
M Zondeki					
Extras (lb 6, w 10)	16				
TOTAL (44.1 overs)	**170**				

TITANS	Runs	Mins	Balls	4	6
AN Petersen c Tsolekile b Willoughby	26	63	49	2	-
GH Bodi c Davids b Willoughby	10	29	25	1	-
*M van Jaarsveld c Puttick b Willoughby	11	24	15	1	-
JG Myburgh not out	59	132	80	5	1
Z de Bruyn c De Lange b Harvey	10	36	31	1	-
G Dros lbw b De Lange	10	32	25	1	-
P de Bruyn lbw b De Lange	8	9	6	1	-
F du Plessis lbw b De Lange	11	9	10	2	-
†CFK van Wyk lbw b Harvey	13	27	19	1	-
BL Reddy not out	7	6	5	1	-
M Morkel					
NE Mbhalati					
Extras (lb 2, w 5, nb 1)	8				
TOTAL (for 8 wkts) (44 overs)	**173**				

Ttn	O	M	R	W
Morkel	8.1	2	24	2 (2 w)
Reddy	9	0	31	2 (4 w)
Mbhalati	9	1	32	3 (2 w)
Z de Bruyn	4	0	20	0 (1 w)
P de Bruyn	4	0	19	0
Du Plessis	4	0	17	0
Van Jaarsveld	4	0	14	1
Dros	2	0	7	0 (1 w)

Cob	O	M	R	W
Dawson	9	1	34	0
Willoughby	9	2	21	3
Harvey	9	2	23	2 (1 w)
Kleinveldt	8	1	45	0 (1 nb, 4 w)
De Lange	9	0	48	3

Fall of Wickets	Cob	Ttn
1st	19 (1)	22 (2)
2nd	25 (2)	46 (3)
3rd	51 (3)	49 (1)
4th	71 (5)	69 (5)
5th	131 (4)	91 (6)
6th	133 (7)	105 (7)
7th	136 (8)	125 (8)
8th	160 (6)	159 (9)
9th	161 (10)	-
10th	170 (11)	-

TITANS v WARRIORS

Standard Bank Cup

Played at Willowmoore Park, Benoni on 16 December 2005

Toss: Titans

Umpires: BG Jerling & S Wadvalla

Referee: MR Magiet

Debuts: Ttn: None. War: None

Result: Titans won by 6 wickets

Man of Match: Alviro Petersen

Points: War: 0; Ttn: 6

Notes: Titans substitute: F du Plessis replaced NE Mbhalati after 28.1 overs of Warriors' innings. Warriors substitute: S de Kock replaced A Jacobs after 1 over of Titans' innings.

WARRIORS	Runs	Mins	Balls	4	6
JP Kreusch c Bodi b Reddy	6	31	19	-	-
CC Bradfield c Myburgh b Steyn	3	27	25	-	-
*RJ Peterson c Dros b De Bruyn	56	127	71	5	1
A Jacobs c De Bruyn b Mbhalati	18	61	50	1	-
†AZM Dyili c Van Wyk b De Bruyn	19	27	30	2	-
LL Gamiet c Van Wyk b Steyn	2	12	10	-	-
MBA Smith c Van Wyk b Steyn	14	45	34	-	-
T Henderson c Petersen b Morkel	25	16	17	3	-
L Meyer not out	18	15	13	3	-
L Mbane not out	2	7	4	-	-
M Ngam					
S de Kock					
Extras (lb 7, w 13, nb 3)	23				
TOTAL (for 8 wkts) (45 overs)	**186**				

TITANS	Runs	Mins	Balls	4	6
GH Bodi c Peterson b De Kock	56	85	57	9	-
AN Petersen lbw b Peterson	72	98	82	10	1
*M van Jaarsveld b Peterson	1	6	6	-	-
JG Myburgh not out	21	35	33	3	-
G Dros c Dyili b De Kock	20	20	19	-	2
F du Plessis not out	9	8	10	2	-
P de Bruyn					
†CFK van Wyk					
BL Reddy					
DW Steyn					
M Morkel					
NE Mbhalati					
Extras (w 6, nb 2)	8				
TOTAL (for 4 wkts) (34.1 overs)	**187**				

Ttn	O	M	R	W
Steyn	9	0	29	3 (1 nb, 5 w)
Reddy	9	0	29	1 (1 nb, 6 w)
Morkel	9	0	42	1 (1 nb, 1 w)
Mbhalati	7	0	31	1 (1 w)
De Bruyn	7	0	27	2
Van Jaarsveld	2	0	11	0
Du Plessis	2	0	10	0

War	O	M	R	W
Henderson	6	1	27	0
Ngam	4	0	26	0 (2 nb, 2 w)
Kreusch	3.1	0	14	0
Meyer	1	0	13	0
Mbane	2	0	13	0 (1 w)
De Kock	9	0	48	2
Peterson	9	0	46	2 (1 w)

Fall of Wickets	War	Ttn
1st	15 (2)	133 (1)
2nd	16 (1)	136 (3)
3rd	74 (4)	139 (2)
4th	101 (5)	174 (5)
5th	112 (6)	-
6th	132 (3)	-
7th	161 (8)	-
8th	166 (7)	-

Warriors v Titans, Port Elizabeth, 23 December 2005. Titans won by 6 wickets.
Cape Cobras v Titans, Paarl, 30 December 2005. Titans won by 19 runs.
Dolphins v Titans, Pietermaritzburg, 2 January 2006. Dolphins won by 8 wickets.

Ga-Ramokoka

WARRIORS

Dolphins v Warriors, Durban, 25 November 2005. Dolphins won by 31 runs (D/L Method).

WARRIORS v EAGLES — Standard Bank Cup

Played at Mercedes-Benz Park, East London on 27 November 2005 — Toss: Warriors
Umpires: SB Lambson & LH Matroos — Referee: NC Pretorius
Debuts: War: None. Eag: None
Result: Eagles won by 6 wickets
Man of Match: Johan van der Wath
Points: Eag: 6; War: 0
Notes: Eagles substitute: PJ Koortzen replaced R Telemachus after 39 overs of Warriors' innings. Warriors substitute: L Mbane replaced AZM Dyili after 1 over of Eagles' innings.

WARRIORS	*Runs*	*Mins*	*Balls*	*4*	*6*
JP Kreusch c Thyssen b Van der Wath	4	29	26	-	-
*CC Bradfield c Bosman b Van der Wath	50	116	85	5	-
T Henderson c McLaren b Van der Wath	0	6	1	-	-
A Jacobs run out (Jacobs)	33	65	48	2	1
AZM Dyili b Thyssen	33	49	41	1	1
SC Pope c Van Wyk b Van der Wath	2	8	3	-	-
BC de Wett not out	31	59	43	2	-
†AM Sodumo c Van Wyk b Telemachus	1	5	6	-	-
D Willemse c Van Wyk b Telemachus	0	1	1	-	-
MW Olivier not out	14	28	17	-	-
M Ngam					
L Mbane					
Extras (lb 4, w 9, nb 1)	14				
TOTAL (for 8 wkts) (45 overs)	**182**				

EAGLES	*Runs*	*Mins*	*Balls*	*4*	*6*
†MN van Wyk b Henderson	0	1	3	-	-
LL Bosman c Kreusch b Olivier	11	34	21	2	-
PJ Koortzen c Kreusch b Henderson	15	23	21	3	-
JA Rudolph b Willemse	40	88	69	4	-
DJ Jacobs not out	80	108	77	7	3
*N Boje not out	21	28	22	3	-
RT Bailey					
CA Thyssen					
JJ van der Wath					
R McLaren					
WA Deacon					
R Telemachus					
Extras (lb 4, w 9, nb 3)	16				
TOTAL (for 4 wkts) (35 overs)	**183**				

Eag	*O*	*M*	*R*	*W*	
Van der Wath	9	0	35	4	(4 w)
Deacon	9	0	26	0	(1 nb, 1 w)
Telemachus	9	0	34	2	(1 w)
McLaren	8	0	39	0	(2 w)
Boje	6	0	29	0	(1 w)
Thyssen	4	0	15	1	

War	*O*	*M*	*R*	*W*	
Henderson	9	0	34	2	
Ngam	5	1	37	0	(1 w)
Olivier	3	0	21	1	(2 nb, 2 w)
Kreusch	7	0	37	0	(1 nb)
Mbane	6	2	21	0	(1 w)
Willemse	5	0	29	1	(3 w)

Fall of Wickets	*War*	*Eag*
1st	19 (1)	0 (1)
2nd	23 (3)	26 (3)
3rd	85 (4)	34 (2)
4th	103 (2)	145 (4)
5th	117 (6)	-
6th	139 (5)	-
7th	140 (8)	-
8th	140 (9)	-

WARRIORS v CAPE COBRAS — Standard Bank Cup

Played at Sahara Oval St George's, Port Elizabeth on 2 December 2005 (D/N) — Toss: Warriors
Umpires: SB Lambson & GH Pienaar — Referee: S Naidoo
Debuts: War: None. Cob: None
Result: Warriors won by 41 runs
Man of Match: Carl Bradfield
Points: War: 6; Cob: 0
Notes: Cape Cobras substitute: H Davids replaced CM Willoughby after 42 overs of Warriors' innings. Warriors substitute: MW Olivier replaced BC de Wett after 9 overs of Cape Cobras' innings.

WARRIORS	*Runs*	*Mins*	*Balls*	*4*	*6*
JP Kreusch b Zondeki	9	37	28	-	-
CC Bradfield not out	86	179	140	8	-
T Henderson c De Lange b Kleinveldt	8	20	9	1	-
A Jacobs c Telo b Kleinveldt	33	50	42	4	-
*RJ Peterson c Willoughby b De Lange	4	12	9	-	-
†AZM Dyili b De Lange	8	16	14	1	-
BC de Wett b Kleinveldt	10	24	18	-	-
LL Gamiet run out (Dawson)	11	13	12	1	-
L Mbane not out	0	3	1	-	-
L Meyer					
D Willemse					
MW Olivier					
Extras (lb 1, w 3, nb 3)	7				
TOTAL (for 7 wkts) (45 overs)	**176**				

CAPE COBRAS	*Runs*	*Mins*	*Balls*	*4*	*6*
AG Puttick c Dyili b Meyer	8	15	17	1	-
DJ Bassage b Henderson	2	19	11	-	-
J-P Duminy lbw b Olivier	22	51	42	4	-
FD Telo lbw b Peterson	53	85	53	7	-
*†TL Tsolekile c Gamiet b Olivier	0	11	11	-	-
H Davids c Kreusch b Olivier	1	6	2	-	-
CD de Lange c and b Willemse	15	37	15	2	-
VD Philander b Peterson	0	2	4	-	-
RK Kleinveldt c Kreusch b Olivier	11	27	24	2	-
AC Dawson not out	6	14	10	1	-
M Zondeki b Olivier	0	2	1	-	-
CM Willoughby					
Extras (lb 3, w 10, nb 4)	17				
TOTAL (30.5 overs)	**135**				

Cob	O	M	R	W	
Dawson	7	1	25	0	
Willoughby	9	1	27	0	
Zondeki	9	0	32	1	(1 nb, 2 w)
Kleinveldt	9	1	38	3	
Philander	3	0	21	0	(2 nb)
De Lange	8	0	32	2	(1 w)

War	O	M	R	W	
Henderson	9	1	18	1	(1 w)
Meyer	5	0	23	1	(3 w)
Mbane	2	0	13	0	
Olivier	5.5	0	53	5	(4 nb, 5 w)
Kreusch	3	0	9	0	(1 w)
Peterson	5	1	11	2	
Willemse	1	0	5	1	

Fall of Wickets	War	Cob
1st	27 (1)	14 (1)
2nd	43 (3)	15 (2)
3rd	106 (4)	71 (3)
4th	114 (5)	83 (5)
5th	131 (6)	87 (6)
6th	156 (7)	116 (4)
7th	171 (8)	116 (8)
8th	-	124 (7)
9th	-	135 (9)
10th	-	135 (11)

Eagles v Warriors, Bloemfontein, 4 December 2005. Warriors won by 8 wickets.
Lions v Warriors, Johannesburg, 9 December 2005. Lions won by 2 wickets.

WARRIORS v DOLPHINS — Standard Bank Cup

Played at Mercedes-Benz Park, East London on 12 December 2005 (D/N) — Toss: Warriors
Umpires: M Erasmus & S Wadvalla (TV: IL Howell) — Referee: A Barnes
Debuts: War: None. Dol: None
Result: Dolphins won by 3 wickets
Man of Match: Lance Klusener
Points: Dol: 5; War: 1
Notes: Dolphins substitute: RP Symcox replaced M Hayward after 41 overs of Warriors' innings. Warriors substitute: L Meyer replaced A Jacobs after 3 overs of Dolphins' innings.

WARRIORS	Runs	Mins	Balls	4	6
CC Bradfield b Klusener	12	34	23	1	-
JP Kreusch run out (HM Amla)	57	85	61	11	-
*RJ Peterson c Brown b Hayward	37	78	53	5	-
A Jacobs c Klusener b Hayward	49	80	73	4	-
LL Gamiet c Brown b Kent	21	38	24	3	-
T Henderson b Tweedie	28	22	14	3	2
†AZM Dyili b Abrahim	3	4	4	-	-
BC de Wett b Tweedie	3	13	9	-	-
L Mbane b Tweedie	4	12	10	-	-
D Willemse not out	1	4	1	-	-
M Ngam not out	1	1	1	-	-
L Meyer					
Extras (lb 2, w 2, nb 3)	7				
TOTAL (for 9 wkts) (45 overs)	**223**				

DOLPHINS	Runs	Mins	Balls	4	6
I Khan run out (Gamiet)	22	69	52	3	-
DJ Watson c and b Ngam	3	18	10	-	-
RP Symcox b Ngam	4	5	2	1	-
HM Amla run out (Meyer/Willemse)	37	71	52	3	-
AM Amla c and b Peterson	10	14	17	2	-
DM Benkenstein st Dyili b Peterson	46	52	44	3	1
JC Kent b Meyer	42	53	53	2	1
†DL Brown not out	17	36	19	1	-
*L Klusener not out	39	22	17	-	5
ZA Abrahim					
ANW Tweedie					
M Hayward					
Extras (lb 3, w 3, nb 1)	7				
TOTAL (for 7 wkts) (44.1 overs)	**227**				

Dol	O	M	R	W	
Klusener	9	0	38	1	(1 nb, 1 w)
Tweedie	9	0	40	3	
Kent	5	0	32	1	(2 nb, 1 w)
Hayward	9	1	47	2	
Abrahim	7	1	34	1	
Benkenstein	6	0	30	0	

War	O	M	R	W	
Henderson	8	2	38	0	
Ngam	6	0	27	2	(1 nb)
Mbane	8.1	0	43	0	
Meyer	6	0	31	1	
Peterson	9	0	34	2	(1 w)
Willemse	6	0	45	0	(1 w)
Kreusch	1	0	6	0	

Fall of Wickets	War	Dol
1st	37 (1)	13 (2)
2nd	103 (2)	17 (3)
3rd	127 (3)	55 (1)
4th	174 (5)	74 (5)
5th	211 (4)	81 (4)
6th	214 (7)	164 (6)
7th	214 (6)	180 (7)
8th	221 (8)	-
9th	222 (9)	-

Titans v Warriors, Benoni, 16 December 2005. Titans won by 6 wickets.
Cape Cobras v Warriors, Paarl, 18 December 2005. Warriors won by 4 wickets.

WARRIORS v TITANS — Standard Bank Cup

Played at Sahara Oval St George's, Port Elizabeth on 23 December 2005 (D/N) — Toss: Warriors
Umpires: MW Brown & KH Hurter (TV: S George) — Referee: A Barnes
Debuts: War: None. Ttn: None
Result: Titans won by 6 wickets
Man of Match: Martin van Jaarsveld
Points: War: 1; Ttn: 5
Notes: Titans substitute: F du Plessis replaced M Morkel after 21 overs of Warriors' innings. Warriors substitute: S de Kock replaced A Jacobs after 17 overs of Titans' innings.

WARRIORS	Runs	Mins	Balls	4	6
CC Bradfield run out (Steyn)	23	57	41	3	-
JP Kreusch run out (Myburgh/Van Wyk)	46	88	69	8	-
*RJ Peterson c Reddy b De Bruyn	90	101	82	9	2
A Jacobs not out	54	90	68	6	-
T Henderson not out	19	21	14	2	-
LL Gamiet					
MBA Smith					
†AZM Dyili					
J Botha					
L Meyer					
M Ngam					
S de Kock					
Extras (lb 2, w 8, nb 4)	14				
TOTAL (for 3 wkts) (45 overs)	**246**				

TITANS	Runs	Mins	Balls	4	6
AN Petersen lbw b Meyer	51	76	57	9	1
GH Bodi st Dyili b Peterson	51	94	64	6	2
*M van Jaarsveld c and b Botha	62	76	67	2	1
JG Myburgh not out	56	76	65	5	-
G Dros c Bradfield b De Kock	8	10	10	-	-
F du Plessis not out	8	6	3	-	1
P de Bruyn					
†CFK van Wyk					
BL Reddy					
DW Steyn					
NE Mbhalati					
M Morkel					
Extras (lb 1, w 9, nb 4)	14				
TOTAL (for 4 wkts) (44 overs)	**250**				

Ttn	O	M	R	W
Steyn	9	0	38	0 (2 nb, 3 w)
Reddy	9	0	48	0 (3 w)
Morkel	5	0	41	0 (2 nb, 1 w)
Mbhalati	7	0	38	0
De Bruyn	9	0	46	1 (1 w)
Van Jaarsveld	2	0	12	0
Myburgh	1	0	9	0
Du Plessis	3	0	12	0

War	O	M	R	W
Henderson	9	1	32	0 (1 w)
Kreusch	5	0	41	0 (1 w)
Ngam	6	0	36	0 (4 nb, 3 w)
Meyer	4	0	32	1 (2 w)
Peterson	7	0	39	1 (2 w)
Botha	9	0	51	1
De Kock	4	0	18	1

Fall of Wickets	War	Ttn
1st	57 (1)	104 (1)
2nd	107 (2)	120 (2)
3rd	204 (3)	222 (3)
4th	-	237 (5)

WARRIORS v LIONS

Standard Bank Cup

Played at Sahara Oval St George's, Port Elizabeth on 2 January 2006
Toss: Warriors
Umpires: JD Cloete & LH Matroos
Referee: CJ Mitchley
Debuts: War: None. Lio: None
Result: Lions won by 17 runs
Man of Match: Stephen Cook
Points: War: 1; Lio: 5
Notes: Henderson scored his off 35 balls in Warriors' innings. Lions substitute: VB van Jaarsveld replaced S Chatterjee after 33.2 overs of Lions' innings. Warriors substitute: S de Kock replaced BB Kops after 28 overs of Lions' innings.

LIONS	Runs	Mins	Balls	4	6
AM Bacher c Peterson b Ngam	41	59	56	5	2
SC Cook c Peterson b De Kock	90	155	105	7	1
*ND McKenzie b Ngam	0	1	3	-	-
†MJ Harris c Jacobs b Peterson	39	70	53	2	2
VB van Jaarsveld not out	52	44	42	5	2
AJ Hall c Smith b Henderson	14	17	11	1	-
DL Makalima not out	2	4	3	-	-
F de Wet					
WL Coetsee					
EO Moleon					
ET Nkwe					
S Chatterjee					
Extras (lb 2, w 20, nb 3)	25				
TOTAL (for 5 wkts) (45 overs)	**263**				

WARRIORS	Runs	Mins	Balls	4	6
CC Bradfield c Moleon b De Wet	12	27	26	2	-
JP Kreusch st Harris b Moleon	32	73	53	5	-
*RJ Peterson lbw b Hall	0	5	3	-	-
A Jacobs b De Wet	3	12	10	-	-
LL Gamiet c Hall b Nkwe	16	62	21	2	-
MBA Smith lbw b Bacher	27	35	32	3	1
†AZM Dyili c McKenzie b Moleon	51	62	49	3	3
T Henderson not out	79	69	48	5	6
L Meyer c McKenzie b Moleon	12	11	9	2	-
S de Kock c Hall b Coetsee	0	4	2	-	-
M Ngam lbw b Hall	3	13	5	-	-
BB Kops					
Extras (lb 3, w 3, nb 5)	11				
TOTAL (42.1 overs)	**246**				

War	O	M	R	W
Henderson	9	1	50	1 (1 nb, 1 w)
Kreusch	3	0	24	0 (4 w)
Kops	3	0	30	0 (4 w)
Ngam	7	2	28	2 (3 w)
Meyer	9	0	44	0 (2 nb, 3 w)
Peterson	9	0	43	1
De Kock	5	0	42	1

Lio	O	M	R	W
De Wet	9	1	41	2 (1 nb, 2 w)
Hall	8.1	1	25	2 (1 w)
Moleon	9	0	46	3
Nkwe	5	1	28	1 (3 nb)
Coetsee	6	0	60	1
Bacher	5	0	43	1 (1 nb)

Fall of Wickets	Lio	War
1st	80 (1)	22 (1)
2nd	80 (3)	23 (3)
3rd	181 (4)	32 (4)
4th	231 (2)	66 (2)
5th	259 (6)	72 (5)
6th	-	112 (6)
7th	-	181 (7)
8th	-	214 (9)
9th	-	227 (10)
10th	-	246 (11)

ALMOST THERE . . . Goolam Bodi's century made sure the Titans beat the Dolphins in their Standard Bank Cup semi-final *Picture: DUIF DU TOIT, Touchline Photo*

SEMI-FINALS

LIONS v EAGLES — Standard Bank Cup Semi-final

Played at Liberty Life Wanderers Stadium, Johannesburg on 6 January 2006 (D/N) — Toss: Lions
Umpires: S George & IL Howell (TV: MW Brown) — Referee: CJ Mitchley
Debuts: Lio: None. Eag: None
Result: Eagles won by 34 runs
Man of Match: Morne van Wyk
Notes: Lions substitute: DJ Terbrugge replaced S Chatterjee after 9 overs of Eagles' innings.

The Lions once again lost their composure in a key game against their nemesis the Eagles, with the visitors making use of their closing overs to push their total beyond the reach of the home side.

Van Wyk and Bosman saw off the new ball with a second-wicket stand of 62 in 11 overs after the Eagles had been sent in to bat, with Bosman scoring at better than a run-a-ball before being deceived by a slower ball from Moleon.

Captain Van Wyk batted through to the 37th over in a composed innings that laid the perfect platform for the Eagles before he was well caught at third man, while Bailey kept the pressure on the Lions bowlers with some delightful innovations. But the chief destroyer was Telemachus, who lashed three fours and a six off 15 balls to ensure a challenging total became a match-winning one.

Lions openers Bacher and Cook put on 76 but struggled to accelerate against the nagging Eagles seamers. The loss of Bacher to a contentious leg-before decision was a terminal blow to the hopes of the Lions, with the rest of the batsmen unable to deal with an asking rate of eight to the over, McLaren finishing with career-best figures.

EAGLES	*Runs*	*Mins*	*Balls*	*4*	*6*
JA Beukes c Harris b Chatterjee	1	21	16	-	-
*†MN van Wyk c Coetsee b De Wet	86	148	101	11	-
LL Bosman b Moleon	40	48	39	7	1
DJ Jacobs c Cook b Moleon	2	17	12	-	-
RT Bailey run out (McKenzie/Harris)	68	87	65	6	1
JJ van der Wath lbw b Coetsee	16	16	17	2	-
R Telemachus not out	31	20	15	3	1
D du Preez not out	13	10	6	1	1
R McLaren					
WA Deacon					
T Tshabalala					
Extras (lb 1, w 4, nb 1)	6				
TOTAL (for 6 wkts) (45 overs)	**263**				

LIONS	*Runs*	*Mins*	*Balls*	*4*	*6*
AM Bacher lbw b McLaren	48	62	61	7	-
SC Cook c Deacon b Du Preez	71	141	76	6	1
*ND McKenzie c Van Wyk b McLaren	6	15	11	1	-
†MJ Harris lbw b Tshabalala	23	30	32	2	-
VB van Jaarsveld run out (McLaren)	22	51	29	1	-
WL Coetsee b Tshabalala	15	13	12	2	-
DL Makalima c Bosman b McLaren	9	11	8	-	-
EO Moleon not out	10	31	7	1	-
F de Wet b McLaren	11	11	9	2	-
ET Nkwe c Du Preez b Telemachus	2	7	6	-	-
DJ Terbrugge c Bailey b Van der Wath	0	4	3	-	-
S Chatterjee					
Extras (b 1, lb 2, w 9)	12				
TOTAL (42.2 overs)	**229**				

Lio	*O*	*M*	*R*	*W*	
De Wet	9	2	37	1	(1 nb)
Chatterjee	4	0	25	1	(1 w)
Terbrugge	5	0	35	0	(1 w)
Moleon	9	0	53	2	(1 w)
Nkwe	3	1	15	0	
Bacher	6	0	35	0	
Coetsee	9	0	62	1	(1 w)

Eag	*O*	*M*	*R*	*W*	
Van der Wath	7.2	0	38	1	(3 w)
Deacon	7	0	37	0	(1 w)
Du Preez	7	0	48	1	
McLaren	9	0	43	4	(3 w)
Tshabalala	9	0	46	2	(2 w)
Telemachus	3	0	14	1	

Fall of Wickets	*Eag*	*Lio*
1st	23 (1)	76 (1)
2nd	85 (3)	96 (3)
3rd	98 (4)	129 (4)
4th	183 (2)	171 (2)
5th	216 (6)	190 (6)
6th	230 (5)	198 (5)
7th	-	203 (7)
8th	-	223 (9)
9th	-	227 (10)
10th	-	229 (11)

TITANS v DOLPHINS

Standard Bank Cup Semi-final

Played at SuperSport Park, Centurion on 8 January 2006
Toss: Titans
Umpires: BG Jerling & MZ Nanabhay (TV: JD Cloete)
Referee: WA Diedricks
Debuts: Ttn: None. Dol: None
Result: Titans won by 10 wickets
Man of Match: Goolam Bodi & AB de Villiers
Notes: Bodi scored his century off 71 balls in Titans' innings. Dolphins substitute: JC Kent replaced DJ Watson after 9 overs of Titans' innings.

The Titans advanced to a second successive final against the Eagles, this time at home, as they demolished the Dolphins, racing to their target in just 157 balls. The Dolphins were unfortunate to lose an important toss and then to come up against De Villiers at his absolute best and Bodi at his cheekiest.

Batting first on a damp, overcast morning, the Dolphins were not able to get any momentum, Reddy and Mbhalati making great use of the conditions. The Amla brothers added 96 in 22 overs, but both were dismissed in successive overs and Klusener was bowled by Mbhalati for a duck four balls later. Benkenstein and Brown did well to haul the Dolphins past 200, but it was never going to be enough as De Villiers and Bodi went on the rampage on a pitch that had flattened out.

De Villiers, who had only flown back to South Africa from Australia the day before, was the initial aggressor with an array of delightful strokes before cramp slowed him down. Bodi then took over and raced to his century with a clinical display of big hitting.

DOLPHINS	*Runs*	*Mins*	*Balls*	*4*	*6*
I Khan c De Villiers b Reddy	15	44	37	-	-
DJ Watson c Van Jaarsveld b Reddy	23	58	43	2	-
HM Amla c Bodi b Steyn	38	97	62	3	-
AM Amla c De Villiers b Mbhalati	53	87	77	5	-
DM Benkenstein not out	31	38	27	4	-
*L Klusener b Mbhalati	0	4	4	-	-
†DL Brown not out	26	30	22	3	-
ANW Tweedie					
ZA Abrahim					
YA Abdullah					
M Hayward					
JC Kent					
Extras (b 4, lb 8, w 12, nb 2)	26				
TOTAL (for 5 wkts) (45 overs)	**212**				

TITANS	*Runs*	*Mins*	*Balls*	*4*	*6*
†AB de Villiers not out	97	112	83	11	2
GH Bodi not out	104	112	71	10	6
*M van Jaarsveld					
JG Myburgh					
G Dros					
JA Morkel					
P de Bruyn					
AM Phangiso					
BL Reddy					
DW Steyn					
NE Mbhalati					
Extras (lb 9, w 7, nb 1)	17				
TOTAL (for 0 wkts) (25.3 overs)	**218**				

Ttn	*O*	*M*	*R*	*W*	
Steyn	9	0	45	1	(2 nb, 2 w)
Reddy	9	0	31	2	(6 w)
Mbhalati	9	1	32	2	(3 w)
Morkel	8	0	38	0	(1 w)
De Bruyn	7	0	42	0	
Phangiso	3	0	12	0	

Dol	*O*	*M*	*R*	*W*	
Tweedie	7	1	42	0	
Abdullah	3	0	24	0	(1 w)
Hayward	3	0	25	0	
Kent	2	0	17	0	(1 nb)
Abrahim	4	0	27	0	
Klusener	2	0	19	0	(2 w)
Khan	2	0	26	0	
Benkenstein	1	0	5	0	
HM Amla	1.3	0	24	0	

Fall of Wickets	*Dol*	*Ttn*
1st	39 (1)	-
2nd	51 (2)	-
3rd	147 (3)	-
4th	148 (4)	-
5th	149 (6)	-

FINAL

TITANS v EAGLES

Standard Bank Cup Final

Played at SuperSport Park, Centurion on 13 January 2006 (D/N)
Toss: Eagles
Umpires: M Erasmus & KH Hurter (TV: MZ Nanabhay)
Referee: MR Magiet
Debuts: Ttn: None. Eag: None
Result: Eagles won by 2 wickets
Man of Match: Johan van der Wath
Notes: Titans substitute: JA Morkel replaced M Morkel after 26.2 overs of Titans' innings.

STANDARD BANK CUP

The Eagles lower-order guided them to a second successive Standard Bank Cup win after a determined Titans fightback with the ball made up for their batting failures. The Free Staters have one of the deepest batting line-ups in the country and it came to their rescue after Morkel's three wickets in 10 balls reduced them to 83-6.

Van der Wath and McLaren withstood some fiery pace bowling before the Eagles charged over the finish line on the back of successive boundaries by Telemachus.

With rain about, causing two delays, the Titans failed to adapt to the conditions batting first and Van der Wath removed key batsmen De Villiers and the experienced Van Jaarsveld in his opening spell.

With the ball zipping about, the diminutive Myburgh showed a lot of courage but it was the fighting spirit of De Bruyn that at least gave the Titans something to bowl at, despite his involvement in the run-outs of Morkel and Reddy.

The Titans bowlers restored respect for the home side in front of a capacity crowd, but they lost their disciplines too often, 36 extras proving crucial in the defeat.

The Titans started poorly in the field with Steyn having Van Wyk dropped twice in his first seven deliveries. They fought back admirably, however, and it was the Eagles tail that eventually had to secure victory in a thrilling finale, Van der Wath once again proving his worth.

The win earned the Eagles R500 000.

TITANS	Runs	Mins	Balls	4	6
†AB de Villiers c Van Wyk b Van der Wath	0	2	4	-	-
GH Bodi c Bosman b Deacon	11	39	21	2	-
*M van Jaarsveld b Van der Wath	4	12	9	1	-
JG Myburgh c Van Wyk b Tshabalala	44	89	63	6	-
G Dros lbw b Telemachus	0	12	7	-	-
P de Bruyn c Bosman b Van der Wath	54	120	92	4	2
AM Phangiso lbw b Boje	0	9	13	-	-
JA Morkel run out (Jacobs)	2	5	7	-	-
BL Reddy run out (Tshabalala/Van Wyk)	6	14	14	-	-
DW Steyn c McLaren b Tshabalala	1	4	7	-	-
NE Mbhalati not out	5	32	20	-	-
M Morkel					
Extras (lb 1, w 12, nb 2)	15				
TOTAL (42.3 overs)	**142**				

EAGLES	Runs	Mins	Balls	4	6
†MN van Wyk lbw b Mbhalati	14	60	40	1	-
DJ Jacobs c Mbhalati b Reddy	8	23	15	2	-
LL Bosman c De Bruyn b Mbhalati	9	24	21	1	-
RT Bailey lbw b JA Morkel	7	53	23	-	-
JA Beukes lbw b JA Morkel	19	59	42	2	-
*N Boje c Bodi b JA Morkel	0	4	2	-	-
JJ van der Wath c Dros b Mbhalati	20	64	42	2	-
R McLaren not out	20	81	39	2	-
WA Deacon c Van Jaarsveld b Steyn	0	9	6	-	-
R Telemachus not out	10	20	12	2	-
T Tshabalala					
Extras (b 1, lb 10, w 19, nb 6)	36				
TOTAL (for 8 wkts) (39.2 overs)	**143**				

Eag	O	M	R	W	
Van der Wath	7.3	0	25	3	(3 w)
Deacon	5	1	20	1	(1 nb, 4 w)
Telemachus	5	1	23	1	
McLaren	7	0	23	0	(1 nb, 1 w)
Boje	9	1	26	1	
Tshabalala	9	0	24	2	(4 w)

Ttn	O	M	R	W	
Steyn	9	1	36	1	(3 nb, 5 w)
Reddy	9	2	24	1	(3 w)
Mbhalati	9	1	39	3	(3 nb, 5 w)
JA Morkel	9	3	19	3	(2 w)
Phangiso	1	0	5	0	
De Bruyn	2	0	8	0	
Dros	0.2	0	1	0	

Fall of Wickets	Ttn	Eag
1st	0 (1)	22 (2)
2nd	12 (3)	42 (3)
3rd	28 (2)	48 (1)
4th	37 (5)	72 (4)
5th	82 (4)	72 (6)
6th	86 (7)	83 (5)
7th	89 (8)	121 (7)
8th	103 (9)	123 (9)
9th	104 (10)	-
10th	142 (6)	-

ANOTHER ONE DOWN . . . Roger Telemachus claims the wicket of Gerald Dros in the Standard Bank Cup final *Picture: LEE WARREN, Touchline Photo*

OTHER LIMITED OVERS MATCHES

JH KALLIS' INVITATION XI v SOUTH AFRICAN XI — Limited Overs Match

Played at Sahara Park Newlands, Cape Town on 16 September 2005 (D/N) — Toss: South African XI

Umpires: M Erasmus & LH Matroos (TV: MW Brown)

Result: South African XI won by 3 runs

Man of Match: Salman Butt

Notes: M Ngam took a hat-trick in South African XI's innings. His victims were Pollock, Ntini, Nel.

SOUTH AFRICAN XI	*Runs*	*Mins*	*Balls*	*4*	*6*
*GC Smith c De Villiers b Donald	69	90	66	8	1
HH Dippenaar c De Villiers b Mohammad Sami	0	1	3	-	-
AJ Hall b Donald	34	78	45	6	-
N Boje run out (Kirsten/De Villiers)	5	17	8	-	-
AG Prince c Johnson b Mohammad Sami	54	114	74	2	1
JM Kemp b Kallis	9	36	29	1	-
†MV Boucher lbw b Klusener	3	13	10	-	-
SM Pollock b Ngam	57	51	61	3	2
M Ntini c Johnson b Ngam	0	1	1	-	-
CK Langeveldt not out	1	6	5	-	-
A Nel c Lara b Ngam	0	2	1	-	-
Extras (lb 3, w 15, nb 8)	26				
TOTAL (49.1 overs)	**258**				

JH KALLIS' INVITATION XI	*Runs*	*Mins*	*Balls*	*4*	*6*
†AB de Villiers c Boucher b Pollock	0	2	4	-	-
Salman Butt c Boje b Hall	102	205	144	8	1
*JH Kallis c Kemp b Langeveldt	10	48	32	1	-
BC Lara c Dippenaar b Ntini	31	79	43	2	1
JN Rhodes lbw b Boje	12	16	10	1	-
G Kirsten c Pollock b Boje	22	28	17	3	1
L Klusener b Hall	44	50	38	5	1
NC Johnson not out	10	28	7	-	1
Mohammad Sami b Hall	6	18	8	-	-
M Ngam					
AA Donald					
Extras (lb 6, w 9, nb 3)	18				
TOTAL (for 8 wkts) (50 overs)	**255**				

Kall	*O*	*M*	*R*	*W*	
Mohammad Sami	8	1	39	2	(2 w)
Ngam	7.1	0	57	3	(2 nb, 3 w)
Klusener	8	0	53	1	(6 nb, 2 w)
Donald	8	0	42	2	(3 w)
Kallis	6	1	17	1	(1 w)
Rhodes	8	0	28	0	
Kirsten	3	0	13	0	(2 w)
Johnson	1	0	6	0	(1 w)

SAXI	*O*	*M*	*R*	*W*	
Pollock	6	0	11	1	(2 w)
Ntini	8	1	19	1	
Nel	9	1	56	0	(1 w)
Langeveldt	7	1	27	1	(2 nb)
Hall	9	0	49	3	(1 nb, 4 w)
Boje	7	0	62	2	
Smith	4	0	25	0	

Fall of Wickets	*SAXI*	*Kall*
1st	1 (2)	1 (1)
2nd	105 (3)	24 (3)
3rd	118 (1)	103 (4)
4th	123 (4)	127 (5)
5th	149 (6)	159 (6)
6th	156 (7)	220 (2)
7th	257 (8)	239 (7)
8th	257 (9)	255 (9)
9th	258 (5)	-
10th	258 (11)	-

JH KALLIS' INVITATION XI v SOUTH AFRICAN XI — Limited Overs Match

Played at SuperSport Park, Centurion on 18 September 2005 — Toss: JH Kallis' Invitation XI

Umpires: M Erasmus & LH Matroos (TV: MW Brown)

Result: South African XI won by 167 runs

Man of Match: Gary Kirsten

SOUTH AFRICAN XI	*Runs*	*Mins*	*Balls*	*4*	*6*
*GC Smith st De Villiers b Salman Butt	79	98	59	11	2
HH Dippenaar run out (Dawson)	54	62	45	8	1
N Boje st De Villiers b Salman Butt	39	68	42	3	-
ND McKenzie c sub b Ngam	61	74	63	7	1
AG Prince not out	84	74	61	8	1
JM Kemp b Mohammad Sami	16	28	16	1	-
†MV Boucher not out	28	25	17	2	1
AJ Hall					
SM Pollock					
CK Langeveldt					
A Nel					
Extras (lb 3, w 18, nb 2)	23				
TOTAL (for 5 wkts) (50 overs)	**384**				

JH KALLIS' INVITATION XI	*Runs*	*Mins*	*Balls*	*4*	*6*
Salman Butt c Kemp b Nel	12	33	27	2	-
†AB de Villiers c Smith b Pollock	19	29	21	4	-
*JH Kallis c Boucher b Langeveldt	19	52	21	3	-
BC Lara b Nel	4	10	8	1	-
G Kirsten c Boucher b Langeveldt	85	102	73	11	1
NC Johnson c Langeveldt b Smith	43	49	37	5	1
L Klusener b Langeveldt	8	25	11	1	-
Mohammad Sami c Nel b Langeveldt	7	7	9	1	-
AC Dawson b Boje	2	7	4	-	-
AA Donald b Boje	1	7	2	-	-
M Ngam not out	1	3	3	-	-
Extras (lb 3, w 5, nb 8)	16				
TOTAL (34.5 overs)	**217**				

Kall	*O*	*M*	*R*	*W*	
Mohammad Sami	7	0	56	1	(4 w)
Ngam	6	0	63	1	(1 nb, 3 w)
Dawson	9	0	66	0	(2 w)
Donald	5	0	35	0	(1 w)
Kallis	7	0	49	0	
Klusener	7	0	48	0	(1 nb, 3 w)
Salman Butt	9	0	64	2	(2 w)

SAXI	*O*	*M*	*R*	*W*	
Pollock	6	0	32	1	(5 nb)
Nel	8	1	44	2	(1 w)
Langeveldt	7	0	49	4	(2 nb)
Hall	6	0	38	0	(2 w)
Boje	3.5	0	25	2	
Smith	4	0	26	1	(2 w)

Fall of Wickets	*SAXI*	*Kall*
1st	109 (2)	39 (2)
2nd	163 (1)	39 (1)
3rd	219 (3)	51 (4)
4th	278 (4)	100 (3)
5th	327 (6)	184 (6)
6th	-	205 (5)
7th	-	213 (8)
8th	-	214 (7)
9th	-	216 (9)
10th	-	217 (10)

STANDARD BANK PRO20

Ken Borland

The third season of the Standard Bank Pro20 proved at least one thing beyond dispute – it's not just the TV networks that love cricket's most abbreviated form. While crowds remained poor for all other domestic cricket, the fans kept flocking to Pro20 matches. Record total crowds of over 150 000 people pitched up for the 18 games of the 2005/06 competition with average match attendances nudging 10 000 at every venue.

The Warriors were quickly knocked out of contention, losing all five of their games, but otherwise the competition reached an exciting conclusion, with the five other teams all in contention for the semi-finals heading into the final round of matches.

The Eagles went on to be well-deserved winners of the title, having won four of their round robin matches and winning both the final and their semi-final in convincing fashion.

Twenty-over cricket may be considered a lottery in some quarters but the Eagles have won 13 of their 20 matches in the competition and have claimed two titles. Clearly the dominant team in South African limited overs cricket are doing something right.

Loots Bosman remained consistently the most dangerous batsman in Pro20 cricket, while Morne van Wyk also gave several attacks a thorough thrashing.

But probably the main reason the Eagles beat most other teams was that they had the two top bowlers in the competition in Cliffie Deacon and Roger Telemachus. The joint leading wicket-takers, with 12 apiece, were also the two most economical bowlers in the series.

The other sides had individual stars – even the woeful Warriors had two of the better bowlers in Tyron Henderson and Justin Kreusch.

AB de Villiers was in excellent form for the Titans and finished as the leading run-scorer (236) despite his team's shock exit at the semi-final stage at the hands of the Cobras.

Neil McKenzie was one of the big success stories with the bat as well, culminating in a shock return to the national side for their Pro20 international against Australia after two years in the wilderness.

Cobras opening bowler Alan Dawson continued to maintain his stellar reputation as a limited-overs expert, playing a key role in the Western Cape team's three wins.

STANDARD BANK PRO20 2005/06

	P	W	L	T	NR	Bonus	Pts	Net RR
Eagles	5	4	1	0	0	1	21	1.39
Titans	5	4	1	0	0	0	21	0.50
Cape Cobras	5	3	2	0	0	0	17	-0.07
Lions	5	2	3	0	0	2	15	0.68
Dolphins	5	2	3	0	0	0	13	0.01
Warriors	5	0	5	0	0	0	3	-2.08

Eagles finish ahead of Titans by virtue of winning the match between them.

STANDARD BANK PRO20

BATTING

Best Strike Rates

Name	Runs	Avg	SR
AM Blignaut (Lio)	145	72.50	170.58
LL Bosman (Eag)	181	25.85	166.05
AB de Villiers (Ttn)	236	47.20	160.54
K Smit (Dol)	165	33.00	151.37
DM Benkenstein (Dol)	143	35.75	140.19

(Qualification: 100 runs)

Most Runs

Name	Runs	Avg	SR
AB de Villiers (Ttn)	236	47.20	160.54
ND McKenzie (Lio)	215	53.75	127.21
MN van Wyk (Eag)	202	33.66	109.18
J-P Duminy (Cob)	199	33.16	104.18
LL Bosman (Eag)	181	25.85	166.05

Best Averages

Name	Runs	Avg	SR
TL Tsolekile (Cob)	107	107.00	115.05
AM Blignaut (Lio)	145	72.50	170.58
ND McKenzie (Lio)	215	53.75	127.21
AB de Villiers (Ttn)	236	47.20	160.54
DM Benkenstein (Dol)	143	35.75	140.19

(Qualification: 100 runs)

Most Sixes

14	AB de Villiers (Ttn)
10	LL Bosman (Eag)
8	AM Blignaut (Lio)

BOWLING

Best Economy Rates

Name	Wkts	Avg	RpO
WA Deacon (Eag)	12	11.33	4.85
R Telemachus (Eag)	12	11.66	5.83
T Henderson (War)	5	21.00	6.17
CM Willoughby (Cob)	4	40.25	6.44
PR Adams (Cob)	5	26.40	6.60

(Qualification: 15 overs)

Most Wickets

Name	Wkts	Avg	RpO
WA Deacon (Eag)	12	11.33	4.85
R Telemachus (Eag)	12	11.66	5.83
AC Dawson (Cob)	11	16.90	7.15
BL Reddy (Ttn)	10	15.00	8.10
JP Kreusch (War)	8	10.25	6.83
ZA Abrahim (Dol)	8	21.75	9.15

Chill
Coca-Cola
Coca-Cola and the Design of the Contour Bottle are registered trademarks of The Coca-Cola Company © 2006.
P69168

Best Averages

Name	Wkts	Avg	RpO
JP Kreusch (War)	8	10.25	6.83
WA Deacon (Eag)	12	11.33	4.85
R Telemachus (Eag)	12	11.66	5.83
BL Reddy (Ttn)	10	15.00	8.10
P de Bruyn (Ttn)	7	16.57	7.17

(Qualification: 5 wickets)

WICKETKEEPING AND FIELDING

Most dismissals

Name	M	Ct	St	R/O	Total
TL Tsolekile (Cob)	8	10	1	2	13
MN van Wyk (Eag)	7	6	2	0	8
MJ Harris (Lio)	6	2	0	6	8
DJ Jacobs (Eag)	7	6	0	1	7
M van Jaarsveld (Ttn)	7	5	0	1	6
P de Bruyn (Ttn)	7	2	0	4	6

ROUND ROBIN MATCHES

DOLPHINS v TITANS — Standard Bank Pro20

Played at Sahara Stadium Kingsmead, Durban on 18 January 2006 (D/N) — Toss: Titans
Umpires: SB Lambson & S Wadvalla (TV: GH Pienaar) — Referee: S Naidoo
Debuts: Dol: YA Abdullah and R Frylinck (Both 20). Ttn: AM Phangiso (20)
Result: Titans won by 9 runs (D/L method), target revised to 136 in 15.1 overs
Master Blaster: Martin van Jaarsveld
Points: Dol: 1; Ttn: 5
Notes: Dolphins substitute: R Frylinck replaced M Hayward after 13 overs of Titans' innings. Titans substitute: Z de Bruyn replaced JG Myburgh after 8 overs of Dolphins' innings.

TITANS	Runs	Mins	Balls	4	6
†AB de Villiers c D Smit b Klusener	27	16	19	4	1
GH Bodi c Kent b Hayward	20	31	18	4	-
*M van Jaarsveld run out (D Smit)	57	59	44	6	1
G Dros c Klusener b Abrahim	29	26	18	2	2
JA Morkel c AM Amla b Abdullah	1	5	4	-	-
BL Reddy c Frylinck b Abrahim	8	8	4	-	1
JG Myburgh b Abrahim	7	11	5	1	-
P de Bruyn not out	19	8	9	1	1
AM Phangiso					
M Morkel					
NE Mbhalati					
Z de Bruyn					
Extras (lb 5, w 4, nb 2)	11				
TOTAL (for 7 wkts) (20 overs)	**179**				

DOLPHINS	Runs	Mins	Balls	4	6
HM Amla b Reddy	19	15	15	4	-
K Smit c Van Jaarsveld b Reddy	2	12	6	-	-
JC Kent c P de Bruyn b Mbhalati	8	7	8	-	1
R Frylinck c Van Jaarsveld b Mbhalati	6	20	8	1	-
AM Amla c M Morkel b JA Morkel	22	30	22	3	-
DM Benkenstein not out	43	31	28	5	1
*L Klusener not out	3	15	6	-	-
†D Smit					
ANW Tweedie					
ZA Abrahim					
YA Abdullah					
M Hayward					
Extras (lb 11, w 8, nb 4)	23				
TOTAL (for 5 wkts) (15.1 overs)	**126**				

Dol	O	M	R	W
Tweedie	4	0	52	0 (1 w)
Abdullah	4	0	36	1 (2 w)
Klusener	4	0	31	1 (1 nb, 1 w)
Hayward	4	0	25	1
Abrahim	4	0	30	3

Ttn	O	M	R	W
M Morkel	2	0	12	0 (1 w)
Reddy	2	0	13	2 (2 w)
Mbhalati	4	0	24	2 (2 w)
JA Morkel	4	0	28	1 (1 nb, 2 w)
Z de Bruyn	2	0	23	0
P de Bruyn	1.1	0	15	0 (1 nb, 1 w)

Fall of Wickets	Ttn	Dol
1st	39 (1)	25 (2)
2nd	60 (2)	26 (1)
3rd	120 (4)	36 (3)
4th	125 (5)	62 (4)
5th	152 (6)	95 (5)
6th	154 (3)	-
7th	179 (7)	-

CAPE COBRAS v DOLPHINS

Standard Bank Pro20

Played at Sahara Park Newlands, Cape Town on 20 January 2006 (D/N) — Toss: Dolphins
Umpires: MW Brown & M Erasmus (TV: LH Matroos) — Referee: WA Diedricks
Debuts: Cob: FD Telo (20). Dol: None
Result: Cape Cobras won by 8 runs
Master Blasters: J-P Duminy & Quinton Friend
Points: Dol: 1; Cob: 5
Notes: Cape Cobras substitute: Q Friend replaced AG Puttick after 8 overs of Dolphins' innings. Dolphins substitute: R Frylinck replaced M Hayward after 12 overs of Cape Cobras' innings.

CAPE COBRAS	*Runs*	*Mins*	*Balls*	*4*	*6*
IJ Harvey c Hayward b Abdullah	13	14	16	2	-
AG Puttick c Klusener b Kent	29	58	33	1	-
J-P Duminy not out	67	70	50	5	2
RK Kleinveldt c Frylinck b Abrahim	20	14	12	3	-
H Davids c K Smit b Tweedie	12	5	5	1	1
R Munnik run out (K Smit/D Smit)	10	5	4	-	1
FD Telo					
*†TL Tsolekile					
AC Dawson					
PR Adams					
CM Willoughby					
Q Friend					
Extras (lb 2, w 8)	10				
TOTAL (for 5 wkts) (20 overs)	**161**				

DOLPHINS	*Runs*	*Mins*	*Balls*	*4*	*6*
K Smit c Kleinveldt b Adams	46	47	36	8	-
HM Amla st Tsolekile b Adams	19	31	23	2	-
JC Kent c Tsolekile b Friend	2	6	7	-	-
AM Amla not out	33	39	27	3	1
DM Benkenstein b Harvey	48	25	25	4	3
*L Klusener run out (Harvey)	1	2	1	-	-
R Frylinck not out	1	1	1	-	-
†D Smit					
ANW Tweedie					
ZA Abrahim					
YA Abdullah					
M Hayward					
Extras (lb 1, w 2)	3				
TOTAL (for 5 wkts) (20 overs)	**153**				

Dol	*O*	*M*	*R*	*W*	
Tweedie	4	0	35	1	
Abdullah	4	0	18	1	(1 w)
Klusener	3	0	27	0	(3 w)
Abrahim	4	0	34	1	(1 w)
Hayward	2	0	19	0	(3 w)
Kent	2	0	17	1	
Frylinck	1	0	9	0	

Cob	*O*	*M*	*R*	*W*	
Dawson	4	0	34	0	
Willoughby	4	0	20	0	
Kleinveldt	2	0	23	0	
Adams	4	0	41	2	(1 w)
Friend	4	0	19	1	(1 w)
Harvey	2	0	15	1	

Fall of Wickets	*Cob*	*Dol*
1st	18 (1)	58 (2)
2nd	94 (2)	61 (3)
3rd	124 (4)	77 (1)
4th	148 (5)	150 (5)
5th	161 (6)	151 (6)

LIONS v WARRIORS

Standard Bank Pro20

Played at Liberty Life Wanderers Stadium, Johannesburg on 20 January 2006 (D/N) — Toss: Warriors
Umpires: KH Hurter & GH Pienaar — Referee: NC Pretorius
Debuts: Lio: AM Blignaut, S Chatterjee and Y Singh (All 20). War: AZM Dyili, L Meyer and MBA Smith (All 20)
Result: Lions won by 8 wickets
Master Blasters: Stephen Cook & Eugene Moleon
Points: War: 0; Lio: 6
Notes: Warriors substitute: BC de Wett replaced M Ngam after 10.1 overs of Warriors' innings.

WARRIORS	*Runs*	*Mins*	*Balls*	*4*	*6*
ML Bruyns c Makalima b De Wet	0	1	2	-	-
JP Kreusch c McKenzie b Moleon	30	38	28	3	1
*RJ Peterson c Chatterjee b Singh	12	6	5	2	-
A Jacobs c Harris b De Wet	0	2	1	-	-
MBA Smith c Van Jaarsveld b Singh	2	12	6	-	-
LL Gamiet c McKenzie b Moleon	5	12	10	-	-
T Henderson c Bacher b Moleon	2	8	5	-	-
†AZM Dyili run out (Makalima/Harris)	23	29	27	1	2
BC de Wett run out (Cook/Moleon)	0	3	0	-	-
L Meyer not out	14	26	16	1	-
M Ntini c De Wet b Moleon	1	5	4	-	-
M Ngam					
Extras (lb 6, w 3)	9				
TOTAL (17.2 overs)	**98**				

LIONS	*Runs*	*Mins*	*Balls*	*4*	*6*
SC Cook c Kreusch b Meyer	35	32	23	6	1
AM Bacher c and b Meyer	34	34	25	5	1
*ND McKenzie not out	12	19	16	1	-
VB van Jaarsveld not out	16	17	13	2	-
†MJ Harris					
DL Makalima					
AM Blignaut					
EO Moleon					
F de Wet					
Y Singh					
S Chatterjee					
Extras (lb 3, w 2)	5				
TOTAL (for 2 wkts) (12.5 overs)	**102**				

Lio	O	M	R	W	
De Wet	4	0	31	2	
Singh	3	0	13	2	
Moleon	3.2	0	9	4	(1 w)
Chatterjee	4	0	17	0	(1 w)
Blignaut	2	0	12	0	(1 w)
Bacher	1	0	10	0	

War	O	M	R	W	
Ntini	4	0	25	0	
Henderson	2	0	28	0	
Meyer	4	0	26	2	(2 w)
Peterson	2.5	0	20	0	

Fall of Wickets	War	Lio
1st	0 (1)	72 (1)
2nd	16 (3)	72 (2)
3rd	18 (4)	-
4th	43 (5)	-
5th	55 (6)	-
6th	56 (2)	-
7th	62 (7)	-
8th	62 (9)	-
9th	94 (8)	-
10th	98 (11)	-

EAGLES v LIONS

Standard Bank Pro20

Played at Goodyear Park, Bloemfontein on 22 January 2006
Toss: Eagles
Umpires: JD Cloete & MZ Nanabhay (TV: SB Lambson)
Referee: A Barnes
Debuts: Eag: D du Preez (20). Lio: None
Result: Lions won by 28 runs (D/L method), target revised to 69 in 7.4 overs
Master Blasters: Neil McKenzie & Cliffie Deacon
Points: Eag: 0; Lio: 6
Notes: Lions substitute: GJ de Bruin replaced SC Cook after 0 overs of Eagles' innings.

LIONS	Runs	Mins	Balls	4	6
SC Cook b Deacon	20	11	16	4	-
AM Bacher b Deacon	2	19	8	-	-
*ND McKenzie not out	85	66	49	5	4
VB van Jaarsveld st Van Wyk b Tshabalala	15	26	25	2	-
AM Blignaut c Deacon b Telemachus	32	17	16	1	2
DL Makalima not out	3	15	8	-	-
†MJ Harris					
EO Moleon					
F de Wet					
S Chatterjee					
Y Singh					
GJ de Bruin					
Extras (lb 5, w 8, nb 4)	17				
TOTAL (for 4 wkts) (20 overs)	**174**				

EAGLES	Runs	Mins	Balls	4	6
*†MN van Wyk b De Bruin	19	27	18	3	-
DJ Jacobs c Blignaut b De Wet	10	20	17	1	-
LL Bosman c Harris b De Bruin	4	6	5	-	-
RT Bailey c Makalima b Moleon	0	6	3	-	-
B Hector not out	1	4	4	-	-
JA Beukes					
R McLaren					
WA Deacon					
R Telemachus					
D du Preez					
T Tshabalala					
Extras (lb 3, w 1, nb 2)	6				
TOTAL (for 4 wkts) (7.4 overs)	**40**				

Eag	O	M	R	W	
Du Preez	4	0	41	0	(1 w)
Deacon	4	0	10	2	
Telemachus	4	0	22	1	(1 w)
Tshabalala	4	0	47	1	(3 w)
McLaren	3	0	35	0	(2 nb, 2 w)
Jacobs	1	0	14	0	

Lio	O	M	R	W	
De Wet	3	0	21	1	(1 w)
Singh	2	0	9	0	(1 nb)
Moleon	1.4	0	6	1	
De Bruin	1	0	1	2	

Fall of Wickets	Lio	Eag
1st	22 (1)	32 (2)
2nd	31 (2)	38 (3)
3rd	73 (4)	38 (1)
4th	128 (5)	40 (4)

TITANS v WARRIORS

Standard Bank Pro20

Played at Willowmoore Park, Benoni on 22 January 2006
Toss: Titans
Umpires: S George & KH Hurter (TV: S Wadvalla)
Referee: CJ Mitchley
Debuts: Ttn: None. War: None
Result: Titans won by 4 wickets
Master Blasters: Albie Morkel & Pierre de Bruyn
Points: War: 1; Ttn: 5
Notes: Titans substitute: Z de Bruyn replaced NE Mbhalati after 3 overs of Titans' innings.

WARRIORS	Runs	Mins	Balls	4	6
JP Kreusch c Bodi b Reddy	73	79	58	7	3
ML Bruyns c Van Jaarsveld b Reddy	1	10	6	-	-
*RJ Peterson b JA Morkel	16	15	11	3	-
T Henderson run out (Van Jaarsveld/P de Bruyn)	7	11	6	-	-
A Jacobs c Mbhalati b P de Bruyn	2	15	7	-	-
LL Gamiet lbw b P de Bruyn	1	5	3	-	-
MBA Smith b P de Bruyn	0	2	4	-	-
†AZM Dyili c Dros b P de Bruyn	0	6	10	-	-
L Meyer b M Morkel	1	3	2	-	-
BB Kops b Reddy	2	2	4	-	-
M Ngam not out	2	9	7	-	-
Extras (lb 2, w 3, nb 2)	7				
TOTAL (19.3 overs)	**112**				

TITANS	Runs	Mins	Balls	4	6
†AB de Villiers c Dyili b Henderson	4	1	3	1	-
GH Bodi c Jacobs b Gamiet	43	81	49	4	-
*M van Jaarsveld c Bruyns b Ngam	1	5	4	-	-
JG Myburgh c Kreusch b Henderson	2	7	9	-	-
Z de Bruyn c Dyili b Henderson	3	6	4	-	-
G Dros c Dyili b Meyer	8	21	18	1	-
JA Morkel not out	46	37	30	8	1
P de Bruyn not out	4	1	1	1	-
AM Phangiso					
BL Reddy					
M Morkel					
NE Mbhalati					
Extras (w 3, nb 2)	5				
TOTAL (for 6 wkts) (19.3 overs)	**116**				

Ttn	O	M	R	W	
M Morkel	4	0	23	1	(2 w)
Reddy	3.3	0	31	3	(1 nb)
Mbhalati	4	0	31	0	(1 w)
JA Morkel	4	0	14	1	
P de Bruyn	4	1	11	4	

War	O	M	R	W	
Henderson	4	0	11	3	(1 w)
Ngam	3	0	12	1	(2 w)
Meyer	4	1	29	1	
Peterson	4	0	22	0	
Kops	2	0	19	0	(1 nb)
Gamiet	2.3	0	23	1	

Fall of Wickets	War	Ttn
1st	18 (2)	4 (1)
2nd	51 (3)	6 (3)
3rd	72 (4)	11 (4)
4th	79 (5)	20 (5)
5th	85 (6)	39 (6)
6th	85 (7)	112 (2)
7th	87 (8)	-
8th	90 (9)	-
9th	93 (10)	-
10th	112 (1)	-

WARRIORS v EAGLES

Standard Bank Pro20

Played at Sahara Oval St George's, Port Elizabeth on 25 January 2006 (D/N) — Toss: Warriors
Umpires: M Gajjar & BG Jerling (TV: S George) — Referee: MR Magiet
Debuts: War: None. Eag: PV Mpitsang (20)
Result: Eagles won by 110 runs
Master Blasters: Roger Telemachus & Cliffie Deacon
Points: Eag: 6; War: 0
Notes: Eagles substitute: PV Mpitsang replaced N Boje after 0 overs of Warriors' innings. Warriors substitute: MBA Smith replaced M Ngam after 16.2 overs of Eagles' innings.

EAGLES	Runs	Mins	Balls	4	6
*†MN van Wyk c Ngam b Meyer	26	33	19	1	2
JA Beukes c Kreusch b Kops	33	23	26	6	-
LL Bosman c De Wett b Peterson	24	28	17	-	2
DJ Jacobs b Peterson	21	36	20	-	1
N Boje b Kreusch	22	10	13	3	-
RT Bailey st Dyili b Kreusch	0	1	2	-	-
R Telemachus c Bruyns b Meyer	34	17	16	2	3
R McLaren not out	7	15	8	-	-
D du Preez not out	0	2	0	-	-
WA Deacon					
T Tshabalala					
PV Mpitsang					
Extras (lb 3, w 3, nb 2)	8				
TOTAL (for 7 wkts) (20 overs)	**175**				

WARRIORS	Runs	Mins	Balls	4	6
JP Kreusch b Deacon	0	2	3	-	-
*RJ Peterson c Jacobs b Deacon	0	5	1	-	-
†AZM Dyili c Telemachus b Mpitsang	13	24	14	-	1
A Jacobs c Van Wyk b Mpitsang	19	17	15	2	1
ML Bruyns run out (Bosman)	1	4	2	-	-
BC de Wett b Tshabalala	15	18	11	2	-
T Henderson run out (Mpitsang)	1	5	3	-	-
MBA Smith not out	9	25	16	1	-
LL Gamiet b Du Preez	2	4	6	-	-
L Meyer c Van Wyk b Du Preez	1	4	5	-	-
BB Kops c Beukes b Tshabalala	0	4	7	-	-
M Ngam					
Extras (lb 1, w 3)	4				
TOTAL (13.5 overs)	**65**				

War	O	M	R	W	
Henderson	4	1	16	0	
Ngam	2	0	21	0	
Kops	3	0	30	1	(2 w)
Meyer	3	0	43	2	(1 nb, 1 w)
Peterson	4	0	34	2	
Kreusch	4	0	28	2	

Eag	O	M	R	W	
Deacon	4	0	26	2	(3 w)
Mpitsang	4	0	24	2	
Du Preez	3	1	9	2	
Tshabalala	2.5	0	5	2	

Fall of Wickets	Eag	War
1st	46 (2)	0 (1)
2nd	62 (1)	2 (2)
3rd	97 (3)	35 (4)
4th	129 (5)	36 (3)
5th	129 (6)	36 (5)
6th	137 (4)	46 (7)
7th	173 (7)	59 (6)
8th	-	62 (9)
9th	-	64 (10)
10th	-	65 (11)

TITANS v CAPE COBRAS

Standard Bank Pro20

Played at SuperSport Park, Centurion on 27 January 2006 (D/N) — Toss: Cape Cobras
Umpires: SB Lambson & S Wadvalla (TV: JD Cloete) — Referee: CJ Mitchley
Debuts: Ttn: None. Cob: None
Result: Titans won by 33 runs
Master Blasters: AB de Villiers & Morne Morkel
Points: Ttn: 5; Cob: 1
Notes: De Villiers scored his fifty off 27 balls in Titans' innings. Cape Cobras substitute: PR Adams replaced Q Friend after 8 overs of Titans' innings.

TITANS	Runs	Mins	Balls	4	6
†AB de Villiers b Adams	51	42	28	4	3
GH Bodi b Harvey	39	38	28	6	1
*M van Jaarsveld c Puttick b Willoughby	32	35	26	2	1
JG Myburgh c and b Munnik	17	16	14	2	-
JA Morkel c Telo b Harvey	6	8	8	1	-
G Dros not out	21	16	11	3	1
BL Reddy c Duminy b Dawson	2	8	5	-	-
P de Bruyn run out (Dawson)	0	2	0	-	-
AM Phangiso					
NE Mbhalati					
M Morkel					
Extras (lb 8, w 4)	12				
TOTAL (for 7 wkts) (20 overs)	**180**				

CAPE COBRAS	Runs	Mins	Balls	4	6
IJ Harvey b Mbhalati	35	41	21	4	2
AG Puttick c De Villiers b M Morkel	7	9	8	-	1
J-P Duminy c Van Jaarsveld b Mbhalati	27	23	25	3	1
R Munnik c and b De Bruyn	4	16	12	-	-
H Davids run out (M Morkel/De Bruyn)	7	5	4	1	-
FD Telo run out (De Bruyn/M Morkel)	34	29	18	2	1
RK Kleinveldt c Van Jaarsveld b De Bruyn	4	8	7	-	-
*†TL Tsolekile run out (De Bruyn)	15	17	13	2	-
PR Adams b M Morkel	3	8	4	-	-
AC Dawson not out	3	6	6	-	-
CM Willoughby not out	2	4	2	-	-
Q Friend					
Extras (lb 3, w 3)	6				
TOTAL (for 9 wkts) (20 overs)	**147**				

Cob	O	M	R	W	
Dawson	4	0	26	1	
Willoughby	4	0	36	1	(2 w)
Kleinveldt	3	0	31	0	(2 w)
Friend	1	0	14	0	
Harvey	4	0	31	2	
Adams	3	0	24	1	
Munnik	1	0	10	1	

Ttn	O	M	R	W	
M Morkel	4	0	17	2	(1 w)
Reddy	4	0	29	0	
Mbhalati	4	0	29	2	
JA Morkel	4	0	37	0	(1 w)
De Bruyn	4	0	32	2	(1 w)

Fall of Wickets	Ttn	Cob
1st	85 (2)	15 (2)
2nd	93 (1)	63 (3)
3rd	127 (4)	74 (1)
4th	145 (5)	82 (5)
5th	154 (3)	82 (4)
6th	176 (7)	98 (7)
7th	180 (8)	134 (8)
8th	-	141 (6)
9th	-	143 (9)

CAPE COBRAS v LIONS

Standard Bank Pro20

Played at Sahara Park Newlands, Cape Town on 29 January 2006
Umpires: M Erasmus & LH Matroos (TV: MW Brown)
Debuts: Cob: None. Lio: None
Result: Cape Cobras won by 5 runs
Master Blasters: Dominic Telo & Charl Willoughby
Points: Lio: 1; Cob: 5

Toss: Cape Cobras
Referee: MR Magiet

CAPE COBRAS	Runs	Mins	Balls	4	6
IJ Harvey c Cook b De Bruin	0	1	3	-	-
AG Puttick c Moleon b Blignaut	7	19	13	1	-
J-P Duminy lbw b Blignaut	31	29	29	1	-
FD Telo run out (McKenzie)	48	37	34	5	1
*†TL Tsolekile not out	38	42	29	4	-
RK Kleinveldt run out (Singh/Harris)	9	5	5	-	1
R Munnik run out (McKenzie/Harris)	19	10	7	1	2
AC Dawson					
PR Adams					
Q Friend					
CM Willoughby					
Extras (lb 2, w 1)	3				
TOTAL (for 6 wkts) (20 overs)	**155**				

LIONS	Runs	Mins	Balls	4	6
AM Bacher b Willoughby	25	32	25	3	-
SC Cook c Friend b Dawson	17	17	12	3	-
*ND McKenzie b Harvey	28	48	30	4	-
VB van Jaarsveld run out (Tsolekile/Adams)	2	8	6	-	-
†MJ Harris c Harvey b Adams	1	7	8	-	-
AM Blignaut not out	42	41	29	6	1
DL Makalima c Tsolekile b Friend	1	6	2	-	-
JL Ontong run out (Dawson)	26	13	8	2	2
GJ de Bruin run out (Harvey/Dawson)	0	1	0	-	-
EO Moleon not out	0	1	0	-	-
Y Singh					
Extras (lb 2, w 6)	8				
TOTAL (for 8 wkts) (20 overs)	**150**				

Lio	O	M	R	W	
De Bruin	4	0	32	1	
Singh	4	0	27	0	
Moleon	4	0	28	0	(1 w)
Blignaut	4	0	31	2	
Bacher	2	0	25	0	
Ontong	2	0	10	0	

Cob	O	M	R	W	
Dawson	4	0	26	1	(1 w)
Kleinveldt	4	0	25	0	(2 w)
Willoughby	4	1	15	1	(1 w)
Friend	2	0	22	1	
Adams	3	0	20	1	(2 w)
Harvey	3	0	40	1	

Fall of Wickets	Cob	Lio
1st	0 (1)	34 (2)
2nd	32 (2)	57 (1)
3rd	49 (3)	62 (4)
4th	106 (4)	66 (5)
5th	118 (6)	105 (3)
6th	135 (7)	114 (7)
7th	-	150 (8)
8th	-	150 (9)

EAGLES v TITANS

Standard Bank Pro20

Played at Goodyear Park, Bloemfontein on 29 January 2006
Umpires: M Gajjar & IL Howell
Debuts: Eag: None. Ttn: None
Result: Eagles won by 6 wickets
Master Blasters: Roger Telemachus
Points: Eag: 5; Ttn: 1
Notes: Eagles substitute: D du Preez replaced T Tshabalala after 17 overs of Titans' innings.

Toss: Titans
Referee: NC Pretorius

TITANS	Runs	Mins	Balls	4	6
†AB de Villiers c Beukes b McLaren	33	35	32	4	-
GH Bodi c Van Wyk b Deacon	0	4	1	-	-
*M van Jaarsveld c Jacobs b Telemachus	28	37	24	3	-
JA Morkel b Telemachus	8	14	12	1	-
G Dros not out	24	40	26	3	-
JG Myburgh c Bailey b McLaren	15	13	13	1	1
P de Bruyn b Du Preez	5	9	7	-	-
BL Reddy c and b Du Preez	0	2	1	-	-
AM Phangiso run out (Beukes)	0	2	1	-	-
M Morkel not out	2	6	3	-	-
NE Mbhalati					
Extras (lb 1, w 12)	13				
TOTAL (for 8 wkts) (20 overs)	**128**				

EAGLES	Runs	Mins	Balls	4	6
†MN van Wyk run out (Reddy)	38	70	56	1	-
JA Beukes st De Villiers b Phangiso	27	55	36	2	-
LL Bosman c Myburgh b De Bruyn	11	8	8	1	-
R Telemachus not out	24	15	11	2	1
DJ Jacobs st De Villiers b Phangiso	6	5	3	1	-
*N Boje not out	4	3	1	1	-
R McLaren					
WA Deacon					
RT Bailey					
D du Preez					
PV Mpitsang					
T Tshabalala					
Extras (lb 10, w 6, nb 6)	22				
TOTAL (for 4 wkts) (18.4 overs)	**132**				

Eag	O	M	R	W	
Deacon	4	0	23	1	(2 w)
Mpitsang	3	0	25	0	(1 w)
Tshabalala	3	0	23	0	
McLaren	3	0	21	2	(1 w)
Telemachus	4	0	21	2	
Boje	2	0	12	0	(1 w)
Du Preez	1	0	2	2	

Ttn	O	M	R	W	
M Morkel	3	0	23	0	(2 nb, 2 w)
Reddy	3	0	21	0	
Mbhalati	4	0	24	0	(2 w)
JA Morkel	2	0	14	0	
De Bruyn	4	0	24	1	(1 nb)
Phangiso	2.4	0	16	2	(1 w)

Fall of Wickets	Ttn	Eag
1st	1 (2)	75 (2)
2nd	65 (1)	92 (3)
3rd	68 (3)	113 (1)
4th	80 (4)	128 (5)
5th	107 (6)	-
6th	122 (7)	-
7th	122 (8)	-
8th	122 (9)	-

DOLPHINS v WARRIORS

Standard Bank Pro20

Played at Sahara Stadium Kingsmead, Durban on 1 February 2006 (D/N)

Toss: Dolphins

Umpires: S George & KH Hurter

Referee: S Naidoo

Debuts: Dol: None. War: MN Ranger (20)

Result: Dolphins won by 11 runs

Master Blasters: Doug Watson & Justin Kreusch

Points: Dol: 5; War: 1

Notes: Dolphins substitute: ANW Tweedie replaced AM Amla after 0 overs of Warriors' innings. Warriors substitute: MN Ranger replaced M Ngam after 0 overs of Warriors' innings.

DOLPHINS	Runs	Mins	Balls	4	6
DJ Watson c Sodumo b Meyer	48	29	23	9	1
K Smit b Ngam	12	12	8	2	-
AM Amla b Peterson	46	44	30	6	1
DM Benkenstein c Meyer b Kreusch	20	23	23	-	1
*L Klusener not out	17	25	17	1	-
JC Kent c Smith b Peterson	5	5	7	-	-
I Khan c Gamiet b Kreusch	1	4	3	-	-
†D Smit b Kreusch	8	7	7	1	-
ZA Abrahim not out	1	2	1	-	-
YA Abdullah					
M Hayward					
ANW Tweedie					
Extras (w 7)	7				
TOTAL (for 7 wkts) (20 overs)	**165**				

WARRIORS	Runs	Mins	Balls	4	6
JP Kreusch c Klusener b Abdullah	22	20	14	4	-
ML Bruyns c Tweedie b Abdullah	2	2	2	-	-
*RJ Peterson c D Smit b Klusener	15	29	19	2	-
T Henderson b Klusener	38	40	28	5	1
A Jacobs lbw b Tweedie	36	43	31	1	2
MBA Smith c Kent b Tweedie	25	22	22	2	-
LL Gamiet not out	3	9	4	-	-
†AM Sodumo not out	4	1	1	1	-
MN Ranger					
L Meyer					
BB Kops					
M Ngam					
Extras (lb 4, w 3, nb 2)	9				
TOTAL (for 6 wkts) (20 overs)	**154**				

War	O	M	R	W	
Henderson	3	0	29	0	(1 w)
Ngam	2	0	24	1	(1 w)
Meyer	3	0	38	1	(1 w)
Kops	4	0	28	0	
Peterson	4	0	23	2	
Kreusch	4	0	23	3	

Dol	O	M	R	W	
Abdullah	4	0	20	2	(2 w)
Tweedie	4	0	31	2	
Klusener	4	0	33	2	(1 nb, 1 w)
Hayward	4	0	35	0	
Abrahim	4	0	31	0	

Fall of Wickets	Dol	War
1st	35 (2)	3 (2)
2nd	79 (1)	33 (1)
3rd	130 (4)	55 (3)
4th	134 (3)	105 (4)
5th	142 (6)	138 (5)
6th	146 (7)	149 (6)
7th	158 (8)	-

TITANS v LIONS

Standard Bank Pro20

Played at SuperSport Park, Centurion on 1 February 2006 (D/N)
Toss: Lions
Umpires: JD Cloete & EC Hendrikse (TV: SB Lambson)
Referee: CJ Mitchley
Debuts: Ttn: None. Lio: JP Campher (20)
Result: Titans won by 6 wickets
Master Blasters: AB de Villiers & Brendon Reddy
Points: Lio: 1; Ttn: 5
Notes: Lions substitute: JP Campher replaced SC Cook after 4 overs of Titans' innings. Titans substitute: Z de Bruyn replaced M Morkel after 0 overs of Titans' innings.

LIONS	Runs	Mins	Balls	4	6
AM Bacher c Phangiso b JA Morkel	52	40	37	6	1
SC Cook c Phangiso b Reddy	13	15	13	2	-
*ND McKenzie c De Villiers b Reddy	66	60	48	7	1
VB van Jaarsveld c Dros b Reddy	35	27	18	6	-
JL Ontong not out	0	5	0	-	-
AM Blignaut not out	7	3	4	1	-
DL Makalima					
†MJ Harris					
EO Moleon					
GJ de Bruin					
Y Singh					
JP Campher					
Extras (lb 2, w 4)	6				
TOTAL (for 4 wkts) (20 overs)	**179**				

TITANS	Runs	Mins	Balls	4	6
†AB de Villiers not out	91	80	52	5	7
GH Bodi c Blignaut b Bacher	36	42	33	6	1
JA Morkel b Bacher	7	6	6	-	-
*M van Jaarsveld run out (Blignaut/Harris)	4	12	8	-	-
G Dros lbw b Blignaut	24	16	11	2	2
JG Myburgh not out	4	2	2	1	-
P de Bruyn					
AM Phangiso					
BL Reddy					
NE Mbhalati					
Z de Bruyn					
M Morkel					
Extras (b 1, lb 6, w 7)	14				
TOTAL (for 4 wkts) (18.4 overs)	**180**				

Ttn	O	M	R	W
M Morkel	4	0	42	0 (3 w)
Reddy	4	0	37	3
Mbhalati	4	0	38	0
JA Morkel	4	0	22	1 (1 w)
Phangiso	1	0	4	0
P de Bruyn	3	0	34	0

Lio	O	M	R	W
De Bruin	3	0	37	0
Singh	3	0	32	0 (1 w)
Moleon	2	0	13	0
Campher	4	0	24	0 (1 w)
Blignaut	1.4	0	25	1 (2 w)
Ontong	2	0	15	0 (1 w)
Bacher	3	0	27	2

Fall of Wickets	Lio	Ttn
1st	28 (2)	93 (2)
2nd	89 (1)	102 (3)
3rd	172 (4)	134 (4)
4th	172 (3)	175 (5)

WARRIORS v CAPE COBRAS

Standard Bank Pro20

Played at Mercedes-Benz Park, East London on 3 February 2006 (D/N)
Toss: Cape Cobras
Umpires: IL Howell & BG Jerling
Referee: MR Magiet
Debuts: War: None. Cob: None
Result: Cape Cobras won by 21 runs
Master Blasters: Rory Kleinveldt & Alan Dawson
Points: War: 1; Cob: 5
Notes: Cape Cobras substitute: VD Philander replaced R Munnik after 0 overs of Warriors' innings.

CAPE COBRAS	Runs	Mins	Balls	4	6
IJ Harvey c Sodumo b Henderson	0	2	4	-	-
AG Puttick c and b Meyer	10	30	19	1	-
J-P Duminy c Meyer b Kreusch	23	23	18	3	-
FD Telo run out (Kops/Peterson)	17	17	9	2	-
H Davids st Sodumo b Peterson	11	14	16	2	-
RK Kleinveldt b Kreusch	46	23	22	2	4
*†TL Tsolekile not out	15	35	19	-	-
R Munnik c Kreusch b Henderson	1	4	5	-	-
PR Adams b Kreusch	13	4	5	1	1
AC Dawson not out	5	2	3	1	-
CM Willoughby					
VD Philander					
Extras (w 3)	3				
TOTAL (for 8 wkts) (20 overs)	**144**				

WARRIORS	Runs	Mins	Balls	4	6
ML Bruyns c Tsolekile b Philander	35	51	38	4	-
JP Kreusch c Tsolekile b Dawson	0	2	1	-	-
*RJ Peterson c Tsolekile b Dawson	6	8	4	-	-
A Jacobs c Tsolekile b Dawson	0	3	2	-	-
T Henderson c Tsolekile b Dawson	0	1	1	-	-
MBA Smith b Harvey	49	61	50	4	1
LL Gamiet c Adams b Philander	4	9	7	-	-
†AM Sodumo run out (Harvey)	4	6	5	-	-
MN Ranger not out	9	13	7	1	-
L Meyer not out	7	5	5	1	-
BB Kops					
Extras (b 1, lb 4, w 4)	9				
TOTAL (for 8 wkts) (20 overs)	**123**				

War	O	M	R	W	
Henderson	4	1	21	2	
Kops	4	0	29	0	(1 w)
Meyer	3	0	16	1	(2 w)
Kreusch	4	0	31	3	
Peterson	4	1	36	1	
Ranger	1	0	11	0	

Cob	O	M	R	W	
Dawson	4	0	18	4	(1 w)
Willoughby	4	0	14	0	
Adams	2	0	16	0	
Kleinveldt	4	0	30	0	
Harvey	4	0	23	1	(2 w)
Philander	2	0	17	2	(1 w)

Fall of Wickets	Cob	War
1st	0 (1)	1 (2)
2nd	34 (3)	15 (3)
3rd	43 (2)	15 (4)
4th	64 (4)	15 (5)
5th	64 (5)	75 (1)
6th	120 (6)	87 (7)
7th	123 (8)	101 (8)
8th	137 (9)	109 (6)

DOLPHINS v EAGLES

Standard Bank Pro20

Played at Sahara Stadium Kingsmead, Durban on 3 February 2006 (D/N) — Toss: Dolphins

Umpires: KH Hurter & ZTA Ndamane (TV: M Gajjar) — Referee: CJ Mitchley

Debuts: Dol: None. Eag: None

Result: Eagles won by 7 wickets (D/L method), target revised to 145 in 15 overs

Master Blasters: Morne van Wyk & Nicky Boje

Points: Eag: 5; Dol: 1

Notes: K Smit scored his fifty off 29 balls in Dolphins' innings. Van Wyk scored his fifty off 28 balls in Eagles' innings. Dolphins substitute: ANW Tweedie replaced K Smit after 0 overs of Eagles' innings. Eagles substitute: D du Preez replaced T Tshabalala after 17 overs of Dolphins' innings.

DOLPHINS	Runs	Mins	Balls	4	6
DJ Watson c Jacobs b Mpitsang	19	12	13	1	2
K Smit c Jacobs b Boje	76	42	41	8	4
HM Amla st Van Wyk b Boje	26	46	18	4	-
DM Benkenstein lbw b Boje	20	13	14	1	1
*L Klusener b Telemachus	23	25	20	2	1
AM Amla b Telemachus	6	10	7	-	-
JC Kent c Bailey b Telemachus	8	9	8	1	-
†D Smit not out	0	1	0	-	-
ZA Abrahim					
YA Abdullah					
M Hayward					
ANW Tweedie					
Extras (lb 4, w 6, nb 2)	12				
TOTAL (for 7 wkts) (20 overs)	**190**				

EAGLES	Runs	Mins	Balls	4	6
†MN van Wyk not out	56	66	33	6	1
JA Beukes c Hayward b Tweedie	19	14	10	2	1
LL Bosman c Benkenstein b Hayward	14	8	8	2	1
DJ Jacobs c Kent b Abrahim	46	40	35	6	-
R Telemachus not out	4	1	1	1	-
*N Boje					
RT Bailey					
R McLaren					
WA Deacon					
D du Preez					
PV Mpitsang					
T Tshabalala					
Extras (lb 3, w 2, nb 4)	9				
TOTAL (for 3 wkts) (14.1 overs)	**148**				

Eag	O	M	R	W	
Deacon	4	0	29	0	
Mpitsang	3	0	32	1	
Telemachus	4	0	37	3	(1 nb)
Tshabalala	1	0	24	0	
Boje	4	0	31	3	(3 w)
McLaren	3	0	29	0	
Du Preez	1	0	4	0	

Dol	O	M	R	W	
Abdullah	3	0	25	0	
Tweedie	2.1	0	32	1	(1 nb)
Hayward	3	0	19	1	(1 nb)
Klusener	3	0	30	0	(2 w)
Abrahim	3	0	39	1	

Fall of Wickets	Dol	Eag
1st	27 (1)	42 (2)
2nd	110 (2)	61 (3)
3rd	146 (4)	144 (4)
4th	148 (3)	-
5th	172 (6)	-
6th	186 (7)	-
7th	190 (5)	-

CAPE COBRAS v EAGLES

Standard Bank Pro20

Played at Boland Park, Paarl on 5 February 2006 — Toss: Cape Cobras

Umpires: M Erasmus & DJ Smith (TV: MW Brown) — Referee: WA Diedricks

Debuts: Cob: None. Eag: PJ Koortzen (20)

Result: Eagles won by 9 runs

Master Blasters: Loots Bosman & Cliffie Deacon

Points: Eag: 5; Cob: 1

Notes: Cape Cobras substitute: R Munnik replaced CM Willoughby after 16 overs of Eagles' innings. Eagles substitute: PJ Koortzen replaced JA Beukes after 13 overs of Eagles' innings.

EAGLES	Runs	Mins	Balls	4	6
JA Beukes b Dawson	3	10	5	-	-
LL Bosman lbw b Kleinveldt	34	32	22	4	1
†MN van Wyk lbw b Dawson	11	8	7	2	-
DJ Jacobs c Telo b Adams	14	24	22	1	-
*N Boje b Kleinveldt	2	2	2	-	-
RT Bailey not out	30	44	35	1	-
R McLaren c Tsolekile b Kleinveldt	0	4	2	-	-
WA Deacon c Puttick b Harvey	9	18	18	-	-
R Telemachus b Dawson	2	2	2	-	-
D du Preez not out	7	4	5	-	-
T Tshabalala					
PJ Koortzen					
Extras (lb 4, w 4)	8				
TOTAL (for 8 wkts) (20 overs)	**120**				

CAPE COBRAS	Runs	Mins	Balls	4	6
AG Puttick c Jacobs b Deacon	16	25	19	2	-
IJ Harvey c Boje b Deacon	4	13	7	-	-
J-P Duminy run out (Jacobs/Boje)	14	31	21	1	-
FD Telo c Du Preez b Deacon	0	1	2	-	-
H Davids lbw b Tshabalala	20	28	29	1	-
*†TL Tsolekile not out	33	33	26	3	-
RK Kleinveldt c Bosman b Koortzen	2	4	5	-	-
R Munnik not out	14	15	11	-	1
VD Philander					
AC Dawson					
PR Adams					
CM Willoughby					
Extras (b 2, lb 2, w 4)	8				
TOTAL (for 6 wkts) (20 overs)	**111**				

Cob	O	M	R	W
Dawson	4	0	30	3 (1 w)
Willoughby	4	0	28	0 (1 w)
Harvey	4	0	29	1
Kleinveldt	4	0	19	3 (2 w)
Adams	4	0	10	1

Eag	O	M	R	W
Telemachus	4	0	21	0 (1 w)
Deacon	4	0	17	3 (1 w)
McLaren	2	1	11	0
Tshabalala	4	0	17	1
Du Preez	1	0	8	0
Boje	4	0	26	0 (2 w)
Koortzen	1	0	7	1

Fall of Wickets	Eag	Cob
1st	11 (1)	9 (2)
2nd	43 (3)	28 (1)
3rd	56 (2)	28 (4)
4th	58 (5)	51 (3)
5th	73 (4)	72 (5)
6th	75 (7)	80 (7)
7th	104 (8)	-
8th	106 (9)	-

LIONS v DOLPHINS

Standard Bank Pro20

Played at Sedgars Park, Potchefstroom on 5 February 2006

Toss: Dolphins

Umpires: BG Jerling & MZ Nanabhay (TV: GH Pienaar)

Referee: A Barnes

Debuts: Lio: None. Dol: None

Result: Dolphins won by 3 wickets

Master Blasters: Andy Blignaut & Adam Bacher

Points: Dol: 5; Lio: 1

Notes: Blignaut scored his fifty off 25 balls in Lions' innings. Dolphins substitute: R Frylinck replaced M Hayward after 12.5 overs of Dolphins' innings. Lions substitute: GJ de Bruin replaced DL Makalima after 12.5 overs of Dolphins' innings.

LIONS	Runs	Mins	Balls	4	6
AM Bacher c K Smit b Kent	24	16	14	4	-
SC Cook c D Smit b Abrahim	45	39	31	6	-
*ND McKenzie b Abrahim	22	33	21	3	-
VB van Jaarsveld c Watson b Abrahim	3	7	5	-	-
JL Ontong c Benkenstein b Klusener	5	9	6	-	-
AM Blignaut not out	61	34	28	3	5
†MJ Harris not out	22	27	17	1	1
DL Makalima					
EO Moleon					
JP Campher					
Y Singh					
GJ de Bruin					
Extras (lb 2, w 2, nb 4)	8				
TOTAL (for 5 wkts) (20 overs)	**190**				

DOLPHINS	Runs	Mins	Balls	4	6
DJ Watson c De Bruin b Blignaut	26	27	14	3	1
K Smit c Ontong b Moleon	29	22	18	4	1
AM Amla run out (Ontong)	28	17	15	5	-
DM Benkenstein b Bacher	12	24	12	1	-
HM Amla c Campher b De Bruin	9	6	6	-	1
*L Klusener c Ontong b Bacher	11	13	11	1	-
JC Kent not out	32	29	18	3	1
R Frylinck b Bacher	29	17	13	2	2
†D Smit not out	3	4	3	-	-
ZA Abrahim					
YA Abdullah					
M Hayward					
Extras (lb 1, w 7, nb 4)	12				
TOTAL (for 7 wkts) (18 overs)	**191**				

Dol	O	M	R	W
Abdullah	4	0	32	0
Hayward	4	0	49	0 (1 w)
Kent	4	0	22	1 (1 nb)
Klusener	4	0	45	1 (1 w)
Abrahim	4	0	40	3 (1 nb)

Lio	O	M	R	W
Singh	2	0	28	0 (1 nb)
Campher	3	0	38	0 (1 nb, 5 w)
Moleon	4	0	48	1
Blignaut	2	0	21	1 (2 w)
Bacher	4	0	23	3
De Bruin	3	0	32	1

Fall of Wickets	Lio	Dol
1st	43 (1)	60 (2)
2nd	89 (2)	65 (1)
3rd	99 (4)	99 (3)
4th	100 (3)	112 (5)
5th	107 (5)	117 (4)
6th	-	128 (6)
7th	-	174 (8)

SEMI-FINALS

TITANS v CAPE COBRAS — Standard Bank Pro20 Semi-final

Played at SuperSport Park, Centurion on 10 February 2006 — Toss: Cape Cobras
Umpires: BG Jerling & MZ Nanabhay (TV: KH Hurter) — Referee: A Barnes
Debuts: Ttn: None. Cob: None
Result: No Result
Notes:Cape Cobras chose to bat, but no play was possible

CAPE COBRAS
AG Puttick, IJ Harvey, J-P Duminy, FD Telo, H Davids, RK Kleinveldt, *†TL Tsolekile, WA Albertyn, AC Dawson, PR Adams, CM Willoughby.

TITANS
†AB de Villiers, GH Bodi, *M van Jaarsveld, JG Myburgh, G Dros, JA Morkel, P de Bruyn, BL Reddy, M Morkel, AC Thomas, NE Mbhalati.

TITANS v CAPE COBRAS — Standard Bank Pro20 Semi-final

Played at SuperSport Park, Centurion on 11 February 2006 — Toss: Cape Cobras
Umpires: BG Jerling & MZ Nanabhay (TV: KH Hurter) — Referee: A Barnes
Debuts: Ttn: None. Cob: None
Result: Cape Cobras won by 22 runs
Master Blasters: Ian Harvey & Rory Kleinveldt
Notes: Cape Cobras substitute: VD Philander replaced FD Telo after 6 overs of Cape Cobras' innings.

Australian Ian Harvey found a rain-reduced seven-overs-a-side game much easier to handle, producing a match-winning innings after his five previous visits to the crease had brought just 52 runs. After hitting three sixes, Harvey was eventually yorked but Philander struck two sixes in the last over to push the Cobras' score beyond reach.

After De Villiers had given the Titans a blazing start, the home side inexplicably sent Van Jaarsveld in at number three, a decision they will surely regret for some time. The Titans captain became bogged down, leaving Albie Morkel to face just four balls at the end of the innings.

Kleinveldt's outstanding penultimate over, in which he conceded just five runs and bowled the big-hitting Dros, was the highlight of the Cobras' effort in the field.

CAPE COBRAS	*Runs*	*Mins*	*Balls*	*4*	*6*
IJ Harvey b M Morkel	45	16	18	5	3
AG Puttick c Reddy b Thomas	19	21	11	2	1
RK Kleinveldt c Dros b Reddy	7	9	3	-	1
J-P Duminy c Bodi b Reddy	4	6	4	-	-
H Davids b Mbhalati	1	4	2	-	-
VD Philander not out	15	5	4	-	2
WA Albertyn not out	1	3	1	-	-
*†TL Tsolekile					
AC Dawson					
PR Adams					
CM Willoughby					
FD Telo					
Extras (w 1, nb 2)	3				
TOTAL (for 5 wkts) (7 overs)	**95**				

TITANS	*Runs*	*Mins*	*Balls*	*4*	*6*
†AB de Villiers c Philander b Willoughby	30	15	13	2	3
GH Bodi c Duminy b Willoughby	1	7	3	-	-
*M van Jaarsveld run out (Adams/Tsolekile)	17	24	13	2	-
G Dros b Kleinveldt	15	10	8	1	1
JA Morkel not out	4	7	4	-	-
P de Bruyn not out	2	1	1	-	-
JG Myburgh					
BL Reddy					
AC Thomas					
M Morkel					
NE Mbhalati					
Extras (lb 3, w 1)	4				
TOTAL (for 4 wkts) (7 overs)	**73**				

Ttn	*O*	*M*	*R*	*W*	
Reddy	2	0	19	2	
M Morkel	2	0	28	1	(1 nb)
JA Morkel	1	0	18	0	(1 w)
Thomas	1	0	14	1	
Mbhalati	1	0	16	1	

Cob	*O*	*M*	*R*	*W*	
Dawson	2	0	21	0	(1 w)
Willoughby	2	0	20	2	
Albertyn	1	0	15	0	
Kleinveldt	1	0	5	1	
Harvey	1	0	9	0	

Fall of Wickets	*Cob*	*Ttn*
1st	60 (1)	18 (2)
2nd	74 (2)	39 (1)
3rd	77 (3)	60 (4)
4th	79 (4)	71 (3)
5th	80 (5)	-

DASHING . . . Loots Bosman hits out as the Eagles head for victory over the Lions in their Standard Bank Pro20 semi-final *Picture: DUIF DU TOIT, Touchline Photo*

EAGLES v LIONS

Standard Bank Pro20 Semi-final

Played at Goodyear Park, Bloemfontein on 13 February 2006 (D/N)
Toss: Eagles
Umpires: S George & KH Hurter (TV: IL Howell)
Referee: CJ Mitchley
Debuts: Eag: None. Lio: None
Result: Eagles won by 34 runs
Master Blasters: Loots Bosman & Roger Telemachus
Notes: The match was originally scheduled for 12 February but was abandoned without a ball bowled (no toss). Bosman scored his fifty off 22 balls in Eagles' innings. Petersen scored his fifty off 27 balls in Lions' innings. Eagles substitute: R McLaren replaced JA Rudolph after 0 overs of Lions' innings. Lions substitute: EO Moleon replaced CK Langeveldt after 18.1 overs of Lions' innings.

The Eagles got away to a hesitant start after choosing to bat first in fine conditions on the reserve day, Rudolph edging the third ball of the match into his stumps, but Bosman then played a dazzling innings. He raced to a thrilling half-century off just 22 balls, the quickest fifty in Pro20 cricket, while Van Wyk produced a more aesthetically pleasing innings as 83 runs were added off just 53 balls.

With such a sound platform, the rest of the order was able to scramble runs in comfort.

The Lions response was mediocre, with Petersen the only batsman to come close to Bosman's jaw-dropping exploits of the first innings. An aggressive Telemachus thoroughly undermined the Lions lower-order, claiming his first four-wicket haul in Pro20 cricket.

EAGLES	*Runs*	*Mins*	*Balls*	*4*	*6*
LL Bosman c Langeveldt b Blignaut	75	54	38	2	6
JA Rudolph b Langeveldt	0	3	1	-	-
†MN van Wyk c Blignaut b Ontong	26	37	27	3	-
HH Dippenaar lbw b Bacher	12	19	11	-	-
*N Boje run out (Ontong/Harris)	32	29	23	4	-
DJ Jacobs not out	18	31	13	1	-
JJ van der Wath run out (Ontong/Harris)	20	7	7	2	1
RT Bailey					
WA Deacon					
R Telemachus					
PV Mpitsang					
R McLaren					
Extras (lb 2, w 3)	5				
TOTAL (for 6 wkts) (20 overs)	**188**				

LIONS	*Runs*	*Mins*	*Balls*	*4*	*6*
AM Bacher c Telemachus b Deacon	8	17	11	-	-
SC Cook b Mpitsang	36	46	28	4	-
*ND McKenzie c Jacobs b Telemachus	2	6	5	-	-
JL Ontong c Mpitsang b Deacon	3	14	9	-	-
AN Petersen not out	51	57	28	3	3
AM Blignaut b McLaren	3	9	8	-	-
VB van Jaarsveld b Telemachus	22	20	17	3	-
†MJ Harris b Telemachus	6	10	8	-	-
EO Moleon c Van Wyk b Telemachus	0	2	3	-	-
F de Wet run out (Boje/Van der Wath)	6	5	2	1	-
GJ-P Kruger not out	2	2	1	-	-
CK Langeveldt					
Extras (lb 6, w 9)	15				
TOTAL (for 9 wkts) (20 overs)	**154**				

Lio	*O*	*M*	*R*	*W*	
Langeveldt	4	0	27	1	(1 w)
De Wet	4	0	46	0	
Kruger	4	0	41	0	
Ontong	2	0	26	1	
Blignaut	3	0	22	1	(2 w)
Bacher	3	0	24	1	

Eag	*O*	*M*	*R*	*W*	
Van der Wath	4	0	38	0	(3 w)
Deacon	4	0	20	2	
Telemachus	4	0	25	4	
Boje	1	0	15	0	(1 w)
Mpitsang	3	0	26	1	(4 w)
McLaren	4	0	24	1	

Fall of Wickets	*Eag*	*Lio*
1st	4 (2)	24 (1)
2nd	87 (3)	29 (3)
3rd	112 (1)	46 (4)
4th	121 (4)	67 (2)
5th	168 (5)	75 (6)
6th	188 (7)	113 (7)
7th	-	142 (8)
8th	-	142 (9)
9th	-	151 (10)

FINAL

EAGLES v CAPE COBRAS

Standard Bank Pro20 Final

Played at Goodyear Park, Bloemfontein on 19 February 2006
Toss: Cape Cobras
Umpires: M Erasmus & IL Howell (TV: KH Hurter)
Referee: MR Magiet
Debuts: Eag: None. Cob: None
Result: Eagles won by 6 wickets
Master Blasters: Davy Jacobs & Cliffie Deacon
Notes: Cape Cobras substitute: WA Albertyn replaced J-P Duminy after 4 overs of Eagles' innings.

After choosing to bat first, the Cobras batsmen were not able to do themselves justice on a slowish pitch.

STANDARD BANK PRO20

Deacon led a disciplined Eagles attack, backed by athletic fielding, and was well-supported by Van der Wath and Telemachus's death bowling. They were able to keep a firm lid on the Cobras' strokeplayers, with only Duminy lasting for long.

Dawson struck two early blows with the ball for the Cobras but Van Wyk and Dippenaar combined for a steadying stand of 35 in six overs. Jacobs then finished things off for the Eagles with a dashing innings.

CAPE COBRAS	Runs	Mins	Balls	4	6
IJ Harvey b Van der Wath	4	4	6	-	-
HH Gibbs c Van Wyk b Deacon	14	24	14	2	-
J-P Duminy c Van der Wath b Mpitsang	33	56	44	1	1
AG Prince c Van Wyk b Deacon	1	9	4	-	-
FD Telo b Telemachus	23	35	29	-	-
VD Philander b Van der Wath	12	11	8	-	1
RK Kleinveldt c Bosman b Telemachus	1	8	3	-	-
*†TL Tsolekile not out	6	13	6	1	-
PR Adams not out	13	9	6	1	1
AC Dawson					
CM Willoughby					
WA Albertyn					
Extras (b 1, lb 2, w 2)	5				
TOTAL (for 7 wkts) (20 overs)	**112**				

EAGLES	Runs	Mins	Balls	4	6
LL Bosman c Philander b Dawson	19	19	11	1	-
JA Rudolph c Tsolekile b Dawson	4	4	4	1	-
†MN van Wyk c Tsolekile b Kleinveldt	26	36	25	4	1
HH Dippenaar c and b Kleinveldt	26	30	29	3	-
DJ Jacobs not out	25	23	18	1	2
JJ van der Wath not out	9	13	8	-	-
RT Bailey					
*N Boje					
WA Deacon					
R Telemachus					
PV Mpitsang					
Extras (lb 2, nb 2)	4				
TOTAL (for 4 wkts) (15.4 overs)	**113**				

Eag	O	M	R	W	
Van der Wath	4	0	35	2	(2 w)
Deacon	4	0	11	2	
Telemachus	4	0	14	2	
Mpitsang	4	0	19	1	
Boje	4	0	30	0	

Cob	O	M	R	W	
Dawson	4	0	31	2	
Willoughby	3	0	28	0	
Adams	4	0	21	0	
Kleinveldt	4	0	26	2	(1 nb)
Prince	0.4	0	5	0	

Fall of Wickets	Cob	Eag
1st	5 (1)	5 (2)
2nd	25 (2)	34 (1)
3rd	29 (4)	69 (3)
4th	72 (3)	80 (4)
5th	82 (5)	-
6th	90 (6)	-
7th	93 (7)	-

STANDARD BANK PRO20 RECORDS

WINNERS

Season	Winners	Runners-up	Margin of victory
2003/04	Eagles	Eastern Cape	7 runs (D/L method)
2004/05	Titans	Warriors	8 wickets
2005/06	Eagles	Cape Cobras	6 wickets

HIGHEST INNINGS TOTALS

225-6	Eagles	v	Lions	Potchefstroom	2004/05
203-5	Titans	v	Dolphins	Benoni	2004/05
200-4	Dolphins	v	Titans	Benoni	2004/05

HIGHEST TOTAL BY A TEAM BATTING SECOND

203-5 (Won)	Titans	v	Dolphins	Benoni	2004/05

LOWEST INNINGS TOTALS

47	Titans	v	Eagles	Centurion	2003/04
65	Warriors	v	Eagles	Port Elizabeth	2005/06
88	Dolphins	v	Western Province Boland	Durban	2004/05

LOWEST TOTAL BY A TEAM BATTING FIRST AND WINNING

(Excluding reduced overs matches)

119-8	Warriors	v	Eagles	Port Elizabeth	2004/05

LARGEST MARGINS OF VICTORY

By runs

130	Eagles	bt	Lions	Potchefstroom	2004/05

By wickets

8 Achieved on 5 occasions by Titans (3 occasions), Eagles and Lions.

STANDARD BANK PRO20

SMALLEST MARGINS OF VICTORY

By runs

3	Eagles	bt	Lions	Bloemfontein	2003/04

HIGHEST MATCH AGGREGATE

403-9 (39.3)	Titans	v	Dolphins	Benoni	2004/05

LOWEST MATCH AGGREGATE (COMPLETED MATCHES)

95-13 (25.4)	Titans	v	Eagles	Centurion	2003/04

BATTING

HIGHEST INDIVIDUAL SCORES

104	LL Bosman	Eagles	v	Lions	Potchefstroom	2004/05
91*	AB de Villiers	Titans	v	Lions	Centurion	2005/06
86	AG Puttick	Western Province Boland	v	Dolphins	Durban	2004/05
85*	JM Kemp	Titans	v	Dolphins	Benoni	2004/05
85*	ND McKenzie	Lions	v	Eagles	Bloemfontein	2005/06
85	T Henderson	Eastern Cape	v	Lions	Potchefstroom	2003/04
84*	LL Bosman	Eagles	v	Dolphins	Durban	2003/04
80*	HD Ackerman	Lions	v	Dolphins	Johannesburg	2003/04
80*	MN van Wyk	Eagles	v	Western Province Boland	Bloemfontein	2004/05

FASTEST CENTURY (BALLS)

41	LL Bosman	Eagles	v	Lions	Potchefstroom	2004/05

FASTEST FIFTY (BALLS)

22	LL Bosman	Eagles	v	Lions	Bloemfontein	2005/06
23	SM Pollock	Dolphins	v	Titans	Benoni	2004/05
23	T Henderson	Warriors	v	Eagles	Bloemfontein	2004/05

MOST RUNS IN A SEASON

236 (avg 47.20, SR 160.54)	AB de Villiers (Ttn)	2005/06

MOST RUNS IN A CAREER

Name	M	Inns	NO	Runs	HS	Avg	SR 100	50
LL Bosman	19	19	1	575	104	31.94	148.191	2
ND McKenzie	16	16	5	425	85 *	38.63	131.570	3
T Henderson	19	17	0	411	85	24.17	152.220	4
MN van Wyk	19	19	3	399	80 *	24.93	110.830	2
J-P Duminy	18	16	4	370	67 *	30.83	106.620	1

BEST BATTING STRIKE RATES IN A CAREER

(Qualification 200 runs)

Name	M	Inns	NO	Runs	HS	Avg	SR 100	50
SM Pollock	10	9	2	245	59	35.00	161.180	1
AB de Villiers	8	7	1	240	91 *	40.00	161.070	2
T Henderson	19	17	0	411	85	24.17	152.220	4
JM Kemp	13	11	5	255	85 *	42.50	150.880	1
LL Bosman	19	19	1	575	104	31.94	148.191	2

MOST SIXES IN A CAREER

LL Bosman	33
T Henderson	20
JM Kemp	18

RECORD WICKET PARTNERSHIPS

1st	151	JA Beukes and LL Bosman	Eagles v Lions (Potchefstroom)	2004/05
2nd	98	AG Puttick and VD Philander	WP Boland v Dolphins (Durban)	2004/05

3rd	83	ND McKenzie and VB van Jaarsveld	Lions v Titans (Centurion)	2005/06
	83	MN van Wyk and DJ Jacobs	Eagles v Dolphins (Durban)	2005/06
4th	73	AM Amla and DM Benkenstein	Dolphins v Cape Cobras (Cape Town)	2005/06
5th	89	JM Kemp and G Dros	Titans v Dolphins (Benoni)	2004/05
6th	83*	AM Blignaut and MJ Harris	Lions v Dolphins (Potchefstroom)	2005/06
7th	57*	AM Amla and L Klusener	Dolphins v WP Boland (Cape Town)	2003/04
8th	52	CA Thyssen and WA Deacon	Eagles v Titans (Centurion)	2004/05
9th	32	AZM Dyili and L Meyer	Warriors v Lions (Johannesburg)	2005/06
10th	19	DJ Terbrugge and GJ-P Kruger	Lions v Eagles (Potchefstroom)	2004/05
	19	JP Kreusch and M Ngam	Warriors v Titans (Benoni)	2005/06

BOWLING

BEST BOWLING

4-9	CM Willoughby	Western Province Boland	v	Dolphins	Durban	2004/05
4-9	EO Moleon	Lions	v	Warriors	Johannesburg	2005/06
4-11	PC Strydom	Eastern Cape	v	Western Province Boland	Cape Town	2003/04
4-11	P de Bruyn	Titans	v	Warriors	Benoni	2005/06
4-13	T Tshabalala	Eagles	v	Lions	Potchefstroom	2004/05
4-18	AC Dawson	Cape Cobras	v	Warriors	East London	2005/06
4-20	DJ Terbrugge	Lions	v	Western Province Boland	Johannesburg	2004/05

ECONOMICAL BOWLING (Qualification 4 overs)

RpO							
2.00	4-1-8-2	T Henderson	Warriors	v	Western Province Boland	Cape Town	2004/05

EXPENSIVE BOWLING

RpO							
18.66	3-0-56-0	AC Thomas	Titans	v	Dolphins	Benoni	2004/05
14.00	4-0-56-1	L Klusener	Dolphins	v	Titans	Benoni	2004/05

MOST WICKETS IN A SEASON

12 (avg 11.33, RpO 4.85)	WA Deacon (Eag)	2005/06
12 (avg 11.66, RpO 5.83)	R Telemachus (Eag)	2005/06

MOST WICKETS IN A CAREER

Name	M	Balls	Runs	Wkts	Avg	RpO	BB	4I
WA Deacon	19	426	358	32	11.18	5.04	3-10	0
T Tshabalala	17	293	329	24	13.70	6.73	4-13	1
T Henderson	19	386	438	22	19.90	6.80	3-11	0
BL Reddy	13	219	268	18	14.88	7.34	3-27	0
RK Kleinveldt	15	298	318	18	17.66	6.40	3-18	0
RJ Peterson	19	364	385	18	21.38	6.34	2-21	0

MOST ECONOMICAL BOWLING IN A CAREER
(Qualification 180 balls)

Name	M	Balls	Runs	Wkts	Avg	RpO	BB	4I
WA Deacon	19	426	358	32	11.18	5.04	3-10	0
SM Pollock	10	186	176	6	29.33	5.67	2-10	0
PC Strydom	12	181	172	8	21.50	5.70	4-11	1
CM Willoughby	15	318	314	10	31.40	5.92	4-9	1
J Botha	14	300	303	5	60.60	6.06	2-12	0

MOST MAIDENS IN A CAREER

T Henderson	4
CM Willoughby	3

STANDARD BANK PRO20

WICKETKEEPING

MOST DISMISSALS IN A MATCH

5 (ct 4, st 1)	MN van Wyk	Eagles	v	Eastern Cape	East London	2003/04
5 (ct 5)	TL Tsolekile	Cape Cobras	v	Warriors	East London	2005/06

MOST DISMISSALS IN A SEASON

13 (ct 11,st 2)	MN van Wyk (Eag)	2003/04

MOST DISMISSALS IN A CAREER

Name	M	Ct	St	Total
MN van Wyk	19	21	8	29
TL Tsolekile	18	17	3	20

MOST RUN OUTS IN A CAREER

MJ Harris	8

FIELDING

MOST CATCHES IN A MATCH

2 This has been achieved on 28 occasions

MOST CATCHES IN A SEASON

6	DJ Jacobs (Eag)	2005/06

MOST CATCHES IN A CAREER

Name	M	Ct
DJ Jacobs	17	9

MOST RUN OUTS IN A CAREER

P de Bruyn	7

TITANS IN ENGLAND 2005

The Titans' victory in the 2004/05 Pro20 final earned them an invitation to play in the inaugural International 20:20 championships in Leicester, England, in September 2005. Six teams competed, including three from England. The Titans' opening match against a Professional Cricketers' Association Masters XI was rained out and the match was decided by an indoors "bowl-out" which the Masters won 6-5.

In what turned out to be their only match on the field, the Titans were defeated by the Sri Lankan champions, Chilaw Marians, whose off-spinner, Janaka Gunaratne, took four wickets. The Marians went on to reach the final where they were beaten by Faisalabad Wolves of Pakistan.

CHILAW MARIANS CC v TITANSInternational 20:20 Club Championship Group B

Played at Grace Road, Leicester on 16 September 2005 Toss: Chilaw Marians CC
Umpires: NG Cowley & NJ Llong (TV: RA Kettleborough)
Debuts: Chil: None. Ttn: PL Harris, M Morkel and JG Myburgh (All 20)
Result: Chilaw Marians CC won by 67 runs
Man of Match: Janaka Gunaratne
Points: Chilaw: 2; Ttn: 0

CHILAW MARIANS CC	*Runs*	*Balls*	*4*	*6*
CS Fernando c De Bruyn b M Morkel	17	11	3	-
†TMI Mutaliph c De Bruyn b Reddy	32	14	4	1
ML Udawatte st Van Wyk b Harris	11	18	2	-
MK Gajanayake b De Bruyn	30	24	1	1
*KHRK Fernando b Harris	0	1	-	-
MMDNRG Perera st Van Wyk b Myburgh	39	18	8	-
LJP Gunaratne c Reddy b Myburgh	9	7	-	1
JMPC Jayasundera run out (Bodi/Van Wyk)	5	6	-	-
OLA Wijesiriwardene c Van Wyk b Myburgh	3	6	-	-
D Hettiarachchi not out	7	5	1	-
PUM Chanaka b Reddy	7	10	-	-
Extras (lb 1, w 8, nb 10)	19			
TOTAL (19.1 overs)	**179**			

TITANS	*Runs*	*Balls*	*4*	*6*
JA Morkel c Gunaratne b Chanaka	0	2	-	-
AN Petersen b Hettiarachchi	29	24	4	-
GH Bodi lbw b Wijesiriwardene	5	5	1	-
JG Myburgh lbw b Chanaka	1	8	-	-
*G Dros st Mutaliph b Hettiarachchi	13	12	1	-
P de Bruyn st Mutaliph b Gunaratne	22	21	2	-
†CFK van Wyk c sub b Gunaratne	24	21	-	-
BL Reddy not out	1	2	-	-
PL Harris b Hettiarachchi	3	6	-	-
M Morkel b Gunaratne	2	5	-	-
NE Mbhalati b Gunaratne	0	3	-	-
Extras (lb 5, w 5, nb 2)	12			
TOTAL (18 overs)	**112**			

Ttn	*O*	*M*	*R*	*W*	
M Morkel	2	0	41	1	(3 nb, 2 w)
Mbhalati	3	0	27	0	(1 nb, 4 w)
Reddy	2.1	0	18	2	(2 w)
JA Morkel	4	0	30	0	
Harris	3	0	23	2	(1 nb)
De Bruyn	2	0	23	1	
Myburgh	3	0	16	3	

Chil	*O*	*M*	*R*	*W*	
Chanaka	4	0	19	2	(1 w)
Wijesiriwardene	3	0	24	1	(1 nb, 1 w)
Hettiarachchi	3	0	14	3	(2 w)
Jayasundera	4	0	29	0	
Gunaratne	4	1	21	4	(1 w)

Fall of Wickets	*Chil*	*Ttn*
1st	44 (1)	0 (1)
2nd	66 (2)	11 (3)
3rd	98 (3)	26 (4)
4th	98 (5)	50 (2)
5th	122 (4)	63 (5)
6th	157 (7)	106 (7)
7th	158 (6)	106 (6)
8th	162 (9)	109 (9)
9th	166 (8)	112 (10)
10th	179 (11)	112 (11)

TWENTY OVERS CAREER RECORDS

As at 30 April 2006

Note: These career records include Standard Bank Pro20, Pro20 Internationals and matches played in other Twenty Overs competitions around the world.

Name	M	Inns	NO	Runs	HS	Avg	SR	100	50	6s	Ct	St	Overs	Mdns	Runs	Wkts	Avg	RpO	BB	4I
YA Abdullah	5	0	0	0	-	-		0	0	0	0	0	114	0	131	4	32.75	6.89	2-20	0
ZA Abrahim	15	3	3	5	2 *	-	83.33	0	0	0	1	0	330	0	454	11	41.27	8.25	3-30	0
PR Adams	12	5	2	50	17 *	16.66	147.05	0	0	2	1	0	207	0	239	9	26.55	6.92	3-19	0
WA Albertyn	3	1	1	1	1 *	-	100.00	0	0	0	0	0	6	0	15	0	-	15.00	-	0
AM Amla	13	13	4	280	47	31.11	107.69	0	0	4	3	0	54	0	104	5	20.80	11.55	2-30	0
HM Amla	14	13	0	229	56	17.61	100.88	0	1	1	3	0	0	0	0	0	-	-	-	0
AM Bacher	17	17	1	364	65	22.75	117.79	0	2	11	3	0	279	0	366	14	26.14	7.87	3-14	0
RT Bailey	9	4	2	33	30 *	16.50	78.57	0	0	0	2	0	0	0	0	0	-	-	-	0
DM Benkenstein	17	17	4	400	53	30.76	134.68	0	1	18	4	0	132	0	175	11	15.90	7.95	3-10	0
JA Beukes	12	11	0	288	57	26.18	101.76	0	1	4	3	0	30	0	24	1	24.00	4.80	1-5	0
AM Blignaut	6	5	3	145	61 *	72.50	170.58	0	1	8	3	0	76	0	111	5	22.20	8.76	2-31	0
GH Bodi	21	14	1	252	47	19.38	102.85	0	0	5	4	0	6	0	6	1	6.00	6.00	1-6	0
N Boje	13	10	4	162	38 *	27.00	119.11	0	0	0	2	0	216	0	290	10	29.00	8.05	3-31	0
LL Bosman	20	20	1	598	104	31.47	147.29	1	2	34	5	0	0	0	0	0	-	-	-	0
ML Bruyns	7	7	0	58	35	8.28	71.60	0	0	0	2	0	0	0	0	0	-	-	-	0
JP Campher	2	0	0	0	-	-		0	0	0	1	0	42	0	62	0	-	8.85	-	0
S Chatterjee	2	0	0	0	-	-		0	0	0	1	0	24	0	17	0	-	4.25	-	0
SC Cook	8	8	0	193	45	24.12	124.51	0	0	1	1	0	0	0	0	0	-	-	-	0
H Davids	12	10	1	96	22 *	10.66	106.66	0	0	2	2	0	0	0	0	0	-	-	-	0
AC Dawson	13	3	3	11	5 *	-	91.66	0	0	0	1	0	275	0	295	17	17.35	6.43	4-18	1
WA Deacon	19	10	3	88	27	12.57	88.00	0	0	1	3	0	426	2	358	32	11.18	5.04	3-10	0
GJ de Bruin	6	2	1	0	0 *	0.00		0	0	0	1	0	102	0	161	5	32.20	9.47	2-1	0
P de Bruyn	10	7	4	79	27 *	26.33	136.20	0	0	3	5	0	157	1	180	11	16.36	6.87	4-11	1
Z de Bruyn	17	13	3	280	76 *	28.00	113.82	0	1	11	0	0	162	0	235	11	21.36	8.70	3-27	0
AB de Villiers	9	8	2	240	91 *	40.00	161.07	0	2	14	5	3	0	0	0	0	-	-	-	0
F de Wet	5	2	0	6	6	3.00	120.00	0	0	0	2	0	90	0	129	5	25.80	8.60	2-25	0
BC de Wett	9	8	0	78	16	9.75	73.58	0	0	0	2	0	0	0	0	0	-	-	-	0

TWENTY OVERS CAREER RECORDS

Name	M	Inns	NO	Runs	HS	Avg	SR	100	50	6s	Ct	St	Overs	Mdns	Runs	Wkts	Avg	RpO	BB	4I
HH Dippenaar	8	8	1	107	28	15.28	84.92	0	0	0	3	0	0	0	0	0	-	-	-	0
G Dros	20	14	4	230	35	23.00	132.94	0	0	13	7	0	0	0	0	0	-	-	-	0
J-P Duminy	18	16	4	370	67 *	30.83	106.62	0	1	8	3	0	84	0	101	3	33.66	7.21	1-3	0
D du Preez	5	2	2	7	7 *	-	140.00	0	0	0	2	0	60	1	64	4	16.00	6.40	2-2	0
AZM Dyili	3	3	0	36	23	12.00	70.58	0	0	3	3	1	0	0	0	0	-	-	-	0
Q Friend	11	3	1	0	0 *	0.00	0.00	0	0	0	1	0	229	0	264	8	33.00	6.91	2-29	0
R Frylinck	3	3	1	36	29	18.00	163.63	0	0	2	2	0	6	0	9	0	-	9.00	-	0
LL Gamiet	12	9	1	56	16	7.00	60.86	0	0	0	1	0	15	0	23	1	23.00	9.20	1-23	0
HH Gibbs	6	6	0	79	56	13.16	129.50	0	1	4	2	0	0	0	0	0	-	-	-	0
MJ Harris	11	8	1	122	35	17.42	91.04	0	0	2	7	0	0	0	0	0	-	-	-	0
IJ Harvey	24	23	3	787	109	39.35	171.08	3	3	29	5	0	455	0	558	26	21.46	7.35	3-28	0
M Hayward	10	2	0	5	3	2.50	83.33	0	0	0	2	0	171	0	249	5	49.80	8.73	3-21	0
B Hector	11	10	1	120	29	13.33	107.14	0	0	1	6	0	18	0	37	0	-	12.33	-	0
T Henderson	19	17	0	411	85	24.17	152.22	0	4	20	1	0	386	4	438	22	19.90	6.80	3-11	0
A Jacobs	19	17	3	284	45	20.28	110.50	0	0	9	6	0	0	0	0	0	-	-	-	0
DJ Jacobs	17	17	3	347	47	24.78	116.05	0	0	10	9	0	6	0	14	0	-	14.00	-	0
JC Kent	14	11	2	89	32 *	9.88	105.95	0	0	3	6	0	120	0	168	7	24.00	8.40	4-25	1
I Khan	9	5	0	30	22	6.00	66.66	0	0	0	3	0	102	0	156	6	26.00	9.17	2-15	0
RK Kleinveldt	15	13	2	143	46	13.00	143.00	0	0	8	3	0	298	1	318	18	17.66	6.40	3-18	0
L Klusener	18	17	7	368	63 *	36.80	132.37	0	2	11	6	0	408	2	566	17	33.29	8.32	2-13	0
PJ Koortzen	1	0	0	0	-	-		0	0	0	0	0	6	0	7	1	7.00	7.00	1-7	0
BB Kops	10	5	2	7	4 *	2.33	46.66	0	0	0	3	0	156	0	194	5	38.80	7.46	2-19	0
JP Kreusch	18	15	2	262	73	20.15	103.55	0	1	4	7	0	92	0	111	8	13.87	7.23	3-23	0
GJ-P Kruger	7	3	2	17	12 *	17.00	73.91	0	0	0	1	0	160	0	226	3	75.33	8.47	1-19	0
CK Langeveldt	7	2	1	2	2	2.00	40.00	0	0	0	4	0	144	0	173	4	43.25	7.20	2-14	0
ND McKenzie	17	16	5	425	85 *	38.63	131.57	0	3	13	5	0	6	0	12	0	-	12.00	-	0
R McLaren	12	7	4	30	10	10.00	81.08	0	0	0	2	0	180	1	204	5	40.80	6.80	2-21	0
DL Makalima	7	4	2	7	3 *	3.50	36.84	0	0	0	3	0	18	0	14	0	-	4.66	-	0
NE Mbhalati	15	1	0	0	0	0.00	0.00	0	0	0	2	0	258	0	334	9	37.11	7.76	3-22	0
L Meyer	5	4	2	23	14 *	11.50	82.14	0	0	0	4	0	102	1	152	7	21.71	8.94	2-26	0
EO Moleon	10	4	2	9	6	4.50	45.00	0	0	0	1	0	156	0	204	9	22.66	7.84	4-9	1
JA Morkel	18	14	4	176	46 *	17.60	125.71	0	0	4	1	0	281	0	363	9	40.33	7.75	2-29	0
M Morkel	8	2	1	4	2 *	4.00	50.00	0	0	0	1	0	126	0	186	5	37.20	8.85	2-17	0
PV Mpitsang	5	0	0	0	-	-		0	0	0	1	0	102	0	126	5	25.20	7.41	2-24	0
R Munnik	10	9	3	96	26 *	16.00	106.66	0	0	6	1	0	54	0	47	5	9.40	5.22	1-5	0

TWENTY OVERS CAREER RECORDS

Name	M	Inns	NO	Runs	HS	Avg	SR	100	50	6s	Ct	St	Overs	Mdns	Runs	Wkts	Avg	RpO	BB	4I
JG Myburgh	8	6	1	46	17	9.20	90.19	0	0	1	1	0	18	0	16	3	5.33	5.33	3-16	0
M Ngam	13	3	1	5	2 *	2.50	33.33	0	0	0	2	0	168	0	245	8	30.62	8.75	2-22	0
M Ntini	10	4	2	12	6 *	6.00	85.71	0	0	0	0	0	216	0	264	7	37.71	7.33	2-26	0
JL Ontong	12	10	1	101	30	11.22	100.00	0	0	3	5	0	138	0	172	4	43.00	7.47	1-20	0
AN Petersen	15	11	4	328	78 *	46.85	127.62	0	3	11	5	0	6	0	11	0	-	11.00	-	0
RJ Peterson	20	18	1	226	42	13.29	96.99	0	0	4	5	0	382	1	414	20	20.70	6.50	2-21	0
AM Phangiso	5	1	0	0	0	0.00	0.00	0	0	0	2	0	22	0	20	2	10.00	5.45	2-16	0
VD Philander	9	6	2	86	40	21.50	114.66	0	0	3	4	0	24	0	35	2	17.50	8.75	2-17	0
AG Prince	7	6	0	81	37	13.50	90.00	0	0	1	2	0	4	0	5	0	-	7.50	-	0
AG Puttick	17	16	2	357	86	25.50	105.30	0	3	4	7	0	0	0	0	0	-	-	-	0
MN Ranger	2	1	1	9	9 *	-	128.57	0	0	0	0	0	6	0	11	0	-	11.00	-	0
BL Reddy	14	7	2	27	10	5.40	108.00	0	0	2	4	0	232	1	286	20	14.30	7.39	3-27	0
JA Rudolph	9	9	1	187	71	23.37	104.46	0	1	2	3	0	1	0	1	0	-	6.00	-	0
Y Singh	5	0	0	0	-	-		0	0	0	0	0	84	0	109	2	54.50	7.78	2-13	0
D Smit	10	4	3	17	8	17.00	106.25	0	0	0	6	0	0	0	0	0	-	-	-	0
K Smit	7	7	0	254	76	36.28	139.56	0	2	7	2	0	0	0	0	0	-	-	-	0
MBA Smith	5	5	1	85	49	21.25	86.73	0	0	1	1	0	0	0	0	0	-	-	-	0
AM Sodumo	9	6	2	33	12	8.25	97.05	0	0	0	6	1	0	0	0	0	-	-	-	0
R Telemachus	19	8	5	70	34	23.33	189.18	0	0	4	7	0	360	1	458	17	26.94	7.63	4-25	1
FD Telo	8	5	0	122	48	24.40	132.60	0	0	2	2	0	0	0	0	0	-	-	-	0
AC Thomas	15	2	2	6	3 *	-	60.00	0	0	0	4	0	270	1	374	12	31.16	8.31	3-20	0
T Tshabalala	17	2	1	9	6 *	9.00	90.00	0	0	0	3	0	293	0	329	24	13.70	6.73	4-13	1
TL Tsolekile	18	12	7	266	52	53.20	118.22	0	1	2	17	3	0	0	0	0	-	-	-	0
ANW Tweedie	6	1	0	10	10	10.00	76.92	0	0	0	1	0	121	0	201	5	40.20	9.96	2-31	0
JJ van der Wath	18	14	3	118	28 *	10.72	100.85	0	0	3	1	0	337	0	443	19	23.31	7.88	2-11	0
M van Jaarsveld	26	23	3	557	61 *	27.85	130.44	0	5	11	16	0	42	0	52	3	17.33	7.42	2-19	0
VB van Jaarsveld	14	13	2	284	64	25.81	127.35	0	2	7	2	0	0	0	0	0	-	-	-	0
MN van Wyk	19	19	3	399	80 *	24.93	110.83	0	2	7	21	8	0	0	0	0	-	-	-	0
DJ Watson	5	5	0	112	48	22.40	147.36	0	0	4	1	0	0	0	0	0	-	-	-	0
CM Willoughby	26	6	4	15	11	7.50	136.36	0	0	1	4	0	551	4	553	25	22.12	6.02	4-9	1

SAA PROVINCIAL THREE-DAY CHALLENGE

Christo Buchner

Northerns scooped both the South African Airways first-class and one-day titles with victories in the finals over Western Province and Boland respectively. What made the victories so much sweeter was that they were both achieved away from home.

Chris van Noordwyk's charges underlined the strength in depth that exists in the north. In the first-class final they thumped Western Province by 100 runs after they amassed totals of 267 and 333-6 declared. In the second innings Kruger van Wyk scored his maiden first-class century.

Johan Myburgh was the shining star with the bat as he amassed 808 runs at an average of 80.80. Gerald Dros, a former Titans captain, scored two hundreds in a total of 565 runs at 70.62. Another former Titan who could not force his way into the franchise side, Pierre Joubert, starred with the ball and claimed 47 wickets at 11.78.

Seventeen teams will contest the 2006/07 competitition in two groups. Namibia, Mpumalanga and Limpopo will join the inland group, while KZN Inland, South Western Districts and Border Kei will be added to the coastal group.

Brian Frost, who heads amateur cricket at Northerns, said the competition was an excellent breeding ground for the franchises. He attributed Northerns' success to a strong club system. Clubs from the province have won the national club championship for the past three seasons.

Zimbabwe entered an Under-23 team in the competition as part of the United Cricket Board's effort to help the Zimbabwe Cricket Union raise standards. They played in five matches, all away from home.

SAA PROVINCIAL THREE-DAY CHALLENGE 2005/06

Pool A	**P**	**W**	**L**	**D**	**Bat**	**Bowl**	**Penalty**	**Pts**
Northerns	10	4	0	6	49.62	35	0	124.62
North West	10	4	1	5	41.98	38	0	119.98
Free State	10	2	5	3	40.62	34	0	94.62
Griqualand West	10	2	4	4	37.36	32	0	89.36
Easterns	10	3	4	3	25.28	32	0	87.28
Gauteng	10	1	2	7	39.18	33	0	82.18

Pool B	**P**	**W**	**L**	**D**	**Bat**	**Bowl**	**Penalty**	**Pts**
Western Province	9	7	1	1	36.24	34	0	140.24
KwaZulu-Natal	9	3	1	5	31.60	32	0	103.60
Border	9	3	3	3	38.42	33	0	101.42
Boland	9	1	3	5	26.94	33	0	69.94
Eastern Province	9	2	4	3	22.20	27	0	69.20
Zimbabwe Under-23	5	0	4	1	8.10	16	0	24.10

Zimbabwe Under-23 did not participate in the second half of the competition. KwaZulu-Natal were awarded 10 points for the match against Boland at Paarl after the match was abandoned due to a dangerous pitch. The match between Gauteng and Griqualand West did not take place and is reflected as a draw.

SAA PROVINCIAL THREE-DAY CHALLENGE

LEADING BATTING AVERAGES

		M	Inns	NO	Runs	HS		Avg	SR	100	50
1	JG Myburgh (Nor)	8	16	6	808	128	*	80.80	52.43	1	7
2	DM van Wyk (Gau)	7	12	5	513	122	*	73.28	55.22	1	4
3	G Dros (Nor)	5	9	1	565	136		70.62	84.96	2	4
4	F du Plessis (Nor)	4	8	2	422	156		70.33	64.92	1	3
5	B Hector (FS)	5	8	1	470	154		67.14	52.98	1	4
6	M Bekker (KZN)	8	9	1	505	138		63.12	82.92	2	3
7	SC Pope (Bdr)	4	7	1	346	102		57.66	59.24	1	2
8	BL Bennett (Bdr)	8	13	0	722	150		55.53	64.06	3	2
9	LL Gamiet (Bdr)	5	9	1	442	105		55.25	48.73	1	2
10	PJ Koortzen (FS)	7	12	1	580	107	*	52.72	59.97	1	3
11	WA Dugmore (Gau)	3	6	0	314	138		52.33	47.64	1	2
12	AJ Seymore (Eas)	6	9	1	410	135	*	51.25	49.93	2	0
13	J Booysen (Eas)	8	13	1	602	134	*	50.16	80.48	1	4
14	JA Beukes (FS)	4	8	0	398	130		49.75	67.45	1	2
15	CFK van Wyk (Nor)	5	5	0	227	104		45.40	54.69	1	2
16	WL Coetsee (NW)	5	9	2	309	108	*	44.14	81.53	1	1
17	W Wyngaard (WP)	9	16	4	529	132	*	44.08	52.42	3	1
18	AM Phangiso (Nor)	8	10	4	260	63		43.33	73.03	0	1
19	HG de Kock (FS)	8	15	2	556	93		42.76	48.47	0	5
20	AJA Gray (WP)	10	20	3	719	112	*	42.29	50.74	2	3

(Qualification: 5 completed innings)

LEADING BOWLING AVERAGES

		M	Overs	Mdns	Runs	Wkts	Avg	RpO	BB	5I	10M
1	P Joubert (Nor)	11	266.5	88	554	47	11.78	2.07	7-32	2	0
2	ZA Abrahim (KZN)	5	106.2	43	274	16	17.12	2.57	3-17	0	0
3	RK Kleinveldt (WP)	3	91.1	19	286	16	17.87	3.13	6-57	1	0
4	M de Stadler (WP)	10	353	115	841	47	17.89	2.38	5-42	1	0
5	WC Hantam (WP)	6	120	27	396	21	18.85	3.30	6-39	1	0
6	U Govender (KZN)	3	73	16	290	15	19.33	3.97	4-50	0	0
7	Q Friend (WP)	7	132.4	30	418	21	19.90	3.15	7-31	1	0
8	S Mhlongo (KZN)	7	130	33	387	19	20.36	2.97	5-25	1	0
9	R Pietersen (GW)	7	136.1	24	493	24	20.54	3.62	6-73	1	0
10	TD Pillay (KZN)	6	158.1	44	381	18	21.16	2.40	5-45	1	0
11	RR Richards (Bdr)	5	157	39	467	22	21.22	2.97	5-30	2	0
12	PSE Sandri (Bol)	6	148.2	34	480	22	21.81	3.23	5-32	1	0
13	S Conrad (WP)	5	158	19	554	24	23.08	3.50	6-45	3	1
14	D du Preez (FS)	5	154	41	372	16	23.25	2.41	5-33	1	0
15	FS Holtzhausen (NW)	8	209.2	40	612	26	23.53	2.92	5-25	1	0
16	S Mjekula (EP)	8	165	34	519	22	23.59	3.14	5-46	1	0
17	GJ de Bruin (Gau)	4	115.5	15	474	20	23.70	4.09	5-47	2	0
18	A Nawab (Gau)	5	119.3	13	498	21	23.71	4.16	6-106	2	1
19	RA Stroh (NW)	7	126	25	428	18	23.77	3.39	4-24	0	0
20	R Frylinck (KZN)	7	155.2	37	500	21	23.80	3.21	6-94	1	0

(Qualification: 15 wickets)

SAA PROVINCIAL THREE-DAY CHALLENGE

LEADING WICKETKEEPERS

		M	Ct	St	Total	
1	RCC Canning (WP)	10	30	1	31	
	HG Kuhn (Nor)	8	31	0	31	*
	C Linde (FS)	10	24	7	31	
4	TA Bula (NW)	10	26	3	29	
5	DR Miller (KZN)	9	26	2	28	

* includes 1 catch as fielder.

LEADING FIELDERS

		M	Ct	
1	DJ Kgamadi (NW)	10	14	
2	DJ van Wyk (FS)	7	11	
3	GE Howell (EP)	8	10	
	FA Steyn (NW)	9	10	
5	AJA Gray (WP)	10	9	
	TD Pillay (KZN)	6	9	
7	R Gobind (KZN)	7	8	
	WC Hantam (WP)	6	8	
	P Joubert (Nor)	11	8	
	AP McLaren (GW)	9	8	*
	LN Mosena (FS)	7	8	
	WE September (Bol)	8	8	

* also took 4 catches as wicketkeeper.

SAA THREE-DAY CHALLENGE AVERAGES

BOLAND

Batting & Fielding

Name	M	Inns	NO	Runs	HS	Avg	100	50	Ct	St
WJ Louw	4	8	1	266	85	38.00	0	1	6	0
H Davids	4	7	0	265	158	37.85	1	1	4	0
WA Albertyn	7	12	2	361	101 *	36.10	1	2	4	0
JG Strydom	5	10	1	301	123	33.44	1	0	1	0
QK Kannemeyer	2	3	0	94	70	31.33	0	1	0	0
PC Laing	5	8	0	243	80	30.37	0	2	4	0
WC Swan	9	16	0	427	93	26.68	0	4	2	0
WE September	8	14	4	263	63 *	26.30	0	1	8	0
R Bailey	3	6	1	125	60	25.00	0	1	2	0
DJ Malan	4	7	0	158	64	22.57	0	1	2	0
C Prinsloo	2	4	0	80	41	20.00	0	0	0	0
L-R Walters	8	15	2	258	56	19.84	0	1	16	1
JM van Wyk	3	5	1	71	33 *	17.75	0	0	0	0
RG Arendse	4	7	0	116	35	16.57	0	0	2	0
PSE Sandri	6	8	4	64	17 *	16.00	0	0	0	0
DL Hobson	1	2	1	15	11 *	15.00	0	0	1	0
WD Hayward	3	5	0	73	47	14.60	0	0	0	0

FA Geldenhuys	1	2	0	28	24	14.00	0	0	0	0
SP Summers	1	2	0	21	21	10.50	0	0	0	0
H Fourie	1	2	0	20	19	10.00	0	0	0	0
GC Stevens	3	5	0	48	18	9.60	0	0	1	0
AW Olivier	1	2	0	18	10	9.00	0	0	0	0
HH Paulse	8	9	4	22	8 *	4.40	0	0	2	0
BL Fransman	5	5	2	6	4 *	2.00	0	0	0	0
NM Northcote	1	1	1	27	27 *	-	0	0	2	0
Totals	99	165	24	3370	158		3	15	57	1
			Extras	303				subs	1	
			Total	3673		26.04			58	

Bowling

Name	Overs	Mdns	Runs	Wkts	Avg	BB	5I	10M
QK Kannemeyer	12	5	15	1	15.00	1-15	0	0
PSE Sandri	148.2	34	480	22	21.81	5-32	1	0
WA Albertyn	127.2	43	318	13	24.46	4-33	0	0
HH Paulse	152.2	22	635	21	30.23	5-65	1	0
BL Fransman	109.5	20	379	12	31.58	3-34	0	0
PC Laing	73	9	301	9	33.44	3-80	0	0
WE September	147	27	552	15	36.80	3-35	0	0
GC Stevens	54.1	11	157	4	39.25	2-22	0	0
JM van Wyk	47	5	205	5	41.00	2-45	0	0
DJ Malan	26.3	1	152	3	50.66	1-22	0	0
SP Summers	15	3	53	1	53.00	1-39	0	0
WC Swan	35	2	149	1	149.00	1-54	0	0
H Davids	11	2	49	0	-	-	0	0
DL Hobson	15	1	85	0	-	-	0	0
Totals	973.3	185	3530	107		5-32	2	0
		b/lb/pen	101	6	run outs			
		Total	3631	113	32.13			

BORDER

Batting & Fielding

Name	M	Inns	NO	Runs	HS	Avg	100	50	Ct	St
BC de Wett	2	4	0	263	182	65.75	1	1	2	0
SC Pope	4	7	1	346	102	57.66	1	2	5	0
BL Bennett	8	13	0	722	150	55.53	3	2	6	0
LL Gamiet	5	9	1	442	105	55.25	1	2	2	0
CC Bradfield	2	4	1	148	80	49.33	0	2	3	0
M Ngam	1	2	1	47	27	47.00	0	0	1	0
DL Brown	3	3	1	90	77 *	45.00	0	1	0	0
MN Ranger	8	11	2	343	96	38.11	0	3	7	0
L Mbane	8	9	2	254	60	36.28	0	1	5	0
GE von Hoesslin	8	13	2	319	101 *	29.00	1	1	17	1
KD Bennett	5	7	1	150	47	25.00	0	0	1	0
AZM Dyili	8	13	1	294	65	24.50	0	2	16	2
MW Olivier	3	2	1	18	9 *	18.00	0	0	0	0
MM Matika	3	5	1	63	21	15.75	0	0	4	0
LL Lwana	6	6	2	53	24	13.25	0	0	3	0
DC Lentz	2	2	0	23	19	11.50	0	0	0	0

S de Kock	6	8	0	85	31	10.62	0	0	1	0
MBA Smith	2	2	0	15	14	7.50	0	0	2	0
MX Pethu	2	4	0	28	15	7.00	0	0	0	0
RR Richards	5	3	0	17	12	5.66	0	0	1	0
WR Hinkel	1	1	1	18	18 *	-	0	0	1	0
Y Pangabantu	5	2	2	1	1 *	-	0	0	0	0
P Fojela	1	1	1	1	1 *	-	0	0	0	0
AM Sodumo	1	0	0	0	-	-	0	0	4	0
Totals	99	131	21	3740	182		7	17	81	3
			Extras	206				subs	2	
			Total	3946		35.87			83	

Bowling

Name	Overs	Mdns	Runs	Wkts	Avg	BB	5I	10M
GE von Hoesslin	1.3	0	9	1	9.00	1-9	0	0
WR Hinkel	27.1	3	66	6	11.00	4-42	0	0
P Fojela	19.1	1	72	6	12.00	4-34	0	0
LL Gamiet	5	0	17	1	17.00	1-14	0	0
RR Richards	157	39	467	22	21.22	5-30	2	0
Y Pangabantu	103	27	302	13	23.23	3-24	0	0
MW Olivier	84.3	10	319	12	26.58	4-68	0	0
BC de Wett	45.4	6	188	7	26.85	7-95	1	0
LL Lwana	77	15	315	11	28.63	3-6	0	0
MN Ranger	143	25	442	14	31.57	6-30	1	0
BL Bennett	76.2	14	292	9	32.44	5-21	1	0
L Mbane	130.3	31	490	15	32.66	5-26	1	0
DL Brown	49.5	10	179	4	44.75	3-83	0	0
S de Kock	86	11	324	7	46.28	2-56	0	0
SC Pope	16	2	65	1	65.00	1-57	0	0
M Ngam	15.3	1	76	1	76.00	1-76	0	0
KD Bennett	20.1	1	95	1	95.00	1-47	0	0
MM Matika	13	3	22	0	-	-	0	0
MBA Smith	12	4	25	0	-	-	0	0
Totals	1082.2	203	3765	131		7-95	6	0
		b/lb/pen	128	2	run outs			
		Total	3893	133	29.27			

EASTERN PROVINCE

Batting & Fielding

Name	M	Inns	NO	Runs	HS	Avg	100	50	Ct	St
CA Ingram	4	7	0	351	169	50.14	1	1	3	0
U Abrahams	7	12	2	354	100 *	35.40	1	2	4	0
SR Adair	4	6	2	128	44	32.00	0	0	9	2
D Willemse	5	6	1	157	58	31.40	0	1	4	0
S Makongolo	1	2	0	61	56	30.50	0	1	0	0
RR Jeggels	9	15	0	396	86	26.40	0	2	3	0
C Baxter	9	16	0	308	67	19.25	0	3	2	0
E Potgieter	3	6	1	79	30	15.80	0	0	4	0
SG Fensham	4	7	1	94	41 *	15.66	0	0	2	0
NG Brouwers	1	2	0	31	30	15.50	0	0	0	0
GE Howell	8	13	2	163	58	14.81	0	1	10	0

WE Bell	3	6	0	74	27	12.33	0	0	1	0
DD Carolus	3	5	1	46	16 *	11.50	0	0	2	0
R Nel	1	2	0	23	23	11.50	0	0	2	0
M Slwana	5	8	0	87	34	10.87	0	0	14	0
L Meyer	5	7	0	73	33	10.42	0	0	2	0
ML Price	6	11	0	110	59	10.00	0	1	1	0
J Theron	6	7	1	52	15	8.66	0	0	1	0
S Mjekula	8	9	6	25	10	8.33	0	0	1	0
LL Tsotsobe	5	6	2	33	12 *	8.25	0	0	1	0
L Dipha	1	2	0	14	9	7.00	0	0	0	0
U Sandi	1	1	1	0	0 *	-	0	0	0	0
Totals	99	156	20	2659	169		2	12	66	2
			Extras	159				subs	2	
			Total	2818		20.72			68	

Bowling

Name	**Overs**	**Mdns**	**Runs**	**Wkts**	**Avg**	**BB**	**5I**	**10M**
CA Ingram	42.3	0	163	8	20.37	4-16	0	0
S Mjekula	165	34	519	22	23.59	5-46	1	0
L Meyer	100	28	265	11	24.09	5-38	1	0
J Theron	122.3	24	387	16	24.18	6-47	1	0
WE Bell	19	1	99	4	24.75	3-57	0	0
U Sandi	10	3	27	1	27.00	1-27	0	0
LL Tsotsobe	123	26	395	14	28.21	4-38	0	0
D Willemse	100	23	299	8	37.37	4-56	0	0
GE Howell	156	28	529	11	48.09	2-27	0	0
DD Carolus	71	20	198	4	49.50	2-25	0	0
L Dipha	23	6	74	1	74.00	1-55	0	0
E Potgieter	1	0	1	0	-	-	0	0
C Baxter	0.5	0	6	0	-	-	0	0
ML Price	4	0	14	0	-	-	0	0
Totals	937.5	193	2976	100		6-47	3	0
		b/lb/pen	144	8	run outs			
		Total	3120	108	28.88			

EASTERNS

Batting & Fielding

Name	**M**	**Inns**	**NO**	**Runs**	**HS**	**Avg**	**100**	**50**	**Ct**	**St**
GH Bodi	1	2	0	158	143	79.00	1	0	2	0
Z de Bruyn	2	2	0	113	107	56.50	1	0	2	0
AJ Seymore	6	9	1	410	135 *	51.25	2	0	7	0
J Booysen	8	13	1	602	134 *	50.16	1	4	6	0
D Wiese	9	15	1	526	168	37.57	1	2	4	0
JA Morkel	1	2	0	70	68	35.00	0	1	1	0
RG Mutch	3	5	2	89	34 *	29.66	0	0	0	0
S Abrahams	1	2	1	26	15	26.00	0	0	0	0
NJ Livi	1	2	0	49	42	24.50	0	0	0	0
S Mandan	6	10	0	228	98	22.80	0	1	2	0
SR Connor	1	2	0	41	24	20.50	0	0	0	0
HA van Straaten	7	11	0	191	68	17.36	0	1	5	0
SP O'Connor	10	17	1	271	41	16.93	0	0	1	0

R Almeida	4	7	0	114	44	16.28	0	0	2	0
TM Bodibe	9	15	3	193	39 *	16.08	0	0	16	3
G Toyana	6	9	0	144	42	16.00	0	0	6	0
AM van den Berg	3	6	0	70	32	11.66	0	0	4	0
M Morkel	1	2	0	23	22	11.50	0	0	0	0
J Theunissen	1	2	0	22	22	11.00	0	0	0	0
BL Reddy	2	4	0	42	16	10.50	0	0	2	0
E Nyawo	5	9	0	88	31	9.77	0	0	4	0
IC Hlengane	9	12	4	55	23	6.87	0	0	4	0
PT Mofokeng	9	9	6	15	4 *	5.00	0	0	4	0
JT Maziya	1	2	0	4	4	2.00	0	0	0	0
W Barresi	3	6	0	9	5	1.50	0	0	5	0
GC Grobler	1	2	1	0	0 *	0.00	0	0	0	0
Totals	110	177	21	3553	168		6	9	77	3
			Extras	158				subs	0	
			Total	3711		23.78			77	

Bowling

Name	Overs	Mdns	Runs	Wkts	Avg	BB	5I	10M
M Morkel	10.5	1	27	3	9.00	3-27	0	0
JA Morkel	37	12	82	7	11.71	4-28	0	0
S Abrahams	28.2	6	93	5	18.60	4-33	0	0
GC Grobler	16	1	72	3	24.00	2-28	0	0
D Wiese	200.3	34	732	26	28.15	4-48	0	0
RG Mutch	70.2	9	282	10	28.20	4-57	0	0
R Almeida	122	26	464	15	30.93	5-18	1	0
IC Hlengane	171.4	27	594	19	31.26	7-107	1	0
AM van den Berg	53	6	182	5	36.40	3-32	0	0
SP O'Connor	130.2	13	547	13	42.07	4-61	0	0
PT Mofokeng	89	16	386	8	48.25	2-36	0	0
BL Reddy	66.1	14	237	4	59.25	3-56	0	0
Z de Bruyn	46	8	150	2	75.00	2-73	0	0
G Toyana	30	4	86	1	86.00	1-30	0	0
J Booysen	1	0	1	0	-	-	0	0
AJ Seymore	2	0	4	0	-	-	0	0
GH Bodi	4	1	23	0	-	-	0	0
JT Maziya	10	0	72	0	-	-	0	0
Totals	1088.1	178	4034	121		7-107	2	0
		b/lb/pen	139	3	run outs			
		Total	4173	124	33.65			

FREE STATE

Batting & Fielding

Name	M	Inns	NO	Runs	HS	Avg	100	50	Ct	St
CA Thyssen	4	5	1	304	157	76.00	1	1	1	0
B Hector	5	8	1	470	154	67.14	1	4	2	0
R Telemachus	1	2	0	116	116	58.00	1	0	1	0
PJ Koortzen	7	12	1	580	107 *	52.72	1	3	7	0
JA Beukes	4	8	0	398	130	49.75	1	2	5	0
HG de Kock	8	15	2	556	93	42.76	0	5	5	0
JF Mostert	3	5	2	112	70	37.33	0	1	1	0

RA Reeves	2	3	1	73	41	36.50	0	0	1	0
DJ van Wyk	7	10	0	351	106	35.10	1	1	11	0
TS Motsamai	8	11	5	171	51 *	28.50	0	1	1	0
LN Mosena	7	13	1	322	78	26.83	0	2	8	0
LL Bosman	1	2	0	48	43	24.00	0	0	0	0
D Elgar	2	4	0	70	32	17.50	0	0	0	0
C Linde	10	16	3	227	56	17.46	0	1	24	7
CA Ingram	2	3	0	42	32	14.00	0	0	2	0
MP Fick	4	6	0	78	29	13.00	0	0	3	0
D du Preez	5	6	0	50	23	8.33	0	0	1	0
JMM Malao	8	8	3	38	18	7.60	0	0	2	0
BK Sekonyane	8	8	0	57	20	7.12	0	0	3	0
SR Sibande	1	2	0	11	6	5.50	0	0	1	0
QG Samson	7	8	3	21	10	4.20	0	0	1	0
AP Abrahams	1	2	0	8	7	4.00	0	0	0	0
GD Perry	1	2	0	1	1	0.50	0	0	0	0
E Nogabe	1	2	1	0	0 *	0.00	0	0	0	0
AJ Schultz	2	2	2	2	2 *	-	0	0	1	0
T Tshabalala	1	0	0	0	-	-	0	0	0	0
Totals	110	163	26	4106	157		6	21	81	7
			Extras	260				subs	0	
			Total	4366		31.86			81	

Bowling

Name	Overs	Mdns	Runs	Wkts	Avg	BB	5I	10M
AP Abrahams	22	2	76	6	12.66	6-36	1	0
AJ Schultz	25	2	105	5	21.00	5-51	1	0
D du Preez	154	41	372	16	23.25	5-33	1	0
JMM Malao	247.4	31	872	30	29.06	5-27	1	0
JF Mostert	34.1	6	118	4	29.50	3-20	0	0
BK Sekonyane	193	43	708	24	29.50	4-80	0	0
R Telemachus	26	3	150	5	30.00	3-43	0	0
RA Reeves	10	1	64	2	32.00	2-25	0	0
TS Motsamai	179	33	585	17	34.41	2-16	0	0
CA Thyssen	18	2	70	2	35.00	2-27	0	0
QG Samson	151	18	702	17	41.29	3-31	0	0
GD Perry	13	3	49	1	49.00	1-49	0	0
MP Fick	26	4	122	2	61.00	1-24	0	0
HG de Kock	33.3	4	123	2	61.50	1-9	0	0
E Nogabe	4	0	22	0	-	-	0	0
PJ Koortzen	9	1	52	0	-	-	0	0
T Tshabalala	14	0	70	0	-	-	0	0
CA Ingram	21	1	71	0	-	-	0	0
Totals	1180.2	195	4331	133		6-36	4	0
		b/lb/pen	103	5	run outs			
		Total	4434	138	32.13			

GAUTENG

Batting & Fielding

Name	M	Inns	NO	Runs	HS	Avg	100	50	Ct	St
DM van Wyk	7	12	5	513	122 *	73.28	1	4	22	5
WA Dugmore	3	6	0	314	138	52.33	1	2	5	0
SC Cook	1	2	0	100	100	50.00	1	0	0	0
CE Knox	3	4	2	92	47 *	46.00	0	0	3	0
ET Nkwe	4	8	2	245	71 *	40.83	0	2	4	0
DR Gain	6	12	2	391	100	39.10	1	3	6	0
WB Motaung	6	11	0	419	114	38.09	2	1	5	0
J Symes	3	5	0	185	133	37.00	1	0	4	0
BC Adams	6	10	3	230	73	32.85	0	1	2	0
BD Snijman	7	13	0	420	114	32.30	1	2	6	0
MR Sekhoto	5	9	1	223	80	27.87	0	1	6	0
BW Buckley	1	2	0	52	41	26.00	0	0	0	0
PG Thompson	2	3	0	76	66	25.33	0	1	3	0
DL Makalima	6	11	0	248	61	22.54	0	2	4	0
DJ Terbrugge	2	4	1	66	28	22.00	0	0	0	0
K Moothosamy	3	5	0	77	42	15.40	0	0	1	0
S Burger	3	5	0	70	31	14.00	0	0	1	0
HW le Roux	4	4	0	49	25	12.25	0	0	5	0
BM Mathebula	3	5	1	46	16	11.50	0	0	1	0
A Nawab	5	6	2	44	19	11.00	0	0	3	0
GJ de Bruin	4	6	1	51	27	10.20	0	0	2	0
AM Omar	3	5	0	39	20	7.80	0	0	5	0
SF Grobler	1	1	0	3	3	3.00	0	0	1	0
JT Mafa	8	6	2	6	4	1.50	0	0	1	0
MT Masinga	1	2	2	69	48 *	-	0	0	1	0
Y Singh	1	1	1	16	16 *	-	0	0	0	0
S Chatterjee	1	1	1	1	1 *	-	0	0	0	0
Totals	99	159	26	4045	138		8	19	91	5
			Extras	212				subs	1	
			Total	4257		32.00			92	

Bowling

Name	Overs	Mdns	Runs	Wkts	Avg	BB	5I	10M
K Moothosamy	4	0	16	1	16.00	1-3	0	0
BD Snijman	41.4	4	161	9	17.88	4-26	0	0
S Burger	84.4	32	244	12	20.33	4-11	0	0
CE Knox	36	9	126	6	21.00	3-31	0	0
MR Sekhoto	12	2	67	3	22.33	2-42	0	0
S Chatterjee	42	9	140	6	23.33	5-81	1	0
GJ de Bruin	115.5	15	474	20	23.70	5-47	2	0
A Nawab	119.3	13	498	21	23.71	6-106	2	1
HW le Roux	70.3	15	296	11	26.90	4-66	0	0
JT Mafa	193.5	24	772	25	30.88	4-46	0	0
WB Motaung	13	1	33	1	33.00	1-15	0	0
DJ Terbrugge	62	13	227	5	45.40	2-38	0	0
J Symes	28.3	3	101	2	50.50	2-13	0	0
BM Mathebula	58	7	282	5	56.40	2-55	0	0
SF Grobler	12	0	65	1	65.00	1-61	0	0

Y Singh	31	8	72	1	72.00	1-44	0	0
PG Thompson	33	4	147	2	73.50	2-46	0	0
ET Nkwe	45	6	191	2	95.50	1-23	0	0
BC Adams	52	6	170	1	170.00	1-71	0	0
MT Masinga	9	1	42	0	-	-	0	0
DL Makalima	17	0	100	0	-	-	0	0
WA Dugmore	34	2	143	0	-	-	0	0
Totals	1114.3	174	4367	134		6-106	5	1
		b/lb/pen	96	3	run outs			
		Total	4463	137	32.57			

GRIQUALAND WEST

Batting & Fielding

Name	**M**	**Inns**	**NO**	**Runs**	**HS**	**Avg**	**100**	**50**	**Ct**	**St**
AG Doherty	4	8	0	308	92	38.50	0	3	1	0
W Bossenger	9	18	2	509	71	31.81	0	4	22	1
AP McLaren	9	18	0	570	131	31.66	2	3	12	0
J Brooker	9	18	0	552	99	30.66	0	5	5	0
AK Kruger	9	18	1	488	103	28.70	1	2	7	0
J Coetzee	9	17	3	383	56*	27.35	0	2	6	0
CN Bennett	5	10	0	266	64	26.60	0	1	3	0
FPG Holtzhausen	3	6	0	143	54	23.83	0	2	4	0
CJ de Jager	4	8	0	185	62	23.12	0	2	0	0
BW Lemmetjies	3	6	0	115	37	19.16	0	0	3	0
D Donaldson	3	6	0	109	42	18.16	0	0	2	0
M Bosman	4	8	0	103	28	12.87	0	0	2	0
NO Arthur	9	17	3	178	45	12.71	0	0	5	0
ES Tsamaisi	2	3	2	10	7*	10.00	0	0	0	0
MC Arthur	2	4	0	36	20	9.00	0	0	1	0
APT Mabuya	2	3	1	18	12*	9.00	0	0	0	0
R Pietersen	7	10	7	24	7	8.00	0	0	1	0
TR Plaatjie	5	9	4	39	25	7.80	0	0	1	0
D Pretorius	1	1	0	1	1	1.00	0	0	2	0
Totals	99	188	23	4037	131		3	24	77	1
			Extras	190				subs	1	
			Total	4227		25.61			78	

Bowling

Name	**Overs**	**Mdns**	**Runs**	**Wkts**	**Avg**	**BB**	**5I**	**10M**
R Pietersen	136.1	24	493	24	20.54	6-73	1	0
W Bossenger	3	0	26	1	26.00	1-26	0	0
J Coetzee	230.4	34	845	31	27.25	5-92	1	0
NO Arthur	187.4	34	658	24	27.41	6-27	1	0
ES Tsamaisi	11	2	59	2	29.50	1-25	0	0
AK Kruger	189	15	827	27	30.62	6-37	3	1
TR Plaatjie	47	8	186	6	31.00	2-39	0	0
D Donaldson	37	3	152	3	50.66	2-64	0	0
BW Lemmetjies	29	1	123	2	61.50	1-37	0	0
D Pretorius	26	3	83	1	83.00	1-83	0	0
FPG Holtzhausen	50.5	7	200	1	200.00	1-22	0	0

AP McLaren	1	0	3	0	-	-	0	0
CN Bennett	5	1	22	0	-	-	0	0
AG Doherty	10	0	44	0	-	-	0	0
APT Mabuya	19	2	95	0	-	-	0	0
Totals	982.2	134	3816	122		6-27	6	1
		b/lb/pen	106	5	run outs			
		Total	3922	127	30.88			

KWAZULU-NATAL

Batting & Fielding

Name	M	Inns	NO	Runs	HS	Avg	100	50	Ct	St
WR Wingfield	4	5	2	214	70	71.33	0	1	0	0
M Bekker	8	9	1	505	138	63.12	2	3	4	0
I Khan	2	3	1	102	61	51.00	0	1	1	0
ZA Abrahim	5	6	3	147	103 *	49.00	1	0	0	0
MD Sanders	5	7	0	290	103	41.42	1	1	0	0
R Gobind	7	11	2	343	112	38.11	1	1	8	0
R Frylinck	7	9	2	253	100 *	36.14	1	1	3	0
ND Hewer	4	3	2	35	23 *	35.00	0	0	1	0
DR Miller	9	12	2	301	64 *	30.10	0	2	26	2
WP Lombard	2	3	2	25	25 *	25.00	0	0	0	0
K Smit	3	4	0	82	46	20.50	0	0	2	0
TD Pillay	6	6	2	70	32	17.50	0	0	9	0
PM Selowa	2	2	0	35	19	17.50	0	0	3	0
T Essack	5	7	0	115	51	16.42	0	1	0	0
W Hauptfleisch	2	4	0	59	50	14.75	0	1	0	0
KC Africa	6	9	1	100	33	12.50	0	0	3	0
U Govender	3	3	1	24	21 *	12.00	0	0	2	0
R Reddy	2	1	0	10	10	10.00	0	0	1	0
TN Harvey	2	4	0	37	19	9.25	0	0	1	0
S Mhlongo	7	6	2	25	21	6.25	0	0	0	0
YA Abdullah	1	1	0	5	5	5.00	0	0	0	0
CS Mabuya	2	2	0	9	5	4.50	0	0	0	0
AI Chinnappa	3	3	0	9	5	3.00	0	0	1	0
FB Lazarus	2	4	0	3	2	0.75	0	0	1	0
Totals	99	124	23	2798	138		6	12	66	2
			Extras	162				subs	2	
			Total	2960		29.30			68	

Bowling

Name	Overs	Mdns	Runs	Wkts	Avg	BB	5I	10M
AI Chinnappa	10	1	33	3	11.00	3-19	0	0
ZA Abrahim	106.2	43	274	16	17.12	3-17	0	0
R Reddy	40.1	12	86	5	17.20	3-32	0	0
U Govender	73	16	290	15	19.33	4-50	0	0
S Mhlongo	130	33	387	19	20.36	5-25	1	0
T Essack	26	10	63	3	21.00	2-19	0	0
TD Pillay	158.1	44	381	18	21.16	5-45	1	0
R Frylinck	155.2	37	500	21	23.80	6-94	1	0
YA Abdullah	19.4	3	101	4	25.25	4-33	0	0

ND Hewer	96	15	328	11	29.81	4-31	0	0
KC Africa	87	22	278	8	34.75	4-31	0	0
WP Lombard	26.2	5	77	2	38.50	1-27	0	0
I Khan	20	2	80	2	40.00	2-50	0	0
R Gobind	3	2	1	0	-	-	0	0
K Smit	1	0	8	0	-	-	0	0
DR Miller	2	0	13	0	-	-	0	0
W Hauptfleisch	4	2	17	0	-	-	0	0
WR Wingfield	9	2	30	0	-	-	0	0
Totals	967	249	2947	127		6-94	3	0
		b/lb/pen	113	4	run outs			
		Total	3060	131	23.35			

NORTHERNS

Batting & Fielding

Name	M	Inns	NO	Runs	HS	Avg	100	50	Ct	St
JG Myburgh	8	16	6	808	128 *	80.80	1	7	7	0
N van Woerkom	2	4	0	308	146	77.00	1	2	1	0
G Dros	5	9	1	565	136	70.62	2	4	7	0
F du Plessis	4	8	2	422	156	70.33	1	3	5	0
AN Petersen	1	2	1	56	48 *	56.00	0	0	4	0
AC Thomas	1	2	1	56	42 *	56.00	0	0	0	0
PL Harris	2	1	0	47	47	47.00	0	0	2	0
CFK van Wyk	5	5	0	227	104	45.40	1	2	12	2
AM Phangiso	8	10	4	260	63	43.33	0	1	2	0
HG Kuhn	8	15	1	576	133 *	41.14	2	3	31	0
P Joubert	11	14	5	352	68	39.11	0	2	8	0
MA Aronstam	7	14	0	473	91	33.78	0	4	1	0
MJ Mokonyama	9	11	2	263	40	29.22	0	0	4	0
N Wagner	4	2	1	29	20	29.00	0	0	0	0
A Paleker	5	7	1	130	48	21.66	0	0	5	1
EE Meyer	3	6	1	100	31	20.00	0	0	1	0
N Chouhan	7	11	1	173	93	17.30	0	1	2	0
SJ Myburgh	4	4	0	44	31	11.00	0	0	4	0
MA Mashimbyi	9	8	2	59	34	9.83	0	0	1	0
NE Mbhalati	1	1	0	8	8	8.00	0	0	0	0
P de Bruyn	1	1	0	4	4	4.00	0	0	0	0
FG Nkuna	10	5	3	7	4 *	3.50	0	0	2	0
L Manzini	2	1	0	0	0	0.00	0	0	1	0
JR Jumat	1	1	1	5	5 *	-	0	0	0	0
AR Beukman	1	1	1	3	3 *	-	0	0	0	0
DW Steyn	1	1	1	1	1 *	-	0	0	0	0
TR Khoza	1	0	0	0	-	-	0	0	0	0
Totals	121	160	35	4976	156		8	29	100	3
			Extras	281				subs	0	
			Total	5257		42.05			100	

Bowling

Name	Overs	Mdns	Runs	Wkts	Avg	BB	5I	10M
CFK van Wyk	1	0	7	1	7.00	1-7	0	0
P de Bruyn	8	1	22	2	11.00	2-22	0	0

P Joubert	266.5	88	554	47	11.78	7-32	2	0
NE Mbhalati	35	15	70	4	17.50	4-35	0	0
N Wagner	85.2	26	245	14	17.50	4-39	0	0
L Manzini	23	4	80	4	20.00	4-22	0	0
TR Khoza	29.3	4	89	4	22.25	3-41	0	0
AC Thomas	21	4	45	2	22.50	2-31	0	0
F du Plessis	60	13	198	8	24.75	3-31	0	0
MA Mashimbyi	162	37	460	17	27.05	3-37	0	0
AR Beukman	21.3	7	55	2	27.50	1-27	0	0
DW Steyn	35	6	116	4	29.00	2-55	0	0
G Dros	81.1	10	264	8	33.00	3-41	0	0
FG Nkuna	175	35	579	17	34.05	4-43	0	0
AM Phangiso	163.4	36	513	15	34.20	5-76	1	0
MA Aronstam	220.3	50	686	17	40.35	5-82	1	0
JG Myburgh	66	15	207	5	41.40	2-45	0	0
N van Woerkom	12	3	43	1	43.00	1-13	0	0
PL Harris	28	8	55	1	55.00	1-8	0	0
EE Meyer	1	0	6	0	-	-	0	0
SJ Myburgh	3	1	11	0	-	-	0	0
JR Jumat	8	1	37	0	-	-	0	0
Totals	1506.3	364	4342	173		7-32	4	0
		b/lb/pen	114	3	run outs			
		Total	4456	176	25.31			

NORTH WEST

Batting & Fielding

Name	**M**	**Inns**	**NO**	**Runs**	**HS**	**Avg**	**100**	**50**	**Ct**	**St**
WL Coetsee	5	9	2	309	108 *	44.14	1	1	2	0
FS Holtzhausen	8	12	4	334	69 *	41.75	0	3	5	0
M Akoojee	10	17	2	626	105 *	41.73	2	2	6	0
FA Steyn	9	16	1	540	116	36.00	2	2	10	0
DJ Kgamadi	10	18	2	575	84	35.93	0	4	14	0
J le Roux	10	17	1	545	110	34.06	2	3	3	0
TA Bula	10	14	2	343	68	28.58	0	3	26	3
RA Stroh	7	11	1	243	52	24.30	0	1	5	0
HM Strydom	1	2	1	24	17	24.00	0	0	1	0
EO Moleon	4	5	2	62	20 *	20.66	0	0	1	0
JP Campher	6	4	2	40	17	20.00	0	0	3	0
R Bhayat	7	8	1	120	44	17.14	0	0	6	0
GH Bhayat	8	8	2	85	61 *	14.16	0	1	6	0
F de Wet	3	2	1	13	11	13.00	0	0	1	0
JS Hermitage	5	6	1	61	17	12.20	0	0	2	0
VCM Mazibuko	3	4	1	33	21	11.00	0	0	2	0
DP Lotter	1	2	0	14	8	7.00	0	0	0	0
F van der Merwe	3	1	0	6	6	6.00	0	0	0	0
Totals	110	156	26	3973	116		7	20	93	3
			Extras	227				subs	0	
			Total	4200		32.30			93	

Bowling

Name	Overs	Mdns	Runs	Wkts	Avg	BB	5I	10M
F de Wet	74	14	209	11	19.00	4-35	0	0
FS Holtzhausen	209.2	40	612	26	23.53	5-25	1	0
RA Stroh	126	25	428	18	23.77	4-24	0	0
VCM Mazibuko	30.2	3	151	5	30.20	3-37	0	0
GH Bhayat	187.5	41	659	21	31.38	3-42	0	0
WL Coetsee	129.3	28	431	13	33.15	3-40	0	0
JP Campher	120.5	15	547	16	34.18	3-54	0	0
J le Roux	8	0	35	1	35.00	1-1	0	0
JS Hermitage	81.2	7	350	9	38.88	3-85	0	0
M Akoojee	47.2	6	181	4	45.25	1-16	0	0
R Bhayat	56	8	257	5	51.40	2-59	0	0
F van der Merwe	54	9	206	4	51.50	2-69	0	0
EO Moleon	87	20	261	5	52.20	2-55	0	0
DJ Kgamadi	1	0	4	0	-	-	0	0
FA Steyn	3	0	17	0	-	-	0	0
Totals	1215.3	216	4348	138		5-25	1	0
		b/lb/pen	122	10	run outs			
		Total	4470	148	30.20			

WESTERN PROVINCE

Batting & Fielding

Name	M	Inns	NO	Runs	HS	Avg	100	50	Ct	St
RK Kleinveldt	3	4	2	136	115 *	68.00	1	0	4	0
VD Philander	1	2	0	92	66	46.00	0	1	0	0
W Wyngaard	9	16	4	529	132 *	44.08	3	1	6	0
AJA Gray	10	20	3	719	112 *	42.29	2	3	9	0
FD Telo	5	9	0	354	72	39.33	0	3	0	0
DJ Bassage	3	6	1	195	108 *	39.00	1	0	4	0
R Munnik	5	8	1	265	75	37.85	0	3	1	0
RCC Canning	10	15	2	473	72	36.38	0	5	30	1
Z Homani	7	13	1	383	118	31.91	1	1	3	0
JM Kuiper	4	6	1	146	81 *	29.20	0	1	1	0
PR Adams	2	2	0	52	47	26.00	0	0	1	0
WC Hantam	6	10	4	151	38	25.16	0	0	8	0
M Williamson	7	14	2	205	44	17.08	0	0	7	0
Q Friend	7	9	1	131	36	16.37	0	0	3	0
M de Stadler	10	11	2	146	37	16.22	0	0	4	0
F Jardine	1	1	0	14	14	14.00	0	0	0	0
JP Geoghegan	2	3	1	23	15	11.50	0	0	0	0
S Conrad	5	6	2	32	11	8.00	0	0	4	0
M Mahlombe	4	3	0	22	20	7.33	0	0	1	0
SG George	1	2	0	7	6	3.50	0	0	0	0
MR Masinda	1	1	0	1	1	1.00	0	0	0	0
LF Simpson	4	5	1	3	2	0.75	0	0	0	0
A Magiet	1	1	0	0	0	0.00	0	0	0	0
MD Walters	1	1	0	0	0	0.00	0	0	1	0
DL Haupt	1	0	0	0	-	-	0	0	0	0
Totals	110	168	28	4079	132 *		8	18	87	1
			Extras	249				subs	2	
			Total	4328		30.91			89	

SAA PROVINCIAL THREE-DAY CHALLENGE

Bowling

Name	Overs	Mdns	Runs	Wkts	Avg	BB	5I	10M
M Mahlombe	56	19	156	11	14.18	3-11	0	0
RK Kleinveldt	91.1	19	286	16	17.87	6-57	1	0
M de Stadler	353	115	841	47	17.89	5-42	1	0
WC Hantam	120	27	396	21	18.85	6-39	1	0
R Munnik	13	1	39	2	19.50	2-14	0	0
Q Friend	132.4	30	418	21	19.90	7-31	1	0
F Jardine	49.5	11	133	6	22.16	5-118	1	0
S Conrad	158	19	554	24	23.08	6-45	3	1
LF Simpson	49.5	9	182	7	26.00	3-22	0	0
VD Philander	37.2	9	108	3	36.00	3-57	0	0
PR Adams	51.2	14	145	4	36.25	2-3	0	0
DL Haupt	21	6	81	1	81.00	1-57	0	0
M Williamson	0.5	0	4	0	-	-	0	0
SG George	1	0	5	0	-	-	0	0
MR Masinda	1	0	8	0	-	-	0	0
JP Geoghegan	11	1	38	0	-	-	0	0
AJA Gray	45	6	165	0	-	-	0	0
Totals	1192	286	3559	163		7-31	8	1
		b/lb/pen	124	10	run outs			
		Total	3683	173	21.28			

ZIMBABWE UNDER-23

Batting & Fielding

Name	M	Inns	NO	Runs	HS	Avg	100	50	Ct	St
C de Grandhomme	5	10	0	279	109	27.90	1	1	4	0
B Mlambo	5	10	0	237	86	23.70	0	1	2	0
GM Strydom	5	9	0	182	56	20.22	0	2	3	0
GM Ewing	3	6	1	101	40	20.20	0	0	1	0
A Mwayenga	5	9	5	70	14 *	17.50	0	0	1	0
S Matsikenyeri	5	10	1	151	53	16.77	0	1	3	0
MA Vermeulen	4	8	0	128	47	16.00	0	0	4	0
IM Chinyoka	2	4	1	34	18 *	11.33	0	0	1	0
TMK Mawoyo	5	10	0	88	35	8.80	0	0	1	0
TN Garwe	1	1	0	8	8	8.00	0	0	0	0
H Matanga	2	4	2	13	8	6.50	0	0	1	0
EC Rainsford	3	6	1	20	10	4.00	0	0	1	0
A Maregwede	5	9	0	35	7	3.88	0	0	13	0
CB Mpofu	4	7	1	17	10	2.83	0	0	0	0
T Hove	1	1	0	2	2	2.00	0	0	1	0
Totals	55	104	12	1365	109		1	5	36	0
			Extras	146				subs	2	
			Total	1511		16.42			38	

Bowling

Name	Overs	Mdns	Runs	Wkts	Avg	BB	5I	10M
EC Rainsford	64.1	18	161	9	17.88	2-16	0	0
GM Ewing	28.4	4	112	5	22.40	3-27	0	0
A Mwayenga	102.1	18	338	14	24.14	5-41	2	0
IM Chinyoka	33.5	4	122	5	24.40	2-42	0	0

GM Strydom	75.1	13	253	8	31.62	3-29	0	0
MA Vermeulen	8	1	34	1	34.00	1-17	0	0
CB Mpofu	78	10	308	8	38.50	3-23	0	0
C de Grandhomme	75.2	14	226	5	45.20	3-26	0	0
H Matanga	56.5	6	162	2	81.00	1-26	0	0
S Matsikenyeri	21	0	94	1	94.00	1-18	0	0
TN Garwe	7	2	42	0	-	-	0	0
Totals	550.1	90	1852	58		5-41	2	0
		b/lb/pen	97	0	run outs			
		Total	1949	58	33.60			

SCORECARDS

Pool A

FREE STATE v GAUTENG — SAA 3-day Challenge Pool A

Played at Goodyear Park, Bloemfontein on 6,7,8 October 2005 — Toss: Free State
Umpires: CJ Conradie & MZ Nanabhay
Debuts: FS: LN Mosena (FC). Gau: HW le Roux (FC)
Close of play: Day 1: FS (1) 70-0 (Ingram 30*, De Kock 34*, 14 overs). Day 2: Gau (2) 82-0 (Cook 56*, Snijman 26*, 13 overs).
Result: Match drawn
Points: FS: 9.24 (bat 5.24, bowl 4, match 0); Gau: 5.84 (bat 3.84, bowl 2, match 0)

GAUTENG	Runs	Mins	Balls	4	6		Runs	Mins	Balls	4	6
SC Cook b Du Preez	0	3	5	-	-	lbw b Motsamai	100	137	126	17	-
BD Snijman c Linde b Schultz	28	82	51	5	-	b Motsamai	50	107	70	9	-
BC Adams c Ingram b Schultz	36	87	69	6	-	not out	30	119	83	1	-
*DR Gain c Ingram b Thyssen	10	60	35	2	-	st Linde b De Kock	22	54	50	2	-
MR Sekhoto b Schultz	80	141	110	14	-	not out	18	35	35	3	-
†AM Omar lbw b Sekonyane	7	15	8	1	-						
K Moothosamy c Linde b Sekonyane	20	48	34	4	-						
S Burger c Du Preez b Thyssen	31	76	47	5	-						
HW le Roux c Linde b Schultz	12	20	20	2	-						
BM Mathebula c and b Schultz	9	10	14	1	-						
JT Mafa not out	2	14	12	-	-						
Extras (b 2, lb 5)	7					Extras (b 2, w 1, nb 4)	7				
TOTAL (67.3 overs)	**242**					**TOTAL (for 3 wkts) (60 overs)**	**227**				

FREE STATE	Runs	Mins	Balls	4	6
CA Ingram b Mafa	32	65	45	5	-
*HG de Kock lbw b Snijman	93	198	164	17	-
DJ van Wyk c Sekhoto b Adams	72	194	139	11	-
PJ Koortzen c Omar b Sekhoto	19	32	32	3	-
CA Thyssen c Sekhoto b Burger	157	167	138	12	8
†C Linde c Le Roux b Mathebula	56	103	82	6	-
D du Preez c Sekhoto b Burger	23	21	12	3	1
LN Mosena lbw b Mathebula	0	3	1	-	-
TS Motsamai not out	0	8	7	-	-
AJ Schultz					
BK Sekonyane					
Extras (b 3, lb 7, w 2, nb 14)	26				
TOTAL (for 8 wkts dec) (101.4 overs)	**478**				

FS	O	M	R	W		O	M	R	W	
Du Preez	15	3	51	1		12	3	48	0	
Sekonyane	18	6	49	2		9	1	62	0	(3 nb)
Motsamai	9	3	33	0		(5) 6	0	16	2	(1 w)
Schultz	14	2	51	5		(3) 4	0	18	0	
Thyssen	7.3	1	27	2		(6) 6	0	19	0	
Ingram	4	0	24	0		(4) 16	1	45	0	(1 nb)
De Kock						7	0	17	1	
Gau	*O*	*M*	*R*	*W*		*O*	*M*	*R*	*W*	
Le Roux	13	0	61	0	(2 nb)					
Mathebula	14	1	92	2	(6 nb, 2 w)					
Mafa	12	2	63	1	(1 nb)					
Burger	23.4	6	117	2	(1 nb)					
Snijman	13	3	47	1						
Adams	23	4	71	1						
Sekhoto	3	0	17	1						

Fall of Wickets

	Gau	FS	Gau
1st	0 (1)	73 (1)	138 (2)
2nd	64 (2)	181 (2)	159 (1)
3rd	65 (3)	215 (4)	199 (4)
4th	109 (4)	247 (3)	-
5th	118 (6)	410 (6)	-
6th	166 (7)	467 (7)	-
7th	205 (5)	469 (8)	-
8th	227 (9)	478 (5)	-
9th	237 (10)	-	-
10th	242 (8)	-	-

NORTH WEST v GRIQUALAND WEST — SAA 3-day Challenge Pool A

Played at Sedgars Park, Potchefstroom on 6,7,8 October 2005 — Toss: Griqualand West

Umpires: IL Howell & SW Liebisch

Debuts: NW: JP Campher (FC). GW: FPG Holtzhausen and R Pietersen (Both FC)

Close of play: Day 1: GW (1) 77-3 (Bosman 28*, Bossenger 4*, 20 overs). Day 2: NW (2) 234-3 (Akoojee 96*, Coetsee 14*, 59 overs).

Result: North West won by 253 runs

Points: NW: 20.62 (bat 6.62, bowl 4, match 10); GW:7.82 (bat 3.82, bowl 4, match 0)

NORTH WEST	Runs	Mins	Balls	4	6		Runs	Mins	Balls	4	6
FA Steyn c Bossenger b Coetzee	74	150	125	12	1	c Lemmetjies b Coetzee	6	2	3	1	-
DJ Kgamadi c McLaren b Pietersen	28	43	33	4	-	c Holtzhausen b Lemmetjies	45	103	87	4	-
M Akoojee lbw b Kruger	15	36	26	3	-	not out	105	267	177	10	-
J le Roux c Bossenger b Coetzee	58	94	84	8	-	c Bosman b Kruger	66	109	92	9	1
WL Coetsee not out	108	160	111	8	1	not out	40	54	36	4	1
R Bhayat lbw b Lemmetjies	1	5	4	-	-						
FS Holtzhausen c Bossenger b Arthur	20	39	42	3	-						
†TA Bula b Coetzee	29	34	38	4	-						
*EO Moleon c Bossenger b Pietersen	19	58	35	2	-						
GH Bhayat c Holtzhausen b Pietersen	9	7	9	1	-						
JP Campher not out	7	6	6	-	-						
Extras (b 4, lb 4, w 2, nb 3)	13					Extras (b 2, lb 7, w 2)	11				
TOTAL (for 9 wkts) (85 overs)	**381**					**TOTAL (for 3 wkts dec) (66 overs)**	**273**				

GRIQUALAND WEST	Runs	Mins	Balls	4	6		Runs	Mins	Balls	4	6
M Bosman c Bula b Campher	28	91	57	5	-	(2) lbw b GH Bhayat	2	20	16	-	-
AP McLaren lbw b GH Bhayat	1	5	3	-	-	(1) b Campher	1	9	3	-	-
AK Kruger c GH Bhayat b Campher	22	32	34	4	-	b GH Bhayat	1	6	3	-	-
J Brooker c Bula b Holtzhausen	20	43	30	4	-	b GH Bhayat	15	20	13	3	-
*†W Bossenger b Moleon	62	114	66	7	1	c Kgamadi b Holtzhausen	30	45	26	4	-
J Coetzee c and b Campher	2	19	13	-	-	not out	56	133	93	6	-
BW Lemmetjies lbw b Coetsee	23	56	56	4	-	c GH Bhayat b Coetsee	35	49	48	3	1
FPG Holtzhausen c Bula b Holtzhausen	52	72	57	6	1	run out (Moleon/Campher)	0	11	11	-	-
NO Arthur c Steyn b Holtzhausen	14	34	33	2	-	b Moleon	3	22	20	-	-
ES Tsamaisi not out	3	24	20	-	-	run out (Bula/Kgamadi)	0	3	1	-	-
R Pietersen b GH Bhayat	6	16	14	-	-	c Le Roux b Coetsee	2	14	13	-	-
Extras (b 1, lb 3, nb 4)	8					Extras (b 9, lb 6)	15				
TOTAL (63.1 overs)	**241**					**TOTAL (41.1 overs)**	**160**				

GW	O	M	R	W		O	M	R	W	
Coetzee	21	3	75	3	(1 nb, 1 w)	17	0	62	1	(1 w)
Pietersen	14	1	69	3	(1 w)	(3) 9	2	47	0	
Tsamaisi	2	1	8	0						
Kruger	9	0	43	1		(2) 18	0	69	1	
Arthur	11	0	51	1	(1 nb)					
Holtzhausen	11	0	55	0	(1 nb)	(4) 12	2	49	0	(1 w)
Lemmetjies	17	1	72	1		(5) 10	0	37	1	
NW	*O*	*M*	*R*	*W*		*O*	*M*	*R*	*W*	
Campher	13	0	61	3		5	1	20	1	
GH Bhayat	10.1	2	26	2	(1 nb)	8	0	46	3	
Moleon	11	2	52	1		(5) 10	2	17	1	
Holtzhausen	15	2	32	3		(3) 3	0	13	1	
Coetsee	14	1	66	1	(3 nb)	(4) 13.1	3	44	2	
Le Roux						2	0	5	0	

Fall of Wickets

	NW	GW	NW	GW
1st	45 (2)	6 (2)	6 (1)	8 (1)
2nd	70 (3)	34 (3)	99 (2)	11 (3)
3rd	167 (1)	70 (4)	209 (4)	12 (2)
4th	192 (4)	78 (1)	-	35 (4)
5th	193 (6)	94 (6)	-	73 (5)
6th	236 (7)	133 (7)	-	132 (7)
7th	296 (8)	183 (5)	-	137 (8)
8th	353 (9)	229 (9)	-	152 (9)
9th	365 (10)	232 (8)	-	152 (10)
10th	-	241 (11)	-	160 (11)

EASTERNS v NORTHERNS — SAA 3-day Challenge Pool A

Played at Willowmoore Park, Benoni on 6,7,8 October 2005 — Toss: Northerns
Umpires: BG Jerling & JEP Ostrom
Debuts: Eas: IC Hlengane and D Wiese (Both FC). Nor: None
Close of play: Day 1: Nor (1) 98-5 (Mokonyama 16*, Joubert 14*, 36 overs). Day 2: Eas (2) 201-8 (Seymore 117*, Abrahams 4*, 86 overs).
Result: Northerns won by 8 wickets
Points: Eas: 5.62 (bat 1.62, bowl 4, match 0); Nor: 15.68 (bat 1.68, bowl 4, match 10)

EASTERNS	*Runs*	*Mins*	*Balls*	*4*	*6*		*Runs*	*Mins*	*Balls*	*4*	*6*
W Barresi b Mbhalati	0	1	2	-	-	c Kuhn b Nkuna	2	24	21	-	-
AJ Seymore c Mokonyama b Mbhalati	3	21	16	-	-	not out	135	431	298	14	-
G Toyana b Mashimbyi	31	84	55	6	-	c Kuhn b De Bruyn	7	67	37	-	-
J Booysen c Kuhn b Mbhalati	9	26	21	1	-	lbw b Joubert	0	2	1	-	-
D Wiese c Mokonyama b Joubert	0	13	2	-	-	c Kuhn b De Bruyn	22	49	50	2	-
*SP O'Connor lbw b Mashimbyi	18	48	39	2	-	c Kuhn b Aronstam	23	56	53	3	-
BL Reddy lbw b Mbhalati	12	39	23	2	-	c Du Plessis b Myburgh	5	14	9	1	-
M Morkel b Aronstam	22	65	59	3	-	(9) b Phangiso	1	32	24	-	-
†TM Bodibe c Myburgh b Joubert	18	111	102	1	-	(8) b Phangiso	8	60	61	1	-
S Abrahams not out	11	60	53	2	-	c Kuhn b Joubert	15	62	60	2	-
IC Hlengane						b Aronstam	11	57	46	1	-
Extras (lb 5, nb 2)	7					Extras (b 2, lb 8, w 1, nb 1)	12				
TOTAL (for 9 wkts dec) (61.3 overs)	**131**					**TOTAL (109.5 overs)**	**241**				

NORTHERNS	*Runs*	*Mins*	*Balls*	*4*	*6*		*Runs*	*Mins*	*Balls*	*4*	*6*
MA Aronstam lbw b Morkel	0	2	2	-	-	c Seymore b Abrahams	20	49	37	3	-
†HG Kuhn c Bodibe b Morkel	0	6	1	-	-	c Booysen b Hlengane	52	120	90	7	-
JG Myburgh c Toyana b Reddy	34	101	66	5	-	not out	90	222	180	12	1
F du Plessis c Bodibe b Morkel	18	50	47	2	-	not out	58	152	115	7	1
P de Bruyn c Booysen b Abrahams	4	28	16	-	-						
MJ Mokonyama c Bodibe b Reddy	17	80	47	2	-						
*P Joubert b Reddy	23	101	80	3	-						
AM Phangiso lbw b Abrahams	7	29	26	1	-						
MA Mashimbyi c Wiese b Abrahams	4	43	26	-	-						
NE Mbhalati lbw b Abrahams	8	28	21	1	-						
FG Nkuna not out	4	7	7	1	-						
Extras (b 1, lb 6, w 1, nb 7)	15					Extras (b 7, lb 3, w 3, nb 7)	20				
TOTAL (55.2 overs)	**134**					**TOTAL (for 2 wkts) (69.1 overs)**	**240**				

Nor	*O*	*M*	*R*	*W*		*O*	*M*	*R*	*W*	
Mbhalati	14	7	35	4		21	8	35	0	(1 w)
Nkuna	11	2	35	0	(2 nb)	12	4	23	1	(1 nb)
Joubert	10.3	8	11	2		(4) 19	4	34	2	
Mashimbyi	7	1	20	2		(3) 14	4	32	0	
Aronstam	9	3	15	1		(7) 16.5	4	38	2	
Phangiso	10	5	10	0		11	1	19	2	
De Bruyn						(5) 8	1	22	2	
Myburgh						7	2	18	1	
Du Plessis						1	0	10	0	
Eas	*O*	*M*	*R*	*W*		*O*	*M*	*R*	*W*	
Morkel	10.5	1	27	3	(6 nb)					
Reddy	22.1	7	56	3		(1) 18	5	64	0	
Abrahams	16.2	6	33	4	(1 nb, 1 w)	(2) 12	0	60	1	(7 nb)
O'Connor	6	2	11	0		8	1	27	0	
Wiese						(3) 7	0	32	0	
Hlengane						(5) 23.1	8	43	1	(1 w)
Toyana						(6) 1	0	4	0	

Fall of Wickets

	Eas	Nor	Eas	Nor
1st	0 (1)	0 (1)	4 (1)	47 (1)
2nd	8 (2)	1 (2)	45 (3)	104 (2)
3rd	28 (4)	35 (4)	46 (4)	-
4th	41 (5)	55 (5)	78 (5)	-
5th	45 (3)	69 (3)	119 (6)	-
6th	70 (6)	107 (6)	129 (7)	-
7th	77 (7)	117 (8)	165 (8)	-
8th	112 (8)	118 (7)	177 (9)	-
9th	131 (9)	127 (10)	222 (10)	-
10th	-	134 (9)	241 (11)	-

GAUTENG v EASTERNS — SAA 3-day Challenge Pool A

Played at Orban Park, University of Johannesburg, Johannesburg on 13,14,15 October 2005 — Toss: Gauteng
Umpires: EC Hendrikse & LJ Willemse
Debuts: Gau: MT Masinga and J Symes (Both FC). Eas: GC Grobler and E Nyawo (Both FC)
Close of play: Day 1: Gau (1) 59-2 (Adams 17*, Gain 0*, 12 overs). Day 2: Eas (2) 126-4 (Bodi 57*, O'Connor 5*, 37 overs).
Result: Easterns won by 133 runs
Points: Gau: 8.8 (bat 4.80, bowl 4, match 0); Eas:16.5 (bat 2.50, bowl 4, match 10)

EASTERNS	Runs	Mins	Balls	4	6		Runs	Mins	Balls	4	6
S Mandan c Symes b De Bruin	0	1	1	-	-	c Masinga b De Bruin	0	1	2	-	-
†W Barresi c Makalima b De Bruin	5	20	13	1	-	lbw b Thompson	0	12	7	-	-
E Nyawo c Omar b De Bruin	0	3	5	-	-	lbw b Burger	31	72	61	6	-
J Booysen c Omar b Burger	67	139	106	14	-	(7) lbw b Burger	95	123	92	13	2
GH Bodi c Omar b De Bruin	15	72	59	2	-	(4) c Thompson b Moothosamy	143	345	239	16	2
D Wiese c Burger b De Bruin	54	96	76	11	-	(5) b Thompson	32	46	32	7	-
*SP O'Connor lbw b Burger	6	12	14	1	-	(6) c Moothosamy b Burger	12	52	39	2	-
R Almeida c and b Symes	19	35	25	4	-	c Omar b De Bruin	3	23	13	-	-
GC Grobler not out	0	4	1	-	-	lbw b De Bruin	0	1	1	-	-
IC Hlengane b Symes	0	1	1	-	-	not out	2	52	34	-	-
PT Mofokeng						b De Bruin	1	17	16	-	-
Extras (b 1, lb 2, w 2, nb 4)	9					Extras (lb 9, nb 5)	14				
TOTAL (for 9 wkts dec) (49.3 overs)	**175**					**TOTAL (88.3 overs)**	**333**				

GAUTENG	Runs	Mins	Balls	4	6		Runs	Mins	Balls	4	6
J Symes lbw b Wiese	27	40	30	5	-	lbw b Almeida	0	2	5	-	-
DL Makalima c Bodi b Wiese	12	22	12	2	-	lbw b Grobler	14	36	23	3	-
BC Adams c Mandan b Almeida	18	56	31	3	-	b Almeida	0	9	6	-	-
*DR Gain lbw b Grobler	20	100	75	4	-	c Barresi b Grobler	5	19	13	1	-
MR Sekhoto b O'Connor	41	112	84	6	-	c Booysen b Wiese	20	37	27	4	-
†AM Omar c Bodi b O'Connor	10	20	15	2	-	(7) lbw b Almeida	2	35	18	-	-
K Moothosamy c Almeida b O'Connor	9	41	23	2	-	(6) c Barresi b Almeida	5	14	9	1	-
S Burger c Barresi b Wiese	16	19	17	3	-	b Wiese	2	9	8	-	-
MT Masinga not out	48	87	72	7	2	not out	21	42	35	1	-
GJ de Bruin c Barresi b O'Connor	0	2	3	-	-	b Almeida	2	5	6	-	-
PG Thompson lbw b Wiese	66	78	57	8	2	c Mofokeng b Wiese	10	18	17	1	-
Extras (b 12, lb 6, w 1, nb 4)	23					Extras (lb 1, w 1, nb 2)	4				
TOTAL (69.1 overs)	**290**					**TOTAL (27.3 overs)**	**85**				

Gau	O	M	R	W			O	M	R	W	
De Bruin	10	1	47	5	(3 nb, 1 w)		23.3	3	103	4	(5 nb)
Thompson	8	1	33	0			13	2	46	2	
Burger	15	8	31	2	(1 nb)	(4)	21	7	35	3	
Masinga	4	1	16	0	(1 w)	(3)	5	0	26	0	
Adams	5	1	12	0		(6)	7	1	31	0	
Makalima	5	0	20	0		(7)	3	0	24	0	
Symes	2.3	0	13	2		(5)	14	3	56	0	
Moothosamy							2	0	3	1	
Eas	O	M	R	W			O	M	R	W	
Almeida	23	8	57	1	(1 nb)		13	6	18	5	
Grobler	10	1	44	1	(2 nb)		6	0	28	2	(2 nb, 1 w)
Wiese	15.1	6	48	4	(1 nb)	(4)	6.3	1	21	3	
O'Connor	12	1	61	4		(3)	2	0	17	0	
Bodi	4	1	23	0							
Mofokeng	2	0	17	0	(1 w)						
Hlengane	3	0	22	0							

Fall of Wickets	Eas	Gau	Eas	Gau
1st	0 (1)	36 (2)	0 (1)	0 (1)
2nd	1 (3)	57 (1)	1 (2)	4 (3)
3rd	13 (2)	61 (3)	49 (3)	21 (4)
4th	56 (5)	114 (4)	106 (5)	22 (2)
5th	117 (4)	130 (6)	143 (6)	27 (6)
6th	127 (7)	137 (5)	285 (7)	50 (5)
7th	175 (6)	154 (8)	297 (8)	52 (8)
8th	175 (8)	162 (7)	297 (9)	52 (7)
9th	175 (10)	162 (10)	331 (4)	56 (10)
10th	-	290 (11)	333 (11)	85 (11)

NORTHERNS v NORTH WEST — SAA 3-day Challenge Pool A

Played at SuperSport Park, Centurion on 13,14,15 October 2005 — Toss: Northerns

Umpires: SB Lambson & SW Liebisch

Debuts: Nor: AR Beukman (FC). NW: JS Hermitage (FC)

Close of play: Day 1: NW (1) 4-0 (Steyn 4*, Kgamadi 0*, 1 over). Day 2: Nor (2) 79-2 (Chouhan 19*, Van Woerkom 10*, 32 overs).

Result: Match drawn

Points: Nor: 8.28 (bat 4.28, bowl 4, match 0); NW: 7.08 (bat 3.08, bowl 4, match 0)

NORTHERNS	Runs	Mins	Balls	4	6		Runs	Mins	Balls	4	6
MA Aronstam c and b Holtzhausen	24	91	54	4	-	c Bula b Holtzhausen	11	50	56	1	-
†HG Kuhn c GH Bhayat b De Wet	7	24	24	1	-	c Steyn b Holtzhausen	24	89	45	2	-
N Chouhan c R Bhayat b De Wet	0	9	5	-	-	c R Bhayat b De Wet	20	88	73	3	-
N van Woerkom lbw b Akoojee	71	135	101	12	-	c R Bhayat b Akoojee	53	155	114	5	-
EE Meyer run out (Kgamadi/Bula)	17	48	36	2	-	c Bula b Holtzhausen	0	4	1	-	-
MJ Mokonyama c Bula b GH Bhayat	13	56	47	1	-	c Moleon b Holtzhausen	32	59	36	5	1
*P Joubert c R Bhayat b GH Bhayat	56	136	85	5	1	b De Wet	33	63	43	3	-
AM Phangiso st Bula b Hermitage	26	68	65	6	-	not out	24	35	32	2	-
MA Mashimbyi b De Wet	34	58	59	2	-	not out	2	13	5	-	-
AR Beukman not out	3	9	4	-	-						
FG Nkuna b De Wet	0	2	3	-	-						
Extras (lb 5, w 2, nb 6)	13					Extras (lb 13, w 3, nb 3)	19				
TOTAL (79.4 overs)	**264**					**TOTAL (for 7 wkts dec) (67 overs)**	**218**				

NORTH WEST	Runs	Mins	Balls	4	6		Runs	Mins	Balls	4	6
FA Steyn c Mokonyama b Van Woerkom	27	141	99	5	-	lbw b Aronstam	105	259	176	14	-
DJ Kgamadi c Kuhn b Nkuna	12	19	11	3	-	c Kuhn b Joubert	6	54	39	-	-
M Akoojee b Joubert	11	27	18	2	-	lbw b Beukman	0	12	9	-	-
J le Roux b Joubert	0	17	14	-	-	c Meyer b Mashimbyi	1	28	21	-	-
R Bhayat b Joubert	0	24	17	-	-	b Mashimbyi	44	85	81	7	-
FS Holtzhausen b Joubert	10	17	17	2	-	c Joubert b Mashimbyi	4	6	6	1	-
†TA Bula c Kuhn b Joubert	37	83	61	6	-	c Van Woerkom b Joubert	18	39	39	2	-
*EO Moleon c Kuhn b Joubert	3	43	37	-	-	not out	1	54	36	-	-
JS Hermitage c Kuhn b Beukman	17	135	93	3	-	b Joubert	0	3	3	-	-
F de Wet c Kuhn b Nkuna	11	23	18	2	-	not out	2	19	18	-	-
GH Bhayat not out	61	106	100	7	2						
Extras (lb 9, w 4, nb 2)	15					Extras (b 4, lb 2, w 1, nb 2)	9				
TOTAL (80.3 overs)	**204**					**TOTAL (for 8 wkts) (71 overs)**	**190**				

NW	O	M	R	W		O	M	R	W
De Wet	13.4	3	35	4 (4 nb)		13	3	32	2 (3 nb, 1 w)
GH Bhayat	17	3	68	2 (1 nb, 2 w)		8	0	41	0
Moleon	13	2	40	0	(4)	15	5	30	0
Holtzhausen	14	2	34	1	(3)	22	6	66	4
Akoojee	12	0	45	1		7	1	28	1
Hermitage	10	2	37	1 (1 nb)		2	0	8	0 (1 w)
Nor	*O*	*M*	*R*	*W*		*O*	*M*	*R*	*W*
Nkuna	16	5	39	2 (2 w)		11	3	37	0
Beukman	13.3	7	28	1		8	0	27	1
Joubert	20	13	39	6 (1 w)		19	5	29	3
Mashimbyi	12	6	21	0 (1 w)		13	1	37	3 (1 w)
Van Woerkom	4	2	13	1 (2 nb)		4	1	11	0 (2 nb)
Aronstam	11	5	17	0		16	3	43	1
Phangiso	4	0	38	0					

Fall of Wickets

	Nor	NW	Nor	NW
1st	13 (2)	17 (2)	35 (1)	38 (2)
2nd	14 (3)	32 (3)	54 (2)	41 (3)
3rd	68 (1)	36 (4)	83 (3)	51 (4)
4th	112 (5)	44 (5)	86 (5)	128 (5)
5th	135 (4)	56 (6)	143 (6)	136 (6)
6th	149 (6)	75 (1)	170 (4)	166 (7)
7th	203 (8)	105 (8)	207 (7)	183 (1)
8th	260 (7)	110 (7)	-	184 (9)
9th	264 (9)	130 (10)	-	-
10th	264 (11)	204 (9)	-	-

GRIQUALAND WEST v FREE STATE — SAA 3-day Challenge Pool A

Played at De Beers Diamond Oval, Kimberley on 20,21,22 October 2005 — Toss: Free State

Umpires: JEP Ostrom & BDA Westraadt

Debuts: GW: None. FS: None

Close of play: Day 1: GW (1) 228-3 (Kruger 103*, Bossenger 10*, 38 overs). Day 2: GW (2) 73-3 (Brooker 32*, Bossenger 0*, 22 overs).

Result: Free State won by 12 runs

Points: GW: 8.94 (bat 4.94, bowl 4, match 0); FS: 18 (bat 4.00, bowl 4, match 10);

FREE STATE	Runs	Mins	Balls	4	6		Runs	Mins	Balls	4	6
SR Sibande c Holtzhausen b Coetzee	6	30	22	1	-	lbw b Coetzee	5	11	13	1	-
*HG de Kock c Bossenger b Kruger	13	47	38	3	-	b Plaatjie	19	53	35	3	-
CA Ingram c Arthur b Coetzee	2	21	18	-	-	c Bossenger b Plaatjie	8	33	26	2	-
PJ Koortzen c Brooker b Plaatjie	38	73	45	5	-	c Bossenger b Kruger	47	128	91	7	-
DJ van Wyk c Bossenger b Pietersen	17	37	21	2	1	c Bossenger b Kruger	34	64	41	5	-
†C Linde c Coetzee b Pietersen	1	8	7	-	-	b Kruger	0	1	1	-	-
D du Preez b Pietersen	0	9	4	-	-	c Holtzhausen b Kruger	0	2	3	-	-
R Telemachus c Bossenger b Plaatjie	116	133	113	15	3	c Coetzee b Kruger	0	7	5	-	-
JMM Malao c Coetzee b Pietersen	0	4	4	-	-	c Bossenger b Kruger	18	60	55	2	-
TS Motsamai not out	51	126	110	7	-	b Holtzhausen	22	37	34	2	-
AJ Schultz not out	0	9	4	-	-	not out	2	18	12	-	-
Extras (lb 3, w 1, nb 2)	6					Extras (b 4, lb 8, w 2, nb 4)	18				
TOTAL (for 9 wkts dec) (64 overs)	**250**					**TOTAL (52 overs)**	**173**				

GRIQUALAND WEST	Runs	Mins	Balls	4	6		Runs	Mins	Balls	4	6
M Bosman lbw b Telemachus	5	22	11	1	-	(2) lbw b Telemachus	22	86	46	4	-
AP McLaren c Linde b Du Preez	16	19	20	3	-	(1) b Du Preez	10	16	18	2	-
AK Kruger c Linde b Du Preez	103	170	126	14	1	b Telemachus	5	20	17	1	-
J Brooker b Malao	70	130	92	8	-	c De Kock b Telemachus	32	62	54	4	-
*†W Bossenger c Sibande b Telemachus	19	44	28	4	-	b Du Preez	5	36	19	1	-
J Coetzee c Koortzen b Du Preez	3	19	12	-	-	c Van Wyk b Motsamai	20	73	66	2	-
BW Lemmetjies c Koortzen b Malao	37	63	34	4	2	c Koortzen b Du Preez	0	20	12	-	-
FPG Holtzhausen c Linde b Motsamai	9	31	26	1	-	c Linde b Motsamai	5	13	8	1	-
NO Arthur c Linde b Malao	1	27	26	-	-	b Du Preez	1	34	11	-	-
TR Plaatjie c Telemachus b Malao	2	8	8	-	-	lbw b Du Preez	1	11	6	-	-
R Pietersen not out	0	2	0	-	-	not out	0	6	3	-	-
Extras (b 4, lb 1, w 2, nb 25)	32					Extras (lb 5, w 3, nb 5)	13				
TOTAL (59.5 overs)	**297**					**TOTAL (42.3 overs)**	**114**				

GW	O	M	R	W		O	M	R	W	
Coetzee	14	3	55	2	(1 nb)	12	3	37	1	(1 w)
Plaatjie	10	4	39	2		11	1	44	2	(1 w)
Kruger	11	2	34	1		(4) 14	3	37	6	(3 nb)
Pietersen	13	0	44	4	(1 w)	(3) 7	1	21	0	
Lemmetjies	2	0	14	0						
Holtzhausen	9	1	39	0	(1 nb)	(5) 8	2	22	1	(1 nb)
Arthur	5	1	22	0						
FS	O	M	R	W		O	M	R	W	
Telemachus	15	0	107	2	(24 nb)	11	3	43	3	(5 nb)
Du Preez	21	5	60	3		18	5	33	5	
Schultz	5	0	33	0		(4) 2	0	3	0	
Motsamai	6	3	26	1	(1 w)	(3) 10.3	2	26	2	(3 w)
Malao	11.5	1	64	4	(1 w)	1	0	4	0	
Ingram	1	0	2	0						

Fall of Wickets

	FS	GW	FS	GW
1st	17 (1)	24 (2)	12 (1)	17 (1)
2nd	23 (2)	28 (1)	35 (3)	29 (3)
3rd	23 (3)	202 (4)	38 (2)	72 (2)
4th	59 (5)	237 (3)	108 (5)	74 (4)
5th	64 (6)	240 (5)	108 (6)	89 (5)
6th	78 (7)	242 (6)	108 (7)	94 (7)
7th	84 (4)	287 (8)	108 (8)	104 (8)
8th	85 (9)	295 (7)	132 (4)	111 (9)
9th	245 (8)	297 (10)	153 (9)	113 (10)
10th	-	297 (9)	173 (10)	114 (6)

FREE STATE v NORTH WEST — SAA 3-day Challenge Pool A

Played at Goodyear Park, Bloemfontein on 27,28,29 October 2005 — Toss: North West

Umpires: CJ Conradie & BM White

Debuts: FS: MP Fick (FC). NW: None

Close of play: Day 1: FS (1) 67-1 (Hector 16*, Van Wyk 18*, 16 overs). Day 2: FS (1) 250-6 (Koortzen 81*, Motsamai 0*, 70.2 overs).

Result: Match drawn

Points: FS: 9.12 (bat 5.12, bowl 4, match 0); NW: 6.72 (bat 3.72, bowl 3, match 0)

NORTH WEST	Runs	Mins	Balls	4	6
FA Steyn c Van Wyk b Samson	52	115	102	8	-
DJ Kgamadi b Samson	24	90	53	2	-
M Akoojee lbw b Samson	59	134	96	10	-
J le Roux b Du Preez	4	31	22	-	-
R Bhayat b Du Preez	0	8	5	-	-
†TA Bula c Linde b Du Preez	9	21	17	1	-
FS Holtzhausen c Koortzen b Malao	28	83	59	6	-
*EO Moleon not out	20	80	62	2	-
JS Hermitage c Van Wyk b Motsamai	7	33	32	1	-
F van der Merwe lbw b Malao	6	11	12	1	-
F de Wet					
Extras (b 6, lb 4, w 1, nb 16)	27				
TOTAL (for 9 wkts dec) (74 overs)	**236**				

FREE STATE	Runs	Mins	Balls	4	6
*B Hector lbw b Holtzhausen	23	102	80	3	-
MP Fick c Bula b Moleon	29	42	25	3	1
DJ van Wyk c Holtzhausen b Van der Merwe	30	76	45	4	-
PJ Koortzen not out	107	247	170	10	-
CA Thyssen b Hermitage	38	88	56	2	3
†C Linde b Hermitage	36	57	58	4	-
D du Preez c Kgamadi b Van der Merwe	3	18	17	-	-
TS Motsamai not out	22	65	62	3	-
JMM Malao					
BK Sekonyane					
QG Samson					
Extras (b 3, lb 10, w 2, nb 3)	18				
TOTAL (for 6 wkts dec) (85 overs)	**306**				

FS	O	M	R	W	
Du Preez	18	7	47	3	
Sekonyane	6	1	40	0	(5 nb)
Motsamai	13	2	46	1	(6 nb)
Samson	14	3	31	3	(5 nb, 1 w)
Malao	15	5	25	2	
Thyssen	4	1	24	0	
Fick	4	1	13	0	
NW	O	M	R	W	
De Wet	19	2	61	0	(3 nb)
Moleon	11	3	43	1	
Van der Merwe	18	1	69	2	(1 w)
Holtzhausen	14	3	35	1	(1 w)
Hermitage	22	1	80	2	
Akoojee	1	0	5	0	

Fall of Wickets

	NW	FS
1st	76 (2)	36 (2)
2nd	94 (1)	83 (1)
3rd	118 (4)	91 (3)
4th	118 (5)	178 (5)
5th	140 (6)	239 (6)
6th	187 (3)	248 (7)
7th	209 (7)	-
8th	227 (9)	-
9th	236 (10)	-
10th	-	-

NORTHERNS v GAUTENG — SAA 3-day Challenge Pool A

Played at LC de Villiers Oval, University of Pretoria, Pretoria on 27,28,29 October 2005 Toss: Gauteng
Umpires: S George & BDA Westraadt
Debuts: Nor: None. Gau: BW Buckley and DM van Wyk (Both FC)
Close of play: Day 1: Gau (1) 38-2 (Dugmore 13*, Makalima 4*, 17 overs). Day 2: Nor (2) 120-4 (Van Woerkom 20*, Mokonyama 13*, 40 overs)..
Result: Match drawn
Points: Nor: 10.76 (bat 6.76, bowl 4, match 0); Gau: 7.38 (bat 4.38, bowl 3, match 0)

NORTHERNS	*Runs*	*Mins*	*Balls*	*4*	*6*		*Runs*	*Mins*	*Balls*	*4*	*6*
MA Aronstam lbw b De Bruin	6	21	19	1	-	c Makalima b Burger	44	70	51	6	-
N Chouhan c Van Wyk b De Bruin	2	31	24	-	-						
JG Myburgh lbw b Burger	12	36	19	2	-	lbw b Burger	14	34	29	2	-
N van Woerkom c De Bruin b Sekhoto	146	279	213	20	1	b Terbrugge	38	125	97	5	-
G Dros c Sekhoto b De Bruin	136	234	195	19	1	b Burger	0	22	11	-	-
†HG Kuhn lbw b De Bruin	0	3	2	-	-	(2) lbw b Burger	18	63	35	2	-
MJ Mokonyama b Sekhoto	17	27	21	3	-	(6) c Van Wyk b Terbrugge	34	91	66	3	-
*P Joubert not out	25	36	22	2	1	(7) not out	17	38	26	2	-
AM Phangiso not out	21	22	17	1	-	(8) not out	22	23	14	3	1
MA Mashimbyi											
FG Nkuna											
Extras (b 4, lb 8, nb 11)	23					Extras (b 4, lb 3, nb 5)	12				
TOTAL (for 7 wkts) (85 overs)	**388**					**TOTAL (for 6 wkts dec) (54 overs)**	**199**				

GAUTENG	*Runs*	*Mins*	*Balls*	*4*	*6*		*Runs*	*Mins*	*Balls*	*4*	*6*
WA Dugmore c Joubert b Dros	56	182	135	7	-	c Dros b Joubert	18	84	65	3	-
BW Buckley lbw b Mashimbyi	11	42	30	2	-	c Kuhn b Joubert	41	72	60	7	-
K Moothosamy c Joubert b Mashimbyi	1	8	5	-	-	lbw b Joubert	42	92	64	6	-
DL Makalima c Dros b Nkuna	4	21	21	1	-	b Joubert	0	8	4	-	-
MR Sekhoto c Kuhn b Nkuna	0	9	6	-	-	c Kuhn b Joubert	33	81	60	5	-
DM van Wyk not out	122	243	197	11	2	not out	56	152	134	7	-
*S Burger c Joubert b Mashimbyi	4	35	22	-	-	c Kuhn b Joubert	17	38	31	2	-
†AM Omar b Joubert	20	44	40	3	-	c Kuhn b Joubert	0	4	2	-	-
DJ Terbrugge b Phangiso	28	49	50	2	1	not out	17	100	73	1	-
GJ de Bruin not out	8	16	11	-	-						
JT Mafa											
Extras (lb 6, w 2, nb 7)	15					Extras (lb 5, nb 5)	10				
TOTAL (for 8 wkts) (85 overs)	**269**					**TOTAL (for 7 wkts) (81.4 overs)**	**234**				

Gau	*O*	*M*	*R*	*W*		*O*	*M*	*R*	*W*	
Terbrugge	20	6	62	0		14	1	76	2	
De Bruin	16	1	67	4	(10 nb)	11	2	31	0	(3 nb)
Moothosamy	2	0	13	0						
Burger	14	5	50	1		(5) 11	6	11	4	
Mafa	11	0	62	0		(3) 7	0	30	0	(1 nb)
Dugmore	13	1	59	0		(4) 8	1	36	0	
Makalima	3	0	21	0						
Sekhoto	6	1	42	2	(1 nb)	(6) 3	1	8	0	(1 nb)
Nor	*O*	*M*	*R*	*W*		*O*	*M*	*R*	*W*	
Nkuna	11	3	33	2	(6 nb)	7	0	25	0	(2 nb)
Mashimbyi	18	2	40	3	(1 nb)	9	0	29	0	
Joubert	13	5	26	1	(2 w)	22	10	32	7	
Aronstam	11	2	45	0		(5) 23.4	5	72	0	
Phangiso	22	2	69	1		(4) 5	1	24	0	
Dros	7	1	27	1		9	2	23	0	
Myburgh	3	0	23	0		2	0	5	0	
Van Woerkom						4	0	19	0	(3 nb)

Fall of Wickets

	Nor	Gau	Nor	Gau
1st	10 (1)	27 (2)	66 (2)	59 (2)
2nd	13 (2)	34 (3)	75 (1)	66 (1)
3rd	41 (3)	39 (4)	88 (3)	68 (4)
4th	306 (5)	44 (5)	104 (5)	139 (3)
5th	308 (6)	122 (1)	150 (4)	140 (5)
6th	331 (4)	156 (7)	163 (6)	169 (7)
7th	344 (7)	195 (8)	-	169 (8)
8th	-	238 (9)	-	-
9th	-	-	-	-
10th	-	-	-	-

EASTERNS v GRIQUALAND WEST — SAA 3-day Challenge Pool A

Played at Willowmoore Park, Benoni on 27,28 October 2005 Toss: Easterns
Umpires: JD Cloete & ZTA Ndamane
Debuts: Eas: HA van Straaten (FC). GW: D Donaldson (FC)
Close of play: Day 1: GW (2) 163-3 (McLaren 51*, Bossenger 37*, 33.2 overs).
Result: Griqualand West won by 258 runs
Points: Eas: 4 (bat 0.00, bowl 4, match 0); GW: 17.34 (bat 3.34, bowl 4, match 10)
Notes: Bossenger retired hurt with his score on 37 and the total on 163-3 in Griqualand West's 2nd innings. Bodibe kept wicket in Griqualand West's 2nd innings. McLaren kept wicket in Easterns' 2nd innings

GRIQUALAND WEST	Runs	Mins	Balls	4	6		Runs	Mins	Balls	4	6
MC Arthur c Wiese b Almeida	20	27	25	2	-	lbw b Wiese	1	4	5	-	-
AP McLaren lbw b Almeida	29	36	29	5	1	c Nyawo b O'Connor	54	132	94	6	1
AK Kruger c Almeida b Mofokeng	39	60	31	7	1	c Nyawo b Almeida	4	7	9	1	-
J Brooker lbw b Wiese	14	29	23	1	-	c and b Hlengane	63	65	64	8	3
*†W Bossenger c Nyawo b O'Connor	5	14	10	1	-	retired hurt	37	38	42	5	-
M Bosman c Hlengane b O'Connor	19	24	14	4	-	c Booysen b Almeida	0	13	11	-	-
J Coetzee b Mofokeng	12	30	24	1	1	not out	43	83	48	8	1
D Donaldson run out (O'Connor)	42	88	64	6	-	c Barresi b O'Connor	16	24	18	4	-
BW Lemmetjies c Booysen b O'Connor	4	6	8	1	-	lbw b Wiese	16	27	22	1	1
NO Arthur c Nyawo b O'Connor	21	58	45	2	-	c Toyana b Mofokeng	11	19	15	1	-
TR Plaatjie not out	2	8	6	-	-	not out	1	7	1	-	-
Extras (lb 7, w 2, nb 1)	10					Extras (lb 5, w 2, nb 2)	9				
TOTAL (46.2 overs)	**217**					**TOTAL (for 8 wkts dec) (54.4 overs)**	**255**				

EASTERNS	Runs	Mins	Balls	4	6		Runs	Mins	Balls	4	6
†W Barresi lbw b Coetzee	2	9	10	-	-	(2) c McLaren b Plaatjie	0	12	7	-	-
HA van Straaten c Donaldson b Plaatjie	6	18	9	1	-	(1) c Donaldson b Kruger	29	71	55	4	-
E Nyawo b Coetzee	0	2	2	-	-	(8) c Coetzee b Kruger	2	11	6	-	-
J Booysen c MC Arthur b Kruger	34	56	35	7	-	c McLaren b Kruger	29	29	20	3	1
G Toyana c Lemmetjies b Kruger	6	24	14	1	-	c Coetzee b Donaldson	13	39	17	2	-
D Wiese b Coetzee	12	20	19	2	-	c Bosman b Coetzee	10	6	8	2	-
*SP O'Connor c Lemmetjies b Kruger	1	8	5	-	-	c Coetzee b Kruger	0	10	7	-	-
TM Bodibe not out	1	19	10	-	-	(3) lbw b Coetzee	21	39	36	3	-
R Almeida b Coetzee	3	4	6	-	-	b Kruger	19	16	13	3	-
IC Hlengane c Bossenger b Kruger	0	4	4	-	-	c McLaren b Kruger	7	21	12	1	-
PT Mofokeng c McLaren b Kruger	0	7	5	-	-	not out	3	8	4	-	-
Extras (lb 3, w 1, nb 1)	5					Extras (w 10, nb 1)	11				
TOTAL (19.4 overs)	**70**					**TOTAL (30.4 overs)**	**144**				

Eas	O	M	R	W		O	M	R	W	
Almeida	13	2	69	2	(1 w)	13	3	46	2	(2 w)
Wiese	9	2	40	1	(1 nb)	10	0	51	2	(2 nb)
O'Connor	14.2	1	65	4		(5) 8	0	41	2	
Mofokeng	10	2	36	2	(1 w)	(6) 2.4	0	14	1	
Hlengane						(3) 12	2	64	1	
Toyana						(4) 9	0	34	0	
GW	O	M	R	W		O	M	R	W	
Coetzee	10	3	25	4		12	2	48	2	(1 w)
Plaatjie	4	0	22	1	(1 w)	4	1	22	1	(1 w)
Kruger	5.4	1	20	5	(1 nb)	(4) 10.4	1	46	6	(1 nb)
NO Arthur						(3) 1	1	0	0	
Donaldson						3	0	28	1	

Fall of Wickets

	GW	Eas	GW	Eas
1st	34 (1)	3 (1)	3 (1)	5 (2)
2nd	50 (2)	3 (3)	8 (3)	47 (3)
3rd	89 (4)	13 (2)	112 (4)	79 (1)
4th	106 (5)	33 (5)	166 (6)	88 (4)
5th	118 (3)	59 (6)	166 (2)	99 (6)
6th	134 (6)	63 (4)	189 (8)	104 (7)
7th	147 (7)	64 (7)	226 (9)	107 (8)
8th	153 (9)	67 (9)	242 (10)	115 (5)
9th	210 (10)	68 (10)	-	135 (9)
10th	217 (8)	70 (11)	-	144 (10)

GRIQUALAND WEST v NORTHERNS — SAA 3-day Challenge Pool A

Played at De Beers Diamond Oval, Kimberley on 3,4,5 November 2005 — Toss: Griqualand West

Umpires: SW Liebisch & BDA Westraadt

Debuts: GW: None. Nor: L Manzini (FC)

Close of play: Day 1: Nor (1) 175-1 (Aronstam 82*, Myburgh 77*, 50 overs). Day 2: Nor (2) 30-1 (Kuhn 6*, Myburgh 5*, 10 overs).

Result: Northerns won by 8 wickets

Points: GW: 8.2 (bat 4.20, bowl 4, match 0); Nor: 19.52 (bat 5.52, bowl 4, match 10)

GRIQUALAND WEST	Runs	Mins	Balls	4	6		Runs	Mins	Balls	4	6
MC Arthur lbw b Mashimbyi	7	13	13	1	-	lbw b Mashimbyi	8	7	9	2	-
AP McLaren b Dros	50	85	57	10	-	c Kuhn b Manzini	22	64	47	3	-
AK Kruger c Kuhn b Nkuna	1	4	3	-	-	c Kuhn b Manzini	28	67	44	6	-
J Brooker c Kuhn b Dros	52	84	67	10	1	c Dros b Manzini	8	26	16	-	-
*†W Bossenger c Kuhn b Dros	9	25	14	1	-	(6) c Kuhn b Manzini	12	29	21	1	-
M Bosman b Aronstam	16	32	28	3	-	(5) lbw b Dros	11	30	21	1	-
J Coetzee lbw b Joubert	54	119	96	9	-	c Phangiso b Dros	36	122	106	3	1
D Donaldson c Kuhn b Joubert	9	25	15	1	-	c Dros b Joubert	32	75	49	4	-
FPG Holtzhausen b Mashimbyi	54	64	58	9	1	run out (Myburgh/Joubert)	23	28	16	5	-
NO Arthur not out	2	3	1	-	-	b Joubert	2	5	7	-	-
TR Plaatjie						not out	1	12	14	-	-
Extras (lb 3, w 2, nb 1)	6					Extras (lb 3, nb 1)	4				
TOTAL (for 9 wkts dec) (58.3 overs)	**260**					**TOTAL (58.1 overs)**	**187**				

NORTHERNS	Runs	Mins	Balls	4	6		Runs	Mins	Balls	4	6
MA Aronstam b NO Arthur	91	204	179	14	-	c Bossenger b Coetzee	18	27	24	3	-
†HG Kuhn run out (MC Arthur)	4	6	3	1	-	b NO Arthur	27	79	68	1	-
JG Myburgh c Brooker b NO Arthur	77	179	142	8	-	not out	51	104	84	8	-
EE Meyer c Kruger b NO Arthur	21	70	62	1	-	not out	17	52	48	2	-
G Dros c Bossenger b Kruger	8	16	14	1	-						
MJ Mokonyama c Brooker b NO Arthur	40	83	57	2	-						
AM Phangiso run out (Holtzhausen/Bossenger)	63	64	49	2	4						
MA Mashimbyi c McLaren b Coetzee	0	3	1	-	-						
*P Joubert c NO Arthur b Coetzee	5	9	7	-	-						
L Manzini run out (Donaldson/Coetzee)	0	1	0	-	-						
FG Nkuna not out	0	1	0	-	-						
Extras (lb 10, w 2, nb 5)	17					Extras (b 6, nb 3)	9				
TOTAL (84.5 overs)	**326**					**TOTAL (for 2 wkts) (36.5 overs)**	**122**				

Nor	O	M	R	W			O	M	R	W	
Nkuna	4	0	28	1	(1 nb)		10	4	37	0	
Mashimbyi	6	0	31	2	(1 w)		7	2	27	1	
Joubert	11.3	1	37	2			12	2	28	2	
Manzini	4	0	26	0			8	1	22	4	(1 nb)
Aronstam	18	1	79	1		(6)	4	0	17	0	
Dros	13	2	41	3	(1 w)	(5)	7.1	1	13	2	
Phangiso	2	0	15	0		(8)	3	0	11	0	
Myburgh						(7)	7	2	29	0	
GW	O	M	R	W			O	M	R	W	
Coetzee	11.5	0	48	2	(1 w)		8	1	21	1	
Plaatjie	3	0	24	0	(1 w)	(5)	2	0	9	0	
Kruger	17	2	75	1	(4 nb)	(2)	6	0	30	0	(3 nb)
NO Arthur	34	2	115	4		(3)	13	5	28	1	
Donaldson	16	3	47	0	(1 nb)						
Holtzhausen	3	1	7	0		(4)	7.5	1	28	0	

Fall of Wickets

	GW	Nor	GW	Nor
1st	13 (1)	10 (2)	9 (1)	23 (1)
2nd	14 (3)	175 (3)	54 (2)	69 (2)
3rd	109 (2)	191 (1)	63 (3)	-
4th	121 (4)	202 (5)	74 (4)	-
5th	124 (5)	219 (4)	84 (5)	-
6th	146 (6)	303 (6)	93 (6)	-
7th	173 (8)	305 (8)	146 (8)	-
8th	258 (9)	323 (9)	175 (9)	-
9th	260 (7)	325 (10)	178 (10)	-
10th	-	326 (7)	187 (7)	-

NORTH WEST v EASTERNS — SAA 3-day Challenge Pool A

Played at Sedgars Park, Potchefstroom on 3,4,5 November 2005 — Toss: Easterns

Umpires: JEP Ostrom & IH van Kerwel

Debuts: NW: None. Eas: SR Connor, NJ Livi and J Theunissen (All FC)

Close of play: Day 1: NW (1) 101-0 (Steyn 74*, Kgamadi 25*, 21 overs). Day 2: Eas (2) 28-2 (Theunissen 17*, Bodibe 0*, 8 overs).

Result: North West won by 10 wickets

Points: NW: 19.62 (bat 5.62, bowl 4, match 10); Eas: 7.2 (bat 5.20, bowl 2, match 0)

EASTERNS	Runs	Mins	Balls	4	6		Runs	Mins	Balls	4	6
HA van Straaten c Bula b De Wet	68	102	75	12	-	c and b De Wet	2	12	4	-	-
J Theunissen c Stroh b De Wet	0	16	12	-	-	run out (De Wet)	22	44	40	3	-
NJ Livi c Steyn b Stroh	42	70	39	9	-	c Bula b De Wet	7	16	8	1	-
J Booysen c and b GH Bhayat	71	102	81	13	-	(6) c Kgamadi b Stroh	0	4	2	-	-
SR Connor c Hermitage b GH Bhayat	17	60	49	3	-	c Kgamadi b Stroh	24	50	41	4	-
*SP O'Connor c Bula b Stroh	41	133	108	4	-	(7) c Kgamadi b Van der Merwe	29	66	57	6	-
BL Reddy c Bula b GH Bhayat	9	26	23	-	-	(9) st Bula b Le Roux	16	12	12	1	2
R Almeida c Kgamadi b Stroh	44	81	67	4	-	c Steyn b Hermitage	22	30	18	3	-
†TM Bodibe c Bula b Hermitage	1	3	3	-	-	(4) run out (Le Roux/Bula/Hermitage)	30	145	87	5	-
JT Maziya c Bula b De Wet	4	15	10	-	-	run out (Stroh)	0	20	14	-	-
PT Mofokeng not out	4	8	6	-	-	not out	4	10	8	1	-
Extras (lb 6, w 2, nb 1)	9					Extras (b 1, lb 4)	5				
TOTAL (78.5 overs)	**310**					**TOTAL (48.3 overs)**	**161**				

NORTH WEST	Runs	Mins	Balls	4	6		Runs	Mins	Balls	4	6
FA Steyn c Bodibe b Mofokeng	116	194	161	18	-	not out	48	49	44	11	-
DJ Kgamadi c Reddy b Almeida	29	117	79	4	-	not out	29	49	27	5	-
M Akoojee c Reddy b Mofokeng	37	85	54	5	-						
J le Roux c Van Straaten b Reddy	109	179	131	14	-						
*RA Stroh run out (Mofokeng)	52	117	90	5	-						
R Bhayat run out (Booysen)	5	10	11	-	-						
†TA Bula c Mofokeng b Almeida	25	31	20	3	-						
JS Hermitage not out	6	7	3	1	-						
F de Wet											
GH Bhayat											
F van der Merwe											
Extras (lb 5, w 4, nb 3)	12					Extras (lb 1, w 1, nb 5)	7				
TOTAL (for 7 wkts) (91 overs)	**391**					**TOTAL (for 0 wkts) (11 overs)**	**84**				

NW	O	M	R	W			O	M	R	W	
De Wet	16.5	2	43	3	(1 nb, 1 w)		11.3	4	38	2	
GH Bhayat	19	4	61	3	(1 w)		14	5	27	0	
Van der Merwe	15	1	75	0		(4)	7	3	24	1	
Stroh	15	2	62	3		(3)	8	2	29	2	
Hermitage	12	1	59	1			7	1	37	1	
Le Roux	1	0	4	0			1	0	1	1	
Eas	O	M	R	W			O	M	R	W	
Reddy	21	2	92	1	(2 nb)	(2)	5	0	25	0	
Almeida	26	1	115	2	(1 nb, 1 w)	(1)	4	0	33	0	(5 nb, 1 w)
O'Connor	16	1	76	0							
Mofokeng	20	6	56	2	(3 w)						
Maziya	8	0	47	0		(3)	2	0	25	0	

Fall of Wickets	Eas	NW	Eas	NW
1st	12 (2)	123 (2)	6 (1)	-
2nd	101 (3)	181 (1)	22 (3)	-
3rd	119 (1)	190 (3)	33 (2)	-
4th	179 (5)	299 (5)	64 (5)	-
5th	214 (4)	309 (6)	64 (6)	-
6th	229 (7)	375 (7)	109 (7)	-
7th	293 (6)	391 (4)	124 (4)	-
8th	298 (9)	-	150 (9)	-
9th	306 (8)	-	157 (8)	-
10th	310 (10)	-	161 (10)	-

FREE STATE v NORTHERNS — SAA 3-day Challenge Pool A

Played at University of Free State Ground, Bloemfontein on 10,11,12 November 2005 Toss: Northerns
Umpires: LM Engelbrecht & BN Harrison
Debuts: FS: JF Mostert (FC). Nor: None
Close of play: Day 1: FS (1) 67-1 (Beukes 48*, Van Wyk 12*, 25 overs). Day 2: Nor (2) 84-3 (Myburgh 44*, Dros 3*, 39 overs).
Result: Match drawn
Points: FS: 6.1 (bat 5.10, bowl 1, match 0); Nor: 9.26 (bat 6.26, bowl 3, match 0)
Notes:Dros scored his fifty off 31 balls in Northerns' 1st innings.

NORTHERNS	Runs	Mins	Balls	4	6		Runs	Mins	Balls	4	6
MA Aronstam lbw b Du Preez	42	93	68	6	-	run out (Mosena)	2	10	6	-	-
†HG Kuhn lbw b Motsamai	80	197	181	7	-	run out (Du Preez/Samson)	17	57	38	2	-
JG Myburgh not out	128	217	167	13	2	lbw b Du Preez	83	301	229	7	-
EE Meyer c Koortzen b Malao	31	73	69	3	-	b Du Preez	14	73	52	1	-
G Dros not out	60	38	35	3	5	c Mosena b Malao	32	113	94	5	-
MJ Mokonyama						lbw b Malao	24	50	49	2	-
*P Joubert						not out	21	82	70	-	-
AM Phangiso						b Motsamai	28	56	52	4	-
MA Mashimbyi						st Linde b Malao	1	11	6	-	-
L Manzini											
FG Nkuna											
Extras (b 8, lb 3, w 1, nb 10)	22					Extras (b 1, lb 1, w 1, nb 8)	11				
TOTAL (for 3 wkts) (85 overs)	**363**					**TOTAL (for 8 wkts dec) (98 overs)**	**233**				

FREE STATE	Runs	Mins	Balls	4	6		Runs	Mins	Balls	4	6
*JA Beukes lbw b Myburgh	130	273	208	19	1	c Manzini b Phangiso	47	94	84	5	2
LN Mosena lbw b Mashimbyi	4	37	24	-	-	b Joubert	29	72	47	3	-
DJ van Wyk c Kuhn b Nkuna	18	71	60	1	-	c Nkuna b Myburgh	28	86	67	1	-
PJ Koortzen lbw b Myburgh	87	179	153	10	-	(5) lbw b Dros	1	4	4	-	-
LL Bosman c Myburgh b Joubert	43	51	38	2	2	(4) b Phangiso	5	16	11	-	-
D du Preez b Joubert	7	11	11	-	-						
†C Linde c Kuhn b Joubert	0	5	5	-	-	(6) not out	21	106	111	1	-
JF Mostert not out	6	19	13	-	-	(7) b Aronstam	8	32	32	1	-
TS Motsamai not out	0	2	1	-	-	(8) not out	0	28	29	-	-
JMM Malao											
QG Samson											
Extras (b 3, lb 3, w 1, nb 3)	10					Extras (b 1, lb 1, nb 1)	3				
TOTAL (for 7 wkts) (85 overs)	**305**					**TOTAL (for 6 wkts) (64 overs)**	**142**				

FS	O	M	R	W			O	M	R	W	
Du Preez	15	3	40	1			25	8	30	2	
Samson	16	0	119	0	(5 nb, 1 w)		15	0	77	0	(2 nb, 1 w)
Motsamai	15	2	46	1	(4 nb)		20	4	45	1	(6 nb)
Mostert	15	4	52	0		(5)	3	0	10	0	
Malao	24	2	95	1	(1 nb)	(4)	35	5	69	3	
Nor	O	M	R	W			O	M	R	W	
Nkuna	11	4	18	1	(1 nb)		5	0	26	0	(1 nb)
Mashimbyi	16	5	51	1	(1 nb)		5	1	6	0	
Joubert	18	3	45	3	(1 nb)		5	0	11	1	
Manzini	7	1	25	0	(1 w)	(5)	4	2	7	0	
Myburgh	10	2	45	2		(7)	10	7	4	1	
Phangiso	10	0	50	0		(4)	19	10	44	2	
Dros	8	0	35	0		(6)	7	1	25	1	
Aronstam	5	0	30	0			8	5	11	1	
Meyer							1	0	6	0	

Fall of Wickets	Nor	FS	Nor	FS
1st	81 (1)	25 (2)	6 (1)	50 (2)
2nd	177 (2)	77 (3)	33 (2)	88 (1)
3rd	272 (4)	241 (1)	77 (4)	106 (4)
4th	-	256 (4)	147 (5)	107 (5)
5th	-	271 (6)	181 (6)	120 (3)
6th	-	275 (7)	185 (3)	130 (7)
7th	-	304 (5)	230 (8)	-
8th	-	-	233 (9)	-
9th	-	-	-	-
10th	-	-	-	-

GAUTENG v NORTH WEST — SAA 3-day Challenge Pool A

Played at Liberty Life Wanderers Stadium, Johannesburg on 17,18,19 November 2005 — Toss: Gauteng
Umpires: SW Liebisch & GH Pienaar
Debuts: Gau: None. NW: DP Lotter and VCM Mazibuko (Both FC)
Close of play: Day 1: Gau (1) 105-5 (Gain 23*, Van Wyk 2*, 38.2 overs). Day 2: Gau (2) 23-2 (Dugmore 4*, Terbrugge 0*, 5 overs).
Result: North West won by 70 runs
Points: Gau: 5.74 (bat 1.74, bowl 4, match 0); NW: 17.6 (bat 3.60, bowl 4, match 10)
Notes:Makalima scored his fifty off 37 balls in Gauteng's 2nd innings.

NORTH WEST	*Runs*	*Mins*	*Balls*	*4*	*6*		*Runs*	*Mins*	*Balls*	*4*	*6*
DJ Kgamadi c Mafa b Mathebula	84	121	94	13	-	lbw b Terbrugge	62	154	128	8	1
*RA Stroh c Van Wyk b Mafa	6	56	38	1	-	c Van Wyk b De Bruin	28	132	84	2	-
M Akoojee lbw b Terbrugge	26	92	56	4	-	c Van Wyk b Snijman	37	92	61	5	-
J le Roux c Snijman b Terbrugge	15	45	34	3	-	c Dugmore b Snijman	22	56	34	3	-
WL Coetsee c Gain b Mafa	49	113	76	9	-	c Dugmore b Snijman	68	106	74	11	-
DP Lotter lbw b Mathebula	6	26	16	1	-	c Van Wyk b De Bruin	8	12	15	1	-
FS Holtzhausen c Van Wyk b Mafa	10	34	20	2	-	not out	57	84	61	10	-
†TA Bula c Motaung b Mafa	0	8	5	-	-	c and b Snijman	0	1	1	-	-
GH Bhayat run out (Motaung/Van Wyk)	2	3	2	-	-						
VCM Mazibuko not out	6	22	23	1	-						
JP Campher											
Extras (lb 8, w 1, nb 17)	26					Extras (b 4, lb 1, w 3, nb 14)	22				
TOTAL (for 9 wkts dec) (57.5 overs)	**230**					**TOTAL (for 7 wkts dec) (74 overs)**	**304**				

GAUTENG	*Runs*	*Mins*	*Balls*	*4*	*6*		*Runs*	*Mins*	*Balls*	*4*	*6*
WB Motaung c Akoojee b Bhayat	11	32	28	2	-	lbw b Bhayat	4	17	11	1	-
BD Snijman c Bula b Holtzhausen	5	26	17	-	-	b Campher	11	9	8	1	1
WA Dugmore b Holtzhausen	1	15	8	-	-	c Stroh b Mazibuko	138	323	225	22	1
*DR Gain not out	42	198	139	6	-	(5) c Bula b Mazibuko	8	50	43	1	-
MR Sekhoto c Bhayat b Stroh	22	51	41	4	-	(6) c Bula b Holtzhausen	9	15	14	2	-
DL Makalima c Bula b Mazibuko	33	40	28	6	1	(7) c Bula b Bhayat	51	58	39	9	2
†DM van Wyk c Bula b Holtzhausen	11	50	47	1	-	(8) c Bula b Stroh	23	70	52	4	-
DJ Terbrugge c Le Roux b Holtzhausen	1	17	8	-	-	(4) c Coetsee b Holtzhausen	20	46	38	2	1
GJ de Bruin lbw b Bhayat	2	7	4	-	-	c Akoojee b Stroh	27	50	40	5	-
BM Mathebula c Stroh b Holtzhausen	0	13	8	-	-	not out	11	30	20	2	-
JT Mafa run out (Holtzhausen/Bula)	0	3	0	-	-	c Kgamadi b Mazibuko	4	10	4	1	-
Extras (lb 2, w 1, nb 6)	9					Extras (lb 7, w 8, nb 6)	21				
TOTAL (53.4 overs)	**137**					**TOTAL (81.2 overs)**	**327**				

Gau	*O*	*M*	*R*	*W*		*O*	*M*	*R*	*W*
Terbrugge	14	4	38	2 (2 nb)		14	2	51	1 (1 nb)
Mathebula	12	2	55	2 (11 nb)	(3)	10	2	37	0 (4 nb)
Mafa	14.5	1	46	4 (4 nb, 1 w)	(4)	15	2	51	0 (3 nb)
De Bruin	11	0	70	0	(2)	18	3	69	2 (6 nb, 2 w)
Dugmore	3	0	5	0		3	0	23	0
Makalima	1	0	3	0		5	0	32	0
Snijman	2	1	5	0		7	0	26	4 (1 w)
Motaung						2	0	10	0
NW	*O*	*M*	*R*	*W*		*O*	*M*	*R*	*W*
Campher	12	1	42	0 (5 nb)		12	2	63	1 (6 nb, 5 w)
Bhayat	11.4	5	25	2		22	5	71	2 (1 w)
Holtzhausen	19	9	25	5		16	5	43	2
Stroh	5	1	23	1	(6)	10	1	51	2
Coetsee	5	3	4	0		12	1	55	0 (1 w)
Mazibuko	1	0	16	1 (1 nb, 1 w)	(4)	9.2	2	37	3 (1 w)

Fall of Wickets

	NW	**Gau**	**NW**	**Gau**
1st	43 (2)	16 (2)	90 (2)	13 (2)
2nd	126 (1)	18 (1)	102 (1)	18 (1)
3rd	143 (3)	18 (3)	160 (4)	55 (4)
4th	159 (4)	49 (5)	171 (3)	72 (5)
5th	178 (6)	96 (6)	181 (6)	86 (6)
6th	204 (7)	116 (7)	304 (5)	172 (7)
7th	210 (8)	122 (8)	304 (8)	235 (8)
8th	212 (9)	125 (9)	-	292 (9)
9th	230 (5)	136 (10)	-	313 (3)
10th	-	137 (11)	-	327 (11)

GRIQUALAND WEST v GAUTENG — SAA 3-day Challenge Pool A

Played at De Beers Diamond Oval, Kimberley on 24,25,26 November 2005 — Toss: Griqualand West
Umpires: CJ Conradie & MZ Nanabhay
Debuts: GW: CN Bennett and CJ de Jager (Both FC). Gau: S Chatterjee and A Nawab (Both FC)
Close of play: Day 1: Gau (1) 91-1 (Snijman 47*, Dugmore 30*, 26 overs). Day 2: GW (2) 32-0 (McLaren 11*, Bennett 19*, 8.2 overs).
Result: Match drawn
Points: GW: 8.52 (bat 5.52, bowl 3, match 0); Gau: 9.54 (bat 5.54, bowl 4, match 0)
Notes: Van Wyk scored his fifty off 36 balls in Gauteng's 2nd innings. McLaren kept wicket when Bossenger bowled in Gauteng's 2nd innings.

GRIQUALAND WEST	Runs	Mins	Balls	4	6		Runs	Mins	Balls	4	6
CN Bennett c Van Wyk b Chatterjee	47	106	71	10	-	(2) c Dugmore b Mafa	38	81	65	8	-
AP McLaren c Adams b Chatterjee	2	14	10	-	-	(1) c Dugmore b Snijman	131	236	174	16	1
CJ de Jager c Nkwe b Chatterjee	62	83	71	10	1	c Van Wyk b Mafa	0	3	2	-	-
J Brooker st Van Wyk b Nawab	33	42	30	6	-	c Dugmore b Chatterjee	6	21	10	1	-
*†W Bossenger c Van Wyk b Chatterjee	66	112	102	11	-	run out (Mathebula/Van Wyk)	53	89	73	5	-
AK Kruger c Nkwe b Mafa	54	105	56	8	1	c Mathebula b Mafa	1	9	4	-	-
J Coetzee c Motaung b Chatterjee	17	46	31	4	-	c Motaung b Mafa	19	15	15	4	-
D Donaldson c Gain b Mafa	5	14	11	1	-	st Van Wyk b Snijman	5	16	10	-	-
NO Arthur c Van Wyk b Mathebula	27	50	38	4	-	not out	1	2	1	-	-
ES Tsamaisi not out	7	48	38	-	-						
R Pietersen not out	0	2	1	-	-						
Extras (lb 2, w 1, nb 3)	6					Extras (b 5, lb 4, w 1)	10				
TOTAL (for 9 wkts dec) (76 overs)	**326**					**TOTAL (for 8 wkts dec) (59 overs)**	**264**				

GAUTENG	Runs	Mins	Balls	4	6		Runs	Mins	Balls	4	6
BD Snijman b Tsamaisi	81	189	117	13	-	lbw b Coetzee	20		31	3	-
WB Motaung b Coetzee	11	12	9	1	1	c Bossenger b Tsamaisi	40		64	5	1
WA Dugmore lbw b Arthur	96	227	208	14	-	c Bossenger b Coetzee	5		18	1	-
*DR Gain c sub (J-PH Triegaardt) b Kruger	53	98	83	3	2	lbw b Arthur	55		55	9	1
ET Nkwe lbw b Kruger	20	59	40	1	-	b Arthur	18		36	2	-
BC Adams c McLaren b Donaldson	6	23	19	-	-	(7) c Pietersen b Arthur	11		25	1	-
†DM van Wyk not out	31	35	28	4	1	(6) not out	66		46	11	1
BM Mathebula c Arthur b Donaldson	10	11	6	-	1	(9) b Arthur	16		5	1	2
A Nawab not out	8	11	5	1	-	(8) c McLaren b Bossenger	0		3	-	-
S Chatterjee						not out	1		5	-	-
JT Mafa											
Extras (b 1, lb 4, w 1, nb 5)	11					Extras (lb 6, w 2)	8				
TOTAL (for 7 wkts) (85 overs)	**327**					**TOTAL (for 8 wkts) (48 overs)**	**240**				

Gau	O	M	R	W			O	M	R	W	
Mathebula	17	2	68	1	(3 nb, 1 w)		5	0	30	0	
Chatterjee	28	8	81	5			14	1	59	1	(1 w)
Nawab	15	2	81	1		(4)	5	1	20	0	
Adams	3	0	23	0		(5)	3	0	10	0	
Snijman	2	0	13	0		(7)	10	0	37	2	
Mafa	11	0	58	2		(3)	15	2	79	4	
Dugmore						(6)	7	0	20	0	
GW	O	M	R	W			O	M	R	W	
Coetzee	6	0	31	1	(1 nb)		10	2	28	2	(1 w)
Kruger	20	1	76	2	(3 nb)		9	0	52	0	
Arthur	19	5	69	1		(4)	15	2	79	4	
Pietersen	14	4	31	0		(3)	4	1	11	0	
Donaldson	15	0	64	2	(1 nb)	(6)	3	0	13	0	
McLaren	1	0	3	0							
Tsamaisi	5	0	26	1	(1 w)	(5)	4	1	25	1	(1 w)
Bennett	5	1	22	0							
Bossenger						(7)	3	0	26	1	

Fall of Wickets

	GW	Gau	GW	Gau
1st	3 (2)	17 (2)	75 (2)	38 (1)
2nd	108 (3)	156 (1)	75 (3)	52 (3)
3rd	121 (1)	215 (3)	94 (4)	74 (2)
4th	155 (4)	266 (4)	198 (5)	142 (4)
5th	253 (5)	269 (5)	209 (6)	157 (5)
6th	281 (6)	279 (6)	246 (7)	203 (7)
7th	291 (8)	296 (8)	262 (1)	204 (8)
8th	295 (7)	-	264 (8)	231 (9)
9th	326 (9)	-	-	-
10th	-	-	-	-

EASTERNS v FREE STATE

SAA 3-day Challenge Pool A

Played at Willowmoore Park, Benoni on 24,25,26 November 2005

Toss: Easterns

Umpires: SB Lambson & BM White

Debuts: Eas: None. FS: RA Reeves (FC)

Close of play: Day 1: FS (1) 378-5 (Linde 18*, Reeves 0*, 85 overs). Day 2: FS (1) 126-1 (De Kock 46*, Hector 54*, 29.2 overs).

Result: Easterns won by 4 wickets

Points: Eas: 14.3 (bat 2.30, bowl 2, match 10); FS: 10.56 (bat 6.56, bowl 4, match 0)

FREE STATE	Runs	Mins	Balls	4	6		Runs	Mins	Balls	4	6
*HG de Kock st Bodibe b Hlengane	50	128	84	8	-	not out	46	130	82	6	-
LN Mosena c Van den Berg b Wiese	0	5	3	-	-	c Bodibe b Almeida	12	42	35	3	-
B Hector c Van den Berg b Almeida	154	313	257	19	2	not out	54	88	62	7	-
DJ van Wyk b Almeida	106	207	155	14	-						
D du Preez c Seymore b Van den Berg	17	22	12	1	1						
†C Linde not out	18	8	9	2	1						
RA Reeves not out	0	2	0	-	-						
T Tshabalala											
TS Motsamai											
JMM Malao											
BK Sekonyane											
Extras (b 1, lb 18, w 4, nb 10)	33					Extras (lb 5, w 6, nb 3)	14				
TOTAL (for 5 wkts) (85 overs)	**378**					**TOTAL (for 1 wkt dec) (29.2 overs)**	**126**				

EASTERNS	Runs	Mins	Balls	4	6		Runs	Mins	Balls	4	6
S Mandan c Linde b Sekonyane	1	14	11	-	-	c Hector b Sekonyane	46	105	75	6	2
AJ Seymore c Van Wyk b Reeves	27	86	55	5	-	c Van Wyk b Motsamai	12	53	34	2	-
AM van den Berg c Linde b Reeves	4	60	41	-	-	b Malao	32	66	33	5	-
J Booysen c Mosena b Motsamai	40	94	62	2	2	not out	134	241	153	10	3
G Toyana c Linde b Sekonyane	0	6	4	-	-	c Linde b Motsamai	42	78	81	6	-
D Wiese c Hector b Malao	44	72	56	6	1	lbw b Malao	8	20	19	-	-
*SP O'Connor c Linde b Du Preez	26	79	60	3	1	b Sekonyane	13	44	37	2	-
†TM Bodibe c De Kock b Malao	7	58	59	-	-	not out	39	84	72	3	1
R Almeida c Reeves b Malao	4	8	4	1	-						
IC Hlengane not out	1	13	2	-	-						
PT Mofokeng c Van Wyk b Malao	1	5	6	-	-						
Extras (lb 4, w 1, nb 5)	10					Extras (b 8, lb 4, w 1, nb 3)	16				
TOTAL (59.2 overs)	**165**					**TOTAL (for 6 wkts) (83.3 overs)**	**342**				

Eas	O	M	R	W		O	M	R	W	
Almeida	19	3	86	2	(2 nb)	11	3	40	1	(3 nb, 2 w)
Wiese	16	1	76	1	(5 nb, 3 w)	9	4	32	0	
Mofokeng	12	1	56	0	(2 nb, 1 w)	5.2	0	37	0	(4 w)
O'Connor	18	4	50	0		4	1	12	0	
Hlengane	6	0	29	1	(1 nb)					
Van den Berg	14	1	62	1						
FS	O	M	R	W		O	M	R	W	
Du Preez	13	5	18	1		17	2	45	0	
Sekonyane	13.5	5	24	2		18.3	5	47	2	(1 nb, 1 w)
Motsamai	9.1	2	19	1	(1 w)	10	1	68	2	
Reeves	5	1	25	2	(2 nb)	(5) 3	0	22	0	(1 nb)
Tshabalala	4	0	24	0	(2 nb)	(6) 10	0	46	0	
Malao	14.2	3	51	4		(4) 25	1	102	2	(1 nb)

Fall of Wickets

	FS	Eas	FS	Eas
1st	0 (2)	7 (1)	22 (2)	17 (2)
2nd	124 (1)	30 (3)	-	90 (1)
3rd	330 (3)	38 (2)	-	100 (3)
4th	354 (4)	45 (5)	-	179 (5)
5th	364 (5)	125 (6)	-	210 (6)
6th	-	125 (4)	-	245 (7)
7th	-	154 (8)	-	-
8th	-	158 (9)	-	-
9th	-	164 (7)	-	-
10th	-	165 (11)	-	-

GRIQUALAND WEST v EASTERNS — SAA 3-day Challenge Pool A

Played at De Beers Diamond Oval, Kimberley on 19,20,21 January 2006 — Toss: Easterns

Umpires: CJ Conradie & BDA Westraadt

Debuts: GW: None. Eas: RG Mutch (FC)

Close of play: Day 1: GW (2) 49-2 (Bennett 15*, Arthur 7*, 12 overs). Day 2: Eas (2) 223-3 (Booysen 38*, Toyana 6*, 42 overs).

Result: Griqualand West won by 114 runs

Points: GW: 17.84 (bat 3.84, bowl 4, match 10); Eas: 5.36 (bat 1.36, bowl 4, match 0)

Notes:Mandan scored his fifty off 35 balls in Easterns' 2nd innings.

GRIQUALAND WEST	Runs	Mins	Balls	4	6		Runs	Mins	Balls	4	6
AP McLaren c Toyana b Wiese	26	29	32	5	-	c Bodibe b Wiese	0	1	2	-	-
CN Bennett c Bodibe b Wiese	31	59	45	7	-	c Bodibe b Hlengane	64	142	105	8	-
CJ de Jager c Bodibe b Mutch	1	9	4	-	-	c Bodibe b Mofokeng	23	29	22	5	-
J Brooker c Bodibe b Mutch	0	3	5	-	-	(5) c Wiese b Hlengane	58	90	70	8	-
*†W Bossenger lbw b Wiese	7	24	15	1	-	(6) c and b Hlengane	1	7	4	-	-
AG Doherty c Seymore b Mutch	92	133	124	14	-	(7) c Toyana b Hlengane	52	79	60	8	-
AK Kruger c Toyana b O'Connor	33	39	35	7	-	(8) c Van Straaten b Hlengane	24	13	14	3	1
J Coetzee c Van Straaten b Wiese	31	52	34	3	1	(9) c Mofokeng b Hlengane	33	33	24	2	2
NO Arthur not out	13	30	20	-	-	(4) b Hlengane	45	72	72	5	1
TR Plaatjie b Mutch	0	1	1	-	-	not out	5	12	12	-	-
R Pietersen											
Extras (lb 5, w 3)	8					Extras (b 6, lb 2, w 1)	9				
TOTAL (for 9 wkts dec) (52.3 overs)	**242**					**TOTAL (for 9 wkts dec) (64.1 overs)**	**314**				

EASTERNS	Runs	Mins	Balls	4	6		Runs	Mins	Balls	4	6
S Mandan lbw b Coetzee	23	29	17	2	1	c Bossenger b Coetzee	98	107	81	17	1
AJ Seymore lbw b Coetzee	5	18	12	1	-	b Arthur	41	99	62	5	-
HA van Straaten c Bossenger b Coetzee	15	37	28	3	-	b Arthur	28	58	40	4	-
J Booysen c and b Kruger	11	5	5	2	-	lbw b Pietersen	84	162	117	9	-
G Toyana c Plaatjie b Coetzee	8	37	27	-	-	c McLaren b Pietersen	28	83	68	2	-
D Wiese c McLaren b Pietersen	15	51	37	3	-	c Bossenger b Arthur	10	17	16	-	-
*SP O'Connor c McLaren b Pietersen	28	73	54	4	-	b Pietersen	1	6	4	-	-
†TM Bodibe b Pietersen	0	12	7	-	-	lbw b Pietersen	3	16	13	-	-
RG Mutch lbw b Arthur	9	20	17	1	-	c Arthur b Pietersen	13	30	18	2	-
IC Hlengane run out (Coetzee/Bossenger)	1	6	4	-	-	b Pietersen	1	6	9	-	-
PT Mofokeng not out	0	4	5	-	-	not out	2	9	5	-	-
Extras (lb 1, w 1, nb 1)	3					Extras (b 4, lb 9, w 2)	15				
TOTAL (35.2 overs)	**118**					**TOTAL (72.1 overs)**	**324**				

Eas	O	M	R	W		O	M	R	W	
Wiese	20	4	61	4	(1 w)	17	2	64	1	
Mutch	12.3	3	57	4	(2 w)	14	0	68	0	
O'Connor	5	0	37	1		(5) 5	0	30	0	
Mofokeng	3	1	20	0		(3) 9	1	37	1	(1 w)
Hlengane	12	0	62	0		(4) 19.1	1	107	7	
GW	O	M	R	W		O	M	R	W	
Coetzee	12	5	48	4	(1 nb)	17	0	85	1	
Kruger	10	0	38	1		11	2	70	0	(1 w)
Plaatjie	2	0	3	0	(1 w)	(4) 4	0	14	0	(1 w)
Arthur	5.2	1	19	1		(6) 15	3	45	3	
Pietersen	6	4	9	3		(3) 19.1	3	73	6	
Doherty						(5) 6	0	24	0	

Fall of Wickets

	GW	Eas	GW	Eas
1st	45 (1)	21 (2)	0 (1)	137 (2)
2nd	54 (3)	28 (1)	35 (3)	147 (1)
3rd	54 (4)	43 (4)	112 (4)	211 (3)
4th	67 (2)	56 (3)	161 (2)	282 (5)
5th	76 (5)	72 (5)	169 (6)	299 (6)
6th	130 (7)	96 (6)	225 (5)	302 (7)
7th	211 (8)	102 (8)	255 (8)	303 (4)
8th	242 (6)	117 (9)	298 (7)	310 (8)
9th	242 (10)	117 (7)	314 (9)	316 (10)
10th	-	118 (10)	-	324 (9)

NORTH WEST v NORTHERNS — SAA 3-day Challenge Pool A

Played at Sedgars Park, Potchefstroom on 19,20,21 January 2006 — Toss: Northerns

Umpires: LM Engelbrecht & SW Liebisch

Debuts: NW: None. Nor: SJ Myburgh and N Wagner (Both FC)

Close of play: Day 1: Nor (1) 95-5 (Wagner 0*, Van Wyk 0*, 25 overs). Day 2: NW (2) 77-5 (Kgamadi 22*, Holtzhausen 8*, 20 overs).

Result: Northerns won by 9 wickets

Points: NW: 6.72 (bat 2.72, bowl 4, match 0); Nor: 18.02 (bat 4.02, bowl 4, match 10)

NORTH WEST	Runs	Mins	Balls	4	6		Runs	Mins	Balls	4	6
FA Steyn run out (Chouhan)	14	23	17	2	-	lbw b Wagner	25	30	26	5	-
DJ Kgamadi c Kuhn b Wagner	72	226	169	6	-	not out	53	261	161	5	-
M Akoojee c Petersen b Joubert	11	62	37	1	-	b Mashimbyi	9	11	11	2	-
J le Roux c Van Wyk b Nkuna	12	37	32	1	-	c Petersen b Wagner	0	8	10	-	-
WL Coetsee lbw b Mashimbyi	9	25	21	2	-	c Myburgh b Joubert	0	11	7	-	-
*RA Stroh c Harris b Joubert	14	48	38	1	-	lbw b Joubert	0	2	1	-	-
FS Holtzhausen not out	25	71	45	5	-	c Harris b Joubert	24	70	48	4	-
†TA Bula c Van Wyk b Wagner	2	10	5	-	-	b Wagner	18	79	49	2	-
VCM Mazibuko c Mashimbyi b Wagner	21	25	22	4	-	lbw b Wagner	0	10	9	-	-
GH Bhayat c Petersen b Wagner	0	7	6	-	-	lbw b Harris	0	17	13	-	-
JP Campher						c Petersen b Joubert	1	6	6	-	-
Extras (b 3, lb 3)	6					Extras (b 4, lb 8, w 3)	15				
TOTAL (for 9 wkts dec) (65.2 overs)	**186**					**TOTAL (56.5 overs)**	**145**				

NORTHERNS	Runs	Mins	Balls	4	6		Runs	Mins	Balls	4	6
HG Kuhn b Coetsee	48	105	72	8	-	c Stroh b Campher	5	28	18	-	-
AN Petersen c Mazibuko b Campher	8	9	7	1	-	not out	48	82	62	6	1
N Chouhan run out (Akoojee/Bhayat)	0	6	1	-	-	not out	11	53	31	2	-
SJ Myburgh lbw b Bhayat	1	10	6	-	-						
MJ Mokonyama b Coetsee	34	69	54	5	-						
N Wagner c Bula b Holtzhausen	20	94	68	3	-						
†CFK van Wyk lbw b Stroh	2	24	15	-	-						
*P Joubert c Campher b Coetsee	68	185	139	11	-						
PL Harris c Campher b Mazibuko	47	73	45	6	2						
MA Mashimbyi c Coetsee b Campher	9	18	14	2	-						
FG Nkuna not out	3	31	19	-	-						
Extras (b 1, lb 1, w 3, nb 6)	11					Extras (lb 5, w 11, nb 1)	17				
TOTAL (72.2 overs)	**251**					**TOTAL (for 1 wkt) (18.2 overs)**	**81**				

Nor	O	M	R	W		O	M	R	W	
Nkuna	9	2	42	1		(2) 4	0	17	0	
Wagner	14.2	4	39	4		(1) 20	9	54	4	
Mashimbyi	11	3	23	1		12	6	32	1	
Joubert	12	3	29	2		11.5	3	22	4	(3 w)
Harris	19	4	47	0		9	4	8	1	
NW	O	M	R	W		O	M	R	W	
Campher	16	4	56	2	(2 nb)	5	0	22	1	(1 nb, 1 w)
Bhayat	10	3	17	1						
Holtzhausen	18	2	70	1	(1 w)	(2) 6	0	20	0	
Mazibuko	7	0	40	1	(3 nb, 2 w)					
Coetsee	13.2	4	42	3	(1 nb)	(4) 3	1	12	0	
Stroh	8	1	24	1		(3) 4	1	15	0	(1 w)
Akoojee						(5) 0.2	0	7	0	

Fall of Wickets

	NW	Nor	NW	Nor
1st	17 (1)	9 (2)	36 (1)	23 (1)
2nd	53 (3)	10 (3)	55 (3)	-
3rd	77 (4)	19 (4)	56 (4)	-
4th	89 (5)	93 (5)	66 (5)	-
5th	129 (6)	94 (1)	66 (6)	-
6th	141 (2)	98 (7)	101 (7)	-
7th	160 (8)	138 (6)	137 (8)	-
8th	186 (9)	210 (9)	139 (9)	-
9th	186 (10)	229 (10)	144 (10)	-
10th	-	251 (8)	145 (11)	-

GAUTENG v FREE STATE — SAA 3-day Challenge Pool A

Played at Liberty Life Wanderers Stadium, Johannesburg on 26,27,28 January 2006 — Toss: Free State
Umpires: JEP Ostrom & BM White
Debuts: Gau: CE Knox (FC). FS: E Nogabe (FC)
Close of play: Day 1: Gau (1) 316-4 (Gain 71*, Van Wyk 76*, 70 overs). Day 2: FS (2) 173-1 (De Kock 65*, Hector 23*, 52 overs).
Result: Gauteng won by 8 wickets
Points: Gau: 21.04 (bat 7.04, bowl 4, match 10); FS: 4.5 (bat 1.50, bowl 3, match 0)

GAUTENG	Runs	Mins	Balls	4	6		Runs	Mins	Balls	4	6
BD Snijman c Van Wyk b Samson	17	29	25	3	-	c De Kock b Samson	15	25	18	2	-
WB Motaung c Mosena b Malao	101	149	123	14	2	c Van Wyk b Samson	5	8	5	1	-
ET Nkwe c De Kock b Sekonyane	25	82	40	3	-	not out	25	27	18	3	1
*DR Gain run out (Samson)	100	202	157	11	-	not out	8	10	7	2	-
MR Sekhoto st Linde b Malao	0	9	8	-	-						
†DM van Wyk b Samson	96	136	143	11	-						
BC Adams not out	28	29	27	1	1						
CE Knox not out	5	11	6	-	-						
HW le Roux											
A Nawab											
JT Mafa											
Extras (b 4, lb 1, w 6, nb 19)	30					Extras (lb 1, nb 1)	2				
TOTAL (for 6 wkts dec) (85 overs)	**402**					**TOTAL (for 2 wkts) (7.5 overs)**	**55**				

FREE STATE	Runs	Mins	Balls	4	6		Runs	Mins	Balls	4	6
*HG de Kock c Sekhoto b Le Roux	13	28	25	3	-	c Van Wyk b Mafa	65	223	170	12	-
LN Mosena c Knox b Le Roux	7	51	28	1	-	st Van Wyk b Nawab	78	159	111	15	-
B Hector c and b Le Roux	0	7	3	-	-	c and b Nkwe	57	117	76	6	1
DJ van Wyk b Mafa	5	8	10	-	-	c Sekhoto b Knox	20	48	35	4	-
MP Fick c Le Roux b Mafa	21	49	23	2	1	c and b Nawab	5	26	12	1	-
†C Linde c Knox b Mafa	0	3	2	-	-	b Le Roux	33	91	80	3	-
RA Reeves c Gain b Nkwe	32	57	39	5	-	c Gain b Nawab	41	46	49	7	-
JMM Malao b Knox	13	51	34	2	-	b Le Roux	1	34	21	-	-
QG Samson c Van Wyk b Nawab	10	21	16	1	-	not out	8	29	23	1	-
BK Sekonyane b Nawab	12	24	19	3	-	b Le Roux	7	14	7	1	-
E Nogabe not out	0	12	8	-	-	c Van Wyk b Le Roux	0	1	1	-	-
Extras (b 4, lb 4, w 1, nb 3)	12					Extras (b 2, lb 1, w 4, nb 7)	14				
TOTAL (34 overs)	**125**					**TOTAL (96.2 overs)**	**329**				

FS	O	M	R	W			O	M	R	W	
Sekonyane	15	3	60	1	(6 nb, 2 w)		3	0	12	0	
Reeves	2	0	17	0	(2 nb)						
Samson	12	0	77	2	(9 nb, 1 w)	(2)	3.5	0	33	2	(1 nb)
Nogabe	4	0	22	0	(2 w)						
Fick	6	0	34	0		(3)	1	0	9	0	
Malao	34	4	135	2	(1 nb)						
De Kock	12	2	52	0	(1 nb, 1 w)						
Gau	O	M	R	W			O	M	R	W	
Le Roux	9	2	45	3	(2 nb)		19.2	7	66	4	
Mafa	11	3	30	3	(1 nb, 1 w)		20	6	65	1	(4 nb)
Nkwe	6	0	23	1			18	2	68	1	(2 nb, 1 w)
Nawab	6	1	19	2		(6)	22	2	72	3	(1 nb)
Knox	2	2	0	1		(4)	8	0	41	1	(3 w)
Motaung						(5)	2	0	2	0	
Adams							7	0	12	0	

Fall of Wickets

	Gau	FS	FS	Gau
1st	42 (1)	21 (1)	130 (2)	13 (2)
2nd	141 (3)	21 (3)	182 (1)	36 (1)
3rd	185 (2)	26 (4)	230 (4)	-
4th	189 (5)	26 (2)	230 (3)	-
5th	360 (6)	27 (6)	246 (5)	-
6th	381 (4)	78 (5)	298 (7)	-
7th	-	88 (7)	314 (6)	-
8th	-	109 (9)	319 (8)	-
9th	-	113 (8)	329 (10)	-
10th	-	125 (10)	329 (11)	-

EASTERNS v NORTH WEST — SAA 3-day Challenge Pool A

Played at Willowmoore Park, Benoni on 26,27,28 January 2006 — Toss: Easterns
Umpires: CJ Conradie & LM Engelbrecht
Debuts: Eas: None. NW: HM Strydom (FC)
Close of play: Day 1: No play. Day 2: Eas (1) 67-3 (Seymore 34*, Toyana 0*, 21 overs).
Result: Match drawn
Points: Eas: 9.16 (bat 5.16, bowl 4, match 0); NW: 6.76 (bat 3.76, bowl 3, match 0)

NORTH WEST	Runs	Mins	Balls	4	6		Runs	Mins	Balls	4	6
FA Steyn c Bodibe b Wiese	10	23	20	2	-	b Mutch	24	19	22	2	1
DJ Kgamadi b Wiese	21	38	41	2	-	b Mutch	6	27	14	-	-
M Akoojee b Hlengane	23	67	57	3	-	c Mofokeng b Hlengane	28	80	71	2	-
J le Roux c Toyana b O'Connor	58	156	125	7	-	lbw b Toyana	16	37	41	1	-
*RA Stroh c Bodibe b Mutch	18	76	75	2	-	not out	30	73	84	1	-
HM Strydom lbw b O'Connor	17	47	40	2	-	not out	7	38	34	-	-
R Bhayat c Seymore b Hlengane	1	4	7	-	-						
†TA Bula not out	65	90	80	6	2						
JS Hermitage st Bodibe b Hlengane	17	69	62	1	-						
VCM Mazibuko b Mutch	6	3	3	-	1						
F van der Merwe											
Extras (lb 1, nb 1)	2					Extras (b 8, lb 4, nb 2)	14				
TOTAL (for 9 wkts dec) (84.5 overs)	**238**					**TOTAL (for 4 wkts) (44 overs)**	**125**				

EASTERNS	Runs	Mins	Balls	4	6
AJ Seymore c Mazibuko b Stroh	133	292	235	20	-
HA van Straaten b Bhayat	0	4	1	-	-
†TM Bodibe b Van der Merwe	1	13	11	-	-
J Booysen c Kgamadi b Stroh	28	66	53	4	-
G Toyana c Akoojee b Hermitage	9	57	36	-	-
D Wiese c Strydom b Stroh	91	139	112	14	-
E Nyawo b Bhayat	26	46	27	4	-
*SP O'Connor not out	9	42	28	-	-
RG Mutch not out	0	4	3	-	-
IC Hlengane					
PT Mofokeng					
Extras (b 3, lb 3, w 3, nb 2)	11				
TOTAL (for 7 wkts dec) (84 overs)	**308**				

Eas	O	M	R	W		O	M	R	W	
Wiese	17	3	57	2	(1 nb)	5	1	24	0	
Mutch	21.5	1	62	2		5	2	19	2	(1 nb)
Hlengane	34	5	78	3		(4) 16	3	35	1	(1 nb)
O'Connor	12	2	40	2						
Toyana						(3) 15	4	30	1	
Seymore						(5) 2	0	4	0	
Booysen						(6) 1	0	1	0	
NW	O	M	R	W		O	M	R	W	
Van der Merwe	14	4	38	1	(1 nb)					
Bhayat	18	5	59	2	(1 w)					
Stroh	18	6	47	3	(1 w)					
Mazibuko	13	1	58	0	(1 nb, 1 w)					
Hermitage	8	0	42	1						
Akoojee	9	3	33	0						
Le Roux	4	0	25	0						

Fall of Wickets

	NW	Eas	NW
1st	22 (1)	0 (2)	25 (1)
2nd	31 (2)	9 (3)	36 (2)
3rd	71 (3)	63 (4)	62 (4)
4th	123 (5)	100 (5)	94 (3)
5th	140 (4)	259 (6)	-
6th	141 (7)	272 (1)	-
7th	153 (6)	307 (7)	-
8th	227 (9)	-	-
9th	238 (10)	-	-
10th	-	-	-

FREE STATE v GRIQUALAND WEST — SAA 3-day Challenge Pool A

Played at Goodyear Park, Bloemfontein on 2,3 February 2006 — Toss: Griqualand West

Umpires: CJ Conradie & BM White

Debuts: FS: None. GW: None

Close of play: Day 1: FS (1) 114-2 (Mosena 46*, Van Wyk 2*, 37 overs).

Result: Free State won by 9 wickets

Points: FS: 16.96 (bat 2.96, bowl 4, match 10); GW: 6.9 (bat 2.90, bowl 4, match 0)

Notes: McLaren kept wicket in Free State's 2nd innings.

GRIQUALAND WEST	Runs	Mins	Balls	4	6		Runs	Mins	Balls	4	6
CN Bennett c Linde b Sekonyane	14	58	37	2	-	(2) c and b Malao	31	97	55	5	1
AP McLaren lbw b Samson	0	8	5	-	-	(1) c Van Wyk b Samson	6	15	13	1	-
CJ de Jager c Mostert b Sekonyane	18	39	29	2	-	c Malao b Sekonyane	15	32	21	3	-
J Brooker c Mosena b Malao	22	67	40	3	-	lbw b Malao	1	5	3	-	-
*†W Bossenger lbw b Fick	8	12	6	1	-	(7) c Samson b Mostert	3	5	5	-	-
AG Doherty run out (Mostert)	21	52	37	3	-	(5) lbw b Malao	0	3	4	-	-
AK Kruger c Fick b Malao	22	44	28	3	-	(6) st Linde b Malao	8	24	11	1	-
J Coetzee not out	46	118	91	3	-	c Van Wyk b Mostert	0	2	4	-	-
NO Arthur b Malao	4	17	11	-	-	c Fick b Malao	11	24	23	1	-
TR Plaatjie c Van Wyk b De Kock	25	50	46	1	3	c Mosena b Mostert	2	3	4	-	-
R Pietersen c Mosena b Mostert	7	10	10	1	-	not out	5	15	10	-	-
Extras (b 1, lb 3, w 1, nb 3)	8					Extras (b 4, lb 7)	11				
TOTAL (56.1 overs)	**195**					**TOTAL (25.3 overs)**	**93**				

FREE STATE	Runs	Mins	Balls	4	6		Runs	Mins	Balls	4	6
*HG de Kock c Brooker b Pietersen	18	44	42	2	-	not out	34	91	66	1	-
LN Mosena c Kruger b Arthur	66	221	144	4	-	(3) not out	46	88	70	4	-
B Hector c Kruger b Arthur	43	86	70	4	-						
DJ van Wyk c McLaren b Kruger	21	54	40	3	-						
CA Thyssen lbw b Coetzee	5	15	12	1	-						
MP Fick c and b Arthur	8	22	12	1	-	(2) c Kruger b Coetzee	0	3	2	-	-
†C Linde c Doherty b Arthur	2	30	20	-	-						
JF Mostert not out	21	61	50	2	-						
QG Samson c Bennett b Arthur	0	15	15	-	-						
JMM Malao lbw b Arthur	0	3	2	-	-						
BK Sekonyane run out (sub - D Donaldson/McLaren)	2	14	10	-	-						
Extras (b 2, lb 4, w 1, nb 5)	12					Extras (lb 7, w 3, nb 1)	11				
TOTAL (68.4 overs)	**198**					**TOTAL (for 1 wkt) (22.5 overs)**	**91**				

FS	O	M	R	W			O	M	R	W	
Sekonyane	14	3	46	2			8	3	19	1	
Samson	13	2	47	1	(3 nb)		3	1	16	1	
Fick	7	2	24	1	(1 w)						
Malao	14	2	54	3		(3)	9.3	3	27	5	
Mostert	6.1	0	11	1		(4)	5	1	20	3	
De Kock	2	0	9	1							
GW	*O*	*M*	*R*	*W*			*O*	*M*	*R*	*W*	
Coetzee	16	2	57	1			6	0	17	1	
Plaatjie	7	2	9	0							
Kruger	12	1	51	1	(5 nb, 1 w)		3	1	9	0	(1 nb)
Pietersen	15	3	48	1		(2)	4	0	19	0	(1 w)
Arthur	18.4	8	27	6		(4)	5.5	1	19	0	
Doherty						(5)	4	0	20	0	

Fall of Wickets

	GW	FS	GW	FS
1st	0 (2)	22 (1)	7 (1)	1 (2)
2nd	35 (3)	106 (3)	44 (3)	-
3rd	40 (1)	146 (4)	49 (4)	-
4th	55 (5)	155 (5)	49 (5)	-
5th	88 (4)	171 (2)	69 (6)	-
6th	89 (6)	171 (6)	72 (7)	-
7th	133 (7)	178 (7)	72 (8)	-
8th	141 (9)	184 (9)	74 (2)	-
9th	184 (10)	184 (10)	77 (10)	-
10th	195 (11)	198 (11)	93 (9)	-

GRIQUALAND WEST v NORTH WEST — SAA 3-day Challenge Pool A

Played at De Beers Diamond Oval, Kimberley on 9,10,11 February 2006 — Toss: North West

Umpires: GH Pienaar & BDA Westraadt

Debuts: GW: None. NW: None

Close of play: Day 1: No play. Day 2: NW (1) 178-2 (Akoojee 79*, Le Roux 42*, 49 overs).

Result: Match drawn

Points: GW: 6.9 (bat 3.90, bowl 3, match 0); NW: 8.74 (bat 4.74, bowl 4, match 0)

GRIQUALAND WEST	Runs	Mins	Balls	4	6		Runs	Mins	Balls	4	6
AP McLaren c Holtzhausen b R Bhayat	31	75	60	4	1	c Holtzhausen b Coetsee	72	113	86	8	2
CN Bennett c Steyn b Campher	0	12	4	-	-	c Akoojee b Holtzhausen	13	39	30	3	-
AG Doherty lbw b Stroh	32	74	51	6	-	b Coetsee	3	36	16	-	-
J Brooker c Kgamadi b Holtzhausen	29	62	30	5	-	c R Bhayat b Coetsee	30	54	46	5	-
*†W Bossenger c Akoojee b Campher	71	179	103	5	-	not out	39	80	66	4	-
AK Kruger b Coetsee	53	54	61	7	1	not out	24	62	39	3	-
J Coetzee c and b Stroh	0	11	8	-	-						
NO Arthur c Bula b Holtzhausen	9	29	32	-	-						
APT Mabuya c Kgamadi b Holtzhausen	5	15	13	-	-						
D Pretorius run out (Bula/Kgamadi)	1	3	2	-	-						
R Pietersen not out	0	11	11	-	-						
Extras (lb 1, nb 13)	14					Extras (lb 3, w 1, nb 5)	9				
TOTAL (60.2 overs)	**245**					**TOTAL (for 4 wkts) (46.2 overs)**	**190**				

NORTH WEST	Runs	Mins	Balls	4	6
FA Steyn lbw b Coetzee	29	84	63	4	-
DJ Kgamadi b Pietersen	17	54	38	1	-
M Akoojee c Bossenger b Pietersen	80	167	131	12	-
J le Roux b Coetzee	42	112	79	5	-
WL Coetsee lbw b Pietersen	2	12	14	-	-
*RA Stroh c Pretorius b Coetzee	9	58	44	1	-
FS Holtzhausen c and b Kruger	17	63	37	2	-
R Bhayat not out	39	117	71	1	1
†TA Bula lbw b Coetzee	59	73	62	7	1
GH Bhayat lbw b Pretorius	1	16	16	-	-
JP Campher c Pretorius b Coetzee	17	11	10	2	1
Extras (lb 5, w 6, nb 4)	15				
TOTAL (93.3 overs)	**327**				

NW	O	M	R	W			O	M	R	W	
Campher	10.2	0	56	2	(12 nb)		8	0	45	0	(5 nb)
GH Bhayat	9	3	40	0	(1 nb)		5	0	16	0	(1 w)
Holtzhausen	13	0	70	3			7.2	2	11	1	
R Bhayat	7	2	26	1			4	0	39	0	
Stroh	8	2	18	2		(7)	4	0	16	0	
Coetsee	13	2	34	1		(5)	12	1	40	3	
Akoojee						(6)	6	1	20	0	
GW	O	M	R	W			O	M	R	W	
Pretorius	26	3	83	1	(1 w)						
Coetzee	27.3	5	92	5	(1 w)						
Pietersen	13	4	29	3	(2 nb)						
Kruger	7	0	42	1	(2 nb)						
Arthur	17	1	70	0							
Mabuya	3	0	6	0							

Fall of Wickets

	GW	NW	GW
1st	8 (2)	43 (2)	40 (2)
2nd	60 (1)	65 (1)	68 (3)
3rd	72 (3)	178 (4)	112 (1)
4th	131 (4)	181 (5)	131 (4)
5th	203 (6)	182 (3)	-
6th	204 (7)	202 (6)	-
7th	230 (8)	210 (7)	-
8th	240 (9)	301 (9)	-
9th	243 (10)	306 (10)	-
10th	245 (5)	327 (11)	-

NORTHERNS v EASTERNS — SAA 3-day Challenge Pool A

Played at Tshwane University of Technology Oval, Pretoria on 9,10,11 February 2006 Toss: Easterns
Umpires: SB Lambson & DJ Smith
Debuts: Nor: None. Eas: None
Close of play: Day 1: No play. Day 2: Nor (1) 147-0 (Kuhn 62*, Chouhan 77*, 40 overs).
Result: Match drawn
Points: Nor: 4.46 (bat 4.46, bowl 0, match 0); Eas: 0 (bat 0.00, bowl 0, match 0)

NORTHERNS	Runs	Mins	Balls	4	6
HG Kuhn not out	133	298	226	12	1
N Chouhan c Booysen b Wiese	93	209	170	12	-
A Paleker not out	28	88	65	2	-
SJ Myburgh					
MJ Mokonyama					
†CFK van Wyk					
*P Joubert					
MA Mashimbyi					
PL Harris					
N Wagner					
FG Nkuna					
Extras (b 7, lb 4, w 1, nb 7)	19				
TOTAL (for 1 wkt) (75.2 overs)	**273**				

EASTERNS
AJ Seymore
HA van Straaten
S Mandan
Z de Bruyn
J Booysen
G Toyana
*SP O'Connor
D Wiese
†TM Bodibe
IC Hlengane
PT Mofokeng

Eas	O	M	R	W	
De Bruyn	23	5	77	0	(5 nb, 1 w)
Wiese	24	3	65	1	(1 nb)
Mofokeng	4	1	17	0	(1 nb)
O'Connor	6	0	27	0	
Hlengane	13.2	1	58	0	
Toyana	5	0	18	0	

Fall of Wickets

	Nor
1st	178 (2)

GAUTENG v NORTHERNS — SAA 3-day Challenge Pool A

Played at Walter Milton Oval, University of Witwatersrand, Johannesburg on 16,17,18 February 2006 Toss: Northerns
Umpires: SW Liebisch & DJ Smith
Debuts: Gau: SF Grobler (FC). Nor: None
Close of play: Day 1: Gau (1) 41-1 (Snijman 19*, Nkwe 18*, 17.5 overs). Day 2: Nor (2) 102-2 (JG Myburgh 14*, Chouhan 2*, 31.4 overs).
Result: Match drawn
Points: Gau: 7.7 (bat 3.70, bowl 4, match 0); Nor: 10.94 (bat 6.94, bowl 4, match 0)

NORTHERNS	Runs	Mins	Balls	4	6		Runs	Mins	Balls	4	6
†HG Kuhn c Nawab b Grobler	111	233	154	10	1	c Snijman b Nawab	50	119	75	6	-
F du Plessis st Van Wyk b Nawab	156	266	203	21	2	c Van Wyk b Mafa	32	105	59	2	-
N Chouhan st Van Wyk b Nawab	15	50	37	1	-	(4) c Van Wyk b Nawab	2	23	20	-	-
JG Myburgh c Gain b Singh	18	36	34	3	-	(3) not out	64	139	109	4	2
A Paleker c Gain b Nawab	5	23	13	-	-	c Thompson b Nawab	0	7	3	-	-
SJ Myburgh b Mafa	31	33	29	1	3	c Grobler b Nawab	12	23	10	1	1
*P Joubert c Makalima b Nawab	17	33	19	2	-	b Nawab	3	9	6	-	-
AC Thomas c Thompson b Nawab	14	12	8	1	1	not out	42	52	42	5	-
AM Phangiso not out	10	13	10	1	-						
MA Mashimbyi c Snijman b Nawab	2	2	2	-	-						
N Wagner not out	9	7	4	2	-						
Extras (b 4, lb 2, nb 3)	9					Extras (b 6, w 2)	8				
TOTAL (for 9 wkts) (85 overs)	**397**					**TOTAL (for 6 wkts dec) (54 overs)**	**213**				

GAUTENG	Runs	Mins	Balls	4	6		Runs	Mins	Balls	4	6
BD Snijman c Kuhn b Joubert	20	84	74	4	-	c Kuhn b Joubert	16	68	56	3	-
WB Motaung c Kuhn b Thomas	4	18	15	-	-	c Du Plessis b JG Myburgh	75	139	128	9	-
ET Nkwe c Paleker b Thomas	26	71	54	3	-	not out	71	196	161	6	1
*DR Gain c Kuhn b Phangiso	64	100	148	6	-	lbw b Du Plessis	4	20	26	-	-
DL Makalima c JG Myburgh b Phangiso	61	95	73	7	2	c Paleker b Wagner	26	60	70	3	-
†DM van Wyk c Paleker b Phangiso	22	46	42	3	-	not out	10	44	37	2	-
SF Grobler lbw b Mashimbyi	3	10	9	-	-						
A Nawab c Du Plessis b Wagner	19	64	42	2	-						
PG Thompson c SJ Myburgh b Phangiso	0	3	3	-	-						
Y Singh not out	16	24	24	2	-						
JT Mafa c Paleker b Phangiso	0	7	2	-	-						
Extras	0					Extras (lb 2)	2				
TOTAL (81 overs)	**235**					**TOTAL (for 4 wkts) (79.4 overs)**	**204**				

Gau	O	M	R	W			O	M	R	W	
Thompson	6	0	42	0			6	1	26	0	(1 w)
Singh	17	3	44	1			14	5	28	0	(1 w)
Mafa	23	3	88	1		(4)	12	1	60	1	
Nkwe	9	2	50	0	(3 nb)	(3)	3	0	11	0	
Nawab	19	0	106	6		(6)	16	4	66	5	
Grobler	11	0	61	1		(7)	1	0	4	0	
Snijman						(5)	2	0	12	0	
Nor	O	M	R	W			O	M	R	W	
Thomas	16	3	31	2			5	1	14	0	
Wagner	9	1	32	1			8	5	10	1	
Phangiso	27	7	76	5		(4)	16.4	4	41	0	
JG Myburgh	2	0	9	0		(6)	19	1	54	1	
Joubert	13	7	29	1		(3)	6	2	9	1	
Mashimbyi	12	2	42	1		(5)	4	1	16	0	
Du Plessis	2	0	16	0			18	7	47	1	
SJ Myburgh							3	1	11	0	

Fall of Wickets

	Nor	Gau	Nor	Gau
1st	252 (1)	5 (2)	96 (2)	36 (1)
2nd	281 (2)	50 (1)	100 (1)	111 (2)
3rd	288 (3)	50 (3)	102 (4)	122 (4)
4th	312 (4)	143 (5)	106 (5)	169 (5)
5th	312 (5)	175 (6)	142 (6)	-
6th	362 (6)	187 (7)	146 (7)	-
7th	368 (7)	213 (4)	-	-
8th	383 (8)	213 (9)	-	-
9th	385 (10)	224 (8)	-	-
10th	-	235 (11)	-	-

NORTH WEST v FREE STATE

SAA 3-day Challenge Pool A

Played at Sedgars Park, Potchefstroom on 16,17,18 February 2006

Toss: Free State

Umpires: JEP Ostrom & BM White

Debuts: NW: None. FS: None

Close of play: Day 1: NW (1) 60-2 (Akoojee 21*, Le Roux 18*, 20 overs). Day 2: FS (2) 137-2 (Hector 24*, Koortzen 33*, 39 overs).

Result: North West won by 4 wickets

Points: NW: 18.08 (bat 4.08, bowl 4, match 10); FS: 6.8 (bat 3.80, bowl 3, match 0)

Notes: Akoojee scored his century off 90 balls in North West's 2nd innings

FREE STATE	Runs	Mins	Balls	4	6		Runs	Mins	Balls	4	6
JA Beukes c Bula b Campher	0	2	3	-	-	b Moleon	47	61	50	10	-
*HG de Kock c and b Akoojee	84	247	199	11	-	c Kgamadi b Holtzhausen	26	76	48	4	-
B Hector c Steyn b Holtzhausen	71	211	148	8	-	lbw b Moleon	68	259	191	5	-
PJ Koortzen lbw b Holtzhausen	12	16	14	1	1	b Coetsee	96	176	117	12	1
CA Thyssen run out (Bula)	35	54	47	4	1	not out	69	101	86	4	2
†C Linde lbw b Coetsee	1	9	11	-	-	not out	38	34	36	4	-
MP Fick b Coetsee	15	53	33	2	-						
TS Motsamai b Bhayat	5	11	10	-	-						
QG Samson b Bhayat	0	4	4	-	-						
JMM Malao not out	3	26	12	-	-						
BK Sekonyane c Steyn b Bhayat	5	15	16	1	-						
Extras (lb 4, nb 5)	9					Extras (lb 8, nb 6)	14				
TOTAL (82 overs)	**240**					**TOTAL (for 4 wkts dec) (87 overs)**	**358**				

NORTH WEST	Runs	Mins	Balls	4	6		Runs	Mins	Balls	4	6
FA Steyn c Linde b Samson	6	23	19	1	-	lbw b Sekonyane	0	1	2	-	-
DJ Kgamadi c De Kock b Samson	14	38	28	3	-	c Linde b Sekonyane	12	41	26	1	-
M Akoojee st Linde b Malao	32	142	100	4	-	b Sekonyane	103	150	101	17	-
J le Roux b Motsamai	110	236	197	14	-	b Fick	28	50	52	5	-
WL Coetsee c Beukes b Sekonyane	0	10	11	-	-	b Sekonyane	33	43	29	5	-
*RA Stroh st Linde b Malao	31	49	64	2	-	c Sekonyane b Samson	41	67	43	-	1
FS Holtzhausen not out	69	97	63	5	3	not out	66	73	54	8	-
†TA Bula c Thyssen b Motsamai	3	13	10	-	-	not out	10	10	8	2	-
EO Moleon c Fick b Malao	19	33	36	2	-						
GH Bhayat not out	0	3	1	-	-						
JP Campher											
Extras (lb 3, w 2, nb 1)	6					Extras (b 7, lb 4, w 5, nb 2)	18				
TOTAL (for 8 wkts) (88 overs)	**290**					**TOTAL (for 6 wkts) (52.1 overs)**	**311**				

NW	O	M	R	W		O	M	R	W	
Campher	8	2	27	1	(3 nb)	8	0	53	0	(2 nb)
Bhayat	16	4	42	3	(2 nb)	9	2	57	0	(1 nb)
Holtzhausen	14	0	51	2		(4) 15	3	49	1	
Moleon	11	5	24	0		(3) 16	1	55	2	(2 nb)
Coetsee	21	7	53	2		(6) 23	5	81	1	
Stroh	7	2	16	0		(5) 13	1	47	0	
Akoojee	5	0	23	1		2	0	4	0	
Kgamadi						1	0	4	0	(1 nb)
FS	O	M	R	W		O	M	R	W	
Sekonyane	19	6	46	1	(1 nb, 1 w)	14	0	80	4	(1 nb)
Samson	8	0	35	2	(1 w)	12.1	3	67	1	
Motsamai	13	3	38	2		3	0	16	0	
Malao	31	3	112	3		10	0	54	0	(2 w)
De Kock	12.3	2	45	0						
Fick	4	0	11	0		4	1	31	1	(1 nb)
Thyssen	0.3	0	0	0						
Koortzen						(5) 9	1	52	0	

Fall of Wickets

	FS	NW	FS	NW
1st	0 (1)	16 (1)	69 (1)	0 (1)
2nd	147 (3)	21 (2)	75 (2)	38 (2)
3rd	163 (4)	118 (3)	233 (4)	91 (4)
4th	186 (2)	121 (5)	295 (3)	184 (5)
5th	189 (6)	170 (6)	-	195 (3)
6th	221 (5)	228 (4)	-	275 (6)
7th	228 (8)	232 (8)	-	-
8th	228 (9)	282 (9)	-	-
9th	233 (7)	-	-	-
10th	240 (11)	-	-	-

NORTHERNS v FREE STATE — SAA 3-day Challenge Pool A

Played at LC de Villiers Oval, University of Pretoria, Pretoria on 23,24,25 February 2006 Toss: Northerns

Umpires: LM Engelbrecht & GH Pienaar

Debuts: Nor: JR Jumat (FC). FS: D Elgar (FC)

Close of play: Day 1: Nor (1) 26-0 (Chouhan 16*, Du Plessis 9*, 9 overs). Day 2: FS (2) 86-4 (De Kock 43*, Linde 0*, 23 overs).

Result: Northerns won by 9 wickets

Points: Nor: 19.16 (bat 5.16, bowl 4, match 10); FS: 6.76 (bat 3.76, bowl 3, match 0)

FREE STATE	Runs	Mins	Balls	4	6		Runs	Mins	Balls	4	6
JA Beukes c Paleker b Nkuna	0	7	10	-	-	c Van Wyk b Joubert	36	64	41	5	-
*HG de Kock c Du Plessis b Nkuna	26	63	44	3	-	c Van Wyk b Phangiso	69	193	133	6	-
PJ Koortzen c Joubert b Nkuna	49	148	105	4	2	lbw b Joubert	0	5	3	-	-
D Elgar c SJ Myburgh b Steyn	6	22	12	-	-	c Van Wyk b Joubert	0	17	8	-	-
LN Mosena c Van Wyk b Nkuna	19	49	47	3	-	lbw b Steyn	1	12	7	-	-
†C Linde lbw b Phangiso	16	63	36	2	-	c SJ Myburgh b Steyn	0	16	17	-	-
JF Mostert b Du Plessis	70	151	157	7	-	lbw b Phangiso	7	41	24	-	-
TS Motsamai b Du Plessis	24	85	73	-	-	c Du Plessis b Phangiso	8	20	16	-	-
BK Sekonyane lbw b Du Plessis	2	25	17	-	-	lbw b Du Plessis	20	36	20	4	-
QG Samson b Steyn	0	5	3	-	-	c Joubert b Phangiso	1	11	9	-	-
JMM Malao not out	0	9	6	-	-	not out	3	11	12	-	-
Extras (b 1, lb 8, w 1, nb 16)	26					Extras (lb 3, w 1, nb 9)	13				
TOTAL (82.2 overs)	**238**					**TOTAL (46.5 overs)**	**158**				

NORTHERNS	Runs	Mins	Balls	4	6		Runs	Mins	Balls	4	6
N Chouhan c Linde b Samson	16	49	43	3	-	c Mosena b Sekonyane	13	34	29	1	-
F du Plessis st Linde b Malao	65	158	111	8	-	not out	57	80	59	6	-
JG Myburgh c Linde b Sekonyane	91	209	157	9	1	not out	10	45	33	1	-
A Paleker c Linde b Motsamai	1	3	4	-	-						
SJ Myburgh c Beukes b Motsamai	0	2	2	-	-						
†CFK van Wyk c Motsamai b Samson	50	144	107	1	-						
*P Joubert b Sekonyane	49	83	57	5	-						
AM Phangiso b Sekonyane	32	36	34	2	1						
JR Jumat not out	5	7	8	-	-						
DW Steyn not out	1	4	1	-	-						
FG Nkuna											
Extras (lb 2, w 1, nb 2)	5					Extras (lb 1, w 1)	2				
TOTAL (for 8 wkts) (87 overs)	**315**					**TOTAL (for 1 wkt) (20.1 overs)**	**82**				

Nor	O	M	R	W			O	M	R	W	
Steyn	19	3	55	2	(15 nb, 1 w)		16	3	61	2	(7 nb, 1 w)
Nkuna	13	2	43	4	(1 nb)		11	3	38	0	(1 nb)
Joubert	11	2	28	0			9	1	26	3	
Jumat	7	1	30	0			1	0	7	0	
Phangiso	17	3	42	1		(6)	7	2	19	4	
Du Plessis	15.2	4	31	3		(5)	2.5	0	4	1	(1 nb)
FS	O	M	R	W			O	M	R	W	
Sekonyane	20	2	66	3	(1 nb, 1 w)		10.1	3	37	1	
Samson	23	5	83	2			4	0	25	0	(1 w)
Motsamai	18	4	61	2			4	1	17	0	
Malao	21	2	78	1	(1 nb)		2	0	2	0	
Mostert	5	1	25	0							

Fall of Wickets

	FS	Nor	FS	Nor
1st	3 (1)	26 (1)	67 (1)	35 (1)
2nd	44 (2)	119 (2)	67 (3)	-
3rd	58 (4)	120 (4)	75 (4)	-
4th	102 (5)	120 (5)	84 (5)	-
5th	113 (3)	204 (3)	90 (6)	-
6th	160 (6)	256 (6)	119 (7)	-
7th	227 (8)	309 (7)	129 (8)	-
8th	236 (7)	310 (8)	148 (2)	-
9th	238 (10)	-	154 (10)	-
10th	238 (9)	-	158 (9)	-

EASTERNS v GAUTENG

SAA 3-day Challenge Pool A

Played at Willowmoore Park, Benoni on 23,24,25 February 2006 Toss: Easterns

Umpires: DJ Smith & S Wadvalla

Debuts: Eas: None. Gau: None

Close of play: Day 1: Gau (1) 4-0 (Motaung 0*, Symes 4*, 1.3 overs). Day 2: Gau (1) 267-7 (Knox 21*, De Bruin 12*, 76 overs).

Result: Match drawn

Points: Eas: 5.84 (bat 1.84, bowl 4, match 0); Gau: 9.2 (bat 5.20, bowl 4, match 0)

EASTERNS	Runs	Mins	Balls	4	6		Runs	Mins	Balls	4	6
S Mandan c Motaung b De Bruin	0	1	1	-	-	b Nawab	41	95	65	8	-
HA van Straaten c Le Roux b De Bruin	4	20	13	-	-	c Van Wyk b Mafa	22	34	23	4	-
AM van den Berg c Makalima b De Bruin	2	9	11	-	-	b Mafa	0	10	7	-	-
Z de Bruyn c Symes b Mafa	6	42	17	-	-	c Le Roux b Knox	107	207	152	13	1
D Wiese c Van Wyk b De Bruin	11	17	16	2	-	c Knox b Nawab	10	10	9	1	1
*SP O'Connor b Le Roux	27	58	50	5	-	c and b Nawab	14	47	40	1	-
E Nyawo c De Bruin b Le Roux	24	54	37	4	-	run out (Snijman)	5	67	52	-	-
†TM Bodibe not out	28	75	72	3	-	c Van Wyk b Snijman	23	97	85	1	-
RG Mutch b De Bruin	33	38	36	3	2	not out	34	78	56	4	1
IC Hlengane c Symes b Nawab	2	15	11	-	-	not out	7	8	8	1	-
PT Mofokeng											
Extras (b 2, lb 1, nb 2)	5					Extras (b 3, lb 1, w 3, nb 5)	12				
TOTAL (for 9 wkts dec) (43.3 overs)	**142**					**TOTAL (for 8 wkts) (82 overs)**	**275**				

GAUTENG	Runs	Mins	Balls	4	6
WB Motaung c De Bruyn b Mutch	13	46	31	1	-
J Symes lbw b De Bruyn	6	17	14	1	-
BC Adams c Bodibe b Mutch	13	12	10	2	-
*BD Snijman lbw b Wiese	114	203	154	15	1
DL Makalima lbw b Wiese	15	40	26	2	-
†DM van Wyk c De Bruyn b Mofokeng	63	185	143	8	-
CE Knox not out	47	114	80	3	-
HW le Roux st Bodibe b Hlengane	5	11	12	-	-
GJ de Bruin c Bodibe b De Bruyn	12	24	24	-	1
A Nawab c O'Connor b Mofokeng	14	32	17	2	-
JT Mafa not out	0	5	1	-	-
Extras (lb 3, w 3, nb 2)	8				
TOTAL (for 9 wkts dec) (85 overs)	**310**				

Gau	O	M	R	W			O	M	R	W	
De Bruin	15	3	55	5	(1 nb)		11.2	2	32	0	(1 nb)
Mafa	9	2	19	1			15	2	51	2	(4 nb, 2 w)
Le Roux	8	2	26	2	(1 nb)	(4)	3	0	26	0	
Knox	5	1	23	0		(3)	10	3	31	1	
Nawab	6.3	1	16	1			21	2	74	3	(1 w)
Motaung							3	1	6	0	
Snijman							2.4	0	8	1	
Symes							12	0	32	0	
Adams							4	0	11	0	
Eas	O	M	R	W			O	M	R	W	
De Bruyn	23	3	73	2							
Mutch	17	3	76	2							
Wiese	13	2	45	2	(1 nb)						
O'Connor	4	0	15	0							
Van den Berg	6	1	23	0							
Mofokeng	12	2	43	2	(1 nb, 3 w)						
Hlengane	10	1	32	1							

Fall of Wickets

	Eas	Gau	Eas
1st	0 (1)	11 (2)	30 (2)
2nd	4 (3)	26 (3)	34 (3)
3rd	9 (2)	37 (1)	97 (1)
4th	22 (5)	78 (5)	111 (5)
5th	26 (4)	210 (4)	153 (6)
6th	70 (6)	240 (6)	185 (7)
7th	79 (7)	248 (8)	212 (4)
8th	131 (9)	268 (9)	268 (8)
9th	142 (10)	307 (10)	-
10th	-	-	-

FREE STATE v EASTERNS — SAA 3-day Challenge Pool A

Played at Goodyear Park, Bloemfontein on 2,3,4 March 2006 Toss: Easterns
Umpires: CJ Conradie & MZ Nanabhay
Debuts: FS: GD Perry (FC). Eas: None
Close of play: Day 1: Eas (1) 162-4 (Morkel 63*, Wiese 51*, 43 overs). Day 2: FS (2) 187-6 (Koortzen 29*, Motsamai 8*, 59 overs).
Result: Easterns won by 2 wickets
Points: FS: 6.58 (bat 2.58, bowl 4, match 0); Eas: 19.3 (bat 5.30, bowl 4, match 10)

FREE STATE	Runs	Mins	Balls	4	6		Runs	Mins	Balls	4	6
JA Beukes c and b Van den Berg	63	124	75	9	-	lbw b Van den Berg	75	129	119	9	-
*HG de Kock c Wiese b Morkel	0	11	8	-	-	c Van den Berg b Morkel	0	14	9	-	-
LN Mosena c Van Straaten b Morkel	28	91	80	1	-	c Mandan b Hlengane	32	90	64	3	-
PJ Koortzen c Seymore b Wiese	42	76	67	7	-	b Hlengane	82	219	166	10	-
D Elgar c Morkel b Van den Berg	32	112	73	4	-	c Seymore b Hlengane	32	68	48	6	-
†C Linde c Bodibe b Wiese	1	6	5	-	-	c Van Straaten b Morkel	4	14	13	-	-
GD Perry lbw b Van den Berg	1	6	5	-	-	lbw b Morkel	0	1	1	-	-
TS Motsamai b Wiese	3	7	7	-	-	b Wiese	36	70	56	7	-
AP Abrahams c Seymore b Morkel	1	13	8	-	-	b Hlengane	7	29	21	1	-
BK Sekonyane lbw b Morkel	1	8	5	-	-	c Hlengane b Wiese	8	20	16	-	1
QG Samson not out	1	13	9	-	-	not out	1	15	8	-	-
Extras (b 4, lb 2)	6					Extras (b 13, lb 2)	15				
TOTAL (57 overs)	**179**					**TOTAL (86.5 overs)**	**292**				

EASTERNS	Runs	Mins	Balls	4	6		Runs	Mins	Balls	4	6
S Mandan c Linde b Samson	18	67	33	4	-	c Linde b Sekonyane	1	6	9	-	-
AJ Seymore c Linde b Samson	8	26	18	2	-	c Koortzen b Abrahams	46	122	91	5	-
HA van Straaten lbw b Motsamai	17	52	30	1	-	b Sekonyane	0	9	5	-	-
AM van den Berg c Linde b Motsamai	1	20	9	-	-	c Sekonyane b Abrahams	31	70	46	3	-
JA Morkel c Beukes b Samson	68	129	103	10	-	c Sekonyane b Abrahams	2	12	7	-	-
D Wiese c Koortzen b Sekonyane	168	293	208	18	4	not out	39	76	57	4	-
*SP O'Connor c Mosena b Sekonyane	22	47	33	2	-	c Beukes b Abrahams	1	6	6	-	-
E Nyawo run out (Mosena)	0	7	5	-	-	c Beukes b Abrahams	0	3	4	-	-
†TM Bodibe lbw b Sekonyane	1	14	10	-	-	lbw b Abrahams	12	38	25	1	-
IC Hlengane lbw b Perry	23	84	76	2	-	not out	0	2	0	-	-
PT Mofokeng not out	0	18	5	-	-						
Extras (b 2, lb 4, nb 5)	11					Extras (lb 1, nb 2)	3				
TOTAL (87.3 overs)	**337**					**TOTAL (for 8 wkts) (41.2 overs)**	**135**				

Eas	O	M	R	W		O	M	R	W
Morkel	16	6	28	4		21	6	54	3
Wiese	16	3	64	3		15.5	2	52	2
O'Connor	5	0	28	0		(4) 5	0	10	0
Mofokeng	4	1	21	0		(3) 5	1	32	0
Van den Berg	16	3	32	3		(6) 17	1	65	1
Hlengane						(5) 23	6	64	4
FS	O	M	R	W		O	M	R	W
Sekonyane	13.3	4	60	3		(2) 11	1	60	2 (2 nb)
Samson	27	4	92	3 (1 nb)					
Motsamai	26	5	90	2 (4 nb)		(1) 16.2	1	38	0
Perry	13	3	49	1					
Abrahams	8	1	40	0		(3) 14	1	36	6

Fall of Wickets

	FS	Eas	FS	Eas
1st	5 (2)	16 (2)	5 (2)	1 (1)
2nd	88 (3)	37 (1)	91 (3)	7 (3)
3rd	106 (1)	43 (3)	114 (1)	66 (4)
4th	150 (4)	44 (4)	174 (5)	74 (5)
5th	154 (6)	167 (5)	179 (6)	87 (2)
6th	155 (7)	213 (7)	179 (7)	89 (7)
7th	160 (8)	213 (8)	255 (8)	89 (8)
8th	173 (9)	228 (9)	282 (9)	131 (9)
9th	175 (10)	315 (10)	286 (4)	-
10th	179 (5)	337 (6)	292 (10)	-

GAUTENG v GRIQUALAND WEST — SAA 3-day Challenge Pool A

At Walter Milton Oval, University of the Witwatersrand, Johannesburg on 2,3,4 March 2006
No play – rain.

NORTH WEST v GAUTENG — SAA 3-day Challenge Pool A

Played at Sedgars Park, Potchefstroom on 9,10,11 March 2006 Toss: Gauteng
Umpires: LM Engelbrecht & SW Liebisch
Debuts: NW: None. Gau: None
Close of play: Day 1: NW (1) 101-5 (Stroh 5*, 29.2 overs). Day 2: Gau (2) 184-0 (Motaung 77*, Symes 93*, 40.3 overs).
Result: Match drawn
Points: NW: 8.04 (bat 4.04, bowl 4, match 0); Gau: 6.94 (bat 2.94, bowl 4, match 0)
Notes:Motaung retired hurt with his score on 77 and the total on 184-0 in Gauteng's 2nd innings and returned at the fall of the 4th wicket.

GAUTENG	Runs	Mins	Balls	4	6		Runs	Mins	Balls	4	6
WB Motaung c R Bhayat b GH Bhayat	41	77	58	6	1	b GH Bhayat	114	247	183	14	-
J Symes c Steyn b Campher	19	40	25	3	-	c Kgamadi b Campher	133	247	184	19	-
ET Nkwe c Hermitage b Campher	50	104	85	7	-	c Bula b GH Bhayat	10	47	29	1	-
*BD Snijman c Steyn b Stroh	4	48	24	-	-	c Bula b Holtzhausen	39	105	49	6	-
DL Makalima c Bula b R Bhayat	32	92	60	2	2	c Steyn b Campher	0	10	5	-	-
†DM van Wyk lbw b Stroh	4	66	41	-	-	c GH Bhayat b R Bhayat	9	30	19	2	-
BC Adams not out	15	60	35	1	-	st Bula b Hermitage	73	158	100	9	1
CE Knox c Kgamadi b Stroh	1	7	8	-	-	b Hermitage	39	78	50	3	-
HW le Roux c Holtzhausen b Stroh	7	25	12	1	-	c Le Roux b Akoojee	25	34	26	3	1
A Nawab c Kgamadi b Campher	2	19	16	-	-	not out	1	10	7	-	-
JT Mafa						b Hermitage	0	3	2	-	
Extras (b 2, lb 6, w 1, nb 13)	22					Extras (b 7, lb 8, w 14, nb 4)	33				
TOTAL (for 9 wkts dec) (58.3 overs)	**197**					**TOTAL (108.2 overs)**	**476**				

NORTH WEST	Runs	Mins	Balls	4	6		Runs	Mins	Balls	4	6
FA Steyn c Van Wyk b Mafa	4	16	15	-	-	c Nkwe b Le Roux	0	1	1	-	-
DJ Kgamadi c Snijman b Knox	46	138	78	6	1	c Motaung b Mafa	15	38	21	2	-
M Akoojee c Adams b Mafa	33	55	40	6	-	not out	17	38	27	1	1
J le Roux c Van Wyk b Mafa	4	10	6	1	-	not out	0	1	0	-	-
*RA Stroh b Mafa	14	101	65	1	-						
FS Holtzhausen c Van Wyk b Knox	4	7	4	1	-						
R Bhayat lbw b Motaung	30	66	50	5	-						
†TA Bula c Snijman b Le Roux	68	117	86	9	-						
JS Hermitage c sub (GJ de Bruin) b Snijman	14	46	29	2	-						
GH Bhayat lbw b Knox	12	22	15	2	-						
JP Campher not out	15	22	15	1	1						
Extras (b 1, w 1, nb 6)	8					Extras (nb 1)	1				
TOTAL (66.1 overs)	**252**					**TOTAL (for 2 wkts) (8 overs)**	**33**				

NW	O	M	R	W		O	M	R	W	
Campher	12.3	3	54	3	(13 nb, 1 w)	11	2	48	2	(4 nb, 2 w)
R Bhayat	11	1	54	1		(6) 16	0	79	1	(1 w)
Holtzhausen	11	3	17	0		22	3	76	1	(1 w)
GH Bhayat	10	2	38	1		(2) 19	3	84	2	
Stroh	13	4	24	4		(4) 13	2	56	0	
Hermitage	1	0	2	0		(5) 19.2	2	85	3	(1 w)
Akoojee						5	1	16	1	
Steyn						3	0	17	0	(1 w)
Gau	O	M	R	W		O	M	R	W	
Le Roux	14.1	4	53	1	(6 nb)	4	0	19	1	
Mafa	14	0	56	4		4	0	14	1	(1 nb)
Nkwe	9	2	39	0						
Knox	11	3	31	3						
Motaung	6	0	15	1	(1 w)					
Nawab	9	0	44	0						
Snijman	3	0	13	1						

Fall of Wickets

	Gau	NW	Gau	NW
1st	43 (2)	15 (1)	215 (3)	0 (1)
2nd	81 (1)	61 (3)	243 (2)	33 (2)
3rd	119 (4)	69 (4)	249 (5)	-
4th	127 (3)	96 (2)	268 (6)	-
5th	162 (6)	101 (6)	302 (4)	-
6th	170 (5)	133 (5)	346 (1)	-
7th	171 (8)	151 (7)	430 (8)	-
8th	193 (9)	191 (9)	472 (7)	-
9th	197 (10)	220 (10)	476 (9)	-
10th	-	252 (8)	476 (11)	-

NORTHERNS v GRIQUALAND WEST — SAA 3-day Challenge Pool A

Played at LC de Villiers Oval, University of Pretoria, Pretoria on 8,9,10 March 2006 — Toss: Northerns

Umpires: ZTA Ndamane & JEP Ostrom

Debuts: Nor: TR Khoza (FC). GW: None

Close of play: Day 1: Nor (1) 72-1 (Aronstam 38*, Myburgh 20*, 23 overs). Day 2: GW (2) 119-4 (Brooker 38*, Coetzee 5*, 34.3 overs).

Result: Match drawn

Points: Nor: 8.54 (bat 4.54, bowl 4, match 0); GW: 6.9 (bat 4.90, bowl 2, match 0)

Notes: G Dros scored his fifty off 30 balls and his century off 59 balls in Northerns' 2nd innings. Paleker kept wicket when Van Wyk bowled in Griqualand West's 2nd innings

GRIQUALAND WEST	Runs	Mins	Balls	4	6		Runs	Mins	Balls	4	6
CN Bennett b Wagner	6	12	11	-	-	(2) c Dros b Nkuna	22	62	48	4	-
AP McLaren c Myburgh b Khoza	119	237	185	10	2	(1) c Chouhan b Wagner	0	11	3	-	-
CJ de Jager lbw b Joubert	55	134	91	6	-	c Van Wyk b Nkuna	11	38	28	1	-
J Brooker c Van Wyk b Joubert	0	3	3	-	-	b Joubert	99	292	235	7	-
*†W Bossenger c Joubert b Dros	46	108	83	3	-	c Myburgh b Khoza	36	67	54	3	-
AG Doherty lbw b Khoza	18	36	35	-	-	(7) lbw b Wagner	90	186	158	8	-
AK Kruger c Mokonyama b Aronstam	31	48	35	3	-	(8) st Paleker b Van Wyk	35	61	36	4	-
J Coetzee lbw b Aronstam	1	10	12	-	-	(6) lbw b Aronstam	10	38	25	1	-
NO Arthur c Myburgh b Aronstam	12	23	19	-	-	c Joubert b Wagner	1	11	13	-	-
APT Mabuya c Chouhan b Khoza	1	7	4	-	-	not out	12	29	20	1	-
R Pietersen not out	0	4	3	-	-	not out	4	2	2	1	-
Extras (b 1, lb 1, nb 4)	6					Extras (b 8, lb 3, nb 1)	12				
TOTAL (79.3 overs)	**295**					**TOTAL (for 9 wkts dec) (104 overs)**	**332**				

NORTHERNS	Runs	Mins	Balls	4	6		Runs	Mins	Balls	4	6
MA Aronstam c Bossenger b Pietersen	50	168	135	6	-	st Bossenger b Arthur	56	112	56	4	-
N Chouhan c Bossenger b Kruger	1	40	21	-	-						
JG Myburgh c Kruger b Pietersen	33	110	78	5	-	not out	29	33	26	1	1
A Paleker b Arthur	23	96	86	2	-						
G Dros c Brooker b Pietersen	78	177	99	5	3	(2) c Bennett b Arthur	130	94	70	7	10
†CFK van Wyk c Bennett b Pietersen	62	128	101	4	-						
MJ Mokonyama not out	31	38	30	1	-						
*P Joubert not out	12	11	8	1	-	(4) not out	21	17	16	-	1
TR Khoza											
N Wagner											
FG Nkuna											
Extras (b 1, lb 9, w 1, nb 18)	29					Extras (b 2, nb 1)	3				
TOTAL (for 6 wkts) (90 overs)	**319**					**TOTAL (for 2 wkts) (27.5 overs)**	**239**				

Nor	O	M	R	W		O	M	R	W	
Wagner	17	2	59	1	(2 nb)	17	5	51	3	
Nkuna	10	0	28	0	(2 nb)	13	1	48	2	(1 nb)
Joubert	11	2	33	2		14	4	35	1	
Dros	10	0	51	1		(5) 8	0	26	0	
Aronstam	20	2	81	3		(4) 27	5	86	1	
Khoza	11.3	1	41	3		18	3	48	1	
Myburgh						6	1	20	0	
Van Wyk						1	0	7	1	
GW	O	M	R	W		O	M	R	W	
Coetzee	23.2	5	66	0	(1 nb)	7	0	50	0	
Kruger	20.4	1	85	1	(16 nb)	5	0	50	0	
Pietersen	16	1	71	4	(1 nb, 1 w)	2	0	21	0	(1 nb)
Arthur	21	4	62	1		(5) 6.5	0	52	2	
Mabuya	9	2	25	0		(4) 7	0	64	0	

Fall of Wickets

	GW	Nor	GW	Nor
1st	9 (1)	21 (2)	13 (1)	179 (2)
2nd	139 (3)	98 (3)	38 (3)	203 (1)
3rd	139 (4)	101 (1)	45 (2)	-
4th	226 (2)	159 (4)	111 (5)	-
5th	242 (5)	263 (5)	138 (6)	-
6th	264 (6)	295 (6)	275 (4)	-
7th	267 (8)	-	287 (7)	-
8th	294 (7)	-	289 (9)	-
9th	295 (9)	-	328 (8)	-
10th	295 (10)	-	-	-

Pool B

EASTERN PROVINCE v BORDER — SAA 3-day Challenge Pool B

Played at Sahara Oval St George's, Port Elizabeth on 6,7 October 2005 — Toss: Eastern Province

Umpires: KH Hurter & ZTA Ndamane

Debuts: EP: S Makongolo and U Sandi (Both FC). Bdr: DC Lentz and RR Richards (Both FC)

Close of play: Day 1: Bdr (1) 184-5 (Mbane 1*, Ranger 8*, 53 overs).

Result: Border won by an innings and 8 runs

Points: EP: 6.52 (bat 2.52, bowl 4, match 0); Bdr: 18.94 (bat 4.94, bowl 4, match 10)

EASTERN PROVINCE	Runs	Mins	Balls	4	6		Runs	Mins	Balls	4	6
C Baxter b Richards	25	142	96	3	-	(2) lbw b Richards	0	10	6	-	-
ML Price c Von Hoesslin b Fojela	3	21	17	-	-	(1) b Fojela	2	17	13	-	-
S Makongolo lbw b Richards	5	11	6	-	-	c Lwana b De Kock	56	139	94	7	-
RR Jeggels b Lwana	46	63	54	9	-	b Richards	8	20	15	2	-
R Nel c Lwana b Ranger	23	43	36	4	-	c Ranger b Fojela	0	6	6	-	-
E Potgieter c Von Hoesslin b Richards	4	17	13	1	-	c Von Hoesslin b Fojela	12	17	19	2	-
*GE Howell c Von Hoesslin b Richards	6	29	18	1	-	c Von Hoesslin b Lwana	5	22	15	1	-
WE Bell c Mbane b Fojela	27	51	46	4	-	lbw b Lwana	0	5	1	-	-
†M Slwana c Von Hoesslin b Richards	0	1	1	-	-	c De Kock b Mbane	5	21	15	-	-
DD Carolus not out	16	34	26	3	-	b Fojela	15	42	32	2	1
U Sandi						not out	0	5	3	-	-
Extras (b 3, lb 7, w 2, nb 9)	21					Extras (b 2, w 2, nb 6)	10				
TOTAL (for 9 wkts dec) (50.4 overs)	**176**					**TOTAL (35.3 overs)**	**113**				

BORDER	Runs	Mins	Balls	4	6
BL Bennett c Slwana b Bell	68	185	143	10	-
†GE von Hoesslin c Baxter b Howell	60	108	92	12	-
MBA Smith c Nel b Sandi	14	18	19	2	-
AZM Dyili c Nel b Carolus	5	23	13	1	-
DC Lentz c Potgieter b Bell	19	48	44	3	-
L Mbane c and b Howell	48	108	88	6	-
*MN Ranger not out	57	121	102	7	1
S de Kock run out (Jeggels/Slwana)	5	12	9	1	-
LL Lwana lbw b Bell	4	1	2	1	-
P Fojela not out	1	4	2	-	-
RR Richards					
Extras (lb 10, w 2, nb 4)	16				
TOTAL (for 8 wkts dec) (85 overs)	**297**				

Bdr	O	M	R	W			O	M	R	W	
Fojela	6.4	1	38	2	(6 nb)	(2)	12.3	0	34	4	(6 nb)
Richards	15	7	30	5	(2 w)	(1)	7	0	28	2	(1 w)
Mbane	7	0	29	0			6	3	13	1	(1 w)
Lwana	7	2	37	1	(2 nb)		5	1	25	2	
Ranger	13	5	31	1	(1 nb)						
De Kock	2	1	1	0		(5)	5	2	11	1	
EP	O	M	R	W			O	M	R	W	
Carolus	32	9	99	1	(2 nb, 1 w)						
Bell	14	1	57	3	(2 nb, 1 w)						
Howell	25	4	90	2							
Sandi	10	3	27	1							
Price	4	0	14	0							

Fall of Wickets	EP	Bdr	EP
1st	13 (2)	101 (2)	3 (2)
2nd	21 (3)	120 (3)	5 (1)
3rd	88 (4)	133 (4)	27 (4)
4th	116 (5)	174 (1)	29 (5)
5th	116 (1)	175 (5)	44 (6)
6th	125 (6)	269 (6)	53 (7)
7th	130 (7)	281 (8)	53 (8)
8th	130 (9)	285 (9)	72 (9)
9th	176 (8)	-	112 (3)
10th	-	-	113 (10)

KWAZULU-NATAL v WESTERN PROVINCE SAA 3-day Challenge Pool B

Played at Chatsworth Stadium, Chatsworth on 13,14,15 October 2005 Toss: Western Province

Umpires: S George & BM White

Debuts: KZN: R Frylinck and DR Miller (Both FC). WP: MR Masinda, LF Simpson, MD Walters and M Williamson (All FC)

Close of play: Day 1: WP (1) 77-5 (Munnik 42*, Kleinveldt 4*, 19.4 overs). Day 2: KZN (2) 119-7 (Frylinck 26*, Abrahim 2*, 28.2 overs).

Result: Western Province won by 10 wickets

Points: KZN: 6.28 (bat 2.28, bowl 4, match 0); WP: 17.88 (bat 3.88, bowl 4, match 10)

KWAZULU-NATAL	Runs	Mins	Balls	4	6		Runs	Mins	Balls	4	6
MD Sanders lbw b De Stadler	31	61	53	7	-	lbw b De Stadler	29	106	77	3	-
K Smit c Wyngaard b Kleinveldt	34	133	79	7	-	lbw b Friend	2	3	3	-	-
W Hauptfleisch b Simpson	4	22	23	-	-	lbw b Friend	0	1	1	-	-
*R Gobind lbw b Simpson	3	21	19	-	-	c Canning b Friend	4	7	7	1	-
FB Lazarus c Munnik b De Stadler	1	4	6	-	-	b Friend	0	7	6	-	-
KC Africa run out (Friend)	15	52	35	2	-	run out (Simpson)	17	32	26	2	-
R Frylinck c Canning b Friend	8	14	15	2	-	(8) b Friend	31	46	29	4	1
†DR Miller b Simpson	20	38	23	3	-	(7) b De Stadler	28	41	26	6	-
ZA Abrahim not out	20	59	46	3	-	lbw b Friend	10	29	26	1	-
TD Pillay c Walters b Munnik	8	37	23	1	-	not out	10	24	10	1	-
S Mhlongo lbw b Munnik	0	1	1	-	-	lbw b Friend	2	17	20	-	-
Extras (b 1, lb 7, w 1, nb 11)	20					Extras (b 4, lb 10, nb 3)	17				
TOTAL (52 overs)	**164**					**TOTAL (38.3 overs)**	**150**				

WESTERN PROVINCE	Runs	Mins	Balls	4	6		Runs	Mins	Balls	4	6
M Williamson lbw b Frylinck	9	20	21	2	-	not out	28	58	48	5	1
AJA Gray c Miller b Abrahim	18	52	35	3	-	not out	41	58	42	5	-
MD Walters b Frylinck	0	1	2	-	-						
W Wyngaard lbw b Abrahim	1	2	3	-	-						
R Munnik c Smit b Frylinck	75	113	75	15	-						
*†RCC Canning c Miller b Frylinck	0	4	3	-	-						
RK Kleinveldt not out	115	188	154	16	3						
M de Stadler c Gobind b Frylinck	0	9	4	-	-						
Q Friend b Abrahim	16	31	15	3	-						
LF Simpson b Frylinck	0	7	6	-	-						
MR Masinda c sub (M Bekker) b Pillay	1	47	21	-	-						
Extras (b 1, lb 4, nb 4)	9					Extras (nb 2)	2				
TOTAL (55.5 overs)	**244**					**TOTAL (for 0 wkts) (14.4 overs)**	**71**				

WP	O	M	R	W		O	M	R	W
Kleinveldt	15	3	42	1 (5 nb)	(2)	7	0	28	0 (2 nb)
Friend	10	2	48	1 (3 nb, 1 w)	(1)	12.3	5	31	7 (1 nb)
Simpson	11	2	22	3 (3 nb)	(4)	6	0	42	0
De Stadler	10	2	30	2	(3)	12	4	27	2
Munnik	6	1	14	2					
Masinda					(5)	1	0	8	0
KZN	O	M	R	W		O	M	R	W
Abrahim	22	4	93	3 (3 nb)		5	2	10	0
Frylinck	20	4	94	6		3	0	24	0
Africa	6	2	28	0		4	0	19	0 (2 nb)
Mhlongo	5	0	19	0					
Pillay	2.5	0	5	1 (1 nb)	(4)	2.4	0	18	0

Fall of Wickets	KZN	WP	KZN	WP
1st	44 (1)	12 (1)	3 (2)	-
2nd	51 (3)	12 (3)	3 (3)	-
3rd	71 (4)	13 (4)	14 (4)	-
4th	72 (5)	47 (2)	18 (5)	-
5th	85 (2)	48 (6)	53 (6)	-
6th	102 (7)	130 (5)	92 (7)	-
7th	117 (6)	136 (8)	95 (1)	-
8th	143 (8)	177 (9)	133 (9)	-
9th	164 (10)	184 (10)	138 (8)	-
10th	164 (11)	244 (11)	150 (11)	-

WESTERN PROVINCE v EASTERN PROVINCE

SAA 3-day Challenge Pool B

Played at Sahara Park Newlands, Cape Town on 20,21 October 2005

Toss: Western Province

Umpires: EC Hendrikse & DJ Smith

Debuts: WP: SG George and M Mahlombe (Both FC). EP: SG Fensham (FC)

Close of play: Day 1: EP (2) 115-5 (Jeggels 39*, Potgieter 16*, 29 overs).

Result: Western Province won by 6 wickets

Points: WP: 15.42 (bat 1.42, bowl 4, match 10); EP: 4 (bat 0.00, bowl 4, match 0)

EASTERN PROVINCE	Runs	Mins	Balls	4	6		Runs	Mins	Balls	4	6
C Baxter c Canning b Kleinveldt	13	22	14	2	-	(2) c Canning b Kleinveldt	17	32	26	3	-
ML Price lbw b Mahlombe	18	94	77	1	-	(1) c Canning b Friend	1	10	7	-	-
WE Bell c Gray b De Stadler	0	25	14	-	-	c Canning b De Stadler	22	32	21	4	-
RR Jeggels lbw b Kleinveldt	0	6	9	-	-	lbw b De Stadler	41	97	84	6	-
*GE Howell lbw b De Stadler	6	61	60	-	-	lbw b Kleinveldt	6	16	17	1	-
SG Fensham c Williamson b Mahlombe	1	18	14	-	-	lbw b De Stadler	10	18	15	2	-
E Potgieter not out	6	36	28	1	-	lbw b Kleinveldt	30	57	45	4	1
L Meyer lbw b De Stadler	0	1	1	-	-	c Williamson b Kleinveldt	33	41	35	5	2
†M Slwana c Kleinveldt b Mahlombe	1	5	7	-	-	c Gray b Kleinveldt	0	19	16	-	-
DD Carolus b De Stadler	7	14	10	1	-	c and b Kleinveldt	2	22	14	-	-
S Mjekula						not out	0	6	5	-	-
Extras (lb 2, nb 5)	7					Extras (lb 4, nb 2)	6				
TOTAL (for 9 wkts dec) (38.1 overs)	**59**					**TOTAL (47.1 overs)**	**168**				

WESTERN PROVINCE	Runs	Mins	Balls	4	6		Runs	Mins	Balls	4	6
M Williamson c Bell b Meyer	2	11	11	-	-	c Howell b Meyer	35	75	57	5	-
AJA Gray c Price b Meyer	7	43	28	1	-	c Potgieter b Howell	6	60	49	-	-
A Magiet c Howell b Meyer	0	18	12	-	-						
W Wyngaard c Slwana b Carolus	0	8	9	-	-	not out	37	70	53	8	-
R Munnik not out	59	118	66	9	2	c Carolus b Mjekula	14	27	21	2	1
*†RCC Canning c Slwana b Carolus	1	4	3	-	-	not out	3	29	18	-	-
SG George c Howell b Meyer	6	20	17	1	-	(3) c Fensham b Howell	1	27	13	-	-
RK Kleinveldt c Slwana b Mjekula	5	18	15	-	-						
M de Stadler c Slwana b Meyer	8	39	30	1	-						
Q Friend c Jeggels b Mjekula	14	17	8	3	-						
M Mahlombe run out (Slwana)	2	11	2	-	-						
Extras (lb 4, w 2, nb 11)	17					Extras (b 4, lb 6, nb 1)	11				
TOTAL (31.5 overs)	**121**					**TOTAL (for 4 wkts) (35 overs)**	**107**				

WP	O	M	R	W	O	M	R	W
Friend	6	2	14	0	4	0	25	1
Kleinveldt	8	3	15	2 (2 nb)	18.1	4	57	6 (2 nb)
De Stadler	13.1	5	17	4	19	7	48	3
Mahlombe	11	6	11	3 (3 nb)	2	0	14	0
Munnik					3	0	15	0
George					1	0	5	0
EP	O	M	R	W	O	M	R	W
Carolus	11	3	25	2	6	4	8	0
Meyer	13	0	38	5 (7 nb)	11	2	30	1 (1 nb)
Mjekula	7.5	0	54	2 (3 nb, 2 w)	8	1	32	1
Howell					10	3	27	2

Fall of Wickets	EP	WP	EP	WP
1st	19 (1)	9 (1)	12 (1)	31 (2)
2nd	27 (3)	16 (3)	40 (2)	49 (1)
3rd	30 (4)	19 (4)	46 (3)	53 (3)
4th	39 (2)	19 (2)	59 (5)	82 (5)
5th	43 (6)	20 (6)	80 (6)	-
6th	45 (5)	28 (7)	132 (4)	-
7th	45 (8)	39 (8)	132 (7)	-
8th	46 (9)	76 (9)	136 (9)	-
9th	59 (10)	112 (10)	166 (8)	-
10th	-	121 (11)	168 (10)	-

BORDER v BOLAND

SAA 3-day Challenge Pool B

Played at Mercedes-Benz Park, East London on 20,21,22 October 2005 Toss: Boland
Umpires: BN Harrison & SW Liebisch
Debuts: Bdr: DL Brown (FC). Bol: None
Close of play: Day 1: Bol (1) 149-4 (Swan 6*, Albertyn 1*, 42 overs). Day 2: Bdr (1) 248-8 (Von Hoesslin 101*, Brown 77*, 85 overs).
Result: Match drawn
Points: Bdr: 7.96 (bat 3.96, bowl 4, match 0); Bol: 6.6 (bat 2.60, bowl 4, match 0)
Notes:Dyili kept wicket in Boland's 2nd innings.

BOLAND		*Runs*	*Mins*	*Balls*	*4*	*6*		*Runs*	*Mins*	*Balls*	*4*	*6*
WJ Louw	c Von Hoesslin b Ranger	43	94	64	8	-	c Smith b De Kock	47	85	69	10	-
C Prinsloo	c Von Hoesslin b Mbane	41	56	43	7	-	c Bennett b Brown	2	36	27	-	-
RG Arendse	b Ranger	34	107	73	5	-	c Smith b Mbane	34	99	67	6	-
H Davids	b Ranger	20	60	51	4	-	(5) c Ranger b Mbane	7	9	13	-	1
WC Swan	lbw b Ranger	14	82	58	2	-	(4) c Ranger b Bennett	93	199	180	12	-
*WA Albertyn	lbw b Lwana	5	25	23	1	-	c Matika b Bennett	34	109	95	2	-
†L-R Walters	lbw b Mbane	8	28	25	1	-	c Matika b Bennett	4	24	26	-	-
JM van Wyk	c Bennett b Ranger	6	50	34	1	-	(9) not out	33	119	100	4	-
WE September	b Ranger	0	8	6	-	-	(8) c Dyili b De Kock	41	101	78	6	1
PSE Sandri	not out	1	21	20	-	-	b Von Hoesslin	2	8	10	-	-
HH Paulse							not out	5	13	17	1	-
Extras	(b 4, nb 4)	8					(b 4, lb 14, w 1, nb 1)	20				
TOTAL	**(for 9 wkts dec) (65.3 overs)**	**180**					**(for 9 wkts) (113.3 overs)**	**322**				

BORDER		*Runs*	*Mins*	*Balls*	*4*	*6*
BL Bennett	lbw b Van Wyk	9	38	24	1	-
S de Kock	lbw b Sandri	0	5	4	-	-
MBA Smith	c Davids b Van Wyk	1	7	8	-	-
AZM Dyili	c September b Paulse	13	51	36	2	-
MM Matika	c Albertyn b Paulse	6	34	25	1	-
DC Lentz	c Louw b Paulse	4	49	39	1	-
†GE von Hoesslin	not out	101	263	179	9	-
*MN Ranger	b September	17	69	52	3	-
L Mbane	c Walters b Sandri	9	5	7	1	-
DL Brown	not out	77	145	138	11	-
LL Lwana						
Extras	(b 6, lb 2, w 1, nb 2)	11				
TOTAL	**(for 8 wkts dec) (85 overs)**	**248**				

Bdr	*O*	*M*	*R*	*W*		*O*	*M*	*R*	*W*	
Lwana	11	3	36	1	(2 nb)	1	0	12	0	
Mbane	17	5	60	2		13	3	36	2	
Brown	15	6	40	0	(2 nb)	11	2	36	1	(1 nb)
Ranger	17.3	5	30	6		(5) 16	6	34	0	
De Kock	5	1	10	0		(4) 19	5	56	2	
Bennett						27	7	74	3	
Smith						12	4	25	0	
Matika						13	3	22	0	(1 w)
Von Hoesslin						1.3	0	9	1	

Bol	*O*	*M*	*R*	*W*		*O*	*M*	*R*	*W*
Van Wyk	17	2	45	2	(1 w)				
Sandri	17	5	47	2					
Albertyn	15	7	30	0					
September	10	1	44	1					
Paulse	16	6	40	3	(2 nb)				
Swan	6	1	18	0					
Davids	4	0	16	0					

Fall of Wickets

	Bol	Bdr	Bol
1st	61 (2)	2 (2)	27 (2)
2nd	95 (1)	7 (3)	72 (1)
3rd	139 (4)	14 (1)	112 (3)
4th	142 (3)	26 (4)	120 (5)
5th	157 (6)	30 (5)	212 (6)
6th	168 (7)	44 (6)	230 (7)
7th	169 (5)	98 (8)	231 (4)
8th	169 (9)	107 (9)	309 (8)
9th	180 (8)	-	311 (10)
10th	-	-	-

KWAZULU-NATAL v ZIMBABWE UNDER-23

SAA 3-day Challenge Pool B

Played at Chatsworth Stadium, Chatsworth on 20,21,22 October 2005 Toss: Zimbabwe Under-23
Umpires: ZTA Ndamane & LJ Willemse
Debuts: KZN: M Bekker, T Essack and TN Harvey (All FC). ZU23: None
Close of play: Day 1: KZN (1) 286-7 (Frylinck 89*, Abrahim 0*, 57.5 overs). Day 2: KZN (2) 143-5 (Bekker 45*, Africa 19*, 37 overs).
Result: KwaZulu-Natal won by 122 runs
Points: KZN: 19.02 (bat 5.02, bowl 4, match 10); ZU23: 5.94 (bat 1.94, bowl 4, match 0)
Notes: Frylinck scored his fifty off 40 balls and his century off 94 balls in KwaZulu-Natal's 1st innings.

KWAZULU-NATAL	*Runs*	*Mins*	*Balls*	*4*	*6*		*Runs*	*Mins*	*Balls*	*4*	*6*
W Hauptfleisch c Vermeulen b Mwayenga	5	33	25	1	-	c Rainsford b Matsikenyeri	50	110	75	8	-
TN Harvey c Maregwede b Mwayenga	4	44	31	-	-	lbw b Rainsford	5	12	9	1	-
T Essack c Maregwede b Mwayenga	35	117	63	4	-	c Maregwede b Mwayenga	11	14	7	2	-
FB Lazarus c Maregwede b Mwayenga	0	6	3	-	-	c Strydom b Mpofu	2	21	11	-	-
†DR Miller c Mwayenga b Strydom	9	26	16	1	-	c Maregwede b Mpofu	6	14	9	1	-
M Bekker c Vermeulen b Strydom	115	172	133	13	4	not out	79	139	98	7	-
KC Africa c Maregwede b Rainsford	5	15	11	-	-	lbw b Mpofu	25	64	61	3	-
R Frylinck not out	100	113	94	14	2	b Ewing	5	11	9	-	-
*ZA Abrahim c Maregwede b Rainsford	4	20	12	-	-	lbw b Ewing	2	12	12	-	-
TD Pillay lbw b Mwayenga	0	6	6	-	-	not out	7	5	8	1	-
S Mhlongo not out	0	1	2	-	-						
Extras (b 5, lb 7, w 1, nb 11)	24					Extras (b 5, lb 2, nb 3)	10				
TOTAL (for 9 wkts dec) (64.1 overs)	**301**					**TOTAL (for 8 wkts dec) (49 overs)**	**202**				

ZIMBABWE UNDER-23	*Runs*	*Mins*	*Balls*	*4*	*6*		*Runs*	*Mins*	*Balls*	*4*	*6*
TMK Mawoyo c sub (WP Lombard) b Frylinck	0	2	4	-	-	c Africa b Pillay	35	90	67	6	-
B Mlambo c Miller b Mhlongo	37	104	66	5	1	b Abrahim	6	27	14	1	-
MA Vermeulen c Frylinck b Mhlongo	17	56	35	3	-	b Pillay	47	91	63	9	-
C de Grandhomme c Miller b Africa	45	170	128	6	-	c Lazarus b Mhlongo	50	108	89	7	-
*†A Maregwede lbw b Pillay	7	24	28	1	-	c Harvey b Pillay	4	8	5	1	-
S Matsikenyeri c Pillay b Africa	28	108	98	2	-	c and b Pillay	4	25	27	1	-
GM Strydom c Bekker b Pillay	0	16	12	-	-	b Abrahim	12	47	35	3	-
GM Ewing c Miller b Africa	0	2	1	-	-	b Abrahim	34	113	81	6	-
EC Rainsford b Africa	0	9	4	-	-	(10) lbw b Frylinck	0	4	4	-	-
CB Mpofu not out	0	9	1	-	-	(9) c and b Pillay	0	25	21	-	-
A Mwayenga c Africa b Pillay	5	5	5	-	-	not out	4	55	44	-	-
Extras (b 4, lb 1, nb 3)	8					Extras (b 14, lb 10, w 3, nb 11)	38				
TOTAL (63.1 overs)	**147**					**TOTAL (73.1 overs)**	**234**				

ZU23	*O*	*M*	*R*	*W*		*O*	*M*	*R*	*W*
Rainsford	11.1	6	24	2 (1 nb)		7	1	33	1 (1 nb)
Mpofu	12	1	68	0 (10 nb)	(3)	7	1	23	3 (1 nb)
Mwayenga	13	4	41	5 (1 w)	(2)	7	0	32	1
Strydom	9	1	50	2	(5)	8	0	36	0
Matsikenyeri	8	0	55	0	(6)	7	0	18	1 (1 nb)
Ewing	6	1	29	0	(7)	9	1	39	2
De Grandhomme	5	1	22	0	(4)	4	1	14	0
KZN	*O*	*M*	*R*	*W*		*O*	*M*	*R*	*W*
Frylinck	11	4	27	1		12	1	48	1 (5 nb, 1 w)
Abrahim	11	5	24	0		9.1	4	17	3 (1 w)
Mhlongo	10	1	27	2 (1 nb)		8	1	35	1 (6 nb)
Africa	11	2	31	4		12	3	36	0 (1 w)
Pillay	20.1	6	33	3 (2 nb)		23	9	45	5
Hauptfleisch						4	2	17	0
Essack						5	3	12	0

Fall of Wickets

	KZN	ZU23	KZN	ZU23
1st	8 (1)	0 (1)	9 (2)	27 (2)
2nd	15 (2)	30 (3)	24 (3)	77 (1)
3rd	16 (4)	60 (2)	47 (4)	109 (3)
4th	32 (5)	69 (5)	65 (5)	117 (5)
5th	132 (3)	140 (4)	96 (1)	145 (6)
6th	143 (7)	142 (6)	169 (7)	180 (4)
7th	286 (6)	142 (8)	181 (8)	180 (7)
8th	297 (9)	142 (7)	193 (9)	196 (9)
9th	300 (10)	142 (9)	-	197 (10)
10th	-	147 (11)	-	234 (8)

EASTERN PROVINCE v ZIMBABWE UNDER-23 — SAA 3-day Challenge Pool B

Played at Pollock Field, Grey High School, Port Elizabeth on 27,28,29 October 2005 — Toss: Eastern Province

Umpires: IH van Kerwel & LJ Willemse

Debuts: EP: None. ZU23: None

Close of play: Day 1: EP (1) 115-1 (Baxter 54*, Price 41*, 39 overs). Day 2: ZU23 (2) 147-4 (De Grandhomme 48*, Matsikenyeri 39*, 59.3 overs).

Result: Eastern Province won by 5 wickets

Points: EP: 17.44 (bat 3.44, bowl 4, match 10); ZU23: 6.24 (bat 2.24, bowl 4, match 0)

ZIMBABWE UNDER-23	*Runs*	*Mins*	*Balls*	*4*	*6*		*Runs*	*Mins*	*Balls*	*4*	*6*
B Mlambo c and b Willemse	86	241	168	11	-	c Slwana b Meyer	18	43	26	3	-
TMK Mawoyo c Baxter b Meyer	3	37	23	-	-	c Slwana b Mjekula	1	28	10	-	-
MA Vermeulen c Jeggels b Mjekula	6	18	11	1	-	b Howell	30	72	61	5	-
C de Grandhomme c Slwana b Mjekula	3	9	10	-	-	run out (Price/Slwana)	109	308	260	17	1
*†A Maregwede c Slwana b Mjekula	0	22	9	-	-	c Slwana b Carolus	2	12	11	-	-
S Matsikenyeri c Mjekula b Howell	8	20	18	-	-	c Willemse b Mjekula	43	135	112	8	-
GM Strydom c Abrahams b Howell	0	9	7	-	-	c Fensham b Mjekula	0	2	3	-	-
GM Ewing c Willemse b Meyer	8	39	32	1	-	b Meyer	40	92	75	6	-
CB Mpofu c Meyer b Willemse	10	74	67	1	-	c Carolus b Mjekula	0	6	5	-	-
A Mwayenga not out	14	29	30	1	1	not out	12	64	48	2	-
EC Rainsford not out	7	19	15	1	-	lbw b Mjekula	10	28	20	2	-
Extras (b 4, lb 5, w 3, nb 5)	17					Extras (lb 3, w 1, nb 6)	10				
TOTAL (for 9 wkts dec) (64 overs)	**162**					**TOTAL (104.1 overs)**	**275**				

EASTERN PROVINCE	Runs	Mins	Balls	4	6		Runs	Mins	Balls	4	6
C Baxter b Mpofu	67	222	174	6	-	b Mpofu	43		87	4	-
D Willemse b Mwayenga	5	58	36	1	-	c Maregwede b De Grandhomme	42	109	80	6	1
ML Price b Strydom	59	159	112	7	1	c De Grandhomme b Mpofu	6	16	22	1	-
U Abrahams c Mawoyo b Strydom	0	30	21	-	-	c Strydom b Mpofu	5	14	13	-	-
RR Jeggels b Rainsford	18	39	27	4	-	c Mlambo b Strydom	61	77	64	1	4
SG Fensham lbw b Ewing	11	81	50	-	-	not out	41		58	1	-
*GE Howell c Matsikenyeri b Rainsford	4	5	3	1	-	not out	6		8	-	-
L Meyer c De Grandhomme b Strydom	1	6	4	-	-						
†M Slwana c sub (IM Chinyoka) b Ewing	34	36	61	3	-						
DD Carolus b Ewing	6	12	19	-	-						
S Mjekula not out	1	1	1	-	-						
Extras (b 5, lb 11)	16					Extras (b 1, lb 5, w 5, nb 1)	12				
TOTAL (84.4 overs)	**222**					**TOTAL (for 5 wkts) (54.1 overs)**	**216**				

EP	O	M	R	W		O	M	R	W
Carolus	14	3	41	0	(4)	8	1	25	1 (1 nb)
Meyer	12	7	17	2 (5 nb, 2 w)	(1)	27	8	85	2 (4 nb)
Mjekula	11	2	32	3 (1 w)	(2)	30.1	12	46	5 (1 nb, 1 w)
Howell	16	5	41	2	(3)	22	3	85	1
Willemse	11	5	22	2		17	6	31	0
ZU23	O	M	R	W		O	M	R	W
Rainsford	16	6	27	2		10	0	31	0
Mpofu	16	2	50	1	(6)	13	1	56	3 (1 nb, 2 w)
Strydom	20	9	29	3	(2)	12.1	0	45	1 (1 w)
Mwayenga	15	1	51	1	(3)	4	0	28	0 (2 w)
Ewing	6.4	1	27	3		7	1	17	0
De Grandhomme	8	1	16	0	(4)	8	1	33	1
Matsikenyeri	3	0	6	0					

Fall of Wickets

	ZU23	EP	ZU23	EP
1st	25 (2)	14 (2)	4 (2)	80 (2)
2nd	47 (3)	146 (3)	28 (1)	94 (3)
3rd	51 (4)	146 (1)	65 (3)	104 (4)
4th	59 (5)	156 (4)	68 (5)	105 (1)
5th	70 (6)	167 (5)	156 (6)	191 (5)
6th	72 (7)	171 (7)	156 (7)	-
7th	88 (8)	172 (8)	233 (8)	-
8th	133 (9)	211 (6)	234 (9)	-
9th	142 (1)	221 (10)	260 (4)	-
10th	-	222 (9)	275 (11)	-

KWAZULU-NATAL v BOLAND

SAA 3-day Challenge Pool B

Played at Chatsworth Stadium, Chatsworth on 27,28,29 October 2005 Toss: Boland

Umpires: SW Liebisch & JEP Ostrom

Debuts: KZN: ND Hewer and R Reddy (Both FC). Bol: None

Close of play: Day 1: KZN (1) 250-6 (Bekker 93*, Abrahim 53*, 52 overs). Day 2: Bol (2) 174-3 (Louw 44*, Swan 1*, 60 overs).

Result: Match drawn

Points: KZN: 10.84 (bat 6.84, bowl 4, match 0); Bol: 5.38 (bat 1.38, bowl 4, match 0)

Notes:Bekker kept wicket when Miller bowled in Boland's 2nd innings

BOLAND	Runs	Mins	Balls	4	6		Runs	Mins	Balls	4	6
C Prinsloo b Africa	11	54	48	2	-	c Miller b Mhlongo	26	99	73	4	-
R Bailey c Reddy b Abrahim	13	42	29	3	-	b Essack	60	114	89	10	1
RG Arendse lbw b Hewer	1	17	9	-	-	lbw b Hewer	35	108	93	4	-
WJ Louw c Bekker b Reddy	21	118	80	3	-	c Miller b Hewer	85	242	186	13	1
WC Swan c Miller b Abrahim	12	60	44	1	-	b Abrahim	20	69	58	3	-
*WA Albertyn run out (Africa/Miller)	0	18	12	-	-	c Africa b Hewer	5	12	8	1	-
†L-R Walters b Hewer	1	4	5	-	-	b Abrahim	20	76	57	2	-
JM van Wyk c Gobind b Reddy	28	37	31	3	1	lbw b Abrahim	4	33	22	1	-
WE September not out	21	19	16	3	1	not out	48	71	57	8	1
PSE Sandri lbw b Abrahim	0	10	3	-	-	not out	17	48	25	2	-
HH Paulse											
Extras (lb 3, w 8)	11					Extras (b 7, lb 5, w 2, nb 2)	16				
TOTAL (for 9 wkts dec) (46.1 overs)	**119**					**TOTAL (for 8 wkts) (111 overs)**	**336**				

KWAZULU-NATAL	Runs	Mins	Balls	4	6
MD Sanders b Van Wyk	16	30	25	3	-
*R Gobind lbw b Sandri	0	5	2	-	-
T Essack c Bailey b Sandri	6	20	10	1	-
WR Wingfield c Arendse b Albertyn	48	73	59	10	-
†DR Miller c Arendse b Albertyn	26	39	23	3	1
M Bekker c Walters b Paulse	138	202	159	24	-
KC Africa c Albertyn b Paulse	0	3	2	-	-
ZA Abrahim not out	103	248	173	10	4
R Reddy c Louw b Sandri	10	50	43	1	-
ND Hewer not out	23	28	21	3	-
S Mhlongo					
Extras (b 6, lb 10, w 1, nb 5)	22				
TOTAL (for 8 wkts dec) (85 overs)	**392**				

KZN	O	M	R	W	O	M	R	W
Abrahim	10.1	4	21	3 (1 w)	24	8	65	3 (1 w)
Hewer	16	3	55	2 (7 w)	20	3	80	3 (1 nb)
Africa	8	3	17	1	(4) 10	2	37	0 (1 nb)
Mhlongo	7	3	12	0	(6) 12	5	23	1 (1 w)
Reddy	5	2	11	2	(3) 19	6	43	0
Essack					(5) 12	3	32	1
Gobind					3	2	1	0
Wingfield					9	2	30	0
Miller					2	0	13	0
Bol	O	M	R	W	O	M	R	W
Van Wyk	12	0	84	1 (4 nb)				
Sandri	20	1	88	3				
Paulse	19	2	98	2 (1 nb)				
Albertyn	13	2	47	2				
Swan	8	0	30	0 (1 w)				
September	13	6	29	0				

Fall of Wickets

	Bol	KZN	Bol
1st	33 (2)	8 (2)	82 (1)
2nd	35 (1)	27 (3)	90 (2)
3rd	35 (3)	27 (1)	167 (3)
4th	62 (5)	76 (5)	206 (5)
5th	62 (6)	111 (4)	212 (6)
6th	63 (7)	112 (7)	264 (4)
7th	93 (4)	318 (6)	266 (7)
8th	102 (8)	342 (9)	283 (8)
9th	119 (10)	-	-
10th	-	-	-

BOLAND v WESTERN PROVINCE

SAA 3-day Challenge Pool B

Played at Boland Park, Paarl on 3,4,5 November 2005

Toss: Boland

Umpires: DJ Smith & BM White

Debuts: Bol: None. WP: FD Telo (FC)

Close of play: Day 1: Bol (1) 78-4 (Swan 12*, September 0*, 26 overs). Day 2: WP (2) 153-3 (Gray 69*, Canning 3*, 49 overs).

Result: Match drawn

Points: Bol: 7.3 (bat 3.30, bowl 4, match 0); WP: 8.56 (bat 4.56, bowl 4, match 0)

WESTERN PROVINCE	Runs	Mins	Balls	4	6		Runs	Mins	Balls	4	6
M Williamson c Walters b Paulse	27	46	32	3	-	lbw b Paulse	1	5	4	-	-
AJA Gray b Paulse	14	33	18	2	-	not out	112	350	263	11	-
W Wyngaard c Walters b Albertyn	8	26	21	1	-	run out (Summers)	31	104	56	4	-
R Munnik b Summers	15	38	15	3	-	(6) c sub (BL Fransman) b September	13	56	45	1	-
FD Telo c Paulse b September	61	113	77	12	-	(4) run out (Fourie)	44	86	55	5	-
*†RCC Canning b September	57	100	89	8	-	(5) b September	33	81	64	4	-
RK Kleinveldt lbw b Albertyn	1	6	3	-	-	not out	15	32	25	2	-
PR Adams c Walters b Paulse	47	94	57	6	1						
M Mahlombe b Paulse	20	61	53	4	-						
M de Stadler not out	13	36	27	1	-						
LF Simpson lbw b Paulse	2	7	5	-	-						
Extras (b 4, lb 2, w 2, nb 5)	13					Extras (b 1, lb 9, w 2, nb 2)	14				
TOTAL (65.2 overs)	**278**					**TOTAL (for 5 wkts dec) (85 overs)**	**263**				

BOLAND	Runs	Mins	Balls	4	6		Runs	Mins	Balls	4	6
R Bailey c Wyngaard b Kleinveldt	1	20	17	-	-	lbw b De Stadler	16	30	27	3	-
JG Strydom lbw b Adams	44	99	74	7	-	c Wyngaard b De Stadler	40	83	62	6	-
RG Arendse c Canning b Kleinveldt	7	33	30	1	-	lbw b De Stadler	3	21	19	-	-
WC Swan c Williamson b De Stadler	15	74	49	-	-	run out (sub)	50	122	96	3	2
H Fourie lbw b De Stadler	1	3	7	-	-	b Kleinveldt	19	51	37	1	-
WE September c and b Kleinveldt	18	65	47	2	-	(9) not out	63	101	110	10	-
SP Summers c Williamson b Kleinveldt	21	22	23	4	-	c Williamson b Kleinveldt	0	2	3	-	-
†L-R Walters b Mahlombe	11	69	66	2	-	(6) b De Stadler	28	53	41	-	-
*WA Albertyn c Kleinveldt b De Stadler	67	167	153	5	-	(8) b Kleinveldt	1	7	7	-	-
PSE Sandri b Adams	10	30	32	1	-	not out	17	80	68	2	-
HH Paulse not out	8	83	59	2	-						
Extras (lb 5, w 6, nb 20)	31					Extras (b 6, lb 1, w 1, nb 7)	15				
TOTAL (89.3 overs)	**234**					**TOTAL (for 8 wkts) (77 overs)**	**252**				

Bol	O	M	R	W	O	M	R	W
Sandri	14	1	77	0 (3 nb, 1 w)	18	3	49	0 (1 nb, 2 w)
Paulse	15.2	1	65	5 (2 nb)	6	0	25	1 (1 nb)
Albertyn	12	2	47	2 (1 w)	(4) 18	3	44	0
Summers	13	3	39	1	(5) 2	0	14	0
September	11	4	44	2	(3) 36	7	100	2
Swan					5	1	21	0
WP	O	M	R	W	O	M	R	W
Kleinveldt	24	6	73	4 (17 nb, 1 w)	19	3	71	3 (6 nb, 1 w)
Simpson	9	1	29	0 (3 nb, 5 w)	3	0	13	0 (1 nb)
De Stadler	26.3	11	45	3	23	5	48	4
Adams	23	4	70	2	(5) 22	7	68	0
Mahlombe	7	3	12	1	(4) 4	2	9	0
Gray					6	1	36	0

Fall of Wickets

	WP	Bol	WP	Bol
1st	42 (2)	7 (1)	1 (1)	31 (1)
2nd	49 (1)	33 (3)	63 (3)	48 (3)
3rd	59 (3)	74 (2)	141 (4)	69 (2)
4th	86 (4)	75 (5)	208 (5)	127 (5)
5th	189 (5)	93 (4)	238 (6)	149 (4)
6th	191 (7)	126 (7)	-	149 (7)
7th	191 (6)	130 (6)	-	156 (8)
8th	244 (9)	160 (8)	-	185 (6)
9th	270 (8)	187 (10)	-	-
10th	278 (11)	234 (9)	-	-

BORDER v ZIMBABWE UNDER-23 SAA 3-day Challenge Pool B

Played at Mercedes-Benz Park, East London on 3,4,5 November 2005 Toss: Border
Umpires: CJ Conradie & BN Harrison
Debuts: Bdr: KD Bennett and Y Pangabantu (Both FC). ZU23: None
Close of play: Day 1: ZU23 (1) 125 all out. Day 2: Bdr (1) 25-0 (BL Bennett 8*, Von Hoesslin 12*, 7.3 overs).
Result: Match drawn
Points: Bdr: 7.48 (bat 3.48, bowl 4, match 0); ZU23: 2.5 (bat 1.50, bowl 1, match 0)

ZIMBABWE UNDER-23	Runs	Mins	Balls	4	6		Runs	Mins	Balls	4	6
B Mlambo b Lwana	4	4	6	1	-	c Von Hoesslin b Pangabantu	5	16	15	-	-
TMK Mawoyo c Von Hoesslin b Mbane	15	45	32	3	-	c Mbane b Lwana	2	11	9	-	-
MA Vermeulen b Pangabantu	19	49	35	3	-	c Gamiet b Lwana	0	15	9	-	-
C de Grandhomme b Mbane	1	11	10	-	-	c Mbane b Lwana	7	20	13	1	-
*†A Maregwede c Dyili b Lwana	6	70	42	-	-						
S Matsikenyeri b Pangabantu	0	9	8	-	-	(5) not out	0	15	4	-	-
GM Strydom lbw b Mbane	30	77	66	5	-						
GM Ewing b Pangabantu	18	56	46	4	-	(6) not out	1	5	4	-	-
CB Mpofu b Mbane	1	15	16	-	-						
A Mwayenga not out	14	38	24	2	-						
TN Garwe b Mbane	8	20	15	1	-						
Extras (lb 9)	9					Extras (b 6)	6				
TOTAL (50 overs)	**125**					**TOTAL (for 4 wkts) (9 overs)**	**21**				

BORDER	Runs	Mins	Balls	4	6
BL Bennett lbw b Strydom	40	125	92	6	-
†GE von Hoesslin c Ewing b Mpofu	13	64	41	1	-
*SC Pope c Maregwede b De Grandhomme	64	132	97	10	1
LL Gamiet not out	49	138	105	7	-
AZM Dyili not out	37	68	49	5	-
KD Bennett					
S de Kock					
DL Brown					
L Mbane					
Y Pangabantu					
LL Lwana					
Extras (b 8, lb 5, w 7, nb 1)	21				
TOTAL (for 3 wkts dec) (64 overs)	**224**				

Bdr	O	M	R	W		O	M	R	W
Lwana	11	3	35	2		5	3	6	3
Pangabantu	17	6	35	3		4	1	9	1
Mbane	16	8	26	5					
Brown	6	0	20	0					
ZU23	O	M	R	W		O	M	R	W
Mwayenga	14	3	34	0	(1 w)				
Mpofu	18	3	64	1	(1 nb)				
Garwe	7	2	42	0	(1 w)				
Strydom	11	2	38	1					
De Grandhomme	10	3	16	1					
Vermeulen	4	0	17	0	(1 w)				

Fall of Wickets

	ZU23	Bdr	ZU23
1st	8 (1)	34 (2)	5 (2)
2nd	34 (2)	82 (1)	7 (1)
3rd	42 (3)	148 (3)	11 (3)
4th	44 (4)	-	20 (4)
5th	45 (6)	-	-
6th	74 (5)	-	-
7th	82 (7)	-	-
8th	88 (9)	-	-
9th	102 (8)	-	-
10th	125 (11)	-	-

EASTERN PROVINCE v KWAZULU-NATAL SAA 3-day Challenge Pool B

Played at UPE No 1 Oval, Port Elizabeth on 3,4,5 November 2005 Toss: Eastern Province
Umpires: EC Hendrikse & LJ Willemse
Debuts: EP: J Theron (FC). KZN: None
Close of play: Day 1: KZN (1) 41-2 (Lombard 25*, Wingfield 5*, 16 overs). Day 2: No play.
Result: Match drawn
Points: EP: 2.96 (bat 1.96, bowl 1, match 0); KZN: 4 (bat 0.00, bowl 4, match 0)

EASTERN PROVINCE	Runs	Mins	Balls	4	6
C Baxter b Abrahim	0	10	10	-	-
D Willemse c Gobind b Pillay	58	187	162	5	1
ML Price lbw b Frylinck	0	13	10	-	-
U Abrahams b Abrahim	1	11	8	-	-
RR Jeggels lbw b Frylinck	4	6	8	-	-
SG Fensham c Miller b Frylinck	11	31	28	2	-
†M Slwana b Reddy	21	75	59	2	1
*GE Howell c Gobind b Reddy	7	23	25	-	-
L Meyer c Miller b Reddy	29	62	65	6	-
J Theron b Pillay	13	39	44	2	-
S Mjekula not out	0	3	4	-	-
Extras (lb 2, nb 2)	4				
TOTAL (70.1 overs)	**148**				

KWAZULU-NATAL	Runs	Mins	Balls	4	6
WP Lombard not out	25	66	55	5	-
*R Gobind c Howell b Mjekula	5	30	21	1	-
T Essack run out (Theron/Slwana)	6	14	11	1	-
WR Wingfield not out	5	20	9	1	-
†DR Miller					
M Bekker					
R Frylinck					
ZA Abrahim					
R Reddy					
TD Pillay					
S Mhlongo					
Extras	0				
TOTAL (for 2 wkts) (16 overs)	**41**				

KZN	O	M	R	W	
Abrahim	14	9	22	2	
Frylinck	15	3	29	3	(1 nb)
Mhlongo	3	0	11	0	(1 nb)
Pillay	22	4	52	2	
Reddy	16.1	4	32	3	
EP	*O*	*M*	*R*	*W*	
Meyer	8	3	26	0	
Mjekula	8	3	15	1	

Fall of Wickets

	EP	KZN
1st	0 (1)	14 (2)
2nd	3 (3)	25 (3)
3rd	5 (4)	-
4th	9 (5)	-
5th	33 (6)	-
6th	84 (7)	-
7th	99 (8)	-
8th	111 (2)	-
9th	148 (10)	-
10th	148 (9)	-

BORDER v KWAZULU-NATAL — SAA 3-day Challenge Pool B

Played at Mercedes-Benz Park, East London on 9,10,11 November 2005 Toss: KwaZulu-Natal
Umpires: S George & LJ Willemse
Debuts: Bdr: None. KZN: None
Close of play: Day 1: KZN (1) 30-2 (Gobind 15*, Pillay 7*, 17 overs). Day 2: Bdr (2) 131-2 (Bennett 77*, De Kock 6*, 40 overs).

Result: Match drawn

Points: Bdr: 8.28 (bat 4.28, bowl 4, match 0); KZN: 9.86 (bat 5.86, bowl 4, match 0)
Notes:Bekker scored his fifty off 34 balls in KwaZulu-Natal's 1st innings. Dyili kept wicket in KwaZulu-Natal's 2nd innings.

BORDER	Runs	Mins	Balls	4	6		Runs	Mins	Balls	4	6
BL Bennett c Miller b Mhlongo	12	63	49	2	-	c Gobind b Lombard	126	250	189	22	1
†GE von Hoesslin c Miller b Africa	19	67	39	2	-	c Gobind b Mhlongo	6	19	11	1	-
SC Pope st Miller b Pillay	34	116	81	6	-	c Gobind b Pillay	36	98	82	5	-
LL Gamiet c Miller b Mhlongo	22	72	56	2	-	(5) c and b Pillay	57	163	135	8	1
AZM Dyili b Frylinck	0	6	5	-	-	(6) lbw b Frylinck	30	68	68	6	-
MM Matika run out (Essack/Miller)	0	17	13	-	-	(7) not out	20	72	48	4	-
*MN Ranger not out	72	177	130	10	-						
S de Kock c Frylinck b Pillay	2	16	5	-	-	(4) c Bekker b Pillay	31	112	93	2	1
L Mbane b Frylinck	60	89	85	10	1						
LL Lwana c Miller b Mhlongo	23	43	34	2	2						
RR Richards st Miller b Lombard	5	10	13	-	-						
Extras (b 1, lb 6, w 4, nb 4)	15					Extras (b 3, lb 4, w 8, nb 6)	21				
TOTAL (84.2 overs)	**264**					**TOTAL (for 6 wkts dec) (103.2 overs)**	**327**				

KWAZULU-NATAL	Runs	Mins	Balls	4	6		Runs	Mins	Balls	4	6
WP Lombard lbw b Richards	0	3	6	-	-	(9) not out	0	2	2	-	-
*R Gobind c Matika b Pope	112	269	218	15	-	(1) c Dyili b Mbane	28	51	32	6	-
T Essack c Dyili b Lwana	5	39	25	1	-	(5) b Richards	1	4	3	-	-
TD Pillay c Richards b Mbane	32	93	62	6	-						
WR Wingfield c Von Hoesslin b Richards	70	143	110	7	1	(4) not out	42	73	46	4	-
R Frylinck c Pope b Richards	18	26	17	2	1	(7) c Von Hoesslin b Richards	2	10	4	-	-
M Bekker c Dyili b Mbane	52	52	39	5	2	(6) c Dyili b Richards	9	27	14	-	-
†DR Miller c Lwana b Mbane	29	28	26	3	-	(2) c Matika b Ranger	51	58	42	9	1
TN Harvey st Von Hoesslin b De Kock	9	10	11	-	-	(3) c Dyili b Richards	19	30	18	2	-
KC Africa not out	1	6	1	-	-	(8) c Von Hoesslin b Richards	4	2	2	1	-
S Mhlongo not out	2	1	1	-	-						
Extras (b 4, lb 3, nb 6)	13					Extras (lb 1, w 1, nb 1)	3				
TOTAL (for 9 wkts) (85 overs)	**343**					**TOTAL (for 7 wkts) (27 overs)**	**159**				

KZN	O	M	R	W		O	M	R	W
Frylinck	23	7	62	2 (1 nb, 1 w)		22	6	67	1 (2 w)
Mhlongo	19	2	71	3 (3 nb, 1 w)		11	3	55	1 (3 nb, 2 w)
Africa	12	5	33	1 (2 w)		11	2	39	0 (2 nb)
Pillay	24	6	64	2		39.2	13	109	3
Lombard	6.2	0	27	1		20	5	50	1 (1 nb)
Bdr	O	M	R	W		O	M	R	W
Richards	25	6	76	3		9	1	53	5 (1 w)
Lwana	15	2	59	1 (5 nb)		2	0	15	0 (1 nb)
De Kock	9	0	42	1					
Mbane	10	2	50	3	(3)	11	0	57	1
Ranger	11	2	46	0	(4)	5	0	33	1
Pope	14	2	57	1					
Bennett	1	0	6	0 (1 nb)					

Fall of Wickets

	Bdr	KZN	Bdr	KZN
1st	33 (1)	0 (1)	15 (2)	71 (1)
2nd	33 (2)	15 (3)	103 (3)	83 (2)
3rd	86 (4)	82 (4)	196 (4)	119 (3)
4th	86 (5)	226 (2)	212 (1)	121 (5)
5th	86 (6)	234 (5)	271 (6)	147 (6)
6th	103 (3)	263 (6)	327 (5)	155 (7)
7th	111 (8)	326 (8)	-	159 (8)
8th	211 (9)	336 (7)	-	-
9th	255 (10)	341 (9)	-	-
10th	264 (11)	-	-	-

WESTERN PROVINCE v ZIMBABWE UNDER-23 — SAA 3-day Challenge Pool B

Played at Sahara Park Newlands, Cape Town on 10,11,12 November 2005 — Toss: Zimbabwe Under-23

Umpires: EC Hendrikse & LH Matroos

Debuts: WP: None. ZU23: None

Close of play: Day 1: ZU23 (1) 68-6 (Strydom 9*, Chinyoka 1*, 39 overs). Day 2: ZU23 (2) 19-3 (Vermeulen 3*, 7.5 overs).

Result: Western Province won by 233 runs

Points: WP: 17.14 (bat 3.14, bowl 4, match 10); ZU23: 4 (bat 0.00, bowl 4, match 0)

Notes: Strydom scored his fifty off 39 balls in Zimbabwe Under-23's 2nd innings.

WESTERN PROVINCE	Runs	Mins	Balls	4	6		Runs	Mins	Balls	4	6
M Williamson c Vermeulen b Chinyoka	9	48	35	1	-	b Rainsford	9	19	14	2	-
AJA Gray c Matsikenyeri b Mwayenga	6	15	9	1	-	c sub (CB Mpofu) b Strydom	51	164	142	7	-
Z Homani c Chinyoka b Mwayenga	74	163	130	12	-	lbw b Chinyoka	10	22	13	2	-
W Wyngaard b Chinyoka	9	49	34	-	-	lbw b Vermeulen	70	173	125	8	-
FD Telo c Mlambo b Rainsford	18	49	41	3	-	c Matanga b Rainsford	50	90	54	3	1
*†RCC Canning c Maregwede b Rainsford	0	22	12	-	-	c Maregwede b Chinyoka	10	29	29	-	-
WC Hantam c Maregwede b De Grandhomme	38	84	59	4	-	not out	13	18	14	2	-
PR Adams c Vermeulen b Matanga	5	24	19	1	-						
M de Stadler not out	25	62	45	5	-						
M Mahlombe c and b De Grandhomme	0	7	2	-	-						
LF Simpson lbw b De Grandhomme	0	1	1	-	-						
Extras (b 5, lb 11, w 6, nb 1)	23					Extras (b 2, lb 10, w 2, nb 1)	15				
TOTAL (64.2 overs)	**207**					**TOTAL (for 6 wkts dec) (65 overs)**	**228**				

ZIMBABWE UNDER-23	Runs	Mins	Balls	4	6		Runs	Mins	Balls	4	6
*†A Maregwede lbw b Hantam	7	47	35	1	-	(2) lbw b Simpson	6	10	10	1	-
B Mlambo c Canning b Hantam	17	44	33	3	-	(1) c and b Hantam	2	12	12	-	-
MA Vermeulen run out (Telo)	6	17	12	1	-	c Canning b De Stadler	3	32	18	-	-
C de Grandhomme c Canning b Mahlombe	13	65	44	2	-	c Canning b Simpson	0	17	19	-	-
S Matsikenyeri lbw b Hantam	2	12	11	-	-	c Wyngaard b Mahlombe	13	61	32	1	-
TMK Mawoyo c Hantam b De Stadler	9	25	22	2	-	lbw b Hantam	0	4	3	-	-
GM Strydom c Wyngaard b Hantam	14	79	60	2	-	c Canning b De Stadler	54	53	48	7	1
IM Chinyoka b Hantam	1	54	51	-	-	not out	18	49	45	2	1
A Mwayenga lbw b Hantam	0	2	2	-	-	c Adams b Mahlombe	2	17	11	-	-
H Matanga not out	0	13	4	-	-	b Adams	8	17	15	1	-
EC Rainsford c Canning b Simpson	3	7	7	-	-	c Mahlombe b Adams	0	6	3	-	-
Extras (lb 2, w 3)	5					Extras (b 1, lb 10, w 4, nb 4)	19				
TOTAL (46.5 overs)	**77**					**TOTAL (35.2 overs)**	**125**				

ZU23	O	M	R	W			O	M	R	W	
Rainsford	10	3	16	2			10	2	30	2	
Mwayenga	15	4	53	2			12	1	32	0	
Chinyoka	15	3	42	2	(1 nb, 4 w)		10	1	46	2	(1 nb)
Strydom	7	0	28	0	(1 w)		8	1	27	1	(2 w)
De Grandhomme	10.2	1	26	3			9	3	19	0	
Matanga	7	1	26	1	(1 w)		11	2	35	0	
Matsikenyeri							1	0	10	0	
Vermeulen							4	1	17	1	
WP	O	M	R	W			O	M	R	W	
Simpson	9.5	4	16	1	(3 w)	(2)	4	1	12	2	(4 nb, 1 w)
Hantam	18	8	39	6		(1)	12	2	53	2	(2 w)
De Stadler	11	6	13	1			10	3	26	2	
Mahlombe	5	2	3	1			6	3	20	2	
Adams	3	2	4	0			3.2	1	3	2	

Fall of Wickets

	WP	ZU23	WP	ZU23
1st	14 (2)	26 (2)	14 (1)	11 (1)
2nd	25 (1)	27 (1)	34 (3)	14 (2)
3rd	70 (4)	37 (3)	127 (2)	19 (4)
4th	115 (5)	39 (5)	181 (4)	20 (3)
5th	131 (6)	56 (6)	199 (6)	21 (6)
6th	133 (3)	58 (4)	228 (5)	92 (5)
7th	154 (8)	69 (8)	-	94 (7)
8th	203 (7)	69 (9)	-	101 (9)
9th	207 (10)	74 (7)	-	121 (10)
10th	207 (11)	77 (11)	-	125 (11)

BOLAND v ZIMBABWE UNDER-23 — SAA 3-day Challenge Pool B

Played at University Oval, Coetzenburg, Stellenbosch on 17,18,19 November 2005 Toss: Zimbabwe Under-23
Umpires: DJ Smith & BM White
Debuts: Bol: PC Laing and NM Northcote (Both FC). ZU23: None
Close of play: Day 1: Bol (1) 129-2 (Strydom 74*, Swan 0*, 38 overs). Day 2: ZU23 (2) 125-5 (De Grandhomme 18*, Mwayenga 0*, 36 overs).
Result: Boland won by 10 wickets
Points: Bol: 18.2 (bat 4.20, bowl 4, match 10); ZU23: 5.42 (bat 2.42, bowl 3, match 0)

ZIMBABWE UNDER-23	Runs	Mins	Balls	4	6		Runs	Mins	Balls	4	6
*†A Maregwede lbw b Fransman	1	50	37	-	-	lbw b Fransman	2	9	7	-	-
T Hove c Swan b Sandri	2	17	8	-	-	(11) absent hurt					
B Mlambo c Strydom b September	32	119	85	3	-	b Fransman	30	67	28	2	1
C de Grandhomme c Laing b Sandri	26	91	61	4	-	b Sandri	25	168	89	2	-
S Matsikenyeri c Northcote b Albertyn	53	118	96	4	1	b Albertyn	0	7	5	-	-
GM Strydom c Davids b Sandri	16	24	24	4	-	run out (Sandri)	56	83	61	7	2
TMK Mawoyo c Bailey b September	12	33	25	2	-	(2) c Northcote b Albertyn	11	91	54	1	-
IM Chinyoka b Fransman	1	7	8	-	-	(9) b Albertyn	14	48	26	3	-
A Mwayenga not out	6	66	41	-	-	(7) lbw b Fransman	13	27	33	2	-
CB Mpofu b Albertyn	0	10	8	-	-	(8) c September b Albertyn	6	62	37	1	-
H Matanga b Sandri	0	4	2	-	-	(10) not out	5	20	16	1	-
Extras (lb 10, w 9, nb 3)	22					Extras (lb 5, w 1, nb 6)	12				
TOTAL (65.5 overs)	**171**					**TOTAL (58.2 overs)**	**174**				

BOLAND	Runs	Mins	Balls	4	6		Runs	Mins	Balls	4	6
R Bailey c De Grandhomme b Chinyoka	35	125	95	5	-	not out	0	3	5	-	-
JG Strydom c Matsikenyeri b Mwayenga	123	280	233	15	-	not out	0	3	0	-	-
WE September c Hove b Matanga	1	16	13	-	-						
WC Swan c Maregwede b Mwayenga	3	25	23	-	-						
H Davids lbw b Mwayenga	2	13	7	-	-						
RG Arendse lbw b Mwayenga	2	16	14	-	-						
PC Laing c Strydom b Mwayenga	65	122	106	8	1						
*WA Albertyn not out	58	111	81	7	-						
†NM Northcote not out	27	68	59	2	-						
PSE Sandri											
BL Fransman											
Extras (b 7, lb 4, w 12, nb 6)	29					Extras (b 4)	4				
TOTAL (for 7 wkts) (104 overs)	**345**					**TOTAL (for 0 wkts) (0.5 overs)**	**4**				

Bol	O	M	R	W			O	M	R	W	
Sandri	16.5	6	40	4	(2 nb)		18	8	56	1	(4 nb)
Fransman	14	5	23	2	(1 nb, 2 w)		17	5	49	3	(2 nb, 1 w)
Albertyn	11	5	23	2	(2 w)		19.2	10	33	4	
Laing	6	2	16	0	(1 w)						
September	18	1	59	2		(4)	4	0	31	0	
ZU23	O	M	R	W			O	M	R	W	
Mpofu	12	2	47	0	(2 w)						
Chinyoka	8.5	0	34	1	(5 nb, 3 w)						
Mwayenga	22.1	5	67	5	(2 w)						
Matanga	38	3	101	1	(2 w)	(1)	0.5	0	0	0	
De Grandhomme	21	3	80	0	(1 nb, 2 w)						
Matsikenyeri	2	0	5	0	(1 w)						

Fall of Wickets

	ZU23	Bol	ZU23	Bol
1st	5 (2)	113 (1)	3 (1)	-
2nd	19 (1)	123 (3)	43 (3)	-
3rd	76 (3)	139 (4)	49 (2)	-
4th	78 (4)	151 (5)	51 (5)	-
5th	106 (6)	157 (6)	125 (6)	-
6th	130 (7)	235 (2)	146 (7)	-
7th	133 (8)	272 (7)	155 (4)	-
8th	168 (5)	-	165 (8)	-
9th	168 (10)	-	174 (9)	-
10th	171 (11)	-	-	-

SAA PROVINCIAL THREE-DAY CHALLENGE

WESTERN PROVINCE v BORDER — SAA 3-day Challenge Pool B

Played at Sahara Park Newlands, Cape Town on 17,18,19 November 2005 Toss: Western Province
Umpires: MW Brown & IH van Kerwel
Debuts: WP: DL Haupt (FC). Bdr: None
Close of play: Day 1: Bdr (1) 71-2 (Von Hoesslin 25*, Gamiet 21*, 24 overs). Day 2: WP (2) 155-2 (Gray 76*, Wyngaard 47*, 48 overs).
Result: Western Province won by 56 runs
Points: WP: 20.28 (bat 6.28, bowl 4, match 10); Bdr: 6.12 (bat 4.12, bowl 2, match 0)
Notes:Dyili kept wicket in Western Province's 2nd innings. Western Province won off the last possible ball of the match.

WESTERN PROVINCE	*Runs*	*Mins*	*Balls*	*4*	*6*		*Runs*	*Mins*	*Balls*	*4*	*6*
AJA Gray lbw b Richards	19	83	53	2	-	(2) c Dyili b Ranger	77	192	142	11	-
M Williamson b Mbane	44	70	52	6	-	(1) c Dyili b Richards	6	21	22	1	-
Z Homani b KD Bennett	118	227	178	16	-	lbw b Richards	15	45	38	2	-
W Wyngaard not out	132	236	196	14	2	not out	101	202	154	8	3
FD Telo c BL Bennett b Ranger	11	11	9	1	-	b De Kock	46	63	54	5	1
WC Hantam not out	18	15	11	1	1	not out	2	10	6	-	-
*†RCC Canning											
M Mahlombe											
M de Stadler											
DL Haupt											
S Conrad											
Extras (lb 15, w 6, nb 1)	22					Extras (lb 15, w 2, nb 1)	18				
TOTAL (for 4 wkts dec) (83 overs)	**364**					**TOTAL (for 4 wkts dec) (69.1 overs)**	**265**				

BORDER	*Runs*	*Mins*	*Balls*	*4*	*6*		*Runs*	*Mins*	*Balls*	*4*	*6*
BL Bennett c Conrad b Hantam	7	17	19	1	-	c Wyngaard b Conrad	150	297	230	15	2
†GE von Hoesslin c Canning b Mahlombe	36	130	98	5	-	c Canning b Haupt	4	36	28	-	-
MM Matika c Williamson b De Stadler	16	43	39	3	-	c Canning b De Stadler	21	38	31	1	-
LL Gamiet lbw b Mahlombe	39	96	82	3	1	b Mahlombe	15	54	33	1	-
KD Bennett c Gray b Conrad	28	81	60	5	-	c Canning b Hantam	8	15	14	1	-
AZM Dyili b Conrad	47	83	77	7	1	b Conrad	65	85	80	8	1
*MN Ranger c Gray b Mahlombe	6	34	30	1	-	c Canning b De Stadler	15	48	40	-	-
S de Kock c Canning b Conrad	11	37	32	1	-	(9) lbw b Conrad	5	31	22	-	-
L Mbane lbw b Conrad	45	46	36	5	1	(8) b Conrad	15	33	23	1	1
RR Richards c and b Conrad	12	25	19	2	-	(11) lbw b Conrad	0	3	4	-	-
LL Lwana not out	1	10	3	-	-	(10) not out	1	12	8	-	-
Extras (lb 6, nb 2)	8					Extras (b 8, lb 9, w 1)	18				
TOTAL (82.1 overs)	**256**					**TOTAL (85 overs)**	**317**				

Bdr	*O*	*M*	*R*	*W*		*O*	*M*	*R*	*W*	
Richards	21	6	60	1		20	5	42	2	(1 w)
Lwana	9	0	42	0	(1 w)					
Mbane	18	4	72	1	(1 w)					
De Kock	9	1	43	0		12	0	64	1	
Ranger	15	1	61	1	(1 nb)	(2) 23	1	76	1	
BL Bennett	3	0	24	0		(5) 4.1	0	30	0	(1 w)
KD Bennett	8	0	47	1		(3) 10	1	38	0	(1 nb)
WP	*O*	*M*	*R*	*W*		*O*	*M*	*R*	*W*	
Hantam	19	3	47	1		10	2	36	1	(1 w)
Haupt	9	4	24	0		12	2	57	1	
De Stadler	22	7	53	1		(4) 25	5	71	2	
Conrad	17.1	5	64	5	(2 nb)	(3) 32	3	111	5	
Mahlombe	15	3	62	3		6	0	25	1	

Fall of Wickets

	WP	Bdr	WP	Bdr
1st	66 (2)	8 (1)	20 (1)	25 (2)
2nd	76 (1)	37 (3)	50 (3)	73 (3)
3rd	310 (3)	98 (2)	157 (2)	131 (4)
4th	329 (5)	115 (4)	252 (5)	143 (5)
5th	-	161 (5)	-	250 (6)
6th	-	180 (6)	-	287 (7)
7th	-	184 (7)	-	299 (1)
8th	-	228 (8)	-	316 (8)
9th	-	253 (9)	-	317 (9)
10th	-	256 (10)	-	317 (11)

BOLAND v EASTERN PROVINCE — SAA 3-day Challenge Pool B

Played at Boland Park, Paarl on 24,25,26 November 2005 Toss: Boland
Umpires: M Erasmus & LJ Willemse
Debuts: Bol: QK Kannemeyer (FC). EP: None
Close of play: Day 1: EP (2) 91-3 (Jeggels 45*, Fensham 0*, 24 overs). Day 2: Bol (2) 165-9 (Sandri 7*, Paulse 0*, 65 overs).
Result: Eastern Province won by 22 runs
Points: Bol: 4 (bat 0.00, bowl 4, match 0); EP: 14 (bat 0.00, bowl 4, match 10)

EASTERN PROVINCE	Runs	Mins	Balls	4	6		Runs	Mins	Balls	4	6
C Baxter c Walters b Sandri	1	29	24	-	-	(2) b Sandri	1	13	10	-	-
ML Price c Walters b Paulse	0	7	6	-	-	(1) b Paulse	5	25	13	1	-
U Abrahams b Sandri	18	51	32	3	-	lbw b Kannemeyer	37	86	60	7	-
RR Jeggels b Paulse	15	47	27	3	-	c Louw b Paulse	47	109	67	6	-
SG Fensham lbw b Albertyn	16	66	47	2	-	c Davids b Sandri	4	41	32	-	-
*GE Howell lbw b Laing	0	13	8	-	-	c Walters b Sandri	26	147	88	4	-
NG Brouwers c September b Laing	1	27	11	-	-	lbw b Laing	30	69	45	4	-
†M Slwana c Davids b Sandri	8	44	31	-	-	b Sandri	18	34	28	4	-
J Theron c Laing b Paulse	15	41	24	3	-	b Sandri	3	24	22	-	-
S Mjekula b Sandri	2	9	4	-	-	not out	5	19	8	1	-
LL Tsotsobe not out	6	7	5	1	-	run out (Laing/Walters)	1	10	11	-	-
Extras (b 2, lb 5, w 2)	9					Extras (b 1, lb 7, w 1)	9				
TOTAL (36.3 overs)	**91**					**TOTAL (64 overs)**	**186**				

BOLAND	Runs	Mins	Balls	4	6		Runs	Mins	Balls	4	6
WJ Louw lbw b Tsotsobe	0	1	1	-	-	c Abrahams b Tsotsobe	2	19	16	-	-
JG Strydom run out (Tsotsobe)	8	36	21	2	-	c Slwana b Theron	17	60	30	3	-
WC Swan c Slwana b Tsotsobe	8	4	5	2	-	lbw b Theron	12	60	51	-	-
H Davids c Slwana b Tsotsobe	9	24	12	2	-	b Theron	0	3	3	-	-
PC Laing b Tsotsobe	0	1	1	-	-	b Theron	13	35	14	2	-
QK Kannemeyer c Howell b Theron	11	62	38	1	-	b Theron	70	201	136	7	-
*WA Albertyn c Slwana b Mjekula	24	79	59	4	-	c Jeggels b Tsotsobe	14	37	29	2	-
†L-R Walters b Theron	5	34	21	-	-	b Howell	8	30	21	1	-
WE September c Abrahams b Mjekula	2	9	9	-	-	b Mjekula	7	40	34	-	-
PSE Sandri not out	7	12	7	-	-	b Theron	10	91	71	-	-
HH Paulse lbw b Theron	1	7	4	-	-	not out	1	22	14	-	-
Extras (lb 4, nb 2)	6					Extras (b 4, lb 12, nb 4)	20				
TOTAL (29.2 overs)	**81**					**TOTAL (69.3 overs)**	**174**				

Bol	O	M	R	W	O	M	R	W
Sandri	11.3	4	24	4	20	5	32	5 (1 w)
Paulse	11	3	43	3 (1 w)	12	1	38	2
Albertyn	7	5	9	1	8	1	28	0
Laing	7	2	8	2	9	1	44	1
September					3	0	21	0
Kannemeyer					12	5	15	1
EP	*O*	*M*	*R*	*W*	*O*	*M*	*R*	*W*
Tsotsobe	12	5	38	4 (1 nb)	17	6	30	2
Mjekula	9	1	27	2 (1 nb)	21	4	52	1
Theron	8.2	4	12	3	19.3	6	47	6
Howell					12	1	29	1 (2 nb)

Fall of Wickets

	EP	Bol	EP	Bol
1st	0 (2)	0 (1)	3 (2)	8 (1)
2nd	2 (1)	8 (3)	10 (1)	28 (2)
3rd	34 (3)	27 (4)	89 (3)	28 (4)
4th	38 (4)	27 (5)	96 (4)	37 (3)
5th	40 (6)	27 (2)	102 (5)	56 (5)
6th	56 (7)	63 (6)	151 (7)	82 (7)
7th	56 (5)	69 (7)	173 (8)	107 (8)
8th	83 (8)	73 (9)	179 (9)	126 (9)
9th	83 (9)	73 (8)	180 (6)	165 (6)
10th	91 (10)	81 (11)	186 (11)	174 (10)

BORDER v EASTERN PROVINCE — SAA 3-day Challenge Pool B

Played at Mercedes-Benz Park, East London on 19,20,21 January 2006 — Toss: Eastern Province

Umpires: BM White & LJ Willemse

Debuts: Bdr: None. EP: SR Adair (FC)

Close of play: Day 1: EP (1) 59-0 (Baxter 31*, Ingram 25*, 10 overs). Day 2: EP (2) 18-0 (Ingram 9*, Baxter 8*, 5 overs).

Result: Border won by 188 runs

Points: Bdr: 20.04 (bat 6.04, bowl 4, match 10); EP: 5.38 (bat 3.38, bowl 2, match 0)

BORDER	Runs	Mins	Balls	4	6		Runs	Mins	Balls	4	6
BL Bennett c Howell b Tsotsobe	92	141	113	13	-	c Adair b Tsotsobe	11	19	18	1	-
CC Bradfield c Adair b Tsotsobe	11	35	23	1	-	c Adair b Theron	80	168	107	14	1
GE von Hoesslin c Ingram b Bell	10	75	45	-	-	c Abrahams b Tsotsobe	21	69	62	4	-
SC Pope b Ingram	102	187	154	11	-	not out	64	127	91	12	-
*MN Ranger b Theron	96	174	168	8	2						
WR Hinkel not out	18	18	14	1	1						
L Mbane						(5) not out	28	42	38	5	-
†AM Sodumo											
MW Olivier											
Y Pangabantu											
RR Richards											
Extras (b 7, lb 6, w 1, nb 9)	23					Extras (b 2, lb 6, w 3, nb 2)	13				
TOTAL (for 5 wkts dec) (84.4 overs)	**352**					**TOTAL (for 3 wkts dec) (52.2 overs)**	**217**				

EASTERN PROVINCE	Runs	Mins	Balls	4	6		Runs	Mins	Balls	4	6
C Baxter c Bennett b Pangabantu	58	93	63	12	-	(2) c Hinkel b Richards	8	33	19	2	-
CA Ingram lbw b Richards	74	199	142	12	-	(1) c Sodumo b Olivier	25	81	63	4	-
U Abrahams c Bradfield b Olivier	7	31	24	1	-	c Sodumo b Olivier	13	38	26	2	-
RR Jeggels lbw b Hinkel	24	40	31	5	-	b Pangabantu	24	41	25	6	-
ML Price c Pope b Hinkel	0	2	2	-	-	c Sodumo b Pangabantu	16	72	46	1	-
*GE Howell run out (Olivier/Richards)	2	12	4	-	-	lbw b Pangabantu	0	7	4	-	-
†SR Adair not out	32	71	56	4	-	c Pope b Hinkel	44	88	79	8	-
WE Bell c Bennett b Olivier	4	14	13	1	-	c Sodumo b Olivier	21	48	34	2	-
J Theron lbw b Hinkel	0	11	9	-	-	b Olivier	0	2	1	-	-
S Mjekula lbw b Olivier	2	11	9	-	-	not out	4	12	10	-	-
LL Tsotsobe b Hinkel	7	12	10	1	-	b Hinkel	0	8	3	-	-
Extras (lb 3, w 1, nb 5)	9					Extras (b 1, lb 2, w 2, nb 2)	7				
TOTAL (59.5 overs)	**219**					**TOTAL (51.2 overs)**	**162**				

EP	O	M	R	W			O	M	R	W	
Tsotsobe	18	4	72	2	(3 nb, 1 w)		12	3	37	2	(1 w)
Mjekula	10	1	35	0		(4)	14	3	48	0	
Theron	18.4	3	58	1	(2 nb)		14	1	61	1	(2 w)
Bell	3	0	21	1	(4 nb)	(2)	2	0	21	0	(2 nb)
Howell	20	2	81	0			6	1	28	0	
Ingram	15	0	72	1			4.2	0	14	0	
Bdr	O	M	R	W			O	M	R	W	
Olivier	15	3	62	3	(5 nb)		16	3	68	4	(2 nb, 1 w)
Richards	17	5	50	1	(1 w)		12	2	35	1	(1 w)
Mbane	5	2	23	0							
Pangabantu	5	1	20	1		(3)	8	1	24	3	
Ranger	4	0	19	0							
Hinkel	13.5	1	42	4		(4)	13.2	2	24	2	
Pope						(5)	2	0	8	0	

Fall of Wickets

	Bdr	EP	Bdr	EP
1st	30 (2)	105 (1)	26 (1)	26 (2)
2nd	105 (3)	121 (3)	77 (3)	48 (3)
3rd	138 (1)	166 (4)	157 (2)	53 (1)
4th	308 (4)	166 (5)	-	78 (4)
5th	352 (5)	172 (6)	-	78 (6)
6th	-	176 (2)	-	103 (5)
7th	-	190 (8)	-	155 (8)
8th	-	191 (9)	-	155 (9)
9th	-	202 (10)	-	158 (7)
10th	-	219 (11)	-	162 (11)

KWAZULU-NATAL v EASTERN PROVINCE SAA 3-day Challenge Pool B

Played at Chatsworth Stadium, Chatsworth on 26,27,28 January 2006 Toss: Eastern Province

Umpires: ZTA Ndamane & DJ Smith

Debuts: KZN: AI Chinnappa and CS Mabuya (Both FC). EP: None

Close of play: Day 1: No play. Day 2: No play.

Result: Match drawn

Points: KZN: 0 (bat 0.00, bowl 0, match 0); EP: 0 (bat 0.00, bowl 0, match 0)

Notes:This was a one innings match for 10 points due to no play on first two days.

KWAZULU-NATAL	Runs	Mins	Balls	4	6
I Khan c Tsotsobe b Theron	61	106	96	6	-
*R Gobind c and b Howell	38	161	110	5	-
K Smit b Willemse	0	4	3	-	-
AI Chinnappa c and b Willemse	4	10	5	1	-
KC Africa run out (Ingram/Willemse)	33	68	64	3	1
M Bekker b Willemse	34	44	38	1	2
CS Mabuya b Ingram	5	5	3	1	-
R Frylinck run out (Willemse/Ingram)	2	5	6	-	-
†DR Miller st Adair b Willemse	0	6	4	-	-
ND Hewer not out	8	12	9	1	-
U Govender c Adair b Ingram	0	8	8	-	-
Extras (b 7, lb 3, w 4, nb 1)	15				
TOTAL (57.3 overs)	**200**				

EASTERN PROVINCE	Runs	Mins	Balls	4	6
CA Ingram c Hewer b Govender	1	17	14	-	-
C Baxter c Gobind b Frylinck	9	51	34	1	-
U Abrahams b Hewer	24	110	61	2	1
RR Jeggels b Frylinck	1	9	10	-	-
†SR Adair b Govender	26	32	26	4	1
*GE Howell c and b Chinnappa	58	86	61	7	1
D Willemse b Chinnappa	25	61	57	2	-
L Meyer lbw b Chinnappa	6	22	13	-	-
J Theron b Hewer	7	18	16	1	-
LL Tsotsobe not out	12	20	19	2	-
S Mjekula not out	1	15	8	-	-
Extras (b 5, lb 5, nb 6)	16				
TOTAL (for 9 wkts) (52 overs)	**186**				

EP	O	M	R	W	
Tsotsobe	6	0	18	0	
Meyer	8	1	20	0	(3 w)
Mjekula	3	0	16	0	
Theron	7	0	26	1	
Willemse	20	4	56	4	
Howell	9	1	35	1	
Ingram	4.3	0	19	2	(1 nb)
KZN	O	M	R	W	
Govender	10.2	0	56	2	(3 nb)
Frylinck	13	5	19	2	
Hewer	16.4	1	52	2	(3 nb)
Khan	5	1	30	0	
Chinnappa	7	1	19	3	

Fall of Wickets

	KZN	EP
1st	80 (1)	6 (1)
2nd	81 (3)	19 (2)
3rd	89 (4)	21 (4)
4th	129 (2)	53 (5)
5th	177 (5)	93 (3)
6th	186 (7)	154 (6)
7th	189 (8)	157 (7)
8th	190 (6)	170 (8)
9th	191 (9)	174 (9)
10th	200 (11)	-

WESTERN PROVINCE v KWAZULU-NATAL SAA 3-day Challenge Pool B

Played at Sahara Park Newlands, Cape Town on 2,3 February 2006 Toss: Western Province
Umpires: EC Hendrikse & IH van Kerwel
Debuts: WP: None. KZN: None
Close of play: Day 1: KZN (1) 103-5 (Pillay 1*, Mabuya 4*, 36 overs).
Result: KwaZulu-Natal won by 10 wickets
Points: WP: 5.28 (bat 1.28, bowl 4, match 0); KZN: 16.5 (bat 2.50, bowl 4, match 10)
Notes: Sanders retired hurt with his score on 15 and the total on 99-4 in KwaZulu-Natal's 1st innings and returned at the fall of the 6th wicket. Miller scored his fifty off 36 balls in KwaZulu-Natal's 2nd innings.

WESTERN PROVINCE	Runs	Mins	Balls	4	6		Runs	Mins	Balls	4	6
DJ Bassage c Pillay b Hewer	0	15	12	-	-	c Bekker b Govender	5	27	13	-	-
AJA Gray c Miller b Hewer	5	41	32	-	-	lbw b Mhlongo	41	131	98	7	-
Z Homani lbw b Mhlongo	13	77	50	2	-	c and b Pillay	17	71	47	1	-
W Wyngaard lbw b Govender	10	40	24	1	-	c Miller b Govender	0	6	6	-	-
M Williamson b Hewer	5	25	15	1	-	c Miller b Mhlongo	20	108	78	1	-
*†RCC Canning b Govender	30	60	51	6	-	c Pillay b Mhlongo	32	58	41	5	-
WC Hantam c Miller b Govender	1	39	27	-	-	lbw b Mhlongo	0	2	1	-	-
Q Friend c Pillay b Mhlongo	18	76	23	2	-	b Govender	22	15	12	5	-
M de Stadler c Pillay b Mhlongo	19	60	53	2	-	lbw b Mhlongo	3	18	11	-	-
S Conrad not out	0	14	4	-	-	c Miller b Govender	11	17	12	2	-
LF Simpson b Hewer	1	5	5	-	-	not out	0	4	0	-	-
Extras (b 1, lb 6, nb 5)	12					Extras (b 4, w 1, nb 2)	7				
TOTAL (48.2 overs)	**114**					**TOTAL (52.5 overs)**	**158**				

KWAZULU-NATAL	Runs	Mins	Balls	4	6		Runs	Mins	Balls	4	6
†DR Miller c Canning b Hantam	22	61	29	3	-	not out	64	67	51	10	1
*R Gobind lbw b Simpson	5	15	14	-	-	not out	31	67	55	4	-
AI Chinnappa c Bassage b De Stadler	5	12	6	1	-						
WR Wingfield st Canning b Conrad	49	117	86	9	-						
M Bekker c Canning b De Stadler	3	11	12	-	-						
MD Sanders lbw b Hantam	25	93	73	3	-						
TD Pillay c Gray b Hantam	13	56	47	2	-						
CS Mabuya c Canning b De Stadler	4	14	11	1	-						
ND Hewer lbw b Hantam	4	10	9	1	-						
S Mhlongo lbw b Conrad	21	58	38	3	-						
U Govender not out	21	51	52	4	-						
Extras (b 1, lb 1, nb 1)	3					Extras (b 4, w 1)	5				
TOTAL (62.4 overs)	**175**					**TOTAL (for 0 wkts) (17.4 overs)**	**100**				

KZN	O	M	R	W			O	M	R	W	
Govender	15.5	5	43	3	(4 nb)		14.5	4	50	4	(1 w)
Hewer	17.2	7	31	4			14	1	54	0	
Mhlongo	13	7	27	3	(1 nb)		16	5	25	5	(2 nb)
Pillay	2.1	0	6	0			7	2	21	1	
Chinnappa							1	0	4	0	
WP	O	M	R	W			O	M	R	W	
Friend	12	5	29	0			4	0	14	0	
Simpson	5	1	27	1	(1 nb)	(3)	2	0	21	0	(1 w)
De Stadler	22	9	42	3		(4)	5	1	27	0	
Hantam	16	2	57	4		(2)	2	0	15	0	
Conrad	7.4	1	18	2			4.4	1	19	0	

Fall of Wickets

	WP	KZN	WP	KZN
1st	3 (1)	12 (2)	14 (1)	-
2nd	11 (2)	27 (3)	51 (3)	-
3rd	33 (4)	53 (1)	52 (4)	-
4th	38 (3)	56 (5)	66 (2)	-
5th	42 (5)	102 (4)	110 (6)	-
6th	67 (7)	107 (8)	110 (7)	-
7th	74 (6)	121 (7)	143 (8)	-
8th	106 (9)	127 (9)	144 (5)	-
9th	113 (8)	134 (6)	152 (9)	-
10th	114 (11)	175 (10)	158 (10)	-

BOLAND v BORDER — SAA 3-day Challenge Pool B

Played at Boland Park, Paarl on 9,10,11 February 2006 Toss: Boland
Umpires: MW Brown & EC Hendrikse
Debuts: Bol: DL Hobson, DJ Malan and AW Olivier (All FC). Bdr: None
Close of play: Day 1: Bdr (1) 79-1 (BL Bennett 31*, De Wett 40*, 17 overs). Day 2: Bol (2) 115-3 (Malan 61*, September 1*, 36 overs).
Result: Border won by 6 wickets
Points: Bol: 9.06 (bat 6.06, bowl 3, match 0); Bdr:20.64 (bat 7.64, bowl 3, match 10)
Notes: Olivier banned from bowling during Border's 1st innings for running on the pitch. Dyili kept wicket in Boland's 2nd innings.

BOLAND	*Runs*	*Mins*	*Balls*	*4*	*6*		*Runs*	*Mins*	*Balls*	*4*	*6*
DJ Malan c Ranger b Olivier	27	115	65	4	-	c De Wett b Pangabantu	64	199	136	11	-
JG Strydom c Bradfield b Olivier	43	79	58	8	-	c Dyili b Olivier	18	42	33	4	-
*WC Swan c Von Hoesslin b Pangabantu	67	175	128	9	-	c Dyili b Richards	15	81	46	1	-
AW Olivier c Bradfield b Olivier	10	54	39	1	-	lbw b BL Bennett	8	27	30	1	-
WJ Louw c Von Hoesslin b Pangabantu	27	88	62	4	-	(6) not out	41	134	106	4	1
PC Laing c Ranger b BL Bennett	80	102	79	9	1	(7) c Ranger b BL Bennett	0	1	3	-	-
†L-R Walters c sub (DL Brown) b Ranger	56	113	72	3	-	(8) c Von Hoesslin b Richards	3	10	7	-	-
DL Hobson not out	11	26	13	1	-	(9) c Ranger b BL Bennett	4	19	10	-	-
WE September not out	11	11	7	1	-	(5) c Mbane b BL Bennett	30	104	65	3	-
BL Fransman						b Olivier	2	23	20	-	-
HH Paulse						lbw b BL Bennett	4	12	10	1	-
Extras (b 1, lb 7, nb 13)	21					Extras (b 4, lb 3, nb 10)	17				
TOTAL (for 7 wkts dec) (85 overs)	**353**					**TOTAL (76 overs)**	**206**				

BORDER	*Runs*	*Mins*	*Balls*	*4*	*6*		*Runs*	*Mins*	*Balls*	*4*	*6*
BL Bennett c Walters b Swan	122	292	174	12	-	c Louw b Fransman	35	28	24	7	-
CC Bradfield c Louw b Paulse	0	11	5	-	-	not out	57	107	79	11	-
BC de Wett c September b Malan	182	245	204	15	7	st Walters b September	18	35	24	2	1
AZM Dyili c September b Laing	4	3	5	1	-	lbw b September	0	1	2	-	-
*MN Ranger c Hobson b September	34	50	46	3	-	c Louw b September	8	16	12	1	-
†GE von Hoesslin c and b September	26	29	37	1	-	not out	10	22	15	1	-
KD Bennett not out	21	30	20	-	1						
L Mbane not out	23	18	26	2	-						
MW Olivier											
Y Pangabantu											
RR Richards											
Extras (b 10, lb 2, w 1, nb 7)	20					Extras (nb 3)	3				
TOTAL (for 6 wkts dec) (85 overs)	**432**					**TOTAL (for 4 wkts) (25.3 overs)**	**131**				

Bdr	*O*	*M*	*R*	*W*			*O*	*M*	*R*	*W*	
Olivier	14.3	1	56	3	(13 nb)		21	1	76	2	(9 nb)
Richards	16	4	53	0		(4)	15	3	40	2	
Pangabantu	15	3	44	2		(2)	13	5	21	1	
Mbane	15.3	3	55	0		(3)	7	1	30	0	(1 nb)
De Wett	7	0	40	0		(7)	2	1	3	0	
Ranger	12	0	58	1		(5)	4	0	8	0	
BL Bennett	5	0	39	1		(6)	14	5	21	5	
Bol	*O*	*M*	*R*	*W*			*O*	*M*	*R*	*W*	
Paulse	15	1	64	1	(2 nb)		2	0	28	0	(1 nb)
Hobson	13	1	73	0		(5)	2	0	12	0	
Fransman	12	1	55	0	(5 nb, 1 w)	(2)	7	0	19	1	(2 nb)
September	12	1	70	2			7	2	35	3	
Laing	14	2	46	1		(3)	4	0	12	0	
Swan	10	0	54	1							
Malan	9	0	58	1		(6)	3.3	0	25	0	

Fall of Wickets

	Bol	**Bdr**	**Bol**	**Bdr**
1st	64 (2)	4 (2)	29 (2)	37 (1)
2nd	93 (1)	311 (3)	92 (3)	73 (3)
3rd	121 (4)	315 (4)	112 (4)	73 (4)
4th	192 (3)	353 (1)	130 (1)	95 (5)
5th	195 (5)	375 (5)	166 (5)	-
6th	317 (6)	392 (6)	166 (7)	-
7th	333 (7)	-	169 (8)	-
8th	-	-	184 (9)	-
9th	-	-	197 (10)	-
10th	-	-	206 (11)	-

EASTERN PROVINCE v WESTERN PROVINCE SAA 3-day Challenge Pool B

Played at Sahara Oval St George's, Port Elizabeth on 9,10,11 February 2006 Toss: Western Province
Umpires: BN Harrison & LJ Willemse
Debuts: EP: None. WP: JP Geoghegan and JM Kuiper (Both FC)
Close of play: Day 1: WP (1) 96-1 (Gray 44*, Homani 1*, 28 overs). Day 2: WP (2) 16-0 (Gray 7*, Bassage 9*, 11 overs).
Result: Western Province won by 9 wickets
Points: EP: 9.18 (bat 5.18, bowl 4, match 0); WP: 16.2 (bat 4.20, bowl 2, match 10)

EASTERN PROVINCE	Runs	Mins	Balls	4	6		Runs	Mins	Balls	4	6
C Baxter c Canning b Friend	0	6	6	-	-	(2) c Hantam b Friend	0	3	3	-	-
*CA Ingram c Kuiper b Conrad	169	280	254	24	2	(1) lbw b De Stadler	39	89	64	3	-
U Abrahams not out	100	293	232	8	3	lbw b De Stadler	7	45	34	-	-
E Potgieter c Conrad b De Stadler	27	10	12	1	3	(6) lbw b Conrad	0	11	5	-	-
L Meyer c Friend b De Stadler	3	7	4	-	-	(8) b De Stadler	1	6	6	-	-
RR Jeggels						(4) c Hantam b Conrad	16	45	37	1	1
†SR Adair						(5) c Hantam b Conrad	4	8	5	1	-
D Willemse						(7) c Hantam b Conrad	16	55	31	2	-
LL Tsotsobe						c Friend b Conrad	7	15	8	-	1
J Theron						not out	14	44	34	-	1
S Mjekula						c Bassage b Conrad	10	20	15	2	-
Extras (b 2, lb 6, w 1, nb 1)	10					Extras (lb 3, nb 5)	8				
TOTAL (for 4 wkts dec) (84.3 overs)	**309**					**TOTAL (39.3 overs)**	**122**				

WESTERN PROVINCE	Runs	Mins	Balls	4	6		Runs	Mins	Balls	4	6
AJA Gray c Adair b Tsotsobe	85	231	153	13	-	b Mjekula	31	103	87	2	-
DJ Bassage c Meyer b Theron	42	98	78	5	-	not out	108	197	155	17	-
Z Homani lbw b Theron	2	29	23	-	-	not out	25	94	58	1	-
W Wyngaard c Potgieter b Theron	4	33	34	-	-						
JM Kuiper c Potgieter b Meyer	11	17	20	1	-						
*†RCC Canning lbw b Tsotsobe	25	57	45	2	-						
WC Hantam not out	30	83	55	5	-						
JP Geoghegan c Adair b Tsotsobe	2	7	9	-	-						
M de Stadler c Theron b Willemse	3	21	15	-	-						
Q Friend c Adair b Mjekula	36	43	32	4	2						
S Conrad b Ingram	1	4	5	-	-						
Extras (b 6, lb 2, w 1, nb 10)	19					Extras (b 7, nb 1)	8				
TOTAL (76.3 overs)	**260**					**TOTAL (for 1 wkt) (49.5 overs)**	**172**				

WP	O	M	R	W		O	M	R	W
Friend	14	4	37	1		9	1	31	1 (2 nb)
Hantam	13	2	49	0		7	1	22	0
De Stadler	22.3	7	65	2		11	2	21	3
Geoghegan	11	1	38	0					
Conrad	24	3	112	1 (1 nb, 1 w)	(4)	12.3	1	45	6 (3 nb)
EP	O	M	R	W		O	M	R	W
Meyer	12	2	35	1	(2)	9	5	14	0
Tsotsobe	15	2	67	3 (3 nb)	(1)	14	2	39	0
Mjekula	7	1	28	1	(4)	7	1	23	1
Theron	16	3	40	3 (7 nb)	(3)	7	2	17	0 (1 nb)
Willemse	25	4	81	1 (1 w)		8	0	43	0
Ingram	1.3	0	1	1		3	0	22	0
Potgieter						1	0	1	0
Baxter						0.5	0	6	0

Fall of Wickets

	EP	WP	EP	WP
1st	0 (1)	85 (2)	2 (2)	61 (1)
2nd	272 (2)	107 (3)	34 (3)	-
3rd	302 (4)	123 (4)	66 (1)	-
4th	309 (5)	138 (5)	70 (4)	-
5th	-	184 (1)	70 (5)	-
6th	-	185 (6)	73 (6)	-
7th	-	187 (8)	74 (8)	-
8th	-	206 (9)	83 (9)	-
9th	-	259 (10)	98 (7)	-
10th	-	260 (11)	122 (11)	-

WESTERN PROVINCE v BOLAND — SAA 3-day Challenge Pool B

Played at Sahara Park Newlands, Cape Town on 16,17,18 February 2006 — Toss: Boland

Umpires: EC Hendrikse & LH Matroos

Debuts: WP: None. Bol: GC Stevens (FC)

Close of play: Day 1: WP (2) 2-0 (Gray 1*, Bassage 0*, 2.1 overs). Day 2: Bol (2) 55-4 (Stevens 5*, Laing 36*, 16 overs).

Result: Western Province won by 398 runs

Points: WP: 18.94 (bat 4.94, bowl 4, match 10); Bol: 5.46 (bat 1.46, bowl 4, match 0)

Notes: De Stadler took a hat-trick in Boland's 1st innings. His victims were September, Fransman, Paulse. Gray scored a century before lunch (102*) on day 1. He scored his century off 80 balls.

WESTERN PROVINCE	Runs	Mins	Balls	4	6		Runs	Mins	Balls	4	6
AJA Gray lbw b Sandri	108	159	98	16	1	lbw b Fransman	22	36	29	4	-
DJ Bassage c Laing b Sandri	8	13	13	1	-	c Walters b Laing	32	102	74	5	-
Z Homani run out (Malan/Walters)	42	92	57	6	-	c Walters b September	16	47	30	2	-
W Wyngaard lbw b Sandri	3	32	25	-	-	not out	104	204	195	6	3
JM Kuiper not out	81	136	81	13	-	c September b Paulse	17	26	25	3	-
*†RCC Canning b Paulse	22	45	34	4	-	c Walters b Stevens	72	117	127	7	-
WC Hantam c Walters b Laing	7	15	11	1	-	b Malan	23	19	13	1	2
JP Geoghegan lbw b September	15	28	22	3	-	not out	6	21	14	-	-
M de Stadler lbw b September	0	9	6	-	-						
Q Friend c Malan b Fransman	1	6	7	-	-						
S Conrad c Swan b Fransman	0	8	6	-	-						
Extras (lb 2, w 1, nb 7)	10					Extras (lb 2, w 1, nb 3)	6				
TOTAL (58.5 overs)	**297**					**TOTAL (for 6 wkts dec) (84 overs)**	**298**				

BOLAND	Runs	Mins	Balls	4	6		Runs	Mins	Balls	4	6
DJ Malan c Canning b De Stadler	18	61	40	2	-	run out (Geoghegan/Canning)	5	21	14	-	-
WD Hayward c Canning b Hantam	10	14	16	1	-	b Friend	0	1	2	-	-
JG Strydom lbw b Hantam	7	22	12	-	-	c Friend b Hantam	1	7	5	-	-
GC Stevens c Canning b Hantam	7	16	16	1	-	c Bassage b Friend	5	75	42	1	-
*WC Swan lbw b De Stadler	33	51	45	5	1	lbw b Hantam	2	4	4	-	-
PC Laing c Gray b Conrad	10	31	21	2	-	c Homani b Friend	46	78	62	9	-
†L-R Walters not out	16	54	35	2	-	c Conrad b De Stadler	4	12	10	1	-
WE September lbw b De Stadler	17	35	33	1	-	b De Stadler	0	7	4	-	-
BL Fransman c Bassage b De Stadler	0	2	1	-	-	not out	0	9	4	-	-
HH Paulse b De Stadler	0	2	1	-	-	b De Stadler	0	4	6	-	-
PSE Sandri absent hurt						absent hurt					
Extras (b 3, lb 2)	5					Extras (b 9, lb 1, nb 1)	11				
TOTAL (36.4 overs)	**123**					**TOTAL (25.2 overs)**	**74**				

Bol	O	M	R	W			O	M	R	W	
Sandri	13	1	67	3	(1 nb)						
Paulse	13	0	67	1	(5 nb, 1 w)	(1)	9	1	28	1	
Fransman	15.5	1	80	2	(1 nb)	(2)	11	3	33	1	(3 nb)
Laing	11	0	67	1		(3)	8	0	28	1	(1 w)
September	6	1	14	2		(4)	23	3	89	1	
Stevens						(5)	25	6	71	1	
Malan						(6)	8	0	47	1	
WP	O	M	R	W			O	M	R	W	
Friend	7	1	18	0			11	2	32	3	(1 nb)
Hantam	8	1	29	3			8	4	26	2	
De Stadler	11.4	2	42	5			6.2	4	6	3	
Conrad	10	2	29	1							

Fall of Wickets

	WP	Bol	WP	Bol
1st	15 (2)	14 (2)	29 (1)	1 (2)
2nd	134 (3)	30 (3)	64 (3)	4 (3)
3rd	161 (4)	42 (4)	76 (2)	6 (1)
4th	184 (1)	42 (1)	102 (5)	10 (5)
5th	230 (6)	79 (6)	231 (6)	60 (4)
6th	242 (7)	89 (5)	274 (7)	69 (7)
7th	278 (8)	123 (8)	-	69 (8)
8th	286 (9)	123 (9)	-	69 (6)
9th	293 (10)	123 (10)	-	74 (10)
10th	297 (11)	-	-	-

KWAZULU-NATAL v BORDER — SAA 3-day Challenge Pool B

Played at Sahara Stadium Kingsmead, Durban on 16,17,18 February 2006 — Toss: KwaZulu-Natal

Umpires: GH Pienaar & S Wadvalla

Debuts: KZN: YA Abdullah and PM Selowa (Both FC). Bdr: MX Petu (FC)

Close of play: Day 1: KZN (1) 183-3 (Smit 4*, Selowa 10*, 55 overs). Day 2: Bdr (2) 264-6 (Gamiet 101*, KD Bennett 20*, 62 overs).

Result: KwaZulu-Natal won by 9 wickets

Points: KZN: 19.52 (bat 5.52, bowl 4, match 10); Bdr: 6.38 (bat 2.38, bowl 4, match 0)

Notes:Gamiet scored his fifty off 39 balls in Border's 2nd Innings.

BORDER	Runs	Mins	Balls	4	6		Runs	Mins	Balls	4	6
BL Bennett b Mhlongo	28	41	34	3	-	lbw b Govender	22	29	18	3	1
MX Pethu c Selowa b Abdullah	2	16	7	-	-	c Miller b Govender	1	12	9	-	-
BC de Wett b Abdullah	0	17	12	-	-	c Govender b Khan	63	142	86	9	1
SC Pope c Selowa b Govender	29	65	37	6	-	lbw b Frylinck	17	61	42	3	-
LL Gamiet c Miller b Mhlongo	28	54	40	3	-	c Miller b Mhlongo	105	193	125	15	-
*MN Ranger c Khan b Abdullah	25	96	59	4	-	b Frylinck	13	52	43	1	-
†AZM Dyili lbw b Abdullah	13	35	28	2	-	b Frylinck	19	32	27	4	-
KD Bennett c Smit b Govender	21	24	20	4	-	c Frylinck b Khan	47	104	60	5	1
LL Lwana c Miller b Govender	0	3	2	-	-	(10) c Govender b Frylinck	24	34	26	3	1
MW Olivier not out	9	27	19	1	-	(9) c Selowa b Govender	9	34	26	2	-
Y Pangabantu						not out	1	10	9	-	-
Extras (lb 4, w 2, nb 8)	14					Extras (b 1, lb 5, nb 7)	13				
TOTAL (for 9 wkts dec) (41.4 overs)	**169**					**TOTAL (77.2 overs)**	**334**				

KWAZULU-NATAL	Runs	Mins	Balls	4	6		Runs	Mins	Balls	4	6
MD Sanders lbw b De Wett	103	185	179	14	2	c BL Bennett b Ranger	69	106	96	10	1
*R Gobind c Pope b De Wett	46	170	109	4	-	not out	71	190	142	10	-
I Khan c Pope b De Wett	4	21	17	-	-	not out	37	83	76	5	-
K Smit c Dyili b De Wett	46	107	67	2	1						
PM Selowa c and b De Wett	16	27	26	1	-						
M Bekker c Dyili b Lwana	22	31	35	1	1						
R Frylinck c sub (DL Brown) b Pangabantu	37	47	38	5	-						
†DR Miller not out	26	33	18	1	2						
YA Abdullah run out (Ranger/Pangabantu)	5	12	15	-	-						
S Mhlongo st Dyili b De Wett	0	5	4	-	-						
U Govender st Dyili b De Wett	3	8	5	-	-						
Extras (b 8, lb 2, w 3, nb 5)	18					Extras (nb 1)	1				
TOTAL (84.4 overs)	**326**					**TOTAL (for 1 wkt) (52.1 overs)**	**178**				

KZN	O	M	R	W		O	M	R	W
Govender	11	0	53	3 (7 nb, 1 w)		21	7	88	3 (3 nb)
Abdullah	9.4	3	33	4		10	0	68	0
Mhlongo	11	3	31	2 (1 nb)		15	3	51	1 (4 nb)
Frylinck	10	0	48	0		15.2	3	63	4
Khan						15	1	50	2
Smit						1	0	8	0
Bdr	O	M	R	W		O	M	R	W
Olivier	6	1	16	0		12	1	41	0 (1 nb)
Pangabantu	21	4	76	1 (1 w)		6	1	21	0
Lwana	10	1	43	1 (2 nb)	(4)	1	0	5	0
Ranger	8	3	16	0 (1 nb)	(6)	11	1	24	1
BL Bennett	15	1	70	0 (2 nb, 2 w)	(7)	7.1	1	28	0
De Wett	24.4	5	95	7	(3)	12	0	50	0
Gamiet					(5)	1	0	3	0
KD Bennett						2	0	6	0

Fall of Wickets

	Bdr	KZN	Bdr	KZN
1st	14 (2)	151 (2)	14 (2)	104 (1)
2nd	31 (3)	164 (1)	42 (1)	-
3rd	31 (1)	167 (3)	86 (4)	-
4th	93 (5)	197 (5)	162 (3)	-
5th	93 (4)	225 (6)	197 (6)	-
6th	121 (7)	289 (4)	227 (7)	-
7th	151 (8)	293 (7)	274 (5)	-
8th	151 (9)	306 (9)	296 (9)	-
9th	169 (6)	310 (10)	330 (8)	-
10th	-	326 (11)	334 (10)	-

BOLAND V KWAZULU-NATAL

SAA 3-day Challenge Pool B

Played at Boland Park, Paarl on 23,24 February 2006

Toss: Boland

Umpires: IH van Kerwel & EC Hendrikse

Debuts: Bol: None. KZN: None

Close of play: Day 1: KZN (1) 101-4 (Bekker 40*, Essack 18*, 29 overs).

Result: Match drawn

Points: Bol: 6.18 (bat 3.18, bowl 3, match 0); KZN: 17.58 (bat 3.58, bowl 4, match 10)

Notes: Match abandoned on the 2nd day due to a dangerous pitch. KwaZulu-Natal awarded 10 points.

BOLAND	Runs	Mins	Balls	4	6
DJ Malan c Miller b Africa	24	68	48	4	-
WD Hayward lbw b Abrahim	47	161	108	6	-
WC Swan lbw b Frylinck	5	31	22	1	-
GC Stevens b Africa	5	38	26	1	-
PC Laing c Miller b Abrahim	29	51	37	6	-
QK Kannemeyer run out (Essack)	13	22	15	2	-
*WA Albertyn lbw b Pillay	17	45	32	2	-
†L-R Walters run out (sub/Miller)	40	96	93	4	-
WE September c Miller b Essack	4	32	43	-	-
BL Fransman not out	4	26	13	-	-
HH Paulse b Essack	0	2	1	-	-
Extras (b 14, lb 3, w 4)	21				
TOTAL (73 overs)	**209**				

KWAZULU-NATAL	Runs	Mins	Balls	4	6
*MD Sanders lbw b Laing	17	72	38	2	-
†DR Miller b Fransman	20	32	29	3	-
AI Chinnappa c Laing b Fransman	0	4	4	-	-
KC Africa b Fransman	0	6	1	-	-
M Bekker c Stevens b Albertyn	53	131	81	8	-
T Essack c September b Laing	51	107	83	9	-
PM Selowa c Walters b Laing	19	51	34	4	-
R Frylinck not out	50	78	50	7	1
ZA Abrahim not out	8	24	25	-	-
TD Pillay					
ND Hewer					
Extras (b 5, lb 3, nb 3)	11				
TOTAL (for 7 wkts) (57 overs)	**229**				

KZN	O	M	R	W
Abrahim	11	7	22	2 (2 w)
Hewer	12	0	56	0 (1 w)
Africa	13	3	38	2 (1 w)
Frylinck	11	4	19	1
Pillay	15	4	28	1
Essack	9	4	19	2
Chinnappa	2	0	10	0
Bol	O	M	R	W
Paulse	12	2	58	0 (1 nb)
Fransman	12	2	34	3 (1 nb)
Albertyn	9	4	20	1 (1 nb)
Laing	14	2	80	3
September	4	1	16	0
Stevens	6	1	13	0

Fall of Wickets

	Bol	KZN
1st	53 (1)	29 (2)
2nd	64 (3)	29 (3)
3rd	87 (4)	33 (4)
4th	114 (2)	42 (1)
5th	137 (6)	150 (5)
6th	143 (5)	150 (6)
7th	167 (7)	193 (7)
8th	182 (9)	-
9th	209 (8)	-
10th	209 (11)	-

BORDER v WESTERN PROVINCE — SAA 3-day Challenge Pool B

Played at Mercedes-Benz Park, East London on 2,3,4 March 2006 — Toss: Border
Umpires: BN Harrison & LJ Willemse
Debuts: Bdr: None. WP: F Jardine (FC)
Close of play: Day 1: WP (1) 97-3 (Telo 7*, 24.3 overs). Day 2: Bdr (2) 134-2 (Gamiet 64*, Dyili 55*, 50.4 overs).
Result: Western Province won by 10 wickets
Points: Bdr: 5.58 (bat 1.58, bowl 4, match 0); WP: 20.54 (bat 6.54, bowl 4, match 10)

BORDER	*Runs*	*Mins*	*Balls*	*4*	*6*		*Runs*	*Mins*	*Balls*	*4*	*6*
KD Bennett c De Stadler b Friend	25	43	28	3	-	c Hantam b Friend	0	1	1	-	-
GE von Hoesslin b Hantam	0	11	10	-	-	run out (sub - F Behardien)	13	56	49	2	-
LL Gamiet c Williamson b Friend	34	74	57	6	-	c Gray b Jardine	93	295	274	9	-
†AZM Dyili c Gray b Hantam	1	15	9	-	-	c De Stadler b Jardine	60	136	116	6	2
*MN Ranger c Hantam b De Stadler	0	5	6	-	-	(11) absent hurt					
MX Pethu c Gray b Friend	15	55	38	2	-	(5) run out (Telo/De Stadler/sub - DJ Bassage)	10	31	27	2	-
DL Brown c De Stadler b Friend	0	1	1	-	-	(6) lbw b Jardine	13	52	46	-	-
S de Kock run out (Telo)	1	17	13	-	-	(7) c sub (F Behardien) b Jardine	30	46	39	4	1
L Mbane b Jardine	26	58	50	5	-	(8) c Canning b Jardine	0	1	2	-	-
M Ngam not out	20	43	40	2	-	(9) c sub (DJ Bassage) b De Stadler	27	30	25	4	1
Y Pangabantu						(10) not out	0	2	0	-	-
Extras (lb 6, nb 1)	7					Extras (lb 1, w 1, nb 1)	3				
TOTAL (for 9 wkts dec) (41.5 overs)	**129**					**TOTAL (96.2 overs)**	**249**				

WESTERN PROVINCE	*Runs*	*Mins*	*Balls*	*4*	*6*		*Runs*	*Mins*	*Balls*	*4*	*6*
AJA Gray c Mbane b Ranger	45	102	75	6	-	not out	4	1	1	1	-
M Williamson c Dyili b Pangabantu	10	39	20	1	-	not out	0	1	0	-	-
Z Homani c Dyili b Ranger	29	53	48	4	-						
FD Telo c Ngam b Brown	72	110	80	12	1						
R Munnik c Von Hoesslin b Brown	52	88	76	11	-						
JM Kuiper c Bennett b Ngam	18	55	34	2	-						
*†RCC Canning not out	64	136	97	7	-						
WC Hantam b De Kock	19	20	16	3	-						
F Jardine c Dyili b Gamiet	14	26	27	1	-						
M de Stadler c Gamiet b De Kock	26	38	35	1	-						
Q Friend b Brown	12	7	7	2	-						
Extras (b 4, lb 6, nb 6)	16					Extras	0				
TOTAL (84.5 overs)	**377**					**TOTAL (for 0 wkts) (0.1 overs)**	**4**				

WP	*O*	*M*	*R*	*W*		*O*	*M*	*R*	*W*	
Friend	19	3	65	4	(1 nb)	1.1	1	1	1	(1 nb)
Hantam	7	2	23	2						
De Stadler	12	5	20	1		(2) 33.2	11	74	1	
Jardine	3.5	0	15	1		46	11	118	5	(1 w)
Williamson						(3) 0.5	0	4	0	
Gray						(5) 15	0	51	0	
Bdr	*O*	*M*	*R*	*W*		*O*	*M*	*R*	*W*	
Ngam	15.3	1	76	1	(3 nb)					
Pangabantu	14	5	52	1						
Mbane	5	0	39	0						
Brown	17.5	2	83	3	(3 nb)					
Ranger	3.3	1	6	2						
De Kock	25	1	97	2						
Gamiet	4	0	14	1						
Bennett						(1) 0.1	0	4	0	

Fall of Wickets	**Bdr**	**WP**	**Bdr**	**WP**
1st	14 (2)	35 (2)	0 (1)	-
2nd	56 (1)	90 (3)	32 (2)	-
3rd	58 (4)	97 (1)	141 (4)	-
4th	59 (5)	203 (5)	159 (5)	-
5th	73 (3)	216 (4)	191 (6)	-
6th	73 (7)	245 (6)	202 (3)	-
7th	76 (8)	271 (8)	202 (8)	-
8th	87 (6)	296 (9)	249 (7)	-
9th	129 (9)	358 (10)	249 (9)	-
10th	-	377 (11)	-	-

EASTERN PROVINCE v BOLAND — SAA 3-day Challenge Pool B

Played at Sahara Oval St George's, Port Elizabeth on 9,10,11 March 2006 — Toss: Eastern Province
Umpires: BN Harrison & LJ Willemse
Debuts: EP: None. Bol: FA Geldenhuys (FC)
Close of play: Day 1: EP (1) 55-1 (Baxter 30*, Abrahams 8*, 15.5 overs). Day 2: Bol (2) 101-4 (Davids 47*, Geldenhuys 12*, 28.5 overs).
Result: Match drawn
Points: EP: 9.72 (bat 5.72, bowl 4, match 0); Bol: 7.76 (bat 4.76, bowl 3, match 0)

BOLAND	Runs	Mins	Balls	4	6		Runs	Mins	Balls	4	6
DJ Malan c Ingram b Theron	15	33	29	2	-	lbw b Tsotsobe	5	22	15	1	-
WD Hayward b Mjekula	16	63	42	2	-	c Adair b Mjekula	0	5	2	-	-
WC Swan b Howell	74	209	148	12	1	lbw b Mjekula	4	12	8	-	-
H Davids c Howell b Mjekula	69	172	121	12	-	st Adair b Howell	158	308	225	26	1
GC Stevens c and b Ingram	13	69	48	1	-	lbw b Dipha	18	58	45	2	-
FA Geldenhuys c Adair b Mjekula	4	16	15	-	-	b Willemse	24	120	64	4	-
*WA Albertyn run out (Dipha/Adair)	35	51	45	4	1	not out	101	212	159	13	-
†L-R Walters c sub (DD Carolus) b Ingram	22	35	37	3	-	not out	32	88	78	6	-
JM van Wyk c sub (DD Carolus) b Ingram	0	6	8	-	-						
BL Fransman c Howell b Ingram	0	2	3	-	-						
HH Paulse not out	3	9	17	-	-						
Extras (b 13, lb 12, w 4, nb 8)	37					Extras (b 4, lb 13, w 6, nb 8)	31				
TOTAL (84.1 overs)	**288**					**TOTAL (for 6 wkts dec) (98 overs)**	**373**				

EASTERN PROVINCE	Runs	Mins	Balls	4	6		Runs	Mins	Balls	4	6
*CA Ingram c Malan b Paulse	15	35	32	2	-	(2) b Stevens	28	69	62	4	-
C Baxter c Albertyn b Van Wyk	65	144	95	15	-	(1) c Albertyn b Paulse	1	10	8	-	-
U Abrahams c Walters b Albertyn	91	251	183	15	-	not out	51	121	78	10	-
L Dipha c Walters b Van Wyk	9	33	27	1	-	lbw b Stevens	5	18	14	1	-
RR Jeggels run out (Fransman/Stevens)	86	161	118	9	1	b Malan	5	12	17	1	-
†SR Adair c Paulse b Stevens	15	20	18	3	-	not out	7	30	22	1	-
GE Howell not out	37	41	32	2	2						
D Willemse not out	11	9	11	-	-						
J Theron											
S Mjekula											
LL Tsotsobe											
Extras (lb 1, nb 6)	7					Extras (b 5, lb 1, nb 2)	8				
TOTAL (for 6 wkts) (85 overs)	**336**					**TOTAL (for 4 wkts) (33.1 overs)**	**105**				

EP	O	M	R	W		O	M	R	W
Tsotsobe	13	3	43	0 (3 nb, 2 w)		16	1	51	1 (2 w)
Theron	12	2	47	1 (4 nb)	(3)	20	3	79	0 (5 nb, 1 w)
Mjekula	18	4	57	3 (1 nb, 1 w)	(2)	11	1	54	2 (3 nb, 1 w)
Dipha	6	2	19	0 (1 w)		17	4	55	1 (1 w)
Howell	21	5	58	1		15	3	55	1
Willemse	7	1	23	0		12	3	43	1
Ingram	7.1	0	16	4		7	0	19	0
Bol	O	M	R	W		O	M	R	W
Paulse	17	3	68	1 (1 nb)		5	2	13	1 (1 nb)
Van Wyk	18	3	76	2					
Fransman	15	3	70	0 (5 nb)	(2)	6	0	16	0 (1 nb)
Albertyn	15	4	37	1					
Stevens	13	1	51	1	(4)	10.1	3	22	2
Davids	7	2	33	0					
Swan					(3)	6	0	26	0
Malan					(5)	6	1	22	1

Fall of Wickets

	Bol	EP	Bol	EP
1st	37 (1)	34 (1)	0 (2)	8 (1)
2nd	54 (2)	126 (2)	6 (3)	52 (2)
3rd	201 (4)	137 (4)	10 (1)	64 (4)
4th	205 (3)	247 (3)	67 (5)	73 (5)
5th	212 (6)	266 (6)	172 (6)	-
6th	259 (5)	316 (5)	300 (4)	-
7th	267 (7)	-	-	-
8th	269 (9)	-	-	-
9th	269 (10)	-	-	-
10th	288 (8)	-	-	-

FINAL

WESTERN PROVINCE v NORTHERNS — SAA 3-day Challenge Final

Played at Sahara Park Newlands, Cape Town on 6,7,8,9 April 2006 — Toss: Northerns

Umpires: ZTA Ndamane & DJ Smith

Debuts: WP: None. Nor: None

Close of play: Day 1: WP (1) 6-0 (Gray 4*, Homani 1*, 1.2 overs). Day 2: WP (1) 290-8 (De Stadler 25*, Conrad 0*, 101.3 overs). Day 3: Nor (2) 230-3 (Van Wyk 83*, Paleker 18*, 85.4 overs).

Result: Northerns won by 100 runs

Notes: Dros scored his fifty off 38 balls in Northerns' 2nd innings.

SAA PROVINCIAL THREE-DAY CHALLENGE

NORTHERNS	Runs	Mins	Balls	4	6		Runs	Mins	Balls	4	6
MA Aronstam lbw b Philander	69	209	187	9	1	c De Stadler b Conrad	40	119	87	5	1
F du Plessis c Homani b Friend	16	27	17	2	-	c Canning b Friend	20	58	39	4	-
JG Myburgh b De Stadler	10	25	18	1	-	run out (Telo)	64	212	170	5	-
A Paleker b Conrad	48	135	116	5	-	(5) run out (Friend/Canning)	25	85	76	2	-
G Dros c Canning b De Stadler	59	143	103	8	1	(6) b De Stadler	62	52	44	2	7
†CFK van Wyk c Homani b Conrad	9	27	17	1	-	(4) c Canning b De Stadler	104	270	175	9	-
MJ Mokonyama b Conrad	11	27	27	-	-	not out	10	19	13	1	-
*P Joubert lbw b De Stadler	2	18	19	-	-						
AM Phangiso b Philander	27	75	57	4	-						
MA Mashimbyi not out	7	30	17	-	-						
FG Nkuna b Philander	0	3	1	-	-						
Extras (lb 3, nb 6)	9					Extras (b 2, lb 4, w 1, nb 1)	8				
TOTAL (95.2 overs)	**267**					**TOTAL (for 6 wkts dec) (100.3 overs)**	**333**				

WESTERN PROVINCE	Runs	Mins	Balls	4	6		Runs	Mins	Balls	4	6
AJA Gray c Dros b Nkuna	27	68	61	5	-	lbw b Mashimbyi	0	1	2	-	-
Z Homani lbw b Joubert	12	77	43	1	-	c Van Wyk b Mashimbyi	10	14	12	1	-
W Wyngaard c Van Wyk b Du Plessis	16	83	67	2	-	c Aronstam b Nkuna	3	19	7	-	-
FD Telo st Van Wyk b Aronstam	43	88	78	3	2	c Dros b Nkuna	9	14	13	1	-
VD Philander run out (Phangiso/Van Wyk)	66	159	122	5	5	lbw b Joubert	26	54	41	1	3
R Munnik lbw b Du Plessis	5	12	12	1	-	c Nkuna b Aronstam	32	85	66	5	-
JM Kuiper b Aronstam	15	35	27	3	-	b Joubert	4	17	12	-	-
*†RCC Canning c Van Wyk b Aronstam	68	174	145	11	-	c Van Wyk b Joubert	56	83	77	6	2
M de Stadler st Van Wyk b Aronstam	37	113	92	3	-	c Myburgh b Aronstam	12	35	26	1	-
S Conrad not out	9	39	23	2	-	c Phangiso b Du Plessis	11	31	14	2	-
Q Friend b Aronstam	4	3	5	1	-	not out	8	5	3	-	1
Extras (b 2, lb 4, nb 9)	15					Extras (b 4, lb 4, nb 4)	12				
TOTAL (111 overs)	**317**					**TOTAL (44.5 overs)**	**183**				

WP	O	M	R	W			O	M	R	W	
Friend	15	2	54	1		(2)	8	2	19	1	
Philander	24.2	7	57	3	(4 nb)	(1)	13	2	51	0	(1 nb)
De Stadler	28	10	74	3			29.3	9	92	2	
Conrad	28	3	79	3	(2 nb)		22	0	77	1	
Munnik							4	0	10	0	
Gray							24	5	78	0	(1 w)
Nor	O	M	R	W			O	M	R	W	
Nkuna	12	2	39	1	(7 nb)	(2)	5	0	23	2	(4 nb)
Mashimbyi	12	3	36	0	(1 nb)	(1)	4	0	17	2	
Joubert	20	8	41	1		(4)	9	5	10	3	
Dros	12	3	23	0							
Phangiso	7	1	31	0	(1 nb)	(6)	3	0	24	0	
Du Plessis	14	1	59	2		(5)	6.5	1	31	1	
Aronstam	34	10	82	5		(3)	17	5	70	2	

Fall of Wickets

	Nor	**WP**	**Nor**	**WP**
1st	24 (2)	42 (1)	36 (2)	0 (1)
2nd	42 (3)	44 (2)	85 (1)	14 (2)
3rd	146 (4)	100 (3)	189 (3)	17 (3)
4th	153 (1)	110 (4)	253 (5)	26 (4)
5th	176 (6)	115 (6)	287 (4)	71 (5)
6th	193 (7)	150 (7)	333 (6)	83 (7)
7th	210 (8)	228 (5)	-	99 (6)
8th	247 (5)	290 (8)	-	121 (9)
9th	267 (9)	313 (9)	-	171 (8)
10th	267 (11)	317 (11)	-	183 (10)

SAA PROVINCIAL ONE-DAY CHALLENGE

SAA PROVINCIAL ONE-DAY CHALLENGE 2005/06

Pool A	P	W	L	T	NR	Penalty	Pts	Net RR
Northerns	10	7	2	0	1	0	40	0.10
Gauteng	10	5	3	0	2	0	34	0.17
North West	10	4	4	0	2	0	31	0.51
Free State	10	3	4	1	2	0	28	0.40
Easterns	10	2	5	1	2	0	25	-0.37
Griqualand West	10	3	6	0	1	0	22	-0.85

Pool B	P	W	L	T	NR	Penalty	Pts	Net RR
Boland	9	7	2	0	0	0	38	0.33
Eastern Province	9	5	3	0	1	0	34	0.73
Western Province	9	6	3	0	0	0	33	0.07
KwaZulu-Natal	9	3	5	0	1	0	24	0.32
Border	9	2	6	0	1	0	18	-0.42
Zimbabwe Under-23	5	0	4	0	1	0	3	-1.89

Eastern Province were awarded the 6 points for the match against KwaZulu-Natal on 29th January as KwaZulu-Natal did not provide a satisfactory venue.
The following games were abandoned without a ball bowled:
Border v Zimbabwe U-23 at East London on 6 November 2005.
Griqualand West v North West at Kimberley on 12 February 2006
Easterns v Gauteng at Benoni on 26 February 2006

LEADING BATTING AVERAGES

		M	Inns	NO	Runs	HS		Avg	SR	100	50
1	DR Gain (Gau)	10	9	4	446	95	*	89.20	70.68	0	4
2	WC Swan (Bol)	11	10	5	395	96	*	79.00	75.52	0	3
3	B Hector (FS)	4	4	1	189	78		63.00	79.41	0	2
4	W Bossenger (GW)	8	8	2	354	157	*	59.00	100.56	1	1
5	K Smit (KZN)	3	3	0	162	75		54.00	123.66	0	2
6	HG Kuhn (Nor)	8	8	1	354	113	*	50.57	78.14	2	1
7	R Frylinck (KZN)	6	5	1	197	82	*	49.25	127.09	0	2
8	F du Plessis (Nor)	7	7	0	332	114		47.42	87.83	1	2
9	M Williamson (WP)	6	6	1	234	94		46.80	65.54	0	2
10	MA Aronstam (Nor)	9	9	1	360	120	*	45.00	73.61	1	2
11	WL Coetsee (NW)	5	5	1	177	130	*	44.25	106.62	1	0
	H Davids (Bol)	5	5	1	177	76		44.25	72.83	0	2
13	FD Telo (WP)	5	4	0	176	90		44.00	99.43	0	2
14	J le Roux (NW)	9	9	3	262	128	*	43.66	101.94	1	0
15	SJ Myburgh (Nor)	4	4	1	128	90	*	42.66	83.11	0	1
16	R Bhayat (NW)	7	6	2	166	76		41.50	99.40	0	1
17	WA Dugmore (Gau)	4	4	1	120	39		40.00	93.75	0	0
	GE Howell (EP)	8	5	1	160	115	*	40.00	136.75	1	0
	CFK van Wyk (Nor)	6	6	3	120	90	*	40.00	76.92	0	1
20	CJ de Jager (GW)	4	4	0	157	70		39.25	94.01	0	1

(Qualification: 3 completed innings)

LL Gamiet (Bdr) scored 217 runs and was dismissed only once.
D du Preez (FS) scored 159 runs and was dismissed only once.

SAA PROVINCIAL ONE-DAY CHALLENGE

LEADING BOWLING AVERAGES

		M	Overs	Mdns	Runs	Wkts	Avg	RpO	BB	4I
1	RR Richards (Bdr)	5	26	3	98	8	12.25	3.76	3-13	0
2	MN Ranger (Bdr)	6	37	2	137	11	12.45	3.70	4-42	1
3	S Burger (Gau)	3	24.2	2	104	8	13.00	4.27	5-44	1
4	S de Kock (Bdr)	5	30	0	121	8	15.12	4.03	3-38	0
5	PC Laing (Bol)	4	26	1	138	9	15.33	5.30	4-42	2
6	QG Samson (FS)	7	33	5	187	12	15.58	5.66	4-25	1
7	VCM Mazibuko (NW)	5	24	3	129	8	16.12	5.37	4-26	1
8	RA Stroh (NW)	6	34	3	156	9	17.33	4.58	2-16	0
9	J Theron (EP)	7	42.3	1	228	12	19.00	5.36	4-50	1
10	JT Mafa (Gau)	9	53	1	277	14	19.78	5.22	4-34	2
11	S Mjekula (EP)	7	44.2	7	181	9	20.11	4.08	4-50	1
12	J Coetzee (GW)	9	70.1	11	283	14	20.21	4.03	4-17	1
13	BL Fransman (Bol)	11	78	8	369	18	20.50	4.73	6-40	3
14	L Meyer (EP)	5	34	6	165	8	20.62	4.85	4-33	1
15	GE Howell (EP)	8	48	6	172	8	21.50	3.58	4-13	1
16	P Joubert (Nor)	12	87.3	6	369	17	21.70	4.21	3-31	0
17	LL Tsotsobe (EP)	5	37.2	3	181	8	22.62	4.84	5-28	1
18	FG Nkuna (Nor)	12	61	4	286	12	23.83	4.68	3-30	0
19	WC Hantam (WP)	7	51	7	221	9	24.55	4.33	5-31	1
20	MA Mashimbyi (Nor)	10	67.2	2	345	14	24.64	5.12	4-57	1

(Qualification: 8 wickets)

LEADING WICKETKEEPERS

		M	Ct	St	Total
1	C Linde (FS)	10	16	4	20
2	RCC Canning (WP)	9	14	3	17
3	DM van Wyk (Gau)	8	12	1	13
4	TM Bodibe (Eas)	9	9	3	12
5	W Bossenger (GW)	8	11	0	11

LEADING FIELDERS

		M	Ct
1	WL Coetsee (NW)	5	6
	BL Fransman (Bol)	11	6
	FS Holtzhausen (NW)	8	6
	WC Swan (Bol)	11	6
5	MA Aronstam (Nor)	9	5
	GE Howell (EP)	8	5
	P Joubert (Nor)	12	5
	WE September (Bol)	11	5
	DJ van Wyk (FS)	7	5
	D Wiese (Eas)	9	5

SAA PROVINCIAL ONE-DAY CHALLENGE

SCORECARDS

Pool A

FREE STATE v GAUTENG — SAA 1-day Challenge Pool A

Played at Goodyear Park, Bloemfontein on 9 October 2005 — Toss: Gauteng

Umpires: MZ Nanabhay & BDA Westraadt

Debuts: FS: ER Bezuidenhout (LO). Gau: HW le Roux and A Nawab (Both LO)

Result: Free State won by 5 wickets

Points: FS: 5; Gau: 1

Notes: Free State substitute: AP Abrahams replaced AJ Schultz after 41 overs of Gauteng's innings. Gauteng substitute: JT Mafa replaced MR Sekhoto after 13 overs of Free State's innings.

GAUTENG	*Runs*	*Mins*	*Balls*	*4*	*6*
SC Cook c Linde b Du Preez	30	32	32	4	-
BD Snijman c Bezuidenhout b Motsamai	2	11	8	-	-
BC Adams c Linde b Schultz	27	72	43	3	-
*†DR Gain not out	95	152	132	6	-
MR Sekhoto lbw b Thyssen	4	22	11	-	-
AM Omar c Van Wyk b Thyssen	6	17	12	-	-
S Burger b Malao	9	21	10	1	-
K Moothosamy c Linde b Du Preez	13	31	18	-	-
HW le Roux not out	9	6	5	-	-
BM Mathebula					
A Nawab					
JT Mafa					
Extras (b 1, lb 3, w 1, nb 1, p 5)	11				
TOTAL (for 7 wkts) (45 overs)	**206**				

FREE STATE	*Runs*	*Mins*	*Balls*	*4*	*6*
CA Ingram c Omar b Mathebula	1	7	6	-	-
*HG de Kock b Burger	18	72	47	3	-
DJ van Wyk c and b Nawab	53	110	80	6	-
PJ Koortzen c Omar b Burger	74	81	68	5	2
CA Thyssen c Mafa b Snijman	18	46	38	-	-
†C Linde not out	13	26	13	-	-
D du Preez not out	14	15	14	2	-
ER Bezuidenhout					
TS Motsamai					
AP Abrahams					
JMM Malao					
AJ Schultz					
Extras (lb 3, w 13)	16				
TOTAL (for 5 wkts) (44.2 overs)	**207**				

FS	*O*	*M*	*R*	*W*	
Du Preez	9	1	38	2	
Motsamai	9	1	37	1	(1 w)
Schultz	8	1	32	1	
Thyssen	9	0	42	2	(1 nb)
Malao	9	0	36	1	
Bezuidenhout	1	0	12	0	

Gau	*O*	*M*	*R*	*W*	
Le Roux	8	0	33	0	(3 w)
Mathebula	7	1	21	1	(1 w)
Burger	6.2	0	31	2	
Mafa	3	0	37	0	(2 w)
Nawab	9	0	33	1	
Adams	8	0	35	0	(3 w)
Snijman	3	0	14	1	(1 w)

Fall of Wickets	*Gau*	*FS*
1st	15 (2)	2 (1)
2nd	36 (1)	58 (2)
3rd	89 (3)	121 (3)
4th	104 (5)	177 (4)
5th	120 (6)	187 (5)
6th	149 (7)	-
7th	194 (8)	-

NORTH WEST v GRIQUALAND WEST — SAA 1-day Challenge Pool A

Played at Sedgars Park, Potchefstroom on 9 October 2005 — Toss: Griqualand West

Umpires: IL Howell & SW Liebisch

Debuts: NW: FA Steyn (LO). GW: D Donaldson, FPG Holtzhausen and R Pietersen (All LO)

Result: North West won by 6 wickets

Points: GW: 1; NW: 5

Notes: Bossenger scored his century off 77 balls in Griqualand West's innings. Coetsee scored his century off 83 balls in North West's innings. Griqualand West substitute: ES Tsamaisi replaced M Bosman after 12 overs of North West's innings.

GRIQUALAND WEST	*Runs*	*Mins*	*Balls*	*4*	*6*
AP McLaren c Coetsee b Mazibuko	31	50	43	5	-
*†W Bossenger not out	157	176	127	21	-
M Bosman c Steyn b Akoojee	32	59	43	2	1
J Brooker run out (Moleon)	7	9	8	1	-
AK Kruger c and b Coetsee	12	21	23	-	-
J Coetzee c Holtzhausen b GH Bhayat	26	30	27	1	1
BW Lemmetjies not out	4	2	1	1	-
D Donaldson					
FPG Holtzhausen					
NO Arthur					
R Pietersen					
ES Tsamaisi					
Extras (lb 3, w 14, nb 2)	19				
TOTAL (for 5 wkts) (45 overs)	**288**				

NORTH WEST	*Runs*	*Mins*	*Balls*	*4*	*6*
FA Steyn c Donaldson b Coetzee	0	2	3	-	-
DJ Kgamadi c Lemmetjies b Coetzee	8	12	9	2	-
M Akoojee lbw b Tsamaisi	71	117	82	8	-
J le Roux c Brooker b Kruger	17	14	10	4	-
WL Coetsee not out	130	138	96	14	3
R Bhayat not out	47	45	37	4	2
FS Holtzhausen					
†TA Bula					
*EO Moleon					
GH Bhayat					
VCM Mazibuko					
Extras (b 6, lb 1, w 10, nb 3)	20				
TOTAL (for 4 wkts) (39 overs)	**293**				

NW	O	M	R	W	
GH Bhayat	9	0	50	1	(3 w)
Moleon	7	0	49	0	(2 w)
Mazibuko	4	0	33	1	(3 w)
Holtzhausen	8	0	55	0	(1 nb, 5 w)
Coetsee	8	0	51	1	
Akoojee	9	0	47	1	(1 nb)

GW	O	M	R	W	
Coetzee	8	1	65	2	
Kruger	6	0	38	1	(3 w)
Pietersen	6	0	30	0	
Donaldson	7	0	40	0	(2 nb)
Arthur	3	0	33	0	(1 w)
Holtzhausen	4	0	23	0	(1 w)
Tsamaisi	2	0	20	1	(1 nb, 2 w)
Lemmetjies	3	0	37	0	(1w)

Fall of Wickets	GW	NW
1st	72 (1)	0 (1)
2nd	191 (3)	10 (2)
3rd	203 (4)	37 (4)
4th	237 (5)	172 (3)
5th	283 (6)	-

EASTERNS v NORTHERNS

SAA 1-day Challenge Pool A

Played at Willowmoore Park, Benoni on 9 October 2005

Toss: Northerns

Umpires: BG Jerling & S Wadvalla

Debuts: Eas: IC Hlengane, M Oosthuizen and D Wiese (All LO). Nor: None

Result: Northerns won by 8 runs

Points: Eas: 1; Nor: 5

NORTHERNS	Runs	Mins	Balls	4	6
MA Aronstam lbw b Abrahams	43	74	64	4	-
†HG Kuhn c Bodibe b Abrahams	20	41	27	3	-
F du Plessis c Bodibe b Abrahams	0	16	4	-	-
P de Bruyn not out	66	126	93	2	-
G Dros c Bodibe b Wiese	0	6	6	-	-
MJ Mokonyama c Bodibe b Hlengane	16	34	23	3	-
*P Joubert c Seymore b Hlengane	22	32	27	1	1
AM Phangiso b Reddy	2	5	4	-	-
AC Thomas c Abrahams b Hlengane	3	9	11	-	-
MA Mashimbyi not out	13	17	14	-	-
FG Nkuna					
Extras (b 3, lb 3, w 9, nb 3)	18				
TOTAL (for 8 wkts) (45 overs)	**203**				

EASTERNS	Runs	Mins	Balls	4	6
W Barresi c Dros b Thomas	0	20	17	-	-
AJ Seymore c Kuhn b De Bruyn	48	87	55	5	-
G Toyana c De Bruyn b Joubert	13	23	13	3	-
J Booysen run out (De Bruyn)	28	40	30	4	-
D Wiese run out (Joubert)	45	81	51	4	1
*SP O'Connor c De Bruyn b Joubert	14	24	18	1	1
BL Reddy c Du Plessis b Aronstam	19	36	41	1	-
M Oosthuizen b Joubert	2	6	5	-	-
†TM Bodibe not out	4	26	13	-	-
S Abrahams st Kuhn b Aronstam	3	6	8	-	-
IC Hlengane c Kuhn b Thomas	8	10	9	1	-
Extras (lb 6, w 4, nb 1)	11				
TOTAL (43.1 overs)	**195**				

Eas	O	M	R	W	
Reddy	9	0	43	1	(2 w)
Oosthuizen	3	0	28	0	(2 nb, 3 w)
Abrahams	9	1	32	3	(1 nb, 1 w)
Wiese	9	1	36	1	(2 w)
O'Connor	6	0	33	0	(1 w)
Hlengane	9	1	25	3	

Nor	O	M	R	W	
Thomas	8.1	1	28	2	(1 w)
Nkuna	3	0	16	0	(1 nb)
Joubert	9	0	40	3	
Mashimbyi	2	0	8	0	
De Bruyn	3	0	19	1	
Aronstam	9	1	43	2	
Phangiso	9	1	35	0	(2 w)

Fall of Wickets	Nor	Eas
1st	53 (2)	9 (1)
2nd	67 (3)	41 (3)
3rd	77 (1)	92 (4)
4th	78 (5)	92 (2)
5th	113 (6)	129 (6)
6th	158 (7)	165 (7)
7th	161 (8)	169 (8)
8th	170 (9)	181 (5)
9th	-	186 (10)
10th	-	195 (11)

GAUTENG v EASTERNS

SAA 1-day Challenge Pool A

Played at Orban Park, University of Johannesburg, Johannesburg on 16 October 2005

Toss: Easterns

Umpires: CJ Conradie & EC Hendrikse

Debuts: Gau: BW Buckley, CE Knox and PG Thompson (All LO). Eas: None

Result: Gauteng won by 7 wickets

Points: Eas: 1; Gau: 5

Notes: Easterns substitute: A Nel replaced AJ Seymore after 0 overs of Gauteng's innings. Gauteng substitute: BW Buckley replaced A Nawab after 0 overs of Gauteng's innings.

EASTERNS	Runs	Mins	Balls	4	6
S Mandan c Omar b Thompson	5	21	17	-	-
AJ Seymore b Burger	54	94	53	9	-
GH Bodi c Omar b Burger	30	34	30	3	1
J Booysen lbw b Burger	0	2	2	-	-
D Wiese c Omar b Knox	12	20	15	2	-
G Toyana c Gain b Thompson	17	50	25	2	1
*SP O'Connor c Moothosamy b Burger	1	10	9	-	-
R Almeida lbw b Thompson	4	11	4	1	-
†TM Bodibe not out	17	63	41	2	-
IC Hlengane c Moothosamy b Burger	17	27	23	1	-
PT Mofokeng lbw b De Bruin	16	31	35	1	-
A Nel					
Extras (lb 5, w 10, nb 1)	16				
TOTAL (42.1 overs)	**189**				

GAUTENG	Runs	Mins	Balls	4	6
DL Makalima b Nel	3	32	17	-	-
BW Buckley c Toyana b Almeida	27	49	36	4	-
BC Adams run out (Booysen)	48	122	78	4	-
*DR Gain not out	81	127	112	11	-
MR Sekhoto not out	20	21	15	4	-
K Moothosamy					
†AM Omar					
S Burger					
CE Knox					
PG Thompson					
GJ de Bruin					
A Nawab					
Extras (lb 5, w 8)	13				
TOTAL (for 3 wkts) (43 overs)	**192**				

Gau	O	M	R	W	
De Bruin	8.1	2	28	1	(1 nb)
Thompson	9	1	40	3	(1 w)
Burger	9	1	44	5	(3 w)
Knox	7	0	43	1	(1 w)
Adams	3	1	15	0	(1 w)
Nawab	6	0	14	0	

Eas	O	M	R	W	
Nel	8	1	35	1	(4 w)
Almeida	8	0	41	1	(3 w)
Wiese	9	0	30	0	(1 w)
O'Connor	3	0	24	0	
Hlengane	9	0	32	0	
Bodi	6	0	25	0	

Fall of Wickets	Eas	Gau
1st	15 (1)	23 (1)
2nd	55 (3)	41 (2)
3rd	55 (4)	161 (3)
4th	93 (5)	-
5th	112 (2)	-
6th	119 (7)	-
7th	130 (8)	-
8th	136 (6)	-
9th	161 (10)	-
10th	189 (11)	-

NORTHERNS v NORTH WEST

SAA 1-day Challenge Pool A

Played at SuperSport Park, Centurion on 16 October 2005

Toss: North West

Umpires: SB Lambson & JEP Ostrom

Debuts: Nor: None. NW: C Jonker (LO)

Result: Northerns won by 6 wickets

Points: Nor: 6; NW: 0

NORTH WEST	Runs	Mins	Balls	4	6
FA Steyn c Dros b Nkuna	14	14	13	3	-
DJ Kgamadi b Thomas	23	27	19	4	-
M Akoojee c Phangiso b Nkuna	3	20	12	-	-
J le Roux c Kuhn b Mashimbyi	14	22	17	3	-
WL Coetsee c Thomas b De Bruyn	29	67	38	4	-
R Bhayat c Kuhn b Joubert	14	31	27	2	-
†TA Bula c Kuhn b De Bruyn	13	22	16	2	-
FS Holtzhausen c Joubert b Thomas	14	33	28	2	-
*EO Moleon c Mokonyama b Mashimbyi	32	71	63	1	-
C Jonker b Joubert	5	30	20	-	-
F de Wet not out	3	11	8	-	-
Extras (w 19, nb 1)	20				
TOTAL (43.2 overs)	**184**				

NORTHERNS	Runs	Mins	Balls	4	6
MA Aronstam c Kgamadi b Moleon	48	77	61	9	-
†HG Kuhn c Bula b Holtzhausen	27	53	25	3	-
F du Plessis c Holtzhausen b Jonker	43	71	59	6	-
P de Bruyn lbw b Coetsee	30	59	43	3	-
G Dros not out	24	23	16	1	2
AM Phangiso not out	2	11	6	-	-
MJ Mokonyama					
*P Joubert					
AC Thomas					
MA Mashimbyi					
FG Nkuna					
Extras (b 1, lb 5, w 5)	11				
TOTAL (for 4 wkts) (35 overs)	**185**				

Nor	O	M	R	W	
Thomas	8	0	45	2	(3 w)
Nkuna	5	0	25	2	
Joubert	9	2	31	2	
Mashimbyi	7.2	0	41	2	(1 nb, 4 w)
De Bruyn	9	1	24	2	(2 w)
Phangiso	5	0	18	0	(2 w)

NW	O	M	R	W	
De Wet	7	0	23	0	(1 w)
Moleon	9	1	37	1	(1 w)
Holtzhausen	6	1	37	1	(3 w)
Jonker	5	0	46	1	
Coetsee	6	0	25	1	
Akoojee	2	0	11	0	

Fall of Wickets	NW	Nor
1st	23 (1)	59 (2)
2nd	40 (2)	99 (1)
3rd	42 (3)	146 (3)
4th	57 (4)	170 (4)
5th	96 (6)	-
6th	112 (5)	-
7th	116 (7)	-
8th	143 (8)	-
9th	173 (10)	-
10th	184 (9)	-

GRIQUALAND WEST v FREE STATE

SAA 1-day Challenge Pool A

Played at De Beers Diamond Oval, Kimberley on 23 October 2005

Toss: Griqualand West

Umpires: JEP Ostrom & BDA Westraadt

Debuts: GW: J-PH Triegaardt (LO). FS: None

Result: Free State won by 90 runs

Points: FS: 6; GW: 0

Notes: Griqualand West substitute: J-PH Triegaardt replaced R Pietersen after 25.5 overs of Griqualand West's innings.

FREE STATE	Runs	Mins	Balls	4	6
CA Ingram c Holtzhausen b Kruger	8	6	11	1	-
*HG de Kock c Bossenger b Coetzee	7	28	19	1	-
DJ van Wyk c and b Holtzhausen	52	105	75	7	-
PJ Koortzen b Donaldson	45	65	45	8	-
SR Sibande run out (Lemmetjies)	0	10	8	-	-
†C Linde c Bossenger b Pietersen	6	22	12	-	-
D du Preez not out	88	69	62	8	5
R Telemachus not out	53	50	40	4	3
JMM Malao					
TS Motsamai					
QG Samson					
Extras (b 1, lb 5, w 2, nb 2)	10				
TOTAL (for 6 wkts) (45 overs)	**269**				

GRIQUALAND WEST	Runs	Mins	Balls	4	6
AP McLaren c Linde b Du Preez	10	2	6	1	1
*†W Bossenger c Linde b Du Preez	17	32	27	3	-
M Bosman b Samson	16	55	26	-	-
J Brooker c Linde b Motsamai	1	5	5	-	-
AK Kruger run out (Du Preez/Linde)	21	15	13	5	-
J Coetzee c Koortzen b Motsamai	0	11	2	-	-
BW Lemmetjies c Malao b Motsamai	8	15	11	2	-
D Donaldson not out	50	90	60	4	1
FPG Holtzhausen c Motsamai b Telemachus	29	44	38	3	-
J-PH Triegaardt st Linde b Malao	10	24	22	-	-
NO Arthur st Linde b Malao	2	12	16	-	-
R Pietersen					
Extras (lb 2, w 7, nb 6)	15				
TOTAL (36.4 overs)	**179**				

GW	O	M	R	W	
Coetzee	9	2	31	1	
Kruger	9	0	66	1	(1 nb)
Pietersen	9	0	82	1	(1 w)
Donaldson	6	1	50	1	(1 w)
Arthur	9	1	16	0	
Holtzhausen	3	0	18	1	(1 nb)

FS	O	M	R	W	
Du Preez	9	1	31	2	
Motsamai	9	0	54	3	(3 nb, 5 w)
Samson	2	0	25	1	(3 nb, 2 w)
Malao	7.4	2	35	2	
Telemachus	5	0	16	1	
Koortzen	4	0	16	0	

Fall of Wickets	FS	GW
1st	9 (1)	10 (1)
2nd	28 (2)	41 (2)
3rd	113 (4)	42 (4)
4th	118 (5)	72 (5)
5th	119 (3)	73 (3)
6th	141 (6)	85 (6)
7th	-	86 (7)
8th	-	141 (9)
9th	-	171 (10)
10th	-	179 (11)

FREE STATE v NORTH WEST — SAA 1-day Challenge Pool A

Played at Goodyear Park, Bloemfontein on 30 October 2005 — Toss: Free State

Umpires: CJ Conradie & BM White

Debuts: FS: MP Fick and LN Mosena (Both LO). NW: JS Hermitage (LO)

Result: North West won by 85 runs

Points: FS: 0; NW: 6

Notes: Free State substitute: LN Mosena replaced QG Samson after 0 overs of Free State's innings. North West substitute: VCM Mazibuko replaced R Bhayat after 0 overs of Free State's innings.

NORTH WEST	Runs	Mins	Balls	4	6
*DJ Kgamadi c Linde b Motsamai	79	167	118	3	-
FA Steyn c Van Wyk b Samson	23	34	34	4	-
M Akoojee c Hector b Malao	47	81	56	4	1
J le Roux c Linde b Thyssen	28	28	29	4	-
R Bhayat lbw b Thyssen	5	18	8	-	-
†TA Bula c Linde b Motsamai	16	17	11	-	1
FS Holtzhausen c Malao b Thyssen	10	21	10	-	-
*EO Moleon b Thyssen	12	19	9	1	-
JS Hermitage not out	0	4	0	-	-
F de Wet not out	2	2	1	-	-
F van der Merwe					
VCM Mazibuko					
Extras (lb 6, w 6, nb 6)	18				
TOTAL (for 8 wkts) (45 overs)	**240**				

FREE STATE	Runs	Mins	Balls	4	6
MP Fick c De Wet b Holtzhausen	7	9	10	1	-
DJ van Wyk c Bula b Moleon	19	56	30	2	-
*B Hector c and b Hermitage	51	115	81	6	1
PJ Koortzen b Van der Merwe	6	19	11	1	-
†C Linde c Kgamadi b Mazibuko	21	24	20	3	1
CA Thyssen lbw b Hermitage	17	30	16	1	-
D du Preez c Holtzhausen b De Wet	2	7	8	-	-
LN Mosena c Holtzhausen b Mazibuko	5	13	8	-	-
TS Motsamai lbw b Hermitage	9	24	17	-	-
JMM Malao c Holtzhausen b Mazibuko	0	3	1	-	-
BK Sekonyane not out	4	12	12	-	-
QG Samson					
Extras (b 1, lb 3, w 10)	14				
TOTAL (35.4 overs)	**155**				

FS	O	M	R	W	
Du Preez	9	1	51	0	
Sekonyane	5	0	35	0	(5 nb)
Samson	6	1	32	1	(4 w)
Motsamai	9	0	47	2	(1 nb, 1 w)
Malao	9	0	25	1	(1 w)
Thyssen	6	0	38	4	
Koortzen	1	0	6	0	

NW	O	M	R	W	
De Wet	6	1	21	1	(2 w)
Holtzhausen	5	0	22	1	(2 w)
Van der Merwe	7	1	37	1	(1 w)
Moleon	7	0	26	1	(1 w)
Mazibuko	5	0	29	3	(4 w)
Hermitage	5.4	0	16	3	

Fall of Wickets	NW	FS
1st	39 (2)	8 (1)
2nd	134 (3)	54 (2)
3rd	173 (4)	69 (4)
4th	198 (5)	100 (5)
5th	200 (1)	129 (3)
6th	223 (6)	132 (7)
7th	236 (7)	135 (6)
8th	238 (8)	146 (8)
9th	-	147 (10)
10th	-	155 (9)

NORTHERNS v GAUTENG — SAA 1-day Challenge Pool A

Played at LC de Villiers Oval, University of Pretoria, Pretoria on 30 October 2005 — Toss: Gauteng

Umpires: S George & BDA Westraadt

Debuts: Nor: L Manzini and AL Ndlovu (Both LO). Gau: DM van Wyk (LO)

Result: Gauteng won by 7 wickets

Points: Gau: 5; Nor: 1

Notes: Gauteng substitute: DM van Wyk replaced JT Mafa. Northerns substitute: AL Ndlovu replaced FG Nkuna

NORTHERNS	Runs	Mins	Balls	4	6
MA Aronstam b Nawab	51	111	74	6	-
†HG Kuhn c Omar b Terbrugge	5	29	17	-	-
JG Myburgh c Mafa b Terbrugge	3	8	8	-	-
EE Meyer c Nawab b De Bruin	13	46	32	1	-
MA Mashimbyi run out (Burger/Omar)	4	12	6	-	-
G Dros c Omar b Mafa	10	34	18	-	-
MJ Mokonyama c Sekhoto b Nawab	1	7	6	-	-
*P Joubert not out	53	72	54	7	-
AM Phangiso c Omar b Nawab	18	34	35	1	-
AL Ndlovu b Burger	5	23	17	-	-
L Manzini c Omar b Terbrugge	0	4	4	-	-
FG Nkuna					
Extras (lb 9, w 5, nb 2)	16				
TOTAL (44.5 overs)	**179**				

GAUTENG	Runs	Mins	Balls	4	6
WA Dugmore c Aronstam b Dros	35	45	39	5	-
DM van Wyk c Dros b Mashimbyi	38	73	53	5	-
K Moothosamy lbw b Phangiso	19	47	29	2	-
DR Gain not out	50	76	62	8	-
MR Sekhoto not out	26	58	64	3	-
DL Makalima					
*S Burger					
†AM Omar					
DJ Terbrugge					
A Nawab					
GJ de Bruin					
JT Mafa					
Extras (lb 1, w 11)	12				
TOTAL (for 3 wkts) (41.1 overs)	**180**				

Gau	O	M	R	W	
Terbrugge	8.5	0	31	3	(1 w)
Burger	9	1	29	1	(2 w)
De Bruin	9	0	49	1	(2 nb)
Mafa	8	0	32	1	(2 w)
Nawab	9	2	25	3	
Dugmore	1	0	4	0	

Nor	O	M	R	W	
Mashimbyi	6	0	31	1	(4 w)
Manzini	6	0	33	0	(2 w)
Joubert	1	0	10	0	(2 w)
Dros	6	0	24	1	(1 w)
Myburgh	7	1	30	0	
Phangiso	9	0	29	1	(1 w)
Aronstam	6.1	2	22	0	

Fall of Wickets	Nor	Gau
1st	24 (2)	61 (1)
2nd	31 (3)	95 (2)
3rd	72 (4)	105 (3)
4th	83 (5)	-
5th	95 (1)	-
6th	99 (7)	-
7th	102 (6)	-
8th	142 (9)	-
9th	178 (10)	-
10th	179 (11)	-

EASTERNS v GRIQUALAND WEST — SAA 1-day Challenge Pool A

Played at Willowmoore Park, Benoni on 29 October 2005 — Toss: Easterns

Umpires: JD Cloete & ZTA Ndamane

Debuts: Eas: E Nyawo and HA van Straaten (Both LO). GW: TR Plaatjie (LO)

Result: Griqualand West won by 4 wickets

Points: Eas: 1; GW: 5

Notes: Easterns substitute: E Nyawo replaced S Mandan during Easterns' innings. Griqualand West substitute: FPG Holtzhausen replaced TR Plaatjie after 35 overs of Easterns' innings.

EASTERNS	Runs	Mins	Balls	4	6
W Barresi c Kruger b Plaatjie	1	10	8	-	-
HA van Straaten c and b NO Arthur	43	109	60	5	1
S Mandan c Bossenger b Coetzee	7	22	14	1	-
J Booysen c Bossenger b Plaatjie	7	6	9	1	-
G Toyana lbw b Coetzee	0	3	3	-	-
D Wiese run out (Kruger)	59	74	56	9	1
*SP O'Connor c and b Lemmetjies	20	69	50	1	-
BL Reddy c Bossenger b Coetzee	5	12	14	-	-
R Almeida lbw b Coetzee	4	9	11	-	-
†TM Bodibe c Bossenger b NO Arthur	0	8	8	-	-
IC Hlengane not out	10	31	32	1	-
E Nyawo					
Extras (lb 9, w 9, nb 4)	22				
TOTAL (43.2 overs)	**178**				

GRIQUALAND WEST	Runs	Mins	Balls	4	6
MC Arthur lbw b Reddy	8	7	8	-	-
AP McLaren lbw b Wiese	43	57	48	9	-
AK Kruger b O'Connor	33	61	33	5	1
J Brooker c Hlengane b Wiese	1	17	12	-	-
M Bosman c Barresi b Wiese	15	44	34	2	-
*†W Bossenger c Bodibe b Almeida	33	84	66	-	-
J Coetzee not out	30	48	46	2	-
D Donaldson not out	4	3	2	1	-
BW Lemmetjies					
NO Arthur					
FPG Holtzhausen					
TR Plaatjie					
Extras (lb 2, w 8, nb 4)	14				
TOTAL (for 6 wkts) (40.4 overs)	**181**				

GW	O	M	R	W	
Coetzee	9	2	17	4	(4 w)
Plaatjie	5	1	23	2	(3 w)
Kruger	8	1	52	0	(4 nb, 2 w)
NO Arthur	9	1	34	2	
Donaldson	8	0	32	0	
Holtzhausen	4	0	10	0	
Lemmetjies	0.2	0	1	1	

Eas	O	M	R	W	
Almeida	7	1	39	1	(1 nb, 2 w)
Reddy	9	0	56	1	(3 nb, 2 w)
Wiese	9	3	25	3	(3 w)
O'Connor	9	0	32	1	(1 w)
Hlengane	5.4	1	24	0	
Toyana	1	0	3	0	

Fall of Wickets	Eas	GW
1st	5 (1)	10 (1)
2nd	23 (3)	87 (2)
3rd	30 (4)	93 (3)
4th	30 (5)	95 (4)
5th	125 (2)	125 (5)
6th	133 (6)	174 (6)
7th	141 (8)	-
8th	146 (9)	-
9th	148 (10)	-
10th	178 (7)	-

GRIQUALAND WEST v NORTHERNS — SAA 1-day Challenge Pool A

Played at De Beers Diamond Oval, Kimberley on 6 November 2005
Toss: Griqualand West
Umpires: SW Liebisch & BDA Westraadt
Debuts: GW: CN Bennett (LO). Nor: H Malan (LO)
Result: Griqualand West won by 2 wickets
Points: GW: 6; Nor: 0

NORTHERNS	Runs	Mins	Balls	4	6
MA Aronstam c Coetzee b Donaldson	25	50	41	3	-
†HG Kuhn c McLaren b Coetzee	17	32	25	3	-
JG Myburgh lbw b NO Arthur	35	84	50	4	2
H Malan c and b Donaldson	2	8	6	-	-
G Dros c McLaren b Donaldson	10	30	22	1	-
MJ Mokonyama c NO Arthur b Donaldson	5	19	14	-	-
*P Joubert not out	22	55	43	2	-
AM Phangiso c McLaren b NO Arthur	2	9	8	-	-
MA Mashimbyi c and b NO Arthur	2	7	6	-	-
BT Mokonyama c Donaldson b NO Arthur	3	12	13	-	-
FG Nkuna c Bennett b Coetzee	1	18	14	-	-
Extras (lb 4, w 6, nb 1)	11				
TOTAL (40.1 overs)	**135**				

GRIQUALAND WEST	Runs	Mins	Balls	4	6
†AP McLaren b Myburgh	8	12	11	1	-
M Bosman c Phangiso b Mashimbyi	1	7	3	-	-
J Coetzee c Joubert b Dros	41	108	72	2	2
*J Brooker c Phangiso b Myburgh	4	8	7	-	-
AK Kruger b Joubert	21	36	37	4	-
D Donaldson lbw b Dros	14	35	23	2	-
MC Arthur run out (BT Mokonyama/Kuhn)	5	7	7	1	-
CN Bennett b Joubert	0	2	1	-	-
FPG Holtzhausen not out	18	29	23	3	-
NO Arthur not out	8	18	13	-	-
R Pietersen					
Extras (lb 10, w 6)	16				
TOTAL (for 8 wkts) (32.5 overs)	**136**				

GW	O	M	R	W	
Coetzee	8.1	0	25	2	(1 w)
Kruger	4	0	23	0	(1 nb, 1 w)
Pietersen	7	0	30	0	(1 w)
Donaldson	9	2	22	4	(2 w)
NO Arthur	9	2	19	4	
Holtzhausen	3	0	12	0	(1 w)

Nor	O	M	R	W	
Mashimbyi	8	2	26	1	(2 w)
Myburgh	6	0	29	2	(2 w)
Joubert	7	1	25	2	(1 w)
Phangiso	5	0	21	0	
BT Mokonyama	2	0	7	0	
Dros	4.5	0	18	2	(1 w)

Fall of Wickets	Nor	GW
1st	41 (2)	12 (2)
2nd	55 (1)	12 (1)
3rd	67 (4)	16 (4)
4th	92 (5)	51 (5)
5th	104 (3)	94 (6)
6th	106 (6)	105 (7)
7th	111 (8)	105 (8)
8th	115 (9)	115 (3)
9th	126 (10)	-
10th	135 (11)	-

NORTH WEST v EASTERNS — SAA 1-day Challenge Pool A

Played at Sedgars Park, Potchefstroom on 6 November 2005
Toss: Easterns
Umpires: JEP Ostrom & IH van Kerwel
Debuts: NW: None. Eas: NJ Livi and J Theunissen (Both LO)
Result: North West won by 155 runs
Points: Eas: 0; NW: 6
Notes: Le Roux scored his century off 93 balls in North West's innings.

NORTH WEST	Runs	Mins	Balls	4	6
FA Steyn c and b O'Connor	49	64	52	6	1
DJ Kgamadi b Reddy	13	29	17	1	-
M Akoojee c Mofokeng b Almeida	76	149	93	4	-
J le Roux not out	128	121	106	11	4
R Bhayat not out	8	7	4	-	1
*RA Stroh					
†TA Bula					
FS Holtzhausen					
F de Wet					
JS Hermitage					
GH Bhayat					
Extras (w 6, nb 3)	9				
TOTAL (for 3 wkts) (45 overs)	**283**				

EASTERNS	Runs	Mins	Balls	4	6
HA van Straaten b Holtzhausen	19	34	26	4	-
J Theunissen c and b Holtzhausen	10	23	16	1	-
NJ Livi c Bula b Holtzhausen	0	3	3	-	-
J Booysen c Bula b Stroh	12	26	18	2	-
D Wiese b GH Bhayat	28	53	37	4	1
*SP O'Connor b Stroh	7	17	6	1	-
†TM Bodibe not out	19	61	42	1	-
BL Reddy b Hermitage	0	6	4	-	-
R Almeida b GH Bhayat	0	2	1	-	-
JT Maziya c GH Bhayat b Hermitage	16	29	22	3	-
PT Mofokeng lbw b De Wet	0	3	2		
Extras (lb 7, w 10)	17				
TOTAL (29.3 overs)	**128**				

Eas	O	M	R	W	
Reddy	9	1	58	1	(1 w)
Almeida	9	1	51	1	(1 nb, 2 w)
O'Connor	9	0	47	1	
Wiese	9	1	50	0	(2 nb, 2 w)
Mofokeng	7	1	61	0	(1 w)
Booysen	2	0	16	0	

NW	O	M	R	W	
Holtzhausen	6	0	30	3	(2 w)
GH Bhayat	9	0	30	2	(7 w)
De Wet	5.3	0	20	1	
Stroh	4	0	21	2	
Hermitage	5	1	20	2	

Fall of Wickets	NW	Eas
1st	21 (2)	27 (2)
2nd	71 (1)	27 (3)
3rd	259 (3)	34 (1)
4th	-	56 (4)
5th	-	72 (6)
6th	-	91 (5)
7th	-	94 (8)
8th	-	95 (9)
9th	-	127 (10)
10th	-	128 (11)

FREE STATE v NORTHERNS — SAA 1-day Challenge Pool A

Played at University of Free State Ground, Bloemfontein on 13 November 2005 — Toss: Northerns
Umpires: LM Engelbrecht & BDA Westraadt
Debuts: FS: None. Nor: None
Result: Northerns won by 17 runs
Points: FS: 1; Nor: 5
Notes: Bosman scored his fifty off 31 balls in Free State's innings. Northerns substitute: BT Mokonyama replaced MJ Mokonyama during Free State's innings.

NORTHERNS	Runs	Mins	Balls	4	6
MA Aronstam not out	120	179	124	8	1
†HG Kuhn c Motsamai b Fick	68	112	96	6	-
JG Myburgh c Koortzen b Malao	4	10	9	-	-
G Dros c Motsamai b Deacon	54	43	38	5	2
AM Phangiso not out	2	10	4	-	-
H Malan					
MJ Mokonyama					
*P Joubert					
MA Mashimbyi					
L Manzini					
FG Nkuna					
BT Mokonyama					
Extras (b 1, lb 4, w 8, nb 1)	14				
TOTAL (for 3 wkts) (45 overs)	**262**				

FREE STATE	Runs	Mins	Balls	4	6
LL Bosman lbw b Myburgh	73	82	56	7	2
MP Fick c Malan b Nkuna	4	15	7	-	-
WA Deacon c Mashimbyi b Joubert	58	86	68	6	1
*PJ Koortzen lbw b Joubert	3	6	6	-	-
DJ van Wyk b Phangiso	21	40	25	1	-
†C Linde run out (Myburgh)	7	20	19	1	-
SR Sibande b Phangiso	6	19	17	-	-
D du Preez not out	55	47	45	2	4
TS Motsamai lbw b Aronstam	2	4	7	-	-
JMM Malao not out	7	29	20	-	-
AJ Schultz					
Extras (b 3, lb 1, w 5)	9				
TOTAL (for 8 wkts) (45 overs)	**245**				

FS	O	M	R	W
Deacon	9	0	50	1 (1 nb)
Du Preez	9	1	51	0 (1 w)
Motsamai	9	0	49	0
Schultz	4	0	31	0 (2 w)
Malao	9	0	47	1 (1 w)
Fick	5	0	29	1 (2 w)

Nor	O	M	R	W
Mashimbyi	5	0	35	0 (2 w)
Nkuna	4	0	25	1
Joubert	9	0	38	2 (1 w)
Phangiso	9	0	39	2 (2 w)
Myburgh	9	0	69	1
Aronstam	9	0	35	1

Fall of Wickets	Nor	FS
1st	143 (2)	23 (2)
2nd	154 (3)	124 (1)
3rd	247 (4)	130 (4)
4th	-	147 (3)
5th	-	168 (6)
6th	-	172 (5)
7th	-	188 (7)
8th	-	193 (9)

GAUTENG v NORTH WEST — SAA 1-day Challenge Pool A

Played at Liberty Life Wanderers Stadium, Johannesburg on 20 November 2005 — Toss: Gauteng
Umpires: SW Liebisch & GH Pienaar
Debuts: Gau: S Chatterjee (LO). NW: JP Campher (LO)
Result: Gauteng won by 1 wicket
Points: Gau: 5; NW: 1
Notes: Gauteng substitute: MR Sekhoto replaced JT Mafa after 0 overs of Gauteng's innings.

NORTH WEST	Runs	Mins	Balls	4	6
DJ Kgamadi lbw b Terbrugge	14	43	40	-	1
*RA Stroh c Van Wyk b Chatterjee	27	105	52	2	-
M Akoojee c Terbrugge b Mafa	6	18	12	1	-
J le Roux b Mafa	14	15	18	3	-
WL Coetsee c Van Wyk b Chatterjee	8	13	12	2	-
PM van Niekerk c Van Wyk b Mafa	3	24	12	-	-
FS Holtzhausen c Van Wyk b De Bruin	16	62	35	-	-
†TA Bula c Van Wyk b Mafa	0	3	3	-	-
GH Bhayat c Makalima b De Bruin	24	33	28	3	1
VCM Mazibuko not out	24	40	33	3	-
JP Campher c Mafa b Snijman	15	30	25	3	-
Extras (lb 4, w 12, nb 8)	24				
TOTAL (43.4 overs)	**175**				

GAUTENG	Runs	Mins	Balls	4	6
WA Dugmore c Bhayat b Mazibuko	38	45	41	7	-
BD Snijman b Mazibuko	18	61	38	3	-
DL Makalima c Bula b Mazibuko	29	42	29	3	2
*DR Gain c Akoojee b Stroh	39	97	79	3	1
WB Motaung b Mazibuko	0	8	5	-	-
MR Sekhoto c Coetsee b Bhayat	8	32	23	1	-
†DM van Wyk lbw b Stroh	4	14	12	1	-
DJ Terbrugge c Coetsee b Holtzhausen	15	39	25	1	1
GJ de Bruin run out (Akoojee/Bula)	1	5	1	-	-
S Chatterjee not out	10	23	16	2	-
BM Mathebula not out	1	4	2	-	-
JT Mafa					
Extras (lb 1, w 11, nb 1)	13				
TOTAL (for 9 wkts) (45 overs)	**176**				

Gau	O	M	R	W
Terbrugge	9	1	20	1 (2 nb)
De Bruin	9	1	30	2 (1 w)
Mafa	8	0	34	4 (1 nb, 5 w)
Chatterjee	9	0	43	2 (1 nb, 3 w)
Snijman	2.4	0	14	1 (1 w)
Mathebula	6	0	30	0 (4 nb, 2 w)

NW	O	M	R	W
Campher	3	0	21	0 (4 w)
Bhayat	7	0	39	1 (1 w)
Holtzhausen	9	2	40	1 (1 w)
Mazibuko	9	3	26	4 (1 nb, 4 w)
Coetsee	9	0	29	0
Stroh	6	1	16	2 (1 w)
Van Niekerk	2	0	4	0

Fall of Wickets	NW	Gau
1st	28 (1)	58 (1)
2nd	36 (3)	76 (2)
3rd	53 (4)	106 (3)
4th	71 (5)	108 (5)
5th	79 (2)	133 (6)
6th	86 (6)	141 (7)
7th	86 (8)	152 (4)
8th	127 (9)	153 (9)
9th	140 (7)	174 (8)
10th	175 (11)	-

GRIQUALAND WEST v GAUTENG — SAA 1-day Challenge Pool A

Played at De Beers Diamond Oval, Kimberley on 27 November 2005 — Toss: Griqualand West
Umpires: MZ Nanabhay & BDA Westraadt
Debuts: GW: CJ de Jager (LO). Gau: None
Result: Gauteng won by 93 runs
Points: Gau: 6; GW: 0
Notes: McLaren kept wicket when Bossenger bowled in Gauteng innings. Gauteng substitute: MR Sekhoto replaced JT Mafa after 38.2 overs of Gauteng's innings. Griqualand West substitute: M Bosman replaced R Pietersen after 23.1 overs of Griqualand West's innings.

GAUTENG	Runs	Mins	Balls	4	6
BD Snijman c Kruger b Coetzee	39	65	48	6	1
WB Motaung c Bossenger b Coetzee	1	17	11	-	-
WA Dugmore c Kruger b Donaldson	39	52	36	6	1
*DR Gain not out	76	125	90	6	1
ET Nkwe lbw b Pietersen	16	35	26	2	-
BC Adams b Pietersen	4	2	3	1	-
†DM van Wyk b Kruger	23	51	36	-	-
MR Sekhoto c Triegaardt b Kruger	0	2	1	-	-
GJ de Bruin not out	30	28	22	2	2
A Nawab					
S Chatterjee					
JT Mafa					
Extras (lb 9, w 1, nb 3)	13				
TOTAL (for 7 wkts) (45 overs)	**241**				

GRIQUALAND WEST	Runs	Mins	Balls	4	6
CJ de Jager c Nawab b Snijman	46	37	37	7	1
CN Bennett c Gain b De Bruin	15	42	25	2	-
D Donaldson c Van Wyk b Nawab	16	61	26	2	-
AP McLaren c Dugmore b Snijman	1	11	10	-	-
J Brooker c Motaung b Chatterjee	6	7	8	1	-
*W Bossenger c Motaung b Chatterjee	1	6	7	-	-
AK Kruger c Van Wyk b Chatterjee	6	8	9	1	-
J Coetzee st Van Wyk b Nawab	25	44	37	2	-
M Bosman c Van Wyk b Adams	20	31	27	2	-
†J-PH Triegaardt b Nawab	0	1	3	-	-
NO Arthur not out	1	3	1	-	-
R Pietersen					
Extras (lb 8, w 3)	11				
TOTAL (31.4 overs)	**148**				

GQ	O	M	R	W	
Coetzee	9	2	33	2	
Kruger	9	2	39	2	(2 nb)
Donaldson	8	0	63	1	(1 w)
Pietersen	9	0	53	2	(1 nb)
Arthur	9	0	36	0	
Bossenger	1	0	8	0	

Gau	O	M	R	W	
De Bruin	6	2	22	1	
Chatterjee	9	1	47	3	(2 w)
Snijman	6	1	22	2	(1 w)
Nawab	5	0	28	3	
Dugmore	4	0	17	0	
Adams	1.4	0	4	1	

Fall of Wickets	Gau	GQ
1st	22 (2)	62 (1)
2nd	81 (1)	62 (2)
3rd	85 (3)	63 (4)
4th	118 (5)	71 (5)
5th	122 (6)	74 (6)
6th	180 (7)	86 (7)
7th	180 (8)	100 (3)
8th	-	144 (8)
9th	-	144 (10)
10th	-	148 (9)

EASTERNS v FREE STATE — SAA 1-day Challenge Pool A

Played at Willowmoore Park, Benoni on 27 November 2005 — Toss: Free State
Umpires: DJ Smith & BM White
Debuts: Eas: None. FS: RA Reeves (LO)
Result: Tied (D/L method), target revised to 175 in 25 overs.
Points: Eas: 3; FS: 3
Notes: Easterns substitute: NJ Livi replaced PT Mofokeng after 9.4 overs of Easterns' innings. Free State substitute: JMM Malao replaced B Hector after 17 overs of Easterns' innings.

FREE STATE	Runs	Mins	Balls	4	6
*HG de Kock c Hlengane b Mofokeng	24	46	34	4	-
LN Mosena c and b Van den Berg	64	120	90	5	1
RA Reeves c Van den Berg b Mofokeng	34	31	27	5	-
B Hector not out	28	67	50	-	-
DJ van Wyk not out	22	24	21	3	-
†C Linde					
D du Preez					
T Tshabalala					
TS Motsamai					
BK Sekonyane					
QG Samson					
JMM Malao					
Extras (b 4, lb 1, w 14, nb 5)	24				
TOTAL (for 3 wkts) (37 overs)	**196**				

EASTERNS	Runs	Mins	Balls	4	6
S Mandan c Linde b Sekonyane	8	8	10	1	-
AJ Seymore b Du Preez	59	98	68	7	-
AM van den Berg b Du Preez	6	15	9	-	-
J Booysen b Motsamai	24	25	14	4	-
NJ Livi b Samson	12	21	13	-	1
G Toyana b Motsamai	6	6	6	1	-
D Wiese c Samson b Tshabalala	25	44	23	-	2
*SP O'Connor not out	10	15	10	-	-
R Almeida run out (Tshabalala)	0	1	1	-	-
†TM Bodibe not out	0	2	0	-	-
IC Hlengane					
PT Mofokeng					
Extras (lb 6, w 13, nb 5)	24				
TOTAL (for 8 wkts) (25 overs)	**174**				

Eas	O	M	R	W
Almeida	5	0	19	0 (2 w)
Wiese	7	2	35	0 (1 nb, 2 w)
O'Connor	5	0	41	0
Mofokeng	9	0	49	2 (4 w)
Van den Berg	9	0	42	1 (1 w)
Hlengane	2	0	5	0

FS	O	M	R	W
Du Preez	5	1	30	2 (1 w)
Sekonyane	4	0	23	1 (1 w)
Samson	5	0	44	1 (5 nb, 3 w)
Motsamai	5	0	33	2
Tshabalala	5	0	26	1
Malao	1	0	12	0 (4 w)

Fall of Wickets	FS	Eas
1st	49 (1)	9 (1)
2nd	105 (3)	22 (3)
3rd	157 (2)	58 (4)
4th	-	95 (5)
5th	-	107 (6)
6th	-	153 (2)
7th	-	173 (7)
8th	-	173 (9)

GRIQUALAND WEST v EASTERNS — SAA 1-day Challenge Pool A

Played at De Beers Diamond Oval, Kimberley on 22 January 2006 — Toss: Easterns

Umpires: CJ Conradie & BDA Westraadt

Debuts: GW: AG Doherty and LA Kruger (Both LO). Eas: RG Mutch (LO)

Result: Easterns won by 5 wickets

Points: Eas: 6; GW: 0

Notes: Booysen scored his fifty off 21 balls in Easterns' innings. Wiese scored his fifty off 23 balls in Easterns' innings. McLaren kept wicket when Bossenger bowled in Easterns' innings.

GRIQUALAND WEST	Runs	Mins	Balls	4	6
*†W Bossenger c Seymore b Wiese	32	8	11	6	1
AP McLaren c Wiese b O'Connor	20	18	13	2	1
AG Doherty c Mutch b O'Connor	3	12	4	-	-
J Brooker c Bodibe b Mutch	12	7	6	2	-
CN Bennett c Wiese b O'Connor	23	17	9	3	1
CJ de Jager c Wiese b O'Connor	14	20	18	2	-
D Donaldson c Wiese b Hlengane	21	27	23	1	-
AK Kruger st Bodibe b Hlengane	35	38	23	1	2
J Coetzee b Wiese	7	13	13	-	-
LA Kruger b Wiese	0	1	1	-	-
NO Arthur not out	0	2	1	-	-
Extras (lb 1, w 4)	5				
TOTAL (20.2 overs)	**172**				

EASTERNS	Runs	Mins	Balls	4	6
S Mandan c De Jager b Coetzee	16	12	10	1	1
AJ Seymore c Doherty b AK Kruger	4	17	9	-	-
HA van Straaten b Donaldson	14	19	10	3	-
J Booysen lbw b LA Kruger	67	45	28	7	5
G Toyana c Brooker b AK Kruger	3	7	5	-	-
D Wiese not out	52	33	23	4	4
*SP O'Connor not out	1	9	5	-	-
†TM Bodibe					
RG Mutch					
IC Hlengane					
PT Mofokeng					
Extras (b 4, lb 1, w 9, nb 2)	16				
TOTAL (for 5 wkts) (14.4 overs)	**173**				

Eas	O	M	R	W
Wiese	4	0	47	3 (1 w)
Mutch	3	0	31	1
O'Connor	5	0	36	4 (1 w)
Mofokeng	5	0	36	0 (1 w)
Hlengane	3.2	0	21	2

GW	O	M	R	W
Coetzee	3	0	24	1 (1 w)
AK Kruger	5	0	58	2 (1 nb, 3 w)
Donaldson	3	0	31	1 (1 nb)
Arthur	1	0	22	0 (1 w)
LA Kruger	1	0	21	1
Bossenger	1.4	0	12	0

Fall of Wickets	GW	Eas
1st	39 (1)	21 (1)
2nd	55 (2)	23 (2)
3rd	57 (3)	53 (3)
4th	73 (4)	65 (5)
5th	102 (5)	142 (4)
6th	112 (6)	-
7th	144 (7)	-
8th	168 (9)	-
9th	168 (10)	-
10th	172 (8)	-

NORTH WEST v NORTHERNS — SAA 1-day Challenge Pool A

Played at Sedgars Park, Potchefstroom on 22 January 2006 — Toss: North West

Umpires: LM Engelbrecht & SW Liebisch

Debuts: NW: NM Serame (LO). Nor: N Chouhan, SJ Myburgh and N Wagner (All LO)

Result: Northerns won by 9 runs

Points: Nor: 5; NW: 1

Notes: Northerns substitute: FG Nkuna replaced HG Kuhn after 2 overs of North West's innings.

NORTHERNS	Runs	Mins	Balls	4	6
MA Aronstam lbw b Campher	4	2	4	1	-
HG Kuhn c Mazibuko b Campher	2	23	12	-	-
AN Petersen c Steyn b Holtzhausen	10	13	11	2	-
N Chouhan c Coetsee b Serame	39	90	51	5	1
SJ Myburgh c Coetsee b Holtzhausen	4	10	6	1	-
†CFK van Wyk not out	90	152	114	5	1
MJ Mokonyama lbw b Stroh	1	2	2	-	-
*P Joubert not out	58	76	72	2	3
MA Mashimbyi					
N Wagner					
L Manzini					
FG Nkuna					
Extras (lb 2, w 11, nb 2)	15				
TOTAL (for 6 wkts) (45 overs)	**223**				

NORTH WEST	Runs	Mins	Balls	4	6
FA Steyn c Wagner b Nkuna	22	43	34	3	-
DJ Kgamadi c Van Wyk b Joubert	18	35	19	4	-
M Akoojee st Van Wyk b Aronstam	23	78	41	3	-
J le Roux c Petersen b Mashimbyi	11	25	18	1	-
WL Coetsee c Mashimbyi b Wagner	10	22	17	1	-
*RA Stroh c Aronstam b Joubert	74	104	88	4	1
FS Holtzhausen c Myburgh b Petersen	19	31	22	2	-
†TA Bula b Mashimbyi	23	33	23	1	-
VCM Mazibuko c Wagner b Joubert	1	4	2	-	-
JP Campher not out	3	14	5	-	-
NM Serame not out	1	3	1	-	-
Extras (lb 2, w 7)	9				
TOTAL (for 9 wkts) (45 overs)	**214**				

NW	O	M	R	W	
Campher	7	0	36	2	(1 nb, 4 w)
Holtzhausen	9	1	35	2	(1 w)
Stroh	9	1	19	1	(4 w)
Coetsee	5	0	44	0	(1 w)
Mazibuko	6	0	41	0	(1 nb)
Serame	9	0	46	1	(1 w)

Nor	O	M	R	W	
Wagner	8	1	29	1	(1 w)
Manzini	3	0	16	0	
Joubert	9	1	31	3	(1 w)
Nkuna	7	1	29	1	(1 w)
Mashimbyi	7	0	37	2	(3 w)
Aronstam	8	0	46	1	
Petersen	3	0	24	1	(1 w)

Fall of Wickets	Nor	NW
1st	4 (1)	35 (2)
2nd	15 (3)	42 (1)
3rd	21 (2)	64 (4)
4th	32 (5)	80 (5)
5th	96 (4)	96 (3)
6th	97 (7)	140 (7)
7th	-	196 (8)
8th	-	198 (9)
9th	-	211 (6)

GAUTENG v FREE STATE — SAA 1-day Challenge Pool A

Played at Liberty Life Wanderers Stadium, Johannesburg on 29 January 2006 — Toss: Free State
Umpires: JEP Ostrom & BM White
Debuts: Gau: MS Templeton (LO). FS: None
Result: No result
Points: FS: 3; Gau: 3

FREE STATE	Runs	Mins	Balls	4	6
*HG de Kock b Mafa	107	167	128	12	-
MP Fick c Snijman b Mafa	10	15	8	1	1
B Hector lbw b Nkwe	78	133	86	10	-
DJ van Wyk c Gain b Nkwe	24	35	25	3	-
†C Linde c Nkwe b Mafa	12	9	9	2	-
RA Reeves c Van Wyk b Mafa	2	8	4	-	-
LN Mosena b Nkwe	7	10	5	1	-
TS Motsamai not out	6	6	6	-	-
QG Samson					
JMM Malao					
BK Sekonyane					
Extras (b 1, lb 7, w 15, nb 1)	24				
TOTAL (for 7 wkts) (45 overs)	**270**				

GAUTENG	Runs	Mins	Balls	4	6
BD Snijman c Van Wyk b Motsamai	9	15	13	-	1
WB Motaung not out	11	26	11	1	-
WA Dugmore not out	8	11	12	2	-
*DR Gain					
ET Nkwe					
†DM van Wyk					
BC Adams					
MS Templeton					
HW le Roux					
A Nawab					
JT Mafa					
Extras (b 1, w 3)	4				
TOTAL (for 1 wkt) (6 overs)	**32**				

Gau	O	M	R	W	
Le Roux	7	0	49	0	
Mafa	9	1	49	4	(1 w)
Nkwe	9	0	57	3	(1 nb, 4 w)
Templeton	6	0	37	0	(9 w)
Motaung	1	0	6	0	
Nawab	9	0	42	0	(1 w)
Adams	4	0	22	0	

FS	O	M	R	W	
Sekonyane	3	0	5	0	(1 w)
Motsamai	3	0	26	1	(2 w)

Fall of Wickets	FS	Gau
1st	16 (2)	20 (1)
2nd	202 (3)	-
3rd	234 (1)	-
4th	250 (5)	-
5th	256 (4)	
6th	258 (6)	-
7th	270 (7)	-

EASTERNS v NORTH WEST — SAA 1-day Challenge Pool A

Played at Willowmoore Park, Benoni on 29 January 2006 — Toss: Easterns
Umpires: CJ Conradie & LM Engelbrecht
Debuts: Eas: None. NW: HM Strydom (LO)
Result: No result
Points: Eas: 3; NW: 3

NORTH WEST	Runs	Mins	Balls	4	6
FA Steyn c Bodibe b Mutch	5	10	10	1	-
DJ Kgamadi c Booysen b O'Connor	18	48	31	-	-
M Akoojee b Hlengane	43	75	73	3	1
J le Roux not out	29	48	43	3	-
*RA Stroh not out	7	10	12	-	-
HM Strydom					
R Bhayat					
†TA Bula					
JS Hermitage					
F van der Merwe					
VCM Mazibuko					
Extras (lb 1, w 3)	4				
TOTAL (for 3 wkts) (28.1 overs)	**106**				

EASTERNS
HA van Straaten
AJ Seymore
NJ Livi
J Booysen
G Toyana
D Wiese
*SP O'Connor
E Nyawo
†TM Bodibe
IC Hlengane
RG Mutch

Eas	O	M	R	W	
Wiese	6	0	19	0	(1 w)
Mutch	6	1	21	1	
Hlengane	8.1	1	26	1	
O'Connor	6	0	30	1	(2 w)
Toyana	2	0	9	0	

Fall of Wickets	NW
1st	7 (1)
2nd	45 (2)
3rd	93 (3)

FREE STATE v GRIQUALAND WEST

SAA 1-day Challenge Pool A

Played at Goodyear Park, Bloemfontein on 4 February 2006

Toss: Free State

Umpires: CJ Conradie & BM White

Debuts: FS: W van der Schyff (LO). GW: None

Result: Free State won by 202 runs

Points: FS: 6; GW: 0

Notes: Griqualand West substitute: W Bossenger replaced R Pietersen after 0 overs of Griqualand West's innings.

FREE STATE	*Runs*	*Mins*	*Balls*	*4*	*6*
*HG de Kock c Brooker b Pietersen	36	85	65	4	-
MP Fick st McLaren b Arthur	57	96	60	2	2
DJ van Wyk b Arthur	32	46	37	2	-
LN Mosena c Tsamaisi b Pietersen	33	47	38	1	-
CA Thyssen c Kruger b Pietersen	37	38	29	1	3
W van der Schyff not out	37	42	37	2	-
†C Linde not out	22	15	14	3	-
JF Mostert					
QG Samson					
JMM Malao					
BK Sekonyane					
Extras (lb 10, w 2, nb 10)	22				
TOTAL (for 5 wkts) (45 overs)	**276**				

GRIQUALAND WEST	*Runs*	*Mins*	*Balls*	*4*	*6*
*W Bossenger c Linde b Sekonyane	0	2	5	-	-
AG Doherty c Linde b Fick	27	72	51	4	-
CN Bennett b Sekonyane	0	9	4	-	-
J Brooker c Linde b Samson	0	6	4	-	-
†AP McLaren c Van Wyk b Samson	0	7	2	-	-
J Coetzee c Van Wyk b Van der Schyff	5	22	11	-	-
AK Kruger c Mosena b Mostert	20	38	23	3	-
D Donaldson b Fick	4	12	8	1	-
NO Arthur not out	1	31	17	-	-
ES Tsamaisi b Mostert	5	13	16	1	-
TR Plaatjie c Thyssen b Malao	7	11	10	1	-
R Pietersen					
Extras (b 1, lb 1, w 3)	5				
TOTAL (25.1 overs)	**74**				

GW	*O*	*M*	*R*	*W*	
Coetzee	9	3	35	0	
Kruger	8	0	60	0	(3 nb)
Pietersen	9	0	51	3	(1 nb, 1 w)
Donaldson	4	0	27	0	(5 nb, 1 w)
Arthur	9	1	45	2	
Tsamaisi	3	0	18	0	
Plaatjie	3	0	30	0	(1 nb)

FS	*O*	*M*	*R*	*W*	
Sekonyane	5	2	13	2	
Samson	6	3	10	2	
Van der Schyff	4	0	22	1	(2 w)
Fick	5	1	16	2	(1 w)
Mostert	4	1	10	2	
Malao	1.1	0	1	1	

Fall of Wickets	*FS*	*GW*
1st	98 (1)	0 (1)
2nd	108 (2)	0 (3)
3rd	172 (3)	3 (4)
4th	180 (4)	7 (5)
5th	237 (5)	24 (6)
6th	-	50 (2)
7th	-	61 (8)
8th	-	61 (7)
9th	-	67 (10)
10th	-	74 (11)

NORTHERNS v EASTERNS

SAA 1-day Challenge Pool A

Played at SuperSport Park, Centurion on 12 February 2006

Toss: Northerns

Umpires: LM Engelbrecht & SB Lambson

Debuts: Nor: None. Eas: None

Result: Northerns won by 5 runs

Points: Eas: 1; Nor: 5

NORTHERNS	*Runs*	*Mins*	*Balls*	*4*	*6*
HG Kuhn c M Morkel b JA Morkel	102	154	116	11	-
SJ Myburgh lbw b De Bruyn	31	56	42	4	-
JG Myburgh c M Morkel b Bodi	71	92	79	6	1
F du Plessis st Bodibe b Bodi	0	8	4	-	-
AM Phangiso st Bodibe b Bodi	8	22	14	-	-
†CFK van Wyk c Wiese b Bodi	1	3	2	-	-
*P Joubert run out (Wiese/Bodi)	6	6	7	1	-
MA Mashimbyi not out	9	14	7	-	-
AC Thomas not out	15	6	7	2	-
MJ Mokonyama					
FG Nkuna					
Extras (lb 2, w 6, nb 8)	16				
TOTAL (for 7 wkts) (45 overs)	**259**				

EASTERNS	*Runs*	*Mins*	*Balls*	*4*	*6*
S Mandan c Thomas b Nkuna	16	23	24	2	1
GH Bodi b Thomas	39	109	57	3	-
Z de Bruyn run out (Phangiso/Van Wyk)	22	41	26	4	-
J Booysen lbw b Du Plessis	40	54	52	4	1
JA Morkel c sub (N Chouhan) b Du Plessis	52	51	41	4	2
D Wiese b Du Plessis	12	13	15	1	-
*SP O'Connor c Kuhn b Du Plessis	10	12	15	1	-
E Nyawo c Thomas b JG Myburgh	11	22	18	1	-
M Morkel b Thomas	35	22	20	2	4
†TM Bodibe b Joubert	1	8	3	-	-
IC Hlengane not out	1	6	1	-	-
Extras (lb 8, w 6, nb 1)	15				
TOTAL (44.2 overs)	**254**				

Eas	*O*	*M*	*R*	*W*	
M Morkel	8	0	60	0	(5 nb, 5 w)
JA Morkel	9	0	38	1	
Wiese	6	0	38	0	(1 w)
De Bruyn	7	0	39	1	
Hlengane	4	0	21	0	
O'Connor	4	0	28	0	
Bodi	7	0	33	4	(3 nb)

Nor	*O*	*M*	*R*	*W*	
Thomas	7.2	0	30	2	(1 nb, 2 w)
Nkuna	5	0	28	1	
Mashimbyi	6	0	32	0	
Joubert	8	0	47	1	(1 w)
Du Plessis	9	0	47	4	
Phangiso	8	0	55	0	(1 w)
JG Myburgh	1	0	7	1	

Fall of Wickets	*Nor*	*Eas*
1st	74 (2)	23 (1)
2nd	216 (3)	74 (3)
3rd	218 (1)	119 (2)
4th	220 (4)	127 (4)
5th	222 (6)	149 (6)
6th	232 (7)	169 (7)
7th	238 (5)	207 (5)
8th	-	213 (8)
9th	-	241 (10)
10th	-	254 (9)

GAUTENG v NORTHERNS — SAA 1-day Challenge Pool A

Played at Walter Milton Oval, University of Witwatersrand, Johannesburg on 19 February 2006 Toss: Northerns
Umpires: LM Engelbrecht & DJ Smith
Debuts: Gau: None. Nor: None
Result: Northerns won by 17 runs
Points: Gau: 1; Nor: 5
Notes: Gauteng substitute: CE Knox replaced JT Mafa during Northerns' innings.

NORTHERNS	Runs	Mins	Balls	4	6
HG Kuhn not out	113	179	135	8	-
F du Plessis c Van Wyk b Mafa	15	37	27	1	-
JG Myburgh c Motaung b Singh	1	12	11	-	-
P de Bruyn b Mafa	0	2	1	-	-
G Dros b Nkwe	7	24	16	1	-
†A Paleker run out (Otto/Van Wyk)	34	67	51	2	1
*P Joubert c Adams b Nkwe	22	21	24	3	-
MA Mashimbyi not out	4	10	8	-	-
AM Phangiso					
FG Nkuna					
L Manzini					
Extras (b 6, lb 4, w 2, nb 3)	15				
TOTAL (for 6 wkts) (45 overs)	**211**				

GAUTENG	Runs	Mins	Balls	4	6
WB Motaung lbw b Mashimbyi	0	4	3	-	-
CE Knox run out (Nkuna)	29	61	44	5	-
DL Makalima run out (Kuhn)	0	16	12	-	-
*DR Gain lbw b Nkuna	0	14	9	-	-
BD Snijman lbw b De Bruyn	54	124	79	2	-
JM Otto c and b De Bruyn	19	20	20	2	1
†DM van Wyk c Myburgh b Joubert	52	87	70	1	1
ET Nkwe lbw b Dros	1	5	2	-	-
BC Adams not out	22	30	22	-	1
Y Singh run out (De Bruyn/Mashimbyi)	1	3	1	-	-
A Nawab c and b Mashimbyi	5	3	3	1	-
JT Mafa					
Extras (b 1, lb 5, w 4, nb 1)	11				
TOTAL (44 overs)	**194**				

Gau	O	M	R	W	
Mafa	9	0	26	2	(1 nb)
Singh	9	2	35	1	(1 w)
Nkwe	9	0	52	2	(2 nb)
Nawab	8	0	39	0	(1 w)
Snijman	4.4	0	14	0	
Adams	4	0	20	0	
Motaung	1.2	0	15	0	

Nor	O	M	R	W	
Mashimbyi	8	0	34	2	(1 nb, 1 w)
Nkuna	7	2	18	1	(1 w)
Manzini	3	0	14	0	
Joubert	8	0	25	1	
De Bruyn	7	0	47	2	
Phangiso	5	0	17	0	
Du Plessis	2	0	13	0	(1 w)
Dros	4	0	20	1	(1 w)

Fall of Wickets	Nor	Gau
1st	31 (2)	3 (1)
2nd	32 (3)	12 (3)
3rd	34 (4)	19 (4)
4th	53 (5)	45 (2)
5th	154 (6)	73 (6)
6th	192 (7)	141 (5)
7th	-	153 (8)
8th	-	185 (7)
9th	-	187 (10)
10th	-	194 (11)

NORTH WEST v FREE STATE — SAA 1-day Challenge Pool A

Played at Sedgars Park, Potchefstroom on 19 February 2006 Toss: North West
Umpires: JEP Ostrom & BM White
Debuts: NW: None. FS: None
Result: North West won by 1 wicket
Points: FS: 1; NW: 5
Notes: Beukes scored his century off 87 balls in Free State's innings. De Wet scored his fifty off 31 balls in North West's innings.

FREE STATE	Runs	Mins	Balls	4	6
JA Beukes lbw b Stroh	127	166	117	16	3
*HG de Kock c Bula b Coetsee	47	108	75	5	-
B Hector b Stroh	32	25	21	3	1
PJ Koortzen b Coetsee	2	10	5	-	-
CA Thyssen c Bhayat b Holtzhausen	43	37	28	1	3
†C Linde b De Wet	25	20	20	2	-
MP Fick not out	1	7	1	-	-
TS Motsamai b De Wet	2	3	5	-	-
QG Samson					
JMM Malao					
BK Sekonyane					
Extras (lb 2, w 4, nb 2)	8				
TOTAL (for 7 wkts) (45 overs)	**287**				

NORTH WEST	Runs	Mins	Balls	4	6
FA Steyn b Samson	14	28	18	1	-
DJ Kgamadi c De Kock b Sekonyane	6	15	14	-	-
M Akoojee c Linde b Sekonyane	1	9	3	-	-
WL Coetsee b Samson	0	5	3	-	-
J le Roux c Linde b Sekonyane	0	6	1	-	-
R Bhayat c sub (LN Mosena) b Samson	76	96	74	6	4
FS Holtzhausen b Sekonyane	30	52	41	3	1
*RA Stroh run out (De Kock/Linde)	2	19	8	-	-
†TA Bula not out	76	82	59	4	3
CO Moleon b De Kock	20	20	17	-	-
F de Wet not out	56	40	32	7	3
Extras (lb 2, w 4, nb 2)	8				
TOTAL (for 9 wkts) (44.4 overs)	**289**				

NW	O	M	R	W	
De Wet	9	1	37	2	(2 nb, 2 w)
Bhayat	4	0	32	0	
Holtzhausen	9	0	63	1	(1 w)
Moleon	9	0	39	0	
Stroh	7	0	59	2	(1 w)
Coetsee	7	0	55	2	

FS	O	M	R	W	
Koortzen	6	0	40	0	
Sekonyane	9	0	38	4	(2 w)
Samson	9	1	51	3	(1 nb)
Motsamai	3	0	18	0	
Fick	4.4	0	53	0	(1 nb, 1 w)
Malao	9	0	47	0	(1 w)
De Kock	4	0	40	1	

Fall of Wickets	FS	NW
1st	139 (2)	14 (2)
2nd	187 (3)	21 (3)
3rd	200 (4)	21 (1)
4th	240 (1)	21 (4)
5th	282 (5)	21 (5)
6th	285 (6)	89 (7)
7th	287 (8)	98 (8)
8th	-	148 (6)
9th	-	187 (10)

Highest 10th wicket partnerships in List A limited overs matches			
106*	IVA Richards and MA Holding	West Indies v England (Manchester)	1984
102*	TA Bula and F de Wet	North West v Free State (Potchefstroom)	2005/06

The 102* by Bula and De Wet is the highest by a team batting second to win a match. They came together with 101 needed in 9.5 overs and got the runs with 2 balls remaining.

NORTHERNS v FREE STATE — SAA 1-day Challenge Pool A

Played at LC de Villiers Oval, University of Pretoria, Pretoria on 26 February 2006 — Toss: Northerns
Umpires: LM Engelbrecht & GH Pienaar
Debuts: Nor: JR Jumat (LO). FS: D Elgar (LO)
Result: No result
Points: FS: 3; Nor: 3
Notes: Northerns substitute: JR Jumat replaced N Chouhan

NORTHERNS	Runs	Mins	Balls	4	6
N Chouhan c Linde b Samson	6	14	10	-	-
F du Plessis c Mostert b Samson	95	106	85	8	2
SJ Myburgh c Sekonyane b Samson	3	20	11	-	-
JG Myburgh st Linde b Mostert	10	22	14	-	1
A Paleker b Abrahams	4	11	8	-	-
†CFK van Wyk b Motsamai	17	25	18	1	-
*P Joubert run out (Linde)	1	4	3	-	-
AM Phangiso b Samson	11	14	7	2	-
DW Steyn not out	6	7	4	-	-
L Manzini not out	2	4	2	-	-
FG Nkuna					
JR Jumat					
Extras (b 2, lb 5, w 5)	12				
TOTAL (for 8 wkts) (27 overs)	**167**				

FREE STATE	Runs	Mins	Balls	4	6
JA Beukes run out (Steyn)	4	12	11	-	-
*HG de Kock run out (Phangiso)	25	44	25	3	-
PJ Koortzen c JG Myburgh b Steyn	5	8	7	-	-
D Elgar c Jumat b Phangiso	24	44	37	1	-
†C Linde c Nkuna b Phangiso	0	6	2	-	-
LN Mosena not out	11	15	14	-	1
JF Mostert not out	2	9	3	-	-
TS Motsamai					
AP Abrahams					
QG Samson					
BK Sekonyane					
Extras (lb 2, w 3)	5				
TOTAL (for 5 wkts) (16.3 overs)	**76**				

FS	O	M	R	W
Sekonyane	6	0	39	0 (2 w)
Samson	5	0	25	4 (2 w)
Motsamai	6	0	27	1 (1 w)
Mostert	5	0	44	1
Abrahams	5	0	25	1

Nor	O	M	R	W
Steyn	4	2	8	1
Nkuna	5	0	31	0 (2 w)
Joubert	2	1	2	0
Phangiso	3	0	18	2
Du Plessis	2.3	0	15	0 (1 w)

Fall of Wickets	Nor	FS
1st	17 (1)	6 (1)
2nd	37 (3)	11 (3)
3rd	68 (4)	43 (2)
4th	87 (5)	43 (5)
5th	130 (6)	74 (4)
6th	133 (7)	-
7th	151 (2)	-
8th	159 (8)	-

FREE STATE v EASTERNS — SAA 1-day Challenge Pool A

Played at Goodyear Park, Bloemfontein on 5 March 2006 — Toss: Easterns
Umpires: MZ Nanabhay & BDA Westraadt
Debuts: FS: GD Perry (LO). Eas: None
Result: Easterns won by 7 wickets
Points: Eas: 6; FS: 0
Notes: Free State substitute: GD Perry replaced D Elgar after 17 overs of Easterns' innings.

FREE STATE	Runs	Mins	Balls	4	6
*HG de Kock c Seymore b Mofokeng	25	56	29	4	-
MP Fick run out (Morkel/Bodibe)	18	21	15	1	1
LN Mosena c Bodibe b Van den Berg	70	121	89	5	-
PJ Koortzen c Mofokeng b O'Connor	13	23	20	1	-
CA Thyssen c Bodibe b Mofokeng	8	23	22	-	-
D Elgar b Van den Berg	26	44	35	1	-
†C Linde c Mofokeng b Van den Berg	3	16	9	-	-
TS Motsamai run out (Wiese)	18	29	23	1	-
AP Abrahams not out	14	28	25	-	-
BK Sekonyane not out	9	7	4	-	-
JMM Malao					
GD Perry					
Extras (lb 2, w 6, nb 1)	9				
TOTAL (for 8 wkts) (45 overs)	**213**				

EASTERNS	Runs	Mins	Balls	4	6
S Mandan not out	115	153	108	10	2
AJ Seymore run out (Linde/Sekonyane)	0	11	4	-	-
AM van den Berg st Linde b Perry	65	106	70	9	-
J Booysen c Mosena b Abrahams	10	19	20	-	-
JA Morkel not out	6	14	10	1	-
D Wiese					
*SP O'Connor					
E Nyawo					
†TM Bodibe					
IC Hlengane					
PT Mofokeng					
Extras (lb 7, w 12, nb 1)	20				
TOTAL (for 3 wkts) (35.1 overs)	**216**				

Eas	O	M	R	W
Morkel	9	0	40	0 (1 w)
Wiese	7	0	48	0 (1 w)
Mofokeng	8	0	39	2 (1 nb, 1 w)
O'Connor	9	0	30	1
Van den Berg	9	0	36	3 (2 w)
Hlengane	3	0	18	0 (1 w)

FS	O	M	R	W
Motsamai	9	0	34	0 (1 w)
Sekonyane	4	0	25	0 (1 nb, 3 w)
Fick	8	0	45	0 (2 w)
Malao	6	0	42	0 (1 w)
Thyssen	1	0	15	0 (1 w)
Perry	5	0	27	1
Abrahams	2.1	0	21	1

Fall of Wickets	FS	Eas
1st	35 (2)	8 (2)
2nd	75 (1)	161 (3)
3rd	100 (4)	189 (4)
4th	116 (5)	-
5th	166 (3)	-
6th	169 (6)	-
7th	172 (7)	-
8th	199 (8)	-

GAUTENG v GRIQUALAND WEST — SAA 1-day Challenge Pool A

Played at Liberty Life Wanderers Stadium, Johannesburg on 5 March 2006 — Toss: Griqualand West

Umpires: ZTA Ndamane & DJ Smith

Debuts: Gau: None. GW: APT Mabuya (LO)

Result: Griqualand West won by 74 runs

Points: Gau: 0; GW: 6

Notes: Gauteng substitute: MR Sekhoto replaced JT Mafa after 19.4 overs of Gauteng's innings. Griqualand West substitute: APT Mabuya replaced AP McLaren after 0 overs of Gauteng's innings.

GRIQUALAND WEST	Runs	Mins	Balls	4	6
CJ de Jager run out (Van Wyk)	70	135	87	5	1
AP McLaren c Makalima b Le Roux	2	6	6	-	-
CN Bennett c Otto b De Bruin	8	23	24	1	-
AG Doherty c De Bruin b Nawab	51	60	52	7	1
*†W Bossenger not out	87	82	75	7	1
J Brooker c and b Nawab	1	3	2	-	-
BW Lemmetjies c Nkwe b Mafa	2	10	10	-	-
J Coetzee not out	14	23	15	1	-
D Donaldson					
NO Arthur					
TR Plaatjie					
APT Mabuya					
Extras (b 2, lb 2, w 10, nb 1)	15				
TOTAL (for 6 wkts) (45 overs)	**250**				

GAUTENG	Runs	Mins	Balls	4	6
*BD Snijman b Plaatjie	9	28	14	1	-
JM Otto c Lemmetjies b Coetzee	4	4	4	1	-
ET Nkwe lbw b Plaatjie	13	15	11	3	-
DR Gain c Bossenger b Arthur	41	70	51	7	-
DL Makalima run out (Brooker)	28	44	28	3	1
†DM van Wyk lbw b Arthur	9	33	31	1	-
MR Sekhoto c and b Lemmetjies	18	52	39	-	-
BC Adams c Bossenger b Lemmetjies	11	10	11	-	1
HW le Roux c Bossenger b Lemmetjies	4	12	9	-	-
GJ de Bruin c Donaldson b Lemmetjies	23	18	19	-	3
A Nawab not out	2	7	6	-	-
JT Mafa					
Extras (lb 1, w 7, nb 6)	14				
TOTAL (36.1 overs)	**176**				

Gau	O	M	R	W
De Bruin	9	2	42	1 (1 nb, 2 w)
Le Roux	7	0	28	1 (2 w)
Mafa	6	0	33	1 (3 w)
Nkwe	4	0	38	0
Nawab	9	1	40	2
Snijman	7	0	37	0 (1 w)
Adams	3	0	28	0 (1 w)

GW	O	M	R	W
Coetzee	7	0	30	1 (2 w)
Plaatjie	7	0	50	2 (1 nb, 1 w)
Donaldson	3	0	28	0 (5 nb, 2 w)
Mabuya	5	1	9	0
Arthur	9	1	33	2 (1 w)
Lemmetjies	5.1	0	25	4 (1 w)

Fall of Wickets	GW	Gau
1st	2 (2)	6 (2)
2nd	24 (3)	22 (3)
3rd	111 (4)	31 (1)
4th	185 (1)	100 (5)
5th	188 (6)	112 (4)
6th	200 (7)	121 (6)
7th	-	135 (8)
8th	-	147 (9)
9th	-	160 (7)
10th	-	176 (10)

NORTH WEST v GAUTENG — SAA 1-day Challenge Pool A

Played at Sedgars Park, Potchefstroom on 12 March 2006 — Toss: North West

Umpires: LM Engelbrecht & SW Liebisch

Debuts: NW: None. Gau: NA Bell (LO)

Result: Gauteng won by 5 wickets

Points: Gau: 5; NW: 1

Notes: Nkwe scored his fifty off 32 balls in Gauteng's innings.

NORTH WEST	Runs	Mins	Balls	4	6
FA Steyn c Makalima b Mafa	137	160	145	18	1
DJ Kgamadi c Gain b Nawab	59	133	81	2	2
R Bhayat run out (Snijman)	16	32	17	-	-
J le Roux not out	21	27	15	2	-
M Akoojee not out	27	22	19	3	-
*RA Stroh					
FS Holtzhausen					
†TA Bula					
GH Bhayat					
JP Campher					
NM Serame					
Extras (w 2, nb 6)	8				
TOTAL (for 3 wkts) (45 overs)	**268**				

GAUTENG	Runs	Mins	Balls	4	6
WB Motaung b GH Bhayat	0	1	2	-	-
*BD Snijman c Steyn b R Bhayat	45	60	42	7	1
ET Nkwe lbw b Stroh	87	132	76	15	-
DR Gain c Steyn b Campher	15	9	10	3	-
DL Makalima c Bula b Stroh	49	55	39	7	-
JM Otto not out	32	46	36	3	1
†DM van Wyk not out	33	38	29	4	1
GJ de Bruin					
A Nawab					
JT Mafa					
NA Bell					
Extras (lb 2, w 7, nb 2)	11				
TOTAL (for 5 wkts) (38.4 overs)	**272**				

Gau	O	M	R	W	NW	O	M	R	W	Fall of Wickets	NW	Gau
De Bruin	9	1	40	0 (1 nb)	GH Bhayat	5	1	32	1 (1 nb)	1st	168 (2)	0 (1)
Mafa	7	0	39	1 (5 nb)	Holtzhausen	5.4	0	51	0 (2 w)	2nd	219 (1)	106 (2)
Nkwe	5	0	27	0	Campher	4	0	39	1 (1 nb, 1 w)	3rd	220 (3)	122 (4)
Bell	9	0	65	0 (2 w)	R Bhayat	3	0	28	1 (1 w)	4th	-	200 (5)
Nawab	9	0	51	1	Akoojee	4	0	31	0	5th	-	203 (3)
Snijman	3	0	21	0	Stroh	8	1	41	2 (3 w)			
Motaung	3	0	25	0	Serame	9	0	48	0			

NORTHERNS v GRIQUALAND WEST — SAA 1-day Challenge Pool A

Played at Tshwane University of Technology Oval, Pretoria on 11 March 2006 — Toss: Northerns

Umpires: JEP Ostrom & DJ Smith

Debuts: Nor: None. GW: None

Result: Northerns won by 5 wickets

Points: GW: 1; Nor: 5

Notes: Dros scored his fifty off 25 balls in Northerns' innings. Griqualand West substitute: TR Plaatjie replaced AG Doherty after 1 over of Northerns' innings.

GRIQUALAND WEST	Runs	Mins	Balls	4	6
CJ de Jager c Aronstam b Manzini	27	52	25	2	1
AP McLaren c Nkuna b Manzini	30	33	26	5	-
D Donaldson c Van Wyk b Nkuna	48	71	76	3	1
AG Doherty c Manzini b Aronstam	14	61	31	1	-
CN Bennett b Aronstam	5	13	15	-	-
*†W Bossenger c Chouhan b Nkuna	27	50	34	2	-
J Brooker c Van Wyk b Nkuna	13	9	10	1	1
AK Kruger b Dros	24	35	25	1	1
J Coetzee not out	28	20	17	1	2
NO Arthur c Van Wyk b Joubert	2	5	4	-	-
APT Mabuya b Joubert	6	7	5	-	-
TR Plaatjie					
Extras (lb 7, w 9, nb 1)	17				
TOTAL (44.3 overs)	**241**				

NORTHERNS	Runs	Mins	Balls	4	6
MA Aronstam c Brooker b Donaldson	10	65	38	1	-
N Chouhan c Bossenger b Plaatjie	5	17	15	1	-
A Paleker b Kruger	47	111	73	6	-
SJ Myburgh not out	90	124	95	8	-
G Dros b Plaatjie	62	44	38	5	4
†CFK van Wyk lbw b Coetzee	0	8	3	-	-
*P Joubert not out	0	6	2	-	-
MJ Mokonyama					
L Manzini					
N Wagner					
FG Nkuna					
Extras (b 1, lb 6, w 8, nb 13)	28				
TOTAL (for 5 wkts) (41.5 overs)	**242**				

Nor	O	M	R	W	GW	O	M	R	W	Fall of Wickets	GW	Nor
Wagner	9	0	48	0 (2 w)	Coetzee	8	1	23	1 (4 w)	1st	61 (2)	10 (2)
Manzini	9	0	44	2 (2 w)	Plaatjie	7.5	1	36	2 (6 nb, 1 w)	2nd	69 (1)	46 (1)
Joubert	8.3	1	43	2 (1 w)	Kruger	9	1	47	1 (2 nb, 1 w)	3rd	131 (4)	124 (3)
Nkuna	9	0	46	3 (1 nb, 2 w)	Donaldson	7	0	58	1 (5 nb)	4th	134 (3)	227 (5)
Aronstam	7	0	40	2	Arthur	8	0	51	0	5th	142 (5)	236 (6)
Dros	2	0	13	1 (1 w)	Mabuya	2	0	20	0	6th	163 (7)	-
										7th	199 (8)	-
										8th	218 (6)	-
										9th	225 (10)	-
										10th	241 (11)	-

Pool B

EASTERN PROVINCE v BORDER — SAA 1-day Challenge Pool B

Played at Sahara Oval St George's, Port Elizabeth on 8 October 2005 — Toss: Border

Umpires: BN Harrison & KH Hurter

Debuts: EP: None. Bdr: DC Lentz and RR Richards (Both LO)

Result: Eastern Province won by 3 wickets

Points: Bdr: 1; EP: 5

Notes: Eastern Province substitute: S Mjekula replaced E Potgieter after 0 overs of Border's innings.

BORDER	Runs	Mins	Balls	4	6
BL Bennett c Baxter b Mjekula	25	72	60	1	-
MBA Smith c Howell b Meyer	0	6	2	-	-
†GE von Hoesslin c Jeggels b Bell	31	84	54	4	-
AZM Dyili c Willemse b Meyer	49	75	54	7	1
S de Kock c Bell b Howell	10	36	28	1	-
DC Lentz lbw b Howell	0	2	3	-	-
*MN Ranger c Howell b Meyer	2	21	12	-	-
L Mbane b Meyer	2	8	4	-	-
P Fojela c Meyer b Carolus	21	27	25	3	-
LL Lwana c and b Mjekula	10	26	23	-	1
RR Richards not out	1	4	1	-	-
Extras (lb 6, w 15, nb 5)	26				
TOTAL (43.4 overs)	**177**				

EASTERN PROVINCE	Runs	Mins	Balls	4	6
C Baxter c Bennett b Richards	14	28	26	1	-
ML Price c Bennett b De Kock	37	119	62	4	-
D Willemse c Von Hoesslin b Richards	10	22	26	1	-
RR Jeggels b Ranger	46	109	82	2	2
*GE Howell lbw b Ranger	14	17	19	2	-
R Nel lbw b De Kock	9	18	15	1	-
L Meyer c and b De Kock	4	16	14	-	-
WE Bell not out	12	21	9	1	-
†M Slwana not out	12	17	12	1	-
DD Carolus					
S Mjekula					
E Potgieter					
Extras (b 2, lb 8, w 9, nb 1)	20				
TOTAL (for 7 wkts) (44 overs)	**178**				

EP	O	M	R	W	
Carolus	8	0	34	1	(7 w)
Meyer	9	1	33	4	(3 nb, 2 w)
Mjekula	6.4	1	17	2	(1 nb, 1 w)
Bell	6	2	18	1	(3 w)
Willemse	5	0	39	0	(2 w)
Howell	9	2	30	2	

Bdr	O	M	R	W	
Fojela	8	0	38	0	(1 w)
Richards	6	1	18	2	(1 nb)
Lwana	6	0	26	0	(2 w)
Mbane	6	1	24	0	(3 w)
De Kock	9	0	38	3	(1 w)
Ranger	9	1	24	2	

Fall of Wickets	Bdr	EP
1st	3 (2)	24 (1)
2nd	63 (1)	44 (3)
3rd	79 (3)	88 (2)
4th	113 (5)	113 (5)
5th	113 (6)	131 (6)
6th	142 (4)	149 (7)
7th	142 (7)	153 (4)
8th	145 (8)	-
9th	174 (9)	-
10th	177 (10)	-

KWAZULU-NATAL v WESTERN PROVINCE — SAA 1-day Challenge Pool B

Played at Chatsworth Stadium, Chatsworth on 16 October 2005 — Toss: KwaZulu-Natal
Umpires: S George & BM White
Debuts: KZN: M Bekker, TN Harvey and DR Miller (All LO). WP: SG George, MR Masinda, LF Simpson, MD Walters and M Williamson (All LO)
Result: Western Province won by 2 runs
Points: KZN: 1; WP: 5
Notes: KwaZulu-Natal substitute: TN Harvey replaced TD Pillay after 0 overs of KwaZulu-Natal's innings. Western Province substitute: SG George replaced MD Walters after 0 overs of KwaZulu-Natal's innings.

WESTERN PROVINCE	Runs	Mins	Balls	4	6
M Williamson c Bekker b Lazarus	94	141	110	10	2
AJA Gray c Miller b Frylinck	1	6	4	-	-
MD Walters run out (Lazarus)	2	19	16	-	-
W Wyngaard b Abrahim	0	4	6	-	-
R Munnik b Frylinck	109	145	105	15	-
RK Kleinveldt c and b Hauptfleisch	16	8	11	3	-
*†RCC Canning not out	26	28	14	4	-
Q Friend not out	4	28	4	-	-
M de Stadler					
LF Simpson					
MR Masinda					
SG George					
Extras (lb 7, w 6)	13				
TOTAL (for 6 wkts) (45 overs)	**265**				

KWAZULU-NATAL	Runs	Mins	Balls	4	6
W Hauptfleisch b Kleinveldt	6	8	10	1	-
K Smit c Wyngaard b Masinda	73	81	60	12	1
†DR Miller lbw b Friend	8	29	16	1	-
TN Harvey run out (Williamson/Canning)	0	3	1	-	-
FB Lazarus c Williamson b Simpson	9	37	20	-	-
*R Gobind c Canning b Simpson	8	16	12	1	-
M Bekker not out	66	102	67	3	1
KC Africa c and b George	23	32	28	2	-
R Frylinck c George b De Stadler	47	52	50	4	1
ZA Abrahim c Munnik b De Stadler	1	4	4	-	-
N Dladla b Friend	5	4	4	-	-
TD Pillay					
Extras (lb 7, w 8, nb 2)	17				
TOTAL (45 overs)	**263**				

KZN	O	M	R	W	
Abrahim	9	2	40	1	(5 w)
Frylinck	9	1	44	2	
Africa	7	1	39	0	(1 w)
Dladla	4	1	24	0	
Pillay	7	0	50	0	
Lazarus	2	0	18	1	
Hauptfleisch	7	0	43	1	

WP	O	M	R	W	
Friend	9	0	34	2	(1 nb, 3 w)
Kleinveldt	9	0	58	1	(1 w)
De Stadler	9	0	70	2	(1 w)
Simpson	7	0	34	2	(1 nb, 3 w)
Masinda	6	0	36	1	
George	5	0	24	1	

Fall of Wickets	WP	KZN
1st	8 (2)	11 (1)
2nd	13 (3)	40 (3)
3rd	14 (4)	40 (4)
4th	171 (1)	100 (5)
5th	203 (6)	112 (2)
6th	254 (5)	114 (6)
7th	-	158 (8)
8th	-	248 (9)
9th	-	250 (10)
10th	-	263 (11)

WESTERN PROVINCE v EASTERN PROVINCE — SAA 1-day Challenge Pool B

Played at Sahara Park Newlands, Cape Town on 22 October 2005 — Toss: Eastern Province
Umpires: EC Hendrikse & DJ Smith
Debuts: WP: FD Telo, DL Haupt and M Mahlombe (All LO). EP: SG Fensham (LO)
Result: Western Province won by 77 runs
Points: EP: 0; WP: 6
Notes: Eastern Province substitute: SG Fensham replaced S Mjekula after 0 overs of Eastern Province's innings.

WESTERN PROVINCE	Runs	Mins	Balls	4	6
M Williamson c Slwana b Howell	35	104	70	3	-
AJA Gray c Slwana b Mjekula	25	51	43	4	-
W Wyngaard b Mjekula	7	30	25	1	-
FD Telo b Mjekula	67	85	56	7	2
R Munnik c Meyer b Nel	29	44	43	2	1
RK Kleinveldt b Meyer	15	14	13	-	2
*†RCC Canning not out	26	18	11	3	1
SG George b Mjekula	22	9	8	3	1
M de Stadler not out	1	4	2	-	-
DL Haupt					
M Mahlombe					
Extras (b 4, lb 5, w 9, nb 1)	19				
TOTAL (for 7 wkts) (45 overs)	**246**				

EASTERN PROVINCE	Runs	Mins	Balls	4	6
C Baxter lbw b Mahlombe	58	119	75	7	-
ML Price c Canning b Kleinveldt	3	8	10	-	-
WE Bell lbw b Kleinveldt	2	2	2	-	-
E Potgieter c Williamson b Mahlombe	19	65	58	1	-
R Nel c Canning b George	15	30	26	2	-
SG Fensham c Gray b George	2	16	15	-	-
*GE Howell c Wyngaard b Mahlombe	5	8	6	-	-
L Meyer c Munnik b George	4	11	8	-	-
RR Jeggels c Munnik b De Stadler	21	49	31	1	-
†M Slwana not out	24	42	44	1	-
DD Carolus not out	0	1	1	-	-
S Mjekula					
Extras (lb 3, w 7, nb 6)	16				
TOTAL (for 9 wkts) (45 overs)	**169**				

EP	O	M	R	W
Carolus	9	1	26	0 (1 w)
Meyer	9	2	52	1 (1 nb, 2 w)
Mjekula	9	2	50	4 (5 w)
Howell	9	1	32	1
Bell	4	0	23	0
Nel	3	0	30	1 (1 w)
Price	2	0	24	0

WP	O	M	R	W
Haupt	9	2	37	0 (5 nb, 3 w)
Kleinveldt	9	0	31	2
De Stadler	9	0	29	1
Mahlombe	9	0	34	3 (1 nb, 2 w)
George	9	0	35	3 (1 w)

Fall of Wickets	WP	EP
1st	44 (2)	9 (2)
2nd	59 (3)	11 (3)
3rd	83 (1)	71 (4)
4th	163 (5)	105 (5)
5th	192 (6)	110 (1)
6th	202 (4)	114 (6)
7th	234 (8)	115 (7)
8th	-	123 (8)
9th	-	169 (9)

BORDER v BOLAND

SAA 1-day Challenge Pool B

Played at Mercedes-Benz Park, East London on 23 October 2005

Toss: Boland

Umpires: BN Harrison & SW Liebisch

Debuts: Bdr: None. Bol: HH Paulse (LO)

Result: Boland won by 6 runs

Points: Bdr: 1; Bol: 5

Notes: Boland substitute: HH Paulse replaced C Prinsloo after 20 overs of Border's innings.

BOLAND	Runs	Mins	Balls	4	6
H Davids b Bennett	76	148	111	7	1
C Prinsloo c De Kock b Pangabantu	15	21	16	1	1
SP Summers lbw b De Kock	70	78	66	10	1
RG Arendse c Von Hoesslin b De Kock	10	13	18	-	-
†WJ Louw c and b Ranger	19	24	19	1	1
WC Swan c Pangabantu b Bennett	16	27	18	2	-
*WA Albertyn b Ranger	15	20	16	-	-
JM van Wyk not out	1	8	2	-	-
WE September lbw b Ranger	3	3	3	-	-
BL Fransman b Ranger	0	1	1	-	-
PSE Sandri					
HH Paulse					
Extras (b 5, lb 7, w 3, nb 1)	16				
TOTAL (for 9 wkts) (45 overs)	**241**				

BORDER	Runs	Mins	Balls	4	6
BL Bennett c Louw b Fransman	28	67	46	4	1
†GE von Hoesslin c Albertyn b Fransman	26	56	42	4	-
MBA Smith c Swan b Fransman	64	116	70	7	2
AZM Dyili c Louw b Fransman	0	2	2	-	-
MM Matika lbw b Albertyn	0	12	7	-	-
DL Brown c Swan b Paulse	5	12	9	1	-
DC Lentz lbw b Paulse	13	22	17	2	-
*MN Ranger not out	56	70	68	2	4
S de Kock not out	32	16	12	3	2
L Mbane					
Y Pangabantu					
Extras (lb 5, w 3, nb 3)	11				
TOTAL (for 7 wkts) (45 overs)	**235**				

Bdr	O	M	R	W
Mbane	5	1	21	0
Pangabantu	9	3	47	1 (1 nb)
Brown	2	0	25	0
Ranger	9	0	42	4
De Kock	9	0	29	2 (1 w)
Smith	7	0	43	0 (2 w)
Bennett	4	0	22	2

Bol	O	M	R	W
Van Wyk	8	2	49	0
Sandri	7	1	21	0 (2 nb)
Fransman	8	0	58	4 (1 nb, 2 w)
Albertyn	7	2	26	1 (1 w)
Paulse	6	2	16	2
Davids	5	0	29	0
September	4	0	31	0

Fall of Wickets	Bol	Bdr
1st	16 (2)	58 (2)
2nd	136 (3)	63 (1)
3rd	156 (4)	63 (4)
4th	193 (5)	76 (5)
5th	205 (1)	85 (6)
6th	234 (6)	108 (7)
7th	237 (7)	183 (3)
8th	241 (9)	-
9th	241 (10)	-

KWAZULU-NATAL v ZIMBABWE UNDER-23

SAA 1-day Challenge Pool B

Played at Chatsworth Stadium, Chatsworth on 23 October 2005

Toss: Zimbabwe Under-23

Umpires: ZTA Ndamane & LJ Willemse

Debuts: KZN: T Essack (LO). ZU23: None

Result: KwaZulu-Natal won by 103 runs

Points: KZN: 6; ZU23: 0

Notes: Smit scored his fifty off 29 balls in KwaZulu-Natal's innings. Zimbabwe Under-23 substitute: H Matanga replaced TN Garwe after 0 overs of Zimbabwe Under-23's innings.

KWAZULU-NATAL	Runs	Mins	Balls	4	6
MD Sanders c Matsikenyeri b Chinyoka	25	40	27	3	-
K Smit c Mawoyo b Mpofu	75	80	52	13	-
†DR Miller lbw b Strydom	9	19	14	-	-
T Essack c Maregwede b Ewing	17	50	25	2	-
FB Lazarus st Maregwede b Ewing	12	25	25	1	-
M Bekker lbw b Matanga	10	20	21	-	-
KC Africa c Ewing b Mpofu	31	53	51	2	-
R Frylinck not out	82	57	51	5	6
N Dladla not out	5	19	11	-	-
*ZA Abrahim					
TD Pillay					
Extras (lb 2, w 15, nb 8)	25				
TOTAL (for 7 wkts) (45 overs)	**291**				

ZIMBABWE UNDER-23	Runs	Mins	Balls	4	6
TMK Mawoyo b Abrahim	20	18	18	4	-
T Hove b Abrahim	5	31	16	-	-
GM Strydom c Essack b Africa	1	4	5	-	-
MA Vermeulen b Essack	65	107	70	7	1
C de Grandhomme c Abrahim b Dladla	17	15	13	4	-
S Matsikenyeri c Miller b Dladla	8	9	8	2	-
*†A Maregwede c Sanders b Essack	0	27	18	-	-
GM Ewing c Essack b Pillay	21	54	42	2	-
IM Chinyoka c Dladla b Pillay	26	35	30	2	2
CB Mpofu c Lazarus b Pillay	15	15	16	2	-
H Matanga not out	1	15	10	-	-
TN Garwe					
Extras (lb 2, w 7)	9				
TOTAL (41 overs)	**188**				

ZU23	O	M	R	W	
Mpofu	9	0	59	2	
Garwe	4	0	32	0	
Chinyoka	9	0	71	1	(8 nb, 1 w)
Strydom	6	1	43	1	(6 w)
Matanga	5	0	18	1	
Ewing	8	0	37	2	
De Grandhomme	1	0	12	0	
Matsikenyeri	3	0	17	0	

KZN	O	M	R	W	
Abrahim	5	0	28	2	(2 w)
Africa	7	1	27	1	(2 w)
Dladla	8	0	50	2	(1 w)
Essack	9	1	33	2	
Lazarus	5	0	18	0	(2 w)
Pillay	7	1	30	3	

Fall of Wickets	KZN	ZU23
1st	81 (1)	25 (1)
2nd	108 (3)	26 (3)
3rd	137 (2)	32 (2)
4th	161 (5)	54 (5)
5th	162 (4)	62 (6)
6th	180 (6)	98 (7)
7th	248 (7)	144 (4)
8th	-	146 (8)
9th	-	162 (10)
10th	-	188 (9)

KWAZULU-NATAL v BOLAND — SAA 1-day Challenge Pool B

Played at Chatsworth Stadium, Chatsworth on 30 October 2005 — Toss: KwaZulu-Natal

Umpires: SW Liebisch & JEP Ostrom

Debuts: KZN: R Reddy (LO). Bol: None

Result: Boland won by 7 wickets

Points: Bol: 5; KZN: 1

KWAZULU-NATAL	Runs	Mins	Balls	4	6
MD Sanders lbw b Swan	53	135	94	4	-
K Smit b Van Wyk	14	35	19	2	-
*R Gobind c Fransman b September	23	45	33	3	-
T Essack c Louw b Albertyn	1	5	5	-	-
M Bekker c Arendse b September	23	33	36	2	-
WP Lombard not out	25	57	44	1	-
KC Africa b Fransman	2	8	14	-	-
†DR Miller b Albertyn	29	25	19	3	1
ZA Abrahim b Van Wyk	14	8	7	-	1
R Reddy					
S Mhlongo					
Extras (lb 3, w 6, nb 1)	10				
TOTAL (for 8 wkts) (45 overs)	**194**				

BOLAND	Runs	Mins	Balls	4	6
C Prinsloo b Lombard	44	79	64	3	1
R Bailey c Smit b Abrahim	18	31	26	2	-
SP Summers c Miller b Mhlongo	23	27	24	4	-
RG Arendse not out	44	91	70	4	-
†WJ Louw not out	57	71	56	7	-
WC Swan					
*WA Albertyn					
JM van Wyk					
WE September					
BL Fransman					
PSE Sandri					
Extras (lb 3, w 5, nb 2)	10				
TOTAL (for 3 wkts) (39.4 overs)	**196**				

Bol	O	M	R	W	
Van Wyk	8	2	38	2	(1 w)
Sandri	5	0	18	0	
Fransman	6	0	37	1	
Albertyn	9	0	49	2	(1 nb, 2 w)
September	9	0	18	2	(2 w)
Swan	8	1	31	1	

KZN	O	M	R	W	
Abrahim	8	0	45	1	(1 w)
Reddy	9	0	32	0	(2 w)
Africa	6.4	0	34	0	(2 w)
Mhlongo	6	0	29	1	(2 nb)
Lombard	7	1	31	1	
Essack	1	0	11	0	
Sanders	2	0	11	0	

Fall of Wickets	KZN	Bol
1st	30 (2)	41 (2)
2nd	78 (3)	79 (3)
3rd	79 (4)	98 (1)
4th	114 (5)	-
5th	124 (1)	-
6th	129 (7)	-
7th	176 (8)	-
8th	194 (9)	-

EASTERN PROVINCE v ZIMBABWE UNDER-23 — SAA 1-day Challenge Pool B

Played at Pollock Field, Grey High School, Port Elizabeth on 30 October 2005 — Toss: Eastern Province

Umpires: IH van Kerwel & LJ Willemse

Debuts: EP: J Theron (LO). ZU23: None

Result: Eastern Province won by 109 runs

Points: EP: 6; ZU23: 0

Notes: Howell scored his century off 65 balls in Eastern Province's innings. Eastern Province substitute: WE Bell replaced SG Fensham Zimbabwe Under-23 substitute: GM Ewing replaced H Matanga

SAA PROVINCIAL ONE-DAY CHALLENGE

EASTERN PROVINCE	*Runs*	*Mins*	*Balls*	*4*	*6*
C Baxter b Mwayenga	2	2	3	-	-
L Meyer c Maregwede b Garwe	6	28	15	1	-
ML Price c Maregwede b Garwe	69	151	106	6	1
U Abrahams c Maregwede b Strydom	9	27	28	1	-
RR Jeggels c Matsikenyeri b Strydom	8	26	16	1	-
SG Fensham c Maregwede b Matanga	7	19	18	-	-
*GE Howell not out	115	74	69	8	6
D Willemse c Hove b Garwe	7	19	11	-	-
†M Slwana not out	3	8	4	-	-
J Theron					
S Mjekula					
WE Bell					
Extras (b 1, lb 1, w 25, nb 1)	28				
TOTAL (for 7 wkts) (45 overs)	**254**				

ZIMBABWE UNDER-23	*Runs*	*Mins*	*Balls*	*4*	*6*
B Mlambo c Baxter b Meyer	0	2	4	-	-
T Hove c Slwana b Mjekula	6	29	15	1	-
MA Vermeulen c Baxter b Meyer	14	20	16	2	-
C de Grandhomme c Slwana b Meyer	1	10	9	-	-
S Matsikenyeri c Slwana b Theron	2	38	20	-	-
GM Ewing c Slwana b Bell	33	99	73	4	-
GM Strydom c Howell b Bell	23	58	45	3	-
*†A Maregwede not out	39	41	32	4	1
A Mwayenga c Slwana b Bell	1	3	3	-	-
IM Chinyoka b Willemse	7	16	11	1	-
TN Garwe b Theron	2	13	9	-	-
H Matanga					
Extras (lb 2, w 12, nb 3)	17				
TOTAL (38.3 overs)	**145**				

ZU23	*O*	*M*	*R*	*W*	
Mwayenga	3	0	13	1	(3 w)
Garwe	8	0	56	3	(1 nb, 10 w)
Chinyoka	9	1	32	0	(2 w)
Strydom	5	2	15	2	(6 w)
Matanga	5	0	25	1	(2 w)
Ewing	9	0	61	0	(1 w)
Matsikenyeri	2	0	14	0	
De Grandhomme	4	0	36	0	(1 w)

EP	*O*	*M*	*R*	*W*	
Meyer	9	2	34	3	(3 nb, 4 w)
Mjekula	9	3	25	1	(8 w)
Theron	6.3	0	26	2	(1 w)
Bell	9	1	26	3	
Willemse	5	0	32	1	

Fall of Wickets	*EP*	*ZU23*
1st	6 (1)	0 (1)
2nd	22 (2)	27 (3)
3rd	53 (4)	33 (2)
4th	71 (5)	33 (4)
5th	85 (6)	46 (5)
6th	191 (3)	94 (7)
7th	229 (8)	99 (6)
8th	-	101 (9)
9th	-	122 (10)
10th	-	145 (11)

BOLAND v WESTERN PROVINCE

SAA 1-day Challenge Pool B

Played at Boland Park, Paarl on 6 November 2005

Toss: Western Province

Umpires: DJ Smith & BM White

Debuts: Bol: QK Kannemeyer and L-R Walters (Both LO). WP: None

Result: Boland won by 5 wickets

Points: Bol: 5; WP: 1

Notes: Boland substitute: QK Kannemeyer replaced BL Fransman after 0 overs of Boland's innings. Western Province substitute: SG George replaced A Magiet after 23 overs of Boland's innings.

WESTERN PROVINCE	*Runs*	*Mins*	*Balls*	*4*	*6*
M Williamson c Swan b Fransman	11	49	34	1	-
A Magiet c Walters b Fransman	6	28	17	1	-
W Wyngaard c September b Fransman	6	9	7	1	-
FD Telo c Swan b Fransman	10	27	12	2	-
WC Hantam c Prinsloo b Swan	53	106	87	3	-
*†RCC Canning b Albertyn	65	91	75	6	-
RK Kleinveldt c and b Fransman	25	18	14	3	1
PR Adams c Prinsloo b Albertyn	2	6	5	-	-
M de Stadler c Smit b Albertyn	7	10	10	-	-
M Mahlombe lbw b Fransman	0	1	2	-	-
DL Haupt not out	3	8	7	-	-
SG George					
Extras (lb 3, w 6, nb 3)	12				
TOTAL (44.3 overs)	**200**				

BOLAND	*Runs*	*Mins*	*Balls*	*4*	*6*
C Prinsloo c Canning b Haupt	88	155	133	9	-
JG Strydom c Adams b Haupt	8	7	6	1	-
RG Arendse run out (Mahlombe/Canning)	16	31	31	2	-
WJ Smit c Canning b De Stadler	19	37	29	4	-
WC Swan not out	49	93	60	4	-
SP Summers st Canning b George	1	8	3	-	-
QK Kannemeyer not out	3	7	6	-	-
*WA Albertyn					
†L-R Walters					
WE September					
PSE Sandri					
BL Fransman					
Extras (lb 5, w 12)	17				
TOTAL (for 5 wkts) (44.4 overs)	**201**				

Bol	*O*	*M*	*R*	*W*	
Sandri	9	1	32	0	(3 nb, 1 w)
Fransman	9	0	40	6	
Albertyn	8.3	1	26	3	(1 w)
Summers	9	0	37	0	(4 w)
September	7	0	40	0	
Swan	2	0	22	1	

WP	*O*	*M*	*R*	*W*	
Kleinveldt	8.4	0	38	0	(1 w)
Haupt	9	0	40	2	(6 w)
Hantam	9	2	36	0	
De Stadler	7	0	34	1	
Adams	6	0	35	0	(1 w)
George	5	0	13	1	(4 w)

Fall of Wickets	*WP*	*Bol*
1st	17 (2)	10 (2)
2nd	24 (3)	47 (3)
3rd	26 (1)	85 (4)
4th	40 (4)	193 (1)
5th	153 (5)	195 (6)
6th	161 (6)	-
7th	177 (8)	-
8th	188 (7)	-
9th	189 (10)	-
10th	200 (9)	-

EASTERN PROVINCE v KWAZULU-NATAL — SAA 1-day Challenge Pool B

Played at Sahara Oval St George's, Port Elizabeth on 6 November 2005 — Toss: KwaZulu-Natal
Umpires: EC Hendrikse & LJ Willemse
Debuts: EP: None. KZN: YA Abdullah (LO)
Result: No result
Points: EP: 3; KZN: 3

EASTERN PROVINCE	*Runs*	*Mins*	*Balls*	*4*	*6*
D Willemse not out	1	7	2	-	-
C Baxter not out	1	7	3	-	-
ML Price					
U Abrahams					
RR Jeggels					
*GE Howell					
SG Fensham					
L Meyer					
†M Slwana					
WE Bell					
J Theron					
Extras (b 1, lb 1, w 1)	3				
TOTAL (for 0 wkts) (0.5 overs)	**5**				

KWAZULU-NATAL
*R Gobind
TN Harvey
WR Wingfield
T Essack
†M Bekker
WP Lombard
R Frylinck
ZA Abrahim
S Mhlongo
R Reddy
YA Abdullah

KZN	*O*	*M*	*R*	*W*
Abrahim	0.5	0	3	0 (1 w)

BORDER v KWAZULU-NATAL — SAA 1-day Challenge Pool B

Played at Mercedes-Benz Park, East London on 12 November 2005 — Toss: KwaZulu-Natal
Umpires: S George & LJ Willemse
Debuts: Bdr: None. KZN: None
Result: Border won by 4 wickets
Points: Bdr: 5; KZN: 1
Notes: Border substitute: LL Lwana replaced Y Pangabantu after 0 overs of Border's innings. KwaZulu-Natal substitute: WP Lombard replaced TN Harvey after 0 overs of Border's innings.

KWAZULU-NATAL	*Runs*	*Mins*	*Balls*	*4*	*6*
*R Gobind c Matika b Pangabantu	11	41	30	1	-
†DR Miller lbw b Richards	0	5	2	-	-
TN Harvey c Pope b Pangabantu	11	11	12	1	-
WR Wingfield c Gamiet b Brown	14	45	38	1	-
T Essack run out (Pangabantu/Dyili)	30	74	39	3	-
KC Africa c Dyili b Brown	9	19	16	1	-
M Bekker c Pangabantu b Brown	9	17	15	1	-
R Frylinck c Mbane b Pope	50	43	37	4	2
R Reddy b De Kock	7	13	12	-	-
TD Pillay c Dyili b De Kock	2	5	6	-	-
S Mhlongo not out	0	9	5	-	-
WP Lombard					
Extras (lb 1, w 4, nb 4)	9				
TOTAL (34.4 overs)	**152**				

BORDER	*Runs*	*Mins*	*Balls*	*4*	*6*
BL Bennett b Pillay	7	30	16	1	-
GE von Hoesslin lbw b Frylinck	1	10	3	-	-
*SC Pope not out	81	141	138	11	1
LL Gamiet lbw b Essack	3	8	4	-	-
†AZM Dyili c Mhlongo b Pillay	1	4	4	-	-
MM Matika st Miller b Essack	0	4	2	-	-
S de Kock c and b Essack	10	26	28	2	-
DL Brown not out	32	78	56	3	-
L Mbane					
LL Lwana					
RR Richards					
Y Pangabantu					
Extras (lb 5, w 13)	18				
TOTAL (for 6 wkts) (41.5 overs)	**153**				

Bdr	*O*	*M*	*R*	*W*
Pangabantu	6	2	13	2
Richards	5	0	13	1
Brown	9	0	48	3 (4 nb)
Mbane	4	0	16	0 (2 w)
Pope	7.4	0	51	1 (2 w)
De Kock	3	0	10	2

KZN	*O*	*M*	*R*	*W*
Frylinck	4	0	12	1
Africa	4	0	26	0 (5 w)
Pillay	9	2	24	2 (1 w)
Essack	9	0	23	3 (1 w)
Reddy	5.5	0	30	0 (1 w)
Wingfield	8	1	18	0 (2 w)
Lombard	2	0	15	0

Fall of Wickets	*KZN*	*Bdr*
1st	2 (2)	6 (2)
2nd	17 (3)	32 (1)
3rd	26 (1)	39 (4)
4th	48 (4)	41 (5)
5th	68 (6)	41 (6)
6th	84 (7)	62 (7)
7th	103 (5)	-
8th	126 (9)	-
9th	132 (10)	-
10th	152 (8)	-

WESTERN PROVINCE v ZIMBABWE UNDER-23 — SAA 1-day Challenge Pool B

Played at Sahara Park Newlands, Cape Town on 13 November 2005 — Toss: Western Province
Umpires: LH Matroos & IH van Kerwel
Debuts: WP: MQ Adams (LO). ZU23: None
Result: Western Province won by 9 wickets
Points: WP: 6; ZU23: 0
Notes: Western Province substitute: M Mahlombe replaced DL Haupt after 0 overs of Western Province's innings.
Zimbabwe Under-23 substitute: TMK Mawoyo replaced A Mwayenga after 30 overs of Zimbabwe Under-23's innings.

ZIMBABWE UNDER-23	*Runs*	*Mins*	*Balls*	*4*	*6*
S Matsikenyeri c Homani b Haupt	7	23	18	1	-
*†A Maregwede c Hantam b Haupt	0	3	1	-	-
T Hove lbw b Haupt	7	36	26	1	-
MA Vermeulen c Adams b Haupt	2	9	6	-	-
C de Grandhomme run out (Adams)	8	23	12	1	-
B Mlambo c Haupt b George	43	85	57	3	1
GM Strydom lbw b De Stadler	42	40	35	6	1
IM Chinyoka c George b Adams	7	21	23	-	-
TMK Mawoyo c Homani b Adams	4	8	6	-	-
CB Mpofu b Adams	21	39	36	4	-
H Matanga not out	7	35	26	-	-
A Mwayenga					
Extras (lb 2, w 11, nb 1)	14				
TOTAL (40.5 overs)	**162**				

WESTERN PROVINCE	*Runs*	*Mins*	*Balls*	*4*	*6*
M Williamson not out	68	137	106	7	-
AJA Gray st Maregwede b Matanga	48	108	76	7	-
MQ Adams not out	23	28	25	2	1
FD Telo					
W Euley					
*RCC Canning					
†Z Homani					
WC Hantam					
SG George					
M Mahlombe					
M de Stadler					
DL Haupt					
Extras (b 4, lb 5, w 13, nb 2)	24				
TOTAL (for 1 wkt) (34.1 overs)	**163**				

WP	*O*	*M*	*R*	*W*
Hantam	7	0	24	0 (1 w)
Haupt	9	1	21	4 (2 w)
De Stadler	8	0	40	1 (4 w)
Adams	7.5	0	53	3 (1 nb, 1 w)
George	9	0	22	1 (3 w)

ZU23	*O*	*M*	*R*	*W*
Mpofu	7	0	40	0 (3 w)
Chinyoka	7	1	26	0 (1 w)
Strydom	6	0	31	0 (3 w)
De Grandhomme	6	2	20	0 (1 nb, 1 w)
Matanga	7	1	30	1 (1 w)
Matsikenyeri	1.1	0	7	0 (1 nb)

Fall of Wickets	*ZU23*	*WP*
1st	2 (2)	122 (2)
2nd	13 (1)	-
3rd	17 (4)	-
4th	20 (3)	-
5th	37 (5)	-
6th	98 (7)	-
7th	118 (8)	-
8th	127 (6)	-
9th	128 (9)	-
10th	162 (10)	-

BOLAND v ZIMBABWE UNDER-23 — SAA 1-day Challenge Pool B

Played at University Oval, Coetzenburg, Stellenbosch on 20 November 2005 — Toss: Boland
Umpires: DJ Smith & BM White
Debuts: Bol: PC Laing (LO). ZU23: None
Result: Boland won by 8 wickets
Points: Bol: 6; ZU23: 0
Notes: Boland substitute: QK Kannemeyer replaced BL Fransman

ZIMBABWE UNDER-23	*Runs*	*Mins*	*Balls*	*4*	*6*
S Matsikenyeri c Walters b Sandri	9	35	21	-	-
B Mlambo c Swan b Sandri	3	21	14	-	-
IM Chinyoka c Davids b Fransman	1	4	4	-	-
C de Grandhomme c and b Laing	24	58	31	3	-
TMK Mawoyo c Davids b Laing	12	28	21	1	-
GM Strydom c Fransman b Laing	52	69	54	4	1
*†A Maregwede c Swan b Laing	5	10	7	1	-
A Mwayenga not out	29	74	64	2	1
CB Mpofu c and b September	2	15	11	-	-
H Matanga lbw b September	0	1	2	-	-
TN Garwe b Fransman	7	18	19	1	-
Extras (lb 11, w 14, nb 2)	27				
TOTAL (41 overs)	**171**				

BOLAND	*Runs*	*Mins*	*Balls*	*4*	*6*
C Prinsloo c Garwe b Mwayenga	1	10	4	-	-
JG Strydom lbw b Matanga	30	36	33	5	-
WC Swan not out	61	121	94	2	1
H Davids not out	53	95	72	6	1
RG Arendse					
PC Laing					
*WA Albertyn					
†L-R Walters					
WE September					
PSE Sandri					
QK Kannemeyer					
BL Fransman					
Extras (b 8, lb 4, w 19)	31				
TOTAL (for 2 wkts) (33.5 overs)	**176**				

Bol	O	M	R	W	
Sandri	6	0	27	2	(1 nb, 5 w)
Fransman	7	1	15	2	(1 nb, 3 w)
Albertyn	6	1	31	0	(2 w)
Laing	9	0	43	4	(1 w)
September	8	2	34	2	
Davids	5	1	10	0	(3 w)

ZU23	O	M	R	W	
Mwayenga	3	0	14	1	(4 w)
Garwe	2	0	19	0	
De Grandhomme	5	0	22	0	(1 w)
Matanga	9	0	33	1	(2 w)
Mpofu	5.5	0	37	0	(2 w)
Matsikenyeri	9	1	39	0	(5 w)

Fall of Wickets	ZU23	Bol
1st	21 (2)	13 (1)
2nd	22 (3)	47 (2)
3rd	27 (1)	-
4th	62 (5)	-
5th	93 (4)	-
6th	102 (7)	-
7th	138 (6)	-
8th	150 (9)	-
9th	150 (10)	-
10th	171 (11)	-

WESTERN PROVINCE v BORDER

SAA 1-day Challenge Pool B

Played at Sahara Park Newlands, Cape Town on 20 November 2005

Toss: Western Province

Umpires: MW Brown & EC Hendrikse

Debuts: WP: None. Bdr: KD Bennett (LO)

Result: Border won by 5 wickets

Points: Bdr: 6; WP: 0

Notes: Border substitute: S de Kock replaced Y Pangabantu after 18 overs of Western Province's innings. Western Province substitute: MQ Adams replaced DL Haupt after 28.1 overs of Western Province's innings.

WESTERN PROVINCE	Runs	Mins	Balls	4	6
M Williamson c Brown b Pangabantu	1	6	3	-	-
AJA Gray lbw b Richards	1	27	13	-	-
Z Homani lbw b Pangabantu	20	35	33	2	-
W Wyngaard c Matika b Brown	9	35	28	1	-
FD Telo c Dyili b Pangabantu	9	24	12	2	-
*†RCC Canning b Ranger	23	77	45	2	-
WC Hantam c Von Hoesslin b Brown	5	43	32	-	-
SG George c Mbane b Matika	5	17	10	-	-
MQ Adams c Gamiet b Richards	21	28	26	-	2
M Mahlombe not out	8	21	15	1	-
M de Stadler lbw b Richards	0	4	5	-	-
DL Haupt					
Extras (lb 4, w 15)	19				
TOTAL (37 overs)	**121**				

BORDER	Runs	Mins	Balls	4	6
BL Bennett c George b De Stadler	42	62	55	4	-
†GE von Hoesslin c Canning b De Stadler	14	27	30	1	-
S de Kock lbw b Mahlombe	0	4	1	-	-
MM Matika c Mahlombe b Adams	22	41	21	4	-
LL Gamiet not out	18	50	41	2	-
KD Bennett c Mahlombe b Adams	20	34	34	2	-
AZM Dyili not out	1	3	4	-	-
*MN Ranger					
L Mbane					
DL Brown					
RR Richards					
Y Pangabantu					
Extras (lb 4, w 1)	5				
TOTAL (for 5 wkts) (31 overs)	**122**				

Bdr	O	M	R	W	
Richards	6	1	13	3	(2 w)
Pangabantu	9	0	33	3	(1 w)
Brown	9	1	23	2	(8 w)
Mbane	5	1	14	0	(1 w)
Matika	4	0	20	1	(1 w)
Ranger	4	0	14	1	(2 w)

WP	O	M	R	W	
Hantam	8	2	30	0	(1 w)
De Stadler	9	2	19	2	
Mahlombe	6	0	25	1	
George	2	0	20	0	
Adams	6	0	24	2	

Fall of Wickets	WP	Bdr
1st	1 (1)	31 (2)
2nd	18 (2)	32 (3)
3rd	30 (3)	74 (1)
4th	44 (4)	88 (4)
5th	44 (5)	121 (6)
6th	67 (7)	-
7th	85 (8)	-
8th	91 (6)	-
9th	121 (9)	-
10th	121 (11)	-

BOLAND v EASTERN PROVINCE

SAA 1-day Challenge Pool B

Played at Boland Park, Paarl on 27 November 2005

Toss: Eastern Province

Umpires: EC Hendrikse & LJ Willemse

Debuts: Bol: None. EP: None

Result: Boland won by 1 wicket

Points: Bol: 5; EP: 1

Notes: Strydom scored his fifty off 35 balls in Boland's innings. Boland substitute: JM van Wyk replaced HH Paulse after 40.5 overs of Boland's innings. Eastern Province substitute: NG Brouwers replaced RR Jeggels after 32 overs of Boland's innings.

EASTERN PROVINCE	Runs	Mins	Balls	4	6
C Baxter b Davids	61	146	98	7	-
ML Price b Paulse	4	14	8	1	-
U Abrahams b Laing	54	78	58	9	-
RR Jeggels c Louw b September	25	27	18	3	1
SG Fensham lbw b September	35	47	50	1	-
*GE Howell c Davids b September	19	16	13	1	1
WE Bell c sub (PSE Sandri) b Davids	6	14	9	-	-
†M Slwana c and b Davids	6	12	9	-	-
J Theron not out	2	8	2	-	-
S Mjekula not out	11	5	6	-	1
LL Tsotsobe					
NG Brouwers					
Extras (lb 1, w 11, nb 1)	13				
TOTAL (for 8 wkts) (45 overs)	**236**				

BOLAND	Runs	Mins	Balls	4	6
C Prinsloo c Slwana b Bell	55	133	97	7	-
JG Strydom c Fensham b Theron	63	75	47	10	-
WC Swan b Theron	7	17	14	1	-
H Davids lbw b Bell	38	57	43	5	-
†WJ Louw c Slwana b Brouwers	19	28	21	2	-
PC Laing run out (Baxter/Brouwers)	16	19	19	-	1
QK Kannemeyer b Theron	3	15	8	-	-
JM van Wyk c Slwana b Bell	7	15	6	-	-
WE September lbw b Theron	0	1	1	-	-
*WA Albertyn not out	5	14	5	-	-
BL Fransman not out	2	7	7	-	-
HH Paulse					
Extras (b 5, lb 4, w 7, nb 6)	22				
TOTAL (for 9 wkts) (44.2 overs)	**237**				

Bol	O	M	R	W	
Paulse	4	0	26	1	(4 w)
Fransman	6	1	24	0	(1 w)
Albertyn	5	0	28	0	
Kannemeyer	7	0	31	0	(1 nb, 3 w)
Laing	4	0	27	1	
September	9	0	44	3	(1 w)
Davids	9	0	44	3	(1 w)
Swan	1	0	11	0	

EP	O	M	R	W	
Tsotsobe	7.2	1	34	0	(1 w)
Mjekula	5	0	35	0	
Theron	9	1	50	4	(2 nb, 1 w)
Howell	9	0	32	0	(1 w)
Bell	9	0	47	3	(2 w)
Brouwers	5	0	30	1	

Fall of Wickets	EP	Bol
1st	15 (2)	109 (2)
2nd	103 (3)	120 (3)
3rd	139 (4)	161 (1)
4th	177 (1)	197 (4)
5th	209 (6)	209 (5)
6th	212 (5)	221 (6)
7th	222 (7)	226 (7)
8th	224 (8)	226 (9)
9th	-	230 (8)

BORDER v EASTERN PROVINCE

SAA 1-day Challenge Pool B

Played at Mercedes-Benz Park, East London on 22 January 2006

Toss: Border

Umpires: BM White & LJ Willemse

Debuts: Bdr: None. EP: SR Adair (LO)

Result: Eastern Province won by 9 wickets

Points: Bdr: 0; EP: 6

Notes: Border substitute: KD Bennett replaced Y Pangabantu after 23.4 overs of Border's innings.

BORDER	Runs	Mins	Balls	4	6
BL Bennett c Abrahams b Tsotsobe	2	2	3	-	-
CC Bradfield b Tsotsobe	1	12	3	-	-
GE von Hoesslin c Adair b Tsotsobe	0	2	2	-	-
SC Pope c Howell b Mjekula	13	37	33	1	-
*MN Ranger c Fensham b Tsotsobe	9	34	19	2	-
†AM Sodumo b Tsotsobe	0	6	4	-	-
DL Brown lbw b Howell	25	71	40	-	-
WR Hinkel c Jeggels b Theron	21	38	34	4	-
L Mbane st Adair b Ingram	10	18	15	2	-
KD Bennett not out	11	18	15	1	-
RR Richards b Mjekula	7	10	6	1	-
Y Pangabantu					
Extras (b 1, lb 2, w 3, nb 1)	7				
TOTAL (28.4 overs)	**106**				

EASTERN PROVINCE	Runs	Mins	Balls	4	6
C Baxter c KD Bennett b Ranger	25	43	33	3	-
CA Ingram not out	73	65	58	12	2
U Abrahams not out	4	22	14	-	-
RR Jeggels					
ML Price					
*GE Howell					
SG Fensham					
†SR Adair					
J Theron					
S Mjekula					
LL Tsotsobe					
Extras (lb 2, w 2, nb 1)	5				
TOTAL (for 1 wkt) (17.2 overs)	**107**				

EP	O	M	R	W	
Tsotsobe	9	1	28	5	(1 nb, 1 w)
Mjekula	7.4	1	15	2	
Theron	4	0	18	1	
Howell	5	0	25	1	(2 w)
Ingram	3	0	17	1	

Bdr	O	M	R	W	
Richards	3	0	19	0	
Mbane	3	0	18	0	
Brown	3	0	24	0	(1 nb, 1 w)
Ranger	4	0	16	1	
Hinkel	3	0	11	0	(1 w)
BL Bennett	1.2	0	17	0	

Fall of Wickets	Bdr	EP
1st	2 (1)	75 (1)
2nd	2 (3)	-
3rd	7 (2)	-
4th	28 (4)	-
5th	28 (5)	-
6th	28 (6)	-
7th	62 (8)	-
8th	80 (9)	-
9th	89 (7)	-
10th	106 (11)	-

WESTERN PROVINCE v KWAZULU-NATAL — SAA 1-day Challenge Pool B

Played at Sahara Park Newlands, Cape Town on 4 February 2006 — Toss: Western Province
Umpires: EC Hendrikse & IH van Kerwel
Debuts: WP: AR Fernandez and JP Geoghegan (Both LO). KZN: CS Mabuya, AI Chinnappa and PM Selowa (All LO)
Result: KwaZulu-Natal won by 63 runs
Points: KZN: 6; WP: 0
Notes: KwaZulu-Natal substitute: AI Chinnappa replaced TD Pillay after 30.4 overs of KwaZulu-Natal's innings. Western Province substitute: SG George replaced DL Haupt after 22.2 overs of KwaZulu-Natal's innings.

KWAZULU-NATAL	Runs	Mins	Balls	4	6
MD Sanders b Hantam	30	79	57	5	-
*R Gobind c Geoghegan b Friend	13	26	25	1	-
WR Wingfield lbw b Hantam	20	36	33	3	-
CS Mabuya c Homani b Hantam	16	34	24	2	1
M Bekker b Hantam	0	7	3	-	-
KC Africa b Geoghegan	1	17	5	-	-
PM Selowa c Hantam b Geoghegan	27	58	47	1	-
†DR Miller c De Stadler b Hantam	17	21	16	2	1
AI Chinnappa c Canning b Geoghegan	14	19	15	2	-
ND Hewer c Hantam b Friend	2	12	5	-	-
S Mhlongo not out	0	2	0	-	-
TD Pillay					
Extras (lb 3, w 5)	8				
TOTAL (38.2 overs)	**148**				

WESTERN PROVINCE	Runs	Mins	Balls	4	6
DJ Bassage b Hewer	0	5	4	-	-
AJA Gray c Miller b Africa	16	59	35	2	-
Z Homani c Miller b Mhlongo	1	13	13	-	-
AR Fernandez lbw b Mhlongo	4	3	3	1	-
SG George c Bekker b Africa	9	28	22	1	-
W Euley b Mhlongo	9	29	9	1	-
*†RCC Canning lbw b Africa	4	4	5	1	-
WC Hantam lbw b Wingfield	13	38	24	1	-
JP Geoghegan lbw b Mhlongo	0	2	1	-	-
Q Friend b Mhlongo	0	3	3	-	-
M de Stadler not out	1	15	4	-	-
DL Haupt					
Extras (lb 10, w 13, nb 5)	28				
TOTAL (19.4 overs)	**85**				

WP	O	M	R	W
Friend	7.2	2	9	2 (1 w)
Haupt	6	0	30	0
De Stadler	7	1	23	0
Hantam	9	1	31	5 (1 w)
Geoghegan	8	0	47	3 (3 w)
George	1	0	5	0

KZN	O	M	R	W
Mhlongo	9	2	29	5 (2 w)
Hewer	6	2	11	1 (2 w)
Africa	4	0	23	3 (5 nb, 1 w)
Wingfield	0.4	0	12	1 (4 w)

Fall of Wickets	KZN	WP
1st	20 (2)	2 (1)
2nd	58 (3)	9 (3)
3rd	67 (1)	13 (4)
4th	73 (5)	30 (5)
5th	84 (4)	42 (2)
6th	86 (6)	47 (7)
7th	111 (8)	60 (6)
8th	137 (9)	60 (9)
9th	148 (7)	60 (10)
10th	148 (10)	85 (8)

BOLAND v BORDER — SAA 1-day Challenge Pool B

Played at Boland Park, Paarl on 12 February 2006 — Toss: Boland
Umpires: MW Brown & IH van Kerwel
Debuts: Bol: DL Hobson, DJ Malan and GC Stevens (All LO). Bdr: None
Result: Boland won by 5 wickets
Points: Bdr: 0; Bol: 6
Notes: Boland substitute: DL Hobson replaced BL Fransman after 17 overs of Border's innings.

BORDER	Runs	Mins	Balls	4	6
BL Bennett c September b Du Toit	1	5	7	-	-
CC Bradfield b September	33	123	62	1	-
BC de Wett b Du Toit	1	18	18	-	-
†AZM Dyili c September b Fransman	14	24	18	3	-
*MN Ranger c Walters b Kannemeyer	23	59	48	3	-
GF von Hoesslin b Stevens	3	10	17	-	-
KD Bennett c Walters b Du Toit	30	45	39	1	2
DL Brown run out (Swan/Walters)	6	15	10	-	-
MW Olivier b Stevens	5	7	10	1	-
RR Richards st Walters b Stevens	5	7	7	1	-
Y Pangabantu not out	0	9	6	-	-
Extras (b 4, lb 5, w 11)	20				
TOTAL (40.2 overs)	**141**				

BOLAND	Runs	Mins	Balls	4	6
DJ Malan c Ranger b Olivier	0	5	6	-	-
WE September c Dyili b Richards	11	27	17	1	-
JG Strydom run out (Dyili)	71	113	73	11	1
GC Stevens c Dyili b Richards	10	21	16	1	-
*WC Swan not out	32	83	54	2	-
QK Kannemeyer lbw b Ranger	0	3	2	-	-
†L-R Walters not out	3	8	7	-	
WJ Louw					
WJ du Toit					
JM van Wyk					
DL Hobson					
BL Fransman					
Extras (lb 3, w 10, nb 2)	15				
TOTAL (for 5 wkts) (28.5 overs)	**142**				

Bol	O	M	R	W		Bdr	O	M	R	W	
Fransman	9	3	20	1	(1 w)	Olivier	7	1	30	1	(2 nb, 3 w)
Du Toit	7.2	2	27	3	(1 w)	Richards	6	1	35	2	(4 w)
Van Wyk	3	0	16	0	(1 w)	Pangabantu	2	0	10	0	
September	9	1	23	1	(1 w)	BL Bennett	7.5	0	36	0	(3 w)
Kannemeyer	3	0	15	1	(3 w)	Brown	4	0	20	0	
Stevens	8	2	18	3		Ranger	2	0	8	1	
Malan	1	0	13	0							

Fall of Wickets	Bdr	Bol
1st	6 (1)	3 (1)
2nd	8 (3)	26 (2)
3rd	35 (4)	48 (4)
4th	81 (5)	129 (3)
5th	91 (6)	134 (6)
6th	94 (2)	-
7th	105 (8)	-
8th	110 (9)	-
9th	124 (10)	-
10th	141 (7)	-

EASTERN PROVINCE v WESTERN PROVINCE — SAA 1-day Challenge Pool B

Played at Sahara Oval St George's, Port Elizabeth on 12 February 2006 — Toss: Eastern Province

Umpires: BN Harrison & LJ Willemse

Debuts: EP: None. WP: S Conrad and JM Kupier (Both LO)

Result: Western Province won by 4 wickets

Points: EP: 1; WP: 5

Notes: Eastern Province substitute: SG Fensham replaced S Mjekula after 39.4 overs of Eastern Province's innings. Western Province substitute: JP Geoghegan replaced S Conrad after 9.5 overs of Western Province's innings.

EASTERN PROVINCE	Runs	Mins	Balls	4	6
C Baxter b Hantam	41	93	73	4	-
*CA Ingram c Canning b De Stadler	39	58	36	7	-
U Abrahams run out (De Stadler)	0	11	8	-	-
RR Jeggels c Canning b De Stadler	1	6	9	-	-
†SR Adair st Canning b Conrad	18	49	24	2	-
E Potgieter c Kuiper b Conrad	31	27	31	3	2
D Willemse c Canning b De Stadler	18	39	31	-	-
L Meyer c Behardien b De Stadler	37	49	40	2	-
SG Fensham not out	13	24	15	-	-
LL Tsotsobe b Friend	1	3	3	-	-
J Theron not out	9	4	3	2	-
S Mjekula					
Extras (lb 9, w 8, nb 3)	20				
TOTAL (for 9 wkts) (45 overs)	**228**				

WESTERN PROVINCE	Runs	Mins	Balls	4	6
AJA Gray lbw b Tsotsobe	46	45	30	9	-
DJ Bassage run out (Baxter)	65	69	53	11	1
JP Geoghegan c Adair b Ingram	29	64	33	2	1
Z Homani b Ingram	12	49	37	1	-
W Wyngaard not out	30	72	53	4	-
JM Kuiper b Willemse	12	10	9	2	-
*†RCC Canning c Adair b Tsotsobe	10	14	15	1	-
WC Hantam not out	13	37	35	2	-
Q Friend					
F Behardien					
M de Stadler					
S Conrad					
Extras (b 2, lb 2, w 8, nb 3)	15				
TOTAL (for 6 wkts) (43.3 overs)	**232**				

WP	O	M	R	W		EP	O	M	R	W	
Friend	9	1	42	1	(1 nb, 2 w)	Meyer	7	1	46	0	(2 w)
Hantam	9	1	49	1	(1 w)	Tsotsobe	9	0	57	2	(1 w)
Behardien	9	0	41	0	(1 nb, 3 w)	Theron	9	0	47	0	(3 nb, 1 w)
De Stadler	9	1	42	4	(1 w)	Willemse	9	2	49	1	
Conrad	9	0	45	2	(1 nb, 1 w)	Ingram	9	0	25	2	
						Potgieter	0.3	0	4	0	

Fall of Wickets	EP	WP
1st	72 (2)	84 (1)
2nd	80 (3)	123 (2)
3rd	81 (4)	159 (3)
4th	94 (1)	164 (4)
5th	142 (6)	181 (6)
6th	144 (5)	197 (7)
7th	187 (7)	-
8th	212 (8)	-
9th	215 (10)	-

WESTERN PROVINCE v BOLAND — SAA 1-day Challenge Pool B

Played at Sahara Park Newlands, Cape Town on 19 February 2006 — Toss: Western Province

Umpires: LH Matroos & IH van Kerwel

Debuts: WP: None. Bol: None

Result: Western Province won by 6 wickets

Points: Bol: 1; WP: 5

Notes: Geoghegan scored his fifty off 35 balls in Western Province's innings. Boland substitute: QK Kannemeyer replaced DJ Malan after 0 overs of Western Province's innings. Western Province substitute: JP Geoghegan replaced S Conrad after 6.1 overs of Western Province's innings.

BOLAND	Runs	Mins	Balls	4	6
DJ Malan c Wyngaard b Hantam	5	21	18	-	-
WE September c Canning b Hantam	7	32	18	1	-
WJ Smit b Behardien	7	6	7	1	-
JG Strydom c Canning b De Stadler	49	46	36	6	2
*WC Swan not out	96	155	103	8	1
PC Laing run out (Zondeki/Conrad)	6	23	16	-	-
GC Stevens c Canning b Conrad	43	47	40	8	-
†L-R Walters st Canning b Conrad	1	5	7	-	-
WJ du Toit b Hantam	15	27	21	-	-
JM van Wyk not out	3	6	4	-	-
BL Fransman					
QK Kannemeyer					
Extras (lb 1, w 9)	10				
TOTAL (for 8 wkts) (45 overs)	**242**				

WESTERN PROVINCE	Runs	Mins	Balls	4	6
AJA Gray st Walters b September	70	134	105	5	2
DJ Bassage c Smit b Du Toit	13	25	19	2	-
JP Geoghegan c Stevens b Kannemeyer	77	75	58	13	1
Z Homani c Strydom b September	44	58	47	7	-
JM Kuiper not out	20	30	20	3	-
WC Hantam not out	11	4	6	2	-
W Wyngaard					
*†RCC Canning					
F Behardien					
M Zondeki					
M de Stadler					
S Conrad					
Extras (b 4, lb 1, w 1, nb 2)	8				
TOTAL (for 4 wkts) (42 overs)	**243**				

WP	O	M	R	W
Zondeki	9	0	44	0 (4 w)
Hantam	9	1	51	3 (2 w)
Behardien	9	0	61	1 (1 w)
De Stadler	9	0	54	1 (1 w)
Conrad	9	1	31	2

Bol	O	M	R	W
Du Toit	9	1	26	1 (1 w)
Fransman	4	0	28	0 (1 nb)
Van Wyk	2	0	24	0
Laing	4	0	26	0
Stevens	9	0	38	0 (1 nb)
September	6	0	44	2
Kannemeyer	8	0	52	1

Fall of Wickets	Bol	WP
1st	13 (1)	17 (2)
2nd	20 (3)	132 (3)
3rd	20 (2)	190 (1)
4th	103 (4)	231 (4)
5th	125 (6)	-
6th	189 (7)	-
7th	193 (8)	-
8th	230 (9)	-

KWAZULU-NATAL v BORDER — SAA 1-day Challenge Pool B

Played at Sahara Stadium Kingsmead, Durban on 19 February 2006 — Toss: KwaZulu-Natal

Umpires: GH Pienaar & S Wadvalla

Debuts: KZN: None. Bdr: MX Pethu (LO)

Result: KwaZulu-Natal won by 11 runs

Points: Bdr: 1; KZN: 5

Notes: Border substitute: MX Pethu replaced Y Pangabantu after 0 overs of Border's innings.

KWAZULU-NATAL	Runs	Mins	Balls	4	6
I Khan c De Wett b Brown	32	27	28	6	-
MD Sanders run out (De Wett/Dyili)	27	60	35	3	-
*R Gobind run out (KD Bennett/Dyili)	73	99	79	6	-
CS Mabuya lbw b Ranger	1	7	2	-	-
M Bekker lbw b Ranger	8	27	25	-	-
AI Chinnappa c KD Bennett b Lwana	6	35	28	-	-
†DR Miller run out (Olivier)	18	36	25	1	-
R Frylinck c and b De Wett	3	10	6	-	-
TD Pillay st Dyili b De Wett	9	24	22	-	-
YA Abdullah st Dyili b De Wett	7	13	8	1	-
S Mhlongo not out	3	9	9	-	-
Extras (b 2, lb 2, w 6, nb 4)	14				
TOTAL (43.5 overs)	**201**				

BORDER	Runs	Mins	Balls	4	6
BL Bennett lbw b Abdullah	0	1	3	-	-
KD Bennett st Miller b Chinnappa	53	135	108	6	1
BC de Wett c and b Abdullah	8	17	19	1	-
SC Pope c Miller b Mhlongo	13	38	21	1	-
LL Gamiet not out	62	116	81	2	-
*MN Ranger c Khan b Pillay	25	29	33	2	-
†AZM Dyili not out	16	9	9	1	1
MX Pethu					
DL Brown					
LL Lwana					
MW Olivier					
Y Pangabantu					
Extras (b 2, lb 1, w 6, nb 4)	13				
TOTAL (for 5 wkts) (45 overs)	**190**				

Bdr	O	M	R	W
Olivier	4	0	30	0 (2 w)
Pangabantu	4	0	23	0
Brown	5	1	32	1 (3 nb, 2 w)
Ranger	9	1	33	2 (1 w)
Pope	6	1	31	0
Lwana	7	0	29	1 (1 nb)
De Wett	8.5	1	19	3 (1 w)

KZN	O	M	R	W
Abdullah	9	1	45	2 (3 w)
Mhlongo	9	1	30	1 (4 nb, 2 w)
Frylinck	5	0	28	0 (1 w)
Pillay	9	0	35	1
Khan	6	0	16	0
Chinnappa	7	0	33	1

Fall of Wickets	KZN	Bdr
1st	42 (1)	1 (1)
2nd	91 (2)	21 (3)
3rd	93 (4)	52 (4)
4th	124 (5)	121 (2)
5th	155 (3)	167 (6)
6th	155 (6)	-
7th	163 (8)	
8th	187 (7)	-
9th	188 (9)	-
10th	201 (10)	-

BOLAND v KWAZULU-NATAL — SAA 1-day Challenge Pool B

Played at University Oval, Coetzenburg, Stellenbosch on 26 February 2006 — Toss: KwaZulu-Natal

Umpires: EC Hendrikse & IH van Kerwel

Debuts: Bol: None. KZN: None

Result: Boland won by 3 wickets

Points: Bol: 5; KZN: 1

Notes: Bekker scored his fifty off 33 balls in KwaZulu-Natal's innings. Boland substitute: QK Kannemeyer replaced WA Albertyn after 15 overs of KwaZulu-Natal's innings. KwaZulu-Natal substitute: KC Africa replaced TD Pillay after 18.1 overs of KwaZulu-Natal's innings.

SAA PROVINCIAL ONE-DAY CHALLENGE

KWAZULU-NATAL	Runs	Mins	Balls	4	6
*I Khan c Louw b Fransman	11	44	19	2	-
MD Sanders c Louw b Fransman	0	12	10	-	-
†DR Miller lbw b Fransman	0	1	1	-	-
M Bekker c Fransman b Laing	58	54	42	10	-
PM Selowa c Smit b Laing	12	56	31	1	-
AI Chinnappa b Fransman	0	7	4	-	-
T Essack c September b Laing	6	14	10	-	-
KC Africa c Louw b Stevens	48	71	51	5	1
R Frylinck c Louw b Kannemeyer	15	23	11	2	1
ZA Abrahim b Laing	1	4	7	-	-
ND Hewer not out	6	30	22	-	-
TD Pillay					
Extras (b 1, w 4, nb 1)	6				
TOTAL (34.3 overs)	**163**				

BOLAND	Runs	Mins	Balls	4	6
†WJ Louw c Abrahim b Hewer	22	38	35	4	-
DJ Malan c Miller b Abrahim	15	18	11	3	-
WJ Smit b Hewer	16	74	43	2	-
JG Strydom lbw b Hewer	0	1	1	-	-
WC Swan lbw b Frylinck	26	55	37	3	-
PC Laing lbw b Frylinck	1	12	3	-	-
GC Stevens lbw b Chinnappa	23	54	43	4	-
QK Kannemeyer not out	29	52	35	3	-
WE September not out	12	17	14	2	-
BL Fransman					
HH Paulse					
*WA Albertyn					
Extras (b 6, lb 5, w 10)	21				
TOTAL (for 7 wkts) (37 overs)	**165**				

Bol	O	M	R	W
Paulse	9	1	52	0 (1 w)
Fransman	9	2	22	4 (1 nb, 1 w)
Albertyn	2	0	27	0
Laing	9	1	42	4 (1 w)
Kannemeyer	5	0	19	1 (1 w)
Stevens	0.3	0	0	1

KZN	O	M	R	W
Abrahim	9	0	41	1 (2 w)
Africa	6	0	28	0 (1 w)
Hewer	8	0	24	3 (3 w)
Frylinck	6	0	27	2 (3 w)
Essack	4	0	14	0 (1 w)
Chinnappa	3	0	13	1
Miller	1	0	7	0

Fall of Wickets	KZN	Bol
1st	6 (2)	31 (2)
2nd	6 (3)	40 (1)
3rd	47 (1)	40 (4)
4th	75 (4)	94 (3)
5th	75 (6)	94 (5)
6th	89 (7)	103 (6)
7th	97 (5)	141 (7)
8th	132 (9)	-
9th	134 (10)	-
10th	163 (8)	-

BORDER v WESTERN PROVINCE

SAA 1-day Challenge Pool B

Played at Mercedes-Benz Park, East London on 5 March 2006

Toss: Western Province

Umpires: BN Harrison & LJ Willemse

Debuts: Bdr: MF Richardson (LO). WP: None

Result: Western Province won by 4 runs

Points: Bdr: 1; WP: 5

Notes: Gamiet scored his century off 91 balls in Border's innings. Border substitute: L Mbane replaced Y Pangabantu after 31 overs of Western Province's innings. Western Province substitute: WC Hantam replaced Z Homani after 38 overs of Border's innings.

WESTERN PROVINCE	Runs	Mins	Balls	4	6
AJA Gray lbw b Pangabantu	5	15	14	1	-
M Williamson c Von Hoesslin b Ngam	25	57	34	2	-
JP Geoghegan c Pethu b Ngam	10	12	10	2	-
Z Homani c Von Hoesslin b Ngam	8	10	9	2	-
FD Telo run out (Ngam/De Kock/Von Hoesslin)	90	128	97	5	-
JM Kuiper lbw b De Kock	29	40	25	3	-
*†RCC Canning b Brown	31	49	36	2	-
F Behardien c Von Hoesslin b Ngam	37	38	35	3	-
F Jardine not out	21	19	12	2	-
S Abrahams not out	1	2	1	-	-
M de Stadler					
WC Hantam					
Extras (lb 2, w 8, nb 4)	14				
TOTAL (for 8 wkts) (45 overs)	**271**				

BORDER	Runs	Mins	Balls	4	6
KD Bennett c Gray b Abrahams	0	2	5	-	-
†GE von Hoesslin c Canning b Abrahams	13	57	26	1	-
MF Richardson b Behardien	69	134	114	8	-
*LL Gamiet not out	134	120	105	14	4
AZM Dyili b De Stadler	29	37	24	1	1
L Mbane not out	5	2	2	1	-
MX Pethu					
DL Brown					
S de Kock					
M Ngam					
LL Lwana					
Y Pangabantu					
Extras (lb 3, w 8, nb 6)	17				
TOTAL (for 4 wkts) (45 overs)	**267**				

Bdr	O	M	R	W
Ngam	9	0	49	4 (3 w)
Pangabantu	9	2	50	1 (1 w)
Brown	9	0	61	1 (2 w)
Lwana	7	0	52	0 (3 nb, 1 w)
De Kock	9	0	44	1 (1 w)
Pethu	2	0	13	0

WP	O	M	R	W
Abrahams	9	2	35	2 (4 nb, 1 w)
Behardien	9	1	53	1 (2 nb, 3 w)
De Stadler	9	0	62	1 (2 w)
Jardine	9	0	45	0 (1 w)
Geoghegan	9	0	69	0 (1 w)

Fall of Wickets	WP	Bdr
1st	11 (1)	0 (1)
2nd	28 (3)	50 (2)
3rd	36 (4)	168 (3)
4th	58 (2)	262 (5)
5th	118 (6)	-
6th	193 (7)	-
7th	235 (5)	-
8th	261 (8)	-

SAA PROVINCIAL ONE-DAY CHALLENGE

EASTERN PROVINCE v BOLAND

SAA 1-day Challenge Pool B

Played at Sahara Oval St George's, Port Elizabeth on 12 March 2006

Toss: Boland

Umpires: BN Harrison & LJ Willemse

Debuts: EP: None. Bol: FA Geldenhuys (LO)

Result: Eastern Province won by 7 wickets

Points: Bol: 0; EP: 6

BOLAND	*Runs*	*Mins*	*Balls*	*4*	*6*
DJ Malan c Adair b Theron	42	75	55	8	-
WE September b Tsotsobe	30	44	33	5	-
WC Swan st Adair b Howell	29	68	41	1	-
H Davids c Jeggels b Theron	7	11	9	1	-
GC Stevens b Howell	0	15	6	-	-
QK Kannemeyer c Adair b Howell	11	39	20	1	-
FA Geldenhuys lbw b Howell	0	2	2	-	-
*WA Albertyn run out (Baxter/Howell)	1	6	5	-	-
†L-R Walters c Howell b Ingram	3	10	10	-	-
BL Fransman not out	14	26	16	2	-
HH Paulse c Baxter b Ingram	1	6	7	-	-
Extras (w 10)	10				
TOTAL (34 overs)	**148**				

EASTERN PROVINCE	*Runs*	*Mins*	*Balls*	*4*	*6*
*CA Ingram run out (Stevens)	60	109	90	8	-
C Baxter c Walters b Davids	46	93	73	7	-
E Potgieter c Fransman b Davids	28	20	16	3	2
U Abrahams not out	4	8	6	1	-
RR Jeggels not out	0	4	1	-	-
L Dipha					
GE Howell					
†SR Adair					
DD Carolus					
J Theron					
LL Tsotsobe					
Extras (lb 2, w 11, nb 1)	14				
TOTAL (for 3 wkts) (31 overs)	**152**				

EP	*O*	*M*	*R*	*W*
Carolus	6	0	27	0
Tsotsobe	6	1	30	1
Dipha	4	0	19	0
Theron	7	0	46	2 (4 w)
Howell	7	3	13	4
Ingram	4	0	13	2 (1 w)

Bol	*O*	*M*	*R*	*W*
Paulse	3	0	15	0
Fransman	4	0	22	0 (1 w)
Kannemeyer	3	0	14	0 (2 w)
September	5	0	25	0 (1 w)
Stevens	9	0	42	0 (1 nb, 1 w)
Davids	6	0	28	2 (3 w)
Swan	1	0	4	0

Fall of Wickets	*Bol*	*EP*
1st	52 (2)	112 (2)
2nd	95 (1)	141 (1)
3rd	107 (4)	148 (3)
4th	115 (5)	-
5th	120 (3)	-
6th	120 (7)	-
7th	126 (8)	-
8th	130 (9)	-
9th	141 (6)	-
10th	148 (11)	-

Semi-finals

BOLAND v GAUTENG

SAA 1-day Challenge Semi-final

Played at Boland Park, Paarl on 25 March 2006

Toss: Gauteng

Umpires: LH Matroos & DJ Smith

Debuts: Bol: None. Gau: None

Result: Boland won by 7 wickets

Notes: Smit scored his century off 99 balls in Boland's innings. Gauteng substitute: CE Knox replaced JM Otto after 10 overs of Boland's innings.

GAUTENG	*Runs*	*Mins*	*Balls*	*4*	*6*
*BD Snijman c Albertyn b Sandri	0	4	6	-	-
WB Motaung c Strydom b Albertyn	37	69	42	6	-
BC Adams lbw b Sandri	13	37	22	2	-
DR Gain c Smit b September	49	104	86	3	-
DL Makalima c Fransman b Albertyn	14	15	14	1	1
JM Otto lbw b September	36	56	58	2	1
†DM van Wyk not out	17	30	23	1	-
HW le Roux not out	22	27	23	-	1
Y Singh					
A Nawab					
JT Mafa					
CE Knox					
Extras (b 4, lb 1, w 10, nb 4)	19				
TOTAL (for 6 wkts) (45 overs)	**207**				

BOLAND	*Runs*	*Mins*	*Balls*	*4*	*6*
C Prinsloo c Snijman b Nawab	7	13	11	1	-
WE September c Van Wyk b Snijman	48	91	58	7	1
JG Strydom c Van Wyk b Mafa	13	8	9	3	-
WJ Smit not out	108	121	104	18	1
WC Swan not out	23	53	32	3	-
QK Kannemeyer					
GC Stevens					
*WA Albertyn					
†L-R Walters					
BL Fransman					
PSE Sandri					
Extras (lb 3, w 5, nb 1)	9				
TOTAL (for 3 wkts) (35.3 overs)	**208**				

Bol	*O*	*M*	*R*	*W*
Sandri	6	0	31	2 (2 nb, 6 w)
Fransman	8	0	43	0 (2 nb, 1 w)
Kannemeyer	5	0	23	0
Albertyn	8	1	41	2
September	9	0	34	2 (2 w)
Stevens	9	0	30	0 (1 w)

Gau	*O*	*M*	*R*	*W*
Singh	5	0	25	0 (2 w)
Nawab	7	0	40	1
Mafa	3	0	27	1 (1 nb)
Le Roux	5	0	17	0 (1 w)
Knox	2	0	16	0 (1 w)
Snijman	6.3	1	33	1
Adams	4	0	21	0
Motaung	3	0	26	0 (1 w)

Fall of Wickets	*Gau*	*Bol*
1st	2 (1)	12 (1)
2nd	44 (3)	26 (3)
3rd	70 (2)	119 (2)
4th	99 (5)	-
5th	162 (6)	-
6th	163 (4)	-

NORTHERNS v EASTERN PROVINCE — SAA 1-day Challenge Semi-final

Played at LC de Villiers Oval, University of Pretoria, Pretoria on 25 March 2006 — Toss: Eastern Province
Umpires: EC Hendrikse & BM White
Debuts: Nor: None. EP: None
Result: Northerns won by 18 runs
Notes: Eastern Province substitute: L Dipha replaced LL Tsotsobe after 16.1 overs of Eastern Province's innings.

NORTHERNS	Runs	Mins	Balls	4	6
MA Aronstam lbw b Carolus	0	2	2	-	-
F du Plessis c Mjekula b Carolus	114	170	133	10	2
JG Myburgh b Theron	31	76	54	4	-
A Paleker c Mjekula b Ingram	44	67	53	4	-
G Dros lbw b Ingram	3	8	10	-	-
MA Mashimbyi b Theron	29	25	14	2	2
*P Joubert b Theron	2	4	3	-	-
†CFK van Wyk not out	1	5	2	-	-
MJ Mokonyama					
L Manzini					
FG Nkuna					
Extras (b 2, lb 10, w 10, nb 1)	23				
TOTAL (for 7 wkts) (45 overs)	**247**				

EASTERN PROVINCE	Runs	Mins	Balls	4	6
*CA Ingram c Joubert b Nkuna	0	1	2	-	-
C Baxter b Mashimbyi	33	73	51	4	-
U Abrahams c Joubert b Manzini	3	13	6	-	-
RR Jeggels c Van Wyk b Nkuna	71	112	72	11	2
L Dipha lbw b Du Plessis	4	23	12	-	-
E Potgieter c Myburgh b Aronstam	27	65	48	-	2
GE Howell c Aronstam b Nkuna	7	10	10	1	-
†SR Adair b Mashimbyi	32	41	30	2	-
J Theron run out (Aronstam)	15	22	16	-	-
DD Carolus not out	11	17	13	1	-
S Mjekula not out	9	10	10	-	-
LL Tsotsobe					
Extras (b 4, lb 4, w 9)	17				
TOTAL (for 9 wkts) (45 overs)	**229**				

EP	O	M	R	W	
Carolus	8	1	30	2	(3 w)
Tsotsobe	6	0	32	0	(1 w)
Mjekula	7	0	39	0	(5 w)
Theron	7	0	41	3	(1 nb, 1 w)
Howell	9	0	40	0	
Ingram	8	0	53	2	

Nor	O	M	R	W	
Nkuna	7	0	30	3	
Manzini	5	0	33	1	(2 w)
Mashimbyi	9	0	44	2	(2 w)
Joubert	8	0	32	0	
Du Plessis	9	1	40	1	(3 w)
Myburgh	2	0	17	0	
Aronstam	5	0	25	1	

Fall of Wickets	Nor	EP
1st	1 (1)	0 (1)
2nd	72 (3)	7 (3)
3rd	179 (4)	83 (2)
4th	188 (5)	103 (5)
5th	229 (2)	137 (4)
6th	239 (7)	145 (7)
7th	247 (6)	175 (6)
8th	-	203 (8)
9th	-	215 (9)

Final

BOLAND v NORTHERNS — SAA 1-day Challenge Final

Played at Boland Park, Paarl on 1 April 2006 — Toss: Northerns
Umpires: ZTA Ndamane & DJ Smith
Debuts: Bol: None. Nor: None
Result: Northerns won by 4 runs
Notes: Boland substitute: DJ Malan replaced BL Fransman after 0 overs of Boland's innings. Northerns substitute: L Manzini replaced MJ Mokonyama after 0 overs of Boland's innings.

NORTHERNS	Runs	Mins	Balls	4	6
MA Aronstam c Albertyn b Stevens	59	115	81	10	-
F du Plessis c and b Stevens	65	87	66	8	2
JG Myburgh b September	29	55	59	-	-
G Dros b Albertyn	68	60	49	2	6
†CFK van Wyk not out	11	33	17	-	-
A Paleker					
MJ Mokonyama					
*P Joubert					
AM Phangiso					
MA Mashimbyi					
FG Nkuna					
L Manzini					
Extras (lb 5, w 1, nb 2)	8				
TOTAL (for 4 wkts) (45 overs)	**240**				

BOLAND	Runs	Mins	Balls	4	6
C Prinsloo c Van Wyk b Mashimbyi	36	60	37	7	-
WE September c Aronstam b Mashimbyi	5	32	22	1	-
DJ Malan c Du Plessis b Joubert	28	63	39	5	-
WJ Smit lbw b Mashimbyi	6	3	3	1	-
H Davids run out (Manzini/Van Wyk)	3	17	8	-	-
WC Swan c Joubert b Mashimbyi	56	91	70	6	-
QK Kannemeyer st Van Wyk b Du Plessis	20	34	35	-	-
GC Stevens b Dros	1	6	5	-	-
*WA Albertyn not out	58	59	46	6	-
†L-R Walters not out	12	23	9	1	-
PSE Sandri					
BL Fransman					
Extras (lb 2, w 5, nb 4)	11				
TOTAL (for 8 wkts) (45 overs)	**236**				

Bol	O	M	R	W	
Sandri	4	1	23	0	(1 nb)
Fransman	8	1	60	0	(1 nb, 1 w)
Albertyn	8	0	42	1	
September	9	0	41	1	
Kannemeyer	5	1	22	0	
Stevens	9	1	28	2	
Davids	2	0	19	0	

Nor	O	M	R	W	
Nkuna	9	1	38	0	(3 nb)
Manzini	2	0	16	0	
Mashimbyi	9	0	57	4	(3 w)
Phangiso	4	0	22	0	
Joubert	9	0	45	1	(1 w)
Du Plessis	6	0	30	1	(1 nb)
Dros	6	0	26	1	(1 w)

Fall of Wickets	Nor	Bol
1st	113 (2)	37 (2)
2nd	138 (1)	60 (1)
3rd	171 (3)	66 (4)
4th	240 (4)	84 (5)
5th	-	102 (3)
6th	-	139 (7)
7th	-	142 (8)
8th	-	187 (6)

SAA ASSOCIATES CHALLENGE

KwaZulu-Natal Inland repeated their double triumph of 2004/05 in winning the South African Airways Associates Three-day and One-day Challenge tournaments and maintaining an unbeaten record in both competitions.

SAA ASSOCIATES THREE-DAY CHALLENGE 2005/06

Pietermaritzburg, 13-14 Oct 2005: KZNI 258-9* (C Bowyer 104, BDM Moses 63, M van Vuuren 28; DJ Pryke 2-44, A Christiaans 5-78, R Swigelaar 2-29). **SWD** 98 (K de Beer 27, F Bonthuys 25; S Marais 4-26, A van Vuuren 2-21, M van Vuuren 2-11) and 132 (C de Swardt 61*, P Stuurman 29; GM Hampson 2-6, M van Vuuren 5-18). **KwaZulu-Natal Inland won by an innings and 28 runs.** KZNI 18.16 pts, SWD 4.

Witbank, 13-15 Oct 2005: Kei 210 (C Mvovo 127*; Q Khurshid 3-36, P van den Berg 5-26) and 169 (M Ntsekwa 32, N Nqxetbwane 28, N Badi 46*; DH Townsend 3-48, Q Khurshid 2-19, D Grobbelaar 2-49, P van den Berg 2-34). **Mpu** 341-5 (J Jordaan 116, L Arendse 101, R Hugo 62*; C Mvovo 2-73) and 42-0. **Mpumalanga won by 10 wickets.** Mpu 17.88 pts, Kei 5.2.

Polokwane, 20-22 Oct 2005: Lim 272-9 (F Walayat 50, S Letsoala 57, I van Zyl 73*; S Marais 2-64, R McMillan 2-28, M Saliwa 3-19, C Bowyer 2-64) and 227 (A Pathan 36, A Galloway 58, J Shokane 27; C Bowyer 6-83, BDM Moses 3-43). **KZNI** 388-5 (R McMillan 32, C Bowyer 102, V Walker-Randall 27, G Addicott 120*, GM Hampson 82*; C Rosendorff 3-68) and 112-2 (C Bowyer 45*, V Walker-Randall 44). **KwaZulu-Natal Inland won by 8 wickets.** KZNI 20.76 pts, Lim 6.44.

Oudtshoorn, 20-22 Oct 2005: SWD 101 (Q Khurshid 7-28) and 287 (W van Dyk 56, P Stuurman 101, H Matthee 30; P van den Berg 4-62, A Milanzi 4-33). **Mpu** 127 (P van den Berg 33; H Matthee 5-36, F Bonthuys 2-21) and 262-3 (P van den Berg 32, D Griebenauw 175*). **Mpumalanga won by 7 wickets.** Mpu 15.54 pts, SWD 5.02.

Umtata, 27-29 Oct 2005: Lim 332 (A Pathan 37, P Haasbroek 71, F Walayat 72, H van Rooyen 41, H Holtzhausen 41*; C Mvovo 2-69, MR Siwani 5-122, T Ngqolo 2-48) and 168 (F Walayat 34, A Galloway 28; Z Mtyupu 2-52, MR Siwani 5-46). **Kei** 217 (MR Siwani 33, K Shah 45, C Mvovo 47, N Badi 28; P Haasbroek 4-54, A Galloway 3-42, F van der Berg 2-29) and 203 (M Ntsekwa 87, Z Mtyupu 40*, C Mvovo 36; I van Zyl 3-39, H Holtzhausen 2-35, F van der Berg 2-14, H van Rooyen 2-12). **Limpopo won by 80 runs.** Lim 19.64 pts, Kei 7.34.

Umtata, 3-5 Nov 2005: KZNI 287-7 (C Bowyer 38, BDM Moses 31, K Padayachee 34, GM Hampson 96*, L Zama 52*; C Mvovo 2-76, T Ngqolo 2-47, MR Siwani 2-63). **Kei** 24-1. **Drawn.** KZNI 4.74 pts, Kei 3.

Witbank, 3-5 Nov 2005: Mpu 367 (P van den Berg 92, D Griebenauw 26, R Hugo 136, L Arendse 40; S Letsoala 2-54, P Haasbroek 3-81) and 154-6 (DH Townsend 34*; S Letsoala 3-59, P Haasbroek 2-41). **Lim** 167 (A Pathan 65, C Rosendorff 35, F van der Berg 29; DH Townsend 5-32, D Griebenauw 3-66) and 350 (P Haasbroek 86, H van Rooyen 41, C Rosendorff 34, I van Zyl 82, A Galloway 41; Q Khurshid 2-86, P van den Berg 2-29, J Jordaan 4-77). **Mpumalanga won by 4 wickets.** Mpu 20.34 pts, Lim 6.34.

Modjadjieskloof, 10-12 Nov 2005: SWD 198 (P Stuurman 44, F Bonthuys 36, G Saaiman 32; I van Zyl 3-45, C Rosendorff 2-36, P Haasbroek 2-49) and 303-6* (C April 73, C de Swardt 83, DJ Pryke 28, K de Beer 41*; I van Zyl 2-54). **Lim** 165 (A Pathan 58, J Potgieter 32, J Shokane 27; DJ Pryke 8-41, A Christiaans 2-32) and 180-8 (P Haasbroek 35, A Galloway 32, I van Zyl 33*; F Bonthuys 2-49, R Swigelaar 2-10). **Drawn.** SWD 6.96 pts, Lim 6.3.

Pietermaritzburg, 17-19 Nov 2005: KZNI 272-7 (R McMillan 25, G Addicott 26, A van Vuuren 77, GM Hampson 56; DH Townsend 2-64, Q Khurshid 2-52, P van den Berg 2-55) and 239 (BDM Moses 33, A van Vuuren 36, M van Vuuren 55; DH Townsend 2-28, P van den Berg 4-42). **Mpu** 276-5 (P Malan 34, J Jordaan 86, D Griebenauw 29, R Hugo 54*, L Mthombeni 29*; GM Hampson 2-59) and 95-4 (P van den Berg 45*; M van Vuuren 2-14). **Drawn.** Mpu 7.52 pts, KZNI 6.44.

Oudtshoorn, 24-26 Nov 2005: Kei 264-9 (T Kraai 38, M Ntsekwa 100, MR Siwani 35, Z Mtyupu 36; W Hartslief 2-48, A Christiaans 5-63, F Bonthuys 2-54) and 289 (K Moerane 57, K Shah 27, M Ntsekwa 37, Z

Mtyupu 73, C Mvovo 48; H Matthee 3-55, R Swigelaar 3-47). **SWD** 281-8 (S-J Avontuur 82, G Moos 67, F Bonthuys 38*; Z Mtyupu 2-48, C Mvovo 2-37, MR Siwani 2-80) and 115-9 (AW Olivier 40, F Bonthuys 27; C Mvovo 2-26, MR Siwani 3-20, K Shah 3-7). **Drawn.** SWD 8.62 pts, Kei 8.28.

Umtata, 19-21 Jan 2006: Kei 176 (S Dwanqube 55, T Ngqolo 47; Q Khurshid 4-14, MJ Neethling 2-28, L Mthombeni 2-19) and 112-7 (S Dwanqube 54; DH Townsend 2-20, MJ Neethling 3-14). **Mpu** 211 (G Donnelly 27, R Hugo 36, MJ Neethling 26, L Mthombeni 31; P Plaatjies 3-39, S Malusi 2-17). **Drawn.** Mpu 7.22 pts, Kei 6.52.

Oudtshoorn, 19-21 Jan 2006: SWD 136-9* (R Swigelaar 47*; GM Hampson 4-21, C Bowyer 2-24) and 265 (AW Olivier 51, C de Swardt 51, R de Reuck 71, S-J Avontuur 28; M Saliwa 4-57, A van Vuuren 2-61, K Padayachee 2-16). **KZNI** 324-6 (R McMillan 151, C Bowyer 25*, BDM Moses 55, A van Vuuren 36, G Addicott 42; F Bonthuys 2-81, AW Olivier 2-36) and 80-2 (C Bowyer 28, BDM Moses 31*). **KwaZulu-Natal Inland won by 8 wickets.** KZNI 19.48 pts, SWD 4.72.

Pietermaritzburg, 26-28 Jan 2006: KZNI 268-4* (R McMillan 135, BDM Moses 102) and 2nd innings forfeited. **Lim** 1st innings forfeited and 146 (A Galloway 31, T Munjamanje 29*; M Saliwa 3-87, GM Hampson 3-29, M van Vuuren 4-29). **KwaZulu-Natal Inland won by 122 runs.** KZNI 14.36 pts, Lim 2.

Witbank, 26-28 Jan 2006: SWD 131-9* (S-J Avontuur 42, P Stuurman 29; DH Townsend 2-13, P van den Berg 3-25, MJ Neethling 2-11) and 172 (AW Olivier 82, R Swigelaar 43*; DH Townsend 2-31, Q Khurshid 4-41, P van den Berg 2-19). **Mpu** 170 (P van den Berg 55, G Donnelly 30; ER Bezuidenhout 2-42, N Nobebe 2-26, F Bonthuys 3-48) and 134-8 (K Erasmus 34, J Jordaan 28; ER Bezuidenhout 3-66, F Bonthuys 2-18). **Mpumalanga won by 2 wickets.** Mpu 16.4 pts, SWD 5.62.

Modjadjieskloof, 2-4 Feb 2006: Kei 132 (A Hlahleni 30, M Ntsekwa 25; I van Zyl 5-42, S Letsoala 2-22, P Haasbroek 2-18) and 272 (A Hlahleni 31, M Ntsekwa 36, C Mvovo 77, N Badi 31; F van der Berg 3-38, T Semenya 2-62). **Lim** 176 (T Pistorius 82, C Rosendorff 54; C Mvovo 2-35, A Hlahleni 2-21, N Badi 2-18) and 163 (F van der Berg 36, I van Zyl 60; C Mvovo 2-37, T Ngqolo 4-41, J Yoli 3-31). **Kei won by 65 runs.** Kei 15.64 pts, Lim 6.52.

Pietermaritzburg, 9-11 Feb 2006: KZNI 302 (R McMillan 54, G Addicott 69, S Woodroffe 82, GM Hampson 39; A Hlahleni 3-70, S Mxoli 4-28) and 251-5* (BDM Moses 101*, G Addicott 56, S Woodroffe 44; T Ngqolo 2-27). **Kei** 197 (S Dwanqube 37, T Kraai 46, M Tshona 35, N Badi 44*; M Saliwa 4-41, S Marais 2-32) and 277 (K Moerane 54, S Dwanqube 95, M Tshona 45; A van Vuuren 4-90, R McMillan 2-27, BDM Moses 3-48). **KwaZulu-Natal Inland won by 79 runs.** KZNI 19.04 pts, Kei 6.94.

Modjadjieskloof, 9-11 Feb 2006: Limpopo v Mpumalanga match abandoned without a ball bowled. Lim 0 pts, Mpu 0.

Oudtshoorn, 16-18 Feb 2006: Lim 151 (P Haasbroek 38, T Pistorius 40; N Nobebe 3-12, F Bonthuys 5-46) and 264 (P Haasbroek 143, C Rosendorff 31*, H Holtzhausen 28; F Bonthuys 5-65, AW Olivier 2-25). **SWD** 176 (C de Swardt 29, F Bonthuys 50, N Nobebe 31; I van Zyl 2-19, S Letsoala 2-17, C Rosendorff 3-28) and 240-8 (R Swigelaar 32, F Bonthuys 87, N Nobebe 29; I van Zyl 2-30, S Letsoala 2-40, H Holtzhausen 3-32). **South Western Districts won by 2 wickets.** SWD 16.52 pts, Lim 6.02.

Witbank, 23-25 Feb 2006: Mpu 154-9* (P van den Berg 44, J Jordaan 29; M Saliwa 2-52, S Marais 3-15, R McMillan 3-6) and 264 (J Jordaan 106, Q Khurshid 36; M van Vuuren 3-64, A van Vuuren 2-52). **KZNI** 214 (R McMillan 29, GM Hampson 32, A van Vuuren 82; DH Townsend 7-53) and 206-8 (R McMillan 96, A van Vuuren 30; Q Khurshid 2-43, P van den Berg 4-61). **KwaZulu-Natal Inland won by 2 wickets.** KZNI 17.28 pts, Mpu 6.08.

Umtata, 2-4 Mar 2006: Kei 137 (C Mvovo 27, M Tshona 50; DJ Pryke 8-38) and 57-8 (DJ Pryke 2-8, W Hartslief 4-15). **SWD** 170 (S-J Avontuur 41, H Levendal 25; M Tshona 4-43, C Mvovo 3-36). **Drawn.** SWD 6.4 pts, Kei 5.74.

SAA ASSOCIATES CHALLENGE

Table	P	W	L	D	Bat	Bowl	Penalty	Pts
KwaZulu-Natal Inland	8	6	0	2	38.26	22	0	120.26
Mpumalanga	8	4	1	3	23.98	27	0	90.98
Kei	8	1	3	4	19.66	29	0	58.66
South Western Districts	8	1	4	3	16.86	31	0	57.86
Limpopo	8	1	5	2	19.26	24	0	53.26

The match between Limpopo and Mpumalanga did not take place and is reflected as a draw in the above table.

Final

Pietermaritzburg, 18-20 Mar 2006: Mpu 144 (P van den Berg 28; M Saliwa 2-35, A van Vuuren 4-40, GM Hampson 3-26) and 102 (M Saliwa 3-39, A van Vuuren 4-15). **KZNI** 323 (R McMillan 116, BDM Moses 45, A van Vuuren 52, GM Hampson 29, M Gqadushe 33; DH Townsend 3-59, Q Khurshid 4-80, P van den Berg 2-36). **KwaZulu-Natal Inland won by an innings and 77 runs.**

LEADING BATTING AVERAGES

		M	Inns	NO	Runs	HS		Avg	SR	100	50
1	R Hugo (Mpu)	6	9	3	356	136		59.33	72.95	1	2
2	R McMillan (KZNI)	9	14	0	707	151		50.50	64.44	3	2
3	D Griebenauw (Mpu)	3	6	1	249	175	*	49.80	75.00	1	0
4	BDM Moses (KZNI)	9	14	3	505	102		45.90	54.95	2	2
5	C Mvovo (Kei)	7	11	2	400	127	*	44.44	59.97	1	1
6	GM Hampson (KZNI)	9	11	2	398	96	*	44.22	77.73	0	3
7	S Dwanqube (Kei)	3	6	0	264	95		44.00	50.57	0	3
8	G Addicott (KZNI)	8	12	3	357	120	*	39.66	70.27	1	2
9	A van Vuuren (KZNI)	8	11	2	351	82		39.00	58.69	0	3
10	J Jordaan (Mpu)	7	14	1	484	116		37.23	52.55	2	1
11	P Haasbroek (Lim)	7	13	0	469	143		36.07	49.52	1	2
12	C Bowyer (KZNI)	9	14	2	428	104		35.66	44.67	2	0
13	P van den Berg (Mpu)	8	15	2	437	92		33.61	44.45	0	2
14	M Tshona (Kei)	2	4	0	132	50		33.00	69.10	0	1
15	A Pathan (Lim)	4	8	0	263	65		32.87	48.88	0	2
16	T Pistorius (Lim)	3	5	0	153	82		30.60	36.95	0	1
17	I van Zyl (Lim)	7	13	3	296	82		29.60	54.71	0	3
18	C de Swardt (SWD)	6	11	1	290	83		29.00	35.06	0	3
19	C April (SWD)	2	4	0	114	73		28.50	36.42	0	1
20	M Ntsekwa (Kei)	7	14	0	396	100		28.28	50.19	1	1

(Qualification: 4 completed innings)

SAA ASSOCIATES CHALLENGE

LEADING BOWLNG AVERAGES

		M	Overs	Mdns	Runs	Wkts	Avg	RpO	BB	5I	10M
1	DJ Pryke (SWD)	3	88.4	30	146	21	6.95	1.64	8-38	2	1
2	P van den Berg (Mpu)	8	207	68	476	34	14.00	2.29	5-26	1	0
3	M van Vuuren (KZNI)	5	100.2	26	249	17	14.64	2.48	5-18	1	0
4	A van Vuuren (KZNI)	8	153.3	45	399	23	17.34	2.59	4-15	0	0
5	DH Townsend (Mpu)	8	259	93	583	33	17.66	2.25	7-53	2	0
6	R McMillan (KZNI)	9	68	11	198	11	18.00	2.91	3-6	0	0
7	Q Khurshid (Mpu)	8	240.4	70	636	35	18.17	2.64	7-28	1	0
8	MR Siwani (Kei)	3	104.5	17	331	17	19.47	3.15	5-46	2	1
9	M Saliwa (KZNI)	9	162	48	474	24	19.75	2.92	4-41	0	0
10	C Bowyer (KZNI)	9	114	27	277	13	21.30	2.42	6-83	1	0
11	S Marais (KZNI)	8	126	32	324	15	21.60	2.57	4-26	0	0
12	F Bonthuys (SWD)	7	205	53	559	25	22.36	2.72	5-46	2	1
13	GM Hampson (KZNI)	9	168.5	47	413	18	22.94	2.44	4-21	0	0
14	T Ngqolo (Kei)	8	119	21	340	14	24.28	2.85	4-41	0	0
15	I van Zyl (Lim)	7	161.5	33	555	22	25.22	3.42	5-42	1	0
16	P Haasbroek (Lim)	7	216.3	58	517	19	27.21	2.38	4-54	0	0
17	C Rosendorff (Lim)	6	87.4	12	304	11	27.63	3.46	3-28	0	0
18	C Mvovo (Kei)	7	180.5	46	482	17	28.35	2.66	3-36	0	0
19	S Letsoala (Lim)	7	143.3	40	421	14	30.07	2.93	3-59	0	0
20	A Christiaans (SWD)	7	157.3	28	458	15	30.53	2.90	5-63	2	0

(Qualification: 10 wickets)

SAA ASSOCIATES ONE-DAY CHALLENGE 2005/06

Pietermaritzburg, 15 Oct 2005: SWD 178-9 in 45 overs (B Carelse 64, P Stuurman 31, DJ Pryke 25; S Marais 2-8, M van Vuuren 2-39). **KZNI** 180-3 in 41.3 overs (R McMillan 71*, C Bowyer 44, BDM Moses 34*; DJ Pryke 2-17). **KwaZulu-Natal Inland won by 7 wickets.** KZNI 5 pts, SWD 1.

Witbank, 16 Oct 2005: Kei 220-8 in 45 overs (M Ntsekwa 57, C Mvovo 53*; DH Townsend 2-36, P van den Berg 2-17, D Griebenauw 2-58). **Mpu** 224-4 in 40.1 overs (J Jordaan 25, P van den Berg 55, D Griebenauw 61, S Nelson 32*; C Mvovo 3-48). **Mpumalanga won by 6 wickets.** Mpu 5 pts, Kei 1.

Polokwane, 23 Oct 2005: Lim 138 in 33 overs (A Galloway 27, F Walayat 28*; M Saliwa 4-37, R McMillan 2-31). **KZNI** 140-0 in 28.1 overs (R McMillan 40*, C Bowyer 85*). **KwaZulu-Natal Inland won by 10 wickets.** KZNI 6 pts, Lim 0.

Oudtshoorn, 23 Oct 2005: SWD 249-6 in 45 overs (AW Olivier 35, K de Beer 95, P Stuurman 57; DH Townsend 2-46). **Mpu** 218 in 43 overs (J Jordaan 32, D Griebenauw 43, L Arendse 60; A Christiaans 2-47, R Swigelaar 3-47). **South Western Districts won by 31 runs.** SWD 5 pts, Mpu 1.

Umtata, 30 Oct 2005: Lim 321-7 in 45 overs (A Pathan 146, A Galloway 36, F Walayat 30, I van Zyl 32, H Holtzhausen 25*; C Mvovo 2-56, K Ayaz 2-46, M Ntsekwa 2-45). **Kei** 116 in 29.3 overs (S Letsoala 2-34, H Holtzhausen 2-28, P Haasbroek 2-12). **Limpopo won by 205 runs.** Lim 6 pts, Kei 0.

Umtata, 6 Nov 2005: Kei v KwaZulu-Natal Inland match abandoned without a ball bowled. Kei 3 pts, KZNI 3.

Witbank, 6 Nov 2005: Lim 227-8 in 45 overs (F Walayat 71, F van der Berg 28, J Shokane 30; Q Khurshid 3-35, D Grobbelaar 2-41). **Mpu** 44-1 in 5.3 overs. **No result.** Mpu 3 pts, Lim 3.

Modjadjieskloof, 13 Nov 2005: SWD 233-6 in 45 overs (C de Swardt 40, K de Beer 46, G Moos 25, P Stuurman 68*; I van Zyl 2-64). **Lim** 236-5 in 43.2 overs (A Pathan 40, P Haasbroek 71, F Walayat 26, A

Galloway 41, C Rosendorff 34*; DJ Pryke 2-29). **Limpopo won by 5 wickets.** Lim 5 pts, SWD 1.
Pietermaritzburg, 20 Nov 2005: KZNI 241-6 in 45 overs (C Bowyer 47, BDM Moses 88*, A van Vuuren 28, GM Hampson 37; Q Khurshid 2-54). **Mpu** 228-8 in 45 overs (P Malan 28, J Jordaan 69, L Arendse 39, R Hugo 29; R McMillan 2-39, GM Hampson 2-41). **KwaZulu-Natal Inland won by 13 runs.** KZNI 5 pts, Mpu 1.
Oudtshoorn, 27 Nov 2005: SWD 235-7 in 45 overs (C de Swardt 77, G Moos 72; K Shah 2-35). **Kei** 119 in 39 overs (C Mvovo 38; H Matthee 4-38, R Swigelaar 4-27). **South Western Districts won by 116 runs.** SWD 6 pts, Kei 0.
Umtata, 22 Jan 2006: Kei 168-7 in 38 overs (K Moerane 79, S Dwanqube 36, S Dyamboti 27; Q Khurshid 4-34). **Mpu** 170-9 in 34.2 overs (C Mvovo 2-30, L Socikwa 3-39). **Mpumalanga won by 1 wicket.** Mpu 5 pts, Kei 1.
Oudtshoorn, 22 Jan 2006: SWD 119 in 38.4 overs (W de Jager 37; M Saliwa 3-24, A van Vuuren 2-21, C Bowyer 3-22). **KZNI** 120-8 in 36.1 overs (BDM Moses 34; H Matthee 5-36). **KwaZulu-Natal Inland won by 2 wickets.** KZNI 6 pts, SWD 0.
Pietermaritzburg, 29 Jan 2006: KZNI 194 in 45 overs (G Addicott 70, A van Vuuren 39; I van Zyl 2-21, S Letsoala 3-32). **Lim** 19-2 in 6.3 overs (GM Hampson 2-13). **No result.** KZNI 3 pts, Lim 3.
Witbank, 29 Jan 2006: Mpu 233-7 in 45 overs (L Arendse 27, S Roodt 76, L Mthombeni 57*; ER Bezuidenhout 3-56). **SWD** 65-1 in 17 overs (C de Swardt 45*). **No result.** Mpu 3 pts, SWD 3.
Modjadjieskloof, 5 Feb 2006: Kei 220-6 in 45 overs (K Moerane 25, S Ndyamboti 66, A Hlahleni 62, C Mvovo 29; S Letsoala 4-34). **Lim** 221-6 in 37.5 overs (A Galloway 63, P Haasbroek 42, F Walayat 64*, F van der Berg 27; N Badi 2-28, S Malusi 2-40). **Limpopo won by 4 wickets.** Lim 5 pts, Kei 1.
Pietermaritzburg, 12 Feb 2006: Kei 169-8 in 45 overs (K Moerane 31, C Mvovo 49*; S Marais 6-25). **KZNI** 173-4 in 25 overs (M van Vuuren 113). **KwaZulu-Natal Inland won by 6 wickets.** KZNI 6 pts, Kei 0.
Modjadjieskloof, 12 Feb 2006: Mpu 179-9 in 45 overs (R Hugo 28, Q Khurshid 32*; S Letsoala 2-25, P Haasbroek 2-33, J Potgieter 2-37). **Lim** 149 in 38.4 overs (P Haasbroek 44, J Potgieter 41; DH Townsend 3-38, P van den Berg 3-14). **Mpumalanga won by 30 runs.** Mpu 5 pts, Lim 1.
Oudtshoorn, 19 Feb 2006: Lim 253-6 in 45 overs (F Walayat 38, A Galloway 114, F van der Berg 35; DJ Pryke 3-24, W de Jager 2-49). **SWD** 233-7 in 45 overs (AW Olivier 64, K de Beer 48, W de Jager 39; S Letsoala 2-46, P Haasbroek 2-32, F van der Berg 2-27). **Limpopo won by 20 runs.** Lim 5 pts, SWD 1.
Witbank, 26 Feb 2006: Mpu 127 in 41.2 overs (P van den Berg 61; M Saliwa 3-11, M van Vuuren 4-32). **KZNI** 129-3 in 11.4 overs (R McMillan 58*, M van Vuuren 54; P van den Berg 3-36). **KwaZulu-Natal Inland won by 7 wickets.** KZNI 6 pts, Mpu 0.
Umtata, 5 Mar 2006: SWD 204-6 in 45 overs (P Stuurman 71*; A Hlahleni 2-29). **Kei** 162-10 in 42.2 overs (S Dwanqube 50, M Ntsekwa 31, M Tshona 30; DJ Pryke 4-19, R Swigelaar 3-30). **South Western Districts won by 42 runs.** SWD 6 pts, Kei 0.

Table	**P**	**W**	**L**	**T**	**NR**	**Penalty**	**Pts**	**Net RR**
KwaZulu-Natal Inland	8	6	0	0	2	0	40	1.69
Limpopo	8	4	2	0	2	0	28	0.61
South Western Districts	8	3	4	0	1	0	23	0.28
Mpumalanga	8	3	3	0	2	0	23	-0.53
Kei	8	0	7	0	1	0	6	-1.83

Final

Pietermaritzburg, 1 Apr 2006: Lim 201-9 in 45 overs (F Walayat 26, C Rosendorff 29, J Shokane 27; M Saliwa 2-17, GM Hampson 3-38, M van Vuuren 2-41). **KZNI** 203-4 in 39.2 overs (M van Vuuren 49, S Woodroffe 26, BDM Moses 51, G Addicott 67*; P Haasbroek 2-42). **KwaZulu-Natal Inland won by 6 wickets.**

SAA ASSOCIATES CHALLENGE

LEADING BATTING AVERAGES

		M	Inns	NO	Runs	HS		Avg	SR	100	50
1	A Pathan (Lim)	4	4	0	218	146		54.50	143.42	1	0
2	BDM Moses (KZNI)	8	7	3	217	88	*	54.25	75.60	0	2
3	P Stuurman (SWD)	8	7	2	257	71	*	51.40	107.98	0	3
4	F Walayat (Lim)	9	9	3	288	71		48.00	70.76	0	2
5	K de Beer (SWD)	4	4	0	191	95		47.75	93.62	0	1
6	G Addicott (KZNI)	7	6	2	179	70		44.75	77.82	0	2
7	R McMillan (KZNI)	8	8	3	206	71	*	41.20	76.29	0	2
8	C Bowyer (KZNI)	6	6	1	204	85	*	40.80	69.62	0	1
9	S Roodt (Mpu)	2	2	0	81	76		40.50	102.53	0	1
10	A Galloway (Lim)	9	9	1	312	114		39.00	89.91	1	1
11	C Mvovo (Kei)	7	7	2	193	53	*	38.60	73.38	0	1
12	M van Vuuren (KZNI)	6	6	0	225	113		37.50	131.57	1	1
13	B Carelse (SWD)	2	2	0	71	64		35.50	68.93	0	1
14	D Griebenauw (Mpu)	3	3	0	106	61		35.33	99.06	0	1
15	C de Swardt (SWD)	7	7	1	196	77		32.66	68.29	0	1
16	G Moos (SWD)	5	4	0	125	72		31.25	80.12	0	1
17	GM Hampson (KZNI)	8	3	1	59	37		29.50	116.66	0	0
18	S Dwanqube (Kei)	4	4	0	117	50		29.25	54.41	0	1
19	K Moerane (Kei)	7	7	1	175	79		29.16	70.00	0	1
20	P van den Berg (Mpu)	8	8	1	188	61		26.85	57.14	0	2

(Qualification: 2 completed innings)

LEADING BOWLING AVERAGES

		M	Overs	Mdns	Runs	Wkts	Avg	RpO	BB	4I
1	DJ Pryke (SWD)	7	47.2	4	127	13	9.76	2.68	4-19	1
2	M Saliwa (KZNI)	8	46.3	7	142	13	10.92	3.05	4-37	1
3	L Socikwa (Kei)	1	8	0	39	3	13.00	4.87	3-39	0
4	S Marais (KZNI)	7	35	3	132	10	13.20	3.77	6-25	1
5	R Swigelaar (SWD)	7	58.2	10	218	14	15.57	3.73	4-27	1
6	H Matthee (SWD)	5	39	7	180	11	16.36	4.61	5-36	2
7	R McMillan (KZNI)	8	25	4	104	6	17.33	4.16	2-31	0
8	S Letsoala (Lim)	9	59.3	5	274	15	18.26	4.60	4-34	1
9	P van den Berg (Mpu)	8	59	13	202	10	20.20	3.42	3-14	0
10	M van Vuuren (KZNI)	6	44.2	2	184	9	20.44	4.15	4-32	1
11	GM Hampson (KZNI)	8	57	8	218	10	21.80	3.82	3-38	0
12	A van Vuuren (KZNI)	7	27.4	2	112	5	22.40	4.04	2-21	0
13	ER Bezuidenhout (SWD)	2	18	1	91	4	22.75	5.05	3-56	0
14	F van der Berg (Lim)	7	11.1	0	70	3	23.33	6.26	2-27	0
15	M Ntsekwa (Kei)	7	8	0	71	3	23.66	8.87	2-45	0
16	C Mvovo (Kei)	7	52.5	4	272	11	24.72	5.14	3-48	0
17	A Hlahleni (Kei)	3	23	1	76	3	25.33	3.30	2-29	0
18	Q Khurshid (Mpu)	8	59	3	305	12	25.41	5.16	4-34	1
19	P Haasbroek (Lim)	9	59.3	3	258	10	25.80	4.33	2-12	0
20	L Mthombeni (Mpu)	6	16	2	80	3	26.66	5.00	1-8	0

(Qualification: 3 wickets)

Section D: Other Cricket

NATIONAL CLUB CHAMPIONSHIPS

Pretoria High School Old Boys successfully defended their title when they won the 2005 National Club Championships, beating the University of Johannesburg in the final at SuperSport Park, Centurion. It was the third successive year a club from the host affiliate, Northerns, had won the title following Pretoria University's win in 2003.

Matches were played in Pretoria, Boksburg and Johannesburg, as well as at Mamelodi Oval and Eersterus Oval, which are both UCBSA World Cup Legacy Projects.

The teams that took part were: Warrenton Cricket Club (Griqualand West), Pam Golding Crusaders Cricket Club (KwaZulu-Natal), Pretoria High School Old Boys (2004 winners, Northerns), Absa Tshwane University of Technology (Northerns), Central Sports Vaal Reefs Cricket Club (North West), Primrose Cricket Club (Western Province), Novel Paarl Cricket Club (Boland), East London Police Cricket Club (Border), CBC Old Boys Boksburg Cricket Club (Easterns), Rotatrim Port Elizabeth Cricket Club (Eastern Province), Absa University of Free State (Free State), University of Johannesburg (Gauteng).

PHSOB lost their opening match against Vaal Reefs but came back strongly to win their remaining four group matches before going on to become the first club since unity to win the title twice in a row.

Leg-spinner Maurice Aronstam was the hero in the final, taking 5-30 as PHSOB defended a moderate total of 196 against the University of Johannesburg, who as Rand Afrikaans University won the title in 1998. The students were well placed when Stephen Cook and William Motaung put on 51 for the first wicket but both openers fell in quick succession and the rest of the batsmen could not master Aronstam, who was named Man of the Match.

RESULTS

Tuesday 20 September 2005
Section One

Port Elizabeth CC 206-9 in 45 overs (D Willemse 31, L Meyer 53, R Esau 51; SP O'Connor 4-31). **CBC Old Boys Boksburg** 178 in 41.2 overs (J Theunissen 38, SR Connor 30; LL Tsotsobe 2-34, J Theron 3-23, D Willemse 4-44). **Port Elizabeth CC won by 28 runs.**

Vaal Reefs 248-9 in 45 overs (FA Steyn 32, J le Roux 82, EO Moleon 34, M Bailey 33*; MA Aronstam 2-34, R van der Merwe 2-38). **Pretoria High School Old Boys** 205 in 42.3 overs (G Steenkamp 77; EO Moleon 3-35, M Eden 2-23, J le Roux 2-35). **Vaal Reefs won by 43 runs.**

Paarl CC 234-7 in 45 overs (L-R Walters 71, B Nicholson 65, L Jansen 34; AK Kruger 2-35, ES Tsamaisi 2-47). **Warrenton CC** 238-5 in 39.5 overs (AP McLaren 128, M Bosman 36, PJ Koortzen 32; GC Stevens 2-49, L Jansen 2-4). **Warrenton CC won by 5 wickets.**

Section Two

Primrose CC 148 in 42.3 overs (A Magiet 33; JP Kreusch 5-19, BC Fourie 3-34). **East London Police** 149-2 in 37.1 overs (JP Kreusch 53, DC Lentz 65*; RK Kleinveldt 2-30). **East London Police won by 8 wickets.**

University of Johannesburg 197 in 44.4 overs (SC Cook 29, JM Otto 40, S Burger 25, J Vorster 26, R Cameron 29*; WA Deacon 3-43, MP Fick 2-22, GD Perry 3-30). **Free State University** 169 in 43.3 overs (CA Ingram 27, MP Fick 35*; GJ de Bruin 3-26, S Burger 3-31, J Vorster 2-40). **University of Johannesburg won by 28 runs.**

Tshwane University of Technology 272-5 in 45 overs (N Chouhan 58, G Morgan 72, R Scheepers 40, JG Myburgh 57*; JC Kent 2-62). **Crusaders** 245-8 in 45 overs (CB Sugden 39, A Perkins 87*, A Angel 65; N Wagner 4-64, R Houbeert 2-24). **Tshwane University of Technology won by 27 runs.**

NATIONAL CLUB CHAMPIONSHIPS

Wednesday 21 September 2005
Section One
CBC Old Boys Boksburg 238-7 in 45 overs (J Theunissen 34, AJ Seymore 92, AM van den Berg 52, SR Connor 26; F Jacobs 2-57, R Andrews 2-36, H Solomon 2-23). **Paarl CC** 150 in 36.3 overs (MD Walters 27, L-R Walters 40; M Oosthuizen 5-36, SP O'Connor 2-16, AM van den Berg 2-10). **CBC Old Boys Boksburg won by 88 runs.**
Vaal Reefs 225-4 in 45 overs (DP Lotter 40, J le Roux 95*, WL Coetsee 25, T Koekemoer 25*; L Meyer 3-34). **Port Elizabeth CC** 226-5 in 44.4 overs (E Nel 58, WE Bell 45, R Nel 33, R Esau 32, L Meyer 29*). **Port Elizabeth CC won by 5 wickets.**
Pretoria High School Old Boys 231-7 in 45 overs (N van Woerkom 57, C Williams 63, M Charlton 34, G Steenkamp 26*; AK Kruger 3-34, FPG Holtzhausen 2-47). **Warrenton CC** 178 in 40.5 overs (AP McLaren 65, FPG Holtzhausen 34, AK Kruger 30; G Steenkamp 2-24, MA Aronstam 3-31, R van der Merwe 2-32). **Pretoria High School Old Boys won by 53 runs.**

Section Two
Primrose CC 162-9 in 45 overs (RK Kleinveldt 77, MS Taliep 27; N Wagner 3-30, PL Harris 2-26). **Tshwane University of Technology** 163-4 in 38.2 overs (N Chouhan 61, G Morgan 60*). **Tshwane University of Technology won by 6 wickets.**
East London Police 219-9 in 45 overs (JP Kreusch 68, A Jacobs 62, KR Peinke 30; R Cameron 2-29, JM Otto 4-44). **University of Johannesburg** 223-9 in 44 overs (DL Makalima 29, S Burger 73, J Vorster 45, R Cameron 27; R Theron 2-24, C Leopperd 2-15, BC Fourie 2-43). **University of Johannesburg won by 1 wicket.**
Free State University 201-9 in 45 overs (CA Ingram 58, E Weirich 29, GD Perry 29*; S Power 4-35). **Crusaders** 191-6 in 45 overs (CB Sugden 71, A Perkins 43*; MP Fick 2-36, AJ Durant 2-22). **Free State University won by 10 runs.**

Thursday 22 September 2005
Section One
CBC Old Boys Boksburg 233-4 in 45 overs (AJ Seymore 130*, J Burger 39*; EO Moleon 2-22). **Vaal Reefs** 237-6 in 43.1 overs (DP Lotter 25, WL Coetsee 62, FA Steyn 85, T Koekemoer 26*; J Spies 2-47, SP O'Connor 2-45). **Vaal Reefs won by 4 wickets.**
Pretoria High School Old Boys 261-5 in 45 overs (MA Aronstam 48, J van Heerden 106*, HG Kuhn 33, C Williams 45). **Paarl CC** 169 in 37.5 overs (L-R Walters 77; G Fawkes 2-21, R van der Merwe 2-10). **Pretoria High School Old Boys won by 92 runs.**
Warrenton CC 109 in 32 overs (LL Tsotsobe 2-28, J Theron 2-17, WE Bell 4-17). **Port Elizabeth CC** 112-2 in 19.1 overs (WE Bell 51*, R Nel 26*; A Moremedi 2-17). **Port Elizabeth CC won by 8 wickets.**

Section Two
Crusaders 204-7 in 45 overs (ET Springer 98*, JC Kent 34; GJ de Bruin 2-49, N Bell 3-7). **University of Johannesburg** 205-6 in 41 overs (BW Buckley 85, DL Makalima 31, J Vorster 46*; S Power 3-32). **University of Johannesburg won by 4 wickets.**
East London Police 206-6 in 45 overs (JP Kreusch 76, KR Peinke 40, S Fredericks 38*). **Tshwane University of Technology** 182 in 41.3 overs (N Chouhan 36, JG Myburgh 41, G Morgan 44; BC Fourie 2-19, KR Peinke 4-30). **East London Police won by 24 runs.**
Free State University 262-3 in 45 overs (CA Ingram 125*, C Linde 53, R McLaren 49*; S Toefy 2-50). **Primrose CC** 212-9 in 45 overs (W Keraan 37, RK Kleinveldt 60; R McLaren 2-25, CA Ingram 2-46, JF Mostert 2-31). **Free State University won by 50 runs.**

Friday 23 September 2005
Section One
CBC Old Boys Boksburg 149 in 42 overs (M Oosthuizen 26; AK Kruger 2-31, TR Plaatjie 2-27, ES Tsamaisi 3-34). **Warrenton CC** 152-1 in 25.1 overs (PJ Koortzen 85*, FPG Holtzhausen 39*). **Warrenton CC won by 9 wickets.**
Pretoria High School Old Boys 216-8 in 45 overs (MA Aronstam 73, J van Heerden 30, HG Kuhn 43; J Theron 4-49). **Port Elizabeth CC** 122 in 35 overs (R Esau 26; C Williams 3-12, R van der Merwe 4-21, MA Aronstam 2-11). **Pretoria High School Old Boys won by 94 runs.**
Paarl CC 227-6 in 45 overs (B Nicholson 25, L-R Walters 34, R Andrews 61*, L Jansen 34; M Bailey 2-35). **Vaal Reefs** 108 in 27 overs (DP Lotter 32; AN Newman 2-23, GC Stevens 2-27, C Philander 5-29). **Paarl CC won by 119 runs.**

Section Two
Crusaders 128 in 44.4 overs (JP Kreusch 4-17, G Young 3-22). **East London Police** 129-4 in 34 overs (DC Lentz 43*, G Young 25*). **East London Police won by 6 wickets.**
University of Johannesburg 198-6 in 45 overs (DL Makalima 66, DM van Wyk 80; S Toefy 2-24). **Primrose CC** 169 in 41.5 overs (RK Kleinveldt 72, MS Taliep 29; GJ de Bruin 6-23). **University of Johannesburg won by 29 runs.**

NATIONAL CLUB CHAMPIONSHIPS

Free State University 239-9 in 42 overs (HG de Kock 100, MP Fick 39, C Linde 26; C Kellerman 2-28, PL Harris 2-52). **Tshwane University of Technology** 199 in 40.3 overs (G Morgan 50, A Letsie 27; WA Deacon 2-25, R McLaren 2-29, MP Fick 2-8, CA Ingram 2-48). **Free State University won by 40 runs.**

Saturday 24 September 2005
Section One
Paarl CC 83 in 35.1 overs (LL Tsotsobe 2-16, S Mjekula 2-21, M Gouws 3-11). **Port Elizabeth CC** 84-4 in 17.5 overs (R Esau 25*; U Ernstzen 3-25). **Port Elizabeth CC won by 6 wickets.**
Pretoria High School Old Boys 250-4 in 45 overs (MA Aronstam 109*, HG Kuhn 63, C Williams 45; RG Mutch 2-41). **CBC Old Boys Boksburg** 128 in 31 overs (AJ Seymore 26, AM van den Berg 32; MA Aronstam 3-27, R van der Merwe 4-20). **Pretoria High School Old Boys won by 122 runs.**
Warrenton CC 172 in 43.4 overs (PJ Koortzen 42, AP McLaren 25, AK Kruger 45*; EO Moleon 2-40, M Bailey 5-29, WL Coetsee 2-23). **Vaal Reefs** 173-2 in 32.5 overs (M Venter 56*, FA Steyn 26, DP Lotter 48*). **Vaal Reefs won by 8 wickets.**

Section Two
Primrose CC 174 in 43.4 overs (MS Taliep 58, RK Kleinveldt 29; JC Kent 2-18, C Park 2-20, A Angel 2-15). **Crusaders** 175-8 in 45 overs (A Angel 38, CB Sugden 55, JC Kent 31; F Jardine 2-15, W Keraan 3-30). **Crusaders won by 2 wickets.**
East London Police 229-4 in 45 overs (JP Kreusch 124, A Jacobs 61*; WA Deacon 2-44). **Free State University** 205 in 42.1 overs (GD Perry 34, WA Deacon 43; BC Fourie 4-20, JP Kreusch 2-32, G Young 3-43). **East London Police won by 24 runs.**
Tshwane University of Technology 197 in 50.5 overs (SJ Myburgh 47, G Morgan 69; GJ de Bruin 2-31, N Bell 4-19, M Oosthuizen 2-29). **University of Johannesburg** 198-4 in 41.1 overs (SC Cook 65, WB Motaung 37, DM van Wyk 53*). **University of Johannesburg won by 6 wickets.**

LOG TABLES

Section One	P	W	L	NR	Pts
PHSOB	5	4	1	0	25
PE CC	5	4	1	0	22
Vaal Reefs	5	3	2	0	17
Warrenton CC	5	2	3	0	11
CBC Old Boys	5	1	4	0	8
Paarl CC	5	1	4	0	7

Section Two	P	W	L	NR	Pts
University of Jhb	5	5	0	0	25
East London Police	5	4	1	0	22
Free State University	5	3	2	0	17
Tshwane UT	5	2	3	0	13
Crusaders	5	1	4	0	8
Primrose CC	5	0	5	0	5

FINAL
Sunday 25 September 2005
Pretoria High School Old Boys 196 in 44.4 overs (N van Woerkom 26, HG Kuhn 52, C Williams 44, R van der Merwe 31; GJ de Bruin 3-41, M Oosthuizen 3-36). **University of Johannesburg** 142 in 40.5 overs (WB Motaung 36; G Fawkes 2-30, MA Aronstam 5-30, R van der Merwe 2-16). **Pretoria High School Old Boys won by 54 runs.**

Leading run-scorers:
1. JP Kreusch (ELPol) 327 (avg 65.40); **2.** G Morgan (TUT) 295 (avg 73.75); **3.**AJ Seymore (CBC Old Boys) 262 (avg 87.33); **4.** MA Aronstam (PHSOB) 258 (avg 51.60); **5.** AP McLaren (Warr) 245 (avg 49.00).

Leading wicket-takers:
1. GJ de Bruin (UJ) 17 (avg 12.05); **2.** R van der Merwe (PHSOB) 16 (avg 8.56), MA Aronstam (PHSOB) 16 (avg 10.50); **4.** JP Kreusch (ELPol) 13 (avg 10.61), **5.** BC Fourie (ELPol) 12 (avg 10.83).

NATIONAL CRICKET ACADEMY

The United Cricket Board of South Africa selected 18 players to attend the 2006 National Cricket Academy at the High Performance Centre, University of Pretoria, from May to August 2006.

Anton Ferreira, the National Coaching Manager and head of the National Academy, said: "The squad of 18 represents the 11th intake of this UCBSA's Elite Player Development Programme and will be the third at the High Performance Centre at Tuks.

"These players all have first-class experience at either amateur provincial or franchise professional levels and the majority have already started making their mark in a big way in various senior competitions.

"The four-month academy will provide an intensive and extensive approach to their development both in cricket and life skills. We want to build their all-round capacities in order to enable them to meet the challenges of the next level of cricket."

The players selected were: Keegan Africa (Dolphins, all-rounder), Craig Alexander (WP, fast bowler), Farhaan Behardien (WP, all-rounder), Werner Coetsee (Lions, off-spinner), Riel de Kock (Free State, batsman), Dillon du Preez (Eagles, all-rounder), Dean Elgar (Free State, batsman), Robert Frylinck (Dolphins, all-rounder), Heino Kuhn (Titans, batsman-wicketkeeper), Corne Linde (Free State, batsman-wicketkeeper), Saidi Mhlongo (Dolphins, fast bowler), Hillroy Paulse (Boland, fast bowler), Abdul Hack Razak (Dolphins, leg-spinner), Pepler Sandri (Boland, fast bowler), Blake Snijman (Lions, batsman), Abongile Sodumo (Warriors, batsman-wicketkeeper), Dominic Telo (Cobras, batsman), Craig Thyssen (Eagles, all-rounder).

SOUTH AFRICAN ACADEMY IN PAKISTAN 2005/06

At the conclusion of the 2005 National Academy, a squad of 15 players was selected to play a series of two four-day and three limited overs matches against the Pakistan Cricket Academy in Pakistan during August 2005.

The squad was led by Francois du Plessis, who was vice-captain of the South African Under-19 team in England in 2003. Of the players, only batsman Myles Williamson did not have first-class experience.

The squad: Francois du Plessis (Titans, captain), Brendon Adams (Boland), Ryan Canning (Western Province), Jandre Coetzee (Griqualand West), Jean-Paul Duminy (Cobras), Ugasen Govender (KwaZulu-Natal), Morne Morkel (Titans), Francis Nkuna (Northerns), Mario Olivier (Boland), Aaron Phangiso (Northerns), Vernon Philander (Cobras), Kyle Smit (Dolphins), Thandi Tshabalala (Eagles), Vaughn van Jaarsveld (Lions), Myles Williamson (Western Province). Coaches, Dave Nosworthy and Yashin Ebrahim Hassan; physiotherapist, Brandon Jackson.

The tour proved a tough learning experience for the South African youngsters, although Duminy showed his class and experience by scoring 355 runs, only being dismissed once, in three innings in the four-day matches, with a highest score of 265 not out. He did not play in the one-day matches because he had been selected to join the South Africa A team in Sri Lanka.

Ryan Canning, who made a century in sharing an unbeaten sixth wicket stand of 349 with Duminy in the second four-day match, scored 167 runs at 83.50 but no other batsman averaged 30, while Tshabalala, appearing as an opening batsman, was the only other player to score a half-century.

Govender, with seven wickets at 22.28, was the most successful bowler, while Morkel and Olivier took six wickets each.

In the one-day matches, Du Plessis notched the only half-century and with 116 runs at 38.66 was the only player to have an average better than 30, while Olivier, Du Plessis and Phangiso took five wickets apiece. Only Philander and Tshabalala conceded fewer than five runs an over.

After gaining a 12-run first innings lead in the first four-day match they collapsed in the second innings and were beaten by nine wickets.

In the second match, the tourists were struggling at 121-5 before Duminy and Canning came together in their remarkable stand. After gaining a first innings lead of 167, the SA Academy batted aggressively in their second innings before declaring, setting their opponents a target of 330 in 68 overs. With the Test batsman Hasan Raza leading the way, the Pakistanis came within six runs of victory with four wickets standing when time ran out.

After losing the first two one-day games, the South Africans won a rain-shortened third match.

Four-day matches

Karachi, 11-13 Aug 2005: SA Acad 248 (M Williamson 31, T Tshabalala 59, J-P Duminy 82*; Yasir Ali 6-59, Mansoor Amjad 3-61) and 118 (VB van Jaarsveld 46; Najaf Shah 3-28, Yasir Ali 4-33, Mansoor Amjad 3-34). **Pak Acad** 236 (Khalid Latif 34, Zulqarnain Haider 76, Mansoor Amjad 25; MW Olivier 3-55, U Govender 4-54, F du Plessis 2-19) and 134-1 (Nasir Jamshed 31*, Shahid Yousuf 83*). **Pakistan Academy won by 9 wickets.**

Lahore, 18-21 Aug 2005: SA Acad 470-5* (K Smit 38, J-P Duminy 265*, RCC Canning 112*; Yasir Ali 2-54, Mansoor Amjad 2-131) and 162-5* (F du Plessis 39, VD Philander 25, RCC Canning 45*; Fahad Masood 2-47). **Pak Acad** 303 (Shahid Yousuf 85, Hasan Raza 57; U Govender 3-43, VD Philander 3-43, FG Nkuna 2-39) and 324-6 (Khalid Latif 50, Shahid Yousuf 111, Hasan Raza 122*; M Morkel 4-78). **Drawn.**

Pakistan Academy won the series 1-0.

Limited Overs matches

Lahore, 24 Aug 2005: Pak Acad 244-8 in 50 overs (Khurram Manzoor 38, Shahid Yousuf 29, Hasan Raza 70, Fawad Alam 28; MW Olivier 2-43, AM Phangiso 2-49, F du Plessis 2-47). **SA Acad** 160 in 39 overs (RCC Canning 35, VB van Jaarsveld 33; Mohammad Irshad 6-21, Mansoor Amjad 3-28). **Pakistan Academy won by 84 runs.**

Lahore, 26 Aug 2005: Pak Acad 280 in 48.3 overs (Agha Sabir 63, Khurram Manzoor 95, Shahid Yousuf 30, Hasan Raza 27; MW Olivier 3-42, AM Phangiso 2-67, F du Plessis 2-54). **SA Acad** 241 in 47.3 overs (K Smit 41, F du Plessis 89, RCC Canning 29; Mohammad Irshad 5-49, Mansoor Amjad 2-32). **Pakistan Academy won by 39 runs.**

Sheikhupura, 28 Aug 2005: SA Acad 164-9 in 25 overs (M Williamson 45, K Smit 32; Mansoor Amjad 4-57). **Pak Acad** 171-5 in 25 overs (Hasan Raza 67*, Shahid Yousuf 56; VD Philander 2-22). **South African Academy won by 4 runs (D/L method), target revised to 176 in 25 overs.**

Pakistan Academy won the series 2-1.

CRICKET SA HIGH PERFORMANCE PROGRAMME

Cricket South Africa announced on 1 April 2006 the names of 22 players who will form part of its High Performance Programme (HPP) aimed at widening the pool of players capable of succeeding at international cricket.

Vintcent van der Bijl, CSA's General Manager of Professional Cricket, said the HPP had been established to elevate the next tier of potential national cricketers to be ready to play at Test and one-day international level. "It is an HPP criterion that players who have been chosen are close to selection for South Africa," he said.

During the 2006 off-season specialist camps were held for batsmen, fast bowlers and spin bowlers, with National Academy players also participating. Among the coaches used were Gary Kirsten (batting), Allan Donald and Robin Jackman (fast bowling), Denys Hobson and Terry Jenner (wrist spinners) and Clive Eksteen and Shafiek Abrahams (finger spinners).

Players were put through detailed physical assessments and put on individual fitness and dietary programmes.

The camps were built on five pillars:

Physical conditioning
Technical development
Game awareness and tactics
Mental conditioning
Personal development

Van der Bijl said: "It is a holistic programme, designed to assist players who the national selectors feel can and will play for SA within two years. The National Academy on the other hand, is designed to develop players who have the potential to play for South Africa within five to eight years and the programme facilitates their development to be complete professional franchise cricketers."

The squad was: Paul Adams (Nashua Cape Cobras), Hashim Amla (Nashua Dolphins), Loots Bosman (Gestetner Eagles), Johan Botha (Warriors), Cliffie Deacon (Gestetner Eagles), J-P Duminy (Nashua Cape Cobras), Paul Harris (Nashua Titans), Davy Jacobs (Gestetner Eagles), Garnett Kruger (Highveld Lions), Neil McKenzie (Highveld Lions), Albie Morkel (Nashua Titans), Mfuneko Ngam (Warriors), Justin Ontong (Highveld Lions), Robin Peterson (Warriors), Andrew Puttick (Nashua Cape Cobras), Dale Steyn (Nashua Titans), Roger Telemachus (Gestetner Eagles), Alfonso Thomas (Nashua Titans), Thandi Tshabalala (Gestetner Eagles), Thami Tsolekile (Nashua Cape Cobras), Johan van der Wath (Gestetner Eagles), Monde Zondeki (Nashua Cape Cobras).

WOMEN'S PROVINCIAL LEAGUE 2005/06

Western Province found form at the right time to win the 2005/06 Women's Provincial League. Having been beaten by Boland in both their round robin encounters, they defeated their neighbours in the final played at Brackenfell.

In the semi-finals, Western Province beat previously unbeaten KwaZulu-Natal, with a key moment coming when top-scorer Johmari Logtenberg was dismissed for 33, the only time she lost her wicket during a season in which she scored 464 runs, with a century and four fifties. This took her career record in the competition to 1090 runs in 20 innings at an average of 155.71.

Group A

Witbank, 2 Oct 2005: Mpu 77 in 33.1 overs (L Reid 4-28, E de Mello Koch 2-2, P Thode 2-5). **Gau** 78-0 in 16.2 overs (K-A Laing 44*). **Gauteng won by 10 wickets.** Gau 6 pts, Mpu 0.

Potchefstroom, 2 Oct 2005: Nor 120 in 26.4 overs (D Mabothe 32; S Plotz 4-37, T Brits 6-28). **NW** 121-6 in 42.2 overs (A Erasmus 27, T Brits 72*; Y Bronkhorst 3-13, C Labuschagne 2-34). **North West won by 4 wickets.** NW 5 pts, Nor 1.

Polokwane, 8 Oct 2005: Limpopo v KwaZulu-Natal match not played, awarded to KwaZulu-Natal by default. KZN 6 pts, Lim 0.

Johannesburg, 9 Oct 2005: Gau 206-5 in 50 overs (K-A Laing 35, T Reeves 74, L Reid 28, K Blair 27*; J Logtenberg 2-38). **KZN** 208-3 in 49.5 overs (N Turner 38, T Chetty 28, J Logtenberg 79*, N Landie 42). **KwaZulu-Natal won by 7 wickets.** KZN 5 pts, Gau 1.

Pretoria, 9 Oct 2005: Mpu 138 in 46.5 overs (T-L Kleynhans 47; S Barnard 2-30, Y Bronkhorst 4-23, M Letsoalo 2-11). **Nor** 139-3 in 39.3 overs (I Marais 51*, Y Bronkhorst 43; J Noeth 2-29). **Northerns won by 7 wickets.** Nor 6 pts, Mpu 0.

Johannesburg, 22 Oct 2005: Gau 149 in 43.3 overs (M Terblanche 57, T Reeves 28; N Motshabi 2-35, T Brits 4-27, R Franken 3-9). **NW** 25 in 17.3 overs (K Blair 5-6, P Thode 2-7, L Reid 2-7). **Gauteng won by 124 runs.** Gau 6 pts, NW 0.

Pretoria, 23 Oct 2005: Lim 124 in 48.5 overs (A Kotze 34; Y Bronkhorst 2-23, L de Beer 2-17, D Mabothe 2-26). **Nor** 125-2 in 33.1 overs (I Marais 26*, Y Bronkhorst 64). **Northerns won by 8 wickets.** Nor 6 pts, Lim 0.

Johannesburg, 29 Oct 2005: Lim 214-6 in 50 overs (H Strydom 72, M Lopez 45, M van Niekerk 42). **Gau** 182-5 in 50 overs (T Reeves 80*, K Blair 29; A van den Berg 2-34). **Limpopo won by 32 runs**. Lim 5 pts, Gau 1.

Durban, 29 Oct 2005: NW 34 in 17.5 overs (D Devnarain 4-8, J Hambrook 2-15, K Naidoo 2-3). **KZN** 35-1 in 6.5 overs. **KwaZulu-Natal won by 9 wickets.** KZN 6 pts, NW 0.

Witbank, 12 Nov 2005: Mpu 70 in 15.4 overs (D Devnarain 7-28, N Ramnath 2-29). **KZN** 73-2 in 15.5 overs (J Noeth 2-10). **KwaZulu-Natal won by 8 wickets.** KZN 6 pts, Mpu 0.

Witbank 13 Nov 2005: Lim 150 in 40.1 overs (H Strydom 38; P Venter 2-16, A Malaka 3-22, C Schmahl 2-14). **Mpu** 93 in 33.4 overs (S Nawrattle 34; A Kotze 3-22, M van Niekerk 2-15, H Strydom 3-14). **Limpopo won by 57 runs.** Lim 6 pts, Mpu 0.

Pretoria 13 Nov 2005: Nor 151 in 38 overs (Y Bronkhorst 79; D Devnarain 2-49, J Hambrook 2-17, J Logtenberg 3-28). **KZN** 153-2 in 39.2 overs (T Chetty 63, J Logtenberg 71*; C Labuschagne 2-37). **KwaZulu-Natal won by 8 wickets.** KZN 6 pts, Nor 0.

Durban, 27 Nov 2005: KZN 275-4 in 50 overs (J Bartholomew 84, T Chetty 67, J Logtenberg 69*; T-L Kleynhans 2-51). **Mpu** 156 in 39.5 overs (J Noeth 83; J Hambrook 3-25, J Logtenberg 5-29, J Bartholomew 2-32). **KwaZulu-Natal won by 119 runs.** KZN 6 pts, Mpu 0.

Potchefstroom, 11 Dec 2005: Mpu 194-7 in 50 overs (C Schmahl 62, S Haven 29, F McEvilly 27*; T Brits 2-29). **NW** 186 in 45.4 overs (L van den Berg 33, R de Kock 27, T Brits 40, L du Plooy 28, L Erasmus 28; C Schmahl 2-27, F McEvilly 2-32, B Qulu 2-13). **Mpumalanga won by 8 runs.** Mpu 5 pts, NW 1.

Durban, 8 Jan 2006: Gau 62 in 34.2 overs (D Devnarain 3-14, J Hambrook 4-7, J Hornsveld 3-11). **KZN** 63-2 in 14.3 overs. **KwaZulu-Natal won by 8 wickets.** KZN 6 pts, Gau 0.

Johannesburg, 14 Jan 2006: Mpu 67 in 24.4 overs (K Blair 6-11, P Thode 3-3). **Gau** 68-2 in 13.3 overs (M Terblanche 37*). **Gauteng won by 8 wickets.** Gau 6 pts, Mpu 0.

Pretoria, 15 Jan 2006: NW 51 in 32 overs (C Labuschagne 2-7, J Knoetze 4-18, L de Beer 2-5). **Nor** 53-1 in 11.2 overs (Y Bronkhorst 27*). **Northerns won by 9 wickets.** Nor 6 pts, NW 0.

Witbank, 22 Jan 2006: Mpu 102 in 30.4 overs (J Noeth 41; M du Preez 6-24). **Nor** 103-5 in 31.4 overs (M du Preez 35*; C Schmahl 3-30). **Northerns won by 5 wickets.** Nor 6 pts, Mpu 0.

Polokwane, 29 Jan 2006: Nor 223-8 in 50 overs (M du Preez 88*, J Knoetze 33; H Strydom 4-20). **Lim** 128 in 40.1 overs (H Strydom 33; J Knoetze 2-28, S Barnard 2-25, C Labuschagne 4-25). **Northerns won by 95 runs.** Nor 6 pts, Lim 0.

Potchefstroom, 29 Jan 2006: NW 128 in 42.2 overs (L van den Berg 26, T Brits 34; P Thode 3-12, C Malindi 2-12). **Gau** 129-5 in 36.4 overs (T Reeves 37; L van den Berg 2-34). **Gauteng won by 5 wickets.** Gau 6 pts, NW 0.

WOMEN'S PROVINCIAL LEAGUE 2005/06

Polokwane, 5 Feb 2006: Gau 153-7 in 45.4 overs (K Blair 36; M van Niekerk 2-13, A Kotze 2-37). **Lim** did not bat. **No result.** Lim 3 pts, Gau 3.
Durban, 12 Feb 2006: KZN 227-6 in 50 overs (T Chetty 41, J Logtenberg 104*; M Letsoalo 4-39). **Nor** 149 in 48.4 overs (Y Bronkhorst 41, M du Preez 31; D Devnarain 4-40, K Naidoo 2-29, J Logtenberg 3-19). **KwaZulu-Natal won by 78 runs.** KZN 6 pts, Nor 0.
Polokwane, 12 Feb 2006: Limpopo v Mpumalanga match abandoned without a ball bowled. Lim 3 pts, Mpu 3.
Potchefstroom, 18 Feb 2006: KZN 186-7 in 50 overs (D Devnarain 44, J Logtenberg 62*; N Motshabi 2-40, R Franken 2-30). **NW** 67 in 32.5 overs (D Devnarain 2-18, K Naidoo 5-14). **KwaZulu-Natal won by 119 runs.** KZN 6 pts, NW 0.
Johannesburg, 19 Feb 2006: Gau 131-6 in 50 overs (M Terblanche 61*; Y Bronkhorst 2-31, C Labuschagne 2-24). **Nor** 81 in 45.3 overs (K Blair 2-15, P Thode 3-6). **Gauteng won by 50 runs.** Gau 6 pts, Nor 0.
Potchefstroom, 26 Feb 2006: North West v Limpopo match abandoned without a ball bowled. NW 3 pts, Lim 3.
Polokwane, 5 Mar 2006: Limpopo v North West match abandoned without a ball bowled. Lim 3 pts, NW 3.
Durban, 12 Mar 2006: KwaZulu-Natal v Limpopo match not played, awarded to KwaZulu-Natal by default. KZN 6 pts, Lim 0.
Pretoria, 12 Mar 2006: Nor 133-8 in 50 overs (Y Bronkhorst 36; C Malindi 2-15, H Nienaber 2-35). **Gau** 88 in 30.2 overs (Y Bronkhorst 7-19). **Northerns won by 45 runs.** Nor 5 pts, Gau 1.
Middelburg, 12 Mar 2006: NW 119 in 28.1 overs (C-Z Brits 67; J Noeth 3-26, C Schmahl 2-18). **Mpu** 121-2 in 27.5 overs (S Nawrattle 29, C Schmahl 38). **Mpumalanga won by 8 wickets.** Mpu 6 pts, NW 0.

Group A	P	W	L	T	NR	Pts
KwaZulu-Natal	10	10	0	0	0	59
Northerns	10	6	4	0	0	36
Gauteng	10	5	4	0	1	36
Limpopo	10	2	4	0	4	23
Mpumalanga	10	2	7	0	1	14
North West	10	1	7	0	2	12

Northerns finish ahead of Gauteng by virtue of more wins.

Group B

Despatch, 29 Oct 2005: EP 193-6 in 50 overs (CS Terblanche 82*, M Strydom 25; G Fritz 2-32, A Taai 2-36). **Bdr** 172-8 in 50 overs (L Jordaan 45, W Croucamp 28*; CS Terblanche 2-23, E Webber 3-32). **Eastern Province won by 21 runs.** EP 5 pts, Bdr 1.
Bloemfontein, 29 Oct 2005: Free State v Western Province match abandoned without a ball bowled. FS 3 pts, WP 3.
Kimberley, 30 Oct 2005: GW 111 in 27.5 overs (L Geyer 32; S Ismail 2-21, A le Breton 4-34, T O'Connell 2-27). **WP** 112-0 in 16.5 overs (AL Hodgkinson 30*, Y van der Westhuizen 57*). **Western Province won by 10 wickets.** WP 6 pts, GW 0.
Kimberley, 6 Nov 2005: GW 95 in 28 overs (B Bezuidenhout 35; SM Benade 3-36, M Loftus 6-18). **FS** 96-1 in 12.2 overs (SM Benade 36). **Free State won by 9 wickets.** FS 6 pts, GW 0.
Cape Town, 6 Nov 2005: WP 95 in 41.3 overs (A Freeman 25*; AE Smith 2-20, B Town 2-15, S Loubser 4-27). **Bol** 97-2 in 21.5 overs (HW Rambaldo 40*). **Boland won by 8 wickets.** Bol 6 pts, WP 0.
Oudtshoorn, 12 Nov 2005: SWD 41 in 24.4 overs (AE Smith 7-15, LZ Jacobs 2-4). **Bol** 42-2 in 4.2 overs. **Boland won by 8 wickets.** Bol 6 pts, SWD 0.
Oudtshoorn, 13 Nov 2005: South Western Districts v Western Province match abandoned without a ball bowled. SWD 3 pts, WP 3.
Kimberley, 19 Nov 2005: GW 54 in 22.4 overs (AE Smith 2-7, S Loubser 4-10, N Christiaans 3-18). **Bol** 55-2 in 7.1 overs (AE Smith 27*; A Mompati 2-21). **Boland won by 8 wickets.** Bol 6 pts, GW 0.
Bloemfontein, 20 Nov 2005: Bol 214 in 48.1 overs (S Loubser 29, B Cartledge 51, AE Smith 46, B Town 26; SM Benade 3-33, A Minnie 2-61). **FS** 130 in 38.2 overs (SM Benade 26, H Labuschagne 37; AE Smith 2-14, S Loubser 2-32, N Christiaans 2-38, LZ Jacobs 2-21). **Boland won by 84 runs.** Bol 6 pts, FS 0.
Oudtshoorn, 26 Nov 2005: SWD 140 in 47.2 overs (C Crause 28; M Loftus 3-15, GJ van Rensburg 4-32, H Labuschagne 2-8). **FS** 141-3 in 30.3 overs (A Minnie 67*; C de Villiers 2-30). **Free State won by 7 wickets.** FS 6 pts, SWD 0.
Oudtshoorn, 27 Nov 2005: GW 109 in 48.4 overs (H Pienaar 2-10, C de Villiers 3-29, C Crause 2-9). **SWD** 110-3 in 24.1 overs (C de Villiers 40*, E Basson 48*; A Krauze 2-29). **South Western Districts won by 7 wickets.** SWD 6 pts, GW 0.
East London, 10 Dec 2005: Bdr 180-9 in 50 overs (W Croucamp 61*; S Loubser 2-22, N Christiaans 2-33, A Petersen 2-32). **Bol** 113 in 38.2 overs (A Petersen 28; E Pienaar 5-20, M Kirchoff 3-29). **Border won by 67 runs.** Bdr 6 pts, Bol 0.
Despatch, 11 Dec 2005: Bol 113 in 36.1 overs (M Seale 2-32, E Webber 2-30). **EP** 104-9 in 50 overs (S Loubser 2-20). **Boland won by 9 runs.** Bol 5 pts, EP 1.
Paarl, 7 Jan 2006: FS 123 in 46.5 overs (SM Benade 37; AE Smith 3-35, S Loubser 4-9, A Petersen 2-29). **Bol** 124-3 in 26 overs (S Loubser 54*, AE Smith 35*). **Boland won by 7 wickets.** Bol 6 pts, FS 0.

WOMEN'S PROVINCIAL LEAGUE 2005/06

Despatch, 7 Jan 2006: EP 91-2 in 17.4 overs (E Webber 28*). **SWD** did not bat. **No result.** EP 3 pts, SWD 3.
East London, 8 Jan 2006: Border v South Western Districts match abandoned without a ball bowled. Bdr 3 pts, SWD 3.
Cape Town, 8 Jan 2006: FS 166 in 50 overs (SM Benade 101; APC Kilowan 2-7, SA Fritz 3-25). **WP** 168-0 in 32.4 overs (AL Hodgkinson 75*, Y van der Westhuizen 78*). **Western Province won by 10 wickets.** WP 6 pts, FS 0.
Paarl, 14 Jan 2006: Bol 268-5 in 50 overs (A Petersen 60, HW Rambaldo 30, AE Smith 56, B Cartledge 34*, B Town 44*; C Crause 2-36). **SWD** 57 in 21 overs (AE Smith 3-24, M Daniels 3-19, S Loubser 3-7). **Boland won by 211 runs.** Bol 6 pts, SWD 0.
East London, 14 Jan 2006: Bdr 331-3 in 50 overs (B Ramjee 80, L Jordaan 147*, W Croucamp 47*; A Mompati 2-60). **GW** 52-9 in 20 overs (E Pienaar 2-23, M Kirchoff 4-22). **Border won by 112 runs (D/L method), target revised to 165 in 20 overs.** Bdr 6 pts, GW 0.
Despatch, 15 Jan 2006: GW 65 in 28 overs (L Esau 2-13, M Kapp 2-11, E Webber 3-11, S Douglas 2-8). **EP** 66-3 in 25.2 overs. **Eastern Province won by 7 wickets.** EP 6 pts, GW 0.
Cape Town, 15 Jan 2006: SWD 99 in 35.3 overs (SA Fritz 2-8, S Ismail 3-14). **WP** 100-3 in 23.4 overs (SA Fritz 38*; C Crause 2-23). **Western Province won by 7 wickets.** WP 6 pts, SWD 0.
Port Elizabeth, 21 Jan 2006: EP 184-8 in 50 overs (M Strydom 65, M Kapp 49*; M Loftus 2-21). **FS** 181 in 49.3 overs (SM Benade 42, A Minnie 99; S Pillay 2-28, M Kapp 3-35). **Eastern Province won by 3 runs.** EP 5 pts, FS 1.
East London, 22 Jan 2006: Bdr 128 in 38 overs (N Ndzundzu 37, M Kirchoff 39; SM Benade 4-24, D Weatherall 2-15). **FS** 86 in 37.1 overs (SM Benade 36; G Fritz 2-19, E Pienaar 2-18, M Kirchoff 4-9). **Border won by 42 runs.** Bdr 6 pts, FS 0.
Paarl, 28 Jan 2006: EP 120 in 45.3 overs (S Pillay 44*; AE Smith 2-20, LZ Jacobs 2-17, CS Terblanche 2-10). **Bol** 121-9 in 37.5 overs (A Petersen 30, S Loubser 27; M Kapp 3-15, L Esau 2-25). **Boland won by 1 wicket.** Bol 6 pts, EP 0.
Kimberley, 28 Jan 2006: GW 77 in 43 overs (E Pienaar 3-14, M Kirchoff 2-15, G Fritz 2-9). **Bdr** 78-2 in 22.2 overs (L Jordaan 42*; A Mompati 2-30). **Border won by 8 wickets.** Bdr 6 pts, GW 0.
Bloemfontein, 29 Jan 2006: FS 96 in 36.2 overs (SM Benade 41; M Kirchoff 2-17, E Pienaar 4-20, A Taai 2-5). **Bdr** 95 in 37.4 overs (W Croucamp 36*; M Loftus 3-15, D Lebeko 2-8). **Free State won by 1 run.** FS 5 pts, Bdr 1.
Cape Town, 29 Jan 2006: EP 85 in 37.5 overs (E Webber 25; SA Fritz 5-13, A le Breton 2-28). **WP** 89-3 in 22.5 overs (SA Fritz 38*; S Pillay 2-20). **Western Province won by 7 wickets.** WP 6 pts, EP 0.
East London, 11 Feb 2006: Bdr 139-9 in 50 overs (L Jordaan 38; SA Fritz 3-17, A le Breton 2-22). **WP** 140-8 in 43.5 overs (Y van der Westhuizen 46; M Kirchoff 2-23). **Western Province won by 2 wickets.** WP 5 pts, Bdr 1.
Despatch, 12 Feb 2006: WP 120 in 46.3 overs (AL Hodgkinson 32, A le Breton 30; S Pillay 5-9). **EP** 121-4 in 38.1 overs (M Strydom 33, J Nel 29). **Eastern Province won by 6 wickets.** EP 6 pts, WP 0.
Stellenbosch, 18 Feb 2006: Bol 127-9 in 50 overs (CS Terblanche 29; E Pienaar 4-24). **Bdr** 128-7 in 41.5 overs (A Taai 32*; S Loubser 2-18, N Christiaans 3-23). **Border won by 3 wickets.** Bdr 5 pts, Bol 1.
Kimberley, 18 Feb 2006: GW 124-8 in 50 overs (S Harmse 26; E Webber 3-24). **EP** 125-2 in 28.4 overs (E Webber 65*; K Moraki 2-30). **Eastern Province won by 8 wickets.** EP 6 pts, GW 0.
Bloemfontein, 19 Feb 2006: EP 186-6 in 50 overs (E Webber 60, M Strydom 27, S Pillay 41*; M Loftus 4-39). **FS** 187-3 in 48 overs (SM Benade 67, H Labuschagne 26, A Minnie 61*). **Free State won by 7 wickets.** FS 5 pts, EP 1.
Cape Town, 19 Feb 2006: Bdr 110 in 44 overs (L Jordaan 32; APC Kilowan 3-21, SA Fritz 3-13, C Esterhuizen 2-35). **WP** 114-6 in 45 overs (AL Hodgkinson 51*; E Pienaar 3-24). **Western Province won by 4 wickets.** WP 5 pts, Bdr 1.
Paarl, 4 Mar 2006: GW 119-8 in 50 overs (S Els 29; S Loubser 2-29, N Christiaans 2-20). **Bol** 120-2 in 17.4 overs (S Loubser 51). **Boland won by 8 wickets.** Bol 6 pts, GW 0.
Oudtshoorn, 4 Mar 2006: SWD 50 in 29.3 overs (G Fritz 4-15, A Taai 2-22, E Pienaar 3-6). **Bdr** 53-0 in 15.4 overs (N Ndzundzu 25*). **Border won by 10 wickets.** Bdr 6 pts, SWD 0.
Oudtshoorn, 5 Mar 2006: EP 184 in 49.2 overs (S Pillay 36, J Nel 31, S Douglas 26; M Rabie 2-30, H Pienaar 2-24, S Coetzee 4-38). **SWD** 46 in 22.3 overs (M Kapp 6-9, S Douglas 2-7). **Eastern Province won by 138 runs.** EP 6 pts, SWD 0.
Cape Town, 5 Mar 2006: GW 81 in 22.4 overs (L Geyer 38; S Ismail 2-7, A le Breton 5-24). **WP** 85-0 in 14.2 overs (A le Breton 42*). **Western Province won by 10 wickets.** WP 6 pts, GW 0.
Kimberley, 11 Mar 2006: GW 166 in 49.5 overs (B Kruger 58*; M Rabie 2-26, A Koen 4-47). **SWD** 74 in 27.4 overs (E Basson 28; L Geyer 2-29, S Harmse 3-9). **Griqualand West won by 92 runs.** GW 6 pts, SWD 0.
Paarl, 12 Mar 2006: Bol 267-5 in 50 overs (S Loubser 45, HW Rambaldo 31, CS Terblanche 86*, AE Smith 45; SA Fritz 2-50, S Ismail 2-39). **WP** 228-9 in 50 overs (O Anderson 27, A le Breton 40, P Enright 50, S Ismail 31; CS Terblanche 2-41, M Vos 2-10). **Boland won by 39 runs.** Bol 5 pts, WP 1.
Bloemfontein, 12 Mar 2006: FS 280 in 45.1 overs (T Khoathela 42, SM Benade 86, E Venter 39, A Minnie 54; S Coetzee 5-24, H Rhodes 2-26). **SWD** 154 in 46 overs (D Lebeko 3-35, A Minnie 2-38, GJ van Rensburg 2-30). **Free State won by 126 runs.** FS 6 pts, SWD 0.
East London, 18 Mar 2006: Bdr 126 in 47 overs (N Ndzundzu 29, L Jordaan 34; S Pillay 2-21, M Seale 2-17, L Pienaar 2-23). **EP** 127-4 in 47.5 overs (E Webber 40*, J Nel 36). **Eastern Province won by 6 wickets.** EP 5 pts, Bdr 1.
Bloemfontein, 19 Mar 2006: GW 74 in 33 overs (SM Benade 2-14, M Loftus 2-4, D Lebeko 3-16, A Minnie 2-24). **FS** 52-0 in 4 overs (A Minnie 28*). **Free State won by 10 wickets (D/L method), target revised to 42 in 20 overs.** They reached their target in 3.3 overs and continued batting until the end of the 4th over. FS 6 pts, GW 0.

WOMEN'S PROVINCIAL LEAGUE 2005/06

Group B	P	W	L	T	NR	Pts
Boland	12	10	2	0	0	59
Western Province	12	7	3	0	2	47
Eastern Province	12	7	4	0	1	44
Border	12	6	5	0	1	43
Free State	12	6	5	0	1	38
South Western Districts	12	1	8	0	3	15
Griqualand West	12	1	11	0	0	6

Semi-finals

Stellenbosch, 25 Mar 2006: Bol 246-6 in 50 overs (S Loubser 25, AE Smith 98*, B Town 40; C Labuschagne 2-36, M Letsoalo 2-35). **Nor** 152-9 in 50 overs (M du Preez 44; S Loubser 2-17, LZ Jacobs 2-28, N Christiaans 2-27). **Boland won by 94 runs.**

Durban, 1 Apr 2006: WP 186-8 in 50 overs (E Auret 26, APC Kilowan 26*; J Hambrook 2-38, J Bartholomew 2-47, J Logtenberg 4-36). **KZN** 107 in 42.3 overs (J Logtenberg 33; C Esterhuizen 4-18, S Hercules 2-9). **Western Province won by 79 runs.**

Final

Brackenfell, 8 Apr 2006: Bol 145 in 50 overs (A Petersen 56; APC Kilowan 2-18, S Ismail 2-35, SA Fritz 4-29). **WP** 148-6 in 44.2 overs (SA Fritz 80*; AE Smith 2-25, B Town 2-33). **Western Province won by 4 wickets.**

LEADING BATTING AVERAGES

		M	Inns	NO	Runs	HS	Avg	SR	100	50
1	CS Terblanche (Bol/EP)	7	7	3	242	86*	60.50	73.78	0	2
2	M du Preez (Nor)	6	6	2	231	88*	57.75	58.48	0	1
3	A Minnie (FS)	11	11	4	392	99	56.00	76.71	0	4
4	SM Benade (FS)	10	10	1	488	101	54.22	72.40	1	2
5	AE Smith (Bol)	14	12	4	375	98*	46.87	94.93	0	2
6	L Jordaan (Bdr)	10	10	2	359	147*	44.87	66.11	1	0
7	H Strydom (Lim)	5	4	0	167	72	41.75	56.22	0	1
8	S Pillay (EP)	11	11	5	249	44*	41.50	51.76	0	0
9	M Terblanche (Gau)	9	9	3	238	61*	39.66	54.10	0	2
10	SA Fritz (WP)	12	9	3	223	80*	37.16	69.04	0	1
11	T Reeves (Gau)	9	8	1	260	80*	37.14	67.77	0	2
12	AL Hodgkinson (WP)	10	10	3	258	75*	36.85	48.67	0	2
13	W Croucamp (Bdr)	10	10	4	218	61*	36.33	81.34	0	1
14	E Webber (EP)	12	12	3	324	65*	36.00	37.76	0	2
15	Y Bronkhorst (Nor)	11	11	1	355	79	35.50	63.96	0	2
16	T Chetty (KZN)	9	8	0	263	67	32.87	66.41	0	2
17	Y van der Westhuizen (WP)	10	10	2	257	78*	32.12	64.57	0	2
18	S Loubser (Bol)	14	11	1	284	54*	28.40	83.52	0	2
19	T Brits (NW)	7	7	1	169	72*	28.16	60.79	0	1

(Qualification: 4 completed innings)

J Logtenberg (KZN) scored 464 runs and was dismissed only once in 9 innings (SR 80.13). She made 1 century and 4 fifties with a highest score of 104*.

Strike-rates are based on matches where details of balls faced are available.

WOMEN'S PROVINCIAL LEAGUE 2005/06

LEADING BOWLING AVERAGES

		M	Overs	Mdns	Runs	Wkts	Avg	RpO	BB	4I
1	P Thode (Gau)	10	21.2	4	33	13	2.53	1.54	3-3	0
2	K Blair (Gau)	9	59	14	133	17	7.82	2.25	6-11	2
3	S Loubser (Bol)	14	121	24	246	30	8.20	2.03	4-9	3
4	E Pienaar (Bdr)	11	98.2	19	245	28	8.75	2.49	5-20	3
5	M Kapp (EP)	8	56	15	144	16	9.00	2.57	6-9	1
6	J Logtenberg (KZN)	9	55	9	169	18	9.38	3.07	5-29	2
7	M Kirchoff (Bdr)	11	78.2	14	199	20	9.95	2.54	4-9	2
8	SA Fritz (WP)	12	86.1	14	249	25	9.96	2.88	5-13	2
9	D Devnarain (KZN)	9	64.4	5	232	23	10.08	3.58	7-28	3
10	AE Smith (Bol)	14	119.3	23	295	28	10.53	2.46	7-15	1
11	J Hambrook (KZN)	8	58.1	7	166	15	11.06	2.85	4-7	1
12	M Loftus (FS)	11	95.4	12	265	22	12.04	2.77	6-18	2
13	T Brits (NW)	7	48.4	3	171	14	12.21	3.51	6-28	2
14	Y Bronkhorst (Nor)	11	89.2	19	284	21	13.52	3.17	7-19	2
15	C Labuschagne (Nor)	8	61	8	211	15	14.06	3.45	4-25	1
16	M Letsoalo (Nor)	10	61.2	16	166	11	15.09	2.70	4-39	1
17	K Naidoo (KZN)	7	53.4	4	154	10	15.40	2.86	5-14	1
18	G Fritz (Bdr)	11	92.1	17	201	13	15.46	2.18	4-15	1
19	N Christiaans (Bol)	13	92.4	11	283	18	15.72	3.05	3-18	0
20	S Ismail (WP)	12	65.1	9	243	15	16.20	3.72	3-14	0

(Qualification: 10 wickets)

WOMEN'S PROVINCIAL LEAGUE RECORDS 2003/04-2005/06

Season	Winners	Runners-up	Margin of victory
2003/04	Boland	Eastern Province	107 runs
2004/05	Gauteng	Border	64 runs
2005/06	Western Province	Boland	4 wickets

Highest innings total:			
331-3	Border v Griqualand West	East London	2005/06
Highest innings total batting second:			
228-9 (Lost)	Western Province v Boland	Paarl	2005/06
227-3 (Won)	Northerns v KwaZulu-Natal	Centurion	2003/04
Lowest innings total:			
22	Limpopo v Northerns	Polokwane	2004/05
Largest margin of victory (by runs):			
266	Northerns v Limpopo	Polokwane	2004/05
Highest individual score:			
155*	J Logtenberg	KZN v FS (Durban)	2004/05
Most runs in a season:			
488 (avg 54.22)	SM Benade (FS)		2005/06
Most runs in a career:			
1134 (avg 56.70)	SM Benade		2003-05
Best bowling in an innings:			
7-15	AE Smith	Bol v SWD (Oudtshoorn)	2005/06
Most wickets in a season:			
30 (avg 8.20)	S Loubser (Bol)		2005/06
Most wickets in a career:			
55 (avg 12.96)	AE Smith		2003-05

RECORD WICKET PARTNERSHIPS

1st	231	E Webber and J Fourie	EP v GW (Kimberley)	2003/04
2nd	151	J Bartholomew and T Chetty	KZN v Mpu (Durban)	2005/06
3rd	232	B Ramjee and L Jordaan	Bdr v GW (East London)	2005/06
4th	147	C van der Westhuizen and Y van der Merwe	Nor v Lim (Polokwane)	2004/05
5th	95	AE Smith and M Lotter	Bol v EP (Paarl)	2004/05
6th	76	Y van der Merwe and C Serwadi	Nor v KZN (Durban)	2003/04
7th	78	L Jordaan and W Croucamp	Bdr v FS (East London)	2004/05
8th	69	SM Benade and M Loftus	FS v WP (Cape Town)	2005/06
9th	64	N Ndzundzu and M Kirchoff	Bdr v FS (East London)	2005/06
10th	30*	CS Terblanche and S Zonke	EP v Bol (Port Elizabeth)	2003/04

DEAF CRICKET WORLD CUP

South Africa participated in the second Deaf Cricket World Cup in Lucknow, India, in November 2005. Nine teams competed in the tournament, organised by the Deaf Cricket International Federation, which was established in April 2004. A previous Deaf World Cup was held in Melbourne, Australia, in 1995/96.

The tournament was played on a round robin basis, with the top four teams going through to the semi-finals. South Africa won three of their eight matches and failed to reach the knock-out stage, which was contested by India, England, Australia and Pakistan. The final was between India and England, with India winning by 79 runs.

Donations from the National Lottery and Jonathan Oppenheimer and support from Transwerk in the form of equipment enabled the SA Deaf Cricket Association to raise funds for the team's participation.

The team was selected after an inter-provincial tournament in March 2005. A preliminary training camp was held in September at which fitness and skills levels were assessed. Several players were able to get assistance from the cricket unions of their home provinces to improve their fitness levels before attending a final camp immediately before the team's departure.

The players had difficulty adapting to slow, hard and grassless pitches, while the outfields were hard and bumpy. Excessive dew played a role and the outfield was invariably wet during the first innings of matches, giving an advantage to teams batting first.

South Africa's poor batting was a major reason why the team finished a disappointing sixth on the log. The batsmen generally failed to adapt to the need to play off the front foot on pitches of low bounce where playing off the back foot was risky. The lack of a reliable opening pair put pressure on the rest of the batting.

Stefan van Zyl, the captain, was the only batsman to finish with an average of more than 20. He scored 143 runs at 23.83 and made the only half-century by a South African. The next most successful batsman was Stephen Lombard, who made 113 runs at 18.83.

The bowlers were more successful, although the fast bowlers struggled to overcome a tendency to bowl too short on slow pitches. Despite conceding too many extras, the bowlers, particularly the spinners, were comparable to those of the more successful teams, while the fielding was good. Avinash Kallichuran took 11 wickets at 19.72. Van Zyl took nine wickets, while Shamiel Howley, Barend van Vreden and Christopher Diab took seven each. All Diab's wickets were taken in one match when he recorded the remarkable figures of 7-16 against Nepal.

A lack of international experience was a major problem, especially as several of the opposition teams had played at this level. A South African deaf team had not played in an international match since the first Deaf World Cup more than nine years before.

The need for more international matches and a long-term selection strategy, ahead of the next Deaf World Cup scheduled for 2009, were two of the issues raised by the team management following the trip to India.

During the World Cup, discussions were held with England with a view to the England team touring South Africa in 2007.

The South African squad in India was: Stefan van Zyl (Northerns, captain), Shamiel Howley (Western Province, vice-captain), Rhyno Cloete (Boland), Paulo da Costa (Gauteng), Christopher Diab (Gauteng), Avinash Kallichuran (KwaZulu-Natal), Gregory Lessing (Gauteng), Stephen Lombard (Northerns), Wocjiech Palinkas (Gauteng), Rishaad Shaik (KwaZulu-Natal), Johannes Rothman (Western Province), Percival Topley (Western Province), Barend van Vreden (Northerns), Kevin Venter (Gauteng), Xolani Wayile (Northerns). Team manager, Rory Hickson; tour manager, Ivan Joubert; coach, Felix Vilakazi; scorer/interpreter, Trudi White; physiotherapist, Fatima Cachalia; delegate, Stephen Venter.

SOUTH AFRICAN SCORES IN BRIEF

At LDA Stadium, 17 November 2005. Pakistan 262 in 49 overs (Mohammad Iqbal 62, Nabeel Anjum 60*, S Howley 2-37). **South Africa** 80 in 26.1 overs (Adnan Ghani 2-25, G Usman 3-23, Mohammad Shakeel 3-10). **Pakistan won by 182 runs**.

At LDA Stadium, 18 November 2005. South Africa 181 in 48.4 overs (S van Zyl 56, N Jayathilake 2-10). **Sri Lanka** 156 in 45 overs (T Sanjeewa 31*, S van Zyl 3-37, B van Vreden 2-32, K Venter 2-12). **South Africa won by 25 runs.**

At LDA Stadium, 19 November 2005. Australia 257-6 in 50 overs (A Watkins 75, N Watkins 78, S van Zyl 3-27). **South Africa** 65 in 25 overs (K Daley 3-10, D O'Halloran 2-18, G Moffat 3-9, T Hall 2-17). **Australia won by 192 runs.**

At Chowk Stadium, 20 November 2005. New Zealand 202-7 in 50 overs (A Brown 92). **South Africa** 79 in 22.3 overs (D Brown 6-43, C Morgan 2-21). **New Zealand won by 123 runs.**

At KD Singh Babu Stadium, 22 November 2005. England 221-8 in 50 overs (S Pichowski 55, M O'Mahony 56, S Howley 2-42). **South Africa** 213 in 50 overs (R Shaik 30, S Lombard 39, S van Zyl 35, P Allen 3-36). **England won by 8 runs.**

At KD Singh Babu Stadium, 23 November 2005. Nepal 48 in 21.2 overs (S Lombard 2-9, C Diab 7-16). **South Africa** 49-0 in 8.2 overs. South **Africa won by 10 wickets.**

At **Gomti Nagar Stadium, 24 November 2005. South Africa** 144 in 37.1 overs (S Lombard 42, S van Zyl 34, G Lessing 32*, Luffar Kabbir 2-22, SM Monjur Iqbal 4-30, Amit Saha 3-27). **Bangladesh** 119 in 40.1 overs (Amit Saha 38*, A Kallichuran 4-23, B van Vreden 3-19). **South Africa won by 25 runs.**

At Gomti Nagar Stadium, 25 November 2005. South Africa 83 in 36.2 overs (Fahimudin Ali 2-11). **India** 84-1 in 17.3 overs (I Yadav 53*). **India won by 9 wickets.**

STUDENTS CRICKET

John Young

The restructuring and amalgamation of South Africa's tertiary institutions was reflected in the format employed for the South African Students Sports Union Cricket Weeks. The A week in Port Elizabeth was expanded to include 16 teams which had previously made up the A and B sections, while a further ten teams competed in the B tournament held in East London.

A SECTION

Having come agonisingly close to the title in 2001 and 2002, the team from Nelson Mandela Metropolitan University took full advantage of their knowledge of local conditions to win the 2005 title. As the University of Port Elizabeth, they had last triumphed in 1997. NMMU captain and all-rounder Grant Howell played a major role in his team's successful week, following in the footsteps of his father Ian who played in the first UPE side to win the universities' title in 1981. Howell senior is now on the international umpires' panel.

In stark contrast to the 2004 week in Johannesburg, during which only one century was recorded, batsmen cashed in on Port Elizabeth's friendly pitches and there were some remarkable run-chases. Seven teams recorded totals over 300 and there were eleven individual centuries: Free State University's Tienie Fick led the way with the week's two biggest scores, 139 and 154, while North West's Eugene Serfontein also posted two centuries.

Chad Baxter from NMMU hit 138 against Walter Sisulu University. All the home team's batsmen showed good form, with Baxter and Lyndon Brown being particularly consistent. Both scored half-centuries in an efficient run-chase in the final against the University of the Western Cape to cap a good week of batting. NMMU's spinners, led by leg-spinner Howell and off-spinner Simon McGillewie, succeeded in tying up the opposition to good effect.

With 16 teams playing a round robin in four pools, interest was maintained into the final two days of cross-pool play-offs. In previous years, one bad result would mean the end of a team's hopes. The winners of the previous tournament, North West, had their colours lowered in dramatic fashion on the first day, falling just one run short of Tshwane University of Technology's total of 221.

Cape Town's teams reversed their bad showings of recent years by securing a position in each semi-final but the University of Cape Town's powerful batting line-up came unstuck in a rain-affected game against the hosts. The University of the Western Cape's outstanding improvement over the last few seasons culminated in their winning a place in the final. A century by Craig Williams set up a thrilling one-run win over Pretoria.

Riaan Osman and the organising committee of the NMMU did a fine job in ensuring eight good pitches every day. Old Grey and Grey High School were used as alternate venues. Mike Gajjar took charge of the umpires and former EP spinner Devdas Govindjee headed a selection panel that also included former EP all-rounder Keith Reid and Faghme Abrahams.

Final log positions (University unless otherwise stated): 1 Nelson Mandela Metropole, 2 Western Cape, 3 Pretoria, 4 Cape Town, 5 Free State, 6 Johannesburg, 7 Witwatersrand, 8 Tshwane University of Technology, 9 Stellenbosch, 10 North West, 11 KwaZulu-Natal, 12 Central University of Technology, 13 Walter Sisulu, 14 Rhodes, 15 Cape Peninsula University of Technology, 16 Durban Institute of Technology.

STUDENTS CRICKET

No representative match took place. A match was planned against a British Universities team but their tour did not happen. Tournament team: Grant Howell (Nelson Mandela, captain), Lyndon Brown, Chad Baxter and Simon McGillewie (Nelson Mandela), Anley Chinnappa (DIT), Tienie Fick and Colin Ingram (Free State), Graeme Marais (Cape Town), Brian Mathebula and William Motaung (Johannesburg), Abraham Ndlovu (Pretoria), Gershwin Rabie and Esmond van Wyk (Western Cape), Pepler Sandri (Stellenbosch), Eugene Serfontein (North West).

A SECTION RESULTS

Monday 5 December

Pool A:

Tshwane University of Technology 221-8 (N Chouhan 71, C Kellerman 60, D Thompson 3-53, A van der Merwe 3-20). **North West** 220 (E Serfontein 118, C Kellerman 4-44, Hobart 3-44). Tshwane won by one run.

Cape Peninsula University of Technology 122 (Parenze 30, G van Wyk 5-15). **Western Cape** 127-3 (A Fernandes 50*, G van Wyk 49*). Western Cape won by 7 wickets.

Pool B:

Walter Sisulu 201-7 (Kray 56, G Stewart 4-42, B Mathebula 3-19). **Johannesburg** 203-2 (D van Wyk 72, W Motaung 81). Johannesburg won by 8 wickets.

Nelson Mandela 233-8 (C Baxter 72, L Brown 67, B Robinson 3-65). **KwaZulu-Natal** 74 (S McGillewie 3-12, M Luscombe 3-14, Grant Howell 3-17). Nelson Mandela won by 159 runs.

Pool C:

Stellenbosch 235 (D Hobson 66, M van Rooyen 55). **Durban Institute of Technology** 178 (A Chinnappa 89, M van Rooyen 4-28, Lopston 3-28). Stellenbosch won by 57 runs.

Witwatersrand 242-8 (W Josselsohn 96, M Street 73, T Rock 4-51). **Cape Town** 243-7 (J Geoghegan 85, J Kuiper 55). Cape Town won by 3 wickets.

Pool D:

Central University of Technology 134 (S Venter 30, D Makua 4-11, Erasmus 3-33). **Pretoria** 135-4 (S Liebisch 47, P van Biljon 34*). Pretoria won by 6 wickets.

Free State 291-7 (T Fick 139, C Ingram 84, P Leyden 3-37). **Rhodes** 196 (A Paterson 79, R Jordaan 4-42). Free State won by 95 runs.

Tuesday 6 December 2005

Pool A:

Cape Peninsula University of Technology 211 (C Pharoah 38, C Booysen 32, T Khoza 4-27). **Tshwane University of Technology** 212-6 (C Kellerman 39 not out). Tshwane won by 4 wickets.

Western Cape 178-7 (E van Wyk 51, A Fernandes 42, A van der Merwe 3-34). **North West** 139 (J Maree 32, E van Wyk 5-20). Western Cape won by 39 runs.

Pool B:

Johannesburg 301-6 (M Otto 110, B Mathebula 36). **KwaZulu-Natal** 165 (D van Wyk 3-23, M van Jaarsveld 3-31). Johannesburg won by 136 runs.

Nelson Mandela 300-4 (C Baxter 138, L Brown 63, M Price 54). **Walter Sisulu** 213-7 (Z Ntyupu 64). Nelson Mandela won by 87 runs

Pool C:

Cape Town 317-5 (G Marais 115, J Geoghegan 80 not out, C Drummond 49). **Stellenbosch** 248 (D Durham 59, C Arkel 4-53). Cape Town won by 69 runs.

Witwatersrand 237-7 (N Winspear 68, K McBain-Charles 44, N Sephton-Poultney 30, W Osterline 3-37). **Durban Institute of Technology** 135 (A. Chinnappa 60, N Sephton-Poultey 6-32, E Leie 4-9). Witwatersrand won by 102 runs.

Pool D:
Pretoria 266-6 (G Lotriet 76, K Pienaar 42, P Haupt 41). **Rhodes** 180 (Brent Bragge 46*, S Liebisch 3-21, K Pienaar 3-27). Pretoria won by 86 runs.
Free State 231-7 (C Ingram 68, T Fick 36, H van Rowenstein 3-48**). Central University of Technology** 224-7 (G McLaren 84 not out, A van Deventer 44). Free State won by 7 runs.

Wednesday 7 December 2005
Pool A:
Western Cape 215-5 (E van Wyk 71, C Williams 64, R Hobart 2-15). **Tshwane University of Technology** 124 (N Chauhan 36, E van Wyk 3-15). Western Cape won by 91 runs.
North West 285-4 (E Serfontein 132, J Danhauser 56). **Cape Peninsula University of Technology** 254 (C Booysen 110, J Moroe 47). C du Toit 4-40). North West won by 31 runs.
Pool B:
Nelson Mandela 243-8 (L Brown 57, C Baxter 50, M Price 43, G Stewart 3-40). **Johannesburg** 202-9 (B Buckley 45, W Motaung 43, G Howell 4-32, A Birch 3-47). Nelson Mandela won by 41 runs.
KwaZulu-Natal 311-8 (W Fynn 82, R McMillian 73, T Krai 3-45**). Walter Sisulu** 127 (N Winspear 37, B Robinson 5-35). Natal won by 184 runs.
Pool C:
Stellenbosch 155 (D Durham 49, C Shuttle 2-34, N Sephton-Poultney 2-37). **Witwatersrand** 157-7 (N Winspear 37, K McBain-Charles 39). Witwatersrand won by 3 wickets.
Cape Town 240-8 (J Kuiper 66, D Cooke 36, S Govender 2-35, A Chinnappa 2-41). **Durban Institute of Technology** 109 (D Govender 45, R Dodds 3-20, K Cox 3-30). Cape Town won by 131 runs.
Pool D:
Pretoria 309-8 (P Haupt 67, B Erasmus 54, K Pienaar 54, P van Biljon 45, C Ingram 3-32). **Free State** 101 (C Linde 36, T Lange 4-23, S Liebisch 3-25). Pretoria won by 208 runs.
Rhodes 215-8 (M Richardson 74, W Briggs 42, H van Rauenstein 4-36). **Central University of Technology** 218-8 (J O'Niell 32, H Poechet 32, H Keeton 5-60). Central University won by 2 wickets.

Thursday 8 December 2005
Cross-pool play-offs.
Semi-final: Western Cape 238-4 (C Williams 101, F Simon 54). **Pretoria** 237-8 (B Erasmus 117, P Haupt 52, G Knott 3-42). Western Cape won by 1 run.
Semi-final: Nelson Mandela 229-6 (L Brown 63). **Cape Town** 97 (B Abrahams 3-14, A Birch 3-26). Nelson Mandela won 143 runs (D/L Method).
Johannesburg 220-6 (B Buckley 48, W Motaung 47, R Tindale 3-52). **Witwatersrand** 206-6 (W Josselsohn 74, R Tindale 50, J Seegers 3-44). Johannesburg won by 14 runs.
Free State 334-6 (T Fick 154, R Jordaan 57, W van der Schyff 48). **Tshwane University of Technology** 171 (N Chauhan 54, J Mostert 2-12, R Jordaan 2-21). Free State won by 171 runs (D/L Method).
North West 217-7 (E Havenga 74, M Botha 49). **Central University of Technology** 167 (Pretorius 65, A van der Merwe 3-9). North West won by 54 runs (D/L Method).
KwaZulu-Natal 123 (D Marais 20, A van Heerden 5-17, Pepler Sandri 3-23). **Stellenbosch** 125-3 (D Durham 56). Stellenbosch won by 7 wickets.
Rhodes 224-8 (W Briggs 62, M Richardson 54, E Parenze 3-45**). Cape Peninsula University of Technology** 222-7 (B Cupido 64*, P Leyden 3-50). Rhodes won by 9 runs (D/L Method).
Durban Institute of Technology 148 (A Chinnappa 64). **Walter Sisulu** 149-5 (T Krai 48). Walter Sisulu won by 5 wickets.

Friday 9 December 2005
The Final:Western Cape 158 (F Simon 52, S McGillewe 3-40). **Nelson Mandela** 161-3 (L Brown 60, C Baxter 59). Nelson Mandela won by 7 wickets.
Cape Town 174 (A Gray 41, J Kuiper 31). **Pretoria** 179-8 (P van Biljon 47, K Pienaar 40, T Rock 3-38). Pretoria won by 2 wickets.

Play-offs: Johannesburg 203-9 (W Motaung 60, R Cameron 47). **Free State** 206-6 (T Fick 53, Corne Linde 50*, H van Zyl 3-82). Free State won by 4 wickets.
Witwatersrand 218-8 (N Winspear 46, R Hobart 3-40**). Tshwane University of Technology** 139 (N Sephton-Poultney 3-32). Witwatersrand won by 79 runs.
North West 153-5 (J Danhauser 54). **Stellenbosch** 156-3 (W Haywood 52, G van Rooy 41). Stellenbosch won by 7 wickets.
Central University of Technology 270 (I O'Niell 62, H van Rauenstein 61, B Robinson 3-37). **KwaZulu-Natal** 271-6 (R McMillian 103, K du Randt 45). KwaZulu-Natal won by 4 wickets.
Rhodes 168-6 (T Pearson 42, M Bana 2-26). **Walter Sisulu** 169-9 (N Nxethwane 24, Z Mtyupu 24) Walter Sisulu won by 1 wicket.
Cape Peninsula University of Technology 305-8 (E Brenzee 65, J Jonus 57, A Chinnappa 3-62). **Durban Institute of Technology** 256 (A Chinnappa 52, M Govender 68, C Pharoah 3-40). Cape Peninsula won by 49 runs.

B SECTION

The B section was played in East London from 28 November to 2 December 2005. Walter Sisulu University earned a place in the A tournament by winning all five of their matches, some by crushing margins. Their score of 300-4 against the University of Venda was a highlight. The teams of Limpopo (Turfloop) and North West (Vaal) put up good opposition but Walter Sisulu retained their unbeaten record to top the log ahead of the latter team.

Log positions (Universities unless otherwise stated): 1 Walter Sisulu, 2 North West (Vaal), 3 Vaal University of Technology, 4 Venda, 5 CIDA, 6 TUT (Soshanguve), 7 Limpopo (Turfloop), 8 Limpopo (Medunsa), 9 Mangosutho Technikon, 10 North West (Mafikeng).

S.A. COUNTRY CRICKET ASSOCIATION

PO Box 1281, Howick 3290. Tel 033 330 4968. Fax 033 330 5650.
E-mail: tchadwick@mweb.co.za
President: Dennis Carlstein. Secretary: Terry Chadwick.

The South African Country Cricket Association Team selected at the 2005 SACCA tournament toured Argentina during December 2005 and won all their five matches.

The 2006 tournament was held in the Grahamstown area from 21 to 26 January. Ten teams participated, divided into two sections.

Border Country won Section A and Boland were the winners of Section B. Boland, who won the 2005 tournament, triumphed again in the final.

Pieter Ferreira of Gauteng was named Player of the Week. The Vereeniging club player scored 236 runs in five innings at an average of 59.00 and took eight wickets. He also top-scored with 75 for the SACCA team against an Eastern Province Invitation team.

The SA Country Cricket Association team selected to play an Eastern Province Invitation team was: Marcel Engelbrecht (Gauteng, captain), Marshal Manas (Boland, vice-captain), Andrew Bowker (EP Grahamstown), Hilton Collett (EP Midlands), Pieter Ferreira (Gauteng), Faan Fourie (North West), Charl Groenewald (KZN Coastal), Mawande Joko (Border Villages), Damien Joseph (Griqualand West), Athi Lwana (Border Villages), Emile Saayman (Boland). 12th man, Lazola Masingata (Border Villages). Manager, Leon Coetzee.

SCORES IN BRIEF
Day One, 21 January
EP Midlands 81 (M Gqadushe 5-22). **Border Villages** 84-1 (L Myanda 31*, D Lwana 37*). **Border Villages won by 9 wickets.**

S.A. COUNTRY CRICKET ASSOCIATION

Border CD 202 (V Makapela 60, A Nel 4-23). **EP Grahamstown** 173 (J Holder 35, B Emslie 35, L Keke 3-37, A Hlahleni 3-31). **Border CD won by 29 runs.**
North West 160 (H Strydom 47, C Groenewald 3-30, M Lyer 3-8). **KwaZulu-Natal Coastal** 110 (M Mzema 2-14, F Fourie 3-21). **North West won by 50 runs.**
Griqualand West 197 (G Meintjies 32, W van Reenen 3-23). **Gauteng** 121 (M Engelbrecht 43, J Kotze 2-12). **Griqualand West won by 76 runs.**
Day Two, 22 January
Border CD 204-3 (M Vuyisa 41, N Yeli 37, M Tshona 36, J Hay 2-13). **EP Midlands** 137 (G Marais 35, G Alexander 32, L Keke 4-23). **Border CD won by 67 runs.**
North West 134-9 (J Kotze 39, D Roats 36, H Strydom 36, L Masingata 2-27). **Border Villages** 135-9 (A Lwana 64, J Kotze 2-13). **Border Villages won by 1 wicket.**
EP Grahamstown 124 (D Childs 3-24, M Manas 2-19, G Ferreira 2-22). **Boland** 130-5 (A Cuttings 47, M Antoni 3-24). **Boland won by 5 wickets.**
Free State 180 (H Jafta 40, E Losper 4-30). **Griqualand West** 181-8 (M Erasmus 49, P Strydom 2-30). **Griqualand West won by 2 wickets.**
KZN Coastal 230-8 (L Jali 44, B Ismail 37, P Ferreira 3-43). **Gauteng** 187 (B Ndimande 55, P Ferreira 61, M Lyer 3-24, R Kazi 2-33, A Maharaj 2-25). **KZN Coastal won by 43 runs.**
Day Three, 23 January
Border CD 194-9 (Campher 48, Mbada 38, Maritz 3-32). **Free State** 169 (D Jafta 56, Schoombie 42, N Joli 4-24). **Border CD won by 25 runs.**
KZN Coastal 186-9 (Lombard 38, Jali 35, Meintjies 2-21). **Griqualand West** 149 (Meintjies 53, Groenewald 3-32). **KZN Coastal won by 37 runs.**
North West 214-7 (Strydom 97, Kahn 42, Swartz 3-35). **EP Midlands** 215-8 (Collett 52, Marais 59, Kahn 3-39). **EP Midlands won by 1 wicket.**
EP Grahamstown 216-7 (Bowker 67, Holder 46, Bana 4-45). **Border Villages** 162 (Masingata 68, C Daniels 3-21). **EP Grahamstown won by 54 runs.**
Gauteng 181-8 (Kidwell 52, Botha 32, Ferreira 3-57). **Boland** 141 (Ferreira 3-3, Engelbrecht 3-24). **Gauteng won by 40 runs.**
Day Four, 24 January
Border CD 159 (B Esterhuizen 63*, M Gqadushe 3-16). **Border Villages** 160-6 (A Lwana 36, Masingata 40, Yoli 2-24, Mbada 2-15). **Border Villages won by 4 wickets.**
KZN Coastal 169-9 (S Faure 4-24, S Pretorius 3-32). **Boland** 170-3 (Huysamen 46, Botha 42). **Boland won by 7 wickets.**
North West 202 (Huisamen 95, Koortzen 40, C Daniels 4-43, Anthony 4-46). **EP Grahamstown** 201-8 (Bowker 71, Anthony 37). **North West won by 1 run.**
Gauteng 252-7 (Ferreira 78*, Ndimane 52, Pietersen 4-29). **Free State** 221-9 (Cinnamon 56, Van Reenen 2-26). **Gauteng won by 31 runs.**
EP Midlands 217 (Murray 57, Collett 57, Joseph 4-37). **Griqualand West** 116 (Du Piesanie 4-38, Marais 3-38). **EP Midlands won by 101 runs.**
Day Five, 25 January
EP Grahamstown 268-7 (A Bowker 48, A Nel 69*, J Hay 4-45). **EP Midlands** 270-7 (H Collett 95*, G Alexander 66, A Bowker 2-1). **EP Midlands won by 3 wickets.**
North West 88 (Tshona 5-25). **Border CD** 90-8 (F Fourie 4-30, C Jonker 4-30). **Border CD won by 2 wickets.**
Gauteng 240-9 (N Pearce 60, M Engelbrecht 50, Bana 3-33). **Border Villages** 241-6 (M Gqadushe 44, A Lwana 69, Masingata 55*). **Border Villages won by 4 wickets.**
Free State 101 (Lombard 4-24). **KZN Country** 102-3 (Jali 35). **KZN Country won by 7 wickets.**
Boland 219 (Botha 44, Loff 58, Joseph 3-42). **Griqualand West** 142 (D Childs 3-20, G Ferreira 3-31). **Boland won by 77 runs.**

Section A	**P**	**W**	**L**	**NR**	**Bon**	**Pts**
Border CD	5	4	1	0	2	22
Border Villages	5	4	1	0	1	21
EP Midlands	5	3	2	0	1	16
North West	5	2	3	0	1	11
EP G'town	5	1	4	0	1	6

Section B		**P**	**W**	**L**	**NR**	**Bon Pts**
Boland	5	4	1	0	3	23
KZN Coastal	5	3	2	0	2	17
Gauteng	5	3	2	0	0	15
Griquas	5	2	3	0	1	11
Free State	5	0	5	0	0	0

Final, 26 January
Border CD 234-8 (Esterhuizen 71, Yoli 53, Charles 2-36). **Boland** 235-3 (Pretorius 79, Cuttings 69, Saayman 55*). C George 54, G Marais 26, W Murray 27). **Boland won by 7 wickets.**
One-day friendly, 27 January
SACCA XI 220-8 (P Ferreira 75, M Engelbrecht 31, Dipha 3-31). **Eastern Province Invitation XI** 223-5 (Jemsana 68, Dipha 63). **EP Invitation XI won by 5 wickets.**

COCA-COLA KHAYA MAJOLA WEEK

Western Province won the Platinum Group in the 12th Coca-Cola Khaya Majola tournament held in East London and three of their players were selected for the South African Schools team that played against the Border Amateur team at the conclusion of the week.

Coca-Cola South Africa reaffirmed its commitment to the United Cricket Board of South Africa, announcing a renewal of their sponsorship until the end of 2007.

South African Schools XI: Dean Elgar (St Dominic's, Free State, captain), Brett Thompson (Grey, Eastern Province), Preston Mommsen (Hilton, KwaZulu-Natal Inland), Grant Mokoena (Queen's, Border), Mduduzi Mbatha (Durban, KwaZulu-Natal), Craig Kieswetter (Bishops, Western Province), Wayne Parnelle (Grey, Eastern Province), Jean Symes (St John's, Gauteng), Ruan Pietersen (Northern Cape, Griqualand West), Mafinki Serame (Milner, North West), Malusi Siboto (Wynberg, Western Province), Craig Alexander (Bellville Tech, Western Province). Manager, Basil Malamba.

South African Colts XI: Gustav Burger (Northern Cape, Griqualand West, captain), Lefa Mosena (St Andrew's, Free State), Pieter Malan (Nelspruit, Mpumalanga), Stitch Seyibhokwe (Dale, Border), Peter Furstenburg (Grey, Eastern Province), Adrian Kritzinger (Bishops, Western Province), Luyolo Thumana (Hudson Park, Border), Kyle Abbott (Kearsney, KwaZulu-Natal), Aviwe Mgijima (Selborne, Border), Sean Davids (Daniel Pienaar, Eastern Province), Johan Bothma (Paul Roos, Boland), Mthokozisi Shezi (Glenwood, KwaZulu-Natal). Manager, Ray Jennings.

Sixteen teams participated, 11 from the provincial Affiliates and five from the Associates.

Western Province won all five of their matches, while Eastern Province and Border both won four out of five. Free State, who finished top in the 2004 Week, failed to win a match.

Preston Mommsen secured his place in the SA Schools team by making centuries against Easterns and Boland, while Pieter Malan made hundreds on the last two days for Mpumulanga in the Gold Group, earning selection for SA Colts.

Mafinki Serame of North West created havoc among Gold Group batsmen and had two five-wicket hauls, including 5-7 against struggling Kei.

Day One, 16 September

Platinum Group

Gauteng 150 in 40.5 overs (C Bekker 30, R Dullabh 20, S Seyibhokwe 3-39, D Allan 2-13). **Border** 141-8 in 45 overs (A Mgijima 78*, S Seyibhokwe 49, R van der Berg 3-20, O Ramela 2-27). **Border won by 2 wickets (D/L Method).**

KwaZulu-Natal Inland 156 in 47.2 overs (P Mommsen 36, K Nelson-Esch 32, D Elgar 4-17, R Ferris 3-22, P Strydom 2-29). **Free State** 152 in 49.1 overs (P Strydom 42, N Harridave 2-10, S Hlatswayo 2-16). **KwaZulu-Natal Inland won by 4 runs.**

Northerns 215-4 in 50 overs (F le Clus 94, D Hewitt 59*, J Potgieter 3-44). KwaZulu-Natal 177 (M Mbatha 68, M Venter 3-25, S Ernst 3-26). **Northerns won by 38 runs.**

Easterns 75 in 39.3 overs (M Siboto 4-10). **Western Province** 76-2 in 16.3 overs (N Dedford 40*). **Western Province won by 8 wickets.**

Boland 101 in 41.1 overs (D Malan 33, K Niewoudt 23, C Dolley 2-21). **Eastern Province** 103-3 in 27.2 overs (B Thompson 42, P Furstenberg 43*). **Eastern Province won by 7 wickets.**

Gold Group

Kei 132-8 in 46 overs (A Dladla 23, T Mpendulo 22, G Burger 4-23, R Pieterson 2-21). **Griqualand West** 112-4 in 35 overs (A Boonzaaier 33*, T Mokwena 24). **Match tied (D/L Method).**

North West 203 (P Letseleme 51, K van Rensburg 37, W Jacobs 3-22, L Arendse 3-28, M Malan 3-36). **Mpumalanga** 141-8 (M Malan 27, A dos Santos 26). **North West won by 62 runs.**

South Western Districts 167 in 40 overs (E Ewerts 73, S Mashela 2-25, M Mphahlele 2-20). **Limpopo** 168-6 in 39.2 overs (T Pistorius 31, T Monyamane 20*). **Limpopo won by 4 wickets.**

Day Two, 17 December
Platinum Group
Eastern Province 202-7 in 50 overs (P Furstenberg 82, W Parnelle 48*, E Partridge 4-51). **Easterns** 159 in 48.1 overs (P van Zyl 43, D Cronje 26, G Gidana 4-24, W Dunlop 2-22). **Eastern Province won by 43 runs.**
Gauteng 161-7 in 45 overs - change of venue resulted in the loss of 5 overs – (J Symes 68, R Bishop 25, O Ramela 22, S Hendrieck 2-12-2). **Western Province** 162-4 in 35.3 overs (T Main 66, R Levi 39*, R van den Berg 2-29). **Western Province won by 6 wickets.**
Northerns 200-8 in 50 overs (S von Berg 60, V Sharma 30, R Cheeseman 3-37, K Nipper 2-20). **KwaZulu-Natal Inland** 103 all out in 37.3 overs (S Ernst 3-13, S von Berg 2-12, M Venter 2-23). **Northerns won by 97 runs.**
Free State 192-6 in 50 overs (D Elgar 99, P Strydom 58, D Allan 2-19, A Mgijima 2-22). **Border** 194-6 in 47.2 overs (S Seyibhokwe 84, L Thumana 44, C van der Schyff 3-33). **Border won by 4 wickets.**
KwaZulu-Natal 195 in 49.5 overs (J Housten 65, J Potgieter 40, M Mbatha 35, K Nieuwoudt 3-33, S van Zyl 3-39). **Boland** 197-8 in 47.2 overs (P Jafta 37, S van Zyl 26, K Abbot 3-23, E Mickleburgh 2-17). **Boland won by 2 wickets.**
Gold Group
Griqualand West 209-5 in 50 overs (A Boonzaaier 73, G Burger 69*, W Booysen 3-27). **Mpumalanga** 138 in 40 overs (L Arendse 68*, R Pietersen 2-17, G Burger 2-27). **Griqualand West won by 71 runs.**
North West 95 in 31.5 overs (E Meyer 6-24, K Carlse 2-12). **South Western Districts** 97-6 in 32.4 overs (E Ewerts 30*, D Lewis 22, M Serame 5-21). **South Western Districts won by 4 wickets.**
Kei 109 in 43 overs (V Mbulawa 29, L Masekela 3-17, S van Heerden 3-19). **Limpopo** 110-9 in 44.1 overs (L Masekela 21, M Songo 3-6, Z Mpikeleli 3-14). **Limpopo won by 1 wicket.**

Day Three, 18 December
Platinum Group
Gauteng 87 in 46.1 overs (W Parnelle 3-8, S Davids 2-15, W Dunlop 2-19). **Eastern Province** 91-6 in 18.4 overs (K Bennett 34, B Thompson 22, J Symes 5-21). **Eastern Province won by 4 wickets.**
Free State 167 in 49.4 overs (K Somiah 46, S Wentzel 32, C Mabuya 2-18, E Mickleburgh 2-21). **KwaZulu-Natal** 168-3 in 44.5 overs (C Nhlapo 60, C Hauptfleish 57*, F Matroos 2-20). **KwaZulu-Natal won by 7 wickets.**
KwaZulu-Natal Inland 202-5 in 50 overs (P Mommsen 105*, I Worth 30). **Easterns** 102 in 31.2 overs (D Cronje 34, T Bodibe 23, O Humphreys 3-20, R Cheeseman 3-35, N Harridave 2-2). **KwaZulu-Natal Inland won by 100 runs.**
Northerns 82 in 28.1 overs (D Allan 4-16, F Genade 2-18, A Mgijima 2-22). **Border** 83-6 in 34.5 overs (L Thumana 29, L Nel 2-11, S Ernst 2-23). **Border won by 4 wickets.**
Western Province 202-9 in 50 overs (C Kieswetter 58, L de Jager 36*, D Malan 5-48). **Boland** 109 in 38 overs (E Linder 45, R van der Ross 4-25, L de Jager 2-8). **Western Province won by 93 runs.**
Gold Group
Kei 62 in 28.5 overs (W Jacobs 5-15, J van Zyl 2-20). **Mpumalanga** 67-2 in 9.2 overs (J van Zyl 20*). **Mpumalanga won by 8 wickets.**
South Western Districts 106 in 40 overs (M Masimela 28, R Pieterson 5-34, S Osman 2-12, J Kotze 2-21). **Griqualand West** 107-4 in 36.1 overs (A Boonzaaier 44, M Masimela 3-15). **Griqualand West won by 6 wicke**ts.
Limpopo 145-9 in 50 overs (T Pistorius 34, T Monyamane 20*, F Kruger 3-14, K van Rensburg 2-16, M Serame 2-20). **North West** 134 in 40.4 overs (T Mostert 29, N Bredenkamp 24, A Jones 2-7, G Rudolph 2-22). **Limpopo won by 11 runs.**

Day Four, 19 December
Platinum Group
Boland 137 in 44.2 overs (K Niewoudt 30, B Aries 23, A Tyali 3-22, F Genade 3-37, A Mgijima 2-33). **Border** 141-6 in 32.2 overs (R Ramoo 57*, G Mokoena 50, J Bothma 3-40, D Malan 2-34). **Border won by 4 wickets.**
KwaZulu-Natal 247-7 in 50 overs (M Mbatha 53, K Abbot 43*, K Maharaj 32, J Botha 3-38, I Hlengani 2-47). **Easterns** 77 (P van Zyl 28, K Abbot 3-11, C Nhlapo 2-13, K Maharaj 2-15). **KwaZulu-Natal won by 170 runs.**
KwaZulu-Natal Inland 134 in 40.5 overs (D Miller 34, K Nelson-Esch 27, T Mbanjwa 5-31, J Symes 3-21). **Gauteng** 135-1 in 28.3 overs (Ryno van den Berg 75*, R Dullabh 49). **Gauteng won by 9 wickets.**
Western Province 197-9 in 50 overs (A Kritzinger 74, C Lewis 38, C van der Schyff 2-23). **Free State** 103 in 38.3 overs (R Ferris 42*, C Alexander 3-22, B Viret 2-30). **Western Province won by 94 runs.**
Eastern Province 187 in 50 overs (B Thompson 71, B Rhodes 42, M Venter 3-34). **Northerns** 188-7 in 48.5 overs (T Digale 84*, L Nel 30, B Rhodes 2-14). **Northerns won by 3 wickets.**
Gold Group
Griqualand West 147 in 49.3 overs (G Burger 70, R Pieterson 30, S van Heerden 3-36, S Mashele 3-26, T Pistorius 2-19). **Limpopo** 108 in 45.3 overs (T Pistorius 34, G de Wee 3-9, A Boonzaaier 2-21). **Griqualand West won by 39 runs.**
South Western Districts 145 in 44 overs (D Lewis 55, S Avontuur 48, A dos Santos 4-36, W Booysen 3-12). **Mpumalanga** 146-1 in 39.1 overs (P Malan 105*). **Mpumalanga won by 9 wickets.**
North West 269-8 in 50 overs (W Erasmus 72, N Bredenkamp 67). **Kei** 41 in 27.5 overs (M Serame 5-7, B Kubedi 3-15). **North West won by 228 runs.**

COCA-COLA KHAYA MAJOLA WEEK

Day Five, 20 December 2005
Platinum Group
Free State 254-7 in 50 overs (D Elgar 81, L Mosena 77, W Dunlop 3-47). **Eastern Province** 255-1 in 43 overs (B Thompson 116*, K Bennett 105). **Eastern Province won by 9 wickets.**
KwaZulu-Natal Inland 224-7 in 50 overs (P Mommsen 103, O Humphreys 35, J Bothma 2-45). **Boland** 208 in 50 overs (D Malan 103*, P Daneel 50, P Mommsen 2-21, K Nipper 2-33). **KwaZulu-Natal Inland won by 16 runs.**
Easterns 238-4 in 50 overs (P van Zyl 75, D van Rooyen 65, D Allan 2-48). **Border** 215-7 in 50 overs (G Ranger 74, G Mokoena 42, N Grobler 3-31). **Easterns won by 23 runs.**
Gauteng 171 in 48.3 overs (R Bishop 52, C Bekker 37, J Potgieter 4-29, M Mbatha 3-20). **KwaZulu-Natal** 174-6 in 30.5 overs (K Abbot 43 ,C Hauptfleish 32*, T Mbanjwa 2-23, C Bekker 2-30). **KwaZulu-Natal won by 4 wickets.**
Northerns 181-9 in 50 overs (J Jumat 52*, V Sharma 50, F le Clus 36, M Siboto 4-46). **Western Province** 182-6 in 47.3 overs (C Kieswetter 90, A Kritzinger 42, M Venter 2-16). **Western Province won by 4 wickets**
Gold Group
Griqualand West 193-5 in 50 overs (G Burger 97, A Boonzaaier 44, K van Rensburg 4-38). **North West** 194-4 in 47.4 overs (T Mostert 61, N Bredenkamp 38, W Erasmus 34, R Pieterson 2-26). **North West won by 6 wickets.**
South Western Districts 94 in 30.3 overs (A Dladla 4-39, C Ndondo 3-20, Z Mpikeleli 2-17). **Kei** 63 in 32.1 overs (M Masimela 4-10, K Carelse 3-15). **South Western Districts won by 31 runs.**
Limpopo 196 in 48.5 overs (T Pistorius 51, G Rudolph 45, R Disilwane 3-24, W Booysen 3-53, W Jacobs 2-32). **Mpumalanga** 200-3 in 49.3 overs (P Malan 104*, H Coetzee 34, W Jacobs 31). **Mpumalanga won by 7 wickets.**

FINAL LOG POSITIONS

1 Western Province, 2 Eastern Province, 3 Border, 4 KwaZulu-Natal, 5 Northerns, 6 KwaZulu-Natal Inland, 7 Gauteng, 8 Boland, 9 Easterns, 10 Free State.

BORDER INVITATION XI v SA SCHOOLS — Limited Overs Match

Played at Mercedes-Benz Park, East London on 21 December 2005 — Toss: Border Invitation XI
Umpires: A Holdstock & C Lazarus
Result: Border Invitation XI won by 111 runs

BORDER INVITATION XI	Runs	Mins	Balls	4	6
ML Bruyns c and b Symes	52	84	59	6	-
BL Bennett c Elgar b Pietersen	28	39	35	5	-
BC de Wett lbw b Siboto	7	18	15	1	-
SC Pope c Symes b Parnelle	39	73	71	3	-
*MN Ranger c Thompson b Pietersen	44	79	76	2	-
†AM Sodumo c Siboto b Serame	24	25	18	-	2
WR Hinkel not out	14	21	14	-	1
BB Kops b Parnelle	2	6	5	-	-
MW Olivier not out	4	9	7	-	-
L Manase					
RR Richards					
Extras (lb 4, w 11)	15				
TOTAL (for 7 wkts) (50 overs)	**229**				

SA SCHOOLS	Runs	Mins	Balls	4	6
PL Mommsen c Sodumo b Kops	7	18	15	-	-
B Thompson c Sodumo b Richards	30	62	42	5	-
*D Elgar run out (Richards/Sodumo)	36	92	53	3	-
G Mokoena c Sodumo b Ranger	10	35	31	-	-
J Symes run out (Richards)	6	5	5	1	-
†C Kieswetter c Bruyns b Ranger	8	23	13	1	-
M Mbatha lbw b Richards	0	9	5	-	-
W Parnelle lbw b Hinkel	3	18	10	-	-
R Pietersen lbw b Hinkel	2	22	16	-	-
M Siboto c and b Hinkel	2	6	7	-	-
NM Serame not out	1	6	7	-	-
Extras (lb 1, w 11, nb 1)	13				
TOTAL (33.5 overs)	**118**				

Sch	O	M	R	W	
Pietersen	9	0	59	2	(3 w)
Parnelle	10	0	39	2	(1 w)
Symes	10	1	27	1	(1 w)
Siboto	10	1	30	1	(1 w)
Serame	9	0	56	1	(1 w)
Elgar	2	0	14	0	(1 w)

Bdr	O	M	R	W	
Olivier	5	0	25	0	(1 nb, 2 w)
Kops	6	1	26	1	(2 w)
Manase	1	0	8	0	
Ranger	10	1	27	2	(1 w)
Richards	8	0	28	2	(6 w)
Hinkel	2.5	0	3	3	
De Wett	1	1	0	0	

Fall of Wickets	Bdr	Sch
1st	65 (2)	19 (1)
2nd	83 (3)	66 (2)
3rd	101 (1)	90 (4)
4th	162 (4)	96 (5)
5th	203 (6)	102 (3)
6th	209 (5)	104 (7)
7th	212 (8)	112 (6)
8th	-	115 (8)
9th	-	117 (10)
10th	-	118 (9)

At United Oval, 21 December 2005. SA Colts 188 in 49.5 overs (P Malan 40, K Peinke 4-41, S de Kock 2-25). **Border Invitation XI** 169-9 in 50 overs (S de Kock 34, A Mgijima 3-19, G Burger 2-58, J Bothma 2-30). **SA Colts won by 19 runs.**

SOUTH AFRICAN SCHOOLS XI CAPS

Note: The names of those who obtained caps before the formation of the United Cricket Board in 1991 are omitted unless they are of special interest. The full list of all players capped until 1976 appeared in the 1977 Annual and all those capped between 1977 and 1998 appeared in the 1999 Annual.

+ International honours * Other first-class cricket # South Africa Under-19

(E) Overseas tour, (C) Captain, (T) Twelfth man, (S) Capped, but did not play, (R) Capped, not in original 12, but played on tour or against England Under-19 in 1997. Two Nuffield Weeks were held in 1970 and 1976, in January and December. They are differentiated by the suffixes (J) and (D).

The team selected at the end of the 1994 and 1995 Coca-Cola Weeks was open to all players under 19. The team selected at the end of the 1995 Week was a South African Schools team with eligibility restricted to those boys still at school. From 1996 onwards, selection was again restricted to boys under 18 on 1 January of that year.

*#Abrahams U (Grey PE)	Eastern Province	1998-99
*Ackerman HM (Dale)	Border	1962-63-63(E)-64-65(C)-66(C)
*#Africa KC (Hilton)	KwaZulu-Natal	2003
*#Alexander CJ (Bellville Tech)	Western Province	2003-04-05(T)
+*#Amla HM (Durban)	KwaZulu-Natal	2000
+*Armitage RLS (St Andrew's G'tn)	Eastern Province	1974
+*Bacher A (King Edward)	Transvaal	1959-60
+*Barlow EJ (Pretoria)	North-Eastern Transvaal	1958
*#Baxter C (St Andrew's G'tn)	Eastern Province	2000-01
*#Benfield MR (St Stithian's)	Transvaal	1993-94(T)
+*Benkenstein DM (Michaelhouse)	Natal	1992(C)
*#Birch ACR (St Andrew's G'tn)	Eastern Province	2003
+*Bland KC (Milton)	Rhodesia	1956-57
*#Bodi GH (Lenasia)	Gauteng	1997
+*Boje N (Grey Bfn)	Orange Free State	1989(T)-90-91(C)
*#Booysen J (Witbank)	Easterns	2002
*#Botha AG (Maritzburg)	Natal	1995
+*#Botha J (Grey PE)	Eastern Province	1999-00(C)
Bothma C (Grey Bfn)	Free State	1999
+*Botten JT (Pretoria)	North-Eastern Transvaal	1956-57
+*#Boucher MV (Selborne)	Border	1994
#Bowyer C (Maritzburg)	KwaZulu-Natal	2003
*Bradfield CC (Kingswood)	Eastern Province	1993
*Brink MM (Brackenfell)	Boland	1993
+*Burger CG de V (Michaelhouse)	Natal	1953-54
+*Callaghan DJ (Grey PE)	Eastern Province	1983-83(E)
+*Carlstein PR (St Andrew's Bfn)	Orange Free State	1956-57-58(C)
Chree K (Grey PE)	Eastern Province	1992
*Coetsee WL (Klerksdorp)	North West	2001(T)
+*Commins JB (Rondebosch)	Western Province	1982
*#Cook SC (King Edward)	Gauteng	2000
*#Creed MW (Grey PE)	Eastern Province	1997
Cronje A (Rondebosch)	Western Province	2002
+*Cronje WJ (Grey Bfn)	Orange Free State	1986-87(C)
+*Crookes DN (Hilton)	Natal	1988(C)
+*Cullinan DJ (Queen's)	Border	1983-83(E)-84(C)
*#De Bruin GJ (Marais Viljoen)	Gauteng	2000
*De Bruin QE (Durban)	Natal	1993

SOUTH AFRICAN SCHOOLS XI CAPS

+*De Bruyn Z (Randburg)	Transvaal	1994
*#De Kock HG (Grey Bfn)	Free State	2001-02(C)
*#De Lange CD (Worcester Gym)	Boland	1999
*#De Nobrega JJ (Bishops)	Western Province	1996
+*#De Villiers AB (Afrikaanse Seuns)	Northerns	2001-02
*De Vos DJJ (Potchefstroom Gym)	Western Transvaal	1992-93
*Dipha L (Grey PE)	Eastern Province	2000
+*#Dippenaar HH (Grey Bfn)	Orange Free State	1995(T)
+*Donald AA (Hoer Tegniese)	Orange Free State	1984(T)-85
*Dros G (St Alban's)	Northern Transvaal	1992
+*Dumbrill R (Durban)	Natal	1957
+*#Duminy J-P (Plumstead)	USSASA U-17	2000(T)
*#Du Toit WJ (Paul Roos)	Boland	1998
Edgar T (Trinity House)	Gauteng	2004
*Ehrke JA (St John's)	Transvaal	1991
+*Eksteen CE (Northcliff)	Transvaal	1984
*#Elgar D (St Dominic's)	Free State	2005(C)
*#Elliott GD (St Stithian's)	Gauteng	1997
*English CV (Kimberley)	Griqualand West	1992
+*Fotheringham HR (Michaelhouse)	Natal	1970(J)(T)-70(D)
*#Gain DR (Hilton)	Natal	1995(C)
+*Gamsy D (Durban)	Natal	1958(T)
+*Gibbs HH (Bishops)	Western Province	1991-92
*Gilder GM (Northwood)	Natal	1992
*#Gobind R (Effingham)	KwaZulu-Natal	1999
+*Goddard TL (Durban)	Natal	1949
Govender D (Durban)	KwaZulu-Natal	2003
+*Greig AW (Queen's)	Border	1965-66
+*Greig IA (Queen's)	Border	1975
+*Griffin GM (Durban)	Natal	1958
Groom R (Kearsney)	Natal	1995
+*Halse CG (Maritzburg)	Natal	1953
*#Hantam WC (Sarepta)	Western Province	2001
*#Hauptfleisch W (Glenwood)	KwaZulu-Natal	1998
*Hayes GL (Queen's)	Border	1975
+*#Hayward M (Daniel Pienaar)	Eastern Province	1995
*#Hearle PK (St Stithian's)	Transvaal	1996(C)
+*Henderson CW (Worcester)	Boland	1990
*Hermitage JS (Richards Bay)	KwaZulu-Natal	2004
+*Hobson DL (Kingswood)	Eastern Province	1970(D)
*#Homani Z (Grey PE)	Eastern Province	1999-00
(Muir)	Eastern Province	2001
*Horan BP (Grey PE)	Eastern Province	1992
*#Hughes BK (Durban)	Natal	1994
*Ingram CA (Woodridge)	Eastern Province	2003(C) (S)
+*Innes GAS (Bishops)	Western Province	1949(T)-50(C)-51(C)
+*Ironside DEJ (Parktown)	Transvaal	1942
+*Irvine BL (Durban)	Natal	1963(C)
#Jantjes C (CBC Boksburg)	Easterns	1996
+*Jefferies ST (Plumstead)	Western Province	1978
+*Jennings RV (King Edward)	Transvaal	1970(D)-72-73
+*Johnson NC (Kingswood)	Eastern Province	1988

SOUTH AFRICAN SCHOOLS XI CAPS

Jones GD (Hilton)	Natal	1994
*#Joubert P (Eldoraigne)	Northern Transvaal	1995-96
+*Kallis JH (Wynberg)	Western Province	1993
*#Karemaker CJ (Centurion)	Northerns	2000
+*#Kent JC (Durban)	KwaZulu-Natal	1997
*#Khan I (Durban)	KwaZulu-Natal	2001(C)
#Kieswetter C (Bishops)	Western Province	2005
+*Kirsten G (Rondebosch)	Western Province	1985(C)
+*Kirsten PN (SACS)	Western Province	1973(T)-74
*#Kleinveldt RK (Plumstead) (Abbott's)	Western Province	2001
+*Koen LJ (Paarl Gym)	Boland	1985
*Koenig SG (Hilton)	Natal	1991
+*Kourie AJ (Jeppe)	Transvaal	1970(J)
*Kruis GJ (St Alban's)	Northern Transvaal	1993
+*Kuiper AP (Bishops)	Western Province	1977(C)
+*Lamb AJ (Wynberg)	Western Province	1973
+*Lance HR (CBC Pretoria)	North-Eastern Transvaal	1958
Le Clus F (Afrikaanse Seuns)	Northerns	2004(C)
*#Le Roux HW (Afrikaanse Seuns)	Northerns	2002
#Levi RE (Wynberg)	Western Province	2004
+*Liebenberg GFJ (Diamantveld)	Griqualand West	1989-90
*#Lumb MJ (St Stithian's)	Gauteng	1997
*Mabuya CS (Durban)	KwaZulu-Natal	2004
MacKay DD (Maritzburg)	Natal	1993
Maier RJ (Kloof)	Natal	1991
+*Markham LA (Glenwood)	Natal	1942
*Masikazana L (Chapman)	Eastern Province	1991-92
Mbatha M (Durban)	KwaZulu-Natal	2005
+*McEwan KS (Queen's)	Border	1970(J)-70(D)(C)
+*McGlew DJ (Maritzburg)	Natal	1948(C)
+*McKenzie KA (King Edward)	Transvaal	1967
+*#McKenzie ND (King Edward)	Transvaal	1993-94(C)
*#McLaren R (Grey Bfn)	Free State	2001
Mfobo M (SACS)	Western Province	1991
*Michau JP (Cradock)	SA Country	1995
*Miller GK (Grey PE)	Eastern Province	1991
#Mokoena G (Queen's)	Border	2005
Mommsen PL (Hilton)	KwaZulu-Natal Inland	2004-05
+*#Morkel JA (Vereeniging)	Gauteng	1998
#Morkel M (Vereeniging)	Transvaal	1995-96
+*#Mpitsang PV (Grey Bfn)	Free State	1997(T)
*Mullins AK (Crestway)	Western Province	1998
*#Munnik R (Tygerberg)	Western Province	1996
*#Myburgh JG (Pretoria)	Northerns	1997
Ndopu MP (St Boniface)	Griqualand West	2001
+*Ngam M (Douglas)	Eastern Province	1997(R)
#Ngxoweni T (Selborne)	Border	1994-95-96
#Niewoudt G (Welkom Gim)	Free State	2004
#Nkomo AN (Wynberg)	Western Province	1997-98
*#Nkuna FG (J Mahlangu)	Northerns	2002-04
+*#Ntini M (Dale)	Border	1995

SOUTH AFRICAN SCHOOLS XI CAPS

*#Omar AM (Topaz)	Transvaal	1994
+*Ovenstone DM (Bishops)	Western Province	1940(C)
#Parnelle W (Grey PE)	Eastern Province	2005
*Paulse HH (New Orleans)	Boland	2004
Penzhorn A (Maritzburg)	KwaZulu-Natal	2002
+*#Peterson RJ (Alexander Road)	Eastern Province	1996(T)-97
*#Phangiso AM (CBC Pretoria)	Northerns	2002
*#Philander VD (Ravensmead)	Western Province	2002-03
+*Pienaar RF (St Stithian's)	Transvaal	1978(C)
*Pietersen C (Northern Cape)	Griqualand West	2001
*Pietersen R (Northern Cape)	Griqualand West	2005
+*Pithey AJ (Plumtree)	Rhodesia	1951-52-53
+*Pithey DB (Plumtree)	Rhodesia	1954
*Pollock GA (King Edward)	Transvaal	1991
+*Pollock PM (Grey PE)	Eastern Province	1959
+*Pollock RG (Grey PE)	Eastern Province	1960-61(C)
+*Pollock SM (Northwood)	Natal	1991
*#Postman IK (Selborne)	Border	2000
+*Pothas N (King Edward)	Transvaal	1990(R)
+*Pringle MW (Kingswood)	Eastern Province	1983-84
+*Procter MJ (Hilton)	Natal	1963-63(E)-64
+*#Puttick AG (Rondebosch)	Western Province	1998(T)
+*Radford NV (Athlone)	Transvaal	1976(J)
#Ramoo R (Selborne)	Border	2004
*#Reddy BL (Springs)	Easterns	2002
+*Rhodes JN (Maritzburg)	Natal	1986-87
+*Richards BA (Durban)	Natal	1962-63-63(EC)-64(C)
+*#Rudolph JA (Afrikaanse Seuns)	Northerns	1997-98-99(C)
+*Rundle DB (St Stithian's)	Transvaal	1982-83-83(E)
+*Rushmere MW (Woodridge)	Eastern Province	1982(C)-83(C)-83(EC)
*#Schorn JR (Hilton)	KwaZulu-Natal	1999-00
+*Schultz BN (Kingswood)	Eastern Province	1989
+*Seeff L (Herzlia)	Western Province	1976(D)
*#Senekal DM (Daniel Pienaar)	Eastern Province	1999
*#September J (Kingswood)	Eastern Province	1994
*#September WE (New Orleans)	Boland	2002(T)-03
#Serame NM (Milner)	North West	2004(T)-05
*Seymore AJ (HF Verwoerd)	Northern Transvaal	1992-93
*Shaw GB (Kingswood)	Eastern Province	1992
#Siboto MP (Wynberg)	Western Province	2005
Sierra R (St John's)	Transvaal	1996
*#Slwana M (Grey PE)	Eastern Province	2003
+*Smith CL (Northlands)	Natal	1976(J)
+*#Smith GC (King Edward)	Gauteng	1998-99
*#Smith GM (St Stithian's)	Gauteng	2001
+*Smith RA (Northlands)	Natal	1979-80
+*Snell RP (Durban)	Natal	1986(S)-87
*Snijman BD (King Edward)	Gauteng	2003
+*Stewart ELR (Westville)	Natal	1987
*#Stigant BG (Grey PE)	Eastern Province	1993
*Still QR (Selborne)	Border	1992
*#Street MR (St John's)	Transvaal	1995-96

SOUTH AFRICAN SCHOOLS XI CAPS

+*Strydom PC (Grey PE)	Eastern Province	1987
*Sugden CB (Michaelhouse)	Natal	1992
*#Symes J (St John's)	Gauteng	2005
+*#Terbrugge DJ (St Stithian's)	Transvaal	1993-94
#Thompson B (Grey PE)	Eastern Province	2005
*#Thyssen CA (Grey PE)	Eastern Province	2000-02
*#Trott IJL (Rondebosch)	Western Province	1998-99
+*#Tsolekile TL (Pinelands)	Western Province	1998(C)
(Abbott's)	Western Province	1999(C)(S)
*Tucker BH (St John's)	Gauteng	1997(C)
*Van Aswegen IG (Hentie Cilliers)	Orange Free State	1994
*Van den Berg AM (Jan Viljoen)	Transvaal	1996
+*#Van der Wath JJ (Ermelo)	Easterns	1996
*#Van Jaarsveld VB (King Edward)	Gauteng	2003
+*Van Ryneveld CB (Bishops)	Western Province	1946(C)
*#Van Wyk DJ (Grey Bfn)	Free State	2003(C)
+*#Van Wyk MN (Grey Bfn)	Free State	1997
Van Wyk R (Afrikaanse Seuns)	Northerns	1997(R)
*Vermeulen VBN (St Stithian's)	Transvaal	1989
(Jeppe)	Transvaal	1990-91
*Volsteedt AK (Grey Bfn)	Orange Free State	1993(C)
*#Vorster CJ (Paarl Gym)	Boland	1994
+*Waite JHB (Hilton)	Natal	1948
+*Watkins JC (Glenwood)	Natal	1940-41-42(C)
*Watson DJ (Maritzburg)	Natal	1991
+*Watson WK (Dale)	Border	1975
+*Wesley C (Durban)	Natal	1956
+*Wessels KC (Grey Bfn)	Orange Free State	1973-75-76(J)(C)
+*Whitfield BJ (Beachwood)	Natal	1976(D)
#Williams M (Grey PE)	Eastern Province	1998
*#Wingfield WR (Durban)	Natal	1995
+*Winslow PL (King Edward)	Transvaal	1947-48

SOUTH AFRICA UNDER-19 CAPS

The following played for SA Under-19 but not for SA Schools:

*Abrahams AP (Highlands North)	Free State	2000
*Adair SR (Grey PE)	Eastern Province	2005
*Adam SM (Durban)	KwaZulu-Natal	1998
*Amla AM (Tongaat)	KwaZulu-Natal	1998
*Bailey RT (Rondebosch)	Western Province	2002
Clark BW (Wynberg)	Western Province	1995
Cowley DJ (Maritzburg)	Natal	1995
Daneel P (Paul Roos)	Boland	2005-06
Das Neves R (King Edward)	Gauteng	2005-06
*Du Plessis F (Afrikaanse Seuns)	Northerns	2003
*Gait AI (Kearsney)	KwaZulu-Natal	1997-98
*Gamiet LL (Selborne)	Border	1996
Hendrieck S (Plumstead)	Western Province	2005
*Henry D (Wynberg)	Western Province	1998
*Hofmeyr S (Wynberg)	Western Province	1996
*Jacobs DJ (Klerksdorp)	North West	2002

SOUTH AFRICA UNDER-19 CAPS

Jaftha R (Bishops)	Western Province	2005
+*Kemp JM (Queen's)	Border	1995
*Khoza TR (Saulridge)	Northerns	2005
*Kops BB (St Thomas)	Eastern Province	2002
Kritzinger A (Bishops)	Western Province	2005
*MacQueen RB (Durban)	KwaZulu-Natal	1996
*Makalima DL (Dale)	Border	2000
*Manase L (Forbes Grant)	Border	2004
*Masimula WB (Eastbank)	Transvaal	1995
*Mitchell I (Queen's)	Border	1996
*Moleon EO (Garlandale)	Western Province	1995
Molutsi K (Monument)	Gauteng	2005
Nkosana S (Grey PE)	Eastern Province	2005
+*Ontong JL (Paarl Gym)	Boland	1998
Pennazza V (Paarl)	Boland	2003-04
*Price ML (St Andrew's G'tn)	Eastern Province	2000
+*Prince AG (St Thomas)	Eastern Province	1995
*Razak AH (Durban)	KwaZulu-Natal	2005
*Samsodien W (Montrose CC)	Western Province	1997-98
Shezi M (Glenwood)	KwaZulu-Natal	2005-06
*Smit D (Northwood)	KwaZulu-Natal	2003
Springer ET (Northwood)	KwaZulu-Natal	2003
*Stevens GC (New Orleans)	Boland	2004
*Tsamaisi ES (St Boniface)	Griqualand West	1998
Van der Merwe R (Waterkloof)	Northerns	2004
Van der Schyff CJ (Grey Bfn)	Free State	2005
*Van Olst M (Grey PE)	Eastern Province	1995
+*Zondeki M (Dale)	Border	2000
*Zondi LE (Glenwood)	Natal	1995

SCHOOLS AND YOUTH CRICKET

John Young

Separate controlling bodies for high and primary schools fell away in the winter of 2005. All USSASA Junior Cricket affiliates had to make provision for a new joint structure. Many cricket festivals and tournaments were held in 2005/06, making for much more contact between schools across provincial boundaries.

Tight finishes were the order of the day in matches between traditional rivals. Potchefstroom Boys' beat Volkskool by one wicket, the same margin by which Centurion pipped Waterkloof. Jeppe bested St Stithian's by four runs while Rondebosch's margin against Wynberg was nine runs. A single run was the difference when SACS beat Hilton and St David's beat Alberton Schools. Afrikaner Boys' High and Grey College achieved that rarest of results, a tie.

High scoring was also common. Northern Cape totalled 332 to win their cup final, Pretoria Boys posted 312-5 against St Stithian's, Rondebosch chased down 257 to beat Wynberg with two balls to spare but possibly the most amazing result came from Johannesburg. The regional South Schools combination must have felt secure with 298 on the board but Parktown Boys went past 300 for the loss of six wickets. Alberton and Hudson Park were other teams to top 300. At the Grey High School Festival in January, Grey College and Wynberg played to the quintessential high-score draw. They amassed 553 runs in the day's play, for the loss of only eleven wickets.

Some fine schoolboy batsmen finished their school careers in 2005. Jean Symes (St John's College), Grant Mokoena (Queen's College) and Richard Levi of Wynberg combined consistent high scoring with powerful shot-making and excellent shot selection. Graeme College's Jon-Jon Smuts came into his own in the first term of his matric year, hitting six centuries in the course of going past Lorrie Wilmot's 1961 record of 3175 runs for the school. Smuts topped 3500 with the fourth term still to come.

At the other end of the achievement scale was the unfortunate tale of Bonteheuwel's Under-13 team who conceded 293 runs in their match against Edgemead CC. Top scorer was Mr Extras with 97!

BORDER

Border youth cricket enjoyed another successful season where cricket was administered by the schools committee in conjunction with the union. The decline of funding for regional fixtures affected the number of rural cricketers who made junior provincial teams. This, and the lack of teachers who have played the game and are able to coach cricket, are the region's biggest challenges.

The Remax/Mercedes-Benz Sixes Festival kicked off the season. The Sixes cup was designed to bring together high schools involved in Saturday fixtures to experience playing cricket at Mercedes-Benz Park and to see their names on the electronic scoreboard. Three formerly disadvantaged teams were involved: United, Western Region and Forbes Grant, and they included players from Fort Beaufort, Alice, Middledrift, King William's Town and Peddie. The other seven teams were Queen's, Grens, Cambridge, Hudson Park, Selborne, Stirling, and Port Rex.

Queen's managed to beat Hudson Park in the final, while Stirling, after narrowly winning their semi-final match, comfortably beat Grens in the plate final. Queen's won a full kit for winning the festival, with Hudson Park, Stirling and Grens getting other equipment. Chase Young from Stirling won a Kookaburra bat for being the player of the tournament.

A fast bowlers' clinic was held at the University of Fort Hare in March 2006 thanks to funding from the national department of Sports and Recreation. Fast bowlers in the age group 15-20 were targeted. Besides local cricketers (Middledrift, Alice and Healdtown), others attended from Queenstown, King William's Town, East London and Mdantsane. Greg Hayes, Anton Ferreira and Justin Price were among the coaches.

Grant Mokoena completed four years at Queen's College in 2005. He excelled in a cricket environment with some of the best school facilities in the country. He dominated schoolboy cricket in 2005 and finished with an average of 82, with a highest score of 165 not out against St Alban's College. He was selected for the SA Schools team and also went to the Under-19 World Cup in Sri Lanka. He was the first player since Justin Kemp ten years earlier to attain honours for cricket at Queen's College.

Hudson Park won the Algie Cup for the fifth time in six years. The Hudson Park Second XI entered this East London schools' competition for the first time – and came second! Hudson Park scored a hat-trick of wins in 2005 against the colleges; Queen's, Selborne and Dale. Luyolo Thumana was a big contributor with the bat (topping the century mark in Hudson Park's huge 324-8 against KZN school Pinetown) and Darryn Allen's off-spin continued to play a big role. Mpilo Njoloza was the star of a last-ball victory on tour against Glenwood Boys. With his team needing one to win, he belted a big six. Another Hudson Park player, Kevin Lloyd, scored 107 not out off 35 balls in an Algie Cup game while Kurt Francis took a hat-trick against Western Region. Stirling's Geone Koopman achieved a milestone in scoring 150 in the Dale College match.

BOLAND

Boland is divided into seven regions in which schools compete against one another. The next level is zonal, after which a regional team is selected which then competes against the other regions to eventually select a Boland provincial squad. Regional games take place over four weeks. Regional festivals have recently been introduced for those age groups that do not compete on provincial level.

A total of 6570 boys from 118 primary schools and 80 high schools participate in Boland youth cricket. Identified cricket high schools play in a knock-out competition sponsored by PYZ. The search is on for a sponsor to introduce this competition at primary school level.

Umpiring and scoring courses on school level are progressing well and interest in scoring has grown among girls. Kim Cupido, scorer for the Under-18 Coca-Cola team, was awarded the junior scoring award. Forty scorers and 30 umpires qualified during the 2005/06 season. Scoring and umpiring courses were held at the juvenile section of Drakenstein prison.

Among the young cricketers to excel during the season were Elton Jantjies (Paarl Gymnasium), William Clift (Paarl Boys' High), Clayton August (New Orleans) and Johan Bothma of Paul Roos Gymnasium. New Orleans Senior Secondary were the winners of the PYZ knock-out competition. The final was played at Boland Park in a day-night 30-over game. New Orleans, who had been semi-finalists since the inception of the competition, bowled out Paul Roos for 143 in the final but the failure of the recognised batsmen from New Orleans ensured a nail-biting finish. Brilliant batting and running between the wickets by Clayton Blommetjies and Clayton August saw them to a first victory in this popular competition.

EASTERN PROVINCE

For the second year, an Executive Committee with two sub-committees ran EP youth cricket. This allowed a greater focus on the playing of the game and improving the standard of play, rather than on the politics of cricket. The High Schools sub-committee dealt with leagues, coaching of squads, trials, umpiring and tournaments. Sub-committee chairman Colin Bartle described this as a step in the right direction.

A workshop was held to tackle the issue of teams not fulfilling fixtures and an improvement was noted. The introduction of composite township teams playing in the leagues worked well and assisted in the identification of talent for provincial teams.

Regular courses and clinics for coaches were held but relatively few teachers participated. Excellent winter programmes were held and it was resolved that more would be organised to try to ensure that so-called fringe players would be given opportunities.

In September both the Cape Schools Week (mainly boys' schools) and the Cape Youth Cricket Festival (mainly co-ed schools and clubs) were held in Port Elizabeth and Uitenhage, bringing together hundreds of cricketers from the Western and Eastern Cape.

Muir College hosted the Under-12 festival in November while Grey High School celebrated their 150th anniversary with two cricket festivals. The Standard Bank-sponsored tournament in January comprised 14 schools from around the country. A Pretoria Boys' High School pair came out tops in the Double Wicket competition played at St George's Park.

The highlight of the Cricket Celebration weekend in March was the match between the Old Grey XI (including Dave Callaghan and Vlam Michau) and the Traditional Rivals XI (Mark Rushmere, Denys Hobson, Kenny McEwan) on the Pollock Field. Graeme and Peter Pollock were special guests, together with Old Grey administrators like Joe Pamensky and Geoff Dakin.

Grey's opening bowler Wayne Parnelle achieved the remarkable analysis of 6-7 against East London school Hudson Park and Alexander Road caused a shock by beating the strong Graeme College XI. Graeme redeemed themselves the next day by beating Grahamstown rivals St Andrew's. Jon-Jon Smuts took many wickets for Graeme but it was his batting that really stood out. Six centuries in the first term, including three in six days, took him to a total of eleven for the school.

Despatch High School's 20-20 competition continued to grow. This season eight teams will take part. The host team's record score of 176-6 will take some beating. Despatch bucked the national trend by relying on spin bowlers like Anru Darr and Dieter Basson. Young Lester Harrop showed potential as a batsman.

FREE STATE

Free State Youth cricket is divided into five areas: North, East, Far North, Goldfields and Southern Free State (Bloemfontein). Regional teams from each of these areas play against one another in September trials to select provincial teams. A new system is to be introduced in 2007 which will see these regional teams playing on a league basis in the fourth and first terms, with the intention of selecting Free State sides at the end of the first term. The hope is that in giving provincial coaches more time to prepare, results will improve at the national weeks.

The number of cricketers is increasing in the province but in some areas other sporting codes are having a negative impact on numbers in the first term. Most youth cricket is played during the week in 35-over matches. The intention is to increase the number of cricketers exposed to 50-over cricket on Saturdays through the regional league and a new "cell" system. Each premier league club will be linked to a number of schools and will select a youth team to play against other "cell" teams. These players will form a feeder system for the clubs.

SCHOOLS AND YOUTH CRICKET

Ninety primary schools are affiliated and there are 65 high schools. Twelve high schools compete in the girls' league and at primary school level girls cricket is growing slowly. Girls like Annelie Minnie and Melissa Loftus seem set to make their mark in the future.

Grey College dominated the Southern Free State leagues and their Under-15 and Under-18B teams once again won the league in Bloemfontein. In the Goldfields, Welkom Gymnasium won the Under-18A and B leagues and St Andrews came up tops in the C league. Witteberg Bethlehem did well in the East area winning the Under-18 league.

At primary school level no league titles are awarded. Schools who have done well in the regions are Goldfields, Dagbreek, Virginia Volkskool (unbeaten for the season) and Naudeville. In the East area schools such as Jordania, Truida Kestell and Harrismith are consistently doing well. In Kroonstad (North), Kroonheuwel Primary had a good season.

GAUTENG

Gauteng high schools are subdivided into nine geographical areas. There are 292 primary schools (922 teams) and 184 high schools (692 teams) in the system.

Primary schools cricket is strong and well organised. Gauteng Primary Schools are at the forefront of organising regional festivals amongst the highveld unions; Northerns, North West, Easterns, Limpopo and Mpumalanga.

The cricket programmes of under-resourced schools are financed by the GCB. The stronger schools from these areas are encouraged to participate as individual schools. These include KwaBhekilanga High (Alexandra), Madiba High (Kagiso), Phafogang High (Soweto), Shakobowa Primary (Soweto) and Hartstraat Primary (Toekomsrus).

The weaker schools are grouped together in five area teams to play in mainstream leagues on Saturdays. The Vaal township schools have been brought into the mainstream development programme. The Central Place Centres and the Cricket World Cup Legacy Project facilities serve an important role in providing facilities for fixtures and programmes.

Thirty-three schools in under-privileged areas have been identified as justifying board funding. A decision has been made to channel funds to committed schools and areas. In Kagiso, 15 of the 21 schools are playing cricket, in Alexandra it is 11 out of 17. The potential for growth in Soweto remains enormous, with 60 of the area's 233 schools offering cricket.

The Chubb Challenge eight-overs challenge culminated in a round of matches at the Wanderers with Parktown High School defeating St David's Inanda by 38 runs in the final.

In the longer version of the game, St David's, for whom Andrew Kirkland had a fine season with the bat, reversed the result against Parktown, winning by a handsome 94 runs. Parktown shocked Johannesburg South Schools by reaching 300 for just six wickets in a remarkable run-chase. Parktown also beat Jeppe, who held their nerve to win by four runs against St Stithian's. St Stithian's were later on the wrong end of massive total of 321-7 put together by Alberton. Alberton also beat St John's.

GRIQUALAND WEST

The 2005/06 cricket season was a promising one for Kimberley and the Northern Cape. In the Under-19A section there was no league winner but many games were won or lost by small margins. Many games were affected by rain.

A highlight of the season was the performance of Floors High, a Kimberley school. They won all their games, most of which were played against Kimberley's best cricketing schools. The other highlight was the annual De Beers Night League competition, played on a knock-out basis. Six teams participated, with Northern Cape coming out on top for the fifth time in six attempts. Abass Mohamed (125) top-scored to help Northern Cape amass 332 in the final against Country Districts A. He was Man of the Match and Man of the Series.

Winter coaching clinics spread from Kimberley to Upington, Kathu and Springbok, with provincial and national players coaching upwards of 600 children in these country areas.

The Kimberley September Festival is growing in stature as more cricketing schools from other provinces show an interest. Paarl Boys' High School were the guests in 2005.

KWAZULU-NATAL

Although KwaZulu-Natal and KwaZulu-Natal Inland are now separate provinces, inter-schools rivalry between the region's cricketing schools remains strong. It was a topsy-turvy season with no one side dominating, although Michaelhouse achieved two wins against Maritzburg College.

Michaelhouse beat Kearsney, Hilton and Westville but went down to Durban High School. DHS in turn lost to Westville, who scored wins over Northwood and Hilton. For Michaelhouse, Jarryd Cairns excelled with the bat while James Brownlee and Matthew Bowes were consistent bowlers. Cameron Delport had a fine season with the bat for Westville.

Pietermaritzburg Oval was the venue of a thrilling Day-Night final between Durban High School (seeking their first trophy) and Maritzburg College, striving for an eighth title in their 12th final appearance. DHS batted first and their 45-over score of 236-9 was anchored by a fine 52 by Mbatha. Barron (73) led a determined College reply but wickets fell regularly and DHS won a famous victory in the last over. Other highlights for DHS included wins over Glenwood, Hilton and Michaelhouse.

The other big game between DHS and Maritzburg was affected by rain and a draw was the result with the match delicately poised. Cayden Lang and Darren Pienaar led the Maritzburg team's batting efforts during the season.

The Maritzburg College England tour included a bad day against Millfield (312 runs conceded) and a number of very good days, including a massive score of 316-5 against Tonbridge, a win against Eton, and victory in a 20/20 tournament hosted by Stowe.

Kearsney College recorded good results during their own festival held in January, with a seven wicket win over St George's and a 101-run victory over the strong SACS team from Cape Town. Kyle Abbott's ability to craft centuries was a major factor in Kearsney's batting strength. St Charles also prospered in the Kearsney Festival, beating both SACS and Johannesburg team St John's. Outstanding all-round performances were turned in by Chris Bestel and Robin Cheesman.

MPUMALANGA

Schools cricket is thriving in Mpumalanga. Bakers Mini Cricket is played by 140 schools with festivals held in three regions. An increasing number of rural schools are showing interest.

Regional leagues for high school, primary schools and girls cricket are running well with trials held for the selection of regional teams. These groups then participate in a trials' week where provincial teams are chosen.

The Mpumalanga primary school winners were Nelspruit (Under-13 boys), Kragbron, Lydenburg and Bergland. Malelane Primary won both the Under-13 and Under-11 sections of schools' competition for schools with fewer than 400 pupils. Nelspruit dominated the high schools division, with their teams winning the Under-14, Under-15 and First Team competitions. The second league was won by HTS Witbank.

SCHOOLS AND YOUTH CRICKET

Pieter Malan of Nelspruit had an outstandingly successful season, scoring several centuries on his way to winning selection to the SA Colts Under-19 team and later making his debut for the senior provincial team. He will spend his matric year in 2006 at Afrikaanse Boys High School in Pretoria.

The provincial Under-17 team showed good progress at the SA Games and the Summer Games. Training of scorers in the linear method resulted in all schools having at least one qualified scorer. This training will be expanded to include primary schools.

Ben Viljoen High School won the girls competition for the second time and an Mpumalanga team did well at the Summer Games. Friendly matches were held at Under-13 and Under-16 level against other provinces.

LSEN (special) schools are widespread through out the province. They play in a separate league and in the provincial second league. An Mpumalanga team played in the National LSEN week during September 2005.

NORTHERNS

The Northerns age group schools' leagues and development programme comprised 172 primary and 67 high schools. In the various high school leagues 253 teams participated with the top Under-19 and Under-15 teams playing 50-over cricket and the rest playing to a 30-over format. To accommodate all the teams, leagues games are held on five days of the week.

Centurion High again had a good season and were undefeated in the A Section of the First team league. Captain and all-rounder Shaun von Berg was consistent. Menlopark High gained promotion to the A Section after dominating the B Section. The school has invested heavily in cricket and made tremendous progress in the last two years. They have an indoor facility, a world class audio-visual room and a cricket technique analysis programme. The schools' XI comprises players who have been playing premier league cricket at the Willowick and PHSOB clubs.

The Under-15 and Under-14 high school sections were won by Pretoria Boys' High and Afrikaanse Boys' respectively. The Annual Double Wicket competition, hosted by Afrikaanse Boys' High, was a great success with Montana High being crowned champions after a long day of competitive cricket.

Primary schools cricket in the province is run by parent committees who appoint the coaches. There were 755 teams participating. Schools choose to play in different terms based on when they play other sports such as athletics. The English schools' league runs in the first and fourth term while the Afrikaans and Area league schools play in the fourth term.

Anton van Wouw Primary School dominated the primary schools leagues by winning the Under-13 Day Night competition and the Under-13 and Under-12 district league-play-offs. Lynwood and Constantia Park were the other primary school league winners.

Umpiring refresher courses were organised before the start of the season. A level-D umpiring course took place during the season for four nights. Level 1 and 2 refresher courses for teachers and school coaches were conducted during the season at SuperSport Park.

A first six-a-side girls' competition for primary and high schools was held at Sinovich Park and a refresher course for girls cricket coaches was held at SuperSport Park.

NORTH WEST

A survey in the North West province has shown that the existence of Cricket Academies at schools has ensured growth at these schools. This applies not only to the number of boys and girls playing cricket, but also to results, which have improved dramatically.

The number of high and primary schools offering year-round cricket coaching and fixtures has increased. Fields College in Rustenburg is one such school. In Klerksdorp, both Wesvalia and Klerksdorp High School offer all-year programmes as do the two primary schools, Goudkoop and President. Potchefstroom has Gymnasium, Volkskool (high schools) and Bailie Park and Central (primary schools).

Klerksdorp High School's Academy, which has been in existence for nearly ten years, maintained its dominance in the North West League with their First team maintaining their unbeaten record in local cricket for an amazing ninth year. They won the Gunn and Moore Trophy in 2005. Klerksdorp's record in producing first-class players continued in 2005 with left-arm fast bowler Jaco Campher making his debut for the Highveld Lions.

A Junior Club league was formed in 2005 in which teams from academies competed at age group level.

A coaches' forum was established and coaching clinics were organised.

The North West Cricket Association and the company Senwes combined to initiate a three-year Spinners' Project in which eight farm schools in the most remote parts of rural North West will be coached and given the opportunity to complete in a Farm Schools league.

SOUTH WESTERN DISTRICTS

Since South Western Districts became part of the mainstream of South African cricket in 2004, significant growth has been experienced in junior cricket. The province has set its sights on producing a first-class cricketer who advanced through the ranks of the school system. The schools are proving a reliable and steady feeder system for clubs.

The successful Bakers Mini Cricket programme involved more than 4600 boys and 1500 girls from 128 schools. Forty-six farm schools were visited and over 2000 pupils reached. From the 78 primary schools and 37 high schools in the province nearly 3000 players (Under-11 to Under-19) participate in the province's most popular summer sport code.

The schools league in the province was run on a friendly basis for the first time but a competition structure will be re-introduced in 2006/07. Nine Under-15 and Under-19 super league schools (Oudtshoorn, Langenhoven Gymnasium, Sentraal, Oakdale, York High, Outeniqua, PW Botha College, Punt High and a combined Mossel Bay schools team) participated in the Saturday league with other schools playing their matches on weekdays. An inter-regional league, with the aim of feeding the provincial team, is also played. Primary schools have an inter-regional league as well as a competition within each of the six regions.

A successful inaugural Pro20 knock-out competition played under lights at the Van Riebeeck Stadium in Mossel Bay was introduced with Oudtshoorn High School beating neighbouring Langenhoven Gymnasium in a pulsating final.

Oudtshoorn High School's Sammy-Joe Avontuur, the vice-captain of the South Western Districts Under-19 team, became the first schoolboy in almost a decade to represent the senior provincial team.

SWD girl cricketers participated for the first time in national tournaments. Four schoolgirls represented the senior SWD women's team: Hedwig Pienaar (Oudtshoorn High

School), Marnizelle Rabie (Morester Secondary School, Oudtshoorn), Bazarin Jansen (Gerrit du Plessis Secondary School, Riversdale) and Vanessa Titus (Dysselsdorp Secondary School).

Three popular pre-season festivals were held in September. Punt High School in Mossel Bay hosted the Die Burger Under-19 tournament, PW Botha College in George the Standard Bank Under-15 tournament, with Langenhoven Gymnasium holding an Under-13 festival. Sammy-Joe Avontuur was the SWD High Schools player of the season whilst the premier wicket-taker, who played three seasons for the SWD Under-13 schools team, Byron Haycock (Outeniqua Primary School), was the SWD Primary Schools player of the season.

WESTERN PROVINCE

WP Youth Cricket saw an exciting early start to the season with 16 teams playing in an Under-13 20-20 Festival sponsored by Feedem Services Group. Feedem also saw to it that the Under-13 Knock-Out quarter-finals, semi-finals and final were held at Newlands. The youngsters from De Kuilen PS, Gugulethu CC, Milnerton CC, Parkdene PS, Peninsula CA, Primrose CC, SACS and WP Prep had their dreams of playing at Newlands Cricket Ground realised.

The Peninsula CA and SACS boys played the final under floodlights in coloured clothing. Peninsula CA scored an impressive 161-1 with a classy 81 not out from James Bredenkamp and 41 not out from Dalton Kannemeyer. The SACS boys scored 101-8 in their 20 overs. Bredenkamp was named Best Batsman and Kannmeyer was Player of the Tournament.

The Rondebosch Boys' High team seemed to have a psychological advantage over Wynberg Boys' in the Under-19 Knock-Out final at Newlands after an excellent season in the all-day league and a day-night win over arch-rivals Bishops. Rondebosch's batsmen did well all season, showing a willingness to chase down any target, but in the KO final, Wynberg's score of 267-7 put the game beyond them. Wynberg were the first team to retain the title.

The Wynberg Under-15 team's total of 132 runs was not enough to outplay Bishops, who carried off the Under-15 Knock-Out trophy for the third consecutive year.

A large number of affiliates, both primary and high schools, play recreational midweek league cricket. In an effort to promote positive cricket in the all-day leagues, specifications were placed on the numbers of overs to be bowled in each session, with the status quo remaining for the compulsory declaration at 65 overs.

With the scrapping of the National B-team tournaments, it was felt that something should be offered at the various age group levels. Regional Festivals at Under-12, Under-14 and Under-18 level were held during November and December. This presented the selectors with an ideal opportunity to identify talent for the trials for the next year.

The development of girls cricket continued and WP hosted teams from Bath, Derbyshire and Warwickshire, who played in a series of matches with WP, Boland and SWD at Bishops. WP Under-19 reached the final before losing against Warwickshire. In the local Under-19 Knock-Out competition, Rustenburg Girls beat Pinelands.

Information about schools cricket will be welcomed by John Young, 18 Garrison Road, Claremont 7708. E-mail john@young.wcape.school.za

NATIONAL UNDER–17 WEEK

The national Under-17 Week was held in Johannesburg from 3 to 6 December 2005. Sixteen teams were divided into four sections, with Western Province and KwaZulu-Natal qualifying for the final, which Western Province won by seven wickets.

Day One, 3 December
Pool One
Griqualand West 147 (S Boomsen 65, R Nel 4-23). **Gauteng** 148-4 (P Platt 78). **Gauteng won by 6 wickets.**
KwaZulu-Natal Inland 292-8 (N Tatham 96, R Viljoen 79, J Brownlee 5-26). **South Western Districts** 164. **KwaZulu-Natal Inland won by 128 runs.**
Pool Two
Boland 216-8. **Northerns** 219-7 (R Van Dussen 50, S Engelbrecht 61). **Northerns won by 3 wickets.**
Border Kei 27 (E Gerber 7-9). **Easterns** 28-3. **Easterns won by 7 wickets.**
Pool Three
Western Province 255 (M Stoop 63, M Vallie 76, L Cronje 3-42). **Border** 240 (A Gqamane 64). **Western Province won by 15 runs.**
Mpumalanga 123 (J Theron 4-19, M Finley 3-16). **Free State** 125-2 (G Whitehead 70). **Free State won by 8 wickets.**
Pool Four
Eastern Province 215 (T Reynolds 84, R Tooth 5-48). **Limpopo** 127 (A Louw 6-18). **Eastern Province won by 88 runs.**
KwaZulu Natal 270-6 (D Jones 139). **North West** 156 (M Lazenby 61, B Varley 5-31). **KwaZulu-Natal won by 114 runs.**

Day Two, 4 December
Pool One
Kwazulu-Natal Inland 193 (G Cloete 4-32). **Griqualand West** 194-9 (A Swanepoel 91, K Vardhan 3-24, R Viljoen 3-39). **Griqualand West won by 1 wicket.**
South Western Districts 124 (T Masilela 3-19). **Gauteng** 128-2. **Gauteng won by 8 wickets.**
Pool Two
Easterns 129. **Boland** 130-5 (D Campbell 54). **Boland won by 5 wickets.**
Northerns 300-8 (R van Dussen 88, J van Wyk 65). **Border Kei** 61 (M Chapman 3-8, E Links 3-3). **Northerns won by 239 runs.**
Pool Three
Western Province 245-8 (S Gomes 78, M Stoop 54). **Mpumalanga** 132 (A Kroff 58, R Jaftha 4-11). **Western Province won by 113 runs.**
Border 217-8 (G Buckley 103, O Pienaar 4-39). **Free State** 161 (N Dick 3-13). **Border won by 56 runs.**
Pool Four
Limpopo 79 (O Rode 4-21). **KwaZulu-Natal** 80-3. **KwaZulu-Natal won by 7 wickets.**
Eastern Province 163 (D Klein 4-25, J Grobler 3-24). **North West** 164-5. **North West won by 5 wickets.**

Day Three, 5 December
Pool One
Griqualand West 96 (B Ferreira 3-13, D van Branden 3-19). **Gauteng** 97-1 (T Moalusi 59*). **Gauteng won by 9 wickets.**
South Western Districts 178-9 (I Fanampe 5-43). **KwaZulu-Natal Inland** 179-9. **KwaZulu-Natal Inland won by 1 wicket.**
Pool Two
Border Kei 86 (C Malan 4-21, L van Wyk 3-14). **Boland** 87-2. **Boland won by 8 wickets.**
Easterns 124 (S Le Roux 5-14). **Northerns** 127-6. **Northerns won by 4 wickets.**
Pool Three
Western Province 222-6 (B Barnes 91*). **Free State** 218-6 (R Rossouw 118*). **Western Province won by 4 runs.**
Mpumalanga 179. **Border** 180-9. **Border won by 1 wicket .**
Pool Four
North West 320 (J Grobler 122, A Joubert 50*). **Limpopo** 158 (D Pretorius 3-44, O Ramaboa 3-21). **North West won by 162 runs.**
KwaZulu-Natal 265-8 (F Mazibuko 61, G Pechey 90, S Goliath 3-19). **Eastern Province** 248-5 (C Armitage 57). **KwaZulu-Natal won by 17 runs.**

Day Four, 6 December
Final: KwaZulu-Natal 188-9 (Z Joseph 3-36). **Western Province** 192-3 (S Gomes 53, M Vallie 62*). **Western Province won by 7 wickets.**

PG BISON UNDER-15 WEEK

The PG Bison Under-15 Week was held in Durban from 10 to 14 December 2005 with 16 teams participating.

Boland were the only unbeaten team, defeating some of the traditional powerhouses of South African cricket before coming up against Free State, who had also won all their first four matches, on the final day. Boland skittled their opponents for 59 to set up a comfortable win.

Day One, 10 December

Border 135 in 34.5 overs (R Alers 21, G Feegan 23, D Deep 4-29, J Ross 3-24). **Gauteng** 102 in 35.4 overs (S Stemela 3-20). **Border won by 33 runs**.

North West 187 in 44.5 overs (C Jacobs 42, V Mabinza 2-15, X Ngumbela 2-35). **Kei** 61 in 26.5 overs (X Ngumbela 23). **North West won by 126 runs.**

South Western Districts 93 in 35.1 overs (E Colyn 21, M Alexander 4-23, C Arendse 3-15). **Western Province** 94-4 in 29.2 overs (N Loizides 34*, J Meredith 23, G Metthee 2-28). **Western Province won by 6 wickets.**

KwaZulu-Natal Inland 114 in 49.2 overs (T Dlehu 3-16, H Savage 2-21, R Heynes 2-17). **Eastern Province** 115-5 in 30.1 overs (C Ackerman 36, D Zwenke 2-19). **Eastern Province won by 5 wickets.**

Northerns 86 in 25.5 overs (L Louw 3-19, W Cliff 2-12). **Boland** 87-3 in 35.2 overs (D Botha 31, F Marais 29). **Boland won by 7 wickets.**

Mpumalanga 117 in 38.4 overs (M Philips 3-32). **Griqualand West** 118-9 in 38.4 overs (Z Vawada 3-33, J Olivier 2-25, F Booysen 2-18). **Griqualand West won by 1 wicket.**

KwaZulu-Natal 183-7 in 50 overs (A Moosa 36, M Alexander 92, A Henning 2-41, E Germishuizen 2-34). **Easterns** 94 in 49 overs (N Nhlapo 22, D White 5-18). **KwaZulu-Natal won by 89 runs.**

Free State 159 in 46.2 overs (J Herbst 40, B Mosena 31, Z McCoffin 3-25, E Redelinghys 3-43). **Limpopo** 101 in 41.3 overs (J Herbst 4-11, S Komari 3-15). **Free State won by 58 runs.**

Day Two, 11 December

KwaZulu-Natal Inland 102 in 45.4 overs (C Saunders 35, W Cliff 3-15). **Boland** 103-1 in 30.5 overs (D Botha 35, E Jantjies 38). Boland won by 9 wickets

Kei 104 in 47 overs (X Ngumbela 27, W Bester 4-11, Kyle van Jaarsveld 2-19). **Griqualand West** 105-4 in 22.4 overs (G Abrahams 31*, Y Nkonzo 2-18). **Griqualand West won by 6 wickets.**

Gauteng 191 in 46.3 overs (J Ross 53, S Landsdale 31, G Matthee 4-30, J van der Vyver 2-14). **South Western Districts** 121 in 38 overs (B Samsodien 33, S Landsdale 4-18, D Deep 3-32). **Gauteng won by 70 runs.**

Northerns 199 in 47.5 overs (W Lues 45, B le Roux 37, S Blom 5-29, R Heynes 2-17). **Eastern Province** 159-7 in 50 overs (K Smuts 37). **Northerns won by 40 runs.**

Border 201 in 47 overs (D Selepe 38, I Hendricks 4-30). **Western Province** 202-7 in 44.2 overs (N Loizides 52*, I Hendricks 66). **Western Province won by 3 wickets.**

Limpopo 108 in 45.4 overs (P Hawken 24, A Baloyi 24, L Fouche 3-16). **KwaZulu-Natal** 109-3 in 32.2 overs (A Moosa 35, M Alexander 32, D Dymond 2-31). **KwaZulu-Natal won by 7 wickets.**

North West 146 in 45.4 overs (D Hees 59, R Pretorius 4-6). **Mpumalanga** 129 in 48 overs (G van Aswegen 23, C van Wyk 3-14). **North West won by 17 runs.**

Free State 220-8 in 50 overs (P Botha 60, S Smith 59, N Mhlangu 3-18, E Germishuizen 2-22). **Easterns** 128 in 45.4 overs (C Ceronie 60, P Botha 3-1, L Letsi 2-18). **Free State won by 92 runs.**

Day Three, 12 December

Griqualand West 126 in 48.1 overs (G Abrahams 23, K van Jaarsveld 22, D Harvey 2-13, J-H Steenkamp 2-23, S Silver 2-19). **North West** 127-4 in 29.3 overs (S Silver 61, H Alli 32, R Williams 2-19). **North West won by 6 wickets.**

Kei 102 in 36.3 overs (S Nkonyeni 32, F Booysen 3-18, B Mabena 3-15). **Mpumalanga** 104-1 in 32.4 overs (P Lee 49). **Mpumalanga won by 9 wickets.**

Gauteng 277-5 in 50 overs (D Hendricks 66, D Conway 54, J Ross 53). **Western Province** 84 (D Deep 3-6, J Scott 3-31). **Gauteng won by 193 runs.**

KwaZulu-Natal 60 in 32.4 overs (B le Roux 37, L Jacobs 3-12, S Smith 2-16, J Kruger 2-25, J Herbst 2-2). **Free State** 62-1 in 10.4 overs (B Mosena 27, J Herbst 20). **Free State won by 9 wickets.**

Easterns 180-7 in 50 overs (B Skade 37*, T Huyser 33, Botikie 3-25). **Limpopo** 181-6 in 49 overs (G Gryvenstein 75, D Dymond 40). **Limpopo won by 4 wickets.**

PG BISON UNDER-15 WEEK

Eastern Province 141 in 47.5 overs (C Faas 29*, K Smuts 24, E Jantjies 4-25). **Boland** 143-8 in 49.1 overs (I Nackerdien 31, J van der Merwe 30, S Blom 2-15, R Heyns 2-23, J McKinnon 2-12). **Boland won by 2 wickets.**
Border 287 in 49 overs (N Mlakalaka 68, R Alers 61, J van der Vyver 3-64, J Olivier 2-55, A Afrika 2-21). **South Western Districts** 170-5 in 50 overs (A Afrika 40, E Colyn 44, L Terblanche 2-28). **Border won by 117 runs.**
Northerns 219-7 in 50 overs (J Esterhuizen 41, S Naidoo 33, R Fortuin 2-36, M Taberer 2-30, R van Niekerk 2-36). **KwaZulu-Natal Inland** 108 in 37.3 overs (D Zwenke 35, S Bergman 3-16, J Esterhuizen 2-21, K Pillay 2-20). **Northerns won by 111 runs.**

Day Four, 13 December
North West 109-8 in 50 overs (J Kruger 3-6, L Jacobs 2-27, S Smith 3-13). **Free State** 110-0 in 27.2 overs (B Mosena 50, H Erlank 41). **Free State won by 10 wickets.**
KwaZulu-Natal 119 in 49.1 overs (M Alexander 31, K van Jaarsveld 3-17). **Griqualand West** 96 in 45.1 overs (S Rosier 28, M Alexander 3-18, K Chetty 2-9, L Fouche 2-6). **KwaZulu-Natal won by 23 runs.**
Kei 47 in 27 overs (G Matthee 3-6, K Moses 3-9). **South Western Districts** 48-1 in 16.2 overs (J van der Vyver 32). **South Western Districts won by 9 wickets.**
Western Province 170-6 in 50 overs (M Alexander 42, N Loizides 53, J McKinnon 2-36). **Eastern Province** 167-7 in 50 overs (J van der Meulen 39, C Faas 37, M Hawkinkels 3-35, C Hamman 3-26). **Western Province won by 3 runs.**
Boland 235-8 in 50 overs (I Nackerdien 60, D Kemp 52, E Schreuder 3-56, S Landsdale 2-28). **Gauteng** 215-8 in 50 overs (D Hendricks 61, J Ross 43, L Louw 2-31). **Boland won by 20 runs.**
Northerns 222-7 in 50 overs (W Lues 52, J Richards 38, L Terblanche 2-38). **Border** 146 in 44.1 overs (C Tsiki 35, G Hirst 31, G van Buuren 3-25, K Pillay 2-18, S Bergman 2-31). **Northerns won by 76 runs.**
Easterns 142 in 49 overs (S Jamison 41*, A Henning 24, A Khumalo 2-20, K Eccles 2-20, C Saunders 2-30). **KwaZulu-Natal Inland** 143-5 in 44.4 overs (K Eccles 46, C King 39, E Badane 2-19). **KwaZulu-Natal Inland won by 5 wickets.**
Limpopo 200-8 in 46 overs (Z McCoffin 43, P Hawken 50, B Viljoen 3-36). **Mpumalanga** 103 in 33.1 overs (D van Reenen 3-21). **Limpopo won by 97 runs.**

Day Five, 14 December
Northerns 193-9 in 50 overs (W Lues 75, J Esterhuizen 33, M Alexander 2-22, C Hamman 2-44, J Buffkins 2-38). **Western Province** 157 in 47.5 overs (N Loizides 62, J Esterhuizen 2-30, G van Buuren 4-33). **Northerns won by 36 runs.**
Border 232-9 in 50 overs (C Dargie 65, R Alers 54, S Rosier 4-38). **Griqualand West** 138 in 39 overs (A Morake 21, C Dargie 5-45). **Border won by 94 runs.**
Mpumalanga 154 in 42.4 overs (F Booysen 49, F de Klerk 28, C Saunders 4-35, J Rayan 2-20). **KwaZulu-Natal Inland** 156-4 in 35.1 overs (M Boote 52, P Lambie 24, P Lee 2-28). **KwaZulu-Natal Inland won by 6 wickets.**
Free State 59 in 20.3 overs (C August 4-18, W Cliff 3-13). **Boland** 60-5 in 16.1 overs (J van der Merwe 24, J Kruger 4-17). **Boland won by 5 wickets.**
Easterns 237-6 in 50 overs (C Ceronie 77, T Huyser 52, K Niewenhuizen 49). **Kei** 47 in 27 overs (E Germishuizen 6-10, S Jamison 2-20). **Easterns won by 190 runs.**
Gauteng 225-8 in 50 overs (D Ratanyake 77, C van Heerden 40, I Lubbe 2-24). **Eastern Province** 217-9 in 50 overs (C Ackerman 83, K Smuts 43, J Ross 3-24, S Landsdale 2-34, C van Heerden 2-49). **Gauteng won by 8 runs.**
KwaZulu-Natal 227-7 in 50 overs (R Hatting 81, K Chetty 45, D Harvey 2-33, W Alexander 2-65). **North West** 175-5 in 50 overs (S Silver 63, David White 4-28, R Hatting 2-15, K Zondo 2-23). **KwaZulu-Natal won by 52 runs.**
South Western Districts 219-8 in 50 overs (J van der Vyver 100, K Moses 31, D Dymond 2-48, E Redelinghys 2-45). **Limpopo** 175-9 in 50 overs (G Grywenstein 51, K Moses 3-37, G Matthee 2-21, A van Tonder 2-34). **South Western Districts won by 44 runs.**

STANDARD BANK UNDER-13 WEEK

Sixteen teams took part in the Standard Bank Under-13 Week, the first step on the inter-provincial ladder for many young hopefuls, in Wellington, Western Cape, from 4 to 8 December 2005.

Day One, 4 December

Boland 197 in 50 overs (L Nel 36, E van der Merwe 33, J Meyer 3-23, N Linde 2-9). **Free State** 186-7 in 50 overs (J Meyer 54, K Rafferty 26*, E van der Merwe 3-34, R Henry 2-36). **Boland won by 11 runs.**

Gauteng 212-8 in 50 overs (T Abendanon 71, K Jennings 31, J Kriel 3-21). **Border** 93 in 23.1 overs (C Diesel 25, P Dikgale 5-43, J van der Merwe 4-12). **Gauteng won by 119 runs.**

Western Province 214 in 44.4 overs (J Crowson 76, D Linegar 71, M Holtshausen 4-36, G Nomyayi 3-34). **Easterns** 173-7 in 50 overs (M Holtshausen 54*, C Bownes 36, G Edmeads 3-30). **Western Province won by 41 runs.**

Limpopo 66 in 35 overs (S Bissoon 3-23, P Subrayan 2-11). **KwaZulu-Natal** 69-1 in 19.3 overs (N Hendrie 41*). **KwaZulu-Natal won by 9 wickets.**

Northerns 248-9 in 50 overs (T de Bruyn 99, D Clarence-Bunn 41, F Lushaba 3-37, T Prinsloo 2-48). **Mpumalanga** 187 in 48 overs (T Prinsloo 76, N Arnoldi 31, A Verster 3-20, C Abrahams 2-18). **Northerns won by 61 runs.**

South Western Districts 111 in 36.5 overs (B Haycock 21, V Prinsloo 2-8, T Mathlare 2-26). **North West** 113-6 in 29.3 overs (R Venter 51*, B Haycock 2-30, G Goliath 2-34). **North West won by 4 wickets.**

Kei 53 in 19.3 overs (C Barnes 5-12, W Wilkinson 4-7). **Griqualand West** 55-1 in 13.1 overs (G Cloete 22*). **Griqualand West won by 9 wickets.**

Eastern Province 205-7 in 50 overs (J Price 85*, L Harrop 30, G Sharpe 3-46, N Platt 2-31). **KwaZulu-Natal Inland** 112-9 in 50 overs (N Platt 28*, G Sharpe 23, J Dolley 4-16, J Ford 2-16). **Eastern Province won by 93 runs.**

Day Two, 5 December

Limpopo 107 in 50 overs (N Linde 4-23, D Vries 2-18). **Free State** 109-3 in 26 overs (N Linde 50*, R Sadler 2-37). **Free State won by 7 wickets.**

Boland 272 in 50 overs (P Kriel 60, J Koegelenberg 48, K Sixolile 2-55, S Vitshima 2-51). **Kei** 39 in 29 overs (E Cook 4-7, A Douman 3-3). **Boland won by 233 runs.**

KwaZulu-Natal Inland 133-9 in 50 overs (G Sharpe 29, J Scott 5-21). **Gauteng** 129-7 in 50 overs (K Jennings 55, D Sartor 34*, N Platt 2-10). **KwaZulu-Natal Inland won by 4 runs.**

KwaZulu-Natal 132 in 40 overs (J Groom 39 *, M Holtshausen 4-21). **Easterns** 136-5 in 36 overs (D Matthews 53, J Lotriet 25*, P Subrayan 2-30). **Easterns won by 5 wickets.**

Mpumalanga 126 in 42 overs (L Wind 38, G Edmeads 4-19, J Crowson 3-11). **Western Province** 128-6 in 29 overs (D Linegar 37, W Mukudam 27, Conrad Viljoen 4-34). **Western Province won by 4 wickets.**

Griqualand West 73 in 34.4 overs (C Herman 5-9, J Price 3-25). **Eastern Province** 75-2 in 17 overs (J Dolley 43*, M Dugmore 2-16). **Eastern Province won by 8 wickets.**

Northerns 198-8 in 50 overs (R Frenz 51, D Clarence-Bunn 31, J Potgieter 2-27, R Vermeulen 2-29). **South Western Districts** 87 in 40.3 overs (R Vermeulen 25, A Verster 4-19). **Northerns won by 111 runs.**

Border 147 in 49.4 overs (C Diesel 58, B Hoogenboesem 3-31). **North West** 148-9 in 45.5 overs (R Venter 53*, S Storm 2-22, L Killsen 2-25). **North West won by 1 wicket.**

Day Three, 6 December

Border 111 in 34.3 overs (C Diesel 24, V Maritz 3-23, W Wilkinson 2-24). **Griqualand West** 113-5 in 44.3 overs (T Mthonxa 43, J Kriel 2-17). **Griqualand West won by 5 wickets.**

KwaZulu-Natal Inland 158-9 in 50 overs (C Hogan 57, M Holtshausen 3-28, P Havanga 2-22). **Easterns** 140 in 41.2 overs (M Holtshausen 63, G Sharpe 3-38). **KwaZulu-Natal Inland won by 18 runs**.

North West 162-9 in 50 overs (D Koertzen 57, S Tshabalala 32, J Groom 4-30, C Savage 3-24). **KwaZulu-Natal** 163-5 in 45.2 overs (J Groom 50*, R Venter 2-23). **KwaZulu-Natal won by 5 wickets.**

South Western Districts 119 in 42 overs (K Pretorius 48, O Fortuin 2-13, N Jordaan 2-30). **Mpumalanga** 121-6 in 45 overs (L Wild 36, N Arnoldi 29, B Haycock 2-32). **Mpumalanga won by 4 wickets.**

Free State 177 in 49 overs (N Linde 58, M Mofokeng 31, J Scott 3-24, R Cartwright 2-26). **Gauteng** 178-3 in 39 overs (J van der Merwe 81*, Q de Kock 48). **Gauteng won by 7 wickets.**

Boland 112-9 in 50 overs (T Kaber 3-24). **Northerns** 113-3 in 42.3 overs (R Frenz 36, A Verster 35*). **Northerns won by 7 wickets.**

Limpopo 219-6 in 50 overs (L Tullis 55, M Dolo 37, A Botha 37, W Nciweni 2-16). **Kei** 35 in 18 overs (T Selobane 5-6, R Serfontein 3-6). **Limpopo won by 184 runs**.

Western Province 246-6 in 50 overs (D Linegar 91, G Edmeades 50, L Harrop 2-29). **Eastern Province** 237 in 48.1 overs (T Wewege 66, B Dolley 39, J Dolley 38, W Mukuddem 4-33, N Lurhafu 2-47). **Western Province won by 9 runs.**

STANDARD BANK UNDER-13 WEEK

Day Four, 7 December
Boland 161-9 in 50 overs (R Henry 32, D Swanepoel 24, S Sunkari 2-24, P Subrayan 2-24, A Dunn 2-26). **KwaZulu-Natal** 128-9 in 50 overs (S Gericke 20, E Cook 2-12, R Engelbrecht 2-18). **Boland won by 33 runs.**
Griqualand West 92 in 30.5 overs (B Hogenboesem 5-25, D Koertzen 3-25). **North West** 93-7 in 33.3 overs (J Brink 23*, T Fredericks 2-11, M Dugmore 2-12). **North West won by 3 wickets.**
Mpumalanga 148-4 in 42 overs (N Arnoldi 77, S Razack 3-25, S Rishen 3-21). **KwaZulu-Natal Inland** 149-4 in 42 overs (J Walsh 55*, N Platt 39, C Viljoen 2-26). **KwaZulu-Natal won by 6 wickets.**
Eastern Province 158 in 48 overs (T Wewege 75, J Dolley 37, K Jennings 6-32, J van der Merwe 3-25). **Gauteng** 161-8 in 43 overs (K Jennings 55, T Abendanon 29, J Price 4-42, J Dolley 3-8). **Gauteng won by 2 wickets.**
Northerns 172 in 49.1 overs (R Frenz 41, G Foxcroft 28, C Fortune 4-23, J Zeeman 2-35). **Western Province** 173-7 in 42.5 overs (J Crowson 50, D Linegar 47*, T Kaber 5-40). **Western Province won by 3 wickets.**
Border 153 in 49.1 overs (B Jonker 42*, L Tsiki 21, P Fourie 3-32, R Saddler 2-16). **Limpopo** 104 in 45.1 overs (P Fourie 28, R Saddler 25). **Border won by 49 runs.**
South Western Districts 184-8 in 50 overs (B Haycock 85*, M Vallabh 40, W Nciwemi 4-14). **Kei** 49 in 27 overs (M Piedt 5-9, G Goliath 2-11). **South Western Districts won by 135 runs.**
Free State 100 in 21.3 overs (N Linde 23, K Rafferty 23, J Lotriet 2-15, D Rankwe 2-29). **Easterns** 101-4 in 22 overs (D Matthews 48, M Holtshausen 22*, J Meyer 2-9). **Easterns won by 6 wickets.**

Day Five, 8 December
Kei 119 in 35 overs (M Gaqela 24, N Arnoldi 3-16, T Prinsloo 3-23). **Mpumalanga** 121-5 in 27.3 overs (C Viljoen 25, S Khela 2-26). **Mpumalanga won by 5 wickets.**
Easterns 31 in 18 overs (T Ntshanyana 3-6, T Wewege 3-6). **Eastern Province** 32-4 (J Lotriet 2-10). **Eastern Province won by 6 wickets.**
Griqualand West 147-9 in 50 overs (G Cloete 38, M Dugmore 30, P Subrayan 2-12). **KwaZulu-Natal** 150-1 in 32.5 overs (N Hendry 80*, R Logan 41). **KwaZulu-Natal won by 9 wickets.**
Border 161-7 in 50 overs (J Godfrey 68, L Tsiki 39, N Linde 4-43, J Meyer 2-17). **Free State** 129 in 48.2 overs (N Marais 59, B Jonker 3-45, J Kriell 2-15). **Border won by 32 runs.**
Gauteng 211-6 in 50 overs (K Jennings 90, C Fortune 2-50). **Western Province** 83 in 28 overs (D Sartor 3-13, K Jennings 3-23). **Gauteng won by 128 runs.**
Northerns 222-6 in 50 overs (D Clarence-Bunn 58*, D Koertzen 2-22, R Venter 2-58). **North West** 140-8 in 50 overs (D Koertzen 50, A Verster 3-14). **Northerns won by 82 runs.**
KwaZulu-Natal Inland 186-6 in 50 overs (N Platt 58*, S Razack 25*, E Cook 2-6). **Boland** 148 in 49.5 overs (E Cook 52*, L Nel 20, G Sharpe 3-16, J Walsh 2-34). **KwaZulu-Natal Inland won by 38 runs.**
South Western Districts 140 in 46.2 overs (G Haycock 63, P Fourie 5-32). **Limpopo** 105 in 46 overs (R Saddler 31, G Haycock 3-24). **South Western Districts won by 35 runs.**

BAKERS MINI CRICKET

The eighth annual Bakers Mini Cricket Seminar took place in the Drakensberg during July 2006. It was attended by representatives from the United Cricket Board of South Africa, National Brands Limited and more than 110 Bakers Mini Cricket coaches. The coaches, many of them volunteers, were able to interact with the sponsors and the UCB, providing feedback and sharing their experiences.

The programme currently involves 100 000 children.

Monique Burger, Bakers Mini Cricket Sponsorship Manager, said: "The opportunity to interact with the coaches and the children and experience their passion for the love of the game is a humbling experience and reinforces the importance of the Bakers Mini Cricket sponsorship, which plays a huge role in growing the game."

SOUTH AFRICAN UMPIRES 2005/06

Umpires who stood in first—class (93), limited overs (102) and Pro20 (21) matches in 2005/06

				Other	Total				Other	Total			Total
	Test	SS	P3	FC	FC	LOI	SB	P1	LO	LO	Pro20	20Int	20
BOLAND													
M Erasmus	-	7	1	-	8	-	6	-	-	6	4	1	5
EC Hendrikse	-	-	8	-	8	-	-	8	-	8	1	-	1
IH van Kerwel	-	-	5	-	5	-	-	7	-	7	-	-	-
BORDER													
S George	-	4	3	-	7	-	6	3	-	9	3	-	3
IL Howell	-	1	1	1	3	2	6	1	2	11	3	1	4
LJ Willemse	-	-	10	-	10	-	-	9	-	9	-	-	-
EASTERN PROVINCE													
MW Brown	-	4	2	-	6	-	5	2	-	7	1	-	1
M Gajjar	-	6	-	-	6	-	3	-	-	3	2	-	2
BN Harrison	-	-	6	-	6	-	-	5	-	5	-	-	-
BG Jerling	-	2	1	1	4	6	6	1	2	15	5	1	6
EASTERNS													
KH Hurter	-	2	1	-	3	2	6	1	-	9	5	1	6
SW Liebisch	-	-	9	-	9	-	-	7	-	7	-	-	-
FREE STATE													
MZ Nanabhay	-	5	3	-	8	-	6	3	-	9	4	-	4
BDA Westraadt	-	-	5	-	5	-	-	8	-	8	-	-	-
GAUTENG													
LM Engelbrecht	-	-	5	-	5	-	-	7	-	7	-	-	-
SB Lambson	-	6	3	-	9	-	5	2	-	7	2	-	2
ZTA Ndamane	-	-	6	-	6	-	-	4	-	4	1	-	1
JEP Ostrom	-	-	7	-	7	-	-	7	-	7	-	-	-
GH Pienaar	-	4	4	-	8	-	3	3	-	6	1	-	1
S Wadvalla	-	7	2	-	9	-	5	2	-	7	2	-	2
BM White	-	-	9	-	9	-	-	10	-	10	-	-	-
GRIQUALAND WEST													
CJ Conradie	-	-	8	-	8	-	-	5	-	5	-	-	-
NORTHERNS													
JD Cloete	-	7	1	-	8	-	5	1	-	6	2	-	2
DJ Smith	-	-	8	-	8	-	-	9	-	9	1	-	1
WESTERN PROVINCE													
LH Matroos	-	5	2	-	7	-	4	3	-	7	1	-	1
INTERNATIONAL													
Aleem Dar (Pak)	1	-	-	-	1	1	-	-	-	1	-	-	-
MR Benson (Eng)	2	-	-	-	2	-	-	-	-	-	-	-	-
SA Bucknor (WI)	2	-	-	-	2	5	-	-	-	5	-	-	-
SJ Davis (Aus)	-	-	-	-	-	3	-	-	-	3	-	-	-
EAR de Silva (SL)	2	-	-	-	2	-	-	-	-	-	-	-	-
BR Doctrove (WI)	2	-	-	-	2	3	-	-	-	3	-	-	-
DB Hair (Aus)	1	-	-	-	1	-	-	-	-	-	-	-	-
DJ Harper (Aus)	1	-	-	-	1	-	-	-	-	-	-	-	-
AL Hill (NZ)	1	-	-	-	1	-	-	-	-	-	-	-	-
JW Lloyds (Eng)	-	-	-	-	-	4	-	-	-	4	-	-	-
IW Shine (NZ)	-	2	-	-	2	-	-	-	-	-	-	-	-
Totals	12	62	110	2	186	26	66	108	4	204	38	4	42

UMPIRES WHO'S WHO 2005/06

All details as at 10 May 2006

BROWN Murray Welsh (EP). B 16/9/66 Grahamstown. Ed St Andrew's (Gmt), UPE. FC debut FS v WP (Bfn) 2002/03, LO debut 2001/02. 29 FC matches. Umpired in 2 FC matches in NZ 2005/06. 28 LO matches, 5 Pro20 matches. Played for EP Schools (1984-1985), UPE (1986-1990).

CLOETE Johannes Daniel (Nor) B 21/7/71 Klerksdorp. Ed Stilfontein HS, Potch Univ. FC debut WT v GW (Potch) 1993/94. 56 FC matches. Umpired in 2 FC matches in NZ 2003/04. 58 LO matches, 8 Pro20 matches. Rugby (Craven Week U-13 1984), Athletics (WT 1988), Indoor Hockey (Potch Univ 1991-1993).

CONRADIE Christoffel Jakobus *(Christo)* (GW). B 4/8/59 Murraysburg. Ed Murraysburg HS. FC debut FS v Gau (Bfn) 2005/06. 8 FC matches, 5 LO matches. Played for West End CC (Kby) (1987-1996).

ENGELBRECHT Lourens Marthinus (Gau). B 17/11/64 Keetmanshoop, South-West Africa. Ed Alberton HS, Technikon SA. FC debut FS v Nor (Bfn) 2005/06. 5 FC matches, 7 LO matches. Played for SAPS (Pretoria), East Rand CC, Alberton CC (1981-1993).

ERASMUS Marais (Bol). B 27/2/64 George. Ed DF Malan HS, Paarl TC, Stell Univ. FC debut SAA v Rest (Pta) 2002/03. 2 Tests as TV Umpire. 23 FC matches. Umpired in 2 FC matches in NZ 2004/05. 22 LO matches, 14 Pro20 matches including 1 international. Played for Bol/BolB (1988-1996). 53 FC matches, 1913 runs (avg 29.43), HS 103* Bol v Warwickshire (Brackenfell) 1991/92, 35 cts, 131 wkts (avg 28.18), BB 6-22 Bol v NZ (Paarl) 1994/95. RHB RFM. Rugby (Bol).

GAJJAR Mookesh *(Mike)* (EP). B 16/8/58 Uitenhage. Ed Uitenhage HS. FC debut EPB v WT (PE) 1993/94. 37 FC matches, 22 LO matches, 3 Pro20 matches. Played for Walmer CC, EP Senior Schools 1976 (SACOS).

GEORGE Shaun (Bdr). B 25/1/68 Port Elizabeth. Ed Chapman SS. FC debut Bol v EP (Paarl) 2004/05. 10 FC matches, 14 LO matches, 4 Pro20 matches. Umpired Women's World Cup final 2005. Played for EP (SACB) (1986-1990). 17 FC matches, 230 runs (avg 10.95), HS 45* EP v Tvl (SACB) (Lenasia) 1989/90, 5 cts, 29 wkts (avg 26.62), BB 3-66 EP v Tvl (SACB) (PE) 1988/89.

HARRISON Bernard Nigel (EP). B 19/3/57 Port Elizabeth. Ed Paterson HS. FC debut Bdr v Bol (EL) 2005/06. 6 FC matches, 5 LO matches. Played for Albany CC (1981-1990), Gelvandale CC (1991-1996).

HENDRIKSE Earl Charles (Bol). B 12/4/67 Stellenbosch. Ed Cloetesville HS. FC debut Kenya v Uganda (Nairobi) 2004. 13 FC matches, 11 LO matches, 1 Pro20 match. Played for Boland CD (1998).

HOWELL Ian Lester (Bdr). B 20/5/58 Port Elizabeth. Ed Grey HS (PE), UPE. Son of EJ Howell (Hon Sec SACUA 1962-1969), Nephew of HC Howell (WP 1949-1954), twin brother of DH Howell (WPB/EP/EPB/Tvl/TvlB/Bdr 1976-1991), father of GE Howell (EP 2004-2005). FC debut Eas v KZNB (Ben) 1998/99. Tests: 6 (2000/01-2005/06). LOIs: 38 (1999/00-2005/06). 12 Tests as TV Umpire, 15 LOIs as TV Umpire. 52 FC matches. Umpired in 2 FC matches in NZ 1999/00. 93 LO matches, 8 Pro20 matches including 1 international. Played for EPB (1981-1983), EP (1982/83), Bdr (1984-1997). 119 FC matches, 3767 runs (avg 26.90), HS 115* Bdr v EP (PE) 1991/92, 69 cts, 243 wkts (avg 35.74), BB 6-38 Bdr v Ntl (EL) 1991/92. LHB LM. Hockey (EP 1979-1981, SAU 1980-1981).

HURTER Karl Heinrich (Eas). B 12/2/64 Port Elizabeth. Ed Pearson HS. FC debut Eas v WPB (Ben) 1997/98. LOIs: 4 (2001/02-2005/06). 5 Tests as TV Umpire, 14 LOIs as TV Umpire. 49 FC matches, 63 LO matches, 11 Pro20 matches including 1 international.

JERLING Brian George (EP). B 13/8/58 Port Elizabeth. Ed PE Tech HS. FC debut Bol v SADF (Wdk) 1988/89. LOIs: 43 (2000/01-2005/06). 6 Tests as TV Umpire, 24 LOIs as TV Umpire. 106 FC matches. Umpired in 1 FC match in NZ 2000/01. 157 LO matches, 14 Pro20 matches including 1 international. Played for SADF EP Command (1978-1981), SADF Rundu Sector (1982-1986).

KOERTZEN Rudolf Eric (Rudi) (ICC). B 26/3/49 Knysna. Ed Despatch HS, PE Technical College. FC debut GW v WPB (Kby) 1981/82. Tests: 73 (1992/93-2005/06). LOIs: 151 (1992/93-2005/06). 12 Tests as TV Umpire, 30 LOIs as TV Umpire. 177 FC matches, 323 LO matches, 1 Pro20 match. Played for Despatch CC (1970-1975), De Beers CC (1976-1981). Soccer (NFL for Drostdy Park 1967-1970), Golf (7 handicap, Uitenhage Golf Club).

LAMBSON Simon Barry (Gau). B 28/8/58 Johannesburg. Ed St Alban's, Wits Univ. FC debut TvlB v GW (Jhb) 1985/86. Tests: 5 (1992/93-1994/95). LOIs: 35 (1992/93-2001/02). 2 Tests as TV Umpire, 23 LOIs as TV Umpire. 141 FC matches. Umpired in 2 FC matches in NZ 2002/03. 236 LO matches, 7 Pro20 matches. Played for Kroonstad Defence.

LIEBISCH Sarel *Walter* (Eas). B 17/2/65 Brakpan. Ed Hoerskool Stoffberg, RAU. FC debut Gau v Nor (Jhb) 2004/05. 13 FC matches, 9 LO matches. Played for RAU (1983-1985), Boksburg CC (1986-1992).

MATROOS Laurence Harvey (WP). B 3/11/57 District Six, Cape Town. Ed South Peninsula HS, Peninsula Tech. FC debut Bol v Gau (Paarl) 2001/02. 1 LOI as TV Umpire. 26 FC matches, 41 LO matches, 5 Pro20 matches. Played for Tramway CC (1987-1991).

NANABHAY Muhammed Zunaid (FS). B 11/1/67 Klerksdorp. Ed Potchefstroom SS, Potch Univ. FC debut Bol v GW (Paarl) 2001/02. LOIs: 1 (2001/02). 2 LOIs as TV Umpire. 29 FC matches, 34 LO matches, 13 Pro20 matches. Played for Potch United Sports Club (1986-1998).

SOUTH AFRICAN UMPIRES 2005/06

NDAMANE Zama Thembekile Anderson *(Zed)* (Gau). B 3/7/64 De Aar. Ed Newell HS, PE Tech. FC debut Kenya v Namibia (Nairobi) 2004. 10 FC matches, 9 LO matches, 1 Pro20 match. Umpired Women's World Cup final 2005. Played for United Brothers CC (1979-1991).
OSTROM Johan Eskil Patrick *(John)* (Gau). B 19/8/56 Johannesburg. Ed Edenvale HS, Pretoria Tech. FC debut Eas v Nor (Ben) 2001/02. 12 FC matches, 15 LO matches.
PIENAAR Gerhardus Hendrik *(Gerrie)* (Gau). B 28/4/59 Johannesburg. Ed Vorentoe HS. FC debut Namibia v Uganda (Wdk) 2004. 15 FC matches, 12 LO matches, 2 Pro20 matches. Played for Sturrock Park CC (1979-1988), Marks Park CC (1989-1995).
SMITH Dennis James (Nor). B 26/11/71 Durban. Ed Durban HS, King Edward VII. FC debut Gau v FS (Jhb) 2004/05. 12 FC matches, 14 LO matches, 1 Pro20 match. Played for NorB (1993-1998), Nor (1993-1998), Eas (1999/00). 28 FC matches, 907 runs (avg 22.12), HSFC 88* NTB v ZimBrd (Vbg) 1993/94, 56 cts, 5 sts. RHB WK.
VAN KERWEL Irvin Henry (Bol). B 27/5/63 Stellenbosch. Ed Luckhoff SS, Athlone CE. FC debut EP v Zim U23 (PE) 2005/06. 5 FC matches, 7 LO matches. Played for Newtons (1980-1994).
WADVALLA Shaid (Gau). B 25/7/49 Zeerust. Ed Chris J Botha HS. Brother of Sikander *(Ziggy)* Wadvalla (Tvl SACB 1990/91, former Gauteng CEO), cousin of A Wadvalla (Tvl SACB/WP SACB 1972-85). FC debut Ntl v EP (SACB) (Dbn) 1989/90. LOIs: 3 (2001/02). 4 Tests as TV Umpire, 10 LOIs as TV Umpire. 86 FC matches. Umpired in 2 FC matches in NZ 1998/99. 89 LO matches, 8 Pro20 matches. Played for Ntl (SACB) (1986/87). 2 FC matches, 26 runs (avg 6.50), HS 14 Ntl v EP (SACB) (PE) 1986/87, 0 Cts, 2 wkts (avg 29.00), BB 2-21 Ntl v EP (SACB) (PE) 1986/87. Also played for Tvl (SACB), Jhb Protea, Crescents.
WESTRAADT Barend Daniel Albertus *(Wessie)* (FS). B 2/4/57 Durban. Ed Cilliers HS (PE), UOFS. FC debut GWB v KZNB (Kby) 1998/99. 16 FC matches, 21 LO matches, 1 Pro20 match.
WHITE Brad Middleton (Gau). B 15/5/70 Port Elizabeth. Ed King Edward VII. FC debut Nor v Eas (Cent) 2004/05. 13 FC matches, 15 LO matches. Played for TvlB (1988-1995), Tvl (1990-1995), Bdr (1996-1999), Eas (2000/01). 78 FC matches, 4000 runs (avg 28.16), HS 180* TvlB v EPB (PE) 1995/96, 76 cts, 25 wkts (avg 34.80), BB 3-23 Bdr v GW (Kby) 1997/98. LHB RM.
WILLEMSE Lawrence Johannes (Bdr). B 24/3/62 Beaufort West. Ed Central HS (Beaufort West). FC debut EP v WP (PE) 2004/05. 15 FC matches, 14 LO matches. Played for SWD CD (1983), Hamiltons CC.

NATIONAL PANEL OF UMPIRES AND MATCH REFEREES 2006/07

National First Class Panel: Murray Brown, Johan Cloete, Marais Erasmus, Shaun George, Earl Hendrickse, Ian Howell, Karl Hurter, Brian Jerling, Barry Lambson, Muhammed Nanabhay, Zed Ndamane, Gerrie Pienaar, Dennis Smith, Shaid Wadvalla.
Emerging Panel: Kevin Adams, Adri Crafford, Christo Conradie, Roderick Ellis, Lourens Engelbrecht, Bernard Harrison, Walter Liebisch, Laurence Matroos, John Ostrom, Irvin Van Kerwel, Wessie Westraadt, Brad White, Lawrence Willemse.
Match Referees Panel: Tiffie Barnes, Wilf Diedricks, Devdas Govindjee, Rushdi Magiet, Enver Mall, Cyril Mitchley, Sagran Naidoo, Nic Pretorius.

TEST UMPIRES IN SOUTH AFRICA 1888/89-2005/06

All details as at 10 May 2006

	Period	Series	Tests		Period	Series	Tests
Adams HV (WP)	1921-27	2	2	Koertzen RE (EP) (b)	1992-2001	10	13
+Aleem Dar (Pakistan)	2004-05	2	3	Lambson SB (Tvl) (b)	1992-94	3	4
Allsop G (Tvl)	1895	1	1	Laver AG (Tvl)	1921-27	3	10
Anderson WP (Tvl)	1961	1	2	*Leaney J (England)	1891	1	1
Ashman RGA (Tvl)	1935-49	4	14	Liebenberg KE (Ntl) (b)	1992-95	4	5
Atfield AJ (Tvl)	1909-13	2	8	+Mahboob Shah (Pakistan)	1993	1	1
Baxter LM (Tvl)	1964-66	2	4	Malan BV (Ntl)	1949-56	3	6
+Benson MR (England)	2005	1	2	Marais W (Ntl)	1956-57	2	5
Beves G (Tvl)	1895	1	2	McCabe AN (Ntl)	1953	1	1
Birkett A (Tvl)	1957	1	2	McMenamin JH (Tvl)	1956-57	2	4
+Bowden BF (New Zealand)	2004	1	1	*Miller AM (England)	1895	1	2
+Bucknor SA (West Indies)	1992-2005	7	14	Mitchley CJ (Gau) (b)	1992-99	10	13
*Butt HR (England)	1895	1	1	+Nicholls EA (West Indies)	2000	1	1

SOUTH AFRICAN UMPIRES 2005/06

Coetzee CMP (EP)	1969	1	3
Collings JC (WP)	1930-35	2	9
Collins DV (WP)	1948-61	6	10
Collins S (WP)	1953	1	1
+Cooray BC (Sri Lanka)	1999	1	1
Coote CD (N Tvl)	1953	1	1
Costello VJ (WP)	1956-64	3	6
+Cowie DB (New Zealand)	1999	1	1
Creese WH (Tvl)	1902	1	1
Deare CR (EP)	1888	1	1
+De Silva EAR (Sri Lanka)	2001-05	2	3
Diedricks WA (Ntl)	1992	1	1
+Doctrove BR (West Indies)	2004-05	2	4
Draper JG (Ntl)	1964-69	3	5
Drew DT (Ntl)	1949-53	2	3
+Dunne RS (New Zealand)	1996-99	4	4
Fell DR (Ntl)	1961	1	1
+Francis KT (Sri Lanka)	1994	1	1
Gibbon GD (EP)	1961	1	1
Goldman G (WP)	1966-69	2	2
Grey FW (Tvl)	1909-22	4	10
+Hair DB (Australia)	1995-2005	6	8
+Harper DJ (Australia)	2002-05	6	8
Harris SL (Tvl)	1909-22	3	4
Hart-Davis JV (Ntl)	1948-49	2	4
Hearne F (WP)	1898-1905	3	6
Hickson JAE (GW)	1888	1	1
+Hill AL (New Zealand)	2005	1	1
Howell IL (Bdr)	2000-01	2	2
+Javed Akhtar (Pakistan)	1997	1	1
+Jayaprakash AV (India)	2000	1	1
+Khizer Hayat (Pakistan)	1994	1	1
Kidson HC (Tvl)	1961-66	3	11
King AC (Ntl)	1930	1	3
+Kitchen MJ (England)	1996-97	2	2
Orchard DL (KZN) (b)	1995-2001	11	15
Page ES (EP)	1927	1	1
Parry G (Tvl)	1961	1	2
Payne FRW (EP)	1953	1	1
*Phillips J (England)	1905	1	5
+Randell SG (Australia)	1995	1	1
Reid JA (Tvl)	1922	1	1
+Riazuddin (Pakistan)	2000	1	1
+Robinson ID (Zimbabwe)	1994-2000	2	2
Routledge WG (Tvl)	1935	1	2
Ryan WT	1930	1	2
Saunders C	1927	1	1
+Sharp G (England)	2000	1	1
+Shepherd DR (England)	1992-2003	4	7
Sickler GL (WP)	1938-48	2	7
Smith DJ (England)	1913	1	1
Smith FE (Tvl)	1902-09	3	5
Soames A (Tvl)	1898-1902	2	2
Taufel SJA (Australia)	2003-04	2	4
Thomas CN (WP)	1891	1	1
Thompson GJ (England)	1922	1	2
+Tiffin RB (Zimbabwe)	1998-2002	4	6
Treadwell GB (Tvl)	1927-30	2	4
+Venkataraghavan S (India)	1995-2003	7	11
Verheyen GA (GW)	1927	1	1
Wade WW (Ntl)	1969	1	1
Wainwright W (England)	1922	1	1
Warner AJ (Tvl)	1969	1	2
Warner JE (WP)	1961-64	2	2
*Warton RG (England)	1888	1	2
Webster HH (EP)	1888	1	1
*White A (England)	1898	1	2
+Willey P (England)	1996-2000	3	3
Woolley WB (WP)	1895	1	1
Unidentified	1895	1	2

* Touring umpire from England accompanying the team. + Neutral umpire provided by the ICC.

(a) Three umpires (two South African and one ICC) stood in all four Tests v India 1992/93.

(b) South African umpires have also stood, as the ICC umpire, in the following Tests:

IL Howell	4 (1 in Aus, 1 in Ban, 1 in Ind, 1 in NZ) 2005.
RE Koertzen	60 (13 in Aus, 10 in Eng, 7 in Ind, 4 in NZ, 6 in Pak, 7 in SL, 8 in WI, 5 in Zim) 1997-2005.
SB Lambson	1 (1 in Eng) 1994.
KE Liebenberg	4 (2 in Aus, 1 in Pak, 1 in WI) 1994-95.
CJ Mitchley	13 (2 in Aus, 4 in Eng, 1 in Ind, 2 in Pak, 1 in SL, 3 in WI) 1994-97.
DL Orchard	29 (2 in Aus, 2 in Ban, 7 in Eng, 1 in Ind, 3 in NZ, 3 in Pak, 5 in SL, 2 in WI, 4 in Zim) 1996-2003.

OBITUARIES

BRIAN VERNON BANFIELD. Born Cape Town 9.5.1934. Died Oudtshoorn, Western Cape 15.3.2006 aged 71. He played cricket for Southern Cape in the 1950s and early 1960s, was for many years the Chairman of the Oudtshoorn Cricket Club and served as the President of the Southern Cape Cricket Union. He headed the organising committee when Kim Hughes' Australian tourists played two matches in Oudtshoorn in November 1986.

EDGAR JOHN BARLOW. Born Pretoria 12.8.1940. Died General Hospital, St Helier, Jersey, Channel Islands 30.12.2005 aged 65. Eddie Barlow was arguably South Africa's greatest cricketing all-rounder. Solidly built, bespectacled and brimming with self-confidence he was an aggressive right-hand batsman, right-arm medium pace bowler, a fine fielder who had the ability to make slip fielding look simple and a competent wicketkeeper. He had little or no respect for reputations and attacked the bowling from the first ball. At times his bowling appeared to be innocuous and then, out of the blue, he would produce the unplayable delivery.

The late Louis Duffus, for many years the doyen of South African cricket writers, wrote, "I am inclined to contend Eddie Barlow had more influence over South African cricket than any single player I know. Perhaps it would be more accurate to say he had more influence on the country's spirit, tempo of batting and approach to the game. He did more than anyone else to break down the timid defensive tactics which for so many years kept South Africa a second-rate cricket country and that to me is a tremendous achievement."

At Waterkloof House Preparatory School (Pretoria) he received advice and guidance from Wilfred MacRobert and at Pretoria Boys High School from Will Hofmeyr, the renowned cricket master. He played first XI cricket with Glen Hall in 1955 and with Jackie Botten in 1955 and 1956 before captaining the side in 1957. He represented NE Transvaal in the 1956, 1957 and 1958 (captain) Nuffield Weeks and regarded being awarded his SA Schools "cap" in the January 1958 tournament in East London as one of the most significant events of his career. He played for the first rugby XV, was a school prefect and won the open mile and 880 yards in the school inter-house athletics meeting. He played hockey for the Old Boys scholars team on Sundays and still holds the Northern Transvaal record for scoring 13 goals in a league game.

His father was for some years the school groundsman. His mother ran the tuck shop.

At Witwatersrand University in Johannesburg he read geography and planned to become a teacher. Keeping wicket for Wits against Wanderers he stumped Johnny Waite for a duck. The University's cricket coach, ex-Transvaal, Western Province and England cricketer Peter Walker, once asked him, "Do you play any other games?" He replied, "I play a lot of rugby" to which Walker commented, "I suggest you concentrate on rugby then".

He played at centre for the Transvaal rugby team (with 12 Springboks), appearing against the 1960 New Zealand All Blacks and the 1962 British Lions.

His fellow-cricketers dubbed him "Bunter" because of his spectacles, which he wore because he was short-sighted, owlish look, stout build and undeniable facial resemblance to the Greyfriars schoolboy Billy Bunter, created by Frank Richards.

He began his career as a batsman who could keep wicket, making his first-class debut at the age of 19 for Transvaal B against Griqualand West at De Beers Stadium, Kimberley, in November 1959 where he made an impressive 72 in his only innings. He played in all six Currie Cup B Section matches for Transvaal B, keeping wicket in two matches.

He was promoted to the Transvaal senior side the following season and hit his maiden first-class century, 110 not out, in the final Currie Cup match of the season against North-Eastern Transvaal at Willowmoore Park in Benoni.

In June and July 1961 he was a member of Stanley Murphy's private team, the Fezelas, on a tour of England, Scotland and Ireland. A youthful side, which included Colin Bland, Denis Lindsay and Peter Pollock, was captained by Roy McLean in an attempt to encourage a more adventurous style of play in South African cricket. He scored 110 against Gloucestershire and made two centuries in non-first-class matches.

He was selected for the first Test against New Zealand at Kingsmead in December 1961, with seven of the South African team making their Test debut. Opening the innings with skipper Jackie McGlew he made 15 and 10 in South Africa's 30-run victory. After scores of 47 and 45 in the second Test at Wanderers Stadium, he scored his first half-century (51) in the Third Test at Newlands. He was third in the South African batting averages with 330 runs (avg 36.66) and took five catches in the series but failed to take a wicket from 43 overs.

At this stage many critics felt he took too many chances with lifting balls outside the off-stump, yet he invariably prospered with his often air-borne cuts to third man.

On his first tour for South Africa in Australasia in 1963/64 he established himself as one of the most exciting players in world cricket scoring 1900 runs (avg 63.33) and taking 28 wickets (avg 31.85) in 18 first-class matches. He hit six centuries in Australia including 209 against a Combined XI in Perth, the highest score by a South African in Australia.

He was at his best in the Tests, heading the batting averages in the five matches against Australia with 603 runs (avg 75.37) and finishing second to Colin Bland in the three Tests in New Zealand with 295 runs (avg 49.16). He was second to Peter Pollock in the Test bowling averages in Australia with seven wickets (avg 32.85).

By scoring 114 in the drawn first Test in Brisbane he became the first South African to score a hundred in his first Test against Australia. With 109 and 54 in the second Test at Melbourne he remains the only South African to score hundreds in his first two Tests against Australia. In the historic fourth Test at Adelaide Oval he played a major role in South Africa's ten-wicket victory which levelled the series. He hit 201 (27 fours, 392 minutes) and 47 not out and took 3-6 in the Australian second innings. With Graeme Pollock (175) he added 341 runs in 283 minutes to set what was then a record for any South African Test partnership.

During the English summer of 1964 he was professional for Accrington CC in the Lancashire League scoring exactly 1000 runs (avg 62.50) the highest aggregate by any batsman in the league and taking 68 wickets (avg 13.75).

Along with most of his team-mates he failed in the innings defeat in the first Test against Mike Smith's England team at Kingsmead in 1964/65, scoring 2 and 0. England were content to hold on to their lead and South Africa were unable to force a result in the remaining four Tests played on lifeless pitches. He scored 558 runs (avg 55.80) in the series, including 138 and 78 at Newlands in the third Test, being subjected to abuse by off-spinner Fred Titmus, who felt he had been caught in the gully during his first innings and should have walked. No England player applauded his century.

He was vice-captain to Peter van der Merwe on the 1965 tour to England and finished fourth in the first-class batting averages with 971 runs (avg 38.84) and was also fourth in the Test batting averages making 184 runs (avg 30.66).

His job took to him to Port Elizabeth for the 1965/66 season and he captained Eastern Province in all six of their Currie Cup matches. He was the province's most successful batsman, amassing 702 runs (avg 63.81), his career-best Currie Cup season aggregate.

He returned to Transvaal in 1966/67 and helped his side inflict the first defeat on an Australian cricket team in South Africa, scoring 79 and 18 and taking two wickets. Appearing in all five Tests he disappointed with the bat, scoring 186 runs (avg 20.66) but took 15 wickets (avg 21.60). In the Second Test at Newlands he took a Test career-best 5-85.

Outside the Tests he was in top form and hit 212 out of 367 in the innings and 60-run victory against Rhodesia at Wanderers Stadium, his highest first-class score in South Africa.

In the English summers of 1967 and 1968 he played in two and four matches respectively for the Rest of the World with his best efforts being 97 and 91 (adding 187 and 66 for the first wicket with West Indian opening batsman Seymour Nurse) against an England XI in Scarborough in 1967 and a brilliant 153 in 145 minutes against Kent at Canterbury the following year, adding 225 for the first wicket with Barry Richards (81) in the second innings.

He joined Western Province in the summer of 1968 after they had finished third in the Currie Cup B Section in 1967/68. With him at the helm the change in fortunes was dramatic as Western Province topped the B Section and gained promotion. In the 1969/70 season his newly promoted charges shared the Currie Cup with Transvaal. The crowds came flocking back to Newlands as the Barlow era produced exciting contests and nail-biting finishes. He believed attack was the best form of defence. Seemingly suicidal declarations turned inevitable draws into thrilling finishes. He used spinners in aggressive and effective roles. Spartan training methods, new to cricket, produced superbly fit players so that fielding reached new heights.

After several near-misses, Western Province won the Currie Cup outright in 1974/75 for the first time since 1955/56. He was a brilliant player and highly successful captain in one-day cricket and led Western Province to victory in the 1969/70, 1970/71 and 1972/73 Gillette Cup finals. His highest score of 186 against Eastern Province in the 1969/70 semi-final at Wanderers Stadium remains the highest one-day score by a Western Province batsman.

Contrary to newspaper reports, then and in the future, he claimed the South African captaincy was never an issue for him. In South Africa's 4-0 clean-sweep against Australia he produced superb performances in all four Tests. In the first he hit 127 and caught four batsmen in the 170-run victory which was their first against Australia at Newlands. At Kingsmead he destroyed the Australian top-order in their first innings total of 157, taking three wickets in ten balls, as the score went from 44-0 to 48-4. He took 3-24 and then 3-63 in the second innings.

A century (110) and two more wickets came his way in the 307-run victory at Wanderers Stadium and he ended the series with scores of 73 and 27 at St George's Park where he put on 157 and 73 for the first wicket with Barry Richards and also took three wickets. Five of his six Test centuries were against Australia, which has only been matched by Graeme Pollock, and his 1149 runs against Australia has been bettered only by Pollock's 1453 runs. Thirty-three of his 40 Test wickets were against the Australians.

Selected to tour England as vice-captain to Ali Bacher on the cancelled tour to England in 1970 he had to be content with playing in the England against the Rest of the World "Test" series. He hit centuries at Lord's (119) and Trent Bridge (142) where he took 5-66 in England's first innings. At Headingley he took 7-64 and 5-78 (12-142 his career-best match figures) and in the first innings took four wickets in five balls (a hat-trick followed by another wicket two balls later). In five matches he topped the bowling averages with 20 wickets (avg 19.80) and totalled 353 runs (avg 39.22).

He was chosen as vice-captain to Ali Bacher for the tour to Australia in 1971/72 but withdrew for business reasons before the tour was called off.

He captained a SA President's XI against Derrick Robins XI in 1974/75 and the SA Invitation XI in three matches against the International Wanderers in 1975/76. There is no doubt he would have been the captain had South Africa played Test cricket in the 1970s.

He played for Derbyshire from 1976 to 1978, becoming the county's fourth captain in five seasons in June 1976. Under his leadership they emerged from mediocrity, helped by a winter fitness programme. His best year was 1976 when he scored 1162 runs (avg 29.05) and hit a career-best 217 against Surrey at Ilkeston. He also took 46 wickets (avg 19.50).

He played World Series Cricket in Australia in the 1977/78 and 1978/79 seasons. As Director of Coaching at Newlands he had laid the foundations for an efficient coaching network and although Western Province won the Currie Cup in 1977/78, by the end of the 1978/79 season concern was being expressed about crumbling morale and playing and coaching discipline. In an important step towards the acceptance of professional cricket he was appointed WPCU's promoter of cricket. He was reinstated as Director of Coaching as well as captain and tied down exciting young players in Le Roux, Lamb and Kirsten with lucrative contracts.

Western Province had one of their worst seasons since he moved to Cape Town when they finished third in the 1980/81 Currie Cup. On the playing side, his protégés rebelled against the disciplined loyalty he demanded, while the administration began limiting his powers. He left without fanfare for Boland. At the time he held the Western Province record for most runs (5024), most 100s (12), most catches (111) and most captaincies (79).

He captained Boland in all their Bowl matches in seasons 1981/82 and 1982/83 and in the former they won the competition. Against Eastern Province B at Uitenhage he carved his way to a remarkable 202 not out, at the age of 41.

Although Boland failed to win the Bowl competition in 1982/83 he ended his career by scoring 472 runs (avg 42.90) and making his 43rd first-class hundred (153) against Orange Free State at Stellenbosch. At the time of his retirement, in Currie Cup matches only Graeme Pollock had scored more than his 7881 runs, only Vintcent van der Bijl and Mike Procter had exceeded his 317 wickets, while Graeme Pollock alone had taken more than his 152 catches.

In 1990 he was given a three-year contract as Senior Coach at Gloucestershire, but stayed for only two years, returning to manage his wine farm in the Cape, after laying the foundations for Gloucestershire's highly successful one-day era. In South Africa he coached Free State in 1991/92 when they won their first major competition, the Nissan Shield. He coached Transvaal in 1992/93 and 1993/94, in the former season winning the Benson & Hedges Series. In 1994 when Bob Woolmer replaced Mike Procter as South Africa's coach he was on the short list along with Duncan Fletcher. He was coach of Griqualand West in 1998/99.

In August 1999 he was appointed Bangladesh's Director of Development on a two-year contract but in April 2000 he suffered a stroke at home in the Gulshan district of Dhaka. It left him partially paralysed and he spent time in hospital in Dhaka, Singapore and Cape Town. At the ICC meeting in June 2000 Test status was conferred on Bangladesh. He returned to Bangladesh but his contract was terminated in December 2000.

He was a liberal voice in the conservative South African political establishment of the 1980s. In 1980 he stood for the Progressive Federal Party against ex-Western Province cricketer John Wiley, a hard-liner in the ruling National Party, in a Parliamentary by-election for the Simon's Town constituency. He became the Director of the South African Sports Office in London in the 1980s, to the dismay of many, arguing that apartheid was starting to crumble and that official sporting contact was preferable to the "rebel" tours.

While playing for Boland he ran a pig farm at Klapmuts in the Western Cape, then a wine farm just outside Cape Town which he sold to his second wife when they were divorced.

In 1996 he bought another wine farm in the Robertson area of the Western Cape to provide for his and wife Cally's retirement. He spent money in improving the farm. After his stroke his insurance company refused to pay his medical bills, due to "non-disclosure" and he had to put the farm up for sale. He received less than its market value and tried in vain to get work as a cricket coach. Due to Hylton Ackerman's efforts in arranging a benefit dinner for him in Cape Town in 2001 he was able to leave South Africa without any debts.

He moved to Cally's mother's home in North Wales and contacted the North Wales Cricket Development Office who employed him as a coach on a part-time basis. In addition to his work with the Welsh development squad, he coached and encouraged young and first team players at Marchwiel & Wrexham Cricket Club.

He died whilst on holiday, visiting his stepdaughter in Jersey, after a fall. He suffered a cut on his nose which wouldn't stop bleeding. After about 20 minutes in the General Hospital in St Helier he had a stroke. He was put on a ventilator but didn't regain consciousness.

The South African players wore black armbands throughout the third Test against Australia at Sydney in January 2006 in his memory. Memorial services were held at Pretoria Boys High School, at Newlands, where a portion of his ashes was scattered, and at St John's Wood Church in London. A portion of his ashes was also scattered on the PBHS wicket.

His first wife, with whom he had a son Craig and a daughter Susan, was Helen Wheelwright; his second Julianne Bailey; and his third in 1998, Cally Carroll.

In 283 first-class matches, he scored 18 212 runs (avg 39.16), with 43 centuries and 86 half-centuries. He took 571 wickets (avg 24.14) and held 335 catches. In 100 List A limited overs matches, he scored 3013 runs (avg 31.71) and took 162 wickets (avg 18.20).

ERIC HERMAN BAUSER. Born Pretoria 7.6.1934. Died Dullstroom, Mpumalanga 27.2.2003 aged 68. A right-hand batsman and a leg-spinner, who gave the ball a tremendous amount of air and bowled extremely slowly, he made three first-class Currie Cup B Section appearances for North-Eastern Transvaal in 1962/63. His debut came against Rhodesia in Salisbury where he took a career-best 4-28.

He was educated at Pretoria Boys High School and was a prolific wicket-taker at club level for Iscor with Syd Burke being one of his team-mates. In three first-class matches he scored 94 runs (avg 31.33) and took seven wickets (avg 28.85).

JAMES THOMAS "JACKIE" BOTTEN. Born Pretoria 21.6.1938. Died Unitas Hospital, Lyttelton, Centurion, Gauteng 14.5.2006 aged 67. A right-hand, hard-hitting, lower order batsman and right-arm fast-medium bowler whose rapid and meteoric rise to fame compared favourably with almost any other player in the history of South African first-class cricket.

He was introduced to the game at Brooklyn Primary School. Denis Lindsay, who remained a close friend for the rest of his life, saw to it that his father, who played three Tests for South Africa, advised him whenever possible.

At Pretoria Boys High School he was a star performer for the First XI, playing alongside future Test cricketers Eddie Barlow and Glen Hall, then captaining the side in his matriculation year in 1956. He remembered four words that Mr Hofmeyr rammed into him, "action, variation, swing, direction". He was selected for the North-Eastern Transvaal Nuffield XI in 1955 but the competition was cancelled due to a polio epidemic. He represented his province in Bloemfontein in January 1956 and took 21 wickets in four matches to earn his South African Schools' XI cap. He was again selected for SA Schools in Bulawayo in January 1957, where took 8-32 against Orange Free State.

He did not play a winter sport at school due to his footballing commitments with Arcadia Shepherds in the National Football League. He captained Northern Transvaal Under-16 to victory in the SA Schools tournament at Durban in 1954. At 18 he played for the provincial side. By 1959 he had played against Preston North End, Bolton Wanderers, Ajax (Holland), Katanga (Belgian Congo) and Beira.

Broad-shouldered and strong, he bowled at a lively pace and could move the ball either way through the air and off the pitch. He had a great out-swinger and varied his pace skillfully, slipping in a devastating slower ball (an off-break which usually beat the batsman in flight), and an in-swinging yorker or occasional in-dipper (a fast off-break) with equal facility.

In 1957/58, aged 19, he made his debut for North-Eastern Transvaal. Record-breaking feats in 1958/59 established him as the spearhead of the attack. Although he ended on the losing side in his first three Currie Cup games he took 22 wickets (avg 13.63). The next match against Border, at Jan Smuts in East London, saw him record match figures of 12-122. Against Griqualand West, on his home ground at Loftus Versfeld, he was virtually unplayable in achieving his career-best innings and match analysis 15-49 (12-6-23-9 and 20-8-26-6), which remain the best innings and match figures for the province. He finished the season with a Currie Cup record of 55 wickets (avg 10.09), which has subsequently only been beaten by five other bowlers. Banned from bowling after taking two wickets in the Border first innings during the final Currie Cup fixture, after the umpires said he was damaging the pitch with his follow-through, he threw the ball and hit an umpire on the shin.

He played for a Combined North-Eastern Transvaal/Griqualand West/Orange Free State team against Transvaal at Bloemfontein, in one of two matches arranged as national trials. He proved that his success was not due to inferior batting in the B Section and in the closing half-hour of the opening day, after the Combined XI had scored 239, he dismissed the top five batsmen and finished with 8-68. His season's total of 63 wickets beat Hugh Tayfield's record of 56 first-class wickets by a South African bowler in a home season, a record which has since been beaten only by Vintcent van der Bijl on three occasions, Joe Partridge and Dale Steyn.

Although he never again quite approached the phenomenal successes of 1958/59 he continued to be a prolific wicket-taken for the province. He had another highly successful season in 1960/61, the only season in which all ten teams played in one Currie Cup log, taking 34 wickets (avg 14.11). In June and July 1961 he was a member of the Fezelas private team in England, Scotland and Ireland. He played in the three first-class matches taking 21 wickets (avg 11.57), including 8-35 from 20.5 overs against Gloucestershire at Bristol.

He played in three first-class matches against Mike Smith's MCC touring side in the 1964/65 season taking 11 wickets in total. He received a long-deserved call-up to international cricket and toured the United Kingdom in 1965. In 12 first-class matches he took 33 wickets (avg 24.78) but with a best of only 3-24 and scored 227 runs (avg 18.91). He appeared in all three Tests and although his bowling figures of eight wickets (avg 42.12) were nothing special, seven of his victims were top-order batsmen. His six Test innings produced 65 runs (avg 10.83) with 33 in the first innings of the first Test at Lord's his highest. He hit his career-best score of 90 against Leicestershire, at Leicester, when putting on 181 runs with Ali Bacher (119), setting a ninth-wicket partnership record for a South African team in England. It was felt by some that he was a better bowler before a coach told him he must get his arm higher. Apparently he did so but his out-swinger was not nearly as effective thereafter.

It was remarkable he was to appear in only three Tests for South Africa but in his prime he had to compete with Neil Adcock, Peter Heine, Peter Pollock, "Goofy" Lawrence and several other fine new-ball bowlers, but there was a strong argument that he should have toured England in 1960 instead of Jim Pothecary or Geoff Griffin and Australia, with Trevor Goddard's 1963/64 side, instead of Clive Halse.

He captained North-Eastern Transvaal from 1969/70 until his retirement at the end of the 1971/72 season. On retiring from first-class cricket only Jack Waddington (317) had taken more than his 280 Currie Cup wickets. He remains the only South African bowler to have twice taken nine wickets in an innings in South African first-class cricket and his returns of 9-23 against Griqualand West in 1958/59 and 9-29 against Rhodesia in 1963/64 have only been bettered in Currie Cup cricket by Ernie Vogler (10-26) and Stephen Jefferies (10-59). Only Vogler (16-38) and "Buster" Nupen (16-136) have achieved better match figures in a Currie Cup match than his 15-49 against Griqualand West.

He was a member of the old North-Eastern Transvaal board and played a role in the embryonic plan to launch the formation of the Northern Transvaal Cricket Union in July 1970. Surprisingly he had a major dispute with Denis Lindsay, a member of Eastern Transvaal CU.

In club cricket he played for Pretoria Boys High School Old Boys and in the mid-late sixties would be bowling at one end with Glen Hall at the other and sides would often get bowled out for under 100. He lived in Pretoria and became a successful property developer.

He died of multiple organ failure, from an infection that set in after a colon operation. He is survived by his wife Louise and their daughters Debbie, Joanne, Lindsey, son Alan, who also attended Pretoria BHS, and twin sister Marie.

In 98 first-class matches, he scored 1775 runs (avg 15.84) and took 399 wickets (avg 20.36), taking five wickets in an innings on 24 occasions, with five ten-wicket returns.

DEREK RUSSELL BRUORTON. Born Grahamstown, Cape Province 5.11.1928. Died Westville, Durban 19.2.2003 aged 74. A right-hand middle order batsman and slow left-arm bowler who played in ten first-class matches for Transvaal. He made his debut against the eventual Currie Cup champions Natal at Kingsmead in December 1951, top-scoring with a career-best 88. In his five Currie Cup appearances he scored 345 runs (avg 43.12) to finish third in Transvaal's Currie Cup batting averages behind Russell Endean and Eric Rowan.

He played in one friendly and four Currie Cup matches the following season.

Educated at St Andrew's College in Grahamstown, he qualified as a doctor at Witwatersrand Medical School and practiced industrial medicine in Natal for 35 years. In ten first-class matches he scored 459 runs (avg 35.30) and took 5 wickets (avg 41.20).

RICHARD HENRY MASON CORIN. Born Wynberg, Cape Town 5.9.1930. Died Boksburg, Gauteng 23.3.1996 aged 65. A right-hand opening batsman and occasional wicketkeeper who played in all six of Transvaal B's Currie Cup matches in 1960/61. This was the only season in which all ten teams played in one competition. His highest score was 75 against Border at the Wanderers Stadium. He kept wicket in three of his appearances. In six first-class matches, he scored 345 runs (avg 28.75), held 14 catches and made one stumping.

RICHARD PETER "DICK" DAVIS. Born Pietermaritzburg 30.12.1919. Died Newlands, Cape Town 20.7.2003 aged 83. A right-hand tail-end batsman and slow left-arm bowler who made his first-class debut for Western Province in 1951/52 and played in Western Province's final three Currie Cup matches of the 1952/53 season in which they won the Currie Cup outright for the first time since 1931/32. His best figures were 3-25 against Orange Free State at Newlands. In four first-class matches, he scored 26 runs (avg 13.00) and took 10 wickets (avg 34.60).

THOMAS ARTHUR DEAN. Born Gosport, Hampshire, England 21.11.1920. Died Alexandria, Eastern Cape 4.6.2004 aged 83. Tall, fair-haired and strong, he bowled leg-spinners and googlies at a lively pace. After being educated at St Charles College, Marist Brothers, in Pietermaritzburg he played for Wanderers CC (Johannesburg). He returned to the county of his birth in 1936 and made his first-class debut in 1939. In his second first-class match against Worcestershire he took four wickets in five balls including the hat-trick and in the next match against Yorkshire he had a spell of five wickets for eight runs. He was a fearless forward short-leg fielder and against Essex at Colchester caught seven catches in a row.

Just as he was reaching his peak the Second World War broke out and he served as a naval gunner in many parts of the world. He never recovered his 1939 form, although in 1946 he had his best bowling analysis of 7-51 (match 10-129) against Derbyshire at Ilkeston.

After a spell as a professional in Devon he took up a coaching position at St Andrew's College in Grahamstown in 1955, where future Springbok captain Peter van der Merwe was the First XI captain. The following year he took over as coach at Grey High School in Port Elizabeth. After 23 years of coaching at Grey he was appointed Secretary of the Eastern Province Cricket Union, a position he held for four years, being the province's first full-time employee. He was groundsman at the same time. He coached the Eastern Province side in the mid-eighties. He made only one first-class appearance in South Africa, the final one of his career, in a friendly for Eastern Province against Border at St George's Park in 1956/57.

Thousands of schoolboys passed under his eagle eye. When asked about the great Graeme Pollock he replied, "I must take the credit for not coaching him. He was a 'freak' and was best left to develop on his own."

In 29 first-class matches he scored 285 runs (avg 8.63), took 54 wickets (avg 31.59) and held 31 catches.

DERRYCK MORRIS DINKELMAN. Born Hillcrest, Natal 1.8.1925. Died Bellville, Western Cape 21.3.1998 aged 72.A left-hand batsman and slow left-arm bowler who made two first-class appearances for Natal, both at The Oval in Pietermaritzburg. Against the 1948/49 MCC touring team he took 5-113 and 3-112. He played rugby for Natal in 1948. In two first-class matches he scored 12 runs without being dismissed and took 9 wickets (avg 26.44).

CHARLES MURRAY SHAND GARDNER. Born Grahamstown, Cape Province 7.10.1913. Died Overport, Durban 2.7.2001 aged 87. A right-hand opening batsman who played in ten Currie Cup matches between 1931/32 and 1936/37, six for Eastern Province and four for Border. He made his highest score of 51 for Eastern Province against Border at the Pirates Ground, Johannesburg, in 1931/32. He gained a law degree at Rhodes University and had a distinguished war career serving in the South African Air Force as Lt Colonel Officer Commanding 40 Squadron, flying Hurricanes and Spitfires in the Western Desert.

In ten first-class matches he scored 295 runs (avg 14.75).

GLENHAM GRANGER. Born Durban 24.2.1927. Died Durban 8.7.2005 aged 78. A leg-break/googly bowler who played for Eastern Province against Transvaal in January 1952, scoring 25 and taking no wickets for 47 runs.

NORMAN HALL. Born Jeppe, Johannesburg 15.12.1901. Died (place unknown) 1.1.1998 aged 96. He played one first-class match for Transvaal against the Australian touring team at The Wanderers in January 1936, scoring 3 and 0 not out and taking 1-74. The scorecard in Duffus' *South African Cricket 1927-1947* recorded his name as "NF Hall" confusing him with Norman F Hall, a motor dealer in Johannesburg. He died aged 96 years 17 days which at the time placed him fifth on the list of oldest known living South African first-class cricketers.

DAVID ERNEST JAMES IRONSIDE. Born Lourenco Marques, Mozambique 2.5.1925. Died Bordesley Green, Birmingham, Warwickshire, England 21.8.2005 aged 80. A tireless right-arm fast-medium bowler whose movement both through the air and off the pitch brought him many wickets off quite a short run. He was strongly built with his most deadly ball a sharp outswinger which he bowled from so close to the stumps that he often knocked the bails off in his delivery stride. It was said he injured his knee in the War with the result his leg swung outwards when he bowled. John Waite stood up to him and took many brilliant stumpings, from off-cutters bowled on the leg stump.

He made his first-class debut for Transvaal in a Currie Cup fixture against Western Province, at Ellis Park in December 1947. He played in six out of seven Currie Cup matches, which saw Transvaal finish runners-up to Natal, taking seven wickets (avg 40.14). His next first-class appearance was in 1951/52, a single Currie Cup appearance, and it was not until 1952/53 that he established himself in the Transvaal side. After being relegated at the end of the previous season, his 29 wickets (avg 18.06) in five Currie Cup matches helped Transvaal regain A Section status. In successive matches at Ellis Park he took 6-29 from 19 overs in the first innings against Rhodesia and a career-best 21.4-5-36-7 against Border.

In 1953/54 accurate, probing bowling against the New Zealanders brought him 6-85 from 33 overs. He clean bowled star batsmen Bert Sutcliffe and John Reid in a drawn game.

Although South Africa won the first Test at Kingsmead by an innings and 58 runs, their first at home for 23 years, he replaced Anton Murray for the second Test at Ellis Park. In a dramatic Test he produced a magnificent performance on Test debut with analyses of 19-4-51-5 and 20.5-10-37-3. He made his highest Test score of 13 in the first innings total of 271. In South Africa's 132-run victory Neil Adcock (match 8-87) bowled one of Test cricket's most lethal spells on the second day as Chapple and Poore were bowled off their chests and Sutcliffe (struck on the head) and Miller (struck on the chest) were put in hospital.

On a dead Newlands pitch he displayed his tenacity and skill in the third Test, taking 4-117 in 46.3 overs in the New Zealand total of 505. He took a further three wickets, at a cost of 70 runs, in the fourth Test at Ellis Park but missed the final Test at St George's Park because of a back injury and was seen no more in Test cricket. In his three Test appearances he scored 37 runs (avg 18.50) in four innings and took 15 wickets (avg 18.33) and one catch.

Over the next two seasons he gave his all for the Transvaal attack, taking 25 wickets (avg 21.84) in 1954/55 and 22 (avg 18.81) in 1955/56.

He was educated at Parktown Boys High and was selected for Transvaal Schools and South African Schools in 1942 and also played soccer at Parktown. Initially he was a leg-break bowler but switched to fast-medium when an opening bowler fell ill.

He joined the SAAF in 1943 where he served as an observer/navigator in the 16th and 19th Squadron Beaufighter squads and saw active service in Italy, Yugoslavia and Egypt.

He played cricket for Wanderers CC (Johannesburg), where he became an honorary life member. He was an active sportsman well into his sixties. He played golf for Wanderers Golf Club off a 10/11 handicap and social tennis. After he retired from cricket he built up his accountancy firm but watched cricket on television and maintained contact with his former Transvaal and South African team-mates, especially John Waite.

He moved to England in 2002 with his second wife Gabriel and died in Heartlands Hospital, after being admitted with a burst abdominal aneurysm. He is survived by his second wife, Gabriel, son Robin, daughters Darryl and Jacqui and grandchildren Robyn and David. His first wife, Joyce, predeceased him in 2001.

In 31 first-class matches, he scored 135 runs (avg 6.42) and took 130 wickets (avg 21.13).

PETER DANIEL JAFFER. Born Cape Town 3.5.1910. Died Cape Town 20.10.1996 aged 86. A middle order batsman who made ten first-class appearances for Western Province between 1949/50 and 1953/54. He made a career-best 128 against Orange Free State at Newlands in 1952/53. He played soccer for South Africa. In ten first-class matches he scored 474 runs (avg 31.60) and took 1 wicket (avg 67.00).

IAN EDWARD FARQUAHAR KIRBY. Born Hopetown, Cape Province 23.10.1922. Died (place and exact date unknown) 2004. A wicketkeeper who was educated at Selborne College in

East London. He served as a Lieutenant with the 114 Squadron, South African Air Force, for four years during World War Two and was awarded the DFC.

He settled in the Orange Free State and made his first-class debut against Border in the Currie Cup match in December 1946 at Ramblers in Bloemfontein. In 1947/48 against Eastern Province at Ramblers he made a career-best 119 when opening the innings. He played in 25 first-class matches until the end of the 1956/57 season. He re-appeared seven years later to captain Orange Free State in their final two Currie Cup B Section matches in 1963/64. He made one rugby appearance for OFS in 1946, won the unofficial provincial tennis singles title and represented OFS at hockey and badminton. He worked in the accountancy profession.

In 27 first-class matches he scored 1376 runs (avg 28.08) including two centuries, held 40 catches and made six stumpings.

JOHN CHRISTOPHER LAURIE. Born King William's Town, Cape Province 7.4.1938. Died Pinelands, Cape Town 13.5.2006 aged 68. A right-hand batsman and right-arm medium seam bowler who played in three Currie Cup B Section matches for Border in 1963/64, scoring 87 runs (avg 21.75) and taking 3 wickets (avg 38.33).

DENIS THOMSON LINDSAY. Born Benoni, Transvaal 4.9.1939. Died Morningside Clinic, Sandton, Johannesburg 30.11.2005 aged 66. A tall, broad-shouldered right-hand attacking batsman who served the game with distinction on and off the field. He was a talented all-round sportsman, quick on his feet and excelled at the hook and cut. However he could produce every shot in the book and some of his most memorable strokes were soaring drives off fast bowlers. A neat and agile wicketkeeper he was equally at home standing up or back.

He was the son of JD (Johnny) Lindsay, also a wicketkeeper, who played for Transvaal and North-Eastern Transvaal (1933/34-1948/49) and in the first three Tests against England in 1947. Johnny also played soccer for Transvaal and Huddersfield Town and hockey for Transvaal. They are one of only five instances of a father and son both playing Test cricket for South Africa and remain the only father and son who have kept wicket for any country in Test cricket. His great-uncle was NV (Nevil) Lindsay who made one home Test appearance against Australia in 1921/22 and played in an "unofficial" Test against SB Joel's XI in 1924/25.

From Merchiston Preparatory School he moved to Maritzburg College. He made his debut for the first XI in 1954 as a 14-year-old. He played for Natal Schools in the January 1957 Nuffield Week in Bulawayo. He attributed much of his success to the sports master "Tiger" Kent. Physically he was a late-developer who blossomed after leaving school. He attended Natal University for 12 months where he represented the Varsity at cricket and soccer and played for Maritzburg Old Collegians under South Africa captain Jackie McGlew.

He returned to the East Rand in 1957 to join his father in the family sports shop and played for Benoni CC (later Benoni Northerns). He made his first-class debut aged 19 years 3 months for North-Eastern Transvaal vs Orange Free State at Willowmoore Park in Benoni in December 1958. In 1959/60 he made his maiden first-class century, 116, batting at number three, in the first innings against Orange Free State at Ramblers, Bloemfontein.

He played for North-Eastern Transvaal (later Northern Transvaal) throughout his career and only six of his 60 Currie Cup appearances were in the A Section.

In June and July 1961 he was a member of the Fezelas private team on a tour of England, Scotland and Ireland. He played in the three first-class matches (147 runs, avg 49.00). Against Essex at Chelmsford he produced one of the most spectacular examples of the new attacking philosophy in the six-wicket victory. With 210 runs required for victory he batted with great vigour throughout his innings of 83 not out. He played the first ball of what proved to be the final over from leg-spinner Bill Greensmith circumspectly back to the bowler. He then sent the next five deliveries soaring over the fence to equal AW Wellard's twice-performed world record feat for Somerset in 1936 and 1938 of five sixes off consecutive balls. Future Test captain Peter van der Merwe said, "It was nearly lunch-time and we needed fewer than 30 runs. Denis hit every one of those sixes dead straight and finished the match so that we could have a relaxing lunch. The success of South African teams in the 1960s owed much to that tour."

A brilliant innings of 77 (16 fours) for NE Transvaal against John Reid's 1961/62 touring New Zealand team earned him a place in the SA Colts side against the New Zealanders at Jan Smuts in East London. John Waite was in a class of his own as the Test wicketkeeper so all he could do was hope to obtain a Test place on the strength of his batting and fielding and, in the meantime, to concentrate on improving his wicketkeeping skills so he was ready to lodge a claim when Waite decided to call it a day.

He was selected as second-string wicketkeeper for the 1963/64 tour of Australia and New Zealand tour but by now was a true all-rounder. In 12 first-class matches he scored 500 runs (avg 35.71) with 28 catches and four stumpings. Against South Australia at Adelaide Oval he scored 104 (140 minutes, 4 sixes, 14 fours), becoming only the fifth South African batsman to score a hundred on first-class debut in Australia. He made three Test appearances against both Australia and New Zealand with 123 runs (avg 41.00) and six catches against Australia and 86 runs (avg 17.20) and four catches, three of them as wicketkeeper, against New Zealand.

In the First Test at Woolloongabba, Brisbane, he made his Test debut as a specialist batsman scoring 17. He was recalled for the fourth Test as wicketkeeper, replacing the injured Waite. Although Waite returned for the fifth Test at Sydney he kept his place in the team as a batsman and made 65 and held two catches in the field. In New Zealand he kept wicket in the final Test at Auckland even though Waite was in the side.

Before the visit of Mike Smith's MCC side in 1964/65 he scored 107 not out for South Africa against The Rest at Wanderers Stadium where 618 runs for four wickets were scored on the first day, the most by one side in a day in South Africa. He and Colin Bland put on 267 for the fifth wicket in the final 99 minutes. He played in the first three Tests, with 50 in the second innings of the Third Test at Newlands his only fifty. He also held six catches.

He took over from Waite as the number one wicketkeeper for the tour to England in 1965. Although South Africa's win in the Second Test at Trent Bridge, Nottingham, was brought about mainly by the performances of Peter and Graeme Pollock, Peter Pollock said later, "A brilliant leg-side stumping in the second innings by Denis to dismiss Colin Cowdrey for 20 off Atholl McKinnon was a key moment in the match." In the three Tests he scored a disappointing 92 runs in six innings (avg 15.33) with a highest score of 40 in the First Test at Lord's. He batted at number three before opening with Tiger Lance in the second innings at Trent Bridge and with Eddie Barlow in both innings at The Oval.

He had a golden summer in 1966/67, scoring a career-best 216 against Transvaal B at Wanderers Stadium before playing in the Test series against Bobby Simpson's Australians. He had passed fifty only twice in his first 20 Test innings, scoring 415 runs (avg 20.75). What followed in the five Tests was astonishing. South Africa was in trouble several times when he came to the wicket and his big innings were played when runs were urgently needed. At least three of them changed the course of the match within a short time. He hit 16 sixes in the five Tests and his 606 runs (avg 86.57) in seven innings, with three hundreds and two fifties, remains the world record for the most runs scored by a wicketkeeper in a Test series.

The First Test at Wanderers Stadium produced arguably the finest moment of his Test career as South Africa's 233-run success was their first home victory over Australia. After top-scoring with 69 out of 199 in the first innings and adding 110 runs for the sixth wicket with Tiger

Lance, Australia scored 325 in reply. He came in to bat in the second innings with the score on 268-5 and with Lance added 81 runs for the sixth wicket and then a record 221 runs with skipper Peter van der Merwe for the seventh wicket which remains the highest seventh wicket stand for South Africa against Australia. His maiden Test century of 182 (227 deliveries, 5 sixes, 1 five, 25 fours) was the highest of his three Test centuries and remains the best by a South African batsman at Wanderers Stadium and also by any South African wicketkeeper. He let loose a barrage of thrilling strokes. South Africa were eventually bowled out for 620, then their highest in Tests and the third-highest second innings total in all Test matches at the time.

In the Australian first innings he equalled the then world Test wicketkeeping record of six dismissals (all catches) in an innings. With two catches in the second innings he set a South African Test record of eight dismissals in a match.

He made 137 in the third Test at Kingsmead and 131 off 95 balls in the fourth Test at the Wanderers Stadium. He held 24 catches in the series.

He did little of note over the next two summers. The visit of Bill Lawry's Australian side from January to March 1970 was to be South Africa's last Test series for 22 years. Prior to the Australians arriving he scored 495 runs (avg 82.50). Dennis Gamsy kept wicket in the first two Tests but Lindsay was recalled for the final two Tests. He made 43 and 60 in the fourth Test at St George's Park as South Africa completed a 4-0 whitewash.

South Africa lost only two of the 19 Test matches he played in. He was in the field for four Tests, taking three catches. In his final four Tests he did not concede a bye as 1580 runs were scored. His Test average of 37.66 remains the highest by a South African wicketkeeper. He was selected for the cancelled tours to England in 1970 and Australia in 1971/72.

He continued to play provincial cricket until 1973/74. He played a role in the Newlands "walk-off" after one ball had been bowled in the Republic Festival Match, between Rest of South Africa and Transvaal in March 1971, along with the Pollock brothers and Vintcent van der Bijl, in seeing Charles Fortune in the commentary box to ask his views on the players' statement before it was released.

His 195 first-class dismissals (168 catches, 27 stumpings) remains the record for North-Eastern/Northern Transvaal and in Currie Cup matches his 181 dismissals has only been exceeded by Noel Day with both totals including 12 catches taken as a fielder.

One-day cricket was only just getting under way as he neared the end of his career and in six Gillette Cup innings for North-Eastern Transvaal and Northern Transvaal he scored 160 runs (avg 40.00) and held three catches.

After his playing career, he was convener of selectors of the Under-13 national squad and filled in as manager/coach of Northern Transvaal at the beginning of the 1993/94 season before Anton Ferreira was appointed full-time coach. He was appointed Honorary Member of Northerns Cricket Union in 1991/92 and received the Christie Vlok Memorial Award in 1991. He coached extensively at numerous schools including Afrikaanse Hoer Seunskool (Pretoria) for three years and had a hand in the future of Jacques Rudolph and AB de Villiers. He regarded the latter as the best prospect he had seen since the days of Barry Richards and Mike Procter. He became Director of Cricket Coaching at Pretoria Boys High School and had hoped to accompany them on their 2005 tour to England but his illness meant he couldn't go.

In 2000 he was appointed to the ICC panel of match referees and he fulfilled this role in seven Tests (2001-2001/02) and 59 Limited Overs Internationals (2000/01-2003/04). He was widely acclaimed in 2001 when he decided to ban the West Indian vice-captain, Ridley Jacobs, for three games after Jacobs claimed a run-out by breaking the wicket but without the ball in his hands. He became a member of South Africa's panel of match referees in domestic cricket and in spite of his illness officiated in SuperSport and Standard Bank matches in November 2005.

During the winter months he kept goal for Benoni United and played hockey for Benoni Northerns. In the latter part of his working life he began to repair and then make cricket bats in partnership with fellow North-Eastern Transvaal cricketer Jim Pressdee.

He was diagnosed with cancer of the bladder early in 2005. He is survived by his wife Val, daughters Kim, Caren, Shelly and Deanne and by six grandchildren.

Peter van der Merwe said: "In the 1966/67 series the Australians knew that if they didn't get Denis early they were in trouble. He was a good team man who played in the true spirit of the game. I remember how Australian fast bowler Dave Renneberg peppered him with bouncers which he frequently hooked for six. The more sixes he hit off him the more beers they shared together after the day's play. He was like Adam Gilchrist, the current Australian wicketkeeper-batsman, renowned for his clean hitting".

In 124 first-class matches he scored 7074 runs (avg 35.54), hitting 12 centuries and 36 half-centuries. He held 292 catches and made 41 stumpings.

MANDLA SOLOMON VICTOR MAKOSANA. Born Cape Town 4.11.1948. Died Cape Town 3.8.2006 aged 57. Solomon Makosana was the President of the Western Province Cricket Association and a member of the General Council of the United Cricket Board of South Africa when he died after a long illness.

He trained as a teacher at Loveday College in Alice and achieved an honours degree in history at the University of Cape Town and a B.Ed at the University of the Western Cape. He taught at schools in Langa and Guguletu before being appointed principal of Nomlinganiselo Primary School in Nyanga. He was an Inspector of Education for the Mitchells Plain district before joining the Amy Biehl Foundation Trust as programme director in 2001, later being appointed Chief Executive Officer. He was the founder of the Black Principals Forum and a member of the Board of the SA Institute of Race Relations.

An opening batsman and slow-medium pace bowler, he played for Langa Cricket Club from 1972 and was involved in formulating the Passmore Trust. He later established Nyanga Cricket Club and also played for Guguletu Cricket Club. He formulated and helped establish the Black Township Forum and became the first black member of the Western Province Cricket Association in 1995/96. He was elected Deputy President in 2005 and took over as President in the same year when Norman Arendse was elected Vice-President of the United Cricket Board.

Cricket South Africa CEO, Gerald Majola, said: "Solomon Makosana was a pioneer of the development of cricket in the Western Cape and throughout South Africa. He was a champion of the previously disadvantaged and his administrative abilities opened many doors for the youth of these communities."

SHARAD MANDAN. Born Johannesburg 8.8.1985. Died Boksburg 2.7.2006 aged 20. A left-hand batsman and leg-break bowler who played in eight first-class matches for Easterns and one for an Easterns/Northerns XI, making his debut against KwaZulu-Natal at Willowmoore Park, Benoni, in October 2004 where he opened the batting and scored 1 and 2.

He played in six of Easterns' ten first-class matches in 2005/06, making a career-best 98 (107 minutes, 81 balls, 17 fours, 1 six, reaching his fifty off 35 balls) in the second innings of the 114-run loss against Griqualand West at De Beers Diamond Oval in Kimberley.

In one-day games he played seven times for Easterns with a career-best 115 not out opening the batting against Free State in what turned out to be his final innings for Easterns on 5 March 2006 at Goodyear Park, Bloemfontein.

He was educated at Wordsworth High School and represented Easterns in the 2001, 2002 and 2003 Coca-Cola Khaya Majola Cricket Weeks. He died instantly when he was involved in a motor accident.

In nine first-class matches he scored 274 runs (avg 18.26) and in seven List A limited overs matches he scored 167 runs (avg 33.40).

STUART VINE MORRIS. Born Rondebosch, Cape Town 26.5.1937. Died Westville, Durban 20.6.1998 aged 61. A left-hand batsman who appeared in four Currie Cup matches for Western Province in 1958/59 and 1959/60, scoring 59 runs (avg 9.83), with a highest score of 27. He was the brother of John (JD Morris - Western Province 1961/62-1962/63) and Richard (RET Morris - Western Province 1967/68-1978/79). The 1960 SA Annual Who's Who incorrectly states his surname as "Vine-Morris" instead of "Morris" with the former being an adopted surname.

GRANVILLE ARTHUR BRUCE MULLER. Born Rondebosch, Cape Town 4.11.1943. Died near Grabouw, Western Cape 5.6.1994 aged 50. A right-hand tail-end batsman and right-arm fast bowler who played in two first-class matches for Transvaal in 1964/65, scoring 1 run (avg 0.50) and taking 0-102. He died in a motor accident while driving back from his holiday house in Hermanus. His mother Helen and eldest daughter Kim also died in the accident.

PETER GRAY OBERG. Born Fulham, London, England 2.9.1921. Died Pinetown, KwaZulu-Natal 11.6.1999 aged 77. A right-hand batsman and wicketkeeper who played in Griqualand West's final four Currie Cup B Section matches of the 1962/63 season, scoring 29 runs (avg 7.25), holding five catches and making one stumping.

NEIL MACLEOD PATERSON. Born King William's Town, Cape Province 19.11.1930. Died Constantia, Cape Town 7.5.2000 aged 69. A competent and enthusiastic umpire who stood in 11 frst-class matches but was known more to thousands of schoolboys as a teacher and headmaster. He played cricket for UCT (1950-52), Old Grey CC (1953-55) and SA Universities (not first-class in 1952). He taught at Grey HS and subsequently at Dale College. He was appointed vice-principal at Lawson Brown High School (PE) and later was principal successively of Muizenberg High (Cape Town), Cambridge High (East London) and SACS (Cape Town) before relinquishing the post in 1983 to become a School Inspector.

PETER KEITH ROBINSON. Born Nottingham, England 15.2.1952. Died Westdene, Johannesburg 11.4.2006 aged 54. One of South Africa's leading cricket journalists, Robinson was diagnosed with cancer of the lung in October last year and underwent surgery. He made a rapid recovery and for months it appeared he had won the battle. In mid-March tumours were discovered on his brain and less than a month later he was dead.

He was educated at Queen's College in Queenstown, Alexandra High in Pietermaritzburg and the University of Natal where he graduated with a BA, majoring in English and Biblical Studies, in 1975.

His long-time colleague and friend John Bishop wrote in the Natal Witness:

"He played first-team cricket and rugby at school but finally found his sporting home as a goalkeeper for the Maritzburg Varsity first soccer team. He was a natural. The job description did not demand that he spend lonely, uncomfortable hours working on his fitness, while his position offered a panoramic view of the action while allowing him to contribute vocally and critically in a loud voice from afar. From there it was just a short step into the world of sports writing.

"He joined The Witness in 1975 as a soccer writer and spent 15 years with the newspaper. Writing under the name Stinkvoet Snyman, he produced a regular column during the 1981 Springbok rugby tour of New Zealand and won a SAB merit award for his efforts.

"In 1989 he moved to The Star in Johannesburg and he started making his name on the international cricket circuit. He became the Argus Group cricket writer while at The Star from 1990-96 and, belatedly and deservedly, won the SAB Sportswriter of the Year award in 1994. After two years with The Sunday Independent, he joined the new sporting daily, Sportsday, as a senior cricket writer and when that newspaper closed he took charge of the South African CricInfo web pages.

"After freelancing for the Mail & Guardian and the London Times, he finally came home to Pietermaritzburg in 2002, rejoining the sports department for a year.

"His desire to return to mainstream cricket writing took him back to Johannesburg in 2003 when he joined another new, but doomed, paper, This Day. When that paper sank Peter spent an enlightening couple of months as news editor of the rapidly-growing Daily Sun tabloid newspaper in Johannesburg before he was appointed Sports Editor of The Citizen in 2005.

"Peter was a lively presence in news rooms and press boxes the world over. He was well suited to the job with an easy, flowing style, able to work quickly and accurately under pressure. He was a gifted writer with a delightful, quirky sense of humour."

He is survived by his wife, Jo, a fellow journalist, who he married in 2004.

LESLIE WALTER ROLFE. Born Cape Town 1.5.1922. Died Witbank, Mpumalanga 5.9.2003 aged 81. A right-hand opening batsman who played in North-Eastern Transvaal's final Currie Cup B Section fixture against Border at Willowmoore Park in Benoni in 1955/56. He scored five and ten. He was selector and team manager for North-Eastern Transvaal during the mid-1960s and was the father of Trevor (TA) Rolfe who played for North-Eastern Transvaal between 1965/66 and 1968/69.

TREVOR ALAN ROLFE. Born Pretoria 13.3.1946. Died 28.5.2005 Reno, Nevada, USA aged 59. A right-hand lower order batsman and right-arm medium bowler who made his first-class debut for North-Eastern Transvaal against Griqualand West at Loftus Versfeld in Pretoria in December 1965. He batted at number eight, making an impressive 64. He took a career-best 3-26 against SA Universities at Berea Park in Pretoria in 1966/67. In 1968/69 he made a career-best 96 against Natal B at Berea Park and with Neville Alistoun (62) set a new provincial record partnership of 131 runs for the eighth wicket.

He moved to the United States in 1974 and bought a Jeep-Nissan dealership in Carson City just outside Reno, Nevada, in 1986. He retired in 1998 and got his golf handicap down to three. He suffered from high blood pressure and borderline diabetes and believing he was about to have a stroke or heart attack and not wanting to be a burden to his family decided to take his own life. He was the son of the North-Eastern Transvaal first-class cricketer Les (LW) Rolfe.

In 15 first-class matches he scored 410 runs (avg 29.28) and took 23 wickets (avg 37.00).

RICHARD LYNN RUTHERFOORD. Born Ubombo, Natal 7.6.1924. Died Harding, Natal 13.10.1985 aged 61. A right-hand batsman and right-arm fast-medium bowler who played one first-class match for a Natal XI against the MCC at The Oval in Pietermaritzburg in February 1949. He scored eight and four not out and took 0-43 in the two MCC innings.

STEFANUS "STEVE" STRYDOM. Born Bloemfontein 26.3.1938. Died Welgemoed, Bellville, Western Cape 29.10.2005 aged 67. A middle order right-hand batsman and right-arm medium bowler who was educated at Grey College, Bloemfontein, where he was a member of a family who were regarded as a sporting institution in Bloemfontein.

He was selected for the OFS Nuffield XI in 1954 and 1956 (the 1955 Week was cancelled due to a polio epidemic) and captained the team in his final year. His first-class debut came in the 1959/60 season. He progressed steadily without producing any fireworks. He scored

45 and 30 for OFS in the drawn match against John Reid's touring New Zealand side in January 1962 and in 1962/63 against Rhodesia in Bulawayo he made a then career-best 67 against the bowling of Joe Partridge, "Goofy" Lawrence and Jackie du Preez.

He did not reappear in first-class cricket until 1965/66. After scoring 66 against Border at Ramblers, he played against Transvaal B at Vereeniging in the only first-class match to have been played on the VBT Company (Brick and Tile) Recreation Ground. The game was played on what was described as a "dream wicket" with 1344 runs scored for the loss of 30 wickets. He made 97 in the first innings but OFS were asked to follow on. He reached what was to become his only first-class century by the close of play and on the final day went on to take his score to 234 in 352 minutes (37 boundaries). He and Neil Rosendorff set a new OFS fourth wicket record partnership of 265 in 243 minutes. He was one of the Cricketers of the Year in the 1966 SA Cricket Annual, the first Afrikaans-speaking cricketer to be awarded the honour.

In first-class matches for OFS he played alongside his brother Piet 12 times, Willie 18 times and all three brothers played in the same side on ten occasions, only the third instance in which three brothers had appeared in the same provincial team. Another brother, Corrie, played for OFS in 1967/68 when Steve was unavailable because of teaching commitments. Steve made a further five appearances in 1968/69 and was captain on three occasions.

He spent all his working life in Bloemfontein, becoming headmaster of Grey College Primary in 1972. In 1978 he became Free State University's first Director of Sport where Ewie Cronje was to be his deputy for more than 21 years.

He represented his province at rugby on 34 occasions between 1960 and 1964 mainly as full-back but with an occasional appearance at fly-half. He played for OFS against the touring Lions (1962), Wallabies (1963) and Wales (1964). His biggest playing disappointment was not being selected for the Springbok tour to the UK in 1964 after playing in the final trial match in the B-side with Lionel Wilson in the A-side. The selectors picked one full-back (Wilson) and opted for another utility back instead of a second full-back.

He became the first South African to referee Test matches abroad, Argentina vs Australia in Buenos Aires in 1979 and the first to referee a Five Nations match, Scotland vs Ireland at Murrayfield in 1985. He refereed six Currie Cup finals, a record equalled later by André Watson, and eight Tests, then equalling the most by a South African. Playing the "advantage" was his forte.

From 1976 to 1993 he was President of the OFS Rugby Union and from 1976 to 1990 he was on the executive committee of the SA Rugby Board. He also served as chairman of the SA Referees' Society. He served on IRB committees as an assessor at the 1999 and 2003 World Cups. He was named Bloemfonteiner of the Year in 1986, became a life member of the OFSRU in 1990 and received a President's Award for services to sport from President Mbeki.

In August 1994 he was diagnosed as having cancer and after a brave 11-year battle died at home. He is survived by his wife Ema (née Joubert) a noted netball and hockey player, son Joubert, who played rugby for Free State Under-20 but made a greater name for himself as an outstanding cricketer for OFS (captaining the side in 31 first-class matches), Transvaal and Northern Transvaal between 1980/81 and 1995/96 and a national cricket selector, daughters Uvain (Burger) and Corli (Witthuhn), both provincial swimmers, and six grandchildren.

In 28 first-class matches he scored 1227 runs (avg 24.05) and took 5 wickets (avg 58.00).

DAVID TALMUD. Born Cape Town 22.12.1913. Died Cape Town 28.6.1999 aged 85. A right-hand batsman who played in two first-class home matches for Griqualand West in 1935/36, scoring 39 runs (avg 13.00). He represented Griqualand West and Western Transvaal at rugby and played hockey for Griqualand West.

CYRIL TAYFIELD. Born Durban 24.11.1932 Died Glenwood, Durban 19.9.2005 aged 72. A right-hand top-order batsman and right-arm fast medium bowler who made his first-class debut for Transvaal in a friendly at Ellis Park, Johannesburg, against North-Eastern Transvaal in November 1951. He played in all six Currie Cup games for Transvaal alongside his elder brother Arthur and had an impressive first season scoring 329 runs (avg 32.90) with a top score of 73 in the drawn game against the eventual Currie Cup winners Natal at Kingsmead, when he used his feet well against an attack which included his other elder brother Hugh. His 18 wickets (avg 21.94) saw him top the Transvaal bowling averages and included a career-best 4-27, from 16 overs, in the five-wicket defeat against Western Province at Ellis Park.

His next appearance in a first-class match was in November 1953, in a friendly against Border at Ellis Park, where he made a then career-best 92. After being relegated in Tayfield's first season, Transvaal were back in the Currie Cup A Section in 1954/55. He made 102 in 164 minutes against Orange Free State at Ellis Park.

He made just three first-class appearances for Transvaal in 1955/56 and none the following season. Two first-class games in 1957/58 included one against the touring Australians at Wanderers Stadium and, in his 21st and final appearance for Transvaal, scored 18 and 13 with both his brothers playing in the side.

Work commitments took him to Kimberley and he was to appear for Griqualand West in 15 first-class matches until he retired in 1963/64. He scored a career-best 112 in the final match of the 1958/59 season, against Orange Free State at De Beers Stadium.

He was educated at Durban High School becoming Head Boy and captain of cricket and rugby. He captained Natal Schools in the 1949, 1950 and 1951 Nuffield Weeks and was selected for the SA Schools team in all three years. Arthur Tayfield was also selected in 1949.

He was a salesman and was the nephew of SH Martin (Natal, Rhodesia 1925/26-1949/50), cousin of H Martin (Transvaal B, New South Wales 1970/71-1971/72) and IR Tayfield (Griqualand West, Natal 1967/68-1979/80).

He had a heart operation in 1986 and complications set in more recently. He is survived by his brother Arthur (Natal, Transvaal 1948/49-1962/63), son Kelvin and daughter Shanda. His wife Esme and brother Hugh (Natal, Rhodesia, Transvaal, South Africa 1945/46-1962/63) predeceased him.

In 37 first-class matches he scored 1457 runs (avg 23.88) and took 56 wickets (avg 26.60).

ALISTAIR INNES "SCOTCH" TAYLOR. Born Johannesburg 25.7.1925. Died Highlands North, Johannesburg 7.2.2004 aged 78. A right-hand opening batsman and occasional leg-break bowler who was educated at King Edward VII in Johannesburg. He was an all-round sportsman, playing soccer at an early age, a member of the school shooting team and representing the First XI at cricket. He went straight from school to train for active service, as a pilot in the South African Air Force, in World War Two.

He obtained a BSc (Mining Engineering) degree from Witwatersrand University in 1949 and his first-class debut was for Transvaal, in a friendly against Natal at Kingsmead, in November of the same year. He became a regular member of the Transvaal side the following season and opening the batting with Eric Rowan amassed 368 runs (avg 40.88) in ten innings as Transvaal went on to win the Currie Cup outright for the first time since 1934/35. He made his maiden first-class century (105) against Griqualand West at Ellis Park in Johannesburg.

He missed the 1951/52 season but appeared in five out of six Currie Cup B Section matches as Transvaal gained promotion in 1952/53. He made a then career-best 164 against Border at Ellis Park and with Eric Rowan put on 274 runs for the first wicket to set a Transvaal opening partnership record which stood until 1988/89. In 1953/54 against the touring New Zealanders at Ellis Park he produced a fighting innings of 64 not out, which rescued Transvaal from a parlous 40-5 and showed his ability against Test-class bowling.

After scoring 461 runs (avg 65.85) from eight Currie Cup innings in 1954/55 he was a strong candidate for a place in the team to tour the United Kingdom in 1955, although he was not selected. He made a career-best 180 against Western Province at Ellis Park.

He captained Transvaal in 1955/56 and 1956/57. In the latter season he batted outstandingly well in making 85 when helping Transvaal beat Natal by three wickets in the first first-class match held at Wanderers Stadium. He was called up for the first Test against England, the first to be held at Wanderers Stadium, after Jackie McGlew's injured shoulder failed to respond to treatment. He made 12 and six in his only Test appearance.

He relinquished the Transvaal captaincy in 1957/58 but took it over again in 1959/60, playing his final first-class match against the touring Cavaliers side the following season.

As well as playing cricket for Old Edwardians he was instrumental in setting up a squash section and played bowls, winning the singles championship and becoming President of the bowls section in 1990 and 1991. He gained Transvaal hockey colours in 1949 as a centre-half and played for the province until 1956, taking part in trials for South Africa. He later became Chairman of the Johannesburg and District Hockey Association and President of the South African Hockey Union.

During World War Two he served as a pupil pilot of single-engine aircraft and later obtained a commercial pilot's licence. He died of a stroke at Randjes Estate Frail Care Centre and is survived by his wife Sheila, his son Neville (also known as "Scotch") and two grandsons. His eldest son, Alistair, died previously aged 25 in a motor accident.

In 52 first-class matches, he scored 2717 runs (avg 31.59), including six centuries, and took 32 wickets (avg 30.81).

ROBERT BASSETT ULLYETT. Born Salisbury, Rhodesia 5.4.1936. Died Sherwood, Durban 19.10.2004 aged 68. A right-hand top-order batsman and right-arm medium bowler. On his day he was a brilliant hooker of the ball and strong on the cut. As a bowler he could move the ball both ways and was a superb all-round fielder. He was an aggressive, confident, player with a good temperament and was not averse to doing a bit of sledging on occasions.

He was educated at Eiffel Flats Junior (Gatooma), Cecil John Rhodes Preparatory (Gwelo) and Chaplin High School (Gwelo). At Chaplin he captained the first XI in 1953 and 1954 and joined Chris Duckworth as the only player to score more than 2000 runs for the First XI. He represented Rhodesia Schools in the 1952, 1953 and 1954 Nuffield Weeks and in the latter was awarded his SA Schools cap. He played rugby for Rhodesia Schools and later played hockey for Rhodesia, representing the country at the 1964 Olympic Games in Tokyo.

He played for Salisbury Sports Club and in December 1957 made his first-class debut in a friendly against Natal at Police A Ground, Salisbury. Against North-Eastern Transvaal at Willowmoore Park in Benoni he took a career-best 7-42.

In 1958/59 Rhodesia played for the first time in the Currie Cup A Section and in the six matches he scored 215 runs (avg 23.88) and took 15 wickets (avg 32.73) including 7-79 against Transvaal at Police A Ground in Salisbury on a damp wicket. Towards the end of 1959 he developed a chipped bone and badly torn muscles in his bowling shoulder. Despite an operation he did not bowl again on a regular basis.

Although Rhodesia had to play in the Currie Cup B Section in 1963/64 he played a part in ensuring they finished top of the log in scoring 449 runs (avg 49.88). He scored his maiden first-class hundred (115) in his first Currie Cup innings for almost three years in the opening match of the season against Border at Police A Ground, Salisbury.

Rhodesia were back in the Currie Cup A Section in 1965/66 when he made a career-best 135 against Eastern Province in Salisbury. In 1967/68, his final season, he scored an unbeaten 126 when Rhodesia beat Orange Free State by an innings and 62 runs at Ramblers in Bloemfontein, losing only one wicket in the match. He and Ray Gripper, who made a Currie Cup record 279 not out, put on an unbeaten 281 for the second wicket, the highest partnership for any Rhodesia wicket. He gave up playing regular cricket after a difference of opinion with the cricket authorities and concentrated on hockey.

The family moved to Durban in 1979 but he returned to Zimbabwe for a few years in the nineties before returning to live in South Africa. He worked in the sports equipment trade. He suffered from prostrate cancer which was diagnosed late and died a short time later in the Highway Hospice. He is survived by his wife Dayne, daughter Susan and sons Clive and Kevin. His son, Kevin, became a world-class men's doubles tennis player, winning many titles in partnership with fellow Zimbabwean Wayne Black, including the 2001 US Open and the 2005 Australian Open.

In 47 first-class matches, he scored 2096 runs (avg 26.53), including four centuries, and took 46 wickets (avg 28.41).

ALLEN EDWARD VAN DER MERWE. Born Kroonstad, Orange Free State 10.9.1949. Died Virginia, Free State 25.3.1998 aged 48. A right-hand batsman who played in three first-class matches for Orange Free State and two for Griqualand West between 1972/73 and 1980/81, scoring 75 runs (avg 8.33). He also played hockey for Orange Free State.

TOBIAS MOSTERT HENRY VAN DER SPUY. Born Mowbray, Cape Town 28.5.1915. Died Claremont, Cape Town 17.6.2006 aged 91. A left-hand batsman and right-arm slow bowler, Henry van der Spuy played in four Currie Cup fixtures for Griqualand West as a schoolboy in 1933/34. He made the first of 22 first-class appearances for Western Province against Vic Richardson's 1935/36 Australian side. When he arrived at the crease he heard Richardson and Jack Fingleton discussing how well Bill O'Reilly was bowling and realised the comments were for his benefit. He said "Dave" Nourse helped shepherd him to 28 not out.

He was a regular member of the side in the next two seasons and scored three centuries, making a career-best unbeaten 121 against Transvaal at Newlands in 1936/37. He took 24 wickets (avg 19.29) in that season, including a career-best 6-95 against Eastern Province.

He served in the SA Artillery during the war. He played in five matches for Western Province in 1946/47 before making six first-class appearances for Orange Free State in 1950/51. He served as a Western Province selector and maintained a keen interest in cricket. He is survived by his daughter Neva, son John (who played for SA Schools in 1967) and five grandchildren. Only 27 South African cricketers are known to have lived longer than his 91 years 20 days. In 32 first-class matches, he scored 1411 runs (avg 30.67) and took 46 wickets (avg 26.69).

HOWARD HUGH "SPARKLE" WATT. Born Rosebank, Cape Town 1.3.1911. Died Howick, KwaZulu-Natal 17.8.2005 aged 94. A fine all-round sportsman who was more famous for his exploits on the rugby field than on the cricket pitch. He was educated at Bishops (Diocesan College) in Cape Town. In 1928, aged 17, his family emigrated to Chicago. In 1932 he played in four matches for an Illinois XVIII against Arthur Mailey's Australian team who were touring Canada and the United States. He bowled Don Bradman for four in the first, also bowling Dick Nutt and Alan Kippax, and 13 in the third. Before the second game in which he was due to play the Australian manager reputedly asked him not to, bowl because they were afraid he would injure Bradman and they were on their way home to host Douglas Jardine's England team.

He returned to South Africa after five years in the United States. He was recognised as the fastest bowler in South Africa but missed out on selection for the Test side. He decided he would have a crack at the rugby Springboks instead. A powerfully-built loose-forward he was selected for the squad which toured Australia and New Zealand in 1937. During the second Test against New Zealand he and the other non-playing members of the squad were so excited that they leapt up and down in the stands and he went through the wooden planking, suffering a sprained ankle. He was due to play in the second Test against the Wallabies but in the last practice before the match he ran into Boy Louw and injured his thigh. He played in seven mid-week matches without playing in a Test.

His first-class cricket debut was for Western Province in a Currie Cup match against Border at Recreation Ground in East London in February 1934. He opened the bowling with Bob Crisp and achieved the analysis of 21-8-29-5. He achieved career-best figures of 6-84 against Griqualand West at De Beers Stadium, Kimberley in 1934/35.

Work commitments meant no first-class cricket until December 1938 when he appeared for North-Eastern Transvaal at Berea Park in Pretoria against Wally Hammond's MCC touring team. World War Two meant he had to wait until December 1945 for his next first-class appearance, a friendly against Transvaal at The Wanderers, which ended in a draw. His final four appearances were in the Currie Cup for North-Eastern Transvaal in 1946/47.

He retained his involvement in sport long after he had stopped playing, being an Orange Free State cricket selector for ten years and coach to the St Helena Rugby Club in Welkom. Prior to his death he was believed to be South Africa's second oldest living first-class cricketer (only DIE Anderson [Transvaal] born 26.1.1910 surviving him) and only 13 other South Africa/Rhodesia first-class cricketers are known to have lived beyond his 94 years 169 days. He was the oldest rugby Springbok and the last survivor of the 1937 touring side.

In 12 first-class matches he scored 115 runs (avg 7.66) and took 44 wickets (avg 24.54).

ROBERT WALTON WIGHTMAN. Born Cape Town 28.3.1933. Died Randburg, Gauteng 22.6.2003 aged 70. A lower-order right-hand batsman who played one Currie Cup match for Western Province against Transvaal at Ellis Park in December 1954. He scored 16 and six and took 2-120.

With acknowledgements to Trevor Chesterfield, Brian de Kock (Old Diocesan Union, Cape Town); Roger Herbert (Pretoria BHS Old Boys Association); Peter Martin (Daily Dispatch, East London); Peter Raath (SA Football Historian) and Robin Thorne.

Full obituaries on the following players will be included in the 2007 Annual:

RAMSEY LOVELL FORWORD. Born Grahamstown, Cape Province 25.9.1925. Died Port Alfred, Eastern Cape 21.3.2006 aged 80. (Eastern Province 1952/53-1956/57).

CHARLES DAVID "BEBE" FRANKLIN. Born Melsetter, Southern Rhodesia 9.5.1920. Died Harare, Zimbabwe 14.7.2006 aged 86. (Rhodesia 1948/49-1950/51).

DESMOND GERARD TOWLERTON LEATHER. Born Louis Trichardt, Transvaal 23.8.1929. Died Waterfall, near Hillcrest, KwaZulu-Natal 19.5.2006 aged 76. (Rhodesia 1964/65).

HAROLD IAN LONG. Born Grahamstown, Cape Province 12.12.1929. Died near Salem, Eastern Cape 24.6.2006 aged 76. (Eastern Province 1952/53-1960/61).

FIXTURES 2006/07

INTERNATIONAL

ICC CHAMPIONS TROPHY

October 2006		
Sat 7	Sri Lanka v Bangladesh (qualifier)	Mohali
Sun 8	West Indies v Zimbabwe (qualifier)	Ahmedabad
Tue 10	Sri Lanka v Zimbabwe (qualifier)	
Ahmedabad		
Wed 11	West Indies v Bangladesh (qualifier)	Jaipur
Fri 13	Zimbabwe v Bangladesh (qualifier)	Jaipur
Sat 14	Sri Lanka v West Indies (qualifier)	Mumbai
Sun 15	England v India (Pool A)	Jaipur
Mon 16	**New Zealand v South Africa (Pool B)**	**Mumbai**
Tue 17	Pakistan v Qualifier 1 (Pool B)	Jaipur
Wed 18	Australia v Qualifier 2 (Pool A)	Mumbai
Fri 20	New Zealand v Qualifier 1 (Pool B)	Mumbai
Sat 21	England v Australia (Pool A)	Jaipur
Tue 24	**South Africa v Qualifier 1 (Pool B)**	**Ahmedabad**
Wed 25	New Zealand v Pakistan (Pool B)	
Mohali		
Thu 26	India v Qualifier 2 (Pool A)	Ahmedabad
Fri 27	**South Africa v Pakistan (Pool B)**	**Mohali**
Sat 28	England v Qualifier 2 (Pool A)	Ahmedabad
Sun 29	Australia v India (Pool A)	Mohali
November 2006		
Wed 1	First Semi-Final, A1 v B2	Mohali
Thu 2	Second Semi-Final, B1 v A2	Jaipur
Sun 5	Final	Mumbai

INDIA IN SOUTH AFRICA

MTN ONE-DAY INTERNATIONAL SERIES, STANDARD BANK PRO20

November 2006			
Thu 16	D/N	South Africa A	Benoni
Sun 19	Day	First MTN ODI	Johannesburg
Wed 22	D/N	Second MTN ODI	Durban
Sun 26	Day	Third MTN ODI	Cape Town
Wed 29	D/N	Fourth MTN ODI	Port Elizabeth
December 2006			
Fri 1	D/N	Standard Bank Pro20 International	Johannesburg
Sun 3	Day	Fifth MTN ODI	Centurion

CASTLE TEST SERIES

Thu 7-10	4-day	South Africa A	Potchefstroom
Fri 15-19		First Castle Test	Johannesburg
Tue 26-30		Second Castle Test	Durban

January 2007			
Tue 2-6		Third Castle Test	Cape Town

PAKISTAN IN SOUTH AFRICA

CASTLE TEST SERIES

January 2007			
Sat 6-8	3-day	South Africa A	Kimberley
Thu 11-15	First Castle Test		Centurion
Fri 19-23		Second Castle Test	Port Elizabeth
Fri 26-30		Third Castle Test	Cape Town

MTN ONE-DAY INTERNATIONAL SERIES, STANDARD BANK PRO20

February 2007			
Fri 2	D/N	Standard Bank Pro20 International	Johannesburg
Sun 4	Day	First MTN ODI	Centurion
Wed 7	D/N	Second MTN ODI	Durban
Fri 9	D/N	Third MTN ODI	Port Elizabeth
Sun 11	Day	Fourth MTN ODI	Cape Town
Wed 14	D/N	Fifth MTN ODI	Johannesburg

ICC CRICKET WORLD CUP 2007

GROUP A (St Kitts & Nevis): Australia, South Africa, Scotland, Netherlands.
GROUP B (Trinidad & Tobago): Sri Lanka, India, Bangladesh, Bermuda.
GROUP C (St Lucia): New Zealand, England, Kenya, Canada.
GROUP D (Jamaica): Pakistan, West Indies, Zimbabwe, Ireland.

SOUTH AFRICAN WARM-UP MATCHES

March		
Mon 5	South Africa v Canada	Trinidad
Fri 9	South Africa v Pakistan	Trinidad

GROUP FIXTURES
(Note: There are reserve days for all World Cup fixtures)

March		
Tue 13	West Indies v Pakistan (Group D)	Jamaica
Wed 14	Australia v Scotland (Group A)	St Kitts
Wed 14	Kenya v Canada (Group C)	St Lucia
Thu 15	Sri Lanka v Bermuda (Group B)	Trinidad
Thu 15	Zimbabwe v Ireland (Group D)	Jamaica
Fri 16	**South Africa v Netherlands (Group A)**	**St Kitts**
Fri 16	England v New Zealand (Group C)	St Lucia
Sat 17	India v Bangladesh (Group B)	Trinidad
Sat 17	Pakistan v Ireland (Group D)	Jamaica
Sun 18	Australia v Netherlands (Group A)	St Kitts
Sun 18	England v Canada (Group C)	St Lucia
Mon 19	India v Bermuda (Group B)	Trinidad
Mon 19	West Indies v Zimbabwe (Group D)	Jamaica
Tue 20	**South Africa v Scotland (Group A)**	**St Kitts**

Tue 20	New Zealand v Kenya (Group C)	St Lucia
Wed 21	Sri Lanka v Bangladesh (Group B)	Trinidad
Wed 21	Zimbabwe v Pakistan (Group D)	Jamaica
Thu 22	Scotland v Netherlands (Group A)	St Kitts
Thu 22	New Zealand v Canada (Group C)	St Lucia
Fri 23	India v Sri Lanka (Group B)	Trinidad
Fri 23	West Indies v Ireland (Group D)	Jamaica
Sat 24	**Australia v South Africa (Group A)**	**St Kitts**
Sat 24	England v Kenya (Group C)	St Lucia
Sun 25	Bermuda v Bangladesh (Group B)	Trinidad

SUPER EIGHT SERIES

March

Tue 27	D2 v A1	Antigua
Wed 28	**A2 v B1**	**Guyana**
Thu 29	D2 v C1	Antigua
Fri 30	D1 v C2	Guyana
Sat 31	A1 v B2	Antigua

April

Sun 1	D2 v B1	Guyana
Mon 2	B2 v C1	Antigua
Tue 3	**D1 v A2**	**Guyana**
Wed 4	C2 v B1	Antigua
Sat 7	**B2 v A2**	**Guyana**
Sun 8	A1 v C2	Antigua
Mon 9	D1 v C1	Guyana
Tue 10	**D2 v A2**	**Grenada**
Wed 11	C2 v B2	Barbados
Thu 12	B1 v C1	Grenada
Fri 13	A1 v D1	Barbados
Sat 14	**A2 v C1**	**Grenada**
Sun 15	B2 v D1	Barbados
Mon 16	A1 v B1	Grenada
Tue 17	**A2 v C2**	**Barbados**
Wed 18	D1 v B1	Grenada
Thu 19	D2 v B2	Barbados
Fri 20	A1 v C1	Grenada
Sat 21	D2 v C2	Barbados

Note: South Africa will be Team A2, provided they qualify for the Super Eight Series.

KNOCKOUT STAGE

April 2007

Tue 24	First Semi-Final, 2 v 3	Jamaica
Wed 25	Second Semi-Final, 1 v 4	St Lucia
Sat 28	Final	Barbados

FIXTURES 2006/07

DOMESTIC

SUPERSPORT SERIES

November 2006

Thu 23-26	Fidentia Warriors v Nashua Cape Cobras	East London
	Nashua Titans v Gestetner Diamond Eagles	Centurion
	Nashua Dolphins v Highveld Lions	Pietermaritzburg
Thu 30-Dec 3	Nashua Cape Cobras v Nashua Titans	Stellenbosch
	Nashua Dolphins v Fidentia Warriors	Durban
	Gestetner Diamond Eagles v Highveld Lions	Kimberley

December 2006

Thu 7-10	Nashua Cape Cobras v Nashua Dolphins	Cape Town
	Fidentia Warriors v Gestetner Diamond Eagles	Port Elizabeth
	Nashua Titans v Highveld Lions	Benoni
Thu 14-17	Nashua Cape Cobras v Highveld Lions	Cape Town
	Gestetner Diamond Eagles v Nashua Dolphins	Bloemfontein
	Nashua Titans v Fidentia Warriors	Centurion

January 2007

Thu 4-7	Nashua Dolphins v Nashua Titans	Pietermaritzburg
	Gestetner Diamond Eagles v Nashua Cape Cobras	Bloemfontein
	Highveld Lions v Fidentia Warriors	Johannesburg
Thu 11-14	Nashua Cape Cobras v Fidentia Warriors	Cape Town
	Nashua Dolphins v Gestetner Diamond Eagles	Durban
	Highveld Lions v Nashua Titans	Potchefstroom
Thu 18-21	Fidentia Warriors v Nashua Dolphins	East London
	Highveld Lions v Gestetner Diamond Eagles	Johannesburg
	Nashua Titans v Nashua Cape Cobras	Benoni

February 2007

Thu 1-4	Nashua Cape Cobras v Gestetner Diamond Eagles	Stellenbosch
	Fidentia Warriors v Nashua Titans	Port Elizabeth
	Highveld Lions v Nashua Dolphins	Potchefstroom
Thu 8-11	Fidentia Warriors v Highveld Lions	East London
	Nashua Dolphins v Nashua Cape Cobras	Pietermaritzburg
	Gestetner Diamond Eagles v Nashua Titans	Bloemfontein
Thu 15-18	Gestetner Diamond Eagles v Fidentia Warriors	Kimberley
	Highveld Lions v Nashua Cape Cobras	Potchefstroom
	Nashua Titans v Nashua Dolphins	Benoni

MTN DOMESTIC CHAMPIONSHIP

September 2006

Fri 29	D/N	Nashua Titans v Nashua Cape Cobras	Centurion

October 2006

Sun 1	Day	Highveld Lions v Gestetner Diamond Eagles	Johannesburg
Wed 4	D/N	Fidentia Warriors v Nashua Dolphins	East London

Fri 6	D/N	Nashua Cape Cobras v Fidentia Warriors	Cape Town
	D/N	Nashua Dolphins v Gestetner Diamond Eagles	Durban
Sun 8	Day	Gestetner Diamond Eagles v Nashua Cape Cobras	Bloemfontein
	Day	Nashua Titans v Nashua Dolphins	Centurion
Wed 11	D/N	Nashua Dolphins v Highveld Lions	Durban
Fri 13	D/N	Nashua Cape Cobras v Nashua Dolphins	Cape Town
	D/N	Fidentia Warriors v Gestetner Diamond Eagles	Port Elizabeth
	D/N	Highveld Lions v Nashua Titans	Johannesburg
Sun 15	Day	Gestetner Diamond Eagles v Nashua Titans	Kimberley
	Day	Highveld Lions v Fidentia Warriors	Potchefstroom
Wed 18	D/N	Fidentia Warriors v Nashua Titans	East London
Fri 20	D/N	Nashua Dolphins v Fidentia Warriors	Durban
	D/N	Highveld Lions v Nashua Cape Cobras	Johannesburg
Sun 22	Day	Gestetner Diamond Eagles v Nashua Dolphins	Kimberley
	Day	Nashua Titans v Highveld Lions	Centurion
Wed 25	D/N	Nashua Cape Cobras v Gestetner Diamond Eagles	Cape Town
	D/N	Fidentia Warriors v Highveld Lions	Port Elizabeth
Fri 27	D/N	Nashua Dolphins v Nashua Cape Cobras	Durban
	D/N	Nashua Titans v Fidentia Warriors	Benoni
	D/N	Gestetner Diamond Eagles v Highveld Lions	Bloemfontein
Sun 29	Day	Nashua Cape Cobras v Nashua Titans	Cape Town

November 2006

Wed 1	D/N	Gestetner Diamond Eagles v Fidentia Warriors	Kimberley
Fri 3	D/N	Fidentia Warriors v Nashua Cape Cobras	East London
	D/N	Highveld Lions v Nashua Dolphins	Potchefstroom
	D/N	Nashua Titans v Gestetner Diamond Eagles	Centurion
Sun 5	Day	Nashua Cape Cobras v Highveld Lions	Cape Town
	Day	Nashua Dolphins v Nashua Titans	Pietermaritzburg
Fri 10	D/N	First Semi Final	TBA
Sat 11		Reserve Day	
Sun 12	Day	Second Semi-Final	TBA
Mon 13		Reserve Day	
Fri 17	D/N	Final	TBA
Sat 18		Reserve Day	

STANDARD BANK Pro20 SERIES

February 2007

Wed 21	D/N	Gestetner Diamond Eagles v Fidentia Warriors	Bloemfontein
Fri 23	D/N	Fidentia Warriors v Nashua Dolphins	East London
	D/N	Highveld Lions v Nashua Cape Cobras	Johannesburg
Sun 25	Day	Nashua Cape Cobras v Fidentia Warriors	Cape Town
	Day	Nashua Titans v Gestetner Diamond Eagles	Centurion
Wed 28	D/N	Nashua Dolphins v Highveld Lions	Durban

March 2007

Fri 2	D/N	Fidentia Warriors v Nashua Titans	Port Elizabeth
	D/N	Gestetner Diamond Eagles v Nashua Cape Cobras	Kimberley
Sun 4	Day	Highveld Lions v Gestetner Diamond Eagles	Potchefstroom
Wed 7	D/N	Nashua Cape Cobras v Nashua Titans	Cape Town
Fri 9	D/N	Nashua Dolphins v Nashua Cape Cobras	Durban
	D/N	Highveld Lions v Nashua Titans	Johannesburg

Sun 11	Day	Gestetner Diamond Eagles v Nashua Dolphins	Bloemfontein
Wed 14	D/N	Fidentia Warriors v Highveld Lions	East London
	D/N	Nashua Titans v Nashua Dolphins	Benoni
Fri 16	D/N	First Semi-Final	TBA
Sat 17		Reserve Day	
Sun 18	Day	Second Semi-Final	TBA
Mon 19		Reserve Day	
Fri 23	D/N	Final	TBA
Sat 24		Reserve Day	

SAA PROVINCIAL COMPETITIONS

(Three-day first-class matches, followed by one-day 45-overs-a-side matches)

POOL A

October 2006

Thu 5-8	Gauteng v Mpumalanga	Johannesburg
	Easterns v Griqualand West	Benoni
	Namibia v Limpopo	Windhoek
Thu 12-15	Free State v Gauteng	Bloemfontein
	Northerns v Powerade Dragons	Centurion
	Limpopo v Mpumalanga	Duiwelskloof
Thu 26-29	Free State v Namibia	Bloemfontein
	Powerade Dragons v Limpopo	Potchefstroom
	Northerns v Easterns	Centurion

November 2006

Thu 2-5	Free State v Northerns	Bloemfontein
	Gauteng v Powerade Dragons	Johannesburg
	Easterns v Mpumalanga	Benoni
Thu 9-12	Griqualand West v Limpopo	Kimberley
	Mpumalanga v Namibia	Witbank
Thu 16-19	Powerade Dragons v Free State	Potchefstroom
	Limpopo v Easterns	Duiwelskloof
	Namibia v Gauteng	Windhoek
Wed 22-26	Griqualand West v Namibia	Kimberley
Thu 30-Dec 3	Northerns v Mpumalanga	Centurion

December 2006

Thu 7-10	Limpopo v Northerns	Duiwelskloof
Thu 14-17	Griqualand West v Free State	Kimberley
	Easterns v Powerade Dragons	Benoni

January 2007

Wed 17-20	Powerade Dragons v Griqualand West	Potchefstroom
Thu 18-21	Free State v Limpopo	Bloemfontein
	Northerns v Gauteng	Centurion
Thu 25-28	Mpumalanga v Free State	Witbank
	Namibia v Easterns	Windhoek

February 2007

Thu 1-4	Griqualand West v Northerns	Kimberley
	Limpopo v Gauteng	Duiwelskloof

FIXTURES 2006/07

Thu 8-11	Mpumalanga v Griqualand West	Witbank
Thu 15-18	Gauteng v Easterns	Johannesburg
Wed 21-24	Powerade Dragons v Namibia	Potchefstroom
Thu 22-25	Easterns v Free State	Benoni
March 2007		
Thu 1-4	Gauteng v Griqualand West	Johannesburg
	Mpumalanga v Powerade Dragons	Witbank
	Namibia v Northerns	Windhoek
POOL B		
October 2006		
Thu 5-8	Kei v Sekunjalo Western Province	Alice
Thu 12-15	KwaZulu-Natal Inland v KwaZulu-Natal	Pietermaritzburg
	South Western Districts v Border	Oudtshoorn
Thu 26-29	Border v Sekunjalo Western Province	East London
	Eastern Province v South Western Districts	Port Elizabeth
	Kei v Boland	Alice
November 2006		
Thu 2-5	Eastern Province v KwaZulu-Natal Inland	Port Elizabeth
	KwaZulu-Natal v Kei	Durban
Thu 9-12	Sekunjalo Western Province v South Western Districts	Cape Town
Thu 16-19	Boland v KwaZulu-Natal	Paarl
	KwaZulu-Natal Inland v Border	Pietermaritzburg
December 2006		
Thu 14-17	South Western Districts v KwaZulu-Natal	Oudtshoorn
January 2007		
Thu 18-21	Sekunjalo Western Province v KwaZulu-Natal Inland	Cape Town
	KwaZulu-Natal v Border	Durban
	Kei v Eastern Province	Alice
Thu 25-28	Boland v South Western Districts	Paarl
	Border v Eastern Province	East London
	KwaZulu-Natal Inland v Kei	Pietermaritzburg
February 2007		
Thu 1-4	Eastern Province v Boland	Port Elizabeth
	KwaZulu-Natal v Sekunjalo Western Province	Durban
Thu 8-11	Boland v Border	Paarl
	South Western Districts v KwaZulu-Natal Inland	Oudtshoorn
Thu 15-18	Sekunjalo Western Province v Boland	Cape Town
	Eastern Province v KwaZulu-Natal	Port Elizabeth
Thu 22-25	Boland v KwaZulu-Natal Inland	Paarl
	Kei v South Western Districts	Alice
March 2007		
Thu 1-4	Sekunjalo Western Province v Eastern Province	Cape Town
	Border v Kei	East London

CROSS-POOL MATCHES
March 2007

Thu 8-11	Four-Day Final	TBA
Sat 17	One-Day Semi-Finals	TBA
Sun 18	Reserve Day	
Sat 24	One-Day Final	TBA
Sun 25	Reserve Day	

UNDER-19 COMPETITION

(Three-day matches, not first-class)
November 2006

Fri 24-26	Eastern Province v Boland	Port Elizabeth
	KwaZulu-Natal v Border	Durban
	Free State v Griqualand West	Bloemfontein
	Northerns v Gauteng	Centurion
Thu 30-Dec 2	Sekunjalo Western Province v Eastern Province	Cape Town
	Border v KZN-Inland	East London
	North West v Free State	Potchestroom
	Gauteng v Easterns	Johannesburg

December 2006

Fri 8-10	Boland v Sekunjalo Western Province	Paarl
	KZN-Inland v KwaZulu-Natal	Pietermaritzburg
	Griqualand West v North West	Kimberley
	Easterns v Northerns	Benoni
Thu 28-30	Sekunjalo Western Province v Boland	Cape Town
	KZN-Inland v Border	Pietermaritzburg
	Free State v North West	Bloemfontein
	Northerns v Easterns	Pretoria

January 2007

Fri 5-7	Boland v Eastern Province	Paarl
	KwaZulu-Natal v KZN-Inland	Durban
	North West v Griqualand West	Potchefstroom
	Easterns v Gauteng	Benoni
Fri 12-14	Border v KwaZulu-Natal	East London
	Eastern Province v Sekunjalo Western Province	Port Elizabeth
	Griqualand West v Free State	Kimberley
	Gauteng v Northerns	Johannesburg

WOMEN'S CHALLENGE

COASTAL
October 2006

Sat 7	Boland v Sekunjalo Western Province	Paarl
	Border v Eastern Province	East London
	Free State v Griqualand West	Bloemfontein
Sat 21	Sekunjalo Western Province v Eastern Province	Cape Town
	South Western Districts v Free State	Oudtshoorn
Sun 22	Boland v Eastern Province	Paarl
	South Western Districts v Griqualand West	Oudtshoorn

FIXTURES 2006/07

November 2006

Sat 4	Griqualand West v Boland	Kimberley
	Border v Sekunjalo Western Province	East London
Sun 5	Free State v Boland	Bloemfontein
	Eastern Province v Sekunjalo Western Province	Port Elizabeth
Sat 18	Griqualand West v Border	Kimberley
	South Western Districts v Boland	Oudtshoorn
Sun 19	Free State v Border	Bloemfontein
	South Western Districts v Sekunjalo Western Province	Oudtshoorn

January 2006

Sat 13	Sekunjalo Western Province v Griqualand West	Cape Town
	Border v South Western Districts	East London
Sun 14	Boland v Griqualand West	Paarl
	Eastern Province v South Western Districts	Port Elizabeth
Sat 27	Eastern Province v Griqualand West	Port Elizabeth
	Sekunjalo Western Province v South Western Districts	Cape Town
Sun 28	Border v Griqualand West	East London
	Boland v South Western Districts	Paarl

February 2007

Sat 3	Eastern Province v Free State	Port Elizabeth
Sun 4	Border v Free State	East London
Sat 10	Boland v Border	Paarl
	Griqualand West v Eastern Province	Kimberley
Sun 11	Sekunjalo Western Province v Border	Cape Town
	Free State v Eastern Province	Bloemfontein
Sat 24	Border v Boland	East London
	Griqualand West v Sekunjalo Western Province	Kimberley
Sun 25	Eastern Province v Boland	Port Elizabeth
	Free State v Sekunjalo Western Province	Bloemfontein

March 2007

Sat 10	South Western Districts v Border	Oudtshoorn
	Sekunjalo Western Province v Free State	Cape Town
Sun 11	Boland v Free State	Paarl
	South Western Districts v Eastern Province	Oudtshoorn
Sat 17	Griqualand West v South Western Districts	Kimberley
Sun 18	Free State v South Western Districts	Bloemfontein
	Sekunjalo Western Province v Boland	Cape Town
Sun 25	Eastern Province v Border	Port Elizabeth
	Griqualand West v Free State	Kimberley

INLAND

October 2006

Sat 7	Gauteng v North West	Johannesburg
	KwaZulu-Natal v KwaZulu-Natal Inland	Durban
Sun 8	Northerns v Limpopo	Pretoria
Sat 21	KwaZulu-Natal Inland v Limpopo	Pietermaritzburg
	Mpumalanga v Gauteng	Witbank
Sun 22	KwaZulu-Natal v Limpopo	Durban
Sat 28	Mpumalanga v North West	Witbank

FIXTURES 2006/07

November 2006		
Sat 4	North West v KwaZulu-Natal	Potchefstroom
	Limpopo v KwaZulu-Natal Inland	Duiwelskloof
Sun 5	Gauteng v KwaZulu-Natal	Johannesburg
	Northerns v KwaZulu-Natal Inland	Pretoria
Sat 18	North West v Northerns	Potchefstroom
	Mpumalanga v KwaZulu-Natal	Witbank
Sun 19	Gauteng v Northerns	Johannesburg
Sat 25	Mpumalanga v KwaZulu-Natal Inland	Witbank
January 2006		
Sat 13	KwaZulu-Natal Inland v North West	Pietermaritzburg
	Limpopo v Mpumalanga	Duiwelskloof
Sun 14	KwaZulu-Natal v North West	Durban
	Northerns v Mpumalanga	Pretoria
Sat 27	Limpopo v North West	Duiwelskloof
	KwaZulu-Natal Inland v Mpumalanga	Pietermaritzburg
Sun 28	Northerns v North West	Pretoria
	KwaZulu-Natal v Mpumalanga	Durban
February 2007		
Sat 3	Limpopo v Gauteng	Duiwelskloof
Sun 4	Northerns v Gauteng	Pretoria
Sat 10	KwaZulu-Natal v Northerns	Durban
	North West v Limpopo	Potchefstroom
Sun 11	KwaZulu-Natal Inland v Northerns	Pietermaritzburg
	Gauteng v Limpopo	Johannesburg
Sat 17	Mpumalanga v Limpopo	Witbank
Sat 24	Limpopo v KwaZulu-Natal	Duiwelskloof
	North West v KwaZulu-Natal Inland	Potchefstroom
Sun 25	Northerns v KwaZulu-Natal	Pretoria
	Gauteng v KwaZulu-Natal Inland	Johannesburg
March 2007		
Sat 10	Mpumalanga v Northerns	Witbank
	KwaZulu-Natal Inland v Gauteng	Pietermaritzburg
Sun 11	KwaZulu-Natal v Gauteng	Durban
Sat 17	North West v Mpumalanga	Potchefstroom
Sun 18	Gauteng v Mpumalanga	Johannesburg
	KwaZulu-Natal Inland v KwaZulu-Natal	Pietermaritzburg
Sun 25	Limpopo v Northerns	Duiwelskloof
	North West v Gauteng	Potchefstroom
Sat 31	First Inland v Second Coastal	TBA
	First Coastal v Second Inland	TBA
April 2007		
Sun 1	Reserve Day	
Sat 7	Final	TBA
Sun 8	Reserve Day	

FIXTURES 2006/07

TOURNAMENTS AND CRICKET WEEKS

September 2006		
Wed 13-17	Associates Club Championships	Witbank
Wed 20-24	National Club Championships	Pretoria
Mon 25	National Club Championships Final	SuperSport Park
November 2006		
Mon 27-Dec 1	SASSU B Week	Polokwane
December 2006		
Sun 3-7	Standard Bank Under-13 Week	Oudtshoorn
Mon 4-8	SASSU A Week	Pretoria
Thu 7-11	Under-17 Boys Week	Bloemfontein
Thu 7-11	Under-19 Girls Week	Kimberley
Sat 9	SASSU XI v Northerns XI	Pretoria
Sat 9-13	PG Bison Under-15 Week	Johannesburg
Mon 11-15	Uner-17 Boys RCASA Week	Graaff Reinet
Sat 16-20	Coca-Cola Khaya Majola Under-19 Week	Stellenbosch
Thu 21	Boland v SA Schools	Paarl
	Boland XI v SA Colts	Stellenbosch
February 2007		
Sat 3-7	Rural Cricket Association of South Africa Week	Potchefstroom
Fri 9	North West XI v RCASA XI	Potchefstroom

FUTURE TOURS

	Tests	ODIs
June 2007		
Afro-Asia Cup in Kenya		
August 2007		
South Africa to Zimbabwe	2	3
September 2007		
ICC Twenty20 World Championship in South Africa		3-5
October 2007		
South Africa to Pakistan	2	5
November/December 2007		
New Zealand in South Africa	2	5
December 2007/January 2008		
West Indies in South Africa	4	5
February/March 2008		
South Africa to Bangladesh	2	
Triangular series Bangladesh/India/South Africa		2-3
March/April 2008		
South Africa to India	3	
May 2008		
Kenya/Scotland in South Africa		2-3
July-September 2008		
South Africa to England	4	5
September 2008		
ICC Champions Trophy in Pakistan		3

FIXTURES 2006/07

November/December 2008		
Bangladesh in South Africa	2	3
December 2008/January 2009		
South Africa to Australia	3	5
February-April 2009		
Australia in South Africa	3	5
June 2009		
ICC Twenty20 World Championship in England		3-5
November 2009-January 2010		
England in South Africa	4	5
February/March 2010		
South Africa to India	3	5
April 2010		
ICC Champions Trophy in West Indies		3
May/June 2010		
South Africa to West Indies	4	5
September 2010		
Zimbabwe in South Africa	2	3
October/November 2010		
South Africa to Pakistan	3	5
December 2010/January 2011		
India in South Africa 3	5	
February/March 2011		
ICC Cricket World Cup in Asia		3-9
September-November 2011		
Australia in South Africa	3	5
December 2011-February 2012		
Sri Lanka in South Africa	3	5
February-April 2012		
South Africa to New Zealand	3	5